Encyclopedia of Psychoanalysis

Encyclopedia
of Psychoanalysis

LUDWIG EIDELBERG, M. D., *Editor-in-Chief*

THE FREE PRESS, NEW YORK

COLLIER-MACMILLAN LIMITED, LONDON

Copyright © 1968 by Ludwig Eidelberg

Printed in the United States of America

Collier-Macmillan Canada, Ltd., Toronto, Ontario

Library of Congress Catalog Card Number: 67-28974.

THIS INVESTIGATION WAS SUPPORTED BY PUBLIC HEALTH SERVICE RESEARCH GRANT NO. MH06631 FROM THE NATIONAL INSTITUTE OF MENTAL HEALTH. In addition, a financial grant from A. L. H. Foundation is gratefully acknowledged.

printing number
2 3 4 5 6 7 8 9 10

To the immortal spirit of Freud

Acknowledgments

We are indebted to the following publishers and authors for allowing us to reprint copyrighted material:

American Imago (Vol. 21, No. 1-2), "Psychoanalysis: Science, Art or Bureaucracy?", Ludwig Eidelberg

Basic Books, extracts from *Selected Papers of Karl Abraham, M.D.,* and *The Life and Work of Sigmund Freud,* Ernest Jones (ed.)

Hogarth Press Ltd., *International Journal of Psychoanalysis* (11, 1930) "Some Unconscious Factors in Reading;" James Strachey, *International Journal of Psychoanalysis* (15, 1934) "The Nature of the Therapeutic Action of Psychoanalysis;" James Strachey, *The Standard Edition of the Complete Works of Sigmund Freud,* James Strachey (ed.), (3, 1962) "The Emergence of Freud's Fundamental Hypotheses"

Hogarth Press Ltd. and Mrs. Katherine Jones, extracts from *The Life and Work of Sigmund Freud,* Ernest Jones (ed.)

Hogarth Press Ltd. and the Estate of Ella Sharpe, extracts from *Collected Papers on Psycho-Analysis,* Ella Sharpe

Hogarth Press Ltd. and Dr. Hilda Abraham, extracts from *Selected Papers on Psychoanalysis,* Karl Abraham

International Journal of Psychoanalysis and J. D. Sutherland (ed.), (30, 1949) "Autoplastic and Alloplastic Adaptation," S. Ferenczi, (4-5, 1960) "The Unconscious Images in the Genesis of Peptic Ulcers," A. Garma, (27, 1946) "Notes on Some Schizoid Mechanisms," M. Klein, (41, 1960) "A Third Contribution to the Study of Slips of the Tongue," Ludwig Eidelberg

International Universities Press, Inc., extracts from *Psycho-Analytic Study of the Child,* Vol. I, Anna Freud; *The Ego and the Mechanisms of Defense,* Anna Freud; *Ego Psychology and the Problems of Adaptation,* Heinz Hartmann; *Essays on Ego Psychology,* Heinz Hartmann; *Studies in Psychoanalysis,* Ludwig Eidelberg; and *An Outline of a Comparative Pathology of the Neuroses,* Ludwig Eidelberg

Journal of the Hillside Hospital (7:98, 1958) "Technical Problems in the Analysis of Masochists," Ludwig Eidelberg, and (8:21, 1959) "A Case of a Schizoid Character," Ludwig Eidelberg

Psychiatric Quarterly (36, 1962) "A Contribution to the Study of the Unpleasure-Pleasure Principle," Ludwig Eidelberg, (31, 1957) "An Introduction to the Study of Narcissistic Mortification," Ludwig Eidelberg, (33, 1959) "A Second Contribution to the Study of the Narcissistic Mortification," Ludwig Eidelberg, (34, 1960) "Primary and Secondary Narcissism," Ludwig Eidelberg and J. N. Palmer

The Psychoanalytic Review (33, 1951) "In Pursuit of Happiness," Ludwig Eidelberg

Pyramid Publications, extracts from *Take off Your Mask,* Ludwig Eidelberg, and *The Dark Urge,* Ludwig Eidelberg

Random House, *Perversions, Psychodynamics and Therapy,* S. Lorand and M. Balint (eds.), "Analysis of a Case of a Male Homosexual," Ludwig Eidelberg

Routledge and Kegan Paul Ltd., extracts from *Man, Morals and Society,* J. Flugel

Editorial Board

Introduction

When Freud created the science of psycho-analysis he and his pupils introduced many scientific terms which initially were defined only vaguely. Later, many new terms, including alterations in old ones, were instituted and concepts borrowed from other sciences or from the common language were altered but never properly redefined. Contributions from many different languages made consistent translation a problem. As well, the terms and concepts of psychoanalysis (or any science), reflecting a dynamic development, were subjected to conflicting interpretations. It is our belief that the proper delineation of psychoanalytic terminology will markedly decrease the misunderstandings that presently exist, misconceptions which seriously complicate the activity of those who report what they discover, criticize what they are taught, and examine the data they receive from their colleagues.

We knew in advance that we would not succeed in assembling all the terms employed in psychoanalysis. Equally, it was to be expected that not all our colleagues would agree with the interpretations that have been rendered. In spite of this and other difficulties, it seemed to us that the need for a psychoanalytic encyclopedia was so great that it was only proper to proceed.* The reader, we agree, will inevitably notice the absence of some

---

*Two other similar efforts were undertaken but never completed: by Adolf G. Störfer, "Samples from a *Dictionary of Psychoanalysis* Now in Progress" (*Z*, 10, 1924), and by Richard F. Sterba, *Psychoanalytic Dictionary* (IntPV, 1936).

definitions, and he will find others to be controversial. In our opinion, it is our warrant to present a controversial interpretation, where the term has been properly defined, in order to provoke discussion that can lead to the detection and correction of errors.

We have not limited ourselves to the terminology used only by a majority of psychoanalysts, for scientific problems are not solved by a vote or ex cathedra decisions. A term which is not presently in wide usage may become so in the near future. Nonetheless, terms which are duplications of older ones probably should be eliminated. It also seems proper to overlook those terms which are used in a manner contradictory to the basic laws of methodology.

We have decided to include not only such analytical terms as *negation* and *sublimation* but more general terms as well, such as *envy*, *jealousy* and *love*. Where an adequate general description of the term can be found in a standard dictionary, we have confined ourselves to the psychological significance of the term. Where this is not the case, a more general exploration of the term has been undertaken to bridge the gap between its common English usage and its psychoanalytic meaning. We should also like to point out that a suggested usage is advanced only to help eliminate an existing semantic misunderstanding. For reasons of accuracy, those quotations which are advanced in support of an interpretation are rendered as they appear in the original (or its translation). This latter circumstance has led to the inclusion of some syntactical differences (e.g. U.S. vs. English spelling). In this, we can only plead the cause of scholarship and point out that elsewhere American usage predominates.

While it is obvious that the interpretations offered in this encyclopedia are the result of a joint effort put forth by all its editors, it seems only fair to suggest that its editor-in-chief be blamed for whatever errors there are that have gone undetected. Finally, we have all tried to abide by Freud's dictum: *We have made up our minds to simplify nothing and to hide nothing. If we cannot see things clearly we will at least see clearly what the obscurities are.**

I would not have succeeded in this effort if it were not for the assistance of Dr. Charles I. Kaufman who was instrumental in helping me obtain a generous grant from the National Institute of Mental Health. I should also like to thank Dr. Sandor Lorand and Dr. Mortimer Ostow for their valuable contributions. I wish especially to thank Mr. Meyer M. Marvald, the Executive Officer of the Downstate Medical Center, Psychiatry Department, for his devoted assistance and his enthusiastic support. To my wife, Marthe, I extend my great appreciation for her six-year editorial labors. I also extend my thanks to Mr. Lee Jacobson and to my Executive Secretary, Miss Michele Robbins, for her assistance. Finally, I wish to draw your

*Freud, S., "Inhibitions, Symptoms and Anxiety." *SE*, 20:124, 1959.

attention to the herculean efforts of two men, Mr. James Strachey and Dr. Alexander Grinstein, whose efforts in the preparation of their respective works, *The Complete Psychological Works of Sigmund Freud* and *The Index of Psychoanalytic Writings*, have made measurably easier the writing of this present volume.

LUDWIG EIDELBERG, M.D.

Prologue[*]

Avec peur et avec reproche

$\mathbf{M}$ost analysts today are convinced that psychoanalysis is a science and that its specific application to the treatment of patients or the examination of various subjects (e.g., anthropology, sociology, aesthetics, etc.) may be referred to as a combination of applied science and art. Many authors have already presented the criteria on which this concept of analysis is predicated, but it may be advantageous to reexamine and clarify some of the original assumptions in such a way as to make them more understandable to the trained analyst and the informed layman.

Although psychoanalysis appears to be more and more accepted by the public at large, it is in large measure merely a kind of lip service. Actually, there exists at present a serious threat to the further development of psychoanalysis, both from without and within. The arguments of both enemy camps have to be investigated: those who openly dispute the scientific character of psychoanalysis, and those who discredit and dilute Freud's ideas by more subtle means.

If one does not regard psychoanalysis as a religion, it is clearly incumbent on each analyst to try to make some contribution of his own to that which we have inherited from the founder of psychoanalysis. Further, apart from whatever each of us does, our societies and institutes are expected to

---

*In an altered form, first published in *Revue Française de Psychanalyse*, Presses Universitaires de France, No. 4, July 1959 and *American Imago*, 21:175–179, 1964.

add their constructive weight by remaining dedicated to the teaching of psychoanalysis and to the stimulation of further research.

Our institutes and societies must learn to navigate cautiously between the shoals of strict and dogmatic adherence to whatever Freud discovered and the shallow waters of the so-called eclectics. Those of us who are in positions of leadership have to decide just how orthodox we ought to be, what papers are to be accepted as properly analytical, and who is to teach in our institutes. In order to achieve further progress, the scientifically minded psychoanalyst must remain aware of the limitations of this young science. Instead of regarding our formulations as final and burying unsolved problems, we should constantly go out of our way to expose and examine them.

The application of psychoanalysis is also an art. The once prevalent notion that science is concerned only about what is true, while art concentrates on expressing beauty has been largely abandoned. Today, most of us would agree that science does not represent the final truth, but simply tries to express as much truth as it is humanly possible to express at a given time in human development. We would agree that art also expresses truth, although it uses another approach. The laws of artistic expression are different from those of science, but the ultimate goal of truth is the same.

There are some who claim that science may be taught, but art may not; yet the theories and techniques of both science and art are being taught all over the world. There are those who insist that science may profit by criticism, but art may not; they consider criticism of art to be a waste of time, a sign of creative impotence. Still, it cannot be denied that we are all inclined to criticize works of art, and some of us even insist on publishing these personal views as if they might have value for others, although such critical statements about art often appear foolish after a while. Similarly, it would be a mistake to assume that the critics of scientific works are always right, even if competent and of high academic standing.

It is not only the enemies of psychoanalysis who dispute its scientific character, but also some of its over-zealous friends. They regard psychoanalysis as the ultimate philosophical system, which contains final answers to all questions, even though it must be admitted that not all patients are cured and some do not even improve (in which respect psychoanalysis resembles other medical therapies).

Psychoanalysis is not a religion and Freud is not considered its prophet. He always wanted his pupils and patients to show a benevolent skepticism toward his teachings and resented an immediate emotional approval. Many things he said he changed when he discovered new facts which made such changes necessary. He certainly was more tolerant with others than with himself. His uncanny ability to separate inner reality from external reality, to differentiate between fantasy and sense organ perceptions, make his writings clear and precise.

Freud was often accused of being rigid and stubborn. The fact is that he was always friendly, willing to listen and examine the arguments of his critics. It is difficult to deny that most of the arguments of his critics represented their resistance to the new discoveries. Freud had to rely on himself as being able to evaluate and modify his views. He was not always right, but he never hesitated to admit it when he discovered that he had been wrong. We may not always agree with what he said but at least we can understand what he meant.

By our own earnest efforts, we may be able to arrive at a better delineation of the structure of the unconscious personality, and thus eliminate some of the contradictions which, aided and abetted by our personal blind spots, keep blurring our own psychoanalytic understanding. But the actual application of psychoanalysis to the problem at hand, the treatment of a patient, must, of necessity, include the presence of a personal equation. Here the analyst may use his artistic ability with a free hand.

Knowledge is not science, although science is based on our ability to utilize knowledge. By the same token, skill is not art. An analyst resembles a teacher more than a doctor, and it stands to reason that a dull teacher is not as effective as an inspired and passionate one. The so-called passivity of the analyst is often confused with a kind of ivory-tower attitude. While it is true that the analyst is not personally involved with his patient, it is also true that he undertakes to work with the patient only on condition that treatment is sought as a means of getting well, not as an excuse for remaining sick.

It is the legitimate aim of psychoanalysis to destroy the patient's resistance to seeing what is going on in the unconscious part of his own personality. This resistance may be torn asunder only by the combined use of the analyst's scientific knowledge of the structure of the unconscious, and his artistic ability to appeal to the patient's total personality, so as to establish close contact with him, arouse his curiosity, decrease his fears, augment his courage, and improve his skill in using words to penetrate his unconscious to further an understanding of himself. The analyst whose own emotions are bottled up, who is afraid to show how he feels about the battle taking place on the couch, who cannot rely on his own unconscious to bring in appropriate material at the right time, who has to consult his notebooks and repeat without conviction what he has been taught, will naturally fail to gain the trust and cooperation of the patient.

If it is true that neurosis occurs when part of the conscious personality of the patient is invaded by derivatives of the unconscious, establishing a state within a state over which the patient has no control, it is obviously necessary, in a therapeutic analysis, to reverse the process. The conscious part of the patient's personality must be helped to invade this unconscious enclave and reassert its rule. This does not imply a sort of professional hypochondriasis so that we always have to examine what is going on within us; it does imply that it is important for us to have the power to make conscious whatever is repressed.

Psychoanalysis, or rather the cluster of psychoanalysts, has grown from the small group of pupils who originally gathered around Freud into a large international organization with many branches throughout the world. The problem of administration, originally handled by Freud himself, has become so complicated that it now takes a number of psychoanalysts, serving as officers of the various organizations, to cope with the task. Most analysts, having chosen their profession because of an intense interest in the study of the unconscious and the treatment of patients, are not particularly interested in problems of administration. The original rules and regulations of the various analytical societies were formulated in such a way so as to guarantee the optimum scientific development of psychoanalysis. However, the execution of these rules takes a considerable amount of energy from those who would prefer to concentrate on purely scientific matters. Fortunately, we do have a number of men and women who don't mind spending part of their time doing the administrative work of the various societies and institutes.

Since our societies are based on democratic principles, with officers elected by secret ballot, their decisions reflect the opinion of the majority of psychoanalysts. To be sure, scientific problems cannot be solved by voting, but such practical questions as who should be admitted as a student, who should be appointed to a teaching post, and which papers deserve to be published, are necessarily decided by the officers, acting as trustees for all the members.

Because many psychoanalysts have little or no interest in administrative affairs, the small minority doing the necessary work inevitably acquire a certain amount of power. While it is true, as Lord Acton put it, that "power corrupts," the continual change-over in leadership is intended to prevent accumulation of too much executive power in the hands of one person or clique. Any small minority, not really interested in the pursuit of science, but only eager to gratify aggression under the mask of taking care of our societies, certainly could play havoc with psychoanalysis should they be permitted to run amok.

Such important details as selection of candidates and teachers, preparation and selection of syllabi, and publication of papers in our journals, could be impaired if personal whims were to influence the decisions of our officers. If friendship and flattery were permitted to influence administration of our groups, the scientific character and integrity of our profession would perish. Fortunately, we have many individuals of fine caliber who may be depended on to do what is fair and just, even if it is sometimes not to their liking.

It cannot be denied that some of our decisions have been, and will continue to be, faulty and that some good men were rejected, while undesirable ones were encouraged to join us. But as we are all human beings, we cannot avoid occasional errors. It is obvious that censorship cannot be applied in our work; freedom to say what we consider proper must be preserved. Any attempt to centralize or organize the opinions of analysts, in such a way as to sacrifice their individual views, could only lead to disaster. The paper curtain of silence which screens out all that is not in keeping with the thinking of a ruling clique, together with the insidious flattery of the fraternity of mutual admiration and citation, could very well ruin our work.

Let us therefore peruse the papers of our younger colleagues with particular care, lest we repeat such shameful examples by rejecting what is true, just because the idea had not occurred to us first, or because we don't happen to like the author. It is well to remember that we all have a tendency to accept, with enthusiasm, things that were stated ever so long ago and have become familiar to us over a long period of time. This thought may be helpful in controlling our resistance against all that is new, without, of course, bending over backwards and applauding everything that comes along, regardless of merit. Modesty, regular attendance at scientific meetings, eagerness to conform, oblige, and appease, and the ability to keep a civil tongue in one's head instead of shouting out in defiance and protest— all these—are not always signs of a creative mentality.

While practical questions, such as how many hours of supervision a student requires or who should serve as a society's officer, can be solved by voting, scientific questions must go unanswered, remaining open to testing and investigation indefinitely. Consequently, we should concentrate on stimulating the curiosity and interest of those who are willing to work for our associations, though it brings them nothing in the way of money or recognition, rather than trying to determine who is most popular or what explanation to unanimously accept.

While it is true that original analytical research does not necessarily increase a member's prestige, and certainly does not enhance his financial status, it is bound to mobilize a certain amount of envy on the part of his colleagues. The picture is not very bright, however, for the young psychoanalyst who, overwhelmed by what he has discovered, naïvely believes that everyone will praise him for his efforts. Only after years of crushing disappointments will he learn, if he has managed to survive, how to disguise what is new without distorting what is true. The knowledge that modesty is a necessary virtue is acquired only slowly.

I belong to those unfortunate beings who do not always react with joy when surprised by an original paper. Indeed, I often experience a distinct hostility and try to reject the paper or at least minimize what it contains. It is only after I realize that my rejection is caused by my resistance and I lay open the unconscious factors responsible for it that I am able to examine the paper in a scientific manner. It seems to me that without such self-analysis I would not have succeeded in understanding and assimilating many contributions of Freud and his pupils.

As a democratically oriented group, we elect officers who make and enforce necessary decisions. They act in line with the guiding principles formulated by us through both participation and neglect. Their work is continuously scrutinized by some members, while others sedulously avoid this responsibility, seeking only to be left in peace. It is not easy to formulate specific recommendations to guide us in this precarious period, nor is it easy to make concrete suggestions about what is proper and necessary for the further development of psychoanalysis. Obviously, we have no alternative but to try again and again to clear away those factors which threaten to obscure our vision, emasculate our drives, and bury the work of Freud.

Caveant consules ne quid detrimentum capiat res publica.

Contents

Acknowledgments vii

Introduction xi

Prologue xv

List of Entries xxiii

Abbreviations xxxi

Alphabetical Entries 1

Bibliography 483

Index 521

List of Entries

A

100 Abraham, Karl
101 Abreaction
102 Absence
103 Abstinence
104 Abstract Thinking
105 Absurdity
106 Abulia
107 Accident Proneness
108 Acrophobia
109 Acting In
110 Acting Out
111 Action (Act)
112 Active
113 Active Play Therapy
114 Active Therapy
115 Activity and
    Passivity
116 Actual Neuroses
117 Adaptation
118 Addiction
119 Adolescence
120 Aerophagia
121 Aesthetic Pleasure
122 Affect
123 Agent Provocateur

124 Agnosia
125 Aggression
126 Aim-Inhibited Drives
    (Instincts)
127 Alcoholism
128 Alimentary Orgasm
129 Alloplastic
130 Altruism
131 Ambiguity
132 Ambivalence
133 Ambivalent Oscilla-
    tion
134 Amentia
135 Amnesia
136 Amphimixis
137 Anaclitic
138 Anaclitic Depression
139 Anagogic
    Interpretation
140 Anal Phase
141 Analytical Insight
142 Analyzing
    Instrument
143 Ananke
144 Anhedonia
145 Animism
146 Anorexia Nervosa

147 Anthropology and
    Psychoanalysis
148 Anticipation
149 Antithetical
150 Anxiety
151 Anxiety Neurosis
152 Anxiety State
153 Aphanisis
154 Aphasia
155 Apperceptive Distor-
    tion
156 Appersonation
157 Applied Psychoanaly-
    sis
158 Arc De Cercle
159 As-If Personality
160 Attraction of the
    Forbidden
161 Autism
162 Autoerotism
163 Autohypnosis
164 Automatic Obedience
165 Automatism
166 Autonomy
167 Autoplastic
168 Autosymbolism
169 Avoidance

xxiii

B

200 Barrier
201 Basic Rule
202 Beating Fantasies
203 Birth Trauma
204 Bisexuality
205 Blushing
206 Body Image
207 Body Language
208 Borderline Cases
209 Boredom
210 Breast Complex
211 Breast Envy
212 Bronchial Asthma

C

300 Caricature
301 Castration Anxiety
302 Castration Complex
303 Catharsis
304 Cathexis
305 Causality
306 Censorship
307 Central Ego
308 Character Neurosis
309 Character Traits
310 Child Analysis
311 Child Psychiatry
312 Choice of a Neurosis
313 Civilization
314 "Civilized Sexual Morality and Modern Nervous Illness"
315 Classification of Jokes
316 Claustrophobia
317 Cloaca
318 Collective Unconscious
319 Color in Dreams
320 Comic
321 Comparative Pathology of the Neuroses

322 Component Instinct
323 Compulsive Masturbation
324 Concept of Time
325 Condensation
326 Conflict
327 Congenital (Connate)
328 Conscience
329 Conscious
330 Content and Form of a Joke
331 Control
332 Conversion and Conversion Symptoms
333 Coprophagia (Coprophagy)
334 Coprophilia
335 Countercathexis (Anticathexis)
336 Counterphobia
337 Countertransference
338 Creativity
339 Criticism
340 Cross Section of Neurosis
341 Crying (Weeping)
342 Curiosity

D

400 Daydreams
401 Day Residues in Dreams
402 Decompensation
403 Defense Mechanisms
404 Deferred Obedience
405 Deferred Reaction
406 Déjà Raconté
407 Déjà Vu
408 Delay of Discharge
409 Delibidinization (Desexualization)
410 Delusions
411 Delusions of Grandeur
412 Delusions of Observation

413 Delusions of Persecution
414 Denial (Disavowal)
415 Depersonalization
416 Depression
417 Derealization
418 Destiny Neurosis (Fate Neurosis)
419 Deuterophallic
420 Discharge
421 Displacement
422 "Dissolution of the Oedipus Complex, The"
423 Doctor Game
424 Dora
425 Dreams
426 Dream-Screen
427 Dream-Work
428 Drugs
429 Dynamic Approach

E

500 Economic Approach
501 Ego
502 Ego-Alien
503 Ego and Self
504 Ego and Sensorium
505 Ego and Sense Organ Perception
506 Ego Boundaries
507 Ego Functions
508 Ego-Ideal
509 Ego Instincts
510 Ego Strength and Weakness
511 Ego-Syntonic
512 Ejaculatio Praecox
513 Ejaculatio Retardata
514 Elation
515 Emotion
516 Emotional Insight
517 Empathy
518 Endopsychic Perception

519 Entitlement (Narcissistic Entitlement)
520 Entropy
521 Envy
522 Epileptic Personality
523 Epistemophilic
524 Eros
525 Erotic Transference
526 Erotogenic Zones
527 Erythrophobia
528 Escapade
529 Ethical Approach
530 Euphoria
531 Evaluation of Psychoanalytic Therapy
532 Exaggeration
533 Exhibitionism
534 External Identification

F

600 Face-Breast Equation
601 Family Romance
602 Fanaticism
603 Fantasy
604 Fascination
605 Fear
606 Feelings in Dreams
607 Feminine Masochism
608 Ferenczi, Sandor
609 Fetishism
610 Fixation
611 Flight into Fantasy
612 Flight into Health
613 Flight into Illness
614 Flight into Reality
615 Forepleasure
616 Fore-Unpleasure
617 Fragmentation
618 Free Will
619 Freud, Sigmund
620 Frigidity
621 Frigidity and Masochism
622 Frustration

G

700 Genital Phase
701 Group Paranoia

H

800 Hair Pulling
801 Hallucinations
802 Happiness
803 Hate
804 Hebephrenia
805 Heredity
806 Hostilodynamics
807 Humiliation
808 Humor
809 Hunger for Stimuli
810 Hypnagogic Phenomena
811 Hypnoanalysis
812 Hypnoid State
813 Hypnosis
814 Hypochondriasis
815 Hysterical Conversion
816 Hysterical Materialization

I

900 Id
901 Idealization
902 Identification
903 Illusion
904 Imitation
905 Impotence
906 Impotence and Masochism
907 Impulse
908 Incest
909 Infancy
910 Infantile Masturbation
911 Inferiority Feelings
912 Influencing Machine
913 Inhibition
914 "Inhibitions, Symptoms and Anxiety"
915 Insomnia
916 Instinct (Instinctual Drive)
917 Instinct of Self-Assertion
918 Instinctual Aim
919 Instinctualization of Smell
920 Instinctual Need
921 Instinctual Vicissitudes
922 Intellectual Activity in Dreams
923 Intellectual Insight
924 Internal Identification
925 Interpretation
926 Intimidation
927 Introego (Undifferentiated Ego Conscience)
928 Introject
929 Introjection
930 Introversion (Fantasy Cathexis)
931 Isakower Phenomenon
932 Isolation

J

1000 Jamais Phenomenon
1001 Jealousy
1002 Joke (Wit)

K

1100 Kleptomania

L

1200 Language
1201 Latency Period
1202 Latent Homosexuality
1203 Latent Psychosis
1204 Laughter
1205 Law and Psychoanaly-
     sis
1206 Law of Constancy
1207 Lay Analysis
1208 Libidinal Phases
1209 Libidinal Types
1210 Libido
1211 Listening with the
     Third Ear
1212 Little Hans
1213 Localization of a Symp-
     tom
1214 Love
1215 Lure of the Past

M

1300 Magic
1301 Making Faces
1302 Maladjustment
1303 Manic-Depressive
1304 Mannerism
1305 Marriage
1306 Masculinity and Femin-
     inity
1307 Masochism
1308 Masochistic Mechanism
1309 Mass (Group)
     Psychology
1310 Mass Hysteria
1311 Masturbation
1312 Masturbation Addicts
1313 Masturbation Equiva-
     lents
1314 Masturbation Fantasies
1315 Matriarchy
1316 Maturation

1317 Megalomania
1318 Melancholia
1319 Menstruation
1320 Mental (Psychic)
1321 Metaphoric Language
1322 Metapsychology
1323 Micropsia
1324 Micropsychophysiology
1325 Misogyny
1326 Mneme
1327 Money
1328 Morality
1329 Moral Masochism
1330 Moral Responsibility
     and Dreams
1331 Motility
1332 Motility in Dreams
1333 Mourning
1334 Mutism
1335 Mystic Union
1336 Mythology

N

1400 Narcissism
1401 Narcissistic Gain
1402 Narcissistic Mortifica-
     tion
1403 Narcissistic Need
1404 Narcissistic Neurosis
1405 Narcissistic Scar
1406 Narcolepsy
1407 Necrophilia
1408 Need for Punishment
1409 Negation
1410 Negative Oedipus
     Complex
1411 Negative Therapeutic
     Reaction
1412 Negative Therapeutic
     Reactions and Maso-
     chism
1413 Negative Tropism
1414 Negativism
1415 Neologism

1416 Neurasthenia
1417 Neuropsychoses of
     Defense
1418 Neuroses (Psychoneur-
     oses)
1419 Neurosis and Psycho-
     sis
1420 Neurosis as a Negative
     of Perversion
1421 Neutralization
1422 Nightmare (Pavor Noc-
     turnus)
1423 Nihilism
1424 Nirvana Principle
1425 Nocturnal Enuresis
1426 Normality
1427 Normal Masturbation
1428 Nuclei
1429 Nymphomania

O

1500 Obesity
1501 Object Choice (Ana-
     clitic and Narcissis-
     tic)
1502 Obliging Dreams
1503 Obsessional Brooding
1504 Obsessive-Compulsive
     Neurosis
1505 Occult
1506 Oceanic Feeling
1507 Oedipus Complex
1508 Omnipotence of
     Thought
1509 Onychophagia
     (Nailbiting)
1510 Optimism
1511 Oral Pessimism
1512 Oral Phase
1513 Organic
1514 Orgasm (Climax)
1515 Orgastic Impotence
1516 Overdetermination
1517 Overt Homosexuality

P

1600 Pain
1601 Pair of Dreams
1602 Pansexualism
1603 Paramnesia
1604 Paranoid Condition (State)
1605 Paranoid-Schizoid Position
1606 Parapathy
1607 Paraphrenia
1608 Parapraxis
1609 Parasitic Superego
1610 Paresis
1611 Passive
1612 Passive-Receptive Longing
1613 Pathognomy
1614 Pathoneurosis
1615 Pavor Nocturnus
1616 Penis Envy
1617 Peptic Ulcer
1618 Perception
1619 Perceptual Consciousness
1620 Persona
1621 Personal Myth
1622 Perversion
1623 Petrifaction
1624 Phallic Character
1625 Phallic Mother
1626 Phallic or Hysterical Character
1627 Phallic Phase
1628 Phallic Pride
1629 Phallic Woman
1630 Phantom Limb
1631 Phobia
1632 Phobic Character
1633 Pity
1634 Pleasure Principle
1635 Pleasure-Unpleasure Principle and Masochism
1636 Polarities
1637 Polycrates Complex
1638 Polymorph Perverse
1639 Positive Tropism

1640 Postambivalent Phase
1641 Postoedipal
1642 Preconscious
1643 Prediction
1644 Pregenitality
1645 Pregenital Masturbatory Equivalent
1646 Pregnancy
1647 Prelogical (Primitive) Thinking
1648 Premenstrual Disorders (Tension)
1649 Preoedipal
1650 Preoedipal Mother Attachment
1651 Prephallic Masturbation Equivalents
1652 Pride
1653 Primal Fantasy
1654 Primal Scene
1655 Primary Identification
1656 Primary Masochism
1657 Primary (Paranosic) Gain in Neurosis
1658 Primary Process
1659 Primitive
1660 Primitive Superego
1661 Progerism
1662 Projection
1663 Projective Counteridentification
1664 Projective Identification
1665 Promiscuity
1666 Protophallic
1667 Protopsyche
1668 Pseudodebility (Pseudoimbecility)
1669 Pseudohallucination (Illusion)
1670 Pseudo-Hypersexuality
1671 Pseudoidentification
1672 Pseudologia Fantastica
1673 Psychiatry
1674 Psychic Apparatus
1675 Psychic Determinism
1676 Psychic (Mental) Energy
1677 Psychic Inertia
1678 Psychic Reality
1679 Psychoanalysis

1680 Psychoanalytic Anthropology
1681 Psychoanalytic Dictionary
1682 Psychoanalytic Methodology
1683 Psychodynamics
1684 Psychogenesis
1685 "Psychopathology of Everyday Life, The"
1686 Psychopathy
1687 Psychosis
1688 Psychosomatic
1689 Psychosomatic Suicide
1690 Psychotic Character
1691 Psychotic Core
1692 Puberty
1693 Pun
1694 Purified Pleasure Ego
1695 Pyromania

Q

1700 Quality
1701 Quantitative Approach

R

1800 Racial Memory
1801 Rage
1802 Rape
1803 Raptus Actions
1804 Rationalization
1805 Rat Man
1806 Reaction Formation
1807 Reading
1808 Reality Principle
1809 Reassurance
1810 Rebelliousness
1811 Rebirth Fantasy
1812 Recovery Wish

1813 Recurrent Dreams
1814 Reflex Act
1815 Regression
1816 Relativity of Reality
1817 Relaxation
1818 Relaxation Principle
1819 Religious Faith
1820 Remorse
1821 Repetition Compulsion
1822 Repression
1823 Rescue Fantasy
1824 Resistance
1825 Respiratory Erotism
1826 Respiratory Introjection
1827 Retention Hysteria
1828 Return of the Repressed
1829 Revenge
1830 Reward by the Super-ego
1831 Rhythm and Periodicity
1832 Rituals
1833 Rorschach Test
1834 Rule of Abstinence

S

1900 Sacrifice
1901 Sadism
1902 Satisfaction (Gratification) of Instincts
1903 Satyriasis
1904 Scapegoat Mechanism
1905 Schizoid Character
1906 Schizophrenia
1907 Schizophrenic Surrender
1908 Schreber Case
1909 Science and Magic
1910 Scopophilia
1911 Screen Memory
1912 Secondary (Epinosic) Gain in Neurosis
1913 Secondary Identification
1914 Secondary Process
1915 Self

1916 Self-Analysis
1917 Self-Esteem and Masochism
1918 Self-Observation
1919 Sensation
1920 Sense of Guilt
1921 Sense of Identity
1922 Sequestration
1923 Sexual Curiosity
1924 Sexual Inhibition
1925 Sexuality
1926 Sexualization and Aggressivization of Anxiety
1927 Sexualization and Aggressivization of Ego Functions
1928 Sexualization and Aggressivization of Speech
1929 Sexualization and Aggressivization of Thinking
1930 Shame
1931 Shamelessness
1932 Short-Term Therapy
1933 Signal Anxiety
1934 Simultaneous Analysis of Mother and Child
1935 Skin Eroticism
1936 Sleep
1937 Slips of the Tongue
1938 Social Compliance
1939 Social Instinct in Man
1940 Social Mindfulness
1941 Society and Self
1942 Somatic Compliance
1943 Somatic Stimuli and Dreams
1944 Speech Functions
1945 Sphincter Control
1946 Sphincter Morality
1947 Spiders
1948 Spoken Words in Dreams
1949 Stage Fright
1950 Stammering (Stuttering)
1951 Stigmata
1952 Strangulated Affect

1953 Structural (Topographic) Approach
1954 Sublimation
1955 Success Neurosis
1956 Suffocation Fears
1957 Suggestion
1958 Suicide
1959 Sunday (Weekend) Neurosis
1960 Superego
1961 Superstition
1962 Supervalent
1963 Supervision
1964 Suppression
1965 Symbiosis
1966 Symbolization
1967 Symptomatic Act
1968 Synthesis
1969 Systematic (Qualitative or Descriptive) Approach

T

2000 Taboo
2001 Teaching Analysis
2002 Technique of Psychoanalysis
2003 Teleology (Finality)
2004 Telepathy
2005 Temperature Eroticism
2006 Thanatos
2007 Thematic Apperception Test (T. A. T.)
2008 Therapy
2009 Thinking
2010 Threshold Symbolism
2011 Tic
2012 Toilet Training
2013 Tolerance of Tension
2014 Torticollis
2015 Totem
2016 Training Analysis
2017 Transference
2018 Transference and Sex
2019 Transference-Love

2020 Transference Neurosis
2021 Transience
2022 Transient Ego-Ideal
2023 Transvestitism
2024 Trauma
2025 Traumatic Neurosis
2026 Traumatic Neurosis and Dreams
2027 Trial Analysis
2028 Trial Identification
2029 Turning Round Upon the Subject's Own Self
2030 Typical Dreams

U

2100 Ulcerative Colitis
2101 Uncanny
2102 Unconscious
2103 Unconscious Action
2104 Unconscious Affects
2105 Unconscious Emotions and Feelings
2106 Unconscious Significance of Speech

2107 Undisguised Dreams
2108 Undoing
2109 Unpleasure
2110 Unpleasure-Pleasure Principle
2111 Uranism
2112 Urination

V

2200 Vagina Dentata
2201 Vaginal Father
2202 Vaginismus
2203 Value
2204 Verbalization
2205 Vertigo
2206 Virginity Taboo

W

2300 War Neurosis
2301 "Wayward Youth"
2302 Weltanschauung
2303 Wet Dream

2304 Wild Psychoanalysis
2305 Wit in Dreams
2306 Wolf Man
2307 Word Association Test
2308 World Salad
2309 Words
2310 Working Through
2311 Writer's Block
2312 Writer's Cramp

X

2400 Xenophobia

Y

2500 Yawning

Z

2600 Zooerasty
2601 Zoophobia

Abbreviations

ActaNeuroBelg	Acta neurologica et psychiatrica Belgica
AdvPsychiat	*Advances in Psychiatry*, M.B. Cohen (ed.)
AHPsa	*American Handbook of Psychiatry*, S. Arieti (ed.). Basic Books, Inc., 1959
AJMS	American Journal of Medical Science
AJP	American Journal of Psychology
AJPt	American Journal of Psychotherapy
Al	Almanach
AMAANP	American Medical Association Archives of Neurology and Psychiatry
AmAnthrop	American Anthropologist
AmIm	American Imago
AmJOrthopsychiat	American Journal of Orthopsychiatry
AmPsych	American Psychologist
ANP	Archives of Neurology and Psychiatry
AnRevMed	Annual Review of Medicine
AnSurvPsa	*Annual Survey of Psychoanalysis: A Comprehensive Survey of Current Psychoanalytic Theory and Practice*, J. Frosch (ed.). International Universities Press, 1952
AnthropQuart	Anthropological Quarterly

AP	Archiv für Psychiatrie und Nervenkrankheiten
APPO	Acta Psychotherapeutica, Psychosomatica et Ortho-paedagogica
ArchKrimin	Archiv für Kriminologie
ASP	Journal of Abnormal and Social Psychology
AU	Allen & Unwin, London, England
BaustPsa	*Bausteine zur Psychoanalyse*, S. Ferenczi, Huber, 1939
BAPA	Bulletin of the American Psychoanalytic Association
BB	Basic Books, Inc., Publishers, New York, N. Y.
BJEP	British Journal of Educational Psychology
BJP	British Journal of Psychology
Bl	Blakiston Division, of McGraw-Hill Book Company, New York, N. Y.
BMC	Bulletin of the Menninger Clinic
BMJ	British Medical Journal
BML	Boston Medical Library
BPAP	Bulletin of the Philadelphia Association for Psycho-analysis
BPV	Berlin Psychoanalytischer Verlag
Br	Robert Brunner, New York, N. Y.
BullN Y AcadMed	Bulletin of the New York Academy of Medicine
C	Zentralblatt für Psychoanalyse und Psychotherapie
CCT	Charles C. Thomas Publishers, Springfield, Ill.
CD	Child Development
Child-FamDig	Child-Family Digest
Cit	Citadel Press, New York, N. Y.
CJM	Cincinnati Journal of Medicine
Cl	Clark University Press
ClinPath	Journal of Clinical Psychopathology
CNP	Zentralblatt für Nervenheilkunde und Psychiatrie
CorUP	Cornell University Press, Ithaca, N. Y.
CP	The Clarendon Press, of Oxford University Press, Inc., New York, N. Y.
CUP	Columbia University Press, New York, N. Y.
CWD	C. W. Daniel Co., Essex, England
D	Dodd, Mead & Co., New York, N. Y.
DAM	Dartmouth Alumni Press
DAW	Deutsche Arbeit und Wirtschaftszeitung
DM	David McKay Co., Inc., New York, N. Y.
D&N	Delachaux and Niestle, Paris, France

DR	Dingwall-Rock, New York, N. Y.
DtschMedWschr	Deutsche medizinische Wochenschrift
DtschZges	Deutsche Zeitschrift für die Gesamte Gerichtliche Medizin
DtschZNerveheilk	Deutsche Zeitschrift für Nervenheilkunde
E	Endocrinology
EJP	Egyptian Journal of Psychology
EvolutPsychiat	Evolution psychiatrique
FS	Farrar, Straus & Co., New York, N. Y. (Farrar, Straus & Giroux, Inc.)
G	Grove Press, Inc., New York, N. Y.
GCB	Garden City Books, New York, N. Y.
GP	Gorham Press, New York, N. Y.
G&S	Grune & Stratton, Inc., New York, N. Y.
H	Heller, Vienna, Austria
HB	Harcourt, Brace & Co., New York, N. Y. (Harcourt, Brace & World, Inc.)
HBP	Harper and Brothers, New York, N. Y. (Harper & Row, Publishers)
HH	Henry Holt & Co., Inc., New York, N. Y.
HPI	The Hogarth Press & the Institute of Psychoanalysis, London, England
Im	Imago
IntJgrpPT	International Journal of Group Psycho-Therapy
IntJPsa	International Journal of Psychoanalysis
IntJPsychol	International Journal of Psychology
IntPV	Internationaler psychoanalytischer Verlag
IUP	International Universities Press, New York, N. Y.
JAbP	Journal of Abnormal Psychology
JAMA	Journal of the American Medical Association
JAPA	Journal of the American Psychoanalytic Association
JCE	Journal of Clinical Endocrinology
JclinPath	Journal of Clinical Pathology
JclinPsychopath	Journal of Clinical Psychopathology
JconsultPsychol	Journal of Consulting Psychology
JCP	Journal of Criminal Psychopathology
JCPs	Journal of Child Psychiatry
JHH	Journal of the Hillside Hospital
JmentDef	American Journal of Mental Deficiency
JMS	Journal of Mental Science
JNMD	Journal of Nervous and Mental Diseases

Abbreviations

JNP	Journal of Neurology and Psychiatry
JP	Journal of Personality
JPediat	Journal of Pediatrics
JPhilos	Journal of Philosophy
JPN	Jahrbücher für Psychiatrie und Neurologie
JPsa	Jahrbuch der Psychoanalyse
JRoyAnthropInst	Journal of the Royal Anthropology Institute
JSP	Journal of Sexology and Psychoanalysis
KP	Kegan Paul, French, Trebner, London, England
L	J. B. Lippincott Co., Philadelphia, Pa.
Log	Loges Press, New York, N. Y.
M	British Journal of Medical Psychology
Mac	The Macmillan Co., New York, N. Y.
MedPr	Medical Press and Circular
MennQ	Menninger Quarterly
Mos	The C. V. Mosby Co., St. Louis, Mo.
MPN	Monatsschrift für Psychiatrie und Neurologie
MRR	Medical Review of Reviews
Mur	Murray, London, England
NeueArb	Neue Arbeiten zur ärztlichen Psychoanalyse
NewDir	*New Directions in Psycho-Analysis*, M. Klein, P. Heimann, & R. M. Money-Kyrle (eds.)
NewEngJMed	New England Journal of Medicine
NMDP	Nervous and Mental Diseases Publishing, Co., New York, N. Y.
Nor	W. W. Norton & Company, Inc., New York, N. Y.
NP	The Noonday Press, New York, N. Y.
NTvG	Nederlandsch Tydschrift voor Geneeskunde
NYMJ	New York Medical Journal
NYSJM	New York State Journal of Medicine
OF-CP	*Collected Papers of Otto Fenichel*. W. W. Norton & Company, Inc., 1953, 1954
OIP	Orgone Institute Press, New York, N. Y.
Ops	American Journal of Orthopsychiatry
OrgPath	*Organization and Pathology of Thought*, D. Rapaport (ed.). Columbia University Press, 1951
OUP	Oxford University Press, Inc., New York, N. Y.
OutPsa	*An Outline of Psychoanalysis*, C. Thompson, M. Mazer & E. Wittenberg (eds.). Random House, Inc., 1955
P	Psyche
PastoralPsychol	Pastoral Psychology

PEA	*Psychoanalytic Explorations in Art*, E. Kris. International Universities Press, 1952
PH	Prentice-Hall, Inc., Englewood Cliffs, N. J.
PL	Philosophical Library
PNW	Psychiatrisch-neurologische Wochenschrift
PPR	Philosophy and Phenomenal Research
PPsa	*Papers on Psycho-Analysis*, E. Jones. W. Wood, 1950
PQ	Psychiatric Quarterly
PQSupp	Psychiatric Quarterly Supplement
PraxKinderPsychol	Praxis der Kinderpsychologie und Kinderpsychiatrie
ProgNeurolPsychiat	*Progress in Neurology and Psychiatry*, E. Spiegel (ed.). Grune & Stratton, 1947–1952
ProgPT	Progress in Psychotherapy
PRSM	Proceedings of the Royal Society of Medicine
Ps	Psychiatry
PsaB	Psychoanalytische Bewegung
PsaP	Zeitschrift für Psychoanalytische Pädagogik
PsaPrx	Psychoanalytische Praxis: Vierteljahrschrift für die aktive Methode der Psychoanalyse
PsaSS	*Psychoanalysis and the Social Sciences*, G. Wilbur, & W. Muensterberger (eds.). International Universities Press, 1955
PsaStC	*The Psychoanalytic Study of the Child*, R. S. Eissler, A. Freud, H. Hartmann, & E. Kris (eds.). International Universities Press, 1945
PsaStudChar	*Psychoanalytische Studien zur Charakterbildung*, K. Abraham, Internationaler Psychoanalytischer Verlag, 1925
PsaT-IUP	*Psychoanalysis Today*, S. Lorand (ed.). International Universities Press, 1944
PsaVkb	*Psychoanalytisches Volksbuch*, P. Federn, & H. Meng (eds.). Huber, 1939
PSM	Psychosomatic Medicine
PsycholBull	Psychological Bulletin
PsycholRev	Psychological Review
PT	American Journal of Psychotherapy
PtPrx	Psychotherapeutische Praxis
PUP	Princeton University Press, Princeton, N. J.
Py	Pyramid Books, Almat Publishing Corp., New York, N. Y.
Q	Psychoanalytic Quarterly
QJSA	Quarterly Journal of Studies on Alcohol

R	Psychoanalytic Review
Re	Rensselaer Publishing Co., New York, N. Y.
RevPsicoanal	Revista de Psicoanálisis
RFPsa	Revue Française de Psychanalyse
RH	Random House, Inc., New York, N. Y.
RPsi	Revista de Psicoanálisis
RP	Ronald Press Company, New York, N. Y.
Sau	W. B. Saunders Co., Philadelphia, Pa.
SchweizANP	Schweizer Archiv für Neurologie und Psychiatrie
SchweizZPsychol	Schweizerische Zeitschrift für Psychologie und ihre Anwendungen
SE	*The Standard Edition of the Complete Works of Sigmund Freud*, J. Strachey (ed.). The Hogarth Press & The Institute of Psychoanalysis, 1953– .
SMS	Southern Medical and Surgical
SocProbl	Social Problems
Soc	American Journal of Sociology
SP	Staples Press, London, England
SPA	*Selected Papers of Karl Abraham*. The Hogarth Press & The Institute of Psychoanalysis, 1942
SPF	*The Selected Papers of Sandor Ferenczi*. Basic Books, Inc., 1955
SPJ	*Selected Papers of Ludwig Jekels*. International Universities Press, 1952
SPsa	*Sex in Psychoanalysis*, S. Ferenczi. Robert Brunner, 1950
TDR	Tulane Drama Revue
TP	Tudor Publishing, Co., New York, N. Y.
UCP	University of Chicago Press, Chicago, Ill.
ULP	University of London Press, London, England
V	The Viking Press, Inc., New York, N. Y.
VS	Verein Studentenwohl, Bonn, Germany
VTB	Visiting Teachers' Bulletin
WarMed	War Medicine
WK	Wiener klinische Wochenschrift
WMW	Wiener medizinische Wochenschrift
WUP	Wayne University Press, Detroit, Michigan
WW	The Williams & Wilkins Co., Baltimore, Md.
WWo	William Wood and Co., Baltimore, Md.
Y	Jahrbuch für psychoanalytische und psychopathologische Forschungen; Jahrbuch der Psychoanalyse

YBPsa	*The Yearbook of Psychoanalysis*, S. Lorand (ed.). International Universities Press, 1945
YUP	Yale University Publications
Z	Internationale Zeitschrift für ärztliche Psycho-analyse; Internationale Zeitschrift für Psycho-analyse
ZdiagnPsychol	Zeitschrift für diagnostische Psychologie und Per-sönlichkeitsforschung
ZNP	Zeitschrift für die gesamte Neurologie und Psychia-trie
ZPSM	Zeitschrift für psychosomatische Medizin
ZPt	Zentralblatt für Psychotherapie und ihre Grenz-gebiete einschliesslich der medizinischen Psy-chologie und psychischen Hygiene
ZPsychol	Zeitschrift für Psychologie
ZPsychopath	Zeitschrift für Psychopathologie
ZpsychosomMed	Zeitschrift für psychosomatische Medizin
ZSW	Zeitschrift für Sexualwissenschaft

Ihr naht euch wieder, schwankende Gestalten!
Die früh sich einst dem trüben Blick gezeigt.

—GOETHE

A

ABRAHAM, KARL, one of the founders of psychoanalysis, was not quite thirty in 1907 when he left Zurich for Berlin to commence his therapeutic work. His training in medical psychology, his extensive reading of the analytic literature, and his personal contact with Freud led him into psychoanalytic practice and, later, teaching. At thirty-three he founded and until his death led the Berlin Psychoanalytical Society. During his lifetime, he took an active part in current controversies that principally raged round the diverging theories of Jung and Rank. He was by nature a teacher, concerned not only with the analytical training of students but with the orientation of nonanalytical colleagues in the principles of psychoanalysis. It is small wonder then that his contributions covered an extensive field and tended to favor certain specific lines of approach.

In all, he published better than a hundred papers and four books during his brief lifetime. Their classification, as is characteristic of most psychoanalytical contributions, could be given under a number of other headings. Early studies of sexuality, for example, concentrating as they did on the history of the infantile libido, could be pigeonholed as studies in child mental development; infantile phantasy studies raise the question of the origin of myths; myths lead one to dream formations; dream formations to the technique of the neuroses, etc.

In his review of Abraham's work, Jones[1] commented on the fact that he was not a voluminous writer, and maintained that considering his early and sustained interest in the psychoses it was surprising that he was content to single out the depressive states for analysis. This comment is of course objective enough. In his personal and professional (expository) reactions, Abraham was ready, fluent and empathetic, regulating his written communications by the strict discipline of economic presentation. How this came about is difficult to determine, but I have no doubt that his early school training aroused a profound interest in philology and this was perhaps partly responsible for his economy of expression. Those who love the origins and meaning of words are not likely to squander their resources in superfluous verbiage.

During the last five years of his life, Abraham's contributions were increasingly frequent and expansive. He was then at the height of his powers, and I have no doubt that had he survived he would have proceeded to reorganize on an adequate scale the relation of analytical practice to analytical theory. This, I venture to think, would have been of inestimable value to the present generation of psychoanalysts whose metaphysical proclivities seem to me to outrun frequently their metapsychological capacities. On the whole, therefore, Abraham's work can best be valued in terms of his therapeutic preoccupations, allowing of course for the fact that clinical discoveries compel even the most matter-of-fact observer to dovetail them into a theoretical framework.

Proceeding on this assumption and classifying his various publications in terms of content and date of

1. Jones, E., "Introductory Memoir." *IntJPsa*, 7:155–189, 1926.

publication, it seems to me incontestable that Abraham was from first to last a clinical observer; thus, we may well subdivide his interests in the following series:

a. Psychoneuroses. Characteristically enough, he was concerned from 1908 on with the relation of dementia praecox to hysteria, with the relation of sexuality to alcoholism, and with the influences of family relationships in the psychology of the neuroses (a theme which continued to fascinate him). Abraham contributed year by year until the time of his death to the clinical features and etiology of the neuroses, paying attention almost impartially to the hysterias and obsessional neuroses. It might be said that the neuroses were his first psychoanalytical love; he contributed to an understanding of their various symptomatic aspects, describing the peculiar difficulties which arose in their treatment. Although a therapeutic optimist almost by nature, he was fully aware of the resistances that arose during their treatment; he dealt with them in a manner that might well be an example to those present day practitioners who are inclined to excuse their failures by attributing them to the depth of the patient's preneurotic (psychotic) difficulties.

b. Sexuality. Abraham returned to the subject of infantile sexuality, sketching out item by item the factors that played a part in the development of the neuroses. As time went on these etiological factors increased in complexity: from 1923 onward he plunged boldly into the vexing question of bisexuality and its relation to character development. In this connection he paid special attention to such clinical conditions as ejaculatio praecox, fetishism, impotence, and the like.

c. Stages of Libidinal Development. As has been suggested, it was inevitable that the foregoing contributions should lead Abraham to a more precise outline of the stages of mental development in children. From about 1917 onward, he was increasingly concerned with the influence of infantile sexual theory and of actual familial relationships on the mental development of the child. In 1925 he was still concerned with so far undocumented sexual theories and hysterical symptoms. He then began to correlate distinct phases in this development with characteristic mental disorders, perhaps his most important contribution to the theory and practice of psychoanalysis. He suggested that on the oral stage

we should differentiate between the wish to suck and the wish to bite; on the anal stage, between the wish to excrete and the wish to retain; and, finally, between the function of the penis urinating and producing sperm. The last of these might have been the forerunner of the separation between the phallic and genital, a concept explored by Freud.

d. Manic Depressive. From 1908 until the time of his death in 1925, Abraham's interest in the psychoses remained unabated. His papers on this subject were at first more factual in nature, but from 1921 onward he set himself the task of seriously placing the psychoses in the overall classification of mental disorders. Contrary to the view of Jones, I find it not at all surprising that he concentrated on the manic-depressive psychoses. Under Freud's caption of *narcissistic neuroses,* these constituted a transitional group of disorders, an understanding of the etiology of the deeper psychoses. In any case, the observations he made on the oral phases of component sexuality inevitably drove him to consider the fixation points of depression. Jumping ahead a few years, we find him in 1925 making his most important contribution to psychoanalysis: an outline of the developmental history of the libido on the basis of a study of mental disorders. Here, he was no doubt profoundly influenced by Freud's earlier work on grief and melancholia, which constituted one of the major steps toward an understanding of ego psychology and the part played in mental development by the aggressive impulses. Abraham's presentation was more systematic and clear-cut; it remains to this day the definitive pioneering work on the part played by the instincts in the formation of mental apparatus.

e. Character Psychology. Allowing for the inevitable overlap of classifications, it is appropriate to single out here Abraham's contributions to what today is referred to as the theory of ego formation. Perhaps the order of the above subheadings should be reversed, for in the early days the conscious part of the personality was little more than a basic mental concept linked indissolubly with the conscious control of impulse (in other words, with conflict). Character studies in fact constituted the earliest attempts to associate specific ego patterns and affective reactions with phases of instinctual development. At first these were somewhat isolated studies. Abraham's contributions to this subject were important, because he added extensively to our knowledge of the oral phase and its various components and substages, and because he sought to systematize the whole series of infantile phases up to and including the genital phase. He correlated these with a progressive series of character (ego) reactions, with the increasing complexity of object relations, their influence on the internal and largely unconscious mental structure and economy of the total ego. Finally, he sought to correlate what were originally called "fixation points" (not just of instinct but of ego structure and function) with a hierarchy of mental disorders. It is this convergence of a number of approaches which, in my opinion, is the outstanding feature of Abraham's work and gives a clue to the master plan of his psychoanalytical research. Abraham had a "tidy" mind and was never happier than when exercising his flair for systematization.

f. Dream Techniques and Interpretation. Here, his contributions were not so copious as those recorded above. Nonetheless, he showed a continuing interest in dream interpretation. His first essay, "Dream and Myth" (1909), belongs strictly to the section on applied analysis. From 1909 until 1923, he published a number of shorter communications on the subject with special reference to symbolism. Like many of his clinical communications, these could also be classified as contributions to psychoanalytic technique. Throughout, psychoanalysis was in a process of both clinical and theoretical expansion: each valid discovery or reliable reconstruction added to the therapeutic resources of both qualified analysts and student candidates.

g. Psychoanalytical Controversies. Abraham played a significant part in those controversies that appeared to him to threaten the scientific standing of psychoanalysis. Strictly speaking, these efforts should come under the heading of administrative activities. With the exception of his "Critique of C. G. Jung" (1914), Abraham did not engage publicly in any psychoanalytical polemics. The recently published correspondence between Freud and Abraham sheds a good deal of light on Freud's conflict with Jung, and, later, with Rank. Here, it is sufficient to mention two points: firstly, Abraham's experience with Jung at Burghölzli enabled him to speak with some authority; secondly, he profoundly disagreed with Freud's view of Jung, and made no bones about

opposing him. Occasionally, he was tempted to give Jung the benefit of the doubt, but, on the whole, as one gathers from the correspondence, from the spring of 1908 (when Freud deplored Abraham's critical reaction to Jung) through the spring of 1914 (when Abraham telegraphed Freud his congratulations on the news of Jung's voluntarily resigning from his post as President of the International Psychoanalytic Association), Abraham stuck to his views and was later proven to be right. This is all the more remarkable when one considers the fact that most of the early analysts could not bring themselves to oppose the man who in their view had given them a new lease on psychological life. To be sure, Abraham had his own personal biases, in his prolonged allegiance to Fliess, who, as Freud remarked in 1911, could possibly sidetrack him from psychoanalysis. The issue here is therefore not so much the scientific matters at stake, for looking back from the present vantage point, these are now seen not to have been particularly important, but the fact that once Abraham was convinced no force could deflect him from his settled conclusions.

h. Applied Psychoanalysis. Apart from Abraham's prentice essay on "Dream and Myth" (1909), his most important contribution was his early biographical essays (Segantini, 1911, and Amenhotep, 1912). Fired no doubt by Freud's example, the early analysts were given to investigations in the field of applied psychoanalysis. In the matter of analytical biography, for example, it can be said that Freud's monograph on Leonardo da Vinci (1909) constituted a breakthrough in the historical reconstruction of the subject's unconscious drives and motivations. Abraham's Amenhotep[2] essay had this additional merit: studies of the unconscious and of the primary processes are not to be judged by the temporal proximity of the subject.

I

Karl Abraham, born in Bremen on May 3, 1877, was the youngest of two sons born to a Jewish

---

2. Abraham's essay on Amenhotep IV (Echnaton), published in 1912, was the first attempt to describe the character of a man who lived well over two thousand years ago. In some respects, it would be fair to say that we now know more about the determining force of Echnaton's character than we do of Abraham's.

teacher of religion who married his cousin.[3] He gave up his religious teaching which was poorly paid to enter business as a wholesale draper, at the urging of his father-in-law, a career which he pursued with undistinguished success but which enabled him to make ends meet. Abraham's father was a kindly, intelligent man, deeply religious and highly respected in the Jewish community, liberal-minded even on some of the ritualistic aspects of his religion; he was nonetheless a patriarchal figure to his children. Abraham's mother came from a comfortable farmstead in the Hildesheim area. She was a warmhearted and devoted mother, was well-educated for her time, with some linguistic and literary gifts. They dwelt in a large, old-fashioned and rambling house with two paternal aunts. It was essentially a familial institution governed by the tradition of hospitality.

Abraham's elder brother, Max, was a weak, asthmatic boy, with whom he had a good relation in his earlier years. Because of his brother's delicate health, his parents did not allow Karl to indulge in any active sports other than that of walking. The inevitable consequence, when freed from parental restrictions, was that he engaged in various active sports and became an Alpinist of some merit. In short, one could say that he was unusually hemmed in by elderly people, profoundly influenced by familial religious traditions,[4] a mother's boy with a muted reaction against maternal discipline and over-solicitude, and yet much affected by what was clearly an oral maternal care for his well-being.

His first step toward extra-familial life took the form of a stay (along with his brother Max) in a small private day school from which he soon graduated to the Bremen Gymnasium where in the course of time he established a reputation for facility in Latin, Greek and, subsequently, an unusual flair for comparative linguistics, as a small notebook written when he was fourteen or fifteen years of age testifies. There was then no opening in the language fields at

the German universities for a relatively poor Jewish boy and, after a family conclave, it was decided that he should train as a dentist, his fees to be paid by his eccentric but relatively affluent uncle, to which proposition Abraham agreed provided he could attend the University and study dental surgery. During his first term at Würzburg, Abraham notified his family that he did not like dentistry and had changed over to the study of general medicine. He started his medical curriculum in 1896, took his finals in Freiburg in 1900, and by 1901 had gained his doctorate in medicine with special reference to embryology and histology.

The Jewish community in Bremen was small and closely knit and it is likely that there was not a great deal of intermingling with the gentile population. At school he encountered some degree of anti-Semitic feeling and did not make any close friends until, during his first university term at Würzburg, he met and was befriended by Ivan Bloch. In any case, he lived in a large family to which, and especially to his mother, he was closely and warmly attached. He did not, I think, feel the need of extra-mural contacts. Here indeed coming events cast their shadow: he was married in January 1906 at the age of 29, and had two children, a daughter born that same year and a son in 1910, and felt little need of contact outside the family circle, excluding of course such professional relations as he freely cultivated. He was a devoted husband and an equally devoted father to his children with whom he was on intimate, often playful, terms; he was understanding, indulgent, yet, at the same time, a guide as well as a friend and a deep source of strength to them. Those who were admitted to his family life, of whom I was privileged to be one, can uniformly testify to the warm consideration and easy hospitality he and his wife displayed. But the guests clearly understood that if they visited him outside office hours, they must be ready to recognize the complete priority of his domestic ties.

It is not quite clear when Abraham became interested in psychiatry, although Jones suggests that at Freiburg he was impressed already by the work of Bleuler. We do know that in April 1901 he obtained his first postgraduate post at the Berlin Municipal Mental Hospital at Dalldorf under Professor Liepmann (the brain histologist and pathologist) and by 1904 had published a number of papers, mostly on histological and neurological

---

3. Abraham's terminal illness was due to lung infection; he thought intermarriage was the source of his original lung weakness.

4. Despite his religious and traditional background and his filial attachment to some father figures, Abraham's first open act of rebellion was to abandon entirely the religion of his forefathers. This act of repudiation was completed when he married an intellectual who had grown up without any religious beliefs. In so doing he violated one of the cherished traditions of Judaism.

subjects, though one written in 1902 was of some significance for his later interests, a paper on the manifestations of delirium tremens in morphinism. During his four years' stay at Dalldorf, he acquired his grounding in clinical psychiatry. By then he was definite in his desire to get on Bleuler's staff and in December 1904 obtained an appointment under him at Burghölzli as an assistant at the University Psychiatric Clinic. When he became first assistant to Bleuler in 1906, he married, feeling that for the first time he would be able to sustain its economic responsibilities.

In Abraham's case there is no doubt that his career was determined to a considerable extent by his desire to set up and support a home of his own. He had known his prospective brother-in-law from his Dalldorf days, meeting his future wife at some of the extra-mural lectures they attended. He found himself at home in her cultural milieu, where he met amongst others Professor Altmann, the Heidelberg sociologist, who later suffered from a manic-depressive psychosis, a situation that seems to have directed Abraham's interest to this particular disorder. After his marriage, it became clear to him that even the post of first assistant to Bleuler would not lead to the economic stability needed to support a family; and, I think, his decision to return to Berlin was much influenced by this consideration.[5]

But dissatisfaction with his material prospects was not the only reason for his decision. Jones has maintained that in effect Burghölzli was not a harmonious psychiatric hunting ground, that there was a good deal of tension between Bleuler and Jung. And as later transpired, it was clear that Abraham was alienated by Jung's personality. As will be seen from his correspondence with Freud, he was clearly in opposition to Jung from 1908 onward, a view that was supported by the comments of Brill, who was also at Burghölzli. More importantly, it was here that he first became familiar with Freud's work, and in 1907 he published his first psychoanalytic paper,

on the significance of early dreams in dementia praecox and in sexual traumas. In October–November, when he decided to resign and move to Berlin, he had already arranged a meeting with Freud which took place in December 1907.

Once established in Berlin, he set about enlisting the support of everyone who showed any interest in analytic ideas. At first his practice was supported by Professor Oppenheim, a relative by marriage, at whose neurological clinic he worked, and by Dr. Wilhelm Fliess, a man for whom Abraham showed the greatest scientific regard. He soon arranged a series of private meetings, held in his own house, made contacts with whatsoever sources seemed likely to nourish psychoanalysis, and took action to counter the opposition which was the common lot of all psychoanalytical pioneers. In 1909 he was joined by Max Eitingon whom he had met at Burghölzli. In March 1910 he founded the Berlin Psychoanalytical Society. This was the first branch of the International Psychoanalytical Association, also founded in March of that same year. Later, he supported Eitingon in the formation of the Berlin Polyklinik in the Potsdamerstrasse and still later, from 1920 on, was a member of the International Psychoanalytic Training Commission, a pet project fostered mainly by Eitingon. He presided over the deliberations of the Berlin Society to the year of his death and contributed freely to the proceedings of that branch. He attended the first Congress of the International Association in April 1908, and read papers at every Congress save his last (1925). After Jung resigned, he became Provisional President of the International Association; he was made Secretary in 1922, President in 1924, and was reelected in 1925. Abraham was on the staff of the *Zentralblatt* and *Zeitschrift* from their foundation and when Jung resigned the editorship of the *Jahrbuch* Abraham produced the sixth and last volume in coeditorship with Dr. Hitschman.

Among his pupils there were many who were later to play an active part in the development of psychoanalysis, including Felix Boehm, Helene Deutsch, James Glover, Melanie Klein, Sandor Rado, Theodor Reik, Ernst Simmel, Alix Strachey, and Edward Glover, the present writer. As a guest of the Berlin Society, I had ample opportunity to observe the skill with which Abraham directed its scientific proceedings. The early meetings were certainly not

---

5. His relations with his wife were governed throughout by their mutual cultural interests. Indeed, it is interesting to reflect that although he was destined to write one of the most illuminating articles on the female castration complex, his views on marital equality of the sexes would, had he lived in Britain, have made him *persona grata* to the Women's Emancipation Movement. When they settled in Berlin, Frau Dr. Abraham played an active part in the didactic psychoanalytic evenings that were held in their home.

unruly, but on the other hand they were not so ritualistic as the later ones. Scientific discussions were apt to degenerate into a welter of contending notions and speculative theories. It was a pleasure to observe the tact and skill with which Abraham kept scientific control of the proceedings, emphasizing in effect the paramount necessity of applying clinical standards during speculative forays. The same could be said of his direction and control of the administrative affairs of the International Association. As Secretary and later President of the Association, Abraham directed these various discussions with an unusual combination of firmness and diplomatic skill. It was quite clear, indeed, that his labors as president of the Bad Homburg Congress in 1925, weakened his already diminishing resistance.

The smooth and progressive course of his career was interrupted by World War I. In 1914–15 he was seconded to the military reserve and worked as a surgeon, first in Berlin, and subsequently in Allenstein in East Prussia. In 1916 he was finally allotted psychiatric beds and built up a psychiatric unit of his own. He was then appointed chief psychiatric physician to the Twentieth Army Corps. During this period, he was still in active correspondence with Freud and published a number of psychoanalytical papers, ranging in content from such matters as early pregenital development and ejaculatio praecox to the analysis of war neuroses. A recurrent attack of dysentery, dating from his East Prussian war experiences, weakened his health in the last six years of his life.

In the spring of 1925, he inhaled an infected foreign body, which induced a severe bronchopneumonia, followed by bronchiectasis. In the autumn, complications set in and despite a serious operation he gradually sank. On Christmas day, 1925, he died in his forty-eighth year at the height of his powers. Almost to the day of his death, he was full of that vital optimistic spirit that had sustained him throughout an active and fruitful life.

II

Leafing through the various obituary and memorial addresses dedicated to his memory (1925 *et seq.*), one cannot but be struck with the unqualified admiration evoked by Abraham's capacities as a teacher of psychoanalysis. His concision, lucidity, objectivity, many-sidedness, and mastery of the arts of exposition, all served to extend his clinical observations, enabling him to provide a psychoanalytic *vade mecum* for students and researchers alike. It is all the more interesting to note, therefore, in the earliest exchange of letters between Freud and Abraham, that he wrote at some length on the subject of sexual traumata. Freud accepted the plausibility of Abraham's conclusions on the subject, but added, "only to me everything seems less clear-cut." It was characteristic of Freud's gentle mode of criticism that he should take the onus on himself. Indeed, Abraham was more dogmatic in his acceptance of Freud's views than Freud himself. Nonetheless, supported by his objective clinical capacities, Abraham was able to turn aside this usual legitimate reservation. The really fascinating issue, whether Freud treated his own conclusions with pessimistic and therefore open-minded reserve, or whether Abraham, being quite incontestably an optimist, brushed aside these reservations to reinforce what he felt to be the irrefragable nature of Freud's findings, is relevant only as a measure of Abraham's veracity. Still, this is certainly not the place to embark on the nature of Freud's reactions to his own discoveries. Personally, I do not think he was a pessimist, but what is quite certain is that Abraham was an optimist, which may account to some extent for the fact that his therapeutic results were so outstanding. For it is probably true that the success of psychoanalytical treatment depends in part on the attitude of the analyst to the sufferings of his patient.

Following this clue, I think it is no coincidence that Abraham was himself an example of those "satisfied oral types," a view of life Abraham described as rose-tinted by an unconscious realization of the comforts of the suckling mother. What is striking about his work is that despite this bias he had an intuitive understanding of the shattering effect on the ego of hate reactions toward the mother engendered by frustration. This was a step forward in analytical comprehension, and led in its time to a dim understanding of the profound influence of ambivalence of feeling on the human race.

Abraham did much to establish the part played by hate and ambivalence in the formation and function of the ego. The release of love-feeling, purged of its sadistic components, served not only to correct ego imbalances but to release both constructive and altruistic energies. Viewed from this point the extensive range of Abraham's interests becomes readily understandable. Despite his obvious interest in the earliest forms of infantile mental life, I think he had in mind a wide conspectus of human development, from infancy to childhood, to adolescence, to early and middle manhood, and, finally, to senescence. These progressive and ultimately regressive phases, the influence of man's inherited instincts, were offered in part as an explanation of the oscillating forces of Love and Hate. No doubt his own outstanding capacities for disciplined observation and his modes of presentation owe much to the balance of forces which he had established in his own mind and which were reflected in his life and character.

Shortly after Abraham's death, Ernest Jones remarked to me that, "The secret of Abraham's life and character was that he was so divinely normal." But what indeed is a *normal* man? Is this the myth that helps man to sustain his manifold and manifest psychological difficulties, his conflicts between individual and social urges? Rather, a rational man may be described as one who is able to resolve the anxieties and guilts that bedevil human adaptation, who can withstand the asperities of life without having to resort to counter-reactions that inhibit his own gifts, faculties and modes of expression. Who shall say? Any or all of these, as well as other standards of "normality," are subject to serious qualification. Psychiatrists or psychoanalysts, looking back over their consulting room experiences, should be the last to pontificate on the matter. All they can do is to record the impressions gained in personal contact and leave the reader to make, if he likes, an ideal ego-image out of these observations, aware of course that ideal images are the most unreliable of psychic phenomena.

When I first met Abraham just after the Christmas of 1920, I was impressed by his physical attributes. He was a slight yet compactly built man just under middle height, in his early forties, youthful yet mature, alert and active, carefully dressed, almost dapper in the best sense of that Dutch equivalent for physical alertness and sartorial trimness. He was easy and friendly in his approach, and possessed of considerable personal charm, yet obviously concerned that he waste no time in social fripperies. He sometimes displayed a punctiliousness of manner that gave some clue to the existence of his deep reserve. Though training candidates are subject to considerable bias, they are not without some capacity to judge the nature of the man who is about to play the most important part in their psychological life.

Karl Abraham was generously endowed with courage, pertinacity and loyalty; he had a strong sense of reality and a strong critical faculty; he was firm in purpose and confidence, fearless and possessed of great integrity; he was staunch in his relations with those with whom he was inevitably bound by personal or professional ties; he was sane in his judgments, unambitious and yet in the scientific sense profoundly ambitious. Endowed with shrewdness and judgment, he had all the attributes of an effective leader and, although ready to overcome opposition through reasoned argument, he could be quite uncompromising, holding and expressing his opinions with firmness and pertinacity. On the other hand, in his private life he showed a light and almost playful sense of humor, together with a warm concern for the feelings of others. Although no idolater, he manifested what might be described as a degree of simple piety in his relations with those elders whose achievements he admired.

We have little or no knowledge of those private egoistic and instinctual factors that govern behavior, and that thereby contribute to an unbiased assessment of character. But we are not entirely without significant evidence. Studying Abraham through direct personal and recorded contacts, supplemented by a study of his writings, I would say that the outstanding feature of his character was his optimism, his realism, his freedom from morbid anxiety, his capacity to sublimate, and his marked absence of ambivalence and egotism. Yet, despite some indications of deep reserve and a trace of austerity sufficient to suggest the existence of deep moral feeling and restraint, he was warm and outgoing in his personal and social contacts. Though he experienced the usual vicissitudes of mental conflict with instinct and was thus given to explosive outbursts of temper in his private life, they were of short duration, ending always in his being in a state of contrition.

If normality is considered as something more than striking averages in human behavior, if it can be measured by degrees of harmonious and elastic adaptation to life and work, if we are prepared to accept a degree of synonymity between the concepts of normality and mental health, then we are safe in accepting Jones' dictum that Abraham was divinely normal, implying thereby that some men are more normal than others. Taking it all-in-all, I think this terse judgment might well pass as an enduring epitaph to Karl Abraham's life and work.

I want to express my appreciation at having been invited to write about Karl Abraham, who in his regrettably short span of professional activity was instrumental not only in setting up a psychoanalytic center in the heart of North Germany, but of promoting and helping to maintain an international organization which is now one of the accepted structures—if not indeed, pillars—of the science of psychoanalysis.

Finally, I am greatly indebted to Dr. Hilda Abraham who, aided by her mother, Frau Dr. Abraham, was able to reconstruct for me her father's family antecedents and background. I have also borrowed from the "Obituary Notice" written by Ernest Jones. This includes a complete bibliography of Abraham's psychoanalytical works. I have also drawn upon the Freud-Abraham letters which have recently been published by Basic Books.

Integer vitae scelerisque purus.

—Edward Glover, M.D., LL.D.

101

ABREACTION is the process of discharging pent-up emotions (unconscious affect) through the recall and verbalization of repressed memories. As a therapeutic tool, it was discovered by Breuer and Freud early in their studies of hysterical patients. Freud and Breuer (1893) explained the therapeutic effectiveness of their treatment as due to the discharge of what had previously been, as it were, "strangulated affects," attached to the suppressed mental acts (abreaction). They likened this response to the fading of a memory or the losing of its affect, and reasoned that it occurred because of a reaction of the voluntary and involuntary reflexes, from tears to acts of revenge. If the reaction is suppressed, the affect remains attached to the memory trace, and an adequate discharge can subsequently take place only if the "mortification" is eliminated so that a cathartic effect occurs. "Language," the authors pointed out, "serves as a substitute for action. . . ."

Further experience led Freud to recognize the insufficiency of abreaction as a real cure for neuroses. It was succeeded by the analytic goal of a fundamental reorganization of the personality. However, one feature of abreaction is still incorporated in analytic therapy, the aspect of *working through*. It is also utilized in other forms of treatment and in sublimations (play and aesthetic experience, among others) which afford spontaneous means of release from emotional tensions.

Related Concepts: ACTING OUT; CATHARSIS.

REFERENCE

Freud, S., & J. Breuer, 1893, "Studies in Hysteria." *SE*, 2:8, 1955.

ADDITIONAL READINGS

Freud, S.: 1893, "On the Psychical Mechanism of Hysterical Phenomena: A Lecture." *SE*, 3, 1962.
1894, "The Neuro-Psychoses of Defense." *SE*, 3, 1960.
1905, "On Psychotherapy." *SE*, 7, 1953.
1914, "Remembering, Repeating, and Working Through." *SE*, 12, 1958.
1925, "Psycho-Analysis." *SE*, 20, 1959.
Gordeon, R. G., "The Phenomenon of Abreaction." *JNP*, 3, 1923.
Hinrichson, O., "Über das 'Abreagieren' beim Normalen und bei den Hysterischen." *ZNP*, 16, 1913.
Loewald, H. W., "Hypnoid State, Repression, Abreaction and Recollection." *JAPA*, 3, 1955.

102

ABSENCE is a lapse or "dissociation" of consciousness. The concept played an important part in the early formulations of Breuer and Freud regarding the development of hysterical symptoms. They supposed, as in hypnoid states, absences to be conducive to the retention of affects in their conversion into symptoms. Freud (1909) considered absences to occur at the climax of every intensive sexual gratification.

The concept of absence is little used in analysis today.

Related Concepts: AUTOHYPNOSIS; HYPNOID STATE.

REFERENCE

Freud, S., 1909, "Some General Remarks on Hysterical Attacks." *SE*, 9:233–234, 1959.

ADDITIONAL READING

Freud, S., & J. Breuer, 1895, "Studies on Hysteria." *SE*, 2, 1955.

103

ABSTINENCE. Although Freud identified abstinence as contributory to neurasthenia, he stressed the role of society in frequently producing or enforcing it to the point of neurosis. Freud (1908) noted that many remain abstinent only with the help of masturbation. Masturbation—if prolonged —despite the gratification of the initial genital desires, appears to be not only the cause of the neurosis but is already its result. The presence of repressed infantile wishes find their expression in masturbation, and, it might be added, always as a symptom of the neurotic patient.

Related Concepts: RULE OF ABSTINENCE; ACTUAL NEUROSIS.

REFERENCE

Freud, S., 1908, "Civilized Sexual Morality and Modern Nervous Illness." *SE*, 9:177–204, 1959.

ADDITIONAL READINGS

Freud, S.: 1895, "On the Grounds for Detaching a Particular Syndrome from Neurasthenia Under the Description of 'Anxiety Neurosis.'" *SE*, 3, 1962.
    1912, "Types of Onset of Neurosis." *SE*, 12, 1958.
    1915, "Observations on Transference-Love." *SE*, 12, 1958.
Kemper, W., "The 'Rule of Abstinence' in Psychoanalysis." *P*, 8, 1955.

104

ABSTRACT THINKING is essential to reality testing and proceeds developmentally from pre-logical to logical, in accordance with the psychical events attendant in the primary and secondary processes. In the primary process, the freely mobilized, unneutralized cathexis is utilized; in the secondary, the bound, neutralized cathexis is employed. It would thus seem that a successful inhibition gives rise to mental activity which utilizes and differentiates between internal and external stimuli, their perception and evaluation, in accordance with the reality principle.

In his earliest definitive statements about thinking and abstract thought, Freud (1911) drew a distinction between the pleasure principle and the reality principle; i.e., thinking instead of acting. He defined thinking as a form of trial action, carried out with a small expenditure of energy, related to perceptual elements in time. Later, in 1915, he pointed out that the unconscious may contain both thing-presentations and object-presentation. In this, thing-presentations were derived from a variety of visual, acoustical, tactile, olfactory, and kinesthetic perceptions. Object-presentations were made up of both thing- and word-presentations. Still later, in 1923, Freud drew a distinction between thinking in pictures, which stood closer to unconscious processes, and thinking in words or other symbol groups (e.g., in numbers). He also felt that word-presentations in dreams occurred only where the words had value in terms of their being recent perceptions and not as abstract thoughts.

The basic capacity for abstract thinking would certainly seem to be an autonomous ego function which can become invested with various conflicts to interfere with its normal functioning. Fenichel (1945) described the instinctualization of the function of abstract thinking in obsessional neuroses as the result of a pathological form of abstraction. "Compulsive thinking is not only abstract, it is also *general*, directed toward systematization and categorization; it is abstract instead of concrete. The patients are interested in maps and illustrations rather than in countries and things."

Abraham (1913) cited several examples of abnormal thinking: "I shall first of all discuss those neurotics who show a keen interest in knowledge or investigation of a concrete nature. In this form of sublimation of scoptophilia the original instinct can sometimes be recognized without any special aids, but in other cases it requires psycho-analytical methods to do this. The two following cases are particularly instructive.

"A very intelligent and cultivated neurotic man had a pronounced desire for universal scientific knowledge. In regard to his very active mental life he noticed that there was always one single problem which especially attracted him in each science which he took up. When I asked him to give an example he mentioned the following:

"What interested him most in chemistry was the *status nascendi*. On going more closely into this it appeared that the moment in which a substance was formed or in which two substances united to form a new one had a positive fascination for him. His interest in procreation (combination of two substances in the formation of a new one) and in birth (*status nascendi*) had been displaced on to scientific problems in a successful way. He unconsciously discovered in each science the problem that was best suited to afford a veiled representation of the interests of his childhood. The field of palaeontology supplied another very instructive example of this sublimatory tendency. The geological period termed pliocene—the period in which man first appeared—particularly engrossed his interest. The child's typical question concerning its own origin had been here sublimated to a general interest in the origin of the human race.

"It would be easy to go on adding to the number of these examples. Those here quoted show that this form of sublimation has an important advantage for the neurotic, namely, that it brings him into close touch with phenomena of the external world. In other cases the repressed pleasure in looking is changed into an unproductive desire for knowledge which is not applied to real events. This constitutes neurotic brooding, which might be termed a caricature of philosophic thinking."

Related Concepts: SECONDARY PROCESS; THINKING.

REFERENCES

Abraham, K., 1913, "Restrictions and Transformations of Scoptophilia in Psycho-Neurotics: with Remarks on Analogous Phenomena in Folk-Psychology." *SPA*, pp. 208–209, 1942.
Fenichel, O., *The Psychoanalytic Theory of Neurosis.* Nor, p. 297, 1945.
Freud, S.: 1911, "Formulation on the Two Principles of Mental Functioning." *SE*, 12:215–226, 1958.
    1915, "The Unconscious." *SE*, 14:159–216, 1957.
    1923, "The Ego and the Id." *SE*, 19:23, 1961.

105

ABSURDITY. Freud studied absurdity in dreams, wit, and other mental processes, demonstrating the meaningfulness of this form of "nonsense." For example, in dreams, absurdity may be a censored expression of embittered criticism. Freud (1900) stated: "If, however, a dream strikes one as *obviously* absurd, if its content includes a piece of palpable nonsense, this is intentionally so; its apparent disregard of all the requirements of logic is expressing a piece of the intellectual content of the dream-thoughts."

In wit and clowning, rebellion against authority figures (representing the infantile superego) emerge, in permissible form, in the guise of nonsense. To reduce an exalted figure to the humiliating position of absurdity may be a source of aggressive pleasure. In religion, the absurd is raised above reason, and accepted as an article of exalted faith.

Related Concepts: CARICATURE; COMIC.

REFERENCE

Freud, S.: 1900, "The Interpretation of Dreams." *SE*, 5:444–445, 662, 1953.

ADDITIONAL READING

Freud, S., 1895, "Obsessions and Phobias: Their Psychical Mechanism and Their Aetiology." *SE*, 3, 1962.

106

ABULIA is an incapacity or inhibition of the will, an extreme indecision and inability to act. Freud (1895) stated: "Phobias and abulias (inhibitions of will) . . . are seen to have been adequately determined by traumatic experiences."

The concept is little used in analysis today.

Related Concept: INHIBITION.

REFERENCE

Freud, S., & J. Breuer, 1895, "Studies on Hysteria." *SE*, 2:87–90, 1955.

ADDITIONAL READING

Freud, S., 1907, "Obsessive Actions and Religious Practices." *SE*, 9, 1959.

107

ACCIDENT PRONENESS is a disposition to-ward self-injury through repetitive accidents, es-pecially where it is unconsciously induced because of masochism. Accident proneness is linked with acting out and symptomatic acts. Dunbar (1948) suggested the existence of a special accident-prone personality type. Fenichel (1945) related accident proneness to the acting-out character and to destiny neuroses. "The patients may appear as restless."

Related Concepts: Acting Out; Masochism; Need for Punishment.

REFERENCES

Dunbar, F., *Synopsis of Psychosomatic Diagnosis and Treatment.* Mos, pp. 381–388, 1948.
Fenichel, O., *The Psychoanalytic Theory of Neurosis.* Nor, p. 506, 1945.

ADDITIONAL READINGS

Alexander, F., "The Neurotic Character." *IntJPsa*, 11, 1930.
Rowson, A. J., "Accident Proneness." *PSM*, 6, 1944.

108

ACROPHOBIA is denotative of a fear of high places, usually involving a specific fear of falling. In this, falling from a high place may represent a punishment (including death or castration) for unconscious sexual or aggressive wishes. The sensa-tion of falling itself is usually representative of the sensation of sexual excitement. As is true of all symptoms, the phobia may represent a compromise formation between defensive and instinctual forces; unconscious wishes are defended against by dis-placement or projection, with a subsequent avoi-dance of the feared object or situation.

Freud (1900) traced the forbidden feelings in-volved in falling, flying and giddiness back to the pleasurable feelings aroused in children when they are swung or dropped (e.g., in a game). He suggested that the incestuous connotations of these feelings may be responsible for the phobia.

Related Concepts: Negative Oedipus Complex; Phobia.

REFERENCE

Freud, S., 1900, "The Interpretation of Dreams." *SE*, 5:394–395 1953.

109

ACTING IN is a discharge by actions instead of words of repressed wishes during the analytical session. For example, a patient getting up from the couch and removing a book from the shelf discharges his pent-up energy. In analysis, this tension should be discharged and explored by talking about it to bring out the unconscious material connected with it. The association connected with the wish to take the book in this instance may indicate and gratify the presence of an unconscious desire to castrate the analyst.

As a reporter and panelist, Kohut (1957) noted: "All those who remarked on it agreed that 'acting out' was a form of resistance which confronts the analyst with a particularly difficult task. It is a resistance because the patient uses it instead of remembering or understanding; he drains the im-pulse rather than recognizing and mastering it. Ludwig Eidelberg differentiated a particular form of acting out that takes place in the analytic session itself (for example, by a patient's inspecting the analyst's bookcase, and the like). These forms of acting out Eidelberg designated with the term 'acting in.' Lorand, too, stressed the technical difficulties that are posed to the analyst by acting-out patients, and he advised that this resistance should be tackled only after a strong transference bond has been established."

Related Concepts: Acting Out; Resistance.

REFERENCE

Kohut, H., "Clinical and Theoretical Aspects of Resistance." *JAPA*, 5:551, 1957.

ADDITIONAL READING

Zeligs, M., "Acting In: A Contribution to the Mean-ing of Some Postural Attitudes Observed During Analysis." *JAPA*, 5, 1957.

110

ACTING OUT is characterized by a discharge of repressed infantile wishes through gratification which occurs outside of analysis, a process which the patient does not usually consciously connect with repressed wishes. The patient thus avoids the verbalization and working through of these wishes in his analysis. For example, a patient suddenly refuses to make his monthly alimony payment to his ex-wife, displacing his resistance against paying his analyst's fees.

As a reporter and panelist, Kanzer (1957) noted: "He referred approvingly to Ekstein's description of acting out as 'experimental recollection' and added that it was also experimental action. Beginning with impulses and proceeding through play, the discharge patterns finally become anchored in reality-tested action. In acting out, this process is not completed; the final action is suffused with primary process energy. The mechanism may be compared to the elaboration of the day residue by the unconscious; whereas the dream is denied access to motility, this is not the case in acting out, which often has somnambulistic elements."

Related Concepts: ACTING IN; RESISTANCE.

REFERENCE

Kanzer, M., "Acting Out, Sublimation and Reality Testing." *JAPA*, 5:142, 1957.

ADDITIONAL READINGS

Bry, T., "Acting Out in Group Psychotherapy." *IntJgrpPt*, 3, 1953.
Carroll, E. J., "Acting Out and Ego Development." *Q*, 23, 1954.
Devereux, G., "Acting Out in Dreams: As a Reaction to a Break-Through of the Unconscious in a Character Disorder." *PT*, 9, 1955.
Durkin, H. E., "Acting Out in Group Psychotherapy." *Ops*, 25, 1955.
Frank, J., "Treatment Approach to Acting-Out Character Disorders." *JHH*, 8, 1959.
Freud, S., 1905, "Fragment of an Analysis of a Case of Hysteria." *SE*, 7, 1953.
Glatzer, H. T., "Acting Out in Group Psychotherapy." *PT*, 12, 1958.
Heilbrunn, G., "Comments on a Common Form of Acting Out." *Q*, 27, 1958.
Kasanin, J. S., "Neurotic 'Acting Out' As a Basis for Sexual Promiscuity in Women." *R*, 31, 1944.
Kohut, H., "Clinical and Theoretical Aspects of Resistance." *JAPA*, 5, 1957.
Roth, N., "Manifest Dream Content and Acting Out." *Q*, 27, 1958.
Sachs, H., "Agieren in der Analyse." *Z*, 15, 1929.

Silverberg, W. V., "Acting Out Versus Insight: A Problem in Psychoanalytic Technique." *Q*, 24, 1955.
Spiegel, L., "Acting Out and Defensive Instinctual Gratification." *JAPA*, 1954.

111

ACTION (ACT) is any motoric movement of the skeletal musculature with the help of which dammed-up energy is discharged and a narcissistic mortification is eliminated. Most psychoanalysts assume that the ego (the conscious as well as the unconscious part) controls action.

Fenichel (1945) stated: "The prerequisite for an action is, besides mastery of the bodily apparatus, the development of the function of judgment. This means the ability to anticipate the future in the imagination by 'testing' reality, by trying in an active manner and in a small dosage what might happen to one passively and in an unknown dosage. This type of functioning is in general characteristic of the ego."

Related Concepts: PARAPRAXIS; TIC.

REFERENCE

Fenichel, O., *The Psychoanalytic Theory of Neurosis,* Nor, p. 42, 1945.

ADDITIONAL READINGS

Freud, S.: 1905, "Three Essays on the Theory of Sexuality." *SE*, 7, 1953.
　　1915, "Instincts and Their Vicissitudes." *SE*, 14, 1957.
　　1933, "New Introductory Lectures on Psycho-Analysis." *SE*, 22, 1964.

112

ACTIVE is the capacity to act, as opposed to being acted upon. All instincts may be regarded as active, because they represent the driving urges of a living organism. Freud, however, separated instincts which have an active aim from instincts which have a passive aim. Eidelberg (1954) further defined active aim as instinctual gratification achieved through the action of the subject, and passive aim as gratification achieved through the action of the object.

Freud originally considered active to be a synonym of masculine, and therefore considered the activity of a woman as expressing her *masculine* part (bisexuality). Later (1933), he recognized that the activity of a woman cannot be referred to as representing her masculine part. The activity of a little girl playing with dolls, of a mother caring for her child, cannot be described as representing their masculine parts. Nonetheless, he still described the female's activity as being dominated by the presence of passive instinctual aims. An examination of the relationship between the mother and her child, Eidelberg (1954) noted, indicates that the mother neither satisfies her passive sexual aim nor her masculine need in taking care of her child.

Freud used the terms active and aggressive synonymously which has lead to a misunderstanding. Behavior may be classed as aggressive in spite of being passive, or active and loving. For example: A man invites his girl friend to a night club and remains seated throughout the night. He is thus both aggressive and passive. If he asks her to dance, he is not aggressive (destructive) necessarily; but he is active.

In his first instinct theory, Freud (1905) described activity and passivity as biological poles which govern mental life. In his second instinct theory (1933), he assigned a more fundamental role to passivity, a manifestation of the need to return to an earlier, inorganic state (Thanatos). Activity, on the other hand, was connected with Eros.

Related Concepts: AGGRESSION; PASSIVE; SEXUALITY.

REFERENCES

Eidelberg, L., *An Outline of a Comparative Pathology of the Neuroses.* IUP, pp. 23–25, 1954.
Freud, S.: 1905, "Three Essays on Sexuality." *SE*, 7:168, 1953.
            1933, "New Introductory Lectures on Psycho-Analysis." *SE*, 22:107, 115, 1964.

ADDITIONAL READINGS

Buxbaum, E., "Activity and Aggression in Children." *Ops*, 17, 1947.
Freud, S.: 1915, "Instincts and Their Vicissitudes." *SE*, 14, 1957.
            1918, "From the History of an Infantile Neurosis." *SE*, 17, 1955.
            1931, "Female Sexuality." *SE*, 21, 1961.
Frumkes, G., "Types of Activity in Psychoanalytic Technique." *AnSurvPsa*, 2, 1951.
Mainx, F., "Foundation of Biology," in *International Encyclopedia of Unified Science.* UCP, 1, 1955.

113
ACTIVE PLAY THERAPY, according to Solomon (1951), is a technique for the treatment of behavior and personality disorders in children based on creating, in effigy, the situations of the child's life to which he makes responses and reveals himself in the third person. For example, a family of dolls is seated around a table. The child patient plays with them and arranges a family scene. By astutely following the leads of the child, much valuable information can be elicited concerning the interpersonal relationships in his home. At deeper levels, preoccupation with oral activity or defensiveness is also demonstrated.

By keeping his third-person position, the child is able to hide behind a cloak of anonymity. Transference-reactions may be evoked by supplying a doll which represents the therapist and putting it into play at appropriate moments.

Related Concept: TRANSFERENCE.

REFERENCE

Solomon, J. C., *An Introduction to Projective Techniques*, Anderson & Anderson, eds. PH, 1951.

ADDITIONAL READINGS

Solomon, J.: "Active Play Therapy." *Ops*, 8, 1938.
            "Active Play Therapy, Further Experiences." *Ops*, 10, 1940.

114
ACTIVE THERAPY. Several psychoanalysts have attempted to shorten or modify the classical psychoanalytic method either because of a personal resistance to some aspect of psychoanalytic theory for practical reasons or in the hope of finding methods of treating psychiatric illnesses which are not ordinarily amenable to classical psychoanalysis. Outstanding among those who experimented with psychoanalytic methods in this way was Ferenczi (1921) who developed a technique called *active psychoanalysis*. He hoped to shorten psychoanalysis to a few months by actively intervening in the patient's mental and actual life by interpretations based on "experience and insight" rather than on

specific material elicited from the patient or through the systematic analysis of resistance and transference.

In active therapy, the patient is urged to face those situations he most dreads in order to accustom himself to those circumstances and to master his anxiety. The patient is then asked to analyze his resultant thoughts. This method, extended and modified, has also been used to treat psychotic patients by Rosen. Schilder extended this therapy to patients suffering from unacceptable thoughts as well as patients unable to face situations. This method has also been adopted by the followers of Pavlov to "decondition" or "desensitize" phobias. None of these methods has met with wide success or acceptance, either as methods of psychoanalysis or as related psychotherapeutic endeavors.

Related Concepts: SHORT-TERM THERAPY; WILD PSYCHOANALYSIS.

REFERENCES

Ferenczi, S., 1921, "Weiterer Ausbau der 'aktiven Technik' in der Psychoanalyse." *Z*, 7:233, 1921.
Freud, S., 1919, "Lines of Advance in Psycho-Analytic Therapy." *SE*, 17:160–161, 1955.

ADDITIONAL READINGS

Ferenczi, S., & O. Rank, *The Development of Psychoanalysis*. NMDP, 1925.
Freud, S., 1937, "Analysis Terminable and Interminable." *SE*, 23, 1964.
Rank, O., *The Trauma of Birth*. NMDP, 1914.

115

ACTIVITY AND PASSIVITY. Metaphorically, Freud (1915) represented this relationship as a series of successive waves or eruptions of lava. The first eruption produces a wave which is unchanged, while the succeeding wave is modified from its outset. Freud characterized this as a change from active to passive, with this new characteristic being added to the later waves.

Economically, the wishes connected with an instinctual aim may under certain conditions (external frustration) seek the discharge of their mental energy by giving up the external object which is not available, displacing or turning the instinctual

energy against the self. The cathexis of the presentations of external objects is withdrawn and shifted to the presentation of the self. In this process, the objectual quality of the energy may be exchanged for narcissistic energy or it may remain objectual in spite of its being used to cathect the presentation of the self. The narcissistic phase may in turn be relinquished by returning to the external object. However, in this return, the object relation is often not an exact repetition of the primary one: it is characterized by a passive aim, substituted for an active aim.

Such vicissitudes of the instincts involving changes of an active aim into a passive aim or the use of the self instead of an external object appears to lead to pathological states only if they take place unconsciously. All neurotic defense mechanisms are characterized by the fact that they do not protect the individual from such dangers as the damming up of instinctual energy or narcissistic mortification but from the conscious recognition of what has happened.

Related Concepts: AGGRESSION; LIBIDO; MASCULINITY AND FEMININITY.

REFERENCE

Freud, S., 1915, "Instincts and Their Vicissitudes." *SE*, 14:127, 129–131, 1957.

116

ACTUAL NEUROSES denotes those phenomena which do not involve psychical mechanisms; specifically, those which arise from the subject's contemporary existence, his current sexual practices, rather than his past life. The actual neuroses were seen as being organically rather than psychologically conditioned. They arose, Freud (1895) noted, from a holding back of sexual excitation; e.g., abstinence when libido is present, unconsummated excitation, and, above all, coitus interruptus.

Later, Freud stated (1917) that the symptoms are the products of entirely somatic processes, affected by what Freud, at that time, called "transformed" sexual libido that has not been adequately discharged. (Neurotic anxiety was seen as transformed sexual libido.) In defining the actual neuroses as the results of disturbances in sexual metabolism, Freud made a speculative analogy to pathological states which arise in the body from chronic intoxications and sudden withdrawals of the toxic substances.

Freud (1898) distinguished three actual neuroses: neurasthenia, anxiety neurosis, and hypochondria. He attributed neurasthenia to excessive discharge of the sexual substances, as in excessive masturbation or too frequent nocturnal emissions. Anxiety neurosis was described as stemming from conditions affording incomplete satisfaction, such as coitus interruptus or abstinence in the face of great sexual desire. Later, Freud (1914) added hypochondria, which he attributed to the "damming up of ego libido." He felt (in 1917) that these occasionally occurred in their pure form; more often, they were intermixed with each other and with a psycho-neurotic disorder. "A symptom of an 'actual' neurosis is often the nucleus and first stage of a psychoneurotic symptom." For example, a headache might originally be a direct sexual-toxic symptom stemming from the practice of coitus interruptus. By condensation and displacement, it can become a substitute-satisfaction for a number of libidinal fantasies and memories, and emerge as a symptom of conversion hysteria.

In recent years, the concept of actual neuroses has been widely discussed, and largely abandoned. Blau (1952), however, has presented evidence in favor of retaining the concept.

Related Concepts: HYPOCHONDRIASIS; NEURASTHENIA; NEUROSIS AND PSYCHOSIS; PATHONEUROSIS.

REFERENCES

Blau, A., "In Support of Freud's Syndrome of 'Actual' Anxiety Neurosis." *IntJPsa*, 33:363–372, 1952.
Freud, S.: 1895, "On the Grounds for Detaching a Particular Syndrome from Neurasthenia Under the Description 'Anxiety Neurosis'." *SE*, 3:108, 1962.
　　1898, "Sexuality in the Aetiology of the Neuroses." *SE*, 3:263–286, 1962.
　　1914, "On Narcissism: An Introduction." *SE*, 3:14: 83–84, 1957.
　　1917, "Introductory Lectures on Psychoanalysis." *SE*, 16:387, 390, 1963.

ADDITIONAL READINGS

Fenichel, O., *The Psychoanalytic Theory of Neurosis.* Nor, 1945.
Nunberg, H., *Principles of Psychoanalysis.* IUP, 1955.

117

ADAPTATION is the integration of instinctual needs with the conditions and demands of the outside world and of the superego, a task performed by the ego through learning and reality testing. Hartmann (1958) stressed the preadaptedness of the inborn ego apparatus, already evolved through the struggles of the species for survival (e.g., perception, memory, thinking and motility). He stated, in 1964, "The reality principle includes both knowledge of reality and acting in regard to it. Biologically speaking, it is part of what we usually term adaptation."

Earlier, Ferenczi speculated (in 1930): "Probably each living being reacts to stimuli of unpleasure with fragmentation and commencing dissolution (death-instinct?). Instead of 'death-*instinct*' it would be better to choose a word that would express the absolute passivity of this process. Possibly complicated mechanisms (living beings) can only be preserved as units by the pressure of their environment. At an unfavourable change in the environment the mechanism falls to pieces and disintegrates as far (probably along lines of antecedent historic development), as the greater simplicity and consequent plasticity of the elements makes a new adaptation possible. Consequently autoplastic adaptation is always preceded by autotomy. The tendency to autotomy in the first instance tends to be complete. Yet an opposite movement (instinct of self-preservation, life-instinct) inhibits the disintegration and drives towards a new consolidation, as soon as this has been made possible by the plasticity developed in the course of fragmentation. It is very difficult to make a conception of the true essence of this instinctual factor and its function. It is as if it could command sources of knowledge and possibilities which go infinitely far beyond everything that we know as faculties of our conscious intelligence. It assesses the gravity of the damage, the amounts of energy of the environment and of the surrounding people, it seems to have some knowledge of events distant in space and to know exactly at what point to stop the self-destruction and to start the reconstruction. In the extreme case when all the reserve forces have been mobilized but have proved impotent in the face of the overpowering attack, it comes to an extreme fragmentation which could be called de-materialisation. Observation of patients, who fly from their own sufferings and have become hypersensitive to all kinds of extraneous suffering, also coming from a great distance, still leave the question open whether even these extreme, quasi-pulverized, elements which have been reduced to mere psychic energies do not also contain tendencies for reconstruction of the ego. . . .

"Contrasted with the form of adaptation described above is alloplastic adaptation, i.e. the alteration of the environment in such a way as to make self-destruction and self-reconstruction unnecessary, and to enable the ego to maintain its existing equilibrium, i.e. its organization, unchanged. A necessary condition for this is a highly developed sense of reality."

Related Concepts: IDENTIFICATION; SOCIAL COMPLIANCE.

REFERENCES

Ferenczi, S., 1930, "Autoplastic and Alloplastic Adaptation." *IntJPsa*, 30:231–232, 1949.
Hartmann, H.: *Ego Psychology and the Problem of Adaptation.* IUP, p. 51, 1958.
    Essays on Ego Psychology. IUP, p. 252, 1964.

ADDITIONAL READING

Romano, J., ed., *Adptation.* CorUP, 1949.

118
ADDICTION is an insatiable recurrent craving for certain substances or activities which eliminates unpleasure or induces a state of euphoria. With drugs, such as the opiates and barbiturates, a physiological dependency develops, in addition to a psychological one, resulting in a need for progressively larger doses in order to achieve the desired effect. In such cases, discontinuing the use of the drug results in the severe disturbance of homeostasis known as the withdrawal syndrome (abstinence).

Although the phenomenon of the physiological dependency has been used to distinguish true addiction from so-called habituation (psychological dependence alone), such a qualitative distinction appears less valid when addiction is viewed in psychoanalytic terms. In a recent study of severe cases of narcotics addiction, Savitt (1963) offered the following explanation: "Object relationships are on an archaic level, and the addict is unable to experience love and gratification through the usual channels of incorporation and introjection. Because of the inability to tolerate delay, he seeks an emergency measure which bypasses the oral route of incorporation in favor of a more primitive one, the intravenous channel."

Eidelberg (1954) has characterized the addict as one who gratifies his infantile omnipotence with the help of the object (drug) he needs. In this way, the internal narcissistic mortification ("It is not true that I cannot control my craving") is denied, and, instead, the external narcissistic mortification ("I depend on the drug") is accepted.

Related Concepts: COMPULSIVE MASTURBATION; FETISHISM.

REFERENCES

Eidelberg, L., *An Outline of a Comparative Pathology of the Neuroses.* IUP, pp. 210–211, 1954.
Savitt, R. A., "Psychoanalytic Studies on Addiction: Ego Structure in Narcotic Addiction." *Q*, 32:43–57, 1963.

ADDITIONAL READINGS

Abraham, K., "Beiträge zur Kenntnis des Delirium Tremens der Morphinisten." *CNP*, 25, 1902.
Freud, S.: 1897, *The Origins of Psychoanalysis: Letters to Wilhelm Fliess.* BB, 1954.
    1928, "Dostoevsky and Parricide." *SE*, 21, 1961.
Gerard, D. L., "Intoxication and Addiction. Psychiatric Observations on Alcoholism and Opiate Drug Addiction." *QJSA*, 16, 1955.
Hárnik, J., "Die Mitwirkung des Ichs in der Psychogenese der Giftsüchte—und was daraus für die Therapie folgt." *ZPt*, 6, 1933.
Kronfeld, A., "Zur Psychologie des Süchtigseins." *PtPrx*, 2, 1935.
Savitt, R., "Extramural Psychoanalytic Treatment of a Case of Narcotics Addiction." *JAPA*, 2, 1954.
Simmel, E., "Alcoholism and Addiction." *Q*, 17, 1948.

119
ADOLESCENCE is that phase of life between childhood and adulthood which is equivalent chronologically to the second decade of life. It has, however, a beginning and an ending, denoted by physical and mental changes not necessarily tied to

a specific span of years. Freud (1905) described adolescence as "a period of final transformations. . . ." A. Freud (1936), described it as follows: "[It is] a breaking out once more with the first approach to puberty, when the distribution of forces inside the individual is upset by qualitative changes in the drives and the ego of childhood, threatened with anxiety by the drive development, enters into a struggle for survival in which all available methods of defense are brought into play and strained to the upmost. . . .

"Normally the organization of the ego and super-ego alter sufficiently to accomodate the new mature forms of sexuality. In less favorable instances a rigid, immature ego succeeds in inhibiting or distorting sexual maturity; in some cases the id impulses succeed in creating utter confusion and chaos in what has been an orderly, socially directed ego during the latency period."

The crisis occurs with the attempt to establish an identity. Erikson (1956) noted: "Identity formation begins where identification with persons of the past ends." When identity experiences have a significantly new and convincing quality, the adolescent moves ahead to adult character forms. In an earlier work, Erikson (1950) noted: "In their search for a new sense of continuity and sameness, adolescents have to refight many of the battles of earlier years, even though to do so they must artificially appoint perfectly well-meaning people to play the roles of enemies; and they are ever ready to install lasting idols and ideals as guardians of a final identity: here puberty rites 'confirm' the inner design for life.

"The integration now taking place in the form of ego identity is more than the sum of the childhood identifications. It is the accrued experience of the ego's ability to integrate these identifications with the vicissitudes of the libido, with the aptitudes developed out of endowment, and with the opportunities offered in social roles. The sense of ego identity, then, is the accrued confidence that the inner sameness and continuity are matched by the sameness and continuity of one's meaning for others."

As A. Freud noted in 1936, a relatively strong id confronts a relatively weak ego. "Adolescents are excessively egoistic, regarding themselves as the centre of the universe and the sole object of interest, and yet at no time in later life are they capable of so much self-sacrifice and devotion. They form the most passionate love-relations, only to break them off as abruptly as they began them. On the one hand they throw themselves enthusiastically into the life of the community and, on the other, they have an over-powering longing for solitude. They oscillate between blind submission to some self-chosen leader and defiant rebellion against any and every authority. They are selfish and materially-minded and at the same time full of lofty idealism. They are ascetic but will suddenly plunge into instinctual indulgence of the most primitive character. At times their behaviour to other people is rough and inconsiderate, yet they themselves are extremely touchy. Their moods veer between light-hearted optimism and the blackest pessimism. Sometimes they will work with indefatigable enthusiasm and at other times they are sluggish and apathetic." Peers and nonparental objects are recathected by identification, which results in intense ego-ideal formations, increased cathexis of ego functions, and as Landauer (1935) pointed out, heightened ego experiences.

Adolescence was characterized by Blos (1962), as follows:

a. Preadolescence. Resolution of the fixation to the preoedipal active, phallic mother, which begins in the oedipal stage (ages three to five, approx.) and continues through the period of preadolescence. The girl, in liberating herself from her mother, temporarily identifies with the active image of her. The boy overcomes his breast envy and his fear of the phallic mother, which he does by identification with her (overt homosexuality).

b. Early Adolescence. Decline of the bisexual tendencies and the establishment of a polarity of active and passive roles. The component instincts (oral, anal, phallic) become fused and genitality assumes primacy.

c. Adolescence Proper. Decathexis of the internalized parents permits the subject to seek the opposite sex.

d. Late Adolescence. Elaboration of an ego identity is accomplished through work, love and sublimation, and the ego boundaries are thereby extended. An individual way of life is thus experienced.

e. Post Adolescence. Harmonization of the entire drive and ego organization and the possibility of parenthood makes its specific contribution to personality growth.

Related Concepts: COMPONENT INSTINCTS; OEDIPUS COMPLEX.

REFERENCES

Blos, P., *On Adolescence.* Mac, pp. 52, 98, 1962.
Erikson, E. H.: *Childhood and Society.* Nor, p. 228, 1950.
    Identity and the Life Cycle. IUP, Psychological Issues, 1:112–113, 1959.
Freud, A., 1936, *The Ego and the Mechanisms of Defense.* IUP, pp. 149–150, 1946.
Freud, S., 1905, "Three Essays on the Theory of Sexuality." *SE,* 7:243, 1953.
Landauer, K., "Die Ich-Organisation in der Pubertät." *PsaP,* 9:380–420, 1935.

ADDITIONAL READINGS

Arlow, J. A., "A Psychoanalytic Study of a Religious Initiation Rite: Bar Mitzvah." *PsaStC,* 6, 1951.
Ausubel, D. P., *Theory and Problems of Adolescent Development.* G&S, 1954.
Blos, P., "Prolonged Adolescence: The Formulation of a Syndrome and Its Therapeutic Implications." *Ops,* 24, 1954.
Buxbaum, E., Report on Panel: "The Psychology of Adolescence." *JAPA,* 6, 1958.
Freud, A., "Adolescence." *PsaStC,* 13, 1958.
Harley, M., "Some Observations on the Relationship Between Genitality and Structural Development at Adolescence." *JAPA,* 9, 1961.
Jacobson, E., "Adolescent Moods and the Remodeling of Psychic Structures in Adolescence." *PsaStC,* 15, 1960.
Mead, M., "Cultural Contexts of Puberty and Adolescence." *BPAP,* 1959.
Root, N. N., "A Neurosis in Adolescence." *PsaStC,* 12, 1957.
Schwartz, L. A., "An Interpretation of the Emotional Needs of the Adolescent." *VTB,* 16, 1941.
Spiegel, L. A.: "A Review of Contributions to the Psychoanalytic Theory of Adolescence: Individual Aspects." *PsaStC,* 6, 1951.
    "Comments on the Psychoanalytic Psychology of Adolescence." *PsaStC,* 13, 1958.
Stein, M. H., "The Adolescent and His Parents." *Child Study,* 1955.

120

AEROPHAGIA denotes the spasmodic swallowing of air, often accompanied by distension of both the stomach and abdomen. A sense of fullness in the lower substernal region, palpitations, and pain in the pericardium and left anterior parts of the chest often result from the gastric accumulation of air. Although aerophagia usually has an emotional origin, the symptoms cited often have a physiological basis which can be reproduced by mechanical inflation of the stomach with air. [Harrison, 1950.]

Aerophagia may result from any emotional stimuli which effects physiological changes resulting in hyperventilation (Arieti, 1959). However, the symptom may be unconsciously produced in order to express symbolically specific unconscious wishes. For instance, a woman may unconsciously fulfill pregnancy wishes by causing her abdomen to extend. Similarly, unconscious cannibalistic wishes may be given symbolic realization. Superego contraventions associated with such wishes may be gratified through the pain which sometimes accompanies the symptom. Further, narcissistic omnipotence can be realized through such a symptom in that it frees the individual of a need for objects; i.e., a woman may symbolically impregnate herself and be independent of the need for a man. The above examples reflect the over-determined and complex symbolic import which the symptom can acquire.

Related Concepts: ANOREXIA NERVOSA; PSYCHO-SOMATIC.

REFERENCES

Arieti, S., ed., *American Handbook of Psychiatry.* BB, vol. 1, 1959.
Harrison, T. R., ed., *Principles of Internal Medicine.* Bl, 1950.

121

AESTHETIC PLEASURE is characterized by the gratification of aim-inhibited instincts. Consequently, although it does not require possession of the object to be enjoyed, it has all the characteristics of end-pleasure. This enjoyment—this kind of ideation—is a purely aesthetic one, which lies only in itself, which has its aim only in itself and which fulfills none of the other ends in life. Thus, an individual who doesn't have aim-inhibited instincts obtains forepleasure through his sense organs, which, after a time, becomes unpleasure, unless he succeeds in physically acquiring the object itself. For instance, if such a man sees a nude in a painting, he is only interested in possessing the model and not the painting; i.e., he is interested in the gratification of his genital desires only. In a normal individual, both aesthetic pleasure and instinctual gratification are possible; the neurotic, on the other hand, may use the aesthetic experience as a defense.

It is not quite clear why Freud (1911) described the activity of the artist as not following the long roundabout path of making real alterations in the external world. The artist's work is considered a work of art because it is not a daydream. Thus, according to Freud: "He is able by making use of special gifts, to mould his phantasy into truth of a new kind"—into aesthetic truth.

Freud regarded the aesthetic experience as dependent more on form than on content, and examined, in detail, certain specific examples as manifested in jokes, humor and comedy. In this, aesthetic pleasure is regarded as a form of forepleasure. He wrote, in 1905: "The pleasure in jokes has seemed to us to arise from an economy in expenditure. . . ."

This may explain the role of *playfulness*, for, as Fischer* noted (quoted by Freud, 1905), "the aesthetic attitude towards an object is characterized by the condition that we do not ask anything of the object, especially no satisfaction of our serious needs, but content ourselves with the enjoyment of contemplating it. The aesthetic attitude is *playful* in contrast to work."

Kris (1952) suggested: "The shifts in cathexis of mental energy which the work of art elicits or facilitates are, we believe, pleasurable in themselves. From the release of passion under the protection of the aesthetic illusion to the highly complex process of re-creation under the artist's guidance, a series of processes of psychic discharge take place, which could be differentiated from each other by the varieties and degrees of neutralization of the energy discharged. All these processes, however, are controlled by the ego, and the degree of neutralization indicates the degree of ego autonomy."

Related Concepts: JOKE (WIT); PLEASURE PRINCIPLE.

REFERENCES

Freud, S.: 1905, "Jokes and Their Relation to the Unconscious." *SE*, 8:10–11, 236, 1960.
    1908, "Creative Writers and Day-Dreaming." *SE*, 9:153, 1959.
    1911, "Formulations on the Two Principles of Mental Functioning." *SE*, 12:224, 1958.

---

* Fischer, K., *Über den Witz.* Heidelberg, 1889.

Kris, E., *Psychoanalytic Explorations in Art.* IUP, 1952.

ADDITIONAL READINGS

Baudouin, C., *Psychoanalysis and Aesthetics.* D, 1924.
Eidelberg, L., *Studies in Psychoanalysis.* IUP, 1952.
Freud, S., 1919, "The Uncanny." *SE*, 17, 1955.
Kanzer, M., & S. Tarachow, "Arts and Aesthetics (part 6)." *AnSurvPsa*, 1, 1950.
Kris, E., "Probleme der Aesthetik." *Z*, 26, 1941.
    & A. Kaplan, "Aesthetic Ambiguity." *PPR*, 8, 1948,
Mayer, F., "Freud und Adler im Licht der Aesthetik." *ZPt*, 4, 1931.
Rank, O., "Beiträge zur Symbolik in der Dichtung." *Z*, 2, 1914.
Reik, T.: "Arthur Schnitzler als Psycholog." *RvHSIm*, 3, 1914.
    "Aesthetik, Literatur, Kunst." *Y*, 6, 1914.
Segal, H., "A Psychoanalytic Approach to Aesthetics." *IntJPsa*, 33, 1952.

122

AFFECT. Originally, Freud insisted that affects could not become unconscious, that only ideas—the abstract concepts of instinctual wishes—could become so. This opinion was based on the conviction that a discharge of instinctual tension could only take place in the *Cs*.

While denying the unconsciousness of an affect, it would appear that Freud considered the anxiety capable of becoming unconscious. A clarification of Freud's idea appeared later (1923). According to Freud, neither the instincts nor the instinctual fusions are directly observed. They do, however, produce two kinds of derivatives which may be examined by psychological methods: (a) ideas, the abstract concepts of instinctual wishes; and (b) affects, the emotions, motoric and secretory discharges connected with instinctual tension.

The recognition that the ego, which is today considered to control all the discharges, may be partly conscious, unconscious or preconscious seems to indicate that unconscious and preconscious feelings are possible. The fact that during sleep feelings and even some acts take place, and the fact that a number of individuals are not aware of having made a slip of the tongue, appears to indicate that Freud's original concept concerning affects should be reexamined.

Critics of Freud did not deny that an idea may disappear and then return. They objected only to the term *unconscious*; they preferred to say that the conscious idea, when it disappeared, ceased to exist as an idea (latent), becoming an idea only when it reentered consciousness. Semantically, the same argument could be used in connection with the concept of unconscious affects.

Related Concepts: EMOTION; UNPLEASURE-PLEASURE PRINCIPLE.

REFERENCES

Freud, S.: 1915, "Papers on Metapsychology." *SE*, 14:178, 1957.
     1923, "The Ego and the Id." *SE*, 19:23, 1961.

ADDITIONAL READINGS

Abraham, K., "Einige Belege zur Gefühlseinstellung weiblicher Kinder gegenüber den Eltern." *Z*, 4, 1917.
Bonnard, A., "Some Discrepancies Between Perception and Affect as Illustrated by Children in Wartime." *PsaStC*, 9, 1954.
Brierley, M., "Die Affekte in der Theorie und Praxis." *Z*, 1936.
Eidelberg, L., *An Outline of a Comparative Pathology of the Neuroses.* IUP, 1954.
Ferenczi, S.: "Lachen." *BaustPsa*, 4, 1913.
     "Die Nacktheit als Schreckmittel." *Z*, 1919.
Freud, S., 1915, "Instincts and Their Vicissitudes." *SE*, 14, 1957.
Glover, E., "The Psychoanalysis of Affects." *IntJPsa*, 20, 1939.
Greenacre, P., ed., *Affective Disorders: Psychoanalytic Contributions to Their Study.* IUP, 1953.
Rapaport, D., "On the Psychoanalytic Theory of Affects." *IntJPsa*, 34, 1953.
Sechehaye, M., "Affects and Frustrated Needs of a Schizophrenic Seen Through Her Drawings." *ActaNeurolBelg*, 1957.

123

AGENT PROVOCATEUR. Heredity was regarded by Charcot as the sole cause of hysteria; any other etiological factor was considered to be merely an incidental precipitating factor, an "agent provocateur" as he termed it. In two early papers on the neuropsychoses of defense, Freud (1894, 1896a) demonstrated that a hysterical symptom in an adult may result from the repression by the ego of an "incompatible idea" and that the symptom serves to support the repression of the idea as well as to give it symbolic expression. He (1896b) extended his concept later that same year, and suggested that the "incompatible idea" assumed traumatic strength because of an associative connection with memories of actual traumatic infantile sexual experiences. The etiological role of these actual infantile seduction experiences were responsible for hysteria, not heredity as Charcot had indicated. Freud felt that a child who had been the passive victim of a seduction was predisposed to developing hysteria in later life and, further, that a child who had actively seduced another child would be predisposed to develop an obsessional neurosis. This concept was never totally rejected but was modified greatly in his subsequent writings.

The term *agent provocateur* was used by Freud to designate any concurrent idea, phantasy, or experience which by association with repressed traumatic infantile fantasies and memory traces served to bring about symptoms, defensive reactions, and even normal phenomena such as dreams.

Related Concept: CAUSALITY.

REFERENCES

Freud, S.: 1894, "The Neuro-Psychoses of Defence." *SE*, 3:45–61, 1962.
     1896a, "Further Remarks on the Neuro-Psychoses of Defence." *SE*, 3:162–174, 1962.
     1896b, "The 'Specific' Aetiology of Hysteria." *SE*, 3:163–167, 1962.

124

AGNOSIA is a concept introduced by Freud (1891) in his preanalytic studies, to describe a type of aphasia in which the recognition of objects is impaired, a defect essentially linked to the ability to form psychic representations from the sensory data of objects. Presumably, this early work foreshadowed later distinctions that Freud made between word-presentations associated with the preconscious and thing-presentations associated with the unconscious. The term agnosia took root in neurology and has become an established concept in that field, where it is usually attributed to brain damage.

Related Concept: APHASIA.

REFERENCE

Freud, S., 1891, "Aphasie," in A. Villaret, *Hand-wörterbuch der Gesamten Medizin*. Stuttgart: Enke, 1:88–90, 1888–1891.

ADDITIONAL READINGS

Freud, S., 1915, "The Unconscious." *SE*, 12, 1957.
Schilder, P., & O. Isakower, "Optischräumliche Agnosie und Agraphie." *ZNP*, 11, 1928.

125

AGGRESSION, also referred to as an aggressive instinct-fusion, is a mixture of Eros and Thanatos, with Thanatos dominating, and is present in all four stages of mental development. In this, the concept of Eros is connected with the need to seek pleasure. Freud said (1933) that Thanatos opposes Eros and aims at the return to an inorganic state. In addition, it appears that Eros makes the subject search for new sources of pleasure, and, therefore, may be considered as closely related to the goal of obtaining pleasure, while the death instinct appears to be aimed at the goal of avoiding unpleasure.

Freud (1923) described the death instinct as a silent one.*

Because Freud recognized aggression as a separate drive (though he originally identified aggression as belonging to the sexual drive), his early assumption that love changes into hate (reversal of the opposite) might better be described as a mobilization of hate resulting from frustrated love (mobilization of the opposite instinct). The individual may seek an aggressive satisfaction independently of sexual aims.

While it is true that Freud used the terms *aggressive* and *active* synonymously (in 1909), in his essay "Three Essays On The Theory of Sexuality" (1905) and in his "New Introductory Lectures" (1933), he used the word active, not as a synonym for aggression, but as representing the most important characteristic of an instinct.

Mainx (1955) noted: "The most general statements about the state of living systems are especially concerned with the energy relations in the living world. The maintenance of the flow equilibrium, in other words, the preservation of the potential differences necessarily present in the living organism, is connected with incessant performance of work; the organism raises in this way the entropy level of its environment; it feeds, so to speak, on 'negative entropy' (Schrödinger). In connection with such considerations and similar ones, it is often customary to speak of the 'activity' of the organism as one of its special characteristics. So long as this word is used only to denote the mutual energy relations between organism and environment, it is meaningful from the point of view of empirical science."

While agreeing that activity in women should no longer be regarded as representative of their masculine counterpart, Freud nonetheless insisted that this female activity was characterized by the presence of chiefly passive aims. He (1933) stated that it must be recognized that a woman's relation to her infant child cannot be referred to as gratification of a passive aim; it seems to indicate clearly the presence of active aims. These active aims cannot be considered the masculine part of her bisexual personality.

Freud (1939) added in a later paper that it was probable that two kinds of instincts could be assumed to be responsible for life and death of the organism; i.e., Eros and Thanatos, respectively. In the female the libido appears to be more repressed than is true for males. Freud suggested that in using a teleological approach one may say that the male may gratify his sexual needs by impregnating his female partner without her permission.

Freud indicated that in normal lovemaking man gratified not only his sexual but also his aggressive wishes. However, Eidelberg (1935) pointed out that the differentiation between sexual instincts and aggressive instincts can be made on the basis of the following definition: "In comparing actions that serve to gratify the sexual instinct fusion, we discover that gratification of the latter is possible only when the object of the aggression displays resistance.

"This fact seems to be genetically connected with the first emergence of the aggressive instinct fusion as a result of the earliest prohibitions and frustrations experienced by the subject."

Eidelberg (1954) further stated that "while psychoanalysis is unable to differentiate directly between the sexual and aggressive instincts, it may separate

---

* Freud never named the energy of the aggressive drive, but two of his pupils have suggested *destrudo* (Weiss) and *mortido* (Federn).

[their derivatives]. . . . Aggressive pleasure is experienced when the subject overcomes the resistance of the object, whereas sexual pleasure is experienced by both the subject and the object, and is achieved by the actions of both."

Related Concepts: ANXIETY; ATTRACTION OF THE FORBIDDEN; DEPRESSION; HATE; PSYCHIC (MENTAL) ENERGY; SENSE OF GUILT.

REFERENCES

Eidelberg, L.: 1935, *Studies in Psychoanalysis.* IUP, p. 135, 1948.
    An Outline of a Comparative Pathology of the Neuroses. IUP, pp. 35, 36, 1954.
Freud, S.: 1909, "Analysis of a Phobia in a Five-Year-Old Boy." *SE*, 10:140–141, 1955.
    1923, "Two Encyclopedia Articles." *SE*, 18:258, 1955.
    1933, "New Introductory Lectures on Psycho-Analysis." *SE*, 22:96, 107, 115, 1964.
    1939, "Moses And Monotheism: Three Essays." *SE*, 23:131, 1964.
Mainx, F., "Foundation of Biology," in *International Encyclopedia of Unified Science*, UCP, 1:26–27, 1955.

ADDITIONAL READINGS

Albino, R. C., "Defences Against Aggression in the Play of Young Children." *M*, 27, 1954.
Bacon, C., "The Role of Aggression in the Asthmatic Attack." *Q*, 25, 1956.
Bandura, A., & R. H. Walters, *Adolescent Aggression.* RP, 1959.
Berna, J., "Kinderanalyse eines Aggressiven." *P*, 9, 1955.
Bowlby, J., "The Abnormally Aggressive Child." *New Era*, 19, 1938.
Freud, A.: "Aggression in Relation to Emotional Development: Normal and Pathological." *PsaStC*, 3–4, 1949.
    "The Problem of Aggression and Its Relation to Normal and Pathological Development." *Harefuah*, 50, 1956.
Freud, S., 1929, "Civilization and Its Discontents." *SE*, 21, 1961.
Gardner, G. E., "The Origin and Nature of Aggressive Behavior." *DAM*, 1955.
Hartmann, H., E. Kris, & R. Loewenstein, "Notes on the Theory of Aggression." *PsaStC*, 3–4, 1949.
Karpman, B., "Aggression." *Ops*, 20, 1950.
Litpon, S., Report on Panel: "Aggression and Symptom Formation." *JAPA*, 9, 1961.
Ostow, M., Report on Panel: "Theory of Aggression." *JAPA*, 5, 1957.
Sterba, R. F., "Die Aggression in der Rettungs-phantasie." *Z*, 25, 1940.
Ziwar, M., "Aggression and Intercostal Neuralgia, a Psychosomatic Study." *EJP*, 1, 1945.

126

AIM-INHIBITED DRIVES are modified instinctual drives which, under the influence of the ego and superego, allow for gratification before the ultimate, original aim is achieved. Ordinarily, such an interruption would be experienced as a frustration; in an aim-inhibited instinct this is not so, for as Freud (1920) pointed out, the aim of an instinct is full discharge with the help of an external object. In amplifying Freud's remarks, Hartmann (1964) noted: "The interest in the aims became predominant, particularly because of their wide variability, characteristic of the human species. Looked at from this point of view (with all its implications for substitute gratification and aim-inhibited expression), it became possible to draw a rather comprehensive picture of the correlations between a person's needs on various levels, his emotions, his ways of solving problems, etc.; and a wealth of concrete features, heterogeneous as they might have appeared from another approach, fell into line. This, of course, also emphasizes the comparative freedom from reactive rigidity, the comparative independence from, and variety of, possible responses to outer and to inner stimuli that we attribute to man to a greater extent than to other species."

Some analysts differentiate between the form of the discharge (e.g., eating) and the external object (e.g., food). For example, feelings of tenderness, while derived from pregenital and genital sexual drives, are not necessarily dependent on *physical* sexual gratifications. In general, enduring object relations become possible independent of fulfillment of the original need. Aim-inhibited drives do not follow the pattern of relatively slow build-up and quick discharge; more constant and prolonged discharge is possible. Rapid fluctuations in drive tension are less characteristic. Destructive instincts may also be aim-inhibited; for example, sarcasm may be an expression of an aim-inhibited wish to devour and bite. Some authors maintain that an aim-inhibited instinct requires countercathexis.

Sublimated drives may allow relatively full discharge of the drive-cathexis; aim-inhibited drives do not.

Related Concepts: AESTHETIC PLEASURE; INSTINCTUAL AIM; SUBLIMATION.

REFERENCES

Freud, S., 1920, "Beyond the Pleasure Principle." *SE*, 18:51–53, 1955.
Hartmann, H., *Essays on Ego Psychology.* IUP, p. 73, 1964.

ADDITIONAL READINGS

Ferenczi, S.: "Denken und Muskelinnervation." *Z*, 1919.
    "Geburt des Intellekts." *BaustPsa*, 1931.
    "Goethe über den Realitätswert der Phantasie beim Dichter." *C*, 1912.
Freud, S.: 1914, "On Narcissism: An Introduction." *SE*, 14, 1957.
    1923, "The Ego and the Id." *SE*, 19, 1961.
Pfister, O.: "Die Rolle des Unbewussten im philosophischen Denken." *Dialectica*, 1949.
    "Psychoanalyse und bildende Kunst." *PsaVkb*, 1926.
Rank, O.: *Art and Artist; Creative Urge and Personality Development*, TP, 1932.
    Der Künstler; Ansätze zu einer Sexualpsychologie. H, 1907.
Starcke, A., "Aanvullende mededeelinger bij de Demonstratie eener Artistieke Productie." *NTvG*, 65, 1921.

127
ALCOHOLISM is an addictive state which develops in a specific character-matrix. For instance, the phobic subject may carry a bottle of alcohol in his pocket to use as a tranquillizer; the homosexual in a heterosexual marriage may drink to make the stress situation tolerable. According to Jellinek (1952), alcoholism begins with a prodromal phase which is characterized by a preoccupation with alcohol, occasional surreptitious drinking, and the use of alcohol as a drug in order to reach a specific psychological state. Occasionally, amnesia for what happened during this state occurs, although the amount of alcohol consumed might not have been excessive. There is a feeling of guilt about drinking and therefore an avoidance of reference to alcohol in conversation. Even in this phase total abstinence is to be recommended for therapy. In the next phase, which Jellinek calls the crucial phase, the desire for alcohol is felt as a physical need, and the fight against this passion leads on one hand to voluntary attempts at abstinence and on the other hand to rationalizations. Lack of self-esteem is overcompensated by grandiosity. There are breakthroughs of repressions and persistent remorse. Life becomes alcohol-centered, and the relationships to other people are reinterpreted; friends who are not alcoholics are dropped; often there is a change of jobs, a loss of outside interests, self-pity, tendency to run away, unreasonable resentment against the family, decrease of libido, alcoholic jealousy, and a need to protect his supply by hiding bottles of alcohol. In the chronic phase (after 7–10 years), there are periods of prolonged intoxication, an impairment of thinking, and an inclination to associate with people below his social level can be observed. A breakdown in the alcoholic's characteristic rationalizations may occur. The subject becomes increasingly selfish, unreliable, and untruthful.

Clinically, alcoholism is characterized by the following: (a) Oral fixation is based on a combination of traumatic experiences in infancy with a probably inherited, stronger and more vulnerable oral-component drive than is average. (b) Narcissistic mortifications lead to self-pity, a persistence of magical thinking, frequent grandiosity, an inclination for dwelling in illusions, an insatiable demand for evidences of love and for omnipotence, and a pseudoconviviality which is hiding a pervasive emotional detachment from people: objects are nothing but deliverers of narcissistic supplies. (c) Feelings of guilt and chronic depression are present with the wish for oblivion and death (often as a result of violence on the part of the father). (d) A defective superego permits impulsivity and the pursuit of immediate pleasure, and a tendency to act out conflicts, probably based on the lack of a desirable father image. (e) The ego is not restrictive. The alcoholic is not willing to accept taboos; there is an absence of neurotic defenses, a facade of invulnerability but in reality great vulnerability; he has a craving for intense relationships, and an inability to compromise: he looks for perfection and cannot accept his imperfections. His aggressiveness is free-floating instead of sublimated, and aimed at breaking dependencies; he is willing to take chances; the mechanisms of denial and projection are predominant, and, therefore, there is a predisposition toward paranoia.

Sperling (1931) assumed that chronic alcoholism was enhanced in a number of cases by an unconscious feeling of guilt which was caused by the sexual education in Western civilization. A high percentage of the wives of alcoholics were frigid or rejecting. Only under the influence of alcohol was the man able to overcome his sexual inhibitions. Many of the alcoholics had their first sexual intercourse relatively late and then infrequently. The same was true for alcoholic women. The rejecting attitude of the partner increased the unconscious feelings of guilt. It was the repetition compulsion which made future alcoholics choose rejecting wives after having experienced a rejecting mother in the oral phase. Some needed alcohol as a precondition for extramarital adventures. In those cases, the arrangement of a situation which carried a conscious feeling of guilt served as a rationalization for an unconscious feeling of guilt.

Abraham (1911) was of the opinion that social influences, faulty education, and inheritance were not enough to explain alcoholism. Ferenczi (1911) emphasized the importance of a fixation at the oral level of psychosexual development. It was obvious that the bottle unconsciously equalled the infant's bottle, and that the greediness characteristic of the oral character was manifested in the intemperateness of the alcoholic. The atmosphere of unhappiness and irregularity in the families of alcoholics necessarily lead to oral deprivation. Knight (1937) observed that the mother of the alcoholic was overprotective and indulgent. The difficult family constellation created specific oral frustrations in childhood which resulted in oral fixation. In boys these frustrations resulted also in a turning away from the frustrating mother to the father, i.e., to more or less repressed homosexual tendencies. Early experiences produced the impulsive character structure which could not tolerate frustration, and which sustained itself through an insatiable need for affection.

Kielholz (1923) pointed out the frequent combination of physical deformation and alcoholism. The role of narcissistic mortification was also emphasized by Fenichel (1945): the alcoholic was seeking elevation in self-esteem. If the alcoholic could not get his narcissistic supplies from companions or from his

wife or from the real life situations, he could get them instantaneously from alcohol. Rado (1933) emphasized the pleasure which the alcoholic experiences. He assumed that the alcoholic established an artificial sexual organization which was autoerotic and modelled upon infantile masturbation. He compared it with the alimentary orgasm of the infant. Sperling (1931) assumed that the pleasure which the alcoholic craved had only a superficial similarity with the alimentary orgasm of the infant and was rather the result of a direct effect of alcohol on the pleasure centers of the cortex. Stanley Rosenman (1955) found the following fantasy as typical for the alcoholic: The sin committed by the alcoholic from which he recoiled was primitive orality. He hated the "good father" whom he held responsible for his degradation and appealed to the rival "bad father" (devil) for relief. Later, the alcoholic bewailed his lack of will power and the devil assumed the role of the castrating castrate who would emasculate him in vengence for his own impotence. Then the alcoholic became the degraded servant of the victorious good father. He turns to A.A. as a prodigal son. Hence, the alcoholic's self-belittling, ritualistic, and humiliating repetition of long-past errors as he addressed an Alcoholics Anonymous audience.

Noyes and Kolb (1959) emphasized the role of anxiety in the causation of alcoholism. This hypothesis is supported by Horton's (1943) findings in primitive societies. He observed that the greater the anxiety concerning drought or flood or crop failure or threatening neighboring tribes, the greater would be the amount of drinking.

Related Concept: ADDICTION.

REFERENCES:

Abraham, K., 1911, "The Psychological Relations Between Sexuality and Alcoholism." *IntJPsa*, 7:2–10, 1926.
Fenichel, O., *The Psychoanalytic Theory of Neurosis*, Nor, p. 376, 1945.
Ferenczi, S., 1912, "On the Part Played by Homosexuality in the Pathogenesis of Paranoia." *SPsa*, pp. 154–186, 1916.
Horton, D., "The Functions of Alcohol in Primitive Societies: A Cross-Cultural Study." *QJSA*, 4: 199, 1943.
Jellinek, E., "Phases of Alcohol Addiction." *QJSA*, 13:673, 1952.

Noyes, A., & L. C. Kolb, *Modern Clinical Psychiatry*. Sau, p. 192, 1959.

Rado, S., "Psychoanalysis of Pharmacothymia." *Q*, 2:1, 1933.

Rosenman, S., "Pacts, Possessions and the Alcoholic." *Im*, 12:241–274, 1955.

Sperling, O., "Alkoholismus und Sexual-Erziehung." *Sexualnot und Sexualreform*, pp. 1–6, 1931.

ADDITIONAL READINGS

Abraham, K., "The Psychological Relations Between Sexuality and Alcoholism." *IntJPsa*, 7, 1926.

Falstein, E. I., "Juvenile Alcoholism: A Psycho-dynamic Case Study of Addiction." *Ops*, 23, 1953.

Glover, E., "The Etiology of Alcoholism." *PRSM*, 21, 1928.

Menninger, W. C.: "The Treatment of Chronic Alchohol Addiction." *BMC*, 2, 1938.

   "Alcoholism: A National Emergency." *MennQ* 1 (2), 1957.

Pfeffer, Arnold, *Alcoholism*. G&S, 1958.

128

ALIMENTARY ORGASM. Rado (1928) noted that the primitive ego of the hungry infant was traumatically flooded by distressing physical sensations and impotent aggressive impulses; sucking at the breast effected a rapid, pleasurable reduction in tension accompanied by restoration of the ego's equilibrium. He observed that the infant subjectively experienced a feeling of bliss at the height of the process of satiation and this he termed *alimentary orgasm*.

Rado considered the alimentary orgasm to be the prototypical experience for subsequent behavior, such as anal expulsion and adult genital orgasm. He suggested that the wish to reexperience the alimentary orgasm was universally persistent and, as a result of propitious superego relationships, reflected itself in such normal states as heightened feelings of self-esteem and religious transport. He considered the wish to reexperience the alimentary orgasm to be a driving one in profoundly regressed persons and related this need to clinical problems of melancholia and mania, as well as to various forms of drug intoxication and addiction.

Related Concepts: GENITAL PHASE; ORAL PHASE; ORGASM (CLIMAX).

REFERENCE

Rado, S., "The Problem of Melancholia." *IntJPsa*, 9:420–438, 1928.

129

ALLOPLASTIC is a form of adaptation directed toward altering the environment rather than the self. The ultimate origin of this urge, this motility, leads to changes in the subject's relationship to the external world, a successor to the autoplastic developmental stage in which the affect is discharged inwardly. Initially dominated by the pleasure principle, the individual's motility evolves into purposeful action under the guidance of the reality principle. Pathological manifestations of alloplastic adaptations are to be found in cases in which motility retains its more primitive and magical functions, as in acting out, compulsions, impulse disorders, flights into reality and psychoses. [Freud, 1924.]

Clinical Example

Eidelberg (1948) cited the following: "The wish to know the analyst socially occurs in many patients, and so we can compare the attitude of this particular man with that of others. The first thing we notice is that he accepted my view at once and without reservation, whereas other patients try to dispute with the analyst or claim to be treated as exceptions. Some accept his refusal, saying: 'You are quite right in not wanting to associate with a person like me', and others maintain that they made the suggestion only out of politeness and are glad that it has been declined. I shall not enumerate all their various reactions, but I think you will agree with me from your own experience that in most cases the refusal to enter into social relations evokes in the patient a more or less obviously aggressive affect, which manifests itself either directly or else shortly afterwards in his associations and dreams. Nothing of the sort happened in this patient of mine and, when I pointed this out to him, he replied that this was just because of his ideal method of adapting himself to reality. By this he meant that he always at once assimilated himself to the person with whom he chanced to be talking and so never had any external conflict. His analysis showed, however, that the contrary was the case: he had a great many conflicts. The external world is not a homogeneous whole and, when he had agreed with A, he could no longer conceal the fact that he had also endorsed the opinions of B, C, and D, which differed from those of A."

Related Concepts: ADAPTATION; INTROVERSION (FANTASY CATHEXIS).

REFERENCES

Eidelberg, L., *Studies in Psychoanalysis.* IUP, p. 108, 1948.
Freud, S., 1924, "The Loss of Reality in Neurosis and Psychosis." *SE*, 19:185, 1961.

ADDITIONAL READINGS

Alexander, F., "The Neurotic Character." *IntJPsa*, 11, 1930.
Ferenczi, S., "Autoplastic and Alloplastic Adaptation." *IntJPsa*, 30, 1949

130

ALTRUISM is the subordination of individual interests to those of others. Identification and the curbing of aggression are significant factors in the transformation from infantile egoism to altruism, a transformation frequently arising as a result of a narcissistic mortification associated with sibling rivalry. Renunciation of the demand for the mother's love, through an altruistic reaction formation, may dispose some to homosexuality in an overt form, or may assume a paranoid tinge. In sublimation, it may lead to positive social feelings. Anna Freud (1936) viewed the masochistic and superego aspects of *altruistic surrender*, and discussed the gratifying and defensive aspects of this behavior pattern. She described a patient of hers, as follows: "She projected her prohibited instinctual impulses on to other people. . . . The patient did not dissociate herself from her proxies but identified herself with them. She showed her sympathy with their wishes and felt that there was an extraordinarily strong bond between these people and herself. Her superego, which condemned a particular instinctual impulse when it related to her own ego, was surprisingly tolerant of it in other people. She gratified her instincts by sharing in the gratification of others, employing for this purpose the mechanisms of projection and identification. The retiring attitude which the prohibition of her impulses caused her to adopt where she herself was concerned vanished when it was a question of fulfilling the same wishes after they had been projected on to someone else. The surrender of her instinctual impulses in favour of other people had thus an egoistic significance, but in her efforts to gratify the impulses of others her behaviour could only be called altruistic."

Related Concept: EGO.

REFERENCE

Freud, A., 1936, *The Ego and the Mechanisms of Defense.* IUP, pp. 136–137, 1946.

ADDITIONAL READING

Freud, S., 1917, "The Libido Theory and Narcissism." *SE*, 16, 1963.

131

AMBIGUITY is denotive of the double meaning of specific words or affects. Freud (1940) noted that in ancient languages contraries are expressed by the same words.

In one sense, the same may be said of affects. Namely, as Freud stated, contrary aims, too, can exist side by side without influencing each other in the unconscious. However, when there is a confluence a compromise occurs whereby these contrary aims are treated as though they were identical. Thus, in the manifest dream one element may stand for another, which is to be understood in terms of the ambiguity of the relationship between the manifest dream and the latent one lying behind it.

Clinically, a study of dreams and parapraxes in terms of their neurotic symptomology reveals many examples of ambiguity. It would seem, as Freud suggested, that they exist owing either to the presence of ambivalent id impulses in consciousness or in the unconscious defense of a nonambivalent wish. For instance, a patient who had ambivalent oral wishes to both love and destroy her mother, had a dream in which a shark appeared, representing both herself and the wish to devour (and possess) her mother.

A sexual phallic wish may lead to hysterical vomiting. The defense of this nonambivalent sexual wish is the aggressive countercathexis (mobilization of the opposite). Slips of the tongue also demonstrate the role ambiguity plays in neurotic expression. Freud (1901) reported that a male patient who wanted to accompany a young lady, intending to say, "May I *begleiten* you," in fact said, "May I beleidigen." In German, the word *begleiten* means "accompany" and *beleidigen* means "insulting." Thus, this slip of the tongue was a confession of aggressive impulses and was intended to provoke rejection.

Equally, ambiguity plays a role in jokes, for they usually end with a word or a phrase having an intended double meaning. Freud (1905) cited an example from Heine.* In reporting on a meeting with Baron Rothschild, Hirsch-Hyacinth says, "He treated me quite as his equal—quite famillionairely." Neither word—familiar nor millionaire—produces laughter, but their condensation with its resultant ambiguity does; the two words represent a slightly disguised wish to be treated familiarly by the rich Baron and his fear of rejection by the Baron.

Kris and Kaplan (1948) emphasized that it was an instrument of artistic style which forced attention from its usual channels and stimulated the primary process, those essential to recreative efforts of the imagination on which aesthetic pleasure depended. The disguise afforded by ambiguity permits forbidden thought contents to escape censorship. Kris distinguished many forms of ambiguity—the conjunctive, disjunctive, additive, etc. Nonetheless, independently of whether the ambiguity is the result of the unconscious id impulse becoming conscious or the result of a nonambiguous wish being warded off by the mobilization of the opposite instinct (love warded off by hate, for instance), it represents a basic characteristic of an unconscious defense mechanism, as shown in the study of dreams, jokes, parapraxes, and neurotic symptoms.

Related Concepts: AMBIVALENCE; ANTITHETICAL; CONDENSATION; JOKE (WIT).

REFERENCES

Freud, S.: 1901, "Psychopathology of Everyday Life." *SE*, 6:68, 1960.
    1905, "Jokes and Their Relationship to the Unconscious." *SE*, 7:16, 1960.

* Heine, H., *Reisebilder.*

    1940, "An Outline of Psycho-Analysis." *SE*, 23:169, 1964.
Kris, E., & A. Kaplan, "Aesthetic Ambiguity." *PPR*, 8:415–435, 1948.

132

AMBIVALENCE denotes the simultaneous existence of strong feelings of love and hate toward the same object. The term was originally used by Bleuler (1911) to describe a variety of other emotional oscillations; some analysts still define it in this broader sense.

Ambivalence is characteristic of the pregenital stage, when sexual and aggressive impulses are mixed. During the oral phase, for instance, the active libidinal aim is cannibalistic, to devour and incorporate the object, while aggression is discharged by shouting or spitting out.

The ambivalent state which exists in the melancholic was described by Freud in 1917. As he pointed out, "the loss of a love object is an excellent opportunity for the ambivalence in love relationships to make itself effective. . . ." For the melancholic, the loss of a love object leads to expressions of self-reproaches where the mourner blames himself for the death of the loved one. The self-torment is characteristic of the ambivalent love-hate attitude toward the object which has now been displaced onto the self.

Some analysts use the term ambivalence to describe the condition of a patient who is unable to make up his mind, whereas others prefer to call such a condition an *ambivalent oscillation* (Eidelberg, 1954). Ambivalent oscillation, as a defense mechanism, serves to protect the patient from the conscious awareness of the presence of an infantile wish and its defense. The patient also maintains the illusion that he can gratify both contradictory wishes at the same time.

Analysts are in general agreement regarding the importance of ambivalence in neuroses—the simultaneous presence of sexual and destructive wishes—but there is a difference of opinion over the source of the aggression involved. Many analysts agree with Freud that there is a separate aggressive instinct; some still follow his earlier instinct theory and maintain that aggression results from a reaction of the ego instincts to some sexual frustration or belongs to the sexual drive.

Clinical Example

After the death of his wife, a patient developed feelings of remorse and melancholia, which lead him to seek psychoanalytic help. In his analysis, he recognized that his feelings of remorse were the result of his unconscious wish to kill his wife, whom he loved and hated, simultaneously. As the death wish was unconscious, the patient reacted to her death as though he had actually killed her.

Related Concepts: AGGRESSION; AMBIGUITY; AMBIVALENT OSCILLATION; DEPRESSION; SADISM.

REFERENCES

Bleuler, E., 1911, *Dementia Praecox, or the Group of Schizophrenias.* IUP, 1950.
Eidelberg, L., *An Outline of a Comparative Pathology of the Neuroses.* IUP, p. 91, 1954.
Freud, S., 1917, "Mourning and Melancholia." *SE,* 14:250–252, 1957.

ADDITIONAL READINGS

Bose, G., "Ambivalence." *Samiksa,* 3, 1949.
Brody, M., "Clinical Manifestations of Ambivalence." *Q,* 25, 1956.
Freud, S.: 1909, "Notes Upon A Case of Obsessional Neurosis." *SE,* 10, 1955.
        1915, "Instincts and Their Vicissitudes." *SE,* 14, 1957.
        1923, "The Ego and the Id." *SE,* 19, 1961.
        1930, "Civilization and its Discontents." *SE,* 21, 1961.
Goldfarb, W., "The Significance of Ambivalency for Schizophrenic Dissociations." *JCP,* 6, 1944.
Odier, C., "A Literary Portrayal of Ambivalency." *IntJPsa,* 4, 1923.

133

AMBIVALENT OSCILLATION is a condition characterized by the subject's inability to make up his mind; quick changes from positive to negative impulses occur with resultant indecision. To differentiate ambivalent oscillation from ambivalence, the latter term is used only to denote the simultaneous existence of strong feelings of love and hate toward the same object.

Ambivalent oscillation, as a defense mechanism, serves to protect the patient from a conscious awareness of the presence of an infantile wish and its defense. The patient also maintains the illusion that he can gratify both contradictory wishes at the same time. If sexual and aggressive infantile wishes, representing active and passive aims, are used to ward each other off, ambivalent oscillation may be employed to eliminate from consciousness the simultaneous presence of these opposing tendencies.

For example, a patient simultaneously wanted to love and to hate his analyst; to give him money and to keep it for himself. These ambivalent feelings were expressed by a state of oscillation between these states. In this way, the patient was able to protect himself against the recognition of his instinct-tensions. His ambivalent oscillation seemed to serve two purposes: it kept the sexual and aggressive infantile wishes from becoming completely conscious, while still providing a partial discharge of their tensions; and it protected him from having to recognize the limitations of his power over others—his lack of power over his own ambivalent feelings. Thereafter, the patient's ambivalent oscillation became unbearable when he insisted that the analyst tell him what was right and what was wrong, a wish which the analyst failed to gratify.

Clinical Example

A patient who suffered from severe doubts about whether little pieces of glass were in the tip of his fingers was cured when the following material became conscious: His doubts started after he broke a bottle in the candy factory his father had founded and where he now worked as an employee following his father's death. Unconsciously, he wished to get little pieces of glass into the candies and to have his brother-in-law, who ran the plant, arrested. The pieces represented feces and his doubts demonstrated his hesitation between his wish to have his brother-in-law arrested by contaminating the candies and his wish to avoid it. The painful doubts were dealt with by his compulsion to show his hands to his sister, and thus to obtain her reassurance that his hands were free of glass.

Related Concepts: ANAL PHASE; LIBIDINAL TYPES; OBSESSIVE-COMPULSIVE NEUROSIS.

REFERENCE

Eidelberg, L., *An Outline of a Comparative Pathology of the Neuroses.* IUP, pp. 91, 92, 93, 1954.

ADDITIONAL READINGS

Eidelberg, L., *Take Off Your Mask*. IUP, 1948.
Freud, S.: 1909, "The Rat Man." *SE*, 10, 1955.
    1926, "Inhibitions, Symptoms and Anxiety."
SE, 20, 1959.

134

AMENTIA. Theodor Meynert used this term to describe various acute psychotic states. At a later date, the Viennese school of psychiatry used amentia as a diagnostic term for acute hallucinatory confusion with a toxic-exhaustive etiology. [Arieti, 1959.] When the term is currently used in the United States and England, it generally denotes a primary mental deficiency. This term is not utilized by modern psychoanalysis and its interest lies primarily in its historical use by Freud.

Freud (1917) suggested that amentia is a reaction to a loss. . . .

The psychotic reaction of a mother, for example, whose child has died would be to deny the death; to hallucinate the presence of the baby and to rock it to sleep. Freud compared the dynamic process involved in amentia to that characteristic of dreams. He felt that in both states the word-presentations of thought processes were regressively transformed into visual representations which then became conscious as sense perceptions. He reasoned that in dreams the withdrawal of cathexis affects all topographical systems equally, whereas in amentia the decathexis, which is primarily in the system *Cs*, affects the perceptions of certain aspects of reality and thus permits the isolated dominance in consciousness of the primary process.

Related Concepts: MANIC-DEPRESSIVE; SCHIZO-PHRENIA.

REFERENCES

Arieti, S., ed., *American Handbook of Psychiatry*.
BB, 2:1233, 1959.
Freud, S., "A Metapsychological Supplement to the Theory of Neurosis." *SE*, 14:233, 1957.

135

AMNESIA is the partial, complete, specific, or generalized loss of memory; often associated with the development of a neurosis. Amnesia may be investigated from a psychological or anatomical point of view. Freud emphasized the importance of hysterical amnesia, the elimination from memory of a traumatic experience through repression, and of infantile amnesia, the lack of memories most people have of their first five-to-eight years of life. The latter is attributed to the need to conceal the beginnings of sexual life, the limitation of the subject's power (infantile omnipotence). [Freud, 1925.]

Amnesia may be differentiated into: (a) anterograde amnesia, lack of memory of events that have transpired since the onset of amnesia; (b) retroactive amnesia, lack of memory of events prior to the onset of amnesia; (c) retrograde amnesia, lack of memory of something previously remembered; and (d) progressive and retrogressive amnesia, gradual loss or recovery of memory.

Related Concepts: REPRESSION; SCREEN MEMORY.

REFERENCES

Freud, S.: 1925, "An Autobiographical Study." *SE*, 20:39, 1959.
    1926, "Inhibitions, Symptoms and Anxiety."
SE, 20:120, 1959.

ADDITIONAL READINGS

Eissler, K. R., "An Unusual Function of an Amnesia."
PsaStC, 1955.
Freud, S.: 1899, "Screen Memories." *SE*, 3, 1962.
    1901, "The Psychopathology of Everyday Life." *SE*, 6, 1960.
    1905, "Fragment of an Analysis of a Case of Hysteria." *SE*, 7, 1953.
    1914, "Remembering, Repeating, and Working Through." *SE*, 12, 1958.
    1917, "Introductory Lectures on Psycho-Analysis." *SE*, 15, 1963.

136

AMPHIMIXIS is a term introduced by August Weismann (1892) to describe the mingling of cellular substances as a result of conjugations. It was used by Freud (1920) to connote the new stimulation of life. The recuperative effect of conjugation can be produced by certain changes of the nourishment of the living organism. In this, Freud concluded that infusoria die as a result of their own vital processes.

He explained Woodruff's findings as resulting from the addition of fresh nourishment to the new generation. Woodruff found that animalculae were damaged by the result of the excretions they produced and succeeded in showing that only the excretions of a certain kind of animalculae were responsible for their death. Freud was aware, of course, that the study of the natural deaths of protozoa would not necessarily elucidate the condition responsible for deaths in higher animals and reasoned that even if the protista were to be considered as immortal, as in Weismann's suggestion, death as a late acquisition related only to the manifest phenomenon and did not explain the processes responsible for it. Freud was thus able to conclude that biology did not negate the death instincts.

Related Concept: ORGASM (CLIMAX).

REFERENCES

Freud, S., 1920, "Beyond the Pleasure Principle." *SE*, 18:48–49, 1955.
Weismann, A., "Essays Upon Heredity and Kindred Biological Problems." *CP*, 2:179–181, 199, 1892.

137

ANACLITIC denotes a dependence on the possession of an external object for gratification. Freud (1914) noted: "We have, however, not concluded that human beings are divided into two sharply differentiated groups. . . ."

Thus, according to Freud, there are two types of object-choice: the anaclitic, "I want to have you," and the narcissistic, "I want to be similar to you or make you similar to me." Freud suggested that the normal masculine object-choice proceeded along anaclitic lines, whereas feminine object-choice depended more on narcissistic factors. In certain perversion, such as homosexuality, as Freud noted, the narcissistic object-choice played the decisive role.

Related Concept: IDENTIFICATION.

REFERENCE

Freud, S., 1914, "On Narcissism: An Introduction." *SE*, 14:87–88, 1957.

ADDITIONAL READINGS

Freud, S.: 1905, "Three Essays on the Theory of Sexuality." *SE*, 7, 1953.
    1927, "The Future of an Illusion." *SE*, 21, 1961.

138

ANACLITIC DEPRESSION is a term introduced by Spitz (1946) to describe a syndrome which can be found in infants deprived of love-objects, especially in institutions. When such children, he stated, do not find normal outlets for their aggressive and sexual drives, they are turned against the self, resulting in a marked impairment of development. Unlike adult depressions, the superego, as yet undeveloped, does not enter into the dynamics of this condition.

Related Concept: DEPRESSION.

REFERENCE

Spitz, R., "Anaclitic Depression." *PsaStC*, 2:313–342, 1946.

139

ANAGOGIC INTERPRETATION. An examination of dream elements which reveal serious and lofty thoughts, often with philosophical or ethical import. Originally described by Silberer (1914), who felt that many, if not all, dreams required two different interpretations, it was later employed by Jung who tried to transform the science of psychoanalysis into a philosophy by eliminating the unconscious infantile material. Silberer referred to the latent infantile sexual material in the dream as the *analytical* approach, and reserved the term *anagogic* for the dream's philosophical meaning.

Freud found the idea of anagogic interpretation to be of little value, saying that the majority of dreams require no higher interpretation and are even insusceptible to it. In the occasional dreams in which Silberer's findings seemed to be confirmed, Freud (1916) felt that the dream material was involved with thoughts of a very abstract nature, which made their representation in the dream very difficult.

Freud (1922) stressed the fact that no valid example of a dream analysis, as Silberer viewed it, had been published, but provided an example of a screen memory in which a patient stressed anagogic interpretation. The patient remembered that when she was an infant, she took a little bird into her hand. Freud contrasted the infantile sexual material that this led to (bird symbolizing genital and so on) with the patient's initial interpretation of the event as an early sign of her feeling that animals have souls, and her protective impulses toward them. This kind of anagogic interpretation of material is usually provided with ease by the patient; the correct analytic interpretation must still be looked for by the technical methods which are specifically psychoanalytical. In so doing, the presence of repressed infantile wishes responsible for the neurosis appears. An anagogic interpretation, therefore, does not increase our understanding of the dream, but, rather, minimizes or denies the presence of unconscious materials.

Related Concepts: DREAMS; DREAM-WORK; INTERPRETATION.

REFERENCES

Freud, S.: 1900, "The Interpretation of Dreams." *SE*, 5:523–524, 1962.
        1917, "A Metapsychological Supplement to the Theory of Dreams." *SE*, 14:228, 1962.
        1922, "Dreams and Telepathy." *SE*, 18:216, 1962.
Silberer, H., *Probleme der Mystik und ihrer Symbolik.* H, 1914.

ADDITIONAL READINGS

Freud, S.: 1914, "On the History of the Psycho-Analytic Movement." *SE*, 14, 1957.
        1916, "Introductory Lectures on Psycho-Analysis." *SE*, 15, 1963.
Friedemann, M., "Anagoge, Übertragungsträume." *PtPrx*, 2, 1935.

140
ANAL PHASE is the second stage of libidinal development, in which the discharge of dammed-up instinctual energy is connected with the act of defecation and the pleasurable organ sensations. From approximately the second year of life to the third, the child's chief interest lies in the retention and expulsion of feces; he regards his excrement as a valuable creation, a prized personal possession, which he has to learn slowly to relinquish. Under favorable conditions, the child repudiates his anal wishes and sublimates the energy into such activities as painting, playing in the sand, being clean and orderly, etc. If the child is *not* permitted to give up his anal interests slowly and a traumatic pressure is experienced, he may use the mechanism of repression in an attempt to immediately eliminate this interest from his conscious mind. The repressed, unconscious anal wishes may thus continue to dominate his life and produce various defense mechanisms.

As compared with the oral stage, in which the infant is preoccupied with sucking the mother's breast and only slowly discovers her importance as the *external* object which is necessary for this gratification, the anal phase permits the infant a certain amount of independence.

According to Freud's first instinct theory, only the libido (not the ego instincts) passes through the anal phase; he consequently used the term *anal-sadistic phase* to indicate the presence of aggressive wishes. After the introduction of the second instinct theory, most psychoanalysts viewed aggression as a separate instinct, and they thus assumed that both libido and destrudo (*narcissistic* as well as *object*) passed through this phase. The libidinal anal wish may be expressed as "I want to give my feces" or "I want to keep my feces," while the aggressive anal wish may be given as "I want to defecate on my parents in order to punish and humiliate them." Exhibitionistic and inspectionistic needs may also be connected with the anal stage.

According to Abraham (1921) two stages of the anal phase may be observed: in the first stage, the feces represented the object in which the child was interested; in the second stage, the child was primarily interested in the act of defecation as it related to a parental object.

Regression to the anal stage may lead to obsessional neurosis or the development of obsessional-neurotic character traits. In addition, it may be helpful to distinguish between a normal character trait (e.g., orderliness) which may be described as a sublimation of the original anal wish, and a neurotic character trait (e.g., extreme pedantry) which may be the result of an unconscious defense of this infantile wish. [Freud, 1908.]

As the term *anal* refers to the wish to defecate or to being constipated, not every symptom connected with the anus should be referred to as being anal. For instance, the unconscious wish, in the male, to use the anus as a vagina, does not represent an anal regression, but, rather, a phallic regression, in which the anus is substituted for a vagina.

Related Concepts: MONEY; OBSESSIVE-COMPULSIVE NEUROSIS.

REFERENCES

Abraham, K., 1921, "Contributions to the Theory of the Anal Character." *SPA*, pp. 370–392, 1942.
Freud, S., 1908, "Character and Anal Erotism." *SE*, 9:169–175, 1959.

ADDITIONAL READINGS

Brodsky, B., "The Self-Representation, Anality, and the Fear of Dying." *JAPA*, 7, 1959.
Freud, S.: 1905, "Three Essays on the Theory of Sexuality." *SE*, 7, 1953.
    1917, "On Transformations of Instinct as Exemplified in Anal Erotism." *SE*, 17, 1955.
Hattingberg, H. V., "Analerotik, Angstlust und Eigensinn." *Z*, 2, 1914.
Hitschmann, E., "Paranoia, Homosexualität und Analerotik." *Z*, 1, 1913.
Jekels, L., "Analerotik." *Z*, 1, 1913.
Lewin, B., "Anal Erotism and the Mechanism of Undoing." *Q*, 1, 1932.
Posinsky, S. H., "The Problem of Yurok Anality." *AmIm*, 14, 1957.
Reik, T., "Zur Analerotik." *Z*, 3, 1915.

141

ANALYTICAL INSIGHT denotes an awareness of the meaning and unconscious origin of behavior and symptoms, especially as a result of working through the resistances in the psychoanalytic situation. Less frequently, the term is used to designate an awareness of mental sickness in the self.

The working through of the resistances is that part of the work, as Freud (1914) pointed out, "which effects the greatest changes in the patient and which distinguishes analytic treatment from any kind of treatment by suggestion. . . ."

Related Concepts: INTERPRETATION; THERAPY; TRANS-FERENCE.

REFERENCE

Freud, S., 1914, "Remembering, Repeating and Working-Through (Further Recommendations on the Technique of Psycho-Analysis II)." *SE*, 12:155–156, 1958.

142

ANALYZING INSTRUMENT is a conception derived from Freud's (1900) description of the analyst's frame of mind in the analytic situation. While listening, the analyst suspends reflective thinking and permits his own unconscious to arrive at a preconscious level. There, influenced by stimuli arriving from the outside—the patient's productions—compromise formations arise between what the patient is communicating and the contents of the alert and receptive analyzing instrument of the psychoanalyst, the ultimate result being verbalizable statements.

The analyzing instrument—proposed by Isakower (1957, 1963), as a technical term—represents an *ad hoc* and implicitly transitory constellation of the psychic apparatus, rendering it optimally suited for the special task of analytic observation and investigation. The analyzing instrument denotes a specific psychological entity; it is an *invariable* element in the analytic procedure, the *variable* elements being the countertransference, the situations that involve empirical devices considered adjuvant, and diverse interventions.

Related Concepts: INTERPRETATION; REGRESSION.

REFERENCES

Freud, S., 1900, "The Interpretation of Dreams." *SE*, 4:101–102, 1953.
Isakower, O.: Report to Curriculum Committee, New York Psychoanalytic Institute, November 1957 (Mimeographed).
    Minutes of Faculty Meeting, New York Psychoanalytic Institute, November 1963 (Mimeographed).

ADDITIONAL READINGS

Lewin, B.: "Sleep, Narcissistic Neurosis, and the Analytic Situation." *Q*, 1954.
    "Dream Psychology and the Analytic Situation." *Q*, 1955.

143

ANANKE is a Greek term for external necessity, what has otherwise been termed *fate*. In this, Freud used the term to designate the counterpart to inner necessity arising from Eros and Thanatos, and described inner necessity and Ananke as the parents of human culture.

He noted (1917): "There is no doubt that the prescribed course of development can be disturbed and altered in each individual by recent external influences. But we know the power which forced a development of this kind upon humanity and maintains its pressure in the same direction to-day. It is, once again, frustration by reality, or, if we are to give it its true, grand name, the pressure of vital needs—Necessity (Ananke)."

Related Concepts: ACCIDENT PRONENESS; EROS; THANATOS.

REFERENCE

Freud, S., "Introductory Lectures on Psycho-Analysis." *SE*, 16:355, 1963.

ADDITIONAL READINGS

Freud, S.: 1910, "Leonardo da Vinci and a Memory of His Childhood." *SE*, 11, 1957.
       1924, "The Economic Problem of Masochism." *SE*, 19, 1961.
       1927, "The Future of an Illusion." *SE*, 21, 1961.

144

ANHEDONIA appears clinically as a chronic state of lack of pleasure—distinct from psychological states having a quality of painfulness—often punctuated by acute anxiety. The concept was first employed by Théophile Ribot, a French psychologist who died in 1916, to designate an absence of pain, an insensibility relating to pleasure alone.

Clinically, Glauber (1949) has described this state as follows: "In psychoeconomic terms it is a consequence of failure of libidinal investment within the conscious ego boundaries due to instinct defusion and the resultant fixation of libido to an unconscious, primitive ego. This ego—the narcissistic ideal ego—is undifferentiated from the magical, omnipotent mother image. This fixation, in turn, is a reaction to specific intolerant environmental conditions during the earliest phases of the child's nurture. . . . Anhedonia can be differentiated from other affective states on the same ego-libido level (anxiety, apathy, depression). Anhedonia may, under certain circumstances, be transformed into any one of these."

Anhedonia is characterized in the following example: A patient is at a social gathering and behaves in an aloof manner, unaware of feeling any pleasure. However, upon his return home, he can mentally reexperience some of the events with considerable pleasurable accompaniment.

Related Concept: PLEASURE PRINCIPLE.

REFERENCE

Glauber, P., "Observations on a Primary Form of Anhedonia." *PQ*, 18:67–78, 1949.

ADDITIONAL READINGS

Kahn, M., "Clinical Aspects of the Schizoid Personality: Affects and Technique." *IntJPsa*, 41, 1960.
Myerson, A., "Anhedonia." *AJP*, 2, 1923.

145

ANIMISM denotes the theory of psychic concepts, of spiritual beings in general. The term owes its present meaning to E. B. Taylor.* Freud (1913) hypothesized that the first picture man formed of the world was a psychological one. It came naturally to primitive man; he transposed the structural conditions of his own mind into the external world. Animism may, as a consequence, be considered a precursor of the spiritual, to religion in general. In Freud's view it is the doctrine of the universality of life, for no race has as yet been discovered which does not employ the concept of spirits and its derivatives.

In primitives, where the process of animistic thought was seen most clearly, the structural condition of his mind was projected into the external world. In this, the body of instruction (prereligious practices) which then sought to control these forces in the external world consisted of what is now known as animism; namely, the magical belief that the *spirit* of the object could be contained. This mode of thinking—the omnipotence of thoughts and

* Taylor, E. B., *Primitive Culture*. London, 1891.

wishes—was the result, in Freud's formulation, of the overevaluation of psychical acts. Dynamically, this act was seen as a projection of man's own emotional impulses, the transformation of an emotional cathexis into persons or things, a sexualization or instinctualization of a process of thinking.

Chronologically, this stage of libidinal development most nearly corresponds to that phase of man's development wherein the world was peopled by demons, and constituted a phase in his development which predated his present institutionalized belief in religious thought and order. It most clearly persists today in the form of superstitious thought, in which the consequence of certain acts or modes of thought are denied sway over the mind by the process of avoidance. Freud (1933) felt that man's first theoretical achievement, the creation of spirits, arose from the same sources as the first moral restrictions to which he was subjected; that is, the observances of a taboo. Thus, the secondary revision of the product of the dreamwork was a system arising in origin in a manner similar to that leading to the development of the animistic system.

Related Concepts: MAGIC; NARCISSISM; PLEASURE PRINCIPLE; RELIGIOUS FAITH; TABOO; TOTEM.

REFERENCES

Freud, S.: 1913, "Totem and Taboo." *SE*, 13:77, 1955.
    1933, "New Introductory Lectures on Psycho-Analysis." *SE*, 22:164–166, 1964.

ADDITIONAL READINGS

Fenichel, O., *The Psychoanalytic Theory of Neurosis.* Nor, 1945.
Jones, E., *The Life and Work of Sigmund Freud.* HPI, 2, 1953.
Kaplan, L., "Animism and Narcissism (A Psycho-Analytic Study)." *JSP*, 1, 1923.

146
ANOREXIA NERVOSA is an inhibition in which the subject stops eating, with consequent loss of weight, often accompanied by amenorrhea and vomiting. The inhibition appears to be connected with the unconscious meaning of food and with the act of eating itself. It signals a fixation or regression at the oral stage, wherein eating represents the act

of devouring and food represents the preoedipal mother. The unconscious defense by the ego and superego thus interferes with this gratification; they punish the patient for having these repressed wishes.

Lorand (1943) described the process as follows: "Loss of appetite: Food implies oral and sexual gratification identified with early fantasies of impregnation. Thus are revived strong feelings of guilt necessitating denial by rejection of food. Food is usually excessively charged with importance in an environment where a patient develops anorexia nervosa. It is the vehicle of love and also of punishment. In this case, food was a constant topic of conversation and the focus of family interests.

"The denial of adulthood in general and especially of sexuality: Adult problems cannot be handled because of constant preoccupation with the problem of food around which the earliest difficulties of the child centered. This preoccupation also excludes adult adjustment to sexual needs. Then, too, genitality has to be denied because of desires and guilt centering around the early oedipus relationship.

"Wasting away: It expresses strong suicidal desires. (This is the end result of the inverted aspect of infantile killing impulses against parents—particularly the mother—which were so outstanding.)

"Menstrual disturbances: Cessation of menstruation is an attempt to eliminate the problem of being preoccupied with genital function which in adulthood implies thoughts of sexual relationship and pregnancy. At times amenorrhea means permanent impregnation, and then again complete rejection of femininity. These are defenses against oedipal guilt.

"Guilt and atonement: Since the symptoms are used to obtain revenge and attention, they become charged with guilt; at the same time the suffering acts as expiatory self-punishment."

Eissler (1943), in describing a case history of a patient suffering from severe anorexia nervosa and amenorrhea, noted the following: "The structure of the patient's personality is discussed. Certain traits, such as the patient's attitude to food, the preponderance of oral traits in her entire personality make-up, her incapacity for appropriation, and the peculiarities of her language are described. Stress was laid on her relationship to her mother which was found to be characterized by a peculiar dependence not encountered in other neuroses, inasmuch as the patient's ego development remained inhibited. This inhibition is shown to be caused by the fact that the mother represents the most important parts of the patient's ego. A short period of relative independence of her mother facilitated the observation of her true mother relation.

"The complete absence of physical affection in the patient's childhood is considered an important factor in the establishment of the disease. The two meanings of the term anorexia nervosa as a symptom and as a disease entity are discussed. The clinical advisability of distinguishing three degrees of anorexia nervosa is suggested. The disease entity anorexia nervosa is differentiated from compulsion neurosis and schizophrenia. The necessity for applying psychotherapy endowed with magic elements in order to establish contact with the patient is demonstrated. The difference between defense and inhibition is sketched and anorexia nervosa classified among inhibitory states."

Related Concepts: DORA; OBESITY.

REFERENCES

Eissler, K. R., "Some Psychiatric Aspects of Anorexia Nervosa." *R*, 30:121–145, 1943.
Lorand, S., "Anorexia Nervosa; Case." *PSM*, 5:282–292, 1943.

ADDITIONAL READINGS

Altschule, M. D., "Adrenocortical Function in Anorexia Nervosa Before and After Lobotomy." *NewEngJmed*, 248, 1953.
Benedek, T., "Dominant Ideas and Their Relation to Morbid Cravings." *IntJPsa*, 17, 1936.
Bernfeld, S., "Die Gestalttheorie." *Im*, 20, 1934.
Dally, P. I., & W. Sargant, "A New Treatment of Anorexia Nervosa." *BMJ*, 1, 1960.
Davis, H. P., "Anorexia Nervosa." *E*, 25, 1939.
Deutsche, F., M. R. Kaufman, & J. V. Waller, "Anorexia Nervosa: A Psychosomatic Entity." *PSM*, 2, 1940.
Dunn, C. W., "Anorexia Nervosa." *Lancet*, 1, 1937.
Flugel, I. C., "The Death-Instinct, Homeostasis, and Allied Concepts." *IntJPsa*, 1953.
Gero, G., "An Equivalent of Depression: Anorexia," in P. Greenacre, *Affective Disorders*. IUP, 1953.
Kohler, A., "Psychische Faktoren bei Gewichtsverschiebungen." *ZpsychosomMed*, 3, 1957.
Linn, L., "Psychoanalytic Contribution to Psychosomatic Research." *PSM*, 20, 1958.
Massermann, J. H., "Psychodynamisms in Anorexia Nervosa and Neurotic Vomiting." *Q*, 10, 1941.
Redlich, F. C., *Psychotherapy with Schizophrenics.* IUP, 1952.
Scott, W., "Notes on the Psychopathology of Anorexia Nervosa." *M*, 21, 1948.
Stephens, D. J., "Annorexia Nervosa: Endocrine Factors in Undernutrition." *JCE*, 1, 1941.
Sylvester, E., "Analysis of Psychogenic Anorexia and Vomiting in a Four-Year-Old Child." *PsaStC*, 1, 1945.
Wall, J. H., "Anorexia Nervosa." *BullNYAcadMed*, 32, 1956.
Wilson, R. R., "A Case of Anorexia Nervosa with Necropsy Findings and a Discussion of Secondary Hypopituitarism." *JCP*, 7, 1954.
Zutt, J., *Psychiatrische Betrachtungen zur Pubertätsmagersucht Klin.* Wschr, 24–25, 1946.

147
ANTHROPOLOGY AND PSYCHOANALYSIS.

Freud contributed five major works to the study of man and his social customs and rules: "Totem and Taboo," "Group Psychology and the Analysis of the Ego," "The Future of an Illusion," "Civilization and Its Discontents," and "Moses and Monotheism." In the first (1913), the relationship of the oedipus complex to the primal parricide, of phobias in children to the infantile return to totemism, and the universal incest prohibition as central to the formation of the patriarchal society were explored at length. In the second (1921), the cohesion of the group was seen as a dynamic process, in which a number of individuals substitute one and the same object for their ego-ideal and subsequently identify themselves with one another in their ego. This group behavior was viewed as resulting from aim-inhibited libidinal processes. In the third (1927), a further investigation into the religious phenomena was undertaken: the overestimation of the importance of psychic reality. In the fourth (1930), Freud sought to answer the question of how culture influences the instinctual endowment of man through the agencies of the life and death instincts, their sublimation and final institutionalization. In the last (1939), he returned to an investigation of the substitutive satisfactions which find theistic presentations.

The application of psychoanalytic theory was employed by Malinowski (1927) in his study of the Trobriand Islanders (during World War I) under conditions that lead to the actual observation of the matrilineal complex. Foremost among the functionalists, he was to view *institutions* as existing to "satisfy, directly or indirectly, the biological needs of man." He finally came to dispute much of psychoanalysis, believing that it was too firmly rooted in the instinct theory, with its Lamarckian conception of adaptation as being genetically determined. Nonetheless, the parallel which could be drawn between the family structure and the formation of myths, legends and fairy tales was clearly rooted for him in psychoanalytic theory. In 1923, he noted: "[The] doctrine of repression due to social influence allows us to explain certain typical latent wishes or 'complexes,' found in folklore by reference to the organization of a given society. Inversely it allows us to trace the pattern of instinctual and emotional tendencies in the texture of the social fabric."

The psychoanalytic approach was used by several of Freud's students in the study of myths, legends and rituals. Róheim (1952) utilized the adaptational point of view and disavowed the theory of primal parricide: he sought to redefine the libido theory in terms of stages of ontogenetic development. The universality of the oedipus complex was supported by Jones (1925): in matrilineal societies, he reasoned, the oedipus complex was repressed. Other authors, such as Erikson (1951), have sought to identify the origin of societal models from other primary sources. Erikson's procedure owes much to Róheim, who spoke of the "projection on the outer world of an arrest of a stage of development," without making clear how this phenomenon functionally affected a society and the individuals who develop within it.

Related Concept: APPLIED PSYCHOANALYSIS.

REFERENCES

Erikson, E., *Childhood and Society*. Nor, 1951.
Freud, S.: 1913, "Totem and Taboo." *SE*, 13:1–163, 1955.
     1921, "Group Psychology and the Analysis of the Ego." *SE*, 18:67–144, 1955.
     1927, "The Future f an Illusion." *SE*, 21:3–58, 1961.
     1930, "Civilization and Its Discontents." *SE*, 21:59–148, 1961.
     1939, "Moses and Monotheism." *SE*, 23:3–140, 1964.
Jones, E., "Mother-Right and the Sexual Ignorance of Savages." *IntJPsa*, 6:109–130, 1925.
Malinowski, B.: "Psychoanalysis and Anthropology," Letter to the editor. *Nature*, 112:650–651, 1923.
     Sex and Repression in Savage Society. KP, pp. 167–170, 1927.
Róheim, G., *Psychoanalysis and Anthropology*. IUP, 1950.

ADDITIONAL READINGS

Arieti, S., "Some Basic Problems Common to Anthropology and Modern Psychiatry." *AmAnthrop*, 58, 1956.
Axelrad, S., "Comments on Anthropology and the Study of Complex Cultures." *PsaSS*, 4, 1955.
Glover, E., "Common Problems of Psychoanalysis and Anthropology." *Man*, 32, 1932.
Kroeber, A. L., *Anthropology, Race, Language, Culture, Psychology, Prehistory*. HB, 1948.
Malinowski, B., "Psychoanalysis and Anthropology." *P*, 4, 1923–24.
Meinertz, J., "Psychologie, Existenz, Anthropologie." *P*, 1953.
Róheim, G., "The Anthropological Evidence and the Oedipus Complex." *AnSurvPsa*, 3, 1952.
Seligman, C. G.: "Anthropological Perspective and Psychological Theory." *JRoyAnthropInst*, 62, 1933.
     "Anthropology and Psychology: A Study of Some Points of Contact." *JRoyAnthropInst*, 54, 1924.
     "The Unconscious in Relation to Anthropology." *BJP*, 18, 1928.

148

ANTICIPATION denotes the expectation of future events, based on the ability to use memories and past experiences. The anticipation of danger is an ego function serving the reality principle. Pathological reactions may be found in neurotic states of anxious expectation, and in excessive dwelling on the past, as in mourning and depression. Anticipation may also be involved in denial mechanisms, as in optimism and elation. The anticipation present in forepleasure guides the individual to end-pleasure. Anticipation may also be involved, according to A. Freud (1936), in the expectation of unpleasure resulting from an increase or decrease of instinctual tension above or below a certain threshold. "Objective anxiety is the anticipation of suffering which may be inflicted on the child as a punishment by outside agents, a kind of 'fore-pain' which governs the ego's behaviour, no matter whether the expected punishment always takes place or not."

Fenichel (1945) summarized his own view, as follows: "The prerequisite for an action is, besides mastery of bodily apparatus, the development of the function of judgment. This means the ability to anticipate the future in the imagination by 'testing' reality, by trying in active manner and in a small dosage what might happen to one passively and in an unknown dosage. This type of functioning is in general characteristic of the ego."

Related Concepts: FOREPLEASURE; FORE-UNPLEASURE.

REFERENCES

Fenichel, O., *The Psychoanalytic Theory of Neurosis.* Nor, p. 42, 1945.
Freud, A., 1936, *The Ego and Mechanisms of Defense.* IUP, p. 155, 1946.

ADDITIONAL READINGS

Arieti, S., "The Processes of Expectation and Anticipation." *JNMD,* 106, 1947.
Bergler, E., "Boredom of Anticipation (Pseudo-Boredom)." *Samiksa,* 4, 1950.
Hill, L. B., "Anticipation of Arousing Specific Neurotic Feelings in the Psychoanalyst." *AnSurvPsa,* 1951.

149
ANTITHETICAL. Freud (1910), in examining the original meanings of language from the standpoint of both dreams and philology, suggested that primal symbols and words originally embraced contrary meanings, which later achieved separate status. For example, the word taboo signifies both *holy* and *unclean*; in each instance, it denotes the *untouchable*. However, it is not only in primitive languages that we find antithetical words. For instance, *affectation* is defined as *aiming at, liking for*; also, *as ostentatious fondness for, artificiality of manner*, and *pretense*.

Related Concepts: AMBIGUITY; AMBIVALENCE.

REFERENCE

Freud, S., 1910, "The Antithetical Meaning of Primal Words." *SE,* 11:159, 1957.

ADDITIONAL READINGS

Freud, S.: 1900, "The Interpretation of Dreams." *SE,* 5, 1953.
        1913, "Totem and Taboo." *SE,* 13, 1955.
        1916, "Introductory Lectures on Psycho-Analysis." *SE,* 15, 1963.
        & J. Breuer, 1893, "Studies on Hysteria." *SE,* 2, 1955.

150
ANXIETY is the unpleasure experienced when the object is unknown and the anticipation of being overwhelmed by an internal or external force is present. The emotion of anxiety, along with the secretory and motoric discharges connected with it, is an affect experienced by the total personality.

On the basis of his clinical studies, Freud (1895) at first concluded that the libido of the repressed wish changes into anxiety.* However, after he introduced the second instinct theory (1920), in which aggression was no longer considered to be a partial sexual drive, he modified his original statement and said that repressed libido may cause anxiety only if its repression has also mobilized aggressive tendencies, which cannot be discharged and then have to be warded off. Consequently, any forbidden wish may produce anxiety. The discovery of the importance of aggression as a decisive factor in the mobilization of anxiety led to the recognition of anxiety as a danger signal. [Freud, 1930.]

The term *anxiety* is used as a synonym for *fear*, although Freud suggested that fear is the reaction to a known specific danger, while anxiety is the reaction to an unknown one. Inasmuch as the real source of the danger is unknown to the neurotic, the use of the word *anxiety* may be employed in connection with neurotic fears.

Neurotic anxiety is the result of the individual's inability to differentiate between the wish and the action, when the wish is repressed and is thereby unconscious. Thus, it resembles the feeling of terror more closely than that of normal anxiety. The full discharge of the repressed wish is experienced as taking place in the present instead of in the future.

_____

* In a letter to Fliess (1897), Freud even then had doubts about his assumption that the libido changes into anxiety: "I have decided, then, henceforth to regard as separate factors what causes libido and what causes anxiety."

The neurotic reacts *as if* the danger of which he is afraid were actually happening.

Freud (1921) described the panic which takes place whenever a disintegration of the mass has occurred and compared the affect of panic to that of neurotic anxiety. His description, thus, of the mass as "impulsive," "changeable," and "irritable," led by the unconscious, corresponds to the behavior of the neurotic.

Normal anxiety results from an anticipation in which the individual recreates, in his fantasy, a memory that is characteristic of anxiety. He recalls a memory of a previous defeat, utilizing it to experience a dangerous threat to the self. He does not attribute this threat to his own aggression. To protect himself against such an external defeat, he mobilizes his aggression and attributes part of it to the dangerous object. Consequently, this dangerous object *attacks* him with his own aggression. As a result, he experiences in his fantasy the threatened defeat, and prepares for flight or fight.

Related Concepts: CASTRATION ANXIETY; FEAR; SENSE OF GUILT.

REFERENCES

Eidelberg, L., *An Outline of a Comparative Pathology of the Neuroses.* IUP, p. 135, 1954.
Freud, S.: 1895, "On the Grounds for Detaching A Particular Syndrome From Neurasthenia Under the Description 'Anxiety Neurosis.'" *SE*, 3:87–120, 1962.
    1921, "Group Psychology and the Analysis of the Ego." *SE*, 18:97, 1955.
    1926, "Inhibitions, Symptoms and Anxiety." *SE*, 20: 79, 124, 1959.
    1930, "Civilization and its Discontents." *SE*, 21:138, 1961.

ADDITIONAL READINGS

Abraham, H. C., "Twin Relationship and Womb Fantasies in a Case of Anxiety Hysteria." *IntJPsa*, 34, 1953.
Boven, W., *Anxiety.* D&N, 1934.
Bowlby, J., "Separation Anxiety." *IntJPsa*, 41, 1960.
Brenner, C., "An Addendum to Freud's Theory of Anxiety." *IntJPsa*, 34, 1953.
Casuso, G., "Anxiety Related to the 'Discovery' of the Penis: An Observation." *PsaStC*, 12, 1957.
Goldstein, K., "Zum Problem der Angst." *ZPt*, 2, 1929.
Harris, I. D., "Typical Anxiety Dreams and Object Relations." *IntJPsa*, 41, 1960.
Isaacs, S., "An Acute Psychotic Anxiety Occurring in a Boy of Four Years." *IntJPsa*, 24, 1943.
Klein, M., "A Contribution to the Theory of Anxiety and Guilt." *IntJPsa*, 29, 1948.
Mitscherlich, A., "The Individual in Anxiety. A Word on the Mass Reactions of our Time." *DAW*, 11, 1956.
Pappenheim, E., & M. Sweeney, "Separation Anxiety in Mother and Child." *PsaStC*, 7, 1952.
Rado, S., "Das Problem der Angst in seinem Verhältnis zur Psychoanalytischen Libidotheorie." *ZSW*, 10, 1923.
Ramzy, I., & R. S. Wallerstein, "Pain, Fear, and Anxiety: Study in Their Interrelationships." *PsaStC*, 13, 1958.
Searles, H. F., "Anxiety Concerning Change, as Seen in the Psychotherapy of Schizophrenic Patients—With Particular Reference to the Sense of Personal Identity." *IntJPsa*, 42, 1961.
Shands, H. C., "Anxiety, Anaclitic Object, and the Sign Function: Comments on Early Developments in the Use of Symbols." *Ops*, 24, 1954.
Sharpe, E., "Anxiety: Outbreak and Resolution." *IntJPsa*, 12, 1931.
Sterba, R., & E. Sterba, "The Anxieties of Michelangelo Buonarrotti." *IntJPsa*, 37, 1956.
Woolf, M., "On Castration Anxiety." *IntJPsa*, 36, 1955.
Zetzel, E., "The Concept of Anxiety in Relation to the Development of Psychoanalysis." *JAPA*, 3, 1955.
Zulliger, H., "Angst in der Spiegelung des Tafeln-Z-Tests." *ZdiagPsychol*, 2, 1954.

151

ANXIETY NEUROSIS is a syndrome described by Freud (1895) as one of the actual neuroses, whose specific symptoms (e.g., general irritability, respiratory disorders, dizziness, etc.) are direct manifestations of anxiety, its rudiments or its equivalents. The symptomatic expectant dread or general apprehensiveness was viewed as a direct *toxic* effect of sexual malpractices involving frustrated excitation; i.e., practices such as coitus interruptus and enforced abstinence, wherein a powerful sexual excitation is insufficiently discharged and not carried through to a satisfying termination. Freud at first assumed that excess libidinal excitation was directly transformed into anxiety. However, after the introduction of the second instinct theory, where he recognized the importance of castration (its connection with aggression), he no longer maintained that excess libido was turned into anxiety.

Today, most analysts recognize the connection between anxiety and aggression, and rarely use the concept of anxiety neurosis.

Related Concepts: ACTUAL NEUROSES; ANXIETY; PHOBIA.

REFERENCES

Freud, S.: 1895, "Obsessions and Phobias: Their Psychical Mechanism and Their Aetiology." *SE*, 3:81–82, 1962.
      1930, "Civilization and Its Discontents." *SE*, 21:138, 1961.

ADDITIONAL READINGS

Freud, S.: 1909, "Analysis of a Phobia in a Five-Year-Old Boy." *SE*, 10, 1955.
      1910, "'Wild' Psychoanalysis." *SE*, 11, 1957.
      1917, "Introductory Lectures on Psycho-Analysis." *SE*, 16, 1963.
      1926, "Inhibitions, Symptoms and Anxiety." *SE*, 20, 1959.

152

ANXIETY STATE is a traumatic neurosis precipitated by a wartime experience; a term used in World War II to describe acute- and chronic-anxiety reactions. Its relationship to the precipitating event is superficial, as in many other traumatic neuroses; it differs from a peacetime neurosis in that a conflict arises as between two ego-ideals; the customary one and the one the war has compelled the soldier to build. In a letter* to Jones (1955), Freud noted: "The war-time ego-ideal is concerned with relations to new objects. . . ."

Related Concepts: REPETITION COMPULSION; TRAUMATIC NEUROSIS.

REFERENCE

Jones, E., *The Life and Work of Sigmund Freud*, HPI, 2:252, 1955.

ADDITIONAL READINGS

Grinker, R., "War Neuroses or Battle Fatigue." *JNMD*, 101, 1945.
McElroy, R. B., "Psychoneurosis, Combat-Anxiety Type." *AJP*, 101, 1945.

---

* October 27, 1918.

153

APHANISIS is the total extinction of the capacity for sexual enjoyment. The concept was introduced by Ernest Jones (1938) as a broadening of the ideas of castration anxiety. He considered fear of aphanisis to lie at the root of all neuroses.

Related Concepts: BIRTH TRAUMA; BREAST COMPLEX; CASTRATION ANXIETY.

REFERENCE

Jones, E., *Papers on Psycho-Analysis*. WWo, pp. 200, 312, 315, 318, 373, 440–441, 445, 1938.

154

APHASIA is a language disorder which occurs as a result of damage to the organic substratum of speech. Freud's work on the subject, in 1891, introduced the functional thinking of John Hughlings Jackson to Germany, and differed sharply from the prevailing German concepts of localized thought. In aphasia, Freud introduced the term *agnosia*, and used, in a neurological sense, many words that were to acquire other meanings in psychoanalysis (regression, association, projection, representation, etc.). While Freud did not directly pursue his interest in aphasia, his concepts were important in their influence on subsequent investigators. Aphasia is chiefly a neurological concept.

Related Concept: AGNOSIA.

REFERENCE

Freud, S., 1891, *On Aphasia, a Critical Study*. IUP, 1953.

ADDITIONAL READINGS

Freud, S.: 1915, "The Unconscious." *SE*, 14, 1957.
      1925, "An Autobiographical Study." *SE*, 20, 1959.
      & J. Breuer, 1893, "Studies in Hysteria." *SE*, 2, 1955.
Stengel, E., "Zur Lehre von den Transcorticalen Aphasien." *ZNP*, 1936.

155

APPERCEPTIVE DISTORTION, according to Bellak (1954), is a broadening of the concept of projection to include nonpsychotic and nonneurotic forms of individual interpretations of stimuli, as, for instance, in the data obtained in projective tests.

Related Concept: PROJECTION.

REFERENCE

Bellak, L., *The Tat and Cat in Clinical Use*. G&S, 1954.

156

APPERSONATION, according to Sperling (1944), is an illusion in which the ego boundaries are extended to include an object (the appersonand), in which stimuli that impinge on the appersonand are then felt as though they impinged on the subject's own person (e.g., a person's relation to a cane is such that if he raps the floor with it, he gets a sensation of the hardness of the floor, as felt at the end of the cane). This illusion usually occurs, in the normal person, in relation to artificial dentures, clothing and jewelry; to his car and house; to his country; etc.

The relationship to another person (or object) is one in which the person is treated like a part of the subject's own body (e.g., one's right arm: one owns it; one makes sacrifices for it, but it has to obey and has no will of its own). This plays a role in identification.

Appersonation may be used as a defense mechanism which permits the gratification of libidinal and aggressive impulses, with diminished feelings of guilt and diminished castration anxiety, or the gratification of suicidal tendencies by the destruction of suicide substitutes. Appersonation is similar to inner identification; it differs from external identification in that no actual acquisition of the characteristics of the object takes place; the ego boundaries are simply extended to include the object.

Related Concepts: IDENTIFICATION; NARCISSISM; OBJECT CHOICE (ANACLITIC AND NARCISSISTIC).

REFERENCE

Sperling, O., "On Appersonation." *IntJPsa*, 25:128–132, 1944.

ADDITIONAL READINGS

Bleuler, E., 1911, *Dementia Praecox, or the Group of Schizophrenias*. IUP, 1950.
Eidelberg, L., *An Outline of a Comparative Pathology of the Neuroses*. IUP, 1954.

157

APPLIED PSYCHOANALYSIS deals with psychic phenomena as they occur outside of clinical practice; thus, the verification of analytical interpretations—e.g., therapeutic change—cannot be obtained. Furthermore, in therapeutic psychoanalysis, the analytical work is made easier by the careful observation of such a phenomenon as transference by the patient to the imago of the analyst and by the analyst's efforts to overcome the patient's resistance. Of greatest importance is the fact that in therapeutic psychoanalysis the subject of the analysis is analyzable only when he considers himself to be sick and wishes to be helped. For instance, the patient who is frightened of crossing the street wants to be cured of his phobia. The symptom of "crossing the street" is thus analyzable. But the normal "crossing of the street" cannot be analyzed. This is true in the case of all neurotic symptoms. The neurotic character trait has to be changed into an ego-alien defense mechanism before it can be analyzed.

Nonetheless, the application of analytical findings to the study of art, history, literature, etc. has a tradition which can be traced back to Freud's earliest studies (1895–1897); in particular, to Freud's letters to Fliess, which contain numerous references to folklore and to anthropology, as well as to works of dramatic art (e.g., *Hamlet*), medieval writings, etc. The first explicit application to a literary work occurred in 1898, when Freud subjected a novel by the Swiss writer C. F. Meyer (1825–1898), *Die Richterin*, to an analytic investigation; an essay he sent to Fliess. More extensive studies by Freud in the field occurred later, in "Delusions and Dreams in Jensen's 'Gradiva'" (1907) and in "Leonardo da Vinci and a Memory of His Childhood" (1910). The following year, Freud published the first psychoanalytic biography, "Psycho-Analytical Notes Upon an Autobiographical Account of a Case of Paranoia," which is better known as the Schreber Case. The last of his studies was undertaken shortly before he died: "Moses and Monotheism" (1939). Freud's most explicit statement as to the far-reaching uses of applied psychoanalysis was given in 1913:

1. Psychological Interest. The study of parapraxes offers itself as the best example for demonstrating the value of the psychoanalytical method in the study of the unconscious processes. As with other phenomena in psychoanalysis it provides a method to trace their etiology to the influence derived from the mental life (rather than the organic) of the individual.

2. Philological Interest. The dream may be considered as the language of the unconscious, in more than one tongue. In this, as the differing psychological conditions govern the various forms of the neurosis, distinguishing one from another, so does the language of the unconscious speak for a given disorder.

3. Philosophical Interest. Psychoanalysis permits the researcher to draw a total picture of the subject, to trace the etiology of the disorder, to form, as it were, an objective portrait of the subject. In the same way, it can help in the investigation of the individual motives which are inherent in all philosophical systems.

4. Biological Interest. The psychological investigation of the etiology of the primary instincts has yet to be fully utilized by the scientists who would investigate behavior, though psychoanalysis may be considered as one of the biological sciences.

5. Developmental Point of View. Theoretical considerations which are inherent in psychoanalysis lend support to an explanation derived from phylogenetic development. The later behavior does not destroy the infantile mode, and thus a psychoanalytic study permits a total portrait to be drawn.

6. Scientific and Aesthetic Interest. Psychoanalysis helps reveal that region which lies half-way between reality and the wish-fulfilling world of the imagination. The study of art as a conventional portrait of reality has yet to reveal its place in the complex structure of man's compensatory mechanisms.

7. Sociological Interest. Psychoanalysis has contributed to the social scientist's knowledge of mass psychology and the relationship of the leader to the group which he dominates.

8. Educational Interest. The knowledge which psychoanalysis has been able to shed on the com-ponent instincts may help educators structure programs which are more conducive to learning by finding methods which do not lead to the repressions of such instincts.

Among the first of Freud's followers, there was an attempt to demonstrate the close correspondence of unconscious phenomena in certain psychoneurotic conditions with other manifestations in nonmedical areas (art, folklore, literature, etc.) and thus to prove the ubiquity of unconscious mental life. For instance, more than one-third of all early scientific meetings of the Vienna Psychoanalytic Society (1906–1908) were devoted to applied psychoanalysis. These early discussions were on Greek, Egyptian and Semitic mythology; anthropology, art and art history; and on poetry, religion, science, and sociology. More recent studies on creativity have been undertaken by Kris (1952) and Greenacre (1958, 1963); on Beethoven by Sterba (1954); on Goethe by Eissler (1963); on Schliemann by Niederland (1965); on Rilke by Siemenauer (1954); and many others.

The investigator working in the field of applied psychoanalysis bases his inquiry almost exclusively on written or printed documents, biographical data, memoirs, letters, diaries, and other recorded or preserved testimony. The margin of possible error is therefore considerable, and the inexperienced or inept investigator can be readily led astray through lack of source material, of a paucity of authentic information, of his reliance on inaccurate sources, or (probably) by his own personal bias and conscious or unconscious propensities. Other potential pitfalls may result from too-general an application of analytic concepts in resorting to what has been called psychoanalytic *reductionalism*, e.g., in attempting to explain individual creativity through the exposition of unconscious processes. Other objections have been raised against the broad use (more precisely, misuse) of Freudian concepts in the attempted uncritical analysis of historical personages, of sociological phenomena, works of art and of literature. Though most investigators agree that the art of the cave dwellers was meant as magic, it is doubtful whether the frescoes on the walls of the Spanish caves can be interpreted by the mere employment of analytic propositions. On the other hand, investigative procedures by experienced workers—such as Róheim's anthropological studies, Reik's exploration of ritualistic customs, Kris' inquiry into the image of the artist and the role of tradition in ancient biographies—have proved illuminatory as well as fruitful. If the subject of investigation is a historical personage, the full availability of, and accessibility to, source material may enable the researchers to arrive, through the employment of analytic exploratory tools, at a high degree of understanding.

Related Concepts: SYNTHESIS; WELTANSCHAUUNG.

REFERENCES

Eissler, K. R., "The Function of Details in the Interpretation of Works of Literature." *PQ*, 28:1, 1959.

Freud, S.: 1907, "Delusions and Dreams in Jensen's 'Gradiva'." *SE*, 9:7–94, 1959.

1910, "Leonardo da Vinci and a Memory of His Childhood." *SE*, 11:63–137, 1962.

1911, "Analytic Notes on an Autobiographical Account of Paranoia." *SE*, 12:9–82, 1962.

1913, "The Claims of Psycho-Analysis to Scientific Interest." *SE*, 13:165–190, 1955.

1939, "Moses and Monotheism." *SE*, 23:7–137, 1964.

Greenacre, P., "*Swift and Carroll: A Psychoanalytic Study of Two Lives.*" IUP, 1955.

Kriss, E.: *The Origins of Psychoanalysis.* BB, 1954.

Explorations in Art. IUP, 1952.

Niederland, W. G., "A Psychoanalytic Inquiry into the Life and Work of Heinrich Schliemann," in *Drives, Affects and Behavior.* IUP, 1965.

Nunberg, H., & E. Federn, *Minutes of the Vienna Psychoanalytic Society.* IUP, 1963.

ADDITIONAL READINGS

Arlow, J. A., "Applied Psychoanalysis: Religion." *AnSurvPsa*, 2, 1951.

Axelrad, S., "On Some Uses of Psychoanalysis." *JAPA*, 8, 1960.

Devereux, G., "Applied Psychoanalysis: Social Sciences." *AnSurvPsa*, 2, 1951.

Heiman, M., ed., *Psychoanalysis and Social Work.* IUP, 1953.

Niederland, W. G., "The First Application of Psychoanalysis to a Literary Work." *Q*, 29, 1960.

Rycroft, C., "A Detective Story. Psychoanalytic Observations." *Q*, 26, 1957.

Schmidl, F., "Psychoanalysis and History." *Q*, 31, 1962.

Wexler, H., "Fate Knocks." *IntJPsa*, 40, 1959.

Winnicott, D. W., *Psychoanalysis and Contemporary Thought.* G, 1959.

158

ARC DE CERCLE is a condition in which the back is arched into a convex position; a conversion symptom that especially occurs in major hysteria. It may represent a partial defense and a partial gratification of an unconscious sexual wish as a position both expressing rejection of coitus and inviting it. Freud (1909) noted that it may represent an invitation to sexual relations.

As with other conversion symptoms, the meaning can be overdetermined; it is usually a defense mechanism of phallic, exhibitionistic libidinal wishes.

Related Concepts: CONVERSION AND CONVERSION SYMPTOMS; EXHIBITIONISM.

REFERENCE

Freud, S., 1909, "Some General Remarks on Hysterical Attacks." *SE*, 9:230, 1959.

ADDITIONAL READING

Weiss, E., "A Contribution to the Psychological Explanation of the 'Arc de Cercle'." *IntJPsa*, 6, 1925.

159

AS-IF PERSONALITY, described by Helene Deutsch (1934), is a schizoid type, in which behavior is seemingly normal, but where actual affective relationships with other people are barred because of pseudoidentification.

For example, a patient asked the analyst to have lunch with him and was told that social intercourse between patient and analyst was not compatible with analysis. The patient said that he was sorry that analysis deprived the analyst of the pleasure of meeting him socially, because he "felt" the analyst's feeling of frustration at not being able to do so. Further analysis disclosed that he had projected his own feeling of frustration onto the analyst and therefore believed that the analyst, and not himself, was frustrated. Consequently, he did not feel sorry about having been rejected, but instead felt sorry for the analyst. He was obviously unwilling to admit the possibility that the analyst may have declined his invitation even if he had not been in analysis. [Eidelberg, 1952.]

Related Concepts: AUTISM; PSEUDOIDENTIFICATION.

REFERENCES

Deutsch, Helene, "Über einen Typus der Pseudo-affektivitaet." *Z*, 20:323–335, 1934.
Eidelberg, L., *Studies in Psychoanalysis.* IUP, pp. 107–115, 1952.

ADDITIONAL READINGS

Bally, G., "Zur Frage der Behandlung schizoider Neurotiker." *Z*, 16, 1930.
Bartemeier, L. H., "A Psychoanalytic Study of Pregnancy in an 'As-If' Personality." *IntJPsa*, 35, 1954.

160
ATTRACTION OF THE FORBIDDEN, according to Eidelberg (1952), is caused by the individual being offered simultaneous gratification of the sexual and aggressive instinct-fusions. Gratification of the aggressive instinct-fusion, as opposed to the sexual instinct-fusion, is possible only when the object of the aggression displays resistance. For example, a Catholic may eat meat on Friday because it gratifies his aggressive defiance of his pious parents, not only his hunger.

Prohibitions and frustrations destroy infantile megalomania and attempts at restitution follow the formula: "I realize that I am not omnipotent, but I want to be at least powerful enough to actively impose what I have passively endured; I want to erase the blemish of my narcissistic mortification by producing a similar mortification in another." Many persons attempt to gratify both the sexual and aggressive instinct-fusions in one action, which is probably related to the earliest prohibitions that simultaneously inhibits the sexual instinct-fusion and destroys the narcissistic feeling of omnipotence. The individual's striking power is decreased when he concentrates simultaneously on aggressive and sexual goals; the risks are higher.

Related Concepts: AGGRESSION; MASOCHISM; SADISM.

REFERENCE

Eidelberg, L., *Studies in Psychoanalysis.* IUP, pp. 135–136, 1952.

ADDITIONAL READING

Servadio, E., "Il Fascino del Proibito." *AnnNeurol*, 52, 1951.

161
AUTISM is a term introduced by Bleuler to describe a primary characteristic of schizophrenia, a preoccupation with the self rather than with outer reality. Kanner (1957) described the syndrome of early infantile autism, marked by the onset, in the second six months of life, of extreme isolation with respect to human contact, but not to inanimate objects which is connected in later years to unusual sensitivities and remarkable feats of memory. The autistic child is analytically regarded as suffering from an incapacity to establish affective relations with the people in his environment. Mahler (1952) contrasted autism with symbiosis, the disturbances of identity which underlies autistic infantile psychosis.

Related Concepts: AUTOEROTISM; NARCISSISM.

REFERENCES

Kanner, L., *Child Psychiatry.* CCT, 3rd ed., pp. 739–742, 1957.
Mahler, M. S., "On Child Psychosis and Schizophrenia: Autistic and Symbiotic Infantile Psychoses." *PsaStC*, 7:286–305, 1952.

ADDITIONAL READINGS

Bergman, P., & S. Escalona, "Unusual Sensitivities in Very Young Children." *PsaStC*, 3, 1949.
Hoop, J. H. van der, "Über Autismus. Dissociation und Affektive Demenz." *ZNP*, 97, 1925.
Kanner, L., "Irrelevant and Metaphorical Language in Early Infantile Autism." *P*, 103, 1946.
Mahler, M. S., "On Child Psychosis and Schizophrenia: Autistic and Symbiotic Infantile Psychoses." *PsaStC*, 7, 1952.
Markuszewicz, R., "Beitrag zum Autisischen Denken bei Kindern." *Z*, 6, 1920.
Ritvo, S., & S. Provence, "Form Perception and Imitation in Some Autistic Children: Diagnostic Findings and Their Contextual Interpretation." *PsaStC*, 8, 1953.

162
AUTOEROTISM denotes the libidinal investment of the self unrelated to an external object. Havelock Ellis (1933, 1938) was the first to employ

this term. He noted: "I devised this term, 'auto-erotism,' in 1898 for those spontaneous solitary sexual phenomena of which genital excitement during sleep may be said to be the type. The term is now generally used, though not always in the exact sense in which I defined it, but sometimes only to connote sexual activity directed towards the self. That is unduly to narrow the term down, and it is not in accordance with the usual sense of the auto-group of terms; thus *automatic* action does not mean action *towards*, but *by*, the self, without direct external impulse. If we narrow the term *auto-erotic* we have no term left to indicate the whole group.

"By 'auto-erotism,' therefore, I mean the phenomena of spontaneous sexual emotion generated in the absence of an external stimulus proceeding directly or indirectly from another person. In a wide sense, which cannot be wholly ignored here, auto-erotism may be said to include those transformations of repressed sexual activity which are a factor of some morbid conditions (as probably in hysteria)."

In characterizing the pleasure stage, Ferenczi (1916) noted: "We have to observe that here the 'period of unconditional omnipotence' lasts until the giving up of the auto-erotic kinds of satisfaction, a time when the ego has already long adjusted itself to the increasingly complicated conditions of reality, has passed through the stages of magic gestures and words, and has already almost attained the knowledge of the omnipotence of natural forces. Auto-erotism and narcissism are thus the omnipotence stages of erotism, and, since narcissism never comes to an end at all, but always remains by the side of object-erotism, it can thus be said that—in so far as we confine ourselves to self-love—in the matter of love we can retain the illusion of omnipotence throughout life. That the way to narcissism is at the same time the constantly accessible way of regression after every disappointment in an object of love is too well known to need proof; auto-erotic—narcissistic regressions of pathological strength may be suspected behind the symptoms of Paraphrenia (Dementia praecox) and Hysteria, whereas the fixation-points of the Obsessional Neurosis and of Paranoia should be found in the line of development of 'erotic reality' (the compulsion to find an object)."

This term in psychoanalysis is often used as a synonym for primary narcissistic libido, the libido used by the infant both in relation to the external object and to the self. Masturbation is not synonymous with autoerotism, but may be a discharge of autoerotic libido and destrudo.

Related Concepts: COMPULSIVE MASTURBATION; INFANCY; LIBIDO.

REFERENCES

Ellis, H., 1933, *Psychology of Sex*. New York: Garden City Books, p. 107, 1954.
Ferenczi, S., 1913, "Stages in the Development of the Sense of Reality." *SPsa*, 233–234, 1916.

ADDITIONAL READINGS

Freud, S.: 1907, "The Sexual Enlightenment of Children." *SE*, 9, 1959.
    1908, "Civilized Sexual Morality and Modern Nervous Illness." *SE*, 9, 1959.
    1910, "Five Lectures on Psycho-Analysis." *SE*, 11, 1957.
    1911, "Psycho-Analytic Notes on an Autobiographical Account of a Case of Paranoia (Dementia Paranoides)." *SE*, 12, 1958.
Kris, E., "Some Comments and Observations on Early Autoerotic Activities." *PsaStC*, 6, 1951.
Spitz, R. A., "Autoerotism Re-Examined: The Role of Early Sexual Behavior Patterns in Personality Formation." *PsaStC*, 17, 1962.

163

AUTOHYPNOSIS is a consciously or unconsciously self-induced hypnoid state, supposed by Breuer and Freud (1895) to be a precondition for the development of conversion hysteria. Autohypnosis is marked by temporary absences, during which the possibility of normal discharge of affect is diminished, and abnormal discharge is fostered through its conversion into somatic symptoms. Constitutional factors, physical and emotional shock, and excessive daydreaming are all considered to be contributory to autohypnotism.

After Freud's advance, from cathartic to analytic therapy, he regarded (in 1896) the hypnoid states as unnecessary constructions in an explanation of hysteria, a factor which led to his split with Breuer.

Related Concepts: ABSENCE; HYPNOID STATE.

REFERENCES

Freud, S., & J. Breuer, 1895, "Studies on Hysteria."
   SE, 2:12, 215–220, 247–248, 1955.
Freud, S., 1896, "The Aetiology of Hysteria." *SE*,
   3:195, 1962.

ADDITIONAL READINGS

Freud, S.: 1909, "Some General Remarks on Hys-
   terical Attacks." *SE*, 9, 1959.
      1910, "Five Lectures on Psycho-Analysis."
   SE, 11, 1957.
      1914, "On the History of the Psycho-Analytic
   Movement." *SE*, 14, 1957.

164

AUTOMATIC OBEDIENCE is the blind carry-
ing-out of commands—for simple actions of all
kinds—without regard to the pleasure principle; a
symptom of schizophrenia, particularly of the
catatonic type. Automatic obedience can be regarded
as a primitive attempt at making contact with the
lost object-world through the mechanism of primary
identification. [Fenichel, 1945.] Metapsychologically, we find a regression, of object and secondary
narcissistic-libido and -destrudo, to primary narcissistic-libido and -destrudo.

In a discussion of child development, Ferenczi
(1916) noted: "Usually one identifies oneself as a
child with the parent of the same sex, and fancies
oneself into all his situations. Under such circumstances obedience is not unpleasant; the expressions
of the all-powerfulness of the father even flatter the
boy, who in his fancy embodies in himself all the
power of the father, and only obeys himself, so to
speak, when he bows to his father's will. This willing
obedience obviously only goes to a certain limit,
varying with the individual; if this is overstepped by
the parents in their demands, if the bitter pill of
compulsion is not sugared with love, a precocious
severing of the 'sexual hunger' from the parents
results, and generally there is an important disturbance of psychical development, as especially
Jung has established (in his work on the part played
by the father)."

Ferenczi also noted that the strictness employed
in the education of children may lead to psychopathic behavior. "The isolation of children in their
sexual exigencies, the resulting exaggerated and false
notions on everything that physiologically or

ideationally has to do with sexuality, the inordinate
strictness in the punishment of sexual habits of
childhood, the systematic training of children to
blind obedience and motiveless respect for their
parents: all these are components of a method of
education, unfortunately prevailing to-day, that
might also be called artificial breeding of neuropaths
and sexually impotent people."

Related Concept: HYPNOSIS.

REFERENCES

Fenichel, O., *The Psychoanalytic Theory of Neurosis.*
   Nor, pp. 423, 438, 1945.
Ferenczi, S., 1909, "Introjection and Transference."
   SPsa, pp. 32, 77–78, 1916.

ADDITIONAL READINGS

Eidelberg, L., *Studies in Psychoanalysis.* IUP, 1952.
Kris, E.: 1934, "The Psychology of Caricature."
   IntJPsa, 17, 1936.
      & E. Gombrich, "The Principle of Caricature."
   M, 17, 1938.

165

AUTOMATISM denotes those automatic actions
which are not under conscious control, the involuntary processes that take place in the preconscious;
a lack of attention-cathexis is a prerequisite to
consciousness. For example, when the attention
cathexis is diverted, automatic reasoning can result
in faulty logic in certain jokes; they reveal hidden
meanings, such as slips of the tongue and other
phenomena of self-betrayal. [Freud, 1905.]

Hartmann (1958) wrote extensively on the concept
of physiological automatic functioning, in respiration for example, and on psychological automatism,
in the part it plays in healthy adaptation. He
reasoned that automatism operates alongside flexible
ego processes and can even give rise to superior ego
and superego functioning (e.g., the automatic
preconscious activity which prevents the driver
from speeding while operating a car). As well,
pathological automatism is involved in compulsion
neurosis, tics, and catatonia. Furthermore, instinctualization of normal automatic functions plays a
role in many neuroses: for example, the ego's control
of motivity can be interfered with in conversion

hysteria. In compulsion neurosis, the conscious attempt to regain control of automatized behavior is referred to as *deautomatization*.

The relationship of automatic actions to the pleasure principle is described by Hartmann, as follows: "Apparently these relatively rigid apparatuses often perpetuate something that was once pleasurable, in that it mastered a task, or removed a disturbance, or the like. We have already stressed that formular abbreviation essentially favors reality relations. It is possible that the 'principles'—as we conceive of them—only trigger the repetition of canalized actions and methods of thought (since they have been structuralized), but do not regulate their subsequent course. Since automatized processes are repetitive, one might think that they are somehow related to the repetition compulsion."

Related Concepts: AUTONOMY; PRECONSCIOUS.

REFERENCES

Freud, S., 1905, "Jokes and Their Relation to the Unconscious." *SE*, 8:151–152, 1960.
Hartmann, H., *Ego Psychology and the Problem of Adaptation*. IUP, p. 95, 1958.

ADDITIONAL READINGS

Fenichel, O., 1928, "Organ Libidinization Accompanying the Defense Against Drives." *OF-CP*, 1, 1953.
Freud, S., 1901, "The Psychopathology of Everyday Life." *SE*, 6, 1960.

166

AUTONOMY. Hartmann (1958) introduced the concepts of *primary* and *secondary autonomy* of the ego functions and apparatus; in which the former is characterized by inborn characteristics of the ego which mature in the course of development; and the latter, by changes of function which persist independently of the original instigating factors and resist regression. For instance, the ability to walk depends essentially on inborn apparatus; the use of walking becomes attached to many aims and goals beyond its original purpose.

The attainment of secondary autonomy is closely associated with the establishment of conflict-free areas of ego functioning; it is characterized by

freedom from conflict, and by the cathexis of the ego with neutralized energy.

Related Concepts: AUTOMATISM; EGO FUNCTIONS.

REFERENCE

Hartmann, H., *Ego Psychology and the Problem of Adaptation*. IUP, p. 100, 1958.

ADDITIONAL READING

Rapaport, D., "The Autonomy of the Ego." *BMC*, 15, 1951.

167

AUTOPLASTIC denotes a form of adaptation directed toward altering the total personality rather than the environment. Thought, fantasy, and affect are substituted for action. As a result of reality testing, the ego may reemerge with new capacities for altering the environment or deriving pleasure from its own functioning (as in aesthetic pleasure). Sleep, laughter, and humor can represent normal autoplastic adaptations. The therapeutic change in analysis results from an autoplastic identification with the analyst.

Pathological autoplasty is to be found in the formation of neurotic symptoms and, especially, in such psychotic formations as delusions and hallucinations, in which the ego is split and fragmented. Ferenczi (1930) noted: "Probably each living being reacts to stimuli of unpleasure with fragmentation and commencing dissolution (death-instinct?). Instead of 'death-*instinct*' it would be better to choose a word that would express the absolute passivity of this process. Possibly complicated mechanisms (living beings) can only be preserved as units by the pressure of their environment. At an unfavourable change in the environment the mechanism falls to pieces and disintegrates as far (probably along lines of antecedent historic development), as the greater simplicity and consequent plasticity of the elements makes a new adaptation possible. Consequently autoplastic adaptation is always preceded by autonomy. The tendency to autonomy in the first instance tends to be complete. Yet in opposite movement (instinct of self-preservation), life-instinct inhibits the disintegration and drives towards a new consolidation, as soon as this has been made possible by the plasticity developed in the course of fragmentation. It is very difficult to make a conception of the true essence of this instinctual factor and its function. It is as if it could command sources of knowledge and possibilities which go infinitely far beyond everything that we know as faculties of our conscious intelligence. It assesses the gravity of the damage, the amounts of energy of the environment and of the surrounding people, it seems to have some knowledge of events distant in space and to know exactly at what point to stop the self-destruction and to start the reconstruction. In the extreme case when all the reserve forces have been mobilized but have proved impotent in the face of the overpowering attack, it comes to an extreme fragmentation which could be called dematerialisation. Observation of patients, who fly from their own sufferings and have become hypersensitive to all kinds of extraneous suffering, also coming from a great distance, still leave the question open whether even these extreme, quasi-pulverized, elements which have been reduced to mere psychic energies do not also contain tendencies for reconstruction of the ego. . . .

"Contrasted with the form of adaptation described above is alloplastic adaptation, i.e., the alteration of the environment in such a way as to make self-destruction and self-reconstruction unnecessary, and to enable the ego to maintain its existing equilibrium, i.e., its organization, unchanged. A necessary condition for this is a highly developed sense of reality."

Related Concepts: ADAPTATION: ALLOPLASTIC.

REFERENCE

Ferenczi, S., 1930, "Autoplastic and Alloplastic Adaptation." *IntJPsa*, 30:231–232, 1949.

ADDITIONAL READINGS

Alexander, F., "The Neurotic Character." *IntJPsa*, 1930.
Freud, S., 1924, "The Loss of Reality in Neurosis and Psychosis." *SE*, 19, 1961.

168
AUTOSYMBOLISM is the direct transformation of abstract dream-content into concrete pictures which can be observed in the dream itself as part of the dream-work. This is particularly striking in the transition between sleeping and waking. Freud (1909) described a dream of Silberer which occurred after he had thought about Kant and Schopenhauer and then had a dream about a hostile secretary refusing to give him information.

Related Concept: HYPNAGOGIC PHENOMENON.

REFERENCES

Freud, S., 1900, "The Interpretation of Dreams." *SE*, 5:503–504, 1953.
Silberer, H., "Report on a Method of Eliciting and Observing Certain Symbolic Hallucination-Phenomena." *OrgPath*, 1909.

ADDITIONAL READING

Silberer, H., "Symbolik des Erwachens und Schwellensymbolik überhaupt." *Y*, 3, 1911.

169
AVOIDANCE is a defense mechanism employed to protect the subject from the recognition of an unconscious wish or from an unconscious narcissistic mortification, or both. The subject responds to certain situations or objects or activities, without being aware of the avoidance, by eliminating an object or a function. The avoided situation or activity is specifically related to unconscious sexual and aggressive impulses. The forgotten traumas are neither remembered nor repeated, according to Freud (1939). They are eliminated from memory, for the trauma represents the basis of the defense mechanism. As a consequence, the patient may develop neurotic symptoms or neurotic character traits. The symptoms and the character traits indicate the presence of a fixation to a certain stage of the development, and are, at the same time, an attempt to deny it. Because the neurotic symptoms and the neurotic character traits represent compromises of opposite tendencies, they lead to conflicts which the individual cannot resolve.

Anna Freud (1936) offered the following explanation: "Instead of perceiving the painful impression and subsequently cancelling it by withdrawing its cathexis, it is open to the ego to refuse to encounter the dangerous external situation at all. It can take to flight and so, in the truest sense of the word, 'avoid the occasions of 'pain.' The mechanism of avoidance is so primitive and natural and moreover so inseparably associated with the normal development of the ego that it is not easy, for purposes of theoretical discussion to detach it from its usual context and to view it in isolation.

"When I was analysing the little boy whom I introduced in the previous chapter as 'the boy with the cap,' I was able to observe how his avoidance of 'pain' developed on these lines. One day, when he was at my house, he found a little Magic Drawing-Block, which appealed to him greatly. He began enthusiastically to rub the pages, one by one, with a coloured pencil and was pleased when I did the same. Suddenly, however, he glanced at what I was doing, came to a stop and was evidently upset. The next moment he put down his pencil, pushed the whole apparatus (hitherto jealously guarded) across to me, stood up and said, 'You go on doing it; I would much rather watch.' Obviously, when he looked at my drawing, it struck him as more beautiful, more skilful or somehow more perfect than his own and decided that he would not compete with me any more, since the results were disagreeable, and thereupon he abandoned the activity which, a moment ago, had given him pleasure. He adopted the role of the spectator, who does nothing and so cannot have his performance compared with that of someone else. By imposing this restriction on himself the child avoided a repetition of the disagreeable impression."

Related Concept: INHIBITION.

REFERENCES

Eidelberg, L., *An Outline of a Comparative Pathology of the Neuroses.* IUP, p. 93, 1954.
Freud, A., 1936, *The Ego and the Mechanisms of Defense.* IUP, pp. 100–101, 1946.
Freud, S., 1939, "Moses and Monotheism." *SE,* 23:76, 1964.

B

200

BARRIER is denotative of physical, physiological, neural, and psychical mechanisms which serve to restrict the perceptual discharge of internal and external stimuli which might otherwise flood the psyche; a shield against stimuli that seek to paralyze the psychical functions. Freud (1920) pointed out that a living organism in its simplified form is an undifferentiated vesicle of a substance susceptible to stimulation. The surface of such a vesicle becomes differentiated, serving as an organ which receives and dampens stimuli from the external world. In this, he observed that the protection against stimuli is an important function, for without a barrier the powerful excitations of the external world would destroy the vulnerable interior of the living organism. The barrier permits the passage of dampened excitations, allowing the organism to *sample* external stimuli; it serves as a guide to the adaptive mechanisms.

The central nervous system is embryologically derived from the primitive ectoderm, which later develops into man's external shield in the form of skin, hair, etc. Various sense organs are left behind on the external shield, while most of the neural system withdraws into the body. A psychically traumatic situation may occur if the resistance to stimuli of the protective envelope is overcome. This may occur in instances such as the experiencing of severe pain or deafening noises. The excessive flood of stimuli may disorganize or completely paralyze psychic functions. When an overwhelming stimulus such as physical pain breaks through the barrier, the ego mobilizes anticathectic or hypercathectic psychical energy in an attempt to prevent a traumatic state. If this defensive maneuver is successful, some degree of psychic impairment results as a consequence of the withdrawal of cathexes from other psychic functions.

Freud felt that the infant had no internal equivalent to the barrier against external stimuli and that internal stimuli such as the instinctual drives were given instant discharge which predisposed the psyche to traumatic flooding. As the ego matures, however, it develops a progressive capacity to bind internal stimuli. In effect, the ego assumes the relationship to internal stimuli that the body surface has to external stimuli. The relative ineffectiveness of the ego to effect this control, Freud hypothesized, was a basic factor in the ability of instinctual drives to induce traumatic and neurotic anxiety states. When a disturbing internal source of unpleasure begins to threaten the barrier, the ego reacts by mobilizing a small amount of anxiety, serving as a signal to indicate a danger and the need for defensive action.

Freud also described the barrier with reference to the primary and secondary processes and to free and bound cathexes. He reasoned that instinctual drive presentations do not find a barrier in the unconscious and seek only discharge. The cathectic energies are thus freely mobilized and undergo displacement, condensation, etc., in accordance with the mode of operation of the primary process. Preconscious and conscious functions utilize bound energies and have the capacity to serve as barriers in order to bind cathexes pressing forward from below. If we imagine a simple living organism,

Freud (1920) reasoned, we will have to assume that the surface of this organism which is in contact with the external world receives stimuli from it. Embryology teaches us that the central nervous system originates from the ectoderm and that the gray matter of the brain which represents a superficial layer has inherited its characteristics. It is possible that as a result of the continuous stimulation by the external world a superficial layer of the living organism is formed which is different from deeper layers. This external layer becomes the site of consciousness and represents the system *Cs.* which is characterized by the fact that it is not capable of permanent changes when stimulated. Freud assumed that the excitations passing from one element of the central nervous system to another had to overcome a certain resistance and that as a result of a repeated excitation this resistance was diminished. In the system *Cs.* he believed the resistance had been eliminated, suggesting that this hypothesis could be related to Breuer's theory of bound and unbound instinctual energy. Consequently, the system *Cs.* could contain only mobile energy and be free of bound energy.

Related Concept: INSTINCT (INSTINCTUAL DRIVE).

REFERENCE

Freud, S., 1920, "Beyond the Pleasure Principle." *SE*, 18:26–27, 1955.

201

BASIC RULE denotes that precept which is to govern the patient's behavior in the psychoanalytic situation; namely, that the patient should *think aloud*, which is achieved by free association, to eliminate normal censorship.

In 1895, in a long footnote to the first of his case histories, Freud noted how neurotic patients seemed to be under a necessity to bring into association with one another any ideas simultaneously present in their minds. This clinical observation climaxed a period of evolution of technique wherein hypnosis, suggestion, pressing of hands, and questioning (from the earlier nondynamic association psychology of the nineteenth century) were used. In 1900 Freud clarified further his technique of free association: its use in the interpretation of dreams, in the penetration into the unconscious. He discarded hypnosis since, among other things, it concealed the important phenomena of resistance, transference, and countertransference. Freud, in his concept, used ideas of psychic determinism, causality, purposive ideas in the unconscious, and the dynamic concept of wish fulfillment.

The basic rule provides an access to the analytical material and is aimed at achieving therapeutic results. The rule is applied by the patient with complete candor, with the assurance that the therapist will maintain the strictest discretion. The free associations are not censored; otherwise, what did not make sense, was offensive or appeared not to be connected with the analysis, etc., might be eliminated. It is this method which permits the patient and the analyst to take from the free associative material what appears to be of consequence; to try to isolate it, and to find those unconscious elements connected with the associations that may help to establish its causal relationship. The analyst who listens is under an obligation to remember what the patient said and to put together what he assumes represents a chain of circumstantial evidence. No patient can obey this rule at once, and if he does he is usually psychotic and unsuitable for psychoanalysis.

Thinking aloud permits the patient some discharge of his tensions and may therefore, without any interpretation from the analyst, produce a therapeutic effect. In addition, verbalization changes ideas and affects into words and thus inner reality becomes external reality (spoken reality). Sometimes a patient may recognize the infantile character of his ideas just as a result of verbalization. From the patient's associations and his specific resistances to certain of those associations, the analyst forms a picture of the patient's problems. It is true that obedience to the basic rule may lead to the experience of exhibitionistic and aggressive pleasure and either increase or eliminate the analytical frustration which is decisive for the continuation of treatment. The analyst thus must deal with the patient's resistances and the gratifications which seduce the patient and permit him to forego the final aim of analysis: namely, to understand and to eliminate neurotic phenomena, to make conscious what is unconscious.

Freud (1909) noticed with surprise that one of his patients asked his permission not to have to describe a torture which he was afraid could be applied to his father. What surprised Freud mostly was the intensity of the fear in relation to the father despite the fact that the father had died many years ago.

The mere communication of the basic rule to the patient may not in itself be sufficient. It has to be repeated, and whatever interferes with it—those unconscious factors responsible for the resistance—must be uncovered and dealt with in the analytical situation. Though psychoanalysis is a science, its practice does not provide scientifically delineated instruments. Thus, the content and form of the explanation offered to the patient as regards the basic rule are of crucial importance, and no exception to the basic rule is permissible.

Related Concept: PSYCHOANALYSIS.

REFERENCES

Freud, S.: 1896, "The Aetiology of Hysteria." *SE*, 3:197–199, 1962.
     1900, "The Interpretation of Dreams." *SE*, 4:280, 1953.
     1909, "Notes Upon a Case of Obsessional Neurosis." *SE*, 10:166, 1955.

ADDITIONAL READINGS

Eidelberg, L., *Take Off Your Mask*. Py, 1948.
Kohut, H., "Beyond the Bounds of the Basic Rule. Some Contributions to Psychoanalysis." *JAPA*, 8, 1960.

202
BEATING FANTASIES. Written in 1919, Freud's paper "A Child Is Being Beaten" was designed to extend the analyst's knowledge of perversions and was, from this point of view, an extension of "Three Essays on the Theory of Sexuality." The paper on beating fantasies concluded with a discussion of the causes for one form of repression. In this, the bisexual constitution of man is one important cause of repression. The dominant sex of an individual whose sexuality is essentially masculine has repressed his subordinate female sexual characteristics.

The differences which arise as between the two sexes in regard to the beating fantasies illustrate his point. In the girl, the first phase of the beating fantasy is represented by the phrase, "My father is beating a child." In effect, the fantasy may be said to mean, "My father does not love this other child; he loves only me." That is, to put it more technically, the child has reached that stage of sexual development in which the incestuous love has achieved a premature choice of an object. The fantasy is in the service of an excitation which involves the genitals but which finds its outlet in masturbation.

In the second phase, the wording runs, "I am being beaten by my father," and is masochistic in its character. This is a direct expression of the girl's guilt, in which sadism has been transformed into masochism as a direct result of the guilt feelings involved. The sexual love is nonetheless present, and it is this convergence of love and guilt that is represented by the beating fantasy of the child's sufferance at the father's hand. *It is not only the punishment for the forbidden genital relationship, but also the regressive substitute for it.*

The third phase for the girl is like the first. It once again seems sadistic in character. The second phase has been repressed. But as Freud noted, "Only the *form* of this phantasy is sadistic; the satisfaction which is derived from it is masochistic. Its significance lies in the fact that it has taken over the libidinal cathexis of the repressed portion and at the same time the sense of guilt which is attached to the content of that portion."

With the boy, the beating fantasy is described as occurring in two phases. The unconscious fantasy, corresponding to the second phase in the girl, arises from the boy's negative oedipal relationship to his father; it takes the form, "I am loved by my father." It is, in effect, an unconscious punishment for the boy's phallic wishes, for the figure of the person doing the beating is changed into the person of the mother while the figure being beaten remains the same. The boy's beating fantasy, Freud thus concluded, is passive from the very beginning; it is derived from the boy's feminine attitude toward the father, and corresponds to the oedipus complex, just as does the female one. *In both cases the beating fantasy has its origin in an incestuous attachment to the father.*

In the case of the girl, what was originally a masochistic situation is transformed into a sadistic one by means of repression, while, in the case of the boy, the situation remains masochistic. "The boy evades his homosexuality by repressing and remodeling his unconscious phantasy." The girl "turns herself in phantasy into a man, without herself becoming active in a masculine way." Thus in both sexes "the masochistic phantasy of being beaten by the father ... lives on in the unconscious after repression has taken place."

The fantasies thus described arose perhaps from accidental causes, between the second and fifth year of life. They were retained for the purposes of autoerotic satisfaction and can only be regarded as primary traits of perversion. This does not mean that infantile perversions necessarily persist into the adult years. They can, as Freud noted, be repressed, be replaced by reaction formation, or be transformed by sublimation. When, however, one of these processes does not take place, the perversion may persist into the mature years.

Related Concepts: HUMILIATION; MASOCHISM; MASTURBATION FANTASIES; REMORSE; SADISM.

REFERENCE

Freud, S., 1919, "'A Child Is Being Beaten': A Contribution to the Study of the Origin of Sexual Perversions." *SE*, 17:181, 189, 191, 198, 200, 1955.

ADDITIONAL READINGS

Bergler, E., "Preliminary Phases of the Masculine Beating Fantasy." *Q*, 7, 1938.
Eidelberg, L., *Studies in Psychoanalysis.* IUP, 1952.
Freud, A., "The Relation of Beating Phantasies to a Day Dream." *IntJPsa*, 4, 1923.
Gero, G., "Sadism, Masochism, and Aggression: Their Role in Symptom Formation." *Q*, 31, 1962.
Loewenstein, R., "A Contribution to the Psychoanalytic Theory of Masochism." *JAPA*, 5, 1957.
Niederland, W.G., "Early Auditory Experiences, Beating Fantasies and Primal Scene." *PsaStC*, 13, 1958.
Schmideberg, M., "On Fantasies of Being Beaten." *R*, 35, 1948.

203

BIRTH TRAUMA. Freud (1900) identified birth as the first experience of anxiety, and thus believed it was prototypic of the affect of anxiety. Rank contended that such a trauma was of encompassing importance. He believed that human behavior resulted in the main from an attempt to undo the psychic trauma through the process of abreaction, that, in fact, neurosis resulted from the failure of this abreactive process. According to Rank, the mother was considered as the primary figure; conflicts arising with the father, including the oedipus complex, were of secondary importance. In effect, all subsequent behavior was the result of the birth trauma. This concept led Rank to a total revision of his psychoanalytic technique: at the very outset of treatment the patient was compelled to affectively reexperience in the transference situation the dramatic moments of birth in the belief that the resulting rebirth would effect a cure. In order to facilitate the therapy, fixed termination dates were set and were adhered to rigorously, gradually reduced in length to three or four months.

Freud looked unfavorably upon the view that, as Rank had noted, birth represented a psychic trauma that could, of itself, account for neurotic disorders. Freud (1926) considered the affect of anxiety at birth to be merely the prototype of an affective state which had to undergo the same developmental vicissitudes as the other affects. He felt that with progressive development the traumatic anxiety states of early infancy were gradually replaced by relatively mild anxiety states which served a signal function; that is, the ego was warned that a current situation was analogous to past danger situations where traumatizing anxiety had been experienced and that avoidance and defensive measures had to be taken.

Rank completely severed his ties with Freudian psychoanalysis and established his own psychoanalytic school. After stimulating a flurry of interest, especially in the United States, his influence quickly waned and has continued to do so over the intervening decades. The few proponents of his views represent at the present time a very small minority among the dissidents from Freudian psychoanalysis. Advances in ego psychology have only strengthened Freud's views on this issue and Rankian concepts have had virtually no effect on the development of modern Freudian psychology or therapeutic technique.

Related Concepts: CASTRATION COMPLEX; OEDIPUS COMPLEX.

REFERENCES

Freud, S.: 1900, "The Interpretation of Dreams." *SE*, 5:400, 1953.
　　　　1926, "Inhibitions, Symptoms And Anxiety." *SE*, 20:151–152, 1959.

ADDITIONAL READINGS

Greenacre, P., "The Biological Economy of Birth." *PsaStC*, 1, 1946.
Rank, O., *The Trauma of Birth*, HB, 1929.

204

BISEXUALITY, Freud viewed bisexuality as a psychological event: all early object relationships were libidinally cathected regardless of sex; they were nondiscriminating and highly plastic. Bisexual dispositions were the inevitable consequence of the sexualization of object relationships. As Freud later stated (1924) in a footnote in his 1905 paper: "Every individual . . . displays a mixture of the character-traits belonging to his own and the opposite sex; and he shows a combination of activity and passivity whether or not these last character-traits tally with his biological ones."

In 1923, with the introduction of the topographic approach, Freud described the bisexual disposition with respect to both libidinal and aggressive drives, culminating in the elaboration of both a positive and negative oedipal complex. Bisexuality tendencies are thus considered to be subject to considerable vicissitudes from one developmental phase to another, as well as within the point of time of a particular life experience. Id contributions to bisexual tendencies can be viewed in terms of libidinal fixations, i.e., a boy who is raised in large part by a male figure will have strong and disturbing homosexual tendencies which may result in overt homosexual behavior.

Normally, ego identifications are important in the genetic origin of bisexual tendencies. Every infant identifies with its mother in the early years. In the case of boys, this effects a preoedipal identification with the mother which can have important developmental consequences. Similarly, girls identify with the father in an attempt to undo their castration anxieties.

In the face of strong libidinal, homosexual fixations, however, ego defenses may fail under the impact of puberty with a resultant shift toward overt homosexual activity. Similarly, certain emotional or situational stresses can result in both ego and libidinal regressions which mobilize previously dormant homosexual tendencies and create neurotic symptoms or perverse sexual activity. Early ego identifications may play a central role in the development of bisexual tendencies. For instance, a boy who loses his mother by death in childhood may defend himself against the loss by effecting an intense identification with the mother. The consequence of this identification may be an undue turning toward the father or the establishment of narcissistic object-choices with young boys.

Superego factors can also play a prominent role in the shaping of an individual's bisexuality: the boy may tend to repress normally strong, positive-oedipal libidinal drives and activate negative-oedipal drives under the duress of intense castration anxieties inculcated by a threatening and punitive father. In general, superego pressures may effect ego libidinal regressions which can fundamentally shift the disposition of bisexual tendencies. Superego considerations can also play a vital role in the ego identifications which are so central to bisexuality. For example, maternal prohibitions directed against a boy's normal inclination to identify with the father can result in an intensification of maternal identification and associated homosexual tendencies. Problems of aggression and masochism are especially pertinent in this regard.

It should be stressed that the vicissitudes of bisexual tendencies are highly complex phenomena whose understanding requires an integrated evaluation of the complementary forces of id, ego, and superego within the context of an individual's development and current life experiences. As regards the vicissitudes of the disposition, Freud (1937) considered the tendency of conflicting male and female characteristics as another proof of the presence of bisexuality.

Case History

"A man, 50 years old, came to my office because of complete impotence. He had had many affairs in the past where he was completely potent; but all these women, although belonging to different social classes, had one thing in common, namely, they all represented an inferior object to him. While he was having these relations, he was aware of the existence of another type of woman, one he was able to admire and respect. He was, however, afraid to meet this type of woman and had succeeded in avoiding it in the past. A few months before he came to me he met a woman of this type and tried again to escape; but either she was too active, or he, getting older, may not have wanted to throw away his last chance of falling fully in love with this type of woman. At any rate he failed to disengage himself. After a short courtship she was willing to become his mistress, but, unfortunately, all attempts to have sexual intercourse failed because of his impotence.

"Whereas in the analysis of other patients usually a great amount of analytical time is needed to show the patient that his impotence with a certain woman is due to the fact that she represents, unconsciously, his mother and that his satisfactory sexual relations with other women are possible because they represent for him a humiliated object, this patient started his analysis with this insight. In one of the opening sessions, he told me that his impotence was caused by the fact that his new girl friend was similar to his mother and added that he had used the picture of his mother in the following masturbation phantasy: He watches his mother sitting on a *bidet* and taking a douche. He remembered that at the age of four he had actually surprised his mother taking a douche when he entered the bathroom and was rebuked by her. This early memory was not suppressed because its infantile material was used, in this case, to cover and deny some other infantile material which was even more dangerous. His masturbation phantasy was based on a cover memory and did not represent a break through of the unconscious wish, but was, like other defense mechanisms, a compromise between the three parts of the personality. The Id wish, responsible for this phantasy was the wish *to be like mother*, to have a vagina, to take a douche, and to be surprised while doing it. This wish was warded off by the unconscious part of the Ego. As a result of this defense, another wish was substituted, namely: 'I want to surprise my mother taking a douche.' This wish, used as a defense, became conscious because it also expressed a denial of the shock connected with the discovery of the existence of the vagina. According to Freud, the little boy may receive many castration threats without being unduly

impressed by them. However, the discovery of the vagina makes him accept the previous threat. The fact that there are human beings without a penis makes the old threat real and *emotionally* effective. In other words, the discovery of the vagina becomes a shock because the boy identifies himself with the woman and, instead of recognizing the vagina as an organ of another sex, he assumes that the woman represents a castrated man. Some of our patients act as if they had accepted the point of view of the little boy and treat women as castrated men. These male neurotics who use some female characteristics as a symbolic castration assume that these female characteristics have the same meaning when they belong to the personality of a normal woman. They do not realize that the feeling of inferiority they experience when they unconsciously try to play the role of a woman is caused by their biological inability to play such a role and not to the inferiority of the female sex. Curiously enough, there are a few analysts who have accepted this neurotic point of view and who regard the normal woman as an inferior creature and expect her to indulge in passive masochistic behavior as an adjustment to the reality." [Eidelberg, 1948.]

Related Concepts: LATENT HOMOSEXUALITY; OVERT HOMOSEXUALITY.

REFERENCES

Eidelberg, L., *Studies in Psychoanalysis.* IUP, pp. 207–208, 1948.
Freud, S.: 1905, "Three Essays on the Theory of Sexuality." *SE*, 7:143–144, 147, 220, 1953.
    1923, "The Ego and the Id." *SE*, 19:33, 1961.
    1937, "Analysis Terminable and Interminable." *SE*, 23:243–244, 1964.

205
BLUSHING is a somatic reaction associated with the feeling of shame or embarrassment, characterized by a hyperemia of the cheeks and face, tingling and turgescence of the skin, and, sometimes, sweating and palpitations. Darwin (1873) and others claimed that the redness of blushing may also appear on abdomen and arms, especially in those who wear no clothes over those parts.

Blushing may, under certain conditions, represent a normal reaction of the individual, and be used to express his conscious feelings. Under pathological conditions, when the individual is unconscious of the meaning of the blushing, it is considered a conversion symptom. In this, blushing is a compromise formation, which partly fulfills forbidden unconscious wishes, and, at the same time, represents a prohibition and punishment for these wishes. Signs of sexual excitement are displaced from the genitals to the face. The accompanying anxiety may be considered a derivative of castration fear.

Although exhibitionistic and scopophilic wishes predominate, a variety of unconscious impulses, including aggressive wishes, may cause shame and blushing. Feldman (1962) stressed the superego contribution to the symptom. According to Feldman and to Bergler (1944), male blushers unconsciously identified with women, as a result of the negative oedipus complex. Eidelberg (1954), however, reported the case of a man who responded to social situations (such as parties) which unconsciously evoked incestuous wishes toward his mother and murderous wishes toward his father (positive oedipus complex) by blushing. His consequent fear of blushing was caused by an anticipation of punishment (castration). Instead of guilt or remorse for his oedipal impulses, he felt shame because of his blushing, and he avoided any situation which would cause him to blush. This indicates that both the positive and negative oedipus complex may lead to the development of the symptom of blushing.

Blushing may be prevented by the subject's avoidance of certain situations. Consequently, a subject, instead of having a conversion symptom, may develop a phobia which would force him to avoid those situations in which the blushing occurs.

Related Concepts: CONVERSION AND CONVERSION SYMPTOMS; EXHIBITIONISM.

REFERENCES

Bergler, E., "A New Approach to the Theory of Erythrophobia." *Q*, 13:43–59, 1944.
Darwin, C., *The Expression of Emotion in Man and Animal.* London: John Murray, p. 326, 1873.
Eidelberg, L., *An Outline of a Comparative Pathology of the Neuroses.* IUP, p. 146, 1954.
Feldman, S., "Blushing, Fear of Blushing, and Shame." *JAPA*, 10:368–385, 1962.

ADDITIONAL READINGS

Feldman, S. S., "On Blushing." *PQ*, 15, 1941.
Fenichel, O., *The Psychoanalytic Theory of Neurosis.* Nor, 1945.
London, L., "Psychopathology of Erythrophobia (Blushing)." *SMS*, 1945.

206

BODY IMAGE. Freud (1923) believed that the sense organ perceptions and the internal perceptions were largely responsible for the development of a body image. In addition, it would appear that the sensations of touch would yield external sense-organ perceptions and might also be responsible for some internal perceptions. The same would appear to be true with respect to the sensations of pain.

Fenichel (1945) elaborated on this, emphasizing that this distinction between outer and inner perceptual data is an important step in the differentiation of self from non-self, and as such is a basic determinant of further ego development. Hartmann, Kris, and Loewenstein (1946) also emphasized the major developmental step of ego formation in the differentiation of self from non-self; Hoffer (1950) stressed the important role of the mouth and the hand in accomplishing this. Greenacre (1958) elaborated on the important role of visual perception and perceptual distortion of the genitals and of the face in the development of the body image. E. Jacobson (1964) stressed that the perception of inner physical sensations becomes the precursor to the perception of the self and the mental self as an object. She noted: "The kernels of the early infantile self-images are the memory traces of pleasurable and unpleasurable sensations, which under the influence of autoerotic and of beginning functional activities and of playful general body investigation become associated with body images."

The body image evolves gradually and is progressively modified through growth, maturation, and development. It does not necessarily correspond to the objective body, and may be distorted by all of the vicissitudes of the primary process. Multiple body images at varying levels of consciousness may coexist simultaneously. However, according to E. Jacobson, "with advancing psychosexual and ego development, with the maturation of physical and mental abilities, of emotional and ideational processes and of reality testing, and with increasing capacity for perception and self perception, for judgement and introspection, the images become unified, organized and integrated into more or less realistic concepts of the object world and of the self."

Related Concepts: EGO BOUNDARIES; SELF.

REFERENCES

Fenichel, O., *The Psychoanalytic Theory of Neurosis.* Nor, p. 36, 1945.

Freud, S., 1923, "The Ego and the Id." *SE*, 19:125–126, 1961.

Greenacre, P., "Early Physical Determinants in the Development of the Sense of Identity." *JAPA*, 6:612, 1958.

Hartmann, H., E. Kris, & R. Loewenstein, "Comments on the Formation of Psychic Structure." *PsaStC*, 2:11, 1946.

Hoffer, W., "Development of the Body Ego." *PsaStC*, 5:18, 1950.

Jacobson, E., *The Self and the Object World.* IUP, 1964.

ADDITIONAL READINGS

Fisher, S., "Body Image and Asymmetry of Body Reactivity." *ASP*, 57, 1958.

Fox, H. M., "Body Image of a Photographer." *JAPA*, 5, 1957.

Keiser, S., "Disturbances in Abstract Thinking and Body-Image Formation." *JAPA*, 6, 1959.

Linn, L., "Some Developmental Aspects of the Body Image." *IntJPsa*, 36, 1955.

207

BODY LANGUAGE denotes those perceptions of specific body functions, sensations, organs, parts, or the body as a whole, which may, in a symbolic way, express unconscious conflicts. Either the unconscious instinctual drives, or the defense against such drives, or both, are unconscious fantasies. Regressive expressions arise from psychic or from primitive somatic discharges. Symbolic expressions may arise as primary conversion symptoms or as secondary cathected responses and fantasies to organic or psychophysiologic conditions. They may also occur as characteristic modes of gait, posture, motor movement, facial expression, etc.

The idea of a body language emerged from Freud's (1908) work on hysteria in which he postulated that there was a *conversion* of psychic excitement and unconscious fantasy into a somatic form of discharge represented by the hysterical symptom. In this formulation, conversion into a body language was linked to hysteria etiologically. Fenichel (1945) elaborated upon the concept of pregenital conversion in an attempt to clarify the observations and manifestations of a body language which may occur in conditions other than hysteria. Deutsch (1959) and his co-workers included all instances and types of somatic illness as expressions of psychic tensions through bodily functions.

Rangell (1959) developed the thesis that "the essence of conversion was the shifting or displacement of psychic energy from the cathexis of mental processes to that of somatic innervations in order for the latter to express in a distorted way the derivatives of repressed forbidden impulses. These somatic changes ... speak symbolically, and via body language express a combination of both forbidden instinctual impulses as well as the defensive forces which bring about the distortion. ... [They are] employed to express repressed forbidden wishes throughout the entire gamut of psychopathological symptomatology. ...

"[The use of body language] consists of and utilizes a number of individual defenses, such as identification, displacement, internalization, symbolization, turning upon the self, and most especially repression."

This hypothesis was further developed by Engel (1962). The specific determinants of conversion symptoms have "sources in the history of the individual's past object relationships and in the type of bodily activities or experiences which have been involved in the gratifications and conflicts that marked these relationships." For Engel, conversion symptoms are translations into body language of the wish and its defense, a correspondence with memories of earlier physical experiences associated with the significant object relationships; it represents memories or fantasies experienced by the object in the past, or, finally, represents a wish that the object experience such a physical symptom.

Related Concepts: LANGUAGE; MANNERISM.

REFERENCES

Deutsch, F., ed., *On the Mysterious Leap from the Mind to the Body*. IUP, 1959.

Engel, G., *Psychological Development in Health and Disease*. Sau, 1962.

Fenichel, O., *The Psychoanalytic Theory of Neurosis*. Nor, p. 311, 1945.

Freud, S., 1908, "Hysterical Fantasies and Their Relation to Bisexuality." *SE*, 9:159, 1959.

Rangell, L., "The Nature of Conversion." *JAPA*, 7:632, 1959.

ADDITIONAL READINGS

Feldman, S., *Mannerisms of Speech and Gestures in Everyday Life*. IUP, 1959.

Silverman, S., "Ego Function and Body Language." *BPAP*, 1960.

208

BORDERLINE CASES. While it is true that an experienced analyst will have no problem in differentiating between neurosis and psychosis he may sometimes encounter cases which represent a mixture of both mechanisms. Fenichel (1945) noted: "It certainly is not true that psychoses represent a kind of higher degree of neurosis. It is possible that the same person may develop both types of mechanisms. There are neurotic persons who, without developing a complete psychosis, have certain psychotic trends, or have a readiness to employ schizophrenic mechanisms whenever frustrations occur. They are sometimes persons who may be called potential schizophrenics; that is, they have not 'broken with reality' yet, though they show certain signs of beginning such a break and, under unfavorable circumstances of life, may develop into psychotics; or they are persons who have 'channelized' their schizophrenic disposition, so to speak, eccentrics who are crazy in one more or less circumscribed area and otherwise retain normal contact with reality."

Related Concept: SCHIZOPHRENIC SURRENDER.

REFERENCE

Fenichel, O., *The Psychoanalytic Theory of the Neurosis*. Nor, p. 443, 1945.

209

BOREDOM, according to Fenichel (1945), "at least in neurotic exaggeration, is a state of excitement in which the aim is repressed; anything the person can think about doing is felt as not adequate to release the inner tension. Bored persons are looking for distraction, but usually they cannot be distracted because they are fixated to their unconscious aim."

Fenichel further defined boredom by quoting Lipps,* who characterized it as a feeling of unpleasure resulting from an intensive need for activity, or from a lack of stimuli, or from the inability to become stimulated, in which the latter is referred to as pathological. In this, the differentiation between pathological and normal forms of boredom is dependent on whether the individual is able to avoid boring stimuli or is able to eliminate boredom by seeking interesting stimuli (elimination of normal boredom); in pathological boredom, the individual sticks to stimuli which are not interesting to him.

A case of pathological boredom was presented by Greenson in 1953. His patient, at first, was extremely bored by her associations and by most of the analytical interpretations. With analytic progress and with the increase of positive transference, Greenson was able to see that the boredom represented a defense against repressed oral incorporating tendencies.

Ferenczi (1912), in another case, reported: "I noticed with one patient that he yawned with striking frequency. I then remarked that the yawning accompanied just those analytic conversations whose content, since it was important to him although disagreeable, would more suitably have evoked interest than boredom. Another patient who came to treatment soon after this brought me what I believe to be the solution of this particular phenomenon. She also yawned often and at inappropriate times, but in her case the yawning was sometimes accompanied with a flow of tears. That gave me the idea that these patients' yawning might be a distorted sign, and in both cases the analysis confirmed my surmise. The censorship effected in both cases the repression of certain disagreeable emotional states that were aroused through the analysis (pain, grief), but it was unable to bring about a complete

---

* Lipps, T., *Grundzüge der Psychologie*. Leipzig, 1913.

suppression, only a displacement of the movements of expression, that was enough, however, to conceal from consciousness the real character of the emotional state." It is still too early to say whether boredom is always connected with the wishes for oral incorporation. Some cases of pathological boredom appear to represent neurotic defenses against the wish to spit out or to vomit.

Winterstein (1930) suggested that in addition to oral there are also anal wishes. Actually, Greenson assumed that boredom could take place at any libidinal stage; thus, this probably included exhibitionistic and scopophilic wishes.

Related Concepts: DEPERSONALIZATION; DEPRESSION.

REFERENCES

Fenichel, O., *The Psychoanalytic Theory of Neurosis.* Nor, pp. 185–186, 1945.
Ferenczi, S., 1912, "Transitory Symptom-Constructions During the Analysis." *SPsa*, pp. 209–210, 1916.
Greenson, R., "On Boredom." *JAPA*, 1:7–21, 1953.
Winterstein, A., "Fear of the New, Curiosity and Boredom." *PsaB*, 2:540–554, 1930.

ADDITIONAL READINGS

Abraham, K., "A Short Study of the Development of the Libido, Viewed in the Light of Mental Diseases." *SPA*, HP, 1927.
Isaacs, S., "The Nature and Function of Phantasy." *IntJPsa*, 29, 1948.
Kris, E., "On Preconscious Mental Processes." *PQ*, 19, 1950.
Lewin, B., *The Psychoanalysis of Elation.* Nor, 1950.
Lewinsky, H., "Boredom." *BJEP*, 13, 1943.
Winterstein A. R., "Angst vor dem Neuen, Neugier und Langeweile." *PsaB*, 2, 1930.

210

BREAST COMPLEX in men was described by Bergler and Eidelberg (1933) as follows: The child reacts to weaning with a violent shock. After all his attempts to recover the breast have failed, the child is obliged to endure this frustration. The child then discovers his penis and uses it as a substitute for the mother's breast. This *breast-penis* is very much loved and carefully protected, particularly against persons who have no penis. Since the vagina is

reminiscent of the mouth, which once wanted to tear off the mother's breast (vagina dentata), it is in the genital region that the danger is most acutely felt. One consequence of the breast complex may be breast envy; which may lead to overt homosexuality, where the penis of the homosexual, and that of his partner, unconsciously represents the breast.

Related Concept: PENIS ENVY.

REFERENCE

Bergler, E., & L. Eidelberg, "Der Mammakomplex des Mannes." *Z*, 19:547–583, 1933.

ADDITIONAL READINGS

Eidelberg, L., *The Dark Urge.* Py, 1961.
Stärcke, A., "The Castration Complex." *IntJPsa*, 2, 1921.

211

BREAST ENVY is the result of the repression of a breast complex in the infant. The subject tries to take away the breast of anyone who represents the preoedipal mother; he ignores the female breasts, and may develop overt homosexual traits, or use other mechanisms to deny the importance of female breasts. For example, some male patients are only able to get sexually excited if the female partner sucks their breast. Breast envy may also be encountered in females who, because they have not accepted their own breasts, continue to resent the original deprivation of the mother's breast.

Sublimated breast envy may contribute significantly to artistic and scientific activities. [Eidelberg, 1952.]

Related Concepts: BREAST COMPLEX; PENIS ENVY.

REFERENCE

Eidelberg, L., *Studies in Psychoanalysis.* IUP, pp. 14–15, 1952.

212

BRONCHIAL ASTHMA. According to Fenichel (1945), bronchial asthma is an organ neurosis of the respiratory system. The id wish responsible for this pregenital conversion is probably the oral wish to incorporate the subject. Since relatively few cases of asthma have been successfully analyzed, it is not clear whether the oral wish is always a sexual one; whether, in fact, the sexual wish becomes aggressive as a result of its defense (mobilization of the opposite). It appears that anxiety is used as a signal of defense.

In bronchial asthma (similar to other conversions on the anal and phallic level), the quantity of the libido is greater than that of the destrudo. It differs from melancholia (a defense mechanism of the oral stage) in that the id and not the superego plays the decisive part (Eidelberg, 1954). As in other conversions, secondary organic changes appear to be responsible for the great danger connected with this symptom. "The mechanism of conversion leads to the formation of a conversion symptom, which may be described as the next step of the unconscious defense.

"The fact that the example described above represents a defense of phallic-exhibitionistic and inspectionistic wishes should not be taken as an indication that conversion is a mechanism characteristic of the phallic stage. Most analysts assume that conversion may be used on all three stages of development, and separate the symptoms due to conversion of oral wishes from those having to do with conversions of anal and phallic wishes. Some analysts prefer to consider conversion as a defense against sexual wishes only, but the great majority assumes that aggressive wishes, in addition to sexual ones, may be dealt with by conversion.

"To sum up, the mechanism of conversion eliminates the consciousness of an infantile wish, or of the product of such a wish and its defense, by allowing a partial discharge of the instinctual energy to take place away from its original destination. Since part of the instinct tension remains blocked, the unpleasure of this tension is not eliminated completely. The patient experiences a mixture of sexual and aggressive emotions, and accepts an internal narcissistic mortification (no power over his conversion symptom) instead of a possible external narcissistic mortification from an object, which possibility is further minimized by an external identification with it."

Related Concepts: TIC; WRITER'S CRAMP.

REFERENCES

Eidelberg, L., *An Outline of a Comparative Pathology of the Neuroses.* IUP, pp. 96–97, 1954.
Fenichel, O., *The Psychoanalytic Theory of Neurosis.* Nor, pp. 250, 321–322, 1945.

C

CARICATURE denotes an emphasis or exaggeration of one feature of a person or thing in order to ridicule it. Caricature may be used as a defense of the ego against the superego; the caricatured object may unconsciously represent the infantile superego. Kris (1952) stressed the resemblance between caricature and verbal puns; he described the magical power of imagery. Distortion by caricature may be a substitute for, or a sublimation of, destructive wishes, and may therefore require distance from immediate emotions and a degree of social approval. The adequate discharge of the inhibited impulse is through laughter, which results from a preconscious comparison. In addition, laughter discharges pent-up energy which is no longer needed for repression.

Related Concepts: COMIC; JOKE (WIT).

REFERENCE

Kris, E., "The Psychology of Caricature." *PEA*, pp. 173–188, 1952.

ADDITIONAL READINGS

Freud, S.: 1905, "Jokes and Their Relation to the Unconscious." *SE*, 8, 1960.
    1927, "Humour." *SE*, 21, 1961.
Kris, E., "Zur Psychologie der Karikatur." *Im*, 20, 1934.
Redlich, F., "The Psychiatrist in the Caricature." *Ops*, 20, 1950.

CASTRATION ANXIETY denotes a fear of loss of, or injury to, the genitals. A common phenomenon in young children, castration anxiety may be caused by the wish to castrate and be castrated. It is often mobilized by a castration threat made by a parent. Although the parental castration threat may be connected with libidinal frustration, it mobilizes aggressive impulses which then cause the anxiety. Castration anxiety is often colored by experiences connected with bowel training and weaning.

Freud originally assumed that dammed-up libido changed into anxiety. He later (in 1926) realized that anxiety is caused by aggression. In other words, he originally regarded castration anxiety as a result of dammed-up libido, but he later recognized that the castration threat produced anxiety and forced the individual to repress certain libidinal wishes.

Related Concepts: ANXIETY; CASTRATION COMPLEX.

REFERENCE

Freud, S., 1926, "Inhibitions, Symptoms and Anxiety." *SE*, 146–147, 1959.

ADDITIONAL READINGS

Abraham, K., & H. Deutsch, *Über Phantasien der Kastration durch Beissen*. BPV, 1923.
Alexander, F., "The Castration Complex in the Formation of Character." *IntJPsa*, 4, 1923.
Freud, S., 1930, "Civilization and Its Discontents." *SE*, 21, 1961.
Stärcke, A., "The Castration Complex." *IntJPsa*, 2, 1921.

302

CASTRATION COMPLEX is the sum of the reactions experienced by all children in connection with castration threats. At first, Freud (1905) had the impression that the castration complex was caused by external traumatic threats, often connected with masturbation or its equivalents. However, he eventually recognized that even in cases in which no threat was issued, the child may have imagined such a threat. He finally concluded that, independently of threats received, the first realization of the lack of a penis in females produced in the male child a strong fear of castration. As a result of such a threat, the boy may have given up his positive oedipal wishes, and developed a negative oedipus complex.

Sexual curiosity and the examination of sexual organs, Freud (1917) reasoned, begins quite early, usually before the third year of life. In the beginning, the child does not have a clear concept of the difference between males and females, and boys assume that the penis is an organ which men and women possess alike. After the boy finds out that the little girl doesn't have a penis, he usually attempts to eliminate this perception (of the lack of a penis) from his consciousness (disavowal). At this stage, the boy is not able to believe that the human being could exist without it. In later years, the boy very often develops castration fears. There is frequently a recall of castration threats made by parents when they catch him masturbating. He develops, as Freud called it, a castration complex which influences his development. It may affect his character, it may be responsible for neurotic symptoms, and it usually appears in his resistance when he is in analysis. Freud was convinced that little girls develop a feeling of inferiority because of the lack of penis and that they react with penis envy by often wanting to become a man. The penis envy plays a great role in the neuroses and is often responsible for frigidity. According to Freud, the little girls often accept a clitoris instead of a penis and use it in masturbation. In normal women, the importance of the clitoris decreases when they grow up and the vagina becomes the main organ responsible for genital gratification. In pathological cases (e.g., in frigidity), the clitoris in a woman may still be the main source of genital pleasure.

Related Concepts: ANXIETY; BREAST ENVY; CASTRATION ANXIETY; NARCISSISTIC MORTIFICATION.

REFERENCES

Freud, S.: 1905, "Three Essays on the Theory of Sexuality." *SE*, 7:157, 158, 195, 1953.
 1917, "Introductory Lectures on Psycho-Analysis." *SE*, 16:317–318, 1963.

ADDITIONAL READINGS

Abraham, K., "Manifestations of the Female Castration Complex." *IntJPsa*, 3, 1922.
Bell, A., "Some Observations on the Role of the Scrotal Sac and Testicles." *JAPA*, 9, 1961.
Bergler, E., & L. Eidelberg, "Der Mammakomplex des Mannes." *Z*, 19, 1933.
Graber, G. H., "Onanie und Kastration." *PsaP*, 2, 1927–1928.
Manchen, A., "Denkhemmung und Aggression aus Kastrationsangst." *PsaP*, 10, 1936.
Riviere, J.: "The Castration Complex." *IntJPsa*, 5, 1924.
 "A Castration Symbol." *IntJPsa*, 5, 1924.
Sachs, L., "A Case of Castration Anxiety Beginning at Eighteen Months." *JAPA*, 10, 1962.

303

CATHARSIS is the discharge of anxiety and tension through the recall, expression and, possibly, further exploration of significant unconscious material. The cathartic method was introduced by Breuer (1895) who discovered that the symptoms of hysteria disappeared when forgotten memories were recalled with appropriate affect during a state of hypnosis. Subsequent to his collaborative work with Breuer, Freud's independent clinical and theoretical development led him to switch from catharsis to psychoanalysis as the favored method of treatment and mental exploration. Current structural theories stress not only the discharge aspects of catharsis (abreaction), but, also, its role in permitting the ego to regain control over the id. Many sublimations (in play, work, and religion), as well as different forms of psychotherapy, including aspects of analysis (working through), involve a degree of catharsis.

In discussing the concept, Freud (1923) noted that his work with Breuer led to the discovery that catharsis came about when the path to consciousness was opened up. The catharsis, as such, was seen as leading to a normal discharge of affect; the affect which previously had been "strangulated" was discharged "along the normal path leading to consciousness."

Related Concepts: ABREACTION; CONVERSION AND CONVERSION SYMPTOMS; STRANGULATED AFFECT.

REFERENCES

Freud, S., & J. Breuer, 1895, "Studies on Hysteria." *SE*, 2:xxii, 8, 1955.
Freud, S., 1923, "Two Encyclopedia Articles." *SE*, 18:235–236, 1955.

ADDITIONAL READINGS

Freud, S.: 1894, "The Neuro-Psychoses of Defence." *SE*, 3, 1962.
　　　1898, "Sexuality in the Aetiology of the Neuroses." *SE*, 3, 1962.
　　　1904, "Freud's Psycho-Analytic Procedure." *SE*, 7, 1953.
　　　1910, "Five Lectures on Psycho-Analysis." *SE*, 11, 1957.

304

CATHEXIS is the psychic energy which is attached to the presentation of an external object or to a presentation of the self. For example, the infant cathects (with object-libido and destrudo) the presentation of the mother's breast; he also simultaneously cathects (with secondary narcissistic- or neutral-libido and destrudo) the presentation of his mouth and the function of sucking. It seems that under normal conditions, object-libido and destrudo cathect the presentation of external objects; whereas narcissistic-libido and destrudo cathect the presentation of the self.

The feelings that become conscious indicate the presence of particular instinctual tensions which may produce pleasure or unpleasure. Freud (1920) reasoned that a closer study of particular tensions present in our feelings might lead to a differentiation of bound or unbound mental energy. In addition, he thought that the feeling of tension of the instinctual energy might be related to changes of the cathexis in a given unit of time.

Related Concepts: COUNTERCATHEXIS (ANTICATHEXIS); LIBIDO; NARCISSISTIC NEED; PSYCHIC (MENTAL) ENERGY.

REFERENCES

Freud, S., 1920, "Beyond the Pleasure Principle." *SE*, 18:62–63, 1955.
Strachey, J., Editorial note. *SE*, 2:xxiii, 1955.

ADDITIONAL READINGS

Eidelberg, L., *Studies in Psychoanalysis.* IUP, 1952.
Freud, S., 1900, "The Interpretation of Dreams." *SE*, 5, 1953.
Holt, R., "A Critical Examination of Freud's Concept of Bound vs. Free Cathexis." *JAPA*, 10, 1962.
Strachey, J., "The Emergence of Freud's Fundamental Hypotheses." *SE*, 3, 1962.

305

CAUSALITY is a hypothesis which describes all phenomena (effects) as the result of other specific phenomena (causes). In psychoanalysis, as in other branches of biology, these phenomena are concerned with living organisms (and their changes), and thus must be distinguished from inorganic matter. In this respect, living organisms are able to retain a basic order despite their changes: the phenomenon of negative entropy. Given this distinction, psychoanalysis was able to employ the causal approach in its investigation of human behavior. For instance, psychoanalysis was to show that a neurotic symptom was the result of a repressed infantile wish and its defenses. This method of investigation does not contradict the final or teleological approach, in which the patient uses his symptoms in order to obtain what is called the secondary gain. Thus, the teleological approach in psychoanalysis cannot be avoided. The *purely* causal approach or the reliance *only* on the descriptive approach are both inadequate, if not wrong.

Aloys Wenzl (1954) has rightly pointed out that the statement, "If these conditions are fulfilled, the event will take place," can be regarded as a representation of the causal approach. If, on the other hand, we say that the condition *aims* at the result, we are using a final approach. Thus, in describing the condition as responsible for the outcome—by using the final approach—it can be said that the condition appeared to aim at this outcome. However, Niels Bohr* has pointed out that even some physicists have expressed the opinion that the microphysical processes are (to some degree) acausal.

Freud (1900) was the first to apply causality to psychology by assuming the presence of instinctual drives which act as the *vis a tergo* responsible for

_____
* See Max Hartmann, *Einführung in die Allgemeine Biologie.* Berlin: Walter de Grayter & Co., 1956.

psychological phenomena. Prior to Freud, psychology was chiefly interested in presenting a final explanation of human behavior. However, Freud used the teleological approach without which the concept of anticipation would not exist. In addition, the fact that an instinctual need leads to an instinctual discharge represents a causal approach. On the other hand, the fact (also) that the individual tries to obtain pleasure from such a discharge represents the teleological approach.

Hartmann (1964) expressed the following view: "We have rejected understanding as *the* method of psychology, have indicated its limitations, and have shown why it must become a source of error for psychological knowledge. We then showed that such error can be avoided only by reliance upon inductive proof. These statements should not be construed to imply the worthlessness of understanding for psychology. Many understandable connections (including the 'as-if' understandable connections) are, as I mentioned before, actually causal connections. We must not forget that the emergence of a voluntary action from an act of will is the paradigm not only of the understanding connection but also of the causal relationship. The concept of causality, however—and this is the crucial point—has freed itself from its origin in the experience of causality. This subjective experience no longer is a valid criterion of causal connections. Understanding connections are, as hypotheses, in many ways indispensable, but their validity must in every case be established empirically. No psychology of the more complex aspects of the mind can fully dispense with understanding. But as long as it is a science, it must not use understanding without having established the limits of its reliability. To ascertain these limits and thereby to determine the sphere within which understanding and causal connections coincide is one of the essential tasks of psychoanalysis."

Related Concepts: MAGIC; OMNIPOTENCE OF THOUGHT; TELEOLOGY (FINALITY).

REFERENCES

Freud, S., 1900, "The Interpretation of Dreams." *SE*, 4:314–316, 1953.
Hartmann, H., *Essays on Ego Psychology*. IUP, pp. 402–403, 1964.
Wenzl, A., *Die Philosophischen Grenzfragen der Modernen Naturwissenschaft*. WK, p. 82, 1954.

ADDITIONAL READINGS

Hoop, J., "Über die kausalen und verständlichen Zusammenhänge nach Jaspers." *ZNP*, 68, 1921.
Marcinowski, J., "Vom finalen und vom kausalen Denken in der Psychologie der Neurosen." *ZPt*, 8, 1935.
Piaget, J., *The Child's Conception of Physical Causality*. HB, 1934.

306

CENSORSHIP is a defensive activity directed against the admission to consciousness of disturbing stimuli from the external world or of forbidden impulse-derivatives from the unconscious. In his study of the resistance to dream interpretation, Freud (1917) observed that there was a counteracting, inhibitory and restricting force ascribable to an *institution* of the mind; namely, the dream censor. He noted that in sleep the censorship activity of the ego was probably weakened but was still operative in the dream, from which rejected, offensive and forbidden wishes tried to break through. This resulted in dream distortion: the transformation of latent dream-content into disguised manifest-content through the various defense mechanisms. A latent thought, one that would be passionately repudiated if the dreamer were awake, was allowed to pass the censor in dreams in disguise. For example, an elderly lady—cited by Freud—brought the idea of sexual traffic with young soldiers into her dream, in which she substituted a low murmur whenever a frank sexual term might have appeared.

Censorship is not a mechanism peculiar to dreams alone. It represents the ego's ever-present counteracting, inhibiting, and restraining force. Freud (1915) postulated the presence of censorship between the unconscious and the preconscious, and between the preconscious and the conscious. The former operated directly against the *Ucs.* derivatives, the latter against the *Pcs.* derivatives of the *Ucs.* derivatives. Both are made up of defensive counter-cathectic systems that Freud, at a later date (in 1933), assigned to the ego functions.

It would seem that the preconscious is separated by a censor from consciousness. It may be that the preconscious is the unconscious part of the ego. It appears also that it is more difficult to overcome the censor between the unconscious and the conscious than between the preconscious and the conscious. This may be accounted for if the material of the preconscious (the unconscious part of the ego) results from a countercathexis against the unconscious id, and therefore represents the lesser evil.

Related Concepts: CONDENSATION; COUNTERCATHEXIS (ANTICATHEXIS); DREAMS.

REFERENCES

Freud, S.: 1915, "The Unconscious." *SE*, 14:191, 1957.
    1917, "Introductory Lectures on Psycho-Analysis." *SE*, 15:141, 143–147, 1963.
    1933, "New Introductory Lectures on Psycho-Analysis." *SE*, 22:71, 72, 1964.

ADDITIONAL READINGS

Freud, S.: 1896, "Further Remarks on the Neuro-Psychoses of Defense." *SE*, 3, 1962.
    1900, "The Interpretation of Dreams." *SE*, 4 & 5, 1953.
    1905, "Jokes and Their Relation to the Unconscious." *SE*, 8, 1960.
    1925, "An Autobiographical Study." *SE*, 20, 1959.

307

CENTRAL EGO. Eidelberg (1960) suggested that the total personality be divided into five parts, instead of the three presently designated in Freud's topographic approach. In this, the ego only is divided as follows: (a) the *external ego*, which contains the presentation of the external world, as reflected by the sense organs; (b) the *body ego*, which is the presentation of the body; and (c) the *central ego*, having all the functions hitherto attributed to the ego alone. Such a division appears to have a heuristic value, for it may help in the differentiation which is made between those individuals whose ego is chiefly interested in sensory perception and those who are chiefly interested in motoric discharges.

Freud (1931) expressed the view in his paper on libidinal types that some individuals had most of their libido concentrated in the id (erotic type); some in the ego (narcissistic type); and, finally, some in the superego (obsessional type). The concept of libido is thus an explanatory one: the observation of the individual cannot be used to detect the quantitative changes supposed to be present in the three libidinal types introduced by Freud. This division into three such types is the result of inherited and not acquired factors, and may be used as the basis for the study of the choice of neurosis. For example, patients belonging to the obsessional type will, if neurotic, develop symptoms in which the quantity of the interference in the superego plays a decisive role (melancholia, obsessional neurosis, anxiety hysteria, etc.); a corresponding role can be projected for the other two. Thus, with the help of this new division of the ego, those individuals belonging to the narcissistic type can be identified as one of three types: (1) those who are chiefly interested in sense organ perceptions, the sensuous type; (2) those chiefly interested in motoric discharges, the athletic type; and (3) those who have their libido concentrated in the central ego, the ego type.

Related Concepts: CHOICE OF A NEUROSIS; LIBIDINAL TYPES; QUANTITATIVE APPROACH.

REFERENCES

Eidelberg, L., "Primary and Secondary Narcissism." *PQ*, 34: 480–487, 1960.
Freud, S., 1931, "Libidinal Types." *SE*, 21: 217–218, 1961.

308

CHARACTER NEUROSIS is a disorder which primarily affects the total personality. It stems from repressed infantile wishes, in which the ego and superego—or rather the total personality—are modified in order to resolve the conflict. The changes within the total personality lead to ego-syntonic processes instead of ego-alien symptoms. There is often little motivation for therapeutic change since the total personality does achieve partial gratification of basic wishes, even though this may be possible only under certain restrictive conditions or with some relinquishment of voluntary control. Rationalization and provocation play important roles in a character neurosis. It frequently appears to the character neurotic that his behavior is consciously determined, that he is as he is as he wants to be, and that he is free of intrapsychic conflict. This appearance of normality is generally attained only by an extravagant and constant expenditure of countercathectic energy or by a high degree of instinctual renunciation, with consequent impoverishment of ego functioning and the formation of rigid, stereotyped patterns of response which present great resistance to therapeutic change. [Freud, 1908.]

A patient suffering from an obsession which forced him to return to the kitchen nine times to check whether a gas jet was off suffered from a symptom neurosis; another patient, who also returned to the kitchen many times to check the gas jet and believed he was doing so only because he was very careful, suffered from a character neurosis. He experienced the waste of time connected with his repeated examination of the gas jets as representing a valuable character trait, rather than as something he was compelled to do against his conscious desires.

If an individual of the narcissistic type develops a neurosis, it will probably be a character neurosis. Eidelberg (1954) noted: "A comparative study of neurotic character traits seems to indicate that they are dominated by the ego. The unpleasure caused by the neurotic character traits seems to be so small that it does not mobilize rejection by the total personality. This lack of rejection may be explained by two factors: (a) the assumption that there is a greater gratification than frustration of the instinct energy, and (b) the internal mortification is minimized. Consequently, the neurotic character trait would be approved and assimilated by the total personality. . . .

"It is obvious that analytic technique had to be modified in order to study the so-called neurotic character traits and transform them into symptoms. In this book, which presents information gained as a result of analytic work, the fascinating problems of analytic technique cannot be discussed. However, it may be permissible to note that in these cases, the neurotic character trait must be isolated and proven to be a liability through a rational discussion in which the patient's contradictions, distortions, and errors are presented to him, and that this discussion does not include infantile wishes, nor does it consist of making unconscious material conscious with the help of interpretations. The intellectual recognition by the patient that his behavior does not make sense will not eliminate this behavior, but it may arouse his curiosity to analyze it.

"Most analysts assume that the basis of 'character' is the habitual set of reactions to external and internal stimuli which the individual uses to solve the problems of instinct satisfaction and adaptation

to external reality. In some cases of patients who have come to us because they are suffering from neurotic symptoms, one is able to see in analysis that the defense mechanisms are not satisfied to create a symptom, but are able to produce character traits in addition, which also serve for the partial gratification and rejection of repressed infantile wishes.

"The various forms of neurotic character traits are usually described in accordance with the developmental stage from which they originate."

Related Concepts: CHARACTER TRAITS; NEUROSIS AND PSYCHOSIS.

REFERENCES

Eidelberg, L., *An Outline of a Comparative Pathology of the Neuroses.* IUP, pp. 165–166, 262, 1954.
Freud, S., 1908, "Character and Anal Erotism." *SE,* 9:167–176, 1959.

ADDITIONAL READINGS

Freud, S., 1931, "Libidinal Types." *SE,* 21, 1961.
Jacobson, E., "The 'Exceptions': An Elaboration of Freud's Character Study." *PsaStC,* 14, 1959.
Kramer, P., "Early Capacity for Orgastic Discharge and Character Formation." *PsaStC,* 9, 1954.
Lubin, A. J., "A Boy's View of Jesus." *PsaStC,* 14, 1959.
Lustman, S., "Defense, Symptom, and Character." *PsaStC,* 17, 1962.
Reich, A., "A Character Formation Representing the Integration of Unusual Conflict Solutions into the Ego Structure." *PsaStC,* 8, 1958.

309

CHARACTER TRAITS. In general, character traits may be described as normal (e.g., orderliness, independence, and frugality) or pathological (e.g., pedantry, parsimony, and obstinacy). They are characterized by the individual's habitual reaction to external and internal stimuli, the result of repressed wishes which are either sublimated or warded off through the employment of the defense mechanisms. More specifically, the infantile wishes are warded off by the ego and the superego. The results of this battle may produce ego-alien or ego-syntonic phenomena. It would seem that those patients who belong to the narcissistic type, for instance, have the ability to modify the results of their defense mechanisms in such a way that they can be assimilated so as to represent ego-syntonic character traits.

From a technical point of view, it is possible to analyze those character traits which appear to be ego-syntonic, which might have been thought unsuitable for analysis. In fact, when the analysis succeeds, the ego-syntonic traits are changed into ego-alien traits. On the other hand, while it is usually possible to analyze neurotic character traits that have been changed into ego-alien phenomena, it is practically impossible to analyze normal character traits which appear to be the result of successful repressions. [Freud, 1913.]

Related Concepts: ADDICTION; PERVERSION; PSYCHOSIS.

REFERENCE

Freud, S., 1913, "The Disposition to Obsessional Neurosis." *SE*, 12:323, 324, 1958.

ADDITIONAL READINGS

Abraham, K., "Über Charakteranalyse." *PsaStud Char*, Al, 1926.
Arlow, J., "On Smugness." *IntJPsa*, 38, 1957.
Michaels, J., *Disorders of Character: Persistent Enuresis, Juvenile Delinquency and Psychopathic Personality.* CCT, 1955.
Reich, W., *Character-Analysis; Principles and Technique for Psychoanalysts in Practice and in Training.* OIP, 1945.
Riviere, J., "A Character Trait of Freud's," in J. M. Sutherland, *Psycho-Analysis and Contemporary Thought.* HPI, 1958.
Valenstein, A., Report on Panel: "The Psychoanalytic Concept of Character." *JAPA*, 6, 1958.

310

CHILD ANALYSIS, a clinical specialty, had its beginning with Freud's report of the case of Little Hans. Published in 1909, the material used in the written record was supplied by the child's father during the many consultations Freud had with him during the course of the analysis. Freud saw the boy only once. In his reconstruction, Freud was able to substantiate certain conclusions he had earlier drawn about infantile sexuality from his analysis of adult patients.

The case of Little Hans was that of a phobia supervened on an anxiety state that developed when the boy was almost five. His neurosis was characterized by a fear of horses; he was afraid of going out into the street for fear of being bitten by them. In the course of the analysis Freud was able to conclude that the boy had displaced his hostile and fearful feelings toward his father onto a substitute. Thus his fear of horses insured that he could remain in his house with his mother. He regarded his father as a competitor, and at the same time, he admired and loved him. To find relief from this conflict, Little Hans displaced his hostile and fearful feelings. Little Hans had arrived at a stage of development to which Freud was to give the name *oedipus complex*, identifying it as "the nuclear complex of the neurosis."

The method of this first recorded child analysis took the form of an intellectual game of hide-and-seek. Little Hans was encouraged to ask questions of both his parents and other adult authorities. In turn, this opened the way to counter-questions on the part of his father. Success was assured when the "game" caught Little Hans' attention, enlisting his enthusiasm. The boy's father was a disciple of Freud's, and was able to conduct the analysis without the usual parental defensive confrontations, despite the fact that much of the boy's hostility was directed to him.

The clinical utility of this technique received its impetus in the early twenties with the work of Anna Freud and Melanie Klein. Much of this early work was corroborative of the conclusions Freud had drawn earlier with regard to infantile sexuality. With the publication of A. Freud's book in 1928 and M. Klein's in 1932, a method was offered which sought to replace the work previously expected from the technique of free association. A. Freud (1928) noted: "Without doubt the play technic worked out by Mrs. Klein has the greatest value for the observation of the child. Instead of losing time and energy in keeping track of the child in its domestic environment, we transplant at one stroke its entire known world to the room of the analyst, and allow the child to move in it under the eyes of the analyst without any interference for the time being. We thus have an opportunity to become familiar with its various reactions, the strength of its aggressive inclinations.

its capacity for sympathy, as well as its attitude toward the different objects and persons which are represented by the dolls. As an advantage over an observation of actual conditions, it may be added that this toy environment is manageable and subject to the will of the child, and that it thus may carry out all its actions upon it, which in the actual world, because of its superior magnitude and strength in contrast to the child, remain limited to a phantasy existence. All these advantages make the application of the Klein play method almost indispensable for intimate knowledge of the small child, who is not yet sufficiently capable of expressing itself in words. . . .

"The affectionate attachment, the positive transference as the analytical term is, is the prerequisite for all subsequent work. In this the child goes even further than the adult, for it has faith only in the person it loves and then accomplishes something only out of love for that person.

"Child analysis requires much more of this attachment than that of the adult. In addition to the analytical intention, it carries out part of an educational one, which we will take up more thoroughly later. Not only child analysis but the whole success of education stands and falls every time with the emotional attachment of the pupil for the educator. Even in the analysis of children, we cannot say that the production of a transference in itself alone satisfies our intention, no matter whether it be of a friendly or hostile nature. We know that with adults we can get along over long periods with a negative transference, which we make use of for our purpose by means of consistent interpretation and reference to its origin. But with the child the negative impulses directed against the analyst—no matter how revealing they may be in many respects—are above all unpleasant. As soon as possible we must seek to weaken and destroy them. The actual productive work will always go hand in hand with a positive attachment."

The technique of classical analysis was not applicable to children much before the age of puberty if free association remained as the primary method: young children are neither willing nor able to embark on it. "It became obvious," as A. Freud (1945) pointed out, "immediately that the classical analytic technique was not applicable to children, at least not before the age of puberty, or at best pre-puberty.

Free association, the mainstay of analytic technique, had to be counted out as a method; young children are neither willing nor able to embark on it. This fact affects dream-interpretation, the second main approach to the unconscious. Children tell their dreams freely; but without the use of free association the interpretation of the manifest dream content is less fruitful and convincing. The child analyst frequently has to supply the links between the manifest dream content and the latent dream thoughts according to his own intimate knowledge of the child's inner situation at the time of dreaming. Furthermore, it is impossible to establish the same outward setting for the analytic hour. Children placed on the analytic couch for the purpose of relaxed concentration are usually completely silenced. Talk and action cannot be separated from each other in their case. Nor can the patient's family be wholly excluded from the analysis. Insight into the seriousness of the neurosis, the decision to begin and to continue treatment, persistence in the face of resistance or of passing aggravations of the illness are beyond the child, and have to be supplied by the parents. In child analysis the parents' good sense plays the part which the healthy part of the patients' conscious personality plays during adult analysis to safeguard and maintain the continuance of treatment. Appropriate substitutes for free association were accordingly the prime necessity in establishing techniques suitable to the varying needs of different phases of childhood. The first divergence of opinion between child analysts arose about this matter. Certain child analysts (Hug-Hellmuth in Vienna, Melanie Klein in Berlin and later in London) developed the so-called play technique of child analysis, a method that promised to give more or less direct access to the child's unconscious. According to this technique, the child's spontaneous play activity with small toys offered by the analyst for free use within the analytic hour, was substituted for free association. The individual actions of the child in connection with this material were considered to be equivalent to the individual thoughts or images in a chain of free association. In this manner the production of material for interpretation became largely independent of the child's willingness or ability to express himself in speech.

"Other child analysts (on the European continent and in the United States) were reluctant to employ this play technique to the same extent. Although such a method of interpretation allowed certain flashes of direct insight into the child's unconscious, it seemed to them open to objections of various kinds. Like all interpretation of symbols (for instance purely symbolic dream interpretations) it had a tendency to become rigid, impersonal and stereotyped without being open to corroboration from the child; it aimed at laying bare the deeper layers of the child's unconscious without working through the conscious and preconscious resistances and distortions. Furthermore these analysts refused to accept such activities as actual equivalents of free association. The free associations of the adult patient are produced in the set situation of analytic transference and, although they are freed from the usual restrictions of logical and conscious thought, they are under the influence of the patient's one governing aim to be cured by analysis. The play activity of the child is not governed by any similar intention. This leads to the further open and controversial question as to whether the relationship of the child to the analyst is really wholly governed by a transference situation. Even if one part of the child's neurosis is transformed into a transference neurosis as it happens in adult analysis, another part of the child's neurotic behavior remains grouped around the parents who are the original objects of his pathogenic past. Considerations of this nature led a large number of child analysts to evolve techniques of a different kind. They worked on the various derivatives of the child's unconscious in dreams and daydreams, in imaginative play, in drawings, etc., including the emotional reactions of the child, both in and outside of the analytic hour. As in adult analysis, the task was to undo the various repressions, distortions, displacements, condensations, etc., that had been brought about by neurotic defense-mechanisms until, with the active help of the child, the unconscious content of the material was laid bare. Such cooperation with the child naturally presupposes the extensive use of speech."

These substitutes for the method of free association accounted for the controversy that has grown up between those who have supported A. Freud and those who have given credence to the work of M. Klein. The technique of play therapy which promised to give more or less direct access to the child's unconscious was undertaken without any great reliance on the child's ability to express himself in speech. Thus, those who used the Klein system were willing to undertake the analysis of children from infancy on. A. Freud, on the other hand, continued to stress the importance of speech to the analytic situation. When this is not the case, she reasoned, neurotic formations may be permitted to occur, for the child continues to possess his original love-objects (his parents), and the transference is not accomplished.

The Klein system analysts accounted for the absence of the transference by an introductory period of instruction. They believed that the individual actions of the child as he handled the play materials were equivalent to the thoughts and actions that result from a chain of free associations, and interpretations were thus offered on only the basis of these substitutive acts.

Bertha Bornstein (1945) cited the case of a child who said (in her second analysis), "I want a piece of milk chocolate. I mean, I want to have a piece of your white breast." Those who follow M. Klein would use a symbolic interpretation to explain the phrase: chocolate = breast. Bornstein noted that it was precisely this "symbolic interpretation and the insistence on sexual topics [which] was gradually understood [to be] a facile way of eluding narcissistic disappointments in everyday occurrences." In the child's second analysis, conducted by B. Bornstein, the defense mechanisms were worked through and the oversexualization was eliminated.

Perhaps the most difficult problem in child analysis is the potential conflict between the authority of the analyst and the parents. "During the course of the analysis the analyst must succeed in putting himself in place of the ego-ideal of the child and he must not begin his analytical work of liberation before he is certain that he can completely control the child at this point. At this crisis the position of authority becomes important to him, as was already mentioned in the introduction to child analysis. Only when the child feels that the analyst's authority can be placed above that of the parents will it be ready to yield the highest place in its emotional life to this new love object, which ranks along with that of the parents." [A. Freud, 1928.]

Related Concepts: CHILD PSYCHIATRY; PSYCHO-ANALYSIS.

REFERENCES

Bornstein, B., "Clinical Notes on Child Analysis." *PsaStC*, 1:151–166, 1945.

Freud, A.: *Introduction to the Technique of Child Analysis*. NMDP, pp. 30–31, 34, 51, 1928.
"Indications for Child Analysis." *PsaStC*, 1:129–130, 1945.

Freud, S., 1909, "Analysis of a Phobia in a Five-Year-Old Boy." *SE*, 10:3–149, 1955.

Klein, M., *Psycho-Analysis of the Child*. HPI, 1932.

ADDITIONAL READINGS

Furrer, A., "Eine Indirekte Kinderanalyse." *PsaP*, 3, 1929.

Gerard, M. W., "Child Analysis as a Technique in the Investigation of Mental Mechanisms. Illustrated by a Study of Enuresis." *P*, 94, 1937.

Glover, E.: "On Child Analysis. (Symposium Contribution)." *IntJPsa*, 8, 1927.
"Examination of the Klein System of Child Psychology." *PsaStC*, 1, 1945.

Greig, A. B., "Child Analysis." *Q*, 10, 1941.

Hoffer, W., "Einleitung einer Kinderanalyse." *PsaP*, 9, 1935.

Jones, E., "Child Analysis." *IntJPsa*, 8, 1927.

Kris, M., "*Child Analysis in Psychoanalysis Today*. IUP, 1944.

Mahler, M. S., *Child Analysis: Modern Trends in Child Psychiatry*. IUP, 1945.

311

CHILD PSYCHIATRY is a branch of general psychiatry. In February 1959, in the U.S.A., it was established as a subspecialty certifiable by The American Board of Psychiatry and Neurology. The requirements for examination by the board to achieve certification are described by Rexford (1962), as follows: (a) graduation from a grade A medical school, (b) an approved internship, (c) at least two years of approved residency training in adult psychiatry, and (d) two years of specialized training in child psychiatry, followed by two years of experience in the field.

The diagnostic criteria, the therapeutic methods, the treatment goals and theoretical concepts from adult psychiatry cannot be directly employed in child psychiatry. The unique components of child psychiatry involve different techniques of therapy, including the therapeutic significance of the child's conflicts and ways of handling them, the immediate and remote meanings of the parent-child relationships (and sibling relationships), the evolvement of social relationships, and the significance of learning. In addition, only part of the analytical material is remembered or reconstructed; only part is directly observable.

Historically, the breakthrough in child psychiatry as a specialty can be traced to a program initiated by the Commonwealth Fund Program for the Prevention of Delinquency in 1922. The program utilized a clinical team, consisting of a psychiatrist, psychologist and social worker. Because emotional disturbances were conceived of as having multiple causation, allied disciplines were necessary in the treatment of the child. Community clinics, termed Child Guidance Clinics, which were an outgrowth of this work, have thus included psychoanalytically trained professional personnel. Prior to the child guidance movement, child psychiatry had little to offer except in the field of organic brain damage and mental retardation. Kanner (1948) referred to the four decades of child psychiatry, as follows: (a) thinking about children (1900–1910), (b) doing things to children (1910–1920), (c) doing things for children (1920–1930), and (d) working with children (1930–1940).

The American Association of Psychiatric Clinics for Children (AAPCC) chartered fifty-four clinics by 1948, approving still more in subsequent years as training centers for child psychiatry (Rexford, 1962). The teaching and practice of child psychiatry occurred within a setting markedly different from the traditional community clinic pattern, for the latter type of clinic frequently included newborns, difficult psychosomatic disorders, and older adolescents. This difference in the scope of the two led directly to the organization of The Academy of Child Psychiatry, in 1953. In conjunction with the American Board of Psychiatry and Neurology, this academy established child psychiatry as a subspecialty of general psychiatry.

In 1963, the prospective clinical child psychiatrist was examined, in the following: (a) Pre-school Child, (b) Grade School Child, (c) Adolescent, (d) Interprofessional and Community Relations, (e) Growth and Personality Development, and (f) History and Literature.

Related Concept: CHILD ANALYSIS.

REFERENCES

Kanner, L., *Child Psychiatry*, 2nd ed. CCT, pp. 3–15, 1948.

Rexford, E., "Child Psychiatry and Child Analysis in the United States." *JCPs*, 1:366–370, 1962.

312

CHOICE OF A NEUROSIS. In Freud's view, neurosis was caused by many factors; as well, he believed that a differentiation should be made between a condition and a cause. As an example, he cited the story of a rich man who was robbed during the night. The "night," according to Freud, should be considered a condition and the robbers' "activity" as the cause of the crime.

He maintained (in 1894) that a passive attitude produced a predisposition to hysteria, while, on the other hand, an active one, an obsessional neurosis. Later, in 1906, he cautioned: "Later on I was obliged to abandon this view entirely, even though some facts demanded in some way or other the supposed correlation between passivity and hysteria and between activity and obsessional neurosis."

In the same paper, he once again stated that no single pathogenic factor was "scarcely ever sufficient; in the large majority of cases a number of aetiological factors are required, which support one another and must therefore be regarded as being in mutual opposition." Further, he stressed the fact that they could not alone be accounted for by heredity or accidental influences. The one thing that remained paramount was that illness "lies solely in a disturbance of the organism's sexual processes."

The choice of a neurosis may be looked for in the organism's libidinal predisposition, and in the influences that have been brought to bear upon that predisposition. In the case of Little Hans (1909), a chronological estimate of the associative chain that culminated in his phobia of horses led more or less directly to an event which occurred during his pregnant mother's confinement. He had witnessed an accident to a horse in the street and had been quite disturbed by it. It acquired its effectiveness, however, from an event that occurred the summer before at Gmunden, an Austrian resort town, where he had been in the habit of playing with the landlord's children (whom he thereafter referred to as "my children," adding that they, too, had been brought by the stork); Fritz, of whom he was fond, had hit his foot and fallen down while playing at horses. Thus an easy associative path was established between Fritz and his father. Nonetheless, as Freud pointed out, "even these connections probably would not have been sufficient if it had not been that . . . the same event showed itself capable of stirring the second of the complexes that lurked in Hans's unconscious, the complex of his mother's confinement."

The repressed hostile and jealous feeling toward his father and the sadistic impulses toward his mother constituted Little Hans's predisposition for his illness. These aggressive and sexual propensities found no outlet, but as soon as there came a time of privation they tried to break out. It was then, Freud noted, that the phobia broke out. A part of repressed ideas, in a distorted form and transformed into another complex, forced their way into his consciousness as the content of a phobia. The choice, as it were, was dependent on the instinctual components that Little Hans had to repress.

In 1934, Eidelberg noted: "The fascinating problem of the choice of the neurosis may be studied, perhaps, in the light of Freud's (1931) concept of the libidinal types. While most analysts agree that hysteria, for instance, arises from phallic wishes, and that obsessional neurosis is caused by anal impulses, the question remains unanswered as to why hysteria produces conversion symptoms in one case, and a phobia in another. It is true that an individual who belongs to the erotic type is characterized not only by his need of love, but also by being less aggressive than individuals who belong to the narcissistic and obsessional types, it may be expected that when such an individual develops hysteria, he will have conversion symptoms. On the other hand, an individual who belongs to the obsessional type will, as the result of a phallic regression, develop an anxiety hysteria. A person who represents the narcissistic type will produce a hysterical character under the same circumstances. Unfortunately, most people belong to mixed libidinal types, and only the few who belong to pure types can be used to study the above suggestions."

Related Concepts: NEUROSIS AND PSYCHOSIS.

REFERENCES

Eidelberg, L., *An Outline of A Comparative Pathology of The Neuroses*. IUP, pp. 260–261, 1954.

Freud, S.: 1894, "The Neuro-Psychoses of Defense." *SE*, 3: 51–52, 1962.

1906, "My Views On The Part Played By Sexuality In The Aetiology of The Neuroses." *SE*, 7:275, 279, 1953.

1909, "Analysis of a Phobia In A Five-Year-Old Boy." *SE*, 10:138–139, 1955.

1931, "Libidinal Types." *SE*, 21:215, 1961.

313

CIVILIZATION, according to Freud (1930), "describes the whole sum of the achievements and the regulations which distinguish our lives from those of our animal ancestors and which serve two purposes—namely to protect men against nature and to adjust their mutual relations."

The fact that many of us complain about certain aspects of civilization does not indicate that civilization was imposed on us in order to interfere with our pursuit of happiness. Rather, like the secondary process which does not contradict the primary process, it aims at increasing our security.

Civilization can provide us with increased security by making us inhibit or modify our instinctual discharges. In addition to developing the mechanisms that control our discharges, Freud pointed out that beauty and order are also the aims of a civilization. They may appear not to be of basic importance, but they permit us to gratify part of our desires in a sublimated manner.

While there are many factors which make the acceptance of civilization difficult, it is the renunciation of aggressive desires which appears to be the most onerous. Menninger (1942), for instance, considered deaggressivization even more important than delibidinization, for the partial gratification of libidinal desires may be directly gratified without threatening or interfering with society. On the other hand, the discharge of aggression represents the greatest danger, and, therefore, requires aim-inhibition and sublimation in an orderly, productive society. Freud (1930) reasoned that the frustration of aggression, not libido, led to feelings of guilt. For example, in order to control aggression, the Old Testament instructed its readers to "Love thy neighbor as thyself"—a command difficult to obey. However, the realization that most men not only love but also hate themselves may decrease the difficulty associated with this command.

Clinically, the frustration of our sexual desires may lead to a conflict with society, the conflict arising from the aggressive drives being added to the original sexual ones. Generally, aggression appears to be inhibited by the fear of punishment, e.g., the little child who incorporates the commands and prohibitions he receives thus avoids an external conflict. These prohibitions and commands which, at first, constitute his infantile superego, are able to control his aggression by making him feel guilty. The little child does not differentiate clearly between action and wish and feels guilty even if he refrains from gratifying his aggression. This may appear paradoxical because it seems to indicate that the little child is punished by feelings of guilt if he gratifies or inhibits his wishes. However, a closer examination indicates that a feeling of guilt represents a signal of danger due to the presence of aggressive wishes. With the help of this signal, the child may inhibit the gratification of his wishes, but, as long as he has these wishes, the danger will remain.

The child matures and learns to differentiate between wish and action. If the inhibition of his wishes is effected by repression, the wish is eliminated from consciousness, but remains in the unconscious. When the wish is rejected or repudiated, the wish disappears. This mechanism requires more time but frees the individual from the presence of infantile hostile wishes, and consequently from the feeling of guilt resulting from these wishes. This can only be achieved by incorporating the external prohibitions and commands in the superego, which remains the custodian of civilized behavior.

Freud rightly points out that the "signal" of having committed an aggressive act is not the feeling of guilt, but remorse. This terminological clarification appears to play an important role in psychoanalytical therapy. Many patients in psychoanalysis who complain of suffering guilt are actually experiencing a feeling of remorse; they do not realize the difference between wish and action. Precisely this, the recognition of the difference between wish and action, represents an important cause for the development of civilization.

Related Concepts: ALTRUISM; SOCIAL COMPLIANCE.

REFERENCES

Freud, S.: 1930, "Civilization and Its Discontents."
SE, 21:77, 89, 138–139, 1961.
Menninger, K., *Love Against Hate.* HB, p. 101, 1942.

ADDITIONAL READINGS

Freud, S.: 1905, "Jokes and Their Relation to the
Unconscious." *SE*, 8, 1960.
1908, "Civilized Sexual Morality and Modern
Nervous Illness." *SE*, 9, 1959.
1910, "Five Lectures on Psycho-Analysis."
SE, 11, 1957.
1912, "On the Universal Tendency to Debasement in the Sphere of Love." *SE*, 11, 1957.
1921, "Group Psychology and the Analysis of
the Ego." *SE*, 18, 1955.

314

**"'CIVILIZED' SEXUAL MORALITY AND
MODERN NERVOUS ILLNESS,"** a paper
written by Freud in 1908, examined the consequences
of the monogamous marriage and found that it led
to many conflicts. Freud considered the taming of
sexuality a difficult task of civilization. "I must
confess that I am unable to balance gain against loss
correctly on this point, but I could advance a great
many more considerations on the side of the loss."
In a later paper (in 1930), he expressed the idea that
civilization interferes chiefly with the aggressive
instincts. "A great theoretical simplification will, I
think, be achieved if we regard this as applying only
to the *aggressive* instincts, and little will be found to
contradict this assumption."

Freud (1908) asked whether the permitted sexual
satisfactions in marriage can represent a compensation for the renunciation of other sexual satisfactions; whether, in fact, the possible effects of such a
renunciation can be made up by cultural gains. "In
general I have not gained the impression that sexual
abstinence helps to bring about energetic and self-
reliant men of action or original thinkers or bold
emancipators and reformers. Far more often it goes
to produce well-behaved weaklings who later become
lost in the great mass of people that tends to follow,
unwillingly, the leads given by strong individuals."
In a later paper (1930), as noted, he returned to this

consideration, concluding as follows: "In all that
follows I adopt the standpoint, therefore, that the
inclination to aggression is an original, self-subsist-
ing instinctual disposition in man, and I return to
my view . . . that it constitutes the greatest impedi-
ment to civilization."

Eidelberg (1948), in discussing the problem of the
attraction of the forbidden, pointed out that the
husband and wife are deprived of the "glamorous"
pleasure connected with extramarital intercourse.
He noted: "This simultaneous gratification is
impeded by two circumstances: the individual's
striking power decreases when he concentrates
simultaneously on aggressive and on sexual goals,
and the risks are higher."

The platonic concept of marriage as the reuniting
of two parts which originally represented one being
is aesthetically attractive, but it cannot be used to
deny that a couple represents two individuals who,
while having many things in common, are not
identical. The institution of marriage which aims at
offering both participants a contract favorable to the
mutual gratification of genital needs and to the rear-
ing of children implies, also, the presence of a similar
approach to a number of problems in which the
husband and wife have sufficient tolerance to endure
their differences. Indeed, as the patriarchal concept
which gave the husband full control keeps on being
abandoned, the ability of husbands and wives to
work out a mutually acceptable compromise becomes essential for the survival of marriage.

Related Concepts: MARRIAGE; MORALITY; SEXUALITY.

REFERENCES

Eidelberg, L., *Studies in Psychoanalysis.* IUP, p. 129.
1948.
Freud, S.: 1908, "'Civilized' Sexual Morality And
Modern Nervous Illness." *SE*, 9:188, 189, 196, 197,
1959.
1930, "Civilization And Its Discontents." *SE*,
21:122, 138, 1961.

315

CLASSIFICATION OF JOKES. The simplest
division of jokes would separate the so-called
innocent jokes from those which are tendentious.

The former aims at producing laughter that is connected with aesthetic pleasure while the latter aims at the discharge of full instinctual energy. The teller of a tendentious joke, if smutty (sexual), aims at the seduction of the listener; if cynical (aggressive), he attempts to humiliate the subject of the joke. The innocent joke, on the other hand, produces laughter in the listener which permits the teller to obtain his sublimated exhibitionistic pleasure. [Freud, 1905.]

Related Concepts: COMIC; HUMOR; JOKE (WIT); LAUGHTER.

REFERENCE

Freud, S., "Jokes And Their Relation To The Unconscious." *SE*, 8:42–43, 1960.

316

CLAUSTROPHOBIA is the fear of the experience of being confined and is pressingly felt when there appears to be no way to escape. Fenichel (1945) described it as a form of anxiety hysteria, as the physical state of sexual or aggressive excitement that is projected. The feeling of suffocation, he reasoned, represents the need to escape the precipitating influence that is represented by the feared place or person, i.e., an "escape from one's own feared excitement as soon as it has reached a certain intensity."

Related Concept: ANXIETY.

REFERENCE

Fenichel, O., *The Psychoanalytic Theory of Neurosis.* Nor, pp. 203–204, 1945.

317

CLOACA. Freud (1905) regarded the anal and phallic processes in the early stages of sexual development to be linked by both "anatomical and functional analogies and relations which hold between them." The excretion and the withholding of feces provides a pleasurable experience for the infant and serves as a forerunner for those sexual activities which later come into action. The sexual activities of this zone, together with those of the genitals (brought into being, at first, by micturition), are the beginning of what is later to become the subject's normal sexual life. The early prohibitions toward bowel functions are the infant's first "glimpse of an environment hostile to his instinctual impulses, on which he learns to separate his own entity from this alien one and on which he carries out the first 'repression' of his possibilities for pleasure. From that time on, what is 'anal' remains the symbol of everything that is to be repudiated and excluded from his life."*

Freud noted that the existence of the vagina is only discovered after the phallic stage has passed. As a result, young children may come to regard their rectum as responsible for the birth of babies. While only a few adult neurotics remain fixated to this concept, many neurotics behave as if the vagina and the rectum were identical. They experience feelings of revulsion in connection with the vagina. The vagina is used as if it were a rectum; and, at the same time, the rectum is used as if it were a vagina. In this, they consider or behave as if the act of defecation represented giving birth to a child and they remain, consequently, bisexual; they are able to play the male and the female roles simultaneously. The male neurotic does not need a female partner, and a female neurotic does not require a male partner in order to react as if she were impregnated.

In the case of a patient who reported that while defecating she had to put her hand around her anus in order to protect it from being torn, her analysis revealed that as a young girl she had read about the birth of a child. In the accompanying description of the obstetrical procedure, the doctor had placed his hand around the entrance of the vagina in order to slow down the emergence of the infant's head, to avoid the danger of the mother being torn.

Related Concepts: ANAL STAGE; LATENT HOMOSEXUALITY.

REFERENCE

Freud, S., 1905, "Three Essays on the Theory of Sexuality." *SE*, 7:186–187, 1953.

* From a footnote added in 1920.

318

COLLECTIVE UNCONSCIOUS. Freud (1913) argued for the assumption of a collective unconscious as universal and contiguous, wherein "psychical processes were continued from one generation to another." In this, the psychical dispositions were inherited and given impetus when roused into actual operation. In proof of this, Freud examined the neurotic and primitive, finding that psychical reality for them both coincided "at the beginning with factual reality: that primitive men actually *did* what all the evidence shows that they intended to do." With the primitive, thought passes directly into action; with the neurotic, inhibitions allow for corresponding actions. The psychical reality, however, is the same.

In one of the last of his contributions, Freud (1939) returned to the problem, again arguing that psychical precipitates were inherited. For example, there are certain innate symbols which derive from the acquisition of speech that are universal, whatever language is being acquired. In a number of important relations, Freud noted, children respond instinctively, "in a manner that is only explicable as phylogenetic acquisition."

According to Hartmann (1964), Freud assumed that not only the instinctual drive might have a hereditary core but that the ego might also have one. Hartmann, then, added: "I think we have the right to assume that there are, in man, inborn apparatuses which I have called primary autonomy, and that these primary autonomous apparatuses of the ego and their maturation constitute one foundation for the relations to external reality. Among these factors originating in the hereditary core of the ego, there are also those which serve postponement of discharge, that is, which are of an inhibitory nature. They may well serve as models for later defenses."

Related Concepts: HEREDITY; UNCONSCIOUS.

REFERENCES

Freud, S.: 1913, "Totem and Taboo." *SE*, 13:158–161, 1955.
　　　　1931, "Libidinal Types." *SE*, 21:215–222, 1961.
Hartmann, H., *Essays on Ego Psychology.* IUP, p. xi, 1964.

319

COLOR IN DREAMS is denotative of a specific element in its manifest content. Some investigators have offered physiological and neurological explanations of color in dreams and organic sources may well be contributory, particularly in such conditions as epilepsy, migraine, and drug intoxication. However, Blum (1964) and Yazmajian (1964) have demonstrated that color may appear in the manifest content of a dream in the absence of a neurophysiological disturbance, and have a definite psychological meaning and function. Color may be present in the *original* dream imagery but fade rapidly as the dream is remembered.

When color is reported spontaneously in the manifest dream content, it has received additional cathexis and serves definite psychological functions. Clinical and experimental evidence indicates that color is more likely to appear in dreams where there is ego or superego reinforcement of voyeuristic or color perceptions. Visual sensory sensitivity, strong external color stimulation or regressive shifts in the perceptual apparatus might also contribute to a heightened perceptual awareness of color. The colors are ultimately derived from perceptual memories, selectively used by the dream work. The dream and its day residue cannot be artificially isolated from the color psychology of waking perception and imagery. Defensive alterations in hue, vividness, amount, or location may occur.

Color in dreams may have a complex multiple function, and frequently be used by the ego for both camouflage and communication. Because of color differences of the skin, mucous membranes of the orifices, and internal body contents such as blood, feces, urine, etc. color may be used to contrast and differentiate inner and outer relationships to the body. Incorporated in the total body image, color may be important in self-representation and identity, including sexual identity. Structurally, dream color may also represent instinctual strivings and superego demands: particular colors may be bound to certain drive-organizations and to specific affects. Repetitive color dreams may be related to traumatic events with visual shock, in which color was involved or defensively incorporated as a screen. Through synaesthesia color may stimulate other sensory modalities such as sound or movement sensation. The metaphorical and colloquial meaning of color may be important in dreams, images, and verbal communications.

Related Concepts: AFFECT; SUBLIMATION.

REFERENCES

Blum, H., "Colour in Dreams." *IntJPsa*, 45:519–529, 1964.
Yazmajian, R., "Color in Dreams." *Q*, 33:176–193, 1964.

320

COMIC denotes that quality of an object which produces in the subject an emotional experience colored by a characteristic pleasure, frequently accompanied by laughter. Freud (1905) quoted Bergson* as saying, "A situation is always comic when it belongs at the same time to two series of events that are absolutely independent, and when it can be interpreted simultaneously in two quite different senses."

According to Freud, pleasure in the comic arises "from an economy in expenditure upon ideation (upon cathexis)." It is similar to the pleasure connected with humor and jokes. Freud noted: "In all three modes of working of our mental apparatus the pleasure is derived from an economy [of expenditure of mental energy]. All three are agreed in representing methods of regaining from mental activity a pleasure which has in fact been lost through the development of that activity."

Eidelberg (1952) suggested that deliberate comic efforts may be connected with feelings of infantile omnipotence, expressed in the comedian's ability to produce laughter and the audience's ability to grasp the comic intent.

Related Concept: JOKE (WIT).

REFERENCES

Eidelberg, L., *Studies in Psychoanalysis.* IUP, pp. 189–190, 1948.
Freud, S., 1905, "Jokes and Their Relation to the Unconscious." *SE*, 8:235–236, 1960.

---

* Bergson, H., *Le rire.* Paris, 1900.

ADDITIONAL READINGS

Jekels, L., "On the Psychology of Comedy. "*TDR*, 2, 1958.
Tarachow, S., "Applied Psychoanalysis: Comedy, Wit and Humor." *AnSurvPsa*, 2, 1951.

321

COMPARATIVE PATHOLOGY OF THE NEUROSES, according to Eidelberg (1954), is a systematic, comparative examination of analytic material, using isolated neurotic symptoms or neurotic character traits as cross sections of neuroses, so that not only different patients, but different symptoms in a single patient may be scrutinized and compared. This comparative study should take place only *after* the completion of a successful analysis, when the case material is being reviewed.

The idea of a comparative pathology of the neuroses originated some thirty years ago in an effort to assimilate the overwhelming mass of material presented to the analyst by his patients. [Eidelberg, 1935.] With the help of the "Special Pathology of the Neuroses" (Deutsch, 1932), some insight was gained into what produces a neurotic symptom; that is, the realization that the factors named by the patient, although they might have mobilized his illness, did not cause it. A study of the "General Pathology of the Neuroses" (Fenichel, 1931) led to a clarification of a variety of defense mechanisms involved in the formation of neurotic symptoms, character neuroses, and perversions. Continuous study of the theoretical concepts by Freud and his pupils led to a further understanding of the pathology of the neuroses. However, it was felt that, in addition to the *special* and *general* *pathology of the neuroses*, a third pathology might be useful, in which certain features of the first two were united and new ones added in the facilitation and the assimilation of analytic observations. The paper by Freud (1925) in which he used a comparative approach to the study of different cases, or different symptoms of the same case, was especially utilized in the formulation of a *comparative theory of the neuroses*.

A case of frigidity is here examined in cross section, showing the structure of an oral conversion, and illustrating the comparative approach. The patient considered herself interested in men, and was unaware of any hostility toward them, until one of her boy friends suggested that she could become a famous toreador if only she would direct her feelings for men toward the bulls.

She was able to masturbate, with a clitorial climax, but without any fantasies. Her ego dealt with the basic id wish, "I want to devour the breasts of my mother," by mobilizing the opposite instinct fusion, and substituting the sexual desire to kiss and caress the breasts of her mother. The wish and its defense were then turned against the self in masturbation, during which the patient would suck the finger she had put in her vagina. Instead of guilt feelings, her superego forced the patient to accept the punishment of lack of sexual climax. The narcissistic mortification of being unable to control mother was denied by the patient's accepting her inability to "control" her vagina ("My vagina doesn't want to have any feelings, and there is nothing I can do about it"). Her total personality resented her frigidity, but partly enjoyed her ability to make men excited and then reject them. In addition, it approved of her masturbation as something which made her self-sufficient.

Related Concepts: Defense Mechanisms; Neuroses (Psychoneuroses).

REFERENCES

Deutsch, H., *Psychoanalysis of the Neuroses.* HPI, 1932.
Eidelberg, L.: "A Suggestion for a Comparative Theory of the Neuroses." *IntJPsa*, 16:439–445, 1935.
    An Outline of a Comparative Pathology of the Neuroses. IUP, pp. 162–163, 1954.
Fenichel, O., *Hysterien und Zwangsneurosen. Psycho-analytische Spezielle Neurosenlehre.* IntPV, 1931.
Freud, S., 1925, "Inhibitions, Symptoms and Anxiety." *SE*, 20:77–178, 1959.

They arise from stimulation and tension in specific erotogenic zones and organs (e.g., mouth and anus) and comprise the pregenital sexual components. In addition, some component instincts are seen as arising from a repetition of a gratification experienced in connection with other organic processes. [Freud, 1905.]

Freud indicated that the separate instincts may displace their libidinal cathexes freely in terms of their object. He described them as extraordinarily plastic, and related to one another like a series of interconnected canals. Each component sexual instinct seeks discharge and satisfaction in accordance with the pleasure principle; even so, a component sexual instinct may be connected with another and thus change its form.

In the course of normal development, these component instincts are organized and fused, particularly in puberty and adolescence, and become subordinated to the primacy of the genital zone. As such, the component instincts then comprise the elements of forepleasure, the purpose of which is to heighten tension and excitation preparatory to the end-pleasure of the sexual act.

The differentiation of abnormal from normal is made on the basis of the intensity of specific component instincts, the extent to which there is a psychic fixation on them, and the use to which it is put during development. Intense persistence and fixation may be manifest in the sexual perversions where the component instinct serves as the source of end-pleasure.

Pregenital impulses and activities are considered to be component instincts. These include scopophilia and exhibitionism, sadism and masochism, as well as a variety of specific oral, anal, and urethral functions. The analysis of specific neurotic symptoms frequently reveals them to be compromise formations, attempts to resolve conflicts arising from the emergence of repressed component instincts into consciousness.

322

COMPONENT INSTINCT is a phenomenon which can be studied only through an examination of its derivatives. The individual component instincts are upon the whole disconnected and independent of one another in their search for pleasure.

Related Concepts: Erotogenic Zones; Forepleasure; Pregenitality.

REFERENCE

Freud, S., 1905, "Three Essays on the Theory of Sexuality." *SE*, 7:167–168, 1953.

ADDITIONAL READINGS

Fenichel, O., *The Psychoanalytic Theory of Neurosis.* Nor, 1945.

Freud, S.: 1915, "Instincts and Their Vicissitudes." *SE*, 14, 1959.

1917, "Introductory Lectures on Psycho-Analysis." *SE*, 15, 1963.

1923, "The Infantile Genital Organization: An Interpolation into the Theory of Sexuality." *SE*, 19, 1961.

"Two Encyclopedia Articles." *SE*, 18, 1955.

323

COMPULSIVE MASTURBATION is characterized by rigid form and lack of pleasure. It appears to serve, like other obsessive symptoms, in the elimination of unpleasure (chiefly, fear). For example, some individuals are only able to fall asleep after masturbation. [Geleerd, 1943.]

Related Concept: MASTURBATION.

REFERENCE

Geleerd, E. R., "The Analysis of a Case of Compulsive Masturbation in a Child." *Q*, 12:520–540, 1943.

324

CONCEPT OF TIME was discussed by Freud in an essay published in 1925. He believed that the discontinuous method of the system *Pcpt.-Cs.* functions could account for the concept of time. He described this process, as follows: "My theory was that cathectic innervations are sent out and withdrawn in rapid periodic impulses from within into the completely pervious system *Pcpt.-Cs.*"

Related Concepts: PRIMARY PROCESS; REALITY PRINCIPLE; SECONDARY PROCESS; UNPLEASURE-PLEASURE PRINCIPLE.

REFERENCE

Freud, S., 1925, "A Note Upon the Mystic Writing Pad." *SE*, 19:231, 1961.

325

CONDENSATION is an unconscious process which results from the blending together of the cathexis of several ideas and affects. In describing its relationship to the mechanism of displacement in his study of dreams, Freud (1940) noted that a single element in the manifest dream can stand for a large number of latent dream thoughts. The psychical intensity may easily be displaced from one element to another, so that one element in the manifest dream may acquire an importance it does not have in the dream thoughts. The dual mechanisms of displacement and condensation, as they are manifested in the dream-work, Freud reasoned, were proof enough for his contention that they comprise the primary processes attributed to the id.

In an earlier work (in 1900), Freud reported the following example of condensation in a dream: "His servant fetched the man back, and the latter remarked: 'It's a funny thing that even people who are "tutelrein" as a rule are quite unable to deal with a thing like this.'"* The first part of the condensation, "tutel," is a legal term for guardianship ("tutelage"), while the second, "tutel," or possibly "tuttel," is a vulgar term for a woman's breast.

Condensation may also be studied in neuroses and jokes. An example which illustrates its function in the joke is reported by Freud (1905) from a story written by Heine: Hirsch-Hyacinth boasts to the poet of his relationship with the wealthy Baron Rothschild. "As true as God shall grant me all good things, Doctor, I sat beside Salomon Rothschild and he treated me quite as his equal—quite *famillionairely.*"

The following clinical example illustrates the use of condensation in neuroses: A patient who couldn't write because of a cramp in his hand discovered its unconscious meaning and cause when he recognized that he tried unconsciously to use his hand as though it were a vagina and his pen as though it were a penis (phallic level). At the same time, on the oral level, the hand represented the greedy, biting mouth, and the pen represented the nipple.

Related Concepts: DISPLACEMENT; DREAM-WORK; AESTHETIC PLEASURE; HUMOR; PRIMARY PROCESS.

---

* Italics removed.

REFERENCES

Freud, S.: 1900, "The Interpretation of Dreams." *SE*, 4:297, 1953.

1905, "Jokes and Their Relationship to the Unconscious." *SE*, 8:16, 1960.

1940, "An Outline of Psycho-Analysis." *SE*, 23:167–168, 1964.

326

CONFLICT is considered external if it takes place between one individual and another or between an individual and the external world; it is called internal when it occurs between various conscious or unconscious tendencies within the individual. Conscious internal conflict takes place between the total personality of the individual and a symptom from which he is suffering; unconscious internal conflict takes place between the id, ego and superego, and leads to an unconscious compromise (neurotic symptom).

It is probable that those patients who belong to the erotic type react to their symptoms with *la belle indifférence*; others, of the obsessional type, show a much stronger reaction (e.g., fright, avoidance, undoing). The narcissistic type assimilates the symptom and transforms it into an ego-syntonic formation (neurotic character trait). A study of the psychotic, on the other hand, reveals that the world he is fighting represents his own projections, an unconscious external conflict. In melancholia there is a conscious conflict between the patient's superego and his total personality; in mania, this conflict is denied.

Other conflicts are also revealed in psychoanalysis; for example, conflicts of thinking versus talking, and of talking versus acting. Freud (1900), for instance, pointed out that conflicts can take place in dreams as well. "The sensation of *inhibition of movement* which is so common in dreams serves also to express a contradiction between two impulses, *a conflict of will*."

Metapsychologically, the following conflicts can be differentiated: *Structural*: between (a) the id and the ego; (b) the id and the superego; (c) the id and the ego on the one side and the superego on the other; (d) the id and the ego and the superego; (e) the ego and the superego; and (f) the ego and the superego and the id. *Economical*: (g) libido versus destrudo; (h) narcissistic libido versus object libido; (i) narcissistic libido versus object destrudo; (j) narcissistic libido versus narcissistic destrudo; and (k) narcissistic destrudo versus object libido. *Systematic*: (l) conscious versus unconscious; (m) preconscious versus unconscious; and (n) preconscious versus conscious. *Dynamic*: (o) active versus passive; (p) active versus passive aim; and (q) male versus female.

Related Concepts: DEFENSE MECHANISMS; MENTAL (PSYCHIC).

REFERENCE

Freud, S., 1900, "The Interpretation of Dreams." *SE*, 5:661, 1953.

ADDITIONAL READINGS

Eidelberg, L., *An Outline of a Comparative Pathology of the Neuroses*. IUP, 1954.
Freud, S.: 1915, "Introductory Lectures on Psycho-Analysis." *SE*, 15, 1963.

1933, "New Introductory Lectures on Psycho-Analysis." *SE*, 22, 1964.
Kaufman, I., "Some Etiological Studies of Social Relationships and Conflict Situations." *JAPA*, 8, 1960.
Loewenstein, R. M., "Conflict and Autonomous Ego Development During the Phallic Phase." *PsaStC*, 5, 1950.
Rangell, L.: "The Scope of Intrapsychic Conflict: Microscopic and Macroscopic Considerations." *PsaStC*, 18, 1963.

"Structural Problems in Intrapsychic Conflict." *PsaStC*, 18, 1963.
Reich, A., "A Character Formation Representing the Integration of Unusual Conflict Solutions into the Ego Structure." *PsaStC*, 13, 1958.

327

CONGENITAL (CONNATE). Most psychoanalysts refer to inherited characteristics as *congenital*, while a few use the term specifically to describe noninherited characteristics present in the individual at birth, including injury or trauma incurred in delivery.

Congenital factors may play a role in the predisposition to mental illness or to particular forms of character formation. Fenichel (1945) noted: "Constitution and experience, as etiological factors, again form a complementary series. The manic-depressive disorders surely give no reason to change this point of view. The organic constitutional influence, which is undoubtedly present, need not be the sole determinant. Psychoanalytic study makes it probable that this constitution consists in a relative predominance of oral eroticism, just as in compulsion neurosis it consists in an enhanced anal eroticism."

Freud (1931) noted: "The precipitating causes of it are frustrations and internal conflicts: conflicts between the three major psychical agencies, conflicts arising within the libidinal economy in consequence of our bisexual disposition and conflicts between the erotic and the aggressive instinctual components."

As a consequence, it may be concluded that a neurosis is not inherited; the choice of neurosis, on the other hand, may be influenced by congenital factors. For instance, an individual inherently belonging to the erotic type, who suffers fixation on the phallic stage, may develop conversion hysteria, whereas another individual, of the obsessional type, in the case of fixation on the phallic stage, may develop anxiety hysteria.

Related Concept: HEREDITY.

REFERENCES

Fenichel, O., *The Psychoanalytic Theory of Neurosis.* Nor, p. 403, 1945.
Freud, S., 1931, "Libidinal Types." *SE*, 21:220, 1961.

ADDITIONAL READINGS

Freud, S., 1913, "The Disposition to Obsessional Neurosis." *SE*, 12, 1958.
Moore, B., "Congenital vs. Environmental: An Unconscious Meaning." *JAPA*, 8, 1960.

jects and therefore is able to obey, even in the absence of the parents. Later, other figures are selected and used to form the individual's conscience. In a normal person, the conscience is assimilated as part of the total personality, and thus helps the individual to differentiate between right and wrong; it is neither rigid nor ego-alien.

Freud responded to frequent assertions that psychoanalysis ignored the moral and ethical aspects of man. He pointed out that the conscience as a function of the superego was, from the beginning, a foundation stone of his hypothetical structure of the mental processes. In this, Freud (1921) quoted LeBon,* as follows: "The first is that the individual forming part of a group acquires, solely from numerical considerations, a sentiment of invincible power which allows him to yield to instincts which, had he been alone, he would perforce have kept under restraint." He then added in his own words: "It has long been our contention that 'social anxiety' is the essence of what is called conscience."

Related Concepts: IDENTIFICATION; SUPEREGO.

REFERENCES

Freud, S.: 1921, "Group Psychology and the Analysis of the Ego." *SE*, 18:74, 75, 1955.
1930, "Civilization and Its Discontents." *SE*, 21:137, 1961.

ADDITIONAL READINGS

Allinsmith, W., "Conscience and Conflict: The Moral Force in Personality." *CD*, 28, 1957.
Bergler, E., "The Battle of the Conscience." *R*, 1953.
Freud, S.: 1923, "The Ego and the Id." *SE*, 19, 1961.
1926, "Inhibitions, Symptoms and Anxiety." *SE*, 20, 1959.
Stärcke, A., "Conscience and the Role of Repetition." *IntJPsa*, 10, 1929.

328

CONSCIENCE, according to Freud (1930), is not a term that can be used synonymously with that of the superego; rather, it represents a part of its function. There are two strata, one coming from an internal authority and the other from an internal source. At first, the conscience appears to be the result of parental criticisms which the child intro-

329

CONSCIOUS. Originally, consciousness was synonymous with mental or psychic, and represented the feelings and ideas and the sensory perceptions of which the individual was aware. Freud, however,

---

* LeBon, G., 1895, *The Crowd: A Study of the Popular Mind.* London, 1920.

enlarged the concept by proving that many unconscious phenomena could be made conscious after the resistance of the individual against such acts was properly dealt with. Consequently, *conscious* is far from being a synonym for *mental;* it is only a quality of it.

Freud (1940) characterized consciousness as a highly fugitive state. "What is conscious," he wrote, "is conscious only for a moment." The apparent contradiction of persistent perceptive qualities is explained by the fact that the stimuli which lead to these perceptions in the preconscious may persist for considerable periods of time and be repeated.

Related Concepts: PRECONSCIOUS; STRUCTURAL (TOPOGRAPHIC) APPROACH; SYSTEMATIC (QUALITATIVE OR DESCRIPTIVE) APPROACH; UNCONSCIOUS.

REFERENCE

Freud, S., 1940, "An Outline of Psycho-Analysis." *SE*, 23:159–160, 1964.

ADDITIONAL READINGS

Aufreiter, J., "Psycho-Analysis and Consciousness." *IntJPsa*, 41, 1960.
Driesch, H., "Bewusstsein und Unterbewusstsein." *DtschemedWschr*, 48, 1922.
Freud, S., 1923, "The Ego and the Id." *SE*, 19, 1961.
Plaut, A., "Aspects of Consciousness." *M*, 32, 1959.
Rioch, D., "Certain Aspects of 'Conscious' Phenomena and Their Neural Correlates." *P*, 111, 1955.
Robbins, B., "Consciousness, Central Problem in Psychiatry." *PT*, 1, 1956.

330

CONTENT AND FORM OF A JOKE. The forepleasure which is experienced in anticipation of listening to a joke is *aesthetic* forepleasure and should be differentiated from the phenomena resulting from the stimulation, for instance, of erotogenic zones. After listening to a joke, as Eidelberg (1960) pointed out, the listener experiences an aesthetic end-pleasure, a full discharge of aim-inhibited instincts.

The joke-teller experiences end-pleasure as a result of two factors: (a) he controls the object (the listener who is made to laugh); and (b) he vicariously enjoys the motoric discharge of his audience (the laughter of the listener). In this context, *aim-inhibited* does not imply unpleasure as a result of increased tension but is used to describe a form of gratification in which the possession of the object is not required. The listener to a joke or the reader of a book does not expect to achieve a full instinctual gratification from such an activity. Croce (1909) pointed out: "By elaborating his impressions, man *frees* himself from them. By objectifying them, he removes them from him and makes himself their superior. The liberating and purifying function of art is another aspect and another formula of its character as activity. Activity is the deliverer, just because it drives away passivity." However, as Freud (1933) noted, we cannot discharge all our instinctual needs by sublimating the libido; there is a limit to what can be sublimated. It is probable that the full gratification of instinctual energy alongside with that of the aim-inhibited instinct improves the quantity and quality of the sublimation.

The following joke is offered for analysis: Catherine the Great finds ten sailors in her bedroom. She says, "I am tired; two must go." An examination of the joke indicates that only those listeners who are able to recognize the dual meaning of the words "two must go" will laugh. Conversely, those listeners who identify with Catherine the Great or the ten sailors—to share in the experiences of the characters of the story—will be disappointed and frustrated by listening to it, for the story offers only a discharge of aim-inhibited energy: it cannot be used for the normal full discharge of the non-aim-inhibited energy. It seems probable that the listeners who will enjoy the end of the story are those who identify not with the characters but with the teller of the joke. They are interested in finding out how the teller will use this joke to produce laughter, not about the possible frustrations of the characters in the story. What amuses the listener—the source of his aesthetic pleasure—is not his participation in the activities of the characters in the joke. The aesthetic pleasure is caused by the recognition of the hidden meaning in the final sentence. This recognition of the final meaning which will produce laughter on the condition that the listener manages to get it without additional help from the teller seems to be caused by the illusion of omnipotence, i.e., the power to fool that part of the personality which seems to believe that Catherine the Great has decided to rest. The pleasure is based on the ability to play with words, on the gratification of the infantile wish to defy the infantile superego which appears to be fooled in this joke.

The experience of aesthetic pleasure—and there is little doubt that the pleasure in jokes has to be considered as representing one form of aesthetic pleasure—makes the individual independent of the possession of the object which is a *conditio sine qua non* for the gratification of the non-aim-inhibited energy and also because it permits us to share the pleasure with a number of individuals who listen to the joke. On the other hand, as Freud (1905) pointed out, we cannot obtain this pleasure by telling a joke to ourselves. However, we are able to laugh even when we are alone and are able to read a joke. It seems that the identification with the author of the joke is of basic importance. The listener requires the teller and the teller requires the listener in order to have this kind of discharge. Thus, it may be concluded that the form of the joke and not its content is of primary importance to the end-pleasure received from it. In this, Eidelberg (1961) noted: "Experiencing aesthetic pleasure of this kind seems to be based on our ability to achieve so much with so little. Freud claimed that it is the saving up of accumulated energy by not using up all that had been prepared that permits us to achieve laughter. As I have pointed out elsewhere, the pleasure we experience while laughing has the characteristics of end pleasure and permits a discharge of accumulated energy via a kind of short cut. The form of the joke, not so much its content, seems to have the magic power to let us return for a little while to our childhood when we could play and did not have to be serious, when fairy tales were believable and reality escapable."

Related Concepts: COMIC; HUMOR; JOKE (WIT).

REFERENCES

Croce, B., *Aesthetic*. NP, p. 21. 1904.
Eidelberg, L.: "A Third Contribution to the Study of Slips of the Tongue." *IntJPsa*, 41:598–601, 1960.
    The Dark Urge. New York: Py, pp. 156–157, 1961.
Freud, S.: 1905, "Jokes And Their Relation To The Unconscious." *SE*, 8:143, 1960.
    1933, "New Introductory Lectures on Psycho-Analysis." *SE*, 22:134, 1964.

CONTROL is the ability of the ego or the total personality to command the drives; it is associated with such concepts as ego strength and ego synthesis. Rapaport (1950) noted: "With the introduction of the concept of countercathexes, psychoanalytic theory introduced the fundamental concept of impulse controls, which is central to our conception of the structure of the ego." The essence of counter-cathexis is the ability to delay the discharge of impulses, the prototype of all defenses.

The control of discharge is an ego function that is related to the active repetition of passive experiences. Pleasurable aspects may be exemplified by aesthetic reactions, while a pathological need to retain controls may inhibit freedom of the imagination and de-automatization of motor activities (compulsive-obsessive neuroses). The ability to relax control by conscious decision plays an important part in sleep and free association. [Fenichel, 1945.]

Related Concepts: EGO STRENGTH AND WEAKNESS; SYNTHESIS.

REFERENCES

Fenichel, O., *The Psychoanalytic Theory of Neurosis*. Nor, pp. 67, 102, 278, 487, 1945.
Rapaport, D., "On the Psychoanalytic Theory of Thinking." *IntJPsa*, 31:164, 1950.

ADDITIONAL READING

Ferenczi, S., *Further Contributions to the Theory and Technique of Psychoanalysis*. HPI, 1926.

CONVERSION AND CONVERSION SYMPTOMS are the result of the transformation of intrapsychic excitation into somatic manifestations. The energy of a mental process is withheld from conscious influences (i.e., repressed) and diverted into symbolic bodily symptoms. Unconscious memories or fantasies, which have an instinctual situation as their subject matter, are "converted" into sensory and motor symptoms, "often taken from the circle of the same sexual sensations and motor innervations that had originally accompanied the phantasy when it was still conscious." [Freud,

1908.] For example, a hysterical patient's repressed wish to become pregnant as a result of performing fellatio, as well as the defensive reaction against that wish, may be expressed, through conversion, by vomiting. Freud (1909) stated that this leap from a mental process to a somatic manifestation "can never be fully comprehensible to us."

Hysterical paralysis is one type of conversion symptom; a so-called functional type of paralysis involving the skeletal musculature. In essence, hysterical paralysis represents a compromise formation between the forbidden instinctual impulse seeking to gain expression and discharge, and the defensive forces of the ego. (After a certain amount of time, a so-called secondary muscular atrophy is superimposed on the paralyzed limb.) Such paralyses may affect any of the peripheral muscles and must be distinguished from neurological paralyses. The paralysis per se frequently expresses materialization; i.e., the repressed thoughts cathect a particular organ representation which is unconsciously used as a substitute. For instance, the paralyzed leg of a hysterical girl expresses her unconscious wish for a penis in that the leg is stiff and, at the same time, it reveals her acceptance of her castration in that she is paralyzed. It also gratifies her unconscious exhibitionistic wishes.

Related Concepts: DEFENSE MECHANISMS; REPRESSION.

REFERENCES

Freud, S.: 1908, "Hysterical Phantasies and their Relation to Bisexuality." *SE*, 9:162–163, 1959.
　　1909, "Notes Upon a Case of Obsessional Neurosis." *SE*, 10:157, 1955.

ADDITIONAL READINGS

Deutsch, F., "Zur Bildung des Konversionssymptoms." *Z*, 10, 1924.
Fox, H. M., "The Theory of the Conversion Process." *JAPA*, 7, 1959.
Lantos, B., "Analyse einer Konversionshysterie im Klimakterium." *Z*, 15, 1929.
Rangell, L., "The Nature of Conversion." *JAPA*, 7, 1959.
Roth, N., "On the Mechanism of Hysterical Conversion." *PT*, 11, 1957.
Schiffer, I., "The Psycho-Analytic Study of the Development of a Conversion Symptom." *IntJPsa*, 43, 1962.

Sperling, M., "Food Allergies and Conversion Hysteria." *Q*, 22, 1953.
Stekel, W., "Geothe Über Einen Fall von Konversion." *C*, 2, 1912.
Wilson, G. W., "The Analysis of a Transitory Conversion Symptom Simulating Pertussis." *IntJPsa*, 16, 1935.

333

COPROPHAGIA (COPROPHAGY) is the actual or symbolic ingestion of feces; the former circumstance occurs rarely, the latter, more commonly. Fenichel (1945) noted: "The impulse to coprophagia, which certainly has an erogenous source (representing an attempt to stimulate the erogenous zone of the mouth with the same pleasurable substance that previously stimulated the erogenous zone of the rectum) simultaneously represents an attempt to re-establish the threatened narcissistic equilibrium; that which has been eliminated must be reintrojected."

Coprophagic fantasies may also give rise to certain types of obsessive undoing and to such activities as reading on the toilet. Symptoms involving disgust at eating certain foods often involve unconscious coprophagic fantasies, in which the disgusting substance is equated with excrement.

Related Concepts: COPROPHILIA; REACTION FORMATION.

REFERENCE

Fenichel, O., *Psychoanalytic Theory of Neurosis.* Nor, pp. 67, 155, 1945.

334

COPROPHILIA denotes the pleasure in handling, seeing, smelling, or otherwise perceiving excrement. Although the manifest perversion is clinically rare, unconscious coprophilic fantasies occur commonly among the determinants of other perversions, such as fetishism, voyeurism, and exhibitionism. Sometimes, the coprophilic tendencies of early childhood are repressed, but later break through the repressive bonds as ego-alien symptoms, sublimated activities, or normal or neurotic character traits. A classical example of a neurotic character trait derived from coprophilic tendencies is miserliness, in which money assumes the symbolic meaning of feces. Excessive cleanliness is often a reaction formation against the wish to smear or play with feces.

Fenichel (1945) suggested that the adult whose sexual excitability is connected with ego functions, in this case, the excretory function (according to Freud's first instinct theory), shows "a specific defense against genital wishes" and denies the danger of castration, because "there is no sex difference in anal functions." Viewed in another way, the symbolic equation penis = feces may be a factor; the male pervert, who watches women defecate, sees something resembling a penis emerging from the female body, while women who are sexually interested in their own anal functions similarly deny their own lack of a penis.

Related Concepts: ANAL EROTISM; COPROPHAGIA.

REFERENCE

Fenichel, O., *The Psychoanalytic Theory of Neurosis.* Nor, pp. 349–350, 1945.

ADDITIONAL READING

Freud, S., 1909, "Notes Upon a Case of Obsessional Neurosis." *SE*, 10, 1955.

335

COUNTERCATHEXIS (ANTICATHEXIS) denotes the psychic energy used by the unconscious ego to block the entrance of id derivatives. Destrudo is used to block libidinal wishes and vice versa. Thus, ideas and affects connected with the energy used in countercathexis may become conscious. For instance, the desire to play with feces may be blocked by the desire to avoid feces or dirt and lead to the conscious experience of the obsessive wish to wash. Although the concept was foreshadowed in an earlier essay (written in 1907), it was developed at length by Freud in 1915, wherein he identified the anticathexis as the sole mechanism of primal repression, a withdrawal of cathexis from the *Pcs*.

Hartmann (1958) noted: "I take as a point of departure here, reaction formations too (and for that matter, all countercathexes) work not with instinctual but with some shade of neutralized energy. Still it may be that countercathexes can be characterized as also energetically differing from other ego functions, which may, at least partly, explain why, according to Freud, they are 'set apart' in the ego. As I mentioned before, it is likely that defense against the drives (countercathexis) retains an element (fight) that allows of their description as being mostly fed by one mode of aggressive energy, and that this mode is not full neutralization. In this sense, countercathexis in repression appears to be a good example to be contrasted, also as to the energy it uses, with the nondefensive ego functions."

Related Concepts: CATHEXIS; PARAPRAXIS; PSYCHIC (MENTAL) ENERGY.

REFERENCES

Freud, S.: 1907, "Obsessive Actions and Religious Practices." *SE*, 9:124, 1959.
    1915, "The Unconscious." *SE*, 14:181, 1957.
Hartmann, H., *Essays on Ego Psychology.* IUP, p. 232, 1958.

336

COUNTERPHOBIA. Some neurotics use a counterphobic mechanism to protect themselves from their phobic terror. They succeed in doing what they are afraid of and derive a certain pleasure from this behavior. The counterphobic mechanism should be differentiated from sublimation. It is often rigid and, according to Fenichel (1945), it appears to be connected with the compulsion to repeat.

Why one patient avoids his fear and another defies it with the help of counterphobic mechanisms is at present unknown.

Related Concepts: AVOIDANCE; SUBLIMATION.

REFERENCE

Fenichel, O., *The Psychoanalytic Theory of Neurosis.* Nor, pp. 480, 484, 1945.

ADDITIONAL READING

Szasz, T., "The Role of the Counterphobic Mechanism in Addiction." *JAPA*, 6, 1958.

337

COUNTERTRANSFERENCE. The term is used by some analysts in connection with all the feelings the analyst experiences for his patients, while others prefer to speak of countertransference only when repressed infantile wishes are involved. The *ideal* analyst should be free from all these infantile emotions, but experience shows that this goal is difficult to achieve, and that analytic work may mobilize unconscious wishes which otherwise might have remained dormant. Whenever a circumstance like this occurs, the analyst should be able to recognize it, and either analyze it himself or ask a colleague to do it for him.

Parin (1960) described the process, as follows: "The countertransference is brought into relation with the analysand's mechanisms of defense in order to gain a clearer theoretical grasp of a process which must be properly understood if the technique of psychoanalysis is to succeed. The term countertransference covers all those reactions of the analyst that tend to cloud his understanding of the patient's unconscious. It has been found that, as a general rule, the patient's unconscious can more easily and speedily provoke countertransference reactions by mobilizing his mechanisms of defense, rather than by cathecting a typical transference figure and projecting it on the analyst."

A short example may be helpful as an illustration: A patient suffering from ejaculatio praecox was in treatment with a female analyst, who forgot her appointment with her patient on two occasions, just at the time when his condition began to improve. She analyzed this parapraxis and discovered that the restored erection of her patient had mobilized her own still unsolved penis envy. Her patient's improvement was dependent on his continuing his analysis, which meant that through an unconscious identification with her patient she would be having sexual intercourse with a woman. She fought against this forbidden homosexual satisfaction by mobilizing an unconscious hostility against her patient. After she had recognized the cause of her trouble, she managed to finish his analysis successfully.

Fenichel (1945) pointed out that while it is true that most analysts may work better with one type of patient than with another such a difference should not interfere with their ability to work. He noted: "An analyst has to have the width of empathy to work with any type. If the reality in this respect differs too much from the ideal state of affairs, the mistake may be the analyst's; it may be rooted either directly in a negative countertransference or in a disappointment because a certain type of patient does not fulfill some expectation that the analyst unduly and unconsciously connects with his work; in such cases the analyst himself should be analyzed more thoroughly."

Ella Sharpe (1950) cautioned: "The analyst must be sufficiently analysed to enable him to detect, and so consciously control, any tendency to regard the patient as the 'bad self' who needs reforming. He is not likely then to experience guilt reactions or anger when, for the patient, he in turn becomes the patient's 'bad self.' I once heard a young male doctor say, with regard to his patients in the hospital, 'They are like a lot of naughty children, they don't know what they are doing half the time, they've first got to be taught.' Fear of his own infantile aggression turned him into a disciplinarian. Unknown resentments against mother and nurses can very easily make an analyst become a strict mother and nurse to patients, just as one can detect a nurse or a teacher meting out the treatment to those under them that they themselves once resented. 'Counter-transference' is often spoken of as if it implied a love-attitude. The counter-transference that is likely to cause trouble is the unconscious one on the analyst's side, whether it be an infantile negative or positive one, or both in alternation. The unconscious transference is the infantile one and, while unconscious, will blind the analyst to the various aspects of the patient's transference. An analyst who is sufficiently analysed will not be afraid to recognise in himself signs that betray impatience, anger, or embarrassment. He will note when he hesitates to give interpretations. Being human, the analyst will feel disappointment and a sense of frustration at his best efforts being thwarted; but, being able to analyse his own reactions in connection with the unconscious infantile imagos, his affects will not trouble him for long. We deceive ourselves if we think we have no counter-transference. It is its nature that matters. We can hardly hope to carry on an analysis unless our own counter-transference is healthy; that healthiness depends upon the nature of the satisfactions we obtain from the work, the deep unconscious satisfactions that lie behind the reality ones of earning a living, and the hope of effecting cures.

"Here are some of the unconscious desires that make for counter-transference that thwart true analytical work and bias interpretation in terms of the analyst's own personality. An unconscious, unsatisfied oral demand on the part of the analyst (which may really be unsatisfied sexual desire) will make him impatient and over-anxious when the patient withholds communication. The analyst's aggression can be aroused until his own attitude approximates to 'You shall' with the inevitably reinforced resistance of the patient 'I won't.' And no words are necessary on the part of either patient or analyst to indicate this impasse. It is unconscious counter-transference. An analyst whose unconscious oral demand causes anxiety will be irrationally pleased at a wealth of material provided by the patient; irrationally, because the talker can so easily talk 'past' the analyst and be oblivious of what is happening. An unawareness of oral aggression will often result in an acute perception of the patient's greed which may well tend to the analyst's selection and concentration on one psychological problem, to the neglect of many others. This runs true of all other problems. A 'flair' for accurate acute prognosis is surely based upon verity of experience, and indicates that paranoidal elements, instead of producing a phantastic pathological creation, are harnessed to realities. It is just when the analyst is swift to see the problem another person is involved in that he must all the more be aware that he could not have this knowledge except on the basis of his own experience. It is one thing to see the problem in another person as a projection of something alien to the self, another thing to know the roots of the problem within; ability to analyse depends upon the latter, while brilliance in diagnosis can sometimes be the limit of the analyst's power. It does not in itself mean ability to analyse the condition. This is the reverse of the difficulties experienced by those whose introjective, rather than projective mechanisms, are dominant. The absorption of the patient's problems into the self, which is necessary to a degree, may lead to a fusion of those problems with the same unmastered ones in the analyst. Hence the blind spots in the analyst render him helpless where they coincide with the patient's. The analyst needs true empathy, but he is impotent as an analyst if he becomes identified

with the patient. It is to be hoped that in the future, when our science and art have evolved further, workers will be so much less afraid of themselves and of each other that it will be possible for a recognized specialization to take place. I mean that certain psychological trends make the analyst more fitted to deal with one type of case than another. Those with more pronounced obsessional traits are probably more handicapped in dealing with obsessionals than those whose mechanisms are not of this type. At our present stage we rather resemble the general practitioner who must do his best for all types of illness. On the other hand it may not work this way at all. An obsessional neurosis truly mastered and understood might give a practitioner facility in dealing with this disorder. Here is something to be found out by experience, vigilance, and honesty with one's self.

"The unconscious satisfactions of an infantile type that the analyst strives for in his work can thwart and prejudice his honestly conscious purpose."

Related Concepts: RESISTANCE; TRANSFERENCE.

REFERENCES

Fenichel, O., *The Psychoanalytic Theory of Neurosis.* Nor, p. 580, 1945.
Parin, P., "Gegenübertragung bei verschiedenen Abwehrformen." *JPsa*, p. 212, 1960.
Sharpe, E., *Collected Papers on Psycho-Analysis.* HPI, pp. 117–119, 1950.

ADDITIONAL READINGS

Benedek, T., "Dynamics of the Countransference." *BMC*, 17, 1953.
Berman, L., "Countertransferences and Attitudes of the Analyst in the Therapeutic Process." *Adv-Psychiat*, 1953.
Bird, H. W., & P. A. Martin, "Countertransference in the Psychotherapy of Marriage Partners." *PS*, 19, 1956.
Brody, M. W., "Transference and Countertransference in Psychotherapy." *R*, 42, 1955.
Cohen, N. B., "Countertransference and Anxiety." *OutPsa*, 1955.
Fliess, R., "Countertransference and Counteridentification." *JAPA*, 1, 1953.
Frank, G. H., "The Literature on Countertransference: A Survey." *IntJgrp PT*, 3, 1953.
Freedman, A., "Countertransference Abuse of Analytic Rules." *BullPhilaAssPsa*, 6, 1956.

338

CREATIVITY is the capacity to produce something new and original. It results from the ability to inhibit an original gratification and to sublimate an instinctual wish. To this must be added the distinction which separates *everyday* creativity from that of the artist or scientist. Freud (1920) provided one such clue in his description of the repetition compulsion. For instance, if a child has experienced pain and anxiety at the dentist's office, he may use this experience in repeating what has happened to him, playing the role of the doctor in pretending to treat his younger brother. One has the impression that in such a play the change from passivity into activity transforms an unpleasant experience into a pleasant game, for in playing the role of a doctor the child succeeds in revenging himself, in using his younger brother instead of the dentist's patient (namely, himself).

This latter experience on the child's part represents everyday creativity, and can be thought of as a precursor to perhaps a *higher* form of activity. To some degree, everyday creativity is characteristic of all human activity. In this, it would appear that Thanatos is connected with the urge to repeat, to return to the inorganic state, while Eros appears to be responsible for the creative urge, in which some new, even original, activity is evolved.

The analytic method is aimed at translating the unconscious repressed wishes and in so doing freeing the patient from neurotic phenomena. The analyst does not analyze "what makes sense." Though he may help uncover the neurotic problems of scientists and artists, he cannot do so for those wishes which have already undergone sublimation. Infantile repressed wishes may lead either to pathological phenomena or become sublimated. Thus, psychoanalysis is only equipped to deal with the wishes that produce neurotic phenomena. For example, a patient who sought analysis because of his inability to play in public without his music, in spite of the fact that he was able to do this when alone, recognized—after his successful analysis—the important role of infantile exhibitionistic wishes. But his analysis did not show why he was a successful composer and virtuoso before his analysis. This example illustrates clearly the well-known limitation of analytical research and therapy.

There is little doubt that sublimation plays a decisive role in scientific and artistic creativity. This may be further characterized by the role that curiosity plays, of the tolerance for frustration, and of the ability to postpone and avoid instinctual gratifications of infantile wishes, which are the conditions of sublimation, and of creativity. The first condition therefore of any achievement is the giving up of infantile omnipotence, and the resulting compromise—the delay—which takes place: better a limited achievement in reality than an unlimited fantasy. It would seem that the artist or scientist gratifies the infantile role to play the mother and the father (perhaps even that of the preoedipal mother who rules the matriarchal society) through the use of the creative activity which characterizes his particular discipline. Consequently, because it will be difficult for the analyst to differentiate between the value of the various forms of sublimation and to decide which have been significant to a given work of art or to a scientific achievement, it may be advisable for him to limit such an evaluation to his own personal set of values.

Related Concepts: APPLIED PSYCHOANALYSIS; EROS; REPETITION COMPULSION; THANATOS.

REFERENCES

Freud, S.: 1905, "Jokes and Their Relation to the Unconscious." *SE*, 8:167, 1960.
       1920, "Beyond the Pleasure Principle." *SE*, 18:17, 1955.

ADDITIONAL READINGS

Eissler, K. R., "Notes on the Environment of a Genius." *PsaStC*, 14, 1959.
Fraiberg, L. B., "Psychology and the Writer: The Creative Process." *LP*. 5, 1955.
Greenacre, P.: "The Childhood of the Artist." *PsaStC*, 12, 1957.
       "The Relation of the Impostor to the Artist." *PsaStC*, 13, 1958.
       "Play in Relation to Creative Imagination." *PsaStC*, 14, 1959.
Kanzer, M., "Contemporary Psychoanalytic Views of Aesthetics." *JAPA*, 7, 1957.
Kris, E., "Psychoanalysis and the Study of Creative Imagination." *BullNYAcadMed*, 29, 1953.
Loomie, L. S., H. Victor, & M. H. Stein, "Ernst Kris and the Gifted Adolescent Project." *PsaStC*, 13, 1958.

Rosen, V. H., "On Mathematical 'Illumination' and the Mathematical Thought Process: A Contribution to the Genetic Development and Metapsychology of Abstract Thinking." *PsaStC*, 8, 1953.

Schneider, D., *The Psychoanalyst and the Artist*. IUP, 1954.

Weissman, P., "The Childhood and Legacy of Stanislavski." *PsaStC*, 12, 1957.

339

CRITICISM. Opponents of Freud claim that he used a dictatorial approach and could not tolerate any criticism of his findings. When he changed his views—for instance, about the aggressive instinct and its relation to anxiety—he admitted his previous error. In this regard, Jones (1957) noted: "Another example, one of many that could be quoted, of Freud's easy tolerance towards his followers' criticism or correction of his conclusions may be mentioned here. In his book, *The Psychopathology of Everyday Life*, he had described how repressed trends could interfere with what he called the 'harmless' conscious intentions. Eidelberg had now written a paper pointing out that the conscious intentions were often not 'harmless,' and that the slip of the tongue or pen could be determined by ego-syntonic reactions against them—in other words the reverse mechanism to that described by Freud. When this paper was for some reason not accepted by the *Zeitschrift* he sent it to Anna Freud, who showed it to her father. She then quoted his opinion. 'Your criticism of the word "harmless" for the trend that is disturbed is thoroughly justified, and further investigation of the apparently "harmless" is undoubtedly important. He suggested that the relation of the two tendencies is probably a variable one. Further investigation along these lines would probably be very rewarding.'"

Those engaged in the practice of psychoanalysis are, of course, aware that their interpretations are subject to critical comments by the patient. No analyst would suggest that the patient should blindly accept his interpretation, for the analyst is not only aware that his interpretation may be wrong, but that an interpretation is only helpful after the resistance against it has been overcome. It is true, to be sure, that such a resistance interferes with the analytical work, but analysis would become not only worthless but even harmful if the therapist gave an analytical interpretation to a patient who was not prepared to accept it.

For example, a paranoid patient dreamt that his analyst cornered him and that the patient's mouth came into contact with the analyst's genitals. The analyst said, "Here you see your homosexual urges." As a result of this interpretation, the patient decided that his analyst had become psychotic. Years later, his latent homosexual wishes were brought to his consciousness by another analyst who was less impatient.

Related Concept: SLIPS OF THE TONGUE.

REFERENCES

Freud, S., 1917, "General Theory of the Neuroses." *SE*, 16:244, 1963.

Jones, E., *The Life and Work of Sigmund Freud*. HPI, 3:213, 1957.

ADDITIONAL READING

Weissman, P., "The Psychology of the Critic and Psychological Criticism." *JAPA*, 10, 1962.

340

CROSS SECTION OF NEUROSIS. According to Eidelberg (1952), the material gained in at least a partially successful analysis can be recorded under five headings: (a) the total personality; (b) the id; (c) the ego; (d) the superego; and (e) the external world. For example, the material gained from the analysis of a paranoid patient is described by Eidelberg (1954), as follows:

Total Personality: He regards his persecutory ideas not as symptoms, but as correct evaluations based on observations of reality. At first, he refuses to examine these ideas, because he considers them self-evidently true.

Id: He wants to be like his mother and be loved by his father.

Ego: If he becomes like mother, it means giving up his penis. Therefore, to avoid castration, the love for father has to be given up. As a defense, the passive sexual wish is replaced by aggressive tension (mobilization of the opposite instinct fusion). At the same time, the passive wish is turned against the self and discharged by masturbation. Finally, the wish to masturbate is projected to the analyst, who is then accused of trying to seduce the patient. The narcissistic mortification caused by his inability to control the sexual wishes is repressed, and, in its place, he accepts the narcissistic mortification of being unable to cope with the external world.

Superego: His guilt feelings, due to the presence of infantile wishes, are exchanged for feelings of shame and remorse.

External World: He is frustrated by lack of interest from his superiors and colleagues.

Related Concepts: COMPARATIVE PATHOLOGY OF THE NEUROSES; STRUCTURAL (TOPOGRAPHIC) APPROACH.

REFERENCES

Eidelberg, L.: *Studies in Psychoanalysis.* IUP, pp. 101–106, 1948.
    An Outline of a Comparative Pathology of the Neuroses. IUP, pp. 149–150, 1954.

ADDITIONAL READING

Waelder, R., "The Principle of Multiple Function, Observations on Over-Determination." *Q,* 5, 1936.

341

CRYING (WEEPING) is the affect characterized by the emotional experience of the feeling of sadness or mourning and the secretory and motoric discharge of mental energy: tears, facial and postural changes usually expressing the acceptance of defeat. Descriptively, crying has the character of a reflex, and, in this respect, may be considered uninhibited; in some subjects, however, the act of crying occurs as the result of a conscious decision. An individual who identifies with a crying person may do so as a result of a preconscious decision (identification).

Normally, an individual cries when he suffers an object-loss, or the loss of the love of the object, or he experiences severe pain (shock). It is often preceded by the feeling of fright at being helpless: an external or internal narcissistic mortification. By mobilizing the subject's aggression, preparing him to fight (defiance), crying may be avoided. In addition to the discharge of mental energy (probably narcissistic libido and destrudo), crying may also

serve as a presentation of unconditional surrender and demand for help from the external world, which may respond with pity or react with embarrassment and contempt. Crying is often considered a sign of weakness; thus, children and even women are permitted to cry more often than men. Many children react with shock when they discover that the omnipotent parents are sometimes unable to refrain from crying.

From an economical point of view, crying represents a discharge of sexual, aggressive, and exhibitionistic wishes. It may indicate, "I am sorry," but it may also represent an accusation, "I have been mistreated." Because of its exhibitionistic meaning, crying may mobilize the feeling of shame, and may be used to inhibit it.

Pathologically, crying may be mobilized as an unconscious defense against laughter, or vice versa. It may also be the result of the displacement from a urethral function to tears. In this case, tears which are shed in public lead to shame, where the shame represents the punishment for infantile exhibitionistic acts. The feeling of shame may be avoided by mobilizing ambition and, thus, achieve a gain in attention (inferiority feelings). Others produce tears to hide their feeling of triumph (crocodile tears).

While laughter is regarded as an emotion which is opposite to that of sadness, the two, under certain circumstances, may be comingled; tears may serve as a reaction formation against laughter.

Case History

Fenichel (1945) provided the following concrete example: "A patient with a tic and who was close to hysteria had been trained 'never to show emotions.' The tic represented the mimetic expression of a suppressed crying of which he was not aware."

Related Concept: LAUGHTER.

REFERENCE

Fenichel, O., *The Psychoanalytic Theory of Neurosis.* Nor, p. 319, 1945.

ADDITIONAL READING

Feldman, S., "Crying at the Happy Ending." *JAPA,* 4, 1956.

342

CURIOSITY is the need to seek new objects and new methods to discharge instinctual drives and to overcome narcissistic mortifications. In addition, perhaps as a result of successful repression, the curiosity itself may be sublimated, and thus lead to the development of an artistic or scientific attitude. In some artists and scientists, a partial sublimation may take place, accounting for the rigidly intolerant attitude toward the work of others.

Curiosity, like many other needs, is controlled by the ego and superego, which inhibits and modifies the original wish. The ego and superego may use various unconscious defense mechanisms (reaction formation, projection, or introjection), or it may use such mechanisms as instinctual vicissitudes (sublimation, normal character traits, and so forth)

to achieve gratification of the original wish. For instance, with the help of reaction formation, the child gives up his curiosity and develops, instead, the opposite attitude: "I am not interested. I want to be left in peace. I don't care to view or examine (to understand) what is going on in me and outside of me." With the help of denial, the child may avoid the recognition of the lack of a penis in the female and may even claim that mother has a penis. [Fenichel, 1945.]

Related Concepts: EXHIBITIONISM; SCOPOPHILIA; SUBLIMATION.

REFERENCE

Fenichel, O., *The Psychoanalytic Theory of Neurosis.* Nor, p. 71, 1945.

D

400

DAYDREAMS, Freud (1900) noted, "are wish-fulfilments; like dreams, they are based to a great extent on impressions of infantile experiences; like dreams, they benefit by a certain degree of relaxation of censorship."

Daydreams are produced by all normal individuals; a satisfaction is obtained for that which is not available in the external world. In this, the daydream appears to give power to the individual which he does not ordinarily have; it allows him to return to a stage of development in which there was no difference between the wish and the action. A study of daydreams, at least in the case of neuroses, indicates that an analytic examination may be permissible and useful.

The case of a male patient who was having an affair with a married woman may serve to illustrate the unconscious meaning of the daydream. In the patient's daydream, he drove into the country in order to make love to his girl friend. To his surprise, after leaving the city, his car was surrounded by the married woman's three brothers, who then began to castrate him. An analysis of this daydream showed that his conscious wish to have sexual intercourse with this woman was interfered with by his unconscious. The woman did not have any brothers; the patient, however, had three, to be exact. With the help of his associations, it was possible to recognize that his mistress represented his mother; consequently, the infantile fears connected with his memory of the competition between himself and his brothers was mobilized. The daydream represented the gratification of his wish, but the consequences of the wish (to sleep with his mother and take her away from his brothers) were his castration fears.

Related Concepts: HALLUCINATIONS; ILLUSION; MASTURBATION FANTASIES.

REFERENCES

Eidelberg, L., *An Outline of a Comparative Pathology of the Neuroses.* IUP, p. 123, 1954.
Freud, S., 1900, "The Interpretation of Dreams." *SE*, 5:492, 1953.

ADDITIONAL READINGS

Fischle-Carl, H., "Tagträume und Wachphantasien." *Al*, 1957.
Freud, S.: 1908, "Creative Writers and Day-Dreaming." *SE*, 9, 1959.
    "Hysterical Phantasies and Their Relation to Bisexuality." *SE*, 9, 1959.
    1916–1917, "Introductory Lectures on Psycho-Analysis." *SE*, 15–16, 1963.
Peller, L., "Reading and Daydreams in Latency. Boy-Girl Differences." *JAPA*, 6, 1958.
Sperber, A., "Über das Auftreten von Hemmungen bei Tagträumen." *Im*, 16, 1930.

401

DAY RESIDUES IN DREAMS denotes the part of the dream which represents an event, experience or thought of the preceding day. It was Freud's belief that in every dream it is possible to find a point of contact with the experience of the previous day. Freud (1900) offered the following example from his own life. He dreamt about a monograph on cyclamens and remembered that he had seen it in a bookshop window. Freud's association revealed that cyclamens were his wife's favorite flowers. Thus, the book on cyclamens mobilized a feeling of guilt when he reflected that he often forgot to bring these flowers to his wife.

The day residue, according to Jekels and Bergler (1934), represents an unconscious feeling of guilt which the dreamer tries to prove unjustified. Eidelberg (1948) offered the following example: A young intern dreamed that the director of the hospital entered his room and said, "Why don't you post a notice on your door saying that information is only given between three and four, and thus avoid being bothered the whole day by relatives of the patients." The analysis of this dream disclosed that the intern had the wish to post such a notice on his door, but rejected this wish because he was afraid that the director would be provoked by such an action and would punish him. Being punished represented the mobilization of aggressive wishes turned against the self in defense of unconscious homosexual desires toward the director. The manifest dream content represented a simple fulfillment of his day wish; analysis of this dream, however, also disclosed the presence of latent homosexual tendencies, which were responsible for the fact that he didn't ask the director to post such a notice. Instead of asking for "favors," he preferred to repudiate his own plans, which would have mobilized his homosexual wishes.

Related Concept: DREAMS.

REFERENCES

Eidelberg, L., 1948, *Take Off Your Mask.* Py, pp. 69–70, 1960.
Freud, S., 1900, "The Interpretation of Dreams." *SE,* 4:169–170, 1953.
Jekels, L., & E. Bergler, 1934, "Instinct Dualism in Dreams." *Q,* 9:394–414, 1940.

402

DECOMPENSATION denotes the loss of an existing compensation through the breakdown of certain ego defenses, characterized by the appearance of anxiety, depression, thought disorder, or other symptom or disablement not previously present. [Knight, 1935.]

For example, a competent and compulsively con-

scientious shop foreman, a widower, suffered a complete disablement as a result of a minor injury to one knee. He took to his bed, wept, and acted as if he would never be able to function again. He had decompensated from his previous compulsive adjustment, with marked regression and suffering. Intensive psychotherapy revealed that joint trouble had heavily charged meaning for him; his wife had died after several years of crippling arthritis. With this insight, the patient was able to reestablish his previous good adjustment; his knee injury cleared up.

Related Concept: RETURN OF THE REPRESSED.

REFERENCE

Knight, R., Unpublished Lectures to Nonpsychiatrist Physicians: "Postgraduate Course in Psychiatry for Physicians." Menninger Clinic, 1935.

403

DEFENSE MECHANISMS are denotative of specific patterns of psychic action, employed to eliminate from the awareness of the total personality any of the external and internal stimuli resulting from the damming up of infantile instinctual tensions and narcissistic mortifications. The defensive measures are initiated to prevent the emergence of instinctual derivatives from the id into consciousness, and to the avoidance of the ego being overwhelmed by a re-experience of the original traumatic narcissistic mortification. The defensive measures affect a balance between the cathexis of the id derivatives and the countercathexis employed by the ego. Normally, the presence of external and internal stimuli produces three conscious derivatives—ideas, emotions, and actions.* The defense mechanisms interfere with the formation of all three; the stimuli are warded off or appear in a disguised form, i.e., they appear consciously as other ideas, emotions, and actions, while the original derivatives are maintained in an unconscious state.

The relative importance of the defense mechanisms has been the subject of some speculation. In ranking the defense mechanisms, unsuccessful

---

* In theory, a "successful" repression proves the exception; the three are eliminated without a consequent countercathetic action.

repression and denial appear to be basic (primary) and, in this consideration, are employed to defend against the conscious awareness of infantile wishes; the other defense mechanisms (secondary) appear to deal with the derivatives of these (primary) instinctual defenses. Some neurotics, like obsessional neurotics, utilize isolation, undoing, and reaction formation as major defenses. In hysteria, repression (secondary) is employed to a large degree. Some defense mechanisms contribute to the ego's permanent modes of adaptation and then may lead to a character formation. Schematically, the following processes characterize the response of the total personality to the defense mechanisms:

"(a) The total personality resents the symptom (the end result of an unconscious defense), because of the unpleasure connected with the presence of the symptom. Consequently, the symptom becomes a foreign body which the total personality tries to get rid of. The unpleasure caused by the symptom may be 'negative' (loss of a function producing pleasure) as well as 'positive' (pain, terror, etc.). It seems that symptoms connected with pain or terror are resented more than symptoms causing a lack of pleasure (such as frigidity).

"(b) The total personality accepts the end result of the defense mechanism and *assimilates* it in the form of a neurotic character trait.

"(c) The total personality accepts the end result of the defense mechanism as its form of genital discharge (perversions).

"(d) The total personality accepts the end result of the defense mechanism as its chief or principal method of eliminating unpleasure (addictions).

"(e) The total personality does not differentiate between inside and outside, and the patient regards his symptoms as being caused by external factors. Consequently, he is unwilling to examine them (psychosis)." [Eidelberg, 1954.]

1. Ambivalence. The simultaneous feeling of love and hate toward the same object; a defensive measure which serves to protect the subject from the conscious awareness of the presence of infantile wishes and their defense. The mixture of sexual and aggressive impulses is characteristic of the anal stage. The term is sometimes employed to describe a patient who cannot make up his mind, which is referred to as ambivalent oscillation. [See **133**.]

2. Ambivalent Oscillation. A condition which is characterized by quick changes from positive to negative impulses which results in indecision. It serves to help the patient maintain the illusion that he can gratify contradictory wishes. If sexual and aggressive infantile wishes, representing active and passive aims, are used to ward each other off, ambivalent oscillation may be employed to eliminate from consciousness the simultaneous presence of these opposing tendencies. For example, a patient simultaneously wanted to love and to hate his analyst; to give him money and to keep it for himself. These ambivalent feelings led to the experience of oscillation between these negative and positive wishes. The patient was thus able to protect himself against the recognition of his instinctual tensions. His ambivalent oscillation seemed to serve two purposes: it kept the sexual and aggressive infantile wishes from becoming completely conscious, while still providing a partial discharge of their tensions; and it protected him from having to recognize the limitations of his power over others, his lack of power over his own ambivalent feelings. [See **134**.]

3. Avoidance. A defensive process employed to protect the subject from the recognition of an unconscious wish and to protect him from an unconscious narcissistic mortification. The subject responds to certain situations or activities by eliminating the activity or object. The temptation which might result in a feared punishment is thus avoided. [See **170**.]

4. Conversion. The transformation of intrapsychic excitation into somatic manifestations. Freud (1905) described the defensive measures as a translation of purely psychical excitations into somatic phenomena. The energy of a mental process is withheld from conscious influences (repressed) and diverted into unconscious *symbolic* bodily symptoms. Unconscious memories or fantasies are converted into sensory and motor symptoms. For example, a hysterical patient's repressed wish to become pregnant as a result of performing fellatio, as well as the defensive reaction against that wish, may be expressed, through conversion, by vomiting. [See **332**].

5. Denial (Disavowal). Aimed at the elimination of traumatic sense organ perceptions, the offensive perceptions mobilized by it being kept from consciousness. It specifically relates to the defense against the claims of external reality. For example, the impotent male patient denies the presence of an attractive woman. [See **414**.]

6. Derealization. A defensive maneuver which is used to protect the ego (total personality) from an external stimulus; it is similar to the mechanisms of repression, denial and negation. Derealization differs from depersonalization in that it is employed to ward off a dangerous external stimulus. It appears that the feeling of the damming up of forbidden wishes and the narcissistic mortification are thus avoided. [See **417**.]

7. Displacement. A defensive process which protects the subject from the consciousness of dangerous derivatives, by shifting the energy attached to one object, activity, or part of the body onto another, with the result that an interest in one object is exchanged for an interest in another. In the case of a man who picked his nose, analysis disclosed that the patient's unconscious wish was to insert his finger into his anus. The wish was warded off by his displacement from his anus to his nose. [See **421**.]

8. Exaggeration. According to Sperling (1963), exaggeration is similar to repression in pushing certain ideas out of consciousness. It differs from repression, for the instinctual drive is, to a certain degree, acted out. The individual defends himself, not by a second action which undoes the first, but, rather, by reacting to a stimulus out of proportion to it. [See **532**.]

9. Fixation. As the result of a traumatic event at a given level of development, an infantile wish may become repressed and thus fixated at a particular stage. It is sometimes described as the result of a defense mechanism employed at a given stage. Withal, it represents an arrested development which causes the libido and destrudo to remain cathected at an infantile stage. For example, in the classical syndrome of melancholic depression, there is an instinctual fixation to orality. Early developmental phases may also persist side by side with later phases and appear in symptoms, character traits, and attitudes. The points of instinctual fixation have an important bearing on the predisposition to different types of neuroses. [See **610**.]

10. Introjection. A defensive measure which allows a patient to eliminate the frustration and narcissistic mortification connected with the loss of an external object. The neurotic cannot accept and

tolerate an object loss without making up for this loss by creating an image of the lost object in the self. As a result of the pathological introjection, the patient is able to deny the external narcissistic mortification—"I have no power over him; I could not prevent his departure"—by accepting instead the internal narcissistic mortification, "I have no power over my hostility; I am responsible for his departure, having provoked it." Concurrently, as Eidelberg (1954) noted, the psychic energy which had cathected originally the presentation of the external object is withdrawn and is used to cathect part of the self instead. The psychic energy seems to remain objectual and does not change into secondary narcissistic energy. [See **929**.]

11. Isolation. The emotional components of a memory or thought are not experienced consciously with any strength. The idea is experienced as though it were relatively neutral, and not as being dangerous, e.g., "I guess you could say that I hate my father." It is a defensive process especially characteristic of obsessionals, in which infantile memories related to infantile wishes and narcissistic mortifications are stripped of their affect. The associative links to the symptom or to similar experiences or strivings are deprived of their cathexis. For example, a woman tells of being seduced as a young girl by an adult man, but does so without any perceptible affect. Only a few moments relating to the seduction itself are recalled; what happened before and after are not subject to recall. Isolation thus involves the basic avoidance of contact, whether libidinal or aggressive. [See **932**.]

12. Negation. A derivative of a repressed wish which enters consciousness under the condition that it is rendered harmless by declaring that what is said is not true, e.g., "It is not true that I hate my mother." The return of the repressed material appears to take place for reasons which are still unknown. It seems that negation takes place only after primary and secondary repression have failed. It may be considered as belonging to the secondary line of defense. Freud (1925) believed that this view of negation suited the fact that in analysis a "no" in the unconscious was not discoverable, i.e., the unconscious can only be recognized by the ego in its expression of the negative formula. [See **1409**.]

13. Projection. A defensive process which is employed by the unconscious part of the ego, through which internal impulses and feelings that are unacceptable to the total personality are attributed to an external object, entering consciousness as a disguised perception of the external world. For example, the unconscious feeling, "I hate you," if unacceptable to the subject's conscious, is perceived through projection, consciously, as "You hate me." In the modified sense of assuming unconsciously that "others feel what I feel," projection may be a normal mechanism in children and primitive social groups, and may contribute to the development of empathy and understanding. However, pathological projection, as manifested in phobia and paranoia, interferes and distorts the individual's understanding of the external world. In addition, an external narcissistic mortification is substituted for an internal narcissistic mortification, allowing the subject to retain an illusion of control over the self. Projection may also be used to externalize parts of the self, e.g., in guilt feeling, "He accuses me" replaces "I feel guilty"; and in the feminine part of the male person, as in paranoid jealousy, it takes the form, it is "she" not "I" who is sexually excited by him. [See **1662**.]

14. Reaction Formation. An infantile wish is warded off and kept in a state of repression through the formation of a character trait representing the opposite instinct fusion. Freud (1926) introduced the term in his study of obsessional neurotics. He regarded the reaction formation as essentially an exaggeration of normal character traits developed during the latency period, which appear later in their altered form, as the result of reinforced instinctual trends that have to be kept in repression. [See **1806**.]

15. Repression (Primary and Secondary). The unconscious instinctual wish and its derivatives, including the affects, memories, and fantasies connected with it, are barred from consciousness. Countercathexis is expended to maintain the repression, and must be expended continuously. Historically, this was the first defense mechanism to be described, and it is considered, by some analysts, to precede all other defenses. If the repression failed, Freud thought, there would be a return of the repressed. Successful repression is postulated when the repressed contents are more or less stripped of their cathexes and, therefore, no pathological defenses are used. *Primary* repression is used to push

back dangerous id derivatives before they can enter consciousness; *secondary* repression is used to eliminate material which was previously repressed, to keep it from re-entering consciousness. [See **1822**.]

16. Reversal into the Opposite. One of four instinctual vicissitudes, according to Freud (1915). It is further identified as a defensive process by many analysts when it takes place on an unconscious level. It protects the individual from an awareness of a dangerous emotion by mobilizing an opposite one. For example, a patient was sometimes compelled to leave her desk and rush into the bathroom to masturbate. Her analysis disclosed that her urge to masturbate represented a defense against the recognition of an unconscious anger. While she resented her sexual drive, she preferred it to her aggressive tension, which she could not discharge and which, accordingly, made her feel helpless. In this, her lack of power over others was hidden behind her lack of power over herself. [See **921**.]

17. Turning Round Upon the Subject's Own Self. A defensive process in which a wish is redirected toward the self, rather than toward the object of the instinctual wish. According to Freud (1915), it represents an intermediate stage in the change of a wish with an active aim into a wish with a passive one. As Freud (1915) noted, the reversal affects only the content, whenever the positive wish is replaced by the aggressive wish, as exemplified in the reversal of love into hate. For example, a patient who could not speak in public suffered from the idea that his listeners would laugh at him. In this, his unconscious exhibitionistic wish, "I want to be ridiculed," was changed into the inspectionistic wish, "I want to watch others laughing." [See **2029**.]

18. Undoing. An action which is performed with the unconscious purpose of magically abolishing the forbidden consequences of another act or thought. For example, a latent homosexual who initially expressed his homosexual desires by sitting on the left side of a theatre, might, in order to undo the first act, deliberately sit on the right side of the theatre. Undoing may be sublimated (e.g., philanthropy and exaggerated kindness). The mechanism of undoing is based on the patient's conviction that his hostile wishes are gratified by thinking and not by acting (infantile omnipotence). [See **2108**.]

Related Concepts: ANXIETY; CONFLICT; COUNTERCATHEXIS (ANTICATHEXIS).

REFERENCES

Eidelberg, L., *An Outline of a Comparative Pathology of the Neuroses*. IUP, pp. 90–112, 230–237, 1954.

Freud, S.: 1905, "Fragment of an Analysis of a Case of Hysteria." *SE*, 7:53, 1953.

    1915, "Instincts and Their Vicissitudes." *SE*, 14:127, 1957.

    1923, "The Ego and the Id." *SE*, 19:42, 1961.

    1925, "Negation." *SE*, 19:235–242, 1961.

Sperling, O., "Exaggeration as a Defense," in a paper read at the Annual Meeting of the American Psychoanalytic Association, 1963.

ADDITIONAL READINGS

Bibring, G. L., T. F. Dwyer, D. S. Huntington, & A. F. Valenstein, "Glossary of Defenses." *PsaStC*, 16, 1961.

Freud, A., *The Ego and the Mechanisms of Defense*." IUP, 1946.

Freud, S.: 1915, "Repression." *SE*, 14, 1957.

    1926, "Inhibitions, Symptoms and Anxiety." *SE*, 20, 1959.

Hendrick, I., "The Ego and the Defense Mechanisms: A Review and a Discussion." *R*, 25, 1938.

Lampl-de Groot, J., "On Defense and Development: Normal and Pathological." *PsaStC*, 11, 1957.

Lustman, S. L.: "Psychic Energy and Mechanisms of Defense." *PsaStC*, 12, 1957.

    "Defense, Symptom and Character." *PsaStC*, 17, 1962.

de Saussure, R., "Mechanisms of Defence and Their Place in Psycho-Analytic Therapy: Discussion." *IntJPsa*, 35, 1954.

Sharpe, E., "Survey of Defence Mechanisms in General Character Traits and in Conduct-Evaluation of Pre-Conscious Material." *IntJPsa*, 11, 1930.

Spitz, R. A., "Some Early Prototypes of Ego Defenses." *JAPA*, 9, 1961.

Sterba, E., "Zwei Arten der Abwehr." *PsaP*, 10, 1936.

404

DEFERRED OBEDIENCE is a reaction to, or acceptance of, a threat or command received early in life, having no effect at the time because it was suppressed or repressed, which may cause a reaction at a later period. Clinically, this is a typical reaction to castration threats. For example, when Little Hans was three-and-a-half years old, he was told by his mother that she would have his "widdler" cut off if he went on playing with it. He calmly replied that then he would "widdle with his bottom." [Freud, 1909.]

There are neurotic cases where deferred obedience has a principal share in determining symptoms and in causing a delayed renunciation of libidinal gratification. Freud (1923) suggested, for example, that Christopher Haizmann, the seventeenth-century painter, was unable to paint following his father's death, because the father had long before opposed the son's wish to become a painter (opposition originally ignored by Haizmann). Deferred obedience made the son dependent again, mobilizing his remorse and self-punishment, which deprived him of his livelihood.

Related Concepts: CASTRATION COMPLEX; DEFERRED REACTION.

REFERENCES

Freud, S.: 1909, "Analysis of a Phobia in a Five-Year-Old Boy." *SE*, 10:35–36, 1955.

    1923, "A Seventeenth-Century Demonological Neurosis." *SE*, 19:87–88, 1961.

ADDITIONAL READING

Freud, S., 1913, "Totem and Taboo." *SE*, 13, 1955.

405

DEFERRED REACTION denotes a specific response to the activation of a suppressed or repressed memory of a past experience which had little effect at the time of its occurrence. For example, the Wolf Man was subject to a primal scene experience when he was one-and-a-half. This was comprehended, and reacted to, only after it was reactivated in a disguised form (in his wolf dream) when he was four. Freud (1917) noted: "It is perfectly possible for a child, while he is not yet credited with possessing an understanding or a memory, to be a witness of the sexual act between his parents or other grown-up people; and the possibility cannot be rejected that he will be able to understand and react to the impression *in retrospect*." Later, however, Freud (1918) pointed out that it is probable—when a patient remembers an observation of parental sexual intercourse—he is confusing the observation of intercourse between animals with that of his parents.

Related Concepts: DEFERRED OBEDIENCE; PRIMAL SCENE.

REFERENCES

Freud, S.: 1917, "Introductory Lectures on Psycho-Analysis." *SE*, 16:369, 1963.
    1918, "From the History of an Infantile Neurosis." *SE*, 17:38, 43–45, 57, 109, 1945.

ADDITIONAL READING

Freud, S., 1909, "Analysis of a Phobia in a Five-Year-Old Boy." *SE*, 10, 1955.

406

DÉJÀ RACONTÉ is a term ascribed to the feeling that something has already been related in the psychoanalytic situation. The patient asserts with great certainty that he has already described a definite episode which, in fact, has not occurred. Freud (1901) explained that this phenomenon was based on the patient's impulse and intention to impart this memory, but which he failed to execute, thus putting forward an explanation as a substitute for the second feeling.

Siegman (1956), in describing a patient with frequent déjà raconté feelings, arrived at the following conclusion: "The ego, reminded of a threat it fears that might be overwhelming, can be reassured (by a trick of perceptual distortion) that this situation was previously mastered successfully, and it is thereby able to cope with it in the present."

Arlow (1959), in discussing the déjà vu experiences, stated: "The other déjà phenomena . . . probably have a similar structure." He saw them as stemming from a "transitory circumscribed disturbance of a specific ego function" which developed as a defensive reassurance that the individual would successfully master a currently threatening situation as he had once before in the past.

Related Concepts: DÉJÀ VU; UNCANNY.

REFERENCES

Arlow, J. A., "The Structure of the Déjà Vu Experience." *JAPA*, 7:611, 1959.
Freud, S.: 1901, "The Psychopathology of Everyday Life." *SE*, 6:260, 1960.
Siegman, A. J., "The Psychological Economy of Déjà Raconté." *Q*, 25:83, 1956.

ADDITIONAL READING

Fliess, R., "The *Déjà Raconté*: A Transference-Delusion Concerning the Castration Complex." *Q*, 25, 1956.

407

DÉJÀ VU is a term ascribed to the feeling of having had the same experience once before, or of having once been in the same place before, which usually occurs in times of stress, fatigue or physical illness. This phenomenon, Freud (1901) noted, "corresponds to the recollection of an unconscious phantasy." The feeling of familiarity in the current scene was accountable to an unconscious association which could be traced back to a pre-existing unconscious fantasy; the unconscious association served to maintain the repression of the former fantasy.

In a letter to Freud (1901), Ferenczi described a patient's déjà vu experience and noted that "it regularly proved to have originated from a forgotten (repressed) portion of a dream of the preceding night."*

Bergler (1942) agreed with this formulation but added that the experience may also have represented a repetition of the superego's need for punishment out of an unconscious sense of guilt. Marcovitz (1952) also agreed with Freud and Ferenczi, but added that the *form* of the experience carried the ego wish for a second chance, to permit a more gratifying outcome of a repressed wish. Arlow (1959) ascribed the déjà vu experience to a transitory circumscribed disturbance of a specific ego function in response to a situation which both symbolized and stimulated the revival of an anxiety producing memory, wish, or fantasy. The specific form of the déjà vu experience represented an ego wish for reassurance and consolation which is expressed by the thought: "Don't worry; you have been in this kind of dangerous situation before and emerged safe and alive. The same will happen now." He compared this to typical dreams of missing trains and examinations.

Related Concepts: DÉJÀ RACONTÉ; ILLUSION; UNCANNY.

---

* Italics removed.

REFERENCES

Arlow, Jacob A., "The Structure of the Déjà Vu Experience," *JAPA*, 7:611, 1959.

Bergler, Edmund, "Contributions to the Psychoanalysis of Déjà Vu." *Q*, 11:165, 1942.

Freud, S., 1901, "The Psychopathology of Everyday Life." *SE*, 6:266–268, 1960.

Marcovitz, Eli, "The Meaning of Déjà Vu." *Q*, 21:481, 1952.

ADDITIONAL READING

Pötzl, O., " Zur Metapsychologie des 'Déjà Vu '." *Im*, 12, 1926.

408

DELAY OF DISCHARGE results from the imposition of ego functions between the occurrences of the stimuli and their discharge. To effect this delay the ego opposes and binds the primitive discharge reactions through countercathexis and neutralization (aim inhibited) of the instinctual drives. Delay in this discharge of mental tensions is especially characteristic of the secondary processes. Hartmann (1964) noted: "Now, the functions of the ego area just touched upon, including those underlying controlled and directed action, often have the character of inhibiting the immediate gratification of the instinctual drives; postponement or displacement of gratification is frequently the consequence of their actitivy. On the other hand, the development of new ego functions, like, for instance, that of acting in the outer world, may open up new avenues for direct and indirect (sublimated) gratifications of instinctual tendencies. Changes in the distribution of psychic energy, in the direction of a stronger investment of the ego functions, go parallel with these developments.

"In stressing the importance of such factors as anticipation, postponement of gratification, and the like, in the development of action, we at the same time give action its place in a general trend of human development, the trend toward a growing independence from the immediate impact of present stimuli, the independence from the *hic et nunc*. This trend can also be described as one toward 'internalization'. The danger signal is an example in question. The signal helps in many cases to master 'inner' danger before it can become danger threatening from outside. Directed and organized action (organized as

to its motivations and as to the way it is brought about) is gradually substituted for the immediate reactions of motor discharge, as mentioned above. Trial activities with whose help we attempt to master a situation, to solve a problem, are gradually internalized: thinking is, in this sense, trial action with small quantities of psychic energy."

The infant, for example, attempts to discharge tension by uncoordinated discharge movements and fixed instinctual or reflex responses. With the later development of the ego, a progressive capacity to bind and tolerate tension and to prevent immediate discharge takes place. This view is consistent with that of the general evolutionary processes: the more differentiated an organism is, the more independent from the immediate environmental stimulation it becomes.

The capacity to delay discharge is of great adaptational value; it facilitates the use of memory and intelligence to form judgments about internal and external reality. These judgments—in conjunction with such trial activities as thinking and playing— allow for realistic, goal-directed activities which are more effective in the achievement of appropriate drive discharge. The adaptational advantages of delay, of thinking, etc., are facilitated by the ego's progressive mastery of the body's motoric apparatus, which permits directed action rather than uncoordinated discharge movements.

Related Concepts: COUNTERCATHEXIS (ANTICATHEXIS); NEUTRALIZATION; REALITY PRINCIPLE.

REFERENCE

Hartmann, H., *Essays on Ego Psychology.* IUP, pp. 40–41, 1964.

409

DELIBIDINIZATION (DESEXUALIZATION) denotes the neutralization of various pregenital libidinal impulses and the employment of the energy in the service of the ego, in the pursuit of aim-inhibited, sublimated activities. According to Freud's first instinct theory, the energy which cathects the self (ego instinct) is free of libido. In his second (1923), the energy cathecting the self is referred to as narcissistic libido. Consequently, it is difficult to accept the terms delibidinization and desexualization. Actually, the original sexual aim connected with the sexual object is lost, when (under normal conditions) the object libido cathects the self. What is lost is neither the libido nor the sexual aim, but the objectual quality of the libido. Therefore, according to Eidelberg (1952), the libido which cathects the self may be referred to as secondary narcissistic libido. For example, the oral sadistic wish to devour may be stripped of its original libidinal aim and expressed, instead, as the need to acquire knowledge; a scopophilic impulse, originally connected with the primal scene, may be diverted to curiosity in the intellectual sphere.

According to Freud (1921), aim inhibition should be regarded as only the first step toward sublimation. Fenichel (1945) emphasized that in a true sublimation there is aim inhibition, desexualization, and a resultant alteration of the ego. He also emphasized the importance of identification in the development of sublimation.

Some authors assume that repression is avoided by sublimation. According to Freud, the inability to sublimate interferes with successful therapeutic completion of psychoanalysis.

Related Concepts: IDENTIFICATION; SUBLIMATION.

REFERENCES

Eidelberg, L., *Studies in Psychoanalysis*. IUP, p. 150, 1948.
Fenichel, O., *The Psychoanalytic Study of Neurosis*. Nor, pp. 141–143, 1945.
Freud, S.: 1921, "Group Psychology and the Analysis of the Ego." *SE*, 18:139, 1955.
　　1923, "The Ego and the Id." *SE*, 19:3–68, 1961.

ADDITIONAL READING

Freud, S., 1915, "Instincts and Their Vicissitudes." *SE*, 14, 1957.

410

DELUSIONS are characterized by firm convictions, not on observable or evaluative external perceptions, which are incorrectable; they are caused by the subject's projection of his own emotions to external objects. As a result, the delusion permits the subject to deny his internal narcissistic mortification (connected with his inability to control certain wishes) and to accept external narcissistic mortifications which are indicative of his inability to deal with threatening external objects.

Freud (1914) reasoned that delusions take place when the psychic energy is withdrawn from the presentation of external objects and concentrated on the presentation of the self. Though neurotics, too, withdraw their psychic energy from the presentation of the object, a presentation of *other* objects takes their place. For instance, in the case of Little Hans, the cathexis of his oedipal wishes was withdrawn from the presentation of his father and cathected, instead, to the presentation of horses. As a result, it was the horse which mobilized the original hostile feelings directed toward the father. Thus, by avoiding the sight of horses, he was able to avoid his hostile wishes and the fear connected with them. In a psychosis, however, such an avoidance is impossible, for the withdrawn psychic energy has cathected the presentation of the self, and, consequently, part of the patient (often the presentation of his superego) becomes the aggressor, punishing him for the presence of these hostile wishes. In normal behavior, the superego, an agency of the psychic apparatus, watches over and criticizes the individual. When a pathological condition intervenes, the patient's superego is projected onto the external world, and the complaint is one of being watched and criticized, not by himself but by others.

Freud (1914) believed there was a psychical agency responsible for self-observation which he attributed to the superego. In pathological cases, the superego is projected onto the external world; the patient attributes his own self-critical comments to an external object.

Clinical Example

A paranoid patient started his analysis by asking about the cause of his troubles. The analyst replied, "Your feelings of guilt." This reply had a magical effect on the patient. He felt cured and decided to terminate his treatment. The next day, at the time he was supposed to see his analyst, he became fearful, believing that his analyst would punish him for his decision to break off the treatment. Panic stricken, he left the city, was picked up by the police while wandering in the country and institutionalized. Two months later, he started treatment again with another analyst.

In his second treatment, the patient's psychotic reaction to the words "feelings of guilt" was analyzed. The interpretation he had first received proved to be correct, if premature. The patient was unable, in his first analysis, to assimilate and integrate this interpretation, warding it off by the delusion that his analyst was persecuting him. His first analyst represented his superego, which criticized him for having deserted the man who helped him. Because the first analyst had helped him, a mobilization of the patient's passive homosexual wishes were warded off by the aggressive wish, "I will desert him." Finally, his superego, projected onto the analyst, punished him through his persecutory delusion.

Related Concepts: DENIAL (DISAVOWAL); DREAMS; HALLUCINATIONS; ILLUSION.

REFERENCE

Freud, S., 1914, "On Narcissism: An Introduction." *SE*, 14:84, 95, 1957.

ADDITIONAL READINGS

Aronson, G. J., "Delusion of Pregnancy in a Male Homosexual with Abdominal Cancer." *AnSurvPsa*, 3, 1952.
Bibring, E., "Klinische Beiträge zur Paranoiafrage." *Z*, 15, 1929.
Cohen, F. I., "The Relationship Between Delusional Thinking and Hostility. A Case Study." *PQ*, 30, 1956.
Freud, S.: 1896, "Further Remarks on the Neuro-Psychoses of Defence." *SE*, 3, 1962.
   1907, "Delusions and Dreams in Jensen's Gradiva." *SE*, 9, 1959.
   1911, "Psycho-Analytic Notes on an Autobiographical Account of a Case of Paranoia (Dementia Paranoides)." *SE*, 12, 1958
   1913, "Totem and Taboo." *SE*, 13, 1955.
   1917, "Introductory Lectures on Psycho-Analysis." *SE*, 16, 1963.
   1924, "Neurosis and Psychosis." *SE*, 19, 1961.
Kaufman, M. R., "Religious Delusions in Schizophrenia." *IntJPsa*, 20, 19,9.
Sharpe, E. F., "Variations of Technique in Different Neuroses. Delusion, Paranoid, Obsession, Conversion Types." *IntJPsa*, 12, 1931.
Stärke, A.: "Rechts und Links in der Wahnidee." *Z*, 2, 1914.
   "The Reversal of the Libido-Sign in Delusions of Persecution." *IntJPsa*, 1, 1920.

DELUSIONS OF GRANDEUR denote a conviction of great personal importance, strongly exaggerated in relation to reality; a symptom of schizophrenia, especially of the paranoid type. Abraham (1908) identified the main characteristic of schizophrenia: a lack of investment of objects with the libido; the libido is turned back on the ego, and this reflex reversion is the source of delusions of grandeur. Freud (1914) accepted this explanation and used it to illustrate his concept of narcissism, stating that the object libido withdrawn from the external world is directed onto the ego, becoming ego libido and inflating the ego. This represents secondary narcissism, superimposed on the original infantile primary narcissism.

Delusions of grandeur usually represent a defense of an unconscious feeling of inferiority, a gratification of infantile omnipotence which takes place after reality testing has been interfered with. Patients suffering from schizophrenia are characterized by a form of megalomania and by a diversion of the object libido to self-presentation. In this, schizophrenics differ from neurotics, for they only displace their libido from one object-presentation to another object-presentation. When a schizophrenic begins to be interested in external objects, this interest represents an attempt at recovery.

Related Concepts: LIBIDO; MEGALOMANIA; NARCISSISM; SCHIZOPHRENIA.

REFERENCES

Abraham, K., 1908, "The Psycho-Sexual Differences Between Hysteria and Dementia Praecox." *SPA*, pp. 64–79, 1942.
Freud, S., 1914, "On Narcissism: An Introduction." *SE*, 14:74, 1957.

ADDITIONAL READINGS

Freud, S.: 1909, "Notes Upon a Case of Obsessional Neurosis. *SE*, 10, 1955.
   1911, "Psycho-Analytical Notes on an Autobiographical Account of a Case of Paranoia (Dementia Paranoides)." *SE*, 12, 1958.
   1917, "Introductory Lectures on Psycho-Analysis." *SE*, 16, 1963.

412

DELUSIONS OF OBSERVATION denote a symptom of paranoid schizophrenia, involving a fixed, false belief on the part of the subject that he is continually being observed, even in his most intimate actions, by unknown powers or persons. The subject usually has hallucinations in which he hears voices announcing the results of their observations. This is not the same thing as delusions of persecution, but it is not far removed from it. It implies that the unknown observers distrust the subject and expect to catch him doing something that is forbidden, for which he will be punished. Freud (1933) stated that delusions of observation are evidence for the self-observatory function of the superego, here split off and projected onto external reality.

Related Concepts: DELUSIONS OF PERSECUTION; DEPERSONALIZATION; HALLUCINATIONS; PARANOID CONDITION (STATE); SCHIZOPHRENIA.

REFERENCE

Freud, S., 1933, "New Introductory Lectures on Psycho-Analysis." *SE*, 22:59, 1964.

ADDITIONAL READINGS

Freud, S.: 1896, "Further Remarks on the Neuro-Psychoses of Defence." *SE*, 3, 1962.
    1914, "On Narcissism: An Introduction." *SE*, 14, 1957.
    1915, "A Case of Paranoia Running Counter to the Psycho-Analytic Theory of the Disease." *SE*, 14, 1957.
    1917, "Introductory Lectures on Psycho-Analysis." *SE*, 16, 1963.
    1919, "The 'Uncanny'." *SE*, 17, 1955.

413

DELUSIONS OF PERSECUTION are those psychotic symptoms which are characterized by the subject's conviction that he is being persecuted, where the subject refuses to ascertain the veracity of the accusations. The subject's delusions may be accompanied by hallucinations which represent erroneous sense organ perceptions but have the character of internal and external perceptions. [Freud, 1922.]

As in other forms of projection, the subject denies the presence of the internal narcissistic mortifica-

tion, "I cannot control my aggression," by accepting the external narcissistic mortification, "I cannot control the hostility of my persecutors." It would appear that only repressed infantile feelings are projected.

Fenichel (1945), described the process, as follows: "This occurs not only in the projection of the hatred which is basic for the delusion; also certain definite attitudes and expressions, which are ascribed to the persecutor, correspond to traits of the patient and especially often to demands of the patient's superego."

Related Concept: PSYCHOSIS.

REFERENCES

Fenichel, O., *The Psychoanalytic Theory of Neurosis.* Nor, p. 430, 1945.
Freud, S., 1922, "Some Neurotic Mechanisms in Jealousy, Paranoia, and Homosexuality." *SE*, 18:246, 1955.

414

DENIAL (DISAVOWAL) is a defense mechanism which is aimed at the elimination of traumatic sense organ perceptions. In this manner, the offensive perceptions and those effects mobilized by it are kept from consciousness. Strachey (1961) pointed out that Freud drew a different distinction between the uses of the two words: " 'Repression' applies to defense against internal instinctual demands and 'disavowal' to defense against the claims of external reality." However, Freud appears to have deviated from his original definition. In 1927, he noted: "If we wanted to differentiate more sharply between the vicissitude of the idea as distinct from that of the affect, and reserve the word 'Verdrängung' ['repression'] for the affect, then the correct German word for the vicissitude of the idea would be 'Verleugnung' ['disavowal']." It seems advisable, therefore, in order to avoid misunderstandings, to make a clear distinction as to whether the concept refers to the defense of external stimuli or the warding off of ideas.

It appears that ideas may try to enter the conscious part of the ego from internal stimuli (instincts) as well as from external sources; the same holds true with respect to affects. Using Freud's former definition of the term denial (defense of external stimuli), Eidelberg (1952) offered the following example: "Many, many years ago, when I started to treat psychotics, I thought that in order to destroy their projection it was necessary to prove to them that they were wrong. In most cases, however, it is impossible to deliver a negative proof. But one day a patient arrived and said that he knew that my wife and my maid had left me and that I was alone. Here, I thought I had finally caught him. When I asked who had opened the door for him, and he answered that the maid had done it, I asked him how he could then say that she had left me. I thought that the patient would be crushed by the way in which I produced the evidence. Little did I know that he had the greatest contempt for my way of reasoning, because I did not understand that what the patient meant was not that my maid and my wife had left me, but that his wife and his maid would leave him. In other words, the patient makes these mistakes because he is not interested in reality. He is not interested in the reality of the external world because he is afraid of his id. The neurotic, too, is afraid of his id, but usually as a result of this fear, he tries to escape from it. He turns his back on the id, whereas the psychotic turns his whole energy to the id." In this, he avoids a split in his total personality.

The analytical examination of various neuroses and psychoses indicates that the denial, in addition to repression, plays an important role. The impotent patient denies his dependency on women; the frigid woman denies her dependency on men. Of course, the denial in neurosis is less visible than in psychosis, for reality testing is not completely eliminated in the former.

Related Concept: REPRESSION.

REFERENCES

Eidelberg, L., "A Discussion of Dr. Wexler's Paper ('The Structural Problem in Schizophrenia: The Role of the Internal Object')," in *Psychotherapy With Schizophrenics*, ed. E. B. Brody and F. C. Redlich. *IUP*, p. 213, 1952.
Freud, S., 1927, "Fetishism." *SE*, 21:153, 1961.
Strachey, J., "Editorial note." *SE*, 21:153, 1961.

ADDITIONAL READINGS

Linn, L.: "Trauma and Denial." *BAPA*, 8, 1952.
　"The Role of Perception in the Mechanism of Denial." *JAPA*, 1, 1953.

Rubinfine, D. L.: "On Denial of Objective Sources of Anxiety and 'Pain'." *YBPsa*, 9, 1953.
　"Maternal Stimulation, Psychic Structure, and Early Object Relations; With Special Reference to Aggression and Denial." *PsaStC*, 17, 1962.

415

DEPERSONALIZATION is a state of mind characterized by a sense of unreality and detachment from the self or the external world, or both. According to Schilder (1935), patients suffering from depersonalization perceive the external world as foreign, strange, and uncanny. Their presentations are usually pale and colorless. Many patients complain that they have no presentations at all; they also complain that they have no feelings, either pleasurable or unpleasurable. An objective examination indicates that their sense organ perceptions and emotions are intact. Some authors regard depersonalization as a symptom which is present in certain forms of neurosis, psychosis, and anatomic lesions of the brain; others consider it to be a mental illness *sui generis*. [Eidelberg, 1954.]

From an analytic point of view, depersonalization appears to be a defense of anal exhibitionistic wishes. These wishes are warded off by mobilization of inspectionistic (scopophilic) wishes directed toward the self. Loss of contact with the external world is caused by the withdrawal of object libido and destrudo from the presentation of external objects. This energy, which is withdrawn, cathects the presentation of the self. The patient experiences anxiety as a result of the loss of the external object. At the same time, he feels guilty for his exaggerated interest in himself. Elements of the id, ego, superego, and external world are expressed in this defense mechanism by which the precipitating infantile anal-exhibitionistic wishes are prevented from becoming conscious. At the same time, the narcissistic mortification, the patient's inability to control his urge to view himself, is used as a disavowal (denial) of the narcissistic mortification, "I cannot force the external world to watch me." The total personality of the patient experiences depersonalization as ego-alien. [Bergler, 1935.]

Depersonalization is often connected with *derealization*, which represents estrangement from the outside world. The two phenomena usually occur simultaneously, and there are no sharp lines of demarcation between them. Depersonalization may be transient and mild; in more severe instances it causes feelings of helplessness and anxiety of great intensity. *Déjà vu, déjà entendu,* and similar phenomena may be regarded as positive counterparts of depersonalization and derealization.

Related Concepts: ANXIETY; DÉJÀ VU; DEREALIZATION; EXHIBITIONISM; SCOPOPHILIA; SELF-OBSERVATION.

REFERENCES

Bergler, E., & L. Eidelberg, "Der Mechanismus der Depersonalisation." *Z,* 21-258, 1935.
Eidelberg, L., *An Outline of a Comparative Pathology of the Neuroses.* IUP, p. 152, 1954.

ADDITIONAL READINGS

Ackner, B., "Depersonalization: I. Etiology and Phenomenology; II. Clinical Syndromes." *JMS,* 100, 1954.
Berman, L., "Depersonalization and the Body Ego With Special Reference to the Genital Representation." *Q,* 17, 1948.
Bird, B., "Depersonalization." *AMAANP,* 80, 1958.
Blank, H. R., "Depression Hypomania, and Depersonalization." *Q,* 23, 1954.
Federn, P., "Depersonalization." *RevPsicoanal,* 11, 1954.
Feigenbaum, D., "Depersonalization as a Defence Mechanism." *RevPsicoanal,* 11, 1954.
Freud, S., 1936, "A Disturbance of Memory on the Acropolis." *SE,* 22, 1964.
Glicksberg, C. I., "Depersonalization in the Modern Drama." *The Personalist,* 39, 1958.
Hartmann, H., "Ein Fall von Depersonalisation." *ZNP,* 74, 1922.
Jacobson, E., "Depersonalization." *JAPA,* 7, 1959.
Nunberg, H., *Principles of Psychoanalysis.* IUP, 1955.
Sadger, I., "Über Depersonalisation." *Z,* 14, 1928.
Salfield, D. J., "Depersonalization and Allied Disturbances in Childhood." *JMS,* 104, 1958.
Schilder, P., *Introduction to a Psychoanalytic Psychiatry.* IUP, 1951.

416

DEPRESSION is a symptom neurosis which is characterized by a decrease of interest in the external world and an increase of aggression against the self; self-criticism, feelings of guilt, remorse, and self-punishment are precipitated by an object loss. The patient tries to eliminate the narcissistic mortification connected with the recognition of his limited power, his inability to protect himself against the loss of the love object. Through the use of the mechanism of introjection, the patient incorporates the lost object and consequently treats himself as if he were the lost object.

Unlike mourning, depression is characterized not only by a greater amount of self-aggression, lack of interest in the external world and disturbances of appetite and sleep, but also by the fact that the lost object unconsciously represents an infantile object. Therefore, its loss mobilizes repressed wishes and unconscious narcissistic mortifications. Unlike melancholia, depression is characterized by the presence of unconscious sexual and aggressive wishes belonging to the phallic stage. Consequently, the lost object unconsciously represents *not* the loss of the mother and her breasts but the loss of the penis. The superego punishes the patient for the presence of unconscious wishes, without leading to a loss of reality testing which occurs in a melancholic depression.

The self-accusations of a depressed patient who blames himself for the loss of the object serves to eliminate the consciousness of his inability to control the object. While it is true that without treatment most depressions disappear after a certain time, many analysts assume that psychoanalytical treatment may not only facilitate the individual's return to normality, but also decrease his suffering.

Edith Jacobson (1953) asserted that a somatic component was essential; the depressed patients gauged their love object and self by the infantile values of omnipotency and invulnerability. Benedek (1956) reasoned that each phase of procreative growth brings about a regression to the oral phase. To her, the ambivalent core of the personality predisposes it to depression whenever regression to the oral level is initiated. Bibring (1953) characterized depression as a state of helplessness of the ego; it resulted from tension in the ego between narcissistic aspirations and its helplessness to achieve them.

Clinical Example

In the case of a forty-eight-year-old man who developed a depression after the death of his wife, his successful analysis disclosed that, because of his death wishes against her, his aggression against himself led to his self-accusations. These wishes were connected with his repressed hostility to his sister when he was five years old. The patient was cured after the wish to be a woman and give up his penis became conscious and his external narcissistic mortification (no power over the life of his wife) was accepted.

Related Concepts: ANACLITIC DEPRESSION; MASOCHISM; MELANCHOLIA; MOURNING; REMORSE; SENSE OF GUILT; SUPEREGO.

REFERENCES

Benedek, T., "Toward the Biology of the Depressive Constellation." *JAPA*, 4:389–427, 1956.
Bibring, E., "The Mechanism of Depression," in *Affective Disorders*, P. Greenacre, ed. IUP, pp. 13–48, 1953.
Jacobson, E., "Contribution to the Metapsychology of Cyclothymic Depression," in *Affective Disorders*, P. Greenacre, ed. IUP, pp. 49–83, 1953.

ADDITIONAL READINGS

Badel, D., "The Repetitive Cycle in Depression." *IntJPsa*, 43, 1962.
Beck, A. T., & M. S. Hurvich, "Psychological Correlates of Depression: I. Frequency of 'Masochistic' Dream Content in a Private Practice Sample." *PSM*, 21, 1959.
Bhaskaran, K., "Some Somatization Patterns in Reactive Depression. A Preliminary Report." *JNMD*, 21, 1955.
Bychowski, G., and M. Klein, S. Nacht, H. Rosenfeld, W. Scott, E. Zetzel, "Symposium on 'Depressive Illness.'" *IntJPsa*, 41, 1960.
Eidelberg, L., *An Outline of a Comparative Pathology of the Neuroses.* IUP, 1954.
Freud, S., 1933, "New Introductory Lectures on Psycho-Analysis." *SE*, 22, 1964.
Jacobson, E., "Depression: the Oedipus Conflict in the Development of Depressive Mechanisms." *Q*, 12, 1943.
Lewin, B., "Reflections on Depression." *PsaStC*, 16, 1961.
Pichon-Rivière, A., "Dentition, Walking, and Speech in Relation to the Depressive Position." *IntJPsa*, 39, 1958.
Rosenfeld, H., "An Investigation into the Psycho-Analytic Theory of Depression." *IntJPsa*, 40, 1959.
Sperling, M., "A Contribution to the Psychodynamics of Depression in Women." *Samiksa*, 4, 1950.
Spitz, R., "Hospitalism." *PsaStC*, 1, 1945.
Stengel, E., "The Treatment of Depressions." *JMS*, 1958.
Weiss, E., "Clinical Aspects of Depression." *Q*, 13, 1944.

417

DEREALIZATION, according to Freud (1936), is a defense mechanism which is used to protect the ego (total personality) from an external stimulus; it is similar to the mechanisms of repression, denial and negation. Derealization differs from depersonalization in that it is employed to ward off a dangerous external stimulus. It appears that the feeling of helplessness (narcissistic mortification) is thus avoided.

Freud analyzed his own experience of derealization which took place when he first viewed the Acropolis. He related: "When, finally, on the afternoon after our arrival, I stood on the Acropolis and cast my eyes around the landscape, a surprising thought suddenly entered my mind: 'So all this really *does* exist, as we learnt at school!' "

As a boy he had not doubted the reality of the Acropolis, only his own ability to travel so far in order to see it. For Freud, seeing the Acropolis meant that he was better than his father; it was an aggressive triumph over his dead father who had never traveled so far from his home. Freud explained his reaction to the Acropolis which he considered to be a derealization. He arrived at the conclusion that this symptom represented a punishment of an infantile wish to defy his father. Consequently, his ability to travel and to see the Acropolis represented an unconscious aggressive triumph over his father, and it was this which eventuated in his self-punishment.

Related Concepts: DÉJÀ VU; DEPERSONALIZATION.

REFERENCE

Freud, S., 1936, "An Experience on the Acropolis." *SE*, 22:240–248, 1964.

418

DESTINY NEUROSIS (FATE NEUROSIS) is a neurotic, self-provoked unconscious condition that leads the subject into repeated setbacks and failures in his life, consciously attributed to external events. Freud (1916) noted that the provocation for those who induce illness in consequence of success is closely connected with the oedipus complex, to the sense of guilt in general. "The superego," he rea-

soned in 1923, "fulfills the same function of protect-
ing and saving that was fulfilled in earlier days by the
father and later by Providence or Destiny." It
would appear that such patients use the mechanism
of unconscious provocation and not projection as a
defense. Instead of imagining an insult, they succeed
in an actual self-induced punishment.

Destiny neurosis and character neurosis are
similar, in that an external agent is held responsible
for the subject's difficulties, or at least, the subject
does not view himself as malfunctioning. H. Deutsch
(1932) viewed destiny neurosis as being more accessible to psychoanalytic therapy than character
neurosis: "The real motive of this fate lies, as we
have seen, in a constant, insoluble, inner conflict.
. . . The distinction between the fate-neurosis and
the so-called *neurotic character* is a fluctuating one
and cannot always be determined. The neurotic
character exhibits more diffuse disharmonies in its
relation to the outer world. These disharmonies are
due to infantile traits which become attached to the
adult personality; but they coincide to so large an
extent with the whole ego-organization that one is
never in a position to trace the unsuccessful repression as clearly as in the fate-neurosis. They are not,
like a symptom or a typical fate-formation, alien
bodies organized against the ego in its entirety."

Case History

Freud (1916) cited two examples of destiny
neurosis. In one, a young woman who had an affair
with an artist for many years became ill when he
finally decided to marry her. She suffered from
persecution mania, pathological jealousy, and
finally became insane. In another case, a man who
was a professor became a melancholic when his
teacher died and he was selected to take over his
position.

Related Concepts: CHARACTER NEUROSIS; MASO-
CHISM.

REFERENCES

Deutsch, H., *Psycho-Analysis of the Neuroses*. HPI,
    p. 47, 1932.
Freud, S.: 1916, "Some Character-Types Met With in
    Psychoanalytic Work." *SE*, 14:316–317, 331, 1957.
        1923, "The Ego and the Id." *SE*, 19:58, 1961.

419

DEUTEROPHALLIC refers to one of two
divisions of the phallic stage. First used by Jones
(1927), the concept was described by him as a phase
wherein a "dawning suspicion that the world is
divided into two classes: not male and female in the
proper sense, but penis possessing and castrated."
The second division is called the protophallic and is
described as a phase marked by innocence or ignorance, at least in consciousness, where the child
confidentially assumes "that the rest of the world is
built like itself and has a satisfactory male organ—
penis or clitoris, as the case may be." Freud (1931)
noted that the concept did not correspond to the
dynamic and chronological development of sexuality. The term is rarely used today.

Related Concepts: PHALLIC PHASE; PROTOPHALLIC.

REFERENCES

Freud, S., 1931, "Female Sexuality." *SE*, 21:243,
    1961.
Jones, E., "The Early Development of Female
    Sexuality." *IntJPsa*, 8:459, 1927.

420

DISCHARGE denotes that process which operates in accordance with the *law of constancy* to effect
an immediate reduction or elimination of any increase in psychical tension resulting from the
impingement of external or internal stimuli. The
results of this discharge are to reduce to nothing, or
to as low a level as possible, the sums of excitation
which flow from the mental processes.

This mental process tends to restore the psyche to a
previously held state. In pathological states, the
discharge may take the form of symptomatic acts;
in normal behavior, as well as in the pathological,
it may take the form of dreams and fantasies. For
both, however, the successful discharge results in a
conscious or unconscious gratification (reduction of
tension) which may, or may not, be associated with
the affect of pain or pleasure. Conversely, an
unsuccessful (or delayed) discharge leads to the
feeling of unpleasure. Equally, however, as Eidelberg
(1954) pointed out, a subnormal level of instinctual
tensions (below a certain threshold) may also lead

to unpleasure. This view is consistent with Freud's later formulation of the pleasure-unpleasure principle (in 1917).

Related Concepts: LAW OF CONSTANCY; UNPLEASURE-PLEASURE PRINCIPLE.

REFERENCES

Eidelberg, L., *An Outline of a Comparative Pathology of the Neuroses.* IUP, 1954.
Freud, S.: 1917, "Introductory Lectures on Psycho-Analysis." *SE*, 16:356, 1963.

421

DISPLACEMENT is a defense mechanism which permits the patient to exchange the original object for another, or to use one part of his body instead of another, the part closely connected with the repressed wish. The original narcissistic mortification, "I have no power over him or over this part of my body," is denied by accepting the narcissistic mortification, "I have no power over another object." [Eidelberg, 1954.]

In the case of a patient who picked his nose in analysis, it became an ego-syntonic habit instead of an ego-alien symptom. The analysis disclosed that his wish was to insert his finger into his anus, smell it, and let others smell it. The wish was warded off by the displacement to his nose. In this case, the selection of the nose was related to the parental prohibition in which he was told that feces had a bad smell. As a result, he used his nose as a defiant gesture: "You wanted my nose to prevent me from smelling feces. I shall defy you and obey you by picking my nose." Thus the patient's anal and exhibitionistic wishes were simultaneously gratified and warded off by the symptom. The narcissistic mortification, "I have no power to disobey my parents," was denied by accepting the narcissistic mortification, "I have no power to control my habit."

Freud (1909) offered the following case history as an example: A patient always paid his bills with clean, smooth bank notes. Asked where he got such new bills, he said that he washed and ironed them; he did not want to pay his bills with dirty notes that might contain bacteria. When asked about his sex life, the patient informed Freud that he knew a number of young girls from respectable families and

would invite them for excursions into the country. He would then invariably arrange to miss the last train and spend the night in a hotel. He used this opportunity to masturbate the young girls. When Freud inquired whether he was not afraid of infecting the girls, the patient was angry and replied that most of the girls enjoyed it. He then terminated his analytical treatment.

Freud concluded this case history by saying that his patient's abuse of girls (who were intrusted to him by their parents) was made possible by displacing the feeling of guilt to his fear of damaging other people through the use of dirty bank notes. This patient would carefully wash and iron all the bank notes he had before he used them, but had no scruples about masturbating young girls.

In manifest dreams, Freud (1900) pointed out, the dream-content replaces the latent repressed wish and represents a displacement of dangerous and forbidden impulses by harmless and ego-syntonic material.

Related Concepts: CHARACTER NEUROSIS; DEFENSE MECHANISMS; DREAMS; WRITER'S CRAMP.

REFERENCES

Eidelberg, L., *An Outline of a Comparative Pathology of the Neuroses.* IUP, p. 98, 1954.
Freud, S.: 1900, "The Interpretation of Dreams." *SE*, 5:655–656, 1953.
    1909, "Notes on a Case of Obsessional Neurosis." *SE*, 10:198, 1955.

422

"DISSOLUTION OF THE OEDIPUS COMPLEX, THE," a paper written by Freud in 1924, deals with an occurrence which is crucial to the child's development. The boy's oedipus complex, in which he desires his mother and wants to get rid of his father as a rival, develops naturally out of the phase of phallic-genital sexuality at age five (approx.), followed by the latency period, and reappearing only with the onset of puberty as genital sexuality.

The threat of castration, in time, forces the boy to give up this attitude. He is prepared for the acceptance of the castration threat by his previous experiences: cutting off of the umbilicus, weaning, and toilet training. Thus, under the threat of castration, supported by his previous experiences, and the discovery that girls lack a penis, he abandons his oedipus complex; it is repressed and in most cases entirely destroyed.

What happens in the case of a girl is almost the opposite. The castration threat prepared the way for the oedipus complex instead of destroying it. Under the influence of her penis envy, she gives up her attachment to her mother and enters the oedipus situation: she is hostile toward her mother and desirous of her father. While the discovery of a lack of a penis in females appears to be responsible for the boy repudiating his oedipal wishes, the girl may, as a result of the same discovery, develop the wish to receive a baby from her father. In other words, the same experience produces different results in boys and girls. In boys it leads to the abandonment of the oedipus complex; in girls it activates oedipal desires. Freud (1931) noted: In women the oedipus complex is not destroyed by castration threats. Therefore, the cultural consequences of the break-up and final solution of the oedipus complex is of lesser importance in women than in men.

The girl at first treats her clitoris as though it were a penis, but the discovery (by observation) that she lacks such an organ leads to feelings of inferiority that are often repressed (unconscious penis envy). The boy, on the other hand, accepts the possibility of castration, for he can see in women that they lack his organ; that is, his recognition that women are castrated and his acceptance of his own possible castration defeats his attainment of satisfaction in the oedipus complex.

Freud (1924) pointed out that the boy—when he realizes that his fixation to his mother may lead to his castration—will try to give up this fixation in order to protect his penis. Consequently, the identification replaces the original fixation to the parents. The infantile libidinal wishes become desexualized and sublimated or their aims are partially inhibited and the original sexual wish is changed into tenderness.

Related Concepts: GENITAL PHASE; PHALLIC PHASE; PREOEDIPAL.

REFERENCES

Freud, S.: 1924, "The Dissolution of the Oedipus Complex." *SE*, 19:173–179, 1961.
1931, "Female Sexuality." *SE*, 21:230, 1961.

423
DOCTOR GAME is played by children to gratify their infantile scopophilic and aggressive wishes. Later, these wishes may be sublimated and changed into the wish to help others. In relating the story of his own impetus to practice medicine, Freud said (in 1926) that he originally had no wish to become a doctor. He did not recall having played the doctor game and considered his infantile sadistic wishes not important enough to lead to the reaction formation which appears to be responsible for the need to help patients. In the beginning, Freud was chiefly interested in physiology and the need to find the truth was more important to him than therapeutic ambition. Freud was convinced that therapeutic ambition, if exaggerated, might injure the patient; the physician who was able to remain detached was better able to care for his patient.

Related Concept: SUBLIMATION.

REFERENCE

Freud, S., 1926, "Postscript to 'The Question of Lay Analysis.'" *SE*, 20:253–254, 1959.

ADDITIONAL READING

Simmel, E., "Doktorspiel, Kranksein und Ärzteberuf." *Z*, 12, 1926.

424
DORA was the first of five* extensive case histories published by Freud. Written in 1901, it was finally issued in 1905 under the title, "Fragment of an Analysis of a Case of Hysteria." The case of Dora, as it is generally called, though incomplete (broken off after only eleven weeks), was written to further his interpretation of dreams and to turn to account the hidden and repressed parts of mental life. The actual case history of Dora was used as a base; the missing parts were supplied from other models. Freud's goal was to describe the commonest cases, their most frequent and typical symptoms.

The patient was commended to Freud's care when she was nineteen by her father, who noted that Dora was subject to fits of depression, was irritable,

---

* The other four were Little Hans, the Rat Man, Schreber, and the Wolf Man.

and suffered from suicidal ideas. The father, in addition, insisted that his daughter was intent upon his breaking off their relationship with Herr K., and more particularly with Frau K., to whom Dora had formerly been quite close. The father professed no more than friendship for his old friend's wife, but events which were to be revealed in the analytic situation proved differently. Indeed, the two families had been intimate for some time, except that the father's supposed friendship for Herr K.'s wife had long since turned into a sexual liaison.

The two families were, each in their own way, deeply unhappy. Dora's mother was cold and frigid, leaving the care of Dora and the other children largely to the nurse when they were young. She was inordinately fastidious, a compulsive house cleaner. She suffered from what Freud called housewife neurosis, an indirect form of gratification for herself and revengeful discomfort for her husband. Dora's father was in his late forties, a man of unusual talents, a manufacturer in comfortable circumstances. His daughter was very attached to him, and in many ways she possessed his salient qualities. She had good critical powers, a girl of intelligence and engaging looks. But she was satisfied neither with herself nor with her family, and was given to revengeful outbursts. Perhaps her most intimate friend was Herr K.'s wife, who enriched Dora's life with many intimacies. She had formed a platonic homosexual relationship with Frau K. and had learned many of the facts (sexual) of life from her.

Herr K. did not seem to mind his wife's extramarital affair with Dora's father. He was enamoured of Dora and, since she was fourteen, had made numerous overt advances toward her. Dora was eighteen when Herr K. declared his love in a long passionate address, outlining his plan to divorce his wife and to marry her. Dora slapped his face, fled, and later complained to her parents. When they put her off, she wrote a long inflammatory letter threatening suicide, among other things. It was this latter threat which led her father to seek treatment for Dora.

Dora believed herself to have been handed over to Herr K., her middle-aged admirer, as the price of his tolerating the relationship between her father and Frau K. She was attracted to Herr K., and, at the same time, rejective of him, refusing to partake, as it were, of an affair within an affair. Freud respected Dora's resentful attitude toward her elder's erotic games. She defended herself logically and formidably, and spun her own "sound and incontestable train of argument." She claimed to detest the K. family and to be resentful of her father's behavior; yet the facts seemed clear to Freud. She was at once in love with her father, the would-be seducer (Herr K.), and with her father's mistress (Frau K.). The latter love, Freud called "the strongest unconscious current in her mental life," but though it was dominant, it was in no way overt.

When Dora was fourteen, Herr K. trapped her in his empty office, kissed and embraced her, which excited her sexually though it disgusted her, too. Thereafter, she suffered a loss of appetite, a fear of passing by any man engaged in affectionate conversation with a lady, a disgust at any form of kissing (even affectionate), a sensation of pressure on the upper part of her body, and fits of coughing or catarrh which persisted for as long as five weeks.

In singling out an event which was first in the order of Dora's recall, Freud was to reconstruct the scene with Herr K., assuming that the girl being kissed felt the erection of the man's penis, which was revolting to her. In her memory the preception of the erected penis was displaced. The obsessional character of her remembrance was formed from the undistorted recollection of the scene. Dora did not like walking past any man who seemed to be in a state of sexual excitement, for she wished to avoid seeing for a second time the somatic sign which accompanied it. The disgust (related to the memory of Herr K.'s amorous embrace) was a symptom of her repression in the erotogenic oral zone, which, in Dora's infancy, had been overindulged, resulting from the pleasure she had received from sucking. "The pressure," Freud noted, "of the erect member probably led to an analogous change in the corresponding female organ, the clitoris; and the excitation of this second erotogenic zone was referred by a process of displacement to the simultaneous pressure against the thorax and became fixed there."

Dora's attacks of coughing and aphonia were coincidental with Herr K.'s absences—at least at their outset. When the person she unconsciously loved was away, she gave up talking; speech had lost its value because she was no longer able to speak to her unrevealed lover. Later on, in an attempt to avoid the coincidence of his absence with the onset of her attacks, their periodicity changed, for otherwise their regularity would have betrayed her secret.

During the course of Dora's incomplete analysis, two dreams were analyzed by Freud; in these he was to discover much of the etiology of her problem. However, before a full disclosure could take place, Dora left analysis. In order to take revenge upon her "lover," she took her revenge on Freud (transference).

Dora identified herself unconsciously with her father, and wanted to serve in that role; namely, to be Frau K.'s lover. "The cough," Freud noted, "which no doubt originated in the first instance from a slight actual catarrh, was, moreover, an imitation of her father (whose lungs were affected), and could serve as an expression of her sympathy and concern for him. But besides this, it proclaimed aloud, as it were, something of which she may then have been still unconscious: 'I am my father's daughter. I have a catarrh, just as he has. He has made me ill, just as he has made Mother ill. It is from him that I have got my evil passions, which are punished by illness.'"

The feeling of disgust she felt when Herr K.'s erect penis pressed against her body (at fourteen) probably meant that she resented the size of her own member. That is, it represented a defense against her consciousness of penis envy. This feeling of disgust persisted, and perhaps was responsible for her refusal to play a feminine role. In this, her father and Herr K., were her competitors. They had what she had not—a penis.

Related Concepts: HYSTERICAL CONVERSION; LATENT HOMOSEXUALITY; OEDIPUS COMPLEX.

REFERENCE

Freud, S., 1905, "Fragment of an Analysis of a Case of Hysteria." *SE*, 7:30, 41–42, 82, 120, 1953.

425

DREAMS. While each dream represents a partial gratification and a partial frustration of an infantile wish, its function is to permit the subject to remain asleep. With the help of unconscious defense mechanisms, each dream tries to deal with external and internal stimuli. A thirsty sleeper who dreams that he is drinking still tries to obtain his wish-fulfillment (Freud, 1933), but finally wakes up because drinking the water in his dream does not eliminate his thirst (convenience dream). Such a dream does not eliminate the dreamer's thirst and, consequently, he has to wake up in order to gratify his need to drink. In spite of the fact that the dream failed to produce the final gratification of the wish to drink, it does indicate that the dream attempts to represent a fulfillment of a wish. Freud (1916) noted that a dream often leads to a failure because it is much more difficult for dream-work to modify the affect than the dream's content, for affects appear to be highly resistive. Whenever such a failure occurs, the dream-work tries to change the unpleasant content of the dream thoughts by imagining a fulfillment of a desire, despite the fact that the affect remains unchanged. Such dreams are characterized by the fact that there is a great difference between the affect of the dream and its content; even a dream with a harmless content, some analysts have pointed out, can be experienced as unpleasant because of the affect.

It appears that end-pleasure and unpleasure are rarely experienced without making the sleeper wake up. However, forepleasure and fore-unpleasure can be experienced in the dream. It is not clear why a pathological hallucination does not fail to gratify the psychotic and force him, in that way, to return to reality. It may be that psychotics experience in their hallucinations only forepleasure or fore-unpleasure. These two phenomena should not be confused with each other: the function of the hallucination is to deny the presence of external perceptions; the dream takes place during sleep, in which there are no external perceptions. After awakening, the sleeper usually has no difficulty in differentiating between his dream and external perceptions. Hallucinations are pathological; dreams are normal phenomena. Sleep may be considered as similar to, but not identical with, the pathological loss of consciousness.

Dreams, according to Freud (1918), are characterized "as another kind of remembering." They are subject to the laws of dream formation. In this, dreams are thought to be of two types, latent and manifest, in which the former represents the related conscious memory, and the latter represents the wish-fulfillment. The manifest dream uses *coded* derivatives to gain admittance to consciousness.

The dream is chiefly visual and uses only a few

acoustical elements. The fact that the dreamer uses visual perceptions instead of words leads to some confusion, for the pictorial presentation in the statement, "*If* I were a father," will be the same in the pictorial presentation, "I am a father." The same would be true of "I *am*" and "I *was*"; the tense does not receive pictorial presentation.

The dreamer may experience (and represent) an internal need and its gratification. The dream, in addition to providing for the instinctual tension, seems also to reject the demands of the id by presenting the ego with the possible punishment connected with the gratification. However, when the stimulus increases past a certain threshold, the dreamer awakens. Thus, the dream is able to prolong the sleep of the dreamer by offering a partial discharge of the instinctual tension, a partial denial of the guilt feelings, and a partial denial of the narcissistic mortification.

Clinical Example

A woman patient offered the following dream: She was in bed with the analyst who caressed her arms, but it felt as if he were fondling her breasts. The analysis of this manifest dream led to the following conclusion: In her session of the day before, the patient had expressed a desire to play with the analyst's penis and had felt guilty for having such a wish (day residue). This feeling of guilt probably interfered with her sleep and mobilized the dream in which the wish to play with the analyst's penis was changed into the analyst playing with her arms. The wish to play with the penis was the result of the mobilization of a sexual desire in order to ward off the aggressive desire to take away the penis from her father. Consequently, the original hostile wish was at first eroticized and then projected to the analyst: "It is not true that I want to be aggressive; the truth is that I want to caress him." Finally, the dream in effect said, reassuringly: "It is not true that I have such a wish; the truth is that the analyst has such a wish and gratifies it by caressing my arms." The emergence of the wish to caress the analyst's penis represented a narcissistic mortification ("I cannot control my sexual wishes"). The conscious memory of this narcissistic mortification was replaced by the external narcissistic mortification ("I cannot control the analyst's sexual desires").

1. Color in Dreams. Color may appear in the manifest content of the dream in the absence of any neuro-physiological disturbances. It may be present in the *original* dream and rapidly fade as the dream is remembered. Clinical and experimental evidence indicates that color is more likely to appear in dreams where there is ego or superego reinforcement of voyeuristic or color perceptions. The colors are ultimately derived from perceptual memories, selectively used in the dream work. Color may be of special importance to maintenance of self-representation and identity. Structurally, it may represent instinctual strivings and superego demands. Particular colors may be bound to certain drives and to specific affects. Repetitive color dreams are probably related to trauma, in which the color is employed or defensively incorporated as a screen [See **319**.]

2. Day Residues in Dreams. A part of the dream represents an event, experience or thought of the preceding day. Freud (1900) explained that these experiences make use of the content of dreams in order to penetrate into consciousness even during the night. According to Bergler and Jekels (1934), the day residue represents an unconscious feeling of guilt which the dreamer tries to prove unjustified. [See **401**.]

3. Dream-Work. The conception of dream work arises, Freud (1900) noted, from a comparison of the remembered manifest dream content and the latent dream thoughts, i.e., the sum of the transforming processes which have been responsible for the change from the latent to the manifest content. Freud identified the processes, as follows: condensation, displacement, representability, and secondary revision. [See **427**.]

4. Feelings in Dreams. The dream feelings are often not connected with the content of the dream. Their presence and the presence of motoric activity appear to contradict the assumption that only ideas are unconscious and indicates that feelings and motoric acts may become unconscious provided they take place in the unconscious part of the ego. These feelings often appear to be connected with the latent dream, and not with the manifest dream. For instance, a latent homosexual wish is accompanied by manifest aggressive feelings. Though the dreamer retains his aggressive feelings, he experiences an erection followed by a nocturnal emission. [See **606**.]

5. Intellectual Activity in Dreams. Those activities in the dream which appear to be the work of judgment are not the result of intellectual activity but the work of the dream thoughts which have been lifted into the manifest content of the dream. The judgments made as the result of recalling the dream form are to a large degree in the latent content of the dream. [See **922.**]

6. Moral Responsibility and Dreams. It was Freud's contention (in 1900) that there was no justification "for people's reluctance in accepting responsibility for the immorality of their dreams. When the mode of functioning of the mental apparatus is rightly appreciated and the relation between the conscious and unconscious understood, the greater part of what is ethically objectionable in our dream and phantasy lives will be found to disappear." [See **1330.**]

7. Motility in Dreams. Voluntary muscle discharges occur during sleep, such as turning or even getting up, which take place without the individual waking up. Freud (1917) believed that dreams were devoid of motor discharge and, for the most part, of motor elements. In this, it must be assumed that he was referring to the individual's inability to move. Actually, the sleeper awakens whenever external or internal stimuli pass a certain threshold. In his remarks on the metapsychology of dreams, Freud contrasted inner perception with reality (external perception), but later recognized that there was no reason to withhold the term *reality* from inner perception provided there was no confusion between inner and external perception. [See **1332.**]

8. Obliging Dreams. Freud (1920) described these dreams, in the beginning of the treatment, as anticipating the result of the treatment. Freud considered these dreams in a case of an overt homosexual female patient as obliging dreams and thought that the patient tried unconsciously to pretend to having been cured of her perversion. [See **1502.**]

9. Pair of Dreams. The result is two dreams occurring in the same night that together carry out what neither could accomplish individually (Alexander, 1925). In such a dual dream they combine to produce a wish fulfillment. Freud (1933) reasoned that the dream-wish contained some illicit action with regard to a particular person. In the first dream the person appears undisguised; in the second, the action is named without disguise. [See **1601.**]

10. Recurrent Dreams. Freud (1900) designated them as "punishment dreams" and not as "wish-fulfillment dreams." They arise, he reasoned, as the result of a conflict between vanity and self-criticism, of a conflict between the masochistic impulses of the mind and an exaggeratedly ambitious fantasy. The conflict receives its presentation in the dream, in which the masochistic element is responsible for the reversal. [See **1813.**]

11. Somatic Stimuli and Dreams. The content of some dreams are the result of somatic stimuli, which serve to fulfill a wish through the utilization of those sensations. In this, repressed instinctual impulses are expressed in the dream, a process which assures the continuation of sleep. With the diminution of repressing forces in sleep, stimuli from external or internal sources might otherwise link up with the unconscious instinctual sources and find expression. The dream serves to furnish an outlet and in that way assists in the maintenance of the sleeping state. [See **1943.**]

12. Spoken Words in Dreams. Isakower (1954) offered the hypothesis that the speech elements in dreams are direct contributions of the superego and that they contribute to the manifest content of dreams. The superego may make a condemning comment on the dream in the phase of waking up, when the process of the dream is itself focused on the reinstatement of the regime of the waking reality. Freud (1900) at first expressed the belief that all spoken communications in the dream were invariably remembered speeches from the dream material itself. [See **1948.**]

13. Traumatic Neurosis and Dreams. The dreams of these subjects usually end in the generation of anxiety, for the function of the dreams fails; i.e., the defense mechanisms implicit in the dream have failed. "It is as though," Freud (1900) noted, "these patients had not finished with the traumatic situation, as though they were still faced by its immediate task which has not been dealt with." [See **2025.**]

14. Typical Dreams. They are dreamt alike by everyone and appear to have the same meaning because they arise from the same source. Although Freud subsumed two classes for such dreams—those with the same content and those which appear to be similar but are not—it would appear that without the help of the subject's associations and their subsequent translation there is no way of arriving at a distinction between the two. In addition, Freud reasoned that typical dreams were largely responsible for the expression of fairy tales, myths, legends, etc. [See **2029**.]

15. Undisguised Dreams. They represent a repressed wish, without disguise, or without sufficient disguise, and are invariably accompanied by the anxiety which interrupts them. The anxiety takes the place of dream distortion, a condition which is typical of other dreaming states. For example, a young girl was kept on a severely limited diet, and later, while asleep, dreamed of the food she could not have until her illness had run its course. [See **2107**.]

16. Wit in Dreams. Freud (1900) believed that dreams become ingenious and amusing when a direct and easy path to the expression of the subject's thoughts is barred. He explained that the presence of wit in dreams, because of the pathological conditions under which dreams were constructed, had nothing to do with whether the subject was witty or not while he was awake. He related their psychological condition to the theory which underlies the construction of all jokes. [See **2305**.]

Related Concepts: DAYDREAMS; FANTASY; HALLUCINATIONS; ILLUSION.

REFERENCES

Alexander, F., "Dreams in Pairs and Series." *IntJPsa*, 6:446–452, 1925.
Freud, S.: 1900, "Interpretation of Dreams." *SE*, 4:165, 235, 274, 298, 445, 579–580, 620, 643, 1953.
        1916, "Introductory Lectures of Psycho-Analysis." *SE*, 15:215, 1963.
        1917, "A Metapsychological Supplement to the Theory of Dreams." *SE*, 14:227, 1957.
        1918, "From the History of an Infantile Neurosis." *SE*, 17:51, 1955.
        1920, "The Psychogenesis of a Case of Homosexuality in a Woman." *SE*, 18:164–165, 1955.
        1933, "New Introductory Lectures on Psycho-Analysis." *SE*, 22:29, 1964.
Isakower, O., "Spoken Words in Dreams. A Preliminary Communication." *Q*, 23:1–6, 1954.
Jekels, L., & E. Bergler, 1934, "Instinct Dualism in Dreams." *Q*, 9:394–414, 1940.

ADDITIONAL READINGS

Abraham, K.: "Technisches zur Traumdeutung." *BPV*, 1920.
        "Ein Beitrag zur Prufungssituation im Traume." *BPV*, 1923.
Demartino, M. F., ed., *Dreams and Personality Dynamics.*" CCT, 1959.
Dement, W. C., "Dream Recall and Eye Movement During Sleep in Schizophrenics and Normals." *JNMD*, 122, 1955.
Eisnitz, A., "Mirror Dreams." *JAPA*, 9, 1961.
Erikson, E. H., "The Dreams Specimen of Psychoanalysis." *JAPA*, 2, 1954.
Feldman, S., "Contributions to the Interpretation of a Typical Dream: Finding Money." *AnSurvPsa*, 3, 1952.
Fisher, C., "Dreams, Images, and Perception. A Study of Unconscious-Preconscious Relationships." *JAPA*, 4, 1956.
Garma, A., "Vicissitudes of the Dream Screen and the Isakower Phenomenon." *Q*, 24, 1955.
Gregory, J. C., "The Dream of Frustrated Effort." *P*, 4, 1923.
Harley, M., "The Role of the Dream in the Analysis of a Latency Child." *JAPA*, 10, 1962.
Kanzer, M.: "The Metapsychology of the Hypnotic Dream." *IntJPsa*, 34, 1953.
        "The Communicative Function of the Dream." *IntJPsa*, 36, 1955.
        "Observations on Blank Dreams with Orgasms." *Q*, 23, 1954.
Kris, E., "New Contributions to the Study of Freud's 'The Interpretation of Dreams': A Critical Essay." *JAPA*, 2, 1954.
Lewin, B., "Reconsideration of the Dream Screen." *Q*, 22, 1953.
Lind, J. E., "The Dream as a Simple Wish-Fulfillment in the Negro." *R*, 1, 1914.
Lorand, S., "Dream Interpretation in the Talmud (Babylonian and Graeco-Roman Period)." *IntJPsa*, 38, 1957.
Maeder, A., "Zur Frage der Teleologischen Traumfunktion. Eine Bemerkung zur Abwehr." *Y*, 5, 1913.
Niederland, W. G., "The Earliest Dreams of a Young Child." *PsaStC*, 12, 1957.
Pfeifer, S., "Der Traum als Hüter des Schlafes." *Z*, 9, 1923.
Prince, M., "The Mechanism and Interpretation of Dreams." *JAbP*, 5, 1910.
Rado, S., "Eine Traumanalyse." *Z*, 9, 1923.
Rangell, L., Report on Panel: "The Dream in the Practice of Psychoanalysis." *JAPA*, 4, 1956.
Richardson, G. A., & R. A. Moore, "On the Manifest Dream in Schizophrenia." *JAPA*, 11, 1963.
Roheim, G., "The Magical Function of the Dream." *IntJPsa*, 30, 1949.

Servadio, E., "A Presumptively Telepathic-Precognitive Dream During Analysis." *IntJPsa.*, 36, 1955.

Tausk, V., "Kleider und Farben im Dienste der Traumdarstellung." *Z*, 2, 1914.

426

DREAM-SCREEN, though rarely described in the literature, is defined by Lewin (1946) as a screen on which a dream appears. Patients reported that the dream was projected on a surface (screen or curtain) which, at some point, usually disappeared. A patient related: "While lying here looking at my dream, it turned over and away from me; rolled up and away from me—over and over like two tumblers."

Related Concepts: DREAMS; ISAKOWER PHENOMENON.

REFERENCE

Lewin, B. D., "Sleep, the Mouth and the Dream Screen." *Q*, 15:419–434, 1946.

ADDITIONAL READINGS

Isakower, O., "A Contribution to the Pathopsychology of Phenomena Associated With Falling Asleep." *IntJPsa*, 19, 1938.

Lewin, B.: "Inferences from the Dream Screen." *IntJPsa*, 29, 1948.

"Reconsiderations of the Dream Screen." *Q*, 22, 1953.

The Psychoanalysis of Elation. Nor, 1950.

Ryecroft, C., "A Contribution to the Study of the Dream Screen." *IntJPsa*, 32, 1951.

427

DREAM-WORK is denotative of those changes which are responsible for the transformation of unconscious thoughts in the content of the dream. The dream, in order to avoid the censorship, Freud (1900) reasoned, has to displace instinctual energy. In addition, the dream-work helps the dream find presentations which are suitable for the presentation or illustration of the dream-thoughts. Condensation is another important mechanism which is often present in the dream. The thoughts expressed in the dreams do not have to obey the rules of logic; the emotions, however, are usually less modifiable.

Related Concept: DREAMS.

REFERENCE

Freud, S., 1900, "The Interpretation of Dreams." *SE*, 5:507, 1953.

428

DRUGS. Four different categories of drugs must be considered separately, although some of the categories overlap in their properties; some drugs possess a variety of properties and are thus included in more than one category.

a. Sedative Drugs. The action of these drugs are characterized by a reduction of anxiety, reduction of the level of arousal, induction of sleepiness, and reduction in susceptibility to stressors. None of the substances exerts any action on instinctual disposition. The newer drugs differ from the older ones in that they are able to reduce the anxiety level with a relatively small tendency to induce sleepiness, and, in some instances, with lesser toxicity and addictive potency. The new drugs differ from each other in their differential effects on levels of alertness, capacity for attention, capacity for thought, induction of sleepiness, level of motor activity, and perceptual thresholds. Nevertheless, the specific spectra of properties are neither sufficiently distinct nor well-known to permit the selective prescription of an individual drug for an individual patient with an individual problem.

b. Addicting Drugs. All addicting drugs deaden psychic pain and thereby produce relief from distress, though they do not all induce somnolence. Because they anesthetize the ego, they permit the individual to detach himself from external and internal stimuli. He thus withdraws into a state which might best be called narcissistic tranquility. The drugs then act to reinforce psychic modes of detachment and to diminish the separation anxiety which such detachment tends to incur. Of course the craving for intoxication develops under the influence of oral impulses, but does not specifically determine craving. The orality may be regarded as a consequence of the regression; partial discharge is achieved through the intake of intoxicating substances. However, it cannot be considered the prime motivation for the drive toward intoxication. This motivation seems to lie rather in the need to avoid pain.

The addictive potency of the drugs which are commonly listed in this category appear to reduce the stressful responsiveness of the individual. This action facilitates the establishment of a state of narcissistic tranquility, the relief from the pain of the stress reaction. The alleviation of stress may for a short time facilitate sexual desire and feelings of potency. The principal component of the withdrawal syndrome created by these drugs establish strong physiologic dependencies, a rebound from the state of reduced stress brought about by the use of the drug.

c. *Hallucinogenic Drugs.* The ego normally corrects the sensations which it receives in such a way as to comply with its objective concept of the environment and with reality testing. Hallucinogenic drugs impair this correction, so that the process of apperception is disturbed and percepts arrive at consciousness distorted by fortuitous external circumstances, by inner needs, by affective orientation, by familiarity, and by the unconscious significance of the percepts to the individual. In even large doses, percepts from the outside fail to reach the level of consciousness. This detachment from the environment, as well as the distortion which precedes it, creates anxiety. Finally, fantasies and hallucinations derived from inner needs invade consciousness, a consciousness which is cut off from external sensations. In addition to these subjective phenomena, there are autonomic changes; perception is often greatly magnified, adding to anxiety and general distress.

A distortion of perception and a greater freedom given to fantasy originating internally has been euphemistically called "consciousness expansion." Nevertheless, the effect of these drugs may very well derive from their ability to alleviate a depression, at least temporarily. The heightened subjectivity brought about by these substances seems to be congenial to the large group of individuals who nowadays find subjective experience to be their chief goal in life. Sensation, experience in itself, seems to be a reliable source of pleasure in the face of cynicism, disillusionment and the failure of traditional values. In some groups, this orientation has led to greater involvement in society, for the purpose of deriving gratification from the personal experiences generated by social contact; in others, it has led to mystical withdrawal.

d. *True Tranquilizers and Energizers.* First, a direct immediate effect upon ego function is not visible.[1] Second, these new drugs seem to affect drive intensity. Third, they influence the clinical course of the illness in a way that drugs previously available have not been able to do. The true tranquilizers have important therapeutic value. The psychoanalyst can bring patients, hitherto inaccessible, into analysis, including, for example, schizophrenics and melancholics. Further, in the event of the reoccurrence of any of these states during the course of an on-going analysis, the condition can be alleviated often without interrupting the patient's daily visits, thus avoiding the need for hospitalization or the administration of shock treatment. Although drugs of this type appear to help resolve major pathologic states, they do not alleviate the conflict situation which brought such a state about.

The theoretical implications are as important—or more important—than the therapeutic implications. First, there is the question of how the actions of these drugs can be described metapsychologically. Sarwer-Foner[2] argued that the effects of these drugs upon somatic function influenced the psychodynamic processes in ways which were therapeutic, if the drug was properly selected, but could be pathogenic if the drug was inappropriate. Winkelman[3] described the results of observations on patients in psychotherapy in terms of the influence of these chemical substances on ego and id functions. However, he did not offer a comprehensive theory. Azima[4] suggested that instinctual drives and energies were influenced by these drugs. He believed that it was the aggressive impulses that were so affected rather than the individual.

In trying to detect the metapsychologic basis for

---

[1] Some of these substances display a sedative effect in addition to their primary tranquilizing or energizing effect. This sedative effect should not be confused with the primary effect of the drug and it is in no way related to it.

[2] Sarwer-Foner, G., "Some Therapeutic Aspects of the Use of the Neuroleptic Drugs in Schizophrenia, Borderline States and in the Short Term Psychotherapy of the Neuroses," in G. Sarwer-Foner, ed., *The Dynamics of Psychiatric Drug Therapy.* Springfield, Ill.: C. C. Thomas, 1960.

[3] Winkelman, N. W., "Chlorpromazine and Prochlorperazine During Psychoanalytic Psychotherapy: Theoretical Formulations Concerning the Ego, Energy Relationships, Anxiety, and the Psychic Therapeutic Process," in G. Sarwer-Foner, ed., *The Dynamics of Psychiatric Drug Therapy.* Springfield, Ill.: C. C. Thomas, 1960.

[4] Azima, H., "Psychodynamic and Psychotherapeutic Problems in Connection With Imipramine (Tofranil)." *JMS,* 1, 1959.

he action of these drugs, Ostow[1] was impressed by the fact that the tranquilizing drugs, given in large enough doses over long enough periods of time, in many individuals, induced melancholia or a melancholic type of schizophrenia, while the energizing drugs, similarly, induced either mania or an excited type of schizophrenia. Ostow reasoned that a drug could deprive the ego of its energies. These considerations led Ostow to develop a concept of ego libido as a significant variable in the natural history of mental illness. Among the factors which increased the supply of ego libido, he listed the following: maturation into adult life, physical well-being, success, object gratification, reward by the superego, mild frustration, and energizing drugs. The factors which reduced ego libido included: aging past the third or fourth decade, failure, object loss, narcissistic blow, detachment from the object or from the real world, superego condemnation, persistant or severe frustration, protracted or intense general adaptation syndrome, and tranquilizing drugs. Ostow also suggested that for those individuals whose regulation of ego libido was defective, pronounced fluctuations of it in a fairly regular sequence over a period of time would determine the natural history of their mental illness. The phase of conflict was the first phase of mental illness, starting in adult life. Classical considerations of pathogenesis and symptom formation were obtained. Primarily, there was an attempt to control a resurgent oedipus complex, which intruded itself into an adult object relation. If the situation was not stabilized by symptom formation, a damming up of libidinal energy occurred and might, in predisposed individuals, create a plethora syndrome. In mild forms, there was a speeding up and intensification of ego activities, a heightening of libidinal drive; generally, with objects other than the primary love object. When the syndrome achieved moderate intensity, more or less major defenses such as detachment were invoked. Even among individuals whose regulation of ego libido was poor, before there was an appreciable plethoric accumulation of libido, a corrective depletion ordinarily set in. The purpose of this depletion, to avoid a situation in which libidinal desire exists, was further intensified by the absence of a suitable

object. The depletion itself constituted a threat to the ego and the ego undertook to defend itself against it. The first form of defense employed by the ego was an intensification of sensual gratification, constituting a paradoxic hypermotivation. In other words, in the presence of a threatening libido depletion, the individual might exhibit erotomania, sexual inversion or perversion, or a symptomatic intensification of some hitherto sublimated activity. If and when this effort failed, or if it was prevented by the superego, the next step was a kind of clinging to the object in an anaclitic way. This clinging, too, represented a paradoxic intensification of motivation. The clinging presented itself as a renewed and strengthened object relation, anaclitic in form, often pregenital in quality if not in actual performance. It might take the form of neurosis or psychosis. When and if this measure failed, it gave way to a phase of angry withdrawal in which the individual repudiated the anaclitic object to whom he had previously turned, including, for example, the psychoanalyst. After the withdrawal, there followed the definitive deficiency which the individual had been fighting against, and in it we see a more or less complete paralysis of the ego; a more or less complete absence of libidinal drive. A good deal of the anger may remain, even though the patient disclaimed object desire; his behavior itself elicited the concern and care of the disappointing object.

One of the chief virtues of this scheme is that it permits the formulation of indications for drug therapy. In the phase of conflict, psychoanalysis alone is effective. There is no drug that can helpfully influence the process or the outcome of the conflict. When there is a plethora syndrome, it will be difficult to deal with it by analytic measures alone and drug therapy may be required. Obviously, in such a situation, tranquilizing drugs are called for. In the depletion states, the transference relationship may serve to support ego libido to a certain extent; interpretation may give the patient better control over the situation. However, in some individuals, interpretation is not sufficient and drug therapy may be required. We can see from this schema that the situation is brought about by a threatening depletion of libidinal energies; and, in this instance, an energizing drug is indicated rather than a tranquilizing drug. If a tranquilizing drug is given in such a state, it will assuredly reduce the hypermotivation, but in

---

[1] Ostow, M., *Drugs in Psychoanalysis and Psychotherapy.* BB, 1962.

many individuals it is likely to precipitate a phase of definitive deficiency as well. Finally, in the state of definitive deficiency, only an energizing drug is called for.[1]

There are many individuals whose ego-libido control remains good so that neither plethora depletion nor deficiency appears. However, many such individuals tend to deal with an intransigent phase of conflict by retreating into a state of narcissism, in which they detach themselves more or less completely in an affective way from all significant objects. The patient may be suffering from a character neurosis, a classical neurosis, or from a psychosis. For example, the individual may simply seem to be an aloof, remote, but an otherwise unremarkable individual; he may phobically avoid contact with other individuals; or he may be a hebephrenic schizophrenic. As a result of the detachment, he achieves a certain amount of tranquility, which reflects itself in psychic changes, and in such phenomena as obesity, in later afternoon torpor, and in hypererotism leading to frequent masturbation. This situation is most difficult to handle therapeutically, and, unfortunately, neither tranquilizers nor energizers are of any value in dealing with it. The reason is, as follows: the state does not reflect or is not brought about by deviation of ego libido. To the contrary, not infrequently such a state is brought about by the administration of a drug to a patient with deviant ego libido, restoring thereby the ego libido status to normal. In effect, the state of narcissism which gave rise to the ego-libido deviation in the first place may thus be reestablished. That is why many patients successfully treated with drugs complain of obesity and afternoon fatigue.

It is quite clear from these considerations that the essential factor in the determination of whether drugs are effective, or which drug is indicated, must be left to an analysis of the state of ego libido. These deviations of ego libido may give rise to any of a number of nosologic entities, depending upon the predisposition of the individual involved. However,

conventional diagnostic terms are irrelevant to the selection of therapeutic drugs and the monitoring of their effects.

—Mortimer Ostow, M.D

429

DYNAMIC APPROACH denotes an examination of the operation and balance of the forces causing psychological phenomena, which, according to Freud, may be viewed in terms of the increase and decrease of instinctual tension and the damming-up or free discharge; concomitantly, the pleasure-unpleasure principle may be viewed in terms of the individual trying to eliminate tension above a certain threshold (homeostasis). The concept of compromise formation is an expression of the dynamic approach. Freud (1915) differentiated between those phenomena caused by external stimuli and those due to internal stimuli. Freud pointed out that in order to file the data gained in analysis a number of complicated postulates were employed. All these postulates are biological and they are based on a teleological approach. The nervous system, for instance, serves the need of elimination of stimuli or at least of reducing their intensity. Consequently, it is assumed that the nervous system aims at the mastery of stimuli. Following the introduction of the concept of instinctual energies, external stimuli are considered to be responsible for making the individual avoid them, while instinctual stimuli, present within the individual, are not to be mastered by avoidance. These inner stimuli may, therefore, make greater demands on the central nervous system than the external stimuli; they cannot be completely avoided, as is the case with certain external stimuli.

Related Concepts: ECONOMIC APPROACH; METAPSYCHOLOGY; SYSTEMATIC (QUANTITATIVE OR DESCRIPTIVE) APPROACH.

REFERENCE

Freud, S., 1915, "Instincts and Their Vicissitudes." *SE*, 14:118–120, 1957.

---

[1] There are some who claim that in agitated depression large doses of tranquilizing drugs together with anti-Parkinsonian drugs will alleviate the depression. This technique must be investigated further.

E

500

ECONOMIC APPROACH, according to Freud (1915), is an examination of the quantity and quality of psychic energy. Although the quantity of psychic energy cannot be measured, it can be estimated in relative terms. In a later paper, Freud (1923) noted: "We have found—that is, we have been obliged to assume—that very powerful mental processes or ideas exist (and here a quantitative or *economic* factor comes into question for the first time) which can produce all the effects in mental life that ordinary ideas do (including effects that can in their turn become conscious as ideas), though they themselves do not become conscious."

Freud (1931) assumed that the differences between the erotic, narcissistic, and obsessional types were caused by the quantitatively different distribution of psychic energy between the id, ego, and superego. Freud identified frustration and internal conflicts, those arising between the three physical agencies and their libidinal economy as the determinants.

Hartmann (1964) discussed the economic approach in terms of the quantitative differences in psychic energy, as follows: "The concept of mental energy was then elaborated in the sense that it is the drives that are the main sources of energy in what Freud calls the 'mental apparatus.' However, a strictly quantifying approach to these energic problems has so far not been developed. Or rather: while it is possible to speak of a greater or lesser degree of, let's say, a resistance (against the uncovering of some hidden material), we have no way of measuring it. To account for the difference in the unconscious and the conscious (and preconscious) processes Freud postulated two forms of energy distribution, conceptualized as, respectively, primary and secondary processes. The primary processes represent a tendency to immediate discharge, while the secondary processes are guided by the consideration of reality. This distinction is again both theoretically significant and clinically quite helpful. The thesis that behavior is to be explained also in terms of its energic cathexis is what we call, in analysis, the economic viewpoint."

Related Concepts: Dynamic Approach; Metapsychology; Systematic (Qualitative or Descriptive) Approach.

REFERENCES

Freud, S.: 1915, "Instincts and Their Vicissitudes." *SE*, 14:152–153, 202, 1957.
1923, "The Ego and the Id." *SE*, 19:14, 1961.
1931, "Libidinal Types." *SE*, 21:220, 1961.
Hartmann, H., *Essays on Ego Psychology*. IUP, p. 327, 1964.

ADDITIONAL READING

Rado, S., "The Economic Principle in Psychoanalytic Technique." *IntJPsa*, 6, 1925.

501

EGO represents that part of the personality which serves as an honest broker between the id, the superego, and the external world; it controls motility and seeks to achieve a reasonable compromise between their needs. The term is also used by many authors to designate the total personality; e.g., certain wishes are ego-syntonic and ego-alien. To these authors, the ego, in this instance, becomes the total personality. Strachey (1961) discussed this double use in Freud's work, noting that he frequently equated the ego and the self. Finally, however, Freud drew a clear distinction—in "Some Additional Notes upon Dream-Interpretation as a Whole"—between the two, i.e., between the two uses of the German word *Ich.*

Metapsychologically, part of the ego is considered to be conscious, and part unconscious. The unconscious part together with the id is responsible for the unconscious defense mechanisms; whereas, the preconscious and conscious are responsible for the decisions and actions of the total personality. In addition to this function, in which the ego is but an aspect of the total personality, we assume that it has an autonomous zone. Economically, under normal conditions, the ego is cathected by secondary narcissistic libido and destrudo; or, according to Hartmann (1958), by neutral (indifferent) libido and destrudo.

Freud (1940), in one of the last of his essays, identified the ego as an intermediary agency of the psychical apparatus between the id and the external world. Its role as regards external events is directed toward bringing about changes in the external world which are to its own advantage. As to internal events, the ego attempts to achieve mastery over the instinctual demands; it achieves this aim by satisfying, postponing, or repressing these instinctual demands. In this, it is guided, as Freud stated, "by consideration of the tensions produced by stimuli, whether these tensions are present in it or introduced into it."

Developmentally, as Glover (1939) noted, the "infant has to abandon an almost animal state of existence in favour of civilized reactions that were established only after thousands of years of painful racial experience. When the pace of this civilizing process is too hot for the infant or when his primitive instincts are too strong, trouble is certain to brew. Either the infant is compelled to make premature adaptations to society, as represented by the grownups in his family, in which case a precocious but essentially weak ego develops: or, in the case where primitive instincts are powerfully charged, the ego is retarded in development and is unable to cope with or master the excitations to which it is subjected. It is at this point that constitutional factors

exert their maximum influence, in particular the capacity to withstand frustration." A. Freud (1936) discussed the ego's capacity to evade stimuli, as follows: "Instead of perceiving the painful impression and subsequently cancelling it by withdrawing its cathexis, it is open to the ego to refuse to encounter the dangerous external situation at all. It can take to flight and so, in the truest sense of the word, 'avoid' the occasions of 'pain'. The mechanism of avoidance is so primitive and natural and moreover so inseparably associated with the normal development of the ego that it is not easy, for purposes of theoretical discussion, to detach it from its usual context and to view it in isolation."

Eidelberg (1957) suggested that the ego may be divided into three parts: (a) external ego, which contains the presentation of the external world, as reflected by the function of our sense organs; (b) central ego, having all the functions hitherto attributed to the ego; and (c) body ego, presentation of the body.

Related Concepts: CHOICE OF A NEUROSIS; ID; SUPEREGO.

REFERENCES

Eidelberg, L., "An Introduction to the Study of the Narcissistic Mortification." *PQ*, 31:657–668, 1957.

Freud, A., 1936, *The Ego and The Mechanisms of Defence.* IUP, pp. 100–101, 1946.

Freud, S., 1940, "An Outline of Psycho-Analysis." *SE*, 23:145–146, 1964.

Glover, E., *Psycho-Analysis.* SP, p. 22, 1939.

Hartmann, H., *Ego Psychology and the Problem of Adaptation.* IUP, pp. 171–172, 1958.

Strachey, J., "Editorial note." *SE*, 19:8, 1961.

ADDITIONAL READINGS

Adatto, C. P., "Ego Reintegration Observed in Analysis of Late Adolescents." *IntJPsa*, 39, 1958.

Alpert, A., & S. Krown, "Treatment of a Child With Severe Ego Restrictions in a Therapeutic Nursery." *PsaStC*, 8, 1953.

Arlow, J.: "Ego Psychology." *AnSurvPsa*, 1, 1950.
    "Ego Psychology and the Study of Mythology." *JAPA*, 3, 1961.

Erikson, E. H., "The Problem of Ego Identity." *JAPA*, 4, 1956.

Federn, P., "Ego Psychology and the Psychoses." *AnSurvPsa*, 4, 1953.

Friend, M. R., "Problems of Early Ego Development (Panel)." *AnSurvPsa*, 2, 1951.

French, T. M., "Defense and Synthesis in the Function of the Ego. Some Observations Stimulated by Anna Freud's *The Ego and the Mechanisms of Defense*." *Q*, 7, 1938.

Freud, A., "The Mutual Influences in the Development of Ego and Id: Introduction to the Discussion." *PsaStC*, 7, 1952.

Freud, S., 1926, "The Question of Lay Analysis." *SE*, 20, 1959.

Gitelson, M., "On Ego Distortion." *IntJPsa*, 29, 1958.

Grauer, D., "How Autonomous is the Ego?" *JAPA*, 6, 1958.

Greenacre, P., "Regression and Fixation? Considerations Concerning the Development of the Ego." *JAPA*, 8, 1960.

Hartmann, H., "Comments on the Psychoanalytic Theory of the Ego." *PsaStC*, 1950.

Hoffer, W., "Development of the Body Ego." *PsaStC*, 5, 1950.

Kris, E., "Ego Psychology and Interpretation in Psychoanalytic Therapy." *Q*, 20, 1951.

Loewenstein, R. M., "Conflict and Autonomous Ego Development During the Phallic Phase." *PsaStC*, 5, 1950.

Marmor, J., "Some Comments on Ego Psychology." *JHH*, 7, 1958.

Peller, L., "The Concept of Play and Ego Development." *IntJPsa*, 1954.

Rank, B., & D. MacNaughton, "A Clinical Contribution to Early Ego Development." *PsaStC*, 5, 1950.

Rapaport, D., "The Theory of Ego Autonomy: A Generalization." *BMC*, 22, 1958.

Saul, L. J., "The Ego in a Dream." *Q*, 22, 1953.

Sterba, R. F., "Das Schicksal des Ichs im Therapeutischen Verfahren." *Z*, 20, 1934.

502

EGO-ALIEN is denotative of those derivatives of the unconscious which give rise to neurotic symptoms, parapraxes, and dreams. In this, they are characterized by symptoms in which the superego and the id play decisive roles. For instance, when the id impulses are warded off with the help of repression and denial, the instinctual impulses are repressed. "That is to say, it [the ego] has withdrawn its interest from them and shut them off from becoming conscious and from obtaining satisfaction by motor discharge" (Freud, 1923). Their derivatives, however, still arouse the resistance of the total personality and the patient is aware that he is suffering from a disorder. In neurotic character traits, on the other hand, the instinctual impulses are modified in such a manner that they are assimilated, i.e., they become ego-syntonic.

Eidelberg (1954) offered the following example of an ego-alien symptom: "The patient's blushing started after puberty. His first sexual intercourse took place when he was twenty-two years old. He did not have a full erection in this attempt, and his emission took place immediately after he entered into the vagina. . . . By mobilization of the opposite instinct fusion, this sexual wish to see his mother urinating was turned into an aggressive one, which was then turned against the self, changing into. 'I want my mother to ridicule me when I urinate.' Finally, the original inspectionistic wish, as well as the aggressive exhibitionistic wish, were mobilized as a countercathexis and displaced to the face." The patient was thus subject to spells of pathological blushing (conversion symptom).

Related Concept: EGO-SYNTONIC.

REFERENCES

Eidelberg, L., *An Outline of a Comparative Pathology of the Neuroses*. IUP, pp. 159–60, 1954.

Freud, S., 1923, "Two Encyclopedia Articles." *SE*, 18:246, 1955.

503

EGO AND SELF. The term ego, originally used as a synonym of self, was employed by Freud after he introduced the structural approach to cover one part of the self. Today, the two are no longer synonyms. Thus, Hartmann (1964) noted: "The one refers to the self (one's own person) in contradistinction to the object; the second to the ego (as a psychic system) in contradistinction to other substructures of personality." It may be further stated that self-cathexis and not ego-cathexis is the opposite of object-cathexis. Despite the fact that Hartmann specifies that the ego interests as hardly ever unconscious and regards them as preconscious or conscious, the clinical approach seems to indicate that the counter-cathexis employed in the defense mechanism is partly unconscious. For instance, a patient suffering from the compulsion to wash his hands every five minutes is aware that he has such a compulsion but the idea that this compulsion is directed against the wish to be dirty is fully unconscious. It seems that even if an obsessional had a vague idea of the unconscious meaning of his compulsion, he would also have to be aware of the presence of the anal wish. The same is true in other neurotic symptoms. An agoraphobic patient knows that he is afraid to cross the street, but develops a strong resistance when the analyst attempts to show him that he is not afraid of being run over by a car but of the presence of his wish to be killed. However, it appears to be true that the resistance against the consciousness of the countercathexis is weaker than the resistance against consciousness of the id wish.

An analysis of slips of the tongue, according to Eidelberg (1960), shows clearly that the resistance against the meaning of the word which was eliminated is greater than the resistance against the substituted word. For instance, a patient took his girl friend out to dinner and wanted to ask for a table. He made a slip, substituting the word *room* for the word *table*. It was relatively easy for the patient to realize that the word *room* represented his wish to have sexual intercourse in addition to eating but only after a strong resistance was he able to realize why he avoided the seemingly innocuous word *table*.

In discussing the strength of the ego, it is necessary to make clear whether part of the personality or the total personality is considered. An overly strong ego which dominates the total personality may actually weaken the self. The harmonic type is an individual who is able to achieve a complete compromise solution which satisfies all three parts of his personality. [Freud, 1931.]

Related Concepts: CENSORSHIP; RESISTANCE; STRUCTURAL (TOPOGRAPHIC) APPROACH.

REFERENCES

Eidelberg, L., "A Third Contribution to the Study of Slips of the Tongue." *IntJPsa*, 41:596–603, 1960.
Freud, S., 1931, "Libidinal Types." *SE*, 21:219, 1961.
Hartmann, H., *Essays On Ego Psychology*. IUP, pp. 127, 136, 1964.

504

EGO AND SENSORIUM. All external stimuli are perceived by the sense organs and are linked with the innervation at the motor end by the mnemic system. The memory traces present in the mnemic system, however, achieve presentation through the system *Pcpt*. Thus, the new stimuli may be received by the system *Pcpt*. because the old stimuli are present in the mnemic system and are temporarily unconscious. Freud (1900) likened the system to a reflex process, calling it the "model of every psychical function." The perceptions which impinge on the psychical apparatus are memory traces, and constitute what is commonly referred to as memory. The system consists of permanent modifications of the elements in the system, of which one end "in the very front of the apparatus receives the perceptual stimuli but retains no trace and thus no memory, while behind it there lies a second system which transforms the momentary excitations of the first system into permanent traces."

Related Concepts: EGO; PERCEPTION; REPRESSION.

REFERENCE

Freud, S., 1900, "The Interpretation of Dreams." *SE*, 5:537–539, 1953.

505

EGO AND SENSE ORGAN PERCEPTION. The infant appears to be able to separate pleasure from unpleasure and later to differentiate between the inside and the outside of his person. Finally, he learns to experience the so-called objective qualities of external objects without reference to them as a source of pleasure or unpleasure.

The ability to form an abstract concept of an external object is achieved with the help of the sense organs. With the sense of smell, however, the ability to form abstract qualities appears to be lacking; the individual does not produce objective data from olfactory stimuli and consequently has to use such statements as *pleasant*, *unpleasant*, etc. In examining sense organ perceptions in their relationship to the ego, it is necessary to separate the actual perception of the senses from the reaction of the total personality. The individual's ability to form and to use *objective qualities* is augmented by his capacity to form an *abstract* of a set of objects. This ability is essential to his recognition of the basic function and meaning of a new object, whether the new object has been previously perceived or not. The concept of *chair-object* does not, for instance, refer to a specific chair but to a class of chair-like items. What is neralized is their quality; that is, that part of the tality which cannot be further divided and which present in all objects belonging to that class. idelberg, 1928.]

Related Concepts: DAYDREAMS; THINKING.

FERENCES

Eidelberg, L., "Die Empfindung Nass und Trocken," in *Zeitschrift für die gesamte Neurologie und Psychiatrie.* Berlin: Verlag von Julius Springer, p. 583, 1928.

506
EGO BOUNDARIES denote phenomenological

cts, according to Federn (1952), in which the ego ppears to extend as far as the feelings of the unity the ego allows. This feeling sharply distinguishes erything that belongs to the ego in an actual mo- ent of life from all other psychic elements. Thus, e feeling of the ego unit is viewed, in Federn's nceptualization, as due to a coherent ego cathexis. this, the ego boundaries are not static but con- nuously changing as the peripheral sensory part of e mental apparatus undergoes changes under the npact of constant stimulation from internal and ternal sources. The organ, changing under the npact of this constant stimulation, retains some ecific trace of the new impression as an engram nemory trace). When these ganglionary elements n no longer be modified by new stimuli, they react nmediately (if briefly) and thereafter return to their evious biological state. Thus, conscious, in his ew, is substituted for the storage of memories.

Federn characterized the ego as a dynamic entity, which the ego boundary is limited by the organ- m's peripheral sensory organs, and that the ego oundary undergoes an increased cathexis when iced with a current problem. Federn extends the go boundary inwardly toward the superego and the l tendencies, but identifies the boundary which xtends toward the outside world as the more nportant, especially as delineated in those persons f importance for the subject in the outside world nd to those boundaries which are derived from the ensation of the subject's own body. These boun- aries do not coincide with body boundaries, for it ay extend beyond them, as illustrated in the act of

a blind person tapping a cane on the floor wherein the hardness and softness (to name only two) of the floor are experienced as occurring at the end of the cane. The ego boundary might, as well, include an actor on the stage, in that any injury to the actor's person is perceived as occurring to the viewer (Sperling, 1944). In a situation of physical trauma, on the other hand, the boundaries of the body are withdrawn (Sperling, 1950). In schizophrenia, as Bleuler (1911) pointed out, a delusional fusion of the subject with another person (object) may occur. This is a condi- tion which is especially true in the case of symbiotic childhood schizophrenia (Mahler, 1958).

Related Concept: EGO.

REFERENCES

Bleuler, E., 1911, *Dementia Praecox or the Group of Schizophrenia.* IUP, 1950.
Federn, P., *Ego Psychology and the Psychoses.* BB, pp. 222, 223, 331, 1952.
Mahler, M. S., "Autism and Symbiosis, Two Extreme Disturbances of Identity." *AJP,* 29:77–83, 1958.
Sperling, O.: "On Appersonation." *IntJPsa,* 25:128– 132, 1944.
        "The Interpretation of the Trauma as a Com- mand." *Q,* 19:352–370, 1950.

507
EGO FUNCTIONS. The principal task of the

ego is self-preservation. The reality testing, which is essential for self-preservation, was originally con- sidered to be a function of the superego. The ego secures the postponement of instinctual discharges with the help of thinking and, thus, permits the reality principle to replace the pleasure principle.

Developmentally, Freud (1925) considered there to be two egos. The first is the pleasure-ego which seeks to introject into it everything that is good and to reject all that is bad. The other develops out of the pleasure ego. This second reality-ego is concerned with testing for the real existence of things. What is perceived is taken into the ego on the basis of "whether something which is in the ego as a presen- tation can be rediscovered in perception (reality)." Freud called it a question, once again, of distin- guishing between what was externally or internally perceived. When this distinction has been arrived at, the pleasure principle has been set aside. The functions which are inherent in what Freud called judgment, both internal and external, have superseded it.

Related Concepts: ID; SUPEREGO.

REFERENCE

Freud, S., 1925, "Negation." *SE*, 19:236–239, 1961.

ADDITIONAL READINGS

Linn, L., "The Discriminating Function of the Ego." *Q*, 23, 1954.
Peto, A., "The Fragmentizing Function of the Ego in the Transference Neurosis." *IntJPsa*, 42, 1961.
Sheppard, E., & L. Saul, "An Approach to a Systematic Study of Ego Function." *Q*, 27, 1958.
Silverman, S., "Ego Functions and Bodily Reactions." *JAPA*, 10, 1962.

508

EGO-IDEAL. Freud (1914) first used the term descriptively, noting that its task was one of watching the actual ego and measuring it by that ideal. Later, in introducing the topographic approach to psychoanalysis, he (in 1923) rechristened it and named it as one aspect of that agency which constitutes the superego. Freud drew a distinction between the ego-ideal and the agency concerned with its enforcement. Still later, in 1933, Freud identified the ego-ideal as the vehicle by which the ego measures itself. Nonetheless, Freud considered the superego to be unconscious, consisting of the conscience and the ego-ideal. Even so, on occasion, he continued to use the two terms synonymously.

Related Concept: SUPEREGO.

REFERENCES

Freud, S.: 1914, "On Narcissism: An Introduction." *SE*, 14:95–96, 1957.
1923, "The Ego and the Id." *SE*, 19:28, 1961.
1933, "New Introductory Lectures on Psycho-Analysis." *SE*, 22:66–67, 1964.
Strachey, J., Editorial note. *SE*, 19:9–10, 1961.

509

EGO INSTINCTS. Freud introduced the term in a paper written in 1910: the ego instincts were identified as the self-preservative instincts, an expres-sion of the nonsexual drives such as eating, defeca-ing, urinating, etc.* With the introduction of th concept of narcissism in 1914, a complication aros Freud advanced the idea that narcissistic-libid cathects the ego, as opposed to object-libido whi cathects the object. Since his original concept was dualistic one, in which the sexual instincts (libid were identified as separate and distinct from the e instincts, Freud (1920) revised his thesis and declar that "narcissistic libido was of course a manifest tion of the force of the sexual instincts . . . to identified with the self-preservative instincts." (T primary instinct of Thanatos [destrudo] was add later.)

In identifying the ego instincts, Freud (191 stated: "No objection can be made to anyone employing the concept of an instinct of play or destruction or of gregariousness." Despite th broadness of this view, he had only one essenti limitation to place upon it. In identifying the sour of those instincts, whether libidinal or self-prese vative, the search was to the primal instincts, f only they could claim importance.

The sexual instincts emanate from a variety organic sources, and their aim is the attainment organ-pleasure. The ego instincts, on the other han provide the path by which they receive presentatio "A portion of them remains associated with eg instincts throughout life and furnishes them wit libidinal components." This is most clearly seen b the onset of illness. "The sick man withdraws h libidinal cathexes back into his own ego, and sen them out again when he recovers." For instance, h withdraws his libidinal interest from his love obje so long as he suffers; he ceases to love.

In sleep, which resembles illness "in implyin a narcissistic withdrawal of the positions of th libido on to the subject's own self," we have, nothing else, Freud (1917) noted, "examples changes in the distribution of libido that are cons quent upon a change in the ego." The egotism sleep fits this concept. "Thus, we know that dream are completely egoistic and that the person wh plays the chief part in their scenes is always to b recognized as the dreamer."

Related Concept: LIBIDO.

---

* In this early paper, *ego* is used to denote the *total person ality*.

REFERENCES

Freud, S.: 1910, "The Psycho-Analytic View of Psychogenic Disturbances of Vision." *SE*, 11:214, 1957.

1914, "On Narcissism: An Introduction." *SE*, 14:82, 83, 1957.

1915, "Instincts and Their Vicissitudes." *SE*, 14:124, 126, 1957.

1917, "A Metapsychological Supplement to the Theory of Dreams." *SE*, 14:223, 1957.

1920, "Beyond the Pleasure Principle." *SE*, 18:50, 1955.

ADDITIONAL READINGS

Eidelberg, L., *An Outline of a Comparative Pathology of the Neuroses. IUP*, 1954.

Freud, S.: 1905, "Three Essays on the Theory of Sexuality." *SE*, 7, 1953.

1923, "New Introductory Lectures on Psycho-Analysis." *SE*, 22, 1964.

Glueck, B., "The Ego Instinct (Symposium on the Relative Roles in Psychopathology of the Ego, Herd and Sex Instincts." *JAbP*, 16, 1921.

510

EGO STRENGTH AND WEAKNESS. The ego, as Freud (1923) pointed out, serves three masters and is consequently menaced by three dangers: from the external world, from the id, and from the super-ego. The ego mediates between the id wishes and the external world. Neurotics utilize the *Pcs.* rationalizations to clothe the id's *Ucs.* and thus disguise the id's conflict with reality. Through the processes of identification and sublimation, the ego strives to do the id's bidding, which results in a defusion of the instincts and a liberation of the aggressive instincts in the superego. In submitting to the ego's dread of the superego, it must succumb to the fear of conscience, to the superior being which turned into the ego-ideal that once threatened castration.

In order to function, the ego requires cooperation from the id and the superego. This cooperation is possible only if at least some of the id needs and some of the demands of the superego are gratified on a conscious level. The reality principle can function only on a conscious level through an examination of external reality, a recognition of instinctual needs, and of the demands of the superego. The consciousness of inner reality eliminates the remnants of the infantile superego and protects the adult from having an ego-alien superego.

The fact that part of the ego is unconscious makes possible its participation in unconscious compromises between the id and the superego, to permit the gratification of infantile wishes and the acceptance of punishment by the superego. As a result of such compromises, the ego is invaded from the id and from the superego and, in trying to deal with the two invaders, has to tolerate the result of the unconscious defenses. Consequently, the analytical aim consists of making the patient face what he prefers to hide, teaching him to reject infantile wishes, and to tolerate infantile narcissistic mortifications. Not only a weak ego but an overly strong ego may result in a weak personality.

Related Concepts: ID; REPRESSION; REPUDIATION; SUPEREGO; TOTAL PERSONALITY.

REFERENCE

Freud, S., 1923, "The Ego and the Id." *SE*, 19:55–58, 1961.

ADDITIONAL READING

Eriksen, C. W., "Psychological Defenses and 'Ego Strength' in the Recall of Completed and Incompleted Tasks." *ASP*, 49, 1954.

511

EGO-SYNTONIC is denotative of that behavior which the individual considers as compatible with the integrity or ethical standards of the self. In outlining the conflicts which lead to neuroses, Freud (1923) noted that disorders occur when conflicts arise between the ego and those sexual impulses which seem not to be in harmony with the ego. "Since these impulses are not *ego-syntonic*, the ego has *repressed them*." In other words, the patient is suffering from ego-alien formations (neurotic symptoms).

The analysis of such patients revealed, as well, that ego-syntonic formations which were accepted by the patient, although they appeared to have a similar structure to neurotic symptoms, represented the end result of unconscious defense mechanisms, in which the ego-part played a decisive role. On the other hand, in symptoms where the superego or id play the decisive role, the end result was ego-alien.

Freud (1917) was forced to try to analyze the character traits (ego-syntonic formations) despite the patient's resentment of such an analysis. There was a strong resistance to an understanding of their unconscious meaning.

Today, a number of ego-syntonic phenomena can be successfully analyzed provided the patient is able and willing to cooperate. These ego-syntonic traits are usually divided in the following manner: (a) neurotic character traits: pedantry, parsimony, obstinacy, etc.; (b) addiction: morphine, cocaine, alcohol, etc.; (c) psychopathy; (d) borderline cases; and (e) psychotic character.

It would seem that the choice between a symptom neurosis and a neurotic character trait or other ego-syntonic formation depends upon the libidinal type to which the patient belongs. Individuals who belong to the narcissistic type will usually use ego-syntonic rather than ego-alien defenses. The unconscious defenses will produce symptoms in patients who belong to the erotic or obsessional type.

Related Concepts: CHOICE OF A NEUROSIS; NARCISSISTIC MORTIFICATION; SYNTHESIS.

REFERENCES

Freud, S.: 1917, "General Theory of the Neuroses." *SE*, 16:350, 1963.
    1923, "Two Encyclopaedia Articles." *SE*, 18:246, 1955.

512

EJACULATIO PRÆCOX is a form of potency disturbance characterized by premature emission of semen before or immediately after intramission of the penis during sexual intercourse. This symptom may show all degrees of severity, and is often associated with disturbances of sensation and lack of rhythmic expulsion. While organic factors may occasionally be present, the majority of cases are undoubtedly psychogenic. In these cases, as Abraham (1917) noted, full genital intercourse is often equated with masturbation; the fixation is on an incestuous object and therefore prohibited by the superego. In addition, there are powerful regressive impulses to wet or soil in an exhibitionistic and defiant manner. There is frequently a history of enuresis, and the manner of ejaculation resembles micturition. Orgastic sensations may be located in the perineum rather than in the shaft of the penis, especially in cases with pronounced feminine identification.

Because of an unconscious sado-masochistic conception of coitus, there is enormous anxiety concerning retaliatory castration and fear of the female genitalia. An additional factor may be a refusal to give love to the object, associated with the wish to disappoint or cheat the partner. Such a refusal may be caused by oral, anal or phallic wishes. The reasons for this particular form of disturbance may be connected with infantile omnipotence which forces the patient to seek premature (immediate) gratification.

"We learn," Abraham noted, "—apart from those reminiscences relating to the strongly accentuated pleasure connected with the voluntary passing of urine in childhood—that it had been a difficult task to train these patients in habits of cleanliness, that even in adult age they often passed urine involuntarily in smaller or larger quantities, that they were bed-wetters up to a late period of childhood, and that they easily react to excitement of any kind with an irresistible desire to urinate. The same persons who have gained control only later on or imperfectly over the functions of the bladder also tend to have a premature and precipitate emission of semen. According to their own account, the physical sensation of premature emission is identical with that of urinary incontinence."

Eidelberg (1954) described ejaculatio praecox as a defense mechanism, in which "the sexual wish to urinate is made aggressive through mobilization of the opposite instinct tension, and becomes, 'I want to soil my mother.' The active wish becomes passive, 'I want to soil myself.' As a result of the aggressive tension, the erection is incomplete. The semen becomes the unconscious representation of urine, and the emission takes place too early."

Related Concepts: IMPOTENCE; NOCTURNAL ENURESIS.

REFERENCES

Abraham, K., 1917, "Ejaculatio Praecox." *SPA*, p. 282, 1927.
Eidelberg, L., *An Outline of a Comparative Pathology of the Neuroses.* IUP, p. 160, 1954.

ADDITIONAL READINGS

Fenichel, O., *The Psychoanalytic Theory of Neurosis.* Nor, 1945.
Freud, S., 1895, "On the Grounds for Detaching a Particular Syndrome from Neurasthenia Under the Description 'Anxiety Neurosis.' " *SE*, 3, 1962.
Tausk, V., "Bemerkungen zu Abraham's Aufsatz," in *Über Ejaculatio Praecox Z*, 4, 1916.

513

EJACULATIO RETARDATA is a form of potency disturbance in the male which is characterized by an unwanted and often unpleasant delay in reaching orgasm; the predominant unconscious motive is to withold the semen (which unconsciously represents food or feces) from the partner. It is related to ejaculatio praecox, and to impotentia ejaculandi, another form of impotence, in which no emission occurs.

Ejaculatio retardata is often connected with narcissistic and sado-masochistic object relations. In addition, ejaculation may be unconsciously equated with the danger of castration, loss of sphincter control, or loss of identity in the union with the partner at orgasm.

Fenichel (1945) noted: "The disturbance *ejaculatio retardata* has, as a rule, more of the character of a true conversion symptom."

Related Concepts: IMPOTENCE; ORGASTIC IMPOTENCE.

REFERENCE

Fenichel, O., *The Psychoanalytic Theory of Neurosis.* Nor, pp. 172–173, 1945.

ADDITIONAL READINGS

Abraham, K., 1917, "Ejaculatio Praecox." *SPA*, 1950.
Balint, M., "Eros and Aphrodite." *IntJPsa*, 19, 1938.
Simmel, E., "Der Coitus Interruptus und sein Gegenstück, der Coitus prolongatus." *Z*, 18, 1932.

514

ELATION is an affective state characterized by strong feelings of self-esteem, optimism, and joy. Elation represents an increased libidinal cathexis of the self-presentation, the additional cathexis being obtained from the superego, from the love of a highly cathected external object, or from both. Ego boundaries are enlarged; the ego moves toward fusion with the superego or with the object.

Elation may be normal or abnormal. Normal elation, for example, may be occasioned by being in love or scoring a triumph. Pathological elation is seen in hypomanic states and in the manic-depressive psychoses. In psychotic states, elation is part of a libidinal defense against destructive impulses with structural regression. In mania, the ego and the ego-ideal are fused together so that the subject enjoys his triumph without considering others and without suffering from self-reproaches (Freud, 1921).

The ego and the superego fusion reproduces, on an intrapsychic level, the original union with the mother's breast; the self representation takes over the libidinal cathexis formerly belonging to the superego. There is regression to the stage of the so-called pleasure ego; the tendency is to perceive sources of pleasure as being within the ego. Libidinal regression to the oral stage occurs. The external world is "devoured" in what may be an insatiable fashion; denial is employed as the major defense against the corresponding wish to be devoured by the superego, or to destroy it and the external objects it represents.

Related Concept: DENIAL (DISAVOWAL).

REFERENCE

Freud, S., 1921, "Group Psychology and the Analysis of the Ego." *SE*, 18:132, 1955.

ADDITIONAL READINGS

Blitzstein, N., "Amphithymia, Some Syndromes of Elations and Depressions." *ANP*, 36, 1936.
Freud, S.: 1917, "Mourning and Melancholia." *SE*, 14, 1957.
       1930, "Civilization and Its Discontents." *SE*, 21, 1961.
Harrison, I., "A Clinical Note on a Dream Followed by Elation." *JAPA*, 8, 1960.
Lewin, B., *The Psychoanalysis of Elation*, Nor, 1950.
Rochlin, G., "The Disorder of Depression and Elation." *JAPA*, 1, 1953.

515

EMOTION is one of the derivatives of the instinctual drive and represents the tension that the individual experiences which forces him to discharge and to eliminate the instinctual need. The word emotion is often used as a synonym of affect and feeling. Freud (1915) described two kinds of instinctual derivatives: ideas and affects (actions).

Ideas are described as representing memory traces. Whereas affects and emotions are present during the discharge, their final manifestations are perceived as feelings.

It is possible to differentiate between affectivity which takes place as a result of internal stimuli (e.g., hunger) and the reaction to external stimuli (e.g., fear caused by a threat). It may also be possible to differentiate between those emotional reactions which are caused by external or internal stimuli and others which appear to be due to the anticipation of such stimuli. In neurotic defense mechanisms, the experienced feeling may represent a defense of the feeling the patient tries to avoid. In this formulation, Freud assumed that affects could only take place in the system *Cs.*, for this system was responsible for the secretory and motoric discharges. He later (in 1923) modified his views, and stated that it was not entirely correct to speak of "unconscious feelings," maintaining that the analogy of unconscious ideas was no longer justifiable. He reasoned that feelings were transmitted into consciousness directly, whereas ideas need "connecting links" before they could be brought into consciousness.

Critics of Freud did not deny that an idea may disappear and then return. They only objected to the term *unconscious*, and preferred to say that the conscious idea, when it disappeared, ceased to exist as an idea (latent), becoming an idea only when it reentered consciousness. Semantically, the same argument could be used in connection with the concept of unconscious affects.

Related Concepts: IDENTIFICATION; INSTINCT (INSTINCTUAL DRIVE); OBJECT CHOICE (ANALYTIC AND NARCISSISTIC); PERCEPTION; SENSATION.

REFERENCES

Freud, S.: 1915, "The Unconscious." *SE*, 14:152, 178, 179, 1957.
     1923, "The Ego and the Id." *SE*, 19:22–23, 1961.

ADDITIONAL READINGS

Blau, A., "A Unitary Hypothesis of Emotion: I. Anxiety, Emotions of Displeasure, and Affective Disorders." *Q*, 24, 1955.

Gross, O., "Die Affektlage der Ablehnung." *MPN*, 32, 1912.
Stevenson, I., & H. Ripley, "Variations in Respiration and in Respiratory Symptoms During Changes in Emotion." *PSM*, 14, 1952.
Szasz, T., "A Contribution to the Psychology of Bodily Feelings." *Q*, 26, 1957.

516

EMOTIONAL INSIGHT denotes an awareness of symptom behavior and the emotional processes which underlie it. This form of insight is a prerequisite to any therapeutic change; it initiates and accompanies the therapeutic process, and is especially related to a reliving of the past in the transference situation. The transference interposes a condition that has taken on all the features of the illness but which is accessible to the analyst's intervention. The repetitive actions which are exhibited lead to the recall of the "forgotten" past once the resistances have been removed. [Freud, 1914.]

Related Concepts: INTERPRETATION; THERAPY; TRANSFERENCE.

REFERENCE

Freud, S., 1914, "Remembering, Repeating and Working-Through (Further Recommendations on the Technique of Psycho-Analysis II)." *SE*, 12:154–155, 1958.

517

EMPATHY is a temporary, conscious identification with an object, in order to understand the object, not to become permanently similar to it or to make it similar to the subject. The subject does not lose its identity but assumes, for a limited time only, the role of the object. In analytical treatment, the analyst experiences empathy with the patient, not to acquire his characteristics, symptoms and wishes, but in order to be able to follow the patient's line of reasoning.

Fenichel (1945), in quoting Fliess, noted that empathy "consists of a temporary identification with an object for the purpose of anticipating what e object is going to do." Anna Freud (1936) pointed out that a complete identification, even if temporary, would result in the subject's losing its identity; in effect, becoming the object. This identification, which she discovered in a case of altruism, destructive of the patient-analyst relationship, for would immobilize the analyst's ability to function.

The ability to empathize with the patient requires, in a sense, that the analyst split his total personality into two parts, in which one part remains to function as the analyst and the other as the patient. This situation is analogous to that of the teacher who partly identifies with the students in order to share better their curiosity (not their lack of knowledge). The same is true of the actor who plays the villain, and is responded to in those terms by the audience; yet, at the same time, the audience enjoys his performance and, later, praises him for it.

Case History

Eidelberg (1948) reported the following conversation between a patient and his analyst:

Patient: "You still don't speak! You don't want to give me any satisfaction. You're too superior. You won't admit that a patient is able to irritate your Serene Highness. You're silent only to make me angry."

As soon as the patient had said that, he grew angrier than ever. "You're quiet simply because you want revenge! This is disgusting and unfair! You're misusing your power, and are making a patient who's dependent on you suffer!"

The analyst decided that it was time to interrupt his silence and said: "Let's try—together—to analyze what you've said. You're angry and upset. You're not interested in research. You'd like to shout at me and call me names. I suggest, instead, that you examine and study your remarks. You want to be cured, and you know you must use your intellect to be cured. I know that a switch from an emotional to an intellectual approach is difficult and painful—but not impossible. A scientist must be able to prevent his emotions from blinding him. He must be able to transform them into a passionate desire—to search for Truth. For instance, you've worked with a microscope; you have spent many hours looking into it, watching the organisms on the slides, studying and drawing them. So I hope you'll under-

stand me when I say, instead of fighting each other, let's fight the problem."

Another patient, a schizophrenic, when visited by his psychiatrist, took a glass from the table and tossed it through an open window. The psychiatrist, without any comment, took another glass and threw it through the same window; contact was established.

Related Concept: IDENTIFICATION.

REFERENCES

Eidelberg, L., 1948, *Take Off Your Mask.* Py, p. 67, 1960.
Fenichel, O., *The Psychoanalytic Theory of Neurosis.* Nor, p. 511, 1945.
Freud, A., 1936, *The Ego and the Mechanisms of Defense.* IUP, pp. 14–31, 1946

ADDITIONAL READINGS

Greenson, R., "Empathy and Its Vicissitudes." *IntJPsa*, 41, 1960.
Kohut, H., "Introspection, Empathy, and Psychoanalysis: An Examination of the Relationship Between Mode of Observation and Theory." *JAPA*, 7, 1959.
Olden, C., "On Adult Empathy with Children." *PsaStC*, 8, 1953.

518
ENDOPSYCHIC PERCEPTION is the knowledge of an event which has taken place without the direct help of the sense organs. Freud (1907) described this phenomenon and illustrated its function in an analysis of a story by Jensen.* The hero of the story, Hanold, an archaeologist, discovered that the sculpture of Gradiva had a real-life embodiment. Freud pointed out that Hanold's scientific interest may be questioned: he may not have been as ignorant of the motives for his research as he was of the origin of his fantasies about Gradiva. "Once he had made his own childhood coincide with the classical past (which it was so easy for him to do), there was a perfect similarity between the burial of Pompeii—the disappearance of the past combined with its preservation—and repression, of which he

---

* Jensen, W., *Gradiva: ein pompejanisches Phantasiestück.* Dresden and Leipzig, 1903.

possessed a knowledge through what might be described as 'endopsychic' perception."

Related Concept: FANTASY.

REFERENCE

Freud, S., 1907, "Delusions and Dreams in Jensen's *Gradiva.*" *SE*, 9:50–51, 1959.

519
ENTITLEMENT (NARCISSISTIC ENTITLE-MENT), according to Murray (1964), denotes those special privileges and expectations to which the patient's early narcissistic orientation *entitles* him; e.g., the schizophrenic who wants to be called Napoleon and the paranoid who feels that he is important enough to be persecuted by the F.B.I. In the psychoanalytic situation, this may take the form of negative transference, in which the patient feels that he can make the analyst represent any object of his choice in order to validate the powerful primitive aggressions raging within him. The need of this narcissistic entitlement is expressed whenever there is a regression to the attitudes and expectations of the pregenital era (Freud, 1914).

Related Concepts: EGO-ALIEN; EGO-IDEAL.

REFERENCES

Freud, S., 1914, "On Narcissism: An Introduction." *SE*, 14:94, 1957.
Murray, J. M., "Narcissism and the Ego Ideal." *JAPA*, 12, 1964.

ADDITIONAL READINGS

Bibring, E., "The Mechanisms of Depression," in P. Greenacre, *Affective Disorders.* IUP, 1953
Bing, J. F., & R. Marburg, "Narcissism." *R*, 3, 1962.
Deutsch, H., "Paper read at Edward Bibring Memorial." *BML*, 1959.
Freud, A., *The Ego and the Mechanisms of Defense.* IUP, 1946.
Freud, S., 1921, "Group Psychology and the Analysis of the Ego." *SE*, 18, 1955.
Hartmann, H., & R. M. Loewenstein, "Notes on the Superego," in *The Psychoanalytic Study of the Child.* IUP, 1962.
Kris, E., "Some Comments and Observations of Early Autoerotic Activities." *PsaStC*, 1962.

520
ENTROPY is the force which, according to th second law of thermodynamics, tends to mak certain physical changes irreversible. Freud (191! used it in connection with the concept of agin. He pointed out that mental plasticity varies great from person to person. Those who lose it prem. turely and are neurotic may discover that "it is im possible to undo developments in them . . . whic have easily been dealt with in other people." Thu in considering "the conversion of psychical energy . we must make use of the concept of an *entrop* which opposes the undoing."

Max Hartmann (1956), in quoting Schrödinge pointed out that the living organism appeared t contradict this law and spoke of negative entrop. As Hartmann noted, the principle of entropy wa also present in organic organisms and was connecte with photosynthesis.

Related Concepts: NIRVANA PRINCIPLE; PSYCHI INERTIA.

REFERENCES

Freud, S., 1918, "From The History Of An Infanti Neurosis." *SE*, 17:116, 1955.
Hartmann, Max, *Einführung in die Allgemeine Bic logie.* Berlin: Walter de Gruyter & Co., p. 78, 195(

521
ENVY is the feeling experienced when one want something belonging to another; the desired objec may be anything: material possessions, persona attributes, etc. The envious person experiences th other's pleasure through partial identification, whil simultaneously realizing that he, the subject, doe not have the desired object.

The feeling of envy may first be experienced whe the child watches its mother suckle a sibling. Th child may want to take the role of the mother wh suckles or that of the rival child, or both. In th phallic phase, the little girl wants to be endowed wit a penis like her father or brother, and to urinate lik them. Envy often involves the conscious or uncon scious impression that the envied object reall belongs to, or has been taken away from, oneself For example, a patient suffered from conscious env because he could not afford a car like his friend's

When the patient's financial situation improved, he bought himself a similar car, and then discovered that it was not the car of which he had been envious. In his analysis, he discovered that the car unconsciously represented his father's penis.

Eidelberg (1954) differentiated envy from jealousy; the latter was applicable only to a triangular situation (real or imagined), involving contradictory impulses over the sharing of a loved object. Bertrand Russell (1952) reasoned that the envious man, instead of deriving pleasure from what he has, obtains pain from what others have. He noted: "Envy, the third of the psychological causes to which we attributed what is bad in the actual world, depends in most natures upon that kind of fundamental discontent which springs from a lack of free development, from thwarted instinct, and from the impossibility of realizing an imagined happiness. Envy cannot be cured by preaching; preaching, at the best, will only alter its manifestations and lead it to adopt more subtle forms of concealment. Except in those rare natures in which generosity dominates in spite of circumstances, the only cure for envy is freedom and the joy of life.

"Of all the characteristics of ordinary human nature envy is the most unfortunate; not only does the envious person wish to inflict misfortune and do so whenever he can with impunity, but he is also himself rendered unhappy by envy. Instead of deriving pleasure from what he has, he derives pain from what others have."

With reference to women, Freud (1917) noted that a deep penetration in the neuroses of women disclosed an "envy for a penis." In others, as he pointed out, there is no such evidence, the wish being replaced by the desire for a child, as though they had understood that it is a substitute for the penis they have been denied. In still others, the infantile wish changes into the wish for a man, and thus they put up with the man as an appendage to his penis.

Related Concepts: JEALOUSY; PENIS ENVY.

REFERENCES

Eidelberg, L., *An Outline of a Comparative Pathology of the Neuroses.* IUP, pp. 141–142, 1954.
Freud, S., 1917, "On Transformations of Instinct as Exemplified in Anal Eroticism." *SE*, 17:129, 1955.
Russell, B., *Dictionary of the Mind.* PL, p. 62, 1952.

ADDITIONAL READINGS

Freud, S.: 1900, "The Interpretation of Dreams." *SE*, 4, 1953.
1905, "Fragment of an Analysis of a Case of Hysteria." *SE*, 7, 1953.
1910, "A Special Type of Choice of Object Made by Men." *SE*, 11, 1962.
1917, "Introductory Lectures on Psycho-Analysis." *SE*, 16, 1963.
1922, "Some Neurotic Mechanisms in Jealousy, Paranoia and Homosexuality." *SE*, 18, 1955.
Fuchs, E., "Neid und Fressgier." *PsaP*, 7, 1933.
Klein, M., *Envy and Gratitude, A Study of Unconscious Sources.* BB, 1957.
Sterba, R., "Zum Oralen Ursprung des Neides." *PsaP*, 3, 1928.

522
EPILEPTIC PERSONALITY denotes a group of character traits often found in patients (particularly hospitalized patients) suffering from idiopathic epilepsy. These traits include: impulsivity, hypersensitivity, excessive pride, marked irritability, aggressiveness on slight provocation, hypochondriasis, unmodulated effect, fixity of opinions, circumstantiality, meticulous attention to detail, unusual verbosity, mental and reactive slowness, unclear and vague thinking, and, often, exaggeration of religious needs.

Formerly, the term was used to describe the existence of a constitutionally determined epileptic personality, but today it is felt that the concept should be used merely as a descriptive term. The psychic changes listed above may be the expression of the same cerebral disorder which causes convulsive manifestations; they may be caused by brain injuries sustained in the course of epileptic seizures; or the effect of antiepileptic medication may, in certain cases, account for some of the symptoms. It is possible, though it has not been demonstrated, there may be a causal relationship between these psychic phenomena and the subthreshold abnormal brain potentials of epileptics. [Strauss, 1959.]

Related Concept: CHARACTER NEUROSIS.

REFERENCE

Strauss, H., "Epileptic Disorders." *AHPsa*, pp. 1125–1126, 1959.

ADDITIONAL READINGS

Bleuler, E., *Texbook of Psychiatry*, Mac, 1924.
Fenichel, O., *The Psychoanalytic Theory of Neurosis*.
Nor, 1945.

523

EPISTEMOPHILIC, according to Freud (1917), refers to that instinct which is aimed at the gaining of knowledge. He contrasted this with the scopophilic instinct which is responsible for the need to look. Today, it appears that what Freud called scopophilic referred not only to the need to watch, and to the gratification of this need, but to all those activities connected with the function of the sense organs (both active and passive aims). Thus, both terms it would seem refer to components of an instinct aimed at forepleasure, for end-pleasure is connected with the full discharge of a basic need and is present when a necessary object has been acquired and the proper action is executed. It is possible, however, that both scopophilic and epistemophilic needs may also lead to end-pleasure, under the condition that the act of observing (or of being observed) and of gathering knowledge by itself represents a final aim toward the achievement of those aims. When this takes place, the scopophilic and epistemophilic instincts may be regarded as aim inhibited. The consequence of this form of gratification may lead to aesthetic or scientific pleasure. Whenever such a gratification takes place, the narcissistic mortification stemming from a lack of knowledge is eliminated.

The epistemophilic needs may also be warded off by defense mechanisms which lead to such symptoms as obsessional brooding or depersonalization. As Freud (1909) noted, brooding may become the principal symptom where the epistemophilic instinct is dominant. The content of thinking itself becomes sexualized. Reaching a successful conclusion to a line of thought is thus experienced as a sexual satisfaction.

Related Concepts: EXHIBITIONISM; FOREPLEASURE.

REFERENCES

Freud, S.: 1909, "Notes Upon a Case of Obsessional Neurosis." *SE*, 10:245, 1955.
        1917, "Introductory Lectures on Psycho-Analysis." *SE*, 16:327, 1963.

524

EROS is a primary instinct,* the aim of which "is to establish ever greater unities and to preserve them thus—in short, to bind them together" (Freud, 1940). His (1920) view was dualistic: "Our speculations have suggested that Eros operates from the beginning of life and appears as a 'life instinct' in opposition to the 'death instinct' [Thanatos] which was brought into being by the coming to life of inorganic substance."

Eros and Thanatos are present, in combination, in all life, producing the sexual instinct fusions when Eros predominates and the aggressive instinct fusions when Thanatos predominates. Their energy—respectively, libido and destrudo—is manifested in derivatives which can be examined in the larger context of human history. "The fateful question for the human species seems to me to be whether and to what extent their cultural development will succeed in mastering the disturbance of their communal life by the human instinct of aggression and self-destruction." [Freud, 1930.]

Related Concepts: INSTINCT (INSTINCTUAL DRIVE); PSYCHIC (MENTAL) ENERGY; THANATOS.

REFERENCES

Freud, S.: 1920, "Beyond the Pleasure Principle." *SE*, 18:53, 60–61, 1955.
        1930, "Civilization and Its Discontents." *SE*, 21:145, 1961.

ADDITIONAL READINGS

Desmonde, W. H., "Eros and Mathematics: Some Speculations." *AmIm*, 14, 1957.
Freud, S., 1933, "New Introductory Lectures on Psycho-Analysis." *SE*, 22, 1964.

525

EROTIC TRANSFERENCE. The erotic stimulation which is sometimes expressed in the analytic situation may be the result of a prolonged sexual frustration, or it may represent a defense against the consciousness of aggressive wishes.

---

* Observable *only* in its fusion with Thanatos.

Case History

Whenever a patient becomes genitally excited, her resistance may increase because of the fear that the analyst may seduce her or because of the fear that after having excited him he may reject her. A frigid woman reacted during analysis as follows: "She started to fidget on the couch. Her complexion grew pink; she was blushing. I was puzzled. What was up? Suddenly she burst out with 'But I can't speak! I'm too excited! I feel an electric current all up and down inside of me!' Her voice grew shrill. 'I'm scared I may get pregnant!'

"That jolted me. Perhaps this *non sequitur* was a clue! I asked, 'But how?'

"She had begun to perspire. 'There's a saying that when a woman feels excitement in her body, she may become pregnant!'

" 'You mean, obviously, that a woman who gets excited while having sexual intercourse—'

"Her voice was even higher than before. 'Intercourse or not, I don't know!' Then she uttered a soft moan, exhaled heavily and began to breathe deeply. After a while, she said in more normal tones, 'Of course I know that one can't get pregnant without having sexual intercourse. But that's what happens when I say whatever goes through my mind. Naturally, not having time to think out what to say, I was bound to make a mistake. . . .'

"I was leaning forward now, glad that she couldn't see me without craning her neck and looking behind her. 'Perhaps your mistake wasn't a mistake at all.'

" 'Oh, obviously it was a silly mistake. I know it. I've had three children, and they weren't the result of sexual excitement, but of sexual intercourse. As I've told you many times, I feel nothing during sexual relations. I'm just bored, and I usually think about the menu for the next day. . . .'

" 'I see,' I said. 'Of course, I also know that there's no pregnancy without intercourse, and that sexual stimulation alone will never produce a child. In spite of this, I wouldn't say that your statement, "I feel an electric current all up and down inside me —I am getting pregnant," is silly. I may *sound* silly, but we may find, by your further associations, that it has some meaning. You may remember what I've always told you: in analysis, one should not reject things which sound silly. Now, let's return to your associations.'

"To the casual observer, had there been one, Mrs. Jensen would have looked quite relaxed, lying there on the couch. Only when you observed her more closely, did you notice the tension in her body —the little tremors which ran down her neck into the shoulders, the tiny twitch of her kneecaps, the uncontrollable trembling of her hands." [Eidelberg, 1948.]

Related Concept: TRANSFERENCE-LOVE.

REFERENCE

Eidelberg, L., 1948, *Take Off Your Mask*. Py, pp. 37–38, 1960.

526

EROTOGENIC ZONES are those parts of the body which serve as substitutes for the genitals and which serve analogously to them. Freud (1914) noted: "We can decide to regard erotogenicity as a general characteristic of all organs and may then speak of an increase or decrease of it in a particular part of the body."

Freud (1905), in agreement with his first instinct theory, believed that excitations of two kinds* arose from the somatic organs, based upon differences of a chemical nature. "One of these kinds of excitation we describe as being specifically sexual, and we speak of the organ concerned as the 'erotogenic zone' of the sexual component instinct arising from it."

Related Concepts: DISPLACEMENT; STIGMATA.

REFERENCES

Freud, S.: 1905, "Three Essays on the Theory of Sexuality." *SE*, 7:168–169, 1953.
        1914, "On the History of the Psycho-Analytic Movement." *SE*, 14:84, 1957.

527

ERYTHROPHOBIA is a fear of blushing, a symptom which is characterized by neurotic avoidance. "Severe cases," as Fenichel (1945) noted, "may be inhibited to such an extent that they withdraw from any social contact; they anticipate

---

* Non-libidinal ego instincts and libidinal sexual instincts.

possible criticisms to a degree that makes them hardly distinguishable from persons with paranoid trends.''

The following case history is offered as an example: The patient was afraid to leave his home without wearing his dark glasses because they had the *magic* power to prevent his blushing. In the beginning, the patient experienced fright in just imagining himself going out without glasses. Later, after some progress was made, he was able to take off his glasses during the analytic session. After additional progress, he was prepared to take off his glasses when he reached the street of his analyst's office.

The material of this successful analysis may be summed up as follows: his fear of blushing started at puberty when he was caught masturbating by his mother. He blushed then and was threatened with mental illness unless he would stop masturbating (which he didn't). During his analysis he had an affair with a girl who was wearing dark glasses and it became possible to show him that he identified with this girl, for his identification gratified his passive feminine wishes.

The infantile wishes responsible for his phobic symptom appeared when he became fully conscious of his desire to replace his mother as his father's wife. Instead of being repudiated, this wish was repressed (probably at the age of five) because of his castration fears. In addition, he had also developed the wish to give up his penis in order to become similar to his mother, who, as he discovered, did not have a penis. The sexual wish appeared to be chiefly responsible for the conversion symptom of blushing. By wishing to become a girl and lose his penis, the patient protected himself from the narcissistic mortification of being deprived of his penis by somebody stronger than himself. While the conversion represented the displaced erection and gratified partly his phallic and his exhibitionistic wishes, the phobia of blushing appeared to be caused by his aggressive wish to eliminate his mother. The projection, "They will laugh about me when I blush," represented a punishment for this aggressive wish; the idea of being ridiculed, a defense of his unconscious scopophilic wishes, which had been mobilized as a countercathexis against his original exhibitionistic phallic needs. With the help of dark glasses, he played the role of a girl and at the same time was able to get the attention he felt he needed.

Related Concepts: BLUSHING; CONVERSION AND CONVERSION SYMPTOMS; PROJECTION.

REFERENCE

Fenichel, O., *The Psychoanalytic Theory of Neurosis.* Nor, p. 180, 1945.

ADDITIONAL READING

Heyer, G. R., "Erythrophobie." *Hippokrates,* 20, 1949.

528

ESCAPADE, a term first introduced by Bychowski (1962), denotes a form of acting out, a partial dissociation of ego identity. In contrast to those cases of multiple personality where the dissociation represents a loss, at least in part, of personal identity, an escapade leaves the sense of self-awareness intact.

Case History

A woman of upper middle class background, analyzed by Bychowski, married and the mother of several children, committed bigamy with a simple working man, moved into his house and assumed all the chores of a simple housewife, including the care of his children. Yet, she never actually forgot her personal identity, telephoned her real home now and then to get information about her children, and was well aware that in "marrying" another man she had committed a criminal act.

Related Concept: ACTING OUT.

REFERENCE

Bychowski, G., "Escapade: A Form Of Dissociation." *Q,* 31:155–174, 1962.

529

ETHICAL APPROACH must be regarded as a part of the therapeutic effort, an endeavour to achieve a standard imposed by the superego which has not been attained by the work of civilization in other ways. In marking off the limits set by this precept, no account is taken of the individual differences which obtain in human activity. Freud (1930) noted: "The behaviour of human beings show differences, which ethics, disregarding the fact that such differences are determined, classifies as 'good' or 'bad'.

So long as these undeniable differences have not been removed, obedience to high ethical demands entails damage to the aims of civilization, for it puts a positive premium on being bad."

Freud (1939) did not deny society its right to set certain limits upon the activities of its citizens; he did note, however, that those activities which appear to be mysterious, grandiose, and mystically self-evident owe their origin to the will of the primary father and its character to a connection with religion. It is to the latter circumstance that civilization, by and large, owes its codification of behavior. Religion long ago recognized that identification with one's fellow men may be used to control human aggression. Freud noted that it was difficult to love another as oneself or to love one's enemies. However, it was psychoanalysis which noted that love for oneself was often connected with a certain amount of self-hatred.

Nonetheless, the quantity of aggression (self-aggression) turned against others can still not be measured. Therefore, psychoanalysis tries to estimate how much is normal and how much is excessive. But certain qualities of aggression can be isolated and in that way considered pathognomic. Contempt, for instance, is a form of aggression, which is often used in dealing with others or with the self. This contempt usually mobilizes the hostility of the object and therefore cannot be used in constructive criticism. A good teacher or a good analyst has no contempt for his pupils or patients. Self-contempt cannot be used successfully in an attempt to improve one's self. It seems that contempt gives the subject who indulges in it an *immediate* gratification, whereas a constructive criticism has to wait until a change for the better can be effected.

Russell (1952) described the moral dilemma which has faced man in the twentieth century, as follows: "There are some who would say that a man need only obey the accepted moral code of his community. But I do not think any student of anthropology could be content with this answer. Such practices as cannibalism, human sacrifice, and head hunting have died out as a result of moral protests against conventional moral opinion. If a man seriously desires to live the best life that is open to him, he must learn to be critical of the tribal customs and tribal beliefs that are generally accepted among his neighbours.

"Science can, if rulers so desire, create sentiments which will avert disaster and facilitate cooperation. At present there are powerful rulers who have no such wish. But the possibility exists, and science can be just as potent for good as for evil. It is not science, however, which will determine how science is used. Science, by itself, cannot supply us with an ethic. It can show us how to achieve a given end, and it may show us that some ends cannot be achieved. But among ends that can be achieved our choice must be decided by other than purely scientific considerations."

Related Concepts: MORALITY; SUPEREGO.

REFERENCES

Freud, S.: 1930, "Civilization and Its Discontents." *SE*, 21:111, 142, 1961.
    1939, "Moses and Monotheism." *SE*, 23:118–120, 1964.
Russell, B., *Dictionary of the Mind.* PL, p. 66, 1952.

ADDITIONAL READINGS

Edel, M., & A. Edel, *Anthropology and Ethics.* CCT, 1959.
Feuer, L. S., *Psychoanalysis and Ethics.* CCT, 1955.
Gerard, R. W., "The Biology of Ethics," in I. Galdston, *Society and Medicine.* IUP, 1955.

530

EUPHORIA is a sustained feeling of elation and well-being, usually without consciously justifiable grounds. Euphoria may be found in conjunction with various somatic diseases, where denial is employed as a major defense. There is either denial of the existence of somatic diseases or denial of superego punishments.

Examples of euphoria have been reported in general paresis, cases of CNS disease and multiple sclerosis, as well as in diseases which do not necessarily have any direct CNS involvement, such as pulmonary tuberculosis. Euphoria may also be produced, in addicts, by the use of certain drugs (e.g., mescaline). [Lewin, 1950.]

Related Concepts: DENIAL (DISAVOWAL); ELATION.

REFERENCE
Lewin, B., *The Psychoanalysis of Elation.* Nor, 1950.

ADDITIONAL READINGS

Freud, S.: 1905, "Jokes and Their Relation to the Unconscious." *SE*, 8, 1960.
      & J. Breuer, 1893–95, "Studies in Hysteria." *SE*, 2, 1955.

531

EVALUATION OF PSYCHOANALYTIC THERAPY

EVALUATION OF PSYCHOANALYTIC THERAPY consists of an examination and verification of the therapeutic changes attributable to the psychoanalytic treatment. Such an examination is difficult, however, for when it is undertaken by the analyst responsible for the treatment the charge may be made that the man liable for the handling of the case may subjectively distort the results achieved. If an evaluation is undertaken by another qualified analyst, a time-consuming study of the case must be made, which has, in the main, proved to be impractical. Though rarely possible, another form of evaluation may be employed. In the Wolf Man case, the patient was treated by Freud and Brunswick on two occasions separated by an interval of twelve years. Brunswick was nonetheless able to verify the record of the case published by Freud in 1918. As can be seen, however, this circumstance is rare, and may even, considering the interval between the analytic situations, be described as an interfering factor. To this must be added the more important circumstance of how *success* shall be evaluated. It cannot be concluded that the Wolf Man in 1914 (the terminal date of his first analysis) was the same patient Brunswick analyzed more than a decade later. Thus, it may be concluded that the analyst responsible for conducting the treatment should conduct the evaluation.

Evaluation

The first step to be undertaken in such an evaluation is the examination and the enumeration of any changes which were registered during the course of the treatment. The inability to measure psychic energy forces the analyst to be satisfied with such evaluative statement as *better*, *good*, *very good*, and *full improvement*. Second, the factors responsible for the therapeutic change must be named. The infantile wishes and narcissistic mortifications which become conscious during the analysis, and the resistances encountered during this procedure, must be described. Any improvement in the patient's symptomatology must be noted. The liberated material and the resistances encountered should be identified. The degree of improvement and its duration should be given. External changes in the life situation of the patient, for which the patient is not responsible, must be registered.* Finally, such elements as transference and countertransference (if any) should not be overlooked.

Value

The concept of value may disturb those critics who would like to make psychology conform to concepts which are useful in exact sciences, but which are not meaningfully employed in a biological science; that is, in psychoanalysis. One such critic, Heinz Hartmann (1964) stated: "In this definition, sublimation is actually a special case of displacement, special in the sense that it includes only those displacements that lead to the substitution of worthy aims. The advantage of this approach was that it clearly stated that the highest achievements of man—art, science, religion—may have and often do have their origin in libidinal tendencies. But some authors... have objected to this definition, pointing out quite correctly that it is always questionable to include value judgments in the definition of a mental process. It was, therefore, a reasonable suggestion to eliminate the element of value judgment and to speak of ego-syntonic aims."

Despite this criticism, it is difficult to deny that the concept of sublimation, for instance, requires an acceptance of the value principle. Freud (1930), who introduced the consideration of value, remarked, as follows: "It is impossible to escape the impression that people commonly use false standards of measurement."

In order not to distort the truth—the final aim of all scientific work—it is essential that the concept of value be discussed. The illusion that it is possible to investigate psychoanalytical phenomena while refraining from evaluating them has to be given up. The facts reported in psychoanalytic work are of practical value only if they occur often and under conditions which can be clearly defined.

---

* There is no doubt that this part of the record may be consciously or unconsciously subject to distortion. When analysts limit their assumption that they must necessarily cure all of their patients, this part of the record may become more reliable.

Related Concepts: PSYCHOANALYSIS; THERAPY.

REFERENCES

Freud, S., 1930, "Civilization and its Discontents." *SE*, 21:64, 1961.

Hartmann, H., *Essays on Ego Psychology.* IUP, p. 217, 1964.

ADDITIONAL READINGS

Berman, L., "Some Problems in the Evaluation of Psychoanalysis as a Therapeutic Procedure." *Ps*, 18, 1955.

Deutsch, H., "Psychoanalytic Therapy in the Light of Follow-Up." *JAPA*, 7, 1959.

Pfeffer, A., "A Procedure for Evaluating the Results of Psychoanalysis." *JAPA*, 7, 1959.

532

EXAGGERATION is a form of behavior in which there is a minor or gross disproportion between the situation and the affect, the command and its execution, or the interpretation of the analyst and the way it is understood by the patient.

The derivatives of the id and superego, if not moderated by the ego, have a tendency to be excessively intense and oblivious to the hierarchy of goals. Only an intelligent mind, which has a concept of adequate minima and the subordination of the means to an end, can avoid or correct exaggeration. The ego may participate in exaggeration in three ways: (a) it may be overwhelmed by the id, e.g., as in psychosis and hysteria; (b) it may be overwhelmed, but may secondarily try to integrate events through the illusion or delusion that what happened was only an exaggeration; or (c) exaggeration may be used as a defense. For example, hatred for the father can be grotesquely distorted, becoming so ego-alien that it is felt as hypocrisy. In fact, although it is the exaggerated expression of a real emotion, the character of its reality is denied. In this, the ego awakens too late to prevent the expression of the id or superego derivative, for by exaggerating it the ego gains the strength to control it.

Reaction formation in compulsion neurosis and hysterical exaggeration acquires the character of exaggeration from the id component. We find more exaggeration in situations where the ego is weak, and less exaggeration where it is strong; children exaggerate more than adults.

As a defense, exaggeration is similar to repression in pushing certain ideas out of consciousness; it is different from it in that the instinctual drive is acted out to a certain extent. In this respect, exaggeration is similar to the mechanism of undoing. However, the individual defends himself not by a second action which undoes the first one, but, rather, by reacting to a stimulus out of proportion to it. [Sperling, 1963.]

Related Concepts: CARICATURE; DEFENSE MECHANISMS.

REFERENCE

Sperling, O., "Exaggeration as a Defense." *Q*, 32:533–548, 1963.

ADDITIONAL READING

Bergler, E., "Hypocrisy: Its Implications in Neurosis and Criminal Psychopathology." *JCP*, 4, 1942.

533

EXHIBITIONISM is characterized by the exposure of the subject in order to obtain instinctual gratification. A normal individual is only able to obtain forepleasure from being looked at, whereas the pervert achieves genital discharge (and pleasure) through being looked at, or requires it as a rigid condition for discharge through sexual intercourse or masturbation.

Freud (1905) noted: "Small children are essentially without shame, and at some periods of their earliest years show an unmistakable satisfaction in exposing their bodies, with especial emphasis on the sexual parts." This common exhibitionistic tendency was referred to by Freud as *component instincts.* They emerge as pairs of opposites, one such set of paired instincts being exhibitionism and scopophilia. Freud assumed that children are of a polymorphous perverse disposition (achieving a normal sexual discharge only later), that "this same disposition to perversions is a general and fundamental human characteristic." As a consequence, the adult pervert accepts an infantile polymorphous perverse wish, whereas a neurotic wards it off. Freud therefore regarded the perversion as a negative of a neurosis. Later, in 1927, he recognized that fetishism (a form of perversion) is not just the result of a simple acceptance of an infantile wish, but represents, rather, a complicated defense, which results in a perverse character trait, not a symptom.

As a result of therapeutically successful analysis of homosexuals and masochists, it has been suggested that all perversions appear to be the result of defense mechanisms leading to ego-syntonic character traits. In addition, the analysis of exhibitionistic perverts disclosed that, while being watched, they unconsciously identified with the viewer and, in that way, unconsciously experienced a forbidden scopophilic gratification. Their exhibitionism therefore represented a denial of the original scopophilic wish, and gratified the demands of the unconscious ego and the superego.

Exhibitionists and scopophilics are interested in the satisfaction of their wishes only under the condition that such satisfaction be forbidden, so that aggressive as well as sexual tendencies can be gratified.

There appear to be more male than female exhibitionists.

Related Concepts: FOREPLEASURE; PERVERSION; SCOPOPHILIA.

REFERENCES

Freud, S.: 1905, "Three Essays on the Theory of Sexuality." *SE*, 7:191-192, 1953.
    1927, "Fetishism." *SE*, 21:149–158, 1961.

ADDITIONAL READINGS

Boehm, F., "Die Heilung eines Exhibitionisten." *ZPSM*, 2, 1955–1956.
Buxbaum, E., "Exhibitionistic Onanism in a Ten-Year-Old." *Q*, 4, 1935.
Christoffel, H.: "Exhibitionism and Exhibitionists." *IntJPsa*, 17, 1936.
    "Male Genital Exhibitionism," in S. Lorand *Perversions: Psychodynamics and Therapy.* RH, 1956.
Clemens, J., *Zur Psychologie des Exhibitionismus.* VS, 1933.
Eidelberg, L.: *Studies in Psychoanalysis.* IUP, 1948.
    An Outline of a Comparative Pathology of the Neuroses. IUP, 1954.
Freud, S., 1900, "The Interpretation of Dreams." *SE*, 4, 1953.
Saul, L., "A Note on Exhibitionism and Scopophilia." *AnSurvPsa*, 3, 1952.
Schmaltz, G., "The Problem of Exhibitionism (Case Report, Symbolism and Theory)." *P*, 6, 1953.
Shindler, W., "Exhibitionistic 'Acting-Out' and Transference in Family Group-Therapy." *Zdiag-Psychol*, 5, 1957.

Sperling, M., "The Analysis of the Exhibitionist." *IntJPsa*, 28, 1947.

534

EXTERNAL IDENTIFICATION refers to those external changes in which the subject becomes similar to the object, or the object to the subject. It may take place on an oral, anal or phallic level. For example, Eidelberg (1948) cited the following case history: "The patient had been an industrious and ambitious pupil who got along very well with his father and teachers. When he began eventually to have sexual relations he succeeded in gratifying his libido with new, non-oedipal, and therefore non-dangerous objects. A conflict had arisen twenty years before the beginning of the treatment, when the patient identified with his respected chief and teacher, who had been dismissed for embezzlement. This meant that identification with a father image could become dangerous, since his father had come into conflict with the outside world. The temptation now consisted in that the patient wanted to embezzle like his chief. This situation was complicated by the fact that his chief often asked him for money, and that the patient became indebted to an official. He began to fear that he would be disciplined because of these debts. He could not bring it upon himself to refuse his former chief's requests for money; yet even social relations with him involved danger for the patient. Agoraphobia appeared for the first time in this conflict situation. It freed him from the necessity of meeting his chief and at the same time represented a partial identification with this man, for the latter also suffered from agoraphobia."

Related Concepts: ANACLITIC; PRIMARY IDENTIFICATION.

REFERENCE

Eidelberg, L., *Studies in Psychoanalysis.* IUP, pp. 91, 109, 1948.

ADDITIONAL READINGS

Eidelberg, L., *An Outline of a Comparative Pathology of the Neuroses.* IUP, 1954.
Fenichel, O., *The Psychoanalytic Theory of Neurosis.* Nor, 1945.
Freud, S., 1921, "Group Psychology and the Analysis of the Ego." *SE*, 18, 1955.

F

600

FACE-BREAST EQUATION denotes the unconscious symbolic formula, under certain circumstances, of the face and the breast, a particularly strong correlation between the nipples and the eyes. Almansi (1960) noted: "The phenomena involved were indissolubly bound to the liberation of large amounts of aggression, specifically, aggression reactive to oral deprivation. It is consistent with psychoanalytic theory that this frustration, in turn, is reacted to with the hallucinatory projection of the satisfaction-giving object, in an attempt to recreate, in part at least, the primitive perceptual cluster consisting of the sensation of the nipple in the mouth and the concurrent vision of the mother's face. The interruption of this cluster by the withdrawal of the nipple is a powerful determinant in the differentiation between the 'I' and the 'non-I,' in the division between what is experienced internally and what is seen as external. And there is much evidence to show that the phenomena described herein relate precisely to a period when the dividing line between the 'I' and 'non-I' was still not sharply drawn. The 'looking and being looked at' motif so clearly expressed in the cartoons and most of the clinical cases presented undoubtedly pertains to this lack of differentiation. In each instance it involves a child, or a man who has been placed in an inferior position, and who is looking at a woman's breasts which, in turn, look at him. This phenomenon embodies both an identification and a projection."

The psychological concomitants of this phenomenon points to its close relationship to orality and to the frustration of oral demands, and suggests that it may embody perceptual experiences and other events of early childhood. It may originate in the transitional state of ego development, when the separation between the *I* and the *non-I* begins to take place and real object relationships are being established. For example, an overt homosexual, who, as a result of his treatment, began to have sexual relations with women, dreamt that he was sucking the breast of his girl friend and felt that he had urine in his mouth.

Related Concepts: BREAST COMPLEX; ORAL PHASE.

REFERENCE

Almansi, R. J., "The Face-Breast Equation." *JAPA*, 8:68, 1960.

ADDITIONAL READINGS

Bergler, E. & L. Eidelberg, "Der Mammakomplex des Mannes." *Z*, 19, 1933.
Spitz, R.: "The Primal Cavity." *PsaStC*, 10, 1955. *No and Yes*. IUP, 1957.

601

FAMILY ROMANCE. While the child's first and only authority is his parents, he must in the process of growing up become independent of them and establish his own superego or develop a neurosis. The birth of a sibling and the oedipal conflict are often responsible for the first stage of estrangement of the child from his parents.

The family romance is also a fantasy which is characteristic of the mass, who searches for a leader in order to become a group. In most legends, Freud (1939) noted, the first family that represents the child's parents is of royal birth. The second one in which the child is brought up is of humble origin. In "the family romance," the contrast between the two families, the royal and the humble one, emphasizes the heroic nature of the child.

Related Concept: DAYDREAMS.

REFERENCES

Freud, S.: 1909, "Family Romances." *SE*, 9:238–239, 1959.
     1939, "Moses and Monotheism." *SE*, 23:13, 1964.

ADDITIONAL READINGS

Frosch, J., "Transference Derivatives of the Family Romance." *JAPA*, 7, 1959.
Toman, W., "Family Constellation as a Character and Marriage Determinant." *IntJPsa*, 40, 1959.

602

FANATICISM is an exaggerated and incorrigible devotion to an idea, cause or person, which may lead to actions endangering oneself or others. It often (but not exclusively) occurs in true paranoia and paranoid schizophrenia. According to Sperling (1944), this excessive cathexis is established by narcissistic libido, not by object libido. The object is appersonated, but little real understanding of the object is achieved; in this way, the ego defends itself against hypercathexis with narcissistic libido (which would lead to hypochondriasis, etc.) after the schizophrenic withdrawal of the object libido. He noted: "Fanaticism in the narrower sense is, on the one hand, the earmark of schizoid or schizophrenic personalities; on the other, it apparently shows such an intense direction of interest towards a person or thing that it is difficult to suppose that we are confronted with that withdrawal of libido from objects which we observe in schizophrenics. It therefore seems important to me to show that in fanaticism, in my experience, it is always narcissistic libido which is turned towards the object; and further, there is an ego-feeling for the object, i.e. it is appersonated."

Related Concept: PARANOIA.

REFERENCE

Sperling, O., "On Appersonation." *IntJPsa*, 25:128–132, 1944.

ADDITIONAL READING

Bolterauer, L., "Contributions to the Psychology of Fanaticism." *IntJPsa*, 33, 1952.

603

FANTASY is the development of memories derived from external perceptions, capable of activation, which are modified and rearranged to create an internal world that supplies a certain amount of gratification—an amount external reality does not. This formation is of special importance during puberty, but appears to decrease in importance under the impact of reality testing in later life. When fantasy formations are sublimated, the external world may be modified to the benefit of all. This may well be in the case of an engineer who builds a bridge, a doctor who treats a patient, and an artist who creates a work of art.

Under pathological conditions, internal perceptions are attributed or treated as if they were a part of the external world. Little Hans, for instance, was afraid of horses, because they unconsciously represented his father, which mobilized his hostility, and also because they represented his omniscient superego. Little Hans was convinced that the horses would know of his hostility, and would punish him for it. [Freud, 1909.]

Related Concepts: NEUROSIS AND PSYCHOSIS; PERCEPTION; SUBLIMATION.

REFERENCE

Freud, S., 1909, "Analysis of a Phobia in a Five-Year-Old Boy." *SE*, 10:79–81, 1955.

ADDITIONAL READINGS

Beres, D., "The Unconscious Fantasy." *Q*, 31, 1962.
Davidson, A., & J. Fay, "Phantasy in Childhood." *JAPA*, 4, 1956.
Faergeman, P., "Fantasies of Menstruation in Men." *Q*, 24, 1955.
Greenacre, P., "The Eye Motif in Delusion and Fantasy." *P*, 5, 1926.
Jarvis, W., "When I Grow Big and You Grow Little." *Q*, 27, 1958.

Joseph, E., "An Unusual Fantasy in a Twin with an Inquiry into the Nature of Fantasy." *Q*, 28, 1959.

Prager, D., "An Unusual Fantasy of the Manner in Which Babies Becomes Boys or Girls." *Q*, 29, 1960.

Singer, M. B., "Fantasies of a Borderline Patient." *PsaStC*, 15, 1960.

604

FASCINATION denotes a strong, sometimes unconscious attraction to and admiration for a person, object or concept; a primitive attempt by the ego to master what is perceived through identification; a regression to an early stage of ego-boundary development. For example, a fascination with narcissistic personalities can frequently be observed in insecure, dependent, immature individuals who attempt to identify with seemingly omnipotent personalities in the hope of being or becoming omnipotent (or close to omnipotent) themselves. Pathological fascination may be manifested in schizophrenics as automatic obedience, corresponding to the primitive imitation of infants. [Bernfeld, 1928.]

Related Concepts: ATTRACTION OF THE FORBIDDEN; IMITATION; NARCISSISM; PERCEPTION.

REFERENCE

Bernfeld, S., Über Faszination." *Im*, 14:76–87, 1928.

ADDITIONAL READINGS

Eidelberg, L., *The Dark Urge*. Py, 1961.

Olden, C., "About the Fascinating Effect of the Narcissistic Personality." *AmIm*, 2, 1941.

605

FEAR is the experience of unpleasure that is characterized by the anticipation of being overwhelmed by an internal or external force—where the object is known. The emotion of fear, along with the motoric and secretory discharges connected with it, is an affect experienced by the total personality.

Normal fear is a danger signal which increases the individual's ability to deal with an external danger. Neurotic fear, on a conscious level, is connected with the phobic object. The analysis of such a fear shows that it is the result of a displacement from an unconscious danger. A patient suffering from neurotic fear behaves *as if* the danger of which he is afraid were actually happening, rather than reacting to a probable (or possible) future danger. The full discharge of the repressed wish is experienced as taking place *now*, instead of in the future.

Freud (1921) described the panic which takes place whenever a disintegration of the mass has occurred and compared the affect of panic to that of neurotic anxiety. His description, thus, of the mass as *impulsive, changeable,* and *irritable,* led by the unconscious, corresponds to the behavior of the neurotic.

The rat fantasy played a great role in the analysis of the Rat Man (Freud, 1909). The patient remembered that when he visited his father's grave he saw a rat and believed that it came out of the father's grave after having eaten the corpse. Rats represented greedy and dirty animals who were hunted and killed, and they therefore mobilized the Rat Man's feelings of pity. In a way, he regarded himself as similar to the rat, as a cruel and persecuted animal.

Related Concepts: ANXIETY; SENSE OF GUILT; SUPER-EGO.

REFERENCES

Freud, S.: 1909, "Notes Upon a Case of Obsessional Neurosis." *SE*, 10:215–216, 1955.

1921, "Group Psychology and the Analysis of the Ego." *SE*, 18:97, 1955.

ADDITIONAL READINGS

Brodsky, B., "The Self-Representation, Anality, and the Fear of Dying." *JAPA*, 7, 1959.

Freeman, L., *Fight Against Fears*. Crown, 1951.

Heilbrunn, G., "The Basic Fear." *JAPA*, 3, 1955.

Janet, P., "The Fear of Action." *ASP*, 16, 1921.

Jones, E., "Fear, Guilt and Hate." *IntJPsa*, 10, 1929.

Nacht, S., "Essai sur la peur." *RFPsa*, 16, 1952.

Ramzy, I., & R. S. Wallerstein, "Pain, Fear and Anxiety: A Study in Their Interrelationships." *PsaStC*, 13, 1958.

606

FEELINGS IN DREAMS are often not connected with the content of the dream. Their presence and the presence of motoric activity appears to contradict the assumption that only ideas are unconscious and indicates that feelings and motoric acts may become unconscious provided they take place in the unconscious part of the ego. These feelings often appear to be connected with the latent dream, and not with the manifest dream. For instance, a latent homosexual wish is accompanied by manifest aggressive feelings. Though the dreamer retains his aggressive feelings, he experiences an erection followed by a nocturnal emission.

Freud (1900) offered the following, as an example: A patient was tormented by his brother for whom he had developed a homosexual attachment. His dream consisted of three parts: (a) the brother was chasing him, (b) two adults were making love to each other, and (c) the brother sold the business which the patient wanted to take over. As a result of this dream, the patient woke up with fear. The analysis of the dream showed that it represented a masochistic wish fulfillment, for the sale of the business meant punishment to the patient.

Related Concept: DREAMS.

REFERENCE

Freud, S., 1900, "The Interpretation of Dreams." *SE*, 4:159, 1953.

607

FEMININE MASOCHISM is a form of masochism in male patients, according to Freud (1924), which indicates an unconscious identification with a humiliated woman (oedipal mother). In examining the masochistic fantasies of such men, the subject who is being tortured represents a woman, i.e., he is either being castrated or is giving birth to an infant. Freud referred to this form of masochism as feminine. The torture the masochist undergoes permits him to retain his genitals and at the same time to eliminate his unconscious feeling of remorse.

The fact that a number of neurotics regard women as being inferior, and that they gratify their need to be punished and humiliated by playing the role of a woman, does not mean that women *are* inferior, or that a normal woman wants to be punished and humiliated. Eidelberg (1959) pointed out that both male and female masochists seek humiliating punishment not only to gratify their unconscious need for

punishment, but also to demonstrate their infantile omnipotence; they are only interested in self-provoked punishments.

Abraham (1910) provided the following case history: "Her masochistic phantasies used to culminate in thoughts of death, in the idea that she must jump out of the window, etc. After the crisis had passed extreme anxiety used to set in, accompanied by anxiety-ideas which varied with the situation of the moment. For example, if the patient happened to be in the street she would have the feeling that she must fall, that she could not get home alone, that she must go up to some man or other and accost him. 'To fall' and 'to accost a man' are equivocal expressions. They not only indicate a state of helplessness and need for assistance, but they point to those prostitution phantasies which are so often met with in hysterical women, but are kept so strictly secret by them.* The patient used to have an impulse to give herself to the first man that came her way, and at times, when she was suffering from frequent attacks of the kind described, she used actually to do so. Her prostitution desires appeared as a special form of masochism, and represented to her, who had in general a high opinion of herself and was even somewhat masterful, the deepest form of humiliation."

Related Concepts: INFANCY; MASOCHISM; NEED FOR PUNISHMENT; PASSIVE.

REFERENCES

Abraham, K., 1910, "Hysterical Dream-States," *SPA*, p. 108, 1942.
Eidelberg, L., "Humiliation in Masochism." *JAPA*, 7:274–283, 1959.
Freud, S., 1924, "The Economic Problem of Masochism." *SE*, 19:162, 1961.

608

FERENCZI, SANDOR, more than thirty years after his death, is still considered to have made a singular contribution to psychoanalysis, second only to Freud's. During his life, he devoted much effort to the development of the psychoanalytic

---

* These phantasies came to expression very clearly in many of the patient's dreams, and were also betrayed in her symptomatic actions.

movement. He was in constant demand as a lecturer, both in Europe and the United States, and contributed many original papers which furthered and deepened our present knowledge. He was understanding and thorough as a teacher, championing the cause of psychoanalysis to both the medical and intellectual circles of his day. In his clinical presentations, he was revered for his clear and precise style, his acuteness and lucidity. Freud described his contribution in the building of psychoanalysis as "pure gold." Yet, at the time of his death, he was almost entirely isolated, having come within a hair's breadth of a fatal break with Freud.[1]

Sandor Ferenczi was born in the city of Miskolc, near Budapest, in 1873. His father was Polish, having moved to Hungary as a young man; his mother also was of Polish extraction. He was the fifth in a family of seven sons and four sisters. When he was a young boy his father's bookstore served as his second nursery. He was an avid naturalist, and was especially fond of birds; in later years he kept a feeding station on the grounds of his villa, where he loved to sit and observe their movements and to listen to their songs. His interest in all the art forms was directly traceable to his early years. In addition to being a book seller, his father ran an artists' bureau, from whom guest artists and lecturers were engaged.

When Sandor was fifteen his father died, and an always close family group moved even closer together. He was especially fond of his eldest brother, a fine musician. Music was always to be heard in the Ferenczi household. In his early twenties, he penned a number of sentimental poems to his mother. One of his sisters recalls that his poetry was much like that of Heine, romantic and lyrical.

After completing his training at the gymnasium, Sandor moved to Vienna to undertake his medical training. It was during this period that he first became interested in psychic phenomena. He experimented with hypnosis, at first with one of his sisters, and later with a clerk in his father's bookstore.

Receiving his medical degree in 1894, he then served a compulsory one-year term in the army as a physician. Soon after his discharge,he took a position in the city hospital of Budapest, where he had

[1] Balint, M., 1933, "Sandor Ferenczi, Obituary." *IntJPsa*, 30:215–219, 1949.

various responsibilities, including running the service which treated the city's prostitutes. It was during this period that he first became interested in the problems of sexual pathology, and turned his attention to the study of nervous and mental diseases. At the turn of the century he opened his own office, during which time he was also chief neurologist for the Elizabeth Poorhouse, and, later, chief of the neurological services in the Workman's Polyclinic. In 1905, he was appointed psychiatric consultant to the Royal Court of Justice, Budapest.

In his preanalytic period, Ferenczi wrote for various Hungarian and German medical journals. During the period 1902–1907, his publications included (a) "The Sensory Regions of the Cerebrum," (b) "On Using Morphine in Older Persons," (c) "Bromismus and Tabes Dorsalis," (d) "Paranoia," (e) "Homosexualitas Feminina," and (f) "The Therapeutic Value of Hypnosis." In all, he published some thirty preanalytic papers.

Ferenczi first met Freud in 1908, after he had written and asked for an appointment. It was the beginning of a friendship, as well as an alliance, that was to continue until his death in 1933. He underwent his analysis with Freud, and thereafter became a central figure in the psychoanalytic movement. In 1909 he accompanied Freud when he came to the United States for a series of lectures at Clark University. Upon that occasion, it was common for Ferenczi to walk beside Freud on his way to the lecture hall, talking and discussing the topic of the day.

In 1910, at the Nurenberg Conference, he proposed the formation of the International Psychoanalytic Association, acting upon Freud's suggestion. Until the year of his death, he attended each conference of the congress and frequently delivered papers which were well attended. At the Fifth International Psychoanalytic Congress in September 1918, the representatives of the Austrian, Hungarian, and German governments were present. Impressed by the work of psychoanalysis, these governments planned to establish clinics for the treatment of war neuroses. In 1919, Sandor Ferenczi was made Professor of Psychoanalysis at the University of Budapest, the first such appointment ever made.

Sandor Ferenczi was an untiring worker, full of enthusiasm and determination. He fought for what he believed would further the aims of psychoanalysis.

The creation of the *International Journal of Psycho-Analysis* is largely ascribable to his efforts. Without waiting for the convening of the next congress, he had set the program in motion, with Ernest Jones as its first editor. The first issue appeared in 1920, the first such journal to be published in English. His importance to the American psychoanalytic movement was furthered by his second visit to the United States, under the sponsorship of the New School for Social Research. He remained in New York for eight months, during which time he spoke to medical and lay audiences: he presented weekly ninety-minute lectures which were primarily designed to acquaint students and friends of psychoanalysis with its basic tenents.

He was married in 1933, a happy if not fruitful union. Mrs. Ferenczi was a highly cultured and charming woman. She had two children by a former marriage who were brought up as though they were Sandor's very own. Mrs. Ferenczi continued living in Budapest after her husband's death, until 1946 when she moved to Switzerland where she died three years later.

II

The first of his psychoanalytic papers, "The Effect on Women of Premature Ejaculation in Man" and "Psychosexual Impotence in Man" (both 1908), were traceable back to his interest in the sexual problems of women, an interest he first expressed in his work with prostitutes in the Budapest Hospital. In these and other papers which were to follow, he made quite clear by clinical illustration the etiology and development of these phenomena. His paper, "The Nosology of Male Homosexuality" (1916), was delivered at the Weimar Congress in 1911. Here, for the first time, he described the fundamental difference between active and passive homosexuals. The latter type does not seek treatment; he is satisfied with the role he plays. The active homosexual, however, is aware of his perversion and thus may try to change his behavior. The passive, homoerotic subject, whose aggression is inhibited, takes over the feminine role and thus wants to be loved by men. In this formulation Ferenczi considered the active homosexual to be typically an obsessive neurotic, wherein the homosexuality is identified as the compulsion. This type of homosexual is "object homo-erotic," is disturbed by his desires and is very aggressive.

In a paper that was to become an important contribution to the study of ego psychology, "Stages in the Development of the Sense of Reality" (1913), Ferenczi identified the four stages, as follows: (a) the period of unconditional omnipotence, (b) the period of magic-hallucinatory omnipotence, (c) the period of omnipotence through magic gestures, and (d) the period of magic words and thoughts. Further, he described the omnipotence of feeling in neurotics as the result of a projection, something that one must obey like a slave. The "magic" which the patient utilizes is an attempt at restoration: the mortified narcissism is "eliminated" through the use of a presumed self-sufficiency. The neurotic utilizes magical thinking to eliminate a disturbing reality, or to effect an apparent change in that reality so that it will no longer prove disturbing. Developmentally, Ferenczi was able to demonstrate that there were three stages in the infant's sense of reality: unconditioned omnipotence; hallucinatory wish-fulfillment; and, finally, magical gestures, an attempt to restore his earlier feelings of omnipotence.

During that same period, Ferenczi wrote a number of short papers on the patient's behavior in the analytic situation. The patient's body movements, gesticulation, modulation, etc. were all inexhaustible sources of information as regards repression and other unconscious processes. To Ferenczi, they were as significant in their way as the information which was obtained through the use of the basic rule (free association). They had also to be understood and interpreted. He observed, for instance, that the dizziness some patients experienced at the end of the analytic hour, or the tendency to fall asleep during it, were all forms of resistance (negative transference). In "Transitory Symptom-Formation," a paper written during this period of Ferenczi's work, he described the symptom as a resistance of the ego, a resistance to those emerging unconscious drives which the analysis itself had mobilized.

III

At the beginning of the First World War, Ferenczi was recalled to active service, serving as chief medical officer to a squadron of Hussars in a small-town garrison. In his "exile," as Ferenczi called it, during the free time he had available he translated Freud's "Three Essays on the Theory of Sexuality" into Hungarian. It was perhaps inevitable that this involvement lead Ferenczi to a further elaboration of his own thinking on sexuality. He submitted his ideas about ontogenetic and phylogenetic theory to Freud when he visited him at his military station. Later, in 1924, his views were published under the title, *Thalassa: A Theory of Genitality*,[2] which is still considered his masterpiece by many.

In *Thalassa*,[3] Ferenczi made use of his background in neurological and embryological research for here he attempted to correlate biological and psychological phenomena—to establish, as it were, a unified theory. As was characteristic of much of his work, it bore the mark of originality; it was no less than an attempt to create a new scientific method. To this he gave the name *bioanalysis*. Freud considered *Thalassa* to be Ferenczi's culminating work. "It was perhaps the boldest application of psychoanalysis that was ever attempted. As its governing thought it lays stress on the conservative nature of the instincts, which seek to re-establish every state of things that has been abandoned owing to an external interference. Symbols are recognized as evidence of ancient connections. Impressive instances are adduced to show how the characteristics of what is psychical preserve traces of primaeval changes in the bodily substance. When one has read this work, one seems to understand many peculiarities of sexual life of which one had never previously been able to obtain a comprehensive view, and one finds oneself the richer for hints that promise a deep insight into wide fields of biology."[4]

In the first issue of the *International Journal of Psycho-Analysis*, Jones[5] reported on Ferenczi's "striking new departure in technique," his presentation of *active therapy*. It was Ferenczi's contention that his formulations were based on those examples provided by Freud of the active measures that were to be taken in the treatment of certain cases of phobias, where the therapy can advance only if the patient is induced to face his phobias as regards his anxiety. Ferenczi noted: "There seems to me little

doubt that the only correct procedure in these cases is to wait until the treatment itself has itself become a compulsion, and then to use this counter-compulsion as a means of forcibly suppressing the compulsion due to the disease."[6]

Ferenczi's first essay was well received, but, with the publication of other papers on active therapy, hostile reactions were soon forthcoming. In a personal communication (1924), the author was informed by Paul Federn that experimentation in technical methods at that time were common, though nobody talked of it. It was Federn's[7] contention that many of his colleagues in Vienna had tried out various methods to further psychoanalytic technique, because all had cases at one time or another which had reached a standstill.

In a book written in 1925, *The Development of Psychoanalysis*,[8] Otto Rank and Sandor Ferenczi tried to synthesize and to summarize the fundamental problems which then faced psychoanalytic therapy, including the role of active therapy. In his review of the work, Franz Alexander[9] noted: "The rich store of the experience acquired during an investigation carried on for thirty years needs to be worked through into general theoretical principles, in order to open up new paths for further research." Though Alexander found that their survey filled a general need, he was nonetheless critical of the technical devices associated with active therapy. By 1925, however, Ferenczi had discarded several of the principal *rules* of his active therapy—namely, those of *command* and *prohibition*—in favor of what he now called positive and negative suggestions. In his paper "Contra-Indications to the Active Psychoanalytic Technique" (1925), he noted that he was always ready to change his mind when there was no opposition to his suggestions. Active therapy was only an auxiliary and pedagogic supplement to *real* analysis. He then proceeded to enumerate the many mistakes he had made, and to discuss his disappointment with the active measures he sometimes employed. The difficulty arose from "putting forward certain injunctions and prohibitions which were far

---

[2] Tr. by H. A. Bunker, *Q*, 1933.
[3] Literally, *sea* (Greek).
[4] Freud, S., 1933, "Sandor Ferenczi." *SE*, 22: 228, 1964.
[5] Jones, E., "Recent Advances in Psychoanalysis." *IntJPsa*, 1:161–163, 1920.

[6] Ferenczi, S., *Further Contributions to the Theory and Technique of Psycho-Analysis*. HPI, pp. 198–217, 1926.
[7] Federn, P., "Sandor Ferenczi, Obituary." *IntJPsa*, 14:467–485, 1933.
[8] NMDP, 1925.
[9] Alexander, F., "Review of Ferenczi and Rank's 'Entwicklungsziele der Psychoanalyse.'" *IntJPsa*, 6:484–496, 1925.

too strong." He warned the analyst that in being too emphatic and forceful, he might repeat some phase of the patient's childhood situation, an experience which would leave the analyst in the position of being the sadistic attacker.

Among those attempts that have been made to explain Ferenczi's active therapy are those by Jones in 1920[10] and by Glover in 1927. In a review of Ferenczi's work, *Further Contributions to the Theory and Technique of Psychoanalysis*, Glover noted: "Whatever the ultimate verdict on his active therapeutic devices, whether they come to be incorporated wholly or partly into a standardized psychoanalytic technique, I venture to think that his original paper on the subject will, in the long run, be valued more for the clinical illustrative material than for the technical conclusions they embody."[11] Despite the criticism, it cannot be denied that his clinical observations helped to clarify for many the fundamental relationship between technical proceedings and theoretical deductions.

Ferenczi contributed enormously to our knowledge of infantile development. In his essay, "The Analysis of Urethro-Anal Habits," he described the pregenital identification of the child with his parents, and suggested that the incipient superego had a pregenital origin, "a sort of physiological forerunner of the ego-ideal or super-ego."

He made further important contributions to an understanding of hysteria, to the phenomenon of materialization, and to the erotogenicity of the body organs. He was among the first to explain the mental processes as they effected bodily symptoms: he focused the thinking of many upon the psychogenic influences in organic diseases. He was the first to undertake a comprehensive psychoanalytic analysis of the tic (1921). In this, he pointed to the similarity between traumatic neuroses and the tic, and the similarity between the tic and catatonia. He reasoned that the tic was a regression of the ego that was far more extensive than was true for the obsessive neurotic or the hysteric.

During the period 1930–1933, Ferenczi contributed several technical papers which further modified his concept of active therapy. In his paper, "The Principle of Relaxation and Neocatharsis," he tried to illustrate how the analyst could consciously

attempt to ease the atmosphere in the analytical situation. He noted that the analyst's indirect contact with the patient through interpretation had to be supplemented by a more direct contact to the childish, more infantile aspects of the patient's behavior. In this and several other controversial papers, "Child Analysis in the Analysis of the Adult" and "Confusion of Tongues Between Adults and the Child," the gap between himself and his colleagues was further widened. Ferenczi was the first to point out the importance of the mother-child relationship. He reasoned that its impact was to be explained in terms of the ego mechanisms of defense. This discussion of the "primary love object" can be seen in various emerging theories which concern the nature of early object relationships.

There was no limit to Ferenczi's interest in the application of psychoanalytic thought. He wrote about sociological problems, about art, and about literature, in such essays as "Philosophy and Psychoanalysis," "Goethe—of the Reality Value of the Poet's Fantasy," and the "Psychology of Mechanics." Of all the Freud disciples, Ferenczi's contributions were the most classic and the most central to the development of psychoanalytic technique and theory. Not only was he an excellent teacher, who, as Freud noted, "made us all his pupils," but he was an outstanding and untiring organizer. In Freud's "On the History of the Psycho-Analytic Movement",[12] Ferenczi was singled out for commendation. Freud (1914) stated: "Hungary, so near geographically to Austria, and so far from it scientifically, has produced only one collaborator, S. Ferenczi, but one that indeed outweighs a whole society."

IV

I should like here to discuss Ferenczi's trip to the United States in 1926, and to suggest that certain errors are present in the reports given by Jones[13] in his biography of Freud and by Oberndorf (1953) in his *A History of Psychoanalysis in America*.[14] I should like to preface my remarks by certain personal observations, since I lived in New York at

---

[10] Jones, *loc. cit.*
[11] *IntJPsa*, 8:417–421, 1927.

[12] *SE*, 14:33, 1957.
[13] Jones, E., *The Life and Work of Sigmund Freud*. HPI, 3, 1957.
[14] G & S, 1953.

the time and was in a position to observe closely the events which took place.

I first met Ferenczi in Czechoslovakia in 1920. Later, I was to invite him to lecture before the Medical Society of Košice, which he gracefully accepted. Thus, in the fall of 1921 I came to spend several days with him. Later he suggested that I try a personal analysis, and in the spring of 1923 I went to Budapest and started my analysis with him.

Ferenczi arrived in New York in the fall of 1926 to teach at the New School for Social Research. During his stay, the New York Society had no official contact with Ferenczi. Oberndorf mentions Ferenczi's classes at the New School and his lecture on "Gulliver's fantasies" in December 1926 before the New York Society of Clinical Psychiatry. He neglected, however, to mention the lecture Ferenczi gave before the American Psychoanalytic Association at their Christmas meeting in New York. Apparently, for reasons which will be disclosed presently, Oberndorf did not want to connect Ferenczi's name officially with the psychoanalytic movement in the United States. At the time, Oberndorf was the secretary of the American Psychoanalytic Association, and Adolf Stern was the president. Both were members of the New York Psychoanalytic Society, and both were present at the Christmas meeting, at the MacAlpin Hotel in New York at which Ferenczi was invited "to give a short résumé of the most important practical and theoretical problems." Members of the American Psychoanalytic Association and those of the New York Society in particular were troubled about problems of didactic analysis. They were, as well, angered with him for his support of lay analysis. The New York Society, in November 1926, supported by a large majority of the members, expressed its opposition to the practice of therapeutic analysis by lay persons. In contrast, Ferenczi emphatically expressed (in agreement with Freud) his support of lay analysis, a fact which some of the medical analysts—particularly Oberndorf—neither forgot nor forgave.

I was then working with Oberndorf on the staff of the Mental Health Clinic of the Mount Sinai Hospital. Oberndorf answered my criticism of the Society's discourteous behavior by saying, "When in Rome do as the Romans do." I could not help thinking that in the past Ferenczi had regularly gone from Budapest to Vienna to help train several of the men who now were ignoring him. Disrespect to a famous teacher was inconceivable to me. To observe it was an extraordinary experience. The fact was— the Society's official position to lay analysis was privately disregarded by many of its members.

In his biography of Freud, Jones reports that the New York Society analysts were offended because Ferenczi did not communicate with them about his trip to New York. Jones confused the New York Society with the American Psychoanalytic Association: their attitudes were quite different. Whereas the American Association invited Ferenczi to speak, the New York Society did not contact him at all. Jones also stated that "relations became more and more strained as the months went by until he was almost completely ostracized by his colleagues." The facts are somewhat different. Leading members of the New York Psychoanalytic Society—Brill, Jelliffe, Feigenbaum, Blumgart, and myself, among others—attended regularly the clinical conferences and seminars Ferenczi gave in New York; we were on the most cordial of terms with him. Jones also claimed that while in New York Ferenczi "trained eight or nine lay people." During his stay Ferenczi did have an analytic practice. But they all were analytic patients. Certainly, Ferenczi did not set up a training program.

Ferenczi left New York in 1927, and I did not see him again until the Congress of 1929. There the question of lay analysis was settled. The European analysts agreed not to accept American physicians or lay persons for training in Europe unless the American Educational Committee agreed, which, in effect, closed the door to lay analysts.

V

Before finishing this brief biography of Ferenczi, I feel it my duty to help to set the record straight concerning Ferenczi's terminal illness and the false impressions of it created by Jones in his biography of Freud. For instance, Jones stated that Ferenczi withdrew from Freud in the autumn of 1929. To the contrary, as the "Ten Letters to Freud"[15] indicate, they remained closely in touch until Ferenczi's death in 1933. If there had been a break it is highly unlikely

---

[15] *IntJPsa*, 30:243–245, 1949.

that the Viennese Psychoanalytic Society would have invited Ferenczi to deliver an address in honor of Freud's seventy-fifth birthday. On that occasion Ferenczi (1931) read his paper "Child Analysis in the Analysis of the Adults."

Jones believed that Ferenczi was intriguing against him. He cited instances in the Freud biography in which Ferenczi was heard to talk behind his back, and accused Ferenczi of lying to Freud. In rereading these passages, I gain the impression that there is a subjective, negative feeling harbored by Jones. In personal discussions with me more than twenty years after Ferenczi's death, Jones frequently expressed irritation and criticism of Ferenczi. Obviously this personal bias disturbed Jones' scientific attitude: he failed to check on the accuracy of reports about Ferenczi's health, relationships and behavior. In a letter written shortly after Ferenczi's death in May 1933, Freud warmly thanked Pfister for his sympathetic letter. Freud went on to recall that his old friend had not been himself during the last two years of his life. Ferenczi was suffering from pernicious anemia with motor disturbances and mentally had changed very much. He finally died of combined lateral sclerosis. Freud concluded his letter by reminding Pfister of the importance of Ferenczi's work, particularly his genital theory.[16]

From 1908 until nearly the time of his death, Sandor Ferenczi played a heroic part, second only to Freud, in building psychoanalysis into a branch of science. He made original and brilliant theoretical and clinical contributions. Among the contributors to psychoanalysis, there is no one with the exception of Freud who offered so many valuable and original ideas. He was an excellent psychoanalyst, a physician interested in offering help to those in pain. He put his heart into his work. His personality kept him surrounded by friends until nearly the time of his death when his relationships became distant and strained. He was nonetheless a pioneer of the heroic period of psychoanalysis, an inspiring teacher, and a man whose contributions have still not been fully assessed.

Per Aspera ad Astra.

—Sandor Lorand, M.D.

---

[16] Pfister, O., *Psychoanalysis and Faith*. BB, pp. 139–140, 1963.

609

FETISHISM is a perversion found primarily in men, in which genital discharge is impossible without the presence of a fetish; usually, a nongenital part of the human body (e.g., foot, hand, hair), an inanimate object (e.g., women's apparel, shoes, gloves, undergarments), or something with a special quality, such as a particular odor (e.g., rubber, leather), or touch (e.g., silk, velvet, fur). The fetish may not even be visible to another person; e.g., Freud's patient whose fetish was the shine on the nose of the object to whom he was attracted. Such a patient usually needs to look at, touch or smell the fetish during, or in preparation for, the sexual act (which may be heterosexual, homosexual, masturbatory, etc.). Often, merely seeing the fetish may result in orgasm. The fetishist usually has a great need to possess the fetish, becoming a chronic collector of the fetishistic objects. He shows similar overestimation of and infatuation for the fetish, much as the lover usually shows for the love object; to a greater or lesser extent, the fetish takes the place of the normal love object.

Freud (1905) at first accepted Binet's* view that the choice of a fetish was the after effect of some sexual impression received in early childhood. He later rejected Binet's theory. Freud (1927) stressed the mechanism of denial and assigned the central dynamic role, in the development of fetishism, to the boy's castration anxiety. The boy initially views the absence of a penis in the woman as evidence that castration is possible, and that he, himself, may be castrated. To avoid the anxiety this generates, he rejects his own perception by attributing the role of the penis to some other object or body-part, frequently something seen at the moment at which the woman's genitals were first viewed (e.g.,underwear), something suitable as a symbolic substitute (e.g., foot, shoe), or something associatively linkable with the experience (e.g., fur, as symbolic of the pubic hair).

Freud later (1940) described this in terms of a split in the ego: part of the ego accepts what it sees and acknowledges the reality of the female genitals; another part, denies the external perception and symbolically invests the woman with a penis-equivalent. By this maneuver, part of the ego does

---

* Binet, A., *Études de Psychologie expérimentale: Le fétichisme dans l'amour*. Paris, 1888.

away with the external evidence which would cast a doubt on the original denial; castration is then impossible (nonexistent), so there is nothing to fear. Yet, the very need for a fetish affirms the fact that some part of the ego *is* aware of the reality. In this way, the fetishist maintains a dual attitude toward this reality.

Other authors, such as Bak (1952) and Greenacre (1955), have emphasized disturbances in the mother-child relationship, as manifested in clinging, the role of touch and smell, increased separation anxiety, visual and respiratory incorporation, etc. as being central to the formation of fetishism.

Freud originally referred to perversion as the negative of neurosis, because he assumed that in the perversion the ego (the total personality) accepted the infantile polymorphic perverse wish. In neuroses, the same drive produced the conflict responsible for the neurosis. In his paper on fetishism (1927), however, he showed that this perversion is not the result of the passive acceptance of an infantile drive, but, rather, a complicated defense of it. Other analysts have demonstrated, with the help of materials gained in therapeutically successful analyses of masochists and homosexuals, that these perversions were also caused by complicated defenses of infantile wishes, although the final result of these defenses appeared ego-syntonic.

Related Concepts: DENIAL (DISAVOWAL); PERVERSION.

REFERENCES

Bak, R., "Psychodynamics of Fetishism." *BAPA*, 8:228, 1952.
Freud, S.: 1905, "Three Essays on the Theory of Sexuality." *SE*, 7:153–155, 162, 167, 171, 1953.
    1927, "Fetishism." *SE*, 21:149–158, 1961.
    1940, "Splitting of the Ego in the Process of Defense." *SE*, 23:276, 1964.
Greenacre, P., "Fetishism and Body Image." *PsaStC*, 8, 1953.

ADDITIONAL READINGS

Abraham, K., "Remarks on the Psychoanalysis of a Case of Foot and Corset Fetishism." *Y*, 2, 1910.
Ansbacher, H. L., "Fetishism: An Adlerian Interpretation." *PQ*, 32, 1958.
Bak, R. C., "Fetishism." *JAPA*, 1, 1953.
Balint, M., "A Contribution on Fetishism." *IntJPsa*, 16, 1935.
Bergman, P., "An Analysis of an Unusual Case of Fetishism." *BMC*, 11, 1947.

Buxbaum, E., "Hair Pulling and Fetishism." *PsaStC*, 15, 1960.
Dudley, G. A., "A Rare Case of Female Fetishism." *IntJSexol*, 8, 1954.
Eidelberg, L., "Neurosis: A Negative of Perversion?" *Q*, 28, 1954.
Grant, V. W., "A Case Study of Fetishism." *ASP*, 48, 1953.
Greenacre, P.: "Certain Relationships Between Fetishism and Faulty Development of the Body Image." *PsaStC*, 8, 1953.
    "Further Considerations Regarding Fetishism." *PsaStC*, 10, 1955.
    "Further Notes on Fetishism." *PsaStC*, 15, 1960.
Lorand, S., "Fetishism in Statu Nascendi." *IntJPsa*, 11, 1930.
Mittelmann, B., "Motor Patterns and Genital Behavior: Fetishism." *PsaStC*, 10, 1955.
Ophuijsen, J., "Mededeelingen over het Fetischisme." *NTvG*, 1928.
Parkin, A., "On Fetishism." *IntJPsa*, 44, 1963.
Payne, S., "The Fetishist and His Ego," in *The Psychoanalytic Reader*, ed. by R. Fliess. IUP, 1948.
Socarides, C., "The Development of a Fetishistic Perversion: The Contribution of Preoedipal Phase Conflict." *JAPA*, 8, 1960.
Sonnenfeld, K., "Hand Kissing and Hand Fetishism." *JSP*, 1, 1923.
Stekel, W., "Über einen Perückenfetischisten." *C*, 1, 1911.
Weissman, P., "Some Aspects of Sexual Activity in a Fetishist." *Q*, 26, 1957.

610

FIXATION denotes the arrested development of a component instinct, which causes the libido or destrudo to remain cathected at that infantile stage or associated with a certain infantile narcissistic mortification, making further advance more difficult, and increasing the likelihood of regression to the point of fixation in the face of later obstacles. For example, in the classical syndrome of melancholic depression, there is an instinctual regression to orality. Early developmental phases may also persist side-by-side with later phases and appear in symptoms, character traits, and attitudes. The points of instinctual fixation have an important bearing on the predisposition to different types of neuroses. It is considered by some analysts to be a defense mechanism.

Freud (1917) also used the term *fixation to trauma* (traumatic neurosis) to denote structural fixations, especially of the ego, where attempts at active mastery of the trauma and persistence (repetition compulsion) or return to earlier levels of ego functioning are manifested by magical thinking, primitive defenses, identification, symbiotic object relationship, etc. It is probable that instinctual fixation and ego fixation are mutually interrelated in a complex and variable manner. Freud (1939), in one of his last essays, pointed out (1939) that each neurotic phenomenon is characterized by a positive and a negative aspect. The positive aspect attempts to bring the trauma back into the consciousness and undo, in that manner, the repression or any repetition of an infantile experience with an adult person. This fixation to an infantile traumatic experience was considered by Freud to be the result of the compulsion to repeat. This fixation may lead to the formation of ego-syntonic character traits, apart from the original experience connected with the pleasure or unpleasure. Consequently, a man who as a child was extraordinarily attached to his mother, as an adult may look for a subject to support him, or a girl who was seduced when she was a child, may unconsciously evoke similar seductions as an adult. The discovery of such mechanisms in analysis may lead to a deeper understanding of the character traits of the patient.

The negative aspects of a neurotic phenomenon appear to aim at the repression of the infantile traumas which are neither remembered nor repeated. They are usually present in the various defense mechanisms as avoidances, inhibitions and phobias. There is no doubt that all the negative reactions contribute to the formation of character traits, for they, too, represent fixations although they aim at the denial of it. Thus, as Freud pointed out, each neurotic symptom represents a compromise formation of two contradictory tendencies and, finally, leads to conflicts which can only be solved by psychoanalysis.

The neurotic symptoms and the neurotic character traits are not flexible. In other words, they are characterized by a great psychic intensity and are independent of other psychic mechanisms which aim at making an adjustment to the external world, following the laws of logic. Here, as Freud noted, neurotic phenomena are only partly influenced by external reality and very often contradict it. Because of their rigidity they cannot be controlled and when-

ever this lack of control reaches a certain threshold the patient may develop a psychosis. In cases in which pathological phenomena do not predominate, they may be held to be responsible for the neurosis; the infantile fixations interfere with the subject's adaptation to external realities and they are regarded justly as signs of an infantile fixation.

Predisposing factors include heredity, excessive gratification, and severe deprivation, or some combination of these factors resulting in a traumatic experience. In ego fixation, there is an excessive attachment of the ego to primitive modes of functioning, e.g., magical thinking in certain neurotic disorders. In id fixation, there is an attachment of the id to component-instinctual pleasures and to infantile love objects, e.g., unconscious oral attachment to the mother, the breasts, etc. In superego fixation, the superego functions on a level which may be described as primitive and cruel, e.g., a sadistic and punitive superego in an obsessive-compulsive neurosis.

Related Concepts: LIBIDINAL TYPES; MENTAL (PSYCHIC) ENERGY; REGRESSION; TRAUMA.

REFERENCES

Freud, S.: 1917, "Introductory Lectures on Psycho-Analysis." *SE*, 16:273–276, 359–367, 1963.
     1939, "Moses and Monotheism." *SE*, 23:75–77, 1964.

ADDITIONAL READINGS

Alpert, A., "Reversibility of Pathological Fixations Associated with Maternal Deprivation in Infancy." *PsaStC*, 14, 1959.
Freud, S.: 1911, "Psychoanalytic Notes on an Autobiographical Account of a Case of Paranoia (Dementia Paranoides)." *SE*, 12, 1958.
     1912, "On the Universal Tendency to Debasement in the Sphere of Love." *SE*, 11, 1957.
     1923, "The Ego and the Id." *SE*, 19, 1961.
Greenacre, P., "Regression and Fixation." *JAPA*, 8, 1960.
Johnson, A., "Factors in the Etiology of Fixations and Symptom Choice." *Q*, 22, 1953.

611

FLIGHT INTO FANTASY denotes a type of defensive behavior, exemplified by people who "fearing their impulses, withdraw and become hypoactive; they feel that as long as they limit themselves to daydreaming, they may be sure that their frightening ideas will not bring about any real injury." [Fenichel, 1945.] Flight into fantasy is closely associated with introversion. In both flight into fantasy and its opposite, flight into reality, it is implicit that the feared fantasies are conscious. For example, a young man gives up his fiancée when he increasingly feels aggressive toward her. Rather than risk acting out these impulses in reality, he stops dating and restricts his sexual life to masturbation, stimulated by highly erotic, sadistically tinged fantasies, involving anonymous women pictured in magazines, disavowing, in that manner, his interest in his fiancée. Unlike reality, fantasy permits gratification of wishes for omnipotence, because no real obstacles must be overcome, and the individual can gratify his desire to play two roles at the same time (e.g., male-female, victor-victim).

From a philosophical point of view, one may question whether reality exists; but it cannot be denied that perception can be separated from fantasy.

Related Concepts: FLIGHT INTO REALITY; INTROVERSION.

REFERENCE

Fenichel, O., *The Psychoanalytic Theory of Neurosis.* Nor, p. 526, 1945.

ADDITIONAL READING

Freud, S., "Introductory Lectures on Psycho-Analysis." *SE*, 16, 1963.

612

FLIGHT INTO HEALTH denotes "an unconscious psychic defense utilized by one already suffering neurotic symptoms who, when faced with the intensified threat of the 'Return of the Repressed' [as in psychoanalysis] reacts by losing his symptoms in order to save himself from further unpleasant truths" (Train, 1953). This phenomenon seems to require a gratifying object relationship, which enables the subject to obtain and utilize narcissistic supplies to repress the unconscious, mollify the superego, and strengthen the ego to deal with reality demands. When it occurs during analysis,

it may be mistaken for therapeutic success by the unwary. From a psychoanalytic point of view, however, it appears to be a *transference cure*, or, more accurately, a *transference remission*. It is a sign of defeat, since the patient flees from further therapy in order to avoid the repressed material. At best, the therapeutic results are unpredictable and uncertain, and relapses are theoretically inevitable if the patient is subjected to stress.

For example, a twenty-eight-year-old married man entered psychotherapy because of anxiety spells related to his fear of succumbing to homosexual drives. He could control this impulse but, when he felt attracted to his subordinates, he suffered intolerable anxiety and sought treatment. During his two years of analytically oriented psychotherapy, he brought up preoedipal material with considerable relief. Later, in connection with oedipal material, dreams indicating homosexual wishes appeared. They were accompanied by asymptomatic behavior when among his colleagues. To all appearances, he was normal and, since he no longer suffered from neurotic symptoms, he insisted on terminating therapy, despite the analyst's interpretation of flight into health. Two years later, the homosexual impulse recurred and the patient returned to therapy, admitting the homosexual transference still required analytic therapy.

Related Concepts: FLIGHT INTO ILLNESS; FLIGHT INTO REALITY; TRANSFERENCE.

REFERENCE

Train, G. J., "Flight into Health." *AJPT*, 7:463–483, 1953.

ADDITIONAL READINGS

Alexander, F., & J. French, *Psychoanalytic Therapy.* Ronald Press, 1946.
Fenichel, O., *The Psychoanalytic Theory of Neurosis.* Nor, 1945.
Gartner, P., "Analytische Deutung einer 'Flucht in die Gesundheit.'" *PsaPrx*, 1, 1931.

613

FLIGHT INTO ILLNESS. This concept is based on the idea that an illness (especially a neurotic one) may represent an escape from the inability to adjust to external or to internal reality. Freud (1909) felt that some hysterical patients inflict various injuries on themselves to prevent them from hurting others, and feel guilty because they have symptoms without organic explanations. Freud thought that the hysterical symptom could be produced by (a) association, (b) by somatic causes, (c) by flights into illness, and (d) by consolation.

Related Concepts: FLIGHT INTO HEALTH; PRIMARY PROCESS; SECONDARY PROCESS.

REFERENCE

Freud, S., 1909, "Some General Remarks on Hysterical Attacks." *SE*, 9:231–232, 1959.

614
FLIGHT INTO REALITY. A normal individual is able to differentiate clearly between external and internal reality. He does not confuse the data acquired by his sense organ perception with the ideas and emotions that become conscious. In neurosis these two realities are often confused. Fenichel (1945) noted: "Neurotics are persons who are alienated from their instinctual impulses. They do not know them and they do not want to know them."

A normal person is "able to remember how he felt as a child. A 'generally frigid' person has forgotten childhood emotions; the hyperemotional person is still a child." Flight into reality is usually used in connection with the flight into external reality. However, as Fenichel noted, in certain cases the external reality becomes transformed into internal reality. The patient feels instead of perceiving.

Related Concepts: FLIGHT INTO HEALTH; FLIGHT INTO ILLNESS.

REFERENCE

Fenichel, O., *The Psychoanalytic Theory of Neurosis.* Nor, p. 477, 1945.

ADDITIONAL READING

Searl, M. N., "The Flight into Reality." *IntJPsa*, 10, 1929.

615
FOREPLEASURE, according to Freud (1905), is an increment of pleasure accompanying increasing tension, particularly connected with the stimulation of the erogenous zones, leading to the end-pleasure connected with the release of the tension (particularly genital discharge). Later, Freud (1908) viewed forepleasure as applicable to the understanding of aesthetic pleasure. The creative writer uses his personal daydreams, presenting them in a form which gives the reader aesthetic pleasure. This aesthetic pleasure represents a forepleasure which seduces the reader into a release of additional instinctual energy. Nonetheless, as Freud pointed out, psychoanalysis knows very little about the technique used by the artist. His *ars poetica* remains the artist's secret.

Eidelberg (1954) suggested a broader use of the term, relating it to the anticipation of various forms of end-pleasure. He noted: "Freud removed this contradiction to his original statement by introducing the concepts of forepleasure and end-pleasure. He said that certain parts of the body, the erotogenic zones, were capable of producing a *pleasurable* increased tension when stimulated. He called this pleasure, 'forepleasure,' reserving the term, 'end-pleasure,' for that which accompanies the final discharge of tension.

"Consequently, an increase of tension could produce either *un*pleasure or *fore*pleasure. Not being able to measure this tension, Freud confined himself to the statement that the tension responsible for the feeling of unpleasure seems to be very high, whereas the tension present during forepleasure is either of lower quantity or characterized by a different rhythm.

"This writer has the impression that the sensation of forepleasure may be derived from other parts of the body, in addition to the erotogenic zones. On the other hand, stimulation of the erotogenic zones may sometimes produce *end* pleasure. For instance, kissing and caressing will produce forepleasure only if the genital act can be anticipated. If for some reason, such as kissing immediately after the genital act, this anticipation is improbable, then *end* pleasure takes place. Similarly, seeing, smelling, and tasting food will produce forepleasure if the eating of food is anticipated. The *act of anticipation*, rather than the localization of the sensation, seems to be of more importance."

Related Concept: FORE-UNPLEASURE.

REFERENCES

Eidelberg, L., *An Outline of a Comparative Pathology of the Neuroses.* IUP, pp. 18–19, 1954.
Freud, S.: 1905, "Three Essays on the Theory of Sexuality." *SE,* 7:149–150, 155–156, 210–212, 234, 1953.
     1908, "Creative Writers and Day-Dreaming." *SE,* 9:153, 1959.

ADDITIONAL READING

Greenson, R., "Forepleasure: Its Use for Defensive Purposes." *JAPA,* 3, 1955.

616

FORE-UNPLEASURE, a term introduced by Anna Freud (1936), denotes the experience connected with the anticipation of unpleasure resulting from an increase or decrease of instinctual tension above or below a certain threshold. She noted: "But in little children there is also an endopsychical conflict, which is beyond the reach of education. The outside world very soon establishes a representative in the child's psyche, in the shape of objective anxiety. The occurrence of such anxiety is not in itself evidence of the formation of a higher institution—the conscience or super-ego—within the ego, but it is its precursor. Objective anxiety is the anticipation of suffering which may be inflicted on the child as a punishment by outside agents, a kind of 'fore-pain'* which governs the ego's behaviour, no matter whether the expected punishment always takes place or not. On the one hand, this anxiety is acute in proportion to the dangerous or menacing behaviour of those with whom the child is in contact. On the other hand, it is reinforced by the turning of instinctual processes against the self, is frequently combined with anxiety originating in phantasy and takes no note of objective changes, so that its connection with reality becomes ever looser. It is certain that in the minds of little children urgent instinctual demands conflict with acute objective anxiety, and the symptoms of infantile neurosis are

---

* In the English translation, the term *fore-pain* is rendered from the German *Vor-Unlust,* which is here given as *fore-unpleasure.*

attempts at solving this conflict. The study and description of these inner struggles are debatable ground amongst scientists: some hold that they are the province of pedagogy, while we feel sure that they lie within the domain of the theory of the neuroses."

The unpleasure due to the presence of an external or internal narcissistic mortification would, if anticipated, lead to fore-unpleasure.

Related Concepts: ANXIETY; DEPRESSION; FORE-PLEASURE.

REFERENCE

Freud, Anna, 1936, *Ego and Mechanisms of Defense.* IUP, pp. 155–156, 1946.

617

FRAGMENTATION denotes a tendency to separate psychological parts, to prevent their unification and integration, or to detach some parts from existing entities. [Silbermann, 1961.] Fragmentation derives its energy from the aggressive drive. It is a normal function of the mind, and runs through a number of progressions, in accordance with the level of drive-development and with the maturation of the ego. Thus, we may speak of fragmentation "at its worst" or at "its primary stage"; of fragmentation "at its best" or at "its secondary stage." Fragmentation at its worst is observable in the id; in pathological states, repression, and regression. Fragmentation at its best is essential to the subject's orientation and differentiation; in concept formation, abstract thinking, artistic and scientific creative activities, etc.

An example of abnormal fragmentation is characterized in the case of a young woman who suffered from severe attacks of anxiety, expressed in explosive outbursts of anger, and an inability to concentrate, study or work, particularly in the late afternoon. After many hours of panic and despair, she would feel as if she had been defeated and had fallen apart. During her hours of relative freedom from anxiety, she was efficient, considerate, apparently composed, witty, and a good mother to her children. She described herself as consisting of two parts, which were only held together by "borrowed energy" as long as she felt accepted and loved, but which fell apart (fragmented) when loneliness overcame her. At those moments, she experienced a loss of identity and felt herself to be a shadow without shape, character, strength, color or content.

Related Concept: DEPERSONALIZATION.

REFERENCE

Silbermann, I., "Synthesis and Fragmentation." *PsaStC*, 16:90, 1961.

ADDITIONAL READINGS

Freud, S., 1920, "Beyond the Pleasure Principle." *SE*, 18, 1955.
Silbermann, I., "Synthesis and Fragmentation." *PsaStC*, 16, 1961.

618

FREE WILL. The problem of free will was given early consideration by Freud (1901). Voluntary movements are usually referred to as being caused by free will, whereas involuntary movements are not so influenced. Psychoanalytic evidence, however, offers proof that conscious emotive or affective states are influenced by involuntary automatic functions. Here, Freud was able to show that internal stimuli are connected with repressed unconscious wishes. The assumption of a free will may represent a necessary illusion to permit us to anticipate what we want and to reject what we dislike.

The concept of free will appears to contradict causal determinism and has therefore been rejected by science. Whenever the illusion of free will is missing, the individual may experience the narcissistic mortification of being helpless. He may be ready to accept the severe limitation of his power, but may refuse to give up planning and anticipation. Each anticipation, of course, represents at best a probability and, in this, forces the individual to admit his inability to predict the future.

It was Freud's thesis that psychical freedom was illusionary. He (1916–1917) categorically stated: "Once before I ventured to tell you that you nourish a deeply rooted faith in undetermined psychical events and in free will, but that this is quite unscien-

tific and must yield to the demand of a determinism whose rule extends over mental life." This process is seen most clearly in the behavior of the neurotic. Hartmann (1964) discussed this phenomenon and noted: "We are all familiar with the obsessional neurotic's fear of losing his self-control—a factor which makes it so very difficult for him to associate freely. The phenomenon which I am thinking of is even more clearly marked in those persons who, for fear of losing their ego, are unable to achieve orgasm. These pathological manifestations teach us that a healthy ego must evidently be in a position to allow some of its most essential functions, including its 'freedom,' to be put out of action occasionally, so that it may abandon itself to 'compulsion' (central control). This brings us to the problem, hitherto almost entirely neglected, of a biological hierarchy of the ego's functions and to the notion of the integration of opposites, which we have already met in connection with the problem of rational conduct. I believe that these considerations relative to the mobility of the ego and the automatic disconnecting of vital ego functions have enabled us to make very considerable progress toward discovering an important condition of mental health. The threads which lead us from this point to the concept of ego strength are clearly visible."

Related Concepts: CAUSALITY; PSYCHIC DETERMINISM.

REFERENCES

Freud, S.: 1901, "The Psychopathology of Everyday Life." *SE*, 6:253, 1962.
     1916–1917, "Introductory Lectures on Psycho-Analysis." *SE*, 15:106, 1962.
Hartmann, H., *Essays on Ego Psychology*. IUP, p. 10, 1964.

619

FREUD, SIGMUND, was born on May 6, 1856, in the small town of Freiberg, in Moravia, 150 miles from Vienna. His father, Jakob, was forty-one at the time of his birth, a wool merchant by trade. Freud was to write in a letter to his wife, Martha (Bernays), three years after their marriage, that he was a man who resembled his father, both physically, and, in some ways, intellectually. He went on to remark that his father was never a notably successful man, always hopeful that something would turn up. If Freud's affection for his father was colored by some regret, this was not the case with his mother. She was twenty when she married, and Sigmund was her first born, at the age of twenty-one. As Freud later wrote: "A man who has been the indisputable favourite of his mother keeps for life the feeling of a conqueror, that confidence of success that often induces real success."[1]

As was true elsewhere in Europe, the introduction of machinery seriously threatened the hand-work which was then traditional in the textile industry. His father's wool business was directly affected, and, in 1859, Jakob moved his family to Leipzig, and a year later to Vienna, to recoup the family fortune. It was during this early period that the essential foundations of Freud's character were drawn. He was the eldest child, the center of the *inner family* "We gather," Jones[2] wrote of this formative period, "that he appears to have been a normal sturdy child, and we can only note the few features that distinguish his circumstances from those of the average run of children. They are few, but important.

"He was the eldest child . . . and for a time therefore the centre of what may be called the inner family. This is in itself a fact of significance, since an eldest child differs, for better or worse, from other children. It may give such a child a special sense of importance and responsibility or it may imbue him with a feeling of inferiority as being—until another child appears— the feeblest member of his little community. There is no doubt that the former was true in Freud's case; responsibility for all his relatives and friends became a central feature of his character. This favourable turn was evidently secured by his mother's life, and, indeed, adoration. Self-confidence was built up to a degree that was very seldom shaken. . . .

"Darker problems arose when it dawned on him that some man was even more intimate with his mother than he was. Before he was two years old, for the second time another baby was on the way, and soon visibly so. Jealousy of the intruder, and anger for whoever had seduced his mother into such an unfaithful proceeding, were inevitable."

A more important occurrence, just before this, was the death of his younger brother, when Freud was nineteen months old and little Julius only eight months. "Before the new-comer's birth the infant Freud had had sole access to his mother's love and milk, and he had to learn from the experience how strong the jealousy of a young child can be. In a letter to Fliess (1897) he admits the evil wishes he had against his rival and adds that their fulfilment in his death had aroused self-reproaches, a tendency to which had remained ever since."[3]

Freud at the age of four left Freiberg with his family and moved to Vienna. At the age of nine Freud entered the gymnasium, which roughly corresponds to four years at an American high school and two years of college. He graduated from the gymnasium at the age of 17, *summa cum laude*. His father permitted him to select his future career, a generous decision which was not the rule at that time. During his medical studies, he became chiefly interested in physiology, working under Ernst Brücke. He wanted to devote his life to the work in the Physiological Institute, but Brücke advised him to give up his theoretical studies because of Freud's bad financial position. Presently Freud entered the general hospital and worked six months in the psychiatric department under Theodor Meynert. At the clinic he acquired a thorough knowledge of psychiatry and neurology, and was the first to make a correct diagnosis of polyneuritis acuta.[4]

In 1885 Freud was appointed lecturer in neuropathology and soon after, as a result of a high recommendation from his former teacher, Brücke, he received a travelling bursary and left for Paris to study with Charcot at Salpêtrière. Charcot was applying hypnotism to the study of hysteria, in which the production of hysterical symptoms could, at will, be removed and, by suggestion, imposed upon male and female subjects. Hysterical paralyses and contractures were produced by hypnotic suggestion which showed the same features as the spontaneous attacks brought about by traumas.[5]

Before Freud left Paris, he decided to use a comparative approach to study the hysterical and the organic paralysis. He discussed this plan with Charcot. Freud wanted to establish that hysterical paralyses and anaesthesias were demarcated "by the

---

[1] Jones, E., *The Life and Work of Sigmund Freud.* HPI, 1:6, 1953.
[2] *Ibid.*, pp. 15–16.

[3] *Ibid.*, p. 16.
[4] Freud, S., 1925, "An Autobiographical Study." *SE*, 20:12, 1959.
[5] *Ibid.*, p. 13.

popular idea of their limits and not according to anatomical facts."[6]

Before returning to Vienna, Freud was to pursue an interest that later led to considerable controversy. In 1884 Freud was in Berlin and there he obtained the little known alkaloid cocaine to study its physiological effects. In the course of his studies, he suggested to Königstein that the anesthetizing properties of cocaine might be used to study diseases of the eye. He thereupon went on a vacation to visit his fiancée. On his return, he found that another colleague, Carl Koller, had completed a series of decisive experiments upon animals' eyes and had presented his findings at the Ophthalmological Congress in Heidelberg. Writing of this incident, Freud noted: "Koller is rightly regarded as the discoverer of local anaesthesia by cocaine, which has become so important in minor surgery." He concluded by stating that he did not blame his fiancée for the interruption of his studies.[7]

Jones commented on this cocaine episode, as follows: "The rather unnecessary initial and concluding remarks suggest that someone ought to be blamed, and there is plenty of evidence that it was himself that Freud really blamed. In another context he wrote: 'I had hinted in my essay that the alkaloid might be employed as an anaesthetic, but I was not thorough enough to pursue the matter further.' In conversation he would ascribe the omission to his 'laziness'. . . .

"The somewhat disingenuous excuse Freud gave for the failure when writing his Autobiography must cover a deeper explanation, since it does not tally very closely with the facts. To begin with, the parting had lasted not two years, but one. In a letter to Wittels Freud even says 'several years'. So in retrospect, as well as at the time, the waiting had seemed terribly long. The cocaine essay was finished on June 18, 1884, and Martha Bernays had left Vienna for Wandsbek only on June 14, 1883. Nor was there any sudden opportunity for visiting her, as his passage rather suggests. From the very time of her departure he planned to do so in the summer holiday of the following year, and there are many references in the correspondence to his difficulty in saving up, gulden by gulden, the sum necessary to cover the cost of the journey. As the time approached he

planned to leave in the third week of July, and since he delivered his manuscript to the editor on the date he had promised, June 20, he was hard put to it to find some other distraction to allay his impatience during the five weeks that remained before he could depart for his holiday. As things turned out he was not able to go before September."[8]

The first we hear of the cocaine topic is in a letter of April 21, 1884, in which he gives news of "a therapeutic project and a hope." In Hanns Sachs' book, *Freud, Master and Friend,*[9] Freud is recalled to have said of Koller: "One day I was standing in the courtyard with a group of colleagues of whom this man was one, when another interne passed us showing the signs of intense pain. (Here Freud told what the localization of the pain was, but I have forgotten the detail.) I said to him: 'I think I can help you' and we all went to my room where I applied a few drops of a medicine which made the pain disappear instantly. I explained to my friends that this drug was the extract of a South American plant, the coca, which seemed to have powerful qualities for relieving pain and about which I was preparing a publication. The man with the permanent interest in the eye, whose name was Koller, did not say anything, but a few months later I learned that he had begun to revolutionize eye surgery by the use of cocaine, making operations easy which till then had been impossible. This is the only way to make important discoveries: have one's ideas exclusively focused on one central interest."

Jones analyzed the incident as follows: "Koller read Freud's essay when it appeared in July, pondered over it, and early in September after Freud had left Vienna for Hamburg appeared in Stricker's Institute of Pathological Anatomy carrying a bottle containing a white powder. He announced to the Assistant there, Dr. Gaertner, that he had reason to think it would act as a local anaesthetic in the eye. The matter was at once easily put to the test. They tried it first on the eyes of a frog, a rabbit and a dog, and then on their own—with complete success. Koller wrote a Preliminary Communication dated early in September, and got Dr. Brettauer to read it, and make practical demonstrations, at the Ophthalmological Congress that took place at Heidelberg on September 15. On October 17 he read a paper in

---

[6] Freud, *op. cit.*, p. 14.
[7] *Ibid.*, pp. 14–15.

[8] Jones, *op. cit.*, pp. 87–88.
[9] Sachs, HUP, p. 71, 1944.

Vienna before the Gesellschaft der Ärzte, which he published shortly afterwards. It contained the sentence: 'Cocaine has been prominently brought to the notice of Viennese physicians by the thorough compilation and interesting therapeutic paper of my hospital colleague Dr. Sigmund Freud.'

"Freud had also called the attention of a closer ophthalmological friend, Leopold Königstein, a man six years older than himself and a Docent of three years' standing, to the numbing powers of cocaine and had suggested that he use it to alleviate the pain of certain eye complaints, such as trachoma and iritis. This Königstein faithfully did, with success, and it was only, some weeks later, early in October, that he extended its use to the field of surgery by enucleating a dog's eye with Freud's assistance. He was just a little too late. At the meeting on October 17 he also read a paper describing his experiences with cocaine, but without mentioning Koller's name. It looked like an ugly fight for priority, but Freud and Wagner-Jauregg managed to persuade him, reluctantly, to insert in his published paper a reference to Koller's Preliminary Communication of the previous month and thus to renounce his own claim. As we shall see, Koller did not reciprocate Freud's chivalrous behavior. . . .

"Koller later emigrated to New York, where, as Freud had predicted, he had a successful career. But even at the beginning of his achievement he committed a 'symptomatic error' which indicated some disturbance in his personality that came to open expression in later years. When publishing the paper he had read in Vienna in October, 1884, he quoted Freud's monograph as dating from August instead of July, giving thus the impression that his work was simultaneous with Freud's and not after it. Both Freud and Obersteiner noticed the 'slip' and corrected it in subsequent publications. As time went on Koller presented the discrepancy in still grosser terms, even asserting that Freud's monograph appeared a whole year *after* his own discovery, which was therefore made quite independently of anything Freud had ever done."[10]

The cocaine incident illustrates a character trait which appeared dominant in Freud. It was difficult for him *not* to be generous and he preferred to blame himself instead of blaming others.

---

[10] Jones, *op. cit.*, pp. 94–95, 96.

II

When Freud returned to Vienna to demonstrate what he had learned with Charcot, he met with the same skepticism he had expressed a year earlier. The Chairman of the Society, Bamberger, declared that what Freud said was incredible. Meinert insisted that Freud should find in Vienna cases similar to those he saw in Paris, and present them at the meetings. Freud tried to do this but the chiefs of the various departments of hospitals refused to give Freud their permission. An old surgeon thought that by explaining to Freud that the word "hysteron" meant "uterus," Freud would be persuaded to give up his idea that male patients also suffered from hysteria.

In 1925, Freud wrote about this incident of the 1886's, making it clear that it was the physician's responsibility to help patients. Unfortunately, as he noted, the single tool available for the treatment of nervous diseases was derived from Erb's electrotherapy. Freud discovered that Erb's methods were of little help, no more than "the construction of fantasy." He thereafter set aside his electrical apparatus and directed his attention to the psychological treatment of patients with neurotic disorders.[11]

Some years later, in a speech delivered on the occasion of the twentieth anniversary of Clark University, in 1909, Freud was to recall the origins of psychoanalysis.[12] Freud contended that Josef Breuer had brought psychoanalysis into being during a time that marked his own student days (1880–1882), and should thus be considered its founder. Specifically, Freud alluded to the case of Frl. Anna O. This intelligent twenty-one-year old had originally been recommended to Breuer for a nervous cough, one of a number of symptoms which had appeared on the death of her father. After several visits, Frl. Anna O. got into the habit of describing the symptoms and hallucinations which troubled her. To Breuer's surprise, one of her symptoms entirely disappeared after she was able to recount the details of its first appearance. One after the other, Breuer encouraged her to discuss each of her symptoms, and many (though not all) fell before the onslaught of what the patient called the "talking

---

[11] Freud, *op. cit.*, p. 16.
[12] Freud, S., 1910, "Five Lectures on Psycho-Analysis." *SE*, 11, 1957.

cure." While still a student at the University, Freud expressed great interest in the case and discussed it over and over again with his revered teacher. This first tentative "professional" association was to mark the beginning of psychoanalysis.

After his own failure to successfully treat patients with electro-therapy, Freud returned to the technique which had so intrigued him five years before. He began by repeating the investigations Breuer had so quickly broken off in the summer of 1882. He discovered that while it was true that with the help of hypnosis he was able to obtain quick and dramatic results, a number of patients would not be hypnotized, and, more importantly, that those who were cured by cathartic hypnosis developed, after a time, some other symptom. With the help of hypnosis, Freud was able to overcome the resistance against the repressed material, and therefore obtained it relatively easily. On the other hand, the technique of hypnosis made impossible the observation and the analysis of the resistance which even today is regarded as the most important problem in dealing with neurotics.

In the beginning Freud was not aware of the importance of sexuality. He wrote of this period in his *Autobiography*: "Nor was I then aware that in deriving hysteria from sexuality I was going back to the very beginnings of medicine and following up a thought of Plato's. It was not until later that I learnt this from an essay by Havelock Ellis."[13] After he discovered the importance of sexuality, he thought that it was the sexuality of a grown-up person. Only after he started to use the method of free association did he discover the phenomenon of infantile sexuality. At first, he thought that the neurotics were seduced by grown-ups and that this seduction represented the causal, traumatic factor responsible for the patient's neurosis. It was not until later that Freud discovered that his patients projected their own incestuous wishes to the grown-up. Freud mentioned this "error" for the first time in a letter to Fliess in 1897. In his autobiographical study, Freud (1925) was to recall that he was at first convinced that the seduction of children actually took place and was responsible for their neuroses. Later, he discovered that these patients reported seductions which hadn't taken place. Consequently, his theory

of seduction had to be abandoned. Finally, he realized that from the child's point of view there was no difference between a real seduction and the wish to be seduced. He thereafter introduced the concept of psychic reality which accounts for this apparent contradiction.[14]

During that early period (1887–1892), Freud and Breuer studied many cases together, and, finally, in 1892, he persuaded the older man to publish their findings. Of this work, Freud (1925) was to remark: "If the account I have so far given has led the reader to expect that the *Studies on Hysteria* must, in all essentials of their material content, be the product of Breuer's mind, that is precisely what I myself have always maintained and what it has been my aim to repeat here. As regards the *theory* put forward in the book, I was partly responsible, but to an extent which it is to-day no longer possible to determine."[15]

In the several years which followed the publication of their joint work, until their final break in 1895, Breuer grew increasingly resistive about Freud's emphasis on the significance of sexuality in the etiology of the neuroses, and began to show "reactions of resentful rejection." We know now that Breuer turned away from the cathartic psychoanalytic method because of the phenomenon of transference. In his introduction to volume two of the Standard Edition to Freud's work, Strachey reckoned the reason for the break, as follows: "Something of the kind can be read between the lines of Breuer's contribution to the *Studies*, and we have the picture of a man half-afraid of his own remarkable discoveries. It was inevitable that he should be even more disconcerted by the premonition of still more unsettling discoveries yet to come; and it was inevitable that Freud in turn should feel hampered and irritated by his yoke-fellow's uneasy hesitations."[16]

III

In September of 1886, shortly after his return to Vienna, in the fourth year of their engagement, Sigmund Freud and his betrothed, Martha Bernays, were married in a Jewish ceremony in Wandsbek,

---

[13] Freud, *op. cit.*, p. 24.

[14] Freud, *op. cit.*, pp. 33–34.
[15] *Ibid.*, p. 21.
[16] Strachey, J., Editorial note. *SE*, 2:xxvi, 1955.

Germany. It was arranged for a weekday so that only a few friends might attend, Freud being opposed to a religious ceremony, as his letters of that period testify. Not a fortuitous beginning, perhaps, but it proved to be a long and happy marriage, running a course of fifty-three years. The bride was twenty-five, the groom thirty.

The first years of their marriage were not without their difficulty. Money was short. Freud had to pawn his gold watch their first summer together. But they were happy years. Even on a slim allowance, Martha always provided for her husband's comfort. He discussed his cases with her, but with the arrival of children to the household and the increasing complexity of his clinical studies he turned the light of his professional interest on others.

In all, three sons and three daughters were to arrive to complete their happiness. Soon after their move to 19 Berggasse, a now well-known address, Minna Bernays joined the family group to remain until her death. "Tante Minna," as she was affectionately called, got on excellently with Freud, and, in later years, took several short excursions with him. There was no sexual attraction on either side, and she seems to have, in every way, been a valuable addition to the growing household.

Freud's wife, Frau Professor, as she was to be known after Freud's promotion in 1902, was well educated and intelligent, though she could not, like her sister, be called an intellectual. She was a *Hausfrau* to be sure, concerned with the health and comfort of her growing family and of her husband, but she did spend many of her evenings reading the current literature. Perhaps she had little desire to participate in Freud's psychoanalytic studies, as has been suggested, yet in his letters written during their summer separations he makes casual allusions to a number of his writings which at least indicates a partial knowledge on her part. The whole of the family atmosphere, as Jones has commented, "was free, friendly and well-balanced. Of few families can so much be said, and it is an eloquent witness to the love that pervaded their relationships."[17]

Freud was altogether an affectionate father, believing in a minimum of restraint and reprimand. His plan was that his children should have every-

thing they should need for their education, but that, once grown, they were to earn their own living, and, in fact, what remained of his estate after his final move to England was left to his wife in trust. Freud believed that there were three things that should not be stinted: education, travel and health. He saw to all three.

During the ten-year period of what he was proud to call his isolation, Freud nonetheless had many close personal friends. It was to the period of his intellectual isolation that he referred. During the nineties, after his break with Breuer, he had only his sister-in-law and Fliess to whom he could turn for discussions of his work. Freud first met Wilhelm Fliess, two years his junior, in Vienna in 1887, and their friendship soon became a close one. They were both educated in the humanities, and their scientific backgrounds were not dissimilar. The chief demand that Freud made upon his friend was that he should listen to Freud's latest findings and pass judgment on them. This Fliess did, and if with no great effect, except in matters of style or syntax, it was apparently sufficient for Freud to have a sympathetic ear in an environment that was almost totally hostile to his writings of the "sexual period." It is to the letters Freud addressed to Fliess in the years that ended the century (1897–1900) that we turn for insight into a period of great intellectual creative effort, and of much neurotic pain. "There is an unmistakable connection between the two facts," Jones writes. "The neurotic symptoms must have been one of the ways in which the unconscious material was indirectly trying to emerge, and without that pressure it is doubtful that Freud would have made the progress he did. It is a costly way of reaching that hidden realm, but it is still the only way."[18]

There is indeed a letter dated in the month (July 1897) Freud began his own analysis, in which he complains of a spell of complete inhibition to writing. In other letters of the period, Freud complains of headaches (migraine) and the two discussed the possibilities of its etiology. He also wrote to Fliess saying that he expected to die of heart failure when he was fifty-one—a prediction that he was to outlive by thirty-two years. He succeeded in giving up his favored cigars for better than fourteen months, a factor that was to prolong his life he said. The years

---

[17] Jones, *op. cit.*, 2:433, 1955.

[18] *Ibid.*, p. 355.

which followed were to prove that he had a sound heart and could sustain a fair quantity of nicotine.

Freud decided that he required self-analysis in order to free himself of some neurotic blank spots and increase his ability to understand his patients, and expected Fliess to examine and comment on his findings. "This Fliess faithfully did," Jones noted. "It was not likely that his comments on the subject matter were of any great value, but he made various suggestions for Freud's writings, concerning questions of arrangement, style and discretion, most of which were gratefully accepted. He acted, in short, as a censor. And a censor, besides his obvious activity in eliminating the objectionable, performs an even more important function in silently sanctioning what he has allowed to pass. This sanction is what Freud at that time needed, not the independent-minded, inflexible Freud we knew in later years, but the very different man he was in the nineties. Fliess bestowed this sanction freely. He admired Freud and had no reason (at first!) to doubt the correctness of Freud's work, so the praise he gladly gave must have been highly encouraging. One example alone of its effect will suffice: 'Your praise is nectar and ambrosia to me' (July 14, 1894)."[19]

The dream interpretation (which Freud discovered while working with Breuer) represented the first important approach to the unconscious; the second was represented by the sexual problems of his patients. In writing of this period Jones noted: "The first forms of sexual excitation in early childhood that Freud recognized were what are now called 'pre-genital' ones and concerned the two alimentary orifices, mouth and anus. These could still be regarded as auto-erotic. It was much harder to admit that the young child might have genital wishes concerning a parent which could in many respects be comparable with adult ones. And to recognize the full richness of the child's sexual life in terms of active impulses was a still further step that Freud took only later with his usual caution."[20]

These repressed infantile wishes were present in the patient and appeared to be mobilized in the psychoanalytical situation. The patient not only remembered what he had repressed, but also tried to repeat with the analyst what had taken place while he was a child. In each analysis, as Freud (1925)

noted, the patient repeats the infantile situation by transferring his infantile emotions to the analyst. These emotions can be positive as well as negative. The patient may use the positive transference when it becomes essential as resistance. The same happens with the negative transference. The transference cannot be avoided; it actually helps the analyst to see what is important for the patient.[21]

His findings in the investigation of dreams Freud summed up in his Autobiographical sketch (1925). "Analysis exploits the dream in both directions, as a means of obtaining knowledge alike of the patient's conscious and of his unconscious processes."[22]

In his later writings, Freud was to assign Fliess the recognition of having been the first to use the terms *latency period* and *sublimation*. Fliess was also designated as the discoverer of what Freud, in "Beyond the Pleasure Principle" (1920), was to call the "grandiose conception" of all vital phenomena, being bound up with the completion of definite time spans (periodicity), to the concept of bisexuality,[23] and to what, later, he called the repetition compulsion.

The reason for their final break is unclear. It would appear that Fliess believed that Freud had robbed him of the clear recognition he thought his due for the discovery of bisexuality, and, to this, we can add little. The last of their correspondence dates from the fall of 1902. Subsequent events were to at least point to the persecutory nature of Fliess' ideas. He was in later years to repeatedly attack Freud in print. Freud did not reply in kind!

It was Freud's custom to send his family away to the country in the late spring while he continued to work on alone in the city, joining his family for July and August. With the improvement of his fortunes in the 1890's he journeyed further afield, setting out on more distant travels, accompanied by his wife, his brother, or, on one occasion, by his sister-in-law. It was in August of 1890 that he and Fliess were to hold the first "Congress"—of two—at Salzburg. In 1891 he went mountain climbing with Fliess, and in the years which followed, he visited him in Berlin several times. In the summer of 1897 he was to take a short walking tour with Minna to Untersberg and

---

[19] Jones, *op. cit.*, 1:327, 1953.
[20] *Ibid.*, p. 355.

[21] Freud, *op. cit.*, p. 42.
[22] *Ibid.*, p. 46.
[23] E.g., in "Three Essays on the Theory of Sexuality" (1905).

Heilbrunn, the period in which he was to begin his own analysis. So, as the century drew to a close, did he embark on the journey that was to take him to fame. In the summer of 1899, in a farm house near Berchtesgaden where his family was to spend many vacations, he was to complete the larger part of his manuscript, "The Interpretation of Dreams." Published in 1900, in a run of six hundred copies that took eight years to sell, it is by all census Freud's major work, certainly his most original.

IV

Freud's emergence from isolation was an undramatic one. His papers and books were variously reviewed in Europe, but his work was largely dismissed or ignored. The beginning of any formal recognition had to wait. In the meantime his work had attracted the attention of at least four men of similar interests—Alfred Adler, Max Kahane, Rudolf Reitter, and Wilhelm Stekel—who began to meet each Wednesday in Freud's waiting room. In the years which followed, they were joined (of those best known) by Paul Federn in 1903, Otto Rank in 1906, and Sandor Ferenczi in 1908. The circle was further enlarged by visits from Max Eitingon and Karl Abraham starting in 1907, Ernest Jones in 1908, and Hanns Sachs in 1910. At the beginning of 1908, there were twenty-two members, not more than eight or ten to be found at any one meeting. That same year the First International Psychoanalytical Congress was held at Salzburg, and the "Psychological Wednesday Society," as it was called, was designated as the Vienna Psychoanalytical Society, the first of many which remained to be founded all over the world.

In 1904, Eugen Bleuler, Professor of Psychiatry in Zürich, informed Freud that his staff—in particular, his assistant, Carl Jung—was finding various applications for psychoanalysis. Jung had succeeded in demonstrating experimentally that the "affective complexes" might interfere with recollected recollections (word association test). Thereafter, Jung and Freud began an active correspondence, and, after meeting with him in 1907, an intense personal as well as professional relationship was established, Freud considered Jung to be one of the most creative of his followers, and Jung manifested great enthusiasm for Freud and his work. When the International Psychoanalytic Association was founded in 1910, Jung became its first president, at Freud's designation. Jung was the logical choice because of "his exceptional talents, the contributions he had already made to psychoanalysis, his independent position, and the impression of assured energy which his personality conveyed."[24] Even so, Jung increasingly disagreed with Freud concerning the relative importance of the instincts of sexuality in the pathogenesis of neuroses. By 1911 he had come to consider libido as merely a form of energy and in his teaching and practice he no longer felt it necessary to go into detail regarding sexuality.

Initially, Jung saw his modification of analytic theory as an attempt to win general and popular acceptance of psychoanalysis by deemphasizing that feature which had been the chief target of critical attack and scorn, and he indicated this to Freud in a letter from America in 1912. However, Freud rejected the idea of this popular acceptance as an advance, and instead felt it "a sacrifice of the hardwon truths of psychoanalysis."[25] He saw Jung's contributions as having only "illuminated an important instance of the sublimation of the erotic instinctual forces and of their transformation into trends which can no longer be called erotic."[26]

The details of the deterioration of the personal and professional relationship between Freud and Jung are recorded by Jones, culminating in the breaking off of personal correspondence in 1912, and of professional relations after the 1913 International Congress. In April 1914, Jung resigned as president of the International Psychoanalytic Association, and later that year he withdrew from the Association altogether.

With increasing recognition came other dissident voices. It was not long after the International Congress of 1910 that Adler, one of the first of Freud's supporters, was to turn into another channel. Adler's theory of neurosis and character formation was manifest in what he called the "masculine protest," and in the compensation for the "feelings of inferiority" to which it gave rise. At first, all such conflicts were thought to arise from the feminine and masculine counterparts of the person-

---

[24] Freud, S., 1914, "On the History of the Psycho-Analytic Movement," *SE*, 14:43, 1957.

[25] *Ibid.*, p. 58.

[26] *Ibid.*, p. 61.

ality, a concept he later modified in terms of "the will for power," as Nietzsche had defined it, arising from pure aggression.

Adler denied the significance of infantile sexuality and libido as motivating forces, as well as the importance of repression and of unconscious mental life. His theory was essentially an elaboration of the psychology of conscious ego. Freud's extensive criticism of Adler's theory is included in his paper "On the History of the Psychoanalytic Movement" (1914). Freud's revision of the instinct theory and his introduction of the concept of a death instinct initiated the more systematic study of aggression which he was to write about at length ten years later, when it was included in analytic theory as a basic drive. The role and vicissitudes of aggression in mental life have been extensively elaborated since that time, but these observations and concepts are far broader than Adler's concept of the will to power.

V

The first public recognition of Freud's work may be traced to the first Congress held in Salzburg in 1908. The Congress was truly an international gathering. Nine papers were read, four from Austria, two from Switzerland, and one each from England, Germany and Hungary. There were forty-two members present, half of whom were practising analysts, or were to become so. By now, of course, the cornerstones of Freud's early work, "Three Essays" and "Interpretation of Dreams", were familiar to all who were present. Indeed, Freud's theory of the mind was gaining increasing recognition in the larger intellectual world beyond 19 Berggasse. Increasing recognition was not bought without strife. Even as the scientific work was successfully proceeding, personal troubles were coming to the fore. Of this time, Freud (1914) wrote: "I could not succeed in establishing among its members the friendly relations that ought to obtain between men who are all engaged upon the same difficult work; nor was I able to stifle the disputes about priority for which there were so many opportunities under these conditions of work in common."[27]

Freud had little interest in problems of adminis-

tration and wanted his energy concentrated on scientific problems. "Once a year," Hanns Sachs related, "we had a business meeting which Freud opened by saying: 'Today we must play high school fraternity' (Heute müssen wir Verein spielen), or words to that effect. Then the treasurer would read some figures and would state that the Society was not in debt. After that someone would move a vote of approbation and propose the re-election of the *Vorstand* which was duly voted, whereupon the scientific work was resumed."[28]

Unfortunately, the psychoanalytical group was troubled by dissensions. The first to leave was Alfred Adler. His ideas of the importance of egoistic impulses interfered with Freud's conception of instinctual drives. Adler refused to accept their presence. Freud (1914) expressed his opinion, as follows: "As we know, the principle of Adler's system is that the individual's aim of self-assertion, his 'will to power' is what, in the form of a 'masculine protest', plays a dominating part in the conduct of life, in character-formation and in neurosis. This 'masculine protest', the Adlerian motive force, is nothing else, however, but repression detached from its psychological mechanism and, moreover, sexualized in addition—which ill accords with the vaunted ejection of sexuality from its place in mental life."[29]

After Adler, Wilhelm Stekel left the psychoanalytic movement. He was originally responsible for the foundation of the psychoanalytical group in Vienna and impressed Freud by his uncanny ability to guess the unconscious meaning of dreams. However, his character was such that he could not be trusted. As Jones noted in his biography of Freud, "Stekel had, however, a serious flaw in his character that rendered him unsuitable for work in an academic field: he had no scientific conscience at all. So no one placed much credence in the experiences he reported. . . . In a paper he wrote on the psychological significance people's surnames have for them, even in the choice of career and other interests, he cited a huge number of patients whose names had profoundly influenced their lives. When Freud asked him how he could bring himself to publish the names of so many of his patients he answered with a reassuring smile: 'They are all made up,' a fact which somewhat detracted from the evidential

---

[27] Freud, *op. cit.*, p. 25.

[28] Sachs, *op. cit.*, p. 62.
[29] Freud, *op. cit.*, p. 54.

value of the material. Freud refused to let it appear in the *Zentralblatt*, and Stekel had to publish it elsewhere."[30]

Jung also left Freud's group and created his own school. Freud wrote about Jung, as follows: "When Jung tells us that the incest-complex is merely 'symbolic', that after all it has no 'real' existence, that after all a savage feels no desire towards an old hag but prefers a young and pretty woman, we are tempted to conclude that 'symbolic' and 'without real existence' simply mean something which, in virtue of its manifestations and pathogenic effects, is described by psycho-analysis as 'existing unconsciously.'"[31]

In spite of the loss of once devoted followers, psychoanalysis continued to grow in importance. In 1909, Freud was invited to Worcester by Stanley Hall, president of Clark University, where he gave five lectures. Freud (1925) refers to his journey to America as follows: "At that time I was only fifty-three. I felt young and healthy, and my short visit to the new world encouraged my self-respect in every way. In Europe I felt as though I were despised; but over there I found myself received by the foremost men as an equal."[32]

VI

The war brought its inevitable dislocations. His sons were in the army, as were several of his colleagues, communication was difficult and, at times, impossible. In 1916, he wrote that he had but three analytic patients, and the next year, one. He believed that his essential contributions to the young science of psychoanalysis was at an end. He attached the highest importance to the seventh chapter of "The Interpretation of Dreams" (1900), the last chapter of "Totem and Taboo" (1913) and the essay in his metapsychological series, "The Unconscious" (1915). What lay ahead he was content to leave to the work of others. It was perhaps understandable after the burst of creative energy he had poured into his metapsychological essays—in particular, his essay a year earlier, "On Narcissism," where he was to confront the problem of accounting for the libidinal character of the ego instincts—that he was pre-

pared to write "Introductory Lectures on Psycho-Analysis" (1916) and to consider his major contributions at an end.

Freud called himself a "cheerful pessimist." Yet, he was eminently a realist, and his metapsychological writings of the period foretell what were to prove major revisions to psychoanalytic thinking. It soon became clear that the resistance met with in treatment was observed to be largely unconscious, but could not be directly related to the concepts inherent in what, later, we came to call the first instinct theory. In the years which followed the war,[33] Freud was to develop the structural (topographic) hypothesis, by which the mental processes were grouped according to their function into the id, ego, and superego, with his previously held constructs of conscious and preconscious-conscious systems now assigned an adjectival reference. Psychic conflict was understood to occur between these faculties of the mind, and a dual instinct theory of Eros and Thanatos was explored by which sexual and aggressive instinct fusions were thought to predominate. As a result, the analyst's interpretations were directed not alone to the instinctual drives, but equally toward the unconscious superego functions and the unconscious defenses and resistance of the ego itself. Emphasis was further placed on the resolution of the transference neurosis, to the undoing of the infantile neurosis, and to the development of the individual toward genital primacy.

In writing of the contributions Freud made to the many fields which encompassed his interests, Kanzer noted: "In retrospect, it may be said that Freud, who broadened science to include the irrational and who drew the techniques of poetry and the dream into the therapeutic armamentarium of the analyst, likewise included religion in certain of its aspects, viz., faith, courage, and love of truth. He deprived these qualities of their supernatural aspects, to be sure, and found that they were vital psychological forces which must be recognized and used in dealing with mental illness and health. Yet this enlightened viewpoint inevitably extends into a sphere where uncertain boundaries between intellectual knowledge and feeling, between tested experience and personal values, constitute dangers to which rationalists and mysticists each in their

[30] Jones, *op. cit.*, 2:153, 1955.
[31] Freud, *op. cit.*, p. 64.
[32] *Ibid.*, 20:52, 1925.

[33] See especially, "Beyond the Pleasure Principle" (1920) and "The Ego and the Id" (1923).

own way succumb. It is the merit of psycho-analysis that, following in the footsteps of Freud, self-scrutiny of its own techniques and assumptions is unending, this providing the best safeguard against the persistence of the demons of the irrational in any guise except as instincts in the service of the ego—an ego, of course, that is committed in turn to the healthy service of the instincts in their social setting."[34]

His work of the period 1914–1926 was indeed revolutionary. The last of his major contributions, "Inhibition, Symptoms and Anxiety" (1926), was written when he was seventy. The topics dealt with in this paper ranged over a wide field: the distinction between repression and defense, the different classes of resistance, and the relationship between anxiety, pain and mourning. Of course, its principal topic was the problem of anxiety. A second theory of this all-important process was given. Here, anxiety was understood as an internalization of previously externally-directed fear. The *instinctual, ego* and *superego* anxieties gradually achieve an anticipatory signal function, in response of which the individual attempts to modify his internal and external environment.

His metapsychological papers of that period can only be briefly summarized, yet they, too, prove to be of primary importance. Mental life was viewed as the end result of a continuous interaction between the complex forces which are integrative within and outside the individual. In this, the genetic approach was understood in terms of the individual development from his earliest years and of the solution of the infantile sexual conflict as the prototype of all subsequent experience. The dynamic approach was confirmed to be the result of the interplay of all the current forces at work within the mind. The economic approach involved the concept of psychic energy, of its continuous variation, i.e., of the relative intensity of the opposing forces within the psychic apparatus. No summary of Freud's work can do him justice. Nonetheless, his more important contributions are, as follows:

(1) Explained how the genital desires of adults develop from early infantile sexual cravings, and how the repression of these infantile cravings may lead to neurosis.

[34] Kanzer, M., "Freud and the Demon." *JHH*, 10:201, 1961.

(2) Showed us that, in addition to external problems, we must learn to solve internal conflicts, which come into existence by the fact that what we want is not always what we should or must want. Each individual has to control various demands of his id, respect the orders and prohibitions of his superego, and teach his ego to act as "an honest broker" in the achievement of a harmonious compromise between himself and the outside world.

(3) Proved that our dreams and parapraxes can be interpreted and used for the understanding and, therefore, for the control of the unconscious parts of our personality.

(4) Exposed our aggression not only as a weapon of defense in the service of our vital needs, but also as a representative of an independent destructive force which we must "tame" in order to survive.

(5) Taught us how to investigate and cure the neurotic patients by decoding the unconscious meaning of their defenses and by encouraging them to repudiate their infantile wishes in order to achieve emotional maturity.

(6) Demonstrated how the study of sublimation can be used to investigate the meaning of scientific and esthetic pleasures.

VII

In his metapsychological period, the year 1923 proved to be the most critical. He was to complete a major work, "The Ego and the Id," and to face the fact of his diminishing physical powers. From the age of forty, Freud had repeatedly written to his friends of his feeling that he would not survive his middle fifties. Finally, in his sixty-seventh year he was to face its eventuality. What at first appeared as a benign growth of the palate and jaw was removed under anaesthesia at a local clinic. A pathological examination found the growth to be cancerous but Freud was not told. Several X-ray treatments followed, but, still, he was rarely free of pain. His daughter, Anna Freud, unmindful of the good reports the doctors offered, urged a further examination and this was finally made by Dr. Felix Deutsch who confirmed her suspicions.

Even then Freud was not given a truthful view of his condition. While Freud vacationed in Rome that summer, Deutsch persuaded Professor Hans Pichler, a noted oral surgeon, to take over the case. Upon

Freud's return, an examination was made in September and Deutsch's views were confirmed. The operations took place on October 4 and 11, opening a cavity between the nasal passage and the mouth. Again, it was performed under local anaesthesia. He had always, thereafter, in order to be able to talk and to eat, to wear a prosthesis, a kind of magnified denture. His daughter Anna, who thereafter attended him regularly as both secretary and nurse—though she had been admitted to membership in the Vienna Psychoanalytic Society in 1922—was asked by her father to treat him with dispassion and to show no outward sign of emotion in her attendance. This proved a difficult task. There were times when their combined strength could not place the "monster" into the cavity.

Professor Pichler attended Freud regularly until, in 1938, his stay in Vienna was no longer tenable. His daughter's choice of surgeon was an excellent one. He was faithful to Freud's dictum that he be told the truth, whatever the consequences. In all he performed all but the last of the thirty-three operations Freud was to undergo. So began sixteen years of pain and anguish—and of continued dedication to the science he had brought into being.

VIII

In 1912 a Committee of the "old guard" was formed which sought to protect Freud and psychoanalysis from those who would change its basic tenets. It was understood that no one of its members would make public any contrary view which had not first been discussed with the rest. The defection of Adler and Stekel, and the suspected defection of Jung, made the formation of such a committee imperative. In response to a query by Ernest Jones, Freud remarked: "What took hold of my imagination immediately is your idea of a secret council composed of the best and most trustworthy among our men to take care of the further development of psycho-analysis and defend the cause against personalities and accidents when I am no more. . . . I know there is a boyish and perhaps romantic element too in this conception, but perhaps it could be adapted to meet the necessities of reality. I will give my fancy free play and leave to you the part of censor.

"I daresay it would make living and dying easier for me if I knew of such an association existing to watch over my creation.

"First of all: This committee would have to be *strictly secret* in its existence and in its actions. It could be composed of you, Ferenczi and *Rank* among whom the idea was generated, Sachs, in whom my confidence is unlimited in spite of the shortness of our acquaintance—and *Abraham* could be called next, but only under the condition of all of you consenting. I had better be left outside of your conditions and pledges: to be sure I will keep the utmost secrecy and be thankful for all you communicate to me. I will not drop any utterance about the matter before you have answered me, not even to Ferenczi. What ever the next time may bring, the future foreman of the psycho-analytical movement might come out of this small but select circle of men, in whom I am still ready to confide in spite of my last disappointment with men."[35]

The group which was to play such a significant role in Freud's life for the next fifteen years held its first meeting in 1913. "Of the five pre-war members," Jones wrote in his biography of Freud, "it was easy to say how Freud's affections were distributed. Ferenczi came easily first, then Abraham, myself, Rank and Sachs, in that order. I may also mention our ages. Ferenczi was the senior, being born in 1873, then Abraham 1877 myself 1879, Sachs 1881, Rank 1885. Rank nad first met Freud in 1906, Abraham in 1907, Ferenczi and myself in 1908, and Sachs in 1910 (although he had attended his lectures for years before)."[36] Max Eitingon, as the sixth member, was suggested in 1919, and quickly accepted.

Of the six members, Sandor Ferenczi was closest to Freud. The extensive correspondence carried on by the members of the Committee contains many of the letters exchanged by Freud and Ferenczi. They reveal a warm friendship, and deal with many of the younger man's personal and domestic as well as his professional problems, a feature that was singularly lacking in Freud's letters to the others. To understand the relationship between the two it must be remembered that Ferenczi underwent his analysis with Freud. It is to the last years of Ferenczi's life (1929–1933) that many investigators have turned to find a growing dissension between the two men.

[35] Jones, *op. cit.*, 2:173–174, 1955.
[36] *Ibid.*, p. 175.

Ferenczi, in those years, was to pursue his investigation of "active therapy," a method which did not go uncriticized by the older man. Yet, there can be no doubt that Freud valued Ferenczi's contribution.

Freud's relationship to Karl Abraham was totally different. The letters exchanged by the two during the life of the Committee bear this out. In analyzing them, Jones noted: "Their scientific content was objective and is the most valuable of the three sets. Abraham's attitude was that of a very senior pupil who could discuss matters seriously and unemotionally. He was learning, but he had no hesitation in saying when he had not yet been able to confirm this or that point from his own experience. Freud must have had a higher opinion of Abraham's intellectual powers than of any of the others, and in my opinion rightly so (I was merely intelligent!). He therefore welcomed confirmation from Abraham most of all. Not that this was always immediately forthcoming, as it would be with some of the others. Abraham once remarked to me that when Freud produced a new theory it took him some time to digest it and he was never satisfied until he could place it in relation to the central Oedipus complex. He was by no means a slow thinker, but he had not Ferenczi's lightning-like divination."[37]

Ernest Jones met Freud in 1905, a relationship which continued in force throughout Freud's life. "Freud's letters to me," Jones writes of that period, "were again different. They were warm, even affectionate, and full of praise for my activity. Much of them was taken up with reports of a treatment he was conducting of a very difficult case, with a mixture of mental and organic symptoms, in a lady who stood in a personal relationship to myself. There would be many comments, often amusing ones, on the extensive reports I would send him of progress in America and England. He did not often volunteer accounts of any new theories, but would answer fully the numerous technical questions I kept putting to him. In the letters to all of us, however, there was always news of what he was writing at the moment, of publications, new editions, difficulties with publishers and the like."[38]

Otto Rank first met Freud in 1906 and became, with Hanns Sachs, the editor of *Imago*. He had little formal education and was of a lower social class

than the other members of the Committee. In many ways, he served as the business agent for the Vienna Society. In point of fact, beginning with the year 1906 and continuing until 1915, Rank was its official and salaried secretary, entrusted with the task of recording its minutes. His service to the Society was interrupted by the war, but with his return he once again took up his manifold tasks. In 1923, Ferenczi and Rank published *The Developmental Aims of Psycho-Analysis*, and, in the last month of the same year, under his own authorship, *The Trauma of Birth*.

Rank's growing neurosis became progressively more evident following the publication of his theory of birth trauma. And, finally, in 1924, he started for the United States—on a journey that was to take him from Vienna forever. He got as far as Paris and turned back. Freud, in writing to Jones, noted: "As you see, an open break has been averted. Rank himself had not intended one, and a scandal would not be in our interest either. But all intimate relations with him are at an end. . . . Not only I, but the two others present at the interview, found it very hard to regard him as honest and to believe his statements. I am very sorry that you, dear Jones, have proved to be so entirely right." Jones replied: "Although his loss bears most of all on you I can genuinely say that I am as sorry I was right as you are yourself. Your words were, it is true, no surprise to me, for bearing the brunt of his neurotic behavior in these last years forced me to think deeply about him and to recognize the situation. My one hope was that you should never know, and my endeavor to prevent this cost me dearly in many ways. But I was throughout very fond of Rank, so that I too suffer an intense regret at the course fate has chosen." Freud then wrote as follows: "The Rank affair is now meeting its end. . . . You must not think that the matter has greatly discomposed me or will have any aftereffect. That is perhaps rather queer when one reflects on what a part Rank has played in my life for a decade and a half. But I know of three explanations for the coolness in my feelings. First it may be a result of age which does not take losses so heavily. In the second place I tell myself that the relationship has so-to-speak been amortized in these fifteen years; it is not the same if someone is disloyal after two or three years or only after he has for years performed superlative work. In the third place, and

[37] Jones, *op. cit.*, p. 177.
[38] *Ibid.*, p. 177.

last not least, perhaps I am so calm because I can trace absolutely no part of the responsibility for the whole process."[39]

Of the last two members of the Committee, Sachs and Eitingon, Jones wrote as follows: "Hanns Sachs was the least closely knit member of the Committee. As a colleague he was an amusing companion, the wittiest of the company, and he had an endless stock of the best Jewish jokes. His interests were primarily literary. When we had, as so often, to discuss the more political aspects of administration, he was always bored and remained aloof, an attitude which stood him in good stead when he emigrated later to America where he wisely confined himself to his technical work. He was completely loyal to Freud, but his spells of apathy did not please Freud, so that he was the member in least personal contact with him.

"Eitingon was marked out, among other respects, in being the only psycho-analyst in the world who possessed private means. He was thus in a position to be of great assistance in various analytical undertakings, and was always generous in doing so. He was entirely devoted to Freud, whose lightest wish or opinion was decisive for him. Otherwise he was rather easily influenced, so that one could not always be sure of what his own opinion was. He felt his Jewish origin more acutely than the others, except possibly Sachs, and was very sensitive to anti-semitic prejudice. His visit to Palestine in 1910 foreshadowed his final withdrawal to that country at the first moment of Hitler's ascendancy more than twenty years later. Eitingon had three special claims to Freud's gratitude which Freud could never forget. He was the first person who, from interest in psycho-analysis, visited him from another country. Secondly, he was of invaluable material assistance to Freud's undertaking at the end of the first world war. Finally, Eitingon's personal devotion was such that Freud could be confident in retaining his friendship in any circumstances. On the other hand one cannot suppose that he thought specially highly of his intellectual abilities."[40]

The committee functioned well for over ten years. It was instrumental in providing that internal unity which is primary to the health of any on-going institution. In the end, its dissolution could be traced to the fate of its individual members, in death, in exile or dissention. "The Committee," Jones wrote, "undoubtedly fulfilled its primary function of fortifying Freud against the bitter attacks that were being made on him. It was easier to dissolve these into jokes when in a friendly company, and we could repel some of them in our writings in a way he did not care to undertake; he was therefore set free for his own constructive work. As time went on other functions became important also. Frequent meetings, either all together or a few at a time, together with a regular correspondence among ourselves, enabled us to keep in touch with what was going on in the world of psycho-analysis. Moreover, a unitary policy formulated by those best informed and possessing considerable influence was invaluable in dealing with the innumerable problems that kept arising, disagreements within a society, the choice of suitable officials, the coping with local oppositions, and the like."[41]

The fortunes of time which were to see Eitingon emigrate to Palestine (now Israel), Hanns Sachs and Rank to the United States, were to strike finally at Freud's own freedom in 1938.[42] His home was invaded by the Nazis and though neither Freud nor his family were molested he no longer felt that he could carry on his work unimpeded. In May 1938, at the invitation of Ernest Jones, Freud emigrated to England. He was a desperately ill man, but weathered the trip though he required several doses of nitroglycerine and strychnine to carry him through. The papers were full of the accounts of his arrival and many articles appeared in the medical journals in praise of his accomplishments. The *Lancet* wrote: "His teachings have in their time aroused controversy more acute and antagonism more bitter than any since the days of Darwin. Now, in his old age, there are few psychologists of any school who do not admit their debt to him. Some of the conceptions he formulated clearly for the first time have crept into current philosophy against the stream of wilful incredulity which he himself recognized as man's natural reaction to unbearable truth." The *British Medical Journal* said: "The medical profession of Great Britain will feel proud that their country has offered an asylum to Professor Freud, and that he has chosen it as his new home."

---

[39] Jones, *op. cit.*, 3:74–75, 1957.
[40] *Ibid.*, 2:181–182, 1955.

[41] *Ibid.*, pp. 184–185.
[42] Karl Abraham died in 1925; Ernest Jones in 1958.

He died as he had lived—a realist to the end. His sixteen years of suffering were at an end, just before midnight on September 23, 1939. His body was cremated at Golders Green, and there remains in one of his favorite Grecian urns.

—Ludwig Eidelberg, M.D.

620

FRIGIDITY is a disturbance in the female's capacity to experience genital sexual pleasure, varying from total genital anesthesia to a partial lack of sexual feeling (such as vaginal anesthesia with clitoral excitability). Most psychoanalysts specifically define frigidity as the incapacity to have a vaginal orgasm, usually associated with impairment of lubrication and sensation, and lack of muscular contraction. There is also conditional frigidity, which is dependent on the type of sex play, special choice of love object, phase of the menstrual cycle, possibility of impregnation, etc. (e.g., a woman who is frigid with her husband, but who can experience vaginal orgasm with her older, fatherly lover, especially if contraception is not practiced).

Constitutional, anatomical, and physiological factors have been mentioned along with psychological inhibitions in relation to frigidity. Abraham (1920) divided it into three stages, as follows: "To disappoint a person is to excite expectations in him and not fulfill them. In her relations with the man the woman can do this by responding to his advances up to a certain point and then refusing to give herself to him. Such behaviour is most frequently and significantly expressed in *frigidity* on the part of the woman. Disappointing other persons is a piece of unconscious tactics which we frequently find in the psychology of the neuroses and which is especially pronounced in obsessional neurotics. These neurotics are unconsciously impelled towards violence and revenge, but on account of the contrary play of ambivalent forces these impulses are incapable of effectually breaking through. Since their hostility cannot express itself in actions, these patients excite expectations of a pleasant nature in their environment and then do not fulfill them. In the sphere of the female castration complex the tendency to disappoint can be formulated in respect of its origin as follows:

"*First stage:* I rob you of what you have because I lack it.

"*Second stage:* I rob you of nothing. I even promise you what I have to give.

"*Third stage:* I will not give you what I have promised."

Common unconscious conflicts influencing frigidity include the rejection of the feminine role concomitant with masculine identification, intense penis envy, oedipal fixation leading to incestuous wish and taboo, and castrating attitudes toward the partner. Fears about impregnation and childbirth, identification with a frigid or disapproving mother, preoedipal conflicts regarding loss of sphincter control, fears of surrender and being overwhelmed by orgastic sensations, fears of fusion with the partner and loss of ego boundaries, and oral conflicts over sucking and biting may also be involved. The psychological meaning of the sexual and reproductive functions and possible disturbances in every single phase of development must all be considered.

Related Concepts: IMPOTENCE; ORGASM (CLIMAX); VAGINISMUS.

REFERENCE

Abraham, K., 1920, "Manifestations of the Female Castration Complex." *SPA*, p. 358, 1942.

ADDITIONAL READINGS

Deutsch, H., "Über Frigidität." *Z*, 15, 1929.
Eidelberg, L.: *Take Off Your Mask*, Py, 1957.
    The Dark Urge. Py, 1961.
Freud, S., 1908, "Civilized Sexual Morality and Modern Nervous Illness." *SE*, 9, 1959.
Moore, B., "Report on Panel—Frigidity in Women." *JAPA*, 9, 1961.
Pichon, E., "Rêve d'une femme frigide." *RFPsa*, 6, 1932.
Robinson, V., ed., "Sexual Anesthesia," in *Encyclopedia Sexualis*. DR, 1936.

621

FRIGIDITY AND MASOCHISM. Repressed masochistic wishes in some cases are the cause of frigidity in women. If a woman regards sexual intercourse as an aggressive act, in which she is being perforated, she protects herself by becoming frigid. [Eidelberg, 1954.] For example, a frigid patient, who was not conscious of her masochistic tendencies, referred to the penis as an aggressive part of the man's body, despite the fact that she should have known, being a doctor, that there are many other parts of the body which can be more successfully used for injuring the female. The masochistic masturbation fantasies present in some women are used by analysts to demonstrate to their patients that they can have genital responses only under the condition that they experience, at the same time, humiliating narcissistic mortifications.

"Frigidity," according to Abraham (1916) "is practically a *sine qua non* of prostitution. The experiencing of full sexual sensation binds the woman to the man, and only where this is lacking does she go from man to man, just like the continually ungratified Don Juan type of man who has constantly to change his love-object. Just as the Don Juan avenges himself on all women for the disappointment which he once received from the first woman who entered into his life, so the prostitute avenges herself on every man for the gift she had expected from her father and did not receive. Her frigidity signifies a humiliation of all men and therefore a mass castration to her unconscious, and her whole life is given up to this purpose."

Related Concepts: FRIGIDITY; MASOCHISM; NARCISSISTIC MORTIFICATION.

REFERENCES

Abraham, K., 1916, "The First Pregenital Stage of the Libido." *SPA*, p. 361, 1942.
Eidelberg, L., *An Outline of a Comparative Pathology of the Neuroses.* IUP, pp. 195–197, 1954.

622

FRUSTRATION denotes the prevention of, or interference with, the satisfaction of instinctual impulses which lead to the damming up of libido and destrudo. External frustration, caused by external objects, should be differentiated from frustration imposed from within. Both may lead to the improvement of reality testing through increased tolerance of the dammed-up energy. Identification with the frustrating external object may lead to internal frustration by the ego and superego. Glover

(1939) noted: "But to grasp the more human aspects of symptomatic regression it is necessary to be familiar with the small child's ideological systems. As has been pointed out the infant has from the first a reality system appropriate to the conditions of life in which it finds itself, but as development proceeds, and as thought-processes become organized, a distinction can be drawn between ideas that focus round reality experiences of pleasure and pain and phantasies that are developed as a response to complete frustration of instinct. These systems of unconscious phantasy have no doubt a compensatory function to perform although the gratification obtained by this means is at best marginal. Even so it is heavily discounted by the anxieties and, later, guilts to which unconscious phantasies give rise. Phantasy formation is fostered by periodic regressions from waking to sleeping life and by numerous misreadings of waking experience to which the small child is naturally prone. So that whilst there is an *appropriate system of reality thinking for each phase* of development, these systems are increasingly infiltrated or at any rate unconsciously associated with *phantasy systems that are also appropriate to the stage of instinctual frustration at which the child has arrived.*"

Freud (1916–1917) stressed the important role of frustration in symptom formation, and noted: "The necessary precondition of the conflict is that these other paths and objects arouse displeasure in one part of the personality, so that a veto is imposed which makes the new method of satisfaction impossible as it stands."

Related Concepts: INHIBITION; INSTINCT (INSTINCTUAL DRIVE); PSYCHOSIS; SENSE OF GUILT.

REFERENCES

Freud, S., 1916–1917, "Introductory Lectures on Psycho-Analysis." *SE*, 16:349–350, 1963.
Glover, E., *Psycho-Analysis.* SP, p. 31, 1939.

ADDITIONAL READINGS

Fenichel, O., *The Psychoanalytic Theory of Neurosis.* Nor, 1945.
Karpe, R., "Die Abstillung als Versagung." *PsaP*, 11, 1937.
Nunberg, H., *Principles of Psychoanalysis—Their Application to the Neuroses.* IUP, 1955.

G

700

GENITAL PHASE. The concept is reserved today for that stage of development which is characterized by the unification of the erotic functions, to that period in which the sexual instincts give rise to the function of propagation. The current concept was offered by Freud in 1933; the original concept received its clearest presentation in 1905 and differed from it, in that "genital" was considered as the third stage of libidinal development, occurring between the third and fifth year of life.

In the present concept, the genital stage is the fourth and final stage of sexual development. The sexual instinctual components distinguished in the earlier stages* (oral, anal, and phallic) proceed side-by-side until there is a maturation of the genitals during puberty, and the normally demanded unification of the erotic functions is established. This unification begins with the oedipal conflict, in which the boy seeks to identify with his father and the girl with her mother. The male becomes aware that the penis is not only the organ responsible for urination; the insertion of the penis into the vagina does not mean "soiling" the partner. The girl, on the other hand, finds that the acquisition of secondary sexual characteristics places her on an equal footing with the male; she is not an inferior, castrated creature.

The consequence of this change would seem to apply as well to the concept of destrudo which also passes through four stages of development. The

exhibitionistic and inspectionistic wishes also pass through the four stages of development. Probably only those wishes belonging to the oral, anal, or phallic stage can be sublimated. The complete gratification of genital desires may, however, interfere with the progress of mental development.

The physiological changes occurring in puberty do not insure a congruent psychological maturation. In many cases, the physiological development takes place before the individual is able to accept the responsibility connected with it. The necessity to prolong the years of training and study may be responsible for such a delayed psychological maturity.

Related Concepts: ACTIVE; AGGRESSION; LIBIDO; PASSIVE; SEXUALITY.

REFERENCES

Eidelberg, L., *An Outline of a Comparative Pathology of the Neuroses.* IUP, p. 33, 1954.
Freud, S.: 1905, "Three Essays on the Theory of Sexuality." *SE*, 7:233, 1953.
　　　1933, "New Introductory Lectures on Psycho-Analysis." *SE*, 22:99, 1964.

ADDITIONAL READINGS

Abraham, K., "Character Formation on the Genital Level of Libido-Development." *IntJPsa*, 7, 1926.
Harley, M., "Some Observations on the Relationships Between Genitality and Structural Development at Adolescence." *JAPA*, 9, 1961.

---

* The term *pregenital* originally employed with the component instincts appears to refer to the phallic stage; thus the oral and anal wishes could be called *prephallic* and not *pregenital.*

701

GROUP PARANOIA denotes those paranoid attitudes which are manifested by a whole assemblage. For example, in the Middle Ages during the plague, the Jews were accused of having poisoned the wells, and irrational mob action was widespread. In group paranoia it seems that the key factor is the acceptance of paranoid leadership, and not the presence of paranoid membership. Hartmann and Stengel (1931, 1932) have emphasized that certain paranoiacs have a specific motivation to establish a following. After the withdrawal of libido from the object world, an attempt at restitution is made by them, where influencing the environment is one of the first steps in the reestablishment of object relationships. For obvious reasons, group paranoia is difficult to examine from a psychoanalytical point of view.

Related Concept: PARANOIA.

REFERENCES

Hartmann, H., & E. Stengel: "Studien zur Psychologie des induzierten Irreseins." *AP*, 95:583–599, 1931.
    "Studien zur Psychologie des induzierten Irreseins." *JPN*, 48:164–183, 1932.

ADDITIONAL READINGS

Bion, W. R., *Experiences in Groups and Other Papers.* BB, 1961.
Freud, A., "An Experiment in Group Upbringing." *PsaStC*, 6, 1951.
Scheidlinger, S., *Psychoanalysis and Group Behavior.* Nor, 1952.

H

800

HAIR PULLING as a symptom is characterized by the pathological pulling of the hair on the body, especially of the head, accompanied by a feeling of relief, and, simultaneously, of anger at the inability to control it. The symptom occurs in children most frequently, more commonly in females than males.

This condition has been described by Edith Buxbaum (1960) as being one which is pathological, and related to fetishism. It stems from severe castration fears which occur pregenitally and render the child incapable of meeting genital-oedipal problems. Phyllis Greenacre (1955) described fetishism, in agreement with Freud (1927), as a disorder which results from a severe preoedipal trauma—"threats not merely by seeing the mother's genitals and observing her apparent castration at the time of special masturbatory arousal . . . but much more than this by witnessing or experiencing bloody mutilating attacks in the form of operations (on the self or others), childbirth, abortions, or accidents."

Buxbaum finds this view to be incomplete. She noted that children go through a "phase in which they are particularly attached to one or the other object—a stuffed animal, teddy bear, blanket or pillow, etc.—and . . . that this kind of fetishism, like other disturbances, must go back to a fixation point in a certain phase of libidinal development . . . when children have intense feelings about such objects."

In one clinical example supplied by Buxbaum, a girl of six named Beryl pulled her hair out and tickled her nose and lips with it while sucking her thumb. The hair in this case represented a part-object, a transitional object, which Beryl gave up when her mother finally learned to stroke and shampoo her hair. Beryl could then continue her libidinal development, to separate herself from her mother, and to reach out to other relationships. Buxbaum summed up the phenomenological factors, as follows: "As long as tactile contacts were disturbed, the ambivalent undifferentiated relationship to the mother's body and to the child's own body existed, and the genital feelings as well as object relations were disturbed."

In addition to the material mentioned by Buxbaum, hair pulling seems to represent an instant gratification of aggressive and exhibitionistic wishes. At the same time, it usually represents a denial of castration and a defense against masturbation (or pseudomasturbation).

Related Concepts: FETISHISM; MASTURBATION.

REFERENCES

Buxbaum, E., "Hair Pulling and Fetishism." *PsaStC*, 15:243–244, 260, 1960.
Freud, S., 1927, "Fetishism." *SE*, 21:152–157, 1961.
Greenacre, P., "Further Considerations Regarding Fetishism." *PsaStC*, 10:187–194, 1955.

ADDITIONAL READING

Barahal, H., "The Psychopathology of Hair-Pulling (Trichotillomania)." *R*, 27, 1940.

HALLUCINATIONS are sensations or perceptions attributed to the sense organs which are erroneously experienced as if they were caused by external objects. Although the subject describes the hallucination as a genuine sensory perception, he is unwilling to examine it. A person who suffers from double vision is able to recognize his error; the person who has hallucinations is not. He considers any attempt to examine them as a hostile interference. Hallucinations must be differentiated from illusions, which the patient may recognize as a wish-fulfillment caused by his desires and not by the external world.

Freud recognized that hallucinations, as with all mental events, have a meaningful emotional content. They represent archaic ideas and memories which emerge from the unconscious and are transformed into visual, auditory, gustatory, tactile, or olfactory sensations. Hallucinations are symptoms which represent both a partial wish-fulfillment and a partial defense of it. They usually contain repressed infantile memories. [Freud, 1900.] Hallucinations are often compared to dreams; they may also be experienced in hypnagogic states.

In structural terms, elements from the id, ego, and superego, as well as elements from the repudiated reality, form the hallucination. For example, a young man, while masturbating, has a hallucination and sees the image of his dead father, who points an accusing finger at him. The exhibitionistic (and other) id wishes, superego threats and elements of a real childhood experience are all reproduced in the hallucination. Reality testing disappears.

There is a controversy today as to whether true hallucinations, in the awake adult, are consistent with the diagnosis of neurosis. Freud maintained that hysterics may also have occasional hallucinations. He hypothesized that infants attempt to satisfy the preemptory demands of internal needs not met by the environment through a so-called hallucinatory fulfillment. The infant subsequently sets up a kind of reality testing and gives up hallucinatory satisfaction of wishes in normal waking life. In negative hallucinations, the perception of real stimuli is blocked and the perceptions are not consciously acknowledged or recognized. Freud regarded negative hallucinations as more primary than positive hallucinations and made the challeng-

ing statement that any attempt to explain hallucinations "would have to start from *negative* rather than positive hallucination." [Freud, 1917.]

In dreams, infantile wishes continue to be hallucinated, and are predominantly visual. Freud (1917) noted that only if the regression has been deep enough and has succeeded in eliminating the reality testing will the hallucination take place. As a result of such a deep regression, the system *Cs.* (*Pcpt.*) will cathect internal rather than external stimuli.

However, hallucinations in dreams disappear after awakening and must, therefore, be differentiated from hallucinations in psychoses. Freud regarded hallucinations in psychoses as representing a restitutional symptom; an attempt at recovery by bringing the libido back to an attachment with objects. This process is a pathological attempt to restore a libidinal cathexis to the representation of objects. Freud (1911) noted a paranoiac usually does not withdraw his interest from the external world as does a patient suffering from Meynert's amentia. It seems that the paranoiac's relation to external objects is due to changes in his libidinal investments.

Related Concepts: DELUSION; ILLUSION.

REFERENCES

Freud, S.: 1900, "The Interpretation of Dreams." *SE*, 5:566–567, 1953.

    1911, "Psychoanalytic Notes on an Autobiographical Account of a Case of Paranoia (Dementia Paranoides)." *SE*, 12:75, 1958.

    1917, "A Metapsychological Supplement to the Theory of Dreams." *SE*, 14:229–234, 1957.

ADDITIONAL READINGS

Bion, W., "On Hallucination." *IntJPsa*, 39, 1958.

Campbell, C., "Hallucinations: Their Nature and Significance." *P*, 9, 1929–1930.

Eidelberg, L., "Psychoanalysis of a Case of Paranoia." *R*, 32, 1945.

Freud, S.: 1896, "Further Remarks on the Neuro-Psychoses of Defense." *SE*, 3, 1962.

    1940, "An Outline of Psycho-Analysis." *SE*, 22, 1964.

Goja, H., "Halluzinationen eines Sterbenden." *Z*, 6, 1920.

Havens, L. L., "The Placement and Movement of Hallucinations in Space: Phenomenology and Theory." *IntJPsa*, 43, 1962.

Jekels, L., "Eine Tendenziöse Geruchshalluzination." *Z*, 3, 1915.

Katan, M., "Further Remarks about Schreber's Hallucinations." *IntJPsa*, 33, 1952.

Schilder, P., "Über Elementare Halluzinationen des Bewegungssehens." *ZNP*, 80, 1923.

Sperling, O., "A Psychoanalytic Study of Hypnagogic Hallucinations." *JAPA*, 5, 1957.

Stern, M., "Blank Hallucinations: Remarks About Trauma and Perceptual Disturbances." *IntJPsa*, 42, 1961.

White, W. A., "Hallucinations." *JNMD*, 31, 1904.

802

HAPPINESS is a feeling of well-being, joy, and gladness. It was Freud's (1930) view that men try to eliminate unpleasure to obtain pleasure. Consequently, it may be said that the pleasure principle dominates the activities of the human being, although he did admit that men are rarely able to achieve this aim of being happy because of external and internal conditions. Even if pleasure is experienced for a long time, it produces contentment, not happiness. According to Freud, the human being is threatened from his own body which grows older and often becomes a source of unpleasure. In addition, the signals of pain and anxiety due to relation to external objects cannot be overlooked. The unpleasure caused by the hostility of others is often more painful than the unpleasure caused by internal sources.

According to Eidelberg (1951), happiness can only be experienced if the individual finds an object suitable for satisfying both object and narcissistic libido at the same time. Such a satisfaction may take place between two individuals who love and are being loved by each other. The gratification of aggressive impulses may lead to pleasure, but not to happiness.

Related Concepts: PLEASURE PRINCIPLE; SATISFACTION (GRATIFICATION) OF INSTINCTS.

REFERENCES

Eidelberg, L., "In Pursuit of Happiness." *R*, 38:222–224, 1951.

Freud, S., 1930, "Civilization and Its Discontents." *SE*, 21:76–77, 1961.

ADDITIONAL READINGS:

Sachs, H., "Psychotherapy and the Pursuit of Happiness." *AmIm*, 2, 1941.

Tridon, A., *Sex Happiness*. Re, 1938.

803

HATE denotes a feeling of intense dislike, aversion, or bitterness toward a particular object; an urge to attain gratification through injury to, or destruction of, the object. Freud (1913) originally placed hate with the ego instincts, in contrast to the unconscious libidinal instincts. The study of compulsive neurotics indicates the presence of a very severe superego and this severity may be due to the quantity of aggression. At first Freud could not agree with Stekel who thought that the study of human development would lead to the conclusion that hate preceded love. Later, in 1920, consideration of the self-destructive nature of the repetition compulsion led him to give hate and love equal status in the id. Hate was placed with the aggressive or death instincts, while love was placed with the sexual instincts. Within the framework of the structural theory, hate was assigned a role in each of the three provinces of the psychic apparatus. In the id, it was synonymous with the aggressive drive. In the ego of the normal individual, it appeared as conscious hatred or as aggression subordinated to constructive ends. In the superego, it took the self as its object and resulted in feelings of guilt or self criticism.

Related Concepts: AFFECT; AGGRESSION; AMBIVALENCE; SENSE OF GUILT.

REFERENCES

Freud, S.; 1913, "The Disposition to Obsessional Neurosis." *SE*, 12:325, 1958.

1920, "Beyond the Pleasure Principle." *SE*, 18:1–64, 1955.

ADDITIONAL READINGS

Freud, S.: 1915, "Instincts and Their Vicissitudes." *SE*, 14, 1957.

1917, "Mourning and Melancholia." *SE*, 14, 1957.

Jones, E., "Fear, Guilt and Hate." *IntJPsa*, 10, 1992.

804

HEBEPHRENIA is a type of psychosis, usually classified as a subgroup of schizophrenia, characterized by childish behavior and mannerisms, and shallow, inappropriate, silly, labile, and unpredictable emotions. Delusions and hallucinations may also be present. Dynamically, hebephrenia can be viewed as a mental condition of psychotic origin; symptomatically, the ego undertakes no activity or effort for the purpose of defending itself but, rather, when beset by conflicts, it "lets itself go." If the present is unpleasant and disturbing, the ego falls back to the past; if more recent modes of adaptation fail, it readily resorts to older ones, taking refuge in infantile types of adaptation and behavior (e.g., passive receptivity). [Fenichel, 1945.]

Related Concepts: PSYCHOSIS; SCHIZOPHRENIA.

REFERENCE

Fenichel, O., *The Psychoanalytic Theory of Neurosis.* Nor, pp. 186, 423, 1945.

ADDITIONAL READINGS

Freud, S., 1911, "Psycho-Analytic Notes on an Autobiographical Account of a Case of Paranoia (Dementia Paranoides)." *SE*, 12, 1958.
Hoffer, W., "Diaries of Adolescent Schizophrenics (Hebephrenics)." *PsaStC*, 2, 1946.

805

HEREDITY is denotative of the total of all elements the organism received from its progenitors through their germ plasm. The biological transmission of characteristics or predispositions, according to Freud (1913), would seem to play a role in the predisposition to mental illness. In growing up, the human being experiences many disturbances (psychic traumata) which are often responsible for neuroses. Not all traumatic experiences produce neuroses. Under certain conditions the individual may remain healthy in spite of them, but if the external condition demands too much the probability of neurotic conflict becomes very great.

In individual human beings, the general features of humanity are embodied in almost infinite variety.

To make a distinction, Freud (1931) contended, a differentiation must be confined to psychological findings. He then distinguished three main hereditary libidinal types; the erotic, the narcissistic, and the obsessional, as follows: The erotic type is characterized by the libido being chiefly concentrated in the id; the narcissistic type, in the ego; and the obsessional type, in the superego. It is true that most people belong to mixed types. Thus, from a descriptive point of view, the pure erotic type appears to be characterized by the fact that individuals belonging to this type are chiefly interested in being loved and in loving. The obsessional type is dominated by fear of his superego, and thus show a high degree of self-reliance. The narcissistic type is characterized by very little tension between the ego and superego. The individuals belonging to this type are often independent, not easily frightened. They impress others as leaders and may often influence the development of civilization.

Freud recognized that most people belong to mixed types (the erotic-obsessional, the erotic-narcissistic, and the narcissistic-obsessional). He also said that the erotic-obsessional-narcissistic type would really not be a type at all, but would represent the ideal harmony.

Related Concepts: CHOICE OF A NEUROSIS; CONGENITAL (CONNATE).

REFERENCES

Freud, S.: 1913, "On Psycho-Analysis." *SE*, 12:209, 1958.
            1931, "Libidinal Types." *SE*, 21:217-219, 1961.

ADDITIONAL READINGS

Freud, S.: 1896, "Heredity and the Aetiology of the Neuroses." *SE*, 3, 1962.
            1905, "Three Essays on the Theory of Sexuality." *SE*, 7, 1953.
            1909, "Analysis of a Phobia in a Five-Year-Old Boy." *SE*, 10, 1955.

806

HOSTILODYNAMICS denotes the hostility and its discharge produced by disharmony in the emotional life (Saul, 1956). This hostility is generated in certain ways, produces certain effects, and behaves according to certain laws (as does heat, in physics).

Related Concept: AGGRESSION.

REFERENCE

Saul, L. J., *The Hostile Mind.* RH, 1956.

ADDITIONAL READING

Saul, L. J., "Inferiority Feelings and Hostility." *P*, 108, 1951.

807

HUMILIATION denotes an unpleasant feeling experienced as the result of being made to feel ashamed, inferior, ridiculous, or unworthy of respect and love. The humiliating action may come from the external world or from the individual's own superego. The feeling of humiliation is the opposite of the feeling resulting from praise or admiration. Freud (1919) described the punishment of the child as a humiliation. A child who is loved by his parents and feels secure in their love develops a feeling of humiliation when punished, for each punishment interferes with the infantile omnipotence.

The study of perverse and moral masochists indicates that they are interested in provoking the unpleasure connected with a humiliating punishment. An external humiliation must be differentiated from an internal humiliation, although it cannot be denied that they often are simultaneously experienced. For instance, some Jews, when they were ordered by the Nazis to wear a yellow star, accepted this external humiliation and actually considered themselves to be inferior. The majority, although humiliated in the same manner, refused to accept the evaluation of their aggressors.

The person engaged in humiliating another often will laugh at him. In this respect, as Freud (1905) noted, a differentiation must be made between voluntary and involuntary humor. The joker makes us laugh at his joke and admire his wit without feeling humiliated. Whereas, the person whom we find ridiculous and who makes us laugh at him feels humiliated, an instance of involuntary humor.

According, to Eidelberg (1959), humiliation appears to be connected with the narcissistic mortification in which the ability to get exhibitionistic pleasure (admiration) fails.

An analytic interpretation may be considered, by a patient, as a humiliation. This may occur whenever the analyst verbalizes his interpretation in an aggressive manner or whenever the patient unconsciously wants to be humiliated. We may say that any exposure of a hidden "weakness" may produce the feeling of humiliation. Anal elements play a decisive role in these feelings (e.g., the colloquial statement, "He was caught with his pants down").

Related Concepts: MASOCHISM; NARCISSISTIC MORTIFICATION; SHAME; SUPEREGO; UNPLEASURE-PLEASURE PRINCIPLE.

REFERENCES

Eidelberg, L., "Humiliation in Masochism." *JAPA*, 7:274–283, 1959.
Freud, S.: 1905, "Jokes and Their Relation to the Unconscious." *SE*, 8:216, 1960.
    1919, "A Child Is Being Beaten: A Contribution to the Study of the Origin of Sexual Perversions." *SE*, 17:187, 1955.

ADDITIONAL READING

Eidelberg, L., "On the Humiliation of the Love Object." *Z*, 30, 1934.

808

HUMOR, according to Freud (1927), is characterized by a certain "grandeur" which the joke doesn't have. Both are a source of aesthetic pleasure, in which a discharge of mental energy takes place as a consequence of their form and not their content. This grandeur is caused by a narcissistic triumph, a victory of the ego. With the help of humor, the individual is able to avoid suffering. Freud illustrated this point, telling the story of a criminal who was being led to his execution, who said, "the week starts badly—it rains."

In cases in which an individual uses his sense of humor in his relation to other people, he behaves in a way an adult would towards a child. He smiles at the trivial sufferings by declaring them nonessential.

The presence of aggression discharged by the superego against the ego or the self is responsible for this pleasure. However, the superego consists not only of the conscience but also of the ego-ideal; with the help of this ego-ideal it may respond in a positive manner to the actions of the individual (praising, consoling, etc.).

According to Kohut (1957), "primal scene experiences, creating overstimulation, dangerous defensive passive wishes, and castration anxiety may lead to the attempt to return to the emotional equilibrium at the beginning of the experience and prepare the emotional soil for the development of the artistic attitudes as an observer and describer. This hypothesis seems particularly compatible with . . . the qualities . . . of detachment and irony . . . more generally . . . it is perhaps a genetic factor in the development of an ironical attitude toward life."

Grotjahn (1957) identified the humorist as belonging to the masochistic type, as follows: "He behaves as if he knows the misery of this world but resolutely proceeds to disregard it. He remains aware of this valley of tears but behaves as if it is still the Garden of Eden. He proceeds not by denying the existence of misery but by pretending to be victorious over it. He illustrates for us the hope for the victory of infantile narcissism over all experience. His victory is only partial and temporary; what he may gain in inner strength and kindness, he will lose in the world of reality and adjustment. He may be free but not necessarily happy or well adjusted to his environment.

"The wit as a person is closely related to the sadist. Under the disguise of brilliance, charm, and entertainment the wit—and we do not mean only the practical joker—is a sadist at heart. He is sharp, quick, alert, cold, aggressive, and hostile. He is inclined to murder his victims in thought; if he inhibits himself and if he does not succeed in transforming his brain child into a joke, he may develop a migraine attack instead.

"The sense of humor develops in stages and gradually during a lifetime. Every step is connected with mastery of a new anxiety, and each conflict mastered at the different developmental stages is marked by a growth of the sense of humor. So people are inordinately proud of it—often even those who have no sense of humor at all. It is the mark of distinction, of having achieved strength and maturity."

Related Concepts: AESTHETIC PLEASURE; FORE-PLEASURE.

REFERENCES

Freud, S., 1927, "Humour." *SE*, 21:162–163, 166, 1961.
Grotjahn, M., *Beyond Laughter*. MH, pp. 257–258, 1957.
Kohut, H., "'Death in Venice' by Thomas Mann. A Story about the Disintegration of Artistic Sublimation." *Q*, 26:223–225, 1957.

ADDITIONAL READINGS

Jacobson, E., "The Child's Laughter. Theoretical and Clinical Notes on the Function of the Comic." *PsaStC*, 2, 1946.
Levine, J., & F. C. Redlich, "Failure to Understand Humor." *Q*, 24, 1955.
Wolfenstein, M.: "A Phase in the Development of Children's Sense of Humor." *PsaStC*, 6, 1951.
         "Children's Understanding of Jokes." *PsaStC*, 8, 1953.
         "Mad Laughter in a Six-Year-Old Boy." *PsaStC*, 1955.
Zwerling, L, "The Favorite Joke in Diagnostic and Therapeutic Interviewing." *Q*, 24, 1955.

809

HUNGER FOR STIMULI. One basic quality of the living substance is the fact that it can be stimulated by an external factor and react to this stimulation under certain conditions. This response of the living organism to an external and internal stimulus may increase or decrease. Fatigue, excitement and certain drugs can alter this response. The hunger for a stimuli leads to excitation. When this does not occur a feeling of unpleasure takes place.

Fenichel (1945) noted: "The striving for discharge and relaxation, the direct expression of the constancy principle, is necessarily the older mechanism. The fact that external objects brought about the desired state of relaxed satisfaction introduced the complication that objects became longed for; in the beginning, it is true, they were sought only as instruments which made themselves disappear again. The longing for objects thus began as a detour on the way to the goal of being rid of objects (of stimuli)."

Related Concepts: REFLEX ACT; UNPLEASURE-PLEASURE PRINCIPLE.

REFERENCE

Fenichel, O., *The Psychoanalytic Theory of Neurosis.* Nor, p. 35, 1945.

810

HYPNAGOGIC PHENOMENA are conditions of the semiconscious state preceding sleep. The first phase (somnolence) is characterized by a reduction in the speed of thinking and an inclination for daydreaming; the second phase, by the phenomenon of dissociation (e.g., repetitions and parapraxes); the third, and last, by hallucinations sometimes reported as visions, which are like dreams and which are terminated on awakening. They are real hallucinations, unlike those images flaring up before sleep which the subject knows as fantasy and not reality, and they are like dreams in that they are divorced from the conscious states. The transition from the waking state to hypnagogic hallucinations is a sudden one.

Unlike dreams, there is no loss of muscle tone in hypnagogic hallucinations; the eyelids close; yet, it is still possible to continue to stand, walk, sit, etc. Spontaneous awakening is easier and the threshold for being awakened is lower. If the process of falling asleep is purposely pathologically slowed down, short hypnagogic states with spontaneous awakening may follow each other several times. Hypnagogic hallucinations are forgotten more frequently than are dreams. They appear more often if one deliberately tries to stay awake.

In order to study hypnagogic phenomena experimentally, Silberer (1951) forced himself to think while in a state of fatigue. He then experienced visual hallucinations in the place of the thought. In these visual hallucinations he could recognize a symbolic (or, according to Jones, metaphoric) representation of the thought which had preceded the hallucination (e.g., he thought of correcting an awkward phrase in an essay and then saw himself smoothing a piece of wood with a plane).

Sperling (1957) maintained that hypnagogic hallucinations start to occur in those developmental periods where there is difficulty in falling asleep, especially during the period of weaning from thumbsucking and of masturbation before falling asleep. Fantasy is substituted for the actual instinctual gratifications. The hypnagogic hallucination continued the fantasy of thumbsucking or masturbation; it demonstrated that there was an interference by the introjected prohibition. The mobilization of signal anxiety by the ego prevented the individual from falling asleep.

Related Concepts: HALLUCINATIONS; SLEEP.

REFERENCES

Silberer, H., "Report on a Method of Eliciting and Observing Certain Symbolic Hallucination-Phenomena." *OrgPath*, pp. 195–207, 1951.
Sperling, O., "A Psychoanalytic Study of Hypnagogic Hallucinations." *JAPA*, 1:115–123, 1957.

811

HYPNOANALYSIS is a method of psychoanalytically oriented psychotherapy which employs a variety of hypnotic procedures as adjuncts. It differs from other hypnotic approaches in that suggestion is used to facilitate insight by uncovering sources of resistance, highlighting transference phenomena, and favoring recovery of traumatic memories. Occasionally, induced half-sleep states are also used as part of this method. [Wolberg, 1945.]

Related Concept: HYPNOSIS.

REFERENCE

Wolberg, L. R., *Hypnoanalysis.* G&S, 1945.

ADDITIONAL READINGS

Lindner, R., "The Jet-Propelled Couch" Harper's Magazine, Dec. 1954.
Taylor, W. X., "Behavior Under Hypnoanalysis and the Mechanism of the Neurosis." *JAbP*, 18, 1923.

812

HYPNOID STATE denotes a peculiar dreamlike condition of consciousness which is characterized by a diminished capacity for association. This early concept owes its importance, as Strachey

(1955) noted, to the fact that it represented a half-way stage in Freud's thinking, "in the process of moving from physiological to psychological explanations of psychopathological states."

Breuer (1893) expressed his view that the psychical processes could only be explained in psychological terms. It was not until 1905 that Freud expressly altered his view, and explicitly repudiated all intention of using the term in any but a psychological sense. As Strachey (1955) noted, this was understandable, since "his earlier training and career as a neurologist led him to resist the acceptance of psychological explanations as ultimate; and he was engaged in devising a complicated structure of hypotheses intended to make it possible to describe mental events in purely neurological terms. This attempt culminated in the 'Project' and was not long afterwards abandoned. To the end of his life, however, Freud continued to adhere to the chemical aetiology of the 'actual' neuroses and to believe that a physical basis for all mental phenomena might ultimately be found. But in the meantime he gradually came round to the view expressed by Breuer that psychical processes can only be dealt with in the language of psychology."

Related Concept: PSYCHOANALYSIS.

REFERENCES

Breuer, J., & S. Freud, "Studies on Hysteria." *SE*, 2:216, 1955.
Strachey, J., Editorial note. *SE*, 2:24–25, 1955.

ADDITIONAL READING

Loewald, H. W., "Hypnoid State, Repression, Abreaction and Recollection." *JAPA*, 3, 1955.

813

HYPNOSIS is a state, usually induced by others, in which the subject's conscious appears not to function, and in which he appears to be asleep, except when carrying out suggestions of the hypnotizer to which he is markedly receptive. Hypnosis is characterized by somnolence, in which the subject, with a certain amount of effort, can resist suggestion and open his eyes; by light sleep, in which the subject is unable to open his eyes and is compelled to obey some or all suggestions, but does not become amnesic; and by deep sleep or somnambulism, which is characterized by complete amnesia after awakening and by posthypnotic symptoms.

Before dealing with neurotic patients analytically, Freud (1892) expanded on Bernheim's theory that all human beings are more or less subject to suggestion, a fact regarded by Freud as a transference phenomenon. Freud also stressed the phylogenetic aspects of hypnosis, and emphasized the archaically tinged relation of the individual to his parents, which are reawakened in hypnosis, especially the subject's compliance to the father (i.e., the idea of a dangerous, overwhelmingly powerful personality toward whom only a passive-masochistic attitude is possible and to whom one's will has to be surrendered). Freud noted that the hypnotized person identifies by incorporating the hypnotist and uses him as a substitute for the ego-ideal (superego). With the exception of the hypnotist, all contact with the external world is cut off, and the hypnotist, who in large part takes over the functions of the subject's superego, is then able (from within) to nullify reality testing. Nonetheless, the subject retains some knowledge that what is happening is more or less a pretense.

In the hypnotic state, the subject expresses an aim-inhibited libidinal relationship with the hypnotist by a willingness to please him. He obeys not only the hypnotist's spoken commands, but also his assumed intentions. The ego undergoes a regression, with a temporary suspension of a number of its functions, particularly reality testing. Magical thinking and omnipotent wishes are projected onto the hypnotist who, for the subject, assumes the infantile aspect of one of his parents.

In obeying the hypnotist, the hypnotized can use all the organs which can be influenced by the sympathetic and parasympathetic nervous symptoms (normally not subject to the subject's will). This means that psychosomatic symptoms may be experimentally produced, and existing psychosomatic symptoms such as asthma may be eliminated, at least temporarily. The range of memory, histrionic ability, contact with the unconscious, and tolerance for pain may also be substantially increased.

In the course of hypnotic treatment, spontaneous hypnosis (the occurrence of a hypnotic state without induction by the hypnotist, or even against his will) serves as a flight from painful reality. Resistance in hypnosis can manifest itself through exaggerated obedience or by awakening.

Through his identification with the hypnotist, the subject unconsciously gratifies his own wish to be omnipotent. In addition, the subject's aim-inhibited unconscious sexual attachment to his parents is a factor in hypnotism, accounting for the indications of sexual excitement in the form of tremors and hysteriform rigidity, as well as the pleasant sensations, which often accompany hypnosis (possibly involving erotic fantasies).

Paranoid manifestations frequently occur in hypnotized subjects, and the psychodynamics of hypnotism may help explain why paranoics frequently complain of having been "hypnotized" by a "persecutor."

The hypnotic relationship is sometimes paralleled, in mass psychology, by the relationship between a leader and his followers. Frequently, the group following a leader manifests the same complete absorption and magical belief in a mysterious and irresistible power, in inhibition of critical judgment, and in an utterly dependent attitude. In addition, the same dependency and need for protection, and fear of the all-powerful father figure are present. [Freud, 1921.]

Related Concepts: AUTOHYPNOSIS; HYPNOANALYSIS.

REFERENCES

Freud, S.: 1892, "A Case of Successful Treatment by Hypnotism with Some Remarks on the Origin of Hysterical Symptoms Through Counterwill." *CPSF*, 5: 33–46, 1950.
     1921, "Group Psychology and the Analysis of the Ego." *SE*, 18:115–116, 1955.

ADDITIONAL READINGS

Bellak, L., "An Ego-Psychological Theory of Hypnosis." *IntJPsa*, 36, 1955.
Eidelberg, L., "Bemerkung zur Physiologie der in der Hypnose suggerierten Sinneseindrücke." *ZNP*, 1928.
Freud, S.: 1893, "On the Psychical Mechanism of Hysterical Phenomena: A Lecture." *SE*, 3, 1962.
     1904, "Psycho-Analytic Procedure." *SE*, 7, 1953.
     1905, "Psychical (or Mental) Treatment." *SE*, 7, 1953.
     1910, "Five Lectures on Psycho-Analysis." *SE*, 12, 1957.

Gill, M., & M. Brenman, *Hypnosis and Related States.* IUP, 1959.
Reiff, R., & M. Scheerer, *Memory and Hypnotic Age Regression, Developmental Aspects of Cognitive Function Explored Through Hypnosis.* IUP, 1959.
Schilder, P., *The Nature of Hypnosis.* IUP, 1956.
Speyer, N., & B. Stokvis, "The Psychoanalytic Factor in Hypnosis. *M*, 17, 1938.
Stengel, E., Review of *The Nature of Hypnosis*, by P. Schilder. *IntJPsa*, 37, 1956.
Wolberg, L., "Hypnosis in Psychoanalytic Psychotherapy." *ProgPT*, 2, 1957.

814

HYPOCHONDRIASIS is a symptom neurosis characterized by continuous complaints of the patient about unpleasant sensations localized in a part of his body. According to Freud (1914), it is an actual neurosis, an illness caused by mental reactions to somatic changes as yet not detected. The mental reactions consist of the withdrawal of libido (and destrudo) from presentations of the external world and the use of this energy to cathect presentations of the self (or parts of it).

The Wolf Man (described by Freud in 1918) developed a hypochondriacal delusion many years after the successful completion of his analysis. Ruth Brunswick (1929), who successfully analyzed this delusion, claimed that no new material was discovered but that the patient's father fixation (transference) was worked through. She suggested that the material was not new for the analyst but perhaps was new (emotionally) for the patient. She suggested that the remnant of transference produced the delusion (a hole in his nose, accompanied by the feeling that life was unbearable). It is evident from Ruth Brunswick's paper that this symptom represented a gratification of his wish to have a vagina (identification with the oedipal mother). The nose may have been selected for the localization of this symptom because it represented his penis; therefore, his symptom showed the condensation of his bisexuality.

These questions remain: Whether the psychic energy connected with presentations of the self is the same in so-called organic illness as in cases without a somatic basis ? Whether the psychic energy, when attached to the self preservation, is still object libido and object destrudo or whether it changes into primary or secondary libido *and* destrudo? Whether the quantity of object libido is smaller than object destrudo in hypochondriasis? Today, only speculations about these problems can be given. Perhaps hypochondriasis is the result of a mechanism similar to conversion: instead of sexual energy it uses aggressive energy.

It may well be that infantile wishes, which contain more Thanatos in their instinctual fusion, produce pain, whereas infantile wishes, with a greater quantity of Eros, lead only to a loss of function. The well-known fact that anxiety is present in hypochondriasis may well be used in favor of this assumption.

Related Concepts: CONVERSION AND CONVERSION SYMP-TOMS; DELUSIONS OF PERSECUTION; MELANCHOLIA.

REFERENCES

Brunswick, Ruth, "Ein Nachtrag zu Freuds Geschichte einer infantilen Neurose." *Z*, 15:1–43, 1929.
Freud, S., 1914, "On Narcissism: An Introduction." *SE*, 14:82, 83, 1957.

ADDITIONAL READINGS

Brautigam, W., "Analyse der Hypochondrischen Selbstbeobachtung. Beitrag zur Psychopathologie und zur Pathogenese mit Beschreibung einer Gruppe von Jugendlichen Herzhypochondern." *Nervenarzt*, 27, 1956.
Carp, E., "Zur Psychoanalytischen Auffassung der Hypochondrie." *ZNP*, 115, 1928.
Kehrer, F., "Über Hypochondrie." *ZPt*, 2, 1929.

815

HYSTERICAL CONVERSION is the transformation of the intrapsychic excitation into somatic manifestations. In hysterical conversion, the psychic energy used in the conversion belongs to the phallic stage. The symptoms affect various functions of the body without *apparently* causing pathological or anatomical changes; in time, however, secondary muscular atrophy may occur.

In hysterical paralysis, a compromise formation occurs between the forbidden instinctual impulse—which seeks to gain expression and discharge—and the defensive forces of the ego. The resulting paralysis may affect any of the peripheral muscles. Psychologically, the paralysis expresses materialization: the repressed thoughts cathect a particular organ presentation which is unconsciously used as a substitute. For example: the paralyzed leg of a hysterical girl expresses her unconscious wish for a penis, in that the leg is stiff, and, at the same time, it reveals her acceptance of castration, in that she is paralyzed. It also gratifies her unconscious exhibitionistic wishes.

Freud (1918) described the Wolf Man, a patient of his who was suffering from phobia, hysterical constipation, and obsessional neurosis. The hysterical constipation was caused by the erotization of his anus, resulting from his identification with his mother. Thus, the infantile wish to have anal intercourse with his father was partly gratified and partly warded off by his constipation. This case illustrates the necessity to differentiate between the localization of a symptom and the regression of the wish to an earlier, infantile stage of development. In this case, for example, the constipation was not the result of the regression to the anal stage. Although the patient had, in addition, such a regression, it was responsible for his obsessional neurosis and not for his constipation which was localized in his anus, caused by regression to the phallic stage. The Wolf Man's feminine attitude toward men led to hysterical intestinal symptoms. These intestinal symptoms consisted of attacks of diarrhea and constipation. In Freud's analysis of the Wolf Man, he identified the reaction to the observation of the parental intercourse as having led to an excitement in the anal zone. Freud pointed out that in other cases a similar observation would have led to an erection as a result of the identification with the father. The Wolf Man, however, identified with his mother and used his rectum instead of the vagina.

Related Concepts: DEFENSE MECHANISMS; PREGENITALITY.

REFERENCE

Freud, S., 1918, "From the History of an Infantile Neurosis." *SE*, 17:80–81, 1955.

ADDITIONAL READINGS

Freud, S., & J. Breuer, 1893, "On the Psychical Mechanism of Hysterical Phenomena." *SE*, 2, 1955.
Wolberg, L. R., "A Mechanism of Hysteria Elucidated During Hypnoanalysis." *Q*, 14, 1945.

816

HYSTERICAL MATERIALIZATION denotes that process whereby a repressed fantasy is symbolically expressed in somatic terms. For example, an unconscious fellatio fantasy may result in *globus hystericus*, or an unconscious wish to be pregnant may produce hysterical vomiting. Hysterical materialization may involve a resexualization of an earlier erotogenic zone, i.e., an upward displacement, as, for instance, when a phallic conflict is expressed by a symptom involving the mouth. It may also involve ego regression to the level of magic gestures; that is, and adaptation is attempted through modification of one's own body rather than through modification of the external world wherein the instinctual tension is probably discharged by the unconscious part of the ego. [Ferenczi, 1950.]

Related Concepts: CONVERSION AND CONVERSION SYMPTOMS; DISPLACEMENT; UNCONSCIOUS.

REFERENCE

Ferenczi, S., *Further Contributions to the Theory and Technique of Psychoanalysis*. HPI, pp. 89–104, 1950.

ADDITIONAL READING

Freud, S., 1894, "The Neuro-Psychoses of Defence." *SE*, 3, 1962.

I

ID. It contains everything that is inherited, that is fixed in the constitution—above all, therefore, the instincts, which originate in the somatic organization; it is in the sevice of the pure pleasure principle, an instinctual cathexis seeking discharge (Freud, 1940). Cut off from the external world, everything which goes on in the id is unconscious and remains so, having no correspondence to space or time. Freud (1923) attributed the term, as to its origin, to Georg Groddeck,* but defined the id as part of the total personality. In 1933, Freud further delineated his idea, and noted that the id contains sexual and aggressive energies, their discharge taking place with the help of the ego, because the ego controls the motility. The study of the id derivatives indicates that there are many contradictory impulses present in the id and that the ego is required to put them in order.

This "kingdom of the illogical," as Freud (1940) called it, is completely unconscious, containing various instinctual impulses which were never conscious, and those which were conscious and were repressed. The id is only interested in the discharge of instinctual tension. However, the actual discharge of this dammed-up energy usually takes place through the conscious part of the personality, although it may also be accomplished through the unconscious part of the ego. The activity of the id is governed by the so-called primary process, in which there is no recognition of *good* and *bad*, or *yes* and *no*. The id has no connection with the external world, but opens toward the ego. It is separated from the ego by its censor, which controls the flow of id derivatives. This censor appears, in psychoanalytic treatment, as resistance. In addition to communicating with the ego, the id also communicates with the superego. Glover (1939) noted: "The Id supplies both ego and superego with the energies with which they operate. It is permanently unconscious. The super-ego is for the largest part unconscious with, however, some conscious facets. The ego has also a deep unconscious part, but a relatively larger proportion of it is preconscious, accessible to consciousness and *via* consciousness, to the influences of external reality. The important point is that the super-ego is much more in touch with and sensitive to the Id than the ego. This accounts for the apparently mystifying nature of symptom formations. The conscious ego is unaware of the Id impulses which stimulate the unconscious super-ego to activity. It is also unaware that super-ego activity has compelled the unconscious ego to make adaptations."

Related Concepts: STRUCTURAL (TOPOGRAPHIC) APPROACH; UNCONSCIOUS.

Freud, S.: 1923, "The Ego and the Id." *SE*, 19:25, 1961.

1933, "New Introductory Lectures on Psycho-Analysis." *SE*, 22:73, 1964.

1940, "An Outline of Psycho-Analysis." *SE*, 23:145–148, 1964.

Glover, E., *Psycho-Analysis.* SP, p. 64, 1939.

---

* Groddeck, G., *Das Buch vom Es.* Vienna, 1923.

183

ADDITIONAL READING

Freud, Anna, 1936, *The Ego and the Mechanisms of Defense*, IUP, 1946.

901
IDEALIZATION is a process "that concerns the *object*. . . . Idealization is possible in the sphere of ego-libido as well as in that of object-libido." [Freud, 1914.] The two may be distinguished in so far "as sublimation has something to do with the instinct and idealization something to do with the object." In technical terms, this overestimation takes place not only in an anaclitic object choice but also in a narcissistic object choice. In most cases both forms of object choice are present, one being, usually, greater than the other.

Generally speaking, love consists in finding one person who has what the individual wants (anaclitic) or is what he would like to be (narcissistic). It appears that love extends the ego boundaries: *I* changes into *we*. Freud (1921) noted that the object we love often may represent our ego-ideal and, by loving this object, we use the object instead of our own ego-ideal.

In love, the object presentation is cathected by object and narcissistic libido, and leads to a decrease in the amount of narcissistic libido used for the presentation of the self. These economical changes are responsible for the overestimation of the object and the underestimation of the self. It seems that what is referred to as a normal love relationship appears to be partly an object relationship, and partly an identification with that object—provided the identification does not play a decisive role.

Related Concepts: OBJECT CHOICE (ANACLITIC AND NARCISSISTIC); SUBLIMATION.

REFERENCES

Freud, S.: 1914, "On Narcissism: An Introduction." *SE*, 14:94–95, 1957.
1921, "Group Psychology and the Analysis of the Ego." *SE*, 18:112–113, 1961.

ADDITIONAL READING

Glover, E., "A Note on Idealization." *IntJPsa*, 19, 1938.

902
IDENTIFICATION is a process, whether conscious or unconscious, in which the subject has the impression that he thinks, feels or acts like the object—or the object has such an impression. Our first interest in an object, as Freud (1921) noted, may be referred to as identification. The object partly represents part of the subject.

Freud (1939) provided the following example of a latent neurosis, in which an identification with the mother did not, for a time, prevent the boy from an apparent success. It began when the patient was a small boy and had repeatedly observed his parents in the sexual act, having slept in the same bedroom with them for a time. Subsequently, after his first spontaneous emission, he suffered from disturbances of sleep, and was extraordinarily sensitive to night noises. Freud identified this disturbance as a true compromise symptom. The boy's prior observations led to a premature sexual aggressive masculinity, wherein he identified with his father and directed his sexual interests to his mother. He began to masturbate and did so until forbidden to do so by his mother. Thereafter, he gave up all sexual activity and became a "model" child, seemingly free of any marked disturbances.

Following the latency period, at the onset of puberty, his manifest neurosis appeared and brought with it his second main symptom, his impotency. His sexual activity remained limited to masturbatory manipulations which were accompanied by sado-masochistic fantasies. His intensified masculinity, brought on by pubescent changes, expressed itself in an extreme hatred for his father. This attitude was later responsible for his failure in the profession his father had chosen for him. After his father's death, he developed an egoistic and despotic personality. His identification with his father, as he had formed a picture of him in his memory, placed him in a rivalry situation with the father, in correspondence to the analogous situation he had with him when he was a small boy.

Though Freud (1933) described identification in terms of an object-attachment, he nonetheless distinguished between identification and object-choice. Whenever the male child identifies with his father he wants to be similar to him. However, if the male child identifies with his mother, the father becomes an object he wants to acquire. The difference, that is, lies between the narcissistic object-like choice and the anaclitic object-choice.

Under normal conditions, little is known about the advantages or disadvantages of the two forms of object-choice. However, under pathological conditions (e.g., in the case of object-loss), an individual preferring the narcissistic mode of object-choice may develop a depression (regression to identification). He appears to have lost not only what he needed, but also something which he regarded as a part of himself. He uses part of his own personality to replace the lost object. Instead of seeking a new object and perhaps discharging the aggression (originally directed toward the lost object), he directs the aggression against himself by being depressed and wanting to die.

Little is known about object-choice in respect to the discharge of aggression. It appears that we hate those who frustrate our wishes (anaclitic object-choice) and those who inflict narcissistic mortifications on us (narcissistic object-choice). It is possible that object destrudo may be discharged through an anaclitic object choice, while narcissistic destrudo may be discharged through a narcissistic object-choice.

From an economic point of view, object libido and destrudo may be discharged by an anaclitic object-choice, while narcissistic libido and destrudo may be discharged in a narcissistic object choice. It appears that only narcissistic libido is used to cathect the presentation of the self. [Eidelberg, 1954.]

1. Alloplastic Identification. A form of adaptation which is directed toward the alteration of the environment rather than the self; a successor to the autoplastic developmental stage. The initial motility in human activity is directed toward the pleasure principle, which, under the guidance of the reality principle is given a more purposeful aim. Pathological manifestations of alloplastic adaptations are to be found in cases in which motility retains its more primitive and magical function: in acting out, compulsions, impulse disorders, flights into reality, and psychoses. [See **130**.]

2. Autoplastic Identification. A form of adaptation which is directed toward the alteration of the total personality rather than the environment; in which thought, fantasy, and affect are substituted for action. The therapeutic changes in analysis result from an autoplastic identification with the analyst. Pathological autoplasty is to be found in the formation of neurotic symptoms, and in such psychotic formations as delusions and hallucinations. [See **168**.]

3. External Identification. Those changes in which the subject becomes similar to the object, or the object to the subject. For example, in the case of a student in his twenties, both ambitious and industrious who, when he began to have sexual relationships, became agoraphobic. His symptom freed him from the necessity of meeting with his chief, a man he identified with his father, who had been dismissed for embezzlement some years before. This unconsciously meant that an identification with a father image was dangerous, for it might lead to a conflict with the outside world. His agoraphobia thus freed him from the necessity of meeting with his father image, who also suffered from agoraphobia. [See **534**.]

4. Internal Identification. A phenomenon in which the subject appears to possess the emotions and feelings of the object with whom he identifies, consciously or unconsciously. In a number of neurotic defense mechanisms, unconscious inner identification is of decisive importance, e.g., persecution mania, pathological jealousy, and impotence. A conscious inner identification is established in the instance of a male spectator and a male actor on the stage; it occurs unconsciously when the spectator's identification is to a female actress assuming the spectator is not an overt homosexual. [See **924**.]

5. Primary Identification. The first object relationship between the mother and the infant, in which there is no differentiation between the subject and the object, i.e., between the infant and the mother. It refers to those early oral relationships in which no differentiation takes place. [See **1655**.]

6. Pseudoidentification. According to Eidelberg (1954), it is a defense mechanism which takes the form of a projection to an object, in which the subject subsequently identifies with the object. For example, a patient avoided expressing a difference of opinion with those with whom he might be talking by immediately and completely identifying with that person [See **1671.**]

7. Secondary Identification. Characterized by a cathexis of the object presentation by narcissistic libido and destrudo. One form of secondary identification appears to be connected with the oral stage of development. In this, the subject becomes more and more similar to the object, treating himself as though he were the object. Secondary identification may also take the form of hysterical identification, in which certain characteristics of the total personality are incorporated into the self. For instance, Freud's patient, Dora, developed a cough like that of the woman she perceived as a rival. [See **1913.**]

Related Concepts: CHOICE OF A NEUROSIS; NEUROSIS (PSYCHONEUROSIS).

REFERENCES

Eidelberg, L., *An Outline of a Comparative Pathology of the Neuroses,* IUP, p. 49, 1954.
Freud, S.: 1921, "Group Psychology and the Analysis of the Ego." *SE,* 18:107–108, 1955.
    1933, "New Introductory Lectures on Psycho-Analysis." *SE,* 22:63, 1964.
    1939, "Moses and Monotheism." *SE,* 23:78–80, 1964.

ADDITIONAL READINGS

Axelrad, S., & L. Maury, "Identification as a Mechanism of Adaptation." *AnSurvPsa,* 2, 1951.
Berezin, M. A., "Enuresis and Bisexual Identification." *JAPA,* 2, 1954.
Eidelberg, L.: *Studies in Psychoanalysis.* IUP, 1948.
    & J. N. Palmer, "Primary and Secondary Narcissism," *PQ,* 34, 1960.
Fenichel, O., *The Psychoanalytic Theory of Neurosis.* Nor, 1945.
Freud, S.: 1914, "On Narcissism: An Introduction." *SE,* 14, 1957.
    1923, "The Ego and the Id." *SE,* 19, 1961.

903

ILLUSION. Two kinds of illusions must be differentiated: (a) those connected with the malfunctioning of our sense organs (double vision resulting from the paralysis of certain eye muscles), which may be referred to as sense-organ illusions; and (b) psychic illusions which denote the anticipation of a future event, not based on the probability of its actual occurrence but on a strong need for instant wish-fulfillment. It is usually possible to differentiate illusion from delusion, because the delusion represents a distortion of a sense-organ perception while an illusion is generally connected with an anticipation. In the case of delusions, their essential characteristic is their contradiction with reality. Illusions need not necessarily be false—that is to say, unrealizable or in contradiction to reality (Freud, 1915). For instance, a middle-class girl may have the illusion that a prince will come and marry her. This is possible; and a few such cases have occurred. That the Messiah will come and found a golden age is much less likely.

Illusions may be considered as necessary for our ability to experience aesthetic pleasure; it does not interfere with the adaptation to reality, serving to enhance it, but should be differentiated from other illusions which prevent such an adaptation. The quantity of mental energy related to inner reality is not by itself pathognomic, for only the confusion between internal and external reality—the inability to separate what takes place within and what belongs in the external world—leads to neurosis.

Religion and Illusion

Freud considered religion to be an illusion, a destructive one because it threatens man's mental development by interfering with his scientific view of the world. Religion is not subject to proof; rather, to belief. Freud stressed the importance of knowledge over belief, and pointed out that mankind's progress is based not on the displacement of infantile omnipotence to God, but on a recognition of its limited ability to deal with inner and external reality.

Science and Illusion

Freud noted (1930) that with the help of science the individual may increase his power over the external world and over himself. He negated the accusation of science being only an illusion and said that we were unable to obtain from other sources what science doesn't give us.

Related Concepts: AESTHETIC PLEASURE; DELUSIONS; HALLUCINATIONS.

REFERENCES

Freud, S.: 1915, "Thoughts for the Times on War and Death." *SE,* 14:280, 1957.

1930, "Civilization and Its Discontents." *SE,* 21:54–56, 1961.

904

IMITATION denotes both the act and the wish to copy an admired and hated object. In this, it is closely related to an external identification and to an identification with an aggressor (A. Freud, 1936). Freud (1920) identified it as an active repetition of what was passively experienced; in his view it represented the compulsion to repeat. Fenichel (1945) noted that alexia was compensated for, in the case of a woman suffering from brain damage, by a learning process that involved outlining the letters of the alphabet by imitating them with head movements. In this sense, imitation was a kind of identification, an awareness that brought perception. Fenichel also noted that in certain cases of conversion symptom imitations served "as an identification, an opportunity for the gratification of the negative Oedipus complex."

The urge to imitate has been identified as the representation of an earlier mechanism, one that occurred prior to the subject's ability to execute orders or to follow verbal instructions. Fenichel contended that, as with other wishes, it could be repressed and rejected, its gratification inhibited and discharged. In support of this thesis, Eidelberg (1948) reported the following experiment: He asked the subject to point to his nose as soon as he said "nose," and to point to a lamp placed to the right as soon as he said "lamp." At the same time the examiner himself pointed to the lamp or to his nose in accordance with the word stimulus. After a few repetitions, during which the subject usually responded correctly, the examiner began to point to the wrong object—to the lamp when he said "nose," and to his nose when he said, "lamp." The subject now pointed to the wrong object. The examiner asked him to pay attention only to the words and to disregard the gestures without, however, looking away. The subject then pointed

to the right object a few times, then again pointed to the wrong object. Despite the warning, he again committed the same error and was unable to heed the injunction to follow only the acoustic stimulus. Thereupon the experiment was modified, as follows:

The subject was asked to respond to the acoustic stimulus by pointing *not* to the nose or the lamp but to the word "nose" or "lamp" written on the blackboard. In this experiment, the subject did not make any mistakes. It was therefore clear, Eidelberg concluded, that it was only the compulsion to imitate the response of the visual perception that forced the subject to disregard the acoustic perception. Psychologically, imitation of motion doubtless was connected with a more primitive layer of the psyche than imitation concerned with a response to an acoustic stimulus. Thus, there were probably many other situations in which the complicated reaction was suppressed while the primitive layer of the psyche asserted a certain independence.

A. Freud offered the following clinical example: "This little boy . . . had been joining in an outdoor game at school and had run full tilt against the fist of the games-master, which the latter happened to be holding up in front of him. My little patient's lip was bleeding and his face tear-stained, and he tried to conceal both facts by putting up his hand as a screen. I endeavoured to comfort and reassure him. He was in a woebegone condition when he left me, but next day he appeared holding himself very erect and dressed in full armour. On his head he wore a military cap and he had a toy sword at his side and a pistol in his hand. When he saw my surprise at this transformation, he simply said, 'I just wanted to have these things on when I was playing with you.' He did not, however, play; instead, he sat down and wrote a letter to his mother: 'Dear Mummy, please, please, please, please send me the pocketknife you promised me and don't wait till Easter!' Here again we cannot say that, in order to master the anxiety-experience of the previous day, he was impersonating the teacher with whom he had collided. Nor, in this instance, was he imitating the latter's aggression. The weapons and armour, being manly attributes, evidently symbolized the teacher's strength and, like the attributes of the father in the animal-phantasies, helped the child to identify himself with the masculinity of the adult and so to defend himself against narcissistic mortification or actual mishaps. . . .

"A child introjects some characteristic of an anxiety-object and so assimilates an anxiety-experience which he has just undergone. Here, the mechanism of identification or introjection is combined with a second important mechanism. By impersonating the aggressor, assuming his attributes or imitating his aggression, the child transforms himself from the person threatened into the person who makes the threat. In *Beyond the Pleasure Principle* the significance of this change from the passive to the active role as a means of assimilating unpleasant or traumatic experiences in infancy is discussed in detail. 'If a doctor examines a child's throat or performs a small operation, the alarming experience will quite certainly be made the subject of the next game, but in the pleasure gain from another source cannot be overlooked. In passing from the passivity of experience to the activity of play the child applies to his playfellow the unpleasant occurrence that befell himself and so avenges himself on the person of this proxy.' What is true of play is equally true of other behaviour in children. In the case of the boy who made faces and the little girl who practised magic it is not clear what finally became of the threat with which they identified themselves, but in the other little boy's ill-temper the aggression taken over from the dentist and the games-master was directed against the world at large."

Related Concepts: ACTION (ACT); IDENTIFICATION.

REFERENCES

Eidelberg, L., *Studies in Psychoanalysis.* IUP, pp. 125–128, 1948.
Fenichel, O., *The Psychoanalytic Theory of Neurosis.* Nor, pp. 37, 222, 1945.
Freud, A., 1936, *The Ego and the Mechanisms of Defense.* IUP, pp. 120–122, 1946.
Freud, S., 1918, "From the History of an Infantile Neurosis." *SE,* 17:36–38, 1955.

ADDITIONAL READINGS

Dollard, J., & N. Miller, *Social Learning and Imitation.* YUP, 1941.
Eidelberg, L., "On the Mechanism of the Imitative Gesture." *JPN,* 46, 1928–1929.

905

IMPOTENCE denotes the inability of the male to perform the sexual act. Most authors differentiate between *impotentia generandi* (inability to have children), which is often caused by pathological anatomical changes, and *impotentia coeundi* (inability to have intercourse), which can usually be examined and effectively treated through psychoanalysis.

Freud (1926) noted that the libido may be inhibited by many factors: by psychic unpleasure; by lack of an erection; by a premature emission; by a complete lack of emission; and by a lack of the emotion present in the experience of the orgasm. In addition, many authors describe a condition (ejaculatio retardata) in which emission takes place only after a very long time, perhaps an hour or more.

Like other symptoms, impotence represents both a partial gratification and a defense of repressed infantile wishes, sexual as well as aggressive. Many things may cause impotence, including an unresolved incestuous fixation on the mother (preoedipal mother), impressions connected with infantile sexuality, problems stemming from fears of castration, and identification with the odedipal mother.

Impotence is sometimes hidden behind neurotic traits, so that the subject is consciously unaware of his impotence. For example, a patient who sought analysis because of his depression said that his sex life was normal. When the analyst became more specific and asked how often the patient had sexual intercourse, the patient replied that he had never actually had intercourse; all the girls he had tried to have sex with had rejected him. After eight months of analysis, his character and approach to women had changed enough so that he succeeded in persuading a girl to share his bed. Only then did he discover, to his horror, that he was completely incapable of having an erection.

Abraham (1917) summarized his own view, as follows: "A rarer neurotic disturbance which is not so well known in medical circles, yet which, although the reverse of ejaculatio praecox, is intimately related to it. I refer to the symptom of impotentia ejaculandi. In many neurotic persons no ejaculation occurs during the sexual act. In this case also there is a sexual disinclination arising from narcissism. In these patients the 'keeping to themselves' is the predominant motive. The effect is the same as in ejaculatio praecox: narcissism gains the upper hand and the woman is disappointed. It need hardly be mentioned here that there is every kind of gradation from normal ejaculation to premature emission on the one hand and to its entire absence on the other. Retarded ejaculation is not an infrequent symptom of many neuroses.

"It is the task of psycho-analytical treatment to free the patient from his narcissistic attitude, and to point out to him the path to a normal transference of feelings. If we can succeed in removing his narcissistic rejection of the female, the path is made free for him to carry out the normal sexual functions. Psycho-analysis acts in a similar manner in removing the female counterpart to ejaculatio praecox—frigidity.

"Naturally, different cases present various degrees of severity of the illness. The milder disturbances of this nature can appear at times in men disposed to them and disappear without any treatment, though there is a constant risk of relapse. A cure, or at least a distinct amelioration of the symptoms, can be obtained by psycho-analysis even in severe and obstinate cases. From the point of view of prognosis those cases are least favourable in which the ejaculatio praecox set in immediately on the attainment of sexual maturity, and has reappeared again and again for a number of years. These are the cases which exhibit an exceptionally marked urethral erotism as opposed to a genital erotism, and in which the pleasure-value of ejaculatio praecox outweighs its displeasure-value. The treatment of this condition may be technically one of the most difficult tasks for the psycho-analyst, since he has to contend with the very considerable amount of narcissism present in such patients. Nevertheless, a persevering and consistent use of the psycho-analytic method will enable him to surmount difficulties even as considerable as these."

Related Concept: FRIGIDITY.

REFERENCES

Abraham, K., 1917, "Ejaculatio Praecox." *SPA*, pp. 297–298, 1942.
Freud, S., 1926, "Inhibitions, Symptoms and Anxiety." *SE*, 20:88, 1959.

ADDITIONAL READINGS

Bien, E., "Zur Aktivanalytischen Therapie der psychischen Impotenz." *ZSW*, 17, 1931.
Bjerre, P., "Zur Impotenzfrage." *PtPrx*, 1, 1934.
Steiner, M., "Die Bedeutung der femininen Identifizierung für die männliche Impotenz." *Z*, 16, 1930.
Stephen, A., "Impotence." *M*, 15, 1936.

906

IMPOTENCE AND MASOCHISM. Many impotent patients manifest unconscious masochistic wishes; they want to have their penises beaten off, crushed, soiled, etc. Consequently, erection and emission are interfered with. Some of these patients are able to masturbate with the help of conscious masochistic fantasies, because, in these fantasies, they play both roles, i.e., they represent both the humiliated man and the humiliating woman.

Freud (1919) noted that patients who masturbate with the help of masochistic fantasies and patients who only can have sexual intercourse by being humiliated may be cured only if the basic origin of their need for punishment and their intolerance of success have been eliminated.

Related Concepts: IMPOTENCE; MASOCHISM.

REFERENCE

Freud, S., 1919, "'A Child Is Being Beaten': A Contribution to the Study of the Origin of Sexual Perversions." *SE*, 17:197, 1955.

ADDITIONAL READINGS

Eidelberg, L., *An Outline of a Comparative Pathology of the Neuroses.* IUP, 1954.
Freud, S., 1924, "The Economic Problem of Masochism." *SE*, 19, 1961.

907

IMPULSE denotes a sudden inclination or desire; the psychological presentation of an instinctual drive (*Trieb*). In impulse neurosis, the individual is subject to ego-syntonic pathological impulses which are extremely intense and often irresistible, probably because of a condensation or fusion of instinctual urges and defensive strivings (countercathexis). Such patients are intolerant of tension, have a low frustration tolerance, and cannot—or can only with great difficulty—postpone immediate reactions or actions (observable in impulsive character neuroses, running away, kleptomania, etc.). [Fenichel, 1945.]

Reich (1949) noted that an impulse, once fully developed, cannot be fully repressed. When an impulse—an instinctual urge—is frustrated, a condition exists which may lead to the formation of an impulsive character disorder. In this, sadistic impulses may be used to defend the subject against imaginary dangers, not excluding those dangers threatening from the impulses themselves.

Related Concepts: ACTING OUT; CHARACTER NEUROSIS; IMPULSE; INSTINCT (INSTINCTUAL DRIVE); PSYCHOPATHY.

REFERENCES

Fenichel, O., *The Psychoanalytic Theory of Neurosis.* Nor, pp. 367–369, 1945.
Reich, W., *Character Analysis.* OIP, p. 151, 1949.

ADDITIONAL READINGS

Bergler, E., "Psychopathology of the 'First Impulse' and 'First Thought' in Neurotics." *PQSup,* 21, 1947.
Reich, W., "Der triebhafte Charakter; eine psychoanalytische Studie zur Pathologie des Ich." *IntPV,* 1925.

908

INCEST denotes heterosexual coition between members of the same family; a virtual taboo of all societies and religions. It has been treated in psychoanalysis primarily in terms of its role in the oedipus complex. The universal sexual prohibition of the son's desire for his mother, and the resulting conflict with the father, has been used by Freud to explain the aetiology of culture and religion. Freud (1913) suggested that the totemic worship which accompanied the practice of exogamy was caused by the taboo prohibiting the desire for the mother and the sister (and mother-in-law). The totem represented the father, which later acquired a societal function, and in this way kept the inhibited hostility under control. Freud (1913) noted: "The first restrictions produced by the introduction of marriage-classes affected the sexual freedom of the *younger* generation."*

This statement indicates that, in this respect, Freud considered the prohibitions of sexual intercourse between sons and mothers as interfering with the freedom of the younger generation. In this, he probably assumed that it was always the son and not his mother who was interested in incest.

It has sometimes been suggested that inbreeding is an intuitive process. Freud stated, in answer, that the horror of incest was the result of an inherited factor. He also was reluctant to accept the idea that inbreeding was responsible for it.

The extraordinary precautions primitives take toward even the possibility of an incestuous relationship is contrasted with the lesser prohibitions of civilized society, which stem from more deeply organized repressions. This difference, however, is less clearly distinguishable in the neurotic for he is compelled to establish phobias, symptoms, and compulsions of great complexity which serve the same purpose as the taboos present in the primitive. Impotence, frigidity and other neurotic phenomena are often the result of unconscious incestuous wishes.

In an earlier paper, Freud (1905) noted that the analytical treatment of neurotics clearly indicates that their sexual desires while repressed have remained related to incestuous objects and are therefore inhibited.

Related Concepts: ANIMISM; CIVILIZATION; OEDIPUS COMPLEX; TABOO; TOTEM.

REFERENCES

Freud, S.: 1905, "Three Essays on the Theory of Sexuality." *SE,* 7:227, 228, 1953.
        1913, "Totem and Taboo." *SE,* 13:4–9, 121, 124, 1955.

ADDITIONAL READINGS

Bally, G., "Das Inzestmotiv." *P,* 1, 1947.
Devereux, G., "The Social and Cultural Implications of Incest Among the Mohave Indians." *Q,* 8, 1939.
Fink, H. K., "Momism and Incest." *Realife Guide,* 2, 1959.
Gordon, L., "Incest as Revenge Against the Pre-Oedipal Mother." *R,* 42, 1955.
Hadley, E. E., "The Origin of the Incest Taboo." *R,* 14, 1927.

---

* In a matrilinear society, the children were considered to be related only to the mother.

Rascovsky, M. W., & A. Rascovsky, "On Consummated Incest." *IntJPs*, 31, 1950.

Weinberg, S., *Incest Behaviour*. Cit, 1955.

Weiner, I., "Father-Daughter Incest." *Q*, 36, 1962.

909

INFANCY is not rigidly equated with a stage of development but is considered to incorporate the oral stage and the beginning of the anal stage; the mental activities, wishes and fears, gestures and actions associated with approximately the first year of life. This period is equivalent to that time when the child is dependent for its nourishment on the mother's breast (or its equivalent) and for its safety on the protection of the parents, in which he cannot move independently nor articulate his wishes and ideas.

When birth is completed, certain reflexes which regulate the delivery of food, oxygen, etc. cease to function. Born into a world where only oxygen is present in sufficient quantity, and available without trouble or delay, the infant can no longer rely on his reflexes alone to satisfy his other vital needs, but has to develop a coordinated action of his whole body. The signal of unpleasure appears to mobilize the forces of the newborn, who then tries to find a way to remove it. There is an increase in certain metabolites and a decrease of others; the instincts mobilized by this unpleasure attempt to restore the original metabolic equilibrium. The action is achieved by the elimination of certain metabolites and the incorporation of others which the infant has to this period not required from the external world. Thus, the infant's first action—to obtain oxygen after the severing of the umbilical cord—is reflexive. His second action, that of satisfying his hunger and thirst, is only achieved with the help of the mother (or surrogate). The mother offers her breast or a bottle. Some time later, the infant will learn to grasp and to suck the breast by himself, eliminating his hunger and thirst in this active way. [Eidelberg, 1954.]

Freud (1905) characterized the derivatives of this activity. The mouth of a child behaves like an erotogenic zone. In that way, the need for food and the need for sensual pleasure are connected with the stimulation of the mouth. Later, Freud (1909)* was

---

* From a footnote added in 1923.

to note that the withdrawal of the mother's breast (weaning), the loss of feces, and perhaps even the separation of which distinguishes birth itself are the prototype of all castration fears. It must be added that the term *castration complex* was confined to those "excitations and consequences which are bound up with the loss of the penis."

The infant does not differentiate between wish and action. He learns to make this distinction because he discovers that wishing alone does not gratify his needs. This attitude, characterized by the infant's belief in his ability to gratify his needs by wishing, is called infantile omnipotence.

In formulating the theory of the libido, Freud made it quite clear that such an instinct did not arrive fully formed. To the contrary, it passes through a rather complicated development before genital primacy is reached. Jones (1955) has briefly described Freud's view of the infant's initial development, as follows: "It begins diffusely from the excitability of many 'erotic zones' of the body. He maintained, for instance, just as a Hungarian pediatrician, Lindner, had twenty years before him, that the infant is impelled to suck not only by hunger, the need for nourishment, but also by the desire for erotic gratification even when it is not hungry. . . . There is an unbroken line in this development, so Freud saw no reasons for refusing it the same name 'sexual' throughout. . . . In all the changes in Freud's conception of aetiology the two factors of 'sexual' and 'infantile' remained constant."

Related Concepts: NARCISSISTIC MORTIFICATION; OEDIPUS COMPLEX; PSYCHIC (MENTAL) ENERGY.

REFERENCES

Eidelberg, L., *An Outline of a Comparative Pathology of the Neuroses*, IUP, p. 30, 1954.

Freud, S.: 1905, "Three Essays on the Theory of Sexuality." *SE*, 7:181–183, 1953.

    1909, "Analysis of a Phobia in a Five-Year-Old Boy." *SE*, 10:8, 1955.

Jones, E., *The Life and Work of Sigmund Freud*, HPI, 2:317–318, 1955.

ADDITIONAL READINGS

Brody, S., "Self-Rocking in Infancy." *JAPA*, 8, 1960.

Freud, A., "Some Remarks on Infant Observation." *PsaStC*, 8, 1953.

Gardner, G., Report on Panel: "Problems in Early Infancy." *JAPA*, 3, 1955.

Mahler, M. S., "On Sadness and Grief in Infancy and Childhood. Loss and Restoration of the Symbiotic Love Object." *PsaStC*, 16, 1961.

Spitz, R. A., "Relevancy of Direct Infant Observation." *PsaStC*, 5, 1950.

Sterba, E., "Analysis of Psychogenic Constipation in a Two-Year-Old Child." *PsaStC*, 3–4, 1949.

910

INFANTILE MASTURBATION takes place prior to the latency period, characterized by lack of genital discharge. Fenichel (1945) noted: "Since the genitals in the infant play only the part of *primus inter pares*, autoerotic activities of little children are by no means limited to genital stimulation. All erogenous zones may be stimulated autoerotically." Freud's concept of infantile sexuality was partially based on the observations of Lindner (1934), who first reported on the masturbatory finger-sucking (*wonnenlutschen*) of infants. By the time the phallic level is reached, boys chiefly use their penis, and girls their clitoris, for masturbation.

With the help of masturbation, the infant (and later the child and the adult) is able to become independent of an external object, and, in that way, eliminate dammed-up instinctual energy and avoid narcissistic mortifications.

Related Concept: MASTURBATION.

REFERENCES

Fenichel, O., *The Psychoanalytic Theory of Neurosis.* Nor, pp. 74–76, 1945.

Lindner, S., "Das Saugen an den Fingern, Lippen, etc. bei den Kindern (Ludeln)." *PsaP*, 8:117–138, 1934.

911

INFERIORITY FEELINGS. Historically, this concept has been identified with Adler's *individual psychology*: it held that the human individual seeks to assert himself, to overcompensate for his inferiority feelings, and to pass from childhood into adulthood by identifying with a masculine or feminine counterpart. In this view, the ego is seen as the self-preserver of the total personality; the ego, thus, may be viewed, conceptually, as that instrument which turns every illness to its advantage.

In psychoanalysis, this view would be described as a secondary gain from illness. Further, in Freudian psychoanalysis, inferiority feelings are viewed as deriving from the ego's relationship to the superego and not to the external world.

The objective facts used by these patients to explain their conscious inferiority feelings appear to be a rationalization. While it is true that there are others who are stronger, smarter and richer, this fact alone does not explain the feeling of inferiority. It seems that the word *inferior*, as used by these patients, is often connected with some kind of feeling of guilt or shame which is only to be justified if the patient falsely claims to be better than he is. Whoever tries to sail under a false flag and to be somebody he is not may rightly be afraid of being unmasked and experience shame. The patient's explanation represents an attempt to cover up some unconscious factor which is responsible for this feeling.

Structural Approach

Students of the psychology of the normal individual may consider the division of the total personality to be an unnecessary complication to their work, and may complain about the difficulty in separating the three parts of the personality from each other. Eidelberg noted (1954): "In pathology, the topographic, or structural approach has proved its value." In this regard, psychoanalysis finds the causes which are responsible for the individual's inferiority feelings to be connected with the three stages of development, as shown in the following example:

a. Oral Stage: *I want to suck; I cannot give anything in return; therefore, I am a parasite and an inferior creature.*

b. Anal Stage: *I want to play with feces and be dirty. Not being able to eliminate the repressed wishes which represent the need and its gratification. I remain dirty and inferior.*

c. Phallic Stage: The girl says, *Without a penis I am an inferior creature. I am envious of all those who have a penis and have to admit that I miss something which I consider important.* The boy says, *I compare my penis with father's and find that it is smaller and, therefore, inferior.*

In all three stages, infantile omnipotence plays

a decisive role. *I am inferior because, unlike my parents, I am unable to do what they do*. It is obvious that the feeling of inferiority is based on the patient's repression or denial of infantile wishes and on the limitation of his power.

When the little girl discovers that the penis is bigger than her clitoris she feels inferior. The neurotic feeling of inferiority should not be confused with the normal ability to accept certain facts the individual cannot change (e.g., blindness) and the ability to compensate for this through the development of other sense organs. [Freud, 1924.]

Inferiority feelings may be regarded as a neurotic symptom, and should be differentiated from an evaluation which is self-critical, i.e., a recognition of those inherent limitations which are characteristic of all individuals. Some can be overcome or decreased, others have to be tolerated or accepted.

Related Concepts: CASTRATION COMPLEX; MEGALOMANIA; OMIPOTENCE OF THOUGHT.

REFERENCES

Eidelberg, L., *An Outline of a Comparative Pathology of the Neuroses*, IUP, p. 68, 1954.
Freud, S., 1924, "The Dissolution of the Oedipus Complex." *SE*, 19:178, 1961.

ADDITIONAL READINGS

Marcinowski, J., "Die Erotischen Quellen der Minderwertigkeitsgefühle." *ZSW*, 4, 1918.
Saul, L., "Inferiority Feelings and Hostility." *P*, 108, 1951.

912

INFLUENCING MACHINE denotes that part of a delusional formation, especially found in paranoid states, involving the idea of being controlled by a machine—an instrument of persecution. Analysis reveals the machine to be an outwardly projected symbol of the patient's genitals and body. In early stages of the disorder, there may be a hypochondriacal investment of organs, depersonalization, and other evidence of changes in the ego boundaries. The deanimation of the body into a machine is related to the automatizing functions of the preconscious and a sense of the uncanny. [Tausk, 1933.]

Related Concepts: CONTROL; PARANOIA; UNCANNY.

REFERENCE

Tausk, V., "On the Origin of the 'Influencing Machine' in Schizophrenia." *Q*, 2:519–566, 1933.

ADDITIONAL READINGS

Elkisch, P., & M. S. Mahler, "On Infantile Precursors of the 'Influencing Machine'." *PsaStC*, 14, 1959.
Freud, S., 1919, "The Uncanny." *SE*, 17, 1955.
Linn, L., "Some Comments on the Origin of the Influencing Machine." *JAPA*, 6, 1958.

913

INHIBITION denotes a restraint or prevention of activity or function by external or internal forces, or both. Neurotic inhibition refers to the partial or complete restraint of an instinctual drive by unconscious forces; it often results in a marked restriction of the individual's mental activities (intellectual, emotional, volitional) or his motoric and visceral functions, through which the instinctual drives and their derivatives are expressed. In describing the inhibition of instinctual impulses, A. Freud (1936) noted: "A person suffering from a neurotic inhibition is defending himself against the translation into action of some prohibited instinctual impulse, i.e. against the liberation of 'pain' through some internal danger. Even when, as in phobias, the anxiety and the defence seem to relate to the outside world, he is really afraid of his own inner processes. He avoids walking in the streets, in order not to be exposed to temptations which formerly assailed him. He keeps out of the way of his anxiety-animal, in order to protect himself, not against the animal itself but against the aggressive tendencies within him which an encounter with it might arouse and against their consequences. In ego-restriction, on the other hand, disagreeable external impressions in the present are warded off, because they might result in the revival of similar impressions from the past. Reverting to our comparison between the mechanisms of repression and denial we shall say that the difference between inhibition and ego-restriction is that in the former the ego is defending itself against its own inner processes and in the latter against external stimuli.

"From this fundamental distinction there ensue other differences between these two psychic situations. Behind every neurotically inhibited activity there lies an instinctual wish. The obstinacy with which each separate id-impulse sets itself to attain its goal transforms the simple process of inhibition into a fixed neurotic symptom, which represents a perpetual conflict between the wish of the id and the defence set up by the ego. The patient exhausts his energy in the struggle; his id-impulses adhere with but little modification to the wish to calculate, to speak in public, to play the violin or whatever it may be, while at the same time the ego with equal persistence prevents or at least mars the execution of his wish."

Glover (1939) described the sexual inhibitions, as follows: "The striking feature of sexual inhibitions is their economy of function. *They protect against unconscious anxieties and guilts without the expenditure of psychic effort necessary for symptom-formation.* Whereas the symptom-formation depends on maintaining an elaborate system of compromises between unconscious instincts and ego-institutions, inhibitions do away with the necessity for compromise and call for activity on the part of the ego only. Inhibitions can affect (a) sexual interest and curiosity, (b) the degree and quality of sexual satisfaction or (c) the actual technique of sexual activities. Inhibition of interest if persistent is extremely significant, it may indeed be a sign of serious maladjustment. But it is rarely regarded as such by the patient himself. Characteristic disturbances of the degree and quality of sexual feeling can be observed in women suffering from *frigidity*. This varies from absence of capacity for orgasm to complete absence of erotic feeling in intercourse (anaesthesia). In the latter case coitus is frequently associated with some degree of pain (dyspareunia) or spasm (vaginismus) and may give rise to a phobia of intercourse. Interference with the technique of sexual activities is more obvious in the male. Minor difficulties are manifested by *inhibition or omission of various forms of fore-pleasure* through which normally a number of infantile forms of sexuality are gratified in a way consonant with adult sexual codes. Mild *impotence*, i.e., difficulty in erection, penetration, sometimes in achieving ejaculation is one of the commonest forms of psychological disturbance. Some degree of *ejaculatio praecox* (or precocious emission) is also common. These varieties of inhibition are the most obvious of all psycho-sexual abnormalities and, in the sense of unconscious protection from anxieties, the most effective. The frigidity of the woman although corresponding to male impotence rarely interferes with the sexual act.

"The significance of these inhibitions varies with their depth and with the amount of unconscious anxiety they conceal. Many of them have the same protective functions as mild conversions or anxiety hysterias. They defend against infantile genital (incestuous) anxieties, i.e., unconscious fear of castration in the male, unconscious conviction of castration and fear of parental seduction and penetration in the female. The underlying disposition in both cases is mildly homosexual. Unconscious (infantile) love drives are charged with sadistic pregenital components (urethral and anal). When these components are overcharged or when the unconscious homosexual interest is overactive, the forms of sexual inhibition are more obvious and more intractable. They then correspond more to obsessional than to hysterical defences. The inhibition is proportionate to the unconscious compulsive and sadistic love attitudes. Some of the deepest and most intractable inhibitions function as substitutes for psychotic defences. They may be part of a depressive guilt system, e.g., a denial of body function based on an animistic conception of the essential 'evil' of the genital organs. Projection anxieties can also give rise to sexual inhibition, but, as a rule, in paranoid and schizoid types, inhibitions are more selective (apparently capricious) and alternate with periods of sexual perversion."

Related Concepts: AVOIDANCE; EGO FUNCTIONS; REPRESSION; RESISTANCE; SUPPRESSION.

REFERENCES

Freud, A., 1936, *The Ego and the Mechanisms of Defense.* IUP, pp. 109–110, 1946.
Glover, E., *Psycho-Analysis.* SP. pp. 252–253, 1939.

ADDITIONAL READINGS

Frenkel-Brunswik, E., "Social Tensions and the Inhibitions of Thought." *SocProbl*, 2, 1954.

Freud, S.: 1900, "The Interpretation of Dreams."
  SE, 4, 1953.
    1905, "Jokes and Their Relation to the
  Unconscious." *SE*, 8, 1960.
    1910, "Leonardo da Vinci and a Memory of
  His Childhood." *SE*, 11, 1957.
    1940, "An Outline of Psycho-Analysis."
  SE, 23, 1964.
Horney, K., "Inhibitions in Work." *Ps*, 7, 1947.
Sperling, O., "Report on Round Table Intellectual
  Inhibitions and Environmental Pressures. "*BAPA*,
  8, 1952.
Waelder, R., *Basic Theory of Psychoanalysis*. IUP,
  1960.

914

**"INHIBITIONS, SYMPTOMS AND ANXI-
ETY,"** a classical paper written by Freud in 1926,
employed the comparative method to examine these
phenomena. Strachey (1959), in his introduction
to this paper, noted: "The topics with which it
deals range over a wide field, and there are signs
that Freud found an unusual difficulty in unifying
the work. This is shown, for instance, in the way
in which the same subject often comes up for discussion at more than one point in very similar
terms, in the necessity under which Freud found
himself of tidying up a number of separate questions
in his 'Addenda,' and even in the actual title of the
book. It is nevertheless true that—in spite of such
important side-issues as the different classes of
resistance, the distinction between repression and
defence, and the relations between anxiety, pain and
mourning—the problem of anxiety is its main
theme. . . . Though on some aspects of the subject
his opinions underwent little modification, on
others, as he tells us in these pages, they were considerably altered."

Total Personality

Freud identified the ego as an organization,
an entity which served to maintain free intercourse
and reciprocity between all parts of the organism.
The desexualized energy is used by the ego to assimilate various impulses and to change mobile energy
into bound energy. Thus, it may be said that the
patient tries, with the help of conscious and unconscious mechanisms, to work out a modus vivendi.

Symptoms

Neurotic symptoms are the result of unconscious
wishes and their defenses and represent a partial
gratification and a partial frustration of infantile
wishes; they are, therefore, compromise formations.
Using a cross-sectional (structural) approach,
each symptom may thus be described as (a) partly
the gratification of an infantile wish (id); and (b)
partly as the frustration due to countercathexis
of the ego and the superego. In addition, the
symptom shows an aspect of the external world.

An analysis of the Wolf Man, who suffered from a
phobia and hysterical conversion symptoms, may
be rendered, as follows:

1. *The id wish*: having sexual intercourse with his
father.

2. *The ego and its defenses*: the erotization of his
bowels (constipation); the repression of the sexual
wish to have intercourse with his father, because
it represented a danger to his masculinity, resulting
in a partial unconscious gratification of the wish
through the use of an enema to relieve his constipation.

3. *The superego*: appeared to ward off the dangerous wish, though it played a small part in the
conversion symptom.

4. *The external world*: characterized by the
epidemic among the sheep; the sufferings of his
mother; his mother's words, "I can't go on living
like this;" his dysentery; his observation of coitus;
his grandfather's story of the wolves; and, finally,
the game with his father, in which the father pretended to be the wolf.

Hysterical conversion symptoms were relatively
easily tolerated by this patient (la belle indifférence).
The Wolf Man was able to control his constipation
with the help of an enema, as noted, which represented his father's penis, and was, in part,
accountable for his later symptoms.

Inhibitions

All neurotic symptoms are pathological phenomena, but inhibitions may be either pathological
or normal. Thus, a separation should be made
between inhibitions and symptoms; and, further,
between those inhibitions which are normal and
those which are not. In this, normal inhibitions are

considered as those which restrict activities linked to conscious danger; and pathological inhibitions, as those which help the patient avoid *dangerous* objects or activities. In the latter, the dangerous object or activity mobilizes unconscious wishes of which the patient is afraid. The patient behaves as if the external object or activity were *in fact* dangerous and exhibits what would be considered a grossly exaggerated reaction. This may be seen in the case of a hysterical symptom, in which the patient fears to cross the street because the act mobilizes his unconscious wish to be killed.

Inhibitions, not unlike some other defense mechanisms (condensation, for one), may represent a normal reaction to danger. This may be seen in the normal caution taken by an individual confronted by a dangerous animal, in which his inhibitions are justified by external reality. In neurotic inhibition, this may take the form demonstrated in the case of the Wolf Man who was afraid to look at a picture of a wolf.

In another classical case, that of Little Hans, a differentiation is made between neurotic inhibitions and neurotic symptoms. Little Hans not only avoided looking at horses, but seemed to avoid even a correct description of the content of his fear. Consequently, one may venture to say that while it is true, as Freud said, that the symptom can no longer be described within the ego, one may suggest that a neurotic inhibition also does not take place within the conscious ego. Instead of trying to localize the symptom with respect to the three parts of our personality, it might be more productive to try to separate the id, ego, superego and external reality aspects in studying symptoms and neurotic inhibitions.

Neurotic inhibitions and neurotic symptoms may be differentiated in pointing out that the latter appear to offer a partial gratification of infantile wishes which are often discharged against the self, while inhibitions protect the patient from discharging such wishes. Little Hans, who had to avoid seeing a horse, appeared to be protected from experiencing hostility and its discharge against the self. However, the inhibition to see the horse may be considered a restriction of his normal activity and may be referred to as an accepted partial castration.

Anxiety

Anxiety is a signal of anticipated danger and, at the same time, represents a repetition in our fantasies of what happened when we were helpless. This repetition, in connection with anticipation, is, however, different from the state of helplessness, because the reality testing permits the normal person to separate clearly what probably would happen from what is actually happening.

According to Freud, three factors appear to be characteristic of anxiety: (a) typical signal of unpleasure—affect of anxiety; (b) somatic discharges—heart palpitations for one; and (c) increased ability to deal with danger (fight or flight). On the other hand, neurotic anxiety is characterized by a decrease in the patient's ability to deal with the problem. Such a decrease, leading even to a collapse, is often explained by the quantity of emotion (affect), which is out of proportion to the encountered danger. Upon closer examination, the neurotic anxiety appears as a signal of an internal danger which is attributed to an external object. Seeing a horse—even from the terrace— mobilized severe anxiety in Little Hans. He explained this by saying that he was afraid of being bitten. Analytical examination, however, showed that what Little Hans was unconsciously afraid of was the experience connected with the mobilization of his repressed hostile wishes. If Little Hans had said, *I am afraid of the horse because I cannot control my wish to beat him*, if he had known that the hostility directed against the horse represented his unconscious hostility towards his father, we would not be entitled to talk about a phobia. Consequently, one may venture to propose that the basic difference between neurotic and normal anxiety is the fact that the former protects the patient from the experience of feelings which he once assumed could not be controlled, whereas normal anxiety is a signal of an external danger.

Both aggressive and sexual wishes may cause anxiety. For instance, the Wolf Man was seized by anxiety whenever he looked at the picture of a wolf. His anxiety protected him from the exeprience of his homosexual wishes towards his father. His homosexuality implied his wish to become a woman and to sacrifice his masculinity.

Without denying the quantitative element in

neurotic anxiety, one may consider that the emotional experience and the somatic aspect of pathological anxiety resemble more the normal reaction to terror than to normal anxiety. While normal anxiety is the result of anticipated danger, terror is connected with the actual experience of a defeat and not with its anticipation. Neurotic anxiety is caused by infantile repressed wishes. Consequently, it is not surprising that the patient behaves as if his wish also represented action, and, therefore, reacts with terror—not anxiety. [Eidelberg, 1954.]

Related Concepts: ANTICIPATION; DEFENSE MECHANISMS; FEAR; NARCISSISTIC MORTIFICATION; REPETITION COMPULSION.

REFERENCES

Eidelberg, L., *An Outline of a Comparative Pathology of the Neuroses,* IUP, pp. 145–146, 240–245, 1954.
Freud, S., 1926, "Inhibitions, Symptoms and Anxiety." *SE,* 20:78, 90, 98, 101, 144, 1959.
Strachey, J., Editorial note. *SE,* 20:78, 1959.

915

INSOMNIA is a symptom neurosis, the prolonged inability to obtain sleep; it often accompanies other neuroses, such as depression and anxiety. Normally, sleep is mobilized by the decrease of instinctual tension and by the conscious decision to sleep. During sleep, the cathexis connected with the consciousness of external and internal stimuli decreases, and the countercathexis which prevents the entry of id derivatives into the conscious ego is partly eliminated. As a result of the entry of id derivatives, sleep is threatened. The dream tries to permit the continuation of sleep by transforming the ego-alien id derivatives, representing the latent dream content, into an acceptable manifest dream.

Sleep does not take place as a result of a decision to sleep. The wish to sleep requires the individual to wait and to accept the limitation of his power to produce sleep immediately. Freud (1900) noted that sleep appears to be the result of external and internal stimuli. The relaxation and rest which take place during sleep are essential for the individual. The dream tries to protect the individual's sleep with the help of the dream-work.

The analysis of cases of insomnia indicates that unconscious fears often prevent the patient from sleeping. These fears are sometimes due to the unconscious wish to die, as if sleep represented the patient's death.* In some cases, the insomnia is a defense against nightmares—caused by hostile wishes becoming conscious. Freud (1900) pointed out that sleep represented symbolically the gratification of a wish to return to the mother's womb. When this unconscious wish is present, the patient is afraid of surrendering to sleep. In some cases, sexual abstinence prevents sleep, and, conversely, a sexual gratification induces it. Equally, aggressive abstinence may interfere with sleep.

Related Concept: HYPNAGOGIC PHENOMENON.

REFERENCE

Freud, S. 1900, "The Interpretation of Dreams." *SE,* 5:678–679, 1958.

916

INSTINCT (INSTINCTUAL DRIVE), in Freud's conception,† is a constant psychic force arising from within the organism, having its source in important somatic processes, with certain goals and objects. Freud (1905) first postulated two groups of instincts: the sexual instincts and the ego instincts. The latter (free of libido), also called

---

* In Greek mythology, Hypnos, the god of sleep, is the brother of Thanatos, the god of death.

† The German term *Trieb,* which appears throughout all of Freud's writings and which has no counterpart in the English language, is usually translated as instinct. *Trieblehre* is rendered *instinct theory,* etc. The linguistic inaccuracy has given rise to much confusion. Therefore, a brief linguistic clarification may be of value. A *Trieb* is a powerful, striving, imperative force within a living organism, deeply rooted in its psychical nature and closely connected with the somatic sources from which it springs. In the causal approach, *Trieb* is further characterized by its intense *vis a tergo* quality, by its great persistency and imperative strivings. The term has been variously described as an innate propensity to certain seemingly rational acts, an innate impulse, and by the use of such descriptive words as "intuitive," "unconscious skill," "natural aptitude," etc. Only a few correspond to the meaning of the word *Trieb* as employed in psychoanalysis. The term should more properly be rendered from the German as *instinctual drive.* The term, closest in conception to what is herein described, was first employed by Freud in 1907 as *instinctual impulse.*

self-preservative drives, were neither clearly defined nor extensively studied. Emphasis was put on the sexual instincts—described in terms of their source, aim, and object—and were classified primarily according to their source, i.e., the somatic processes arising in the various erotogenic zones—oral, anal, phallic, and genital. The sexual excitations arising from these zones, or from their respective organs, were called *component instincts*.

The pressure of an instinct refers to the force which requires a discharge of the instinctual energy. While every instinct is active, the aim of the instinct may be a passive or an active one. The aim of an instinct is always its complete satisfaction, but there are also instincts which are inhibited in their aims and can be only partly satisfied. The object which is essential may be part of the subject or may be an external object. Strong connections between this object and the instinct are referred to as fixations. The sources of the instinct are usually not open to analytical investigation. They are probably caused by certain physiological processes. [Freud, 1915.]

Later, in his second instinct theory, Freud (1920) introduced the classification of erotic instincts and destructive instincts. The destructive instincts were described in their relationship to the three stages of development. The second instinct theory was further remodeled in 1923, especially the theory of aggression, with the introduction of the structural division of the mind into id, ego, and superego. The id was viewed as the vital stratum from which the instincts arose. The two sets of instincts— sexual and aggressive—while moving toward satisfaction in their own spheres entered into a variety of relationships, both associative and antagonistic, with each other; i.e., in a fusion and defusion of instincts.

Freud (1920) postulated the presence of two primary instincts, Eros and Thanatos. They produce psychological derivatives only after mixing with each other into aggressive and sexual instinct fusions. These two instinctual fusions are often referred to as aggressive and sexual instincts. Freud (1940) assumed the presence of two basic instincts and thought that they may either combine with each other or replace each other.

Related Concepts: INSTINCTUAL VICISSITUDES; LIBIDO; PASSIVE.

REFERENCES

Freud, S.: 1905, "Three Essays on the Theory of Sexuality." *SE*, 7:168, 1953.
    1915, "Instincts and Their Vicissitudes." *SE*, 14:122–123, 1957.
    1920, "Beyond the Pleasure Principle." *SE*, 18:36–43, 1955.
    1923, "The Ego and the Id." *SE*, 19:23–28, 1961.
    1940, "An Outline of Psycho-Analysis." *SE*, 23:148–149, 1964.

917

INSTINCT OF SELF-ASSERTION is one of the fourteen primary instincts in McDougall's (1925) classification: it represents a primary motivation, a hereditary innate (action impulse). This view of self-assertion as a separate isolated drive does not appear acceptable in the light of psychoanalytic theory, which views instincts as biologically conditioned phenomena which cannot be further resolved from a psychological standpoint. Indeed, self-assertion finds its roots not only in the aggressive instinct, but also in many other psychological factors; among these are patterns of identification, self-image and self-esteem, reaction formations to castration anxieties and homosexual leanings, and many other ego and superego derivatives.

According to Fenichel (1945), the term *instinct of self-assertion* is synonymous with self-esteem, which he defines as "the awareness of how close the individual is to the original omnipotence." This equation is extremely questionable, as self-esteem and self-assertion—although interdependent and very closely connected psychologically—appear to be two separate psychic entities, the former being a feeling one holds toward oneself, and the latter being an outbound force.

From a psychoanalytic point of view, self-assertion is basically connected with narcissistic libido and destrudo. Normal self-assertion requires the acceptance of the normal limitations of the power of the individual, and freedom from repressed infantile narcissistic mortification.

Adler (1927) assigned self-assertion a particularly important place in the economy of the psyche, relating it to the helpless infant's strivings to overcome biological limitations. The different solutions of this problem account for individual behavioral variations. These solutions, adopted in early infancy, tend to remain fixed and characteristic of the person throughout life. Horney (1939) placed particular emphasis on the central position of self-assertion in the etiology of neurosis. According to her, the nuclear conflict is based on the principle of individual competition, out of which hostilities, fears, and emotional isolation develop, while, simultaneously, the need for love becomes particularly intensified.

Related Concepts: AGGRESSIVE INSTINCT; NARCISSISM.

REFERENCES

Adler, A., "The Feeling of Inferiority and the Striving for Recognition." *PRSM*, 20:1181–1886, 1927.
Fenichel, O., *The Psychoanalytic Theory of Neurosis.* Nor, p. 406, 1945.
Horney, K., *New Ways in Psychoanalysis.* Nor, 1939.
McDougall, W., "Instinct and the Unconscious." *JAbp*, 20:43–47, 1925.

918

INSTINCTUAL AIM. The excitation in an organ, according to Freud (1905), may be regarded as the source of an instinct; with the help of gratification, the internal source responsible for the excitation is eliminated. Eidelberg (1954), in discussing the aim of an instinct, suggested that a separation be made between the object which is needed for gratification and the form in which gratification is achieved (e.g., the wish to eat is gratified by finding food and incorporating it). He noted: "At first, the baby is interested chiefly in filling his mouth. Later, he discovers the pleasure connected with the act of defecation, and still later, he arrives at the phallic stage (age three to five years). At this level (originally called 'genital') the boy is preoccupied mainly with his penis, and the girl with her clitoris. Fixation or regression to one of these stages is followed, usually, by repression of the wishes connected with them, and these repressed wishes are consequently available for the formation of neurotic symptoms.

"The genital stage is reached after the latency period, approximately at the age of thirteen or fourteen years. At this stage, the boy discovers that his penis produces not only urine, but also seminal fluid. The girl develops her breasts and, with the help of menstruation, accepts the vagina as her sexual organ.

"Exhibitionistic and inspectionistic wishes usually are present in all four stages.

"This writer is in agreement with analysts who describe a parallel development of the aggressive and sexual instinct fusions. Aggression on the oral level appears to be expressed by crying or 'spitting out.'At the anal stage, it is manifested by withholding feces, soiling in defiance of prohibitions, and by the wish to take the feces of others. On the phallic stage, aggressive tensions are discharged by using urine to soil, and by the wish to castrate."

Related Concepts: DYNAMIC APPROACH; INSTINCT (INSTINCTUAL DRIVE); UNPLEASURE-PLEASURE PRINCIPLE.

REFERENCES

Eidelberg, L., *An Outline of a Comparative Pathology of the Neuroses.* IUP, p. 33, 1954.
Freud, S., 1905, "Three Essays on the Theory of Sexuality." *SE*, 7:168, 1953.

919

INSTINCTUALIZATION OF SMELL. The olfactory sense is an important part of an early perception and of the autonomous ego function. Coprophilic interests and anal fixations represent the importance of smell in character formation. Smell conflict may also involve all levels of instinctual development and be related to all parts of the body (sense organ perceptions). There are characteristic odors in the body folds, especially around the mouth, armpits, rectum and genitals which may be cathected with infantile sexuality.

Object loss may be defended against by inhaling the odor of the article belonging to that object, a loss which is restituted through the respiratory introjection of what represents the object. Smell may be used to seduce or charm the object and to whet the appetite. This may be external, as with perfume, or internal, as is the case with genital odors. Other bodily functions, such as flatus and halitosis, may be used to attack the object.

The sense of smell may be highly developed, as is the usual case when it serves as a compensatory mechanism for other sensory deficits, or it may be lessened by the defensive activities of denial and repression. Smell is used as a primitive form of reality testing; the external world is introjected for libidinal gratification and for adaptive use. There are strong cultural taboos against odors, and deodorants and perfumes are examples of the defensive elaborations which, in part, determine the vicissitudes of olfaction. Olfactory stimuli may be depreciated or displayed in the normal series of component instinctual acts which contribute to foreplay excitement (forepleasure). However, Freud (1930) pointed out, that in spite of the undeniable depreciation of olfactory stimuli, there exist even in Europe peoples among whom the strong genital odours which are so repellent to us are highly prized as sexual stimulants and who refuse to give them up.

Related Concepts: COMPONENT INSTINCT; COPRO-PHILIA.

REFERENCES

Fenichel, O., *The Psychoanalytic Theory of Neurosis.* Nor, p. 73, 1945.
Freud, S., 1930, "Civilization and Its Discontents." *SE*, 21:106, 1961.

920

INSTINCTUAL NEED denotes the specific manifestation of an instinctual drive experienced as a tension, based on somatic inheritance, combining elements of somatic and psychic origin. Its psychological elaboration originates in the unconscious part of the mind (Freud, 1915). A better name for the stimulus which is caused by an increase or a decrease of instinctual energy might be the term "need." The elimination of this need could be referred to as "satisfaction."

The presence of this need leads to a cathexis of the ego, in order to achieve discharge in thought or action. Where the need is held unacceptable to the ego and superego, as Freud (1923) noted, they attempt to keep it unconscious or they may allow discharge through a compromise formation, i.e., a neurotic symptom. Whereas the normal person tries to achieve full discharge by a compromise action (between ego, superego, and external world),

the neurotic achieves partial gratification in a form in which the content of the wish remains unconscious.

Related Concept: INSTINCT (INSTINCTUAL DRIVE).

REFERENCES

Freud, S.: 1915, "Instincts and Their Vicissitudes." *SE*, 14:118–120, 1957.
        1923, "The Ego and the Id." *SE*, 19:38–39, 54–57, 1961.

921

INSTINCTUAL VICISSITUDES are those changes which the instincts or instinct fusions undergo when constitutionally determined dispositions are subjected to external influences. It was Freud's observation (in 1915) that the instincts underwent the following vicissitudes: (a) reversal into its opposite, (b) turning around upon the subject's own self, (c) repression, and (d) sublimation.

In discussing the instinctual vicissitudes and the defense against the instincts, Eidelberg (1948) noted: "Instinctual vicissitudes and neurotic defense mechanisms are the consequences of instinctual inhibition and narcissistic mortification. While instinctual vicissitudes are intended to eliminate the inhibition and mortification by means of specific changes, the neurotic defense mechanisms are intended to prevent their coming into consciousness.

"The instinctual vicissitudes are oriented to the future and the outside world. 'Since I have suffered a narcissistic mortification and an instinctual inhibition,' the ego seems to say, 'I shall attempt, through appropriate change of my behavior, to achieve instinctual gratification and remove the narcissistic mortification.'

"Neurotic defense mechanisms are directed to the past and to the inner life. 'It is not true,' the ego says, 'that I have suffered a narcissistic slight and that I must endure an instinctual inhibition.'

"The instinctual vicissitudes are conscious or can become conscious processes; the neurotic defensive mechanisms are unconscious. The instinctual vicissitudes are plastic and adjust themselves to new situations; the neurotic defense mechanisms are rigid."

Related Concept: DEFENSE MECHANISMS.

REFERENCES

Eidelberg, L., *Studies in Psychoanalysis*. IUP, p. 117, 1948.
Freud, S.: 1914, "On Narcissism: An Introduction." *SE*, 14:93–94, 1957.
1915, "Instincts and Their Vicissitudes." *SE*, 14:126–127, 1957.

922
INTELLECTUAL ACTIVITY IN DREAMS.

It was Freud's (1900) belief that all activity in the dream rightly belonged to the dream thoughts. Any judgment expressed in a dream, even a judgment after awaking, should be regarded as a part of the latent content of the dream and in that way be used in the interpretation.

Related Concepts: ACTIVE; THINKING.

REFERENCE

Freud, S., 1900, "The Interpretation of Dreams." *SE*, 5:445, 1953.

923
INTELLECTUAL INSIGHT

denotes an awareness of symptom behavior, divorced from the emotion which accompanies it. It does not ordinarily lead to therapeutic change. For instance, a subject may conclude, whether on direct or indirect evidence, that he hates a sibling, yet, he still does not feel any conscious hatred.

Hartmann (1964) noted: "Moreover, if we state, let's say, that a certain thought is reality syntonic in a given situation, this may refer to either one of two meanings. It may mean that the thought is true in the sense that it corresponds to reality. On the other hand, it may also mean that its use, in a given reality situation, leads to a successful mastery of this situation. That in a larger sector of human behavior there is no simple correlation between the degree of objective insight and the degree of adaptiveness of the corresponding action is not in need of being proved. Objective knowledge of and practical orientation in reality do not necessarily coincide. We all know that action in line with 'common sense,' which is practically orientated, can be more efficient. But it is hard to state in general terms where it will be efficient and where, on the other hand, the kind of thinking we call scientific is called for."

Developmentally, a degree of avoidance of outer reality, which might in the adult world lead to a difficulty, as A. Freud (1936) noted, is a condition of childhood. "In the theory of education the importance of the infantile ego's determination to avoid 'pain' has not been sufficiently appreciated, and this has contributed to the failure of a number of educational experiments in recent years. The modern method is to give to the growing ego of the child a greater liberty of action, above all, to allow it freely to choose its activities and interests. The idea is that thus the ego will develop better and sublimation in various forms will be achieved. But children in the latency-period may attach more importance to the avoidance of anxiety and 'pain' than to direct or indirect gratification of instinct. In many cases, if they lack external guidance, their choice of occupation is determined not by their particular gifts and capacities for sublimation but by the hope of securing themselves as quickly as may be from anxiety and 'pain.' To the surprise of the educationist the result of this freedom of choice, is, in such cases, not the blossoming of personality but the impoverishment of the ego."

Related Concepts: INTERPRETATION; THERAPY; TRANSFERENCE.

REFERENCES

Freud, A., 1936, *The Ego and the Mechanisms of Defense*. IUP, pp. 111–112, 1946.
Hartmann, H., *Essays on Ego Psychology*, IUP, p. 253, 1964.

924
INTERNAL IDENTIFICATION

is denotative of an identification in which no external change takes place, but in which the subject appears to possess the emotions or feelings of the object with whom he identifies himself; it may take place on an oral, anal, or phallic level. As with other forms of identification, it may occur consciously or unconsciously, e.g., with the former, a relationship may be established between the male spectator and the male actor in a play, and, in the latter, with a feminine lead in the play, assuming the spectator is not an overt homosexual.

In a number of neurotic defense mechanisms, such as persecution mania, pathological jealousy, and impotence, unconscious inner identification is of decisive importance. [Eidelberg, 1954.]

Related Concepts: EXTERNAL IDENTIFICATION; PSEUDOIDENTIFICATION.

REFERENCE

Eidelberg, L., *An Outline of a Comparative Pathology of the Neuroses*. IUP, p. 50, 1954.

ADDITIONAL READING

Freud, S., 1921, "Group Psychology and the Analysis of the Ego." *SE*, 18, 1955.

925

INTERPRETATION denotes the analyst's explanation to the patient of the unconscious meaning of the neurotic manifestations as they contribute to the gain of insight and, ultimately, to the reintegration of the patient's personality. For example, a patient who is habitually late for his analytic appointment is told that this is done to show rebelliousness and control in a struggle for power. This explanation could lead to insight about the patient's conflict over his passive strivings vis-à-vis a parent. During analysis, the patient is induced to remember what he has repressed. The analyst on the other hand has to try to reconstruct from this memory what has happened in childhood which has led to the repression or denial.

Hartmann (1964) described the technical principles involved, as follows: "The necessity for scrutinizing our patients' material as to its derivation from all the psychic systems, without bias in favor of one or the other, is nowadays rather generally accepted as a technical principle. Also we meet many situations in which even the familiar opposition of defense and instinct is losing much of its absolute character. Some of these situations are rather well known, as is the case in which defense is sexualised or—equally often—'aggressivized' (if I may use the expression); or instances in which an instinctual tendency is used for de-

fensive purposes. Most of these cases can be handled according to general rules derived from what we know about the dynamics and economics of interpretation as, for instance: resistance interpretation precedes interpretation of content, etc. In other cases these rules do not prove subtle enough; unexpected and sometimes highly troublesome quantitative or qualitative side effects of interpretations may occur. This, then, is a problem that clearly transcends those technical situations I gave here as illustrations. If such incidental effects occur, our dosage or timing may have been wrong. But it may also be—and this is the more instructive case—that we have missed some structural implications though correctly following quantitative economic principles. It may be that we have considered this quantitative aspect of a resistance only and have not considered precisely enough how the same quantity may involve the various functions of the ego and the superego in a different degree. While concentrating on the analysis of a resistance, we are actually working on many parts of the field at the same time. But we are not always mindful of the possible side effects if we focus too exclusively on the duality 'defense-warded-off impulse' only. General rules about the dynamics and economics of interpretation are incomplete as long as we do not consider that, besides the quantitative factors, the resistances represent also the ways in which the various psychic functions, directly or often indirectly, participate in defense—'participation' pointing to intersystemic and intrasystemic correlations, including also their genetic aspects, which here refers to the memory systems. Of course, we do know something about how to handle different forms of resistance differently even when they appear to be equivalent when looked at from the economic angle. I made my point only because I feel that this structural aspect of interpretation is still less completely understood and less explicitly stated than its dynamic and economic aspects. One day we shall probably be able to formulate more systematically the rational element of our technique, that is 'planning' the predictable outcome of our interventions, with respect to these structural implications."

Id interpretations are the exposure of infantile wishes and should be distinguished from *ego interpretations* which deal with the unconscious defense of this wish. *Construction* and *reconstruction* are terms which describe the analyst's efforts to fill those blanks in the patient's memory which defy recall. Prior to interpretation, a patient may be confronted with some facet of his behavior which the analyst considers symptomatic; e.g., when the patient keeps on looking at his watch while on the couch. As a rule, interpretations are given when the patient's resistance has been weakened and enough material has been accumulated to establish the validity of the interpretation in accordance with the rules of psychoanalytic technique. In some cases, the interpretation mobilizes additional resistances.

Clinical Example

"A patient suffering from psychosexual impotence brought to me on one occasion a dream composed of two fragments. In the first one the only occurrence was that instead of a Hungarian newspaper 'Pesti Hirlap,' which came regularly to him, he received the Vienna 'Neue Freie Presse,' to which as a matter of fact one of his colleagues had subscribed. The second part of the dream dealt with a brunette whom he ardently desired to marry. It turned out that in the dream he acquired not the foreign newspaper but, in the hidden sense of the dream, a foreign woman to whom in fact a colleague had 'subscribed.' This woman had long excited his interest, for it seemed to him that just this person would be able to get his sexuality, which was struggling with strong inhibitions to function. The thought associations that came from this idea made it plain that he had been deceived in his hopes of another woman, with whom he had entered into the same relation. This woman, being a Hungarian, had been concealed in the dream behind the name of the paper 'Pesti Hirlap.' Of late he had occupied himself in seeking free sexual associations, which led to no obligations, instead of a more stable relationship. When we know the great freedom with which the dream avails itself of symbols, we are not surprised to learn that my patient also applied the word 'Press' in a sexual sense. The second part of the dream shows, as though to confirm our interpretations, that the patient had often been obliged to think, not without anxiety, that relations which lasted too long, like that between him and his friend, could easily lead to a *misalliance*. One does

not know what Freud has shown in his monograph, namely that the psychic motive and means of presentation of wit are almost exactly the same as those that come out in dreams, might consider us guilty of a cheap joke in saying that the dream succeeds in condensing in the words 'Neue Freie Presse' all the patient's thoughts and wishes relating to the pleasures of which his illness had robbed him and the means of benefit that he had in mind, namely, the stimulus of the new, and the greater freedom for which he was striving." [Ferenczi, 1916.]

Related Concepts: ANALYTICAL INSIGHT; REPRESSION; TECHNIQUE OF PSYCHOANALYSIS.

REFERENCES

Ferenczi, S., *Sex in Psycho-Analysis*. GP, pp. 114–115, 1916.
Freud, S., 1937, "Constructions in Analysis." *SE*, 23: 258–259, 1964.
Hartmann, H., *Essays on Ego Psychology*. IUP, pp. 150–151, 1964.

ADDITIONAL READINGS

Eissler, K., "The Function of Details in the Interpretation of Works of Literature." *PQ*, 28, 1959.
Feldman, S., "Blanket Interpretation." *PQ*, 27, 1958.
Fenichel, O., *The Psychoanalytic Theory of Neurosis*. Nor, 1945.
Freud, S.: 1910, "'Wild' Psycho-Analysis." *SE*, 11, 1957.
     1911–1915, "Papers on Technique." *SE*, 12, 1958.
     1914, "Déjà Raconté in Psycho-Analytic Treatment." *SE*, 13, 1955.
     1919, "Lines of Advance in Psycho-Analytic Therapy." *SE*, 17, 1955.
Isaacs, S., "Criteria for Interpretation." *IntJPsa*, 20, 1939.
Nunberg, H., *Principles of Psychoanalysis—Their Application to the Neuroses*. IUP, 1955.
Sterba, R. F., "The Abuse of Interpretation." *Ps*, 4, 1941.
Taylor, J., "A Note on the Splitting of Interpretations." *IntJPsa*, 40, 1959.

926

INTIMIDATION sometimes denotes a defense against anxiety, as Knight (1942) pointed out— whether vocal, physical or facial—frequently accompanied by fantasies of belligerent content, all intended to frighten and impress others. The anxiety appears only after redoubled efforts to frighten and impress do not seem to be effective. This kind of intimidation is usually associated with pronounced unconscious passive homosexual wishes. The neurotic anxiety is the result of the inability to differentiate between wish and action, and thus more closely resembles the feeling of terror.* The full discharge of the repressed wish is experienced as if the feared danger were actually taking place.

Case History

A young college boy had an acute schizophrenic episode and was hospitalized, recovering rapidly. The episode was precipitated by his being hypnotized by an amateur hypnotist. Before being brought out of the trance, he fiercely fought all his fraternity brothers who tried to help. Later, in analysis, he revealed that all through his teens he had feared physical fighting, but had secretly practiced shadow boxing before a mirror, had tried out many belligerent facial expressions, habitually carried one shoulder a little higher than the other, walked with a catlike gait and a sharp shifting gaze, and, at all times, in his pocket carried a boxer's protective mouthpiece, which he practiced getting out of his pocket and into his mouth with all possible speed as he squared off. The analyst's first attempts to bring out his fears of homosexuality were taken as accusations, and he rose up from the couch belligerently threatening to punch the analyst's nose. When the analyst did not appear impressed, he became anxious.

Related Concepts: ANXIETY; DENIAL (DISAVOWAL); PASSIVE; REACTION FORMATION.

REFERENCE

Knight, R. P., "Intimidation of Others as a Defense Against Anxiety." *BMC,* 6:4–14, 1942.

ADDITIONAL READING

Fenichel, O., *The Psychoanalytic Theory of Neurosis.* Nor, 1945.

---

* *Anxiety* is sometimes employed as a synonym for *fear.* Freud suggested that fear is the reaction to a known danger; anxiety, to an unknown one.

927

INTROEGO (UNDIFFERENTIATED EGO CONSCIENCE) denotes the pregenital organization within the ego of introjected images of parental attitudes and prohibitions. It provides the infant's ego with a means of sharing the power of its parents and their protection against prephallic instinctual demands. For example, a patient with obsessive fears of what his mother would think of his masturbation was able during his analysis to reevoke early introjected images of his mother as a threatening nun-like figure. [Weissman, 1954.]

Related Concept: SUPEREGO.

REFERENCE

Weissman, P., "Ego and Superego in Obsessional Character and Neurosis." *Q.* 23:529–543, 1954.

ADDITIONAL READINGS

Weissman, P.: "Pregenital Compulsive Phenomena and the Repetition Compulsion." *JAPA,* 4, 1956. "Characteristic Superego Identifications of Obsessional Neurosis." *Q,* 28, 1959.

928

INTROJECT, according to Bychowski (1945), denotes the presentation of the love-hate object in the self. When the ego fails to assimilate the introjects, it seeks to destroy the internalized love-hate object (or its surrogate). The attempt of the ego to rid itself of the internalized object may then be followed by an attempt to replace it once again with an even more powerful introjected imago. In this, the compulsive destructive acting out which may result does not succeed in destroying the internalized object and the ego is thus forced to maintain the compulsion, inevitably turning the destructive impulses against the self.

Case History

Bychowski cited the case of a woman who, as a child of four, lost her father, and then, as a consequence, introjected his legs which had become paralyzed during his illness. The introject reactivated his paralysis for her (as an adult), and, as a result, she experienced pains and weakness in her own legs. This hysterical reaction was accompanied by bursts of destructive acting out toward her husband and toward her analyst, both of whom were substitutes for her parental imago.

Related Concept: IDENTIFICATION.

REFERENCE

Bychowski, G., "The Ego of Homosexuals." *IntJPsa*, 26:1–14, 1945.

ADDITIONAL READING

Bychowski, G., *Psychotherapy of Psychosis.* G & S, 1952.

929

INTROJECTION. The normal process (a) by which the infant incorporates prohibitions and commands, forms a presentation of external objects, and builds his infantile superego (precursor of the superego); and (b) the neurotic defense mechanism which is used by the neurotic to eliminate the frustration and narcissistic mortification connected with the loss of an external object.

In the first (a) process, through the sense organs, all external stimuli are analyzed after being perceived and are stored in the mental apparatus. Those connected with prohibitions and commands are used to form the infantile ego-alien superego. The infant learns to do what is expected of him to be loved, and what is to be avoided under threat of punishment. His superego, which is at first ego-alien, represents his parents (or other authorities) and permits the infant to conform to their demands even in their absence.

In the second (b), where introjection is employed as a defense mechanism, the neurotic cannot accept and tolerate an object loss without making up for this loss by creating an image of the lost object in the self. This unconscious mechanism becomes conscious only after a resistance to acknowledge its presence has been overcome in analysis. As a result of the pathological introjection, the patient is able to deny the external narcissistic mortification—"I have no power over him; I could not prevent his departure"—by accepting instead the internal narcissistic mortification, "I have no power over my hostility; I am responsible for his departure, having provoked it." Concurrently, as Eidelberg (1954) noted, the psychic energy which originally cathected the presentation of the external object is withdrawn and is used to cathect part of the self instead. The psychic energy seems to remain objectual and does not change into the secondary narcissistic energy.

Abraham (1924) provided the following example: "Dr. Elekes of Klausenburg has recently communicated to me the following peculiarly instructive case from his psychiatric practice in an asylum. A female patient was brought to the asylum on account of a melancholic depression. She repeatedly accused herself of being a thief. In reality she had never stolen anything. But her father, with whom she lived, and to whom she clung with all an unmarried daughter's love, had been arrested a short while before for a theft. This event, which not only removed her father from her in the literal meaning of the word but also called forth a profound psychological reaction in the sense of estranging her from him, was the beginning of her attack of melancholia. The loss of the loved person was immediately succeeded by an act of introjection; and now it was the patient herself who had committed the theft. This instance once more bears out Freud's view that the self-reproaches of melancholia are in reality reproaches directed against the loved person.

"It is easy enough to see in certain cases that object-loss and introjection have taken place. But we must remember that our knowledge of these facts is purely superficial, for we can give no explanation of them whatever. It is only by means of a regular psycho-analysis that we are able to perceive that there is a relationship between object-loss and tendencies, based on the earlier phase of the anal-sadistic stage, to lose and destroy things; and that the process of introjection has the character of a physical incorporation by way of the mouth. Furthermore, a superficial view of this sort misses the whole of the ambivalence conflict that is inherent in melancholia. The material which I shall bring forward in these pages will, I hope, help to some extent to fill in this gap in our knowledge. I should like to point out at once, however, that our knowledge of what takes place in normal mourning is equally superficial; for psycho-analysis has thrown no light on that mental state in healthy people and in cases of transference-neurosis. True, Freud has made the very significant observation that the serious conflict of ambivalent feelings from which the melancholiac suffers is absent in the normal person."

Related Concepts: DEPRESSION; DESTRUDO; LIBIDO; MELANCHOLIA; NARCISSISM; SUPEREGO.

REFERENCES

Abraham, K., 1924, "A Short Study of the Development of the Libido, Viewed in the Light of Mental Disorders." *SPA*, pp. 434–435, 1942.
Eidelberg, L., *An Outline of a Comparative Pathology of the Neuroses.* IUP, pp. 99–102, 1954.

ADDITIONAL READINGS

Brody, E. B., "Superego, Introjected Mother, and Energy Discharge in Schizophrenia: Contribution from the Study of Anterior Lobotomy." *JAPA*, 6, 1958.
Cameron, N., "Introjection, Reprojection, and Hallucination in the Interaction Between Schizophrenic Patient and Therapist." *IntJPsa*, 42, 1961.
Foulkes, S. H., "On Introjection." *IntJPsa*, 18, 1937.
Knight, R. P., "Introjection, Projection and Identification." *Q*, 9, 1940.
Kovacs, S., "Introjektion, Projektion und Einfühlung." *C*, 2, 1912.
Matte Blanco, I., "On Introjection and the Processes of Psychic Metabolism." *IntJPsa*, 22, 1941.
Stephen, K., "Introjection and Projection: Guilt and Rage." *M*, 14, 1934.

930
INTROVERSION (FANTASY CATHEXIS).
Jung coined the term in his description of dementia praecox. He noted (in 1924): "There is a turning inwards of the libido whereby a negative relation of subject to object is expressed. Interest does not move towards the object, but recedes towards the subject."

According to Freud (1914), we may only "legitimately" use the term to describe a universal psychic tendency to direct libido away from satisfaction through action in reality, and onto fantasies. Freud (1912) regarded introversion as an invariable and indispensable precondition of *every* onset of a psychoneurosis. He wrote (1917): "An introvert [will develop symptoms] unless he finds some other

outlets for his dammed-up libido." Freud rarely used the term introversion in his later works.

Related Concepts: DAYDREAMS; FANTASY; FLIGHT INTO FANTASY.

REFERENCES

Freud, S.: 1912, "The Dynamics of Transference." *SE*, 12:102, 1958.
     1914, "On Narcissism." *SE*, 14:74, 1957.
     1917, "Introductory Lectures of Psycho-Analysis." *SE*, 16:374, 1963.
Jung, C. G., *Psychological Types.* HB, p. 567, 1924.

ADDITIONAL READINGS

Fenichel, O., *The Psychoanalytic Theory of Neurosis.* Nor, 1945.
Freud, S., 1912, "On the Universal Tendency to Debasement in the Sphere of Love." *SE*, 11, 1957.

931
ISAKOWER PHENOMENON,
or rather a group of interrelated subjective experiences, was first described and introduced into psychoanalytic literature in 1936 by Isakower (hence, the eponym). The most common condition in which the phenomenon can be observed is in a certain phase in the process of falling asleep. In this hypnagogic state, sensations very different from those of waking life are experienced in a peculiar combination of perceptions localized in certain regions of the body, principally the mouth, the skin and the hand, and, at the same time, as occurrences in the external world, in that border-region of it which immediately surrounds the body.

These phenomena can, under certain conditions, be observed in the transitional states of falling asleep and waking up, and also in states of fever. They are furthermore closely related to the experience of déjà vu and to certain pathological conditions, e.g. some types of aura ('dreamy states') associated with epileptic attacks, and to psychotic states preceding a full-fledged delusion of world cataclysm. The phenomenon has a two-fold significance: (a) it represents a revival of an archaic phase of developments, and (b) it affords a detailed study of the changes within the organization of the different parts of the ego in various states of consciousness.

Related Concepts: HYPNAGOGIC PHENOMENON; SLEEP.

REFERENCE

Isakower, O., 1936, "A Contribution to the Patho-psychology Associated with Falling Asleep." *IntJPsa*, 19:331–345, 1938.

ADDITIONAL READING

Azima, H., & E. D. Wittkower, "Anaclitic Therapy Employing Drugs: A Case of Spider Phobia with Isakower Phenomenon." *Q*, 26, 1957.
Fenichel, O., "Frühe Entwicklungsstudien des Ichs." *Im*, 23, 1937. *The Collected Papers of Otto Fenichel.* Nor., 1954.
Garma, A., "Vicissitudes of the Dream Screen and the Isakower Phenomenon." *Q*, 24, 1955.
Heilbrunn, G., "Fusion of the Isakower Phenomenon with the Dream Screen." *Q*, 22, 1953.
Lewin, B., "Reconsideration of the Dream Screen." *Q*, 22, 1953.

932

ISOLATION is a defense mechanism especially characteristic of obsessional neurosis, in which elements belonging together are split apart and kept apart. Infantile memories related to infantile wishes and narcissistic mortifications are stripped of their affect (instead of being repressed as in hysteria), or the associative connective links to the symptom or to similar experiences or strivings are deprived of their cathexis. Freud (1926) noted that the individual to avoid unpleasure may decide to refrain from perceiving or from doing anything.

For example, a woman patient related without any emotion her experience of having been seduced as a young girl by an adult man. Only a few moments of the seduction were remembered: what happened before, many details during, what happened after the experience, and the related circumstances were not subject to conscious recall because of a partial repression.

Isolation involves a basic avoidance of contact, both libidinal and aggressive. It complies with the fundamental taboo of touching found in the obsessive compulsive; ultimately, the taboo against oedipal and preoedipal contact. A. Freud (1936) noted: "We learn that the mode of defence adopted in symptom-formation by the ego of the obsessional neurotic is that of isolation. It simply removes the instinctual impulses from their context, while retaining them in consciousness. Accordingly, the resistance of such patients takes a different form. The obsessional patient does not fall silent; he speaks, even when in a state of resistance. But he severs the links between his associations and isolates ideas from affects when he is speaking, so that his associations seem as meaningless on a small scale as his obsessional symptoms on a large scale."

Related Concept: DEFENSE MECHANISMS.

REFERENCES

Freud, A., 1936, *The Ego and the Mechanisms of Defense.* IUP, pp. 37–38, 1946.
Freud, S., 1926, "Inhibitions, Symptoms and Anxiety." *SE*, 20:120, 163–164, 1959.

J

JAMAIS PHENOMENON, "the erroneous reaction, 'I've never experienced anything like that before,' is frequently observed in varying degrees.... It varies in intensity from a simple, easily correctible phenomenon to a firmly fixed and unchangeable conviction" (Silberman, 1963). The jamais phenomenon is a defense mechanism of the ego, by which an event is torn out of the context of experience, removed from consciousness, and rigidly warded off. As a result, there appears a lacuna in memory, a break in continuity, an unawareness of causality and sequence. Fragmentation is the dynamic factor in the jamais phenomenon. The strength and duration of the jamais phenomenon indicates the level of regression. When it is implacably maintained and the repressed content rigidly fixed in isolation, the pathology is serious. Normal and neurotic individuals do not defend their jamais impressions with the same vigor and rigid persistence as psychotic patients. In contrast to the déjà experience, the jamais experience is ego-alien.

For example, a patient saw a toy in a window, which he said was different from any toy he had ever seen before. With an inexplicable sense of excitement, he bought it for his young son. Both father and son played with the toy and enjoyed it because of its novelty. The toy turned out to be the very popular pegboard American children know so well, a toy actually seen many times by the patient. This jamais phenomenon was particularly interesting, because the patient reported that, as a child, he had been puzzled by a recurring fantasy, in which his mother had a red hole in her arm, a hole large enough to admit an electric plug or a thick wooden peg.

Related Concept: Déjà Vu.

REFERENCE

Silbermann, I., "The 'Jamais' Phenomenon in Reference to Fragmentation." *Q*, 32:184, 1963.

JEALOUSY denotes a suspicion or fear of rivalry or unfaithfulness; an affective state frequently compounded of the anticipation of grief, or grief itself, over the loss of a loved object, enmity toward the rival, and a certain amount of self-criticism. Jealousy may be present, to some degree, in everyone.

Freud (1922) described jealousy of abnormal intensity as existing in three layers: the first being *competitive* jealousy, which occurs when the love object is viewed as turning toward a rival. It is usually more pronounced than warranted, being based on the unconscious conflicts of early life rooted in the oedipus complex and sibling rivalry. It is generally experienced bisexually. The jealous man suffers because of the unfaithfulness of the woman he loves, from a hatred of his rival and, at the same time, experiences pain because of his unconscious love for the rival and his hostility against the woman who is unconsciously his competitor.

Freud's second layer, that of *projected* jealousy, involves the defense mechanism of projection:

the subject projects his own unfaithful impulses onto his love object, "I don't want to be unfaithful, she does." The third layer—*delusional* jealousy—involves the projection of homosexual impulses onto the love object: "I (a man) don't love him, she does."

Eidelberg (1954) differentiated *envy* from *jealousy*; he viewed the latter as specifically involving conflicts over sharing a loved object in a triangular situation. For example, the little boy is jealous (not envious) when he realizes that his mother prefers his father as a bedmate. He makes a partial identification with his mother and in that way experiences her pleasure in having his father as a partner, but, at the same time, he suffers the painful recognition of his exclusion.

Ferenczi (1916), in describing the jealousy of many alcoholics, noted: "There is no doubt that this was a case of alcoholic delusions of jealousy. The conspicuous feature of homosexual transference to myself, however, allows of the interpretation that his jealousy of men signified only the projection of his own erotic pleasure in the male sex. Also, the disinclination for sexual relations with his wife was probably not simply impotency, but was determined by his unconscious homosexuality. The alcohol, which might well be called a *censure-poison*, had evidently for the most part (though not quite) robbed his homosexuality, which had been spiritualised into friendliness, assiduity and complaisance, of its sublimations, and so caused the crude homosexual erotism that thus came to the surface—intolerable as such to the consciousness of a man of ethical high standing—to be simply imputed to his wife. In my opinion the alcohol played here only the part of an agent destroying sublimation, through the effect of which the man's true, sexual constitution, namely the preference for a member of the same sex, became evident."

Case History

"This patient, who had always been a rather jealous husband, experienced an increase of this jealousy after his wife became frigid. As a result of the disappointment caused by her lack of interest in him, the patient became more attached to his business partner and friend. While on a business trip, they spent one night together in the same room, and during that night the patient had an emission dream which disturbed him profoundly, although he could not remember its content. As a result of identification with his oedipal mother, the patient wanted to play the role of his father's wife. This passive homosexual wish was partly satisfied in his marriage because his wife was also the unconscious representation of his father, and he was able to satisfy and deny his homosexual cravings at the same time in his sexual relations with her. Her frigidity eliminated this form of gratification, and led to the damming up of libido. The passive feminine wish, 'I want to have sexual intercourse with my business partner,' was changed into, 'She [his wife] wants to have sexual intercourse with him.' Presently, by mobilization of the opposite instinct fusion, the sexual emotion was substituted by aggressive feelings. By projection, the patient was able to satisfy his feminine tendencies and protect himself from an overt homosexual experience. Instead of feeling guilty because of the satisfaction of these forbidden wishes, this patient suffered from jealousy. The *narcissistic mortification*: 'I cannot control my feelings for my partner' is avoided by acceptance of the idea: 'My wife is overwhelmed by her sexual desire.' The *total personality* partly resented this jealousy, and the patient tried to free himself from it." [Eidelberg, 1954.]

Related Concepts: ENVY; OEDIPUS COMPLEX; PARANOID CONDITION (STATE); PROJECTION.

REFERENCES

Eidelberg, L., *An Outline of a Comparative Pathology of the Neuroses.* IUP, p. 142, 150–151, 1954.
Ferenczi, S., 1912, "On the Part Played by Homosexuality in the Pathogenesis of Paranoia." *SPsa*, pp. 161–162, 1916.
Freud, S., 1922, "Some Neurotic Mechanisms in Jealousy, Paranoia and Homosexuality." *SE*, 18:223, 1955.

ADDITIONAL READINGS

Fenichel, O., "A Contribution to the Psychology of Jealousy." *OF-CP*, 1, 1953.
Freud, S.: 1900, "The Interpretation of Dreams." *SE*, 4, 1953.
    1901, "The Psychopathology of Everyday Life." *Se*, 6, 1960.
    1907, "Delusions and Dreams in Jensen's *Gradiva*." *SE*, 9, 1959.
    1931, "Female Sexuality." *SE*, 21, 1961.

Loewenstein, R. M., "Un Cas de jalousie pathologique." *RFPsa*, 5, 1932.

Riviere, J., "Jealousy as a Mechanism of Defense."
IntJPsa, 13, 1932.

1002

JOKE (WIT)* is a brief story which usually
ends with a word or phrase which represents a
double meaning, leads to a pleasurable experience,
and generally culminates in laughter.

The following is an example of a joke: Catherine
the Great finds ten sailors in her bedroom. She says,
"I am tired; two must go." An examination of this
joke indicates that only those listeners who are able
to recognize the dual meaning of the words "two
must go" will laugh, for, in effect, "eight stay here"
is inherent in the remark.

In agreement with other writers (Lipps, Fischer,
Heymans and Richter), Freud (1905) recognized
that pleasure derived from a joke represents an
aesthetic pleasure, which is connected with the
discharge of sublimated energy. He pointed out that,
from a psychoanalytic point of view, it is caused by
the economy of expenditure and forepleasure
principle; further, he recognized that the pleasure
depends more on the form than on the content of
the joke. For instance, if the punch line of the joke
is changed to "eight stay here," form alone deprives
the joke of its double meaning, though the content
remains the same; namely, that she is sending two
away, but keeping eight.

Eidelberg (1960) suggested that this pleasure is not
a forepleasure but rather an end-pleasure, and that
it appears to be connected with infantile omnipotence; namely, the ability of the joker to find the
words which will produce laughter in the listener,
and of the ability of the listener to grasp the second

---

* *Joke* is a better translation of the German word *Witz;*
generally translated *wit*. [Strachey, 1960.]

surprising meaning of the joke. Sometimes, a statement or poem may have such an effect. Freud
pointed out that, in addition, a similar reaction of
the listener may take place without the author intending to stimulate laughter, and often without his
recognition that what he said was funny. The
following poem* illustrates the point: "Between
mankind and poor dumb beasts there stretches/A
chain of souls impossible to see./Poor dumb beasts
have a will—*ergo* a soul too—/Even though they
have a soul smaller than we."

The technique of a joke, Freud (1905) noted,
depends on the various mechanisms used—condensation, displacement, mobilization of the opposite instinct fusion—which appear similar to those
present in the unconscious defenses. They differ
from them, however, in that they do not mobilize
the strong resistance which protects the hidden
meaning of a pathological defense mechanism from
becoming conscious.

Related Concepts: COMIC; HUMOR.

REFERENCES

Eidelberg, L., "A Third Contribution to the Study of
Slips of the Tongue." *IntJPsa*, 41:596, 1960.
Freud, S., 1905, "Jokes and Their Relation to the
Unconscious." *SE*, 8:236, 1960.
Strachey, J., Editorial note. *SE*, 8:7, 1960.

ADDITIONAL READINGS

Abraham, K., "Dreikäsehoch; zur Psychoanalyse
des Wortwitzes." *Im*, 5, 1918.
Eidelberg, L.: "A Contribution to the Study of Wit."
R, 32, 1945.
    "Ein Beitrag zum Studium der ästhetischen
Lust." *P*, 10, 1962.
Kanzer, M., "Gogol—A Study on Wit and Paranoia."
JAPA, 3, 1955.

---

* Kempner, F., 1891, "Against Vivisection."

K

1100

KLEPTOMANIA is characterized by obsessive stealing, usually without sufficient economic motivation, traceable to profound frustrations during the oral, anal, or phallic stage. The stolen objects are substitute pleasures for those previously denied. The act is one of revenge on the images of those held responsible for the supposed malfeasance. In women, kleptomania represents an active castration tendency directed against the penis of the male, with incorporative aims. Kleptomania represents an exhibitionistic and masochistic provocation of external punishment for both sexes. [Eidelberg, 1958.]

Related Concepts: ACTING OUT; ATTRACTION OF THE FORBIDDEN; PENIS ENVY; PSYCHOPATHY.

REFERENCE

Eidelberg, L., "Psychoanalyse einer Psychopathin." *P*, 12:448, 1958.

ADDITIONAL READINGS

Baudouin, C., "Ein Fall von Kleptomanie." *PsaP*, 4, 1930.
Bornstein, B., "Enuresis und Kleptomanie als passagere Symptome." *PsaP*, 8, 1934.

L

1200

LANGUAGE. The analyst and his patient are able to work together only if they use the same language. Both listen and speak and try to understand each other. In addition to the words used, some ideas are communicated with the help of the intonation, gestures, mannerisms, etc. (nonverbal). The analyst uses the material communicated to him to uncover ideas and affects which the patient is not aware of because they were repressed. In addition to the decoding and the bringing of the unconscious into consciousness, the skillful analysis of the resistance and transference is of basic importance. The basics of semantics are essential to analytic practice: the translation from unconscious into conscious can only take place if conscious errors have been eliminated.

Freud (1893) pointed out that affects are discharged by various voluntary and involuntary reflexes (from tears to the acts of revenge). Fenichel (1945) pointed out that "the sensations that form the basis of the superego begin with the auditory stimuli of words."

Isakower (1939) further delineated this view: "It follows from this that the auditory sphere is one of the most important apparatuses for the regulation of relations with the environment and with the introjected representations of interests in that environment, an arrangement absolutely specific for the human species. Research on the brain also seems to furnish indirect evidence of this, since it establishes that it is in the region of the radiations of the auditory tract that the cyto-architectonic formation of the cerebral cortex shows the relatively greatest difference between men and the anthropoids in the building-up of the layers.

"There is much to be said for the view that at earlier stages of development a close connection exists between the linguistic and logical concept 'right-wrong' ('correct—incorrect') on the one hand and the moral concept 'right—wrong' ('good—bad') on the other. Certainly this fact has a great deal to do with the way in which education in speech takes place, but even so it is worthy of note that the linguistic branch of education cannot be thought of as isolated from the rest.

"Moreover it is probable that the function of judgement in its beginnings is to be conceived of as a single unit in judging processes both in the external world and in the internal world, and that consequently these two differently directed parts of the function are not easy to separate. The problem of reality-testing is closely bound up with this. Freud, as we know, first ascribed reality-testing to the super-ego, but later (in *The Ego and the Id*) decided upon a correction, assigning it to the ego as its specific task, in accordance with the relations of the ego to the world of perception. On the other hand there is good reason to ascribe to the super-ego function something of the character of perception, when one considers that the ego can take itself as an object, in self-observation, which is indisputably a super-ego function. It is this which seems to speak for the view that at least in an early stage in the development of the ego the function of reality-testing can hardly be separated off sharply from the function which has to judge the individual's

215

own methods of behaviour as 'correct or incorrect' and 'right or wrong.'"

In Hayakawa's (1939) view, language is the most highly developed form of symbolism. He noted: "It has been pointed out that human beings, by agreement, can make anything stand for anything. Now, human beings have agreed, in the course of centuries of mutual dependency, to let the various noises that they can produce with their lungs, throats, tongues, teeth and lips systematically stand for specified happenings in their nervous systems. We call that system of agreement *language*." Croce (1909) defined it somewhat differently: "We must here note an error into which have fallen those very philologists who have best discerned the activistic nature of language, when they maintain that although language was *originally a spiritual creation*, yet that it afterwards increased by *association*. But the distinction does not hold, for origin in this case cannot mean anything but nature or character; and if language be spiritual creation, it must always be creation; if it be association, it must have been so from the beginning. The error has arisen from having failed to grasp the general principle of Aesthetic, known to us: that expressions already produced must descend to the rank of impressions before they can give rise to new impressions. When we utter new words we generally transform the old ones, varying or enlarging their meaning; but this process is not associative, it is *creative*, although the creation has for material the impressions, not of the hypothetical primitive man, but of man who has lived long ages in society, and who has, so to say, stored so many things in his psychic organism, and among them so much language."

1. Body Language. Those perceptions of specific bodily function which in a symbolic way express unconscious conflicts. The idea of a body language emerged from Freud's work on hysteria (in 1908), in which he postulated a *conversion* of psychic excitement and of unconscious fantasy into a somatic form of discharge, represented by the hysterical symptom. Generally, all instances of somatic illness may be expressions of psychic tensions; specifically, they may be considered as symbolic expressions which may arise as primary conversion symptoms or as secondary cathected responses and fantasies to organic or psycho-

physiologic conditions. They may also occur as characteristic modes of gait, posture, facial expression, etc. [See **207.**]

2. Mannerisms. A term employed by Feldman (1959) to express a language habit; a gesture which is used to both reveal and conceal unconscious processes. In this, he identified nonverbal communications as belonging to mannerisms of speech because they replace speech and vice versa. Thus, the "working through" of a physical gesture or verbal cliché is considered as an important element in the analytic treatment. "If they are neglected, a valuable opportunity to reach more fundamental conflicts might be missed." [See **1304.**]

3. Metaphoric Language. The deliberate use of a word or words out of normal context in order to convey a conceptual similarity or allegory. Metaphors reflect a form of primary process thinking which psychotics may use without recognition. Abnormal metaphoric thinking may also appear in dreams, and in temporary states of regression in neurotics. [See **1321.**]

Related Concept: ACTION (ACT).

REFERENCES

Croce, B., 1909, *Aesthetic*. NP. pp. 144–145, 1958.
Feldman, S., *Mannerisms of Speech and Gesture in Everyday Life*. IUP, pp. 5, 232, 1959.
Fenichel, O., *The Psychoanalytic Theory of Neurosis*. Nor, p. 107, 1945.
Freud, S.: 1893, "On the Psychical Mechanism of Hysterical Phenomena: Preliminary Communication." *SE*, 2:8, 1955.
    1908, "Hysterical Fantasies and Their Relation to Bisexuality." *SE*, 9:159, 1959.
Hayakawa, S. I., *Language in Action*. HB, p. 30, 1939.
Isakower, O., "On the Exceptional Position of the Auditory Sphere." *IntJPsa*, 20:343–344, 1939.

ADDITIONAL READINGS

Ekstein, R., "Language of Psychology and of Everyday Life." *PsycholRev*, 49, 1942.
Fromm, E., *The Forgotten Language: An Introduction to the Understanding of Dreams, Fairy Tales and Myths*. G, 1957.

1201

LATENCY PERIOD denotes that phase of emotional development between the resolution of the oedipal phase (fourth or fifth year) and the onset of prepuberty (eleventh or twelfth year). It is characterized by a sublimation or lessening of sexual and aggressive drives, which, in combination with other maturative factors, favors the consolidation and strengthening of ego and superego functions. Other objects (playmates, teachers, etc.) are substituted for parents and siblings. During the latency period, Freud (1905) pointed out, such feelings as disgust and shame act as inhibitions of the gratification of infantile wishes. He also expressed the opinion that these feelings are determined by heredity and that education only modifies them.

Ferenczi (1916) discussed the latency period in neurotics, as follows: "Apprehension about the smallness and consequent incapacity of the copulatory organ—or, as we psycho-analysts are accustomed to say, 'the complex of the small penis'—is especially common among neurotics, and far from rare among the healthy. In every case in which I have analysed this symptom the explanation was as follows: All those who suffered later in this way had in their earliest childhood occupied themselves to an unusual degree with the phantasy of coitus cum matre (or with a corresponding older person); in doing so they had naturally been distressed at the idea of the inadequacy of their penis for this purpose.* The latency period interrupted and suppressed this group of thoughts; when, however, the sexual impulse unfolded itself afresh in puberty, the interest was again directed towards the copulatory organ, the old distress once more emerged, even when the actual size of the organ was normal or exceeded the average. While, therefore, the penis developed in the normal way, the idea of the penis remained at an infantile level. The deflection of attention from the genital region led the individual to take no note of the changes in it."

Related Concept: PUBERTY.

---

* "The condition for this apprehensive phantasy is the ignorance of the extensibility of the vagina; children only know that coitus takes place in an opening through which they once passed *in toto* at birth."

REFERENCES

Ferenczi, S., 1911, "On Obscene Words." *SPsa*, pp. 145–146, 1916.
Freud, S., 1905, "Three Essays on the Theory of Sexuality." *SE*, 7:177–178, 1953.

ADDITIONAL READINGS

Bornstein, B.: "On Latency." *PsaStC*, 6, 1951.
    "Masturbation in the Latency Period." *PsaStC*, 8, 1953.
Freud, S., 1924, "The Dissolution of the Oedipus Complex." *SE*, 19, 1961.
Peller, L., "Reading and Daydreams in Latency. Boy-Girl Differences." *JAPA*, 6, 1958.

1202

LATENT HOMOSEXUALITY can be detected in all normal people, the result, as Freud (1937) noted, of a struggle between two rival trends. In short, every human being is bisexual: a male individual represses his female sexual needs, a woman, her male desires. As a result, most individuals have unconscious or latent homosexual wishes. Because they are latent they do not interfere with the individual's normal heterosexual functions.

Pathologically, latent homosexuality is usually connected with the negative oedipus complex: unconscious infantile wishes remain unconscious by being warded off by various neurotic symptoms or character traits. In the case of the Wolf Man, Freud (1918) applied the idea clinically. Here, the fear of castration was connected with the image of the father in competition with the castration threats emanating from the mother. The Wolf Man manifested an irrational fear of wolves as an unconscious defense against the unconscious wish to copulate with his father. His mother represented the castrated wolf and his father the wolf that mounted her. The Wolf Man's fear was caused by his unconscious identification with his mother, and by his unconscious wish to be copulated by his father.

Related Concepts: NEGATIVE OEDIPUS COMPLEX; OBJECT CHOICE (ANACLITIC AND NARCISSISTIC); OVERT HOMOSEXUALITY.

REFERENCES

Freud, S.: 1918, "From the History of an Infantile Neurosis." *SE*, 17:47, 1955.
         1937, "Analysis Terminable and Interminable." *SE*, 23:244, 1964.

1203

LATENT PSYCHOSIS, a term borrowed from Eugen Bleuler, has been reexamined by Bychowski (1960) with reference to modern ego psychology; he proposed the term as a substitute for *borderline psychotic*. This condition is characterized by Bychowski, in the case of the latent schizophrenic, as follows: "Here the depressive core is masked by a façade compounded out of character traits and neurotic symptomatology. Obsessive compulsive character structure underlies obsessive or phobic symptoms, interspersed with trends of hysterical emotionality and suggestibility. Depressive reactions may occur at the slightest provocation. Time and again, the picture becomes enriched by a hypomaniac excitability."

Related Concept: PSYCHOTIC CORE.

REFERENCE

Bychowski, G., "The Structure of Chronic and Latent Depression." *IntJPsa*, 41:504-508, 1960.

ADDITIONAL READING

Bychowski, G., *Psychotherapy of Psychosis*. G&S, 1952.

1204

LAUGHTER is an involuntary motoric discharge which results often when, for whatever reason, an individual, anticipating a narcissistic mortification, achieves a triumph. Freud (1905) described laughter as a discharge of psychic energy. Freud considered laughter as a sign of pleasure, and he was inclined to refer to this pleasure as the release of the previously existing cathetic energy.

In identifying the etiology of laughter, Eidelberg (1961) noted: "We go back to the stage of development when thinking was not differentiated from acting and words had the power to give us complete gratification of our instinctual needs. Listening and understanding a joke serves but one purpose—that of gaining almost instant end-pleasure. We might say a joke permits us a temporary return from the reality of the adult to the simple pleasure realm of the child. By laughing, we agree not to bother about the problem involved, but rather to laugh it off."

Laughter may also be used as a defense against crying and against embarrassment.

Related Concepts: COMIC; HUMOR; JOKE.

REFERENCES

Eidelberg, L., *The Dark Urge*, Py, pp. 156–157, 1961.
Freud, S., 1905, "Jokes and Their Relation to the Unconscious." *SE*, 8, 146–149, 1960.

ADDITIONAL READINGS

Brody, M., "The Meaning of Laughter." *Q*, 19, 1950.
Gregory, J. C., "The Nature of Laughter." *P*, 4, 1923.
Grieg, J. Y., *The Psychology of Laughter and Comedy*. D, 1923.
Grotjahn, M., *Beyond Laughter*. Bl, 1957.
Jacobson, E., "The Child's Laughter; Theoretical and Clinical Notes on the Function of the Comic." *PsaStC*, 2, 1946.
Kris, E., *Psychoanalytic Explorations in Art*. IUP, 1952.
McDougall, W., "A New Theory of Laughter." *P*, 2, 1922.
Stärcke, A., "Ein einfacher Lach-und Weinkrampf." *Z*, 5, 1919.

1205

LAW AND PSYCHOANALYSIS. In two papers written some years apart, Freud (1906, 1931) discussed the problem of what psychoanalysis could contribute by way of application to legal proceedings. He pointed out that the criminal, in contrast to the psychoanalytic patient, is intent upon consciously witholding the truth from the investigator. The patient, contrarily, consciously assists in combating his resistance and in uncovering his "secret".

The patient works with the psychoanalyst to

uncover what is hidden even from himself because he has something to gain; but the criminal does not assist the investigator and thus makes the work of the discovery difficult, if not impossible. The danger is that the patient in a self-accusative manner may appear to be guilty when, in fact, he is innocent of any wrong doing. Thus, as Freud pointed out, it is a fair question to ask whether the conscious resistance is betrayed by exactly the same indications as the unconscious resistance. The patient's secret is usually a wish, whereas the criminal's relates to an act. It was Freud's belief that the processes used to achieve therapeutic results in psychoanalysis with patients could not—as then proven—be used to achieve the same results with criminals. He concluded his paper (written in 1906) with the suggestion that experimental work having no bearing on the outcome of legal cases be collected and that these conclusions then be put to the test of how the court's verdict compared with it.

Related Concepts: METHODOLOGY; SYNTHESIS.

REFERENCES

Freud, S.: 1906, "Psycho-Analysis and the Establishment of the Facts in Legal Proceedings." *SE*, 9:108, 1959.

1931, "Expert Opinion in the Halsmann Case." *SE*, 21:251–253, 1961.

1206

LAW OF CONSTANCY denotes a principle which governs all mental processes, a tendency toward stability which Freud (1920) employed from a concept first advanced by Fechner. The purpose of such a mechanism was to reduce to nothing, or to as low a level as possible, the sums of excitation which flow from the mental processes.

Originally, the pleasure-unpleasure principle was considered to be identical with the Nirvana principle (in 1914). Unpleasure is experienced when an increase of instinctual tension took place; pleasure, a decrease. In 1924, Freud rejected this idea: the two principles exist in the human being at the same time and are responsible for the achievement of equilibrium. Thus, the two forces (i.e., classes of instinct), Eros and Thanatos, which are responsible for the maintenance of this equilibrium, are identified as the unpleasure-pleasure principle, on the one hand, and the Nirvana principle on the other.

Those who disagreed with Freud's concept of the death instinct maintained that the constancy principle held true for all instinctual drives, that the stimulus of hunger and need for objects associated with the pleasure principle are still derived genetically from the principle of constancy.

Related Concepts: NIRVANA PRINCIPLE; PLEASURE PRINCIPLE; UNPLEASURE-PLEASURE PRINCIPLE.

REFERENCES

Freud, S.: 1914, "Instincts and Their Vicissitudes." *SE*, 14:120, 1957.

1920, "Beyond the Pleasure Principle." *SE*, 18:9, 1955.

1924, "The Economic Problem of Masochism." *SE*, 19:159–160, 1961.

1207

LAY ANALYSIS. Freud's view on the matter of the suitability of nonmedical practitioners is clear. He deemed the study of medicine a circuitous way of approaching the profession of analysis. Nonetheless, in 1926, the year Freud published "The Question of Lay Analysis," four out of five aspirants who sought psychoanalytical training were doctors. He noted, in a postscript, a year later that as long as there are no special schools for training analysts, individuals who had a preliminary knowledge of medicine would make the best candidates.

Historically, the societal requirements which predated the practice of psychoanalysis were to influence the outcome of this question. In most countries, those who were not licensed physicians were not permitted to treat human ailments. The confusion arose, therefore, as to the domain of psychoanalytical treatment. Since it was a treatment for neurosis, it was not, in an earlier day, prohibited. As the precepts and practice of psychoanalysis grew in influence and importance, however, medical societies came to consider such a practice as a part of medical psychiatry, and subject, therefore, to the same training and licensing requirements.

Congruently, other disciplines, principally clinical psychology and social work, developed techniques which, in character, were similar to those of psychoanalysis. Thus, in most Western countries, the distinction was no longer quite so clear. In the U.S., for instance, most of the states (there being no federal statute) containing large population centers passed licensing legislation which tended to "legitimize" the practice of therapeutic non-medical analysis.

Apart from the implied legal question, the essential difficulty was the growth of these disciplines in influence and importance *outside* of Freudian psychoanalysis. Freud foresaw this difficulty, which may, in part, account for his belief that the "threat" to psychoanalytical therapy lay in another direction. In a letter dated shortly before his death (1938), he wrote that he still objected to psychoanalysis being absorbed by psychiatry.

The decisive argument from a scientific point of view has, again, been offered by Freud. A scientist interested in the study of X-ray, Freud wrote, does not require patients. He may work on guinea pigs which the analyst is unable to do. Consequently, any scientist interested in studying psychoanalysis requires human beings suffering from neuroses.

Today, the question of lay analysis is still unsolved. The one central factor remains to plague those who would broaden the practice while, at the same time, maintain its standards. Jones (1957) provided a decisive view of this question: "If the intending students of psychoanalysis were to be told that the study of medicine was irrelevant, would it not in time become irrelevant? How many of them would be quixotically inclined to spend tedious years of toil and expense in an unnecessary direction? That might lead to the majority of analysts being lay. In that event one might have to envisage the practice of psychoanalysis becoming increasingly divorced from the science of medicine, to its great practical and theoretical detriment. Moreover, its prospects of ever becoming recognized as a legitimate branch of science would be reduced perhaps to the vanishing point. Psychiatry, in its broadest sense, i.e., the psychological aspects of medicine, is certainly its nearest link to the other branches of science, one more accessible than pure (academic) psychology."

Related Concept: PSYCHOANALYSIS.

REFERENCES

Freud, S., 1926, "The Question of Lay Analysis." *SE*, 20:254, 257, 1959.
Jones, E., *The Life and Work of Sigmund Freud.* HPI, 3:312, 1957.

ADDITIONAL READINGS

Alexander, F., "Diskussion zur Laienanalyse." *Z*, 13, 1927.
Hitschmann, E., "Diskussion der Laienanalyse." *Z*, 13, 1927.
Horney, K., "Discussion on Lay Analysis." *IntJPsa*, 8, 1927.
Jokl, R. H., "Diskussion der Laienanalyse." *Z*, 13, 1927.

1208
LIBIDINAL PHASES are the stages of development of the hypothetical energy of sexual instinct-fusion. According to Freud (1940), there are four stages of development, which are characterized by the erotogenic zones of the mouth, the anus, the phallus and the genitals. They are connected with certain aims, as in sucking the breast, in defecating and evacuating the feces, in urinating and playing with the phallus (penis in men, clitoris in women) and, finally, in the mature genital discharge. The libido is discharged by active-passive (passive aim) and self-erotic manifestations. In addition, inspectionistic and exhibitionistic activities are attached to the four stages of development. It appears that the destrudo (the energy) of an aggressive instinct-fusion passes through similar stages.

The mouth represents an erotogenic zone for the infant. Sucking and later eating represent the gratification of oral needs. The fact that the infant often sucks a pacifier indicates that he is not only concerned with the incorporation of calories. When the infant begins to have teeth, the need to bite expresses his sadistic desires. The second stage of development is usually referred to as the sadistic-anal, and is characterized by the infant's interest in excreting or retaining his stools. Finally, the third stage is referred to as the phallic, in which the boy is interested in his penis and the girl in her clitoris. The boy's interest in his penis appears to be responsible for his positive oedipus complex, which is finally dissolved by the fear of castration. The girl reacts with penis envy, if she considers her clitoris to be an inferior organ to the penis.

Freud pointed out that the stages are not clear-cut, and that the fourth stage, the genital phase, is achieved only with puberty. This stage is characterized by the boy discovering that the penis produces semen and serves not only to excrete but to secrete. The girl discovers the presence of her vagina when she begins menstruation, developing narcissistic pride in her breasts at the same time.

Related Concepts: ACTIVE; AGGRESSION; PASSIVE.

REFERENCE

Freud, S., 1940, "An Outline of Psycho-Analysis." *SE*, 23:153–155, 1964.

1209

LIBIDINAL TYPES denote a personality classification, devised by Freud (1931), based on hypothetical differences in the distribution of libidinal energy to the main parts of the psychic apparatus. Three main libidinal types are designated: the *erotic* type, where the major allocation of libido remains in the id which is its source; the *obsessional* type, where there is a preponderance of libido in the superego; and the *narcissistic* type, where the ego has the greatest share of libido. Implicit in this classification are the assumptions that this distribution of libidinal energy remains relatively constant throughout life, represents a basic, perhaps innate quality, and is not caused by pathological traumas.

The erotic type focuses his main interest on loving and being loved (with the latter concern usually more prominent). He embodies the instinctual claims of the id. Persons of this type dread loss of love, and are dependent on their objects. When a person of this type develops a neurosis, it is likely to be an hysterical disorder.

In the obsessional type, dread of the superego, rather than fear of losing external love, is predominant. These people may be capable of considerable self-reliance. When a neurosis develops, it is most likely to be of the obsessional type.

In the narcissistic type, self-preservation is the primary goal. Often, there is considerable aggression

available to the ego, and with this goes a tendency to be active. These people may include "personalities" or leaders. Psychoses and "acting-out disorders" are the more frequent forms of mental illness in this group.

Mixed types are more frequently found than the pure forms just described. Freud considered the *erotic-narcissistic* to be the most common type. In this type, love of objects and love of self moderate each other. The *erotic-obsessional* type is characterized by dependence on the love of present objects, as well as the love of past objects and ideals (through the superego). The *narcissistic obsessional* type is considered the most valuable for civilization; activity and self-reliance are coupled with regard for the superego and society. Independent thinkers, scientists, and innovators are most apt to be in this group. A combination of all three types would be no "type" at all, but an idealized norm.

Eidelberg (1957) suggested that the total personality may be divided into five parts, instead of three, by splitting the ego into (a) sensory ego, which contains the representation of the external and internal perceptions, (b) central ego, which has all the functions hitherto attributed to the ego, and (c) body ego, which contains the presentation of the body. Consequently, in Eidelberg's view, there are five libidinal types; the two additional types are the *sensuous type* and *athletic type*.

While the characteristics mentioned by Freud are present in both normal and neurotic people, it may be advisable to try to separate the two. For example, a neurotic of the erotic type seems to be chiefly interested in concealing the importance of his instincts from his consciousness, and not in satisfying the demands of his id; whereas, a normal person of this type is chiefly interested in gratifying his id. The same kind of relationship holds true for the behavior of normal and neurotic persons belonging to the other libidinal types. Thus, a neurotic of any type, if cured, is still of that type.

The concept of libidinal types may be used to study the choice of neurosis. For example, a patient who has regressed to the phallic stage and belongs to the erotic type will develop a conversion symptom; whereas a patient who has the same kind of regression, but belongs to the obsessional type, will develop anxiety hysteria.

Related Concepts: CATHEXIS; CHOICE OF A NEUROSIS.

REFERENCES

Eidelberg, L., "An Introduction to the Study of the Narcissistic Mortification." *Q*, 31:657–668, 1957.
Freud, S., 1931, "Libidinal Types." *SE*, 21:215–223, 1961.

ADDITIONAL READINGS

Eidelberg, L., *An Outline of a Comparative Pathology of the Neuroses.* IUP, 1954.
Feigenbaum, D., "Notes on the Theory of Libidinal Types." *Q*, 1, 1932.

1210

LIBIDO is the psychic energy responsible for man's sexual activity. Although Freud employed the term as early as 1895, it was not until 1905 that he provided an adequate description, stating that the energy of the libido represents the energy of the sexual instinct.

In Freud's early formulation, the sexual instincts contained libido and the ego instincts did not. He altered this view in 1924: both instincts (sexual and ego) contained libido. The sexual instincts contained object-libido and the ego instincts contained secondary narcissistic-libido. These two forms appear to be the result of a splitting of the primary narcissistic-libido (autoerotic libido). An infant does not differentiate between the inside and outside; he regards his mother and her breasts as a part of his own body; thus, the presentation of her and himself is cathected by primary narcissistic-libido. After he learns to differentiate, the presentation of the mother is cathected by object-libido and the self by secondary narcissistic-libido.

The splitting of the primary narcissistic-libido into object-libido and secondary narcissistic-libido is the result of reality testing. It seems, under normal conditions, that the presentations of external objects are cathected by object-libido while the presentations of the self are cathected by secondary narcissistic-libido. Eidelberg (1954) noted: "It seems improbable that the total amount of our libido may become either narcissistic or objectual, although object libido may change into narcissistic libido, and *vice versa*. It appears that such a change takes places only within certain limits. It is not clear whether, under normal conditions, the total amount of primary narcissistic libido is transformed into secondary narcissistic libido and object libido. It may well be that a certain quantity of primary narcissistic libido is present in the normal adult. Little is known about the factors responsible for the change of narcissistic libido into object libido. It seems probable that an external frustration may turn object libido into narcissistic libido, while an internal frustration, such as the inability to satisfy hunger by sucking the thumb, may stimulate the change of narcissistic libido into object libido. When the hunger tension has been discharged by the incorporation of food, the cessation of eating is explained as due to a change of object libido into secondary narcissistic libido. Whenever we are interested in an external object, the representation of this object becomes cathected by object libido. When this interest is satisfied, the object libido is withdrawn, turned against the self, and becomes secondary narcissistic libido (under normal conditions)."

In a paper published in 1940, Freud discussed the two primary instincts, Eros and Thanatos. They mix with each other to produce two instinct fusions: (a) the sexual instinct fusion in which Eros plays a decisive role as compared to Thanatos, and (b) the aggressive instinct fusion in which Thanatos contributes most of its energy. Libido is the energy of Eros, or the energy of the sexual instinct-fusion. However, the terms Eros, Thanatos, and libido are explanatory, and are not subject to proof by external or internal perceptions; they are perceived only in terms of their derivatives, ideas, and affects.

Related Concepts: EROS; THANATOS.

REFERENCES

Eidelberg, L., *An Outline of a Comparative Pathology of the Neuroses.* IUP, pp. 22–23, 1954.
Freud, S: 1895, "On the Grounds for Detaching a Particular Syndrome from Neurasthenia Under the Description 'Anxiety Neurosis.'" *SE*, 3:102, 1962.
　　　1905, "Three Essays on the Theory of Sexuality." *SE*, 7:135, 1953.
　　　1924, "A Short Account of Psycho-Analysis." *SE*, 19:203, 1961.

1211

LISTENING WITH THE THIRD EAR, a term used by Reik (who borrowed it from Nietzsche), refers both to the innate and acquired sensitivity with which the analyst listens to his patient in an attempt to guess the meaning which lies buried beneath the spoken words. The analyst, in effect, hears his own *voix intérieure*, litetally, his own interior voice.

For example, while listening to a patient who was an enthusiastic horsewoman, Reik remembered an incident which had taken place during the First World War in which a sergeant had shouted to an older reservist: "God have mercy on your wife if you cannot ride her better than you ride that mare." His next association was to the Amazons, a mythical race of female warriors who were excellent horse-women. Reik then realized that the patient's interest in horseback riding represented a disavowal of her femininity. Instead of being "ridden," she was the "rider," a reversal from passive femininity to active masculinity. Reik's early impression was subsequently confirmed.

Related Concept: PSYCHOANALYSIS.

REFERENCE

Reik, T., *Listening with the Third Ear.* FS, 1948.

ADDITIONAL READING

Sherman, M., "Clues to the Third Ear." R, 46, 1959.

1212

LITTLE HANS. In the first published case history of a child analysis, Freud (1909) was able to demonstrate the therapeutic application of psychoanalysis, to substantiate certain conclusions he had drawn earlier about infantile sexuality from his analysis of adult patients. Published under the title, "Analysis of a Phobia in a Five-Year-Old Boy," the material used in the written record was supplied by the boy's father from the many consultations Freud had with him during the course of the analysis. Freud saw the boy only once.

The case of Little Hans was that of a phobia supervened on an anxiety state that had developed when the boy was almost five, nine months after the birth of a sibling. Freud classified the case as one of anxiety hysteria. The therapeutic results were excellent. When Freud saw the boy some years later (in 1922), he was free of symptoms, appeared healthy and outgoing.

Little Hans's neurosis was characterized by a phobia of horses. He refused to go out into the street for fear of being bitten by them. In his mind, he was afraid that they might come into his room and bite him as a punishment for his wish (and only then) that they fall down and die. In the course of his analysis, Freud was able to conclude that the boy had displaced his hostile and fearful feelings onto a substitute for his father.

A chronological estimate of the associative chain that culminated in Little Hans's phobia lead more or less directly to the event of his pregnant mother's confinement. He had witnessed an accident to a horse and had been quite disturbed by it. It acquired its effectiveness, however, from an event that had occurred the summer before at Gmunden, an Austrian resort, where he had been in the habit of playing with the landlord's children (whom he thereafter referred to as "my children," adding that they, too, had been brought by the stork); Fritz, of whom he was fond, had hit his foot and fallen down while they were playing at being horses. Thus an easy associative path was established between Fritz and his father. Nonetheless, as Freud pointed out, these connections probably would not have been sufficient except for the second of the complexes that lurked in Hans's unconscious, the complex of his mother's confinement. From that moment on the way was clear for the return of the repressed: the pathogenic material was transposed into Little Hans's horse complex.

Little Hans's first formulation—"The horse will bite me"—was derived from another event which had happened at Gmunden that summer. It related not only to the hostile wishes he had against his father, but to the warning he had received against onanism from his mother (who had playfully threatened to send for the doctor to have his penis cut off). In this, it seemed evident to Freud that Hans's hostility toward his father screened his lustful desire for, and fear of, his mother.

Writing about this case at a later date, Freud (1913) noted that little Hans regarded his father as a competitor for his mother's favors toward whom he had directed his "budding" sexual wishes. In this, Freud identified the motive for the displacement. The boy was not able to achieve uninhibited sway over his mind; it had to contend with his affection and admiration for the very same persons. To find relief from this conflict, Little Hans displaced his hostile and fearful feelings.

Little Hans had arrived at the stage of development which is typical of the male child in his relationship to his parents. To this conflict, Freud was to give the name *oedipus complex*, and to identify it as "the nuclear complex of the neurosis." The "crime" of Oedipus the king was that he killed his father and married his mother. Both of these acts have been identified as the two basic wishes of children—"the insufficient repression or the reawakening of which forms the nucleus of perhaps every psychoneurosis."

Related Concepts: ANXIETY; AVOIDANCE; FEAR.

REFERENCES

Freud, S.: 1909, "Analysis of a Phobia in a Five-Year-Old Boy." *SE*, 10:3–149, 1955.
    1913, "Totem and Taboo." *SE*, 13:128–129, 132, 1955.

ADDITIONAL READINGS

Baumeyer, F., "Bemerkungen zu Freuds Krankengeschichte des 'Kleinen Hans.' " *PraxKinderpsychol*, 1, 1953.
Fliess, R., "Phylogenetic versus Ontogenetic Experience. Notes on a Passage of Dialogue Between 'Little Hans' and His Father." *IntJPsa*, 37, 1956.

1213

LOCALIZATION OF A SYMPTOM. Freud pointed out that the localization of a neurotic symptom should not be confused with the regression to an infantile stage of development. For instance, all hysterical conversion symptoms—hysterical blindness, hysterical paralysis and hysterical vomiting, to name several—represent partial gratifications and partial frustrations of repressed phallic wishes.

A clinical example may suffice to illustrate the point. The Wolf Man suffered from hysterical

constipation, developing this symptom as a defense against his wish to have anal intercourse with his father. His repressed feminine wishes cathected the anal zone and led, consequently, to his constipation and diarrhea. Freud (1918) pointed out that the Wolf Man's symptoms were hysterical in nature, or, to be exact, represented a conversion hysteria.

This conversion symptom was the result of his use of his rectum for the localization of his conversion and did not represent a regression to the anal stage. His inability to defecate without an enema and his need for the enema represented the partial gratification and the partial frustration of the phallic wish, and, as such, was responsible for the erotization of this part of his body. The Wolf Man, as well, had suffered a regression to the anal stage, but the result of this regression was his obsessional neurosis, not his constipation.

The "choice" of localization depends partly on constitutional factors (perhaps that part of the body with the lowest somatic resistance) and partly on accidental factors—experiences in which a particular function or part of the body is traumatically affected.

Related Concepts: CHOICE OF A NEUROSIS; CONVERSION AND CONVERSION SYMPTOMS; WOLF MAN.

REFERENCE

Freud, S., 1918, "From the History of an Infantile Neurosis." *SE*, 17:78, 80, 113, 1955.

1214

LOVE is an affective state, an attitude of the total personality toward an object, characterized, in its most mature form, as follows: by the wish to possess the object and identify with it, by feelings of tenderness toward the object, by the wish to care for and to give pleasure and satisfaction to the object, by genital sexual desires toward the object (which may be aim-inhibited), by idealization of the object, by the wish to be loved in return by the object, by the experience of pleasure when the object is near, and by a high intensity of cathexis of the representation of the object; it may be distinguished from attitudes related to it: as with friendship, sympathy, empathy, fondness, affection, loyalty, etc. As Freud (1915) noted, it is a manifestation of the sexual instincts; its expression follows the development of the libido, with characteristic qualities in each libidinal phase. It may undergo regression, or any of the instinctual vicissitudes. It may be mobilized as a defense, mainly against aggressive feelings. In an aim-inhibited form, love may be mainly altruistic (for example, the love of mankind or the love of an ideal).

Freud (1914) designated two basic types of love. In the narcissistic type, one may love oneself, what one once was, what one would like to be, or someone or something who is similar to one, whom one would want to become similar to or make similar to oneself. The anaclitic type loves the mother who feeds him and the father who protects him; at a later time, he substitutes an object he wants and needs. Adult love includes both types. Where love is based primarily on identification, regression of loving has probably occurred. However, no love can be completely free of some elements of identification nor would this be desirable.

During pregenital libidinal phases, the object is treated as something to be devoured and incorporated into the self, something to be controlled and forced to behave as though it were a part of the self. The infant's dependence on its mother results in awareness and cathexis of objects other than the self. It is then that object-love appears. At first, object-love exists only when there is need fulfillment by possession or identification with the object. Gradually, love becomes less dependent on constant narcissistic supplies and instinctual gratifications.

The most mature form of love is that of the genital phase, in which some of the sexual instincts become sublimated and aim-inhibited; it no longer depends exclusively on genital sexual satisfaction. Narcissistic cathexis is partly surrendered to the object which is idealized; the ambivalence is solved to the extent that the aggressive drives are separated from loving. Genital love is dependent on the intersystemic harmony characteristic of the successful resolution of the oedipus complex.

In love, secondary narcissism is replenished by the love given by the object, the act of loving, and the ego-superego systems of the subject. Genital love is both active and passive; at its deepest level, the one who gives love is actively repeating the role of the nursing mother. Parental love represents an aim of the genital phase, in which the specific genital sexual aim is inhibited. It is based, to a large extent, on a narcissistic object-choice, i.e., the object is what the subject once was (what he would have liked to be), and that which was once a part of himself. Yet, there is no doubt that parental love may be of the most mature form. Sibling love is a mixture of narcissistic and anaclitic love. It is based partly on a sublimation of, or reaction formation to, sibling rivalry and partly on an identification with the loving attitudes of the parents. Homosexual love often depends, to a large extent, on a narcissistic type of object-choice; often the object also represents a part of the self. Neurotic self-love takes place when the self is loved as though it were an object, but where no true object relationship exists.

Related Concepts: GENITAL; IDENTIFICATION; NARCISSISM; OBJECT CHOICE (ANACLITIC AND NARCISSISTIC).

REFERENCES

Freud, S.: 1914, "On Narcissism: An Introduction." *SE*, 14:88–91, 100–101, 1957.
      1915, "Instincts and Their Vicissitudes." *SE*, 14:137–138, 1957.

ADDITIONAL READINGS

DeForest, I., "Love and Anger. Two Activating Forces in Psychoanalytic Therapy." *Ps*, 7, 1944.
Eidelberg, L.: "Vorläufige Mitteilung: Zur Erniedrigung des Liebesobjekts." *Z*, 20, 1934.
      The Dark Urge, Py, 1961.
Freud, S., 1923, "The Ego and the Id." *SE*, 19, 1961.
Hitschmann, E., "Freud's Conception of Love." *YBPsa*, 1953.
Jekels, L.: "Mitleid und Liebe." *Im*, 22, 1936.
      & E. Bergler, "Transference and Love." *Q*, 18, 1949.
Richardson, H. B., "Love and Psychodynamics of Adaptation." *R*, 43, 1956.

1215

LURE OF THE PAST is characterized by a fascination for and a desire to return to the contented, carefree, dependent period of early infancy.

This wish is most often the result of a retrospective falsification of the memories of childhood.*

In psychopathology, the lure of the past finds expression in the regression attendant on all mental and emotional illnesses. It expresses the wish to revert to the safety of the first libidinal objects, to an omnipotent narcissistic condition, and to the polymorphous perverse sexuality of childhood. The repetition compulsion, according to Freud (1920), leads to active repetition of what was passively experienced in the past. It appears as a transference in the psychoanalytic situation.

Servadio (1953) noted: "The person who most typically experiences the lure of the forbidden is he who does *not* feel a particular attraction for a certain kind of action so long as this can be considered licit; whereas he is impelled to act when the action appears unlawful. One of my patients in the beginning of his analysis stated that he did not particularly enjoy sexual intercourse whenever it could be performed under circumstances which did not imply a prohibition; and, conversely, that he looked for situations in which he would run the risk of being punished or reproached, either by an impersonal authority or by individuals; or in which, in any case, he would have the feeling that he was doing something wrong."

Related Concepts: REGRESSION; REPETITION COMPULSION.

REFERENCES

Freud, S., 1920, "Beyond the Pleasure Principle." *SE*, 18:16–17, 35–36, 1955.
Servadio, E., "The Lure of the Forbidden." *IntJPsa*, 34:325, 1953.

ADDITIONAL READINGS

Baudouin, C., "La Réactivation du Passé." *RFPsa*, 14, 1950.
Fenichel, O., *The Psychoanalytic Theory of Neurosis.* Nor, 1945.

---

* In religion and mythology, a parallel may be found in the many tales which relate to a *primal* golden age of the human race.

M

Freud, S.: 1914, "On Narcissism: An Introduction." *SE*, 14, 1957.

1919, "The Uncanny." *SE*, 17, 1955.

1926, "Inhibitions, Symptoms and Anxiety." *SE*, 20, 1959.

Nunberg, H., "Homosexualität, Magie und Aggression." *Z*, 22, 1936.

Reik, T., *Dogma and Compulsion: Psychoanalytic Studies of Religion and Myths*. IUP, 1951.

Roheim, G., *Magic and Schizophrenia*. IUP, 1955.

Schneider, E., "Experimentelle Magie." *Z*, 7, 1921.

1300

MAGIC denotes the illusory possession of supernatural powers, the supposed achievement of gratification through irrational, supernatural forces; a belief that wishing alone will make a desired event occur. In neurotics, this may lead to compulsive memorizing of long lists of names of feared persons or things. Magic may be ascribed to almost anything: to numbers, touch, symmetry, facial expression, gestures, etc.

Magical thinking is a component of superstition, social custom, and certain mental disorders, as Freud (1913) noted, in which primary process thinking prevails or in which thoughts and feelings remain close to (or regress to) primary process types of thinking. The rituals of obsessive-compulsive neurotics are magic ways of producing some effect or warding off some danger. The common defense mechanisms of undoing, and sometimes isolation, are magic ways of wiping out, or at least separating, some events by a magical kind of action, behavior, or thought.

Related Concepts: DEFENSE MECHANISMS; OMNIPOTENCE OF THOUGHT.

REFERENCE

Freud, S.: 1913, "Totem and Taboo." *SE*, 13:59–78–88, 91–92, 115, 117, 1955.

ADDITIONAL READINGS

Freud, S.: 1909, "Notes upon a Case of Obsessional Neurosis." *SE*, 10, 1955.

1301

MAKING FACES may represent a magic gesture, in which an individual who feels ugly because of his unconscious wish to be castrated denies that this castration took place. This device may also be used to deceive those whom he considers intent on castrating him by making them believe that he has already been castrated. Making an ugly face may also impart a feeling of power through possession of the ability to frighten others, i.e., to deny the presence of a wish to be admired (*oderint dum metuant*).

Fenichel (1945) noted: "What is the unconscious meaning of the game of making faces? (1) The active play of being ugly is enjoyed as a proof that the person controls beauty and ugliness, that is, that one is not castrated for good, since one can bring about and undo castration at will. (2) Being ugly means being able to frighten others, that is, being powerful, which is felt as a reassurance. (3) To play the part of the ugly (castrated) one is an archaic means of misleading the powers that want to make one ugly (to castrate). (4) To play being ugly (castrated) serves as a magical gesture, an attack on the spectator: 'I show you how ugly (how castrated) you ought to be.'"

Related Concept: Exhibitionism.

REFERENCE

Fenichel, O., *The Psychoanalytic Theory of Neurosis.* Nor, p. 319, 1945.

ADDITIONAL READINGS

Coriat, I., "A Note on the Medusa Symbolism." *AmIm*, 2, 1941.
Ferenczi, S., *Further Contributions to the Theory and Technique of Psychoanalysis.* HPI, 1926.
Freud, S., 1940, "Medusa's Head." *SE*, 18, 1955.

1302

MALADJUSTMENT denotes the inability to maintain a harmonious relationship with the environment; usually the result of intrapsychic conflict within the total personality. Since maladjustment results from the presence of unconscious conflicts, leading to an inability to react appropriately, emotionally and intellectually, it can be viewed as the manifest expression of such conflict, which results in an inadequate and more or less unhappy way of life. Maladjustment is present in most neurotic and psychotic disturbances. [A. Freud, 1949.]

Related Concepts: Adaptation; Conflict; Neurosis and Psychosis.

REFERENCE

Freud, A., "Certain Types and Stages of Social Maladjustment." *YBPsa*, 5:225–237, 1949.

ADDITIONAL READING

Hartmann, H., *Ego Psychology and the Problem of Adaptation.* IUP, 1958.

1303

MANIC-DEPRESSIVE disorders belong to a group of affective psychoses which are characterized by a predominating mood of depression or elation,

increased or decreased activity, and exaggeration or diminution of ideas and feelings. The nonpsychotic, basic personality structure has been referred to as cyclothymic and elation and depression in such individuals is seen in its muted forms, in optimism-pessimism and enthusiasm-dejection. Manic-depressive psychosis accounts for five to fifteen per cent of first admissions to mental hospitals, although the number of patients has been decreasing in recent years, due probably to cultural factors and to better diagnostic differentiation from schizophrenia. There is strong evidence for constitutional factors in the periodicity of the illness: high familial incidence and high correlation of illness in identical twins.

Manic-depressive psychosis is much more frequent in the highest social and professional class, and like other depressive illness is more commonly found in women. The illness appears with onset of acute self-limited changes of mood and early maturity, separated by asymptomatic intervals of varying duration. The disorder may become continuous, and some observers have noted progression to schizophrenia. Recent clinical studies have traced initial periods of depression with crying commencing in early childhood. While some manic-depressive patients have mainly depressions, others may display only recurrent manic attacks, and the classical circular, alternating form is relatively rare. Attenuated attacks may occur as hypomania with increased gaiety, affability, buoyant self-confidence and seemingly boundless energy. A previously brooding and inhibited person may become demanding, effusive, and unconventional in speech and manner. Sudden oscillations of emotion and capriciousness are common. The psychomotor-retardation of the depression gives way to manic overactivity. In the psychotic form delusions often reflect the mood of triumphant elation or profound depression. Self-depreciation, self-accusation, remorse, and hypochondriasis may alternate with grandiose, boastful, and assertive feelings.

The psychoanalytic theory of depression has been well delineated and includes libidinal regression and oral cannibalism, internalized aggression, ego regression and increased narcissism, omnipotence of thought, primitive defenses (especially introjection and denial), archaic sadistic superego, and introjection of the ambivalently loved object.

The onset of the disorder has been characterized as consisting of an internalized struggle between the ego and superego and between the self and the preoedipal maternal surrogate.

In mania, the superego is fused with the ego, as were the self and the object in the oral symbiotic union. Whereas in melancholy the ego feels powerless, in mania the ego has regained omnipotence through union with the superego by participating in the omnipotence of the object. The mirthful mood of mania has been economically explained as due to the release in psychic tension between the ego and superego. The manic exaggeration has defensive qualities which betray the lack of genuine freedom. The patient suffers, has sleep and work disturbances, and may develop exhaustion or stupor. The apparent hypergenitality of the typical manic has an oral character which aims at the incorporation of all objects. The hunger for new objects coexists with a rapid destruction of objects in fantasy, corresponding to cycles of introjection and projection, or of oral incorporation and elimination. The object representation is split into good and bad. The bad object is expelled from the ego while the good object is introjected into the superego.

Clinical Example

Abraham (1924) cited the following: "I had a patient in whom certain events brought on a parathymic condition when he was already well forward in his analysis. It passed off much more lightly than his earlier attacks of depression had done, and resembled in some of its main features an obsessional condition. This state was followed by a very slight deviation in the direction of mania. It passed over after a few days, and then the patient told me that during that short period he had felt the desire to indulge in some form of excess. He said: 'I had the feeling that I must eat a great deal of meat— that I must go on eating till I was absolutely glutted'. He had thought of it as a yielding to a kind of intoxication or orgy.

"In this instance it was quite evident that the patient's manic state was ultimately nothing else than an orgy of a cannibalistic character. His words, quoted above, are convincing evidence of the correctness of Freud's view that in mania the ego is celebrating the festival of its liberation. That celebration takes the form in phantasy of a wild excess in eating flesh, as to whose cannibalistic significance enough has already been said, I trust, to leave no room for doubt.

"Like melancholia, the reactive manic parathymia takes a certain length of time in which to work itself off. Gradually the narcissistic requirements of the ego diminish and larger quantities of libido are set free and can be transferred to external objects. Thus, after both phases of the illness have passed off, the libido is able to attain a relatively real relation to its objects. That this relation remains incomplete has already been fully shown in the chapter dealing with the fixation of the libido in the anal-sadistic phase.

"In this phase we must consider a point which has already been discussed in connection with melancholia. Freud has drawn a very instructive parallel between mania and the celebration of a festival by the ego; and he has associated that festival with the totem-feast of primitive people, that is, with man's 'primal crime' which consisted in killing and eating the primal father. What I must here point out is that the criminal phantasies of the manic patient are for the most part directed against his mother. A striking illustration of this was given by one of my patients who had a delusion during his manic excitement that he was the emperor Nero. He afterwards accounted for this by the fact that Nero had killed his own mother, and had also had the idea of burning the city of Rome (as a mother-symbol). Let me once more add that those emotions directed towards the mother are a secondary kind; they were in the first instance aimed at the father, as became quite evident in the course of the analysis referred to above.

"We are now, therefore, able to some extent to understand the reactive state of exaltation following upon melancholia as a pleasurable emancipation on the part of the individual from the painful relation in which he has hitherto been to his introjected object of love. But we know that an attack of mania can come on without having been preceded by a melancholia. However, if we remember what has been said in the previous chapter, we shall not be quite at a loss to account for this fact. In that chapter we showed that certain definite psychological traumas in the early childhood of the patient caused a state of mind in him which we called the 'primal parathymia'. In 'pure' mania, which is frequently of periodic occurrence, the patient seems to me to be shaking off that primal parathymia without having had any attack of melancholia in the clinical sense. But lack of suitable data forbids me to make any definite statements in this connection."

Related Concept: DEPRESSION.

REFERENCE

Abraham, K., 1924, "A Study of the Development of the Libido Viewed in the Light of Mental Disorders." *SPA*, pp. 473–475, 1942.

ADDITIONAL READINGS

Freud, S., 1917, "Mourning and Melancholia." *SE*, 14, 1957.
Kanzer, M., "Manic-Depressive Psychoses with Paranoid Trends." *IntJPsa*, 33, 1952.
Scott, W.: "A Note on the Psychopathology of Convulsive Phenomena in Manic Depressive States." *IntJPsa*, 27, 1946.
    "On the Intense Affects Encountered in Treating a Severe Manic Depressive Disorder." *IntJPsa*, 28, 1947.
Thompson, C. M., "Analytic Observations During the Course of a Manic-Depressive Psychosis." *R*, 17, 1930.

1304
MANNERISM, a term employed by Feldman (1959) to express a language habit, is defined as a gesture which is used to both reveal and conceal unconscious processes; a form of communication. In this, he identified nonverbal communication as belonging to mannerisms of speech because they replace speech and vice versa. Thus, the "working through" of a physical gesture or verbal cliché is considered as an important element in the analytic treatment. "If they are neglected, a valuable opportunity to reach more fundamental conflicts might be missed."

In working through the mannerisms, strong resistance is at first encountered, but when some insight into the meaning of these unconscious phenomena is achieved, significant progress can be expected. Feldman noted: "Some habits are disadvantageous to the patient and their cure is a deeply cherished secondary gain of psychoanalytic treatment. The nuclear complex ... of neurosis can be found in the patient's habitual actions which should be analyzed."

Related Concepts: REPRESSION; RESISTANCE.

REFERENCE

Feldman, S., *Mannerisms of Speech and Gestures in Everyday Life.* IUP, pp. 5, 232, 1959.

ADDITIONAL READINGS

Berne, E., "Concerning the Nature of Communication." *PQ*, 27, 1953.
Darwin, C., *The Expression of the Emotions in Man and in Animals.* London: Murray, 1873.
Feldman, S., "Mannerisms of Speech: A Contribution to the Working Through Process." *Q*, 17, 1948.
Loewenstein, R., "Some Remarks on the Role of Speech in Psychoanalytic Technique." *IntJPsa*, 37, 1956.
Rangell, L., "The Psychology of Poise." *IntJPsa*, 37, 1954.

1305
MARRIAGE is legally defined in most societies as the union between two heterosexual partners especially joined to serve the sexual aims of the two parties and, as well, to serve in the support of the progeny that derives from it. Psychologically, it may not be possible to define a happy marriage, for, as Freud (1919) pointed out, the constituent elements can no longer be separated out to form a synthesis of the behavior involved. Psychoanalysis is specifically directed toward an understanding of the resistances which divide the minds of neurotic patients, in which the symptoms are broken up into their elements and the resistances are removed. In the normal adult, however, the great unifier— the ego—does not allow for such an intervention. This, coupled with the fact that original aims have long since been sublimated (or perhaps repressed, or both), does not allow the analyst to directly perceive how such a psycho-synthesis occurred. In *Anna Karenina,** Tolstoy observed: "Happy families are all alike; every unhappy family is un-

_____
* Published by Random House, N.Y.

happy in its own way." This might well be paraphrased with respect to marriage.

From a societal point of view, marriage is no doubt valuable and it is therefore not surprising to find that such arrangements as free love, temporary marriage, trial marriage, etc. do not long survive as substitute instrumentalities. No doubt while many marital problems are caused by neurotic manifestations like frigidity, promiscuity, impotence, alcoholism, etc., it is still necessary to admit that even two normal people can become unhappy in their marriage.

Nonetheless, pathological conditions may, in fact, be responsible for the unhappy marriage. As Freud (1919) pointed out, the marriage partners may exchange their neuroses for an unhappy marriage. The course of a marriage may be altered, as Freud later (in 1933) noted, by the birth of a child. The wife's identification with her own mother may be revived and the circumstances of her parents' "bad" marriage may be reproduced (compulsion to repeat).

Clinical Example

"David was married to a cold and unattractive woman, ten years his senior. While he complained about the choice he had made, he hesitated to divorce the woman whom he disliked intensely. Analysis disclosed that his frigid wife was the only woman with whom he was potent. Before and during his marriage he had tried to have sexual intercourse with women he found desirable but failed to have an erection. His passive feminine desires interfered with his masculine role. When he was attracted to a pretty woman, he not only wanted to have her but also to be like her. This wish to have a vagina in addition to a penis made the execution of the sexual act impossible.

"The patient was potent with his homely wife because he had no wish to identify himself with her. While he consciously resented being tied to a woman so different from the ones he pictured in his daydreams, he was reluctant to leave her because it meant depriving himself of the only outlet for his genital desires. Confronted by the choice of being impotent or unhappily married, he preferred to remain with his unattractive and aggressive spouse who allowed him to discharge his hostility and remain free of guilt feelings. . . .

"A neurotic choice of mate may be the result of various unconscious defense mechanisms. Fixation or regression to one of the three stages of development generally lies at the core of the problem. Thus, defense mechanisms that are directed against an awareness of phallic wishes may be separated from defense mechanisms originating at the anal or oral stages. All three types of defense mechanisms can interfere with the choice of mate by making a person select someone who helps partly to gratify and partly to deny the presence of infantile wishes. In other words, whenever a neurotic choice is made, the patient, instead of choosing a person with whom he could be happy, has selected an object he needs in order to avoid recognizing what he is afraid of. The defense mechanisms used to achieve this aim lead to various pathological formations that are ego accepted and can therefore be differentiated from neurotic symptoms." [Eidelberg, 1956.]

Related Concept: PROMISCUITY.

REFERENCES

Eidelberg, L., "Neurotic Choice of Mate," in *Neurotic Interaction in Marriage*, V. W. Eisenstein, ed. BB, pp. 57, 60, 1956.
Freud, S.: 1919, "Lines of Advance in Psycho-Analytic Therapy." *SE*, 17:161, 163, 1955.
        1933, "New Introductory Lectures on Psycho-Analysis." *SE*, 22:133–134, 1964.

ADDITIONAL READING

Eisenstein, V. W., ed., *Neurotic Interaction in Marriage*. BB, 1956.

1306

MASCULINITY AND FEMININITY. Freud used three approaches in the study of this concept: (a) analytically, he considered *masculine* to be a synonym for active, and *feminine,* for passive; (b) biologically, the presence of spermatozoa or ova, respectively, characterized the male from the female; and (c) sociologically, he described a man and a woman as mixtures of both male and female characteristics, in which male qualities were dominate in men, and female qualities, in women. Freud (1905) noted: "Since I have become acquainted with the notion of bisexuality I have regarded it as the decisive factor."

For many years, Freud (1925) referred to *male* as active and *female* as passive, and considered the libido *male*. In addition, he introduced the concept of active and passive aims, i.e., the subject's activity may seek active or passive forms of gratification. As he considered an individual a mixture of both sexes, he referred to activity in women as representing their masculine part, and to passivity in men as indicative of their feminine traits.

However, Bergler and Eidelberg (1933) pointed out that the use of the concept activity = masculinity would imply that the mother who takes care of her infant is obviously not only active (but also gratifying an active aim) and would then have to be described as expressing masculine traits. In addition, the hypothesis that masculine libido is responsible for male and female behavior would lead to the assumption that a sensuous and seductive woman, engaged in love-making, sought the gratification of her masculine libido and that her behavior indicated the masculine aspect of her personality.

Little children do not know the difference between male and female, and assume that both sexes possess a penis. When they discover the lack of a penis in women, they often assume that the penis has been removed. Consequently, boys often respond to this discovery with fears of castration; and girls with penis envy.

According to Max Hartmann, who quotes Cleveland, the *Trichonympha* may copulate, the weaker one playing the female role; the stronger, the male role. This observation is similar to a suggestion expressed by Ferenczi (1924) in *Versuch einer Genitaltheorie* (translated).

Related Concepts: ACTIVITY AND PASSIVITY; BISEXUALITY; FETISHISM; SEXUALITY.

REFERENCES

Eidelberg, L., & E. Bergler, "Der Mammakomplex des Mannes," *Z*, 19:574, 1933.
Ferenczi, S., 1924, "Theory of Genitality." *Q*, 2:361–403, 1933.
Freud, S.: 1905, "Three Essays on the Theory of Sexuality." *SE*, 7:220, 1953.
    1925, "Some Psychical Consequences of the Anatomical Distinction Between the Sexes." *SE*, 19:255, 1961.
Hartmann, Max, *Einführung in die allgemeine Biologie*. Sammlung Göschen, Band 96, Berlin: Gruyter, 1956.

1307

MASOCHISM. A distinction is made between the moral masochist* who accepts defeat under the condition that his actions are unconsciously self-provoked and the masochistic pervert who, while also seeking physical or mental unpleasure, achieves a genital discharge under the condition of being humiliated and punished. The masochistic pervert denies the pleasure he obtains and believes that the pleasure of his experiences are not directly related to the punishment he unconsciously seeks. The punishment produces a genital stimulation; or, more properly, without the punishment a genital stimulation is blocked. After this stimulation by punishment has taken place, the genital pleasure is experienced consciously in masturbation or in intercourse. Generally, most masochistic perverts are also moral masochists. In the latter condition the masochistic behavior which leads to unpleasure represents a discharge of countercathetic energy, in the following ways: (a) by identification with the aggressor (whose activity is provoked by the patient), (b) by the sexualization of a defeat, and (c) by having the power to provoke the aggressor. [Eidelberg, 1954.]

Freud at first (1905) viewed masochism as sadism turned on the self. The concept of pain as a condition for genital pleasure, rather than as a direct source of pleasure, eliminated the contradiction between masochism and the pleasure principle. Study of beating fantasies led to the concept of masochism as a form of anal-sadistic regression of oedipal strivings, under the influence of the superego and the unconscious need for punishment. After the introduction of the structural theory, the defensive aspects of masochism and its role in preserving object relations were stressed. Equal emphasis was placed on the multiple functions of masochistic character formation in a great variety of mental disorders. According to Freud (1924), patients who appeared to have too strict a conscience were referred to as moral masochists (masochistic character trait). This type of masochism is not related to erotism; rather, it is a norm of neurotic behavior, a concern with unpleasure itself. Moral masochists are often referred to as those

---

* Usually connected with pseudomoralistic attitude, employed as a rationalization.

who cannot tolerate success. Like other neurotics, they prefer punishment and humiliation to a feeling of guilt or remorse because, as a result of punishment, they are "permitted" to continue to sin. Consequently, such behavior is good neither for the individual nor his morality. The superego of such an individual is referred to as being sexualized and sadistic.

The unpleasure of the masochistic pervert differs from the unpleasure which the normal individual tolerates in accordance with the reality principle; rather, it is an unpleasure which the masochist requires to gratify his unconscious need for punishment. By unconscious identification with the sadistic partner, the masochist gratifies his own sadistic impulses. Through this form of *folie à deux*, the masochist is able to retain his illusion of infantile omnipotence. The *provocation* which the masochist unconsciously exercises is used to control the aggressor and thus helps the masochist to maintain the illusion of his omnipotence. Unprovoked defeat may be unacceptable, for it represents a narcissistic mortification. At the same time, the sadistic component-drive finds gratification in whatever aggression is contained in the provocation.

In comparing the analytic technique employed in the treatment of masochistic perverts and moral masochists (masochistic character), Eidelberg (1955) noted: "We may say that in dealing with the perversion we do not have to prove to the patient that he is responsible for the punishment he suffers. On the other hand, it is quite difficult to induce the masochistic pervert to decrease the amount of his masochistic gratification in order to dam up the instinctual energy so that it will produce more psychological derivatives in the analysis. In the treatment of both the perversion and the masochistic character, the problem of the recognition, and final elimination, of the infantile omnipotence is of decisive importance.

"To fail in his analysis, to be dismissed as incurable is more important to the masochist than to get cured. Only God knows how, in spite of this, some masochists are prepared to allow the analyst to assist in their cure. The recognition that *they* have the power to wreck the treatment, and that the analyst depends on their good will, may sometimes induce them to appear charitable and surrender their unlimited power to obtain self-punishment in exchange for a limited ability to succeed.

"Some analysts have attempted to solve the complicated problem of masochism by saying that the masochist does not 'really' crave unpleasure, but that he wants something which merely appears as unpleasure to others. This is a mistake! While it is true that different people consider different things as pleasant, and while most of us agree that the fact that we dislike something should not be used as proof that everybody else must dislike it too, there are also objective criteria for what analysis considers to be unpleasure.

"First, any increase of our instinctual tension above a certain level is experienced as unpleasure, although this level varies with different individuals. Secondly, a narcissistic mortification, caused by an external object which has the power to overcome us and to force us to act contrary to our wishes, produces the experience of unpleasure. Consequently, we refer to an individual as a masochist only if he finds that he is interested in aims which are not only unpleasant to us, but are also unpleasant to him. A masochistic pervert, who has to be beaten in order to achieve a genital stimulation, experiences the pain inflicted on him as unpleasant, but he accepts this unpleasure because, without it, he is unable to obtain a genital discharge.

"The patient with a masochistic character trait resents the humiliations he provokes, but at the same time, he *enjoys the power* he has to force the external object to punish him. Furthermore, this punishment, although painful, represents not only hostility, but also love and attention. A normal person may accept, in jest, being ridiculed, and may enjoy being laughed at as a sign of his ability to make the listener laugh. However, different from the masochist, he is aware of what he is doing.

"It is easy to see that a child, having feelings of remorse because he has been naughty, looks for punishment. Such a punishment frees him from the unpleasure connected with the feeling of remorse, and is preferable to it. We also can understand that an adult, tortured by his superego because of the 'crime' he committed, may surrender voluntarily to the authorities and accept their punishment.

"The masochist's need of punishment becomes

understandable if he discovers the crimes he keeps on committing in his unconscious. Like other neurotics, he does not differentiate in his unconscious between wishes and actions. Consequently, whenever he has a hostile wish, he develops a feeling of remorse instead of a feeling of guilt. In other words, instead of rejecting his prohibited infantile wish, he gratifies it partly, with the help of his neurotic character trait, and he needs punishment to free himself from this consequent feeling of remorse. Whereas a normal person, after recognizing the presence of an aggressive wish may reject this wish, aided by the feeling of guilt, and feel proud of his moral achievement, the neurotic reacts to his wish as if this wish represented an act, and he is therefore unable to remain moral. Instead, he has no other choice but to accept punishment for the presence of his hostile wishes."

1. Feminine Masochism. A form of masochism in male patients that arises from an unconscious identification with a humiliated woman. Their masochistic fantasies place them in a characteristically feminine situation, to signify being castrated, being copulated with, etc. [See **607.**]

2. Frigidity and Masochism. A repressed masochistic wish is the causal agent in frigidity. The woman comes to regard sexual intercourse as an aggresssive act of perforation, from which she seeks protection by becoming frigid. Commonly, frigid women have masochistic masturbation fantasies, i.e., they experience a narcissistic mortification, a humiliation which permits a genital discharge to occur. [See **621.**]

3. Impotence and Masochism. Many impotent males manifest masochistic wishes and are only able to achieve genital discharge through the employment of masochistic fantasies while masturbating. In this, they play both roles, the humiliated man and the humiliating woman. [See **906.**]

4. Masochistic Mechanism. A process wherein the subject renders external frustrations harmless by actively creating his own humiliating frustrations, i.e., in utilizing a self-produced defeat. Here, the subject enjoys the power he has in his fantasy to force an external object to punish him. [See **1308.**]

5. Moral Masochism. In the analytic situation, it leads to a negative therapeutic reaction. The patient sets himself against recovery, and the approach of a therapeutic improvement is dreaded as though it were a danger. His unconscious sense of guilt is experienced as a resistance to recovery, an expression of his need for punishment at the hands of the parental imagos. Moral masochism is characterized by an acceptance of defeat under the condition that actions are unconsciously self-provoked, leading to unpleasure. [See **1329.**]

6. Negative Therapeutic Reaction and Masochism. A component action of moral masochism, in which the patient sets himself against therapeutic change. The patient strives for unpleasure, believing that his guilt must be endured. He seeks to provoke a punishment from the parental representative, the analyst, and thus to defy him. [See **1412.**]

7. Pleasure-Unpleasure Principle and Masochism. The masochist seeks unpleasure in order to avoid a punishment which he fears even more (e.g., castration). He thus avoids a feeling of guilt or remorse or an external narcissistic mortification. [See **1635.**]

8. Primary Masochism. A basic instinct which does not produce psychological derivatives and which is referred to as being *silent*. Combined with the life instincts, however, it produces the sexual and aggressive instinct-fusions. [See **1656.**]

9. Self-Esteem and Masochism. Some masochists appear to be lacking in self-esteem and accuse themselves of all kinds of deficiencies; an unconscious denial of infantile omnipotence. [See **1917.**]

Related Concepts: DEPRESSION; EXHIBITIONISM; PARANOIA; PROJECTION; SADISM; SCOPOPHILIA.

REFERENCES

Eidelberg, L.: *An Outline of a Comparative Pathology of the Neuroses.* IUP, pp. 174–179, 198–199, 1954.

    1955, "Technical Problems in the Analysis of Masochists." *JHH*, 7:107–108, 1958.

Freud, S.: 1905, "Three Contributions to the Theory of Sexuality." *SE*, 7:157–160, 1953.
 1924, "The Economic Problem of Masochism." *SE*, 19:157–170, 1961.

ADDITIONAL READINGS

Adams, W. R., "The Masochistic Character: Genesis and Treatment." *BPAP*, 9, 1959.

Berliner, B., "The Role of Object Relations in Moral Masochism." *Q*, 27, 1958.

Bernstein, I., "The Role of Narcissism in Moral Masochism." *Q*, 26, 1957.

Bieber, I., "The Meaning of Masochism." *PT*, 7, 1953.

Blumstein, A., "Masochism and Fantasies of Preparing to be Incorporated." *JAPA*, 7, 1959.

Brenner, C., "Psychopathology of the Masochistic Character: Illustrative Cases." *JNMD*, 123, 1956.

Brown, B. S., & M. Nyswander, "The Treatment of Masochistic Adults." *Ops*, 26, 1956.

Gardiner, M. M., "Feminine Masochism and Passivity." *BPAP*, 5, 1955.

Glatzer, H. T., "Analysis of Masochism in Group Psychotherapy." *IntJgrpPt*, 9, 1959.

Richter, H., "The Basis of Masochism." *Nervenarzt*, 25, 1954.

Stein, M. H., reporter, "The Problem of Masochism in the Theory and Technique of Psychoanalysis." *JAPA*, 4, 1956.

1308

MASOCHISTIC MECHANISM is denotative of a psychic process in which the subject renders external frustrations harmless by actively creating his own humiliating frustrations, instead of passively enduring them. This mechanism may cease to operate after it has been thoroughly analyzed, because the self-produced defeats can replace the real ones so long as they appear to be real to the subject. "Metapsychologically," as Eidelberg (1948) noted, "this masochistic mechanism belongs to the already familiar mechanisms, such as projection, introjection, repression, and reaction formation."

Elsewhere, Eidelberg (1958) described the mechanism, as follows: "We refer to an individual as a masochist only if he finds that he is interested in aims which are not only unpleasant to us, but are also unpleasant to him. A masochistic pervert, who has to be beaten in order to achieve a genital stimulation, experiences the pain inflicted on him as unpleasant, but he accepts this unpleasure because, without it, he is unable to obtain a genital discharge.

"The patient with a masochistic character trait resents the humiliations he provokes, but at the same time, he *enjoys the power* he has to force the external object to punish him. Furthermore, this punishment, although painful, represents not only hostility, but also love and attention. A normal person may accept, in jest, being ridiculed, and may enjoy being laughed at as a sign of his ability to make the listener laugh. However, different from the masochist, he is aware of what he is doing."

Related Concepts: MASOCHISM; PERVERSION.

REFERENCES

Eidelberg, L.: *Studies in Psychoanalysis*. IUP, p. 40, 1948.
 "Technical Problems in the Analysis of Masochists." *JHH*, 7:107–108, 1958.

1309

MASS (GROUP) PSYCHOLOGY. Freud (1921) identified mass psychology as the oldest form of human psychology. In using Darwin's hypothesis of the primal horde, Freud did not dogmatically identify the original organization of primitive society; he did point out, however, that the matriarchal form may have occurred after a breakdown of the patriarchal society. He noted that the mother deities had male priests who were castrated for the mother's protection. But he also admitted (as did Bachofen, Graves, and others) the possibility that the matriarchal society was the first primitive organization.

Each form of the mass may thus be the result of an individual or a mass to replace the father of the primal horde, for it is only with the establishment of the patriarchal form of society that individual efforts met with success. "It was then, perhaps, that some individual, in the exigency of his longing, may have been moved to free himself from the group* and take over the father's part." This struggle is best exemplified in the birth of the heroic myth, in which the poet or story teller creates a hero who is a man "who by himself had slain the father—the father who still appeared in the myth as a totemic monster." The very act of this creation—that of the hero

* The German word *Masse* might be more properly translated as *mass*, not *group*.

—may have set its creator free from the mass, at least in his imagination.

In the analytic situation the therapist does not completely disregard the problem of the mass; however, no matter how he may concentrate on the individual's problem, the patient's tie with other individuals and with the mass will intervene. Nonetheless, in the therapist's examination of the individual, there is a differentiation to be made as between the patient's autistic and narcissistic needs and his social needs. The group or the mass is not interested in the discovery of the truth; rather, it requires illusions and cannot exist without them, for the unreal is always more important than the real. Thus, the differentiation between truth and untruth is often completely lacking.

In the study of the unconscious, Freud was able to show that fantasy or delusion of a wish, representing at the same time not only a need but its gratification, is of basic importance. The neurotics are dominated not by external but by internal reality. In hysteria, we find often a symptom which is based on the fantasy of the original trauma; in obsessional neurosis, the feelings of guilt and remorse are caused by an unconscious wish. In groups and in neurotics the reality testing plays an inferior role.

In discussing Le Bon's* thesis, Freud took exception to the notion that whenever living beings are gathered together, they accept a leader—*any* leader —because a group cannot exist without such a master. Such a leader has to love chiefly himself while the members of the mass must have the illusion that the leader loves all of them equally. As noted, Freud used Darwin's concept of the primitive horde ruled by the powerful father, wherein the sons were not permitted to have sexual relations with the female members of the mass. The sons' relation to the father was described as one of identification, being ambivalent in nature. Consequently, the sons wanted to become similar to the father and therefore tried finally to eliminate him.

Freud did not describe the emotional relationship of the female members of the horde to the leader. He did not mention whether they were competing with each other and felt envy or jealousy. However, he did point out that finally one female member was responsible for the termination of the rule of the

powerful father. It was Le Bon's contention that man's thirst for obedience is the real cause of the acceptance of a master. It is possible, according to Freud, that the youngest son became a hero protected by his mother. The prehistoric woman is often described as the prize of a battle, in which she may have taken an active part as its instigator.

McDougall* claimed that the regression present in the group can be avoided if the group is highly organized. Freud agreed that this regression could be avoided. The individual living outside of the group possessed his own self-consciousness, differentiating between himself and his competitor. However, after he became a member of the mass he lost his individuality. Instead, the mass accepted some of the qualities of the individual it incorporated, a fact which appears to be in accordance with Trotter's statement that the formation of organized masses tends to be similar to the multicellular structure of higher organisms. Trotter thus considered gregariousness as analogous to multicellularity.

Freud accepted Trotter's[†] suggestion of a herd instinct. However, Trotter, like McDougall, seemed to overlook the importance of the role of the leader, while Freud emphasized that for the group to exist it had to have a leader. He studied the relationship between the members of the group and the leader in two organizations—the army and the church— and pointed out that while in the army the soldiers seemed to identify chiefly with other soldiers while insisting on being justly and equally treated by the leader, in the church, the individual identifies with the leader. While there is no doubt that highly organized groups show less regression that unorganized ones, Freud pointed out that in religion and in science those outside of the group are treated as enemies. Basically, every religion offers love only to those who accept it, and, conversely, is cruel to heretics. Believers in religion cannot escape this aggressive approach, while those who do not believe are free of this kind of cruelty.

In addition, Freud described the panic which takes place whenever a disintegration of the mass has occurred and compared the affect of panic to that of neurotic anxiety. His description, thus, of the mass as "impulsive," "changeable," and "irritable,"

---

* Le Bon, G., 1895, *The Crowd: A Study of the Popular Mind*. London, 1920.

* McDougall, W., *The Group Mind*. Cambridge, 1920.
† Trotter, W., *The Instincts of the Herd in Peace and War*. London, 1916.

led by the unconscious, corresponds to the behavior of the neurotic.

Related Concepts: IDENTIFICATION; MYTHOLOGY.

REFERENCE

Freud, S., 1921, "Group Psychology and the Analysis of the Ego." *SE*, 18:80–81, 86–87, 98, 99, 116, 118, 123, 135, 136, 137, 1955.

1310

MASS HYSTERIA denotes the behavior of a large group of people, which is similar to the behavior found in individuals having hysterical character traits, frequently characterized by irrational actions and fears that interfere with the function of the whole group; a reaction to a danger signal which is excessive, paralyzing, uncoordinated, irrational, or even paranoid (e.g., the public's reaction to the famous radio program depicting a fictional invasion from Mars, which was regarded as actual by many listeners). An important factor in mass hysteria is the failure or absence of adequate leadership (mob action). Sometimes, the wrath of the masses turns against their leader, and he tries to divert their aroused destructive tendencies toward an underling, a minority group, or other scapegoat.

Freud (1921) supplied the following example of hysteria in a group. A girl in a boarding school receives a letter from her lover and experiences jealousy because of it; i.e., she produces hysterical symptoms. As a result, some of her friends will produce exactly the same symptoms, for they, too, wish to play the same role (identification). They also would like to have a lover and, as a result, accept the punishment connected with it. Their symptoms are not the result of their sympathy with the subject suffering from the hysterical symptoms. Such an identification takes place under the condition that very little sympathy exists between the girl and her "friends."

Related Concept: GROUP PARANOIA.

REFERENCE

Freud, S., 1921, "Group Psychology and the Analysis of the Ego." *SE*, 18:107, 1955.

ADDITIONAL READINGS

Allport, G. W., & L. Postman, *The Psychology of Rumor*. HH. 1947.
Cantril, H., *The Invasion from Mars*. PUP, 1940.
Kris, E., "Danger and Morals." *Ops*, 14, 1944.
Sperling, O., "Failure of Leadership." *PsaSS*, 1955.

1311

MASTURBATION denotes the use of the self as the object of erotic stimulation and gratification. Masturbation is universally practiced in infancy and youth, and is regarded as a normal psychosexual manifestation during that period. Masturbation by adults, apart from periods of transition or sexual deprivation, is considered a pathological symptom. According to Eidelberg (1954), masturbation by adults under most circumstances may be considered a perversion. The significance of masturbation is neglible from a physical viewpoint; its meaning and importance depend on the fantasies expressed by or accompanying it, the fantasy life bound up with it, and the anxieties and conflicts resulting from it. As the main expression of sexuality in infancy and youth, it is part of an attempt to master intense impressions, and to anticipate and prepare for future excitements. The discharge of genital wishes is frequently accompanied by mobilization of fear and guilt leading to masturbatory conflicts.

In the phallic phase, the fantasies centering on the oedipal constellation are an integral part of masturbation; in adolescence and later life, the original guilt linked with these fantasies is displaced onto the act of masturbation itself. The sense of guilt accompanying masturbation makes it a psychosexual phenomenon of prime importance. Masturbation, as with some other defense mechanisms, may be used by neurotics as a proof of potency, a defense against aggressive wishes (mobilization of the opposite wish and self-castration), and a provocation for punishment (masochistic provocation).

Ontogenetically, at the primary narcissistic stage of development in earliest infancy, autoerotism undergoes gradual changes with ego maturation and the awareness of environmental objects and their functioning. If genital masturbation has been repressed, regressive substitutes may be used, as when an older child or adult favors oral, anal, urethral, or other masturbation equivalents. During adolescence, absence of masturbation suggests that sexual urges have been overwhelmed by fear and guilt. Girls tend to relinquish masturbation at an earlier age than boys; penis envy often plays a role in this development or may affect the form of their masturbation.

The first objective appraisal of masturbation as a common psychosexual phenomenon occurred only with the emergence and development of psychoanalysis (Freud, 1905). A review of the preanalytic literature reveals a primarily moralistic attitude or, later, a sadistically tinged "antimasturbatory" attitude. With the further development of psychoanalytic theory and technique, the significance of masturbation, and the struggle against it, was seen in the larger framework of character formation, resolution of the oedipus complex, maturation of the ego, and development of the superego.

In an essay written in 1912, Freud summarized the problem, as follows:

(a) The masturbation fantasy must be analyzed because it represents an important approach to the understanding of the masturbator;

(b) The masturbation as such does not produce pathological results;

(c) The sense of guilt felt by the masturbator may be caused either by the lack of full gratification or social factors;

(d) All children go through the stage of masturbation; and

(e) It is still too early to say whether the mechanism of masturbation represents a danger or whether the actual neuroses are caused by masturbation.

Related Concepts: AUTOEROTISM; EROTOGENIC ZONES; OMNIPOTENCE OF THOUGHT.

REFERENCES

Eidelberg, L., *An Outline of a Comparative Pathology of the Neuroses.* IUP, p. 205, 1954.
Freud, S.: 1905, "Three Essays on the Theory of Sexuality." *SE*, 7:185–190, 192, 219–221, 234, 272, 274, 1953.
     1912, "Contributions to a Discussion on Masturbation." *SE*, 12:245–246, 1958.

ADDITIONAL READINGS

Arlow, J., "Masturbation and Symptom Formation." *JAPA*, 1, 1953.
Bornstein, B., "Masturbation in the Latency Period." *PsaStC*, 3, 1953.
Eidelberg, L., "A Contribution to the Study of the Masturbation Fantasy." *IntJPsa*, 26, 1945.
Hug-Hellmuth, H. von, "On Female Masturbation." *C*, 3, 1912.
Landauer, K., "Die Onanieselbstbeschuldigungen in Psychosen." *PsaP*, 2, 1927–1928.
Meng, H., "Das Problem der Onanie von Kant bis Freud." *PsaP*, 2, 1927–1928.
Reich, W., "Über Spezifität der Onanieformen." *Z*, 8, 1922.
Roheim, G., "Masturbation Fantasies." *PQ*, 20, 1945.
Spitz, R. A., "Authority and Masturbation: Some Remarks on a Bibliographical Investigation." *Q*, 21, 1952.
Stekel, W., "Ein Fall von Larvierter Onanie." *C*, 3, 1913.
Tamm, A., "Prophylaxe und Behandlung der Onanie." *PsaP*, 4, 1930.
Tausk, V., "On Masturbation." *PsaStC*, 6, 1951.

1312

MASTURBATION ADDICTS are those individuals who continuously discharge instinctual tension through masturbation. Simmel (1930) believed that some individuals used drugs instead of masturbation. The use of drugs may at first represent genital masturbation, which regresses to the oral stage. As with masturbation, the drug eliminates the need for a partner.

Fenichel (1945) used the term masturbation addicts to refer to "extreme types" of "compulsive masturbators," who are "frequently chronic neurasthenics. Masturbation may become the uniform response to any kind of stimulus. . . . In severe cases of 'sexual addictions,' sexuality loses its specific function and becomes an unsuccessful nonspecific protection against stimuli." Masturbation may also be used to deny an external narcissistic mortification.

Related Concepts: ADDICTION; ALCOHOLISM; MASTURBATION.

REFERENCES

Fenichel, O., *The Psychoanalytic Theory of Neurosis.* Nor, pp. 191, 384, 1945.

Simmel, E., "Zum Problem von Zwang und Sucht," Report, Fifth General Medical Congress for Psychotherapy, Baden-Baden, 1930.

ADDITIONAL READING

Crowley, R., "Psychoanalytic Literature on Drug Addiction and Alcoholism." *R,* 26, 1939.

1313

MASTURBATION EQUIVALENTS denotes those autoerotic activities in which bodily areas and parts, other than the genitals, are sexualized and used to achieve sexual pleasure and discharge (e.g., mouth, breast, anus, urethra, skin, and musculature; motor activity in general, or, of a specific type; the organs of sensation and perception). After genital masturbation, or its equivalent, has been repressed, another body area becomes a regressive substitute for it.

Masturbation equivalents often constitute a compulsion. They are frequently viewed by the subjects as an antimasturbatory measure, and may have been initiated as such, but they eventually acquire the content, both cathetic and ideational, of the original, repressed masturbation. Fenichel (1945) noted: "Since the genitals in the infant play only the part of *primus inter apres*, autoerotic activities of little children are by no means limited to genital masturbation. All erogenous zones may be stimulated autoerotically. If, however, an adult or an older child indulges predominantly in various kinds of anal, oral, urethral, muscular (etc.) masturbation equivalents, analysis regularly reveals that this represents a regressive substitute for genital masturbation after the latter had been repressed."

Related Concepts: AUTOEROTISM; COMPULSIVE MASTURBATION; NORMAL MASTURBATION.

REFERENCE

Fenichel, O., *The Psychoanalytic Theory of Neurosis.* Nor, pp. 75–77, 1945.

1314

MASTURBATION FANTASIES. An analysis of these fantasies, like the acts of perverts, indicates that they are ego-syntonic. The individual may have a number of such fantasies, but they usually show a similar structure. The fantasies bound up with masturbation are extremely significant, more significant, in fact, than the physical act, and examination of them can be an important contribution to an understanding of the patient.

Eidelberg (1948) provided the following example and analysis of a masturbatory fantasy: "Since puberty he had masturbated with the following fantasy: A brutal landlord forces a young woman who is unable to pay her rent to have sexual intercourse with him. The patient at first avoided describing in detail the masturbation with this fantasy calling it vaguely a fantasy of sexual intercourse which produced a satisfactory climax without ejaculatio praecox. The analysis of this patient and his fantasy allows the following interpretation of its unconscious meaning: The patient identified himself partly with the brutal landlord or, to use descriptive language, disguised as the landlord he satisfied his sadistic wishes. Obviously, only in uniting in one action his aggressive as well as his sexual tendencies, was he able to achieve an orgasm. The successful sexual discharge was dependent on his ability to humiliate the woman he was having intercourse with.

"The patient's behaviour was due to the fact that when, as a boy of four, he exhibited his penis in front of his mother, she not only frustrated his wish by refusing to admire his performance, but, in addition, she punished him severely. As a result of this behaviour of his mother, he had suffered, not only a damming up of his exhibitionistic wishes, but, in addition, a narcissistic mortification. As a result, so to speak, of this double blow, he became interested, not only in finding an object which would allow him the satisfaction of the suppressed libidinal wishes, but in one which would also take the punishment for the humiliation he suffered as a child. Thus, the landlord who forced the young woman to have sexual intercourse with him was not only seeking a sexual pleasure, but, was also seeking an aggressive pleasure, so that he might avenge himself for the humiliation he had suffered in the past. The masturbation fantasy enabled the patient to repeat in an active way the trauma he had suffered in a passive way from his mother....

"An even greater resistance was encountered when the deeper part of his masturbation fantasy was examined. The results were as follows: The young woman in the fantasy represents, not only his mother, but also that part of the patient which, by identification with her attitude toward her husband, has become *passive feminine*. In other words, the patient satisfies his wishes, not only by playing the role of the brutal landlord, but also by being, at the same time, the raped young woman. This young woman was able to satisfy her sexual wishes without feelings of guilt because, consciously, she did not enjoy the sexual intercourse and accepted it only under pressure. The fact that she was raped and humiliated served as a kind of camouflage for the presence of his sexual pleasure."

Eidelberg concluded: "In each of these examples a genital discharge is achieved, while the patient imagines acts which deviate more or less from what is considered to be normal sexual intercourse. In order to facilitate the study of these masturbation phantasies, we have separated the examination of the structure of these phantasies from that of the accompanying masturbation. The study of these phantasies shows that, in addition to a manifest content which looks like a simple wish fulfillment of the conscious personality of the patient, there is also a latent content, unconscious to him. The analysis of this latent content shows that these phantasies are the result of an unconscious defense by the Ego and the Super Ego against the infantile wish from the Id. These phantasies represent, like other defense mechanisms, a partial satisfaction of an infantile wish and a denial of an infantile narcissistic mortification. The satisfaction and the denial of a narcissistic mortification suffered in infancy are unconscious to the patients. In addition to this unconscious satisfaction and this unconscious denial of a narcissistic mortification, these phantasies lead to a conscious genital stimulation. As a result of this stimulation, the patients masturbate and experience a genital discharge. The masturbation produces a conscious genital pleasure, and a conscious feeling of being independent of an external object and of being able to control and use their phantasies. These phantasies are accepted by the total personality of the patient and are used as a

stimulation for masturbation because their structure differs from the structure of phantasies which are rejected and because the patient who accepts them belongs constitutionally to the narcissistic type."

Related Concept: DAYDREAMS.

REFERENCE

Eidelberg, L., *Studies in Psychoanalysis*. IUP, 204–205, 222–223, 1948.

1315

MATRIARCHY. Freud, in examining the life of the primitive man—using the basic works of a number of men, including Frazer, Ellis, Darwin, Cameron and Bachofen—concentrated on the study of the patriarchal society, drawing his conclusions about the primitive from his work concerned with child development. He (1913) thought that the oedipus complex might have represented a repetition of the phylogenetic experiences related to the archaic father, his death at the hands of the sons, and the establishment of the brother-clan society. He left open the question of whether the matriarchal society followed the fatherless society or preceded it.

Graves (1957) suggested in his studies on European mythology that the matriarchal society preceded the patriarchal. "Ancient Europe had no gods. The Great Goddess was regarded as immortal, changeless, and omnipotent; and the concept of fatherhood had not been introduced into religious thought. She took lovers, but for pleasure, not to provide her children with a father."

Graves claimed that the change took place when man discovered the importance of impregnation as a cause of pregnancy. "Once the relevance of coition to child-bearing had been officially admitted—an account of this turning point in religion appears in the Hittite myth of simple-minded Appu—man's religious status gradually improved, and winds or rivers were no longer given credit for impregnating women." After the religious change occurred, man achieved a role in society he did not have previously. "Achaean invasions of the thirteenth century B.C. seriously weakened the matrilineal tradition. It seems that the king now contrived to reign for the term of his natural life; and when the Dorians arrived, towards the close of the second millennium, patriarchal royalty became the rule."

Eidelberg (1961) suggested that there may be another factor responsible for the change from the matriarchal to the patriarchal form of society; namely, the discovery that a male could force the female to have sexual intercourse, and thus impregnate her against her wish. The female could not play this role.

Ontologically, the infant finally discovers the importance of the father when the oedipus complex begins to develop. The male child transfers his aggression, originally cathected to the presentation of his mother, to his father, and, under favorable conditions, identifies with him. He, thus, becomes the father's rival; he wishes to be like his father and to possess his mother. The girl, conversely, transfers her positive feelings to her father and identifies with her mother.

In later years (1931), after the discovery of the preoedipal phase, Freud had to reformulate the basic concept of the early infantile fixation. The first relation of the male and female infant is to the mother; the father does not exist as a significant figure. In this, the preoedipal mother must be differentiated from the so-called oedipal mother who often plays a secondary role, and who is responsible for the development of the positive and negative oedipus complex. The preoedipal mother represents the active mother, and, consequently, the identification with this active mother does not lead to passivity but to activity in both sexes.

The activity of a girl which is a resultant of her identification with the preoedipal mother represents a feminine, not a masculine activity. When the oedipal stage develops, the preoedipal stage is partly repressed, instead of repudiated; both sexes remain unconsciously fixated to the preoedipal mother. Thus, the boy has difficulty in dealing with his aggression, because it is directed (still) toward the mother; and the girl has difficulty in learning to love her father, instead or her preoedipal mother.

Phylogenetically, the rule of the woman came first, and the man played a secondary role. This stage resembles the preoedipal situation in infancy where the nursing mother represents the most important object to the male and female infant. The matriarchal situation changed into a patriarchal form as a result of the discovery of sexual intercourse.

It is questionable whether a child living in a matriarchal society would develop an oedipus complex. Malinowski (1924) noted: "The oedipus complex leads to the repression of the wish to kill the father and marry the mother. Whereas, in a matriarchal society we find the wish to marry the sister and to kill the mother's brother."

In trying to determine whether a particular society is more or less a patriarchy or a matriarchy, it is necessary to differentiate between those which are ruled by a woman playing the role of a man (pseudo-matriarchy) and those in which the female ruler is the symbol of eternal love and the eternal mother.

Related Concepts: AMBIVALENCE; BREAST COMPLEX; IDENTIFICATION.

REFERENCES

Eidelberg, L., *The Dark Urge*. Py, p. 11, 1961.
Freud, S.: 1913, "Totem and Taboo." *SE*, 13:149, 1955.
⠀⠀⠀⠀⠀1931, "Female Sexuality." *SE*, 21:226, 1961.
Graves, Robert, *The Greek Myths*. New York: George Braziller, pp. 11–13, 1955.
Malinowski, B., *Mutterrechtliche Familie und Ödipus-Komplex*. Im, 10: 228–277, 1924.

1316

MATURATION denotes the progressive development of the functions of the psychic apparatus, which is dependent on the genetically determined growth of the central nervous system, in accordance with the environment. Drives are experienced and modified through the successively maturing erogenous zones. When the ego and superego functions (which depend on sufficient development of motor control, perception, memory, affects, thinking, and their synthesis) lose their infantile character, a mature total personality, relatively independent of external objects, is established.

Hartmann (1958) noted: "There is still another fact we must take into consideration when we try to check on what relations actually exist between developmental level and adaptation. The idea of a disharmonious precocity in the development of certain tendencies is familiar to us as a factor which is frequently pathogenic. But there is also the possibility that precocious development of certain ego functions, among them rational thought processes, might be a causative element in the genesis of obsessional neurosis. Facts like these and some others mentioned before make me inclined to formulate conditions of health in terms of the equilibrium that exists between the substructures of personality on the one hand, and between these and the environment on the other hand."

Anna Freud (1936) summarized her view, as follows: "This estimate of the normality or abnormality of particular instinctual aims depends, however, on a standard of values which belongs to adult life and has little or nothing to do with the ego of the adolescent. The inner defensive conflict goes on and not much attention is paid to these values. In adolescence, the attitude of the ego towards the id is primarily determined by quantitative and not by qualitative considerations. The point at issue is not the gratification or frustration of this or that instinctual wish but the nature of the psychic structure in childhood and latency, as a whole and in general. There are two extremes in which the conflict may possibly end. Either the id, now grown strong, may overcome the ego, in which case no trace will be left of the previous character of the individual and the entrance into adult life will be marked by a riot of uninhibited gratification of instinct. Or the ego may be victorious, in which case the character of the individual during the latency-period will declare itself for good and all. When this happens, the id-impulses of the adolescent are confined within the narrow limits prescribed for the instinctual life of the child. No use can be made of the increased libido and there has to be a constant expenditure on anti-cathexes, defence-mechanisms and symptoms in order to hold it in check. Apart from the resulting crippling of the instinctual life, the fact that the victorious ego becomes rigidly fixed is permanently injurious to the individual. Ego-institutions which have resisted the onslaught of puberty without yielding generally remain throughout life inflexible, unassailable and insusceptible of the rectification which a changing reality demands.

"It would seem natural to suppose that the issue of the conflict in one or another of these extremes or its happy solution in a new agreement between the psychic institutions and, further, the many different phases through which it passes are determined by a quantitative factor, namely, the variations in the absolute strength of the instincts. But this simple explanation is contradicted by analytic observation of the processes in individuals at puberty. Of course it is not the case that, when the instincts become stronger for physiological reasons, the individual is necessarily more at their mercy or, on the other hand, that with a decline in the strength of the instincts those psychic phenomena become more prominent in which the ego and the super-ego play a greater part than the id. We know from the study of neurotic symptoms and pre-menstrual states that, whenever the demands of instinct become more urgent, the ego is impelled to redouble its defensive activities. On the other hand, when the instinctual claims are less pressing, the danger associated with them diminishes and with it the objective anxiety, the anxiety of conscience and the instinctual anxiety of the ego. Except in cases in which the latter is entirely submerged by the id, we find the converse of the suggested relation. Any additional pressure of instinctual demands stiffens the resistance of the ego to the instinct in question and intensifies the symptoms, inhibitions, etc., based upon that resistance, while, if the instincts become less urgent, the ego becomes more yielding and more ready to permit gratification. This means that the absolute strength of the instincts during puberty (which in any case cannot be measured or estimated independently) affords no prognosis of the final issue of puberty. The factors by which this is determined are relative: first, the strength of the id-impulses, which is conditioned by the physiological process at puberty; second, the ego's tolerance or intolerance of instinct, which depends on the character formed during the latency-period; third—and this is the qualitative factor which decides the quantitative conflict—the nature and efficacy of the defence-mechanisms at the ego's command, which vary with the constitution of the particular individual, i.e. his disposition to hysteria or to obsessional neurosis, and with the lines upon which he has developed."

Related Concepts: NEUTRALIZATION; SUBLIMATION.

REFERENCES

Freud, A., 1936, *The Ego and the Mechanisms of Defense*. IUP, pp. 163-165, 1946.
Hartmann, H., *Ego Psychology and the Problem of Adaptation*. IUP, p. 60, 1958.

ADDITIONAL READINGS

Freud, S.: 1905, "Three Essays on the Theory of Sexuality." *SE*, 7, 1953.
1923, "The Ego and the Id." *SE*, 19, 1961.

1317

MEGALOMANIA denotes an excessive self-esteem which sometimes leads to delusions of grandeur. Megalomania is based on sexualization of the ego and superego functions, and on the impairment of reality testing. As a result of a denial of internal and external narcissistic mortifications, the representations of the ego and the superego are probably cathected by object-libido and object-destrudo.

Fenichel (1945) described the delusional symptoms of megalomania as follows: "The belief in one's omnipotence is but one aspect of the magical-animistic world that comes to the fore again in narcissistic regressions."

Abraham (1908) noted: "The auto-erotism of dementia praecox is the source not only of delusions of persecution but of megalomania. Under normal conditions, when two persons have transferred their libido on to one another each over-estimates the value of the other whom he loves (Freud calls this 'sexual over-estimation'). The mental patient transfers on to himself alone as his only sexual object the whole of the libido which the healthy person turns upon all living and inanimate objects in his environment, and accordingly his sexual over-estimation is directed towards himself alone and assumes enormous dimensions. For he is his whole world. The origin of megalomania in dementia praecox is thus a reflected or auto-erotic sexual over-estimation—an over-estimation which is turned back on to the ego. Delusions of persecution and megalomania are therefore closely connected with each other. Every delusion of persecution in dementia praecox is accompanied by megalomania.

"The patient's auto-erotic isolation from the external world not only affects his reactive behaviour but also his receptive attitude. He shuts himself off from the sense-perceptions of reality that flow towards him. His unconscious produces sense-perceptions of a hallucinatory nature, and these correspond to repressed wishes. He thus carries his self-isolation so far that in a certain measure he boycotts the external world. He no longer gives it anything, or accepts anything from it. He grants himself a monopoly for the supply of sense-impressions."

Related Concepts: DELUSIONS OF GRANDEUR; OMNIPOTENCE OF THOUGHT.

REFERENCES

Abraham, K., 1908, "The Psycho-Sexual Differences Between Hysteria and Praecox." *SPA*, p. 75, 1942.
Fenichel, O., *The Psychoanalytic Theory of Neurosis*. Nor, p. 421, 1945.

1318

MELANCHOLIA is a psychosis, characterized by "a profoundly painful dejection, cessation of interest in the outside world" (Freud, 1917).

Abraham (1924) provided the following summary of a case history to support his thesis, as follows: "A careful analysis of the self-criticisms and self-reproaches—especially those of a delusional nature—uttered by melancholic patients will show that the process of introjection takes two forms:

"1. The patient has introjected his original love-object upon which he had built his ego ideal; so that that object has taken over the role of conscience for him, although, it is true, a pathologically formed one. Our material goes to show that the pathological self-criticism of the melancholiac emanates from this introjected object. One of my patients used to be continually taking himself to task and repeating the same reproaches against himself; and in doing this he copied exactly the tone of voice and actual expressions that he had often heard his mother use when she had scolded him as a little boy.

"2. The content of those self-reproaches is ultimately a merciless criticism of the introjected object. A patient of mine used to pass judgement on himself in the following words: 'My whole existence is based on deceit'. This reproach turned out to be determined by certain elements in the relationship of his mother and father.

"I will give an example to illustrate the way in which these two forms of introjection work in with one another. The patient I have just spoken about used to say that he was utterly incapable and could never lead a useful life. Analysis showed that this complaint was an exaggerated criticism of his father's quiet and inactive character, in contrast to whom his mother was for him the ideal of practical efficiency. He felt that he himself took after his father. His criticism of himself therefore stood for an unfavourable judgement passed by his introjected mother on his introjected father. We have here a very instructive instance of a twofold process of introjection.

"If we take this view we are able to understand another symptom this patient had—a delusional self-reproach. During his last period of depression he had been put in an asylum. One day he declared that he had introduced lice into the place. He grew more and more agitated and bewailed the enormity of his act, saying that he had infected the whole house with lice. He tried to demonstrate the presence of the lice to the house-physician. He saw them in every particle of dust and in every shred of material. The analysis of this delusion brought to light the special symbolic importance of lice to him. In dream-symbolism and all other forms of phantasy small animals represent children. A house which is full of lice thus means a house (his father's and mother's house) which is full of children. As a child the patient had been deprived of his mother's love because a great many younger brothers and sisters had been born. One of the determinants of his introjected complaint had been the thought, 'My wicked mother, who once pretended to love me so much, has filled the whole house with children'. Furthermore, if we consider that the house is a symbol of the mother, we can see that he is also blaming his father for having procreated the children. Thus in this example also the patient's accusations against both his parents have been condensed into a single accusation directed against himself."

The four preconditions of melancholia are real or emotional loss of a loved object, ambivalence, regression to an oral cannibalistic and narcissistic phase, and discharge of aggression against the self (danger of suicide). The ambivalently loved object is introjected, and the libido is withdrawn into the self which serves to establish an identification with the abandoned object. The "object-loss is transformed into an ego-loss and the conflict between the ego and the loved person into a cleavage between the critical activity of the ego as altered by identification." That is, a conflict between ego and superego becomes manifest. In melancholia, the ego is paralyzed because it finds itself incapable of meeting the danger (Bibring, 1952). In extreme instances the person may commit suicide "if owing to the return of object cathexis it can treat itself as an object."

Case History

A patient whose wife died of cancer developed a melancholia: he believed that he could have saved her life if he had insisted on her monthly check-up. He considered himself a murderer and tried to commit suicide, but after several months of institutionalization his symptoms decreased in severity and he was released, and thereafter he sought treatment. His psychoanalysis disclosed that he had harbored unconscious death wishes against his wife from the day of their marriage. He did not, however, differentiate between wish and action; he experienced remorse rather than feelings of guilt. The idea, "I killed my wife," was used to deny the external narcissistic mortification, "I was helpless to prevent her dying." He accepted instead the *internal* narcissistic mortification, "I have failed to eliminate my unconscious death wishes."

Related Concepts: DEPRESSION; ELATION; MOURNING.

REFERENCES

Abraham, K., 1924, "A Short Study of the Development of the Libido, Viewed in the Light of Mental Disorders." *SPA*, pp. 461–462, 1942.
Bibring, E., "Das Problem der Depression." *P*, 6:82–101, 1952.
Freud, S., 1917, "Mourning and Melancholia." *SE*, 14:244, 249, 1957.

ADDITIONAL READINGS

Federn, P., "Die Geschichte einer Melancholia."
    Z, 9, 1923.
Rado, S., "The Problem of Melancholia." IntJPsa,
    9, 1928.
Wisdom, J., "Comparison and Development of the
    Psycho-Analytical Theories of Melancholia."
    IntJPsa, 43, 1962.

1319

MENSTRUATION. Psychological reactions
to menstruation are varied: it may lead to feelings
which are similar to that of giving birth, to an
intensification of genital excitement (although some
women are *less* genitally excitable during menstruation); it may also represent loss of anal and
urethral control, oedipal guilt, castration, frustration
of wishes for a child, or humiliation. Some women
are depressed during menstruation. The intensity
of the psychic determinants may cause menstrual
dysfunctions. Menstruation may serve as a reminder
of the infantile belief in castration, and thus pave
the way for feelings of inferiority, penis envy, and
the masculinity complex. Menarche is an important
experience leading to the recognition of the genital
stage. [Fenichel, 1945.]

The menstruation which perhaps in a primitive
excited the sexual desires, Freud (1930) noted, decreases this desire today. It may well be that when the
primitive began to use his hind legs for locomotion,
the olfactory stimuli lost their importance. Of course,
even today, a little child is not disgusted by excreta.

Related Concepts: GENITAL; MATURATION.

REFERENCES

Fenichel, O., *The Psychoanalytic Theory of Neurosis*.
    Nor, pp. 240–242, 411, 1945.
Freud, S., 1930, "Civilization and Its Discontents."
    SE, 21:99–100, 1961.

ADDITIONAL READINGS

Faergeman, P. M., "Fantasies of Menstruation in
    Men." Q, 24, 1955.
Silbermann, I., "A Contribution to the Psychology
    of Menstruation." IntJPsa, 31, 1950.
Vorwahl, H., "Erwartung und Eintreffen der Men-
    struation im Seelenleben der Mädchen." PsaP,
    5, 1931.

1320

MENTAL (PSYCHIC). Mental was often used
as a synonym for *consciousness* before Freud
discovered that mental phenomena may both lose
and regain the state of consciousness, and the
term was subsequently defined as that which can
become conscious. It is still true, however, that
illnesses with no sign of pathological or anatomical
changes in the central or peripheral nervous systems
are often referred to as "mental," "nonorganic,"
"functional," or "psychic." One disadvantage of this
categorization of illnesses is that the pathological
anatomical changes may not actually be absent,
but, rather, may be unrecognizable. For instance,
Parkinson's disease was originally referred to as a
"mental" illness, only because the anatomical
changes characteristic of this disease (located in
the middle brain) were not then known. Freud, while
describing the mental changes in neurosis, always
insisted that one day the organic nature of this
illness would be discovered.

The mental phenomena can be examined either
through sense-organ perception (chiefly with the
help of language and gestures) or through inner
perception. Many psychoanalysts divide mental
phenomena, which they consider to be derivatives
of an instinctual fusion, into ideas, emotions,
and motoric and secretory discharges. Only the
latter can be directly observed. Ideas and emotions
can be recognized either by inner perception or
through the communication of another individual
(or may be deductively inferred from their actions).
The evaluation of data received through words
and gestures is more difficult than the evaluation of physiological data (e.g., increase of blood
sugar).

As Freud (1913) noted, the psychical reality, not
the factual reality, is preferred by the neurotic. The
deeds which provoke the neurotic's behavior are not
to be found, rather, it is to be understood in terms
of the energy which is held back from discharge.

Related Concepts: ORGANIC; PSYCHIC (MENTAL)
ENERGY; SOMATIC COMPLIANCE.

REFERENCE

Freud, S., 1913, "Totem and Taboo." SE, 13:159,
    1955.

ADDITIONAL READINGS

Eidelberg, L., *An Outline of a Comparative Pathology of the Neuroses.* IUP, 1954.

Freud, S.: 1905, "Three Essays on the Theory of Sexuality." *SE*, 7, 1953.

1933, "New Introductory Lectures on Psycho-Analysis." *SE*, 22, 1964.

1321

METAPHORIC LANGUAGE denotes the deliberate use of a word or words out of normal context in order to convey a conceptual similarity or allegorical meaning. Metaphors reflect a form of primary process thinking which psychotics may use without recognizing them as metaphors. Abnormal metaphoric thinking may also appear in dreams, and in temporary states of regression in neurotics.

Sharpe (1940) noted: "Metaphor evolves alongside the control of the bodily orifices. Emotions which originally accompanied bodily discharge find substitute channels and materials. Spontaneous metaphor used by a patient proves upon examination to be an epitome of a forgotten experience. It can reveal a present-day psychical condition which is based upon an original psycho-physical experience. In metaphor that is the expression of vital emotion the repressed psycho-physical experiences have found the verbal images in the pre-conscious that express them. The earliest of all verbal images are the sounds of words and hence the importance of phonetics and the value of listening to a patient's *phonetic* associations. The person who speaks vitally in metaphor *knows*, but does not know in consciousness what he knows unconsciously. An examination of metaphors used by patients reveals, as one would expect, a preponderance of images based upon experiences of the pre-genital stages and the repressed Oedipus wishes. They reveal also something of the early incorporated environment. Metaphor gives information concerning instinctual tension. The metaphors of depression denote the zero hour, exhaustion and immobility, giving us the physical setting which first accompanied the psychical feelings; prolonged crying, bed-wetting, loneliness and exhaustion. Other metaphors give pictures of futile activity, achievement of no goal; continual thwarting and obstructing of the self. Others again reveal pent-up energy, a straining at the leash, desire and fear of 'letting go,' as in the bow and arrow image. Information is to be gained by noting the type of image that comes most frequently from any given patient. I have found that a wealth of auditory imagery is often accompanied by a marked absence of visual, and, when visual imagery prevails, auditory ones are lacking, thus giving one an indication of the connection of conflicts with a particular sense."

Related Concept: PRIMARY PROCESS.

REFERENCE

Sharpe, E. F., 1940, "Psycho-Physical Problems Revealed in Language: An Examination of Metaphor," in *Collected Papers on Psycho-Analysis.* HPI, pp. 168–169, 1950.

1322

METAPSYCHOLOGY denotes the comprehensive study of mental processes, of which a full account would incorporate explanations derived from each of four approaches: systematic, dynamic, economic, and structural (topographic). This general picture of the mind, as Strachey (1960) noted, was first explored in the "Project" of 1895; in 1900, in the seventh chapter of "The Interpretation of Dreams"; and in the metapsychological papers of 1915–1917: "Instincts and Their Vicissitudes," "Repression," "The Unconscious," "A Metapsychological Supplement to the Theory of Dreams," and "Mourning and Melancholia." In these, the systematic approach divided the psyche into conscious and unconscious parts, of which the preconscious contained everything unconscious that could become conscious. The dynamic approach was understood in terms of the conflict which arose between the system *Cs.* and *Ucs.*,[*] from which it was possible to investigate certain phenomenological derivatives (symptom formation). To this, Freud added the economic approach which sought to investigate the quantity and quality of the energy used.

The structural[†] approach was touched upon in

---

[*] Modified after the introduction of the structural approach.

[†] Also called the topographic approach by Freud (1940); *structural* is the preferred usage in this work.

Freud's metapsychological papers, but explored more fully in "Two Encyclopedia Articles" (1923) and in "The Ego and the Id" (1923). Here, the total personality was divided into the id, ego, and superego; the id containing the instinctual forces; the ego, the organized part of the id; and the superego, the precipitates of the ego's first attachment to objects (as well as being heir to the oedipus complex). Thus, metapsychology may be described as combining descriptive (systematic) and explanatory terms, an explanation which seeks to denote mental processes comprehensively.

Related Concept: PSYCHOANALYSIS.

REFERENCES

Freud, S., 1937, "Analysis Terminable and Interminable." *SE*, 23:225–227, 1964.
Strachey, J., Editorial note. *SE*, 6:259, 1960.

ADDITIONAL READINGS

Bonnard, A., "The Metapsychology of the Russian Trials Confessions." *IntJPsa*, 35, 1954.
Brierley, M., "Notes on Metapsychology as Process Theory." *IntJPsa*, 25, 1944.
Eidelberg, L., *An Outline of a Comparative Pathology of the Neuroses*. IUP, 1954.
Eissler, K. R., "On the Metapsychology of the Preconscious: A Tentative Contribution to Psychoanalytic Morphology." *PsaStC*, 17, 1962.
Freud, S., 1915, "Repression." *SE*, 14, 1957.
Hartmann, H., E. Kris, & R. Loewenstein, "Comments on the Formation of Psychic Structure." *PsaStC*, 2, 1946.
        "Contributions to the Metapsychology of Schizophrenia." *PsaStC*, 8, 1953.
Isaacs, S., "Notes on Metapsychology as Process Theory: Some Comments." *IntJPsa*, 26, 1945.
Rapaport, D., & M. Gill, "The Points of View and Assumptions of Metapsychology." *IntJPsa*, 40, 1959.
Sterba, R. F., "Metapsychology of Morale." *BMC*, 7, 1943.

1323

MICROPSIA is a visual abnormality in which objects appear to be much smaller than they actually are. Micropsia may appear as a neurotic defense against envy and intense frustration, especially in orally fixated individuals. In psychotic states, with endopsychic perception of changes and imminent disintegration within the ego, micropsia may represent an attempt to stave off feelings of self-estrangement by projection. [Inman, 1938.]

Related Concept: PERCEPTION.

REFERENCE

Inman, W. S., "A Psycho-Analytical Explanation of Micropsia." *IntJPsa*, 19:226–228, 1938.

1324

MICROPSYCHOPHYSIOLOGY denotes that process of observing and understanding the changes and dynamic flow of psychic processes in minute, microscopic detail which is akin to the study of physiology in organic functioning. This can best be done by observing such states *in statu nascendi*. For example: the microscopic observation of the "leap" from the psychic to the somatic in conversion; the leap or transition into a delusion, an obsession, or even fantasy. [Rangell, 1959.]

Related Concept: PSYCHODYNAMICS.

REFERENCE

Rangell, Leo, "The Nature of Conversion." *JAPA*, 7:632–662, 1959.

1325

MISOGYNY denotes a hatred of women. Psychoanalysis has shown that some men who hate women have suffered severe trauma when frightened by the castration threats expressed by their mothers; others, fixated at the negative oedipus complex, hate women because of their inability to become women. The preoedipal fixation to the mother may also mobilize their hatred as a result of the trauma of weaning or their inability to identify with the preoedipal mother (e.g., breast envy).

A similar phenomenon is the hatred of women for men, which may also be connected with the oedipal or preoedipal constellation; it may represent the wish to be independent of a sexual object or at least independent of a male sexual object. In this connection, it is interesting to note that in Greek mythology female goddesses interested in hunting and war (e.g., Artemis and Pallas Athena) were supposed to be virgins; and differed in this from other female goddesses (e.g., Aphrodite) who were married and had many lovers.

Before developing a castration complex, Freud (1910) noted, when the male child considers women to have a penis, he begins to show the scopophilic desire, for in his examination of the genitals of others he is comparing them with his own. His erotic attraction to his mother leads him to search for her female penis. After he discovers that she doesn't have a penis, his original love may change into disgust, perhaps to become one of the causes responsible for his impotence, homosexuality or misogyny.

Related Concepts: AGGRESSION; BREAST ENVY; OMNIPOTENCE OF THOUGHT.

REFERENCE

Freud, S., 1910, "Leonardo Da Vinci and a Memory of His Childhood." *SE*, 11:96, 1957.

1326

MNEME denotes an associative trace; literally, a memory trace, a residue, or an image. In constructing a schema of the psychical apparatus, Freud (1900) noted that the mnemic system in the psychical apparatus links the stimulus at the sensory end (perception) with the innervation that takes place at the motor end. The mnemic elements contain the record, therefore, of associations which describe the identity of each individual. Freud* reported a case history to illustrate his view, as follows: "Among the early recollections of a rather unintelligent patient figured a scene with her brother. All she remembered was that her brother wanted to show her something and dragged her off. A curtain then closed the scene. Freud told her that the essential part of this scene would come to her in a single word. When this was of no avail, he told her (in order to take her censor by surprise) that the word would emerge letter by letter and that, with each pressure of his hand, one letter would emerge. Ten or eleven letters came to her mind in this way. (Of one letter, she was not quite sure.) Under further pressure of his hand she arranged the letters in a

---

* *Minutes of the Vienna Psychoanalytic Society*, Nunberg, H., & E. Federn, eds. IUP, p. 50, 1962.

certain sequence. First, she gave the vowels a fixed position; then the consonants. The resulting word was *medchnfogl;* [*Mädchenvogel* = girl bird].*

"In reference to [Helen] Keller, Freud says that Meisl is correct in pointing out a similarity [between her unawareness and] the remaining unconscious of childhood memories. It is difficult for strong impressions to remain unconscious. It is easy for memories. Memory has a stronger effect than perception."

Related Concepts: PERCEPTUAL CONSCIOUSNESS; UNCONSCIOUS.

REFERENCE

Freud, S., 1900, "The Interpretation of Dreams." *SE*, 5:539-543, 1953.

ADDITIONAL READING

Jelliffe, S. E., "The Mneme, the Engram and the Unconscious. Richard Semon: His Life and Work." *JNMD*, 57, 1923.

1327

MONEY. The analysis of people who are pathologically stingy, wasteful, etc., shows that money sometimes unconsciously represents feces and serves as a gratification of anal drives. Fecal matter represents something which is or was part of the self. It is a prized possession, which may be retained (hoarded) or rapidly evacuated (spent). Its bulk and other qualities may be scrutinized and cherished; its elimination is subject to many regulations. It may be viewed by the infant as a gift to be bestowed on those who are loved, or as as mode of attack on those who are hated (ambivalence). It has the power to control external objects; it is itself a controlled object and may, by association, represent external objects which can be sadistically expelled and destroyed or kept alive through retention. [Freud, 1908.]

Money, or its counterpart in other societies, is dealt with in ways which parallel early attitudes toward feces. Ferenczi described the typical childhood development, from the interest in fecal matter

---

* What her brother showed her, and what she obviously denied, was his penis. The nonsense word may refer to an associative term, *vögeln*, which is a vulgar term for coitus.

through an interest in odorless things of a similar consistency (like mud and clay), or in objects such as sand and stones, or in objects like marbles and buttons, or finally, in an interest in shiny coins, i.e., money. The symbolic equation—breast = feces = penis = baby—increases our understanding of the unconscious meaning of money. Ferenczi (1914) observed: "Children originally devote their interest without any inhibition to the process of defaecation, and that it affords them pleasure to hold back their stools. The excrementa thus held back are really the first 'savings' of the growing being, and as such remain in a constant, unconscious inter-relationship with every bodily activity or mental striving that has anything to do with collecting, hoarding, and saving.

"Faeces are also, however, one of the first toys of the child. The purely auto-erotic satisfaction afforded to the child by the pressing and squeezing of the faecal masses and the play of the sphincter muscles soon becomes—in part, at least—transformed into a sort of object-love, in that the interest gets displaced from the neutral sensations of certain organs on to the material itself that caused these feelings. The faeces are thus 'introjected,' and in this stage of development—which is essentially characterised by sharpening of the sense of smell and an increasingly adroit use of the hands, with at the same time an inability to walk upright (creeping on all fours)—they count as a valuable toy, from which the child is to be weaned only through deterrents and threats of punishment.

"The child's interest for dejecta experiences its first distortion through the smell of faeces becoming disagreeable, disgusting. This is probably related to the beginning of the upright gait. The other attributes of this material—moistness, discolouration, stickiness, etc.—do not for the time being offend his sense of cleanliness. He still enjoys, therefore, playing with and manipulating moist street-mud whenever he has the chance, liking to collect it together into larger heaps. Such a heap of mud is already in a sense a symbol, distinguished from the real thing by its absence of smell. For the child, street-mud is, so to speak, deodourised dejecta."

A child who is forced to defecate (laxative or enema) experiences a narcissistic mortification, which, if repressed, may lead to a compensatory, internal narcissistic mortification. For example, a young woman in analysis became infuriated when her fee was due. She complained that the analyst picked her brain, drained her thoughts, and extracted exorbitant fees. Her associations revealed that she regarded the fee collection and the analysis as if she were once again the victim of forcibly given enemas, which robbed her of her feces.

We speak of someone being "money hungry" (reflecting its oral connections). In fairy stories, "devil's gold," which later changes into feces, symbolically expresses the power to corrupt and control. Phallic aspects further appear in associations with money and power ("He had a roll as big as your fist," etc.).

Related Concept: ANAL PHASE.

REFERENCES

Ferenczi, S., 1914, "The Ontogenesis of the Interest in Money." *SPsa*, pp. 321–322, 1916.
Freud, S., 1908, "Character and Anal Erotism." *SE*, 9:167–176, 1959.

1328

MORALITY is the code used to control the discharge of instinctual wishes: to avoid conflict between an individual and the group, between individuals within the group, and between one group and another. Although psychoanalysis is not alone in the investigation of mental functions, it does, rather more specifically, differentiate between certain basic propositions—true and false, just and unjust—independently of whether what is true appears to be pleasurable or unpleasurable, or both. In this respect, it is necessary to acknowledge that the scientific approach must be limited to a study of the methods by which moral concepts are established, and admit that what appears moral to one individual may be immoral to another.

Freud at first considered the oedipal complex and its resolution to be the origin of the superego. The boy discovered that his wish to have his mother and eliminate his father had to be repudiated and sublimated because of the threat of castration. Contrarily, the little girl had to give up her oedipal wishes and accept her lack of a penis. Later, Freud discovered the importance of the preoedipal stage, and so reformulated his theory. In addition to the oedipal stage, which resolution is responsible for the formation of the superego, the preoedipal was also thought to act as a precursor to the development of morality. The original fixation to the preoedipal mother, was slowly resolved by the boy concentrating his love on his mother and his hostile wishes on his father; the opposite condition, of course, applying to the girl. Thus, the final resolution of the oedipus complex appears to lead to the incorporation of both parents through the formation of the superego. Its prohibitions slowly lose their ego-alien character and the infantile superego is finally assimilated, becoming, in normal adults, the mature ego-syntonic superego. Thus, Freud (1930) regarded morality as a therapeutic attempt to achieve, by means of the command of the superego, something which had so far not been achieved by means of any other cultural activity. Unless the external prohibitions and commands were accepted and assimilated by the individual through the formation of the superego, the society would perish.

Related Concepts: INHIBITION; SUBLIMATION; SUPER-EGO.

REFERENCE

Freud, S., 1930, "Civilization and Its Discontents." *SE*, 21: 145, 1961.

ADDITIONAL READINGS

Bettelheim, B., & E. Sylvester, "Delinquency and Morality." *PsaStC*, 5, 1950.
Flugel, J., "Psychoanalysis and Morals." *YBPsa*, 2, 1946.
Piaget, J., *The Moral Judgment of the Child.* HB, 1933.

1329

MORAL MASOCHISM. With the introduction of the topographic approach in 1923, Freud showed that the derivatives of primary masochism are feminine, erotogenic and moral masochism. Of the latter form, Freud noted that there are patients in analysis who are disturbed by any sign of satisfaction as to the progress of the treatment. They cannot accept success, exhibiting what is known as a "negative therapeutic reaction."

Freud identified this factor as "moral"; that is their sense of guilt and its punishment are maintained, for they find satisfaction in their illness. These patients do not feel guilty, but are ill instead. Their sense of guilt is expressed only as a resistance toward recovery. In returning to this problem a year later (in 1924), Freud stated that upon closer examination there was a distinction to be drawn between what he called "an unconscious sense of morality" and moral masochism. In the former the ego submits to the superego's sadism, while in the latter it submits to the ego's own masochism which seeks punishment, whether from the superego or from the parental imagoes. Freud was thus able to define the "unconscious sense of guilt" in terms of the need for punishment from the external parental powers.

Clinical Example

Eidelberg (1948) provided the following case history: "The patient left for a short vacation. After his return he declared that for the first time in his life he had enjoyed his vacation. Half a year before, during the summer holidays, he had borne badly an interruption of treatment, and the guilt feelings he experienced in every vacation period had on this occasion been particularly violent. He had noted slight signs of improvement before he went away; but had not paid particular attention to them; now the change was so great that it could not be overlooked.

"After the patient had informed me of this successful result of therapy, he had violent outbreaks of rage against me and the analysis. He declared that the whole treatment was a fraud, that I had him lured into analysis by false statements, etc. Nevertheless, it was possible to resume analysis after several hours, through appeal to his reason. The connection between his aggression and the improvement was clearly established; I told him that we must ascribe the aggression as an attempt to maintain the status quo. Since he had been accustomed to a certain amount of masochistic gratification, deprivation of it resulted inevitably in disorders; these, however, should be only temporary. Gradually the masochistic gratification would yield to normal gratification; at the same time the stage at which the former had been withdrawn while the latter was still to come, was unpleasant.

"Shortly afterward it was possible to discover another reason for the patient's fury. He formulated it as follows: 'If I recover, it will mean that I was wrong and you were right—in other words, I am again the little child who must give in.'

"I replied that he himself wanted to recover, that otherwise he would not have submitted to analysis or would have interrupted it after a short time. The analyst, I insisted, is merely an instrument, an agency acting on the patient's behalf; there are many neurotics who avoid any type of treatment and who cannot be helped by analysis.

"It became clear that the uncertainty involved in any real action was felt by the patient to be particularly unpleasant. He would have liked to undertake something, but only if I guaranteed in advance that he would be successful. I explained to him that such certainty does not pertain in real actions, that the normal individual is capable of assuming a certain amount of risk, that failure is not a disgrace, and that by examining one's failures and changing one's behavior accordingly (reality adjustment), one can in the end achieve success.

"A few more weeks passed before the patient finally made up his mind to translate these ideas into practice and to attempt resumption of his relation with his woman friend. On discovering that he was impotent with her, he wished to withdraw again; but in the interval his character had been changed to such an extent that he was unable to withdraw. He stayed with her, and after several unsuccessful attempts found himself potent.

"This effect of therapy resulted again in violent outbreaks of rage. The patient reproached me with having compelled him to have intercourse against his will. He declared that when he now attempted to escape his old masturbatory fantasies, he failed; he charged that I had promised him the opportunity of freely choosing, after analysis, between sickness and health, but instead he was compelled to choose health. Once again I was able to analyze the patient's aggression. Such outbursts of rage recurred a few times; whenever the patient was forced to admit improvement, he tried to interrupt the treatment."

Related Concepts: NEGATIVE THERAPEUTIC REACTION; SUPEREGO.

REFERENCES

Eidelberg, L., *Studies in Psychoanalysis.* IUP, pp. 22–23, 1948.
Freud, S.: 1923, "The Ego and the Id." *SE,* 19:49–50, 1961.
      1924, "The Economic Problem of Masochism." *SE,* 19:169–170, 1961.

1330

MORAL RESPONSIBILITY AND DREAMS. It was Freud's (1900) contention that there was no justification for the reluctance of patients to accept the immorality of their dreams. It was his contention that this reluctance would disappear once the relationship between the conscious and unconscious life was understood, and drew a distinction between psychical and external reality.

Related Concept: SUPEREGO.

REFERENCE

Freud, S., 1900, "The Interpretation of Dreams." *SE,* 5:620, 1953.

1331

MOTILITY is described as the discharge of energy controlled by *Cs.*, in Freud's first formulation, and as a function of the ego in his second. The difference stems principally from a conceptual change which Freud introduced when he recognized that not only the wish but the defense is unconscious; the change also explained such clinical phenomena as sleep walking and parapraxes. In his second theory (1923), the total personality is divided into the id, ego, and superego—the structural approach. In his first concept (1900), he differentiated between the *Ucs.* and *Cs.*, with the preconscious as a part of *Cs.*—the topographic or systematic approach. Freud also employed the term topographic in his description of the structural approach. In this, the ego was considered to contain elements which were unconscious, conscious and preconscious. Thus, the involuntary motoric discharges were thought to occur on an unconscious level, while the voluntary motoric system activities could be considered as being controlled usually in the preconscious and conscious ego.

All conversions differ from voluntary movements in that they represent a partial gratification and a partial frustration of the wish involved. A normal action may also be a compromise of various tendencies, but it finally serves to gratify the total personality: it is ego-syntonic, seeks pleasure, does not deny inner and external reality, and, therefore, can easily be differentiated from a neurotic motoric discharge.

The motility may be interfered with by inhibitions which may be either normal or based on neurotic phenomena, the avoidance of the street in agoraphobia, for instance. Analytically, the so-called voluntary actions take place on a preconscious level without being considered pathological; closing the eyes to protect them from an external threat, to cite another example.

Eidelberg (1948) pointed out that in so far as the urge to imitate appears to be greater than our ability to make conscious decisions and act accordingly, we often encounter a phenomenon in which a voluntary action is inhibited by this need. The hypotonia or hypertonia of muscles affected by neurotic paralysis differs from that present in so-called organic cases. In this, physiology and neurology have added little to the understanding of functional symptoms.

Related Concept: Tic.

REFERENCES

Eidelberg, L., *Studies in Psychoanalysis.* IUP, pp. 125–128, 1948.

Freud, S.: 1900, "The Psychology of the Dream-Processes." *SE,* 5:615, 1953.

    1923, "The Ego and the Id." *SE,* 19:7–9, 1961.

ADDITIONAL READINGS

Fries, M. E., & P. J. Woolf, "Some Hypotheses on the Role of the Congenital Activity Type in Personality Development." *PsaStC,* 8, 1953.

Mittelmann, B.: "Motility in Infants, Children, and Adults: Patterning and Psychodynamics." *PsaStC,* 9, 1954.

    "Motility in the Therapy of Children and Adults." *PsaStC,* 12, 1957.

    "Intrauterine and Early Infantile Motility." *PsaStC,* 15, 1960.

1332

MOTILITY IN DREAMS denotes those voluntary muscle discharges that occur during sleep, such as turning or even getting up, which take place without the individual waking up. Freud (1917) reasoned that dreams were without motor discharge or motor elements for the most part. It is obvious that the term *paralysis,* which he employed, was not meant to be identical with neurological or functional paralysis. As he pointed out, some limited movement does take place in sleep which would be impossible in paralysis. In this, it is assumed that he was referring to the individual's inability to move; the sleeper wants to rest, not to move. Freud used the word paralysis to indicate something *similar* but not identical to this phenomenon.

Actually, the sleeper wakes up whenever external or internal stimuli pass a threshold; in paralysis, this is not the case. In his remarks on the metapsychology of dreams, Freud contrasted inner perception with reality (external perception); he later recognized that there was no reason to withhold the term *reality* from inner perception, provided there was no confusion between inner and external perception.

Related Concept: DREAMS.

REFERENCE

Freud, S., 1916–1917, "Introductory Lectures on Psycho-Analysis." *SE,* 16:388, 1963.

1333

MOURNING is the grief experienced over the actual loss of a love-object (or an abstraction: such as loss of liberty or one's country), characterized by dejection, by cessation of interest in the outside world, by temporary loss of the capacity to love, and by inhibition of activity. Although mourning may involve serious deviations from the normal course of a person's life, it is not regarded as a pathological condition. Normally, after a short period of time, libido and destrudo bound to the lost object are gradually detached; the ego once more becomes free and uninhibited. Under pathological conditions, depression and melancholia may also result from object-loss, if the external narcissistic mortification caused by it is partially or completely denied.

Mourning may be postponed or a substitute-object found. For example, Freud (1899) showed how a premonitory fantasy protected the ego against the awareness of mourning for a lost object of the past. Stein (1953) pointed out the defensive character of certain premonitory fantasies, in which the loss of a substitute-object may then be anticipated and mourned with less pain.

Freud (1916) emphasized the strength with which the libido clings to its objects, frequently not renouncing them as lost, even though a substitute lies at hand. Those in mourning sometimes believe that all perishable possessions have lost their worth. They endeavour, by the renunciation of everything, to end the painfulness of mourning. Its metapsychological aspects were described by Freud in 1917. He noted that a libidinal position is not given up unless a substitute is already at hand. The memories and expectations are hypercathected by bound libido. When this compromise with reality testing is carried out, and the work of mourning completed, the ego once again becomes free and uninhibited.

Related Concepts: DEPRESSION; MELANCHOLIA.

REFERENCES

Freud, S.: 1899, "A Premonitory Dream Fulfilled." *SE*, 5: 623–625, 1953.
1916, "On Transience." *SE*, 14: 305–307, 1957.
1917, "Mourning and Melancholia." *SE*, 14: 244–245, 1957.
Stein, M., "Premonition as a Defense." *Q*, 2:69–74, 1953.

ADDITIONAL READINGS

Bowlby, J.: "Processes of Mourning." *IntJPsa*, 42, 1961.
"Note on Dr. Max Schur's Comments on Grief and Mourning in Infancy and Early Childhood." *PsaStC*, 16, 1961.
Freud, A., "Discussion of Dr. John Bowlby's Paper." *PsaStC*, 15, 1960.
Klein, M., "Mourning and Its Relation to Manic-Depressive States." *IntJPsa*, 21, 1940.
Rosner, A., "Mourning Before the Fact." *JAPA*, 10, 1962.
Solnit, A. J., & M. H. Stark, "Mourning and the Birth of a Defective Child." *PsaStC*, 16, 1961.

1334

MUTISM denotes the inability or refusal to speak. In hysteria, speech may be prevented by hysterical paralysis, frequently based on conflicts of libidinal or aggressive impulses. In certain types of schizophrenia, especially catatonia, mutism may be present as a result of the withdrawal of a cathexis from the outside world; there is no need for communication. In psychotic or severely neurotic patients, mutism may serve as a defense against intense aggression. They may view words as being invested with magical qualities; especially, omnipotence and other characteristics of primary process thinking (concreteness) may be responded to as though they were dangerous to release. Speech may be seen as part of oral aggression; mutism protects against biting, devouring, tearing to pieces, or hostile impulses in general. Mutism may also be used as a defense against being spoken to. Some patients regard silence on the part of the analyst as aggression. [Reik, 1928.]

Related Concepts: AGGRESSION; INHIBITIONS.

REFERENCE

Reik, T., "Das Schweigen," in *Wie man Psychologe wird. Al*, pp. 72-85, 1928.

1335

MYSTIC UNION denotes an attempt by the schizophrenic patient to attain a likeness to God, or to others who represent position and power. In the reconstruction of his ego, the patient tries to build a self which is in keeping with his self-assertive and self-exaltative strivings, and with his desire to extend his power. This striving toward an exaltation of the personality may be sought through an identification with God (or surrogate). The original driving force is an over-estimation of the self. It follows the psychological law of affective transformation (an inclination also found in primitive man). The affective tone is expressed by increasing the dimensions of the emotionally stressed objects. The union with God is consummated as a sexual union, a form of magic identification of the self with the numen. In the autistic fantasy world of schizophrenics, the ego is elevated to a dominating role. From this concentration in the self, the ego becomes filled with cosmic significance and comes to embrace the whole universe. The self becomes the world. The *world destruction* fantasy of schizophrenics is thus only an image of the revolution that is taking place in their inner world. Freud (1911) described this process in his analysis of the Schreber case.

In schizophrenics, *cosmos identification* of the self with the universe is similar to the identification of earthly with heavenly things that occurs in primitive peoples. All religious theories of the universe contain the idea that existence and events, as they appear on earth, correspond to cosmic existence and events. Man as the image of God is a cosmos in miniature and shares the fate of the cosmos: this fundamental idea is expressed, for example, in astrology, which connects the course of the life of the individual with the laws of the cosmos.

The primitive ego retains the notion of limitless extension. This tendency to regression to primordial states carries with it the foundation for mystic unity. A mystic union involves identification with equations made early in life. Fenichel (1945) noted: "A person sensing himself in a landscape does not simply feel love or hatred for the natural objects, but generally experiences a kind of identification with the landscape, the *unio mystica* with 'father's penis' or 'mother's womb'." In discussing suicide, Fenichel mentions one unconscious motivation as being "the oceanic longing for a union with the mother."

Related Concepts: IDENTIFICATION; OCEANIC FEELING; RELIGIOUS FAITH.

REFERENCES

Fenichel, O., *The Psychoanalytic Theory of Neurosis.* Nor, pp. 206, 401, 1945.
Freud, S., 1911, "Psycho-Analytic Notes on An Autobiographical Account of a Case of Paranoia (Dementia Paranoides)." *SE*, 12:51-52, 1958.

ADDITIONAL READINGS

Freud, S.: 1914, "On Narcissism: An Introduction." *SE*, 14, 1957.
    1927, "The Future of an Illusion." *SE*, 21, 1961.

1336

MYTHOLOGY denotes those legends about the origin of life, the mystery of the supernatural life and death, which are personified in the guise of gods, demi-gods, spirits, etc. Freud (1932) noted that the study of myths was like the reconstruction the analyst undertakes when he seeks to unravel the patient's dreams. Bearing in mind the distortions which may be expected to occur in transition from historical facts to the contents of a myth, they are "no worse than those which we acknowledge every day, when we reconstruct from the patients' dreams the repressed but extremely important experiences of their childhood."

In one sense the myth speaks for the instinctual life. "Instincts," Freud (1938) stated, "are mythical entities, magnificent in their indefiniteness." This statement does *not* indicate that his opinion relating to his theory of instincts was merely a myth. On the contrary, Freud considered the theory of instincts to be a valuable explanatory concept. His use of the word mythology seems to indicate that he believed that each myth contained valuable material which, if scientifically evaluated, could facilitate an approach to the ultimate truth. Obviously, Freud did not believe that Zeus had a villa on Mount Olympus, but he did believe that the legends of Zeus and Hera contained an aspect of what was important for the study of what the Greeks wanted to have, were frustrated about, and projected to the image of Zeus. Thus, an analytical study of mythology reveals those infantile wishes which appear to be responsible for their creation.

It is not always easy to draw a sharp line between myth and religion, unless one arbitrarily uses the word religion in connection with what is worshipped. Independently of whether "truth" is what is expressed in myths or religion, a psychoanalytical examination reveals certain phenomena which occur in both. For instance, Reik (1960) noted that Eve's birth appeared to represent a denial of the recognition that men are born from women and not vice versa. This recognition may have represented a threat to the patriarchal Jewish society; it may have reminded it of a prior allegiance to the matriarchal goddess Astarte. The various rapes committed by Greek gods and demi-gods on their female partners are but a reaffirmation of the power of the male.

The Jewish prayer in which the man thanks the Almighty for having created him as a man and not as a slave, or as a woman, appears to indicate a similar denial. In Graves's (1955) examination of Greek mythology, there are many examples of the patriarchal myth-figure which obscures the importance of women (e.g., Athene being born from the head of Zeus).

Related Concepts: Animism; Religious Faith; Taboo; Totem.

REFERENCES

Freud, S.: 1932, "The Acquisition and Control of Fire." *SE*, 22:187, 1964.

Freud, S.: 1933, "New Introductory Lectures on Psycho-Analysis." *SE*, 22:95, 1964.

Graves, R., *Adam's Rib*. New York: Thomas Yoseloff, 1955.

Reik, T., *The Creation of Woman*. George Braziller, Inc., pp. 73–78, 1960.

ADDITIONAL READINGS

Almansi, R. J., "Applied Psychoanalysis: Religion, Mythology and Folklore." *AnSurvPsa*, 4, 1953.

Arlow, J., "Ego Psychology and the Study of Mythology." *JAPA*, 9, 1961.

Posinsky, S., "The Death of Maui." *JAPA*, 5, 1957.

Roheim, G., "Mythology of Arnhem Land." *AmIm*, 8, 1951.

Tarachow, S., "Mythology." *AnSurvPsa*, 1, 1950.

N

1400

NARCISSISM. Primary narcissism (autoerotic) is typified by the newborn's relationship to his parents, in which no differentiation is made between himself and the external world. "At this stage," Eidelberg and Palmer (1960) noted, "the infant does not differentiate between himself and the external world. Consequently the energy responsible for this early relationship is called primary narcissistic or autoerotic libido and destrudo. After the infant begins to differentiate between himself and the external object, the imago of the external object he faces and is interested in, is cathected by object libido and destrudo, whereas the image of the external object he remembers, and of the self, is cathected by secondary narcissistic libido and destrudo." Fenichel (1945) ascribed this lack of differentiation to the fact that no distinction was made between the ego and instinctual behavior at this stage of development.

When the feeling of omnipotence is renounced, the imago of the external object is cathected by object-libido and destrudo and the image of the external object—as well as the self—is cathected by secondary narcissistic libido and destrudo. In this there is no description (by Freud and others) as to whether the total amount of primary libido and destrudo is divided and changed into secondary narcissistic libido and destrudo and object-libido and destrudo; equally, there is no indication as to whether a part of the original primary narcissistic libido and destrudo remains unchanged, where it is stored, or how it becomes visible in the adult. Secondary narcissistic libido and destrudo may,

under certain conditions, change *partly* into object-libido and destrudo and vice versa.

In Freud's first instinct theory, the sexual instincts were responsible for the survival of the human race; they were differentiated from the ego instincts which take care of the individual. An example of a function of the ego instincts is urination, while sexual intercourse is representative of the activity of the sex instincts. Thus, according to the first instinct theory, ego instincts were free of libido. But the first instinct theory was abandoned by Freud in favor of the second instinct theory, in which the sex instincts were separated from the aggressive instincts, and the ego instincts were endowed with narcissistic libido and destrudo. As regards this distinction, Freud (1917a) noted that egoism implies an advantage for the individual, whereas narcissism is only used when a libidinal satisfaction takes place. Consequently, it is possible for an individual to be egoistic and still have powerful object cathexis; i.e., he discharges his libidinal impulses with the help of objects. Conversely, an egoist will avoid anything which represents a disadvantage to his ego. At the same time, an egoist may be narcissistic, having very little interest in external objects. This may be true not only in reference to direct sexual gratification but also in reference to instincts which are aim-inhibited. The word "love" is sometimes used to refer to the aim-inhibited instincts, in contrast to those which lead to direct sexual gratification. The egoism is usually constant, the narcissism, on the other hand, represents a variable factor. Altruism (frequently the opposite of egoism) does not require that a direct sexual gratification be obtained with the help of an external object. Nonetheless, in all the cases where a human being is completely in love, altruism is present, too, as is the need for direct libidinal gratification. Usually a sexual object appeals to the subject's narcissism and becomes responsible for what Freud called sexual over-evaluation of the object. If altruism replaces egoism, the object becomes highly important: one could say that it has absorbed the ego. Further, in the same year (1917b) he noted that in dreams the individual appears egoistic. One is therefore not surprised that incipient illness appears at first in the dream.

Related Concepts: Libido; Narcissistic Mortification; Narcissistic Scar.

REFERENCES

Eidelberg, L., & J. N. Palmer, "Primary and Secondary Narcissism." *PQ*, 34:480, 1960.
Fenichel, O., *The Psychoanalytic Theory of Neurosis.* Nor, p. 36, 1945.
Freud, S.: 1917a, "Introductory Lectures on Psycho-Analysis." *SE*, 16:417–418, 1963.
     1917b, "A Metapsychological Supplement to the Theory of Dreams." *SE*, 14:223, 1957.
     1940, "An Outline of Psycho-Analysis." *SE*, 23:150–151, 1964.
Strachey, J., Editorial note. *SE*, 19:64, 1961.

ADDITIONAL READINGS

Abraham, K., 1920, "The Narcissistic Evaluation of Excretory Processes in Dream and Neurosis." *SPA*, 1942.
Andreas-Salome, L.: "Narzissmus als Doppelrichtung." *Im*, 7, 1921.
     "The Dual Orientation of Narcissism." *Q*, 3, 1962.
Balint, M., "Primary Narcissism and Primary Love." *Q*, 29, 1960.
Bing, J., F. MacLaughlin, & R. Marburg, "The Metapsychology of Narcissism." *PsaStC*, 14, 1959.
Cronin, H. J., "Phallic Symbolism in a Narcissistic Neurosis." *R*, 20, 1933.
Fox, H. M., "Narcissistic Defenses During Pregnancy." *Q*, 27, 1958.
Glover, E., *Psychoanalysis.* SP, 1949.
Hartmann, H., "Comments on the Psychoanalytic Theory of the Ego." *PsaStC*, 5, 1950.
Kapp, R. O., "Sensation and Narcissism." *IntJPsa*, 6, 1925.
Leuba, J., "Introduction to the Clinical Study of Narcissism." *RFPsa*, 13, 1949.
Meng, H., "On the Psychology of the Instinctual Narcissist." *PsaP*, 9, 1935.
Rank, O., "A Contribution to the Study of Narcissism." *Y*, 3, 1911.
Reich, A., "Narcissistic Object Choice in Women." *JAPA*, 1, 1953.

1401

NARCISSISTIC GAIN. The normal individual is interested in the discharge of objectual and narcissistic mental energy. Under certain conditions, it may be possible to isolate an action in which only narcissistic energy is discharged: the so-called functional pleasure is experienced as a result of a correct function of the body. Descriptively speaking, this narcissistic gain or gratification appears to be milder when compared with the gratification of object-libido and object-destrudo. As long as the functions of the organs are intact, the individual is scarcely aware of having a narcissistic gratification; but when he recovers from an illness and is once again able to breathe, to walk, and to think the narcissistic gratification becomes vivid. Not only the discharge of narcissistic energy but also a charge of it (rest) represents a source of narcissistic gain; both are normal as long as they are not used instead of an objectual discharge.

Freud (1923) described the etiology of this phenomenon, and suggested that it represents a kind of sublimation. It is probable that desexualization represents a kind of sublimation and that the sublimation begins by transforming object libido into narcissistic libido.

Eidelberg and Palmer (1960) described this occurrence, as follows: "Most analysts assume today that secondary narcissistic libido and destrudo are responsible for the so-called intrapsychic functions of the total personality which, according to Freud, may be divided into id, ego and super-ego. The term, intrapsychic, refers to functions of the individual from which the external world is excluded. The act of recognition of an instinctual need, its evaluation, acceptance or rejection, the control of the body, the memory, and the ability to achieve a harmonious compromise between the id and the super-ego, require a discharge of secondary narcissistic libido and destrudo under normal conditions. On the other hand, talking, eating and other activities which involve an external object appear to be possible only if, *in addition*, object libido and object destrudo are available."

Related Concept: NARCISSISM.

REFERENCES

Eidelberg, L., & J. N. Palmer, "Primary and Secondary Narcissism." *PQ*, p. 3, 1960.
Freud, S., 1923, "The Ego and the Id." *SE*, 19:30, 1961.

ADDITIONAL READINGS

Glover, E., *Psychoanalysis*. SP, 1949.
Hartmann, H., "Comments on the Psychoanalytic Theory of the Ego." *PsaStC*, 5, 1950.

1402

NARCISSISTIC MORTIFICATION is the emotional experience that results from a sudden loss of control over external or internal reality, or both, with a resultant response of fright or terror, but not of fear. Freud (1917) characterized fear as a condition that draws attention to the object; anxiety, to a state where the object is disregarded. The feeling of fright (terror or horror) is a reaction, not to the *anticipated* danger of a blow, but to a defeat which caught the subject by surprise. The unpleasure characteristic of fright is that of feeling weak, even of collapsing. In this, it differs from the unpleasure of fear or anxiety which appears to produce an increase of instinctual tension. Fright, on the other hand, appears to represent an unpleasure which is connected with a decrease of instinctual tension below a certain threshold. Whereas the unpleasure that Freud described appears to be due to the frustration of wishes connected with the need for an external object, and represents the damming up of object-libido and object-destrudo, fright seems to be connected with the inability to discharge narcissistic libido and destrudo. [Eidelberg, 1957.]

While the unpleasure due to object instinctual tension is removed by a discharge of the object instinctual energy, a narcissistic mortification is eliminated only by achieving the independent aim of regaining the lost control and unblocking the dammed-up narcissistic libido. Consequently, a complete discharge of sexual, as well as aggressive, object instinct-fusions may be experienced as unsatisfactory, because it still leaves unappeased the need to regain an *active* control over others and over the self. Internal stimuli, unlike external stimuli, usually appear as the result of a *slow* increase of tension, but, under certain conditions, they are able to surprise and overwhelm the total personality.

Detection of a narcissistic mortification (as with other elements in the unconscious) may be interfered with by the mechanisms of denial and repression. If the terror produced by the narcissistic mortification is not too severe, as Eidelberg (1959) noted, it results in a healthy, creative impulse leading to the development of a coordinated action of the total personality, an attempt to solve an internal or external problem. Should the terror be too great, or last too long, the individual becomes "paralyzed" and must resort to denial or repression in order to protect himself from being completely overwhelmed. Such denial or repression having taken place, a self-created narcissistic mortification is substituted for the original "real" narcissistic mortification.

Under pathological conditions, the patient's need to keep the narcissistic mortification he experiences from becoming conscious does not eliminate the feeling of fright. The patient attempts to project and thus to displace the object, but not the feeling, attributed to or responsible for its mobilization. The projection does not eliminate the original unpleasure, but does permit the individual to attribute the cause of this unpleasure to an external, not internal, source. The unpleasure connected with being overwhelmed by hostile wishes (internal narcissistic mortification) is avoided not by accepting the same unpleasure but by attributing it to an external enemy.

In melancholia, with the help of introjection, the patient who suffers the loss of an external object is able to say, "It is not true that I am frightened because she left me and died; the truth is that I feel remorse because, unable to control my hostility against her, I refused to take her to the doctors who would have cured her."

Under normal conditions, the individual is able to recognize and often to overcome a narcissistic mortification he has suffered and to therefore experience the feeling of triumph (sometimes connected with laughter). However, under certain pathological conditions, the narcissistic mortification may remain unconscious. The patient may not only protect himself from any knowledge of the source of his narcissistic mortification, but may even succeed in substituting a narcissistic gratification—which is the experience of triumph that replaces the unpleasure connected with his feeling of terror (counterphobic mechanism and mania)—for the narcissistic mortification.

Related Concept: NARCISSISTIC SCAR.

REFERENCES

Eidelberg, L.: "An Introduction to the Study of the Narcissistic Mortification." *PQ*, 31:657–668, 1957.
    "A Second Contribution to the Study of the Narcissistic Mortification." *PQ*, 33:636–646, 1959.
Freud, S., 1917, "General Theory of the Neuroses." *SE*, 16:395, 1963.

ADDITIONAL READINGS

Eidelberg, L., *The Dark Urge.* Py, 1961.
Freud, S., "Extracts from the Fliess Papers." *SE*, 1, 1966.
Marcinowski, J., "Die erotischen Quellen der Minderwertigkeitsgefühle." *ZSW*, 4, 1918.

1403

NARCISSISTIC NEED represents the wish for additional libidinal cathexis. In order to gratify this wish, a certain amount of libido which cathects the object-presentation is withdrawn and used to cathect the ego-presentation.

According to Eidelberg (1954), a normal individual uses secondary narcissistic libido to cathect the presentation of the ego and object-libido to cathect the object-presentations. Under pathological conditions, object-libido may be used to cathect the ego-presentation and secondary narcissistic libido may be discharged with the help of external objects. For example, the patient who appears to be preoccupied with his tooth, as the result of a toothache, is fulfilling a narcissistic need. For the duration of the toothache, the presentation of the tooth is cathected with libido withdrawn from the presentation of external objects. Normally, this object-libido changes into secondary narcissistic libido.

Related Concepts: NARCISSISM; NARCISSISTIC MORTIFICATION.

REFERENCE

Eidelberg, L., *An Outline of a Comparative Pathology of the Neuroses.* IUP, pp. 22–23, 1954.

1404

NARCISSISTIC NEUROSIS is a term used by Freud in his early writings, in a manuscript dated May 31, 1897 (1917a). In this, narcissistic neurosis is characterized by regression from object relationships to identification. Object-libido is withdrawn and reinvested in the self, with a loss of cathexis of the external object. The resulting symptomatology is an attempt to reestablish object-cathexis. Freud (1917b) considered melancholia and paranoia to be examples of narcissistic neuroses. In Freud's view, narcissistic neurosis was not amenable to psychoanalysis, because the patients failed to develop a transference neurosis. Today, most analysts regard melancholia as resulting from a defense against oral cannibalistic wishes and consider some cases suitable for psychoanalytic treatment.

Related Concepts: MELANCHOLIA; PARANOID CONDITION (STATE); PSYCHOSIS.

REFERENCES

Freud, S.: 1917a, "Mourning and Melancholia." *SE*, 14:240, 1957.
    1917b, "Introductory Lectures on Psychoanalysis." *SE*, 16:427–428, 446–447, 1963.

1405

NARCISSISTIC SCAR. According to Freud (1920), loss of love, and failure, especially during the painful extinction of the oedipus complex, may create a "permanent injury to self-regard in the form of a narcissistic scar." Severe narcissistic mortifications or injuries may lead to a narcissistic scar, which, in turn, may cause a character distortion manifested by feelings of inferiority and inadequacy or by a "perverse fixation." Early bodily deformity may also lead to the formation of narcissistic scars, and may, as Freud (1919) pointed out, result in a character disorder. Niederland (1961) described a patient with hidden bodily deformities who showed evidence of an unresolved narcissistic injury; that is, to put it another way, a narcissistic scar, with a narcissistic character disorder of considerable severity. A narcissistic scar should not be confused with a narcissistic mortification.

Related Concepts: NARCISSISM; NARCISSISTIC MORTI-FICATION.

REFERENCES

Freud, S.: 1919, "A Child Is Being Beaten." *SE*, 17:193, 1955.
　　　　 1920, "Beyond the Pleasure Principle." *SE*, 17:20–21, 1955.
Niederland, W. G., 1961, Panel Discussion on Narcissism. *JAPA*, 10:594–596, 1962.

ADDITIONAL READINGS

Freud, S., 1915, "Some Character Traits Met with in Psycho-Analytic Work." *SE*, 14, 1957.
Marcinowski, J., "Die erotischen Quellen der Minderwertigkeitsgefühle." *ZSW*, 4, 1918.

1406

NARCOLEPSY is a disorder characterized by attacks of compulsive sleepiness or by a transitory loss of consciousness; it may be due to organic brain disease. However, psychotherapeutic cures have been reported (Pond, 1952; Spiegel and Oberndorf, 1946).

Fenichel (1945) considered psychogenic narcolepsy to be a syndrome involving hysterical conversion and the transitory elimination of all consciousness. This kind of defense can be mobilized in relation to forbidden impulses, whose content can be as varied as the fantasies involved in hysterical symptoms in general. In addition to its defensive aspects, the narcoleptic attack (a compromise formation, like all symptoms) may also represent a partial gratification. It may represent orgasm, or present itself as a state of temporary helplessness that can mean an invitation to seduction or attack. Narcolepsy may be both the expression of, and the defense against, hostile impulses and death wishes turned back on the self. A narcoleptic patient, like all patients with dramatic hysterical symptoms, has many opportunities for the exploitation of his illness through secondary gain.

Related Concepts: CONVERSION AND CONVERSION SYMPTOMS; EPILEPTIC PERSONALITY.

REFERENCES

Fenichel, O., *The Psychoanalytic Theory of Neurosis.* Nor, p. 226, 1945.
Pond, D., "Narcolepsy." *JMS*, 98:595–604, 1952.
Spiegel, L., & C. Oberndorf, "Narcolepsy as a Psychogenic Syndrome." *PSM*, 8:28–35, 1946.

ADDITIONAL READING

Murphy, W. F., "Narcolepsy—A Review and Presentation of Seven Cases." *P*, 98, 1941.

1407

NECROPHILIA is a perversion characterized by a sexual object relationship with a corpse. The primary form of the object relationship may not result in intercourse, but may take the form of sado-masochistic practices; oral activity is common. It may represent an unconscious attempt to preserve the lost object, to deny the object-loss; a kind of perverse mourning. [Brill, 1941.]

The object generally represents the mother (or other parental object), for death itself is frequently depicted in fantasy as a devouring mother earth. The usual oral activity is an attempt to incorporate the object, an object which cannot demand or frustrate; it is otherwise all giving. It corresponds in character to the earliest ego state of the child in which eating, being beaten, and sleeping are all equated with death.

The act may represent an attempt to restore the object. The necrophile may thus act out the primal scene on the "defenseless, sleeping" parental figure (Tarachow, 1960). The act can be carried out without fear of reprisal. The aggressive impulses, since the object is dead and thus cannot be further destroyed, are denied at the outset. The subject is able to dramatize—to live out, as it were—the murderous fantasies which have heretofore been repressed.

Related Concepts: MASOCHISM; PERVERSION; SADISM.

REFERENCES

Brill, A. A., "Necrophilia." *JCP*, 3:51–73, 1941.
Tarachow, S., "Judas the Beloved Executioner." *Q*, 29:528–554, 1960.

ADDITIONAL READINGS

Bierman, J., "Necrophilia in a Thirteen-Year-Old Boy." *PQ*, 31, 1962.
Segal, H., "A Necrophilic Phantasy." *IntJPsa*, 34, 1953.

1408

NEED FOR PUNISHMENT denotes the seeking of pain in apparent disregard of the pleasure principle. Feeling a need for punishment, instead of feeling guilt or remorse, may indicate a relative failure to neutralize instinctual wishes toward an object and to fully incorporate it within the ego. As the infantile repressed wishes lead to partial unconscious gratification, the subject reacts with remorse instead of feelings of guilt. And as the remorse can be eliminated either through undoing or punishment, he often prefers punishment. Consequently, because all repressed infantile wishes represent the wish and its gratification, it leads to the need for punishment. By making the infantile wish conscious, psychoanalysis permits the patient to accept the responsibility and the feelings of guilt; to reject the archaic wish and its unconscious gratification; and thus to avoid punishment. After a correct interpretation, it is most clearly revealed that dreams and slips of the tongue represent not only wish-fulfillments but also the consequences of it.

Ultimately, the need for punishment does not contradict the pleasure principle, as the desired punishment appears to be easier to endure than remorse. It may be referred to as a drive motivated by the wish to eliminate unconscious feelings of guilt and remorse provoked by the gratification, real or fantasied, of a forbidden, usually aggressive, unconscious wish. The punishment may be sought after, e.g., the criminal who unconsciously wishes to be caught and imprisoned by society. It may be left to the hands of fate, like neurotic character types who provoke, or passively accept, various failures. While essentially unconscious, the drive for punishment may also be consciously experienced (e.g., in depression and masochism). [Eidelberg, 1954].

From a descriptive point of view, quantitative and qualitative differences must be distinguished. The need for punishment may lead to depressive states, e.g., parapraxes, and compulsions; relatively, however, psychopathy may be viewed as an extreme

instance. Freud (1916) described a number of cases where patients reported that in their early youth they committed a number of crimes. Their analysis made clear that the crimes were committed because they had to defy a prohibition. In a way, their sense of guilt was present before their crimes were committed.

Related Concepts: DEPRESSION; MASOCHISM; SUPER-EGO.

REFERENCES

Eidelberg, L., *An Outline of a Comparative Pathology of the Neuroses.* IUP, pp. 174–175, 1954.
Freud, S., 1916, "Some Character-Types Met with in Psycho-Analytic Work." *SE*, 14:332, 1957.

ADDITIONAL READINGS

Freud, S., 1924, "The Economic Problem of Masochism." *SE*, 19, 1961.
Reik, T., "Geständniszwang und Strafbedürfnis; Probleme der Psychoanalyse und der Kriminologie." *IntPV*, 1925.

1409

NEGATION is a defense mechanism with the help of which the repressed material, after its return to consciousness through verbalization, is rendered "harmless" by declaring that what was just said is not true. The return of the repressed material appears to take place for reasons which are still unknown. It seems that negation takes place only after primary and secondary repressions have failed. It may, therefore, be considered to belong to the "secondary line of defense." As Freud (1925) noted, the defense mechanism of negation represents a good illustration of the fact that the word "no" does not exist in the unconscious. As a result of analytical interpretation, the patient says, "I never thought of that."

For example, a patient, an editor, who was asked for his opinion on a book submitted to his publisher, said, "I don't envy the author who had to write this book." When, in analysis, he was reminded that he was asked by his publisher for a professional opinion and not for his feelings about the subject, the patient got angry at first, but presently admitted that, for many years, he had wanted to write a book on this very subject and that his reply represented a negation of his unconscious envy. In analyzing this incident—from his associations—it became clear that the words "I don't envy" represented a defense of an infantile wish to incorporate the breast of his mother and the envy connected with his inability to gratify this wish; to accept the fact that she had breasts which he wanted but could not have.

"I don't" meant "It is not true that I suffer because I have not written this book." This suffering was connected with the narcissistic mortification which exposed the limitation of his power. Thus, the patient had to refrain from becoming aware of his archaic, anachronistic wishes and narcissistic mortification. Only after his resistance was overcome was he able to recognize the unconscious meaning of his "lack" of envy.

Related Concepts: DEFENSE MECHANISMS; DENIAL (DISAVOWAL); THINKING; UNDOING.

REFERENCE

Freud, S., 1925, "Negation." *SE*, 19:237–239, 1961.

ADDITIONAL READINGS

Olinick, S., "Questioning and Pain, Truth and Negation." *JAPA*, 5, 1957.
Penrose, L., "Some Psychoanalytical Notes on Negation." *IntJPsa*, 8, 1927.
Sugar, N., "On the Question of Mimic Affirmation and Negation." *Z*, 26, 1941.

1410

NEGATIVE OEDIPUS COMPLEX. Normally, after the preoedipal phase, the infant arrives at the oedipal stage: the boy transfers his aggression (or at least a part of it) from the preoedipal mother to the oedipal father, attaching his libidinal tendencies to the oedipal mother; the aggressive instincts of the girl, on the other hand, remain cathected to the mother (who then becomes the oedipal mother), her libidinal drives attaching themselves to the oedipal father. Under certain conditions, however, the boy transfers his positive feelings to his father, his aggression remaining attached to his mother with whom he identifies; the girl transfers her aggression to her father and attaches her libidinal drives to the oedipal

mother. Whenever such a constellation takes place we speak of a negative oedipus complex.

In the case of the Wolf Man, Freud (1918) discovered that the phobia involved both of the parents. The patient's mother represented the castrated wolf, whereas the father represented the wolf which climbed upon her. The patient realized that in order to satisfy his passive feminine wishes he had to give up his penis.

Perhaps the chief clinical finding in this case, Strachey (1955) reasoned, "was the evidence revealed of the determining part played in the patient's neurosis by his *primary* feminine impulses.* The very marked degree of his bisexuality was only a confirmation of views which had long been held by Freud and which dated back to the time of his friendship with Fliess. But in his subsequent writings Freud laid greater stress than before on the fact of the *universal* occurrence of bisexuality and on the existence of an 'inverted' or 'negative' Oedipus complex."

Related Concepts: BISEXUALTIY; LATENT HOMOSEXUALITY; PREOEDIPAL.

REFERENCES

Freud, S., 1918, "From the History of an Infantile Neurosis." *SE*, 17:47, 1955.
Strachey, J., Editorial note. *SE*, 17:6, 1955.

1411

NEGATIVE THERAPEUTIC REACTION denotes an increase in neurotic behavior after an improvement has been derived from analytic treatment. The desire for recovery has succumbed to the patient's masochistic needs. After the resistance has been uncovered and eliminated, the patient becomes hostile. Whenever the patient's symptoms disappear or decrease in intensity, during the analytical treatment, the patient begins to feel worse. Originally, Freud (1923) thought that the patient wanted to prove the inferiority of the physician and only in

---

* The anal zone was used to permit the Wolf Man to play the female role. He also suffered from hysterical constipation and required an enema, administered to him by a man. In this, the man represented his father, and the enema represented the act of copulation.

later years did he recognize that there are a number of people who cannot tolerate even a partial success. Later, in amplifying his view, Freud (1924) reasoned that the negative therapeutic reaction, which is characteristic of all masochistic patients, might disappear, when some other suffering developed (organic illness or external defeat).

Clinical Example

A masochistic patient, after he had informed his analyst of his therapeutic progress, violently raged against his analyst and his analysis. He declared that the whole treatment was a fraud, that the analyst had lured him into analysis by false statements, etc. Nevertheless, it was possible to resume analysis after several hours, once the negative therapeutic reaction had been analyzed.

The patient tried to eliminate the existence of real defeats by producing self-provoked defeats. He complained about every unconsciously self-provoked defeat, though its existence protected him from the recognition of the limitation of his power. In his analysis, the patient failed to provoke the analyst to terminate his treatment and finally admitted that the analyst had succeeded in helping him although he wanted to remain sick. [Eidelberg, 1954.]

Related Concepts: MASOCHISM; MASOCHISTIC MECHANISM; OMNIPOTENCE OF THOUGHT.

REFERENCES

Eidelberg, L., *An Outline of a Comparative Pathology of the Neuroses.* IUP, p. 174, 1954.
Freud, S.: 1923, "The Ego and the Id." *SE*, 19:49, 1961.
          1924, "The Economic Problem of Masochism." *SE*, 19:166, 1961.

ADDITIONAL READINGS

Eidelberg, L.: *Studies in Psychoanalysis.* IUP, 1948.
          "Technical Problems in the Analysis of Masochists." *JHH*, 7, 1958.

1412

NEGATIVE THERAPEUTIC REACTIONS AND MASOCHISM. A patient who accepts an interpretation as correct will experience increased positive transference toward his analyst; in the analysis of masochists, however, a negative therapeutic reaction is observed. [Freud, 1923.]

A patient of Eidelberg's (1948) remarked that for the first time he had enjoyed his vacation. After reporting this success, which he attributed to his treatment, he started to shout and accused the analyst of having changed his character, instead of having dealt with his symptoms. It was possible to analyze this negative therapeutic reaction and to ultimately terminate the treatment successfully.

Related Concepts: MASOCHISM; SADISM.

REFERENCES

Eidelberg, L., *Studies in Psychoanalysis.* IUP, p. 22, 1948.
Freud, S., 1923, "The Ego and the Id." *SE*, 19:49, 1961.

1413

NEGATIVE TROPISM, according to Solomon (1954), is a retreat or withdrawal from an external source of threat or displeasure. For example, a young man too bashful to ask a girl for a date and too timid to get into a fight, even when threatened, turns away from both.

Related Concept: AGGRESSION.

REFERENCE

Solomon, J. C., *A Synthesis of Human Behavior.* G & S, pp. 11, 197, 214, 1954.

1414

NEGATIVISM is behavior which is characterized by responses exactly opposite to those normally elicited by a given stimulus, sometimes referred to as *negative attitude* or *negative behavior.* It is related to resistance, and is the opposite of automatic obedience.

The "age of resistance," "spite period of childhood" or "period of negativism," is a normal phenomenon, usually occurring from approximately the ages of eighteen months to four years, following a relatively submissive period; a defense against submission. This attitude of persistent resistance or opposition to the environment of the preschool child is considered a normal feature of the child's development. It is usually stimulated by parents who do not allow the child to solve his own problems or make up his own mind. The negative effects of repeated adult interference may produce this state, since this period of negativism coincides with the training of the child for cleanliness and control. Most investigators believe it manifests itself when a child begins to get a feeling of himself as an independent agency; he enjoys trying out his powers. This infantile negativism has been compared, by some, to the sulkiness and sullenness observed in early puberty; it chiefly consists of hostility to the environment and is associated, at the same time, with the formation of strong outside attachments. This resistance diminishes with age, and, so, may be considered a normal phase of maturation. It appears at the same age level under very different educational conditions and in various primitive cultures. [A. Freud, 1952.]

Simple resistance is an educational problem; prolonged negativism is neurotic or psychotic. When negativism is a fixed attitude of opposition directed against everybody, it is a serious phenomenon closely related to morbidity. The basic disturbance lies in the child's failure to adapt to his environment, due to insecurity and anxiety. His inability to form relationships with people leads to hostile refusal, isolation, and a failure to develop normal functions (e.g., enuresis and speech disorders). Neurotic negativism is characterized by a combination of social-contact disturbances, partial inhibition of psychic development, inner insecurity, and faulty training.

Negativism is a frequent and disagreeable symptom of schizophrenia (Bleuler, 1911). When the patients should get up, they want to remain in bed; if they should remain in bed, they want to get up. Neither on command, nor in accordance with the rules of the hospital, do they want to get dressed or undressed, come to meals, or leave their meals; but if they can perform the same acts outside of the required time or somehow contrary to the will of the environment, they often do them. Many resist all influences with excited scolding and fighting. In some cases the patient can be brought to do the desired

act if one forbids him to do it, or orders him to do the opposite (command negativism).

However, even the most pronounced negativism is not absolute; it may be greater toward some people than toward others. The pronounced character of negativism in schizophrenics may be due to a fundamental cause of which we are ignorant. Their deficient understanding of the environment, the countermeasures of confinement, naturally produce a hostile attitude. In women, sexuality with its marked ambivalence can contribute its influence, and lead the patients to reject what they really want. Although negativism appears to represent a conscious effort to achieve independence, unconsciously, it gratifies the wish to obey and remain dependent.

Related Concepts: NEGATION; RESISTANCE.

REFERENCES

Bleuler, E., "Antwort auf die Bemerkungen Jungs zur Theorie des Negativismus." *Y*, 3:475–478, 1911.
Freud, A., "A Connection Between the States of Negativism and of Emotional Surrender." *IntJPsa*, 33:265, 1952.

ADDITIONAL READINGS

Ausubel, D., "Negativism as a Phase of Ego Development." *Ops*, 20, 1950.
Bleuler, E., *The Theory of Schizophrenic Negativism.* NMDP, 1912.
Freud, S., 1925, "Negation." *SE*, 19, 1961.
Gross, O., "Zur Differentialdiagnostik Negativistischer Phänomene." *PNW*, 37, 1904.
Mahler, M., "On Child Psychosis and Schizophrenia." *PsaStC*, 1952.

1415

NEOLOGISM denotes an often preconsciously or unconsciously coined word which is new and unusual; it is usually made by condensing and combining two or more regular words. Neologisms often have a special meaning to the subject which is not easily understandable to the object. Neologisms are formed in accordance with the laws of the primary process. They may occur whenever the secondary process is not securely in control of the primary process (in psychosis, dreams, early childhood, etc.).

The unconscious sources of neologisms are subject to analysis. Freud (1908) showed that in his dream the sentence, "It's written in a positively norekdal style," referred to a paper which he considered inferior because it was grandiose. The word "norekdal" was a condensation of two characters in an Ibsen play, namely, Nora and Ekdal.

Related Concept: PARAPRAXIS.

REFERENCE

Freud, S., 1900, "The Interpretation of Dreams."*SE*, 4:296, 1953.

ADDITIONAL READING

Jones, E., "The Psychopathology of Everyday Life." *PPsa*, 1938.

1416

NEURASTHENIA is a syndrome characterized by fatigue and feelings of physical and mental weakness, frequently accompanied by aches, pains, insomnia, etc. In 1895, Freud related neurasthenia to the libido theory. The fact that anxiety neurosis may be present together with neurasthenia does not contradict Freud's concept that these two illnesses should be separated. In both neuroses the source of the increased tension appears to be somatic. In neurasthenia, as Freud (1898) later pointed out, the infantile material which is characteristic of psychoneurosis is not found. Freud thought that excessive masturbation lead to neurasthenia, whereas anxiety neurosis may be the result of coitus interruptus.

Related Concepts: ACTUAL NEUROSIS; ANXIETY.

REFERENCES

Freud, S.: 1895, "On the Grounds for Detaching a Particular Syndrome from Neurasthenia Under the Description 'Anxiety Neuroses.'" *SE*, 3:114, 1962.
    1898, "Sexuality in the Aetiology of the Neuroses." SE, 3:268, 1962.

ADDITIONAL READINGS

Brill, A., "Diagnostic Errors in Neurasthenia." *MRR*, 36, 1930.
Freud, S., 1906, "My Views on the Part Played by Sexuality in the Aetiology of the Neuroses." *SE*, 7, 1953.

Meng, H., "Neurasthenie, Neuropathie, Psychopathie des Kindesalters." *PsaVkb*, 1926.
Schilder, P., "Über Neurasthenia." *Z*, 17, 1931.

1417

NEUROPSYCHOSES OF DEFENSE. In a short paper published in 1894, Freud grouped together hysteria, obsessions and certain cases of acute hallucinatory confusion under the name of *neuropsychoses of defense*. The concept represented an early use of the principle of constancy; the mind defends itself against overstimulation; unbearable ideas or experiences are removed from consciousness or deprived of their powerful affect.

In his paper on the neuropsychoses of defense, Freud (1896) provided an early classification of defense mechanisms of the specific neuroses and psychoses. Defense was seen as a common denominator: this concept of neurosis was a dynamic one, involving a struggle and compromise formation between repressed and repressing forces. In hysteria, the affect of the traumatic idea or experience was "converted" into a motor innervation or a hallucinatory sensation; in phobias, the affect was changed into anxiety and then was displaced onto another object; in obsessions, the idea was separated from its affect; in hallucinatory psychosis, the traumatic experience was rejected as if it had never occurred (flight into psychosis); and in paranoia, the unwelcome idea was projected onto other people.

These preliminary expositions of the specific neuroses were centered around Freud's conclusion that the responsible etiological event necessitating defense was a traumatic sexual seduction (usually by an adult) of a child; a passive experience in the case of hysteria, and an active experience in the case of obsessions (although a passive experience precedes it). The sexual trauma was viewed as occurring before puberty, although the neurosis broke out after puberty. Freud (1914) later abandoned this theory, recognizing that in many cases the significant childhood sexual trauma had occurred only in fantasy, not in actuality. The term is now obsolete.

Related Concepts: CONVERSION AND CONVERSION SYMPTOMS; DEFENSE MECHANISMS; DISPLACEMENT; PROJECTION; REPRESSION.

REFERENCES

Freud, S.: 1894, "Neuro-Psychoses of Defence." *SE*, 3:45–70, 1962.

    1896, "Further Remarks on the Neuro-Psychoses of Defence." *SE*, 3:162–188, 1962.

    1914, "On The History of the Psycho-Analytic Movement." *SE*, 14:16, 1957.

1418

NEUROSES (PSYCHONEUROSES) are denotative of emotional disturbances resulting from inadequate resolution of unconscious intrapsychic conflict, characterized by impaired effectiveness in functioning. Although there is some disagreement over the exact boundaries of the neuroses and their quantitative properties, most psychoanalysts today agree with Freud (1905) that the neuroses are a result of a fixation on, or a regression to, some phase of infantile sexuality, the degree of psychopathology being directly related to the earliness of the fixation or the depth of the regression.

Freud (1895) originally divided the neuroses into actual neuroses and psychoneuroses. In the actual neuroses, intrapsychic conflict result in dammed-up libido (the affective component Freud first thought was anxiety) which could seek indirect discharge through symptoms (e.g., the conversion symptom). Actual neuroses, which included neurasthenia and anxiety neuroses, were ascribed directly to increased tension resulting from physiologically based sexual frustrations. Freud referred less and less to the concept of the actual neuroses, finally abandoning it, as have most contemporary analysts.

The conflicts causing neuroses were first formulated by Freud in terms of the sexual (erotic) forces versus the self-preservative forces (ego instincts). However, when it became clear that the sexual drives were invested in the self and the self-preservative forces were not free of libido, this formulation had to be revised. Freud's (1923) dual instinct theory stated that all drives are composed of a fusion of two primary instincts, Eros and Thanatos; thus, two instinct-fusions—sexual and aggressive—were responsible for all the derivatives.

From a structural viewpoint, neurotic conflict may be viewed in terms of the id, ego, and superego striving for unconscious gratification. Neuroses resulting from attempts to resolve this conflict by repressing the instinctual wishes are unacceptable to the ego and often result in superego prohibitions. Failure of the repression, because of heightened instinctual forces or weakened defensive forces, results in the unconscious wishes, which have retained their energy, pushing toward consciousness. Anxiety often results from this threatened breakthrough of the repressed wishes, acting as a signal for the ego to attempt to bind the energy of the derivatives of the unconscious drives in neurotic symptoms, which act as compromises, simultaneously satisfying (partly) both the repressed wish and the repressing agencies. The unacceptable wishes achieve some degree of discharge in a disguised form.

The conditions necessary for the occurrence of neuroses include: revival of infantile (repressed) instinctual impulses and infantile narcissistic mortifications (precipitated by current happenings); ego development of counter cathectic measures (defenses) against the instinctual forces; and the failure of the defenses to maintain the repressions, bringing about a return of the repressed and leading to secondary repressions. The development of symptoms may simultaneously discharge the instinctual energy and act as a defense, by the ego, of the emergence of the impulses into consciousness. An intensification of the defenses may lead to the formation of symptoms or to neurotic character traits.

Related Concepts: ACTUAL NEUROSIS; ANXIETY; SENSE OF GUILT.

REFERENCES

Freud, S.: 1895, "On the Grounds for Detaching a Particular Syndrome from Neurasthenia Under The Description 'Anxiety Neurosis.'" *SE*, 108, 1962.

    1905, "Three Essays on the Theory of Sexuality." *SE*, 7:237–241, 1953.

    1923, "The Ego and the Id." *SE*, 19:40–47, 1961.

ADDITIONAL READINGS

Alexander, F., "Neurosis and the Whole Personality." *IntJPsa*, 7, 1926.

Eidelberg, L., *An Outline of a Comparative Pathology of the Neuroses.* IUP, 1954.

Fraiberg, S., "A Critical Neurosis in a Two-and-a-Half-Year-Old Girl." *PsaStC*, 7, 1952.

Freud, S.: 1896, "Further Remarks on the Neuro-Psychoses of Defence." *SE*, 3, 1962.

1900, "The Interpretation of Dreams." *SE*, 5, 1953.

1914, "On Narcissism: An Introduction." *SE*, 14, 1957.

Kolansky, H., "Treatment of a Three-Year-Old Girl's Severe Infantile Neurosis: Stammering and Insect Phobia." *PsaStC*, 15, 1960.

Root, N. N., "A Neurosis in Adolescence." *PsaStC*, 12, 1957.

Wolff, M., "The Problem of Neurotic Manifestations in Children of Preoedipal age." *PsaStC*, 6, 1951.

1419

NEUROSIS AND PSYCHOSIS. In two papers written in 1924, Freud examined the differences between neurosis and psychosis, and suggested the following definition: neurosis represented the outcome of a conflict between the ego and the id; in narcissistic neurosis, such as melancholia (depression), between the ego and superego; and in psychosis, between the ego and outer world. It may be proper to examine Freud's (1924a) basic formulations in detail. The conflict between the id and ego or superego which finally becomes conscious to the patient only occurs during the course of treatment. The patient slowly discovers, as it were, that the symptoms of his neurotic disorder are the result of a conflict between the id wishes and the defenses of his ego and superego. The patient is not aware at first of this conflict. What he suffers from is a conflict between himself and his symptoms. The symptom permits a partial gratification and a partial frustration of the repressed wishes to take place. The quantity of the gratification may, of course, depend on the disorder; it appears to be greater in conversions than in phobias and obsessions. The strength of the defense, from a structural point of view, may depend chiefly on either its superego aspects, as in anxiety neurosis, or in the ego aspects, as in neurotic character traits.

It is the differentiation between the inner and external reality which appears decisive. The neurotic appears to be able to tolerate a *split* in his personality and to recognize the symptom as a foreign body which he cannot eliminate. The psychotic, conversely, appears unable to *accept* such a split and denies it by accepting instead the conflict between himself and the external world. The loss of reality in psychosis takes place as a result of the introjection of the world. The external world against which he fights is not the real world but a manifestation into which he has projected his infantile wishes and their defenses.

Neurosis

In neurosis, the ego, in the service of the reality principle, undertakes to repress the id impulses. The neurosis itself occurs as a result of the "compensation" which must be paid for the damage done to a part of the ego; that is, as Freud (1927a) noted, it occurs "in reaction to the repression and in a miscarriage of it." The neurotic symptom which results is the consequence of an unconscious defense of an infantile repressed wish, and represents a compromise between the id and the ego and superego. Subsequently, a compromise occurs, as well, between the patient and the external world. A neurotic symptom, therefore, represents a compromise between the demands of the id, ego, and superego and the external world.

The neurotic's total personality tries to isolate the symptom which represents a foreign body. In conversion symptoms this usually leads to a mild rejection (la belle indifférence); in the symptom of depression it produces anguish; in phobias and obsessional neuroses there is a mobilization of secondary defense mechanisms. The phobic patient uses the secondary defense mechanisms of avoidance and inhibition of certain activities to protect himself against the emotion of fright; the obsessional patient uses his obsession to free himself of compulsive doubts. The patient with a neurotic character trait accepts it as a part of his own personality, perhaps as a consequence of the fact that the ego plays a quantitatively greater role: for instance, a moral masochist uses unconscious provocation as a defense mechanism instead of projection and, consequently, fights the real aggression which he has provoked. In contrast, the paranoid patient fights against an imagined aggressor (his own projected hostility).

The patient with a neurotic character disorder uses rationalization as a defense mechanism to deny the real unconscious causes of his behavior, to produce what appears to be a pseudo-explanation.

Psychosis

In psychosis, Freud (1924b) noted, something analogous to the process of what happens in a neurosis occurs. The psychotic tries to deal with his unconscious wishes by projecting them onto the external world. Because his reality testing is faulty, he attributes his wishes to external objects. In addition, with the help of negative hallucinations, he denies the reality of the external world: "It is not true that I am hostile; the truth is that the external world is hostile." In phobia, a projection takes place but there is a basic difference between the projection in phobia and the projection in paranoia. The paranoid patient says: "They hate me; I am afraid of them." The phobic patient says: "I am afraid I may be run over by a car." The phobic recognizes his fears as being pathological and, as a result, tries to attribute them to external sources (e.g., to the car). The paranoid starts by perceiving his own hostility as a defense against his hostility to the external object, for unlike a phobic patient he is unable to avoid the object. The difference between the two may be accounted for by the patient's relationship to the object. In the phobic patient, the dangerous wish is mobilized by certain objects (but not others), and as long as he avoids them he is free of the resultant fear. In the paranoid, on the other hand, the projection takes place independently of the object. That is, it seems that in phobia the psychic energy is withdrawn from the presentation of an external object, and displaced to the presentation of *other* objects. In paranoia the displaced energy cathects the self.

Related Concepts: BORDERLINE CASES; CHARACTER TRAITS; PSYCHOPATHY; PSYCHOTIC CHARACTER.

REFERENCES

Freud, S.: 1924a, "Neurosis and Psychosis." *SE*, 19:149, 1961.
　　　1924b, "The Loss of Reality in Neurosis and Psychosis." *SE*, 19:184–185, 1961.

ADDITIONAL READINGS

Deutsch, H., *Psychoanalysis of the Neuroses.* IUP, 1951.
Federn, P., "The Four Statutes of Compulsive Neurosis." *Z*, 19, 1938.
Fleming, J., "Observations on the Defenses Against a Transference Neurosis." *Ps*, 9, 1946.
Greenschpoon, R., "A Famous Case of Compulsion Neurosis." *R*, 24, 1937.
Hitschmann, E., "Psychoanalysis of Compulsion Neuroses." *ZNP*, 1932.
Meng, H., "On the Problems of Neuroses, Psychology of Psychoses, Endocrine System." *P*, 13, 1959.

1420

NEUROSIS AS A NEGATIVE OF PERVERSION is a construct which originated in the early writings of Freud. He then reasoned (in 1905) that perverts accepted those sexual trends which the neurotic tried to repress. Clinically, the view was held that perverts could not be treated in analysis, because they satisfied their infantile wishes consciously without any interference from their ego or superego. In later years, however, Freud (1927) recognized that perversion was not caused by a breakthrough from the id; still, some analysts continued to describe perversion as being caused by a lack of defense against instinctual wishes. They reasoned that experience gained in the treatment of neurotics had shown that a successful analysis was possible only if the patient suffered from his symptoms, wanted to destroy them, and was willing to cooperate in seeking out the unconscious elements responsible for them. Most analysts were prepared to accept the correctness of an analytic interpretation only if a therapeutic change took place (in addition to the presence of a sufficiently convincing chain of circumstantial evidence). Thus, the material gained from the treatment of perverts, in whom no change took place, appeared to be of little value. If perversion were a negative of neurosis, there could be little or no expectation to cure perverts by the analytic method. In this, the pervert had repressed nothing and there was, therefore, nothing for the analyst to decode and uncover. Consequently, many analysts have refused to treat perverts, or have limited their treatment to the accompanying neurotic symptoms only.

Fenichel (1931) characterized the problem in the form of two questions: Under what circumstances does the ego approve of an action that is otherwise warded off? Why is a neurosis produced in one case and a perversion in another? It was Fenichel's belief that the construct of the "neurosis as a negative of the perversion" had to be corrected. He reasoned that Freud was correct in his belief that a partial repression of the infantile sexuality took place, and added that it was his belief (Fenichel's) that it covered a much larger portion—the remaining part of the infantile sexuality—which remained hidden from the pervert's consciousness. The part that is admitted to consciousness and gratified he characterized, as follows: (a) the fact that it is connected with very strong pregenital fixations, and (b) by its potency in explicitly disavowing the danger of castration.

Eidelberg (1948) did not, however, believe that acceptance of the perverted act by the ego satisfactorily resolved the problem posed by Fenichel. He noted: "If the absence of defense on the part of the ego is explained by a quantitatively large component instinct, this means that the relation between the component instinct and the pervert's ego is basically different from that obtaining in neurosis, in which a quantitative increase of the component instinct results not in the elimination but in a strengthening of the ego's defense. . . .

"Direct observation in analysis does not confirm the assertion that the component instinct is weaker in serious compulsion neurosis than in homosexuality. Fenichel's second assertion that the pregenital actions are particularly suitable for disavowing the oedipal goal and are therefore accepted by the pervert's ego—does not explain why the neurotic, who would also like to disavow the oedipal goal, does not look for the same way out but wards off the preoedipal drives. Moreover, it is difficult to agree with the hypothesis that the pervert's ego attaches so much importance to disavowing the oedipal instinctual goal with the first assertion, according to which the ego is so small as compared with the instinct that it renounces all defense. One is led to suppose that the same ego which is so weak with regard to the component instincts is extremely strong with regard to the oedipal instinctual goals— and this supposition is equally unsupported by observation."

The problem of the ego-approval of the component instinct in perversion does not seem satisfactorily solved by any formulation made to date. What is approved—the perverted action—is *not* identical with the component instinct, and does not amount to a simple gratification of it. It appears rather that the component instinct must undergo extensive change and masking in order to be gratified by the perverted action. This masking is conditioned by the defense of the pervert's ego, which resists the gratification of a component instinct as energetically as does the ego of a neurotic. Thus the perverted action, like the neurotic symptom, results from a conflict between the superego, the ego and the id. It represents a compromise and contains elements both of instinctual gratification and of frustration. At the same time it satisfies the demands of the superego. Just as in the case of the symptom, the instinctual gratification takes place in a masked form, its real content remaining unconscious. The perverted action differs from the neurotic symptom, first, in the manner of gratification of the id impulse (by means of an orgasm), and, second, in the ego's wishes for omnipotence—which is satisfied by ego-syntonic action.

Eidelberg reasoned that both perverts and neurotics warded off the component instincts. He noted: "The difference between them consists not in the fact that the one approves of and the other rejects the component instinct, but in *the different attitude of the ego toward the defense mechanisms*. In every neurosis, the ego regards the neurotic's symptom, which is a result of its defense activity, as a foreign element, and disavows it to a quantitatively varying extent; in a perversion on the other hand, the perverted action, which is also the result of the ego's defensive activity, *is approved by the ego*.

"This difference in ego attitude is determined, first, by the fact that in the formation of the perverted action the infantile megalomania of the patient's ego is accorded much greater consideration than in the formation of the neurotic symptom, and second, by the fact that in the perverted action the wishes of the three psychic systems are harmoniously gratified in a compromise form.

"As regards the genesis of perversions and other psychic illnesses, two factors must be considered: the presence of regression to one of the three developmental stages, and the libidinous type to which a given patient belongs."

Related Concept: DEFENSE MECHANISMS.

REFERENCES

Eidelberg, L., *Studies in Psychoanalysis*. IUP, pp. 3–4, 29–30, 1948.
Fenichel, O., *Perversionen, Psychosen, Charakter-störungen*. IntPV, 19, 1931.
Freud, S.: 1905, "Fragment of an Analysis of a Case of Hysteria." *SE*, 7:50, 1953.
    1927, "Fetishism." *SE*, 21:157, 1961.

1421

NEUTRALIZATION is the result of the aim-inhibition of an instinct, and, according to Freud (1923), represents a *kind* of sublimation; however, Hartmann (1964) regards this as a synonym of sublimation. With the maturation and development of the psychic apparatus, the gradual deaggressivization and desexualization of the aggressive and libidinal drives take place. When the original instinctual aims, whether aggressive or libidinal, come under the influence of the secondary process, part is turned against the self.

Freud (1923) distinguished between sublimation and the desexualization of libido, but wonders whether "all sublimation does not take place through the mediation of the ego, which begins by changing the sexual object-libido into narcissistic libido and then, perhaps, goes on to give it another aim." It must be noted that while Freud speaks of "indifferente Energie," which is assumed to be desexualized libido and sublimated energy, he also includes a third, which is rendered by the translator as *neutral* energy. With this, Hartmann (1964) noted: "Again the term is sometimes used for the nondefensive, in contradiction to the defensive, ego functions, and their aims and cathexis." Thus, sublimation refers to the process now denoted as *neutralization*.

More recently, Hartmann, Kris and Loewenstein have stressed that neutral energy is derived from the undifferentiated ego-id matrix at birth, which then becomes available to the ego following structuralization. A second source of neutral energy results from deaggressivization and delibidinization of the primitive drives. Thus, neutralization develops under the influence of secondary-process activity and object-constancy, and is closely related to instinctual fusion and sublimation. Should regression occur, deneutralization follows with resultant reinstinctualization.

Related Concepts: AIM-INHIBITED DRIVES (INSTINCTS); SUBLIMATION.

REFERENCES

Freud, S., 1923, "The Ego and the Id." *SE*, 19:30, 1961.
Hartmann, H., *Essays on Ego Psychology*. IUP, p. 227, 1964.

ADDITIONAL READING

Kris, E., "Neutralization and Sublimation: Observations on Young Children." *PsaStC*, 10, 1955.

1422

NIGHTMARE (PAVOR NOCTURNUS). Freud (1900) never denied that disorders of internal organs may provoke certain dreams. However, Freud maintained that a nightmare represented a gratification and, it may be added, the consequences of such a gratification are punishment for infantile repressed wishes. It appears that aggressive wishes play a decisive role in the psychogenesis of a nightmare. Sexual intercourse, if observed by children, produces anxiety in them and appears as something uncanny. According to Freud, night terrors are the result of increased sexual impulses.

M. Sperling (1958) distinguished two forms of pavor nocturnus in children: the psychotic form, involving hypermotility, hallucinations, and a retrograde amnesia on awakening; and the neurotic form, characterized by nightmares, from which the child awakens still experiencing anxiety and with a vivid memory of the dream, which may be caused by conflicts about homosexual, sado-masochistic, and aggressive impulses. The psychotic type may continue into puberty, at which time serious character disorders, perversions or even psychotic states may become manifest. The neurotic form may be revived later in life.

Related Concept: DREAMS.

REFERENCES

Freud, S., 1900, "The Interpretation of Dreams." *SE*, 5:585, 1953.
Sperling, M., "Pavor Nocturnus." *JAPA*, 6:79–94, 1958.

ADDITIONAL READINGS

Kanzer, M., "Repetitive Nightmares After a Battle-field Killing." *PQ*, 23, 1949.

Rangell, L., "A Treatment of Nightmares in a Seven-Year-Old Boy." *PsaStC*, 5, 1950.

Schacter, N., "The Nightmare: Its Psychosomatic Constellation." *RFPsa*, 23, 1959.

1423

NIHILISM is a symptom of an acute psychotic disorder, characterized by delusions of world destruction and chaos. With the withdrawal of cathexis from the object world, a regression to primary narcissism probably occurs, involving the dissolution of ego boundaries. The resultant fantasies, then, are delusional projections to the outer world of the unconscious wish to destroy and to be destroyed. In many cases of paranoia, Freud (1911) noted, the patient experienced a world catastrophe. It seems that the cause of this catastrophe was the patient's withdrawal of his instinctual energy from external objects; his delusions represented an attempt at recovery and reconstruction.

Related Concepts: DEPERSONALIZATION; LIBIDO.

REFERENCE

Freud, S., 1911, "Psycho-Analytic Notes on an Auto-biographical Account of a Case of Paranoia (Dementia Paranoides)." *SE*, 12:69–71, 1958.

1424

NIRVANA PRINCIPLE is denotative of that tendency to reduce all internal tensions to the lowest possible level, and constitutes a regulating principle of mental life.* Freud (1920) considered the Nirvana principle to be a tendency which found expression in the pleasure principle.

Originally, the Nirvana principle and the pleasure-unpleasure principle were treated as synonyms. An increase of tension meant unpleasure, whereas a decrease meant pleasure. Later, Freud (1924) modified this view. In addition to the increase and the decrease, qualitative factors like rhythm were respon-

sible for the differentiation between pleasure and unpleasure. Furthermore, the Nirvana principle was closely related to the death instinct, whereas the pleasure principle was connected with libido.

Related Concepts: LAW OF CONSTANCY; PLEASURE PRINCIPLE; PRIMARY MASOCHISM.

REFERENCES

Freud, S.: 1920, "Beyond the Pleasure Principle." *SE*, 18:55–56, 1955.

1924, The Economic Problem of Masochism." *SE*, 19:159–160, 1961.

ADDITIONAL READINGS

Freud, S., 1915, "Instincts and Their Vicissitudes." *SE*, 14, 1957.

Low, B., *Psycho-Analysis. A Brief Account of the Freudian Theory.* AU, 1920.

1425

NOCTURNAL ENURESIS is a conversion symptom, usually hysterical in nature, caused by sexual and aggressive phallic wishes. It appears that exhibitionistic and scopophilic needs and their defenses are of basic importance. Consequently, the feeling of shame (reaction formation) is often present. Enuresis is often referred to as a masturbation equivalent.

Abraham (1927) noted: "A condition in neurotic women which owes one of its most important determinants to the castration complex is *enuresis nocturna*. The analogy between the determination of this symptom in female and male neurotics is striking. I may refer to a dream of a male patient of fourteen who suffered from this complaint. He dreamt that he was in a closet and urinating with manifest feelings of pleasure, when he suddenly noticed that his sister was looking at him through the window. As a little boy he had actually exhibited with pride before his sister his masculine way of urinating. This dream which ended in enuresis, shows the boy's pride in his penis; and enuresis in the female frequently rests on the wish to urinate in the male way. The dream represented in this process in a disguised form ended with a pleasurable emptying of the bladder.

"Women who are prone to *enuresis nocturna* are regularly burdened with strong resistances against the female sexual functions. The infantile desire to urinate in the male position is associated with the

---

* Though not specifically identified, Freud discussed the problem in the "Project," as early as 1895: "The principle of neuronic inertia, which asserts that neurones tend to divest themselves of quantity."

well-known assimilation of the ideas of urine and sperma, and of micturition and ejaculation. The unconscious tendency to wet the man with urine during sexual intercourse has its origin in this."

Related Concept: CONVERSION AND CONVERSION SYMPTOMS.

REFERENCE

Abraham, K., 1927, "The Female Castration Complex." *SPA*, p. 351, 1942.

ADDITIONAL READINGS

Blau, A., "Nocturnal Enuresis." *JAMA*, 154, 1954.
Marcuse, M., "Das Bettnässen (Enuresis Nocturna) als Sexualneurotisches Symptom." *ZSW*, 11, 1924.
Michaels, J. J., "Enuresis—A Method for Its Study and Treatment." *Ops*, 9, 1939.

1426

NORMALITY. No clear definition of normality or of mental health is possible, though a differentiation between the normal and the pathological is essential in analytical treatment. Attempts at such a definition are based on the concepts of the defense mechanism, the repression, the regression, etc., but, as Hartmann (1964) reasoned, "these conceptions of health approach the problem too exclusively from the angle of the neuroses, or rather they are formulated in terms of contrast with the neuroses. Mechanisms, developmental stages, modes of reaction, with which we have become familiar for the part they play in the development of the neuroses, are automatically relegated to the realm of the pathological." Hartmann does nonetheless admit that the arbitrary nature of such an approach is less evident in the literature of psychoanalysis than in its application to social conditions, artistic activity, etc.

The study of what is normal is relegated to a study of the derivatives of behavior. Here, "we distinguish three kinds of derivatives—ideas, affects, and motor discharge reactions. This means that an instinct fusion is observable in one of these three forms, or that a given quality of the instinct fusion can manifest itself by way of an idea, an affect, or a motor discharge reaction. In classificatory terms, the sphere in which the instinct fusions dwell is called the id; that in which their derivatives dwell,

the ego." [Eidelberg, 1948.] It is precisely the latter that allows for a quantitative evaluation. In a treatment situation—the starting point for all psychoanalytic investigation—the analysis is limited by those claims the patient makes upon the analyst.

Thus, in one sense, it was necessary to arrive at a definition of illness before any reasonable satisfactory attempt could be made to define normality. Freud (1910) discussed the etiology of his early discoveries and his consequent conclusions. The nature and the purpose of a neurotic illness became clearer after the discovery of the infantile libidinal impulses. The human being develops a neurosis when an external factor leads to a frustration of instinctual needs or when he is unable to adapt to external reality. In not being able to obtain a full satisfaction because of his frustrations, the patient tries to escape into an illness that offers him partial gratifications for his infantile wishes.

Whenever a neurosis develops from the lack of satisfaction in reality, the phenomenon of regression results, characterized by the patient's return to an infantile stage. Freud was convinced that the experience gained in the therapy of the neurotics could be used in the study of phenomena which result from the sublimation of infantile fantasies. He thought that healthy people had similar problems to that of neurotics, and he thus regarded health as a result of a quantitative factor, deriving from the strengths of the infantile energy and the strengths of the mature ego.

From a practical point of view, most analysts agree that an individual who is able to love, to be loved and to work may be considered normal. While it is true that the presence of repressed infantile wishes interfere with mental health, the decisive factor in determining whether an individual is normal and healthy is the quantitative evaluation of the blocked, repressed mental energy.

Related Concepts: DEFENSE MECHANISMS; EGO-SYNTONIC; INSTINCT (INSTINCTUAL DRIVE).

REFERENCES

Eidelberg, L., *Studies in Psychoanalysis.* IUP, p. 116, 1948.
Freud, S., 1910, "Five Lectures on Psycho-Analysis." *SE*, 11:49–50, 1957.
Hartmann, H., *Essays on Ego Psychology.* IUP, pp. 13–14, 1964.

1427

NORMAL MASTURBATION. Most authors agree that a normal adult will discharge sexual drives through masturbation only if external objects are not available. In adolescence, masturbation is considered normal. Patients who have *never* masturbated may have a bad prognosis because of this repression of genital outlet. The psychoanalysis of neurotics shows that masturbation may be connected with a number of pathological phenomena. [Fenichel, 1945.]

Related Concept: MASTURBATION.

REFERENCE

Fenichel, O., *The Psychoanalytic Theory of Neurosis.* Nor, pp. 75–76, 1945.

1428

NUCLEI. The nuclear theory was presented by Glover (1939) to explain the formational processes of the ego. In this, he noted: "The early formation of ego nuclei within a primary narcissistic organization depends on corporeal experience of motor and sensory innervations and of motor or sensory expression of affect which vary with the rise or fall of instinctual excitation. These corporeal experiences also vary with fluctuation in the physiological and erotogenic activity of the organ concerned so that the early nuclei of the ego are 'body nuclei' contained as it were within a skin nucleus. These constitute the first internal differentiations of narcissism but as recognition of object increases, the narcissistic phase gives place gradually to a phase of distinction between the ego and its objects. Differentiation of objects is heightened by experience of different degrees and kinds of object cathexis."

Related Concept: STRUCTURAL (TOPOGRAPHIC) APPROACH.

REFERENCE

Glover, E., *Psycho-Analysis.* SP, p. 184, 1939.

1429

NYMPHOMANIA denotes an abnormal, insatiable desire for sexual relationships by the female; often referred to as a perversion. A form of pseudo-hypersexuality, it usually masks a type of frigidity that is characterized by inadequate and incomplete satisfaction. Such subjects are usually impulse ridden, unable to tolerate any frustration or delay. They are in a constant search for oral narcissistic supplies. They have little or no regard for the object of their erotic desires; their erotomania is nonetheless an attempt to preserve some kind of object relationship.

Nymphomania may represent a defense against unconscious hostility and, at the same time, permit the gratification of sadistic impulses. The frequent oral character of this disorder—of the nymphomaniacal instinctual organization—combined with its ego defects, is expressed as an impulsive, insatiable desire to devour the male's penis. The nymphomaniac can't be raped; she uses the illusion of sexual control (omnipotence) to deny her fear of sexuality. Her promiscuity represents both an avoidance of, and an endless search for, the incestuous object, and for the preoedipal, all-loving and all-satisfying object. Nymphomania may replace, or be replaced, by compulsive masturbation: the blame is then projected onto the object which is held to be responsible for the nymphomaniac's failure to find satisfaction. Nymphomania is often a defense against homosexual urges, and against early infantile fantasies of fusion and symbiosis.

Clinical Example

"The author treated a young girl, who had been previously married and divorced, who was unable to refuse sex relations to any man who became her escort for an evening. She worried about what she called a 'weakness', and wanted to learn how to develop sufficient will power to become discrete. She had gotten into difficulties with married men on numerous occasions.

"Her early history disclosed excessive masturbation through manual manipulation of the clitoris. She admitted an inability ever to achieve an orgasm during coitus. She experienced no pleasurable sensations in the vagina (anesthesia vaginalis). Her promiscuity was an attempt in fantasy to meet some man perhaps who would succeed in having her experience an orgasm during sexual intercourse.

"Frigid wives often become unfaithful for the

same reason—the hope of finding the ideal sexual partner.

"As is often the case with prostitutes, women who suffer from promiscuity or nymphomania have a strong latent homosexual component. They run to many men to convince themselves that they are not lesbians. Their sexual excesses with many men represent a form of pseudo-heterosexuality which accounts for their frigidity." [London and Caprio, 1950].

Related Concepts: FRIGIDITY; PERVERSION; SATYRIASIS.

REFERENCE

London, L., & F. Caprio, *Sexual Deviations.* Washington: The Linacre Press, pp. 615–616, 1950.

ADDITIONAL READING

Hollander, M., "Prostitution, the Body, and Human Relatedness." *IntJPsa*, 42, 1961.

O

OBESITY, aside from the constitutional factors resulting from inheritance, represents a partial gratification and a partial defense of various instinctual needs. Developmentally, they were described by H. Bruch (1941, 1950), in part, as follows: a. *Oral Stage*. Wishes for oral gratification where food is a substitute for the object cathected with oral libido. Eating may satisfy the unconscious wish for reincorporation of the object or part object (e.g., breast or penis) for the purpose of securing a symbiotic fusion between the ego and the object, either to protect against separation from the object or to destroy it. b. *Anal Stage*. Coprophagic fantasies. c. *Phallic Stage*. Where the wish for food is connected with an unconscious pregnancy fantasy, in which the mouth is regressively cathected with phallic libido (mouth equals vagina), the food becomes equivalent to a baby, and obesity may equal pregnancy. In the male, the fantasy may be the incorporation of the father's penis in order to achieve an oedipal triumph in the positive oedipus complex.

In addition, obesity may represent the gratification of delusional fantasies involving grandiosity and omnipotence. Eating may counteract fantasies of ego and libidinal depletion, and may be used as a defense against feelings of ego dissolution, castration, separation anxiety, castration anxiety, or the fear of death; it may also be used as a defense against anorexia.

Related Concepts: ADDICTION; COPROPHAGIA (COPRO-PHAGY).

REFERENCES

Bruch, H., "Obesity in Childhood and Personality Development." *Ops*, 11:467–475, 1941.
    "The Psychology of Obesity." *CJM*, 31:273–281, 1950.

ADDITIONAL READINGS

Brosin, H. W., "The Psychiatric Aspects of Obesity." *JAMA*, 155, 1954.
    "Developmental Obesity and Schizophrenia." *Ps*, 21, 1958.
    "Obesity," in *The Pediatrics Clinics of North America*. Sau, 1958.
    "The Importance of Overweight." *JAPA*, 6, 1958.
Stunkard, A., "Obesity and Denial of Hunger." *PSM*, 21, 1959.

OBJECT CHOICE (ANACLITIC AND NARCISSISTIC). According to Freud (1914), a differentiation should be made between two kinds of object-choice: the anaclitic, "I want to have you," and the narcissistic, "I want to be similar to you or make you similar to me." Freud suggested that, normally, masculine object-choice favors the anaclitic form, whereas feminine object-choice depends more on narcissistic factors. In certain perversions, such as homosexuality, narcissistic object-choice plays the decisive role.

Originally, the sexual impulses are connected with the ego instincts. Only later do they separate, the original object the child requires representing the object he is attached to because it gratifies his need.

This object is referred to as anaclitic. In addition, children select objects which are similar to them, a narcissistic one. In most cases, there is a mixture of both types of objects. Freud thought that anaclitic love played a greater role for males than for females. The anaclitic object is usually over-estimated. In the female, more often, there is a narcissistic object choice.

It seems that the narcissism of a beautiful woman who basically loves herself and the narcissism of a child fascinate many men. However, even those narcissistic women who remain cool towards men experience anaclitic love when they have children. Summing up, Freud said that the narcissistic type is characterized by the selection of an object which is either himself, or which he would like to be, or which he was. In making an anaclitic object, we select the woman who feeds us or the man who protects us.

Related Concepts: IDENTIFICATION; LOVE.

REFERENCE

Freud, S., 1914, "On Narcissism: An Introduction." *SE*, 14: 87–90, 1957.

ADDITIONAL READINGS

Fries, M. E., "Some Factors in the Development and Significance of Early Object Relationships." *JAPA*, 9, 1961.
Ritvo, S., Report on Panel, "Object Relations." *JAPA*, 10, 1962.
Rosen, V. H., "Abstract thinking and Object Relations: With Special Reference to the Use of Abstraction as Regressive Defense in Highly Gifted Individuals." *JAPA*, 6, 1958.

1502

OBLIGING DREAMS. Freud (1920) described a series of dreams—of an overt homosexual woman—whose latent content represented the gratification of the infantile wish to fool her father, the displacement from her father to Freud. The analyst who objects to the term *obliging dreams*, Freud went onto note, should remember that the wish to please the father may be of infantile nature and may be expressed in a manifest form by producing a dream in which the patient behaves as if she were already cured.

Related Concept: DREAMS.

REFERENCE

Freud, S., 1920, "The Psychogenesis of a Case of Homosexuality in a Woman." *SE*, 18:165–166, 1955.

1503

OBSESSIONAL BROODING (in obsessional neurosis) interferes with thinking and other activities resulting from the sexualization and aggressivization of the thought processes. Freud (1909) noted that whenever the thought process becomes sexualized, thinking replaces sexuality and may represent a gratification of the libido.

Eidelberg (1948) noted: "We then turned to another element of the patient's work inhibition, which was his difficulty in reading. He had become aware of this difficulty long before he had undertaken any treatment. His symptom was that he had to re-read frequently the same word, and to note compulsively the letters out of which it was composed. This disturbance appeared at about thirteen years of age. At that time, he had noticed that some of his school mates possessed a larger vocabulary than he. Accordingly, he bought a dictionary and attempted to increase the amount of words he knew, but his studies were in vain as it soon became apparent that he was not making any progress. He became increasingly depressed about this until his mother, who had noticed his upset condition, advised him to burn the dictionary. Although the patient had already decided to do this, he could no longer carry out his intention, as soon as he had received the same advice from his mother. As the first association to this incident, he had the idea that the minute observation of the various words and letters represented symbolically a sexual play with the various parts of a beautiful woman's body."

Related Concept: AMBIVALENT OSCILLATION.

REFERENCES

Eidelberg, L., *Studies in Psychoanalysis.* IUP, p. 57, 1948.
Freud, S., 1909, "Notes Upon a Case of Obsessional Neurosis." *SE*, 10: 245, 1955.

ADDITIONAL READINGS

Abraham, K., *Aus der Analyse eines Falles von Grübelzwang*. BPV, 1912.

Eidelberg, L., *An Outline of Comparative Pathology of the Neuroses*. IUP, 1954.

1504

OBSESSIVE-COMPULSIVE NEUROSIS is characterized by repetitive ideas and actions which are ego-alien, and which are used as a defense against an ambivalent oscillation. This ambivalent oscillation leads to an inability to make decisions; the subject develops compulsive doubts in the form of a symptom or in the form of a neurotic character trait. The subject does not understand the real meaning of his obsessional thoughts and actions. In this regard, Freud (1913) noted the striking agreement between the obsessional prohibitions of neurotics and the taboos of the primitives, both of which are lacking in apparent motive and puzzling in origin.

The subject's obsessive thoughts and actions represent a compromise between defensive prohibitions, atonements, and disguised substitute gratifications. In addition, they are used to deny traumatic narcissistic mortifications and to give the subject the illusion of omnipotence. In the latter instance, the omnipotence is often projected to another person, who appears to have the magic needed to solve the subject's problems.

Unlike hysterical symptoms (which are caused by defenses of phallic wishes), obsessive-compulsive symptoms are caused by defenses of anal wishes. The superego plays a quantitatively greater role and behaves in a sadistic manner toward the subject. The subject uses the punishment which the superego inflicts to avoid the feelings of remorse. In his unconscious, such a patient is unable, even with the help of the signal of guilt, to reject the dangerous desires; he behaves *as if* he had actually acted upon them. In addition, the infantile content often appears to be conscious, although deprived of its emotional character through the mechanism of isolation. Another defense mechanism which plays a great role in this type of neurosis is undoing, for it is the undoing which helps the subject atone for and expiate his hostile wishes.

The obsessional is usually worried that "something terrible" will happen to somebody else: the phobic patient, to himself. He suffers from compulsive doubting The creation of doubt, Freud (1909) noted, is used by the patient to deny external and internal reality and in that way forces him to withdraw from the external world.

Related Concepts: AMBIVALENCE; CHARACTER TRAITS; OMNIPOTENCE OF THOUGHT; TABOO.

REFERENCES

Freud, S.: 1909, "Analysis of a Phobia in a Five-Year-Old Boy." *SE*, 10:232, 1955.
        1913, "Totem and Taboo." *SE*, 13:26, 1955.

ADDITIONAL READINGS

Bergler, E., "Bemerkungen über einer Zwangsneurose in ultimis. Vier Mechanismen des narzisstischen Lustgewinns im Zwang." *Z*, 22, 1936.

Berman, L., "The Obsessive-Compulsive Neurosis in Children," in L. Bender, *A Dynamic Psychopathology of Childhood*. CCT, 1954.

Bonnard, A., "The Mother as a Therapist in a Case of Obsessional Neurosis." *PsaStC*, 5, 1950.

Bornstein, B., "Fragment of an Analysis of an Obsessional Child. The First Six Months of Analysis." *PsaStC*, 8, 1953.

Dai, B., "Obsessive-Compulsive Disorders in Chinese Culture." *SocProbl*, 4, 1957.

Gero, G., & L. Rubinfine, "On Obsessive Thoughts." *JAPA*, 3, 1955.

Gordon, A., "Obsessive Hallucinations and Psychoanalysis." *JabP*, 12, 1917.

Hitschmann, E., "Die Zwangsbefürchtung vom Tode des gleichgeschlechtlichen Elternteils." *PsaP*, 5, 1931.

Kasanin, J. S., "The Psychological Structure of the Obsessive Neuroses." *JNMD*, 99, 1944.

Niederland, W. G., "The Psychoanalysis of a Severe Obsessive-Compulsive Neurosis." *BullPhilaAssPsa*, 8, 1958.

Sokolnicka, E., "Analysis of an Obsessional Neurosis in a Child." *IntJPsa*, 4, 1922.

Tausk, V., "Über eine besondere Form von Zwangsphantasien." *Z*, 4, 1916.

Weissman, P., "Characteristic Superego Identification of Obsessional Neurosis." *Q*, 28, 1959.

Young, J. C., "Study of a Severe Case of Obsessional Neurosis." *M*, 1, 1921.

1505

OCCULT denotes the seemingly meaningful correspondence which occurs between thoughts, dreams, symptoms and events in the external world that cannot be accounted for in causal terms and which, if attributed to chance, lose their dynamic significance; extrasensory, telepathic, or clairvoyant communication. For example, a patient of Freud's, in the course of his associations, mentioned that his girl friend called him "Mr. Foresight." This happened to bear a striking correspondence to the name of a favored visitor, Dr. Forsyth, who had a few minutes earlier left Freud's office. Freud, after examining various possibilities which might account for the correspondence, made the assumption that *if* one could postulate the patient's telepathic awareness of Dr. Forsyth's visit one could structure the otherwise meaningless communication in terms of presumptive transference strivings, "After all, I'm a Forsyth too." [Freud, 1933.]

The class of events termed occult, or the class of so-called psi phenomena, includes, in addition to presumptive telepathic phenomena, seemingly premonitory or prophetic dreams and visions which appear not to fit into the normal time framework of everyday events. If such dreams or other manifestations are structured dynamically and without regard to the temporal anomalies involved, as Eisenbud (1954) noted, they may make a good deal of sense in psychoanalytic terms. Conversely, detailed psychoanalytic investigation can "sometimes diminish rather than augment the probability that the correspondence between certain events, whose extraordinary relationship in time constitutes merely one aspect of their occult nature, can be ascribed to known and accepted causal processes." He described (in 1956) the relationship of the presumptive manipulation of time in certain ostensibly prophetic dreams to various dynamic situations such as the oedipus complex.

Related Concepts: Déjà Vu; Perception; Telepathy.

REFERENCES

Eisenbud, J., "Behavioral Correspondences to Normally Unpredictable Future Events." *Q*, 23:205–233, 355–389, 1954.
     "Time and Oedipus." *Q*, 25:363–384, 1956.
Freud, S., 1933, "New Introductory Lectures on Psycho-Analysis." *SE*, 22:47–48, 1964.

ADDITIONAL READINGS

Deutsch, H., "Okkulte Vorgänge während der Psychoanalyse." *Im*, 12, 1926.
Devereux, G., ed., *Psychoanalysis and the Occult.* IUP, 1953.
Servadio, E., "Psychoanalyse und Telepathie," in G. Devereux, *Psychoanalysis and the Occult.* IUP, 1953.

1506

OCEANIC FEELING denotes a feeling of oneness with God, nature, or the universe; it is the source of all religious feeling. Freud (1930) cited Grabbe's* play, in which the principal character says: "Indeed, we shall not fall out of this world. We are in it once and for all." Here, the playwright is expressing the idea of being one with the world as a whole. It is the source of the religious spirit: the inseparable bond between the self and the external world as a whole. It is equated with that primitive feeling of oneness, the limitless extension of the self both inward and outward. Freud compared this desire with the normal's growth to maturity. While the majority of men accept genital primacy and a dependence on a specific love object, a minority transfer it to all men rather than to an individual. This all-embracing love for others (and the world) is then equated with what is *good* and *just*.

Freud (1913) predicated the founding of the family on a need for permanent sexual satisfaction. Man's acceptance of genital erotism as the central part of his life made him dependent on his love-object. While the majority accepted this state, a minority found their happiness independent of the object, one not attached to individual objects but to all men equally, the sexual aim being inhibited. This fulfillment of the pleasure principle has been linked with religion. The all-embracing love for others and the world is frequently regarded as the highest state of mind of which man is capable.

The oceanic feeling, according to Lewin (1946), is genetically derived from the incomplete separation of the ego from the environment; i.e., basically, on the fusion or near-fusion of the ego and the maternal breast. In his view, the feeling connected with the dream-screen and the class of blank

---

* Grabbe, C. D., *Hannibal.*

dreams (reflective of infantile breast experiences) are based on a blending of early infantile images, sensations, feelings and vague memory traces of the breast-infant closeness with later experiences of breast-infant separation (partial or transient separation, mother-child "in weaning", etc.).

Niederland (1954) emphasized the historical fact that at a time when ocean travel did not exist the desert was a place more prone than others to set the stage for such experiences, that it therefore cannot be coincidental that the Jewish, Christian and Moslem religions originated in or around the vast and almost boundless expanses of Arabia and other deserted or semideserted areas. This corresponds to the all-encompassing quality of the oceanic feeling in which, according to Eissler (1963), "the ego widens to engulf reality."

Related Concepts: MYSTIC UNION; RELIGIOUS FAITH.

REFERENCES

Eissler, K., "Goethe, a Psychoanalytic Study." WUP, 1963.
Freud, S.: 1913, "Totem and Taboo." *SE*, 13:147–152, 1955.
    1930, "Civilization and Its Discontents." *SE*, 21:64–65, 1961.
Lewin, B., "Sleep, the Mouth, and the Dream Screen." *Q*, 15:419–434, 1946.
Niederland, W. G., "Jacob's Dream." *JHH*, 3:73–98, 1954.

1507

OEDIPUS COMPLEX denotes the emotional relationship of the child to his parents; more specifically, in the female to the transference of her affection to her father and identification with the mother, and in the male to the identification with the father and desire (anaclitic love) for the mother. With the male the oedipus complex is repressed, and in the most normal cases entirely destroyed, with a severe superego set up as its heir. In the female it is never entirely abandoned; the preoedipal attachment to the mother persists. As Freud (1925) noted, in boys the oedipus complex is destroyed by the castration complex, in girls it is made possible and led up to by the castration complex: As might be expected, the oedipal conflict is directly related to the individual's biological development. Freud

(1923) noted that the child's sexuality reaches its first climax in the third to fifth year, and that, after a period of inhibition, in puberty, it once again sets in.

In females the oedipus complex is not eliminated by fear of castration. Consequently, it may persist much longer and may be only slowly abandoned. In boys, as a result of the dissolution of the oedipus complex, there is an identification with the father and the preservation of positive feelings for the mother.

The persistence of the oedipus complex is most easily demonstrated in neurotic behavior. It accounts for disturbances of misjudgment and dissatisfactions, and manifests itself most dramatically in the choice of love-objects. The neurotic misjudges all object relationships; he sees, as it were, only representatives of past objects. The nature of the disturbance is of course determined by the specific nature of the oedipal conflict.

Related Concepts: ANACLITIC; INCEST; NARCISSISM; OBJECT CHOICE (ANACLITIC AND NARCISSISTIC); NEGATIVE OEDIPUS COMPLEX; PREOEDIPAL; SUPEREGO; TOTEM.

REFERENCES

Freud, S.: 1923, "The Ego and the Id." *SE*, 19:33–34, 1961.
    1925, "Some Psychical Consequences of the Anatomical Distinction Between the Sexes." *SE*, 19:256–257, 1961.

ADDITIONAL READINGS

Behn-Eschenburg, H., "The Antecedents of the Oedipus Complex." *IntJPsa*, 16, 1935.
Dalmau, C. J., "Post-Oedipal Psychodynamics." *R*, 44, 1957.
Eisenberg, S., "Time and the Oedipus." *Q*, 25, 1956.
Jacobson, E., "Depression; the Oedipus Conflict in the Development of Depressive Mechanisms." *Q*, 12, 1943.
Keiser, S., "A Manifest Oedipus Complex in an Adolescent Girl." *PsaStC*, 8, 1953.
Lampl de Groot, J., "Re-Evaluation of the Role of the Oedipus Complex." *IntJPsa*, 33, 1952.
Levin, A. J., "The Oedipus Myth in History and Psychiatry; A New Interpretation." *Ps*, 11, 1948.
Lewis, H., "The Effect of Shedding the First Deciduous Tooth Upon the Passing of the Oedipus Complex of the Male." *JAPA*, 6, 1958.
Meiss, M. L., "The Oedipal Problem of a Fatherless Boy." *PsaStC*, 7, 1952.

Reich, W., "Die Charakterologische Überwindung des Oedipus-Komplexes." *Z*, 17, 1931.

Spielrein, S., "The Manifestations of the Oedipus Complex in Childhood." *Z*, 4, 1916.

1508

OMNIPOTENCE OF THOUGHT denotes the belief that thoughts alone are able to gratify our wishes without the help of corresponding actions and an available external object. There is a general overevaluation of all mental processes; thus, all psychical acts are subject to its will. This phenomenon is characteristic of infantile behavior, and, to some degree, of the behavior of the primitive and of the neurotic.

The infant seeks to eliminate the various unpleasures from which he suffers; initially he appears to believe that he can gratify his needs by wishing alone (hallucinatory manner). He begins by learning to recognize that the sensation of hunger does not disappear as a result of his wish to eat; that an external object is required (his mother) to satisfy his hunger. Thus, the difficult road to external reality begins. Because his power is limited, he has to learn that "I want" is not a synonym for "I have."

Freud (1913) identified the overevaluation of thinking as the probable result of a regression or fixation to the narcissistic stage, which follows the autoerotic phase. Having discovered the importance of psychic reality, he arrived at the conclusion that all neurotics and most primitives overestimate the importance of thoughts (inner reality) as compared to external reality. It may be suggested that today the neurotic is not considered to be totally different from the normal.

Freud (1909) pointed out that obsessional neurotics are similar to the primitives in their behavior; they do not differentiate between thought and action. They differ from primitives by being afraid that something evil would happen, not to them, but to others, if they refrain from using their magic compulsion. The actual belief in omnipotence is a sign of the delusion. In its latent form it may be encountered in many neuroses. For example, the omnipotence becomes conscious when a patient accuses himself of being responsible for the suicide of a woman because he rejected her.

In 1913 Freud still used the concept of the first instinct theory and consequently explained anxiety as the result of the transformation of dammed-up libido. One may suggest that it would be profitable to try to rewrite Freud's basic formulation in order to do justice to his new views, wherein aggression appears as an equal partner of sex, and the ego instincts are no longer considered to be free from libido.

Ferenczi (1927) wrote of infantile omnipotence and pointed out that as long as the individual is interested in loving himself, he can retain the illusion of being omnipotent. In mania, he uses himself as a love object; in melancholia, as the object he hates. Both avoid the recognition of the limitation of their power. Earlier, Ferenczi (1913) noted that obsessional thoughts appeared to be substitute wish-fulfillments. "Leaving aside the fact that analysis reveals such obsessive thoughts and actions to be the substitutes of wish-impulses that are logically correct, but which on account of their intolerableness have been repressed, and turning our attention exclusively to the peculiar manifestation of this obsessional symptom, we must admit that it constitutes a problem in itself.

"Psycho-analytical experience has made it clear to me that this symptom, the feeling of omnipotence, is a projection of the observation that one has slavishly to obey certain irresistible instincts. The obsessional neurosis constitutes a relapse of the mental life to that stage of child-development characterised, amongst other things, by there being as yet no inhibiting, postponing, reflecting thought-activity interposed between wishing and acting, the wish-fulfilling movement following spontaneously and unhesitatingly on the wishing—an averting movement away from something disagreeable, or an approach towards something agreeable."*

Eidelberg (1954) suggested that the emotional experience connected with the recognition of the limitation of the child's power should be called "infantile narcissistic mortification." Whenever

---

* "It is well known that small children almost reflexively stretch out their hands after every object that shines or in any other way pleases them. They are to begin with also incapable of foregoing any 'naughtiness' that yields them any kind of pleasure, whenever the stimulus causing this appears. A young boy who had been forbidden to bore his finger into his nose answered his mother, 'I don't want to, but my hand does and I can't prevent it.' "

this experience is denied or repressed, the child behaves as if he had not accepted the fact that wishing is not identical to acting and that a fantasy cannot be used instead of an external object. The neurotic uses his defense mechanism to retain the unconscious belief in omnipotence. Consequently, the aim of a therapeutic analysis can only be reached if the infantile repressed wish and the infantile narcissistic mortification become conscious.

Related Concepts: DELUSIONS; HALLUCINATIONS; ILLUSION; PRIMARY PROCESS; SECONDARY PROCESS.

REFERENCES

Eidelberg, L., *An Outline of a Comparative Pathology of the Neuroses.* IUP, p. 37, 1954.
Ferenczi, S.: 1913, "Stages in the Development of the Sense of Reality." *SPsa*, pp. 215–216, 1916.
    Bausteine für Psychoanalyse. IntPV, p. 79, 1927.
Freud, S.: 1909, "Notes Upon a Case of Obsessional Neuroses." *SE*, 10:233–235, 1955.
    1913, "Totem and Taboo." *SE*, 13:26, 80, 85, 87, 1955.

ADDITIONAL READINGS

Bruch, H., "Parent Education or the Illusion of Omnipotence." *Ops*, 24, 1954.
Fenichel, O., *The Psychoanalytic Theory of Neurosis.* Nor, 1945.
Hyroop, M., "The Factor of Omnipotence in the Development of Paranoid Reactions." *PT*, 5, 1951.
Mannheim, R., "'Allmacht der Gedanken' bei Kindern." *PsaP*, 2, 1927–1928.
Reik, T., "Die 'Allmacht der Gedanken' bei Arthur Schnitzler." *Im*, 2, 1913.
Silverberg, W. V., "The Factor of Omnipotence in Neurosis." *Ps*, 12, 1949.

1509

ONYCHOPHAGIA (NAILBITING). As with other neurotic symptoms, nailbiting represents both a partial discharge and a partial frustration of various infantile wishes. At the same time, it is used to deny an external narcissistic mortification ("It is not true that I have no control over the external object I want to incorporate") by *accepting* an internal narcissistic mortification ("It is true that I have no control over my wishes").

According to Solomon (1955), nailbiting is related to the biting-clawing impulse of the infant.

It is an attempt to integrate gross aggressions, seeking discharge through oral-sadistic channels, with a strong need to deny these aggressions. Hostile aggression is released through biting the nails (the claws), the external object is spared damage, and guilt is expiated by the infliction of pain on the self.

Related Concept: AUTOEROTISM.

REFERENCE

Solomon, J. C., "Nailbiting and the Integrative Process." *IntJPsa*, 6:393–395, 1955.

ADDITIONAL READINGS

Eidelberg, L., *An Outline of a Comparative Pathology of the Neuroses.* IUP, 1954.
Wechsler, D., "The Incidence and Significance of Fingernail Biting in Children." *R*, 18, 1931.

1510

OPTIMISM. The optimist, according to Abraham (1924), is usually an individual whose experiences on the oral stage have molded his character. He may be a normal individual who faces life with the anticipation of success. Or he may refrain from working, expecting the others to take care of him. "In certain other cases the person's entire character is under oral influence, but this can only be shown after a thorough analysis has been made. According to my experience we are here concerned with persons in whom the sucking was undisturbed and highly pleasurable. They have brought with them from this happy period a deeply-rooted conviction that everything will always be well with them. They face life with an imperturbable optimism which often does in fact help them to achieve their aims. But we also meet with less favourable types of development. Some people are dominated by the belief that there will always be some kind person— a representative of the mother, of course—to care for them and to give them everything they need. This optimistic belief condemns them to inactivity. We again recognize in them, individuals who have been over-indulged in the sucking period. Their whole attitude towards life shows that they expect the mother's breast to flow for them eternally, as it were. They make no kind of effort, and in some cases they even disdain to undertake a bread-winning occupation."

Anny Angel (1934) described three cases of optimistic behavior. The first of the three, a patient with optimistic character traits, used these to deny an unconscious castration anxiety. The third patient was considered normal by the author; the patient protected her optimism, not by denial, but by an underestimation of the external danger.

Related Concepts: CHARACTER NEUROSIS; PESSIMISM.

REFERENCES

Abraham, K., 1924, "The Influence of Oral Erotism on Character-Formation." *SPA*, pp. 399–400, 1942.
Angel, A., Einige Bemerkungen über den Optimismus." *Z*, 20:191–199, 1934.

1511

ORAL PESSIMISM denotes a pathological character formation originating in oral erotism, determined either by frustration of unusually pronounced oral satisfactions, or by exceptional oral deprivations. Oral pessimism and oral sadism are assumed to represent alternate oral-erotic stages. Oral pessimism is characterized by acute depressions and chronic depressive attitudes, while oral sadism is exemplified in redress-demanding attitudes of behavior. Fixation at the level of oral wishes manifests itself as a general disinclination to care for oneself and a tendency to require this care from others. This demand will express itself in either extreme passivity or intensely active, oral-sadistic behavior. Often, oral pessimism is a defense against optimism; the pessimist avoids recognition of the limitations of his omnipotence, in connection with knowledge of the future, and he gratifies his aggression by pretending to be able to predict the future. [Bergler, 1934.]

Abraham (1924) noted: "This optimism, whether it is allied to an energetic conduct in life or, as in the last-mentioned aberration, to a care-free indifference to the world, stands in noteworthy contrast to a feature of the anal character that has not been sufficiently appreciated up to the present. I refer to a melancholy seriousness which passes over into marked pessimism. I must point out,

however, that this characteristic is to a great extent not directly of anal origin, but goes back to a disappointment of oral desires in the earliest years. In persons of this type the optimistic belief in the benevolence of fate is completely absent. On the contrary, they consistently show an apprehensive attitude towards life, and have a tendency to make the worst of everything and to find undue difficulties in the simplest undertakings."

Related Concepts: NARCISSISTIC MORTIFICATION; OPTIMISM.

REFERENCES

Abraham, K., 1924, "The Influence of Oral Erotism on Character-Formation." *SPA*, p. 400, 1942.
Bergler, E., "Zur Problematik des 'oralen' Pessimisten demonstriert an Christian Dietrich Grabbe." *Im*, 20:330–375, 1934.

1512

ORAL PHASE is the first stage of libidinal development, approximately from birth to the ninth or twelfth month of age, At first, the infant is chiefly interested in the breast of its mother and gratifies its wishes by sucking the breast or the substitute milk bottle. At this stage of development, the child regards the breast as if it represented part of his own body (primary identification); later, usually in connection with weaning, he begins to realize that the breast of the mother, while highly important, represents as external object. [Freud, 1905.] Metapsychologically, he begins to cathect the presentation of the breast with object-libido and the presentation of his mouth with secondary narcissistic libido.

Abraham (1924) subdivided the oral stage into two parts: in the first oral-erotic phase, the infant wants to suck the breast; in the second oral-sadistic phase, he tries to bite it off. Freud (1933) noted: "In the first sub-stage what is in question is only oral incorporation, there is no ambivalence at all in the relation to the object—the mother's breast. The second stage, characterized by the emergence of the biting activity, may be described as the 'oral-sadistic' one; it exhibits for the first time the phenomenon of ambivalence, which becomes so much clearer afterwards, in the following sadistic-anal phase. The value of these new distinctions is to be seen especially if we look for the dispositional points in the development of the libido in the case of particular neuroses, such as obsessional neurosis or melancholia. You must here recall to mind what we have learnt about the connection between fixation of the libido, disposition and regression."

After Freud (1920) introduced the second instinct theory, in which aggression was no longer described as a part of a libidinal wish, but was considered an independent instinct, some authors suggested that the child, in the oral stage, is interested in both libidinal and aggresssive gratifications. They referred to the desire to devour the breasts as a gratification of aggressive and sexual wishes (sadistic) and considered crying, shouting, and spitting out as serving the gratification of aggressive wishes only. As Eidelberg (1954) pointed out, the oral stage may be referred to as representing the oral component of the libido and destrudo which finally achieves complete maturity on the genital level. In addition to such oral wishes as devouring, spitting out, and shouting, we also find exhibitionistic and scopophilic wishes in the oral stage (to look at the breast and to be looked at by others).

The term *oral* is sometimes used to describe a neurotic or normal character trait. Abraham (1924) discussed the two, as follows: "The character-trait of ambition, which we meet with so frequently in our psycho-analyses, has been derived long ago by Freud from urethral erotism. This explanation, however, does not seem to have penetrated to the deepest sources of that characteristic. According to my experience, and also that of Dr. Edward Glover, this is rather a character-trait of oral origin which is later reinforced from other sources, among which the urethral one should be particularly mentioned.

"Besides this, it has to be noted that certain contributions to character-formation originating in the earliest oral stage coincide in important respects with others derived from the final genital stage. This is probably explicable from the fact that at these two stages the libido is least open to disturbance from an ambivalence of feeling.

"In many people we find, beside the oral character-traits described, other psychological manifestations which we must derive from the same instinctual sources. These are impulses which have escaped any social modification. As examples a morbidly intense appetite for food and an inclination to various oral perversions are especially to be mentioned. Further, we meet many kinds of neurotic symptoms which are determined orally; and finally there are phenomena which have come into being through sublimation. These latter products deserve a separate investigation, which, however, would exceed the limits of this paper; hence I shall only briefly give a single example.

"The displacement of the infantile pleasure in sucking to the intellectual sphere is of great practical significance. Curiosity and the pleasure in observing receive important reinforcements from this source, and this not only in childhood, but during the subject's whole life. In persons with a special inclination for observing Nature, and for many branches of scientific investigation, psycho-analysis shows a close connection between those impulses and repressed oral desires.

"A glance into the workshop of scientific investigation enables us to recognize how impulses pertaining to the different erotogenic zones may support and supplement one another if the most favourable results possible are to be achieved. The optimum is reached when an energetic imbibing of observations is combined with enough tenacity and ability to 'digest' the collected facts, and a sufficiently strong impulse to give them back to the world, provided this is not done with undue haste. Psycho-analytical experience enables us to recognize various kinds of divergencies from this optimum. Thus there are people with great mental capacity for absorbing, who, however, are inhibited in production. Others again produce too rapidly. It is no exaggeration to say of such people that they have scarcely taken a thing in before it comes out of their mouths again. When they are analysed it often proves that these same persons tend to vomit food as they have eaten it. They are people who show an extreme neurotic impatience; a satisfactory combination of forward-moving oral impulses with retarding anal ones is lacking in the structure of their character.

"In conclusion, it seems to me particularly important to allude once more to the significance of such combinations. In the normal formation of character we shall always find derivatives from all the original instinctual sources happily combined with one another."

Related Concepts: CHARACTER TRAITS; LIBIDO.

REFERENCES

Abraham, K., 1924, "A Short Study of the Development of the Libido Viewed in the Light of Mental Disorders." *SPA*, pp. 404–405, 1942.

Eidelberg, L., *An Outline of a Comparative Pathology of the Neuroses.* IUP, p. 32, 1954.

Freud, S.: 1905, "Three Essays on the Theory of Sexuality." *SE*, 7:179–185, 198, 205, 222, 232–233, 1953.

1920, "Beyond the Pleasure Principle." *SE*, 18:33–44, 1955.

1933, "New Introductory Lectures on Psycho-Analysis." *SE*, 22:99, 1964.

ADDITIONAL READINGS

Abraham, K., "The Influence of Oral Eroticism on Character Formation." *IntJPsa*, 6, 1925.

Bibring-Lehner, G., "Über eine orale Komponent bei männicher Inversion." *Z*, 25, 1940.

Bruch, H., "Transformation of Oral Impulses in Eating Disorders; A Conceptual Approach." *PQ*, 35, 1961.

Cremerius, J., "Die Bedeutung der Oralität für den Altersdiabetes und die mit ihm Verbundenen Depressiven Phasen." *P*, 11, 1957.

Feldman, S. S., "A Syndrome Indicative of Repressed Oral Aggression." *Samiksa*, 7, 1953.

Friedman, L. J., "Defensive Aspects in Orality." *IntJPsa*, 34, 1953.

Gero, G., "Zum Problem der Oralen Fixierung." *Z*, 24, 1939.

Glover, E., "Notes on Oral Character Formation," *IntJPsa*, 6, 1925.

Hendrick, I., "Ego Defense and the Mechanism of Oral Ejection in Schizophrenia: The Psychoanalysis of a Pre-Psychotic Case." *IntJPsa*, 12, 1931.

Keiser, S., "Orality Displaced to the Urethra." *JAPA*, 2, 1954.

Marmor, J., "Orality in the Hysterical Personality." *JAPA*, 1, 1953.

Rascovsky, A., "Beyond the Oral Stage." *IntJPsa*, 37, 1956.

Spielrein, S., "Verdrängte Munderotik." *Z*, 6, 1920.

Sullivan, H. S., "The Oral Complex." *R*, 12, 1925.

Szasz, T. S., "Oral Mechanisms in Constipation and Diarrhea." *BAPA*, 6, 1950.

Wulff, M., "Über einen interessanten oralen Symptomenkomplex und seine Beziehungen zur Sucht." *Z*, 18, 1932.

1513

ORGANIC. In psychoanalysis and psychiatry, the term organic usually refers to pathological anatomical changes in the central or peripheral nervous systems. Illnesses with no sign of such pathological, anatomical changes are referred to as *nonorganic, functional, mental* or *psychic.* One disadvantage of this categorization of illnesses is that the pathological anatomical changes may not actually be absent, but, rather, they may go unrecognized. For instance, Parkinson's disease was originally referred to as a "functional" illness, because the anatomical changes characteristic of this disease were not known then. In describing the mental changes in neuroses, Freud (1893–1895) noted that in neurasthenia the psychical apparatus played no role. In obsessional neurosis there is a plenitude of psychological data; in neurasthenia this is lacking.

Furthermore, the word *mental* or *psychic* appears to refer more to the method or approach of the examination than to the nature of the phenomenon involved. Consequently, as Eidelberg (1954) suggested, instead of referring to a symptom as being organic or mental, we should name the method used in the investigation and differentiate between material gained from an anatomical, histological, physiological, or psychoanalytic approach. For instance, a patient suffering from a fractured leg (organic symptom) may, in analysis, reveal the presence of an unconscious wish to get hurt (accident proneness).

From a semantic point of view, *organic* may refer to whatever can be examined by sense-organ perception. Consequently, the material gained in analysis, which reaches the analyst with the help of his sense organs, cannot be referred to as *nonorganic.* While it is true that a urinalysis may require less time and skill than the examination of a patient's unconscious wishes, both depend on the doctor's ability to use his sense organs. With the progress of science, the range of phenomena subject to such investigations will be extended through new methods of investigation (e.g., improvements in microscopy).

Related Concepts: MENTAL (PSYCHIC); SOMATIC COMPLIANCE.

REFERENCES

Eidelberg, L., *An Outline of a Comparative Pathology of the Neuroses.* IUP, pp. 14–15, 1954.
Freud, S., 1893–1895, "Studies on Hysteria." *SE*, 2:257–258, 1955.

ADDITIONAL READINGS

Freud, S.: 1917, "Introductory Lectures on Psycho-Analysis." *SE*, 16, 1963.
1933, "New Introductory Lectures on Psycho-Analysis." *SE*, 22, 1964.

1514

ORGASM (CLIMAX) is the experience of an intensive end-pleasure received at the genital stage of development. Nonetheless, the pleasure and full discharge of tension are also available at other stages of development; still, the orgasm is characteristic of the genital stage.

The climax is usually associated with an emission of semen in the male and a vaginal discharge in the female. However, some patients who have an emission or discharge do not experience the emotion of climax (orgastic impotence in males and orgastic frigidity in females).

The unconscious fear of being overwhelmed often interferes with the climax or orgasm. Fenichel (1945) noted: "A fear of death may represent a 'fear of one's own excitement.' 'Dying' has become an expression for the sensations of an overwhelming panic, that is, for the distorted conception which these patients have formed of orgasm."

Related Concepts: FRIGIDITY; IMPOTENCE.

REFERENCE

Fenichel, O., *The Psychoanalytic Theory of Neurosis.* Nor, p. 209, 1945.

ADDITIONAL READINGS

Devereux, G., "The Significance of the External Female Genitalia and of Female Orgasm for the Male." *JAPA*, 6, 1958.
Laforgue, R., "De l'angoisse à l'orgasme." *RFPsa*, 4, 1930–1931.
Lorand, S., "Contribution to the Problem of Vaginal Orgasm." *IntJPsa*, 20, 1939.
Tannenbaum, S. A., "Orgasm in the Female." *JSP*, 2, 1924.

1515

ORGASTIC IMPOTENCE denotes a lack of climax (orgasm) which occurs despite normal erection and ejaculation (Freud, 1926). For example, a patient who complained of being bored while having a seminal emission, disclosed that he was unconsciously afraid of being overwhelmed by the loss connected with ejaculation and that he avoided this experience by mobilizing the wish to urinate. In this case, urination meant the expression of contempt for his partner who had to be punished for having excited him.

Reich (1949) contended that a neurosis would not develop unless there was a disturbance of the genital function, and, further, that a cure was "not possible without the elimination of this disturbance." More recently, Hartmann (1964) stated: "The phenomenon which I am thinking of is even more clearly marked in those persons who, for fear of losing their ego, are unable to achieve orgasm. These pathological manifestations teach us that a healthy ego must evidently be in a position to allow some of its most essential functions, including its 'freedom,' to be put out of action occasionally, so that it may abandon itself to 'compulsion' (central control). This brings us to the problem, hitherto almost entirely neglected, of a biological hierarchy of the ego's functions and to the notion of the integration of opposites, which we have already met in connection with the problem of rational conduct. I believe that these considerations relative to the mobility of the ego and the automatic disconnecting of vital ego functions enabled us to make very considerable progress toward discovering an important condition of mental health. The threads which lead us from this point to the concept of ego strength are clearly visible."

Related Concepts: FRIGIDITY; IMPOTENCE.

REFERENCES

Freud, S., 1926, "Inhibitions, Symptoms and Anxiety." *SE*, 20:88, 1959.
Hartmann, H., *Essays on Ego Psychology.* IUP, p. 11, 1964.
Reich, W., *Character Analysis.* OIP, p. 300, 1949.

ADDITIONAL READING

Fenichel, O., *The Psychoanalytic Theory of Neurosis.* Nor, 1945.

1516

OVERDETERMINATION is descriptive of the fact that a phenomenon may be caused by more than one factor, some being more important than others. For example, Freud (1916–1917) explained slips of the tongue as due to two essential factors; the more important one being the cause of the slip, and the less important, as representing its condition. He used the following analogy: A rich man while walking though the forest at night was attacked by robbers. Freud named the night and the forest as conditions facilitating such an attack but pointed out that this condition by itself would not rob the merchant of his money. Only the robber (the cause) was able to achieve this.

With reference to symptomatology, Freud (1900) noted that it had at least two determinants, one arising from each of the systems involved in the conflict. With the introduction of the structural approach, Freud (1923) recognized that the symptom was not a breakthrough of the neurosis but represented a compromise formation between the id, ego and superego. Eidelberg (1954) suggested that the results of unconscious defense mechanisms should be described as compromise formations among four, rather than three, factors; id, ego, superego, and external world.

Flugel (1945) noted: "The compromise involved in such symptoms is, of course, an example of the mechanism of 'over-determination,' which is itself of wide application and not confined to the sphere of neurosis. Even over-determination in the particular sense of satisfying through one action both gratification of an id impulse and the need for punishment is sometimes to be found outside neurosis—for instance in the practice of confession, which is itself, as we have seen, a sort of equivalent of punishment."

Related Concept: CAUSALITY.

REFERENCES

Eidelberg, L., *An Outline of a Comparative Pathology of the Neuroses.* IUP, p. 239, 1954.
Flugel, J., *Man, Morals and Society.* IUP, p. 157, 1945.
Freud, S.: 1900, "The Interpretation of Dreams." *SE,* 5:569, 1953.
    1916–1917, "Introductory Lectures on Psycho-Analysis." *SE,* 15:45, 1963.

ADDITIONAL READING

Gessmann, "Das Problem der Überwertigkeit." *ZNP,* 64, 1921.

1517

OVERT HOMOSEXUALITY is a perversion characterized by dependence on a partner of the same sex for erotic stimulation and gratification; also called "inversion" or "contrary sexual sensation." In childhood, the choice of the sexual object is less limited by the sex of the object than it is in adulthood. This childhood trait is preserved and accentuated in the homosexual. Bisexual predispostion may be the basis of the original freedom of object-choice, as frequently reflected in the invert's choice of an object that represents a compromise between male and female; e.g., female mental characteristics and a male body—genitals. [Freud, 1908.] Physical sexual characteristics, mental sexual characteristics (masculine or feminine attitude) and the kind of object-choice, up to a certain point, may vary independently of one another (Freud, 1920). "Absolute inverts" rely exclusively on the same sex as the object-choice. "Amphigonic bisexual inverts" are capable of choosing objects of either sex. "Contingent inverts" choose a homosexual object only under certain external conditions (inaccessibility of any normal sexual object).

Innate, constitutional factors in homosexuality are outside the scope of psychoanalytic investigation, but Freud (1905) considered it doubtful that an innate predisposition went beyond the assumption of general unspecific constitutional determination. In a later paper (in 1910), Freud noted that all overt homosexuals have a strong fixation to the infantile mother on the oral stage. In order to remain faithful to her, the homosexual runs away from other women and transfers, in effect, the sexual excitation from women to men, making a narcissistic object-choice. A disturbance may have occurred in childhood because of the absence, inadequacy, or excessive cruelty of the father. The narcissistic object-choice of the homosexual is connected to the high value which he sets on the male organ and his inability to tolerate its absence in the love-object. Another probably related factor is the need to eliminate the female breasts in the object.

According to Eidelberg (1948), the homosexual's mother fixation appears to be a fixation to the preoedipal mother, an identification with both mother and infant (himself). What is approved by the total personality in the homosexual is not identical with an open gratification of the component instinct (Freud originally assumed the neurosis to be a negative of perversion). The preoedipal mother is the object the homosexual seeks; he wants to be such a mother and to have an infant and vice versa. Eidelberg cited the following fragment of a case history: "*The patient became aware that there was a connection between his greediness for food—even more for drink—and his early oral frustration.* He admitted that his behavior was often reminiscent of that of an insatiable suckling. *Thus his hatred for women was connected with this first disappointment.* Peculiar sensations in the oral region and at the fingertips, which the patient had reported before, now became understandable. The sensations consisted of an unpleasant feeling of dryness in these regions, and to overcome it he often greased his skin, lips, and anus. At this point we discussed the connections between mouth, hand, and anus. The patient's predilection for milk and dairy products was a *fixation on the first happy period of his life, while his aversion for meat and butcher shops was associated with the beginning of the biting stage and the subsequent weaning.* He never ordered a meat dish in a restaurant, on the ground that it was too expensive. On the basis of his associations it was possible to prove that he was not concerned over expenses but over the loss of his mother's breast after the appearance of his first teeth. It was as though he wished to say: *So long as I renounce meat, and therefore biting, I am allowed to remain unmolested at my mother's breast.* The patient's behavior when he ate candy proved that this renunciation was only partly successful. Actually he did not remain a complete suckling; against his will he had grown teeth, and he could inhibit their functioning only temporarily. Since his libido could not be completely gratified by his eating habits, inhibitions and conflicts were produced.

"We now could give a more complete explanation of the patient's enuresis nocturna. As a result of his oral frustration, his hatred for his mother, and his identification with her, his penis became a substitute for a breast; what had previously been passively received was now actively given. The mutual masturbation in his homosexual relationship, the sucking of nipples and penis, signified playing the game of mother and child. The patient represented the *phallic mother*, was active in relation to the friend who sucked his penis; sometimes his friend played the role of the phallic mother. . . .

"During the analysis of the oral phase, the patient's homosexual orientation underwent considerable change. His tie to his friend grew gradually weaker; he renounced the homosexual relationship; his indifference to, or hatred for, women began to yield to erotic interest. He had dreams in which he saw himself lying with a naked woman and sucking her breast. The favorable course of the treatment forshadowed complete cure."

The first love-object of both sexes is the mother. The girl who has a strong attachment to her father, may have had an equally strong prior attachment to the preoedipal mother (Freud, 1931). Some women may be fixated at the original mother attachment, never achieving the changeover to the father. The outcome of the castration complex in the girl may be threefold: she may take her father as the love object and arrive at the oedipus complex in its feminine, passive form; she may turn away from sexuality altogether; or she may identify with the preoedipal mother, denying (disavowing) aggression against her mother's breasts by loving them. Also of considerable importance is the transformation of aggressive impulses, especially against the pregnant mother, into a masochistic attitude. Oral-sadistic elements also play a great role in female homosexuality. Early in his investigations, Freud noted the female homosexual's preference for contact with the mucous membrane of the mouth.

The prognosis for psychoanalytic treatment of homosexuals and other perverts, who want to be cured, is no worse than the prognosis for patients suffering from neurotic character traits.

Related Concepts: IDENTIFICATION; LATENT HOMOSEXUALITY; OEDIPUS COMPLEX; PERVERSION.

REFERENCES

Eidelberg, L., *Studies in Psychoanalysis.* IUP, pp. 10–12, 1948.
Freud, S.: 1905, "Three Essays on the Theory of Sexuality." *SE*, 7:137–144, 229–230, 1953.

Freud, S.: 1908, "On the Sexual Theories of Children." *SE*, 9:206, 1959.

    1910, "Leonardo da Vinci and a Memory of his Childhood." *SE*, 11:99, 1957.

    1920, "The Psychogenesis of a Case of Homosexuality in a Woman." *SE*, 13:145–174, 1955.

    1931, "Female Sexuality." *SE*, 21:223–246, 1961.

ADDITIONAL READINGS

Bose, G., "Genesis of Homosexuality." *Samiksa*, 4, 1940.

Deutsch, H., "On Female Homosexuality." *Q*, 1, 1932.

Eidelberg, L., "Dynamics and Therapy of Homosexuality." *BAPA*, 8, 1952.

    "Neurosis, a Negative of Perversion?" *PQ*, 38, 1954.

    An Outline of a Comparative Pathology of the Neuroses. IUP, 1954.

Freud, A., "Clinical Observations on the Treatment of Manifest Male Homosexuality." *Q*, 20, 1951.

Hartmann, H., "Kokainismus und Homosexualität." *ZNP*, 95, 1925.

Saul, L., & A. Beck, "Psychodynamics of Male Homosexuality." *IntJPsa*, 42, 1961.

Wiedeman, G., "Survey of Psychoanalytic Literature on Overt Male Homosexuality." *JAPA*, 10, 1962.

Winterstein, A., "On the Oral Basis of a Case of Male Homosexuality." *IntJPsa*, 37, 1956.

P

1600

PAIN denotes (a) specific bodily sensations transmitted through certain nerve endings and nerve tracts to particular areas in the brain; or (b) unpleasant affects, which may be designated as *psychic* pain, in contrast to sensory or somatic pain. In a fundamental sense, pain may be considered the reaction to intolerably strong stimulation. In the infant and in extreme situations later in life, such stimulation may result in a traumatic situation. In infancy, the bodily and psychic reactions cannot be separated. With further maturation, terror is distinguished from pain, and both serve the ego: terror as a signal of the danger of being overwhelmed by an external or internal aggressor, and pain as a warning of injury or loss to the body; both mobilize aggression.

Psychic pain, the affect of pain, develops as a separate entity with the shift of psychic interest from the subject's own body to external objects, i.e., with the development of object-relations. Psychic pain may then be experienced when the cathected love-object is lost or fails the individual, much as bodily pain is produced by damage to or loss of part of the body.

In childhood, some painful bodily sensations may produce sexual excitement which forms the basis of erogenous masochism (perhaps as a defense against pain and aggression by mobilization of sexual impulses). Excitation of the erogenous zones of the skin and muscles beneath the skin (especially of the buttocks) may be produced by pain-provoking stimuli. [Fenichel, 1945.]

Related Concepts: NARCISSISTIC MORTIFICATION; UNPLEASURE.

REFERENCE

Fenichel, O., *The Psychoanalytic Theory of Neurosis.* Nor, pp. 61, 257, 1945.

ADDITIONAL READINGS

Eidelberg, L., *An Outline of a Comparative Pathology of the Neuroses.* IUP, 1954.
Ramzy, I., & R. S. Wallerstein, "Pain, Fear, and Anxiety. A Study in Their Interrelationships." *PsaStC*, 13.
Szasz, T., *Pain and Pleasure.* BB, 1957.

1601

PAIR OF DREAMS are the result of two dreams occurring in the same night which combine to produce a wish-fulfillment. Franz Alexander (1925) described those dreams which occur during the same night, the first containing a person who is undisguised, in which the hidden action is only hinted at, while in the second the action is without disguise, but the person is disguised or replaced by another. In still other pairs, the first dream represents a punishment, and the second, a sinful wish-fulfillment.

Related Concept: DREAMS.

REFERENCE

Alexander, F., "Dreams in Pairs and Series." *IntJPsa*, 6:446, 1925.

1602

PANSEXUALISM denotes a belief in the "fact" that all human behavior can be explained on the basis of sexuality. One of the most common criticisms directed against Freudian psychoanalysis is its alleged reduction of all psychic phenomena to sexuality. This criticism is unfounded. Freud used the concept *sexual* in two different ways: as encompassing sexuality in the commonly accepted sense, and in reference to an energy aimed at uniting small units into bigger ones (opposing, in this way, the destructive drive). This latter, broader interpretation is fundamental to such concepts as the sexual instincts, pleasure principle, etc. [Freud, 1933.] Moreover, Freud never denied the existence of nonsexual interests; from the very beginning he distinguished the sexual drives from the self-preservative drives, and, subsequently, from the aggressive drives.

There are several possibilities which permit a harmless discharge of the repressed wishes after they become conscious in analysis. The majority of such wishes are simply eliminated by the mature mental activities. Repression which has been used by the child to eliminate the dangerous impulses from his conscious mind is replaced by condemnation. This can be achieved in analysis because the patient who is being analyzed is no longer a child and therefore is able to deal with impulses that originally threatened him. In addition. Freud (1910) pointed out that by changing the unconscious wishes into conscious ones the patient was able to use sublimation as a method which permitted the subject to change his infantile impulses which were not acceptable and were unconscious into others; i.e., they were aim-inhibited and thus could become conscious. Consequently, successful analysis not only eliminates the disturbing neurotic symptom but opens the door to sublimation.

Related Concepts: INSTINCT (INSTINCTUAL DRIVE); SUBLIMATION.

REFERENCES

Freud, S.: 1910, "Five Lectures on Psycho-Analysis." *SE*, 11:53–54, 1957.
        1933, "New Introductory Lectures on Psycho-Analysis." *SE*, 22:95, 110, 111, 1964.

ADDITIONAL READINGS

Freud, S., 1925, "An Autobiographical Study." *SE*, 20, 1959.
Redl, F., "'Pansexualismus' und Pubertät." *PsaP*, 9, 1935.

1603

PARAMNESIA is a distortion of memory, involving false recollections which are not recognized as such. For example, in the first edition of "The Interpretation of Dreams," Freud gave Schiller's birthplace as *Marburg*, instead of the correct *Marbach*, which he really knew and should have recalled (Freud, 1901). The associations connected with Marbach and Marburg (the name of a friend of his father's) led to unfriendly and critical thoughts toward his father, and the connection to these conflict producing thoughts motivated the parapraxis. The result was a compromise formation serving both the repressing and the instinctual forces. The paramnesia here involved the (temporary) conviction that Marburg was the correct town.

Displacement to a substitute memory is not a chance one: it may be connected by associative links to the accurate forgotten memory, and may serve the purpose of avoiding a conflict connected with the repressed affectively charged material. Paramnesia is often found as a part of delusional paranoid formations. There is a similarity between paramnesic impressions and screen memories. In the latter, indifferent but real memories, as Freud (1901) noted, are preserved because of their associative connection with other repressed and affectively charged memories. As in paramnesia, the substitute memory serves as a partial gratification and as a partial frustration of infantile wishes.

It was Freud's contention (in 1905) that amnesia and paramnesia sometimes stand in complementary relationship to each other. Some patients consciously keep certain things secret. Others keep them secret as a result of repression, and, finally, there are distortions of memories due to both factors.

Related Concepts: AMNESIA; PARAPRAXIS; SCREEN MEMORY.

REFERENCES

Freud, S.: 1901, "Psychopathology of Everyday Life." *SE*, 6:43–45, 217, 1960.
1905, "A Case of Hysteria." *SE*, 7:17, 1953.

ADDITIONAL READINGS

Freud, S.: & J. Breuer, 1895, "Studies on Hysteria." *SE*, 2.
1921, "Psycho-Analysis and Telepathy." *SE*, 18, 1955.

1604

PARANOID CONDITION (STATE) is a psychosis characterized by delusions of persecution and megalomania, not as systematized or elaborate as in paranoia nor as fragmented and bizarre as in paranoid schizophrenia.

Freud provided the first genetic and dynamic understanding of the syndrome. He initially (1896) formulated the paranoid psychosis as a defense psychosis, stressing the mechanism of projection, in which an internal perception is perceived as coming from without. Later (1923), Freud gave greater prominence to aggression in the genesis of paranoia, and emphasized that an ambivalent attitude is present from the outset. He reformulated the change of love into hate, in terms of a reactive shifting of cathexis at a primitive ambivalent level. In persecutory paranoia, the patient is warding off a strong homosexual wish; as a result of this defense, love changes into aggression. Freud considered this change of love into aggression as being caused by a primary ambivalent feeling toward the original loved homosexual object. The hostility may also be caused by a rivalry. As well, Freud recognized that the fact that love can change into hate may be due to the presence of indifferent energy which, under certain conditions, becomes either erotic or destructive.

More recently, Knight (1940) emphasized the paranoid's excessive need for love in order to neutralize his tremendous unconscious hostility. Melanie Klein (1948) believed that persecutory delusions are connected with the paranoid position, and that these delusions constitute a phase of development through which every infant passes during the first or second year of life. In this phase, the infant feels persecuted by sadistic objects which represent its own projected sadism, and it fears retaliation for its sadistic fantasies. Ruth Brunswick (1928) successfully analyzed a female patient suffering from delusional jealousy and was able to demonstrate that it represented a defense of the patient's preoedipal attachment to her mother.

Related Concepts: PARANOID-SCHIZOID POSITION; PSYCHOSIS.

REFERENCES

Brunswick, R., "Die Analyse eines Eifersuchtswahnes." *Z*, 14:458–507, 1928.
Freud, S.: 1896, "Further Remarks on the Neuro-Psychoses of Defense." *SE*, 3:174–185, 1962.
1923, "The Ego and the Id." *SE*, 19:9, 43–44, 1961.
Klein, M., *Contributions to Psycho-Analysis. 1921–1945*. HPI, pp. 252, 256, 284, 289, 291–292, 1948.
Knight, R. P., "The Relationship of Latent Homosexuality to the Mechanism of Paranoid Delusions." *BMC*, 4:149–159, 1940.

ADDITIONAL READINGS

Ackerman, N., "Paranoid State with Delusions of Injury by 'Black Magic.'" *BMC*, 2, 1938.
Bose, G., "The Paranoid Ego." *Samiksa*, 2, 1948.
Bleuler, E., *Dementia Praecox or the Group of Schizophrenias*, IUP, 1950.
Brunswick, R. M., "The Analysis of a Case of Paranoia (Delusions of Jealousy)." *JNMD*, 70, 1929.
Eidelberg, L., "Psychoanalysis of a Case of Paranoia." *R*, 32, 1945.
Studies in Psychoanalysis. IUP, 1952.
Feigenbaum, D., "Analysis of a Case of Paranoia Persecutoria: Structure and Cure." *R*, 17, 1930.
Fischle-Carl, H., "Zur Behandlung der Paranoia." *Al*, 1958.
Gaupp, R., "Zur Lehre von der Paranoia." *Nervenarzt*, 4, 1947.
Grant, V. W., "Paranoid Dynamics: A Case Study." *P*, 113, 1956.
Hitschmann, E., "Paranoia, Homosexualität und Analerotik." *Z*, 1, 1913.
Kanzer, M., "Gogol—A Study on Wit and Paranoia." *JAPA*, 3, 1955.
Landauer, K., "Paranoia." *PsaVKb*, 1926.
Niederland, W. G., "The 'Miracled-up' World of Schreber's Childhood." *PsaStC*, 14, 1959.
Payne, C. R., "Some Freudian Contributions to the Paranoia Problem." *R*, 1, 1914.
Rycroft, C., "The Analysis of a Paranoid Personality." *IntJPsa*, 41, 1960.

1605

PARANOID-SCHIZOID POSITION. M. Klein (1950) believed that two forms of anxiety should be distinguished: persecutory and depressive. "I arrived at the further conclusion that at the beginning of his post-natal life the infant is experiencing persecutory anxiety both from external and internal sources: external, in so far as the experience of birth is felt as an attack inflicted on him; and internal, because the threat to the organism, which, according to Freud, arises from the death instinct, in my view stirs up the fear of annihilation—the fear of death. It is this fear which I take to be the primary cause of anxiety."

According to Freud, the inability to differentiate between inside and outside—the result of a deficiency in reality testing and of the presence of infantile omnipotence in adults—is not considered by him to be neurotic or psychotic when it takes place in an infant. The conflict in these two views is best summarized in Klein's (1950) statement: "It is true that I have occasionally used the term id more loosely in the sense of representing the death instinct only or the unconscious." It appears doubtful that Freud, who gave precise definitions of the three terms—id, death instinct, and unconscious—would have agreed with her. Lorand (1957) noted: "Surely one of the prime requisites of an adequate theory is economy of explanatory concepts—a good theory should give the simplest explanation which does justice to the facts. This requirement appears to be violated by Kleinian theorists."

Related Concepts: INTROJECTION; PROJECTION.

REFERENCES

Klein, M., "On the Criteria for Determination of a Psycho Analysis." *IntJPsa,* 31:78, 1950.
Lorand, S., Book review, *New Directions in Psycho-Analysis,* M. Klein, et al., eds. *IntJPsa,* 38:283–285, 1957.

1606

PARAPATHY is a synonym for psychoneurosis, used by Stekel (1931) because he felt the old term emphasized the role of the nervous system, even in functional mental diseases. He wanted to empha-size the disordered emotions (*para* means wrong, perverted, beyond, etc.). The term is rarely used.

Related Concept: PSYCHONEUROSIS.

REFERENCE

Stekel, W., "Parapathie und Phimose." *PsaPrx,* 1:37–39, 1931.

1607

PARAPHRENIA was a term used by Freud (1911) in an effort to clarify descriptive classifications of the psychoses. He suggested that the term *paraphrenia* replace both *dementia praecox* and *schizophrenia* as distinct from the related *paranoia.* Freud later changed his mind about the use of paraphrenia, although he retained the conviction that paranoia be held distinct from dementia praecox, on the basis of differences between both fixation points and restitutional mechanisms of the two kindred illnesses. He chose (1914) to use paraphrenia as a common designation for paranoia and dementia praecox (or schizophrenia), calling these "the paraphrenias." The term has not been adopted in the analytic literature, and Freud himself did not use it much after 1918.

Related Concepts: PARANOIA; SCHIZOPHRENIA.

REFERENCES

Freud, S.: 1911, "Psycho-Analytic Notes on an Autobiographical Account of a Case of Paranoia (Dementia Paranoides)." *SE,* 12:76, 1958.
    1914, "On Narcissism: An Introduction." *SE,* 14:82, 1957.

ADDITIONAL READING

Freud, S., 1913, "The Disposition to Obsessional Neurosis." *SE,* 12, 1958.

1608

PARAPRAXIS is a disturbance caused by unconscious conflict in the performance of a commonplace mental function or voluntary motor act; it generally results in the substitution of an erroneous performance for an intended one (e.g. slips of the tongue, forgetting of names and words, accidental actions and perceptions, errors of thought, etc.). If not for the unconsciously determined error, the intended function could easily have been completed. The investigation of these disturbances by Freud (1901) led to the now hackneyed figure of speech, "a Freudian slip." Freud demonstrated that the error could be investigated by psychoanalytic methods and that it was the result of a partial breakthrough of repressed wishes. He used the analysis of parapraxes to demonstrate the ubiquitous nature of repression and psychic determinism, and, later, to show how mechanisms similar to those found in dreams determined the setting and form of the parapraxes. He maintained that neurotic symptom formations were based on the same mechanisms as the symptomatic errors. His emphasis was on the substituted form of the act, rather than the intended one.

For example, a woman who says, "my husband can eat what I want," although she wanted to say, "my husband can eat what he wants," has made a slip which represents two conflicting tendencies; the first is conscious, the second, unconscious. With the help of the slip, the unconscious tendency, "my husband can eat what I want," becomes conscious and makes her say (confess) that the husband can eat what she wants.

The conscious intention, "he can eat what he wants," Freud (1916–1917) called the interfered with intention. Whereas the unconscious wish, "he can eat what I want," Freud called the interfering tendency. He thought that the analyst should concentrate on the study of the interfering tendency.

Eidelberg (1952) showed how the "slip" served functions of the superego, the ego, and the id; a full understanding involved the study of the interfered-with tendency as well as with the interfering one. For example, a patient who had been analyzed for many months related the following: He had entered a restaurant with a girl and approached the headwaiter to ask for a table; instead, he said, "Do you have a room?" In this instance, his associations showed that he was preoccupied with the idea of going to bed with his girl friend and considered it a waste of time to dine first. Further associations indicated that this slip represented a punishment; by admitting what he wanted in public

he had to accept a certain amount of embarrassment. In addition, eating had an infantile meaning for him and, in his unconscious, he wanted to be forced to feed his girl friend. All the wishes connected with the word "room" represented a countercathexis mobilized as a defense. The word "table" had to be omitted, because it would have been used for the infantile gratification of a repressed oral, aggressive, and scopophilic wish connected with identification with the preoedipal mother. "Table" represented an unconscious defense of this oral wish. While it is true that the word "room" expressed phallic and exhibitionistic desires, "table" represented something more dangerous; namely, the wish to be a wet nurse, forced to feed his girl friend. In addition, this slip of the tongue was used to avoid the consciousness of a certain narcissistic mortification; namely, that his girl friend had the power to force him to feed her. Therefore, what Freud originally called the "harmless" word (*table*) had to be eliminated and the unconsciously less dangerous word (*room*) substituted for it. Jones (1957) noted: "Eidelberg had now written a paper pointing out that the conscious intentions were often not 'harmless' and that the slip of the tongue or pen could be determined by ego-syntonic reactions against them—in other words, the reverse mechanism to that described by Freud."

Related Concepts: DREAMS; WIT.

REFERENCES

Eidelberg, L., *Studies in Psychoanalysis.* IUP, pp. 154–173, 1948.
Freud, S., 1901, "The Psychopathology of Everyday Life." *SE,* 6:53–105, 222–238, 250–257, 268–279, 1960.
　　　 1916–1917, "Introductory Lectures on Psycho-Analysis." *SE,* 15:62–63, 1963.
Jones, E. *The Life and Work of Sigmund Freud.* HPI, 3:213, 1957.

ADDITIONAL READINGS

Brenner, C., "A Reformulation of the Theory of Parapraxes." *BPAP,* 5, 1955.
Bryan, C., "A Slip of the Tongue." *IntJPsa,* 4, 1923.
Dattner, B., "A Historical Slip." *C,* 1, 1911.
Federn, P., "The Ego-Cathexis in Parapraxis." *Im,* 19, 1933.
Freud, S.: 1898, "The Psychical Mechanism of Forgetfulness." *SE,* 3, 1962.

Freud, S.: 1913, "The Claims of Psycho-Analysis to Scientific Interest." *SE*, 13, 1955.

    1915, "The Unconscious." *SE*, 14, 1957.

Hartmann, H., & S. Betlheim, "On Parapraxes in the Korsakow Psychosis," in *Organization and Pathology of Thought.* CUP, 1951.

Jekels, L., "A Case of Slip of the Tongue." *Z*, 1, 1913.

Jones, E., "An Example of the Literary Use of a Slip of the Tongue." *C*, 1, 1911.

Pfeifer, S., "Repeated Slips of the Tongue During Analysis." *Z*, 9, 1923.

Reik, T., "Fehlleistungen im Alltagsleben." *Z*, 3, 1915.

Sachs, H., "Eine Fehlhandlung zur Selbstberuhigung." *Z*, 3, 1915.

Sugar, N., "Zur Frage der Unbewussten Verständigung und der 'Ansteckenden' Fehlhandlung." *Z*, 26, 1941.

Szalai, A., "Die 'Ansteckende' Fehlhandlung." *Z*, 19, 1933.

that only patients who preserve an infantile passive masochistic attitude will surrender to the hypnotist's orders.

Related Concepts: EGO; HYPNOSIS; SUPEREGO.

REFERENCES

Ferenczi, S., 1909, "Introjection and Transference." *SPsa*, pp. 70–71, 1916.

Freud, S., 1921, "Group Psychology and the Analysis of the Ego." *SE*, 18:127–128, 1955.

Rado, S., "The Economic Principle in Psychoanalytic Technique." *IntJPsa*, 6:35–44, 1925.

Sperling, O., "The Interpretation of the Trauma as a Command." *Q*, 9:352–370, 1950.

ADDITIONAL READING

Sperling, O., "Psychodynamics of Group Perversion." *Q*, 25, 1956.

1609

PARASITIC SUPEREGO denotes a foreign body of commands and standards, which coexists (if temporarily), and is in conflict, with the superego. Rado (1925) has shown that the hypnotists' suggestions establish a parasitic superego in the mind of the subject. According to Sperling (1950), a similar mechanism may be found in war neurosis, when enemy propaganda or the soldier's interpretation of what the enemy wants him to do conflicts with his superego as formed in childhood, synthesized with later influences.

This mechanism also operates in group perversion, where the example of, and seduction by, the leader leads to a perverse act, in contradiction to previously held superego values and prohibitions. It seems that only people who have retained an infantile superego can acquire a parasitic superego. The related mechanism, described by Freud (1921), may be considered different from a parasitic superego insofar as it consists of a group of individuals putting one object (the leader) *in the place* of their ego-ideal. In addition, Freud discussed an idea first advanced by Ferenczi. The latter discovered that when a hypnotist orders the hypnotized subject to sleep he represents the parents; he thought that the hypnotist played the role of the loving and friendly mother and the threatening father. The command to sleep represents the withdrawal of interest from the external world. It appears

1610

PARESIS may result from somatic changes in the central and peripheral nervous systems or it may be the result of unconscious defense mechanisms, in which the voluntary movements of the involved parts are eliminated with no detectable physical changes. General paralysis designates a disorder of the central nervous system resulting from syphilis which usually develops from ten to thirty years after the initial infection. Its symptoms are both mental (behavior changes, impaired memory, etc.) and physical (paralysis, epileptiform attacks, etc.). Cerebrospinal fluid shows a positive Wassermann and a typical colloidal gold curve pattern. [Brain, 1948.]

An inherited cerebro-nervous system with syphilitic involvement, juvenile paresis, is usually observed in children twelve to fourteen years old. Its symptoms are similar to those of general paresis. Freud (1905a, 1905b) did not claim that neurosis was the sign of hereditary syphilis, in spite of the fact that syphilis in the father was found to be present in many neuropathic children.

Freud did not discuss this topic further in any of his later writings and this concept has been abandoned.

Related Concepts: CONVERSION AND CONVERSION SYMPTOMS; PATHONEUROSIS.

REFERENCES

Brain, W. R., *Diseases of the Nervous System*. OUP, pp. 411–420, 1948.
Freud, S.: 1905a, "Fragment of an Analysis of a Case of Hysteria." *SE*, 7:21, 1953.
　　　1905b, "Three Essays on the Theory of Sexuality." *SE*, 7:236, 1953.

1611

PASSIVE is a term originally used by Freud (1909) to designate "feminine" characteristics: he regarded the libido in both males and females as masculine; the individual represented a mixture of both characteristics. His reasoning was apparently based on a biological observation: spermatozoids were active and ova passive. The term active was also synonymous with that which was aggressive, e.g., sadism was characterized as masculine and masochism as feminine. As late as 1933, Freud still considered female activity to be characterized by passive aims. As Bergler and Eidelberg (1933) pointed out, however, a mother suckling her child seems to gratify both an active and a passive aim. The differentiation to be made is between the activity of the subject and that of the object, between that which is active and that which is passive: acted upon, or acted toward.

In the biological sciences, the recognition of the difference is of basic importance. In this, Mainx (1955) noted: "The most general statements about the state of living systems are especially concerned with the energy relations in the living world. The maintenance of the flow equilibrium or, in other words, the preservation of the potential differences necessarily present in the living organism, is connected with incessant performance of work; the organism raises in this way the entropy level of its environment; it feeds, so to speak, on 'negative entropy' (Schrödinger). In connection with such considerations and similar ones, it is often customary to speak of the 'activity' of the organism as one of its special characteristics. So long as this word is used only to denote the mutual energy relations between organism and environment, it is meaningful from the point of view of empirical science. Unfortunately, the use of such words and ones similar to them often leads more or less consciously to anthropomorphic ideas, like the ideas of active 'forces' in physics, which have long been superseded."

Related Concepts: ACTIVE; AGGRESSIVE; LIBIDINAL TYPES; MASCULINITY.

REFERENCES

Bergler, E., & L. Eidelberg, "Der Mammakomplex des Mannes." *Z*, 19:572, 1933.
Freud, S.: 1909, "Analysis of a Phobia in a Five-Year-Old Boy." *SE*, 10:140, 1955.
　　　1933, "New Introductory Lectures on Psycho-Analysis." *SE*, 22:115, 116, 1964.
Mainx, F., *Foundations of Biology*, UCP, 1(9):26–27, 1955.

ADDITIONAL READINGS

Hart, H. H., "Masochism, Passivity and Radicalism." *R*, 39, 1952.
Keiser, S., "The Fear of Sexual Passivity in the Masochist." *IntJPsa*, 30, 1949.
Pavenstedt, E., "The Effect of Extreme Passivity Imposed on a Boy in Early Childhood." *PsaStC*, 11, 1956.

1612

PASSIVE-RECEPTIVE LONGING denotes the desire to achieve a state of primary narcissism and passive object-love, like the infant, who, under the pressure of powerful narcissistic and erotic needs, wants gratification from the object without returning anything and without having to strive for it. The passive-receptive orientation finds expression in all stages of libidinal development, particularly the oral and anal stages, and is closely correlated with the wish to receive the object inside the body, i.e., incorporating it. Important corollaries of this disposition are oral and anal fixations, femininity in men (often accompanied by the fantasy of being a woman), masochistic tendencies, hunger for love, dependency, inability to tolerate frustration, intense pleasure in warmth, passivity, and omnipotent thinking. In the infant, the passive-receptive state is followed by one of passive-receptive mastery, in which satisfaction of instinctual needs is achieved by overcoming the difficulties connected with the early traumatic frustrations. Regression to passive-receptive attitudes can be studied in hypnosis, is common in neurosis, and is particularly outstanding in addiction. [Fenichel 1945.]

Related Concept: MATURATION.

REFERENCE

Fenichel, O., *The Psychoanalytic Theory of Neurosis*, Nor, pp. 119, 170, 192, 1945.

1613

PATHOGNOMY is the examination of the correlation between particular signs, symptoms or character traits and a specific disease or basic internal conflict. In psychoanalysis, a number of these specific correlations have been established, especially between fixation points and regressions and certain mental disorders. Some symptoms are indicative of a specific conflict (e.g., repressed phallic wishes lead to hysteria, whereas anal wishes appear to be responsible for obsessions).

Eidelberg (1954) noted: "The fascinating problem of the choice of the neurosis may be studied, perhaps, in the light of Freud's concept of the libidinal types. While most analysts agree that hysteria, for instance, arises from phallic wishes, and that obsessional neurosis is caused by anal impulses, the question remains unanswered as to why hysteria produces conversion symptoms in one case, and a phobia in another. If it is true that an individual who belongs to the erotic type is characterized not only by his need of love, but also by being less aggressive than individuals who belong to the narcissistic and obsessional types, it may be expected that when such an individual develops hysteria, he will have conversion symptoms. On the other hand, an individual who belongs to the obsessional type will, as the result of a phallic regression, develop an anxiety hysteria. A person who represents the narcissistic type will produce a hysterical character under the same circumstances. Unfortunately, most people belong to mixed libidinal types, and only the few who belong to pure types can be used to study the above suggestions."

Related Concept: CHOICE OF A NEUROSIS.

REFERENCE

Eidelberg, L., *An Outline of a Comparative Pathology of the Neuroses*. IUP, pp. 260–261, 1954.

ADDITIONAL READINGS

Eidelberg, L., *Studies in Psychoanalysis*. IUP, 1948.
Fenichel, O., *The Psychoanalytic Theory of Neurosis*. Nor, 1945.

1614

PATHONEUROSIS is a neurosis which develops in connection with a somatic disease. The somatic disease mobilizes intrapsychic conflicts by disrupting the previous intrapsychic balance. It unconsciously comes to represent the gratification of a drive and punishment by the superego, or both. Pathoneurosis also includes neurotic reactions to the limitations imposed by somatic disease, particularly various attempts at denial of the real inhibitions or incapacities of physical function.

Fenichel (1945) cites a case of eunuchoidism, psychoanalytically treated by Carmichael,* as follows: "The organic disturbance manifested itself at puberty, and mental difficulties started when the patient became aware of it. He unconsciously interpreted his disease as 'castration'." His anal and compulsive character became more pronounced, he tried to deny the existence of any sexual feeling, and he blanked out all infantile sexual memories, in addition to other pathoneurotic symptoms.

Related Concept: NEUROSES (PSYCHONEUROSES).

REFERENCE

Fenichel, O., *The Psychoanalytic Theory of Neurosis*. Nor, p. 259, 1945.

ADDITIONAL READING

Freud, S., 1914, "On Narcissism: An Introduction." *SE*, 14, 1957.

---

* Carmichael, H. T., "A Psychoanalytic Study of a Case of Eunuchoidism." *Q*, 10:243–266, 1941.

1615

PAVOR NOCTURNUS is a fear reaction which occurs at night in sleep; it was described by Freud (1900) as a nocturnal anxiety attack with hallucinations. The anxiety is a result of warded-off and distorted sexual impulses.

M. Sperling (1958) distinguished two forms of pavor nocturnus in children: the psychotic form, involving hypermotility, hallucinations, and a retrograde amnesia on awakening; and the neurotic form, characterized by nightmares, from which the child awakens still experiencing anxiety and with a vivid memory of the dream, which may be caused by conflicts about homosexual, sado-masochistic, and aggressive impulses. The psychotic type may continue into puberty, at which time serious character disorders, perversions or even psychotic states may become manifest. The neurotic form may be revived later in life.

According to Jones (1948), nightmares may be considered as pathological behavior. "The most obvious of these is of course the fact that dreams belong to normal phenomena, neuroses to abnormal. On this matter, however, there is a great deal to say. In the first place, certain dreams are decidedly pathological in nature. For instance, nightmares and other severe anxiety-dreams occur only in subjects who show other evidences of an anxiety-neurosis (commonly included under the heading of neurasthenia), and there is reason to believe that increased knowledge of dreams will show that certain types are indicative of definite forms of neurosis or insanity. . . .

"Many neurotic symptoms—e.g., night terrors, noctambulic wanderings, nocturnal paralyses, certain kinds of nocturnal epileptiform fits—definitely belong to the region of sleep, and others, such as various automatic and twilight conditions, occur in mental states that are hard psychologically to distinguish from sleep. On the other hand, there is a most intimate connection, both in essence and appearance, between night-dreams and daydreams or reveries. Some of the most typical dreams, particularly night-mare, occur by day (day-mare) as well as by night, and in all stages between deep sleep and full waking; often the subject is quite unable to tell whether he was awake or asleep at the time or in an intermediate state half-way between the two."

Related Concepts: ANXIETY; NIGHTMARE.

REFERENCES

Freud, S., 1900, "The Interpretation of Dreams." *SE*, 5:585, 1953.
Jones, E., *Papers on Psycho-Analysis*. WW, pp. 270–271, 1948.
Sperling, M., "Pavor Nocturnus." *JAPA*, 6:79–94, 1958.

ADDITIONAL READINGS

Klein, M., *The Psychoanalysis of Children*. Nor, 1932.
Schneider, E., "The Origin of Pavor Nocturnus in a Child: An Addendum." *PsaP*, 2, 1927–1928.

1616

PENIS ENVY denotes the female's conscious or unconscious envy of the penis; a normal occurrence in little girls during the phallic phase of development. The onset of penis envy may occur from the beginning of the second year to the end of the third year, depending on various factors (e.g., observations of playmates, birth of boy siblings, time of exposure to primal scene, etc.). Prior to the phallic phase, both boys and girls deny the anatomical differences between the sexes or attribute no meaning to them. In the phallic phase, the little girl often takes her mother as a love-object, competing with the father, and expresses her active phallic strivings through the wish to protect, care for, and impregnate the mother. In this connection, the lack of a penis becomes painfully meaningful and is felt as a narcissistic mortification. The little girl may have fantasy of once having had a penis, that it was lost as a result of her active phallic wishes toward her mother or was taken away from her and given to the preferred boy. She might imagine that she still has a penis, but that it is hidden and will one day grow longer than the little boy's. With the final recognition and acceptance of not having a penis, the little girl blames her mother for the loss and turns to her father, with the expectation of obtaining a penis from him, a hope later replaced by the wish to receive a child from him—a doll, a gift in general. [Freud, 1924, 1925.]

Freud (1933) claimed that the castration complex in females starts with the discovery of the penis in males. The girl reacts with an envy for the boy's penis; she feels inferior and this inferiority feeling may produce various neurotic symptoms which prevent her from reaching genital maturity. Freud thought that envy and also jealousy played a much greater role for the female than for the male. The little girl believes for a time that she will grow a penis because she thinks that her mother has a penis. When she discovers that her mother does not have a penis, she reacts with a feeling of contempt for all females.

Abraham (1919) defines penis envy in the adult woman as "a hostile feeling against the male associated with the impulse to deprive him of what he possesses. The union of these two reactions constitutes envy which represents a typical expression of the anal-sadistic developmental phase of the libido."

Penis envy has its roots in the oral and anal periods of development. Insofar as the mother's breast is felt as a part of the infant's own body, weaning means that a part of the body is taken away. In a similar way, as Freud noted (in 1909), the fecal mass is felt as a part of the infant's own body, and having to surrender it to the mother, on her command, may be experienced as an anal castration.

The substitution of a child, a doll, or a gift for the penis has been mentioned above, but a considerable number of women are unable to carry out this adaptation to the feminine role and may pursue active masculine strivings throughout their lives. They may become vengeful towards men or by denying their feminine role entirely, in the pursuit of the illusory penis, they may turn to overt homosexuality. Other women may find sublimated outlets to gratify their masculine strivings, such as the pursuit of a career, while renouncing children and any pleasure from the vagina.

Among the neurotic symptoms in which penis envy plays an important role are as follows: enuresis nocturna, in which the female expresses the wish to urinate in the male way; redness and swelling of the nasal mucous membrane, representing a symbolic penis; kleptomania; vaginismus; nymphomania; and preference for a passive feminine (castrated) man as a partner. Penis envy may also occur without the wish to be a man, i.e., with the wish to be a woman with a penis. This phenomenon has its root in orality; specifically, in the wish to have

all the possessions of a woman and all the possessions of a man (hermaphroditism).

Penis envy may also occur in males, i.e., as the wish to have a bigger penis. In many cases, it represents a defense against the consciousness of the breast complex.

Related Concepts: BREAST COMPLEX; CASTRATION COMPLEX; ENVY.

REFERENCES

Abraham, K., 1919, "Concerning the Female Castration Complex." *SPA*, pp. 338–369, 1942.
Freud, S.: 1909, "Analysis of a Phobia in a Five-Year-Old Boy." *SE*, 10:8, 1955.
     1924, "The Dissolution of the Oedipus Complex." *SE*, 19:178, 1961.
     1925, "Some Psychical Consequences of the Anatomical Distinction Between the Sexes." *SE*, 19:256–257, 1961.
     1933, "New Introductory Lectures on Psycho-Analysis." *SE*, 22:125–127, 1964.

ADDITIONAL READINGS

Barrett, W. G., "Penis Envy and Urinary Control; Pregnancy Fantasies and Constipation; Episodes in the Life of a Little Girl." *Q*, 8, 1939.
Bergler, E., & L. Eidelberg, "Der Mammakomplex des Mannes." *Z*, 19, 1933.
Freud, S.: 1905, "Three Essays on the Theory of Sexuality." *SE*, 7, 1953.
     1931, "Female Sexuality." *SE*, 21, 1961.
     1940, "Medusa's Head." *SE*, 18, 1955.
Horney, K., "The Dread of Women." *IntJPsa*, 13, 1932.
Kouretas, D., "Sur un cas de Névrose à Base d'Envie du Penis." *RFPsa*, 14, 1950.
Müller-Braunschweig, C., "The Girl's First Object Cathexis in Relation to Penis Envy and Femininity." *P*, 13, 1959.

1617

PEPTIC ULCER is a psychosomatic disorder with pathological changes of the mucous membrane of the stomach or duodenum resulting in pain, discomfort and possible complications of stenosis, hemorrhages and perforations. Many somatic factors have been implicated, including abnormal gastric motility and hyperacidity; the proof for constitutional factors lies in the inherited tendency toward high blood and urine peptogenic levels.

From a psychoanalytic viewpoint, this disorder is not limited to a particular personality type, but is always associated with an oral regression and usually with a serious oral fixation. This leads to marked ambivalence with urges to both incorporate and destroy through biting, as well as oral envy, impatience, greed, and aggressive attempts to ward off passive-dependent yearnings. In object relationships, there is a frequent identification with both a suckling mother and a suckling child (breast = penis equation). Castration anxiety may be expressed as a fear of being eaten and a fear of starvation. The ego shows a marked intolerance of affect, especially anxiety and anger, and an inability to tolerate frustration or postpone gratification. In the face of frustration or conflict, there is a marked rapid psychological, and perhaps physiological regression in the form of resomatized aspects of emotions. A sadistic maternal superego has been postulated, which orally assaults the patient, biting and digesting the self, and cathecting the food with harmful psychic contents. Garma (1960) summarized his own view, as follows: "Although patients suffering from peptic ulcer do not show any apparent inhibitions in their genital behaviour, their sexual object is generally someone who frustrates them genitally. The conflict with this frustrating person antedates the appearance of their ulcer. Owing to their conflicts these patients suffer a harmful oral-digestive regression of their genitality. This regression results in intensification of their cruel superegos, especially in their maternal aspects. In the unconscious there is a reactivation of the mental representations of a mother who sucks, bites, and digests them from within and also forces them into harmful alimentary behaviour, such as eating harmful food, depriving themselves of good food, and cathecting food with bad psychic contents. This psychic constellation brings on various functional and organic disorders in the digestive tract of these patients, finally producing ulcers. Owing to this genesis of ulcers, the sole etiological and most efficient treatment for peptic ulcer patients is prolonged psycho-analysis." Freud (1933) himself used the example of the stomach digesting the self as a patho-phsyiological manifestation of the aggressive instinct.

Case History

"One duodenal ulcer patient expressed his oral-digestive regression in saying that 'When I think of being with women I feel something like a bug wriggling and gnawing inside my stomach' and that 'these worries damage my stomach'. When he had improved through his psychoanalytic treatment he compared his overcoming this fear to 'the removal of a fly from my food'. According to what the patient said, 'This fly had a bad effect on my stomach, because my brain, my mind, rejected the fly, although the stomach itself would not have reacted at all'. The fly was an image of his maternal superego that sucked and poisoned him digestively.

"Another duodenal ulcer patient was never breast fed by his mother but by five successive wet-nurses. His mother was very domineering towards her husband and children. The patient chose his fiancée out of an unconscious wish for masochistic submission to a bad genital object with his mother's characteristics. He would often call her 'Mummy' by mistake and regarded her as phallic just as he did his real mother. He even entertained the idea that she had been obliged to undergo an operation for hermaphroditism. His submission to her made him accept her quite groundless reproaches about his being homosexual.

"Once his ulcer symptoms became worse when he was upset at hearing his fiancée praise other men. He reacted by feeling castrated and forced by his fiancée and his mother to eat bad food. For him this stood for their bad breasts. Thus on this and other similar occasions he used to take alcoholic drinks of inferior quality, and each time two glassfuls, representing the women's two bad breasts. When somewhat better, he substituted two cups of coffee for the two glasses of alcohol. He had very demonstrative dreams, with very plainly regressive oral-digestive, masochistic contents. In one of them he was forced to chew up in his mouth (which in the latent dream content meant his stomach and duodenum) a very sharp razor-blade 'like the one a madman used for cutting off his penis'. This blade also had the symbolic meaning of maternal teeth that bit into his digestive tract and provoked his ulcer.

"In situations of genital conflict with his fiancée, later to become his wife, one gastric ulcer patient had various phantasies, the latent meaning of which was that of submitting to his father in passive anal coitus. In these phantasies the father entered by his anus into his intestine and ascended along it until he reached the inside of his duodenum and stomach. But on the way he had turned into a lioness with a lion's mane. In other words, the father turned into an animal clearly symbolic of the phallic mother. This lioness bit into his stomach and by this oral aggression provoked his ulcer.

"These contents of oral-digestive aggression carried out by a maternal superego upon a person who is experiencing situations of genital failure, are also seen in descriptions of ulcer patients reported by other psycho-analysts. Thus H. B. Levey describes an ulcer patient who, on one occasion, after having temporarily usurped an older brother's place at the table, slept badly and had phantasies connected with a boyhood memory of being scolded by his mother who pulled his ear. Thereupon he identified himself with Christ and felt he was being eaten up at a Catholic Mass." [Garma, 1960.]

Related Concepts: PSYCHOSOMATIC; SOMATIC STIMULI AND DREAMS.

REFERENCES

Freud, S., 1933, "New Introductory Lectures on Psycho-Analysis." *SE*, 22:106, 1964.
Garma, A., "The Unconscious Images in the Genesis of Peptic Ulcer." *IntJPsa*, 41:446, 449, 1960.

ADDITIONAL READINGS

Cushing, M., "Psychoanalytic Treatment of Ulcerative Colitis." *BAPA*, 8, 1952.
Garma, A., "The Predisposing Situation to Peptic Ulcer in Children." *IntJPsa*, 40, 1959.
Szasz, T. S., "Factors in the Pathogenesis of Peptic Ulcer." *PSM*, 11, 1949.
Van Der Heide, C., "A Study of Mechanisms in Two Cases of Peptic Ulcer." *PSM*, 2, 1940.

1618

PERCEPTION denotes an internal experience arising from sensations and feelings; an external perception, from sensory phenomena; both are controlled by the ego. Internal perception is further divided into perceptions from the id (desires) and from the superego (feelings of guilt). External perceptions become directly conscious and are brought about by an assignment of meaning to otherwise undifferentiated sensory experiences. Internal perceptions, on the other hand, arise from residual memories (ideas) stored in the psychic apparatus, in the unconscious part of the ego, which must become preconscious and establish a connection to an external presentation to enter consciousness. [Freud, 1923.]

The infant learns slowly to differentiate between himself and the external world; consequently, the primary narcissistic libido and destrudo are divided into (a) objectual libido and destrudo which cathects the external object presentation, and (b) secondary narcissistic libido and destrudo which cathect the presentation of the self. In addition, he begins to separate what he likes from what he dislikes, and, finally, he discovers that an emotional reaction to sense organ perceptions may be separated from the pure perceptions—often referred to as "objective data." For example, the statement, "I want this steak," is to be separated from the remark, "This *is* a steak." independently of whether the subject wants it or not.

Hartmann (1964) viewed this developmental process, as follows: "The child learns to recognize 'things' probably only in the process of forming more or less constant object relationships. We assume that progress in neutralization is involved in both steps, and that with regard to this factor both steps have a common origin. Further, the development of what one calls 'intentionality'— the child's capacity to direct himself toward something, to aim at something, in perception, attention, action, etc., a process that according to Freud probably presupposes hypercathexis—could be viewed as one ego aspect of developing object relations. Actually, intentionality is among the first achievements of the child we would not hesitate to characterize as true ego functions. Others among the especially developmentally interesting, but little explored object-directed ego tendencies should be systematically approached in the same way."

Related Concepts: HALLUCINATIONS; ILLUSION.

REFERENCES

Freud, S., 1923, "The Ego and the Id." *SE*, 19:20, 23, 1961.
Hartmann, H., *Essays on Ego Psychology*. IUP, p. 173, 1964.

ADDITIONAL READINGS

Eidelberg, L.: "A Contribution to the Physiology of Sense Perceptions Suggested in Hypnosis." *ZNP*, 1, 1928.
          "The Perception of Wet and Dry." *ZNP*, 3, 1928.
Fisher, C., "Dreams, Images and Perception: A Study of Unconscious-Preconscious Relationships." *JAPA*, 4, 1956.
Rubinfine, D. L., "Perception, Reality Testing and Symbolism." *PsaStC*, 16, 1961.
Spiegel, L. A., "The Self, the Sense of Self, and Perception." *PsaStC*, 14, 1959.
Spitz, R., "The Primal Cavity: A Contribution to the Genesis of Perception and Its Role for Psychoanalytic Theory." *PsaStC*, 10, 1955.

1619

PERCEPTUAL CONSCIOUSNESS, according to Freud (1933), is a superficial part of the central nervous system. This system receives stimuli from the external world. In addition, Freud (1900) differentiated between the reception of stimuli by this system of the psychic apparatus and the recording of its memory traces. He further postulated that the human organism was able to erect barriers against excessive stimuli by withdrawing the cathexis from the perceptual-consciousness system. Structurally, the capacity to perceive appears to represent a function of the ego. Freud suggested that the system which receives the external stimuli did not retain them; rather, these stimuli were recorded in another system.

Recent work by Fisher and Paul (1959) tends to corroborate the selectivity of consciousness in perception; some perceptions may be incorporated as memory traces without reaching consciousness.

The term "perceptual consciousness" is rarely used today; its conceptual components are discussed under other headings: e.g., the ego, perception, the unconscious, etc.

Related Concepts: PERCEPTION; SENSATION; SYSTEMATIC (QUALITATIVE OR DESCRIPTIVE) APPROACH.

REFERENCES

Fisher, C., & I. H. Paul, "The Effect of Subliminal Visual Stimulation on Images and Dreams: A Validation Study." *JAPA*, 7:35–83, 1959.
Freud, S.: 1900, "The Interpretation of Dreams." *SE*, 5:537–538, 1953.
          1933, "New Introductory Lectures on Psycho-Analysis." *SE*, 22:75, 1964.

ADDITIONAL READING

Fenichel, O., *The Psychoanalytic Theory of Neurosis.* Nor, 1945.

1620

PERSONA, according to Jung (1928), is the aspect of the individual's personality, the mask which he habitually shows to his environment as the result of conscious adaptation and unconscious identification. Introverts identify too much with a single persona; extroverts easily change their persona in different environments.

Related Concept: IDENTIFICATION.

REFERENCE

Jung, C. G., *Two Essays on Analytical Psychology.* London: Balliere, Tindall & Cox, 1928.

1621

PERSONAL MYTH is a defensive act involving screen and distorted autobiographical memories; the distorted personal history becomes part of the self-image to which the individual becomes attached. According to Kris (1952), by keeping certain memories out of consciousness, the myth acts as a substitute for a repressed family romance from which it derives some of its cathexis. Among the factors predisposing the individual toward the development of a personal myth is the occurrence of a severe trauma during the oedipal phase, following a relatively undisturbed preoedipal development.

Related Concepts: DENIAL (DISAVOWAL); FAMILY ROMANCE; SCREEN MEMORY; SELF.

REFERENCE

Kris, E., "The Personal Myth." *JAPA*, 4, 1956.

PERVERSION. Most psychoanalysts define perversion as a habitual deviation from the prevaling sexual norm. They view perversion as the result of a specific defense mechanism, in which genital discharge is permitted or achieved; it is not the result of a breakthrough of an infantile wish. Neurotic character traits and perversions are both ego-syntonic; but unlike neurotic character traits, perversions lead to genital discharge and conscious pleasure.

Although Freud initially described neurosis as the negative of perversion, he later (1927) discovered that fetishism (a perversion) was not a breakthrough of an infantile wish, but was, rather, the result of a complicated defense mechanism which permitted the fetishist to deny the lack of a female penis. In a way, the fetishist is protected from becoming a homosexual. His fetish represents the female penis, a penis which is in his possession.

Among the commonly recognized forms of perversion are fetishism, masochism, overt homosexuality (male and female), exhibitionism, voyeurism (inspectionism), transvestitism, sodomy (bestiality), pedophilia, and necrophilia. According to Eidelberg (1954), a study of perversions shows the following: "They are caused by the presence of infantile wishes and unconscious defenses, the end result of this defense is accepted by the total personality. Different from patients who are suffering from symptom neuroses, perverts approve of their form of genital gratification, but in deviation from character neurotics, they are aware of being peculiar, queer, or better than normal, although not normal. Similar to the character neurotics, they are unable to separate love from hate. They try to destroy or humiliate the object they are attracted to. At the same time, they select their objects in such a way as to make sure that the love they receive will be connected with some form of hostility.

"Perversions are not caused by a simple breakthrough of the id, and a passive acceptance by the ego of the infantile wishes. In the structure of the perversion, it seems that the energy used as countercathexis is not altogether substituted for that of the original wish, but is used to 'dilute' it. Therefore, perversions can be analyzed and cured by a modified technique. The analysis of perverts seems to indicate that, in comparison with 'normals,' they are more interested in having a genital outlet than in loving and being loved, and that they discharge a greater amount of aggression against their partners than the 'normals' do toward their love objects. While many perverts consider themselves better than normal and claim that their life is more 'gay,' their climax more intense, their intellect superior, and their moral standards higher than that of the common man who cares only about his family, some of them do suffer from feelings of inferiority and want to be analyzed.

"For example, the fetishist who could have sexual intercourse only with women who were menstruating was freed from this rigid condition of intercourse when he discovered that this perversion served as an unconscious defense against his wish to devour his mother. Another pervert was able to have intercourse only after having been beaten. His masochism was eliminated when he recognized that the punishment he needed in order to attain a genital outlet represented an unconscious defense against his wish to defecate on his father."

Later, Eidelberg (1956) noted, in regard to the pervert's ability to sublimate, the following: "The experience of most analysts in the analysis of perverts does not indicate that the limitation of the perversion paralyzes their ability to sublimate. The opposite appears to be the case. However, the handling of unconscious infantile omnipotence, important in each analysis, appears to be of special significance in a case of perversion. The idea that one may play two roles at the same time, either by masturbating or by selecting a partner who represents the self, seems to be the result of an unconscious fear of not being able to survive after being cut off from the parents. It is my opinion that, in manifest homosexuality, the identification and the fixation on the pre-Oedipal mother is especially important. The phallic and the anal material present in such cases should not be regarded as trivial or banal and no short cut to the examination of the oral stage should be attempted. Neither should the experience we have gained in the treatment of other homosexuals nor the findings communicated to us by our colleagues cause us to neglect the study of the concrete material a particular patient offers. In other words, knowledge should not blind us to new discoveries. One may say, perhaps, that, in analyzing a patient, we should be as naive as possible and suppress for a time what we have learned from other cases. Our ability to recognize in the new patient what we have heard described before no doubt helps us to proceed with our work, but this knowledge should not be used *instead* of examination of the concrete material presented to us by the patient on the couch."

Related Concept: CHARACTER NEUROSIS.

REFERENCES

Eidelberg, L.: *An Outline of a Comparative Pathology of the Neuroses.* IUP, pp. 249–250, 1954.
    "Analysis of a Case of Male Homosexuality," in *Perversions, Psychodynamics and Therapy*, Lorand, S. and M. Balint, eds. RH, pp. 288–289, 1956.
Freud, S.: 1905, "Three Essays on the Theory of Sexuality." *SE*, 7:149–150, 155–162, 170–171, 1953. 1927, "Fetishism." *SE*, 21:154, 1961.

ADDITIONAL READINGS

Aarons, Z. A., "A Study of Perversion and an Attendant Character Disorder." *Q*, 28, 1959.
Abraham, K., "Über die Beziehungen zwischen Perversion und Neurose. Referat über die erste von Freud's *Drei Abhandlungen zur Sexualtheorie*." *BPV*, 1911.
Arlow, J., "Psychodynamics and Treatment of Perversions." *BAPA*, 8, 1952.
Boehm, F., "Sexual Perversions." *IntJPsa*, 2, 1921.
Eidelberg, L., "Neurosis, a Negative of Perversion?" *PQ*, 28, 1954.
Eissler, K. R., "Notes on Problems of Technique in the Psychoanalytic Treatment of Adolescents: With Some Remarks on Perversions." *PsaStC*, 13, 1958.
Gillespie, W.: "The General Theory of Sexual Perversion." *IntJPsa*, 37, 1956.
    "The Structure and Aetiology of Sexual Perversion," in S. Lorand *Perversions: Psychodynamics and Therapy*. RH, 1956.
Lorand, S., "The Therapy of Perversions," in *Perversions: Psychodynamics and Therapy*, RH, 1956.
Nacht, S., "The Ego in Perverse Relationships." *IntJPsa*, 37, 1956.
Sachs, H., "Zur Genese der Perversionen." *Z*, 9, 1923.
Sadger, J., "Ein Fall von Multipler Perversion mit Hysterischen Absenzen." *Y*, 2, 1910.
Sperling, O., "Psychodynamics of Group Perversions." *PQ*, 25, 1956.

1623

PETRIFACTION of the viewer is frequently mentioned as a possible punishment for scopophilic acts in mythology and religious lore. In this context, petrifaction represents the outcome of aggression consummated through the eye, as in the myth of the Medusa head (Coriat, 1941).

The scopophilic acts which bring about punishment by petrifaction are, or represent, peeping on the parents' sexual activities and the terrifying sight of the "castrated" female genitalia. Petrifaction thus embodies the wish to "peek": the fascination exerted by the object peeked at, the defense against peeking, and the punishment for it. Symbolically, petrifaction means death, castration, and erection, and serves as a reassurance that the beholder still possesses a penis. On a somatic level, it relates to the feeling of paralysis and the stiffening of the body musculature (especially the respiratory muscles) connected with terror. A similar fantasy is the belief that a grimace may "freeze" and "stick" on the face. [Fenichel, 1937.]

Related Concepts: CASTRATION COMPLEX; SCOPOPHILIA.

REFERENCES

Coriat, I. H., "A Note on the Medusa Symbolism." *AmIm*, 6:281–285, 1941.
Fenichel, O., "The Scoptophilic Instinct and Identification." *IntJPsa*, 18:6–34, 1937.

1624

PHALLIC CHARACTER is a formation resulting from a fixation at the phallic stage, in which an attempt to deny castration anxiety is made, often through an identification of the self with the phallus. Fear of castration may lead to passivity, and an accentuation of some phallic characteristics, or it may lead to an over-confident, aggressive, and exhibitionistic manner (counterphobic). Patients with phallic character traits are extremely sensitive to narcissistic mortifications and are constantly on guard against them. They often manifest potency disturbances. They live as if they were unafraid of castration. [Eidelberg, 1954.]

Related Concepts: FRIGIDITY; IMPOTENCE.

REFERENCE

Eidelberg, L., *An Outline of a Comparative Pathology of the Neuroses.* IUP, pp. 166–173, 1954.

ADDITIONAL READINGS

Horney, K., "On the Genesis of the Castration Complex in Women." *IntJPsa*, 5, 1924.
Loewenstein, R., "Phallic Passivity in Men." *IntJPsa*, 16, 1935.
Lorand, S., *Clinical Studies in Psychoanalysis.* IUP, 1950.
Reich, W., *Character Analysis.* OIP, 1949.

1625

PHALLIC MOTHER identifies the commonly held belief, on the part of the male child, that his mother has a penis. In other cases, as a result of the repression of the breast complex, the boy displaces the cathexis from the breast to his own penis; he thus denies his breast envy and creates the image of the mother with a penis (instead of the breast) and therefore does not have to feel humiliated by the lack of it. The phallic mother is a recurrent image in the analysis of overt homosexuality and melancholia, and is plainly connected with fetishism. Freud (1927) noted that the fetish which represents the penis is actually a female penis, the penis which was lost in childhood and is now returned with the help of the fetish.

As early as 1910, Freud provided a historical example which served as a precursor to the idea that the male homosexual was fixated at the oral stage (preoedipal mother). The object of the fixation was the mother's breast which represented her penis. In analyzing a dream of Leonardo da Vinci's, in which a bird* placed its tail into his mouth and struck him "many times with its tail against his lips." Freud summarized his view of what the bird meant, as follows: The vulture in Leonardo's fantasy represented the actual memory, and appeared to be connected with his later life. The fantasy of the vulture whose tail is in the mouth of the child represents the mother's breast that the child has sucked but, at the same time, represents also the mother's "penis." Freud at first could not understand how a

* Freud identified the bird as a vulture; later translations of Leonardo's journals have rendered the word as "kite."

male genital should be confused with the female breast. However, in utilizing his experiences in translating absurd dreams, he suggested that such mixtures of male and female attributes may take place, not only in dreams but also in mythology. For instance, the Egyptian deity Mut is characterized by the head of a vulture, whose body, as the breasts indicate, is female, but she also has an erect penis. Similarly, in Leonardo's fantasy, Mut is a mixture of male and female characteristics. It appears that the power responsible for the invention of such deities (and of the Leonardo fantasy) have something in common; namely, the mixture of male and female elements.

Related Concepts: BREAST COMPLEX; PHALLIC WOMAN.

REFERENCES

Freud, S.: 1910, "Leonardo da Vinci and a Memory of his Childhood." *SE*, 11:82, 93–94, 96, 1957.
1927, "Fetishism." *SE*, 21:152–153, 1961.

ADDITIONAL READINGS

Alexander, F., "Kastrationskomplex und Charakter; eine Untersuchung über passagere Symptome." *Z*, 8, 1922.
Bergler, E., & L. Eidelberg, "Der Mammakomplex des Mannes." *Z*, 19, 1933.
Stärcke, A., "Der Kastrationskomplex." *Z*, 7, 1921.

1626

PHALLIC OR HYSTERICAL CHARACTER is denotative of that formation which appears to be the result of unconscious defenses of sexual and aggressive wishes present in the phallic stage of development. Pathogenetically, an identification of the self with the phallus may be made in order to deny the castration anxiety. The fear of castration may thus lead to passivity, and to the accentuation of other phallic characteristics; or in defiance of it, it may lead to an over-confident, aggressive and exhibitionistic behavior. [Eidelberg, 1954.]

Clinical Example

A woman patient who had been married and divorced several times thought that her several husbands were responsible for her unlucky marriages. Her analysis showed that she had experienced a trauma at the age of five, having found her father in bed with her governess. This memory was repressed and came slowly back to consciousness after the resistance against this material was overcome. The patient identified herself with her father and developed the wish to take away her mother from him (negative oedipus complex). As a result of the defense against her latent homosexual wishes, she developed the need to seduce married men, and to take them away from their wives. Once this was accomplished, she lost interest in the man. The patient did not feel guilty or remorseful about her sexual adventures, but accepted and used the resulting divorces as a punishment, proving her inferiority.

Related Concepts: FRIGIDITY; IMPOTENCE.

REFERENCE

Eidelberg, L., *An Outline of a Comparative Pathology of the Neuroses.* IUP, pp. 166–173, 1954.

1627

PHALLIC PHASE is the stage of libidinal development in which the boy's penis and the girl's clitoris acquire primacy as the physical localization of sexual excitation and the primary zones of discharge of sexual fantasies. The phallic phase follows the anal phase and undergoes repression during the latency period; it normally occurs between the ages of three and six. During this period, libidinal investment progresses to a form related to, although not identical with, adult genital sexuality. [Freud, 1905.]

The phallic phase is characterized, in the male, by pride in the penis, a belief in its unique possession, and by castration anxiety resulting from castration threats. In the female, in addition to the presence of oedipal problems, the discovery of the clitoris (and comparison of it with the penis) leads to penis envy and feelings of inferiority. The interrelationships of these factors, for both sexes, constitutes a crucial aspect of character formation and potential neurotic development. During this stage, as Freud (1923) pointed out, infantile masturbation is most active, and its repression and, more importantly,

the repression of connected oedipal fantasies, crystallize the vital processes of the superego formation and leads to the latency period. The degree to which the oedipal wishes become aim-inhibited, and further susceptible to sublimation (when these conflicts are reworked during adolescence) will determine the relative freedom from neurosis.

Both boys and girls initially share typical phallic evolution and fantasies, believing that everyone has, or will have, a penis; the little girl enviously hoping that her clitoris will become one. Ultimately, after the phallic phase, cathexis must shift from the incestuous object to a nonincestuous, heterosexual object. In a sense, the oedipal wishes are doomed to abandonment because they are not fulfilled. Another major factor contributing to their dissolution is castration anxiety, which may result, in general, in increased femininity. While both the oedipus complex and castration anxiety may be considered universal phenomena, the child's narcissism and masturbatory preoccupation with its own genitals renders it more sensitive to the narcissistic mortification that not everyone has, or will get, a penis.

From its phallic orientation, the child divides people into two categories: those with a penis, and those without a penis (an inferior group). This division may remain permanent and result in a fixed feeling of loathing for all those who represent the castrated group (women). A complex cluster of fantasies is constructed in an attempt to deny the "castrate" state of the female. One common fantasy is that there is really a penis concealed inside. The most important fantasy, however, connects the castration with the boy's own sexual sensations in that area. Since these are coupled with his aggressive wishes toward his father, he assumes that castration of the mother was performed by the father, perhaps during intercourse, in retaliation for the aggressive feelings he directed toward his father. Henceforth, castration will be connected with threatened punishment for all sexual wishes which retain their unconscious bond with the oedipus complex.

To escape castration, as Freud (1925) noted, the boy may abandon his aggressive oedipal rivalry and develop a negative oedipus complex. The girl, faced with the fact of her mother's "castration," may develop contempt for her mother and renounce her as an object of identification, and identify, instead, with her father. As heir to the oedipus complex, a new mental structure is established, the superego. The enriched ego is now capable of greater independence, and, for the first time, it has the capacity for true sublimation.

A conscious fantasy that the mother has a phallus may occur prior to awareness of the anatomical differences between the sexes. [Freud, 1925]. Afterwards, in an attempt to deny castration anxiety, the fantasy may be retained in the unconscious. It may take various forms, most of them based on the idea that the phallus is somewhere concealed in the mother's body. This fantasy is a defense against the preoedipal mother.

Freud (1905) originally called the third stage of libidinal development the genital phase, Later, he (1923) recognized that the genital phase would be more properly characterized by the male's recognition of the penis as an organ of impregnation and the female's discovery of the vagina, occurring in puberty. He then renamed the third stage the phallic phase.

Freud initially regarded aggression as a part of the libidinal drives and discussed phallic-sadistic tendencies from this point of view. However, as a result of his later view that aggression represented an independent instinct, most analysts today assume that the aggressive wishes common to the phallic phase (to castrate; to rip, pierce, or tear with the penis; to soil with urine) result from the basic vicissitudes of the energy of this independent instinct (destrudo or mortido), which pass through stages similar to those of the libido.

Some analysts, notably M. Klein (1937) and her followers, believe that the oedipus complex occurs well before the phallic phase, and they ascribe a much earlier role to vaginal sensations.

Related Concepts: OEDIPUS COMPLEX; PSYCHIC APPARATUS.

REFERENCES

Freud, S.: 1905, "Three Essays on the Theory of Sexuality." *SE*, 7:176–179, 199, 233, 1953.
    1923, "The Infantile Genital Organization: An Interpolation into the Theory of Sexuality." *SE*, 19:142–144, 1961.

Freud, S.: 1925, "Some Psychical Consequences of the Anatomical Distinction Between the Sexes." *SE*, 19:245, 250–252, 254–255, 257, 1961.
    1931, "Female Sexuality." *SE*, 21:232, 237–239, 241, 1961.

Klein, M., *The Psychoanalysis of Children*. HPI, 1937.

ADDITIONAL READINGS

Brunswick, R., "The Pre-Oedipal Phase of the Libido Development." *Q*, 9, 1940.

Freedman, A., "Observations in the Phallic Stage." *BPAP*, 4, 1954.

Freud, S., 1924, "The Dissolution of the Oedipus Complex." *SE*, 19, 1961.

Greenacre, P., "Respiratory Incorporation and the Phallic Phase." *PsaStC*, 6, 1951.

Horney, K., "On the Genesis of the Castration Complex in Women." *IntJPsa*, 5, 1924.

Jones, E., "The Phallic Phase." *PPsa*, 1950.

Katan, A., "Distortions of the Phallic Phase." *PsaStC*, 15, 1960.

Keiser, S., "Orality Displaced to the Urethra." *JAPA*, 2, 1954.

Kestenberg, J., "On the Development of Maternal Feelings in Early Childhood; Observations and Reflections." *PsaStC*, 11, 1956.

Loewenstein, R.: "Phallic Passivity in Men." *IntJPsa*, 16, 1935.
    "Conflict and Autonomous Ego Development During the Phallic Phase." *PsaStC*, 5, 1950.

Lorand, S., *Clinical Studies in Psychoanalysis.* IUP, 1950.

Reich, W., *Character Analysis*. OIP, 1949.

1628

PHALLIC PRIDE denotes an exaggerated self-esteem connected with, and dependent on, the importance of the phallus. Phallic pride is most often seen in those who attempt to cope with intense castration anxiety by an accentuation of some phallic aims.

Reich (1949) advised that to the unconscious of such a subject the penis serves as an instrument of aggression and vengeance. History generally reveals a serious disappointment with the opposite sex, in which the mother was the stronger of the two parents. There is a consequent identification with the mother's role: the mother is introjected and the boy turns to his father and develops an active homosexual trend, while the mother is retained only as an object with narcissistic attitudes. A woman, in this circumstance, unconsciously castrates or renders her lover (or makes him appear) impotent.

Related Concepts: PHALLIC PHASE; PHALLIC WOMAN.

REFERENCE

Reich, W., *Character Analysis*. OIP, pp. 203–204, 1949.

ADDITIONAL READING

Bergler, E., & L. Eidelberg, "Der Mammakomplex des Mannes." *Z*, 19, 1933.

1629

PHALLIC WOMAN denotes a fixation at the phallic stage; the woman unconsciously seeks to deny the absence of a penis. She reacts with intense unconscious penis envy, and unconsciously attempts to castrate all men. Often, there is an identification of the self with the phallus in order to deny castration.

As Freud (1924) noted, there is no doubt that there is a difference in the development of girls and boys. Yet, they both experience an oedipus complex, a superego and a latency period. The little girl begins to treat her clitoris as a penis but thereafter discovers the difference between the penis and clitoris and develops inferiority feelings. Not having a penis may protect her from castration. The female oedipus complex appears to be similar and it culminates in the wish to receive a gift (a baby) from the father. As this wish is not fulfilled the female oedipus complex has to be given up or repressed.

Related Concepts: PHALLIC MOTHER; PHALLIC PHASE.

REFERENCE

Freud, S., 1924, "The Dissolution of the Oedipus Complex." *SE*, 19:177–179, 1961.

ADDITIONAL READINGS

Brunswick, R., "The Pre-Oedipal Phase of the Libido Development." *Q*, 9, 1940.
Freud, S., 1931, "Female Sexuality." *SE*, 21, 1961.
Horney, K., "On the Genesis of the Castration Complex in Women." *IntJPsa*, 5, 1924.
Lorand, S., *Clinical Studies in Psychoanalysis*. IUP, 1950.

1630

PHANTOM LIMB denotes the recurring or continuing sensation, often felt by amputees, that the amputated limb (arm, leg, occasionally breast) is still present. The phantom limb sensation may include the whole amputated limb or be limited to a part of it, particularly the hand or the foot (the parts which have a larger cortical representation). It may be felt as being of natural size or smaller, as static or capable of movement. It may be felt as stable or it may eventually shrink. Pathogenetically, the phantom limb sensation is dependent on the peripheral innervation and the paresthesia, and on the pain and kinesthetic sensations derived from the amputated peripheral nerves and the amputation neuroma, and on the central mechanisms which condition the recognition of posture. However, it is generally accepted that organic mechanisms alone cannot account for the phantom limb sensation; to a great extent it is dependent on emotional factors, i.e., the wish to maintain the integrity of the body and the need to preserve the integrity of the body scheme. The phantom limb sensation may be viewed, therefore, as a reactivation of the perceptive pattern of the body image, under the impact of emotional forces. The changes in shape and size of the phantom limb suggest that subjective impressions of any organ are deposited from childhood perceptions (external and internal) and that after the amputation, by a regressive process, previous images of the lost organ are produced. [Schilder, 1950.]

Related Concept: BODY IMAGE.

REFERENCE

Schilder, P., *The Image and Appearance of the Human Body*. IUP, pp. 63–70, 1950.

1631

PHOBIA is a symptom neurosis, characterized by a pathological fear of a particular object or situation, and the consequent attempts to avoid them. The feared situation or object leads to the feeling of fright by providing stimuli to the activation of repressed wishes, usually oedipal, and the defenses against these wishes. Because the source of this fright is unconscious, the attempt to escape it by avoiding the external situation may allay the fear, but it will not cure the phobia.

Four basic mechanisms appear to be operative in phobias: mobilization of the opposite instinct fusion, projection, displacement, and avoidance. A libidinal wish is warded off by mobilization of an aggressive drive. An unconscious wish is projected to an external object and then displaced to a different (secondary) object, which is then feared and avoided. The primary object relationship may still be maintained in the unconscious; the superego is appeased by the restrictions on freedom by avoidance of the secondary object. Often, phobias provide considerable instinctual gratification through secondary gain, making therapy more difficult. For example, a young woman with agoraphobia, connected with death wishes toward her mother, required the constant company of her mother in order to accomplish her daily activities. She derived considerable aggressive pleasure from the inconvenience she caused her mother.

Contributors have emphasized the role of the aggressive and exhibitionistic wishes, and pregenital conflicts. The original classification of phobia as an anxiety hysteria, primarily resulting from *libidinal* phallic conflicts, is open to doubt; phobia has been described as being caused by wishes belonging to the *aggressive* phallic phase. Eidelberg (1954) noted: "Whereas a normal person differentiates between a probable danger in the future and an actual defeat, the neurotic cannot separate possibilities from probabilities, and reacts to the unconsciously anticipated defeat as if it were taking place in the present.

"Most phobic symptoms appear to represent the end result of an unconscious defense against wishes belonging to the phallic stage of development. Descriptively speaking, each patient who suffers from a phobia seems to be afraid of certain objects (horses, dogs, chickens), or of a certain activity (crossing a street, looking through the window, etc.). Because of this fear, he avoids the external object or the activity which mobilizes the fear. If forced to see or to do what he is afraid of, he is overcome by panic and may collapse. His fear may be differentiated from normal fear because:

"(a) His explanation of what he is afraid of does not make sense at all, or his fear appears to be out of proportion.

"(b) His fear paralyzes him instead of increasing his ability to deal with the problem.

"(c) His fear seems to be caused by a discharge of unconscious object destrudo against the self.

"Different from normal fear, the aggression responsible for neurotic fear is unconscious, and probably contains object destrudo. As a result, the patient is not aware that he is attacking himself. His behavior becomes understandable when we recognize that he is not afraid of the horse, or of being run over by a car, but that he is afraid of the aggression which is mobilized by the phobic object or activity. The aggression the patient is afraid of is due to his own object destrudo, but he is not aware of this fact. The object destrudo (or, according to some authors, primary narcissistic destrudo) appears as countercathexis of an aggressive or sexual wish on the phallic level. In addition, the infantile inspectionistic wishes of this stage appear to be blocked and replaced by exhibitionistic impulses.

The repressed wishes in phobia belong to the negative or positive oedipus complex. Consequently, the phobic object represents unconsciously the father, the mother, or both. The panic-producing object is often referred to as a castrating, or castrated object (i.e., it threatens castration, or it shows the result of castration). The conscious fear of being run over or bitten represents the unconscious wish to castrate and to be castrated. It seems that the phobic object or activity mobilizes phallic wishes, and that the neurotic fear represents an unconscious defense against them. The phobic symptom is rejected by the total personality of the patient."

In addition, it appears that the phobic patient is afraid that something will happen to him; the obsessional, that something will happen to another person.

The study of a classic case of phobia, Little Hans, is summarized by Eidelberg (1954), as follows: "(1) Fear of the horse was due to the fact that the horse was the unconscious representation of his father. (2) The fear of his father was caused by the hostility he had mobilized in Little Hans when he expelled him from his mother's bed. (3) Unable to destroy his father and sleep with his mother, and unable to give up these desires, Little Hans had to repress them. (4) As a result of this repression, the forbidden impulses remained active in the unconscious, where they were kept under control by fear. By projection, 'I hate father,' was changed into, 'Father hates me." (5) By displacement of his wishes onto the horse, Little Hans succeeded in remaining free from fear at home. (6) From the economic standpoint, repression of the libidinal wish mobilized destrudo which was then discharged against the self."

1. Acrophobia. A neurotic fear of high places; a specific fear of falling. Freud (1900) traced the phobia back to the pleasurable feeling aroused in a young child when he was swung or dropped, i.e., to the subsequent incestuous connotation of these feelings. He suggested that it was here that the root might be found. Falling from a high place may represent a punishment for sexual or aggressive wishes. [See **108.**]

2. Agoraphobia. A pathological fear of open spaces, characteristically appearing in connection with the activities of walking in the street, traveling, stage fright, etc. It may represent a compromise formation between defensive and instinctual forces; unconscious wishes are defended against by displacement and projection, with a subsequent avoidance of the feared object or situation.

3. Claustrophobia. A fear of being confined; characterized by an extreme fear when there appears to be no means of escape. Fenichel (1945) described it as a form of anxiety hysteria: the physical state of sexual or aggressive excitement is projected onto and, thus, represented by a feared external object or situation. The symptom is characterized by an increase in anxiety (or fear) which is projected onto the confining object (room, train, etc.) that precipitated the excitement. The need for a sudden escape is an expression of an unconscious desire to avoid a feared sexual or aggressive wish. [See **316.**]

4. Erythrophobia. The fear of blushing, a conversion symptom which is characterized by neurotic avoidance. In severe cases, there is a withdrawal from all social contact, hardly distinguishable from paranoid trends. In less severe cases, the symptom is indicative of a subject's fear (unconscious) that his masturbatory practices may be found out; his behavior may be governed by scopophilic compulsions, i.e., by sexual or aggressive strivings. [See **527.**]

5. Zoophobia. A fear of animals which is especially common in children. Typically, the phobia is restricted to one or two animals having a specific unconscious meaning. In the case of Little Hans, for instance, his fear of horses was generated by the ambivalent wishes he had toward his father in the resolution of his oedipal conflict. Here, he desired his mother and feared the consequent castration by his father. He projected his contrary wishes toward his father (he at once feared and revered him) onto the horses, and responded to the horses as though they were the hostile and fearful object, at the same time repressing his prior affection for horses. [See **2601.**]

Related Concepts: NEUROSIS AND PSYCHOSIS; PHOBIC CHARACTER.

REFERENCES

Eidelberg, L., *An Outline of a Comparative Pathology of the Neuroses.* IUP, pp. 145–146, 242–244, 1954.
Fenichel, O., *The Psychoanalytic Theory of Neurosis.* Nor, p. 180, 1945.
Freud, S.: 1900, "The Interpretation of Dreams." *SE,* 5:394–395, 1953.

ADDITIONAL READINGS

Alexander, V. K., "A Case of Phobia of Darkness." *R,* 44, 1957.
Bornstein, B., "The Analysis of a Phobic Child. Some Problems of Theory and Technique in Child Analysis." *PsaStC,* 3–4, 1949.
Colm, H. N., "Phobias in Children." *PPR,* 46, 1959.
Eisenberg, L., "School Phobia: A Study in the Communication of Anxiety." *P,* 114, 1958.
Eisenbud, J., "Analysis of a Presumptively Telepathic Dream," in G. Devereux, *Psychoanalysis and the Occult.* IUP, 1953.
Eisler, E. R., "Regression in a Case of Multiple Phobia." *Q,* 6, 1937.
Ferber, L., Report on Panel: "Phobias and Their Vicissitudes." *JAPA,* 7, 1959.
Freedman, A., "The Feeling of Nostalgia and Its Relationship to Phobia." *BPAP,* 6, 1956.

Friedjung, J. K., "Ein Beispiel einer kindlichen Phobie." *C*, 2, 1912.

Gardiner, M. M., "A Fleeting Phobia in a Girl of Three." *BPAP*, 4, 1954.

Greenson, R., "Phobia, Anxiety and Depression." *JAPA*, 7, 1959.

Hall, G. S., "Thanatophobia and Immortality." *AJP*, 25, 1915.

Kolansky, H., "Treatment of a Three-Year-Old Girl's Severe Infantile Neurosis: Stammering and Insect Phobia." *PsaStC*, 15, 1960.

Lewin, B., "Phobic Symptoms and Dream Interpretation." *Q*, 21, 1952.

Lorand, S., "A Horse Phobia: A Character Analysis of an Anxiety Hysteria." *R*, 14, 1927.

Mallet, J., "Contribution to the Study of Phobias." *RFPsa*, 20, 1956.

Rangell, L., "The Analysis of a Doll Phobia." *IntJPsa*, 33, 1952.

Reich, W., "Über kindliche Phobie und Charakterbildung." *Z*, 16, 1930.

Scottlander, F., "Phobie; eine Untersuchung über die Hintergründe der Neurose." *P*, 1, 1947.

Sperling, M.: "Mucous Colitis Associated with Phobias." *Q*, 19, 1950.

"Animal Phobias in a Two-Year-Old Child." *IntJPsa*, 34, 1953.

Stengel, E., "Air-Raid Phobia." *M*, 20, 1944.

Wegrocki, H. G., "A Case of Number Phobia." *IntJPsa*, 19, 1938.

Yates, S. L., "Phobias." *M*, 11, 1932.

1632

PHOBIC CHARACTER is a type of neurotic character formation in which instinctual conflict is typically dealt with through the use of the defense mechanisms employed in phobic symptom formation, i.e., projection, displacement, and avoidance. Persons of a phobic character are extremely inhibited, restricted, and fearful. They tend to avoid situations which might provide instinctual temptations, but they do not regard this as pathological. Fenichel (1945) noted: "Phobic characters would be the correct designation for persons whose reactive behavior limits itself to the avoidance of the situations originally wished for."

Neurotic character traits (including phobic character traits) are ego-syntonic, unlike neurotic symptoms. From an economic viewpoint, the quantity of destrudo in neurotic character traits appears to be greater than it is in conversion symptoms. Structurally, the superego appears to play a greater role in phobias, while the ego appears to be dominant in phobic character formation. [Eidelberg, 1948.]

Related Concept: PHOBIA.

REFERENCES

Eidelberg, L., *Studies in Psychoanalysis*. IUP. pp. 93–95, 1948.

Fenichel, O., *The Psychoanalytic Theory of Neurosis*. Nor, p. 527, 1945.

ADDITIONAL READINGS

Deutsch, H., *Psychoanalysis of the Neuroses*. HPI, 1932.

Eidelberg, L., *An Outline of a Comparative Pathology of the Neuroses*. IUP, 1954.

Freud, S.: 1909, "Analysis of a Phobia in a Five-Year-Old Boy." *SE*, 10, 1955.

1918, "From the History of an Infantile Neurosis." *SE*, 17, 1955.

1926, "Inhibitions, Symptoms and Anxiety." *SE*, 20, 1959.

Lewin, B., "Phobic Symptoms and Dream Interpretation." *Q*, 21, 1952.

1633

PITY is the normal reaction of compassion for someone who is suffering or who is unhappy, based, as a rule, on an identification with the sufferer; sometimes a reaction formation against an aggressive wish toward the sufferer.

Jekels (1952) distinguished two forms of pity. The first form is a feminine-masochistic identification with the sufferer, as a gratification of a childhood beating fantasy, which is a regressive form of passive-feminine libidinal wishes for the father. Fate, representing the superego, symbolizes the beating father. In the second form of pity, the defense against castration anxiety causes a rejection of the passive-feminine wish. Instead of the wish to be beaten, there is the wish to be loved. But this passive wish is also not acceptable to the subject, and is, instead, projected to the sufferer (object). The sufferer is treated by the subject as he wishes his superego (the father) to treat him; but he does it actively, pitying and actively loving the sufferer. In some cases, pity mobilizes the wish to help; in others, it is expressed in the urge to suffer with the object of the pity.

Related Concepts: MASOCHISM; REACTION FORMATION; SADISM.

REFERENCE

Jekels, L., "The Psychology of Pity." *SPJ*, pp. 88–97, 1952.

ADDITIONAL READINGS

Ekman, T., "Phaenomenologisches und Psychoanalytisches zum Problem des Mitleids." *Z*, 26, 1941.
Reik, T., "Zur Psychoanalyse des Mitleids." *PsaP*, 2, 1927–1928.

1634

PLEASURE PRINCIPLE refers to the final aims of the subject—the teleological approach. From a causal approach, the instinct-tensions are responsible for the subject's wishes and their gratification. Hartmann (1964) discussed the problem, as follows: "The idea that pleasure and unpleasure are dominant forces in motivating human behavior had, of course, not escaped the attention of earlier thinkers; it goes far back in the history of philosophy and has been strongly emphasized especially by a school of British philosophers. Bentham, to quote at least one of them, said that nature has put man under the control of two sovereign masters, pain and pleasure. We find also in the pre-Freudian literature references to a development toward a more adaptive state of affairs. Freud has never claimed property rights in this respect; on the contrary, in discussing the pleasure principle, he said that 'Priority and originality are not among the aims that psycho-analytic work sets itself'. Originality was not the aim of his work, although it was, in the case of Freud, invariably its outcome. It was with Freud's pleasure and reality principles in a way as with his concepts of the unconscious mental processes. While the terms had been used before, the decisive achievements of finding a method to study these processes, of filling the terms with specific psychological meaning, and of assigning them their place in a coherent structure are Freud's.

"If the infant finds himself in a situation of need, and if attempts toward hallucinatory gratification have proved disappointing, he will turn toward reality; and the repetition of such situations will gradually teach him better to know reality and to strive for those real changes that make gratification possible. This is what Freud says in the 'Two Principles.' It gives us a solid basis and point of departure for the following considerations. In the case described, the first step, the turning toward reality in search of gratification, simply follows the pleasure principle. We attribute to functions of the ego both the cognition and the purposive change of reality involved in the process. But the reality principle, according to Freud, means also that uncertain pleasure is renounced, with the purpose of ascertaining, in a new way, that an assured pleasure will come later. This clearly presupposes two other ego functions of the greatest importance—postponement and anticipation."

The infant uses hallucinatory satisfactions whenever he experiences an instinctual need. Only after this form of gratification proves to be disappointing does he discover the importance of an external real object (reality principle). Freud (1917) stated that all human beings appear to seek pleasure and avoid unpleasure. He thought at first that an increase of tension was responsible for unpleasure and that a decrease led to pleasure.

In what appears to be a contradiction, the increase in tension which occurs as a result of the stimulation of autoerotogenic zones does not produce unpleasure but produces pleasure. The pleasure connected with the increase of tension Freud identified as forepleasure. He noted that, finally, only a full discharge of tension is able to produce the pleasure—called end-pleasure. Thus, Freud proposed the existence of two kinds of pleasure: forepleasure and end-pleasure.

Eidelberg (1954) suggested that forepleasure can be experienced without the stimulation of the erotogenic zones. The forepleasure is found not only in connection with the sexual act but in a number of other activities, whenever end-pleasure is anticipated. In addition, he noted that the stimulation of erotogenic zones immediately after the sexual act does not produce forepleasure. A complete discharge does not necessarily lead to the experience of pleasure. The pleasure is only obtained if the gratification of the instinctual tension takes place—when the object is pleasing and the form of the discharge of tension is also pleasing.

The recognition that the elimination of unpleasure

does not lead necessarily to the sensation of pleasure is not of primary importance. The aim of the elimination of unpleasure is not identical with the aim of the experience of pleasure. Pleasure can often only be obtained if the individual is willing to tolerate a degree of temporary unpleasure. Certain subjects are more interested in obtaining pleasure and will, therefore, tolerate unpleasure to a greater degree. This behavior pattern may be contrasted with that of those subjects who are more interested in avoiding unpleasure, even if it means foregoing pleasure. Thus, Eidelberg suggested that instead of one pleasure-unpleasure principle, two separate principles should be considered: (a) the pleasure principle; and (b) the unpleasure principle.

Eidelberg also suggested that the experience of narcissistic mortification which is responsible for a kind of unpleasure seems to be caused not by an increase in tension but by a lowering of tension below the normal threshold. This unpleasure is illustrated in the case of an overseas traveller who, in passing through customs, suddenly finds that his passport is missing, and experiences a feeling of weakness (fright).

Related Concepts: NIRVANA PRINCIPLE; REALITY PRINCIPLE.

REFERENCES

Eidelberg, L., *An Outline of a Comparative Pathology of the Neuroses.* IUP, pp. 19–20, 1954.
Freud, S.: 1905, "Three Essays on Sexuality." *SE*, 7:210, 1953.
      1917, "General Theory of the Neuroses." *SE*, 16:356, 1963.
Hartmann, H., *Essays on Ego Psychology*, IUP, pp. 241–242, 1964.

ADDITIONAL READINGS

Brunswick, D., "The Physiological Viewpoint." *IntJPsa*, 41, 1960.
Buchenholz, B., "Pleasure, Preliminary Report of an Investigation." *JNMD*, 123, 1956.
Hartmann, H., "Gedächtnis und Lustprinzip. Untersuchungen an Korsakoffkranken." *ZNP*, 126, 1930.
Kanzer, M., & L. Eidelberg, "The Structural Description of Pleasure." *IntJPsa*, 41, 1960.
Mitscherlich, A., "Lust und Realitätsprinzip in ihrer Beziehung zur Phantasie." *P*, 6, 1952.
Saussure, R. de, "The Metapsychology of Pleasure." *IntJPsa*, 40, 1959.
Szasz, T., *Pain and Pleasure: A Study of Bodily Feelings.* BB, 1957.

1635
PLEASURE - UNPLEASURE PRINCIPLE AND MASOCHISM.

Masochism appears to contradict Freud's pleasure-unpleasure principle. If unpleasure is no longer a signal of danger but represents a source of pleasure, the individual is deprived of the protection of this important signal. [Freud, 1924.]

Closer analysis of masochistic patients presenting neurotic symptoms, neurotic character traits, or perversions reveals that they seek punishment and humiliation because they are unconsciously convinced that this is the only way they can avoid something worse (e.g., castration). In other words, the masochist seeks self-produced or self-provoked punishment to avoid feelings of guilt or remorse, or to avoid unprovoked external narcissistic mortifications over which he has no control.

Eidelberg (1954) noted: "Whenever an individual avoids pleasure, the 'price' of which appears too high, or endures unpleasure in order to obtain more or better pleasure later, he is acting in accordance with the reality principle, which represents a modified unpleasure-pleasure principle. In other words, a masochist is not an individual who accepts unpleasure in order to obtain some pleasure later on, or avoids pleasure because of its actual or potential punitive consequences. In order to qualify for the diagnosis of masochist, one has to seek unpleasure although it will not bring pleasure in the future, and to neglect pleasure which is presently available without any threat of punishment. As long as the term, 'pleasure,' describes the subjective experience of an individual, what appears to be pleasure to one person may be unpleasure to another. For example, the fact that I dislike peanut butter sandwiches does not allow me to call a man who eats such sandwiches a masochist. Only if he dislikes peanut butter and keeps on eating it, refusing other food which is available, is it allowable to call him a masochist. If such a definition is accepted without further qualification, it might be possible to refer to any neurotic as a masochist. The phobic, the obsessional neurotic, the patient who suffers from a conversion, they all avoid pleasure and accept unpleasure. However, only a few analysts would classify all neurotics as masochists. Most analysts use this term only if unpleasure is looked for, and pleasure avoided, not as the result of a symptom, but by voluntary action."

Related Concept: NARCISSISTIC MORTIFICATION.

REFERENCES

Eidelberg, L., *An Outline of a Comparative Pathology of the Neuroses.* IUP, pp. 174–175, 1954.
Freud, S., 1924, "The Economic Problem of Masochism." *SE*, 19:159, 1961.

1636

POLARITIES. Freud (1915) noted that there were three polarities which were connected with each other in variously significant ways, defined as follows: (a) subject (ego) and object (external world); (b) pleasure and unpleasure; and (c) active and passive.

The object is brought to the ego from the external world, in the first instance by the instincts of self-preservation (ego instincts). In the beginning, whatever represents the external world is hated, and whatever represents the subject is loved. Later, the child discovers that some external objects are required to gratify his needs, and, consequently, the equation *external object = unpleasure* is given up.

Originally, the pleasure-unpleasure phenomenon represented one aim: an increase of tension producing unpleasure, with a decrease leading to the experience of pleasure. Freud (1905) pointed out that under certain conditions (stimulation of erotogenic zones) an increase of tension produces pleasure. He called this pleasure *forepleasure*, and differentiated it from end-pleasure. Consequently, he assumed that a decrease of tension produced end-pleasure and an increase of tension lead to the experience of unpleasure. Thus, the polarity—unpleasure versus end-pleasure—meant that the individual had to decide whether he wanted to experience unpleasure or seek end-pleasure. Freud noted that there were two basic reasons responsible for the individual's decision to seek unpleasure. First, in order to obtain end-pleasure, a certain amount of tolerance of unpleasure becomes a *conditio sine qua non*. The individual has to recognize that instant end-pleasure is not avail-able and that he must decide, therefore, whether it is more important to avoid unpleasure (even if it means foregoing end-pleasure) or to pursue end-pleasure even at the expense of tolerating unpleasure. Second, the decision to accept or even seek unpleasure became clear when Freud discovered that many patients were willing to exchange feelings of guilt, remorse, anxiety and depression for some kind of unpleasure connected with punishment and humiliation. For instance, the masochist accepts and requires unpleasure as a condition which permits him to obtain end-pleasure.

The polarity which appears to dominate human life is the antithesis between active and passive. The normal individual is able to arrive at a healthy compromise. The neurotic oscillates between the two aims, often using passivity to deny his need for activity, and vice versa.

Finally, Freud's recognition that two basic drives—the sexual and the aggressive—are the driving forces responsible for the individual's behavior lead him to a further understanding of many neurotics, who try to find a form of discharge for both energies, at the same time and with the same object, instead of separating these two forms of gratification. It appears that repression and denial lead to an imbalance of polarities, and it is this imbalance which is responsible for neurotic conflicts. In the restoration of this balance, psychoanalysis permits the individual to face the problems connected with the gratification of his needs and to make decisions in accordance with external and internal reality.

Related Concepts: ACTIVITY AND PASSIVITY; AGGRESSION; UNPLEASURE-PLEASURE PRINCIPLE.

REFERENCES

Freud, S.: 1905, "Three Essays on Sexuality." *SE*, 7:149–150, 209–210, 1953.
            1915, "Instincts And Their Vicissitudes." *SE*, 14:133–134, 136–137, 1957.

ADDITIONAL READING

Heyer, G. R., "Die Polarität, ein Grundproblem im Werden und Wesen der Deutschen Psychotherapie." *ZPt*, 7, 1934.

1637

POLYCRATES COMPLEX is descriptive of that behavior in individuals who, having enjoyed great success, grow alarmed in the belief that it will lead to a disaster of some consequence which can only be overcome through the act of a voluntary sacrifice (Flugel, 1945).

According to Herodotus, Polycrates (tyrant of Samos) was visited by Amasis of Egypt and told by him that his happiness would arouse the envy of the Gods, unless appeased by a sacrifice of something highly valued by him. Deciding that the ring on his finger was the most valuable of his possessions, Polycrates cast it into the sea as a sacrifice. But, a few hours later, as he was dining, a fish was brought to the table and in its belly was the self-same ring. Considered a bad omen, his friends departed; he was left to face his doom alone.

Freud (1919) noted that Polycrates left in horror after he had discovered that the ring which he had offered to God had been returned to him. The fear of punishment by the gods may be regarded as being caused by Polycrates' own unconscious need of punishment or unconscious feeling of guilt. In offering his sacrifice, Polycrates tried to save his life and his wealth. In this, he was acting in a manner which resembles the behavior of those patients who because of the unconscious feeling of guilt cannot tolerate success or at least cannot tolerate a certain quantity of success which they feel they do not deserve. These patients use unconscious provocation for self-punishment to eliminate their feelings of guilt. The fact that in Herodotus' presentation the gods are described as being envious may represent the projection of the child's envy originally directed toward the parents. Thus, the child instead of being envious accuses the parents of having such feelings. In the case of Polycrates, the gods by being called envious are in a way made more human. An omnipotent god should actually never feel envy. Also the prohibition of eating the apple which was given by God to Adam was based on the idea that Adam, by eating this apple, could learn to differentiate between good and bad and therefore become godlike. Thus, children are treated the same as Adam when they are told to obey the orders and prohibitions of their parents, rather than supplied understandable reasons for their actions.

Related Concepts: MASOCHISM; NEED FOR PUNISHMENT; SENSE OF GUILT.

REFERENCES

Flugel, J., *Man, Morals and Society*, IUP, p. 153, 1945.

Freud, S., 1919, "The Uncanny." *SE*, 17:239, 1955.

1638

POLYMORPH PERVERSE behavior refers to the infantile interest in obtaining gratification from such activities as viewing, touching, smelling, exhibiting, sucking, defecating, and urinating. Freud (1905) claimed that children can easily be seduced and become polymorph perverse.

The infantile sexual aims develop into normal sexual behavior as a result of changes in inhibitions occurring in the course of maturation. The first three stages of this psychical development were first referred to by Freud as oral, anal, and genital. Later, however, in 1923*, he recognized the existence of the phallic phase, which he identified as occurring before the genital, separated from it by a period of latency.

The polymorph behavior occurring during the child's sexual maturation is distinguished from the perversions of adults whose defense mechanisms can be traced back to a repression of libidinal and aggressive trends. Shame, disgust and pity restrict the activity of the sexual instincts. Freud considered that perversions represent at the same time various sexual inhibitions and sexual dissociations.

It appears, on the other hand, that adult perversions, as Eidelberg (1954) noted, are the ego-syntonic results of unconscious defense mechanisms, in which a genital discharge is sought, and a partial gratification and a partial frustration of infantile wishes is obtained, along with the denial of the original infantile narcissistic mortification. The subject's perversion is not a breakthrough of infantile wishes but a compromise between unconscious id wishes and their unconscious defense by the ego and superego. Freud originally assumed that infantile wishes represented sexual

---

* Footnote added to "Three Essays on the Theory of Sexuality" (1905).

discharges, for aggression was considered to be a part of sexuality. Later in 1920, in his second instinct theory, Freud identified it as an independent instinct (instinct fusion). It became obvious that the infantile perversions represented sexual as well as aggressive gratifications. The wish to suck, defecate and urinate may have served, at first, to gratify the subject's infantile sexuality only. In the second phase, however, after the child had been weaned and toilet trained, the original sexual discharge was prohibited, and occurred in private only. The child was taught that his excreta smelled badly and that it should not be regarded as a gift bestowed on his parents; eating was substituted for devouring (cannibalism). Thus, the restriction on the original sexual wishes of the pervert activities, also represented a gratification of the child's aggressive impulses.

Related Concepts: AGGRESSION; ATTRACTION OF THE FORBIDDEN; COMPONENT INSTINCT; PERVERSION; SEXUALITY.

REFERENCES

Eidelberg, L., *An Outline of a Comparative Pathology of the Neuroses.* IUP, pp. 190–193, 1954.
Freud, S.: 1905, "Three Essays on the Theory of Sexuality." *SE*, 7:191, 231–232, 1953.
　　　1920, "Beyond the Pleasure Principle." *SE*, 18:53–55, 1955.

1639

POSITIVE TROPISM denotes an attraction to a source of gratification or an object which will help to discharge tension or afford pleasure (Solomon, 1954). For example, during the critical learning period following birth, the human infant turns toward the mother, regardless of her attitude, because of a basic innate need. This innate need, a positive tropism, has been confirmed in the laboratory with the newborn of many species.

Related Concept: LOVE.

REFERENCE

Solomon, G. S., *A Synthesis of Human Behavior.* pp. 7, 21, 1954.

1640

POSTAMBIVALENT PHASE is the final genital stage of development, in which an ability for real object love is achieved, after the more ambivalent feelings of the earlier pregenital phases have been overcome. In the second half of the oral phase—and in the anal phase—the process of achieving satisfaction destroys the object (e.g., by biting and defecating); object relationships follow this model and are, therefore, highly ambivalent.

The whole person can be the love object only in the final genital phase. According to Abraham (1925), this development of sexuality for both sexes is paralleled by a purification of love from the admixture of destructive and selfish components. He noted: "The final stage of character-formation shows traces everywhere of its association with the preceding stages. It borrows from them whatever conduces to a favorable relation between the individual and his objects. From the early oral stage it takes over enterprise and energy; from the anal stage, endurance, perseverance, and various other characteristics; from sadistic sources, the necessary power to carry on the struggle for existence. If the development of his character has been successful the individual is able to avoid falling into pathological exaggerations of those characteristics, whether in a positive or a negative direction. He is able to keep his impulses under control without being driven to a complete disavowal of his instincts, as is the obsessional neurotic. The sense of justice may serve as an illustration; in a case of favourable development this character-trait is not heightened to an excessive punctiliousness and is not liable to break out in a violent way on some trivial occasion. We have only to think of the many actions done by obsessional neurotics in the way of 'fairness': suppose the right hand has made a movement or touched an object, the left hand must do the same. We have already said that ordinary friendly feelings remain entirely distinct from exaggerated forms of neurotic overkindness. And similarly it is possible to steer a middle course between the two pathological extremes of either delaying everything or always being in too great a hurry; or of either being over-obstinate or too easily influenced. As regards material goods, the compromise arrived at is that the individual respects the interests of others up to a certain point, but at the same time secures his own existence. He preserves to some extent the aggressive impulses necessary for the maintenance of his life. And a considerable portion of his sadistic instincts is employed no longer for destructive but for constructive purposes.

"In the course of this general alteration of character, as presented here in rough outline, we also observe that the individual achieves a steady conquest of his narcissism. In its earlier stages his character was still in a large measure governed by his narcissistic impulses. And we cannot deny that in its definitive stage it still contains a certain proportion of such impulses. Observation has taught us that no developmental stage, each of which has an organic basis of its own, is ever entirely surmounted or completely obliterated. On the contrary, each new product of development possesses characteristics derived from its earlier history. Nevertheless, even though the primitive signs of self-love are to some extent preserved in it, we may say that the definitive stage of character-formation is *relatively* unnarcissistic.

"Another change of great importance in the formation of character is that in which the individual overcomes his attitude of ambivalence (I speak again in a relative sense). Instances have already been given to show in what way a person's character avoids extremes on either side after it has attained its final stage of development. I should also like to draw attention here to the fact that as long as a severe conflict of ambivalent feelings continues to exist in a person's character, there is always a danger both for him and for his environment that he may suddenly swing from one extreme to its opposite.

"Thus if a person is to develop his character more or less up to that point which we have taken to be its highest level, he must possess a sufficient quantity of affectionate and friendly feeling. A development of this sort goes hand in hand with a relatively successful conquest of his narcissistic attitude and his ambivalence."

Related Concepts: AMBIVALENCE; LOVE; POSTO-EDIPAL.

REFERENCE

Abraham, K., 1925, "Character-Formation on the Genital Level of the Libido." *SPA*, pp. 415–416, 1942.

1641

POSTOEDIPAL, according to Peller (1954), is the period following the resolution of the oedipal complex; approximately the years between six and twelve. As a concept, *postoedipal* might replace *latency*, for many analysts today do not assume that sexuality is completely latent in this phase; rather, they believe that the manifestations of sexuality are less overt, genital sexuality is less dominant, and incestuous fantasies are repressed.

Related Concept: LATENCY PERIOD.

REFERENCE

Peller, L. E., "Libidinal Phases, Ego Development and Play." *PsaStC*, 9:178–198, 1954.

1642

PRECONSCIOUS denotes that division (system) of the total personality which contains those unconscious mental elements which are latently conscious; i.e., capable of becoming conscious with relative ease. Freud (1900) defined preconscious elements as verbal images which could be hypercathected and made available to consciousness with little or no effort, and which could then be decathected again, remaining in latent form as a result of loss of attention. He also postulated the presence of other latent elements, in the psychic apparatus, that could gain awareness only after removal of a resistance. Freud accepted this as a censor existing between the preconsious-conscious system, in addition to a more formidable censorship between the unconscious and preconscious; unconscious elements may only gain access to the preconscious by overcoming considerable resistance (e.g., by analysis) or by achieving a partial breakthrough in disguised form (e.g., as in symptom formation). Freud stated that unconscious memory traces became preconscious by attaching themselves to verbal images; i.e., the object- or thing-presentation acquires a verbal presentation which is cathected in the preconscious.

Freud's early systematic approach (in 1900) attempted to provide a conceptual model of the psychic apparatus that would emphasize the unconscious source of all mental activity. According to this, many unconscious elements never succeeded in reaching a preconscious state, but nevertheless continued to affect it. Certain mental activities of an automatic nature become conscious only in rare circumstances, yet they continue to subserve a vital function in everyday activities (e.g., as in automatic driving).

As a result of the evolution of analytic theory and the development of the structural hypothesis (id, ego, and superego), Freud (1923) made a further delineation between the system unconscious and the system preconscious-conscious. He suggested that the unconscious elements follow the laws of primary process, whereas the system preconscious-conscious is subject to the law of secondary process. The unconscious, therefore, has unbound mobile or deneutralized energy at its disposal, whereas the preconscious system is mainly cathected with bound energy.

More recent contributions (e.g., Kris, 1950) have attempted to elaborate Freud's views on the preconscious, to encompass it in our further understanding of ego psychology. Today, we consider the preconscious as not only composed of latent elements on the road to consciousness, but as a complex system composed of diverse elements, ranging from the most logical abstract thought processes to the most primitive fantasies; a system influenced by both pleasure and reality principles, governed, in the main, by secondary process. Although primarily utilizing bound neutralized energy in its more intellectual functions, the preconscious also has fantasy elements in it which are cathected with deneutralized libido and aggression.

Under certain circumstances, as in creative productions utilizing a controlled type of ego regression, the preconscious may be temporarily dominated by primary process modalities. From the metapsychological standpoint, the preconscious forms a vital part of the continuum from unconscious to conscious. Structurally, it falls under the domain of the ego and its synthetic function. Dynamically, it is sometimes allied with, and sometimes in conflict with, the id and the superego. Economically, it is primarily subject to secondary process and neutralized energy, although it has at its disposal considerable reserves of deneutralized libido and aggression. Finally, under the sway of both pleasure and reality principles, it is the mediator between the id and the external world.

Related Concepts: REALITY PRINCIPLE; STRUCTURAL (TOPOGRAPHIC) APPROACH; UNPLEASURE-PLEASURE PRINCIPLE.

REFERENCES

Freud, S.: 1900, "The Interpretation of Dreams." *SE*, 5:507, 541–542, 574–577, 1953.
     1923, "The Ego and the Id." *SE*, 19:15, 18, 19–25, 1961.
Kris, E., "On Preconscious Mental Processes." *Q*, 19:540, 560, 1950.

ADDITIONAL READINGS

Brenner, C.: *An Elementary Textbook of Psychoanalysis*. IUP, 1955.
     "The Concept 'Preconscious' and the Structural Theory." *BPAP* 9, 1959.
Eissler, K., "On the Metapsychology of the Preconscious: A Tentative Contribution to Psychoanalytic Morphology." *PsaStC*, 17, 1962.
Federn, P., *Ego Psychology and the Psychoses*. BB, 1952.
Fenichel, O., *The Psychoanalytic Theory of the Neurosis*. Nor, 1945.
Freud, S.: 1915, "The Unconscious." *SE*, 14, 1957.
     1917, "A Metapsychological Supplement to the Theory of Dreams." *SE*, 14, 1957.
Glover, E., *On the Early Development of the Mind*. IUP, 1956.
Hartmann, H., E. Kris, & R. Loewenstein, "Comments on the Formation of Psychic Structure." *PsaStC*, 2, 1946.

1643

PREDICTION. The normal individual is aware of his limited powers and therefore restricts his predictions to the probable or the possible; he would otherwise have to be omniscient. In psychoanalysis, the analyst is interested in prediction in connection with the problem of prognosis, but he avoids predicting what problems will be brought up by his patient and how the patient will react to them. The passive role the analyst plays is, in part, a restriction placed upon him to avoid selecting a solution which he personally would prefer and thus advising the patient to follow his example. Instead, the analyst has to insist that the patient decide for himself what appeals to him after his blind spots (his resistances) have been eliminated. Nonetheless, certain guide posts are given by the patient as to the possible role he will play in the future.

The planning present in the teleological approach in psychoanalysis cannot be overlooked, even if it is assumed that one day all causes will be known and the hypothesis of free selection can be abandoned. The anticipation in all predictive acts—independent of free will and its philosophical meaning—is to be employed with caution. [Freud, 1912.]

Hartmann (1964) reflected the view of many when he wrote: "One obvious limitation of our predictive potential is, of course, the great number of factors determining, according to psychoanalytic theory, every single element of behavior—what Freud has termed 'overdetermination.' Still, our technique is constantly directed by tentative predictions of the patient's reactions. Also, studies in developmental psychology by means of direct child observation, such as have been conducted by E. Kris and other psychoanalysts are guided by the formulation of expectations and their checking in individual cases. Here I just want to point to one way in which psychoanalytic hypotheses can be used vis-à-vis individual cases and how they may be confirmed in experience. I may mention here that problems of validation of psychoanalytic hypotheses ought not to be equated, as has too often been done, with the problem of therapeutic success.

"A further difficulty results from the fact that psychoanalytic theory must also deal with the relation between observer and observed in the analytic situation. There are personality layers, if you will excuse this term, that in the average case the observed cannot reach without the help of the observer and his method of observation. But the insight of the observer ought not to be confused with the insight of the observed. Some of these problems belong in a theory of psychoanalytic technique. But there is also the problem of the 'personal equation.' "

Related Concept: Synthesis.

REFERENCES

Freud, S., 1912, "Recommendations to Physicians Practising Psycho-Analysis." *SE*, 12:114, 1958.
Hartmann, H., *Essays in Ego Psychology*, IUP, p. 337, 1964.

ADDITIONAL READING

Kris, M., "The Use of Prediction in Longitudinal Study." *PsaStC*, 12, 1957.

1644

PREGENITALITY denotes those object-relations, fantasies, and conflicts characteristic of the pregenital phases of libidinal organization, i.e., prior to the establishment of genital primacy.* During the pregenital period, a greater capacity for object relations evolves, from autoerotism through phases of transitional and part objects. Incorporative and projective mechanisms become less important. The instinctual aim of incorporation of the object is partially replaced by the aim of possessing and controlling the object. Other aspects of ego function develop: verbalization becomes possible, and the reality principle is established to a greater degree. Concomitantly, precursors of the superego are formed. The pregenital conflicts greatly influence the outcome of the oedipus complex and, in turn, are reorganized by it.

Syndromes primarily connected with pregenital drives and conflicts are characterized by intense ambivalence conflicts (e.g., depressions, addiction, and homosexuality). Abraham (1924) noted: "In the first period of his extra-uterine life his libido, is, according to our view, predominantly attached to the mouth as an erotogenic zone. The first vital relation of the infant to external objects consists in sucking up into its mouth a substance that is suitable for it and accessible to it. In its embryonic life, the first organ that is formed in connection with the earliest simple process of cell-division is the so-called blastopore, an organ which is permanently retained and keeps its function in low forms of the animal world such as the Coelenterata.

"It is a long time before the sexual organs (in the narrower sense of the word) of the child take over the leading part in its sexual life. Before this state is reached the intestinal canal, and especially

* In 1933, in "New Introductory Lectures on Psycho-Analysis," Freud noted that the third stage refers to the discovery of the importance of the penis in males and the clitoris in females (phallic phase). The genital stage is reached only in puberty.

the apertures at either end, becomes possessed of an important erotogenic significance, and sends out strong stimuli to the nervous system. This state also has its prototype in the embryo. For a time there exists an open connection between the intestinal canal (rectum) and the caudal part of the neural canal (*canalis neurentericus*). The path along which stimuli may be transmitted from the intestinal canal to the nervous system might thus be said to be marked out organically.

"But what is most clearly visible is the biological prototype of the child's oral sadistic (cannibalistic) and anal-sadistic phases. Freud has already alluded to this fact; and I will quote the passage here: 'The sadistic-anal organization can easily be regarded as a continuation and development of the oral one. The violent muscular activity, directed upon the object, by which it is characterized, is to be explained as an action preparatory to eating. The eating then ceases to be a sexual aim and the preparatory action becomes a sufficient aim in itself. The essential novelty, as compared with the previous stage, is that the receptive passive function becomes disengaged from the oral zone and attached to the anal zone.' He goes on to speak of parallel processes in the field of biology but does not specify which they are. In this connection I should like to lay particular stress on a striking parallel between the organic and the psychosexual development of the individual.

"At first the blastopore is situated at the anterior end (cephalic end) of the primitive streak. In the embryos of certain animals we can observe that the original mouth opening closes up at the anterior end and becomes enlarged at the posterior end. In this way it gradually approaches the tail, which is in process of formation, and finally comes to rest there as the anus. This direct derivation of the anus from the blastopore appears as the biological prototype of that psychosexual process which Freud has described and which occurs somewhere about the second year of the life of the individual.

"At about the same time as the anus is being formed in the embryo we can observe the muscular system of the body developing. In this process the jaw muscles are far in advance of the limb muscles. The development of the anus and of the jaws is closely connected. We may also remark that in extra-uterine life the jaw muscles are able to perform powerful and effective movements much earlier than other muscles, such as the muscles of the trunk or of the limbs.

"We recognize as the fourth stage of the psychosexual development of the individual that in which he has as his sexual aim the retention and control of his object. Its correlate in biological ontogenesis is to be found in the formation of the intestinal mechanisms for retaining what has been taken into the body. These consist in constrictions and enlargements, annular contractures, branching passages, divagations ending blindly, manifold convolutions, and finally the voluntary and involuntary sphincter muscles of the anus itself. At the time that this complicated arrangement for the retention of objects is being formed there is as yet no sign of the appearance of the uro-genital apparatus.

"We have seen that the genital organization of the libido falls into two stages which correspond to two stages in the development of object-love. Here once more the organic development of the individual supplies the model. The genital organs are at first 'indifferent', and it is only later on that they become differentiated into 'male' and 'female'. This applies to the generative glands as well as to the organs of copulation. In the same way we have detected a gradual process of differentiation in the psycho-sexual life of the individual."

Related Concepts: LIBIDINAL TYPES; LIBIDO.

REFERENCE

Abraham, K., 1924, "A Short Study of the Development of the Libido, Viewed in the Light of Mental Disorders." *SPA*, pp. 499–501, 1942.

ADDITIONAL READINGS

Brunswick, R., "The Pre-Oedipal Phase of the Libido Development." *PsaR*, 1948.
Lewin, B., *The Psychoanalysis of Elation*, Nor, 1950.

1645

PREGENITAL MASTURBATORY EQUIVALENT denotes an ego-syntonic act in which oral, anal and phallic wishes are partly frustrated and partly gratified. For instance, a patient who often sucked his tongue reported that he felt the need to do so usually after he had experienced some humiliating frustration. The analysis of his activity showed that the patient was able to eliminate an external narcissistic mortification by using his tongue as an object so as to become, in this way, self-sufficient. [Eidelberg, 1954.]

Abraham (1910) noted: "The patient had been accustomed in early youth to indulge in day-dreaming, and when the activity of a vivid phantasy was at its height, to make use of masturbation as an outlet for the accumulated excitement. When he tried to abandon the practice of masturbation his day-dreaming had to find a different end. It now formed an introduction to a dream-state just as earlier it had been an introduction to masturbation. The second and third stages—that of removal from reality and of mental blankness—corresponded to the increasing sexual excitement and to its culminating point, the moment of ejaculation. The final stage of anxiety and weakness was transposed unaltered from the act of masturbation. Those symptoms are familiar to us as the regular consequence of masturbation in neurotics.

"The comparison we have made requires further confirmation as regards the second and third stages. A stage similar to the removal from reality in the dream-state is also found in masturbation, in which the increasing sexual excitement leads to an exclusion of all external impressions. In the dream-state this effect is chiefly evident on the mental plane. The patient was aware of his attention being entirely 'turned inwards'. This auto-erotic seclusion from the outer world gave him a feeling of isolation. He 'withdrew from the world'. His ideas transplanted him into another world which was founded on the model of his repressed wishes. So great was the power of his repressed wishes when once they emerged from the unconscious that he accepted their fulfilment in phantasy as reality and perceived reality as the empty fabric of a dream. His entire surroundings, and even his own body, seemed strange and unreal to him.

"The feeling of being isolated is peculiar to many neurotics who retire from the world in order to indulge in sexual practices in solitude. The patient remembered a favourite phantasy from his early youth which related to a secret underground room, hidden away somewhere in a forest, to which he wished to escape in order to be alone with his phantasies. Later on, anxiety appeared in the place of this wish. And anxiety of being alone in a closed room still dominated him as a grown-up man.

"The disappearance of thought—the mental blankness—that characterizes the third stage corresponds roughly to the marked 'loss of consciousness' which takes place, especially in neurotics, at the climax of each sexual excitation; and there then occurs a marked sensation of giddiness or of something akin to giddiness but difficult to describe. The patient definitely stated that he had the same sensation during masturbation at the moment of ejaculation. This short suspension of consciousness corresponding to the moment of emission is also met with in hysterical attacks.

"It need no longer surprise us to find that the dream-state is pleasurable up to the stage of mental blankness; for this would tend to confirm its derivation from masturbation, which is also pleasurable up to the corresponding stage, and afterwards often produces the liveliest feelings of distress in neurotics. It is also very interesting to remember that the patient under discussion used frequently to interrupt his dream-state prematurely, *i.e.* before the onset of mental blankness. This is a kind of attempt to renounce the habit of having dream-states. Neurotics frequently do exactly the same when they wish to give up masturbation. In their opinion it is the loss of semen which is the harmful thing in masturbation, and they content themselves with breaking off the act before emission. They then indulge in the consoling idea that they have not *really* masturbated."

Related Concepts: COMPULSIVE MASTURBATION; MASTURBATION FANTASIES.

REFERENCES

Abraham, K., 1910, "Hysterical Dream States." *SPA*, pp. 98–99, 1942.
Eidelberg, L., *An Outline of a Comparative Pathology of the Neuroses.* IUP, p. 32, 1954.

ADDITIONAL READING:

Fenichel, O., *The Psychoanalytic Theory of Neurosis.* Nor, 1945.

1646

PREGNANCY is the culminating goal of the genital drives and receives rich contributions from all libidinal phases. A girl becomes feminine when the wish for a penis is replaced by the wish for a baby. At first the girl wishes the baby to be a gift from her father and when she finally recognizes that this wish cannot be fulfilled her oedipus complex is abandoned. [Freud, 1933.]

Fantasies about pregnancy are universal and represent a focal point of childhood preoccupations. Oral and anal processes predominate in these fantasies; any bodily orifice (mainly mouth, anus, and umbilicus) may be involved. When the individual's associations are aggressive, pregnancy and childbirth are viewed as mutilating events. Coupled with castration anxiety, pregnancy may be held to produce castration for either partner. Underlying all pregnancy fantasies is the symbolic equation: breast = feces = penis = baby. Each of these highly cathected objects was formerly viewed as a part of the self and each underwent a painful separation from the self. Prior to the oedipus complex, the wish for a baby exists, but is based mainly on narcissistic and pregenital needs. The oedipus complex reworks the earlier drive patterns into the specific infantile genital wish to be given a baby by the father or to give a baby to the mother. Then, when freed from the incestuous object, the adult genital wish evolves. Where a close link with oedipal objects is retained, and castration anxiety or penis envy are strong (as in hysterical disorders), pregnancy will unconsciously be forbidden and resisted. Neurotic symptoms may develop as a result of regressively revived conflicts from any of the contributing levels. Fears of mutilation, or having deformed babies, are generally the result of phallic conflicts. Somatic disturbances during pregnancy, like vomiting, diarrhea, and appetite change, may be influenced by revived pregenital fantasies. Anal-sadistic elements produce expulsive and retentive conflicts toward pregnancy. Oral-sadistic conflicts may produce the fear of being devoured by the fetus.

Related Concepts: Birth Trauma; Identification; Oedipus Complex; Sexuality.

REFERENCE

Freud, S., 1933, "New Introductory Lectures on Psycho-Analysis." *SE*, 22:128–129, 1964.

ADDITIONAL READINGS

Bibring, G., T. Dwyer, D. Huntington, & A. Valenstein, "A Study of the Psychological Processes in Pregnancy and of the Earliest Mother-Child Relationship." *PsaStC*, 16, 1961.
Deutsch, H., *The Psychology of Women.* G&S, 1945.
Hofstätter, P., *Über eingebildete Schwangerschaft.*" Vienna: Urban & Schwarzenberg, 1954.
Jarvis, W., "Some Effects of Pregnancy and Childbirth on Men." *JAPA*, 10, 1962.

1647

PRELOGICAL (PRIMITIVE) THINKING denotes that thought processes of the early mental apparatus which is still under the domination of the pure pleasure principle (primary process); characteristic of the mode of functioning of the id, as opposed to that of the ego and the total personality under the control of the reality principle. The transition from prelogical to logical thinking may be slower (and accomplished at a later age) than the transition from predominantly primary process to secondary process thinking. Prelogical thinking is present in the older child and in the daydreams of adults. [Hermann, 1929.]

Related Concepts: Fantasy; Primary Process; Secondary Process.

REFERENCE

Hermann, I., "'Das Ich und das Denken.' Eine psychoanalytische Studie." *Im*, 15:325–348, 1929.

ADDITIONAL READINGS

Tauber, E., & M. Green, *Prelogical Experience. An Inquiry Into Dreams and Other Creative Processes*, BB, 1959.
Varendonck, J., *The Evolution of the Conscious Faculties.* Mac, 1923.

1648

PREMENSTRUAL DISORDERS (TENSIONS). A few days prior to each menstrual period, women show manifestations of tension, usually connected with unconscious infantile sexual fantasies.

Conflicts over female castration may be revived, with menstruation signifying the loss of the penis, and, later, the loss of anticipation of a baby; premenstrual and menstrual depression are often the result of that symbolic castration. Sadistic concepts of sexuality may be revived by the anticipation of the flow of blood. Menstruation may reawaken oedipal guilt and fear of approaching sexual maturity. It may also be considered evidence of masturbation. Such relations may stem from unconscious oedipal fantasies. Pregenital factors also influence reactions to menstruation: it may be viewed as the retention and expulsion of something dirty, or the loss of control over excretory functions or aggression. The bleeding is sometimes viewed as evidence of internal illness; this may be the expression of oral-sadistic conflicts, i.e., a devouring malady. Fenichel (1945) noted: "There is no doubt that in menstrual or premenstrual mental disorders in women, a somatic factor always plays a part."

Related Concepts: CASTRATION ANXIETY; CASTRATION COMPLEX; MENSTRUATION.

REFERENCE

Fenichel, O., *The Psychoanalytic Theory of Neurosis.* Nor, p. 240, 1945.

1649

PREOEDIPAL denotes the stage of development in which the external object choice is the mother, and is represented by her image, the so-called phallic mother; the stage of development in which the importance of the father is not recognized. Freud (1931) discovered the importance of the infant's first relationship to the mother, and reformulated his basic concept of this infantile fixation. In this, the preoedipal mother was differentiated from the oedipal mother.

In the oedipal stage, the girl must give up her preoedipal love object, the mother, and accept in its place a new love-object, the father; the boy's first love-object, on the other hand, remains unchanged. Thus, Freud stressed the greater importance of the preoedipal phase for the female. The original attachment of the girl to her mother was known long before the importance of the preoedipal stage had been discovered. It was understood that

what the little girl ascribed to her father was originally experienced with the phallic preoedipal mother. [Freud, 1933.]

The necessity to transfer the original positive attachment from the mother to the father (preoedipal stage) interferes with the formation of the oedipal complex in girls, On the other hand, the boy, in order to develop the positive relation to the oedipal mother, has also to relinquish the hostile feeling which at the preoedipal stage was attached to the mother. From a clinical point of view, it is necessary to distinguish in the analysis of a male patient whether his fixation to his mother is oedipal or preoedipal in nature.

Eidelberg (1948)* described the case of a mammary complex which details this preoedipal conflict, as follows:

"The child obviously reacted to weaning with a violent shock. After all his attempts to recover the breast had failed, the child was obliged to endure this frustration. First an aggression that up until then (early oral phase) had been gratified (sucking the mother's breast) was inhibited. This inhibition resulted in a quantitative increase of the aggression. Part of this aggression, together with a corresponding component of the libido, was used for identification with the mother, which was ambivalent from the outset. Another part was transferred to the penis, a third remained with the mother, and a fourth cathected the anal zone by way of the oral incorporation of the breast. . . .

"The relation to the mother, who is equally loved and hated, seems to be the most unpleasant one. In it the child becomes acquainted with the disadvantages of the ambivalent attitude and attempts to overcome the difficulties by separating the two instincts; as Freud conjectured in his essay on feminine sexuality, he transfers his hatred to the father. As a substitute for the breast, the penis has a number of disadvantages: there is only one penis, while there are two breasts; the penis is smaller than the breast; it cannot be reached by the mouth; it does not give nourishment; the child is forbidden to play with it with his hands. Yet it is there, seems really to belong to the child, who has become independent of his mother through possessing it.

"The attempt to transfer large quantities of

* Also, with E. Bergler, "Der Mammakomplex des Mannes." *Z,* 19, 1933.

hatred to the father is unsuccessful. In children who later fail to resolve the mammary complex, the first tie to the mother was too intense; furthermore the father, as weaker personality, was unable to draw large amounts of libido to him. As a result, the Oedipus complex did not reach normal intensity. The castration fear remains predominantly associated with the mother, the identification with the father is only weak. If the course of the subsequent development is marked by frustrations and regression, the libido regresses much more than normally, namely, to the oral phase. During the so-called passing of the Oedipus complex, the fact that the father-hatred and castration anxiety are of relatively low intensity makes itself felt. The child succeeds in identifying with the mother only by replacing the breast with the penis. In order to avoid the disadvantages resulting from a comparison between the two objects, he eliminates the breast from awareness, and invests the penis with large quantities of libido."

Related Concepts: MATRIARCHY; OEDIPUS COMPLEX.

REFERENCES

Eidelberg, L., *Studies in Psychoanalysis*. IUP, pp. 13–15, 1948.

Freud, S.: 1931, "Female Sexuality." *SE*, 21:225–226, 235, 237, 1961.

⸺ 1933, "New Introductory Lectures on Psycho-Analysis." *SE*, 22:119, 121, 1964.

ADDITIONAL READINGS

Beres, D., "Vicissitudes of Superego Functions and Superego Precursors in Childhood." *PsaStC*, 13, 1958.

Blos, P., "Preoedipal Factors in the Etiology of Female Delinquency." *PsaStC*, 11, 1957.

Brunswick, R., "The Preoedipal Phase of the Libido Development." *Q*, 9, 1940.

Bunker, H. A., "Tantalus: A Preoedipal Figure of Myth." *Q*, 22, 1953.

Glatzer, H. T., "Notes on the Preoedipal Phantasy." *Ops*, 29, 1959.

Gottesman, A., "The Preoedipal Attachment to the Mother; A Clinical Study." *IntJPsa*, 39, 1958.

Lampl-de Groot, J., "The Pre-Oedipal Phase in the Development of the Male Child." *PsaStC*, 2, 1946.

Servadio, E., "The Role of the Pre-Oedipal Conflicts." *RFPsa*, 18, 1954.

Silbermann, I., "Two Types of Preoedipal Character Disorders." *IntJPsa*, 38, 1957.

Sprince, M. R., "The Development of a Preoedipal Partnership Between an Adolescent Girl and Her Mother." *PsaStC*, 17, 1962.

Wolff, M., "The Problem of Neurotic Disturbances in Children of Preoedipal Age." *PsaStC*, 6, 1951.

1650

PREOEDIPAL MOTHER ATTACHMENT denotes the character, the quality, and the vicissitudes of the instinctual aims directed toward the mother; the fantasies concerning her, prior to the full development of the oedipus complex. Preoedipal attachment to the mother normally lasts into the early part of the phallic phase. During the oral and anal phases, attachment to the mother is intense; she is the most important object in the child's life, an active, omnipotent, and all-giving figure; the father is regarded as an intruder and rival. During the anal phase, both the boy and the girl wish to receive an anal baby for the mother and, also, to give her one. The all-powerful aspect of the mother gives rise, during the early phallic phase, to the fantasy of the phallic mother. Intense castration anxiety promotes the retention of this fantasy. Both the boy and the girl must ultimately renounce the mother as a primary object, and must decathect the fantasies to her. Fixation to the phallic mother is of great influence in the genesis of overt homosexuality. The preoedipal mother is often imagined as having a penis (phallic mother). The degree to which the preoedipal conflicts have been solved will greatly influence the fate of the oedipus complex. [Freud, 1933.]

Case History

"Mr. Wurmer was having an affair with a girl who loved him very much and whom he liked. He seemed to have normal sexual relations and regarded his climax as superior to that which he used to have in his homosexual relations. It was difficult to say whether his rather cool attitude toward his girl friend was pathological and could, therefore, be changed by analysis. Not being able to measure the emotions of our patients, it is very difficult to say how much emotional involvement should be regarded as normal.

"However, independently of the lack of such a

quantitative approach, I had the impression that the quality of his attachment was narcissistic in nature. The patient had accepted and 'forgiven' his girl friend's lack of penis. He even seemed to have lost his envy of her breasts and was prepared to be content without insisting on being man and woman, child and mother, at the same time. But, in spite of his success in his business and the satisfactory love affair with his girl friend, he did not appear to be happy.

"Not being able to prove to the patient that he used his girl friend as an extension of his own body (and refrained from using her as an independent external object), I was already prepared to interrupt his treatment and wait for some change in the external reality which would make him more accessible. Just at this time, a dream occurred which perturbed him. In this dream, he was sucking the breasts of his girl friend and he felt the taste of urine coming from her breasts. The interpretation of this dream, which he described as a nightmare, showed that the breasts of his girl friend represented his own penis. In spite of the fact that the oral material had already been worked through, and that his interest in men had disappeared after he had recognized that their penis represented and denied his fixation to the breast, this additional piece of evidence appeared to have caused a great emotional response.

"The fact that his penis represented the loved and hated breasts seemed to have become clearer now than before. During the analysis of his oral stage of development, I had represented his pre-Oedipal mother and his transference to me contained both love and hate. When this material was worked through, his intense fear of women and his disgust with the female breast decreased to such an extent that he was able to have sexual intercourse with the girl who was 'in love' with him before he had started his analytic treatment. It appeared now that his therapeutic progress had caused us to overlook an important stage in his development; it was the period when his infantile desires were turned inward upon himself, before he succeeded in accepting his younger brother as his love object. Consequently, his self-centred love and hate had escaped the attention it deserved and was projected on to his girl friend. As she no longer represented his pre-Oedipal mother, he was able to meet her without fear but, as long

as she represented himself, his reaction to her remained narcissistic. While it is true that, in so-called normal love, the representation of the external object is cathected not only with objectual but also with narcissistic libido, this patient's objectual libido belonged to an infantile stage." [Eidelberg, 1956.]

Related Concepts: OEDIPUS COMPLEX; PHALLIC MOTHER; PREOEDIPAL.

REFERENCES

Eidelberg, L., "Analysis of a Case of a Male Homosexual," in *Perversions*, *Psychodynamics and Therapy*, Lorand, S., & M. Balint, eds. RH, pp. 280–282, 1956.
Freud, S., 1933, "New Introductory Lectures on Psycho-Analysis." *SE*, 22:124–130, 1964.

ADDITIONAL READINGS

Brunswick, R., "The Pre-Oedipal Phase of the Libido Development." *PsaR*, 1948.
Eidelberg, L., *Studies in Psychoanalysis*. IUP, 1948.
Servadio, E., "The Role of the Pre-Oedipal Conflicts." *RFPsa*, 18, 1954.
Silbermann, I., "Two Types of Preoedipal Character Disorders." *IntJPsa*, 38, 1957.

1651

PREPHALLIC MASTURBATION EQUIVALENTS denote those autoerotic activities in which bodily areas and parts, other than the genitals, are sexualized and used to achieve sexual pleasure and discharge (e.g., mouth, breast, anus, urethra, skin, musculature, motor activity in general or of a specific type, and the organs of sensation and perception). After genital masturbation, or some component of it has been repressed, another body area becomes a regressive substitute for it.

Masturbation equivalents often constitute a compulsion. They are frequently viewed by the subjects as an anti-masturbatory measure, and may have been initiated as such, but they eventually acquire the content, both cathectic and ideational, of the original repressed masturbation. [Fenichel, 1945.]

Related Concepts: AUTOEROTISM; MASTURBATION.

REFERENCE

Fenichel, O., *The Psychoanalytic Theory of Neurosis.*
Nor, pp. 76–77, 320, 1945.

1652

PRIDE denotes a feeling of self-esteem, as a rule, resulting from the accomplishment or anticipation of a successful performance (real or fantasied). Pride is originally rooted in the narcissism of infancy, and then in identifications with loving and supporting objects. When free of dependence on external objects, pride can lead to narcissistic ego enrichment, to aid goal-directed activity, despite obstacles and frustrations. Pride may be attached to specific instinctual patterns; oral, anal, phallic, and genital pride may be delineated. Excessive pride may represent a reaction formation; abnormally proud people generally strive to preserve narcissistic illusions of omnipotence.

Although generally used to designate a normal feeling of self dignity, regarded as an asset, pride sometimes refers to an exaggerated feeling of self-importance which is an overcompensation for inferiority feelings, and consequently, a liability. [E. Jacobson, 1954.]

Related Concept: NARCISSISM.

REFERENCE

Jacobson, E., "The Self and the Object World."
PsaStC, 9:75–128, 1954.

1653

PRIMAL FANTASY is denotative of certain early childhood sexual fantasies, such as parental intercourse, seduction by parents, and castration. Freud (1918) suggested that such fantasies are accepted by the child as real; further, that they are used by the child to fill the gaps in his knowledge of actual sexual experiences.

In accordance with the Lamarckian concept of the inheritance of acquired traits, it was Freud's personal conviction that such fantasies derive from inherited memory traces of actual experiences in man's phylogenetic past which are activated by ontogenetic experience. Although the psychic importance of childhood sexual fantasies is universally accepted by analysts, the concept of "inherited" primal fantasies is not.

Related Concepts: CASTRATION COMPLEX; TRAUMA.

REFERENCE

Freud, S., 1918, "From the History of an Infantile Neurosis." *SE*, 17:57, 1955.

1654

PRIMAL SCENE, according to Freud (1917), is the child's observation (or fantasies) of parental intercourse. These memories or fantasies (primal fantasies) may be heavily influenced by the child's prevalent prephallic drives. They may involve excitations which are overwhelming to the young child; they have the effect of a traumatic experience, and result in repression (successful or unsuccessful).

Whether the primal scene was a fantasy or a real experience was eventually recognized as irrelevant by Freud, as both have equal psychical reality. Under the impact of the oedipus complex, the repressed fantasies serve as organizing factors for previous libidinal fixations and pathogenic influences on the ego. The child, regardless of its own sex, may identify with the father, the mother, or both. The repressed fantasies may be of great importance in later neurotic development and sexual identification. Among the more common childhood interpretations of intercourse is the child's view of it as a sadistic, destructive encounter. It may be used as an explanation for sex differences, i.e., as the way in which the father *castrated* the mother.

Among the recollections of neurotics, Freud (1917) noted, often are found the memories of observations of the parents having sexual intercourse, or the memory of having been seduced by an adult, and the fears connected with castration threats. These memories can often be checked and proven to be correct, though Freud discovered that these "memories" were sometimes fantasies (internal reality).

Quite often children who discover pleasure in masturbation are threatened with castration. Their parents admit to having made such threats and a number of patients admit to having a memory of such a threat. However, it happens that the threat which was expressed by the mother is often displaced to the father. In *Struwelpeter*, the well-known book by Hoffmann, the threat of castration is modified into the threat of having the thumbs cut off as a punishment for sucking them. In many cases in which no threats were uttered, the child imagines such a punishment, often as a result of the discovery of the lack of penis in females. The small child which the adults often consider incapable of understanding sexual intercourse sometimes may be a witness of sexual acts.

In all cases where the memory of sexual intercourse was described in detail, something which would have been difficult for the child to perceive, Freud assumed that the patient confused an actual observation of intercourse between animals with the intercourse of his parents. Probably, such a memory represented the child's gratification of scopophilic wishes.

In the mythology of the Dogon, God created the earth and copulated with her, and as this act was not completely satisfactory, he excised her clitoris (Parin et al., 1963).

Related Concepts: Libido; Trauma.

REFERENCES

Freud, S., 1917, "Introductory Lectures on Psycho-Analysis." *SE*, 16:368–369, 1963.
Parin, P., F. Morgenthaler, & G. Parin-Matthey, *Die Weissen denken zu viel.* Zürich: Atlantic Verlag, p. 27, 1963.

ADDITIONAL READINGS

Fenichel, O., *The Psychoanalytic Theory of Neurosis.* Nor, 1945.
Freud, S., 1918, "From the History of an Infantile Neurosis." *SE*, 17, 1955.
Izner, S., "On the Appearance of Primal Scene Content in Dreams." *JAPA*, 7, 1959.
Niederland, W. G., "Early Auditory Experiences, Beating Fantasies, and Primal Scene." *PsaStC*, 13, 1958.
Wälder, J., "Analysis of a Case of Night Terror." *PsaStC*, 2, 1946.

1655

PRIMARY IDENTIFICATION, according to Freud (1921), is the first object relationship between the infant and its mother.* At this stage of develop-

---

* He referred to it as primary narcissistic identification (autoerotic).

ment, the child does not differentiate between the object and himself, and regards the breast as a part of himself. After a few months (as a result of weaning), he begins to differentiate between external reality and himself. Thereafter, the presentation of the external object is cathected by object libido and destrudo, whereas the presentation of the self is cathected by secondary narcissistic libido and destrudo. Consequently, the early oral relationship, in which such differentiation does not take place, may be referred to as primary identification. [Eidelberg and Palmer, 1960.]

Related Concepts: Identification, Narcissism.

REFERENCES

Eidelberg, L., & J. N. Palmer, "Primary and Secondary Narcissism." *PQ*, 34:480–487, 1960.
Freud, S., 1921, "Group Psychology and the Analysis of the Ego." *SE*, 18:105–110, 1955.

ADDITIONAL READINGS

Freud, S.: 1914, "On Narcissism: An Introduction." *SE*, 14, 1957.
1923, "The Ego and the Id." *SE*, 19, 1961.

1656

PRIMARY MASOCHISM. A basic instinct which does not produce psychological derivatives and is referred to as being *silent* (*stumm*). [Freud, 1920.] However, this primary masochism, Thanatos or death instinct, may combine with Eros, or life instinct, to form an aggressive or sexual instinct-fusion. In the aggressive instinct-fusion, the quantity of Thanatos is greater than the quantity of Eros; in the sexual instinct-fusion, the reverse is true. In the literature, the aggressive instinct-fusion is usually referred to as aggression or aggressive drive, and the sexual instinct-fusion is referred to as sexual or libidinal drive.

Sexual instinct-fusions and aggressive instinct-fusions may be simultaneously discharged in neurosis. This simultaneous presence of the two instinctual fusions should not be confused with the fusion of Eros and Thanatos.

Related Concepts: Aggression; Eros; Masochism; Repetition Compulsion; Sadism.

REFERENCE

Freud, S., 1920, "Beyond the Pleasure Principle." *SE*, 18:3, 38–41, 44, 46–47, 49–57, 60, 63, 1955.

ADDITIONAL READINGS

Freud, S.: 1923, "The Ego and the Id." *SE*, 19, 1961.
1924, "The Economic Problem of Masochism." *SE*, 19, 1961.
1926, "Inhibitions, Symptoms and Anxiety." *SE*, 20, 1959.
1930, "Civilization and Its Discontents." *SE*, 21, 1961.

1657

PRIMARY (PARANOSIC) GAIN IN NEUROSIS is denotative of the gain to the ego resulting from the relief of instinctual pressures (drives) through the partial discharge of drive-energy that occurs with the formation and maintenance of neurotic symptoms. This discharge of repressed drive-energy produces an unconscious gratification. There is also a secondary, or epinosic gain which is the gratification the total personality obtains from the environment because of the disease. Both paranosic and epinosic gain operate as part of what Freud (1923) designated as ego-resistance. Some causes responsible for the neurosis were no doubt present before its outbreak. Freud differentiated between a primary and a secondary advantage resulting from a neurosis. A certain psychic effort is avoided in the neurosis, and, consequently, we speak of a "flight into illness."

Related Concepts: RESISTANCE; SECONDARY (EPINOSIC) GAIN IN NEUROSIS.

REFERENCE

Freud, S., "Fragments of an Analysis of a Case of Hysteria." *SE*, 7:43, 1953.

1658

PRIMARY PROCESS, described by Freud as (a) the mechanism of displacement of energy cathecting one idea to another, and (b) the mechanism of condensation of cathexis of several ideas into one, was at first related to the system *Ucs.*, and, later, to the id. In addition to the primary process, Freud (1915) stated that the id was also characterized by (c) the "exemption from mutual contradiction," (d) "of timelessness," and (e) of "replacement of external by psychical reality." It would seem that all five mechanisms are also present in the unconscious part of the ego and superego. Thus, the primary process which controls the life of the embryo appears to remain after birth in the unconscious part of the personality. In this, the primary process is intimately connected with the pure pleasure principle, for its immediate aim is to eliminate unpleasure, while failing to differentiate between external and internal reality.

The condensation and the displacement, the two mechanisms which are characteristic of the primary process, appear to be aimed at the instant discharge and at keeping unconscious the meaning of this discharge. Consequently, only after the patient's resistance has been overcome, does he begin to realize the hidden meaning of the primary process. Whereas conscious condensation permits us to save mental energy by blending two concepts into one, and conscious displacement helps us to find an available object, even if inferior, instead of one which cannot be had, unconscious condensation and displacement prevent us from facing certain problems and dealing with them effectively by means of the secondary process.

Related Concepts: AESTHETIC PLEASURE; SECONDARY PROCESS; STRUCTURAL (TOPOGRAPHIC) APPROACH; SYSTEMATIC (QUALITATIVE OR DESCRIPTIVE) APPROACH; UNPLEASURE-PLEASURE PRINCIPLE.

REFERENCE

Freud, 2., 1915, "The Unconscious." *SE*, 14:186–188, 1957.

ADDITIONAL READING

Burstein, A. G., "Primary Process in Children as a Function of Age." *ASP*, 59, 1959.

1659

PRIMITIVE. The development of man was seen by Freud (1913) as falling into four stages; the two most recent were religious and scientific, and the two earliest were preanimistic (animatism) and animism. In the preanimistic stage, the outer world was thought to determine the well-being or misfortune of man in a more or less direct way, while in the stage of animism man populated the world with demons and souls and thus through projection delegated some part of his own being to the spirits around him.

The primitive's attitude resembles that of the unconscious; his exaggerated belief in the power of thought—the basis of all magic—was an index of his pronounced narcissism. This attitude of the primitive, Freud (1913) postulated, was correlated to the 'omnipotence of thought' that was to be found in neurotic fantasies and in the mental life of young children. This ritualistic conceptualization was derived from man's exaggerated belief in the power of his own thoughts. It was, however, the phenomenon of death, above all, which impelled man to alter his attitude toward life, which led to his invention of demons, the precursor of his later mythology and its codification into religious doctrine.

Though Freud accepted Darwin's concept of the primal horde, he was well aware that no anthropological evidence has been discovered to substantiate the doctrine that man's first society consisted of a primitive living in a group, in which there was one male and a number of females who were directly subservient to him. Freud thought that the most primitive organization of individuals consisted of bands of males. These bands, he thought, may have originated after the father, the original ruler of the band, had been killed.

Freud considered as primitive those who were ignorant of the importance of impregnation and believed that sexual intercourse was not connected with begetting children. Graves (1955) assumed that the discovery of the importance of the genital act was responsible for the patriarchal system superseding the matriarchal.*

Freud (1913) cautioned those who would investigate the primitive. Primitives are not necessarily telling the truth when they report their beliefs.

---

* It is interesting to note that even after this discovery the mechanics responsible for impregnation remained unknown for a long time. It was Descartes, according to Lewinsohn (1958), in a posthumously published treatise, who expressed the view "that the process of generation resembled chemically that of beer-brewing, in which the froth of beer could be used as yeast for other beers: 'the semina of the two sexes mingle and act as yeast, each on the other.'" [The importance of the spermatazoa we owe to Hamm and Leeuwenhoek.]

Therefore, there are many difficulties in evaluating the material gained from a study of primitives.

Related Concepts: MASS (GROUP) PSYCHOLOGY; TABOO; TOTEM.

REFERENCES

Freud, S., 1913, "Totem and Taboo." *SE*, 13:75, 76, 90, 102, 103, 141, 1955.
Graves, R., *The Greek Myths.* New York: George Braziller, pp. 11–13, 1955.

ADDITIONAL READING

Devereux, G., "Primitive Genital Mutilations in a Neurotic's Dream." *JAPA*, 2, 1954.

1660

PRIMITIVE SUPEREGO. The primitive superego, according to Bychowski (1945), is the primary image of the self which, at an early age, imposed on the ego the demands of a primitive grandiosity. The feeling of weakness and passivity is compensated for with an increase in the original narcissistic grandiosity. Thus, elements of primary narcissism and megalomania served to maintain the archaic superego. In this, the primitive ego-ideal contained the primary narcissism, while the primitive superego was characterized by the punitive and hostile demands of the early introjects. The greater the correspondence between the ego-ideal and the superego to their original introjects, the more nearly they represented the external world from which they came. In this early form of identification, Fenichel (1945) noted, "narcissistic needs and sexual needs become differentiated."

Related Concept: SUPEREGO.

REFERENCES

Bychowski, G., "The Ego of Homosexuals." *IntJPsa*, 26:1–14, 1945.
Fenichel, O., *The Psychoanalytic Theory of Neurosis.* Nor, pp. 40–41, 1945.

ADDITIONAL READING

Bychowski, G., *Psychotherapy of Psychosis.* G&S, 1952.

1661

PROGERISM, according to Solomon (1954), is a chronologically premature state of resignation to old age. For example, a man in his fifties, who has lost all hope of attaining financial success, wards off feelings of depression or anxiety by accepting the role of a useless old man (although still in good health). He can then be dependent on others, punish his environment, and await his end.

Related Concept: DEPRESSION.

REFERENCE

Solomon, J. C., *A Synthesis of Human Behavior.* G&S, p. 227, 1954.

1662

PROJECTION is a defense mechanism employed by the unconscious part of the ego, through which internal impulses and feelings that are unacceptable to the total personality are attributed to an external object, and then enter consciousness as a disguised perception of the external world. Projection is the most important symptom in paranoia. With the help of this symptom, an internal perception is eliminated and attributed to an external object. However, projection appears not only in paranoia but also in neurosis, e.g., in phobia. [Freud, 1911.]

In the modified sense of assuming unconsciously that "others feel what I feel," projection is a normal mechanism in children and primitive social groups, and contributes to the development of empathy and understanding. However, pathological projection, as manifested in phobia and paranoia, interferes and distorts the individual's understanding of the external world. In this, an external narcissistic mortification is substituted for an internal narcissistic mortification, allowing the subject to retain an illusion of control over the self. Projection may also be used to externalize parts of the self; e.g., in guilt feeling: "He accuses me" replaces "I feel guilty;" and in the feminine part of the male person, as in paranoid jealousy, "It is she, not I, who is sexually excited by him." In different stages of libidinal organization, projection may unconsciously represent spitting out, defecating, urina-

ting, ejaculating, and being born. The projection of internalized objects is of prime importance in the theories of M. Klein (1919).

Case History

"One day, a patient of mine, a man of forty, suffering from many neurotic character traits and symptoms, accused me of trying to hypnotize him. Analysis disclosed that this unconscious wish to be hypnotized was a defense against the infantile wish to play the role of his mother in intercourse with his father. The original sexual wish was replaced, in part, by the aggressive wish, 'I want to be castrated.' At the same time, this passive wish became partly active, and could be expressed as, 'I want to masturbate and castrate myself.' In that way, the wish to be hypnotized meant, 'Being masturbated and castrated,' and was already the result of an earlier defense mechanism. By projecting this wish onto me, the patient was able to protect himself from a recognition of his own desires, and of his lack of power over them: 'It is not true that I want to be seduced and therefore have the fear that I may find a man who will do it. The truth is that the analyst wants to seduce me.'

"The unconscious wish to love or hate one's self may undergo the following changes as the result of projection:

"(1) I want to love myself: into, He wants to love me.

"(2) I want to love myself: into, He wants to be loved by me.

"(3) I want to love myself: into, He wants to love a third person.

"(4) I want to love myself: into, He wants to be loved by a third person. Very often, the words, 'I want to,' are eliminated, and since the neurotic does not differentiate between wish and act, 'He loves me', appears instead of, 'He wants to love me.'

"Sometimes, the words, 'He thinks,' are added, and instead of saying, 'He loves me,' the patient will say, 'He thinks that I love myself, or him, or want him to love me, or to be loved by me.'

"In many cases studied so far, this writer has the impression that projection is used to ward off a wish turned against the self, but it is not claimed that this is always so, nor is it denied that in certain cases, the idea of, 'He hates me,' may represent a projection of the thought, 'I hate him.' " [Eidelberg, 1954.]

Related Concepts: DEFENSE MECHANISMS; INTROJECTION.

REFERENCES

Eidelberg, L., *An Outline of a Comparative Pathology of the Neuroses.* IUP, pp. 104–106, 1954.
Freud, S., 1911, "Psycho-Analytic Notes on an Autobiographical Account of a Case of Paranoia (Dementia Paranoides)." *SE*, 12:66, 1958.
Klein, M., *The Psycho-Analysis of Children.* HPI, 1949.

ADDITIONAL READINGS

Bellak, L., "The Concept of Projection." *Ps*, 7, 1944.
Feigenbaum, D., "On Projection." *Q*, 5, 1936.
Freud, S.: 1914, "On Narcissism: An Introduction." *SE*, 14, 1957.
　　　　1915, "Instincts and Their Vicissitudes." *SE*, 14, 1957.
Jelgersma, G., "Projection." *IntJPsa*, 7, 1926.
Kaufman, M. R., "Projection, Heterosexual and Homosexual." *Q*, 3, 1934.
Knight, R., "Introjection, Projection and Identification." *Q*, 9, 1940.
Weiss, E.: "Regression and Projection in the Super-Ego." *IntJPsa*, 13, 1932.
　　　　"Projection, Extrajection and Objectivation." *Q*, 16, 1947.

1663

PROJECTIVE COUNTERIDENTIFICATION, according to Grinberg (1962), is a specific reaction of the analyst which results, in part, from the patient's excessive use of projective identification. The analyst is unconsciously and passively led to play the sort of role the patient hands over to him. For example, in the course of the patient's analysis, the analyst observed a strange and uncommon reaction in himself. Throughout a number of sessions, every time the patient spoke about the possibility of getting married, the analyst was overcome by an intense drowsiness, which interfered with his relationship to the patient and the subject of discussion. However, the analyst remembered that drowsiness had been a frequent characteristic of this patient at the beginning of his analysis.

Grinberg summarized his view, as follows: "This . . . deals with the disturbance in technique arising from the excessive interplay of projective identification and what is termed 'projective counteridentifications'. The latter came about specifically, on some occasions, as the result of an excessive projective identification, which is not consciously perceived by the analyst, who, in consequence, finds himself 'led' into it. The analyst then behaves as if he had *really and concretely* acquired, by assimilating them, the aspects that were projected on to him. The various considerations are supported by relevant clinical examples."

Related Concepts: COUNTERTRANSFERENCE; PSEUDO-IDENTIFICATION.

REFERENCE

Grinberg, L., "On a Specific Aspect of Countertransference due to the Patient's Projective Identification." *IntJPsa*, 43:436–440, 1962.

ADDITIONAL READING

Grinberg, L., "Aspectos magicos en la transferencia y contratransferencia. Identificacion y contra-identificación proyectivas." *RPsi*, 15, 1958.

1664

PROJECTIVE IDENTIFICATION, M. Klein (1946) believed, was an early defense mechanism which was a combination of splitting off parts of the self and projecting them on to another person. She noted: "As regards normal development, it may be said that the course of ego development and object relations depends on the degree to which an optimal balance between introjection and projection in the early stages of development can be achieved. This in turn has a bearing on the integration of the ego and the assimilation of internal objects. Even if the balance is disturbed and one or the other of these processes is excessive, there is some interaction between introjection and projection. For instance, the projection of a predominantly hostile inner world which is ruled by persecutory fears leads to the introjection—a taking back—of a hostile external world. *Vice versa*, the introjection of a distorted and hostile external world reinforces the projection of a hostile inner world.

"Another aspect of projective processes, as we

have seen, implies the forceful entry into the object and control of the object by parts of the self. As a consequence, introjection may then be felt as a forceful entry from the outside into the inside, in retribution for violent projection. This may lead to the fear that not only the body but also the mind is controlled by other people in a hostile way. As a result there may be a severe disturbance in introjecting good objects—a disturbance which would impede all ego-functions as well as sexual development and may lead to an excessive withdrawal to the inner world. This withdrawal is, however, not only caused by the fear of introjecting a dangerous external world but also by the fear of internal persecutors and an ensuing flight to the idealized internal object.

"I have referred to the weakening and impoverishment of the ego resulting from excessive splitting and projective identification. This weakened ego, however, becomes also incapable of assimilating its internal objects, and this leads to the feeling that it is ruled by them. Again, such a weakened ego feels incapable of taking back into itself the parts which it projected into the external world. These various disturbances in the interplay between projection and introjection, which imply excessive splitting of the ego, have a detrimental effect on the relation to the inner and outer world and seem to be at the root of some forms of schizophrenia."

Related Concept: PSEUDOIDENTIFICATION.

REFERENCE

Klein, M., "Notes on Some Schizoid Mechanisms." *IntJPsa*, 27:103–104, 1946.

ADDITIONAL READINGS

Abraham, K., "The Psycho-Sexual Differences Between Hysteria and Dementia Praecox." *SPA*, 1942.
Fairbairn, W. R. D.: "A Revised Psychopathology." *IntJPsa*, 22, 1941.
    "Endopsychic Structure Considered in Terms of Object Relationships." *IntJPsa*, 25, 1944.
    "Object Relationships and Dynamic Structure." *IntJPsa*, 27, 1946.
Freud, S., 1911, "Psychoanalytic Notes Upon a Autobiographical Account of a Case of Paranoia." *SE*, 3.

Heimann, P., "A Contribution to the Problem of Sublimation and its Relation to the Processes of Internalization." *IntJPsa*, 23, 1942.
Klein, M.: *The Psycho-Analysis of Children*. HP, 1932.
    "A Contribution to the Psycho-Genesis of Manic-Depressive States." *IntJPsa*, 16, 1935.
Winnicott, D. W., "Primitive Emotional Development." *IntJPsa*, 26, 1945.

1665

PROMISCUITY commonly denotes the uninhibited genital discharge by heterosexual partners living in an essentially monogamous society. It is viewed psychoanalytically as an indiscriminate discharge involving a strong fixation to the oedipal and preoedipal stage. As such, it represents both an avoidance of, and an endless search for, the incestuous object: the all-loving, all-satisfying object. Promiscuity is sometimes linked with perversion and may serve as a defense against homosexual, if unconscious urges; a defense against infantile fantasies of fusion and symbiosis.

There is a separation between the erotic and affective components. In this, Glover (1945) has described the matter as follows: "[It occurs] because the primitive sexual components were too strong, or the associated hatreds and jealousies were too violent, or the unconscious conscience too stringent."

Promiscuous wishes and actions appear either as unconscious needs leading to repressions or as a countercathexis to hide some other archaic desires. The inability to love is caused (nominally) by a fear of getting involved, and it is this factor which appears to be responsible for the promiscuity encountered in many neurotics. Furthermore, these patients whose day dreams involve the enjoyment of sexual intercourse with many objects usually reveal that all the gorgeous lovers they embrace in their masturbation fantasies represent themselves. The inability to establish a normal relationship with another person based on their ability to fall in love and become temporarily dependent on another object is avoided in the patient's promiscuous fantasies.

According to Graves (1955), it would seem that the matriarchal society exempted the queen who could take as many lovers as she wanted. This privilege was taken from the female (of whom the queen was the surrogate) when the matriarchal society was superseded by the patriarchal. With the rise to dominance of the Judaeo-Christian monogamous God, the number of wives was limited to one object: procreation was stressed, not pleasure. This would seem to correspond to the change over from the matrilineal to patrilineal form of society, in which impregnation, and its source, were recognized as stemming from the male. In this recognition the male gained the upper hand, and man achieved a role in society he did not have previously. Thus, it may be claimed that the prohibition which characterizes most religious practices (from the birth of Judaism) was in support of the male role in society.

Related Concept: LOVE.

REFERENCES

Glover, E., *The Psycho-Pathology of Prostitution.* London: Institute for the Scientific Treatment of Delinquency, p. 4, 1945.
Graves, R., *The Greek Myths.* New York: George Braziller, pp. 11–13, 1955.

1666

PROTOPHALLIC refers to one of two divisions of the phallic stage. First used by Jones (1927, 1933), the concept was described as a phase marked by innocence or ignorance, at least in consciousness, where the child confidentially assumes "that the rest of the world is built like itself and has a satisfactory male organ—penis or clitoris, as the case may be." The second division is called the deuterophallic phase, wherein a "dawning suspicion that the world is divided into two classes" takes place. Jones noted that the two were not male and female in the proper sense, "but penis possessing and castrated." Freud (1931) described the concept as one which did not correspond to the dynamic and chronological development of sexuality. Presently, the term is rarely employed.

Related Concepts: DEUTEROPHALLIC; PHALLIC PHASE.

REFERENCES

Freud, S., 1931, "Female Sexuality." *SE,* 21:243, 1961.
Jones, E.: "The Early Development of Female Sexuality." *IntJPsa,* 8:459, 1927.
    "The Phallic Phase." *IntJPsa,* 14:1, 1933.

1667

PROTOPSYCHE denotes a chronological region of the mind which corresponds to primitive ontogenetic and phylogenetic stages of development, in which adaptation has not achieved a modification of the outer world; a modification of the subject's own body. Rarely employed, it was first used by Ferenczi (1919) to describe that reflexive process (preliminary stage) to which the highest psychic elaboration always remains inclined to regress. He noted: "The puzzling leap from mental to bodily in the conversion symptom and the reflex wish-fulfilling phenomenon of materialization becomes less amazing. It is simply regression to the protopsyche."

Related Concepts: ALLOPLASTIC; CONVERSION AND CONVERSION SYMPTOMS; IDENTIFICATION; REGRESSION.

REFERENCE

Ferenczi, S., 1919, *Further Contributions to the Theory and Technique of Psychoanalysis.* BB, pp. 89–103, 1952.

1668

PSEUDODEBILITY (PSEUDOIMBECILITY) denotes a consciously or unconsciously simulated feeblemindedness or retardation, as opposed to actual mental retardation; extreme intellectual inhibitions, serving as a defense against anxiety and guilt. Denial plays a dominant role in this neurotic trait, often representing a need to disavow forbidden knowledge of the self or of others. Pseudodebility may manifest itself as extreme naïveté, permitting gratification of forbidden wishes and avoidance of punishment. [Mahler-Schoenberger, 1942.]

Fenichel (1945) noted "People become stupid *ad hoc* . . . where understanding would cause (castration) anxiety or guilt feelings."

Related Concept: INHIBITION.

REFERENCES

Fenichel, O., *The Psychoanalytic Theory of Neurosis.* Nor, p. 180–181, 1945.
Mahler-Schoenberger, M., "Pseudo Imbecility: A Magic Cap of Invisibility." *Q*, 11:149–164, 1942.

ADDITIONAL READINGS

Bergler, E., "Zur Problematik der Pseudo-Debilität." *Z*, 18, 1932.
Bornstein, B.: "A Case of Cured Stupidity. Report on a Psychoanalytic Case History." *PsaP*, 4, 1930.
"Psychogenesis of Pseudodebility." *Z*, 16, 1930.

1669

PSEUDOHALLUCINATION (ILLUSION) denotes a hallucination which the subject recognizes as a pathological phenomenon; although sensation is vividly experienced, the subject realizes it does not come from an external source. Many analysts question the use of the term pseudohallucination, feeling that it describes a true hallucination. The realization that it *is* a hallucination is only preliminary or transitory.

As defined, it often represents a transition toward a real hallucination; it is found in schizophrenia and organic psychosis. If hallucinations are experienced by neurotics (a moot point, with the exception of hypnagogic hallucinations), they are pseudohallucinations. A minimal economic shift in the mental balance of someone subject to pseudohallucinations can result in the complete inability to test reality, and genuine delusions and hallucinations may take place. [Fenichel, 1945.]

Related Concepts: DELUSIONS; HALLUCINATIONS; HYPNAGOGIC PHENOMENON.

REFERENCE

Fenichel, O., *The Psychoanalytic Theory of Neurosis.* Nor, p. 444–445, 1945.

1670

PSEUDO-HYPERSEXUALITY may derive from an increase of sexual activity (e.g., in puberty) or it may be the result of an unconscious defense mechanism. The aggressive oral wish to vomit, to spit out, and to starve may be blocked and kept unconscious by the mobilization of a sexual wish that leads to overeating, tongue biting, teeth grinding, and to the inability to listen or to the inability to talk. Similar defenses may be used on the anal level, as in diarrhea and prolonged defecation, or on the phallic level leading to an increase in the frequency of urination. On the genital level, an increase in the frequency of sexual intercourse may be caused by an unconscious defense of homosexual or pervert activities.

Fenichel (1945), in describing the symptoms of a patient suffering from a series of severe neurotic difficulties of a cyclothymic character, summarized his findings, as follows: "It was the expression of a deep oral-sadistic excitement.... The genital behaviour did not correspond to genuine genital impulses but rather to the striving of the ego to master the dangerous oral-sadistic temptations."

Related Concept: PSEUDOIDENTIFICATION.

REFERENCE

Fenichel, O., *The Psychoanalytic Theory of Neurosis.* Nor, p. 518, 1945.

1671

PSEUDOIDENTIFICATION, according to Eidelberg (1948), is a defense mechanism which takes the form of a projection to an object, in which the subject subsequently identifies with the object. For example, a patient of Eidelberg's avoided expressing any difference of opinion with those with whom he might be talking by immediately and completely identifying himself with that person. Eidelberg noted: "He considered that in so doing he had discovered the ideal way of adapting himself to reality. He deliberately refused to have an opinion of his own and accepted that of others with the utmost alacrity. He himself described his attitude as lacking in character, but he was proud of this lack. His point of view was that, as he only pretended to adopt other people's opinions and adhered to them only so long as he was with those same people, he was in fact a person of independence and immune from attack."

In another instance, this patient claimed that he had defended the analyst at the meeting of the Bar Association by saying that criminals are actually neurotics and should therefore be analyzed and not imprisoned. When the analyst asked the patient how he knew what the analyst felt about the subject he claimed that he felt it. Actually, the patient had projected his own wishes to the analyst and had thereafter accepted the ideas which he attributed to the analyst. He thus did not feel responsible for his view, assuming that the immediate acceptance of an idea belonging to the other person protected him from an external conflict. In this case, the patient originally had the idea that criminals should not be prosecuted, but his superego objected to the idea. This internal conflict with his superego's point of view was then projected to the person of the analyst. The resulting external conflict (the superego disguised as the analyst) was finally eliminated by his accepting the point of view his analyst presumably held without contradiction.

Pseudoidentification may be mobilized by external frustration, which leads to the damming up of object-libido and destrudo, and which inflicts, at the same time, a narcissistic mortification. With the latter, the mortification is projected on to the object: "I am getting annoyed" becomes "He is getting annoyed, I am sorry for him." In addition, the dammed-up instinct is also projected: "I love him" becomes "He loves me." Finally, the product of the projection is accepted ostensibly and for the time being. Eidelberg provided the following case history, as an example: "The patient tried to turn the analytic hour into a friendly meeting and to this I responded with marked reserve. One day he suggested that he should introduce me to friends of his, a man and a woman. I declined, giving as my reason that I must observe the rules of the technique of analysis. He did not appear offended, but replied as follows: 'I am sorry that you feel obliged because of this technical rule to forego the pleasure of associating with such an interesting person as myself. I think it is very praiseworthy of you to make this sacrifice in my interest. I will return your kindness by looking you up after the analysis, when I no longer need your services.' "

Related Concepts: IDENTIFICATION; PROJECTION.

REFERENCE

Eidelberg, L., *Studies in Psychoanalysis*. IUP, pp. 107, 108, 1948.

ADDITIONAL READINGS

Bally, G., "Zur Frage der Behandlung schizoider Neurotiker." *Z*, 16, 1930.
Deutsch, H., "Über einen Typus der Pseudoaffektivität." *Z*, 20, 1934.

1672

PSEUDOLOGIA FANTASTICA is a clinical syndrome characterized by the creation of elaborate fantasies believed to be true by the subject; it may be found to occur in both psychoses and neuroses. Numerous circumstantial details are marshalled in an attempt to support the "truth" of the fantasy.

The mendacious elaboration of fantasy is primarily a defensive maneuver, an attempt to effect denial (disavowal), in making the object the "witness" by getting him to believe in the truth of the denying fantasy. However, these lies also contain the content to be denied, and can thus reveal the truth in a manner which is similar to that revealed by screen memories. H. Deutsch (1922) noted that the content of these fantasies consisted in screen stories of something which actually had happened. They may be compared to myths, which contain historical facts distorted by wish-fulfillments in a manner that denies unpleasant realities.

Related Concepts: DELUSIONS; DENIAL (DISAVOWAL); FANTASY; SCREEN MEMORY.

REFERENCE

Deutsch, H., "Über die Pathologische Lüge." *Z*, 8:153–167, 1922.

ADDITIONAL READING

Fenichel, O., "Zur Oekonomie der Pseudologica Phantastica." *Z*, 24, 1939.

1673

PSYCHIATRY is the medical speciality dealing with mental disorders; specifically, psychoses, but, more recently, neuroses as well. In most states in the

U.S., psychoanalysis is not legally divisible from psychiatry and is, thus, not recognized as a separate science. Psychiatrists do not have to meet the rigid requirements set up by the International Psycho-Analytical Institute for its members. Thus, the training received by psychiatrists is of a quite different order (e.g., there is no requirement for a didactic or personal analysis) and, until recent times, their principal clinical training was restricted to mental institutions, which tended to emphasize the study of psychotic disorders to the exclusion of all others. Though changes have occurred, many of the differences still remain. Freud, writing in 1917, noted that psychiatry does not use the methods of psychoanalysis. It refrains from trying to make any conclusion from the content of the delusion, and in relying on heredity it provides only a very general etiology of psychiatric diseases without trying to locate their specific causes. This fact does not indicate a basic difference between psychoanalysis and psychiatry; rather, it shows that psychiatry and psychoanalysis need each other. Psychoanalysis, too, does not deny the importance of heredity, for it asserts that the genetic factors combine with the acquired factors. Therefore, Freud arrived at the conclusion that psychiatric work is not opposed to psychoanalysis and that only some psychiatrists oppose it.

Pre-Freudian psychiatry offered a descriptive approach to the many forms of mental illness which is still used today. Psychoanalysis employs the psychiatric terminology in differentiating neurosis from psychosis and in separating obsessional neurosis from hysterical neurosis. However, only after Freud extended the concept of psychology to cover the unconscious processes was it possible to use a psychological (i.e., psychoanalytical) approach to study the structure of mental disorders, its causes, therapy and prevention.

The pre-Freudian psychiatrists chiefly employed physiological examinations in the determination of the etiology of neurosis and psychosis. In spite of many physiological examinations, it cannot be said that the riddle of mental disorder was solved. On the other hand, the fact that psychoanalysis increased our understanding of psychosis and neurosis does not mean that physiological examinations will not in the future provide a fuller understanding of mental disorders.

Related Concepts: METHODOLOGY; TRAINING ANALYSIS.

REFERENCE

Freud, S., 1917, "Introductory Lectures on Psychoanalysis." SE, 16:254–255, 1963.

ADDITIONAL READINGS

Arieti, S., American Handbook of Psychiatry. BB, 1959.
Bunker, H., "American Psychiatric Literature During the Past Hundred Years," in One Hundred Years of American Psychiatry. CUP, 1944.
Eissler, K., "Some Comments on Psychoanalysis and Dynamic Psychiatry." JAPA, 4, 1956.
Knight, R., & C. Friedman, eds., Psychoanalytic Psychiatry and Psychology: Clinical and Theoretical Papers. IUP, 1954.
Linn, L., A Handbook of Hospital Psychiatry. A Practical Guide to Therapy. IUP, 1955.
Szurek, S., "Teaching and Learning of Psychoanalytic Psychiatry in Medical School." Q, 26, 1957.

1674

PSYCHIC APPARATUS was first used by Freud to describe the interrelated processes of the mind; a functional, not an anatomical concept: perception, memory, and motility. Freud (1900) described mental phenomena as being unconscious, preconscious and conscious. In this, the differentiation was referred to as a qualitative one. The perception system (Pcpt.) which is responsible for receiving external stimuli does not have a memory. Consequently, the mnemic images of these memories have to be traced to another system. In the dream, it is the system of the Ucs. which appears to be responsible for its formation.

Freud made a distinction in those early years between secondary and primary processes, assigning the former to conscious-preconscious and the latter to the unconscious. He considered neurosis to be the result of a conflict between the unconscious and the conscious-preconscious. He referred to this concept as a qualitative, systematic or descriptive approach. Later, in 1923, he introduced the topographic* or structural concept, in which he assumed

* In 1900, and thereafter, he used the term as a synonym for systematic. After 1923, the term topographic was used synonymously with structural.

a division into id, ego, and superego. Accordingly, the id was considered as unconscious; the ego and superego, as partly conscious, partly preconscious, and partly unconscious. The id has no direct contact with the external world. All instincts operate within the id. However, in order to discharge the instinctual energy, they require the cooperation of the ego. The ego mediates between the id, the superego and the external world. The superego represents not only the conscience but also the ideal ego. [Freud, 1940.]

The apparatus, activated by inner energies, operates both intrasystematically and in relation to the external world. Energic activities of the apparatus are presumed to operate in accordance with the law of constancy, so that it may be viewed as a device for mastering excitations. The components of the psychic apparatus include the ego apparatus and its subdivisions, the perceptive and muscular apparatus, etc. Hartmann (1958) stressed the "inborn equipment" of the apparatus and its relation to personality functions.

Related Concepts: ECONOMIC APPROACH; EGO; ID; LAW OF CONSTANCY; METAPSYCHOLOGY; SUPEREGO.

REFERENCES

Freud, S.: 1900, "The Interpretation of Dreams." *SE*, 5:536–542, 603–605, 1953.
　　　1923, "The Ego and the Id." *SE*, 19:22–27, 1961.
　　　1940, "An Outline of Psycho-Analysis." *SE* 23:197–207, 1964.
Hartmann, H., *Ego Psychology and the Problem of Adaptation*. IUP, pp. 11–12, 1958.

ADDITIONAL READINGS

Glover, E., *Selected Papers on Psychoanalysis*. IUP, 1956.
Klein, M., "On the Development of Mental Functioning." *IntJPsa*, 39, 1958.

1675

PSYCHIC DETERMINISM is a concept which seeks to explain every change in the psyche as being causal and not subject to free will. Freud (1916) was of the opinion that there was "a deeply rooted faith in undetermined psychical events" which was "quite unscientific and must yield to the demand of a determinism whose rule extends over mental life." For instance, we see the sun moving around our earth. The fact that the perceptions responsible for this statement are based on an illusion does not contradict the astronomical facts; namely, that the opposite takes place.

Conceptually, psychoanalysis does not deny that a normal individual behaves *as if* he had a limited freedom of action. For example, we eat or we starve, but we assume that we have the freedom to choose the kind of food and time needed to eat it. If this emotional experience of freedom is referred to as descriptive, it will not contradict the hypothesis that with the expansion of our present knowledge this "freedom" may be found to be considerably narrower than presently supposed. For instance, psychoanalysis has succeeded in showing that the determination of a neurotic symptom is explained by the presence of repressed infantile wishes and their defenses. Independent of such philosophical formulations and reservations, the analyst is able to help the patient gain freedom from his unconscious defenses. This freedom is not absolute, but permits a greater choice of aims and methods, still within the framework of "biological causality."

Instead of seeking gratification of his infantile wishes, the patient learns to face what he wants, accept what he ought to, and agree to what he has to do, and aim at a reasonable compromise in what he will do. Thus, the man or woman who can only have intercourse with a humiliated object, the compulsive who washes his hands every twenty minutes, and the phobic patient who can only cross the street when accompanied by a companion are freed of their unconscious inhibitions. In spite of the fact that the successful analysis *appears* to increase the freedom of choice, the individual remains dependent in his action on various factors that are at present unknown, but which decisively influence his life.

Related Concepts: CAUSALITY; PSYCHIC (MENTAL) ENERGY; TELEOLOGY (FINALITY).

REFERENCE

Freud, S., 1916, "Introductory Lectures on Psycho-Analysis." *SE*, 15:106, 1963.

1676

PSYCHIC (MENTAL) ENERGY is one of the basic explanatory concepts introduced by Freud. According to his first instinct theory (1900), the energy of the sexual instincts was referred to as libido whereas the energy of the ego-instincts was originally considered to be free of libido and not further classified; later, the concepts of ego-libido and narcissistic libido were added.

In Freud's (1923) second instinct theory, libido is referred to as the energy of Eros (primary instinct) or the energy of the sexual instinct-fusion, while destrudo or mortido is referred to as the energy of Thanatos or of the aggressive instinct-fusion. It may be considered significant that Freud never named the energy of the destructive instinct. "We are without a term analogous to libido for describing the energy of the destructive instinct" (Freud, 1939).

Libido and probably destrudo appear at first in the newborn as primary narcissistic libido and destrudo. After the difference between the self and the external world is established, the infant uses objectual libido or destrudo to cathect presentations of external objects and uses secondary narcissistic libido and destrudo to cathect the presentation of the self. The change from object-libido and object-destrudo into secondary narcissistic libido and destrudo is referred to as delibidinization or deaggressivization. It may be correct to ask what remains of object libido after its delibidinization? Perhaps the process of change which occurs in object-libido and narcissistic libido should be described simply as object-libido losing its objectual quality. [Eidelberg, 1954.]

Freud reasoned that the mental energy may be present as free energy or as bound energy. In this regard, Hartmann (1964) noted: "The concept of mental energy was then elaborated in the sense that it is the drives that are the main sources of energy in what Freud calls the 'mental apparatus.' However, a strictly quantifying approach to these energic problems has so far not been developed. Or rather: while it is possible to speak of a greater or lesser degree of, let's say, a resistance (against the uncovering of some hidden material), we have no way of measuring it. To account for the difference in the unconscious and the conscious (and preconscious) processes Freud postulated two forms of energy distribution, conceptualized as, respectively, primary and secondary processes. The primary processes represent a tendency to immediate discharge, while the secondary processes are guided by the consideration of reality. This distinction is again both theoretically significant and clinically quite helpful. The thesis that behavior is to be explained also in terms of its energic cathexis is what we call, in analysis, the economic viewpoint."

Related Concepts: ECONOMIC APPROACH; META-PSYCHOLOGY; PSYCHIC APPARATUS.

REFERENCES

Eidelberg, L., *An Outline of a Comparative Pathology of the Neuroses.* IUP, pp. 22–23, 1954.
Freud, S.: 1900, "The Interpretation of Dreams." *SE*, 5:537–543, 1953.
       1923, "The Ego and the Id." *SE*, 19:23–25, 1901.
       1939, "Moses and Monotheism." *SE*, 23:150, 1964.
Hartmann, H., *Essays on Ego Psychology.* IUP, p. 327, 1964.

ADDITIONAL READINGS

Brody, E. B., "Superego, Introjected Mother, and Energy Discharge in Schizophrenia: Contribution from the Study of Anterior Lobotomy." *JAPA*, 6, 1958.
Lustman, S. L., "Psychic Energy and the Mechanisms of Defense." *PsaStC*, 12, 1957.

1677

PSYCHIC INERTIA is denotative of a tendency to fixation which Freud (1937) related to the phenomenon of the "resistance of the id," and which elsewhere (1926) he attributed to the power of the compulsion to repeat. As Freud (1915) pointed out, the term *psychic inertia* is actually another term for *fixation*. It implies the resistance not against everything, but against progress and recovery.

Patients who remain highly fixated to the infantile wishes may often remain uncured by analysis. But there is also another type of patient who appears to have a highly mobile libido. He produces often very quick results but, unfortunately, they are not durable. [Freud, 1937.]

Related Concepts: FIXATION; REPETITION COMPULSION.

REFERENCES

Freud, S.: 1915, "A Case of Paranoia Running Counter to the Psycho-Analytic Theory of the Disease." *SE*, 14:272, 1957.

    1926, "Inhibitions, Symptoms and Anxiety." *SE*, 20:160, 1959.

    1937, "Analysis, Terminable and Interminable." *SE*, 23:241, 1964.

1678

PSYCHIC REALITY denotes those fantasies (wishes, fears, and other forms of mental activity) which are a part of what Freud termed *inner reality*. At first Freud (1895) believed that what his patients reported as seductions in early childhood had actually occurred. Only later (in 1906) did he discover that they had never taken place and represented the child's wishes. This discovery at first confused him, until he realized that for a child a wish may be equal to an actual experience. Freud called this kind of infantile experience psychic reality.

The recognition that wishes and fantasies, fears and feelings of guilt were not to be overlooked did not mean, of course, that internal and external reality were not to be distinguished. The abandonment of the pleasure-unpleasure principle in favor of the reality principle proved that the difference between fantasy (inner reality) and external reality was of decisive importance, for the fantasy of a wish fulfillment did not gratify the subject's needs. While it is true that forepleasure and fore-unpleasure take place as a result of anticipation and may for a time give rise to a partial gratification or a partial frustration, this forepleasure and fore-unpleasure cease to exist if external reality does not finally intervene.

Normal individuals who are able to derive pleasure from anticipation make a clear distinction between their fantasies and the actual achievement of what they want. This is not only true for pleasure but also for unpleasure. The anticipation of unpleasure, like the anticipation of pleasure, is basically different from the experience of pleasure and unpleasure caused by the external world.

In introducing the term *psychic reality*, Freud made clear that, in addition to external reality, there exists an internal reality which must be regarded as influencing our behavior: mental activities which lead to the charge or discharge of libido and destrudo, even if external stimuli are not present. These changes are covered by the rule of psychic determinism and cannot be overlooked or regarded as being without importance. By temporarily inhibiting or postponing instant gratification, inner reality is created: thinking, dreaming, remembering and anticipating.

Freud (1913) thought that the primitive was uninhibited and all his impulses led to action, not to thinking. Thus, one may venture to say (to paraphrase Freud) that after the deed was inhibited, the need became conscious and thus created thoughts and words.

Related Concepts: PLEASURE; REALITY PRINCIPLE; UNPLEASURE.

REFERENCES

Freud, S.: 1906, "Sexuality in the Neuroses." *SE*, 7:274–275, 1953.

    1913, "Totem and Taboo." *SE*, 13:161, 1955.

ADDITIONAL READING

Eidelberg, L., *An Outline of Comparative Pathology of the Neuroses*. IUP, 1954.

1679

PSYCHOANALYSIS, the science which investigates the interaction of conscious and unconscious processes, has as its aim the discovery and formulation of laws involving the function of the mental system.

Originating with the work of Breuer and Freud in the treatment of a patient with hysterical symptoms, previously forgotten "reminiscences" of early traumatic experiences were recalled under hypnosis. The "strangulated affects" associated with them were discharged and the neurotic symptoms disappeared. Later, hypnosis was discarded and replaced by suggestion and exhortation to remember: the cathartic method of therapy. In turn, free association was substituted, and remains the basic technique still employed.

Freud was the first to understand that seemingly senseless communications of the patient are translatable by treating them as coded derivatives of the unconscious. Increasingly, he recognized the importance of internal conflicts based on infantile and childhood sexual instincts, independent of external traumatic events. The therapeutic aim became "to make the unconscious conscious," with the analyst playing an active role, either interpreting directly the nature of the various unconscious drives or reconstructing the repressed material. When the patient was "in a state of positive transference," such interpretations could be accepted by him; when he was unable to accept the analyst's interpretations, he was thought to be "in a state of resistance," and interpretations were generally suspended until this resistance was eliminated.

Continual observations in the treatment of patients forced a major revision of psychoanalytic theory. The central role of the ego function was recognized, as was the unconscious nature of the resistances to the therapy. Subsequent new theoretical concepts led to a change in the theory and technique of psychoanalytic therapy. The analyst's interpretations were directed not alone toward the content of the instinctual drives, but equally toward the unconscious superego functions, and those unconscious defenses and resistances of the ego itself. Emphasis was placed on the development and resolution of the transference neurosis, and on the internal psychic structural changes as a sign of therapeutic progress. The analysis of character traits and functions was intensified, as was the relationship of the individual to his external environment and reality. The psychoanalytic method thus led to the discovery of unconscious mental processes, their dynamic relationship to the conscious and emotional life; to the phenomenology of psychosexual and aggressive development; and to the etiological factors of certain of the psychopathological states: e.g., the existence and manifestation of the repetition compulsion and of the transference process.

Freud defined psychoanalysis as "any therapy which recognizes the significance of unconscious resistance, of the transference, and of the infantile genetic roots of neurosis." The broad and varied applications of psychoanalysis to the treatment of other conditions and the introduction of psychoanalytic theory into general dynamic psychiatry, including the various attempts to modify or shorten the therapy, have led to a decreasing distinction between psychoanalysis and dynamic psychotherapy. Today, psychoanalysis as a method of

treatment can be defined in terms of (a) general therapeutic techniques and goals, and (b) specific characteristics of the analytic situation. This includes the development, elaboration, and resolution of a regressive transference neurosis; the undoing of the infantile amnesia; the modification of psychic structures (in so far as it is possible); the development of the individual toward genital primacy; the exploration of the primary process; and the preparation of the individual to carry on the work of analysis after treatment is terminated.

I

The general theory of psychoanalysis evolved gradually, with progressive modifications and changes as new observations were made. Initially, Breuer and Freud postulated that the patient was in "a hypnoid state" when the traumatic events occurred. They attempted thereby to explain the observed phenomenon of repression. This was followed by "the seduction theory," in which neurosis was seen as the result of overt active or passive childhood sexual seduction.

The discovery of infantile sexuality, Freud's own self-analysis, and his discoveries in connection with dreams led to the development of the systematic approach. Mental phenomena were conceived as distributed between the system conscious-preconscious and the system unconscious. Conflict was understood as occurring between the sexual instincts of the unconscious and the ego-instincts (self-preservative instincts) of the conscious-preconscious. Anxiety was understood to be a direct result of dammed-up or inadequately discharged libido, which might also be converted directly into physical disturbances of the sensory-motor systems. Neuroses were divided into the psychoneuroses and the actual neuroses, and later into the transference neuroses and the narcissistic neuroses.

The period 1911–1917 was known as the metapsychological period, during which attempts were made to elaborate and refine the systematic theory. While these were successful in some areas, it became clear that the theory could not account for many clinical observations. Such states as the resistances to treatment, the negative therapeutic reaction, the role of guilt (the need for punishment), and aggression in mental life were observed to be largely unconscious. Yet, they could not be related directly to the sexual instincts as the topographic hypothesis required.

These factors forced a new and sweeping revision of the basic theory in the period 1920–1926, and led to the development of the *structural hypothesis*. In this theory, mental processes were grouped according to their functions: id, ego, and superego. Conscious, preconscious and unconscious were given an adjectival connotation (qualitative). Psychic conflict was understood to occur between these functional groups, and a dual instinct theory of libido and aggression (life instinct and death instinct) was proposed. A second theory of anxiety was given to accompany the structural hypothesis (*topographic*): anxiety was understood as an internalization of a previously externally directed fear. In this, instinctual anxiety resulted from the anticipation of being flooded by excessive tension and stimulation from the organism's own drives. Ego anxiety resulted from the internalized perception of a danger situation which was once thought to be external, and was responded to by the various fantasies and distortions of the primary process. Superego anxiety resulted from the internalized threats of punishment or loss of love on moral grounds, now experienced as the sense of guilt. Fear was related to realistic external danger and was proportional to the nature and severity of the external danger. These anxiety reactions gradually achieved an anticipatory and signal function, in response to which the individual attempted to modify the internal or external environment, or both.

II

Mental life and behavior are viewed as the end result of a continuous interaction between all the various complex forces which are integrated by the individual from outside and within the organism. (a) The *genetic approach* seeks to explain the behavior of the individual in terms of previous developmental stages and modes of adaptation; i.e., a complete understanding of current behavior requires an understanding of his antecedents, including those of the remote past. In psychoanalytic theory, the individual's development in infancy and earliest childhood, his solution of the infantile neurosis and of conflicts over infantile sexuality, are

the prototypes of all subsequent development and experience. (b) In the *dynamic approach*, the individual's present behavior is understood to be the result of the interplay of all the current forces within the mind, which appear to be genetically determined. These current forces continue to exert an influence on behavior as long as their activity persists. (c) The concepts of psychic energy, of the continuous variation in the relative intensities of forces within the mental apparatus, are explained by the *economic approach*. When opposing forces coexist, their net effects are a reflection of their mutual interaction and relative intensity. (d) The major development of ego psychology, stimulated initially by the work of Anna Freud and of Heinz Hartmann, carried on by numerous investigators, led to the development of the *adaptational approach*. This concept emphasizes the central and crucial role of the ego in organizing and integrating both normal and pathological mental life and behavior. It stresses the interrelatedness of the internal and external environments of the organism, and the existence of a constantly fluctuating dynamic equilibrium of biological, psychological and social forces which must be maintained in a state of balance for adaptation to occur.

III

In adults, the psychoanalytic situation involves four or five weekly sessions, fifty minutes in length, for a period of seldom less than two years. The patient reclines on a couch with the analyst sitting out of his direct view. The patient uses the basic method of free association, and the analyst relies primarily on the tools of interpretation. Within the limitations of the countertransference, the analyst maintains a neutral participant-observer role. He seeks to carry out the treatment without transference gratifications; in a state of abstinence.

After the elimination of the patient's resistance, repressed memories become conscious. Thereafter, the analyst is able to show the patient that he is still preoccupied with infantile wishes and narcissistic mortifications. By interpretation and reconstruction, the analyst tries to demonstrate to the patient that his neurotic symptoms or character traits (representing partial frustrations and partial gratifications of his infantile trends) protect him from becoming conscious of infantile threats that have remained unresolved despite his age. Schematically, each psychoanalysis can be divided into two parts: The patient and the analyst try to examine and isolate the problems which appear not to make sense. This part of the analytic procedure is relatively simple in symptom neuroses, but quite complicated in character neuroses, perversions and psychopathy. The second part of the analysis consists of helping the patient to use the material he brings up, and to understand its unconscious meaning. The seemingly senseless material becomes meaningful; it is recognized as belonging to the archaic history of the patient's childhood and infancy. As a result, the patient begins to think, feel and behave like a mature individual. The infantile needs, the neurotic feelings of guilt, self-punishments and anxiety become obsolete.

IV

Applied psychoanalysis began with Freud's study of anthropological data from the psychoanalytic point of view in "Totem and Taboo." This has been followed by numerous studies, by Freud and many others, on the application of the psychoanalytic method to the study of the arts, history, social phenomena, mythology, education, etc. Today, the impact of psychoanalytic thinking extends far beyond the immediate therapy of symptom neurosis which was the impetus for its origin.

ADDITIONAL READINGS

Alexander F., *Fundamentals of Psychoanalysis*. Nor, 1948.

Brill, A., "Basic Principles of Psychoanalysis." *Q*, 18, 1949.

Freud, Anna, 1936, *The Ego and the Mechanisms of Defense*. IUP, 1946.

Fromm-Reichmann, F., "Psychoanalytic Psychotherapy with Psychotics. The Influence of the Modification in Technique on Present Trends in Psychoanalysis." *Ps*, 6, 1943.

Frosch, J., "Special Problems of Psychoanalytic Therapy." *AnSurvPsa*, 1, 1950.

Gardner, G. E., "The Therapeutic Process. II. The Therapeutic Process from the Point of View of Psychoanalytic Theory." *Ops*. 22, 1952.

Hartmann, H., *Ego Psychology and the Problems of Adaptation*. IUP, 1958.
      Essays on Ego Psychology. IUP, 1964.

Hawkins, M., "Psychoanalysis of Children." *BMC*, 4, 1940.

Hermann, I., "Psychoanalyse und Logik: Individuell-logische Untersuchungen aus der Psychoanalytichen Praxis." *IntPV*, 1924.

Neiditsch, S., "Die Psychoanalyse in Russland während der letzten Jahre." *Z*, 7, 1921.

Putnam, J. J., "Psychoanalyse und Philosophie." *C*, 3, 1913.

Servadio, E., "Psychoanalyse und Telepathie." *Im*, 21, 1935.

Strachey, J., "The Nature of the Therapeutic Action of Psychoanalysis." *IntJPsa*, 15, 1934.

Zulliger, H., "Psychoanalysis and the Form-Interpretation Test." *IntJPsa*, 31, 1950.

1680

PSYCHOANALYTIC ANTHROPOLOGY is employed to examine and explain life in general, and to further an understanding of the customs and social rules in particular. This psychoanalytical approach utilizes the scientific data gathered in the study of neurotics, separated from its therapeutic factors, in such a manner that its validation must be limited to circumstantial evidence. Anthropology may be described as a science *in statu nascendi* which developed in various directions. It may concentrate on sociological phenomena of various cultures or may even examine religion, philosophy and art and try to explain the connection between these phenomena and human society.

Freud (1913) introduced psychoanalytic anthropology in writing "Totem and Taboo." He applied what he had discovered in his treatment of neurotics to the study of the unconscious factors responsible for the behavior of primitive people. One of the fundamental results of psychoanalytic anthropology was his examination of *taboo* as a cultural and psychic factor.

In his paper, "Psychology of the Mass and Analysis of the Ego," Freud (1921) studied the relationship of the individual to others, and the psychology of the mass, with special emphasis on the importance of the leader. These examinations in ego psychology were continued by such writers as Hartmann, Kris, and Loewenstein.

In "Civilization and Its Discontents," Freud (1930) expressed the idea that culture is based chiefly on the control of aggression. In other papers, he applied psychoanalysis to the problems of anthropology, in particular: "The Future of an Illusion" and

"Moses and Monotheism," written in 1927 and 1937, respectively.

Freud's pupils (Jones, Rank, Reich, Marie Bonaparte, Winterstein, and Róheim) used the psychoanalytical approach in studying myth, legend, and ritual. These writers also used anthropological findings and applied them to the study of the individual.

Ethnologists like Malinowski have accepted one part of psychoanalysis and used it to explain their theories of culture. Kardiner and Linton introduced the idea of the basic personality structure; i.e. the dependence of the basic personality features on certain cultures. Erickson succeeded in describing a psychoanalytical theory of culture. Finally, other authors like Parin and Morgenthaler examined North African cultures, applying these psychoanalytic theories.

1681

PSYCHOANALYTIC DICTIONARY. The need for such a work was foreseen as long ago as 1924.* In that year, Storfer published seven samples from a work in progress; the dictionary, however, was never completed. The next attempt to produce a dictionary of psychoanalytic terms was undertaken by R. Sterba in 1936. Unlike the earlier work, Sterba completed all the concepts through the letter *F*. Here, Freud (1936) recognized the importance of the work, and, equally, the many difficulties it presented.

REFERENCES

Freud, S., 1936, "Preface to Richard Sterba's Dictionary of Psycho-Analysis." *SE*, 22:253, 1964.

Sterba, R., *Handwörterbuch der Psychoanalyse. IntPV*, 1936.

Storfer, A. J., "Samples from a *Dictionary of Psychoanalysis*." *Z*, 10:350–372, 1924.

1682

PSYCHOANALYTIC METHODOLOGY. Psychoanalysis uses explanatory and descriptive terms in much the same way as do other scientific methods.

---

* A glossary of terms was published in 1924 by the Hungarian Psychoanalytic Society. Unfortunately, all copies were destroyed during the Nazi occupation. [Private communication, S. Lorand to ed.]

The descriptive terms are the result of the analyst's sense-organ perceptions, while the explanatory terms are based on heuristic hypotheses derived from these observations. The aim of the analytical method is to establish a circumstantial chain of evidence which fully explains such phenomena as parapraxes, dreams, psychoneuroses, etc. When such a chain is established and a subsequent therapeutic change occurs, the analytical interpretation can be considered to have been validated.

The presence of those mental factors which are characteristic of the patient's behavior is brought to consciousness by *free association*. In this, the patient must be willing to try to say what goes through his mind while engaged in the analytic situation. This basic rule provides an access to the analytic material and is aimed at achieving therapeutic results. When the patient or the analyst notice something of significance, they try to isolate it, and to find the unconscious element connected with the free association in order to establish its causal relationship.

The analytical method is also used in the study of educational, social and aesthetic problems. Freud repeatedly emphasized that such an application of what was discovered to take place in the formation of a neurosis should only be used with great caution. While it is true that psychoanalytical research proved valuable when applied to various subjects, it also mobilized justified criticism whenever the analyst failed to follow Freud's advice. In this regard, Hartmann (1964) noted:

"It is obvious that the most serious errors can occur if we allow ourselves to be guided solely by the self-evidence of psychological understanding when we judge a psychological connection. For example: we meet a man who appears to be strong and in good health and who abhors and fights anything sickly, weak or half-hearted. The man's own health and well-being makes this attitude understandable; we experienced this meaning-connection as directly self-evident. But now, let us assume, we 'get to know the man better,' and we learn from him or from someone else that he suffers from a serious defect which he is loath to admit, and which has until now remained concealed from us, and that he is basically not only in very poor health but psychologically also a very insecure person. Now, too, we understand,

and the connection between the man's own weakness and insecurity and his abhorrence of these things in others is clear to us, and the insight in this connection is accompanied by an experience of self-evidence. We should not think of this example as merely an exception. Everyone encounters such cases in his daily life. We must then say: the experience of self-evidence has deceived us; or: self-evidence opposes self-evidence and the decision as to truth or falsity obviously cannot be derived from self-evidence. The understandable connection has, in a concrete case, proved to be a pseudo connection. But it is precisely the exposing of such pseudo connections which plays so great a role in psychoanalysis."

Psychoanalysis has given a better understanding of the technique of jokes and of the problem of aesthetic pleasure. Nonetheless, psychoanalysis does not offer a prescription of how to create beauty or how to recognize a work of art. Psychoanalysis, like other sciences, has contributed and will continue to contribute to an understanding of basic human problems, provided it stays within the limits of the scientific method and avoids the formulation of a *Weltanschauung*. Freud (1927) did not believe that modifications of scientific ideas and theories should be considered as revolutionary. A law which at first appeared to be generally accepted has many times, in a later age, turned out to be only a special example or has been partly contradicted by another law. Consequently, what represents the truth is in the beginning a general outline which requires additional study to render an understanding of truth more exact. On many subjects, science has no other choice but to use a trial hypothesis, which may be rejected if it is proven incorrect. Freud also pointed out that scientific examination which can take place with the help of our own sense organs should not be rejected, simply because they do not appear to represent the real nature of what is not apparent.

Related Concept: METHODOLOGY.

REFERENCES

Freud, S., 1927, "The Future of an Illusion." *SE*, 21:55, 1961.
Hartmann, H., *Essays on Ego Psychology*, IUP, pp. 380–381, 1964.

1683

PSYCHODYNAMICS is the approach in psychoanalysis which explains all mental phenomena as resulting from those conflicts which arise between the various "parts" of the personality. For example, such phenomena as parapraxes and dreams are understood to be compromise formations of id wishes, ego and superego defenses. Thus, a description of the interaction and counterreaction between these forces present in each part of the total personality—their origin, aim and objectual presentation—would constitute a dynamic approach. Elsewhere, this approach is defined in terms of processes, of development, of progression or regression (Fenichel, 1945).

At first, Freud (1900) employed a systematic approach in describing mental activity, dividing the personality into the system conscious-preconscious and the system unconscious. Later, he (1923) introduced the topographic approach (also referred to as structural), and divided the total personality into id, ego and superego. The boundaries of the topographic cut across the lines separating the systems of conscious-preconscious and unconscious, exempting the id which was totally unconscious. This conceptualization lent itself to a more precise description of the repressed and repressing factors; thus, the demands of id wishes and of their ego defenses could then both be understood to be unconscious.

Freud (1933) admitted that the division of the mental apparatus into id, ego and superego would be easier to accept if one could assume that the id was always unconscious; the ego, conscious; and the superego, preconscious. This, however, is not the case: analytical observation shows that the id is completely unconscious, with the ego and superego partly conscious, preconscious and unconscious.

Case History

An unconscious cannibalistic wish prevented a patient from asking the waiter for a table, and thus he avoided the unconscious mobilization and consequent damming up of his cannibalistic wishes. This patient, instead of saying, "May I have a table?" asked, "May I have a room?" The word "room" implied his wish to go to bed with the lady he had invited to dinner. The patient's slip of the tongue was used as a countercathexis and represented a defense of his cannibalistic needs.

Related Concepts: ECONOMIC APPROACH; STRUCTURAL (TOPOGRAPHIC) APPROACH; SYSTEMATIC (QUALITATIVE OR DESCRIPTIVE) APPROACH.

REFERENCES

Fenichel, O., *The Psychoanalytic Theory of Neurosis.* Nor, p. 11, 1945.
Freud, S.: 1900, "The Interpretation of Dreams." *SE*, 5:536–540, 1953.
      1933, "New Introductory Lectures on Psycho-Analysis." *SE*, 22:72–73, 1964.

ADDITIONAL READINGS

Eidelberg, L., *An Outline of a Comparative Pathology of the Neuroses.* IUP, 1954.
Guntrip, H., *Personality Structure and Human Interaction. The Developing Synthesis of Psychodynamic Theory.* IUP, 1961.

1684

PSYCHOGENESIS is a hypothesis which allows for the use of a psychological approach in demonstrating the causes which are responsible for a certain event. A compulsion to wash every five minutes, for instance, may represent a defense against an unconscious anal wish. If such a psychogenetic approach is correct, the analyst may anticipate that he will discover during the analysis some traumatic experiences in his patient's childhood which, when the resistance against them is overcome, will demonstrate to the patient that his act of washing is directed not against dirt but against the wish to be dirty. Finally, after such a wish becomes conscious and is repudiated by the patient, his compulsion to wash will disappear.

The hysterical blindness resembles the blindness of a hypnotized individual who has accepted the order to be blind. Certain experiments which mobilize emotions may be used to demonstrate that the patient denies having seen the objects used in such experiments; he reacts as if he had seen them. As a result of a dissociation between conscious and unconscious systems, a patient may develop hysterical blindness. This blindness must be regarded as an expression and not as a cause of his hysteria. [Freud, 1910.]

Related Concept: CAUSALITY.

REFERENCE

Freud, S., 1910, "The Psycho-Analytic View of Psychogenic Disturbance of Vision." *SE*, 11:211–212, 1957.

1685

"PSYCHOPATHOLOGY OF EVERYDAY LIFE, THE," published in 1901, has been translated into many languages, a popular work which helped prevent psychoanalysis from passing unnoticed. The medical world reacted either with iron silence or with hostility (with very few exceptions).

In this book, Freud offered a number of examples, of his own and of his pupils. Unfortunately many of these examples depend on a play on words and are therefore not suitable for translation. Therefore, Brill, his first American translator, substituted a number of English examples for those supplied by Freud.

The first mention of Freud's interest in the study of parapraxis (Fehlleistung), occurs in Freud's letter to Fliess (1898). Freud's interest in the study of the unconscious causes of parapraxes continued almost to the end of his life. Strachey (1960) noted that Freud's "belief is in the universal application of determinism to mental events. This is the truth which he insists upon in the final chapter of the book: it should be possible in theory to discover the psychical determinants of every smallest detail of the processes of the mind. And perhaps the fact that this aim seemed more nearly attainable in the case of parapraxes was another reason why they had a peculiar attraction for Freud."

According to Freud, certain errors (parapraxes) are characterized by the fact that they take place within normal limits; they are only temporary. In addition, whenever a parapraxis occurs, we don't know what caused it; only analysis will be able to bring into the open the unconscious material responsible for a given parapraxis. As far as superstition goes, Freud believed that the exploration of the unconscious would elucidate what appears to us as mysterious. Freud quoted an experience, in which he had met a couple about whom he was thinking at that moment. A closer examination of this phenomenon disclosed that he had seen the couple when he was still far away but for certain reasons had denied this sense organ perception.

Freud never claimed that all errors have an unconscious meaning, but he insisted that many of them could be analyzed. He concluded: "The phenomena can be traced back to incompletely suppressed* psychical material."

Related Concepts: DREAMS; JOKE (WIT); PUN; SUBLIMATION.

REFERENCES

Freud, S., 1901, "The Psychopathology of Everyday Life." *SE*, 6:239–254, 257–258, 264, 272, 279, 1960.
Strachey, J., Editorial note. *SE*, 6:xiii–xiv, 1960.

1686

PSYCHOPATHY. Many psychopaths cannot be psychoanalyzed because they suffer from the results of their defense mechanisms without realizing they are sick. The psychopaths who enter psychoanalytic treatment do so because of other neurotic troubles. It would appear that by modifying the technique of analytical treatment the analyst may be able to help such patients establish transference and, thus, to create an analytical condition conducive to treatment. At first, the patient may be unwilling to admit that his troubles are self-provoked and be skeptical about his ability to change his behavior. Only when the patient in the course of treatment discovers that he is using his superego, not as an integrated ego-syntonic agency, but as an ego-alien authority projected to the external world, will he begin to try to understand the unconscious causes of his neurosis.

In reviewing the case history of a Miss Smith, Eidelberg (1958) observed: "A few weeks after Miss Smith started her treatment, she began to arrive late for her appointments. I explained to her the reasons why we must insist that the patient be on time, and suggested that she was late because of some unconscious resistance. My suggestion infuriated her, and she accused me of being completely lacking in the tolerance and empathy an

* Here used as a synonym of *repression*.

analyst ought to have. After having listened for a time, I interrupted her flow of free associations, and asked her to try to criticize her own accusations. She was surprised that I had dared to interrupt her. She thought that free associations commanded the absolute respect of the analyst, and that the patient always may use them for the discharge of tension. The idea that free association is used only to obtain an insight into the unconscious, and that the elimination of the censorship should be temporary, was foreign to her. I asked her whether she did not feel guilty because of the hostility she expressed. Miss Smith denied any feeling of guilt, and again expressed surprise that I expected her to feel guilty. She thought that a patient should not feel guilty because of any free associations, and regarded my question as a non-analytical attempt to humiliate her. She objected strongly to my explanation that the freedom to say whatever went through her head did not mean that the patient should destroy his faculty of self-criticism. Rather, we want him to verbalize the idea he has, *and* to criticize it. Consequently, a patient obeying the 'analytic rule' should not eliminate his feelings of guilt, but must express his hostile ideas *in spite* of these feelings.

"Instead of bringing up material which would explain her lateness, Miss Smith preferred to be on time. She could not, as she said, afford the luxury of fighting a war on two fronts. Her lover had begun to lose interest in her, and she thought that she had to try to keep me, at least. She would not repeat the mistake of Hitler, whom she greatly admired, but whom she criticized for having declared war on Russia. She regarded a dictatorship as the only sensible way to govern, and condemned democracy because of its dependence on the majority. Using such examples as literary best sellers, she tried to prove that the judgment of the majority is always inferior. Fortunately, her interest in politics was small and she preferred to use other forms of resistance. In her analysis, however, she wanted to preserve her dictatorial ideas by insisting that either she or I must dominate the other. In the transference situation, it became possible to show her that while she enumerated her objections to the democratic form of government, she meant to condemn not the inferior tastes of the majority, but the use of a rational approach.

She could not deny that a dictatorship would not protect her from the low mentality of the masses, because she knew too many examples in which the masses were prepared to accept a dictator, and in which the dictator was in favor of the popular demands of the intellectually uninterested citizens.

"At this stage of her analysis, her conflict with her lover was probably decisive in her decision to stay with me. On the other hand, this conflict may have been provoked by her being in analysis. Her lover resented her treatment. He felt that analysis offended the dignity of the human soul. Not being able to understand and study psychoanalysis, he preferred to rely on his intuition. Even a superficial appraisal of the therapy Miss Smith sought frightened him because it meant the acceptance of the limitations of his mental power. It is possible that his rejection of Miss Smith represented his defense against his jealousy, as my patient suggested, but in her analysis, we obviously were unable to analyze the unconscious motives of others.

"In the beginning of her treatment, Miss Smith avoided the examination and the discussion of her affair, and the possible unconscious motives responsible for it. Now, as this affair was breaking up, she wanted me to help her keep her lover, and was prepared, therefore, to cooperate. I made my point clear by saying that analysis could not teach her how to retain the love, or even the attention of Mr. Z., but that it might help her free herself from this involvement in case we were to find out that Mr. Z. was not available, through no fault of hers.

"A dream gave us more insight into the unconscious mechanisms of her infatuation. She dreamed that she was having sexual intercourse with her friend, after which he walked out, leaving his penis in her vagina. The patient suggested that this dream referred to her friend abandoning her for his former homosexual partner. Leaving the penis in her vagina meant that her friend had castrated himself in order to return to his homosexual practices. Having been reminded that her dreams should be used to examine *her* wishes, she resented, but could not deny, that this dream indicated her wish to take away the penis of her friend. After this idea was verbalized, many associations appeared in which the passionate violence of her sexual intercourse appeared to be connected with such a castrating urge. Admiration for her boy friend in general, and for his penis in particular, which appeared at first as a legitimate need for a male partner, seemed now to be caused by the desire to deprive her partner of his penis, becoming a male herself.

"It is my impression that whenever a patient is dominated by a desire connected with a part of the body of a love object, this partial interest represents not only the wish to have an object with such an attribute, but also indicates the desire to become similar to the object. Furthermore, the wish of a female to have a penis, and the wish of a male to have breasts, means not only the wish to change one's own sex for the other, but rather to acquire the opposite sex *in addition*.

"Miss Smith's need to have sexual intercourse every day was not only a sign of her physical desires, but also was due to the idea that she must perish if deprived of a penis for too long a time. A criminal activity, her stealing, meant getting this penis. Her lack of a feeling of guilt was caused by her unconscious conviction that her penis had been stolen from her, and she was therefore entitled to get it back. The urge to have a penis often produces a 'penis envy,' which may cause various symptoms, neurotic character traits, or perversions. In this case, however, the patient seemed to be aware of her penis envy before she received my interpretation. While she resented my suggestion that her dream indicated her wish to castrate men, she seemed to have accepted this urge, and considered it proper to castrate her unfaithful friend. The only reason why she was prepared to refrain from the discharge of such a hostile desire was her fear of external punishment. She claimed that, as a result of her analysis, her courage had been diminished, and she thought that she had 'lost face' by not attacking Mr. Z. physically, and thus had lost an opportunity to regain his affection.

"As analytic therapy is based on the idea that an infantile wish will be rejected by the total personality when brought into consciousness, an acceptance of such an infantile wish by the total personality seems to threaten our therapeutic efforts. The psychopath appears to be an individual who does not bother to repress his infantile wishes, and behaves as if he had no superego. However, in analysis—if the psychopath is in need of our help—we usually are able to find out that he, too, has unconscious wishes, in which consciousness is prevented by strong unconscious resistances.

"In this case, the wish to castrate, which appears horrible to the total personality of the neurotic patient, was accepted and approved of by Miss Smith. The technical problem was obviously not to try to induce the patient to reject this wish, but to find out whether the wish was not being used to hide another wish, even more frightening. I communicated this idea to my patient, but either I was wrong, or her resistance was too severe, and I failed to obtain any material in this connection. My attempts to examine the deeper part of the dream mobilized her hostility. She wanted to know why I should try to persuade her that the wish to castrate could be used as a screen for some other desire. It is obvious that whenever an analyst makes a suggestion, asks a question, or explains a problem, he acts in that way because he thinks that what he is saying is true, and because he believes that stating the truth, while it may be unpleasant or even frightening, will finally help the patient.

"The psychopath, similar to the character neurotic, suffers because the external world has more power than he has, and his conflict with the external world therefore leads to his defeat. One of the reasons why he may be prepared to cooperate with us is the hope that he may become stronger after his treatment, and be able to defy external authorities more successfully. At the same time, he is suspicious that the analyst is on the side of society, and is trying to 'tame' him.

"In such a situation, I make no bones about being in favor of the social structure of the society in which I live. This does not mean that I am in favor of all the laws we have today, nor does it imply that I am blind to the many injustices and abuses to which the individual is exposed. I regard many of the orders and prohibitions we are expected to obey as *malum necessarium*, but I think that their sudden lifting would lead to chaos. Having made my point of view clear, I usually succeed in showing to the patient the fact that I am not interested in persuading him to accept my approach. Should he decide, after his unconscious wishes have become conscious, to fight against me or the society to which I belong, he will have to do so outside the analytic situation. Differences of opinion do not necessarily mean hostility, but a hostile patient will exploit such a difference as a means and a justification for achieving a hostile discharge against himself or others. We have to have agreement from our patients on the answer to only one question, i.e., as to whether they should be allowed to retain their method of solving their problems unconsciously, or whether a conscious decision should replace the unconscious one.

"Similar to character neurotics, the psychopath approves of himself and does not feel sick. In order to be cured, the patient has to be prepared to accept the split within himself which would be implied by the development of a faculty of self-criticism. In this case, Miss Smith had started her critical self-examination before she came to me, and from a technical point of view, she had to be encouraged to retain this healthy split between the reasonable and unreasonable parts of her personality. It happens often enough that the patient, under the pressure of analysis, discovers the assets of his neurosis and tries to present a united front against our efforts to analyze him.

"No patient likes his unconscious wishes. Facing them, he gets scared, and he would rather be neurotic than to be dominated openly by the dynamic power of his infantile drives. The psychopath does not *suffer* from the end-results of his unconscious defense mechanisms, or he is not aware of such suffering. His psychopathic character trait protects him from recognizing that what he is doing is the result of a power beyond his conscious control. Unlike the psychotic, he is aware of being different from others, perhaps superior to them, and he realizes that he provokes at least some of the conflicts he is continually experiencing. However, he is not aware that his behavior does not express a simple gratification of what he wants, but serves to discharge *unconscious* wishes under a mask.

"Under normal conditions, the conscious decision to gratify a wish represents a fair compromise between the id, the ego, the superego, and the external world, but the neurotic is able to act without being aware of what these divisions of his personality are interested in. In this particular case, it was the superego which the patient most obstinately refused to see, while she was prepared to accept the id and the ego. In most of the interpretations I tried to give her, she was quite ready to acknowledge the presence of aggressive wishes. For instance, in the dream in which her friend walked out, leaving his penis in her vagina, she had no difficulty in accepting my interpretation that the dream represented a satisfaction of her castration impulses. However, she refused to investigate the possibility that this wish to castrate represented a defense against some other desire. One has the impression that she was in favor of, and accepted, any interpretation which showed how aggressive she was.

"The analysis of her attitude to men showed that, with men who were interested in loving her and being loved by her, she was a complete failure. Having no conscious desire for love, it was relatively easy for her to pretend to be involved, and to reject any man who would fall for her. If she met a masochist, she would keep on teasing him, even allowing him to undress her, but she would prevent a genital approach. Should the man turn out to be more active, she would give in very soon, 'make herself cheap,' pretend that she was raped, and hate the man for having humiliated her. Everything was permitted, as long as it would not make her happy. She had heard that patients fall in love with their analysts, and often referred to me as a prostitute who made his living by offering himself to any stranger prepared to pay the price, insisting that the difference between her former practise and mine was that I had a license.

"In addition to her inability or unwillingness to recognize that she had positive desires also, she kept on denying the presence of her superego. She considered her decision to give up her criminal activities as being caused solely by the recognition that she could make more money and take fewer risks by being a legitimate business woman. Analytical experience shows that all patients have a superego, although many of them succeed in behaving as if they did not. Furthermore, we know that the part of the personality which the patient hides is usually the one which is of the greatest importance to him.

"One day, a symptom which neither the patient nor I had considered psychosomatic disappeared. She had complained for years about a pain in her right arm which had been diagnosed as rheumatic and treated without any success. A few days before her depersonalization started, the patient brought in a dream, the content of which she forgot, with the exception of the image of a penis which looked like an arm. Now, the patient suddenly 'understood' that she used her arm to satisfy her unconscious wish to have a penis. In the beginning of her treatment, I had tried to point out to her that she was holding her arm in a rather unusual and obviously uncomfortable position while lying on the couch, but she had rejected with scorn my suggestion that she might analyze the meaning of the way she held her arm. Now, without my help, she had arrived at the conclusion that her arm was kept outstretched and stiff to simulate an erect penis, and she suffered the pain in her muscles as a result. A few days after she had arrived at this interpretation and had relaxed her arm, the pain disappeared completely.

"The resistance against the recognition of the connections between her symptom, the wish to have a penis of her own, and her provocation of men, was relatively mild. On the other hand, she resisted strongly my interpretation that her symptom indicated, in addition, the presence of a wish to love the penis of her father, and the punitive action of the superego.

"I have the impression that, as a result of the partial acceptance of this interpretation, and the superficial recognition of the importance of her superego, her psychopathic behavior decreased in intensity. Unfortunately, instead of becoming more normal, she developed the symptom of depersonalization.

"During the analysis of her depersonalization, her psychopathic character traits continued to be analyzed. In summing up the results of this work, I may say that her psychopathic behavior was caused by an unconscious defense against a sexual wish belonging to the phallic stage. In her criminal activities, and in her role as a prostitute, she partly gratified and partly warded off this wish. To steal meant to castrate men. Having sex with men who had to pay her meant depriving men of money and punishing them for their ability to humiliate her by refusing to 'surrender' the penis.

"At the same time, her psychopathic behavior gratified and controlled her infantile exhibitionistic wishes. Stealing meant, 'Nobody sees what I do.' Watching people before she decided to steal represented a discharge of inspectionistic energy used in countercathexis. The same meaning was present in her 'watching' of the penis of the men with whom she had sexual intercourse."

Related Concepts: BREAST ENVY; PENIS ENVY.

REFERENCE

Eidelberg, L., "Psychoanalyse einer Psychopathin." *P*, 12:447–459, 1958.

ADDITIONAL READINGS

Greenacre, P., "Conscience in the Psychopath." *Ops*, 15, 1945.
Karpman, B., "From the Autobiography of a Liar; Toward the Clarification of the Problem of Psychopathic States." *PQ*, 23, 1949.

1687

PSYCHOSIS denotes a major category of mental illness, characterized by severely impaired reality testing, and, possibly, severe regression, distortions of perception, hallucinations, delusions, and lessened control over instinctual wishes. The psychoses include the so-called organic psychoses, where brain pathology is demonstrable; and the so-called functional psychoses of melancholia, paranoia, and schizophrenia, where organic causation is debatable and as yet unproven.

Although Freud's contributions to the subject of psychosis are fragmentary, no one else has contributed more to our understanding of this still obscure subject. One of the basic tenets of psychoanalysis is that all mental events are meaningful and can be understood genetically. Freud, Abraham, and others have been able to interpret the significance of psychotic symptoms, language, and behavior. Freud (1896) demonstrated that a paranoid patient's hallucinations "were nothing else than parts of the content of repressed childhood experiences." This was in keeping with an attempt to see psychosis and neurosis as phenomena involving *defenses* against unbearable experiences and feelings. The withdrawal from reality, Freud (1894) noted, was the way that "the ego has fended off the incompatible idea through a flight into psychosis."

In his classic study of the Schreber case, Freud (1911) introduced his major formulations about psychosis. These deal primarily with the break with external reality seen in acute psychosis (mainly schizophrenia and paranoia, lumped together by Freud in his designation *paraphrenia*). In the hypothetical first step in breaking with reality, the patient withdraws his libido. End-of-the-world fantasies were seen as a projection of this internal catastrophe, and megalomania was ascribed to the detached libido turning back onto the ego.

Freud felt that the dispositional fixation points for psychotic patients were in very early development, "to be looked for in a stage of libidinal development before object choice is established— that is the phase of auto erotism and narcissism" (Freud, 1913). Abraham (1924) felt that schizophrenia involved fixation at and regression to the first oral stage of libido development, melancholia regression to the second oral stage, and paranoia regression to the first anal stage. Freud called these diseases *narcissistic neuroses*, in contrast to the *transference neuroses*; he felt that psychoanalysis offered little therapeutic promise for these patients, since the capacity to form a transference to the physician seemed to be lacking. Most analysts today would modify this statement.

The withdrawal of libido from the external world was given a more specific meaning in Freud's (1915) paper on the unconscious. The internalized object-cathexes (*thing-cathexes* of the system *Ucs.*) are given up. The cathexes of *word-presentations* in the system *Pcs* are retained "or rather recathected as part of the attempt at restitution."

In the light of the new structural hypothesis of the mind, Freud (1924) attempted to outline the difference between neurosis and psychosis. The neurosis was the result of a conflict between the id and the ego; the psychosis, of a conflict between the external world and the ego. Freud here brings in factors that we have still not weighed and understood properly: the impulses derived from the psychotic id (are they stronger, or qualitatively different?), and the mysteries of the psychotic's ego weaknesses.

Freud (1933) increasingly stressed the importance of structural damage over the factor of intolerable reality. He suggested that a crystal breaks in accordance with its structure, which is an example of the structural approach in analysis. The total personality of mental patients is split in a similar way.

Schematically speaking, the symptom neurotic is able to criticize himself, and able to admit that the description of his complaints does not make sense because he treats the external world as part of himself. The character neurotic and the pervert deny that their conflicts are caused by their unconscious defenses against unconscious wishes, but, with analytic help, they may succeed in changing their minds. Unlike psychotics, they are able, and often willing, to engage in such self-examination. Most psychotics, on the other hand, are unable and unwilling to examine their troubles. A phobic patient may say: "I cannot cross the street. I am afraid of a bus. I agree that my fears are out of proportion, but still I cannot cross the street. However, I am prepared to examine my fear." A character neurotic will say: "I do not cross the street because, unlike the idiots who risk their lives and get killed, I enjoy staying home." But he is prepared to examine his decisions and their causes. The psychotic, however, says, dogmatically: "The bus drivers are after me and I must hide at home. You should examine them, not me!" [Eidelberg, 1954.]

Related Concepts: AUTOEROTISM; DEFENSE MECHANISMS; DELUSIONS; HALLUCINATIONS; MELANCHOLIA; PARANOIA; PRIMARY PROCESS; SCHIZOPHRENIA.

REFERENCES

Abraham, K., 1924, "A Short History of the Development of the Libido, Viewed in the Light of Mental Disorders." *SPA*, pp. 418–502, 1942.
Eidelberg, L., *An Outline of a Comparative Pathology of the Neuroses.* IUP, pp. 214–216, 1954.
Freud, S.: 1894, "The Neuro-Psychoses of Defence." *SE*, 3:59, 1962.
1896, "Further Remarks on the Neuro-Psychoses of Defence." *SE*, 3:181, 1962.
1911, "Psycho-Analytic Notes on an Autobiographical Account of a Case of Paranoia (Dementia Paranoides)." *SE*, 12:318, 1958.
1913, "The Disposition to Obsessional Neurosis." *SE*, 12:318, 1958.
1915, "The Unconscious." *SE*, 14:196–203, 1957.
1917, "Introductory Lectures on Psycho-Analysis." *SE*, 16:422, 1963.
1924, "The Loss of Reality in Neurosis and Psychosis." *SE*, 19:151, 1961.
1933, "New Introductory Lectures on Psycho-Analysis." *SE*, 22:16, 59, 154, 1964.

ADDITIONAL READINGS

Bychowski, G., "The Problem of Latent Psychosis." *JAPA*, 1, 1953.
Ekstein, R., J. Wallerstein, & A. Mandelbaum, "Countertransference in the Residential Treatment of Children; Treatment Failure in a Child with a Symbiotic Psychosis." *PsaStC*, 14, 1959.
Freud, S.: 1913, "On Beginning the Treatment." *SE*, 12.
1917, "Mourning and Melancholia." *SE*, 14, 1957.
1920, "Beyond the Pleasure Principle." *SE*, 18.
1930, "Civilization and Its Discontents." *SE*, 21.
Geleerd, E. R., "A Contribution to the Problem of Psychoses in Childhood." *PsaStC*, 2, 1946.
Isaacs, S., "An Acute Psychotic Anxiety Occurring in a Boy of Four Years." *IntJPsa*, 24, 1943.
Mahler, M.: "On Child Psychosis and Schizophrenia: Autistic and Symbiotic Infantile Psychoses." *PsaStC*, 7, 1952.
& P. Elkisch, "Some Observations on Disturbances of the Ego in a Case of Infantile Psychosis." *PsaStC*, 8, 1953.
Malamud, W., "The Application of Psychoanalytic Principles in Interpreting the Psychoses. *R*, 16, 1929.
Romm, M., "Transient Psychotic Episodes During Psychoanalysis." *JAPA*, 5, 1957.
Schultz-Hencke, H., "Die Struktur der Psychose." *ZNP*, 175, 1943.

1688

PSYCHOSOMATIC. Fenichel (1945) differentiated between two categories of functional disturbances. "One of them is physical in nature and consists of physiological changes caused by the inappropriate use of the function in question. The other one . . . is an expression of a fantasy in a 'body language' and is directly accessible to psychoanalysis in the same way as a dream." Glover (1949) defined the term as "the organic changes consequent on affective changes, the organic manifestation of dammed-up instinct and physical consequences of unconscious attitudes or unconsciously determined behaviour patterns."

Freud introduced the concept of nonpsychogenic symptoms in 1910. The fact that analysis examines only what is called mental and neglects the organic factor is not due to the analyst's contempt for the latter. Freud always pointed out the importance of the organic factor and he spoke of "somatic compliance," a term used to indicate the choice of the organ affected by the neurotic symptom.

In this, it would appear that Freud referred to those psychogenic symptoms caused by the unconscious gratification of repressed wishes, provided the gratification involved an organ or its function. An analytical interpretation may, however, be restorative; the patient suffering from writer's cramp may be cured once he has recognized that his cramp is the result of his wish to use the hand as a vagina and his pen as a penis. This unconscious attempt at bisexuality may appeal to the patient because it makes him independent of a woman. A similar process holds true of conversions from the oral or anal stage, independently of the organ involved. All conversions, despite the unconscious gratification, produce a certain degree of unpleasure. In addition, there is a secondary organic change. For instance, in prolonged hysterical coughing the patient may develop a nonpsychogenic pharyngitis which will require a treatment even after the hysterical symptom has been eliminated.

Related Concept: CONVERSION AND CONVERSION SYMPTOMS.

REFERENCES

Freud, S., 1910, "The Psycho-Analytic View of Psychogenic Disturbances of Vision." *SE*, 11:217–218, 1957.

Glover, E., *Psycho-Analysis.* SP, p. 348, 1949.

ADDITIONAL READINGS

Alexander, F., & H. Visotsky, "Psychosomatic Study of a Case of Asthma." *PSM*, 17, 1955.

Arlow, J. A., "Psychoanalytic Studies in Psychosomatic Medicine." *AnSurvPsa*, 3, 1952.

Beache, F. A., "Psychosomatic 'Phenomena in Animals'." *PSM*, 14, 1952.

Bieber, I., "The Psychosomatic Symptom," in J. Wortis, *Basic Problems in Psychiatry.* G&S, 1953.

Davidson, H. B., "The Psychosomatic Aspects of Educated Childbirth." *NYSJM*, 53, 1953.

Fries, M. E., "Psychosomatic Relationships Between Mother and Infant." *PSM*, 6, 1944.

Grinker, R., "Brief Psychotherapy in Psychosomatic Problems." *PSM*, 9, 1947.

Groen, J., "Psychosomatische Forschung als Erforschung des Es." *P*, 4, 1951.

Grotjahn, M., "Psychoanalytic Contributions to Psychosomatic Medicine—A Bibliography." *PSM*, 6, 1944.

Lofgren, L., "A Case of Bronchial Asthma with Unusual Dynamic Factors, Treated by Psychotherapy and Psycho-Analysis." *IntJPsa*, 42, 1961.

Roose, L. J., "The Influence of Psychosomatic Research on the Psychoanalytic Process." *JAPA*, 8, 1960.

Schwartz, L. A., "Psychosomatic Aspects of Cardiospasm With Case Presentation." *Samiksa*, 3, 1949.

Stern, E., "Zum Problem der Spezifizität der Persönlichkeitstypen und der Konflikte in der Psychosomatischen Medizin." *PSM*, 4, 1957.

Sperling, M., "Psychosis and Psychosomatic Illness." *IntJPsa*, 36, 1955.

Strauss, A., "Unconscious Mental Processes and the Psychosomatic Concept." *IntJPsa*, 36, 1955.

Tarachow, S., "A Psychosomatic Theory Based on the Concepts of Mastery and Resolution of Tension." *R*, 32, 1945.

Uexkull, T. von. "Möglichkeiten und Grenzen Psychosomatischer Betrachtung." *Nervenarzt*, 26, 1955.

Weiss, E., "Psychosomatic Aspects of Hypertension." *JAMA*, 120, 1942.

Wisdom, J. O., "On a Differentiating Mechanism of Psychosomatic Disorder." *IntJPsa*, 41, 1960.

1689

PSYCHOSOMATIC SUICIDE, according to M. Sperling (1955), is a phenomenon observed especially in patients with ulcerative colitis and bronchial asthma. "It occurs in a situation of intense frustration. Frustration leads to an acute increase of destructive impulses which have to be repressed abruptly as long as the psychosomatic relationship prevails." Clinically this manifests itself in an acute and severe exacerbation of the somatic symptoms leading to a fulminant attack of ulcerative colitis or status asthmaticus, which prove resistant to medical treatment.

Clinical Example

A 48-year-old man with chronic bronchial asthma was in status asthmaticus in the hospital. He was in an oxygen tent and medical treatment seemed ineffective. His case history had been discussed in a conference. The impression gained was that this man psychologically was in a state of acute frustration and rage resulting from the relationship with his wife (unconsciously, a mother substitute). A direct interpretation of his unconscious suicidal impulses was then given to the patient; namely, that he was extremely disappointed in his wife and that this, because his religion forbade suicide, was his way of suiciding. This interpretation had an immediate effect. The severe asthmatic attack which had resisted all medical intervention was interrupted immediately. [Sperling, 1955.]

Related Concept: SOMATIC COMPLIANCE.

REFERENCE

Sperling, M., "Psychosis and Psychosomatic Illness." *IntJPsa*, 36:4, 1955.

1690

PSYCHOTIC CHARACTER is a term which is sometimes employed to describe borderline cases where the pathological behavior appears to be ego-syntonic. As with neurotic character traits, there is a confusion in the distinction to be made between internal and external reality. The behavior of the psychotic character differs from the psychotic in that he is able to establish a relationship to a number of individuals who remain unaware of his disorder. Because the psychotic character gratifies the repressed wishes of others—especially those of omnipotence—he is sometimes elevated to a position of leadership, wherein the group uses him as a superego. In this, the psychotic character represents a potential danger, in that he uses the group as an extension of his own personality. The attitude of the psychotic character "reminds us of patients suffering from 'folie à deux,' only that instead of being satisfied with finding and conquering one person, he is able to influence a large group of people," especially those interested in finding a demigod. "The psychotic character, because of his lack of self-criticism, is ideally suited for such a role." [Eidelberg, 1954.]

Related Concept: CHARACTER TRAITS.

REFERENCE

Eidelberg, L., *An Outline of a Comparative Pathology of the Neuroses.* IUP, p. 217, 1954.

1691

PSYCHOTIC CORE. According to Bychowski (1963), the personality of the psychotic patient contains a nucleus of psychotic ego supported by various defenses of a neurotic or characterological nature. In this, the primitive archaic ego functions with fluid boundaries, possessing a heavy investment of primary narcissism colored by the grandiosity of primitive nonneutralized aggression and destructive hostility. The libidinal fixations are pregenital and the defense mechanisms are massive projections which have the characteristics of paranoid position: introjection, denial, a turning against the self.

Related Concept: LATENT PSYCHOSIS.

REFERENCE

Bychowski, G., "The Psychoanalysis of the Psychotic Core." *Psychiatric Research Report 17*, American Psychoanalytic Association, November 1963.

ADDITIONAL READINGS

Bychowski, G.: *Psychotherapy of Psychosis.* G&S, 1952.
     "The Structure of Chronic and Latent Depression." *IntJPsa*, 41, 1960.

1692

PUBERTY is the period when genital maturity is reached and secondary sex characteristics are developed. The start of puberty is marked by menarche in the female, and the ejaculation of sperm in the male. Puberty extends roughly from age twelve to age fifteen. Psychoanalytically, puberty is the second major phase of instinctual thrust (the infantile sexual period being the first). While some authors use *puberty* and *adolescence* as synonyms, others divide this stage into *prepuberal*, *puberal*, and *postpuberal* periods, including only the latter two periods in adolescence.

During prepuberty, latency defenses are intensified, and there is an increased concern with reality and activity, and the formation of transient identifications. With the onset of puberty proper, the intersystemic equilibrium of the latency period is shattered. Oedipal conflicts are revived, with mounting instinctual pressure and counterreactions, and there are transitory regressions to preoedipal levels, rapid cathectic shifts (often with increased narcissism), and rapidly fluctuating identifications and object-choices. These processes may be manifested by "crushes," both homosexual and heterosexual; shifting and intense passions and moods; revivals of instinctual patterns more or less renounced in latency; ascetic traits and intellectualism; idealism; absorption with fads; espousal of "causes"; rapid shifts in interests, ideals, and objects; narcissistic preoccupation with the self; and antisocial and delinquent acts. Where earlier conflicts have been largely unresolved, regression may become fixed. [A. Freud, 1958.]

This period of marked intensification of oedipal conflicts, as Freud (1905) noted, with severe masturbatory pressure, is normally followed by structural and instinctual reorganization. Genital dominance is established, incestuous objects are renounced, the superego is wrested free of its dependence on the parents, and a greater capacity for instinctual neutralization and fusion is developed. In puberty the autoerotic sexuality changes. In the genital stage, the girl develops breasts, discovers her vagina, whereas the boy discovers that his penis is able to produce semen. At the same time, what has been more or less autoerotic is not acceptable as an external object.

Related Concepts: ADOLESCENCE; LATENCY PERIOD; PHALLIC PHASE.

REFERENCES

Freud, A., "Adolescence." *PsaStC*, 13:255–278, 1958.
Freud, S., 1905, "Three Essays on Sexuality." *SE*, 7:207–208, 1953.

ADDITIONAL READINGS

Deutsch, H., *The Psychology of Women*, G&S, 1, 1944.
Freud, A., *The Ego and the Mechanisms of Defense*. IUP, 1946.
Freud, S., 1933, "New Introductory Lectures on Psycho-Analysis." *SE*, 22, 1964.
Spiegel, L., "A Review of Contributions to a Psychoanalytic Theory of Adolescence." *PsaStC*, 6, 1951.

1693

PUN denotes a condensed joke that produces aesthetic pleasure when the listener discerns its inherent double meaning. It differs from the joke in that its story content is implied rather than given. In spite of the fact that many people regard the pun as a low form of the joke, Freud (1905) thought that some puns were of high quality.

Fowler (1926) noted: "The assumption that puns are *per se* contemptible, betrayed by the habit of describing every pun not as a *pun*, but as a *bad pun*, or a *feeble pun*, is a sign at once of sheepish docility and desire to seem superior. Puns are good, bad, and indifferent, and only those who lack the wit to make them are unaware of the fact."

In Heine's "The Baths of Lucca," Hirsch-Hyacinth, a character who serves as a comic foil, boasts to the poet that Baron Rothschild and he are good friends. He says: "I sat beside Salomon Rothschild and he treated me quite as his equal—quite famillionairely." This joke contains a pun, namely the word *famillionairely*.

Related Concepts: AESTHETIC PLEASURE; JOKE (WIT).

REFERENCES

Freud, S., 1905, "Jokes and Their Relation to the Unconscious." *SE*, 8:45, 47, 1960.
Fowler, H., 1926, *A Dictionary of Modern English Usage*. Revised by Ernest Gower, 2nd ed. LCP, p. 492, 1965.

ADDITIONAL READING

Stoddart, W. H., "A Pun Symptom." *IntJPsa*, 10, 1929.

1694

PURIFIED PLEASURE EGO is a primitive ego state, according to Freud (1915), "which places the characteristic of pleasure above all others." Ferenczi (1916) described the infant's discovery of external reality, as follows: "If we try, not only to feel ourselves into the soul of the new-born babe (as the nurses do), but also to think ourselves into it, we must say that the helpless crying and struggling of the child is apparently a very suitable reaction to the unpleasant disturbance that the previous situation of being satisfied has suddenly experienced as a result of the birth. We may assume, supported by considerations which Freud has expounded in the general part of his *Traumdeutung*, that the first consequence of this disturbance is the hallucinatory re-occupation of the satisfying situation that is missed, the untroubled existence in the warm, tranquil body of the mother. The first wish-impulse of the child, therefore, cannot be any other than to regain this situation. Now the curious thing is that—supposing normal care—this hallucination is in fact realised. From the subjective standpoint of the child the previously unconditional 'omnipotence' has changed merely in so far, that he needs only to seize the wish-aims in a hallucinatory way (to imagine them) and to alter nothing else in the outer world, in order (after satisfying this single condition) really to attain the wish-fulfilment. Since the child certainly has no knowledge of the real concatenation of cause and effect, or of the nurse's existence and activity, he must feel himself in the possession of a magical capacity that can actually realise all his wishes by simply imagining the satisfaction of them. (*Period of magical-hallucinatory omnipotence*.)

"That the nurse guesses the hallucinations of the child aright is shewn by the effect of her actions. As soon as the first nursing measures are carried out the child calms itself and goes to sleep. *The first sleep, however, is nothing else than the successful reproduction of the womb situation (which shelters as far as possible from external stimuli)*, probably with the biological function that the processes of growth and regeneration can concentrate all energy on themselves, undisturbed by the performance of any external work. Some considerations, which cannot be presented in this connection, have convinced me that also every later sleep is nothing else than a periodically repeated regression to the stage of the magical-hallucinatory omnipotence, and through the help of this to the absolute omnipotence of the womb situation. According to Freud, one has to postulate for each system subsisting by the pleasure-principle arrangements by means of which it can withdraw itself from the stimuli of reality. Now it seems to me that sleep and dreams are functions of such arrangements, that is to say, remains of the hallucinatory omnipotence of the small child that survive into adult life. The pathological counter-part of this regression is the hallucinatory wish-fulfilment in the psychoses.

"Since the wish for the satisfying of instincts manifests itself periodically, while the outer world pays no attention to the occurrence of the occasion on which the instinct is exerted, the hallucinatory representation of the wish-fulfilment soon proves inadequate to bring about any longer a real wish-fulfilment. A new condition is added to the fulfilment: the child has to give certain *signals*—thus performing a motor exertion, although an inadequate one—so that the situation may be changed in the direction of his disposition, and the 'ideational identity' be followed by the satisfying 'perceptual identity.'

"The hallucinatory stage was already characterised by the occurrence of uncoordinated motor discharges (crying, struggling) on the occasion of disagreeable affects. These are now made use of by the child as magic signals, at the dictation of which the satisfaction promptly arrives (naturally with external help, of which the child, however, has no idea). The subjective feeling of the child at all this may be compared to that of a real magician, who has only to perform a given gesture to bring about in the outer world according to his will the most complicated occurrences.

"We note how the omnipotence of human beings gets to depend on more and more 'conditions' with the increase in the complexity of the wishes. These efferent manifestations soon become insufficient to bring about the situation of satisfaction. As the wishes take more and more special forms with development, they demand increasingly specialised signals. To begin with are such as imitations of the movement of sucking with the mouth when the infant wants to be fed, and the characteristic expressions by means of the voice and abdominal pressing when it wants to be cleansed after excreting. The child gradually learns also to stretch out its hand for the objects that it wants. From this is developed later a regular gesture-language: by suitable combinations of gestures the child is able to express quite special needs, which then are very often actually satisfied, so that—if only it keeps to the condition of the expression of wishes by means of corresponding gesture—the child can still appear to itself as omnipotent: *Period of omnipotence by the help of magic gestures*."

All sources of pleasure for the infant are introjected and all sources of unpleasure are projected. Kahane (1962) noted: "The first pleasurable charges are probably the first intake of breath and sucking at the mother's breast." Self and pleasure are then equated, as are nonself (external) and unpleasure (formerly indifference). The infant's ego becomes aware of the need for external objects in order to survive, and thus starts to distinguish between self and nonself. Eventually, frustration associated with the necessity of having objects for instinctual gratification facilitates the establishment of the adult reality ego and the reality principle. The hypomanic ego is a regression to the stage of the pleasure ego. The ego is orally fused with those parts of the superego which bring pleasure. Ego and pleasure are one. The hypomanic ego may be used as an illustration of the pleasure ego.

Related Concepts: EGO; EGO BOUNDARIES; NARCISSISM.

REFERENCES

Freud, S., 1915, "Instincts and Their Vicissitudes." *SE*, 14:136, 1957.
Ferenczi, S., 1913, "Stages in the Development of the Sense of Reality." *SPsa*, pp. 221–225, 1916.
Kahane, M., "Etiology and Therapy of the Neuroses." *MVPsaS*, 1:99, 1962.

ADDITIONAL READINGS

Freud, S.: 1911, "Formulations on the Two Principles of Mental Functioning." *SE*, 12, 1958.
    1925, "Negation." *SE*, 19, 1961.
Lewin, B., *The Psychoanalysis of Elation.* Nor, 1950.

1695

PYROMANIA is a compulsion to set fires, usually neither for practical reasons nor for material profit. However, psychoanalytic investigation of cases of arson for profit, spite, etc. may reveal underlying dynamics similar to those found in pyromania. Pyromania may occur in the feeble-minded, in subjects in confused or delirious states, and in delusional subjects (particularly paranoids, who may relate the setting of fires to religious ideas of godlike power or purification). Frosch and Wortis (1954) classify pyromania as a symptom-impulse disorder, characterized by one, or several, more-or-less isolated impulsive acts, usually of a recurrent nature, which represent the main problem of the subject. Phenomenologically, the pyromanial impulse may appear suddenly, and be acted out immediately, or it may be preceded by moodiness and anxiety. It may be carried out in a twilight state. The quantity of moral inhibitions to be overcome varies from case to case.

Pathogenetically, pyromania is closely connected with urethral eroticism, and associated consciously (or unconsciously) with enuresis and general urinary incontinence. This might account for the fascination with matches and fires so often found in children. The relationship between pyromania and urethral eroticism is established, on a somatic level, by the burning sensation which may be experienced in the urethra during urination, the sensation of heat present in the genitals during sexual excitement, and the reciprocally exclusive character of erection and urination. On a psychological level, fire is equated with love and sexual excitement (flame equals phallus), a finding corroborated by the observation that the sight of fire causes sexual excitement in the pyromaniac. Aggressive urethral impulses may also represent powerful motivating factors (urinating equals attacking and destroying with the urine). The destructive character of fire may be a symbol for the powerful nature of the sexual urge.

The unconscious libidinal and aggressive factors underlying pyromania indicate possible ties with masturbatory activities. Pyromaniacs are often compulsive masturbators, who succeed in mobilizing libidinal and sadistic fantasies through pyromania. The libidinal component of pyromania may also explain the fire fantasies sometimes experienced by frigid women.

According to Freud (1932), fire mobilizes both sexual feelings and a desire to eliminate the fire by urinating on it.

Related Concepts: NOCTURNAL ENURESIS; URINATION.

REFERENCES

Freud, S., 1932, "The Acquisition of Power over Fire." *SE*, 22:192, 1964.
Frosch, J. & B. Wortis, "Contribution to the Nosology of Impulse Disorders." *AJP*, 3:132–138, 1954.

ADDITIONAL READINGS

Bleuler, E., *Textbook of Psychiatry.* Mac, 1924.
Lewis, N., & H. Yarnell, *Pathological Fire Setting.* NMDP, 1951.

Q

QUALITY, derived from the perceptions and memory traces, becomes conscious as pleasure and unpleasure in terms of a "qualitative something" that occurs in the course of mental events (Freud, 1923). This *something* may take the form of a qualitative change in a stimulus (as does a quantitative reduction) and so tend to characterize the pleasure-unpleasure principle. Freud (1933) noted that the instinctual cathexis seeking discharge from the id does so with a complete disregard for the quality of what is cathected On the other hand, the ego with the help of the quality of the object inhibits the instant discharge and, guided by the reality principle, utilizes not only a *specific* but the *form* of the discharge.

In the ego, we find an agency which can be approached from the external world, from the id and from the superego. In this, it is the quantitative and qualitative differences in the stimuli, whether from the inside or the outside, which determine the nature of their subsequent function.

Freud (1900) earlier discussed quality with reference to the perceptual. Consciousness, according to Freud, is nothing else but the perception of psychic qualities. Their qualities may either come from the id, or from the superego or from the external world, or from all three.

Gill (1963) objected to Freud's formulation: *Ucs.* contents do not become conscious "except via the preconscious." He considered it misleading, since *Ucs.* contents can in effect be invested with quality by virtue of being linked with strong sensory images, and can in certain circumstances (e.g., the psychoses) become conscious directly. The supplantation of the systematic approach by the structural approach negates the difficulties to which this idea may give rise.

Related Concepts: CONSCIOUS; PRECONSCIOUS; QUANTITY; STRUCTURAL (TOPOGRAPHIC) APPROACH.

REFERENCES

Freud, S.: 1900, "Interpretation of Dreams." *SE*, 5:615–616, 1953.
    1923, "The Ego and the Id." *SE*, 19:22, 1961.
    1933, "New Introductory Lectures on Psycho-Analysis." *SE*, 22:74–75, 1964.
Gill, M., *Topography and Systems in Psychoanalytic Theory.* IUP, pp. 15–20, 63–67, 1963.

QUANTITATIVE APPROACH. Freud (1900) believed that a quantitative difference existed in all mental functions, which was capable of being increased, decreased, displaced, or discharged. He distinguished between internal and external excitation, reasoning that both operated on a quantitative basis. As Strachey (1953) noted, Freud assumed that "their actions were wholly determined by the magnitude of the nervous excitation impinging upon them."

Freud gave up his attempt to use a physiological approach in the examination of such problems as quantity and quality, and introduced an economical approach, in which the quality and the quantity of the instinctual drives and their derivatives were examined. In his paper, "The Economic Problem of Masochism," he pointed out that the pure change of the quantity of the instinctual tension cannot account for the experience of pleasure or gratification. While Freud (1924) admitted that an increase of tension may often produce unpleasure, while a decrease of tension may lead to pleasure, he was aware that under certain conditions pleasure may be connected with an increase of tension and unpleasure with a decrease.

In his paper, "Libidinal Types," Freud (1931) suggested that the proportion between the libidinal and the aggressive instinctual tension may not be the same in each individual. He postulated three types of innate forms which he named the erotic type, the narcissistic type, and the obsessional type. This hypothesis which may be verified by the observation of the instinctual derivatives permits us to study various problems which (without this quantitative hypothesis) are not otherwise accessible to analytical work. Freud suggested that people who belong to the erotic type become hysterics when they have their choice of a neurosis. On the other hand, people belonging to the narcissistic type may, when sick, develop a psychosis or become criminals.

Eidelberg (1948) noted: "The impossibility of obtaining exact quantitative data is often cited as an argument proving that psychoanalysis is not a natural science. But psychoanalysis does not renounce the quantitative method. Since it must operate without units of measurement, it resorts to the device of comparison. The problem is to apply this comparative method in such a way that the results obtained by it can be verified.

"For instance, in analyzing an obsessional neurotic we note the frequency with which his symptoms manifest themselves, the time needed to eliminate them, etc. We know that in certain processes a quantitative change, when sufficiently great, brings a qualitative change in its wake. In this respect psychoanalysis proceeds like other natural sciences, which also define qualities in terms of quantity (e.g., in relation to the theory of color).

"It is a much more complicated task to compare two patients with regard to the quantitative factor. While it may be possible, for an experienced analyst, to compare similar symptoms in different patients, quantitative comparison of two different symptoms —for instance, an obsessional symptom and a hysterical conversion symptom—seems impossible. . . .

"1. The three libidinous types represent different mixtures of eros and thanatos. In the erotic type, the eros component predominates; in the narcissistic type, the two components are approximately equal; in the obsessional type, the thanatos component predominates.

"2. In the course of the individual's life, the erotic component decreases and the amount of thanatos increases. As result there is a small displacement of the instinct fusion from the id to the superego, in such a way that during childhood a great share of eros is assigned to the id, during the middle years to the ego, and during old age to the superego.

"3. The quantitative difference between eros and thanatos is constitutionally determined in every individual; it seems to be one of the causes of the formation of different libidinous types."

Related Concepts: COMPARATIVE PATHOLOGY OF THE NEUROSES; ECONOMIC APPROACH; QUALITY.

REFERENCES

Eidelberg, L., *Studies in Psychoanalysis.* IUP, pp. 147, 153, 1948.

Freud, S.: 1900, "The Interpretation of Dreams." *SE*, 5:602, 1953.

     1924, "The Economic Problem of Masochism." *SE*, 19:160, 1961.

     1931, "Libidinal Types." *SE*, 21:220, 1961.

Strachey, J., Editorial note. *SE*, 4:xvi–xviii, 1953.

ADDITIONAL READING

Bernfeld, S., & S. Feitelberg, "Über psychische Energie, Libido und deren Messbarkeit." *Im*, 16, 1930.

R

1800

RACIAL MEMORY is denotative of the phylogenetic transmission of certain general developmental patterns and reactions; specific mental and emotional contents originating in situations which have repeatedly occurred in the past; and events which owing to their overwhelming emotional impact may leave unconscious memory-traces. The belief in such a heritage was repeatedly expressed by Freud in several contexts, particularly in connection with the primal horde theory. He (1913) felt that religious ceremonials and individual psychological reactions still bear witness to the unconscious persistence of memories of archaic situations, anxieties, feelings of guilt, and various reaction formations which are beyond contemporary experience. Freud (1918) similarly explained the universality of certain symbolic expressions—especially speech symbolism—and certain primordial fantasies, especially those connected with parental coitus and related castration fears. He agreed with Jung in saying that the phylogenetic experiences modify our behavior, but he insisted that it would be wrong to neglect the actual experiences of the individual.

In Freud's opinion, these were manifestations of the inheritance of acquired characteristics, which he conceptualized along Lamarckian lines and believed to be generally valid in both the psychological and biological fields. This hypothesis is subject to doubt and criticism; indeed, while the validity of Freud's basic assumption is uncertain at present, the general nonacceptance of Lamarckian theories in scientific circles makes their tenability most problematical on a theoretical level.

A superficially similar, but substantially different, version of racial memory was advanced by Jung (1916), in terms of the archetypes of the collective unconscious: systems of ideational and symbolic contents common to all humanity; primordial patterns appearing in the language of the unconscious as personified or symbolized picture forms, corresponding to the concept of the "pattern of behavior" in biology.

Related Concepts: COLLECTIVE UNCONSCIOUS; HEREDITY.

REFERENCES

Freud, S.: 1913, "Totem and Taboo."*SE*, 13:125–126, 141–146, 1955.
   1918, "From the History of an Infantile Neurosis." *SE*, 17:97, 1955.
Jung, C. G., *Psychology of the Unconscious: A Study of the Transformations and Symbolisms of the Libido.* KP, 1916.

ADDITIONAL READINGS

Freud, S.: 1931, "Libidinal Types." *SE*, 21, 1961.
   1939, "Moses and Monotheism." *SE*, 23, 1964.
Glover, E., *Freud or Jung.* AU, 1950.

1801

RAGE is an affective state characterized by intense anger, whether outwardly manifested or controlled. Rage is an archaic type of reaction to frustration, a massive emergency discharge, intended to release a flood of unmastered excitation in a total or partial absence of ego-control. Its most obvious and uncontrolled expression is most often found in children, in adults whose personalities have retained infantile characteristics (e.g., epileptics and psychopaths), and in adults in severely regressed states (e.g., psychotics). The primitive character of rage is also indicated by its diffuse and undifferentiated character, and its demonstrability in the earliest postnatal phases; e.g., an infant, if physically restrained, is liable to stiffen its body, move its extremities violently, and hold its breath, causing its face and body to redden. The infant's rage reaction results from the frustration of instinctual urges and needs, which threatens homeostasis. This rage reaction persists in the growing child, but becomes increasingly more complex and differentiated as the whole psychic structure becomes progressively more delineated. For example, the painful tension resulting from hunger may engender hostility in the infant, which he may then project, giving him a hostile image of the environment, particularly of the mother. His rage against her may be turned into fear of retaliation, and his cannibalistic wish to bite her may be turned into a fear of being devoured. Each phase of libidinal development contributes to the process of differentiation of the rage reaction. In addition, each phase creates new potential sources of frustration and the consequent onset of rage. The libidinization of rage may involve it as a component of sexuality and therefore make it dependent on the vicissitudes of the libido.

The difficulty in tolerating the painful tensions connected with frustrations and the attendant rage eventually leads to mastery through the use of two mechanisms: (a) active forgetfulness which Glover (1939) called "oblivescence," a mental turning away which tends to obliterate the awareness of the frustrated impulse and the discomfort originating from it, and (b) an increasing ability to accept partial or substitute gratifications. Glover noted: "What cannot be endured must be cured. Either the infant must bring about changes in the environment or he must learn to regulate his own reactions to environment and so reduce the states of tension that arouse fear and hostility. Now the infant's capacity to alter his environment is very strictly limited. It is true that he can to some extent bribe or intimidate his guardians into affording him more gratification. But experience soon teaches him that blandishments are not to be depended on and that although demonstrations of rage occasionally produce good results, they are even more likely to lead to increased frustration if not actual punishment. And so his energies are directed to mastering his own states of excessive excitation. *He develops a number of psychic mechanisms to assist him in his emotional impasse.* No doubt these mechanisms are derived from inherited psychic tendencies, but they are already well established before their operation is detected by the observer. Some differences of opinion exist as to the order of emergence of these mechanisms but there is no doubt that from very early times the child can exploit a capacity for 'active forgetfulness' or '*oblivescence*' a mental 'turning-away' by which it may succeed to some extent in remaining unaware, not only of its own frustrated impulses, but of any discomfort arising from their frustration. True, it will still desire to eat and will complain if hungry, but the love and hate components of its cannibalistic systems can be obliterated, and may then give no indication of their presence except in the form of functional eating difficulties."

Eventually, the ego may defend itself, against the dangers connected with rage, through use of any of its defense mechanisms, particularly repression, reaction formation, identification, or projection. Clinically, this may result in postponement of affect, apathetic states, formation of a reactive character structure, or, if the rage is deflected inward to the ego, the self-destructive elements of the sadistic impulse may result in an abnormal fear of death. If rage reactions cannot be mastered, a state of rage readiness may persist. Partial repression of rage may lead to its invasion of the fantasy life, causing anxiety and symptom formation. Rage may be considered as a manifestation of the aggressive instinct; under ideal conditions, rage is sublimated and its discharge becomes both acceptable and beneficial to the total personality. [Fenichel, 1945.]

In pathological states, Glover noted the following: "In depression, misery is accompanied by self-hatred which may culminate in suicide. In relatively mild cases the self-hatred may be confined to feelings of worthlessness: in melancholia delusional self-accusations take grotesque forms which nevertheless are significantly concerned with 'sins' of a sexual or aggressive nature. In mild cases of mania on the other hand the patient experiences a sense of freedom and release, as if a grievous burden had been lifted from him, or he were rid of a heavy obligation. He now feels that instead of being unloved, as in the depressive phase, he is loved by everybody: nevertheless he is quick to react with irritability or rage to any apparent disparagement or interference. In other words the pathological 'mourning' of the depressive becomes the 'festival' of the maniacal phase. All this falls into perspective when it is realised that the gross and savage caricature of conscience exhibited by the depressive is overthrown by the maniac who then produces a caricature of the sanguine and facile ego of a child, whose mind has not yet been subjected to super-ego organisation and domination. In other words the ego presented by the depressive is really a totalitarian super-ego: the super-ego of the maniac for the time being has disappeared."

Related Concepts: AGGRESSION; SADISM.

REFERENCES

Fenichel, O., *The Psychoanalytic Theory of Neurosis.* Nor, pp. 208, 238, 267, 1945.
Glover, E., *Psychoanalysis*, Sp, pp. 24–25, 207, 1939.

ADDITIONAL READING

Greenacre, P., "The Predisposition to Anxiety." *Q*, 10, 1941.

1802

RAPE is most commonly defined as sexual intercourse in which the male has forced the female to submit. From a psychoanalytical point of view, rape represents, as far as the male is concerned, a gratification of libidinal and aggressive wishes. The female suffers an external narcissistic mortification and may at the same time have a genital gratification and even achieve a climax. Some authors also use "rape" to describe some extra-genital activities (e.g., oral rape, in which the mother forces the child to eat by closing its nostrils; or anal rape, in which an enema is given, forcing the child to defecate).

Under normal conditions, in accordance with the pleasure-unpleasure principle, the individual tries to obtain an instinctual satisfaction and avoid narcissistic mortification. In rape, the rapist is not only interested in achieving an instinctual discharge, but he also needs to inflict a narcissistic mortification on the raped object. Analysis of such cases indicates that the rapist unconsciously identifies with his victim, whereas, in the case of masochism, the raped individual unconsciously identifies with the sadistic partner.

The analyst rarely deals with an actual rapist, but fantasies of rape are not uncommon, and often accompany masturbation. Eidelberg (1961) noted: "Recognition of the importance of the archaic wish to rape and be raped, an understanding of the factors responsible for the perseverance of this wish, helps us to free ourselves of a need which interferes with our growing up. Of course this insight does not solve all our problems. It cannot cure all diseases nor shield us from the inevitable frustrations of life. What it does do is make it possible for us to find a way to love and to work.

"The wish to rape and be raped may be directed not only against someone or something outside, it may also be turned inward against oneself. Some patients want to rape themselves or be raped by parts of themselves. Instead of trying to achieve a compromise by finding out what it is they need or have to do or want to do, these patients go right on attacking themselves and loving themselves.

"Some of my patients use masturbation as a form of self-rape. When sexually aroused, they try to fight against the wish to masturbate, submitting to it only as a last resort. Some of them masturbate in a very aggressive way and hurt themselves. Some react with remorse; some succeed in eliminating this feeling by unconsciously provoking a variety of punishments.

"Among the patients who were afraid of being raped, there were some that used this fear of external danger to deny the internal danger of being overwhelmed by their own emotions. Other patients were suspicious of their own wishes and were afraid they might lose their heads. They denied it by fearing someone would rape them.

"It appears that denying what is true is the primary aim of every neurotic. In order not to know what horrifies or disgusts him, the patient is willing to believe or accept as probable a number of frightening and humiliating ideas, since their very presence helps him hide what he was originally afraid of."

Related Concepts: Masochism; Masturbation Fantasies; Sadism.

REFERENCE

Eidelberg, L., *The Dark Urge.* Py, p. 137, 1961.

ADDITIONAL READING

Heyer, G. R., "Hypnose und Notzucht." *ZSW*, 15, 1928.

1803

RAPTUS ACTIONS denote extremely violent, impulsive actions, mostly of a highly destructive (often self-destructive) type, which appear with relatively little warning in deeply regressed patients in a state of semiconsciousness or automatism. In the course of a raptus, patients may commit suicide, autocastration, arson, and other crimes of senseless ferocity. Raptus actions may be followed by complete amnesia or by a reawakening of consciousness accompanied by surprise and horror. Raptus actions are usually reactions to unbearable tensions, which the patient must get rid of at any cost. They result from the breakthrough of strong aggressive impulses; extemely tense, anxious, and depressed patients thus give vent to their feelings with sudden violent motor discharges. [Fenichel, 1945.]

Related Concepts: Affect; Impulse.

REFERENCE

Fenichel, O., *The Psychoanalytic Theory of Neurosis.* Nor, p. 439, 1945.

1804

RATIONALIZATION is an unconscious process wherein ego-alien thoughts, behavior, feelings, and motivations are justified or rationally interpreted in an ego-syntonic way: a compromise is effected between primary and secondary processes, yielding to the impulses or defenses; a justification acceptable to the total personality. For example, the oedipally (positive) attached son justifies his unwillingness to marry by the rationalization, "I must take care of my mother," or the alcoholic rationalizes his drinking by saying, "I drink only to keep myself warm in the cold environment in which I work." The tendency to give a rational and apparently legitimate reason for an unconsciously motivated phenomenon is a general human characteristic. Rationalizations are frequently encountered in everyday life and are practically a constant feature in neurosis. Rationalizations, being unconscious, differ from conscious lying; the patient avoids facing his ego-alien impulses and their defenses.

Rationalizations may utilize somatic factors (particularly in hysteria), superego attitudes, projective mechanisms (particularly to rationalize aggressive behavior), etc. An event may be erroneously interpreted as being in accordance with ethical standards; thus, a weak superego may help the ego to reinforce unconscious resistances, a maneuver classified by Fenichel (1945) as *moralization*.

According to Glover (1938), idealization is another form of rationalization: ego-alien drives are permitted, with the excuse that an ideal requirement will consequently be fulfilled. A secondary advantage is the enhancement of feelings of omnipotence and self-esteem. This glorification of instinctual activity is particularly prominent in manic states where the functions of the superego appear to have been usurped by a kind of second ego-ideal which welcomes instinctual expressions (such a duality of ideals may be rooted in an original division of the parental figures into one "good" and one "bad"). A similar phenomenon is that of superego corruptibility, whereby a meritorious deed is used to justify a succeeding unworthy one.

Often a posthypnotic suggestion can be used to demonstrate the concept of rationalization: an individual is hypnotized and receives the order to climb on a chair, to imitate a rooster, and to forget that he has received such an order. Thereafter, the subject is awakened and, on a prearranged signal (e.g., a whistle), proceeds to climb on the chair and to imitate a rooster. Asked what he is doing, the subject usually invents some story; e.g., he heard about a man who imitated a rooster and wanted to show what the man did.

In psychoanalysis, rationalization plays a decisive role in various forms of resistance. The patient does not use the rationalization to ward off the id derivatives; it serves to assimilate defense mechanisms. Consequently, the analyst must overcome the patient's resistance, showing him that his explanation is only pseudorational.

Related Concepts: CHARACTER NEUROSIS; DEFENSE MECHANISMS.

REFERENCES

Fenichel, O., *The Psychoanalytic Theory of Neurosis.* Nor, p. 486, 1945.
Glover, E., "A Note on Idealization." *IntJPsa,* 19:91–96, 1938.

ADDITIONAL READINGS

Alexander, F., *Psychoanalysis of the Total Personality.* NMDP, 1930.
Glover, E., *Psycho-Analysis.* SP, 1949.
Hollitscher, W., "The Concept of Rationalization." *IntJPsa,* 20, 1939.
Hsu, E. H., "An Experimental Study of Rationalization." *JAbP,* 44, 1949.
Jacobson, E., "Beitrag zur asocialen Characterbildung." *Z,* 16, 1930.
Jones, E., "The Psychopathology of Everyday Life." *PPsa,* 1913.

1805

RAT MAN. The Rat Man, a patient of Freud's, was a lawyer nearly thirty years of age who had suffered from obsessional impulses and fears since early childhood, with a severe exacerbation in the four-year period prior to his analysis, which began in 1907 and lasted eleven months. Despite the inadequacies of psychoanalysis at that time and the brief treatment the results were positive. A long follow-up was not possible, because the patient was killed in the First World War.

The first month of treatment was given in a protocol before the Vienna Psychoanalytic Society over the period of two evenings in 1907, as follows (in part):

"The basic conflict in this case lies, roughly speaking, in the patient's struggle between his drive toward man and that toward woman (his drive toward man is stronger).

"He has repressed death wishes against his father (obsessional ideas actually are obsessional wishes).

"This case shows with special clarity something that is never lacking in a case of obsessional neurosis:

"That it concerns repressed, bad, aggressive, hostile and cruel feelings (sadistic and murderous wishes). This cruel component justifiably can be called 'masculine'; yet it is equally present in women. Hence, the relationship of sexuality to neuroses

yields a theoretical conclusion: the unconscious in man cannot be basically different from that in woman. Neurosis develops at the expense of active drives which are repressed."

From time to time over the next several years Freud was to expand his views. The case was finally published in 1909. Here, Freud described the complex meaning of the patient's obsession with rats in terms of his bisexuality, anal birth fantasies and regression from the oedipal conflict because of unbearable castration anxiety and guilt. The patient reported that while he was talking to an army Captain who impressed him as being cruel, he had the idea that a certain horrible punishment would be inflicted on a person dear to him. The patient at first tried to avoid describing this torture and asked Freud to permit him to refrain from such a description; but Freud explained to him that he didn't have the power to grant him this privilege. Finally, the torture was described as having a rat put on the anus of the tortured individual and biting through his intestines. The patient then added that he was also afraid that this torture may be used on his father. This fear was very intensive in spite of the fact that the patient's father had been dead for many years.

Freud was able to show that the Rat Man (as with other obsessionals) was worried about those who were near and dear to him, and not about himself (in this he differed from a phobic patient). Freud also pointed out the intensity of his death wishes, and the constant presence of the patient's doubts (ambivalence). The compulsion, according to Freud, is a defense against the intolerable doubts the patient is suffering from. These doubts caused by ambivalence appear of basic importance in the obsessional neurosis.

The cardinal features of the obsessional-compulsive neurosis was contrasted with other mental disorders: in hysteria, unconscious fantasies and feelings might be repressed with subsequent amnesia; in obsessional states such unacceptable thoughts might be present in consciousness along with dissociation or isolation of affect. He further noted the employment of the ellipse in obsessional thinking, in which an important intermediate thought may be deleted. Action may be paralyzed, to be replaced by thought and the thought, in turn, may be sexualized and thus represent a masturbatory struggle. In the obsessional patient's terror of his thoughts he recognized the importance of omnipotence of thought.* He delineated the connections between obsessional thinking, ritualistic acts, religious ceremonials, superstitions and magical incantations. He observed the importance of ambivalence in the obsessional, the struggle between love and hate, sadism and protection of the object. "Doubting" represented the mental struggle due to the patient's deep ambivalence just as the compulsive acts represented the doing and undoing of forbidden instinctual acts. Whereas ambivalent meanings were condensed in the hysterical symptom which was a compromise between various psychic forces, the compulsive acts occasionally appeared in isolated forms. Freud contributed two technical insights for unraveling clouded obsessions. Distorted obsessions often appear in dreams in an unaltered form and the first of a series of obsessions is probably the original, with all in the series being identical in unconscious meaning.

In summary, Freud noted that by a regression to an earlier stage of development preparatory acts were submitted for final decisions, wherein thinking replaces acting, which has the force of a compulsion. This first kind of regression, from acting to thinking, is facilitated by an early, premature repression of the sexual instinct of looking and knowing (the scopophilic and epistemophilic instinct). Thus, a thought process is obsessive or compulsive when, in consequence of an inhibition that is the result of opposing impulses of hate and love, it is undertaken with an expenditure of energy (both quality and quantity) which normally is reserved for action alone—an obsessive or compulsive thought represents an act regressively. The consequence is that obsessive thoughts are distorted and displaced, following the same rules as those existent for dream work.

Related Concepts: OBSESSIONAL-COMPULSIVE NEUROSIS; OMNIPOTENCE OF THOUGHT; UNDOING.

REFERENCES

Freud, S.: 1907, "Beginning of a Case History." *MVPS*, 1:232, 1962.
　　　1909, "Notes Upon a Case of Obsessional Neurosis." *SE*, 10:153–320, 1955.

* Which might better be translated *omnipotence of wishes.*

1806

REACTION FORMATION is denotative of a defense mechanism whereby an infantile wish is warded off and kept repressed through the formation of a character trait representing the opposite instinct fusion. Freud (1926) noted that this defense mechanism may also play a role in the formation of normal character traits, but that they were usually lacking in hysteria. The presence of the reaction formation, which is responsible for changing love into hate, activity into passivity, is often the result of the function of the superego. The obsessional neurotic has an over-strict superego which fights not only his erotic but, even more so, his aggressive wishes. The basic reason responsible for the reaction formation is the regression of the instinctual energy to the anal stage.

Freud (1905) assumed that a character trait could be formed by (a) a breakthrough of the original infantile wish, (b) sublimation, and (c) reaction formation. It is doubtful whether the breakthrough of an original instinctual demand, according to Eidelberg (1954), can produce a neurotic character trait; it is usually the result of reaction formations. An example of this process in a neurotic patient would be, as follows: A patient, under analysis, who is overly clean, fussy, pedantic and obstinate discovers that these traits are a reaction formation against an infantile anal wish to play with feces. His mother had deprived him of the pleasure connected with defecation and as the mobilization of any such wish caused him to anticipate parental displeasure, he introjected the mother's prohibition, substituting the wish, "I want to be overclean," for his anal wish, "I want to be dirty." As a consequence, the infantile anal wish was not given up, but remained repressed, and the fight between this wish and its prohibitions continued unconsciously. This led to a "waste" of libidinal and aggressive energy (countercathexis) and to a lack of full instinctual discharge—the denial of a narcissistic mortification. It was Freud (1926) who pointed out, in the case of Little Hans, that the phobia was characterized by the fact that the reaction formation was not employed; rather, that oedipal wishes required different mechanisms to be carried out.

Related Concepts: COUNTERCATHEXIS (ANTICATHEXIS); DEFENSE MECHANISMS; SUBLIMATION.

REFERENCES

Eidelberg, L., *An Outline of a Comparative Pathology of the Neuroses.* IUP, pp. 106–108, 1954.
Freud, S.: 1905, "Three Essays on the Theory of Sexuality." *SE*, 7:178, 232, 238–239, 1953.
    1926, "Inhibitions, Symptoms and Anxiety." *SE*, 20:102, 115–116, 157–158, 1959.

Blanchard, P., "Psychoanalytic Contributions to the Problem of Reading Disabilities." *PsaStC*, 2, 1947.
Freud, S., 1901, "The Psychopathology of Everyday Life." *SE*, 6, 1960.
Rosen, V., "Strephosymbolia: An Intrasystemic Disturbance of the Synthetic Function of the Ego." *PsaStC*, 10, 1955.

1807

READING is a complex ego function, involving the synthesis of visual and auditory perception: the capacity for controlled symbol formation, resulting from the sublimation of instinctual aims, mainly scopophilic, exhibitionistic, and oral. The ability to read is dependent, in part, on connecting sound and motor images with the innovation of speaking. Freud (1915) pointed out that there are various forms employed in reading. For instance, when he read the galley proofs of his papers, he had to eliminate his interest in their content in order to find the misprints which might be present there.

Neurotic reading disturbances may result if reading is involved in unconscious conflicts. Reading disturbance may symbolize castration, based on the unconscious equation, eye or head = phallus. Reading may express the unconscious wish to castrate or to devour, and may therefore be prohibited. The wish to deny knowledge of castration, and the prohibition of masturbatory activity, or sexual curiosity in general can impede reading. Visual and auditory functions may be associated with the parents; they may be involved with primal-scene fantasies, and it may be impossible to use them together. Looking may be involved in oral-sadistic conflicts. [Jarvis, 1958.]

Related Concepts: AUTONOMY; EGO FUNCTIONS; SUBLIMATION.

REFERENCES

Freud, S., 1915, "The Unconscious." *SE*, 14:211–213, 1957.
Jarvis, V., "Clinical Observations on the Visual Problem in Reading Disability." *PsaStC*, 13:451–470, 1958.

ADDITIONAL READINGS

Abraham, K., "Restrictions and Transformations of Scotophilia in Psycho-Neurotics; with Remarks on Analogous Phenomena in Folk-Psychology." *SPA*, 1942.

1808

REALITY PRINCIPLE denotes the psychical changes which first occur in the life of the child when fantasy is separated, to some degree, from reality. It does not represent a change of aims, but rather a change of method by which the child achieves his aim by acting rather than wishing. This transition from a reliance on the pure pleasure principle to the reality principle is probably never completed. The transition from the pleasure principle to the reality principle occurs only slowly. After the child discovers that the hallucinatory gratification of his wishes does not eliminate his need, he has no choice but to learn to find the necessary object and the method to get it. [Freud, 1911.]

The reality principle represents not one but two goals: elimination of unpleasure and the gain of pleasure. Furthermore, a temporary tolerance of unpleasure must be accepted in order to obtain pleasure. The following conditions seem to interfere with the functioning of the pure pleasure principle: (a) the fact that the individual is not omnipotent prevents an instant gratification (lack of an available and suitable object); (b) the discharge of tension may lead to some external punishment; and (c) the discharge of one instinctual drive may impair the discharge of another. Thus, unless the pure pleasure principle is given up, the reality principle cannot be effected.

Eidelberg (1952) suggested that the pleasure-unpleasure principle be divided into two principles: the pleasure principle and the unpleasure principle. Consequently, the reality principle should also be formulated in terms of its two goals. He noted: "The teleological suggestion of the pleasure-unpleasure principle was later modified by Freud when he explained that the pure pleasure principle seems to dominate only the life of the newborn. In addition to avoiding unpleasure and gaining pleasure, the child will have to examine the external world to find out what is true. He cannot withdraw his interest completely from an object which produces unpleasure, nor can he concentrate solely on objects giving pleasure. Instead, while trying to gain pleasure and avoid or overcome unpleasure, he must learn to examine unpleasant as well as pleasant facts. The assumption of a tendency to differentiate between true and false is necessary because the child is not only interested in the avoidance of unpleasure, but has also the ability to *deny* unpleasure when it is actually present. Such denial is in the interest of the pure pleasure principle, and is an attempt to withdraw interest immediately from any object producing unpleasure."

"The reality principle modifies, but does not eliminate, the original pleasure principle. Activities having to do with reality also require and use up instinctual energy, as, for example, in the recognition of unpleasure, its classification, recall of past experiences in which such unpleasure was eliminated and pleasure gained, the decision to plan for future action, examination of the external world for the selection of proper objects, and the choice of ways to obtain them."

Hartmann (1964) characterized the reality principle, as follows: "In our literature two meanings are currently attached to the term reality principle. Used in one sense, it indicates a tendency to take into account in an adaptive way, in perception, thinking, and action, whatever we consider the 'real' features of an object or a situation. But in another, maybe we could say, narrower sense, we refer primarily to the case in which it represents a tendency to wrest our activities from the immediate need for discharge inherent in the pleasure principle. It is in this sense that we speak of the reality principle as the natural opponent, or at least modifier, of the pleasure principle. This poses a problem. One cannot state in a general way that reality-syntonic behavior curtails pleasure. This would be a quite illegitimate generalization, and not only because—as Freud repeatedly emphasized and I have just quoted— behavior under the guidance of the reality principle is aimed at gaining, in a new way, assured pleasure at a later stage, while giving up momentary pleasure. In this case, its timing determines whether or not discharge is reality syntonic. But beyond this consideration of expected or assured gains, there is also the fact that the activities of the functions that constitute the reality principle can be pleasurable in

themselves. I remind you at this point of the pleasurable potentialities of sublimated activities. Organized thought or action, in which postponement is of the essence, can become a source of pleasure. While this, at first sight, seems to complicate things, there is no way denying it; indeed, it becomes perfectly clear if we think of the reality principle in terms of ego functions. If I have emphasized here the double meaning of the term reality principle, it was in order to forestall possible misunderstandings; failure to note the double meaning has occasionally led to a misrepresentation of Freud's thinking on the subject. In opposing reality principle and pleasure principle, he certainly did not mean to negate the pleasures we derive from the world outside; and he repeatedly commented on the advantages the ego provides for instinctual gratifications, aside from its different role as an opponent of the drives."

Related Concepts: HAPPINESS; INSTINCT (INSTINCTUAL DRIVE); PAIN; PLEASURE PRINCIPLE; SATISFACTION (GRATIFICATION) OF INSTINCTS; TELEOLOGY (FINALITY).

REFERENCES

Eidelberg, L., *An Outline of a Comparative Pathology of the Neuroses.* IUP, p. 41, 1954.
Freud, S.: 1911, "Formulations on Two Principles of Mental Functioning." *SE*, 12:220–223, 1958.
  1940, "An Outline of Psycho-Analysis." *SE*, 23:146, 1964.
Hartmann, H., *Essays on Ego Psychology.* IUP, pp. 244–245, 1964.

ADDITIONAL READINGS

Frumkes, G., "Impairment of the Sense of Reality as Manifested in Psychoneurosis and Everyday Life." *IntJPsa*, 34, 1953.
Hartmann, H., "Notes on the Reality Principle." *PsaStC*, 11, 1956.
Marcus, E., "Zum 'Lust- und Realitätsprinzip.'" *C*, 4, 1913.
Mitscherlich, A., "Lust- und Realitätsprinzip in ihrer Beziehung zur Phantasie." *P*, 6, 1952.
Rycroft, C., "Beyond the Reality Principle." *IntJPsa*, 43, 1962.

1809

REASSURANCE is denotative of that process wherein a reduction of unpleasant emotions (mainly anxiety) is achieved through a deliberate increase in self-esteem and in the functional capacity of the ego; it sometimes aids in the maintenance of repression, and permits a partial discharge of instinctual wishes. As an ego-supportive technique, it is sometimes employed as a psychotherapeutic measure. It offers the patient a supportive ego, signs of love from a superego figure, and a model for identification. Its effectiveness is, in the main, dependent on a positive transference. It does not rely on greater insight and, in this respect, differs from the results of analytic interpretation. Reassurance is essentially not a psychoanalytic technique (although it is sometimes employed as an auxiliary aid in controlling excessive anxiety). Alfred Adler* and his followers gave it a prominent role.

Reassurance may also be given by the self, in winning the love of the superego and in encouraging ego activity, or by employing techniques related to denial (disavowal). This can be done consciously; e.g., self-encouragement given in the face of some danger. When connected with powerful unconscious conflicts the need for reassurance may itself become unconscious and exert strong influence on character traits. An oral narcissistic character constantly reassures himself that he has objects who love and protect him; an obsessional character must reassure himself that his ambivalence is under control; a counterphobic character reassures himself that he has no need to be afraid; and a phallic character tries to reassure himself against the danger of castration and shame. [Fenichel, 1954].

Related Concepts: ANXIETY; DENIAL (DISAVOWAL); SHAME; SUPEREGO.

REFERENCE

Fenichel, O., "The Counter-Phobic Attitude." *OF-CP*, pp. 163–173, 1954.

ADDITIONAL READING

Glover, E., *The Technique of Psychoanalysis.* IUP, 1955.

---

* Ansbacher, H. & R., *The Individual Psychology of Alfred Adler.* BB, 1956.

1810

REBELLIOUSNESS may result from the transference of an infantile object relationship to a present object, accompanied by the revival of repressed instinctual conflicts. In general, any conflict which mobilizes aggressive instincts may result in rebelliousness. A reaction against parental authority may be transferred, with the rebelled-against figures representing the parents. A man may repetitively defy and attempt to defeat his oedipal rival; at the same time, his rebelliousness reassures him against the danger of castration. Defenses against unconscious homosexual wishes—as well as other feared submissive wishes derived from the oral, anal, and phallic stages—may produce rebelliousness.

Neurotic rebelliousness may mask a need to be overcome by the rebelled-against object. A masochistic character may seek, and even provoke, attacks on himself through rebelliousness. He unconsciously wishes to be attacked, and thus derives libidinal and aggressive gratifications from the results of his actions. Unconscious wishes to be raped, punished, beaten or devoured may all contribute to rebelliousness.

An unconscious need to rebel differs from rebellion against external injustice in that the latter aims to overcome and correct the injustice, while the unconscious rebel wishes to rebel more than to correct, and may even be disappointed if his rebellion succeeds in its apparent aim. Unconscious rebellion is against an infantile object and can never be satisfied in reality. To be an effective rebel against real injustice, one must be free of the unconscious compulsion to rebel. This zeal of the neurotic rebel may aid him in assuming leadership in justified rebellion, but his unconscious needs may well result in a disservice to the goal of the group.

Freud (1930) believed that the suppression of sexuality was true for each civilization; i.e., various taboos were used to limit the sexual gratification. In our present civilization, sexual intercourse is "accepted" only under the proviso that the conditions of monogamy and legitimacy be met.

Related Concept: AGGRESSION.

REFERENCE

Freud, S., 1930, "Civilization and Its Discontents." *SE*, 21:104–105, 1961.

1811

REBIRTH FANTASY is a wishful fantasy of flight from the world. Frequently connected with the fantasy of return to the womb, it also gratifies an unconscious incestuous wish. In the male, it may be a mutilated and censored version of the homosexual wishful fantasy. The fantasy serves the purpose of denying death, and appears to be at the root of many religious beliefs of resurrection and life after death.

In his analysis of the Wolf Man, Freud (1918) discovered the presence of the rebirth fantasy. The fantasy led at first to the Wolf Man's wish to play the female role; i.e., to be impregnated by his father and thus to sacrificing his penis. He discovered that this patient used his intestines instead of his "uterus" and considered his feces as representing his anal children. Freud also pointed out that the rebirth fantasy may be connected with having incestuous intercourse with the mother.

Related Concepts: DELUSIONS; WOLF MAN.

REFERENCE

Freud, S., 1918, "From the History of an Infantile Neurosis." *SE*, 17:100–102, 1962.

1812

RECOVERY WISH. The factors involved in the formation of this drive are multiple, and their qualitative and quantitative variations in each case, in conjunction with the characteristics of those forces which tend to perpetuate neurotic illness, try to form a great number of highly different individual patterns. Generally speaking, the wish for recovery will be stronger if moral masochistic leanings are minimal, if the ego is relatively stable, if the superego formation has followed a more normal course (with little sexualization), and if no deep regression has taken place. The ability to successfully sublimate libidinal and aggressive drives, and primitive narcissistic defeats, is also important, as is an ability to be active or passive as required by external or internal reality. Other significant elements are the patient's self-esteem, the pattern of his identifications, and his motives for illness, particularly the presence or absence of important epinosic gains. Finally, the patient's social situation and the sum of the external circumstances surrounding him and his illness often represent important factors influencing his wish to get well.

As Nunberg (1955) noted, analysis is initially made possible by the convergence of the conscious wish for recovery, the unconscious infantile need for help, and the unconscious wish to satisfy the repressed strivings. Later on, the wish to get well is incorporated in the transference, which thus becomes one of the main driving forces of the treatment.

A genuine recovery wish must be distinguished from the drive to confess, from efforts to dispel anxiety by talking about one's problems, and from the pursuit of narcissistic gratification through analysis. Assessment of the patient's wish for recovery, as Waldhorn (1960) indicated, is an important element in determining the prognosis, need for, and course of the analytical treatment.

Related Concepts: FLIGHT INTO REALITY; TRANSFERENCE.

REFERENCES

Nunberg, H., *Principles of Psychoanalysis.* IUP, 1955.
Waldhorn, H. F., "An Assessment of Analyzability." *Q,* 39:478–506, 1960.

1813

RECURRENT DREAMS. Freud (1900) reported that he had frequent dreams which involved his conducting chemical experiments. According to his interpretation, the experiments were connected with his discovery of psychoanalysis; it represented, in a way, a punishment for his having made it.

Related Concept: DREAMS.

REFERENCE

Freud, S., 1900, "The Interpretation of Dreams." *SE*, 5:475–476, 1953.

1814

REFLEX ACT. Freud (1900) used the neurological concept of the reflex, in which the motoric act takes place as a result of a sensory stimulation. However, he recognized that mental activity cannot be described within the framework of neurological reflexes and he introduced, therefore, the concept of a reflex act in order to describe mental phenomena. The psychic activity begins with a stimulation from an external or internal source. On the other hand, action starts in the central nervous system and proceeds to a motoric end. However, in both dreams and neuroses, the motoric system, as it were, moves backward to reach the perceptual system and thus to produce a hallucinatory (or mimetic) phenomenon. The dream may succeed in replacing distressing ideas with contrary ones and in suppressing the unpleasurable effects connected to them. The resultant dream serves as a wish fulfillment. A wish, in this view, is described as a drive mobilized by unpleasure, aiming at pleasure.

Glover (1939) interpreted this latter statement to mean the following: "Freud operated with certain basic conceptions which enabled him to describe psychic phenomena without departing from biological criteria. Thus his theory of mental structure and function is based on the old physiological *concept of a reflex arc*. Mind corresponds to the *central system* of this arc, a system whose function it is to regulate excitations arriving by afferent paths and to secure as far as possible their appropriate discharge through efferent channels. By adopting this analogy, mind can be regarded as an instrument or *apparatus* and can be thought of as having a psychic locality and *structure*, which can then be sub-divided into a number of component parts (mental *institutions*). This constitutes the *topographic* approach to the problem."

Related Concept: STRUCTURAL (TOPOGRAPHIC) APPROACH.

REFERENCES

Freud, S., 1900, "The Interpretation of Dreams." *SE*, 5:537, 542, 556, 598, 1953.
Glover, E., *Psycho-Analysis*. SP, p. 15, 1939.

1815

REGRESSION, according to Eidelberg (1954), indicates "that, under certain conditions, the repressed wish or its energy may 'regress,' to be discharged on an earlier stage of development.

"A patient, who had suffered a traumatic experience on the phallic stage, had regressed to the anal level of development and was prevented from having intercourse by severe doubts as to whether or not he would be able to find the entrance of the vagina. He feared that he might introduce his penis into the girl's anus by mistake.

"It seems that regression, by interfering with the normal development and disposition of instinctual energy, makes it more difficult to become aware of an infantile wish, and mobilizes other defense mechanisms."

The progression of the development of the instinctual fusions is not always smooth. Fixation of the energy involved on various levels occur which prevent or interfere with normal development. As a result, Freud (1917) differentiated between two forms of regression: one in which the libido returns to the original object, and a second, in which it returns to the infantile sexual organization. Regression may also serve as a defense by hiding the original wish and offering the ego and superego a wish less likely to result in anxiety and guilt (e.g., by offering a preoedipal wish to replace an anxiety-laden oedipal wish). Freud likened the process of regression to an army which has left some of its number (cathected libido) at rear bases and, in the face of a strong enemy (psychic conflict), is retreating to those previously established strongholds at the rear.

Instinctual regression is often accompanied by ego and superego regression. Revival of an infantile wish also revives the infantile object. Ego regression is also apparent in other ways; for instance, in increased narcissism and movement toward the stage of infantile omnipotence. However, every regression reactivates the primary process: old defenses and ego mechanisms are revived (e.g., regression to an anal level increases magical thinking and may result in greater use of a mechanism such as undoing). To some degree any ego function may be involved in regression. Morality itself may undergo regression. For example, the morality of the anal organization is much more characterized by the exaggeration typical of reaction formation than is the morality of the genital organization, and, as a result, it is far more corruptible and inconsistent. In a more general way, when regression occurs, less neutralized energy is available for the functions of the ego and superego. Instinctual diffusion occurs with regression; the ego and superego must cope with an influx of infantile aggressive energies, sublimations falter, and adaptation through defense mechanisms is more likely. In psychosis, the influence on the ego is pervasive.

Some authors view regression as a normal process under certain conditions. For example, regressions occur regularly during puberty and are probably necessary to accomplish the psychic reorganization characteristic of that period. Organic disease may produce regression which, with its heightened narcissism, may help in the healing process. Object-loss produces regression which may aid in mourning and the preparation for subsequent object-relationships. Regression always carries back characteristics of the later level to the earlier level; thus, it may allow reworking of some of the earlier conflicts by a more mature ego organization, thereby enhancing later progress (this occurs in the process of psychoanalytic treatment). Regression may aid ego functions: the essential quality of these regressions in the service of the ego (total personality) is that they are controlled; they are circumscribed, transient, and reversible. They do not submerge ego function, and ego control is maintained over the id derivatives; i.e., no countercathexis is necessary: the id derivatives are accessible to consciousness. Regressions of this type aid creative thinking, intuition, and imagination. Greater communication exists between the ego and id; the mobile cathexes of the primary process become available for secondary process utilization. [Kris, 1952.] Group formation involves controlled regression, occurring in both ego and superego; identification tends to replace object relationships of a more mature type (an external object, the leader, takes the place of the individual's superego which has been internalized). Freud (1921) recognized the problem of maintaining such group regression in the service of civilization.

Any ego function may undergo regression: when a tired child stops walking and crawls, there is a regression of motility; sleep and dreams involve extensive regression; sensory deprivation induces regressions in the perceptual systems, etc. The concept of pathological regression is indisputably linked with that of intrapsychic conflict. It is not clear if this is true in all cases of regression, particularly when the regression is in the service of the ego.

Related Concepts: FIXATION; PSYCHIC APPARATUS; REPRESSION; UNCONSCIOUS.

REFERENCES

Eidelberg, L., *An Outline of a Comparative Pathology of the Neuroses*. IUP, p. 108, 1954.
Freud, S.: 1917, "Introductory Lectures on Psycho-Analysis." *SE*, 16:341, 1963.
    1921, "Group Psychology and the Analysis of the Ego." *SE*, 18:117, 122, 1955.
    1925, "An Autobiographical Study." *SE*,
Kris, E., *Psychoanalytic Explorations in Art*. IUP, 1952.

ADDITIONAL READINGS

Alexander, F., "Two Forms of Regression and Their Therapeutic Implications." *Q*, 25, 1956.
Arlow, J. A., & C. Brenner, "The Concept of Regression and the Structural Theory." *Q*, 1960.
Sprague, G. S.: "Regression in Catatonia." *JNMD*, 91, 1940.
    "Deeper Levels of Regression." *PQ*, 16, 1942.

1816

RELATIVITY OF REALITY is that impression of external reality which varies from individual to individual (Laforgue, 1940). The more normal individual is less likely to distort reality, while neurotic and psychotic individuals are constantly battling their inner conflicts and thus repeatedly distort external reality because of their pathological defenses. Unsuccessfully repressed impulses tend to develop derivatives that impair the objective testing of reality. "We should not take it for granted," Hartmann (1964) noted, "that recognition of reality is the equivalent of adaptation to reality. The most rational attitude does not necessarily constitute an optimum for the purposes of adaptation. When we say that an idea or system of ideas is 'in accordance with reality,' this may mean that the theoretical content of the system is true, but it can also signify that the translation of these ideas into action results in conduct appropriate to the occasion. A correct view of reality is not the sole criterion of whether a particular action is in accordance with reality. We must also reflect that a healthy ego should be able to make use of the system of rational control and at the same time take into account the fact of the irrational nature of other mental activities."

Related Concepts: REALITY PRINCIPLE; SENSE OF REALITY.

REFERENCES

Hartmann, H., *Essays on Ego Psychology*. IUP, pp. 9–10, 1964.

Laforgue, R., "The Relativity of Reality; Reflections on the Limitations of Thought and the Genesis of the Need of Causality." *NMDP*, Monograph No. 66, p. 92, 1940.

1817

RELAXATION is an affective state characterized by a tolerance of fantasies and external perceptions, and relative harmony between ego, superego, id, and external reality; a more or less pleasurable, tension-free state. Although abatement of effort is generally associated with relaxation, this need not be the case; either active or passive aims may be dominant. High degrees of instinctual gratification and functional pleasure of the ego may even be derived. It is most likely, however, that activity will be within the conflict-free sphere of the ego, mainly aim-inhibited instincts will be gratified, and mainly neutralized energies will be employed. High levels of cathexis, rapid rates of discharge of sexual or aggressive energies, or a high level of countercathexis, are probably inconsistent with a state of relaxation. Although instinctual pressure is not great during relaxation, the ego must be able to bind energies, delay and regulate discharge, tolerate frustration, and accept substitutes (Hartmann, 1958).

An inability to relax may result from high levels of anxiety, guilt, and instinctual or environmental pressure; it may appear as a symptom of any psychoneurosis. This inability is most clearly seen in the absence of specific activities or duties, i.e., when customary anxiety-regulating activities are not employed, and the danger of eruption of unconscious wishes is increased. A common alternative to relaxation is boredom, perhaps resulting from anxiety over forbidden instinctual gratification, with resultant extensive repression of derivative fantasies (Ferenczi, 1919). As a pervasive symptom, Fenichel (1953) noted, boredom is related to apathy and depression. Boredom is like hunger that can never be satisfied; it results in a restless, fruitless search for satiation. Defenses against incorporative wishes are of a major importance in such syndromes. The ability to relax normally probably requires a degree of oral optimism which offers promise of ultimate gratification.

Relaxation may be a highly efficient mechanism of the total personality. The relative tolerance of fantasy or its derivatives, and the diminution of intense countercathexes, makes it highly desirable, at least as a preliminary phase of most activity. Successful sexual activities or creative efforts, for example, may suffer if a state of relaxation does not initially exist.

Related Concepts: ANXIETY; FANTASY; REPRESSION.

REFERENCES

Fenichel, O., "On the Psychology of Boredom." *OF-CP*, pp. 292–302, 1953.

Ferenczi, S., 1919, "Sunday Neuroses." *SPF*, 2:174–176, 1950.

Hartmann, H., *Ego Psychology and the Problem of Adaptation*. IUP, p. 197, 1958.

ADDITIONAL READINGS

Greenson, R., "On Boredom." *JAPA*, 1, 1953.

Lewin, B., *The Psychoanalysis of Elation*. Nor, 1950.

1818

RELAXATION PRINCIPLE denotes an experimental modification of psychoanalytic technique—proposed by Ferenczi (1930). It is characterized by indulgence, tenderness, and affectionate behavior on the part of the analyst. Ferenczi first tried to heighten the tensions of the patient, thereby forcing fantasies into consciousness by increasing active frustration of nonverbal outlets for libidinal and aggressive discharge. He felt, however, that this sometimes increased resistances, while the opposite approach might make the repressed fantasies and defences accessible to analysis. He believed that an atmosphere of indulgence could revive the shock experienced by the patient during childhood in response to trauma, especially to the repressed incestuous behavior of his parents toward him. Ferenczi recognized the problems involved in this approach, but felt that they could be overcome. On the whole, these recommendations were not approved by Freud, and most analysts today would consider this analytic role to be transference manipulation; they would not consider it justified or useful in a case suitable for psychoanalytic treatment.

Related Concepts: ANACLITIC; TECHNIQUE OF PSYCHOANALYSIS; TRANSFERENCE.

REFERENCE

Ferenczi, S., "The Principles of Relaxation and Neocatharsis." *SPF*, 3:108, 115, 1930.

1819

RELIGIOUS FAITH is denotative of the belief in a force which is superior to the human; a force which controls fate, sometimes influenced by human behavior, as in prayer. All formal religious doctrines supply information as to the nature of God, the nature of what is considered *good* or *bad*, and enumerate the consequences which will follow when its rules and practices are abridged. Although critical of religious faith, Freud (1930) was not in favor if its abolition. He never denied the ethical and aesthetical gains connected with religions, only objecting whenever it interfered with the pursuit of scientific aims.

Related Concepts: OMNIPOTENCE OF THOUGHT; TABOO; TOTEM.

REFERENCE

Freud, S., 1930, "Civilization and Its Discontents." *SE*, 21:94, 1962.

ADDITIONAL READINGS

Allport, G. W., "The Roots of Religion." *PP*, 5, 1954.
Bunker, H. A., "Psychoanalysis and the Study of Religion." *AnSurvPsa*, 2, 1951.
Casey, R. P., "The Psychoanalytic Study of Religion." *ASP*, 33, 1938.
Clar, W. H., *The Psychology of Religion*. Mac, 1958.
Fromm, E., "Faith as a Character Trait." *Ps*, 5, 1942.
Gaines, C. H., "Psychoanalysis and Faith." *NAmerRev*, 219, 1924.
Hiltner, S., "Religion and Psychoanalysis." *R*, 37, 1950.
Jones, E., "Psychoanalysis and Religion." *PsaVkb*, 1957.
Lorand, S., "Psycho-Analytic Therapy of Religious Devotees. (A Theoretical and Technical Contribution.)" *IntJPsa*, 43, 1962.

1820

REMORSE, according to Freud (1930), should be differentiated from a feeling of guilt. Remorse relates to the "deed that has been done." That is, the feeling of guilt may be understood as an emotional signal indicating the presence of aggressive wishes, whereas the feeling of remorse informs us that these wishes have been gratified.

Eidelberg (1954), however, noted that many neurotics experience a feeling of remorse in connection with their unfulfilled aggressive wishes. As a result of their feeling of infantile omnipotence, they do not differentiate between their wishes and their actions. Consequently, an obsessional neurotic tries to undo not only what he has done, but also what he only wanted to do.

Related Concept: AGGRESSION.

REFERENCES

Eidelberg, L., *An Outline of a Comparative Pathology of the Neuroses*. IUP, 1954.
Freud, S., 1930, "Civilization and Its Discontents." *SE*, 21:131, 137, 1961.

1821

REPETITION COMPULSION refers to an active repetition of a passively experienced unpleasure. Fine (1962) pointed out that this active repetition "helps the individual to master the anxiety involved in passively suffering some trauma" (narcissistic mortification). In some cases cited by Freud, an aggressive pleasure was achieved; in others, at least unpleasure was eliminated. To this, Eidelberg (1954) added that in the compulsion to repeat, the passive role may also be repeated.

Freud (1926) regarded the repetition compulsion as operating to promote the dominating function of the mental apparatus, i.e., to bind tension and eliminate excitation. He viewed it as an expression of the Nirvana Principle, and as a derivative of the ultimate aim of the aggressive (death) instincts, the return to an inorganic state.

Clinical manifestations of the repetition compulsion may be seen in children's play, traumatic neuroses, the transference neurosis, and neuroses in general (especially the fate neuroses). Children's play is frequently devoted to the active repetition of passively experienced traumatic events; for example, the game of doctor played by a child who has just received an injection. In the dreams of someone with a traumatic neurosis, the trauma is repeated over and over. In the transference, the painful repressed wishes of the infantile neurosis are revived and repeated.

The compulsion to repeat is connected with the experience of the uncanny, according to Freud (1919). During one of his visits to Italy, he realized while walking through a street that it was inhabited by prostitutes. He tried quickly to get out of this part of the city but after a time he found himself again walking along the street he had wanted to avoid.

Related Concepts: AGGRESSION; IDENTIFICATION; IMITATION; NIRVANA PRINCIPLE; UNCANNY; UNPLEASURE-PLEASURE PRINCIPLE.

REFERENCES

Eidelberg, L., *An Outline of a Comparative Pathology of the Neuroses.* IUP, p. 143, 1954.
Fine, R., *Freud: A Critical Re-Evaluation of His Theories.* DM, p. 175, 1962.
Freud, S.: 1919, "The Uncanny." *SE*, 17:236–237, 238, 1955.
    1926, "Inhibitions, Symptoms and Anxiety." *SE*, 20:153–154, 159, 1959.

ADDITIONAL READINGS

Bibring, E., "The Conception of the Repetition Compulsion." *Q*, 12, 1943.
Biermann, G., "Geständnis- und Wiederholungszwang im Sceno-Test." *ZdiagnPsychol*, 3, 1955.
Hermann, I., "Randbemerkungen zum Wiederholungszwang." *Z*, 8, 1922.
Kubie, L. S., "A Critical Analysis of the Concept of a Repetition Compulsion." *IntJPsa*, 20, 1939.

1822

REPRESSION is a defense mechanism, in which undesirable instinctual demands are expelled and kept from the conscious mind. Except for some adult cases of severe shock leading to a traumatic neurosis, repressions are produced only in the child. Freud (1962a) noted that whenever the ego is invaded by an impulse which it cannot deal with, it reacts by eliminating this impulse from its conscious mind (repression).

Freud felt that repression is used only after other mechanisms or instinctual vicissitudes (e.g., turning into the opposite or turning against the self) have been unsuccessfully employed. The mechanism of rejection (repudiation) becomes available only later in life, when the ability to reject the gratification of a wish without eliminating the wish from the conscious mind is developed. Of primary interest, however, is Freud's conviction that repression affects the memory and not the original perception. In a letter to Pfister written in 1910, he noted: "I can answer your theoretical doubts in accordance with your own inclination. There need have been no shameful or horrible incident, but only subsequent repression made it so. All repressions are of *memories*, not of experiences; at most the latter are repressed in retrospect. With the complexes one must be very careful; indispensable as the idea (of complexes) is in various performances, when one is theorising one should always try to find out what lies behind the complex, not make a frontal attack, which is too vague and inadequate."

Freud originally considered repression as functioning to eliminate from the system *Cs.* whatever produced unpleasure. He differentiated between primary repression, which originally expelled the dangerous instinctual derivative from the system *Cs.*, and secondary repression, which prevented the expelled derivative from returning to consciousness. After the introduction of the structural approach, Freud (1926b) recognized that all defense mechanisms, including repression, are the result of an unconscious wish, and an unconscious countercathexis employed by the ego; consequently, repression represented a conflict between the id and the unconscious part of the ego and the superego.

In comparing conversion hysteria with phobia, Freud (1905) noted that it was only in the latter that repression succeeded in completely blocking the instinctual derivatives. He regarded the conscious anxiety present in phobia to be the affect of the instinct altered under the pressure of repression. Later, he (1915) recognized that anxiety was a cause of repression, rather than a result of it, and he gave up his hypothesis that libido changed into anxiety. Freud (1933) also differentiated between an unsuccessful repression, in which some of the instinctual derivatives enter the conscious mind (leading to neurosis), and a successful repression, in which the repressed wish remains unconscious (which may be the case in sublimation).

Related Concepts: DENIAL (DISAVOWAL); ISOLATION.

REFERENCES

Freud, S.: 1905, "Fragment of an Analysis of a Case of Hysteria." *SE*, 7:41–42, 1953.
　　　1910, *Psychoanalysis and Faith*. BB, p. 31, 1963.
　　　1915, "Papers on Metapsychology." *SE*, 14:155–157, 178–179, 182–184, 1957.
　　　1926a, "The Question of Lay Analysis." *SE*, 20:202–203, 1959.
　　　1926b, "Inhibitions, Symptoms and Anxiety." *SE*, 20:77–178, 1959.
　　　1933, "New Introductory Lectures on Psycho-Analysis." *SE*, 22:81–90, 1964.

ADDITIONAL READINGS

Blumgart, L., "A Short Communication on 'Repression.'" *R*, 4, 1916.
Bose, G., *The Concept of Repression*." Calcutta: Bose, 1921.
Brenner, C., "The Nature of Development of the Concept of Repression in Freud's Writings." *PsaStC*, 12, 1957.
Bunker, H., "Repression in Prefreudian American Psychiatry." *Q*, 14, 1945.
Freud, S., 1930, "Civilization and Its Discontents." *SE*, 21, 1961.
Grinker, R., "A Comparison of Psychological 'Repression' and Neurological 'Inhibition.'" *JNMD*, 89, 1939.
Jacobson, E., "Denial and Repression." *JAPA*, 5, 1957.
Johnson, A. M., "Some Etiological Aspects of Repression, Guilt and Hostility." *Q*, 20, 1951.
Lundholm, H., "Repression and Rationalization." *M*, 13, 1933.
Malinowski, B., *Sex and Repression in Savage Society*. HB, 1928.
Tausk, V., "Compensation as a Means of Discounting the Motive of Repression." *IntJPsa*, 5, 1924.

1823

RESCUE FANTASY denotes the wish to be rescued or to rescue someone else; it appears in a manifest or latent form in many patients. It seems to represent an immediate elimination of the infantile helplessness or the magic ability to save others from such predicaments. Freud (1901) recalled a scene from Daudet's *Le Nabab*, where a poor accountant, without friends and rather lonely, was walking through the streets of Paris, feeling low. His name was Jocelyn. Suddenly a carriage with two horses passed by, and the horses got wild and Jocelyn courageously brought them under control. He thus saved a great man who later became his friend. Freud did not remember the exact details and upon his return home he looked up the book by Daudet and found that the character called Jocelyn did not exist. Though the story was correctly related, the name was not. The name Jocelyn was Joyeuse. Freud explained this paramnesia by pointing out that Joyeuse was the feminine form of his name in French. He pointed out that he was not a man to look for a protector.

An indication that his unconscious wish to be protected and his unconscious defense of this wish were responsible for the elimination of the name Joyeuse used by Daudet. Freud did not explain why the name Jocelyn was used in its place. It is possible that the name Jocelyn was substituted for Joyeuse, because it had a bisexual inuendo. It may have referred to Lamartine's novel, *Jocelyn*, in which the hero, a seminarian, befriends a girl disguised in boys' clothes.

Abraham (1922) pointed out that the fantasy of the son's rescue of his mother was caused by the presence of infantile sexual wishes. The saving of the father, on the other hand, seems to represent the gratification of aggressive wishes. This, no doubt, takes place on the level of a positive oedipus complex. In the case of a negative oedipus complex the opposite will occur. Whenever preoedipal wishes are involved the saving or killing of the preoedipal mother will be of decisive importance. While Abraham claimed that saving meant unconsciously killing, today one would say that the saving represented the denial of the unconscious wish to kill.

Related Concepts: BISEXUALITY; NARCISSISTIC MORTIFICATION.

REFERENCES

Abraham, K., "Vaterrettung und Vatermord in den Neurotischen Phantasiegebilden." *Z*, 8:71, 1922.
Freud, S., 1901, "The Psychopathology of Everyday Life." *SE*, 6:149–510, 1960.

ADDITIONAL READING

Harnike, J., "Nachtrag zur Kenntnis der Rettungs-phantasie bei Göthe." *Z*, 5, 1919.

1824

RESISTANCE is the dynamic power which interferes with the progress of analysis. An examination of resistances and of transferences, as Freud (1912) remarked, is what analysis consists of, and little else. When the resistances have been overcome, the unconscious desires which were repressed (so that they might not be faced) are made conscious. The resistance is that part of the patient's personality which resents the basic aim of the analysis: to undo the repression and to make unconscious wishes—their gratification and their frustration—conscious.

Freud (1926) identified five kinds of resistance, each differing in its dynamic nature, emanating from three directions—id, ego, and superego. Of the five, the first three have their source in the ego.

a. Repression resistance is the first, an expenditure of energy to maintain the repression with the help of anticathexis.

b. The second, transference resistance, which is of the same nature as the first, has a different and clear effect in analysis. It succeeds in establishing a relationship to the analytic situation or to the analyst himself and thus reanimates a repression which should only have been recalled.

c. The third is of a quite different nature. It proceeds from a gain derived from the illness, an assimilation of the symptom into the ego. It stems from the patient's unwillingness to renounce any satisfaction or relief that has been obtained principally in the analysis.

d. The fourth stems from the id and is the resistance which requires "working through."

e. The last, coming from the superego, seems to originate from the sense of guilt or the need for punishment which opposes every move toward success.

As already noted, resistance is that force which separates the unconscious part of the personality from the conscious. However, it must be recognized that a not dissimilar mechanism is at work *outside* of the analytic situation. In this, the resistances encountered may be described, not as an "artifact" of analysis, but as a function which occurs independently of the treatment whenever an attempt is made to translate unconscious into conscious. Thus, resistance may be further defined as that condition, which mobilizes the opposite instinct fusion when dangerous impulses threaten to become conscious. The power responsible for this aim—that of keeping the repressed content from becoming conscious—is called resistance.

This resistance can be studied from several points of view. Phenomenologically, a differentiation between resistance which appears as a prolonged silence may be made from a resistance in which the patient talks without interruption, becoming indignant whenever the analyst tries to comment.

Systematically, a differentiation is made between conscious and unconscious resistances, an investigation which does not permit a separation to be made between the repressing elements and the repressed impulses.

Structurally, the role which the various parts of the personality play in the formation of resistance may be investigated. Such an approach may help to differentiate the resistance caused chiefly by the ego from the resistance caused chiefly by the superego or the id.

An economical approach will help reveal what instinct-fusion (aggressive or sexual) is responsible for the resistance. From this point of view, it is assumed that the energy of the instincts is used to keep the repressed impulses from becoming conscious and that this aim is achieved by the mobilization of the opposite instinct fusion or by a turning against the self. In other words, it is assumed that the instinct-fusions are mobilized by specific stimuli to restore the basic equilibrium of the metabolites, or to protect the ego under traumatic conditions from the conscious experience of unpleasure. Here, analysts who are in favor of the second instinct theory will try to separate the resistance which represents a derivative of a sexual instinct fusion from the resistance caused by the aggressive instinct fusions. For example, a depressed patient who attacked and blamed himself for mistakes he had committed showed great resistance when the analyst explained that self-criticism is healthy only if it is based on those factors which the patient is able to control. In this instance, the patient continued to blame himself for the suicide of his brother even when the analysis revealed that he was in no way responsible for his death. In spite of these findings the patient felt guilty, an indication that his self-accusation was caused by something else. He developed a strong resistance against any suggestion that he was both hostile and loving toward his brother. His hostility was mobilized and accepted by him to hide and protect him from the more dangerous derivatives of the sexual instinct-fusion.

In this example, analysts who still use the first instinct theory may consider it as a proof that love and hate belong together as derivatives of the sexual instinct. The analysts who favor the second instinct theory will describe the presence of the aggression as a result of the mobilization of the counter-cathexis used by the defense mechanism to keep the sexual derivatives repressed.

In addition, the energy responsible for a given resistance is either narcissistic or objectual in nature. This is illustrated in the case of a patient who appeared interested in the analyst and claimed that opening and closing the window indicated a hatred for him. Though the analyst indicated that the patient had no power to read his analyst's mind, his intellectual understanding did not eliminate his emotional response. When the hatred the patient felt was demonstrated, the mechanism of his projection began to emerge from unconscious obscurity. Though the analyst had no concrete means by which to prove that the patient's behavior was narcissistic and not objectual, he could point out that the patient was treating him as though he were an extension of the patient's own body.

In translating the unconscious into the conscious, the analyst usually finds—in addition to dammed-up infantile wishes—narcissistic mortifications which have been caused by the patient's internal or external "enemies." This condition is illustrated in the history of a patient whose mother closed his nostrils in order to force him to open his mouth so that he might be fed. He succeeded in denying this external narcissistic mortification by inflicting an internal mortification on himself; namely, by blaming himself for those things for which he could not blame others.

In addition, some recognition must be given to the phenomena of *acting out* and *acting in*. Whenever the patient "acts" instead of "talks," his analysis becomes impossible.

Finally, an examination should be made of the resistances which result from the fear of being over-whelmed by instinctual demands (with their resultant discharges) and the resistances caused by fear or frustration and rejection. For example, a female patient who was afraid to verbalize her sexual wishes to avoid seduction by the analyst was at the same time also afraid that he wouldn't—an indication of his rejection.

Related Concepts: ACTING IN; ACTING OUT; COUNTER-CATHEXIS; COUNTER TRANSFERENCE; TRANSFERENCE; TRANSFERENCE NEUROSIS.

REFERENCES

Freud, S.: 1912, "A Note on the Unconscious in Psychoanalysis." *SE*, 12:264, 1958.
　　　1926, "Inhibitions, Symptoms and Anxiety." *SE*, 20:160, 1959.

ADDITIONAL READINGS

Adler, A., "Beitrag zur Lehre vom Widerstand." *C*, 1, 1911.
Bouvet, M., "Resistance and Transference." *RFPsa*, 23, 1959.
Brody, S., "Some Aspects of Transference Resistance in Prepuberty." *PsaStC*, 16, 1961.
Deutsch, H., "A Discussion of Certain Forms of Resistance." *IntJPsa*, 20, 1939.
Eidelberg, L.: "A Contribution to the Study of the Phenomenon of Resistance." *PQ*, 26, 1952.
　　　Studies in Psychoanalysis. IUP, 1952.
Evans, W. N., "Evasive Speech as a Form of Resistance." *Q*, 22, 1953.
Freud, S., 1900, "The Interpretation of Dreams." *SE*, 4, 1953.
Giovacchini, P. L., "Resistance and External Object Relations." *IntJPsa*, 42, 1961.
Graber, G. H., "Die Widerstandsanalyse und ihre Therapeutischen Ergebnisse." *ZPt*, 11, 1939.
Jokl, R. H., "Der Widerstand Gegen die Psychoanalyse." *WMW*, 1, 1930.
Krause, M., "Defensive and Nondefensive Resistance." *Q*, 30, 1961.
Laforgue, R., "Les Resistances de la fin du Traitement Analytique." *RFPsa*, 6, 1933.
Lorand, S., "Resistance." *Q*, 27, 1958.
Reik, T., "Some Remarks on the Study of Resistances." *IntJPsa*, 5, 1924.
Sterba, R., "Character and Resistance." *AnSurvPsa*, 2, 1951.
Weizacker, V. von, "Two Types of Resistance." *P*, 4, 1950.

1825

RESPIRATORY EROTICISM is the use of the respiratory apparatus for the gratification of libidinal drives other than those usually subsumed under the physiological functions of the respiratory system. While partial instincts of the respiratory system are not readily recognized, their existence is indicated in some of the breathing play of children, and in some of the pleasures of smoking (inhaling) in adults. Aggressive components may also be discharged through the respiratory system. [Wulff, 1913.]

Related Concepts: BRONCHIAL ASTHMA; RESPIRATORY INTROJECTION.

REFERENCE

Wulff, M., "Zur Psychogenität des Asthma bronchiale." *C*, 3:202–205, 1913.

1826

RESPIRATORY INTROJECTION is the fantasy of incorporating an object, or part of an object, by means of inhalation through the respiratory tract. Air is external to the self, transcends the self boundaries, and may become a part of the self, providing a ready medium for incorporative fantasies. Such fantasies are often connected with early oral fantasies, but may serve other libidinal drives. [Fenichel, 1953.]

Elsewhere, Fenichel (1945) noted: "'Respiratory introjection' is closely tied up with the 'taking in of odors,' that is, with anal eroticism on the one hand and with the idea of identification with dead persons ('inhaling the soul') on the other."

Related Concepts: BRONCHIAL ASTHMA; RESPIRATORY EROTISM.

REFERENCES

Fenichel, O.: *The Psychoanalytic Theory of Neurosis.* Nor, pp. 250–251, 1945.
　　"Respiratory Introjection." *OF-CP*, pp. 221–241, 1953.

1827

RETENTION HYSTERIA. Breuer and Freud (1895) divided hysteria into hypnoid hysteria, retention hysteria, and defense hysteria. Retention hysteria was described as resulting from excitation which is denied an outlet (suppression), that is "retained" and converted into somatic phenomena. This was seen as a simple failure to react sufficiently to traumatic stimulation and did not involve the concept of defense. Theoretically, therefore, little or no resistance was to be expected in attempting to cure it by abreaction. Freud expressed doubts about retention hysteria and hypnoid hysteria, implying they might ultimately be forms of defense hysteria, which "originates through the repression of an incompatible idea from a motive of defence." In defense hysteria, resistance was to be expected; Freud had encountered it in *all* his cases of hysteria. The term "retention hysteria" soon disappeared from his writings.

Related Concepts: ACTUAL NEUROSIS; REPRESSION; RESISTANCE.

REFERENCE

Breuer, J., & S. Freud, 1895, "Studies on Hysteria." *SE*, 2:211, 285–286, 1955.

1828

RETURN OF THE REPRESSED. Repressed material which tries to return, or does return, to consciousness may be responsible for symptom formations, and thus a secondary repression becomes necessary. Self-criticism, shame, morality are the result of a successful defense of infantile wishes. However, when the neurosis occurs, the repressed wishes try to break into consciousness and usually appear as compromise formations. [Freud, 1896.]

Jones (1912) was of the opinion that the return of the repressed material leads a secondary defense. "To complete the list of our conclusions the considerations should be recalled that were brought forward at the beginning of this paper. There I called attention to the various layers of secondary defence that covered the three attitudes of fear, hate and guilt, and pointed out that the defences themselves constituted a sort of 'return of the repressed.' We have seen how deep must be the primary layers of these three emotional attitudes, and also that two stages can be distinguished in the development of each of them. The relationship of the secondary layers would appear to be somewhat as follows. Any one of these primary attitudes may prove to be unendurable, and so secondary defensive reactions are in turn developed, these being derived, as was just indicated, from one of the other attributes. Thus a secondary hate may be developed as a means of coping with either fear or guilt, a secondary fear attitude ('signal' anxiety) as a means of coping with guilty hate, or rather the dangers that this brings, and occasionally even a secondary guilt as a means of coping with the other two. These secondary reactions are therefore of a regressive nature, and they subserve the same defensive function as all other regressions."

Clinical Example

"A stern and early toilet training, combined with narcissistic mortifications on the phallic stage, seemed to represent the causes responsible for his anal regression and fixation. He had been below average in school, and had started to earn money after high school. He advanced slowly, but finally, through his steady work and frugal life, he became a successful, independent, real estate operator. When his treatment started he was a well-to-do man. As he had no insight into the neurotic nature of his stinginess, an analysis of the unconscious motives responsible for it could be attempted only after he began to realize that his approach to money matters interfered with business. For instance, the taxi fare between his home and his office varied between 60 and 65 cents. He spent the time in the taxi hoping and praying that the meter would show only 60 cents. The energy devoted to this attempt to decrease his fare obviously could be used in some other way. The same was true with his habit of washing his hands every hour on the hour. Sometimes he had to interrupt an important business meeting to go and wash his hands. As he was in a hurry, he could not dry them properly and they would get dirty again (return of the repressed), but he still had to wait until the next hour to wash them again." [Eidelberg, 1954.]

Related Concept: NEUROPSYCHOSES OF DEFENSE.

REFERENCES

Eidelberg, L., *An Outline of a Comparative Pathology of the Neuroses.* IUP, pp. 181–182, 1954.
Freud, S., 1896, "Further Remarks on the Neuro-Psychoses of Defence." *SE,* 3:169–170, 1962.
Jones, E., 1912, *Papers on Psycho-Analysis.* WW, p. 317, 1950.

1829

REVENGE is the need of the offended and humiliated to retaliate by punishing the aggressor; it involves the magical assumption that the original act of aggression can be undone. Freud (1893–1895) thus assumed that the *need* for revenge was unconscious. The need for revenge, which in the primitive was very strong, has been partly eliminated by civilization's progress. Instead of self-justice, the civilized man leaves it to the judge to punish the criminal.

The wish for retaliation and revenge is usually characterized by persistence and intensity. Accordingly, it may occur at any level of development. The wish for revenge may be related to hostility toward the parental figures, based on the conflict between the child's feeling of omnipotence, his narcissistic demands, and the parents' restraining influence. This may, in turn, as A. Freud (1949) pointed out, lead to a fear of retaliation which may result in anxieties, feelings of guilt, and consequent retaliatory action from the child's archaic superego. The anxiety engendered by fear of retaliation often leads to a repression of the aggressive drives. Identification with an ungiving parent is often prominent in the revengeful person. Sibling problems, castration conflicts in both the male and female, or the need to undo humiliations and frustrations in a magical fashion may play a dominant role. The intensity of the unconscious aggressive motives explains why certain neurotics lead a life of hostility which is acted out against the self and others, and why there may be considerable difficulty in eradicating such feelings through psychoanalysis. It should also be noted that the satisfaction of a need for revenge represents, in many cases, an important secondary gain of a neurotic process.

Ontogenetically, the *law of talion* has generally served as the basis of the primitives' system of justice. It nonetheless continues to operate in a more modern form. The presence of the regression is no doubt responsible for the need for revenge and civilization tries with the help of the reaction formation to keep this need under control.

Related Concepts: AGGRESSION; INSTINCT (INSTINCTUAL DRIVE); NARCISSISTIC MORTIFICATION; REPETITION COMPULSION.

REFERENCES

Freud, A., "Aggression in Relation to Emotional Development." *PsaStC*, 3:37–42, 1949.
Freud, S.: 1893–1895, "Studies in Hysteria." *SE* 2:205–206, 1955.
          1930, "Civilization and Its Discontents." *SE*, 21:112, 1961.

1830
REWARD BY THE SUPEREGO denotes the "happiness and self-satisfaction [which is] the result of the superego's approval of ... some behavior or attitude on the part of the ego which the superego particularly approved" (Brenner, 1955). This virtuous feeling is the opposite of punishment by the superego or loss of the superego's love, leading to the feeling of guilt induced by the superego's disapproval of the ego, its increase induces an increase in the narcissistic cathexis of the ego. As the loss of self-esteem which depends on feelings of guilt tends to bring about feelings of inferiority. Viewed in terms of the general economy of the psyche, this increase in the ego's narcissistic libidinal cathexis represents a compensation for the renunciation of instinctual satisfaction or aggressive impulses, connected with the frustration of object-libido and destrudo.

Since the infantile superego represents the introjected image of the parents, its relationship to the ego remains that of the parent to the child; the approval or guilt with which the superego rewards the ego for its behavior, represents, therefore, a repetition of infantile situations in which the child received either acceptance or disapproval from the parents for his actions. The reward by the superego involves both a positive element (the joy caused by the feeling of being loved by the parents) and a negative one (avoidance of the unpleasure caused by feelings of guilt or anxiety). The normal, independent superego—the result of assimilation of introjects of various authorities—is able to reward the individual without causing him to feel inferior, as though he were a child.

Related Concepts: CONSCIENCE; DEFENSE MECHANISMS.

REFERENCE

Brenner, C., *An Elementary Textbook of Psychoanalysis*. IUP, p. 136, 1955.

1831
RHYTHM AND PERIODICITY refers to regular repetitions which are characteristic of every biological phenomenon. In the field of biology proper, examples of rhythmic periodicity are the regular oscillations of body temperature, pulse, respiration, metabolic phenomena, menses, sucking, urinating and defecating, and the events which accompany the day and night cycle. In the field of normal psychology, rhythm and periodicity are already evident in the earliest stages of life (e.g., nursing, thumbsucking, and rhythmic stimulation of the genitals). Later, they occur in repetitive games and rhythmic activities (e.g., repetitive jumping). In the normal adult, rhythm and periodicity are evident in such things as the periodic character of dream activity, the common predilection for dances, songs, and certain sports, and the normal oscillation of moods. Pathological periodic behavior may be found in infants, in the form of head-knocking and stereotyped self-rocking. Later in life, rhythms and repetitive phenomena are prominent in the perseverations of the compulsive neurotic; in the stereotypes of the schizophrenic; in the extreme oscillations of mood characteristic of mania and melancholia; in the tendency to repeat traumatic events in dreams and symptoms; in traumatic neurosis; and in the compulsion to repeat past situations, characteristic of psychoneuroses. [Fenichel, 1945.]

Many rhythmic activities can be explained as autoerotic actions or masturbatory equivalents. Such activities may be conditioned by the need to establish (either in an autoerotic or autoaggressive fashion) a close personal relationship with one's own body or by the need to recreate a missing object relationship or ward off the anxiety attendant upon the presence of a stranger (Spitz, 1937). At times they may serve the purpose of promoting the maturational process, by testing reality and establishing mastery over the body and the environment.

The repetition of the trauma in the neuroses constitute attempts at achieving belated mastery over the traumatic event. The oscillations in mood which are characteristic of manic-depressive psychotics are the ultimate result of oral vicissitudes; basically, they are reproductions of the alternative cycle of hunger and satiety. Where repetition is conditioned by the tendency to find an outlet for the repressed, it is the result of an unending cycle, whereby, as the repressed wish tends to come to the surface, anxiety is mobilized, superego demands are intensified and further repression ensues which, in turn, brings about the re-emergence of the repressed impulse and renewal of the cycle. This condensation of instinctual drives and antiinstinctual forces is seen with particular clarity in obsessive-compulsive neuroses, in which the repetitive character of the symptoms seems to express the continuously shifting balance of forces between the id and superego.

In order to account for the ever-recurring tendency toward repetition which he found in traumatic neuroses, neurotic symptoms, and transference (and impressed by its obvious parallels to the rhythmic periodicity of the instincts), Freud (1920) hypothesized the existence of a new principle of mental functioning, which he called the repetition compulsion. The general concept of an inborn, biologically conditioned tendency to repeat appears to be most useful, as it emphasizes the importance of the general biological and instinctive matrix underlying rhythmic and periodic phenomena, and affords a unified conceptual framework for their understanding.

In the child, repetitive rhythmic actions are pleasurable until—coinciding with the formation of the superego—boredom sets in. In the adult, rhythmic activities may again cause pleasure if the superego is weakened of if the activities are approved by the superego. It must finally be noted that there is a direct relationship between rhythmic activities and regression; regression may bring about a return to the infantile rhythmic propensity and rhythm may facilitate regression (as seen, for example, in hypnosis).

Related Concept: REPETITION COMPULSION.

REFERENCES

Fenichel, O., *The Psychoanalytic Theory of Neurosis.* Nor, pp. 291–295, 1945.
Freud, S., 1920, "Beyond the Pleasure Principle." *SE*, 18:62, 1955.
Spitz, R., "Wiederholung, Rhythmus, Langeweile." *Im*, 23:171–196, 1937.

1832

RITUALS are those ceremonial acts which are typically found in cases of obsessive-compulsive neurosis. In many ways it is similar to the religious rites and practices to which the term generally refers. It is characterized by rigidity of pattern, repetitiveness, and stereotypical execution; e.g., the bedtime ritual of an obsessive-compulsive neurotic may involve placing the pillow, sheets, blankets, and nightclothes in a particular position, with no variation from night to night. Any deviation from the ritual is bound to create severe anxiety.

Although similar in pathogenesis, it is useful to distinguish between rituals and other obsessive-compulsive manifestations; obsessive thoughts constitute a series of obsessive phenomena of increasing severity from most severe to least, in the following order: obsessive thoughts, words, actions, and rituals.

Many ritualistic actions have been observed. The most common are those connected with cleansing, washing, bedtime preparations, eating, and toilet habits. Rituals involving the touching of objects or parts of the body are also common. Ritualistic peculiarities have been described in connection with the handling of money or gifts, the act of walking (e.g., stepping on or avoiding cracks in the pavement), checking lights, doorlocks, gas jets, etc. Rituals are often connected with counting, i.e., performing certain actions a fixed number of times. There are brief and simple rituals, as well as extremely lengthy, repetitious, and complex ceremonials, which may seriously interfere with everyday life.

In general, as Fenichel (1945) noted, the behavior of obsessional patients shows a tendency to progress from simple expressions to those of ceremonial complexity. If, however, a ritual recedes in severity, isolated forms of compulsive action may remain as a residual. At times, no clear-cut distinction can be made between ritual and other compulsive manifestations, such as obsessional actions and minor obsessional habits.

From a dynamic standpoint, rituals represent, in symbolic form, condensed derivatives of instinctual drives—either libidinal or aggressive—and their defenses. Thus, ceremonials may represent a forbidden wish or an unconscious fantasied crime, and (at the behest of the superego) a way of annulling or counteracting the wish, or represent a reparation. The defense mechanism most prominent here is undoing. Either the instinctual wish or the superego injunction, or both, may be represented in a ritual, or it may represent a compromise between the instinctual demand and the prohibition. The meaning of a ritual may undergo changes in the course of time.

Most commonly, the unconscious nucleus of a ceremonial is found in problems connected with the oedipus complex, masturbation, anal-sadistic derivatives (especially aggressive impulses), and homosexual fantasies. Both the libidinal and the aggressive instincts may be involved in the same act.

Numerous psychic mechanisms participate in ritual formation. Among the most important are the characteristic ambivalence of obsessive-compulsive neurotics, their rigidity and primitive superego structure, and their tendency to utilize reaction formations and displacement (facilitating the symbolic representation of the conflict). A tendency toward superstitious thinking and a belief in magic are also important. Indeed, belief in the omnipotence of thought, whereby wishes and intentions are equated with action, and belief in the possibility of undoing by magical acts, are at the very core of ritualism.

Ritualistic practices are often found in acts involving the group (mass psychology), ranging from the rituals of religious and fraternal ceremonials to those practiced (especially) in totalitarian and autocratic regimes. The psychodynamics underlying these social rituals are basically similar to those underlying individual ritualistic behavior.

Related Concepts: OBSESSIVE-COMPULSIVE NEUROSIS; REPETITION COMPULSION; TABOO.

REFERENCE

Fenichel, O., *The Psychoanalytic Theory of Neurosis.* Nor, pp. 268, 302, 1945.

ADDITIONAL READING

Glover, E., *Psycho-Analysis.* SP, 1949.

1833

RORSCHACH TEST. First described by Hermann Rorschach,* a Swiss psychiatrist, the test is a projective instrument used primarily as an aid in diagnosis and prognosis. In its present form the test consists of ten ink-blot patterns: five in monochrome, two in black and red, and the remainder in color. The ten cards are presented to the subject one at a time, the examiner saying only, "What might this be?" The examiner then records the subject's responses in full, after which the cards are again presented to make a record of where the subject saw each thing mentioned. Thereafter, each card is scored with respect to three principal features: *location,* based on the whole blot or a portion; *quality,* whether the response was determined by the form of the blot, its color, shading, or movement; and *content,* literally, whether what is seen is a human or animal figure, etc. The scores from the responses received are totaled with respect to the individual elements, the relationship of the elements being of decisive value. For example, a subject providing an unusually large number of "whole responses" might be interpreted, by way of simplification, as a person given to grandiose or egocentric ideas. However, no interpretation is given on the basis of a single set of responses. In general, the use of "form" represents objectivity; affective values are presented in terms of "color responses"; and the use of both, as the integration of objective and emotional tendencies. To give an unusual number of color responses indicates loss of control through dominating affect, while a rich inner life is indicated by a high "human-movement" score. The artistic type of person most characteristically responds with both color and human movement; the rigid type, with neither. [Murphy, 1947.]

Diagnosis may be complicated by extreme reac-

* Rorschach, H., 1921, *Psychodiagnostics.* Berne: Hans Huber, 1942.

tions in one area or by the total record. Rapaport and Schafer (1945) noted: "The test has a welter of variables, all of which may occur in adjustments and in maladjustments of different types and degrees of severity (neuroses, psychoses, character disorders, addictions, organic lesions of the central nervous system and psychosomatic disorders). In many cases the test has indications to show in what setting a certain sign occurs, e.g., whether an increased ideational productivity refers to creative ingenious-ness or is in a setting which must be considered indicative of intensive phantasying, phobias, obses-sions, delusions, confusion, etc."

The test is utilized as a diagnostic tool, most effectively employed when it is used with other tests, properly applied and interpreted by an examiner familiar with the broadest aspects of dynamic psychiatry. A. Freud (1945) noted: "The various tests so far devised assess circumscribed aspects of ego development; they are nearly indispensable in cases where a differential diagnosis has to be made between mental deficiency and defective awareness of reality through excessive denial. The Rorschach test goes furthest in inquiring into the state of libido development and its disturbances."

Related Concept: WORD ASSOCIATION TEST.

REFERENCES

Freud, A., "Indications for Child Analysis." *PsaStC*, 1:149, 1945.
Murphy, G., *Personality.* H&R, pp. 674–675, 1947.
Rapaport, D., & R. Schafer, "The Rorschach Test: A Clinical Evaluation." *BMC*, 9:73–77, 1945.

ADDITIONAL READINGS

Allen, R. M., *Elements of Rorschach Interpretation.* IUP, 1954.
Brown, F., "The Present Status of Rorschach Inter-pretation." *JAPA*, 5, 1957.

Morgenthaler, W., "Erinnerungen an Hermann Rorschach, Die Waldauzeit." *SchweizZ-Psychol*, 1958.
Phillips, L., & J. Smith, *Rorschach Interpretation: Advanced Techniques.* G&S, 1953.
Piotrowski, Z., *Perceptanalysis.* Mac, 1957.
Schafer, R., *Psychoanalytic Interpretation in Rorschach Testing.* G&S, 1954.
White, R., "What is Tested by Psychological Tests?" in *Relation of Psychological Tests to Psychiatry.* G&S, 1952.

1834

RULE OF ABSTINENCE denotes the analyst's deliberate refusal to satisfy the patient's desires and longings (sexual as well as aggressive) so that their dammed-up energy may serve, instead, as the driving force in the therapeutic process, impelling the patient to talk instead of allowing him to gratify his wishes by acting out or acting in. Freud (1919) suggested that analysis should take place in abstinence, that only infantile wishes should be controlled. Even that is often difficult to achieve.

The abstinence of the gratification of infantile wishes does not interfere with the gratification of adult wishes, such as working and loving.

Related Concepts: ABREACTION; ABSTINENCE; ACTING IN; ACTING OUT.

REFERENCES

Freud, S.: 1915, "Observations on Transference–Love (Further Recommendations on the Technique of Psycho-Analysis III)." *SE*, 12:165, 1958.
          1919, "Lines of Advance in Psycho-Analytic Therapy." *SE*, 17:162, 163, 1955.

ADDITIONAL READING

Kemper, W., "The 'Rule of Abstinence' in Psycho-analysis." *P*, 8, 1955.

S

1900

SACRIFICE, in its most general connotation, denotes a self-imposed deprivation of something having either material or moral value. Oral and anal factors contribute considerably to the psychological motivations for sacrifice (particularly anality, with the symbolic equation of stool equaling gifts). The most important factor underlying all forms of sacrifice is connected with the oedipal constellation. It is reasonable to believe that the original sacrifice was a human one, representing the ceremonial killing of the father, followed later, by the sacrifice of the first-born son, representing the masochistic expiation and retaliation for the former act. This symbolic parricide, which was often represented in religious rites as the killing of the god, was originally performed on a victim of importance (often, the king), and, by successive substitutions, on victims of lesser importance (e.g., criminals, slaves, or captives) until it became transformed into offerings of inanimate effigies, animals, fruits of the land, and money, or simple prayers, incense, or abstention. The general principle underlying all sacrifices is the warding off of danger through establishing a loss, in advance, which is qualitatively or quantitatively smaller than the loss which is feared. According to Fenichel (1945), "a greater hurt is averted by voluntarily submitting the ego to an earlier and lesser one."

While religious feasts led to the gratification of instinctual satisfaction, the sacrifice implied a frustration. A child was killed (later an animal) and the individual offering the sacrifice suffered in order to prove his religiosity. [Freud, 1913.]

In individual psychology, the making of a sacrifice is underlined by the same basic factors and motivations: a dependency on magical thinking, an archaic superego structure, the wish to gain favor and avert danger, a need to bribe the superego with an offering of lesser value than the advantage hoped for, punishment, and the wish to magically undo an evil deed or thought. Sacrifice is directly sought as a lesser evil, because the time and manner of "punishment" are determined, in all details, by the subject himself (unconscious provocation).

Sacrifice for the sake of another person is often motivated by the wish to gain the other's interest and love. Often, feelings of guilt, either toward the other person or displaced from other subjects, may represent a strong determining factor for this wish.

Related Concepts: MASOCHISM; SCAPEGOAT MECHANISM.

REFERENCES

Fenichel, O., *The Psychoanalytic Theory of Neurosis.* Nor, p. 74, 1945.

Freud, S., 1913, "Totem and Taboo." *SE*, 13:37, 134–136, 1955.

1901

SADISM denotes the conscious or unconscious infliction of physical or mental unpleasure, pain, or humiliation, in order to obtain gratification or pleasure; the ability to experience a specific kind of pleasure connected with the simultaneous gratification of both libidinal and aggressive tendencies.

The term is also used to describe some intrapsychic processes. A harsh and archaic superego is endowed with sadism.

Sadism and masochism occur in pairs of opposites in the individual, and represent the active and passive aspect of partial instinctual drives which pass through psycho-sexual developmental stages. They may be considered as normal partial instincts present in all children. At first, sadistic impulses manifest themselves in the oral biting stage, as oral sadism; they then find powerful expression as anal sadism; and, during the phallic phase, as phallic sadism. In the course of development, sadistic impulses may undergo sublimation, modifications or reaction formations, and contribute to character formation.

In 1920, Freud identified both as component instincts. He viewed masochism as complementary to sadism, a component instinct that has been turned round upon the subject's own ego. That is, masochism is usually sadism turned against the self. However, Freud did not exclude the possibility of primary masochism.

In perversion, the sadist obtains a genital discharge and an aggressive discharge against the object who is being humiliated. Most sadists are interested in finding a masochistic partner, so that their activities represent both a gratification of their own sadistic wishes and a gratification of the masochistic wishes of the partner with whom they unconsciously identify. However, some sadists use objects who are not interested in playing a masochistic role, and have to be forced to endure it. Sadists of this group may commit rape or homicide.

Individuals who experience sadistic pleasure without genital involvement, may limit their activities to masochistic objects or to objects whom they are able to force to accept sadistic discharge. With some neurotics, infantile wishes are connected with the experience of sadistic pleasure and are warded off and repressed because of this. Their symptoms can only be eliminated if, as a result of analysis, the unconscious wish becomes conscious and is rejected or sublimated.

Case History

In 1939 Freud detailed the development of a sadistic attitude in a male patient. It began when the patient was a small boy and had repeatedly observed his parents in the sexual act, having slept in the same bedroom with them for a time. Subsequently, after his first spontaneous emission, he suffered from disturbances of sleep, and was extraordinarily sensitive to night noises. Freud identified this disturbance as a true compromise symptom. The boy's prior observations led to a premature sexual aggressive masculinity, wherein he identified with his father and directed his sexual interests to his mother. He began to masturbate and did so until forbidden to do so by his mother. Thereafter, he gave up all sexual activity and became a "model" child, seemingly free of any marked disturbances.

Following the latency period, at the onset of puberty, his manifest neurosis appeared and brought with it his second main symptom, his impotency. His sexual activity remained limited to masturbatory manipulations which were accompanied by sado-masochistic fantasies. His intensified masculinity, brought on by pubescent changes, expressed itself in an extreme hatred for his father. This attitude was later responsible for his failure in the profession his father had chosen for him. After his father's death, he developed an egoistic and despotic personality. His identification with his father, as he had formed a picture of him in his memory, placed him in a rivalry situation with the father, in correspondence to the analogous situation he had had with him when he was a small boy.

Related Concepts: Masochism; Oedipus Complex; Primary Masochism; Rape.

REFERENCES

Freud, S., 1920, "Beyond the Pleasure Principle." *SE*, 18:54–55, 1955.
    1939, "Moses and Monotheism." *SE*, 23:78–80, 1964.

ADDITIONAL READINGS

Feldman, A. B., "Zola and the Riddle of Sadism." *AmIm*, 13, 1956.
Ruffler, G., "The Analysis of a Sado-Masochist," in S. Lorand, *Perversions: Psychodynamics and Therapy.* RH, 1956.
Sadger, J., "Über den Sado-Masochistischen Komplex." *Y*, 5, 1913.

1902

SATISFACTION (GRATIFICATION) OF INSTINCTS denotes the elimination of unpleasure caused by dammed-up psychic energy of the instinctual drives by motoric action which restores the organism to its original balance (law of constancy). Freud's original thesis, given in 1916, equated the pleasure principle with the law of constancy. Later (1919) he recognized that the two are not to be regarded as identical, but, rather, as modifications of the Nirvana principle. Freud originally regarded the Nirvana principle as identical with the pleasure-unpleasure principle. Only later (in 1939) did he suggest that the seeking of pleasure represented the pleasure principle, while the wish to die is connected with the Nirvana principle.

The elimination of unpleasure depends on the individual's ability to find what he requires, to select an object that is both pleasing and available, and, finally, to develop activities which permit him to obtain what he needs. Thus, instincts which are considered to be located in the id are discharged only when there is a close cooperation between the ego and the superego. In this, instinctual gratification may be conscious, preconscious, or unconscious. Within this continuum, a partial gratification can be achieved even in sleep.

The elimination of a narcissistic mortification may produce a narcissistic gratification and under certain conditions a narcissistic pleasure. For instance, the infant, unable to summon his mother by wishing alone, discovers that by crying, and, later, by calling her, he may overcome the limitation of his power. Learning to walk, in a later stage, will finally cancel the narcissistic mortification connected with the inability to move.

Thus, it may be better to refer to the discharge of tension as instinct *satisfaction* (or *gratification*), reserving the word *pleasure* for gratification in which the individual has selected an object pleasing to, and in a form appealing to, the total personality. In addition, the overcoming of a narcissistic mortification may be referred to as narcissistic gratification. Eidelberg (1951) noted: "In deviation from Freud we think that the pregenital instincts are capable of what we call End Pleasure (Pleasure with discharge of tension as different from Fore Pleasure, Pleasure with increased tension)."

Related Concepts: NARCISSISTIC MORTIFICATION; PLEASURE PRINCIPLE; REALITY PRINCIPLE.

REFERENCES

Eidelberg, L., "In Pursuit of Happiness." *R*, 38:243–244, 1951.
Freud, S.: 1916, "Introductory Lectures on Psycho-Analysis." *SE*, 16:375, 1963.
     1919, "The Economic Problem of Masochism." *SE*, 19:159–160, 1961.

1903

SATYRIASIS denotes an abnormal, insatiable desire for sexual relationships by the male; often referred to as a perversion. A form of pseudo-hypersexuality, it usually masks a type of impotence that is characterized by inadequate and incomplete satisfaction. Such subjects are usually impulse ridden, unable to tolerate any frustration or delay. While seeking narcissistic supplies, such men attempt to dominate a succession of objects in orally parasitic and sado-masochistic relationships. Orgastically impotent, their behavior is actually an exaggeration of normal activity and represents an obsessional interest with the multiple functions of discharge and defense. The erotomania may replace or be replaced by compulsive masturbation, wherein the blame is projected onto the object in their fantasy, who is then held to be responsible for their failure to find satisfaction. [Fenichel, 1945.]

The Don Juan type of behavior represents both an avoidance and an endless search for the incestuous object, for the preoedipal or oedipal object-love of the mother. The persistent search for object-love may also be viewed as an attempt to find restitution for the traumatic object-loss.

Related Concepts: FRIGIDITY; PERVERSION.

REFERENCE

Fenichel, O., *The Psychoanalytic Theory of Neurosis.* Nor, p. 244, 1945.

1904

SCAPEGOAT MECHANISMS denotes the projection of the subject's own feelings of sinfulness and guilt onto another person in an effort to obtain self-purification. The scapegoat is also the object of the aggression which has been deflected onto him, so that persecution of the scapegoat usually follows the projection. The scapegoat mechanism may develop in many psychiatric disorders, where patients tend to project ego-syntonic thoughts and feelings which they have repressed and which they are unable to recognize in themselves. This is particularly prevalent in latent homosexuality. The need to find a scapegoat is not solely a phenomenon of individual psychology; it plays a prominent role in mass psychology, where groups accept the same scapegoat. For example, the anti-Semite projects his own instinctual drives and aggressions (against Jesus Christ), which have undergone partial repression, onto the Jew, either independently or at the command of a leader. [Fenichel, 1940.]

It was Freud's claim (in 1939) that hatred of the Jews was rooted in the remotest past, operating from the unconscious of those expressing a bigoted attitude. It was as though they believed there was truth in the claim that the Jews were the first-born of God. This hatred is further supported by the custom which has set the Jews apart until recent times; namely, that of circumcision, with its consequent castration anxieties. Finally, as Freud pointed out, those who excel in their expressed prejudice have become Christians only in late historic times, driven to it by bloody coercion. They have, as it were, not gotten over their grudge; they have displaced it onto those people who were the source of Christian thought and belief. At the bottom, their hatred for the Jews is a hatred for all that is Christian.

Related Concept: PROJECTION.

REFERENCES

Fenichel, O., "Psychoanalysis of Anti-Semitism." *AmIm*, 1:24–39, 1940.
Freud, S., 1939, "Moses and Monotheism." *SE*, 23:91–92, 1964.

1905

SCHIZOID CHARACTER identifies a character neurosis in which traits and mechanisms of a schizophrenic type are predominant. Fenichel (1945) described this syndrome, as follows: "There are neurotic persons who, without developing a complete psychosis, have certain psychotic trends, or have a readiness to employ schizophrenic mechanisms whenever frustrations occur."

Eidelberg (1959) discussed the treatment for this form of character neurosis, as follows: "From a technical point of view, it may be permissible to say that in this case . . . a logical discussion of the pathological traits was used, and appeared helpful in our attempts to prepare the patient for the analysis of his unconscious. Different from other cases of character neurosis, a schizoid personality may require more patience and flexibility from his analyst. Similar to other cases, the establishment of a workable transference appears to be the first target. However, while in other cases this goal is achieved by, so to speak, a negative means . . . in this case it was necessary to show the patient that his analyst did not have contempt for him, and to persuade him that the analyst did not deserve the contempt the patient had for him. Before any unconscious causes of his behavior could be approached, the conscious part of his personality had to change. This superficial change was not the result of my ability to prove to the patient that he was wrong, but rather the result of some form of identification. In other words, while we kept on discussing aesthetic and scientific problems, he began to like my approach, and began to identify with me. As a result of this identification, the problem of preventing the patient from remaining infantile and helping him to develop his own superego became even more decisive than in other cases. He had to learn that normal identification does not require a complete surrender of his own personality. On the contrary, his urge to become an identical copy of his mother was recognized as one of the important reasons for his hatred of her. The normal adult accepts from his elders and teachers only what he considers useful. Without becoming a photographic copy of one of them, he assimilates what he has incorporated into his own personal form of character."

Related Concepts: CHARACTER NEUROSIS; PSYCHOSIS.

REFERENCES

Eidelberg, L., "Schizoid Character." *JHH*, 8:34, 1959.
Fenichel, O., *The Psychoanalytic Theory of Neurosis.* Nor, pp. 443–444, 1945.

ADDITIONAL READINGS

Khan, M., & R. Masud, "Clinical Aspects of the Schizoid Personality: Affects and Technique." *IntJPsa*, 41, 1960.

Segal, H., "A Note on Schizoid Mechanisms Underlying Phobia Formation." *IntJPsa*, 35, 1954.

Silverberg, W. V., "The Schizoid Maneuver." *Ps*, 10, 1947.

Tillman, C., "Detecting Schizoid and Pre-Schizophrenic Personalities." *BMC*, 5, 1941.

1906

SCHIZOPHRENIA is a descriptive term introduced by Eugene Bleuler in 1911 to replace Kraepelin's concept of *dementia praecox*: the psychosis exclusive of the manic-depressive psychosis. It was meant to include those cases characterized by a splitting—a disintegration—of the personality; most especially, by a discrepancy between affect and thinking. These cases were described as exhibiting disturbances of thinking and affect, autism, and a break with external reality. Four main types (following Kraepelin) were described: catatonia, characterized by psychic regression and motor rigidity; hebephrenia, characterized by early onset, severe regression, and a shallow inappropriate affect; simplex, characterized by a lack of interest in the real world with arrest of mental and emotional development; and paranoia, characterized by systematized delusions with a relative lack of psychic deterioration. It is generally felt that these categories, while useful, are inadequate to cover the vast and complex variations in the functional psychotic disorders they are intended to differentiate.

Freud introduced a dynamic viewpoint and included cases of schizophrenia and paranoia into a syndrome he called *paraphrenia*. He insisted that schizophrenic language, symptoms and actions were meaningful; they could be understood according to the laws of primary process thinking, and were connectable genetically with the life experiences of the patient. In his early papers on psychopathology, Freud (1914) attempted "to explain all neurotic and psychotic phenomena as proceeding from abnormal vicissitudes of the libido." He viewed psychosis as a defense against traumatic experiences where the outcome was a withdrawal from an unbearable reality. Even in these early papers, Freud (1894)

pointed out that the mechanism of projection was the characteristic mechanism of paranoid delusions.

In his study of the Schreber case, Freud (1911) introduced his major premise regarding paraphrenia. The focus of attention was placed here on the break with reality and the ensuing "clamorous" symptoms of schizophrenia. The first step (analogous to repression) was the withdrawal of libido from objects in the external world. This decathexis of external reality was expressed by a catastrophic feeling of loss, with a consequent projection of anxieties into end-of-the-world phantasies. The detached libido returned back to the ego* resulting in the formation of megalomaniacal traits. Most of what Freud called the "clamorous" symptoms were associated with the hypothetical second step, the restitutional phase, in which an attempt was made to reconstruct the lost object world. The patients' delusions and hallucinations represented an "attempt at recovery" of the lost objects. Freud stated that the clinical picture was complicated by the fact that "the detachment of the libido . . . might just as easily be a partial one, a drawing back from a single complex." In other words, a part of the ego remained relatively intact.

The libidinal cathexis that brought about the restoration was described by Freud (1915) as follows: the internalized ideas of real objects were given up in the break with reality, i.e., the thing-cathexes of the system *Ucs.* were given up in the first step of withdrawal. The subsequent restitution was not accomplished by the recathexis of primal thing-cathexes, but by the recathexis of the word-presentations of objects, located in the system *Pcs.*

Freud's reformulation of both his libido theory and his hypothetical structure of the mind in the 1920's influenced his attempt to understand schizophrenia. Thereafter, he tried to differentiate between neurosis and psychosis in terms involving the new structural hypotheses, recognizing the ego as the intermediary, controlling, defensive apparatus between the impulses derived from the id and the frustrating forces that stem from the environment. Most subsequent psychoanalytic work has focussed on attempt to define the ego-defects involved in schizophrenia.

Other analysts, notably Hartmann (1953), tried to examine the functions and the structures of the

---

* After 1914 this was expressed as object-libido turning back into ego-libido.

ego in schizophrenia. "What is most obviously lacking is the organized ego-integrated stability of defenses." Primitive defense mechanisms—turning against the self, reversal into the opposite, projection, and the detachment of libido—"are more characteristic of schizophrenia than those like repression that demand a maintainance of countercathexis."

Schizophrenia has also been studied from the point of view of specific defects in ego functioning, in defenses, reality testing, and language. Eissler (1953) pointed out that in schizophrenics anxiety does not act effectively as a signal to forestall danger. M. Mahler (1952) investigated the faulty early object-relationships, drawing attention to her studies of the apparently unrelated diseases that comprise childhood schizophrenia. Hartmann attempted an economic explanation of the defects: he ventured to suggest that the schizophrenic ego's capacity for neutralization was deficient. The ego's capacity to defend itself against instinctual drives was largely dependent on its capacity to neutralize aggression. The sexualization and aggressivization of ego functions that arose through the failure in neutralization lead to the disturbances present in ego functions.

Related Concepts: PRIMARY PROCESS; PSYCHOSIS.

REFERENCES

Eissler, K., "Notes Upon the Emotionality of a Schizophrenic Patient and Its Relation to Problems of Technique." *PsaStC*, 8:191–251, 1953.
Freud, S.: 1894, "The Neuro-Psychoses of Defense." *SE*, 3:45–70, 1962.
    1911, "The Case of Schreber." *SE*, 12:9–84, 1958.
    1914, "The History of Psychoanalysis." *SE*, 14:7–66, 1957.
    1915, "The Unconscious." *SE*, 14:166–216, 1957.
Hartmann, H., *Essays on Ego Psychology*. IUP, pp. 185–186, 1964.
Mahler, M., "On Child Psychosis and Schizophrenia: Autistic and Symbiotic Infantile Processes." *PsaStC*, 7:286–303, 1952.

ADDITIONAL READINGS

Ausubel, D. P., "Relationships Between Shame and Guilt in the Socializing Process." *PsycholRev*, 62, 1955.
Bally, G., "Das Schuldproblem in der Psychotherapie." *SchweizANP*, 70, 1952.

Barabal, H. S., "A Psychoanalytic Approach to Schizophrenic Anxiety"' *PQ*, 32, 1958.
Bellak, L., "On the Etiology of Schizophrenia (Dementia Praecox). A Critical Review of the Literature of the Last 10 Years." *JNMD*, 105, 1947.
Bion, W. R.: "Notes on the Theory of Schizophrenia." *IntJPsa*, 35, 1954.
    "Development of Schizophrenic Thought." *IntJPsa*, 37, 1956.
Branch, C. H., "Schizophrenia and Related Problems." *JNMD*, 127, 1958.
Brody, E. B., & F. C. Redlich, "Psychotherapy With Schizophrenics: A Symposium." *AnSurvPsa*, 3, 1952.
Eissler, K. R.: "Remarks on the Psychoanalysis of Schizophrenia." *AnSurvPsa*, 2, 1951.
    "Notes Upon Defects of Ego Structure in Schizophrenia." *IntJPsa*, 35, 1954.
Fromm-Reichmann, F., "Basic Problems in the Psychotherapy of Schizophrenia." *Ps*, 21, 1958.
Hartmann, H., "Contribution to the Meta-Psychology of Schizophrenia." *PsaStC*, 8, 1953.
Knight, R. P., "Psychotherapy in Acute Paranoid Schizophrenia with Successful Outcome: A Case Report." *BMC*, 3, 1939.
Krapf, E., "The Social Therapy of Schizophrenia." *P*, 12, 1958.
Lidz, T., "The Familial Environment of the Schizophrenic." *P*, 13, 1959.
Menninger, K. A., "Reversible Schizophrenia." *P*, 1, 1922.
Nelken, L., "Analytische Beobachtungen über Phantasien eines Schizophrenen." *Y*, 4, 1912.
Richter, H., "Object Relationship in Schizophrenia." *Nervenarzt*, 29, 1958.
Rosenfeld, H. A., "Notes on the Psychopathology of Schizophrenia." *P*, 10, 1956.
Sechehaye, M. A., *Symbolic Realization; a New Method of Psychotherapy Applied to a Case of Schizophrenia*. IUP, 1951.
Spielrein, S., "Über den Psychologischen Inhalt eines Falles von Schizophrenie (Dementia Praecox)." *Y*, 3, 1911.
Storch, A., "Die Welt der beginnenden Schizophrenie und die Archaische Welt. Ein Existenzial-Analytischer Versuch." *ZNP*, 127, 1930.
Sullivan, H. S., "The Onset of Schizophrenia." *P*, 7, 1927.

1907

SCHIZOPHRENIC SURRENDER. This term was first proposed by Campbell (1941) and applies to that psychotic condition wherein there is an apparent, passive giving in, where the ego undertakes no activity for the purpose of defending itself.

Technically, this surrender may be described as the slow withdrawal of libidinal cathexis from the external world back onto the ego arising from the restitutional phase of the psychosis.

Related Concept: PSYCHOSIS.

REFERENCE

Campbell, C. M., "Clinical Studies in Schizophrenia: A Follow-Up Study of a Small Group of Cases of Deterioration with Few Special Trends." *AJP*, 99:475–483, 1943.

1908

SCHREBER CASE. A case history of a paranoid schizophrenic, Freud drew his data from a work published in 1903, *Memoirs of My Nervous Illness*, written during a period when its author, Daniel Paul Schreber, was a patient in an asylum in Saxony. Released in 1902, Schreber returned to his duties as a judge and carried on his life with no apparent outward symptomatology, until his wife's near-fatal illness in 1907 when he had a further break with reality and was again institutionalized. Thereafter, he remained in a disordered state and was largely inaccessible until his death in 1911.

Freud distinguished two essential delusional elements in Schreber's system: his transformation into a woman and his favored relationship to God. These interrelated "ideas" led Schreber into the belief that the world would be destroyed in more or less two-hundred years and that he, after being changed into a woman, would give rise to a better race of men through his physical union with God.

It was Freud's (1911) belief that the exciting cause of Schreber's illness was the appearance in him of a feminine (that is, a passive homosexual) wishful phantasy, which took as its object the figure of his doctor. An intense resistance to this phantasy arose on the part of Schreber's personality, and the ensuing defensive struggle, which might perhaps just as well have assumed some other shape, took on, for reasons unknown to us, that of a delusion of persecution. The person he longed for now became his persecutor, and the content of his wishful phantasy became the content of his persecution.

Schreber's struggle with Professor Flechsig, director of the inpatient department at the Psychiatric Clinic in Leipzig, again typifies Schreber's father complex. Schreber's persecutor was Flechsig who became God, the one who wanted to impregnate him.

The most striking characteristic of the paranoiac is the process of projection: he repressed an internal perception which, after undergoing a certain kind of distortion, entered his consciousness in the form of an external perception. In persecution, love changes into hate; by itself, this is not only characteristic of paranoia. It is also present in other symptoms.

Successive studies by a number of authors have helped to amplify the present record. In a paper published in 1956, Baumeyer reproduced a number of the original case records. In papers published in 1951, 1959, and 1963, Niederland supplied and interpreted early childhood data, and explained many of the pathogenic origins of Schreber's disorder. In 1959, he noted: "In correlating certain formations of Schreber's delusional system with experiences in his early life, it has been possible to arrive at the kernel of 'historical truth' in the genesis of such formations, thus illuminating hitherto unintelligible aspects of the Memoirs." These include the origin of the "divine miracles", the "cursorily made little men," the intense castration fears experienced by Schreber and other heretofore obscure features of his pathology.

Related Concepts: DELUSIONS; PARANOIA; PROJECTION; PSYCHOSIS.

REFERENCES

Baumeyer, F., "The Schreber Case." *IntJPsa*, 37:6, 47, 50, 51, 61, 1956.

Freud, S., 1911, "Psycho-Analytic Notes on an Autobiographical Account of a Case of Paranoia (Dementia Paranoides)." *SE*, 12:16–17, 41, 47, 55–56, 63, 66, 1958.

Niederland, W. G.: "Three Notes on the Schreber Case." *Q*, 10:579–591, 1951.

    "Schreber—Father and Son." *Q*, 28:151–169, 1959.

    "The Miracled-Up World of Schreber's Childhood." *PsaStC*, 14:383–413, 1959.

    "Further Data and Memorabilia Pertaining to the Schreber Case." *IntJPsa*, 44:201–207, 1963.

Schreber, D., 1903, *Memoirs of My Nervous Illness*. London: William Dawson, 1955.

ADDITIONAL READINGS

Fairbairn, W. R., "Considerations Arising Out of the Schreber Case." *M*, 29, 1956.

Katan, M.: "Schreber's Delusion of the End of the World." *Q*, 18, 1949.

    "Schreber's Pre-Psychotic Phase." *IntJPsa*, 34, 1953.

    "Schreber's Hereafter." *PsaStC*, 14, 1959.

Macalpine, I., & R. A. Hunter, "The Schreber Case. A Contribution to Schizophrenia, Hypochondria, and Psychosomatic Symptom Formation." *Q*, 22, 1953.

Shengold, L., "Chekhov and Schreber: Vicissitudes of a Certain Kind of Father-Son Relationship." *IntJPsa*, 42, 1961.

White, R. B., "The Schreber Case Reconsidered in the Light of Psychosocial Concepts." *IntJPsa*, 44, 1963.

1909

SCIENCE AND MAGIC. Freud (1933) expressed the view that a scientific *Weltanschauung* must submit itself to the truth and reject illusion. In this, he believed that psychoanalysis should adhere to the scientific *Weltanschauung* and not try to create one of its own. However, in psychoanalysis, as in all science, there was always the danger that belief in the omnipotence of science itself could prove to be a danger. As Freud (1913) pointed out, the animistic stage (followed by a religious phase) is now being dominated by our scientific age. Science teaches us that we are not omnipotent; we have only to study the natural laws to increase our actual power. In fact, the emotional acceptance of man's limitations —of his omnipotence—is a requirement of science, whatever its form. Without it, science cannot investigate the rational world.

Related Concept: WELTANSCHAUUNG.

REFERENCES

Freud, S.: 1913, "Totem and Taboo." *SE*, 13:88, 1955.

    1933, "New Introductory Lectures on Psycho-Analysis." *SE*, 22:181–182, 1964.

1910

SCOPOPHILIA is denotative of the act of looking to obtain instinctual gratification. A scopophilic* tendency is common in children, and was identified by Freud as a "component instinct." It emerges as pairs of opposites, one such set of paired instincts being scopophilic and exhibitionistic. Freud (1905) assumed that children are of a polymorphous perverse disposition (achieving abnormal sexual discharge only later), that "this same disposition to perversions is a general and fundamental human characteristic." Abraham (1913) added: "We assume with Freud that a considerable part of the scoptophilia of a healthy person succumbs to repression and sublimation in childhood. Some of the important psychological phenomena which owe their origin in a great part to this process are the desire for knowledge (in a general sense), the impulse towards investigation, interest in the observation of Nature, pleasure in travel, and the impulse towards artistic treatment of things perceived by the eye (for example, painting).

"In many neurotics we have to assume a constitutional intensification of the scoptophilic instinct. Nevertheless, the pleasure in looking can increase in importance as a result of an inhibition of sexual activity. In that case, instead of active sexual behaviour there appears a greater tendency to look on inactively at things from a distance. The results of this neurotic pleasure in looking may be very diverse. It may be in part preserved in its original form, in part altered through sublimation in the sense described above, and finally in part employed to form neurotic symptoms. The stronger the instinct is, the greater must be the work of sublimation in order to prevent the development of neurotic disturbances, and the more severe will such disturbances be if the formation of symptoms does take place."

Freud postulated that an adult pervert accepted an infantile polymorphous perverse wish, whereas a neurotic warded it off; therefore, he regarded the perversion as a negative of a neurosis. Later (1927), however, he recognized that fetishism was not the

---

* The correct form is *scopophilia*, which has been used in all the more recent translations of Freud (including the *Standard Edition*), and in most recent psychoanalytic literature by others; it was originally translated as *scoptophilia*. [Personal communication, J. Strachey to ed.]

result of the simple acceptance of an infantile wish: it represented, rather, a complicated defense, which resulted not in a symptom but in a perversion.

As a result of therapeutically successful analyses of homosexuals and masochists, Eidelberg (1954) suggested that all perversions are the result of defense mechanisms leading to ego-syntonic compromise formations. The analysis of scopophilic perverts disclosed that, while watching, they unconsciously identified with the watched object and, thus, experienced an unconsciously exhibitionistic gratification. Their scopophilia therefore represented a denial of the original exhibitionistic wish; it gratified the demands of the unconscious ego and of the superego. There appear to be more male than female scopophilic perverts. Scopophilics and exhibitionists are interested in the satisfaction of their wishes only if such satisfaction is forbidden, so that aggressive as well as sexual tendencies are gratified.

It seems that looking—similar in function to other sense organ derivatives—may represent the gratification or discharge of narcissistic and object-libido and destrudo.

Sense organs other than the eyes may also be used to achieve perverse pleasure (e.g., hearing or smelling). Originally, the sense organs were supposed to serve to discharge ego and libidinal instincts. Since the introduction of the concept of ego or narcissistic libido (and destrudo), those functions of sense organs which lead to narcissistic satisfaction or pleasure are separated from others which, as a result of a discharge of object libido and object destrudo, produce aggressive or sexual forepleasure.

The act of looking may also produce aesthetic end-pleasure. In describing the vicissitudes of instincts, Freud (1915) distinguished three stages. At first, activity is satisfied at looking at the external object; then, in turning against the self to study the self, there develops the desire to be looked at.

Related Concepts: EXHIBITIONISM; FOREPLEASURE; PERVERSION.

REFERENCES

Abraham, K., 1913, "Restrictions and Transformations of Scoptophilia in Psycho-Neurotics; With Remarks on Analogous Phenomena in Folk-Psychology." *SPA*, p. 208, 1942.
Eidelberg, L., *An Outline of a Comparative Pathology of the Neuroses.* IUP, p. 204, 1954.

Freud, S.: 1905, "Three Essays on the Theory of Sexuality." *SE*, 7:156–157, 166, 169, 191–194, 1953.
    1915, "Instincts and Their Vicissitudes." *SE*, 14:119, 129, 1957.
    1927, "Fetishism." *SE*, 21:149, 158, 1961.

1911

SCREEN MEMORY is denotative of that period of infantile amnesia which is made manifest in isolated fragments. It illustrates the forgotten years of childhood and is similar to the way the manifest dream represents the latent dream-thoughts. Since the memories which return come back as a cover for other associated but repressed memories, their actual representation may be true or false, or, what is more probable, a mixture of both.* In the analytic situation, the analyst takes them seriously, even if he suspects that what the patient remembers is not what actually happened, but, in one sense, what he wanted to happen.

The traumatic experiences of early childhood, up to and about the fifth year of life, are totally forgotten. These memories are not normally available for recall, falling within the period of what Freud (1939) called "infantile amnesia." These memories relate to sexual and aggressive experiences, in which there was no clear distinction between them, and to early injuries to the ego (narcissistic mortifications). It is precisely to this period in time that the psychoanalytic situation directs its attention. The process of analysis allows for a recall of these forgotten experiences which have been decisive in the life of the patient.

Case History

Eidelberg (1961) provided the following from the case of a frigid adult, who related:

"'Of course! Aunt Marie! I can see her now, quite clearly.' Her voice grew reminiscent. 'I can hear her voice. . . . It was a day just like today—very warm.

---

* Freud's letter to Pfister, in 1910, stated: "I can answer your theoretical doubts in accordance with your own inclination. There need have been no shameful or horrible incident, but only subsequent repression made it so. All repressions are of *memories*, not of experiences; at most the latter are repressed in retrospect. With the complexes one must be very careful; indispensable as the idea (of complexes) is in various performances, when one is theorising one should always try to find out what lies behind the complex, not make a frontal attack, which is too vague and inadequate."

We were in our garden. I can see and smell the white lilies. It was then that she tried to explain the facts of life to me. She was embarrassed, and what she said was not very clever. I had just had the curse, for the first time.... She said, "Now you're a young lady. Now you must stop playing with boys. You'll have to be very careful, or you could become pregnant!"'

"'Just by playing?' I asked her.

"'Yes. By playing with—well, when you're bleeding. . . .' She was very embarrassed.

"'A few days later, I was in the garden with my cousin Carl. We kissed, and we necked a little, and then, suddenly, he was lying on me. He lifted my skirt, and then I felt, for the first time, the same electric feeling I had today! I remember the whole scene very clearly. He started to undress me, and I embraced him, trembling with delight. Suddenly, the image of my aunt appeared, and again I heard her warning! I grew frightened, and ran away from Carl. I dashed inside the house, and went to bed. No one understood why. I stayed in bed until my next period came, and then I felt relieved. . . .'"

It is impossible for the analyst to say how much of what she said actually happened or was imagined. The fact is that after this memory returned and was worked through, the frigidity of the patient disappeared.

Related Concepts: REPRESSION; RESISTANCE; TRANSFERENCE.

REFERENCES

Eidelberg, L., *Take Off Your Mask.* Py, pp. 40–41, 1948.
Freud, S.: 1910, *Psychoanalysis and Faith: Dialogues with the Reverend Oskar Pfister.* BB, p. 31, 1963.
    1939, "Moses and Monotheism." *SE*, 23:74–75, 1964.

1912

SECONDARY (EPINOSIC) GAIN IN NEUROSIS is the subject's use of a neurosis as a source of gratification, derived from external factors. There is also a primary, or paranosic, gain connected with partial gratification and partial frustration of the original wish associated with the resolution of an intrapsychic conflict between the id, ego, and superego by a symptom compromise (Freud, 1917).

For example, a woman developed conversion hysteria as an outcome of intrapsychic conflict; her hysterical vomiting forced her husband, who had neglected her, to pay more attention to her, which in turn encouraged her to continue vomiting.

Whenever secondary gain is pronounced, and no replacement for it can be found in reality, the prognosis for successful treatment is poor. Both paranosic and epinosic gain operate as part of what Freud called *ego-resistance*.

Related Concepts: PRIMARY (PARANOSIC) GAIN IN NEUROSIS; RESISTANCE.

REFERENCE

Freud, S., 1917, "Introductory Lectures on Psycho-Analysis." *SE*, 16:383–385, 1963.

1913

SECONDARY IDENTIFICATION is characterized by a cathexis of the object-presentation by narcissistic libido and destrudo. One form of secondary identification appears to be connected with the stage of the oral phase of development (e.g., oral, melancholic, or total identification, in which the whole object is incorporated in the self). In this, the subject becomes more and more similar to the object and treats himself as if he were the object. Secondary identification may also take the form of hysterical identification, in which certain characteristics of the total personality are incorporated into the self. For example, Freud's (1905) patient, Dora, developed a cough like that of a woman she perceived as a rival.

Related Concept: IDENTIFICATION.

REFERENCE

Freud, S., 1905, "Fragment of an Analysis of a Case of Hysteria." *SE*, 7:82–83, 1953.

ADDITIONAL READINGS

Eidelberg, L., *An Outline of a Comparative Pathology of the Neuroses.* IUP, 1954.
Freud, S.: 1921, "Group Psychology and the Analysis of the Ego." *SE*, 18, 1955.
    1933, "New Introductory Lectures on Psycho-Analysis." *SE*, 22, 1964.

1914

SECONDARY PROCESS denotes the sum of the mechanisms which control the primary mechanisms and other activities of what was originally called the system *Ucs.* and today is referred to as the *id*.

Instead of insisting on immediate discharge of the dammed-up (mobile) energy to eliminate unpleasure, the secondary process attempts to control this discharge by inhibiting, postponing or modifying the instinctual gratification. The discharge takes place after the probable results of the gratification have been anticipated. In order to obtain such a discharge, in accordance with the reality principle, the original bound energy is changed into mobile energy.

For example, an individual, experiencing the feeling of hunger, inhibits the incorporation of food until he finds food which is suitable, guided by the memory of previous acts of eating. The dammed-up libido (or destrudo) which cathects the presentation of food and seeks discharge, is controlled and thereby achieves its gratification under the guidance of the ego (total personality). This control is caused by the ego's ability to differentiate between fantasy and external reality.

Strachey (1955) noted: "Freud argued that the 'primary psychical processes' do not by themselves make any distinction between an idea and a perception; they require, in the first place, to be inhibited by the 'secondary psychical processes', and these can only come into operation where there is an 'ego' with a large enough store of cathexis to provide the energy necessary to put the inhibition into effect. The aim of the inhibition is to give time for 'indications of reality' to arrive from the perceptual apparatus. But, in the second place, besides this inhibiting and delaying function, the ego is also responsible for directing cathexes of 'attention' on to the external world, without which the indications of reality could not be observed."

Related Concepts: EGO; PRIMARY PROCESS; REALITY PRINCIPLE; UNPLEASURE-PLEASURE PRINCIPLE.

REFERENCES

Freud, S., 1917, "A Metapsychological Supplement to the Theory of Dreams." *SE*, 14:220, 1957.
Strachey, J., "Editorial note." *SE*, 18:35, 1955.

1915

SELF denotes that concept of one's own person as distinguished from objects in the external world; the totality of self-presentations cathected in the ego (as opposed to object-presentations). Spiegel (1954) defined the self "as a frame of reference or zero point to which representations of specific mental and physical states are referred and against which they are perceived and judged." Others define the self as synonymous with the whole person.

The development of a sense of the self is strongly influenced by psychosexual and ego development, and by maturation from birth on. Partially as a result of perception, the infant soon develops a body ego in which he first begins to differentiate various aspects of his body image from objects in the external world. With the accumulation of identifications in the ego, as well as within the superego, multiple self-presentations are formed, the totality of which gradually form a stable concept of the self. The concept of the self is made more permanent as a result of the achievement of object constancy.

Flugel (1945) characterized this phenomenon, as follows: "[The child] does not clearly recognize the difference between a disagreeable outer stimulus and an unpleasant tension in himself (such as that caused by being cold, wet, or hungry). Everything connected with a state of tension, e.g. his own hunger sensations on the one hand and the breast that does not easily supply milk on the other, are regarded as 'bad' in the same way; just as the feeling of satisfied hunger and the satisfying nipple are regarded as 'good' in the same way.

"Associated with this fundamental absence of the distinction between the subjective and the objective, between the self and the not-self, are two further confusions of detail with important consequences. There is no adequate distinction between sensations and their accompanying feelings and impulses, nor —more important still—between these feelings and impulses and the associated outer objects. In other words the child does not distinguish between the cognitive and orectic aspects of his own experience, not between his own orexis and the outer world. Thus the sensations of hunger are not separated from the distress and anger aroused by these sensations, nor is anger, with its accompanying tendency to suck or bite aggressively, separated from the mother's breast which is failing to satisfy the hunger—and similarly in other situations. When distress is not alleviated and unsatisfied desire persists, the child begins to feel overwhelmed by his own inner tension, and it is this condition which gives rise to what psycho-analysts have sometimes described as fear of the instincts (i.e. of uncontrollable instinctual tension). In the earlier days of psycho-analysis the instincts which were thought of as arousing fear were mainly sexual, but as psycho-analysts began to concern themselves more and more with aggression, the accent in this connection passed from the sexual to the aggressive elements. The 'English School,' intensified and hastened this process by drawing attention to the importance of these aggressive elements in very early life. A vivid impression of the way in which the infant can come to feel threatened and overmastered by its own aggressiveness is conveyed, for instance, by Rivière: 'The child is overwhelmed by choking and suffocating; its eyes are blinded with tears, its ears deafened, its throat sore; its bowels gripe, its evacuations burn it'.* Thus the child's autogenous aggression, the biological purpose of which, as manifested for instance in crying, is no doubt to get others to relieve its needs, may threaten to destroy its owner, and it is the impotence of the child in face of the mounting tension which makes uncontrolled and unrelieved aggression appear as a situation of acute danger. If at these earliest stages there is at the same time no clear distinction between such distressful and alarming inner conditions and the associated outer objects or circumstances, it is easy to see that the first step has been taken towards the creation of an outer 'bogy' of ill-defined but intense and almost unimaginable evilness.

"A later and more definite step in the same direction occurs as soon as the mechanism of projection comes into play. The origins of this mechanism— of such immense importance to mental development and, especially in later life, to psychopathology— are perhaps to be found in the primal lack of distinction between the self and the not-self. In any case, however, when the distinction does actually begin to be drawn, the line of demarcation is not logical or consistent and the not-self will include many elements (both of 'badness' and 'goodness') which

a more experienced and sophisticated mind would unhesitatingly consider to be subjective and to belong to the person's own inner orectic life. Soon, however, other tendencies (our understanding of which admittedly still leaves much to be desired) begin to exercise a more selective influence in leading the child to ascribe some of his own experiences to the outer world and thus to cause projection. The most important factor in this selective influence (and here psycho-analysts are in pretty general agreement) is the attempt to identify pleasure with the self and unpleasure with the not-self."

In those instances where a psychic conflict promotes ego and libidinal regression and culminates in a withdrawal of object cathexis, there is also a fluctuation in self-presentation, affecting one's sense of identity and sense of self.

Related Concepts: DEPERSONALIZATION; SELF-OBSERVATION.

REFERENCES

Flugel, J., *Man, Morals and Society*. IUP, pp. 109–111, 1945.
Spiegel, L., "The Self, the Sense of Self and Perception." *PsaStC*, 14:1959.

ADDITIONAL READING

Wolberg, L. R., "The Problem of Self-Esteem in Psychotherapy." *NYSJM*, 43, 1943.

1916

SELF-ANALYSIS. Although Freud (1912) did not advise his patients to analyze themselves, he did express the opinion that a future analyst should prepare himself for his profession by conducting his own self-analysis. The analysis of his own dreams appeared to Freud to be the best way to become an analyst. However, he learned that many people are prevented from doing this by their resistance to such an analysis. He therefore suggested a didactic analysis, including courses in the theory and practice of psychoanalysis, as an essential component of a training program. In being analyzed, the future analyst not only learns the technique but gets rid of those unconscious blocks which would interfere with his recognition of patient's problems; a technique

---

* Rivière, J., "On the Genesis of Psychical Conflict in Earliest Infancy." *IntJPsa*, 17, 1936.

which also prevents the analyst from projecting his own problems onto the patient or from becoming sick himself.

In one of his last papers, Freud (1937) recognized the necessity of a training analysis and suggested that every analyst should periodically undergo analysis. However, for practical reasons this advice doesn't appear to have been generally accepted.

Related Concept: TECHNIQUE OF PSYCHOANALYSIS.

REFERENCES

Freud, S.: 1912, "Recommendations to Physicians Practising Psycho-Analysis." *SE*, 12:116–117, 1958.
       1937, "Analysis Terminable and Interminable." *SE*, 23:249, 1964.

1917

SELF-ESTEEM AND MASOCHISM. Some masochists appear to be lacking in self-esteem; they accuse themselves of all kinds of deficiencies. Although supported by the subject's life experiences, closer examination reveals that his self-accusation represents an unconscious denial of his infantile omnipotence.

For example, a patient who claimed that he went to prostitutes, because all the "nice" girls he was interested in rejected him, had to admit, in analysis, that the rejections about which he complained were all unconsciously self-provoked (Eidelberg, 1948).

Related Concepts: MASOCHISM; MASOCHISTIC MECHANISM; MORAL MASOCHISM.

REFERENCE

Eidelberg, L., *Studies in Psychoanalysis.* IUP, p. 31, 1948.

1918

SELF-OBSERVATION denotes the act of, or capacity for, self-scrutiny; a prerequisite for self-awareness and self-knowledge. From a practical standpoint, it is useful to distinguish between self-observation of the body and its functioning, and self-observation of thoughts, feelings, and psychic functioning. Under normal circumstances, there is little conscious self-observation of the body, except in cases of illness. Self-observation of psychic functioning is normally more common: it, too, may increase with the advent of mental illness, particularly in the early, less severe stages of psychosis when ego functioning is not as yet too severely impaired.

From the standpoint of ego psychology, the self-scrutinizing function of the mind constitutes one of the ego's specialized functions. This implies a splitting of the ego into two parts, one looking at the other. In this way, by taking preconscious and unconscious processes as objects of scrutiny, self-observation can reestablish mental links which have been lost.

There appears to be an inverse relationship between self-observation and the normal state of consciousness, a shift of cathexis inward from the external world. In some pathological states, particularly in the course of psychotic processes, a part of the ego which has become the object of self-observation, becomes projected, thereby alienating mental processes from the self.

The tendency to self-observation first manifests itself in relation to the child's own body. Freud (1915) noted that "the active aim appears before the passive, that looking precedes being looked at." Later in life, with the development of a well-formed, mature ego, it is applied to psychological functioning, varying in significance and importance in different individuals, in accordance with congenital factors, the presence of stress, and, in all probability, with other factors which cannot as yet be fully assessed.

The difference between normal and pathological self-observation may be exemplified by the difference between the self-observation found in the analytic situation and the self-observation which is typical of obsessive-compulsives. In the former, what occurs is merely a temporary splitting of the ego in the service of the ego itself; in the latter, the split is in the interest of the defense and denial of narcissistic and instinctual drives, and is of a more permanent character, having become a part of the character structure. The suppression of self-knowledge is characteristic of many neurotic patients, which is basically related to their attempts to keep instinctual drives and their derivatives under repression.

Related Concepts: DEPERSONALIZATION; NARCISSISM.

REFERENCES

Freud, S.: 1914, "On Narcissism: An Introduction."
  SE, 14:98–100, 1957.
      1915, "Instincts and Their Vicissitudes." *SE*,
  14:129, 1957.

REFERENCES

Fenichel, O., *The Psychoanalytic Theory of Neurosis.*
  Nor, pp. 17, 161, 227, 262, 1945.
Freud, S., 1933, "New Introductory Lectures on
  Psycho-Analysis." *SE*, 22:75–76, 1964.

1919

SENSATION is produced by external and internal stimuli. The sense organ perceptions of the external world form the individual's image of the external world. Through inner perception, the individual learns that he is hungry, thirsty, sleepy, etc. While it is impossible to prove the existence of the world, he is usually able to differentiate between fantasy and sense organ perceptions (except in some cases of extreme mental illness).

The consciousness of external and internal stimuli takes place automatically, although elimination of certain stimuli (e.g., closing the eyes) can occur voluntarily. Acknowledgement of the presence of certain sensations caused by either internal or external stimuli can also be consciously avoided. Suppression is one mechanism in which the knowledge of a sensation is eliminated by a voluntary decision. Repression and denial are mechanisms through which the individual avoids conscious awareness of certain sensations, without consciously making such a decision. Repression, suppression or denial do not eliminate the stimulus; they only prevent the knowledge of the sensation caused by the stimulus from becoming conscious (a similar process takes place if anesthetics are given). [Fenichel, 1945.] In sleep, too, some stimuli are not perceived or their perception is warded off. Freud (1933) pointed out that a small discharge of instinctual energy takes place in each perception. The ego can be isolated from the id and the superego. In self-observation, the superego scrutinizes the ego. The ego, on the other hand, acts as the "honest broker" between the id, superego, ego and the external reality.

Related Concepts: EGO; EMOTION; ID; REPRESSION; SUPPRESSION.

1920

SENSE OF GUILT denotes an unpleasant feeling caused by the superego's criticism of, and interference with, particular drives or their form of expression. Freud originally assumed that sexual drives produce a feeling of guilt, but he later recognized this as true only if they are connected with aggressive impulses.

The feeling of guilt may be conscious, partly conscious (i.e., the feeling is experienced consciously, but the real cause is unconscious), or unconscious. In the latter case, we may assume that it results from the patient's need for punishment. Even if the patient is not conscious of having such a need, his continuous provocation of external punishment or self-punishment makes it apparent to the analyst (as in psychic masochism, and accident proneness).

Guilt is often confused with remorse. Remorse, as Freud (1930) noted, is related "only to a deed that has been done." In other words, the feeling of guilt may be understood as an emotional signal indicating the presence of aggressive wishes, whereas the feeling of remorse informs us that such feelings have actually been gratified. Thus, an individual who succeeds in rejecting an aggressive wish, after he has been warned of its presence by a feeling of guilt, is freed of this feeling, provided he has rejected (and not only repressed, but suppressed) the aggressive impulse. On the other hand, if he gratifies his aggressive wish, he will experience a feeling of remorse, which can only be eliminated by undoing what he has done and renouncing its repetition in the future.

According to Eidelberg (1954), many neurotics experience a feeling of remorse in connection with their aggressive wishes, because, as a result of their infantile omnipotence, they do not differentiate between their wishes and their actions. Consequently, an obsessional neurotic has to undo not only what he has done, but what he wanted to do.

Related Concepts: AGGRESSION; MELANCHOLIA; RE-MORSE; SEXUALIZATION AND AGGRESSIVIZATION OF EGO FUNCTIONS.

REFERENCES

Eidelberg, L., *An Outline of a Comparative Pathology of the Neuroses.* IUP, pp. 153–154, 1954.
Freud, S., 1930, "Civilization and Its Discontents." *SE*, 21:130–131, 1961.

ADDITIONAL READINGS

Freud, S.: 1914, "Mourning and Melancholia." *SE*, 14, 1957.
⎯⎯ 1924, "The Economic Problem of Masochism." *SE*, 19, 1961.
Jones, E., "Fear, Guilt, and Hate." *IntJPsa*, 10, 1929.
Klein, M., "A Contribution to the Theory of Anxiety and Guilt." *IntJPsa*, 29, 1948.
Nunberg, H., "The Feeling of Guilt." *Q*, 3, 1934.

1921

SENSE OF IDENTITY is the awareness of being a person separate and distinct from all others; it is based on the integration of the body image with the vicissitudes of the libido, childhood identifications, and developmental changes from both endowment and the social role (Greenacre, 1958). Both ego and superego functions are involved in giving the individual his sense of identity.

Metapsychologically, the borders of the self (total personality) are hypercathected and the distinction from the "not I" is emphasized. This hypercathexis is first generated by the experience of separation from the mother and the sensation of being alone. The increasing locomotor and visual experiences between the eighteenth month and third year of life add to the sense of separateness. Excessively prolonged fusion or closeness of the growing child with the mother tend to interfere with the development of the feeling of separateness and, therefore, with his sense of identity. Development of a normal sense of identity might also be prevented by repression and denial of infantile narcissistic mortifications.

Related Concepts: SELF-OBSERVATION; SYMBIOSIS.

REFERENCE

Greenacre, P., "Early Physical Determinants in the Development of A Sense of Identity." *JAPA*, 6:612–627, 1958.

ADDITIONAL READINGS

Erikson, E., *Identity and the Life Cycle.* IUP, 1959.
Kramer, P., "On Discovering One's Identity. A Case Report." *PsaStC*, 10, 1955.
Lichtenstein, H., "Identity and Sexuality: A Study of Their Interrelationship in Man." *JAPA*, 9, 1961.
Lynd, H. M., *On Shame and the Search for Identity.* HB, 1958.
Mahler, M., "Autism and Symbiosis, Two Extreme Disturbances of Identity." *IntJPsa*, 39. 1958.
Wheelis, A., *The Quest for Identity.* Nor, 1958.

1922

SEQUESTRATION, according to Saul (1958), is a process through which the individual consciously detaches the pathological part of his personality from the normal part. For example, a young man refers to the dictates of his superego as the voices of his father and his father's father; and he says, referring to his id impulses, that he sees intellectually that he has a body, but he has no experience of any urges, needs or desires arising from it. He tries to avoid having to deal with those parts of his psyche which he cannot control.

Related Concepts: ISOLATION; PSEUDOIDENTIFICATION.

REFERENCE

Saul, L., "Technique and Practice of Psychoanalysis." L, p. 125, 1958.

1923

SEXUAL CURIOSITY. Seeing and touching represent the first activities in the discharge of the sexuality. However, the normal person uses them only to gain forepleasure and remains interested in the genital act for the gain of end-pleasure. For neurotics touching or seeing may lead to end-pleasure. Freud (1905) pointed out that shame appears to be a reaction formation which controls scopophilic tendencies which the small child does not have. Shame is an acquired characteristic.

Sexual curiosity can be sublimated into a desire to acquire all forms of knowledge. As a result of the repression of sexual curiosity, an inhibition of its sublimation may develop which manifests itself as an intellectual inhibition (Freud, 1926).

Related Concepts: INFANCY; SCOPOPHILIA; SUBLIMATION.

REFERENCES

Freud, S.: 1905, "Three Essays on the Theory of Sexuality." *SE*, 7:156–157, 191–192, 1953.
     1926, "Inhibitions, Symptoms and Anxiety." *SE*, 20:87–89, 1959.

1924

SEXUAL INHIBITION is denotative of those prohibitions, threats and punishments connected with weaning, toilet training and castration threats. Under certain conditions, the inhibitory factor may lead to trauma and may result in repression or disavowal or other mechanisms of defense and, thus, to the formation of the various neurotic phenomena, of neurotic symptoms, of neurotic character traits, of addiction, and of borderline cases. Ferenczi (1908) summarized his view, as follows: "I may sum up as follows my view on male psycho-sexual impotence: I. Male psychosexual impotence is always a single manifestation of a psychoneurosis, and accords with Freud's conception of the genesis of psychoneurotic symptoms. Thus it is always the symbolic expression of repressed memory-traces of infantile sexual experiences, of unconscious wishes striving for the repetition of these, and of the mental conflicts provoked in this way. These memory-traces and wish-impulses in sexual impotence are always of such a kind, or refer to such personalities, as to be incompatible with the conscious thought of adult civilised human beings. The sexual inhibition is thus an interdiction on the part of the unconscious, which really is directed against a certain variety of sexual activity, but which, for the better assuring of the repression, becomes extended to sexual gratification altogether.

"2. The sexual experiences of early childhood that determine the later inhibition may be serious mental traumata. When the neurotic predisposition is marked however, unavoidable and apparently harmless childhood impressions may lead to the same result.

"3. Among the pathogenic causes of later psychosexual impotence, incestuous fixation (Freud) and sexual shame in childhood are of specially great significance.

"4. The inhibiting effect of the repressed complex may manifest itself at once in the first attempts at cohabitation, and become fixed. In slighter cases the inhibition becomes of importance only later, in cohabitation accompanied by apprehension or by specially strong sexual excitement. An analysis carried to a sufficient depth, however, would probably be able in all such cases to demonstrate beside (or, more correctly, behind), the current noxious influence that is acting in a depressing way also repressed infantile sexual memories and unconscious phantasies related to these.

"5. Full comprehension of a case of psychosexual impotence is only thinkable with the help of Freud's psycho-analysis. By means of this method cure of the symptom and prophylaxis against its return is often to be obtained even in severe and inveterate cases. In mild cases suggestion or a superficial analysis may be successful.

"6. The psychoneurosis of which the sexual inhibition is a part manifestation is as a rule complicated by symptoms of an 'actual-neurosis' in Freud's sense (neurasthenia, anxiety-neurosis)."

Related Concepts: FRIGIDITY; IMPOTENCE; INHIBITION; LIBIDINAL TYPES; SEXUAL CURIOSITY; SEXUALIZATION AND AGGRESSIVIZATION OF THINKING.

REFERENCE

Ferenczi, S., 1908, "The Analytic Interpretation and Treatment of Psychosexual Impotence." *SPsa*, pp. 32–34, 1916.

1925

SEXUALITY. Freud (1905) drew a clear distinction between the concepts of sexual and genital, for the former includes *all* functions which are directed towards the obtainment of pleasure from whatever zone or organ of the body, while the latter is brought into the service of reproduction connected with a love object. Accordingly, the concept *sexual* is not confined to adult genital activity but is enlarged to include any activity which is erotic. The sexual instinct, in both its bodily and psychic aspects, does not appear in a finished form, but goes through several complex stages before genital primacy is reached.

There is an unbroken line in this development. It

begins diffusely with the erotic gratification connected with sucking, grasping, etc. which are attached to the vital somatic functions. It has, as yet, no sexual object, and is thus autoerotic. Its sexual aim is dominated by the autoerotogenic zone. Later, between the ages of two and four to five, a choice of a sexual object is made, and there is a splitting of the primary narcissistic libido (autoerotic libido). An infant does not differentiate between the inside and outside regarding his mother and her breasts as a part of his own body; the presentation of the self is cathected by primary narcissistic libido. After he learns to make this differentiation, the presentation of the object is cathected by object-libido and the self by secondary narcissistic libido.

From the age of approximately four onward, before the phase of puberty, a period of latency or near-latency ensues. At the cost of infantile sexual impulses, the mental forces predominate, impeded in their course by the construction of what Freud metaphorically called *dams*. The flow does not cease; it is diverted wholly or in part to other ends. In short, the reproductive processes are deferred. They are either sublimated or they give rise to perverse impulses, or both. The perverse impulses which arise from the autoerotogenic zones lead to feelings of unpleasure. The dams of which Freud writes are thus "constructed" to suppress this unpleasure (reaction formation). The sublimated drives, on the other hand, are responsible for the more organized, civilized forms of behavior. With the arrival of puberty at least two decisive alterations occur which call a halt to the former period of latency: the primacy of the genital zone is asserted and the process of finding an object takes place. This is accomplished by the mechanism of exploiting forepleasure. What were formerly self-contained sexual acts become preparatory to new sexual aims. An object-choice, in brief, is now possible; a differentiation into masculine and feminine counterparts occurs. The oedipal conflict, in which the boy responds to his identification with his father and the girl with her mother prepares the way for the primacy of the genital zone. The sexual instinctual components distinguished in the early phases proceed side-by-side until there is a primacy of the genitals, and the normally demanded unification of the erotic function is established.

At any stage of sexual development, a point of fixation can occur and a neurosis develop. The sexual instincts are prevented from seeking gratification by psychical obstructions and are thus blocked from attaining their aim. They find their way subsequently into other channels; i.e., in parapraxes, dreams, neuroses, etc.

Mature sexuality is threatened from three directions: from the first by a fixation or regression to the pregenital stages which mobilizes defense mechanisms and thus prevents a normal discharge of genital desires; from the second by latent homosexual wishes which interfere with mature heterosexual performance; and from the third by the presence of aggressive wishes which combine with sexual needs to mobilize fear and feelings of guilt.

Related Concepts: AGGRESSION; ANAL PHASE; ATTRACTION OF THE FORBIDDEN; GENITAL PHASE; LATENT HOMOSEXUALITY; ORAL PHASE; PHALLIC; POLYMORPH PERVERSE.

REFERENCE

Freud, S., 1905, "Three Essays on the Theory of Sexuality." *SE*, 7:177–178, 233, 1953.

ADDITIONAL READINGS

Abraham, H., "A Contribution to the Problems of Female Sexuality." *IntJPsa*, 27, 1956.
Abraham, K., "Beobachtungen über die Beziehungen zwischen Nahrungstrieb und Sexualtrieb." *BPV*, 1913.
Greenacre, P., "Special Problems of Early Female Sexual Development." *PsaStC*, 5, 1950.
Kestenberg, J. S., "Vicissitudes of Female Sexuality." *JAPA*, 4, 1956.
Money-Kryle, R., *The Development of the Sexual Impulses.* HB, 1932.
Tausk, V., "Zur Psychologie der Kindersexualität." *Z*, 1, 1913.
Teslaar, J. S. van, "Religion and Sex. An Account of the Erotogenetic Theory of Religion as Formulated by Theodore Schroeder." *R*, 2, 1915.
Wolff, M., "Sexuelle Neugierde eines kleinen Mädchens." *PsaPrx*, 3, 1933.
Wulff, M., "Beiträge zur infantilen Sexualität." *C*, 2, 1912.

1926

SEXUALIZATION AND AGGRESSIVIZA-TION OF ANXIETY are the processes by which anxiety, ordinarily employed by the ego as a signal of danger, becomes the source of unconscious aggressive gratifications. Anxiety is then sought, usually in an unconscious manner, rather than avoided through defensive maneuvers. Generally, the unconscious gratification comes from one of two sources: triumph over the threatening danger or object, or masochistic pleasure derived from the anxiety experience. Submission to the superego, with the pleasure of atonement, may also result from the discomfort of anxiety. Counterphobic characters, according to Fenichel (1954), generally show a need to deny unconscious anxiety, along with a concomitant pleasure in experiencing conscious anxiety and overcoming danger. Some persons unconsciously seek out and experience anxiety in order to repeat the infantile parent-child relationship in which they were reassured by the parent (e.g., the patient who repeatedly visits the doctor for reassurance about fears of illness). [Fenichel, 1953.]

Humor, in general, represents a sublimation of anxiety. An example of the relationship between masochism and anxiety is given in the case of a young woman who unconsciously sought situations where she could be anxious about the payment of bills, taxes, etc. Her anxiety experience was a substitute for an anal rape by her father, achieved through anxious fantasies about forced extraction of money from her. Anxiety as an aspect of an aggressive (masochistic) relationship with the superego is seen in the case of a student who was unconsciously impelled to experience anxiety before each examination; atonement to his superego was a necessary prerequisite to his passing any test.

Related Concepts: ANXIETY; ATTRACTION OF THE FORBIDDEN; COUNTERPHOBIA; SEXUALIZATION AND AGGRESSIVIZATION OF EGO FUNCTIONS.

REFERENCES

Fenichel, O.: "Defense Against Anxiety, Particularly by Libidinization." OF-CP, p. 303, 1953.
    "The Counterphobic Attitude." OF-CP, p. 163, 1954.

ADDITIONAL READING

Freud, S., 1926, "Inhibitions, Symptoms and Anxiety." *SE*, 20, 1959.

1927

SEXUALIZATION AND AGGRESSIVIZATION OF EGO FUNCTIONS. Psychoanalytic theory has always postulated a separation between the energies employed for the ego functions and those used for instinctual gratifications with the help of outside objects. Hartmann (1958) noted that there is a conflict-free sphere in the ego which operates with neutralized (indifferent) energies derived from the sexual and aggressive instincts. In this, the ego functions probably have neither an instinctual aim nor an object, and are primarily uninvolved in instinctual conflict. When non-neutralized energy, whether aggressive or sexual, is employed for ego functions—with the retention of the instinctual aim, object and quality—the sexualization or aggressivization of the ego functions may be said to have occurred.

After the introduction of the second instinct theory, Freud (1926) discussed the eroticization and aggressivization of the ego functions. Many activities which appear to be harmless, like walking or writing, may become inhibited whenever they come to represent an unconscious gratification of infantile wishes.

Under normal conditions, the ego functions (e.g., thinking and talking) lead to a discharge of secondary narcissistic libido or destrudo (or, according to Hartmann, to the discharge of neutral libido or destrudo). Under pathological conditions, such functions are probably connected with the discharge of object-libido and destrudo. The term sexualization, though still used, appears to have originated with the concept of the first instinct theory; in this, the ego instincts were free of libido.

Related Concept: NEUTRALIZATION.

REFERENCES

Freud, S., 1926, "Inhibitions, Symptoms and Anxiety." *SE*, 20:89–90, 1959.
Hartmann, H., *Ego Psychology and the Problem of Adaptation.* IUP, 1958.

1928

SEXUALIZATION AND AGGRESSIVIZATION OF SPEECH is denotative of those processes by which speech becomes a source of unconscious infantile sexual or aggressive gratification. The speech apparatus, or the spoken words and their content, may be employed to gratify sexual or aggressive wishes directed toward an infantile object. Speaking may represent a biting attack, an expression of oral sadism. Silence may correspond to a longed-for state of fusion with the breast, or a defense of oral aggression. Words may be offered as anal gifts, expelled as a fecal attack, aggressively withheld in defiant constipation, or allowed to burst or slip out in regressive incontinence. Urethral-phallic influences can convert speech into a stream of words, to be exhibited and regulated, guided by unconscious purposes rather than communicative needs. Talking can become a phallic battle; to be interrupted or to be silent may signify a dreaded castration (therefore, something to be avoided). Stammering is a common neurotic disturbance of speech, and slips of the tongue are transient intrusions of conflict in speech. The unique, individual, ego-syntonic qualities of speech, characteristic of individual styles, may represent the constant influence of unconscious conflicts. [Fenichel, 1945.]

Freud (1905) discussed the intentional bringing into prominence of sexual facts and relations by speech. He did not hesitate to use the word sexuality in the study of many mental phenomena. In his analysis of jokes, he pointed out that smut represented a sexual aggression.

Related Concepts: PARAPRAXIS; STAMMERING (STUTTERING).

REFERENCES

Fenichel, O., *The Psychoanalytic Theory of Neurosis.* Nor, pp. 312–317, 1945.
Freud, S., 1905, "Jokes and Their Relationship to the Unconscious." *SE*, 8:97–98, 1960.

1929

SEXUALIZATION AND AGGRESSIVIZA-TION OF THINKING is denotative of those processes by which the ego function of thinking becomes a source of unconscious infantile gratification. The wishes may be derived from any libidinal phase. Thoughts may represent milk, to be given or aggressively withheld. Thinking, especially "freely,"

may reawaken fears of oral incorporation as oral sadistic drives are released. Thoughts, representing feces, may be manipulated in unconscious anal masturbation, or aggressively withheld or forced on the outside object, or even on the self. An incontinence of thoughts may result in sloppy or loose thinking. The forgetting of thoughts may be a form of soiling. An idea equated with an anal or phallic baby may undergo a difficult birth. Thoughts may express urethral and phallic aims and conflicts. Thinking, in general, may have an oedipal meaning, to know the forbidden, to intrude on the forbidden domain of the parents. The sexualization and aggressivization of thought may produce a specific neurotic inhibition or a special style of thinking. It is marked in cases of obsessional neurosis. [Freud, 1926.]

Clinical Example

"His symptom was that he had to re-read frequently the same word, and to note compulsively the letters out of which it was composed. This disturbance appeared at about thirteen. At that time, he had noticed that some of his school mates possessed a larger vocabulary than he. Accordingly, he bought a dictionary, and attempted to increase the amount of words he knew, but his studies were in vain, as it soon became apparent that he was not making any progress. He became increasingly depressed about this until his mother, who had noticed his upset condition, advised him to burn the dictionary. Although the patient had already decided to do this, he could no longer carry out his intention, as soon as he had received the same advice from his mother. As the first association to this incident, he had the idea that the minute observation of the various words and letters represented symbolically a sexual play with the various parts of a beautiful woman's body." [Eidelberg, 1948.]

Related Concepts: CREATIVITY; EGO FUNCTIONS.

REFERENCES

Eidelberg, L., *Studies in Psychoanalysis.* IUP, p. 57, 1948.
Freud, S., 1926, "Inhibitions, Symptoms and Anxiety." *SE*, 20:121–122, 1959.

1930

SHAME is a painful affect related to feelings of guilt or inadequacy, fears of being ridiculed, humiliated or exposed; it is a defense against the wish to exhibit, based on the anticipation of rejection by the external world or the superego. Freud (1905) regarded shame (and morality) as historical precipitates.

According to Eidelberg (1954), shame may be described as an emotional signal warning us of exhibitionistic wishes and the possible dangers of gratifying them. When an individual anticipates that his attempt to gain attention may fail, that he may receive scorn instead of admiration, he may utilize the feeling of shame to inhibit his exhibitionistic wishes. In this sense, shame is connected with anxiety. Shame may also be experienced after an unsuccessful attempt to gain attention, and it is probable that the shame resulting from anticipation occurs only on the basis of previous experiences in which the wish to gain attention was frustrated. In addition, shame may be experienced when weaknesses (real or fancied) are exposed (hence, the expression, "He was caught with his pants down").

We may differentiate between external shame, when the individual is ridiculed by external objects, and internal shame, when he is attacked by his own superego.

Related Concepts: EXHIBITIONISM; HUMILIATION; SENSE OF GUILT.

REFERENCES

Eidelberg, L., *An Outline of a Comparative Pathology of the Neuroses*. IUP, p. 140, 1954.
Freud, S.: 1905, "Three Essays on the Theory of Sexuality." *SE*, 7:162, 1953.
        1926, "The Question of Lay Analysis." *SE*, 20:210–211, 1959.

1931

SHAMELESSNESS is a character trait representing a reaction formation against strong unconscious feelings of shame, probably resulting from a failure to develop inhibiting mechanisms or a counterphobic mechanism (Fenichel, 1945). As a rule, shamelessness involves a pact with the superego; the wish used as countercathexis is allowed expression instead of the original id impulse. Sometimes, the wish may be expressed shamelessly only under certain conditions. For example, as a reaction to his sadistic wishes, an attorney was shamelessly ruthless in the courtroom, but extremely passive in his relations with women. In a gross form, shamelessness is typically seen in mania and general paresis. [Sterba, 1929.]

Freud (1905) believed that clothing, because it concealed the body, mobilized curiosity. This curiosity may appear in normal individuals who seek to view or to expose their bodies in order to gain forepleasure or in perverts who obtain end-pleasure by such acts.

Related Concepts: COUNTERPHOBIA; EXHIBITIONISM; SCOPOPHILIA.

REFERENCES

Fenichel, O., *The Psychoanalytic Theory of Neurosis*. Nor, p. 164, 1945.
Freud, S., 1905, "Three Essays on the Theory of Sexuality." *SE*, 7:156–57, 1953.
Sterba, E., "Nacktheit und Scham." *PsaP*, 3:58–67, 1929.

1932

SHORT-TERM THERAPY designates any of a number of treatment methods which seek the elimination of neurotic symptoms—of bringing repressed material into consciousness—by means that are less costly and of shorter duration than is true for classical psychoanalysis. These methods have been numerous, employing hypnosis (Wolberg, 1954), dramatization (Grinker, 1945), and transference manipulation by the therapist (Alexander, 1948). However, no effort to shorten psychoanalysis to date has withstood the test of time.

Freud (1937) tried to shorten the time required for analytical treatment by giving the patient a time limit; he adhered to this but he realized that this approach (while sometimes speeding up the analysis) had many disadvantages.

Short-term therapy also refers to psychotherapeutic techniques which are directed toward the relief of immediate and pressing conflicts, usually of an acute nature, and directed to the support offered to parents in dealing with their children and of children in need of guidance. There is no conflict between these methods and those of classical psychoanalytic theory as long as no false claims are made for the methods employed and these methods are not called psychoanalysis. The conflicts between proponents of new methods of treatment and classical psychoanalysts have always arisen when short therapy techniques were called psychoanalysis.

Alexander (1948) proposed the use of a corrective emotional experience in which unconscious transference relationships were alleged to be made tractable and conscious when the therapist played an appropriately dramatic role. Like all other attempts to shorten the length of psychoanalyses, this method proved unsuccessful.

Related Concepts: ACTIVE THERAPY; WILD PSYCHO-ANALYSIS.

REFERENCES

Alexander, F.: *Fundamentals of Psychoanalysis.* Nor, 1948.
Freud, S., 1937, "Analysis Terminable and Interminable." *SE*, 23:218–219, 1964.
Grinker, R., & J. Spiegel, *Men Under Stress.* Bl, 1945.
Wolberg, L., *Hypnoanalysis.* G&S, 1954.

1933

SIGNAL ANXIETY is the sign of an impending danger which takes place when the individual has experienced a prior defeat, and anticipates the defeat taking place again. The act of anticipation requires, from an economical point of view, the use of aggressive energy which is discharged against the self. In Freud's (1926) view, anxiety appeared as an original reaction to the infant's helplessness which the infant later repeated as a warning signal in case of an external or internal danger.

Eidelberg (1954) noted that there is a basic difference between the emotion experienced when the individual is overwhelmed by external or internal reality (terror) and the emotion experienced in anticipation of a narcissistic mortification. With the latter, the characteristic feeling of anxiety serves as a signal to the total personality to mobilize its resources so as to deal (combating, escaping, or surrendering) with the aggressor.

Related Concepts: ANXIETY; NARCISSISTIC MORTIFICATION.

REFERENCES

Eidelberg, L., *An Outline of a Comparative Pathology of the Neuroses*, IUP, p. 135, 1954.
Freud, S., 1926, "Inhibitions, Symptoms and Anxiety." *SE*, 20:166–167, 1959.

1934

SIMULTANEOUS ANALYSIS OF MOTHER AND CHILD, according to M. Sperling, is a method whereby mother and child are treated in separate sessions by the same analyst, preferably without the child knowing of the mother's treatment. She introduced this technique in 1946 for the treatment of young children suffering from severe ulcerative colitis.

The onset of the clinical manifestations of ulcerative colitis in young children occurs typically between the ages of one and one-half to three, a period which corresponds to the time of toilet training, when the child has to give up soiling, to give up the pleasure in his excretion, and to acquire bowel control. It is also the age during which the child undergoes an important psychological transformation, turning from a passive and completely dependent infant into the overtly aggressive and even destructive toddler, i.e., when he begins to show strivings for self-assertion and independence from his mother. An unusual preoccupation with bowel functions and the restriction of the child's aggressive drives during this phase interfere with his satisfactory development and provide the basis not only for a bowel disturbance as a reaction to certain experiences but also for a disturbance that may affect the child's ability to handle and to express aggression adequately in later life.

The repressed anal-erotic and anal-sadistic needs of the mother can be gratified "legitimately" through the illness of the child. For instance, the mother of a four-year-old boy who developed ulcerative colitis at the age of eighteen months reported with pride that at the age of one her son had already shown an unusual concern about cleanliness. Her reaction to his developing ulcerative colitis can be described best in her remark, "I am such a clean woman and my child has such a messy disease." In the analyst's playroom, he was afraid even to touch clay and had to wash his hands immediately when he touched it. His illness made it necessary for both of them to handle the forbidden and consciously abhorred fecal matter continually.

In further psychoanalytic work with adult patients suffering from ulcerative colitis, Sperling (1959) could show that this specific relationship between mother and child in ulcerative colitis may be transferred later to another person. Such a mother-substitute may be a sibling, a sweetheart, the wife or husband, or even the patient's own child. It is always one person with whom the patient has this exclusive relationship. The degree of security or insecurity of this relationship is indicated by the decrease or increase of the patient's symptoms. The onset and recurrences of ulcerative colitis occur whenever there exists a threat of separation from this person—mother or mother-substitute, or the danger of loss of this relationship.

Related Concepts: ANAL PHASE; PSYCHOSOMATIC.

REFERENCES

Sperling, M.: "A Psychoanalytic Study of Ulcerative Colitis in Children." *Q*, 15:302–329, 1946.
    "A Study of Deviate Sexual Behavior in Children by the Method of Simultaneous Analysis of Mother and Child," in *Dynamic Psychopathology in Childhood*, L. Jessner and E. Pavenstedt, eds. G&S, pp. 221–242, 1959.

ADDITIONAL READINGS

Burlingham, D., "Child Analysis and the Mother." *PQ*, 4, 1935.
Johnson, A., & S. Szurek, "Collaborative Psychiatric Therapy of Parent-Child Problems." *AmJOrthopsychiat*, 12, 1942.
Levy, K., "Simultaneous Analysis of Mother and Child." in *The Psychoanalytic Study of the Child*. IUP, 1960.

1935

SKIN EROTICISM. Cutaneous contact, touch, as well as temperature and pain sensations, are sources of erotogenic stimulation.* Fenichel (1945)

* The word *feeling* refers to both an internal perception (e.g., thirst) and to an external perception (e.g., touching).

noted: "After the achievement of genital primacy these sensory stimulations function as instigators of excitement and play a corresponding part in forepleasure. If they have been warded off during childhood they remain isolated, demanding full gratification on their own account and thus disturbing sexual integration."

Nominally identified with the oral phase of libidinal development, skin eroticism—the sensations from the mouth, hand and skin—all combine to form what Spitz (1955) called "a unified situational experience in which no part is distinguishable from the other." This description corresponds to Freud's (1905) definition of the skin as the erotogenic zone par excellence.

The pleasure derived from painful stimulation of the skin is the erotogenic basis of all types of masochism. The part played by forepleasure, according to Fenichel, becomes of primary concern, "a procedure that often makes masturbation more gratifying for them than an actual realization of their perverse activities which could not have fulfilled all the anticipated details." The sexual aim is thus no longer directed toward end-pleasure. The fantasy tries to overcome the fear that blocks the capacity for end-pleasure; rather, the fantasy is directed toward controlling the fear so that pleasure can take place.

Related Concepts: EROTOGENIC ZONES; TEMPERATURE EROTICISM.

REFERENCES

Fenichel, O., *The Psychoanalytic Theory of Neurosis.* Nor, p. 70, 1945.
Freud, S., 1905, "Three Essays on the Theory of Sexuality." *SE*, 7:156, 209–210, 1953.
Spitz, R., "The Primal Cavity: A Contribution to the Genesis of Perception and Its Role in Psychoanalytic Theory." *PsaStC*, 4:215–240, 1955.

1936

SLEEP is the gratification of the need to rest which is served by weakening or decreasing the cathexis of the presentations of inner and external perceptions and of the motoric apparatus. The necessary precondition, Freud (1925), noted, is the concentration of the ego upon the wish to sleep and the withdrawal of psychical energy from all the interests of life. In this, sleep represents a return to a state which is similar to that which existed in the womb: a return to the intrauterine life that has been abandoned.

Psychoanalysis has studied this phenomenon by investigating the pathology of insomnia, and by an examination of dream content. The dream appears to protect the sleeper from awakening; a dream state is made possible by a reduction of endopsychic censorship. Insomnia, on the other hand, prevents the gratification of the need to sleep, because of the unconscious meaning of such a need (e.g., dying).

The repression decreases in sleep because the discharge of the infantile energy is to a large degree prevented. However, whenever an important increase of instinctual tension takes place, sleep is terminated and the patient awakens. [Freud, 1933.]

Related Concepts: ABSENCE; DREAMS; INSOMNIA.

REFERENCES

Freud, S.: 1925, "An Autobiographical Study." *SE*, 20:45, 1959.

    1933, "New Introductory Lectures on Psycho-Analysis." *SE*, 22:16, 19, 21, 1964.

ADDITIONAL READINGS

Fraiberg, S., "On the Sleep Disturbances of Early Childhood." *RP*, 15, 1958.

Jekels, L., "A Bioanalytical Contribution to the Problem of Sleep and Wakefulness." *Q*, 14, 1945.

1937

SLIPS OF THE TONGUE are a form of parapraxes which result from a partial breakthrough of repressed wishes (Freud, 1916–1917). He emphasized the substitutive form of the act, rather than the intended form, i.e., a second purpose was made to feel itself felt alongside of the first. More recently, Eidelberg (1948) indicated that "slips" may represent an unconscious defensive maneuver rather than a simple breakthrough of an unconscious impulse. He stressed the need for analyzing the associations of the consciously intended tendency as well as those of the unconscious interfering tendency. He cited clinical material in which the apparently "innocent" conscious intention was associated with deeply forbidden unconscious infantile fantasies. These fantasies impelled the ego to unconsciously and to defensively mobilize an opposing impulse which deceptively appeared to be the forbidden one. In effect, his patients "confessed" to a lesser crime in order to hide the greater one associated with the consciously intended tendency.

Yazmajian (1963) suggested that all slips result from unconscious conflict, but that in some slips the associative chains of the word components are not in opposition; instead they constitute a complementary unit derived from a single unconscious fantasy. His clinical findings indicated that the unconscious intention of the ego was to bring the two words involved in such slips into conscious apposition, and served to represent the unconscious fantasy in a condensed symbolic form. In effect, he suggested that the word components of such slips can be approached as though they were a dream-pair, or two elements of the manifest content of a single dream. Each half of a dream-pair, or two elements in a single dream, often have associative chains which are not individually meaningful or reveal only part of a fantasy. By fusing the two dreams, there is often a complete formulation of the unconscious fantasy which the ego could originally express only after defensively splitting the total fantasy.

The stress of the above studies was on the relationship of the word components and their associative chains to unconscious ego activities. In subsequent contributions, Eidelberg (1960) explored slips of the tongue in the context of the operations of the total personality and of his concept of narcissistic mortification. He pointed out that the unconscious motivation of some slips is to avoid an internal narcissistic mortification, whereas in others it is to avoid an external one. He felt that careful metapsychological investigation of slips illuminated more general problems involved in infantile wishes and omnipotence; in neurotic symptoms; in forepleasure and endpleasure; in instinctual gratification and instinctual satisfaction; in aesthetic pleasure; and in wit.

Eidelberg also noted that the reactions of patients to the commission of slips often reflected their basic character structures as developmentally influenced by their attempts to maintain their infantile omnipotence. For example, he described as the erotic type those persons who are slightly disturbed by their parapraxes without however minding too greatly. This kind of reaction was compared to "la belle indifférence" of the conversion hysteric. The narcissistic type denoted those individuals who are proud of their slips and almost enjoy them as though they were jokes. Persons who are so much afraid of committing a slip that they avoid talking altogether were termed obsessional types.

At a seminar, Yazmajian (1963) demonstrated that in many instances the associative chains of the word components of slips are of secondary importance. In some cases the very process of slip formation became instinctualized and assumed a symbolic value. The ego unconsciously utilized the technique of slip formation for the symbolic expression of oral, anal, phallic, and genital drives and fantasies, as well as certain ego identifications and superego demands. Yazmajian also demonstrated the way in which some slips are utilized consciously for symbolic purposes. In this, he considered the previously overlooked fact that there are really two broad groups of slips: those in which the individual is aware of having committed a slip and those in which he is apparently unaware of having done so. He felt that those slips which occurred on a purely mental level without verbalization could be regarded as a third group. In one case it was clinically shown that both the creation of a slip and its immediate repression was unconsciously intended by a patient because of the symbolic castrative meaning attached to the act of repression. Since the act of repression was an integral part of the total form of the slip, the analysis of its symbolic meaning was essential to its full understanding. The case of a patient was cited who was apparently unaware of having made a slip. Upon questioning, she remarked that she was aware of having committed a slip but "didn't want to bother correcting it." The unconscious symbolic implication of this conscious attitude required analysis since the ego unconsciously intended it to be part of the total form of the slip. Slips involving the reversal of time sequences were created by one patient in order to symbolically negate time itself. A case history was cited which demonstrated the use of a slip as a means of unconscious communication to the analyst of a taboo transference yearning.

Related Concepts: PARAPRAXIS; REPRESSION.

REFERENCES

Eidelberg, L.: *Studies in Psychoanalysis.* IUP, pp. 154–161, 174–202, 1948.
    "A Third Contribution to the Study of Slips of the Tongue." *IntJPsa*, 41:596–603, 1960.
Freud, S., 1916–1917, "Introductory Lectures on Psycho-Analysis." *SE*, 15:62–63, 1963.
Yazmajian, R.: "Verbal and Symbolic Processes in Slips of the Tongue." Presented at State University Downstate Medical Center, Division of Psychoanalytic Education, November 6, 1963.
    "Slips of the Tongue." Presented at Midwinter Meeting of the American Psychoanalytic Association, December 6, 1963.

ADDITIONAL READINGS

Devereux, G., "A Primitive Slip of the Tongue." *AnthropQuart*, 30, 1957.
Seyler, C. A., "Slips of the Tongue in the Norse Sagas," *IntJPsa*, 36, 1955.
Winterstein, A. R., "Drei Fälle von Versprechen." *C*, 2, 1911.

1938

SOCIAL COMPLIANCE, a term coined by Hartmann (1944), is analogous to somatic compliance; it is descriptive of the way in which the social structure determines, at least in part, the adaptive chances of a particular form of behavior. Thus, it facilitates certain modes of energy discharge with a predisposition toward characteristic trends in personality development in a given culture.

In a later work, Hartmann (1964) noted: "From these considerations, it appears that the intimate analytic study of an individual's interaction with his social environment can be included among the methods of sociology. Analysis has taught us as much about the various family structures as it has about biological human needs. The attention of analysts has been perforce directed to the object relationships of childhood, for these are infinitely more important to the development of personality than those of later life; the general and legitimate prevalence of the genetic point of view among analysts has reinforced this attitude. This is a second point, besides the general theory of action, where psychoanalytic data and hypotheses are indispensable to sociology but in which there has been a divergence of interest between the two fields.

This statement in no way denies, indeed is far from denying, that our patients' current social environment constantly enters the analytic picture. It simply explains why this aspect has been less energetically studied, and why our knowledge about the current milieu appears less clearly in our largely genetic psychological concepts. I agree with Parsons that in this regard our descriptions of analytic work could be more explicit. If a concerted attempt in this direction were systematically made, it would probably yield a more complete insight into the psychological meaning of specific social structures than could be obtained through any other method."

Related Concepts: CHOICE OF A NEUROSIS; PSYCHO-SOMATIC; SOMATIC COMPLIANCE.

REFERENCES

Hartmann, H., "Psychoanalysis and Psychology." *PsaT-IUP*, pp. 326–341, 1944.
　　Essays on Ego Psychology. IUP, p. 93, 1964.

1939

SOCIAL INSTINCT IN MAN manifests itself in the pleasure the individual takes in the company of the members of his family, friends, or with people who speak his own language, etc. It is recognizable in the earliest human responses and persists up to the end as a craving for social contact. The so-called social instincts do not represent a sublimation of the original infantile energy but have a close relationship to it. Freud (1923) regarded the affectionate relationship between parents and children and between married people as belonging to this class. In his view (1911), after the heterosexual choice has been made, the homosexual tendencies are not eliminated, rather they become aim-inhibited and are responsible for a love of mankind in general. He also considered tenderness and the so-called social identifications as reaction formations against the aggressive wishes (Freud, 1922).

In tracing the origin of the libido involved in social instinct, Sperling (1955) showed that the love for either parent could be deflected onto a sibling and, later, transferred to society as a whole, and could therefore be considered a heterosexual as well as a homosexual function. It was Sperling's contention that narcissistic libido may also be involved by the mechanism of appersonation. The mechanism of appersonation facilitated the transition from an egotistical community of interests to an anaclitic love of the members of the family. [Sperling, 1944.]

Related Concept: SOCIAL COMPLIANCE.

REFERENCES

Freud, S.: 1911, "Psycho-Analytic Notes on An Autobiographical Account of a Case of Paranoia (Dementia Paranoides)." *SE*, 12:61, 1958.
　　1922, "Some Neurotic Mechanisms in Jealousy, Paranoia and Homosexuality." *SE*, 18:231–232, 1955.
　　1923, "Libido Theory." *SE*, 18:258, 1955.
Sperling, O.: "On Appersonation." *IntJPsa*, 25:128–132, 1944.
　　"A Psychoanalytic Study of Social-Mindedness." *Q*, 24:265–266, 1955.

1940

SOCIAL MINDFULNESS is a form of altruism in which a highly sublimated love is directed toward society. Socially mindful people give time to the study of social conditions and search for the causes of and solutions to social problems. Sperling (1955) observed that often they feel personally responsible for the improvement of social conditions. If ambition, economic gain, popularity, political advantage or social hunger—the desire to be accepted by the group—play a dominant role, the results may be spurious, i.e., behavior which is superficially similar to genuine social mindfulness only as long as the particular need is served. Freud (1911) pointed out that those manifest homosexuals who reject the direct genital gratifications often excel in their sublimation of social activities.

Related Concept: ALTRUISM.

REFERENCES

Freud, S., 1911, "Psycho-Analytic Notes on an Autobiographical Account of a Case of Paranoia (Dementia Paranoides)." *SE*, 12:61–62, 1958.
Sperling, O., "A Psychoanalytic Study of Social Mindedness." *Q*, 24:256–269, 1955.

1941

SOCIETY AND SELF. When the infant is born, the family he enters represents the objects of the external world. The family helps him to survive, for without such help the infant would die shortly after his birth. At first, his mother, then both parents, family and friends constitute the society he learns to love and hate. Freud (1939) noted that the superego is the successor and representative of the parents who supervised his actions in the first period of life.

The orders and commandments the child receives become memories which guide him and help him gratify those wishes which are acceptable and inhibit others which are not. Thus, each wish has two aspects: (a) *I like it* or *dislike it*, and (b) *they like it* or *dislike it*. Memories of received-praise or punishment form the nucleus of the infantile superego. At first they are ego-alien in that they represent a foreign body; slowly they become assimilated and, thus, ego-syntonic. It appears that an unsuccessful repression of infantile wishes interferes with this integration and permits an adult to retain his infantile superego.

Erikson (1950) viewed ego-identity, as follows: "With the establishment of a good relationship to the world of skills and tools, and with the advent of sexual maturity, childhood proper comes to an end. Youth begins. But in puberty and adolescence all sameness and continuities relied on earlier are questioned again, because of the rapidity of body growth which equals that of early childhood and because of the entirely new addition of physical genital maturity. The growing and developing youths, faced with this physiological revolution within them, are now primarily concerned with what they appear to be in the eyes of others as compared with what they feel they are, and with the question of how to connect the roles and skills cultivated earlier with the occupational prototypes of the day. In their search for a new sense of continuity and sameness, adolescents have to refight many of the battles of earlier years, even though to do so they must artificially appoint perfectly well-meaning people to play the roles of enemies; and they are ever ready to install lasting idols and ideals as guardians of a final identity: here puberty rites 'confirm' the inner design for life.

"The integration now taking place in the form of ego identity is more than the sum of the childhood identifications. It is the accrued experience of the ego's ability to integrate these identifications with the vicissitudes of the libido, with the aptitudes developed out of endowment, and with the opportunities offered in social roles. The sense of ego identity, then, is the accrued confidence that the inner sameness and continuity are matched by the sameness and continuity of one's meaning for others as evidenced in the tangible promise of a 'career.'

"The danger of this stage is role diffusion. Where this is based on a strong previous doubt as to one's sexual identity, delinquent and outright psychotic incidents are not uncommon. If diagnosed and treated correctly, these incidents do not have the same fatal significance which they have at other ages. It is primarily the inability to settle on an occupational identity which disturbs young people. To keep themselves together they temporarily overidentify, to the point of apparent complete loss of identity, with the heroes of cliques and crowds. This initiates the stage of 'falling in love,' which is by no means entirely, or even primarily, a sexual matter—except where the mores demand it. To a considerable extent adolescent love is an attempt to arrive at a definition of one's identity by projecting one's diffused ego images on one another and by seeing them thus reflected and gradually clarified. This is why many a youth would rather converse, and settle matters of mutual identification, than embrace."

Related Concepts: AIM-INHIBITED DRIVES (INSTINCTS); FEAR; INSTINCT (INSTINCTUAL DRIVE); REPRESSION; SUBLIMATION; SUPEREGO.

REFERENCES

Erikson, E., *Childhood and Society*. Nor, pp. 227–228, 1950.
Freud, S., 1939, "Moses and Monotheism." *SE*, 23:117, 1964.

1942

SOMATIC COMPLIANCE is the predisposition of an organ to respond as a locus for psychogenic symptoms; it is based in constitutional factors.

In the case of Dora, a patient who entered treatment suffering from aphonia (among other symptoms), Freud (1905) discovered that it first arose in coincidence with the absence of her "suitor." When the person she unconsciously loved was away, she gave up talking; speech had lost its value because she was no longer able to speak to her loved one. Later on, in an attempt to avoid the coincidence of his absence with the onset of her attacks, their periodicity changed, for otherwise their regularity would have betrayed her secret. To this, Freud was to add the evidence of the inordinate gratification she received as a child from oral activities; an "overindulgence," he called it. Hysterical symptoms occur because of a certain degree of somatic compliance. When this is not forthcoming, something other than a hysterical symptom arises; of a similar nature, perhaps a phobia or an obsession; in short, a mental symptom.

Related Concept: CHOICE OF A NEUROSIS.

REFERENCE

Freud, S., 1905, "Fragment of a Case of Hysteria." *SE*, 7:41–42, 1953.

1943

SOMATIC STIMULI AND DREAMS. Freud (1900) considered bodily sensations to be among the dominant dream stimuli. As such, somatic stimuli are not themselves capable of supplying the dream content. "It forces the dream-thoughts to make a choice from the material destined to serve the purpose of representation in the dream-content, inasmuch as it brings within easy reach that part of the material which is adapted to its own character, and holds the rest at a distance."

Since the dream serves to fulfill a wish, even though it be painful or disagreeable, it must utilize those sensations which will serve this purpose. Somatic factors are responsible for the content of the dream. The gratification of a wish may produce unpleasure to the total personality. Whenever the somatic wish cannot be gratified by the dream the patient awakens. Freud, in a footnote added in 1919, noted that Rank had studied the stratification of symbols in arousal dreams: what appeared in the dream as a sexual stimulus was originally due to the increased tension of the pressure in the bladder.

Related Concept: DREAMS.

REFERENCE

Freud, S., 1900, "The Interpretation of Dreams." *SE*, 5:235, 402–403, 1953.

1944

SPEECH FUNCTIONS, according to Freud (1940), bring the thoughts and ideas of the ego into a firm connection with the memory traces of visual and auditory perceptions. With the acquisition of speech a decisive step is taken toward the development of reality testing; it allows for a more precise communication with objects and for trial actions by way of anticipation (Fenichel, 1945). Inhibitions of speech—from mutism, stuttering and slips of the tongue to occasional lapses stemming from a given situation—interfere with these normal processes and are thus classed as clinical symptoms resulting from repression or other pathogenic causes.

The style of speech, the choice of words, and the metaphors employed are all influenced by the developmental history of the ego and of the instincts. It may communicate an infantile mode of defense; it may have libidinal and aggressive connotative characteristics; it may be equated with milk, feces, urine, semen, etc. In hysterical aphonia, the tongue may be cathected by phallic libido and thus serve as a phallic symbol. Words may acquire the significance of introjected objects, e.g., the conflict between the object and ego is expressed as a conflict between the patient and his speech production. Speech may have an exhibitionistic, narcissistic meaning in terms of attacking, seducing or charming the object, and may be especially threatening where there is a fixation to the omnipotence of words. Because obscene words retain much of their original magical significance, they may arouse defensive maneuvers. Affective speech may be inhibited, as well, where there is an intolerance of affect, and result in halting or incomplete productions. This may result, as Fenichel pointed out, from an obsessive tendency to doubt everything and to prepare for action instead of acting, which in severe cases may lead to a kind of paralysis. If it is due to a defect in the function of the superego (which is primarily introjected through the auditory sphere), the capacity to make a decision may be impaired; the fear of aggressive feelings may overwhelm the subject. When these functional disorders of speech are more than simple inhibitions, they are typical examples of pregenital conversion neuroses.

In slips of the tongue, as Eidelberg (1948) noted, a phrase or word that was to have been spoken is interfered with and results in another word or phrase taking its place. This "substitution" has both a conscious and unconscious significance; the latter represents a gratification of infantile instinctual wishes emanating from the id and the unconscious part of the ego which sets up a defense to prevent the unconscious wish from achieving satisfaction. This defense is two-fold: the instinct-fusion pressing for satisfaction is turned against the self, and the opposite type of instinct-fusion is mobilized. An analysis of the word or phrase which is eliminated should not be overlooked. Jones (1957) noted: "Eidelberg had now written a paper pointing out that the conscious intentions were often not 'harmless', and that the slips of the tongue or pen could be determined by ego-syntonic reactions against them—in other words, the reverse mechanism to that described by Freud."

In the psychoanalytic situation, speech serves as a means of discharge and as a binding of affects. Verbalization substitutes discrete discharges for more global ones, which may lead to overt destructive acts or to illness. The act of speech objectifies preconscious and conscious inner processes and strengthens the function of the reality principle.

Related Concepts: NEOLOGISM; SLIPS OF THE TONGUE; STAMMERING (STUTTERING).

REFERENCES

Eidelberg, L., *Studies in Psychoanalysis.* IUP, pp. 161, 1948.
Fenichel, O., *The Psychoanalytic Theory of Neurosis.* Nor, pp. 46, 47, 182, 1945.
Freud, S., 1940, "An Outline of Psycho-Analysis." *SE*, 23:162, 1964.
Jones, E., *The Life and Work of Sigmund Freud.* HPI, 3:213, 1957.

1945

SPHINCTER CONTROL, one of the principal stages of psychosexual development, is achieved through the voluntary regulation of the anal and urinary sphincters. The renouncement of the "immediate" instinctual pleasure connected with these bodily functions serves as a prototype for the control of some instinctual wishes, the child's need to renounce instinctual gratification to satisfy the demands of a loved object. Freud (1908) was the first to draw attention to the correlation between those whose pleasure in anal sensations had been unusually great in infancy and the character traits which were likely to occur later in life, namely those of orderliness, miserliness, and obstinacy.

In his developmental scheme, Erikson (1959) included the anal phase and sphincter control in the stage of autonomy versus shame and doubt. Erikson emphasized the significance of the fact that only the child himself can fulfill these functions, and that his voluntary cooperation must be obtained in developing sphincter control.

Related Concept: SUPEREGO.

REFERENCES

Erikson, E., *Identity and the Life Cycle.* IUP, 1: 39–41, 1959.
Freud, S., 1908, "Character and Anal Erotism," *SE*, 9:167, 19.

ADDITIONAL READINGS

Abraham, K.: 1924, "A Short Study of the Development of the Libido." *SPA*, 1, 1953.
  1921, "Contributions to the Theory of Anal Character." *SPA*, 1, 1953.
Ferenczi, S., *Psychoanalysis of Sexual Habits.* BB, 1952.
Freud, S., 1905, "Three Contributions to the Theory of Sexuality." *SE*, 7, 1953.

1946

SPHINCTER MORALITY, according to Ferenczi (1925), results from the child's compliance with parental demands for regulation of fecal matter; it is a precursor of the superego. At this phase of development, the child begins to distinguish between internal impulses and external reality. Sphincter pleasure and magical mastery are relinquished because of the fear of object-loss and because of an identification with the continent object. There is a conflicted oscillation between compliance and defiance, and between incontinence and autonomy. There are further developments in the concept of time, of delay, of future consequences, and the beginnings of such values as right and wrong, good and bad. Reaction formation and reversal defense against anal drives are important forerunners of the superego regulation. To be good is to be clean, to be bad is to be soiled or dirty. Later concepts of morality including chastity and honesty have roots in sphincter responsibility and cleanliness. Early anal and urethral identifications are important, according to Ferenczi, "not only in the sense that the child constantly compares his achievements in these directions with the capacities of his parents, but in that a severe sphincter morality is set up which can only be contravened at the cost of bitter self-reproaches and punishment by conscience."

The expression "to do one's duty" is illustrative of the unconscious connection between the sense of responsibility and the infantile regulation of defecation. Shame, disgust, and humiliation are affects associated with sphincter morality; guilt appears only with the later development of an internalized superego. The pregenital archaic superego equates the struggle over impulse control and sphincter control, and repeats with the ego the sadomasochistic struggle over defiance and compliance.

"In the archaic superego the aggressive energy attaching to the prohibiting introspect is least neutralized and very closely approximates instinctual qualities. It is such predominance of an archaic superego that may be of importance in the genesis of observational neurosis" (Weissman, 1954).

Related Concepts: ANAL PHASE; EGO-IDEAL.

REFERENCES

Ferenczi, S., 1925, "Psychoanalysis of Sexual Habits," in *Further Contributions to the Theory and Technique of Psychoanalysis*. HPI, pp. 259–271, 1926.
Weissman, P., "Ego and Superego in Obsessional Character and Neurosis." Q, 23:529–543, 1954.

1947

SPIDERS are symbolically employed in folklore, in dreams, and in phobias. Abraham (1922) noted: "The fact that . . . dreams contain a special use of spider symbolism indicates that there are probably still further meanings of this symbol. Perhaps this communication of mine will stimulate others to publish similar and supplementary analyses.

"The significance of the spider in folk psychology has not been sufficiently considered from the psychoanalytical point of view. The fact that it serves both as a good and a bad omen may be regarded as an expression of a generally widespread ambivalent attitude towards this insect. There is no doubt that it produces a feeling of 'uncanniness' in many people."

Occasionally, as Sterba (1950) noted, the spider may assume a masculine connotation and signify the revenging oedipal father or, in the transference, the analyst who drains the patient financially and sits and waits, poised for his destruction. In birth fantasies, the spider may symbolize the child, or, like other vermin, siblings. The many different symbolic meanings of the spider help explain the ambivalence with which it is often viewed, and the frequency with which it has been regarded as a good or a bad omen. These meanings, and the fact that the female spider of some species kills the male after copulation, indicate why spiders may be related to the idea of death or of love followed by death, and why spider fantasies often have an oral connotation and correspond to the sexual fantasy of being devoured.

In the dream, Abraham noted, the spider symbolism indicated the following: "In the first place the wicked mother who is formed like man, and in the second place the male genital attributed to her. In this the spider's web represents the pubic hair and the single thread the male genital. . . . The spider in this case also represented the dangerous mother, but in a special sense. The patients' unconscious phantasies were concerned with the danger of being killed by his mother during incestuous intercourse." Nunberg laid stress on the fact that the spider kills its victim by sucking its blood, and that this sucking served as a castration symbol in the case observed, i.e., it gave expression to the typical phantasy of losing the penis during the sexual act.

Clinical Example

Abraham provided the following case history: "I was standing beside a cupboard in the office with my mother or my wife. As I was taking a pile of deeds out of the cupboard a big, hairy, long spider fell out at my feet. I felt very glad that it did not touch me. A little later we saw the spider sitting on the floor, looking almost bigger and more horrible than before. It flew up and came whirring at me in a big semicircle. We fled through the door into the next room. Just as I was pulling the door to, the spider reached me on a level with my face. Whether it got into the next room, or was shut out in the office, or was crushed in the door I do not know.

"For some weeks prior to this dream the patient's resistances towards the female sex, or to be more correct, towards the female sex-organs, had come to light, together with his tendency to make himself into a woman by way of castration phantasies, and on the other hand to turn his mother into a man. He brought me a drawing of the spider as it appeared in the dream, and was himself astonished to recognize in his drawing the oval shape of the external female sex-organs, the hair surrounding it, and in the middle, where the body of the spider was, something that was unquestionably very like a penis.

"The spider's falling down in the dream represents the fall of his mother's penis, which becomes detached on his going to the cupboard (mother symbol). His relief at not having come in contact with the spider, i.e., the maternal genitals, comes from his horror of incest. In real life the sight of the female sex-organs, and still more any manual contact with them, used to horrify him. The subsequent increase in size of the spider, which also rises up and flies in a semicircle through the air, is an obvious symbol of erection: the maternal phallus attacks the dreamer. The doubt at the conclusion of the dream as to whether it was crushed in the door, is significant. We here find a phantasy of crushing the penis such as we meet with in the phantasies of neurotic women with a marked castration complex. This feature also reminds us of the first dream in which the spider was also crushed.

"We thus arrive at the conclusion that the spider has a second symbolic meaning. It represents the penis embedded in the female genitals, which is attributed to the mother. In support of this I may quote the dream of another patient, in which the dreamer attempted to enter a certain dark room filled with a number of small animals. From certain allusions in the manifest content of the dream, but particularly from the patient's associations, there was no doubt that the room represented the mother's body. As he entered it a butterfly fluttered towards

him. For the sake of brevity I need only mention that, just as in other dreams, the wings of the butterfly had the significance of female genitals; this symbolic use of the wings is based, among other things, on the observation of their opening and closing. The body of the butterfly, which is concealed between the wings, was unmistakably a male genital symbol. The idea of a hidden female penis also came out in this patient's neurotic phantasies.

"The 'wicked' mother who, according to Freud's view, is represented by the spider, is clearly a mother formed in the shape of a man, of whose male organ and masculine pleasure in attack the boy is afraid—just as young girls are timid in regard to men. The patient's feeling towards spiders can be best described by the word 'uncanny'."

Related Concept: SYMBOLIZATION.

REFERENCES

Abraham, K., 1922, "The Spider as a Dream Symbol." *SPA*, pp. 327–332, 1942.
Sterba, R. F., "On Spiders, Hanging, and Oral Sadism." *AmIm*, 7:21–28, 1950.

1948

SPOKEN WORDS IN DREAMS. Freud (1900) descriptively offered it as an invariable rule: when a spoken utterance is used in a dream it has originated from a spoken speech in the dream material. The wording of the speech may either be preserved in its entirety or have undergone only slight alteration. Isakower (1954) contended that the "speech elements in dreams are direct contributions from the superego and contribute to the manifest content of the dream."[*] Further, in analyzing a patient's dream, he was to note that in the crossover toward wakefulness the spoken words were utilized in the "warding off the abortive attempt of the superego at a first interpretation of his dream. Under ordinary circumstances, when the dream work has its way, the secondary reaction takes care of the superego contributions also. It is understood that the secondary reaction is largely a function of the superego anyway. . . .

---

[*] Italics removed.

"*One might say that focusing the mental eye on the dream during (and immediately after) the process of waking up assists reinstating the regime of the waking reality*. In this phase of transition the superego may assert itself with exaggerated vigor, and may appear giving off an emphatically condemning comment on the whole dream."

Related Concept: HYPNAGOGIC PHENOMENON.

REFERENCES

Freud, S., 1900, "The Interpretation of Dreams." *SE*, 4:183-185, 1953.

Isakower, O., "Spoken Words in Dreams." *Q*, 23:1-6, 1954.

1949

STAGE FRIGHT is an anxiety state induced by acting before an audience, or, in a more general sense, by the assumption of any position in the limelight. This phobic type of reaction may be related to both erythrophobia and fear of crowds, and is generally both a defense and a gratification of voyeuristic-exhibitionistic impulses. The subject looks and is looked at, responds to, and evokes a response. The desire to exhibit may defend against both castration anxiety and object-loss, while the audience may reassure him against these dread outcomes. An unconscious primal scene excitement may be simultaneously attributed to the observers. There may be a confession of weakness and temptation as well as unacceptable instinctual impulses directed toward the object-audience. The object then serves as an external superego in which the subject's worthiness is judged to provide a heightened self-esteem, an absolution from guilt; or, conversely, to impose punishment, humiliation and castration on the subject. Certain affects connected with nuclear conflicts may be especially involved, such as shame, embarrassment, ridicule, etc.

Stage fright, Fenichel (1945) pointed out, is, "as a rule, the result of other previous instinctual conflicts." The exhibitionism which is warded off is a defense of the anxieties, guilt and inferiority feelings which first attended the exhibitionistic behavior. The audience's role is one of proving to the subject that no castration has taken place and thus of contradicting the feeling that exhibitionistic acts will lead to castration.

The watching audience leads to overstimulation and to the fear that he may be exposed. The resultant regression may lead to the acting out of forbidden unconscious fantasies. When there is a poorly integrated body image and sense of identity in the subject, there may be a danger of identity diffusion depersonalization, and loss of identity. For the actor, the omnipotence of words and gestures provides immediate fantasied gratifications, while defensively controlling the audience. If there is apprehension that the audience cannot be controlled and manipulated, there is the danger of an overwhelming narcissistic mortification. The actor who functions in a normal manner loses his fear (stage fright) when he starts to act. This change from passivity to activity frees him from whatever pathological symptoms may be present preceding his appearance on the stage.

Related Concepts: ACTING OUT; EXHIBITIONISM; FEAR; PHOBIA.

REFERENCE

Fenichel, O., *The Psychoanalytic Theory of Neurosis.* Nor, pp. 201–202, 1945.

1950

STAMMERING (STUTTERING). Stammering and stuttering are compromise formations, gratifying both anal exhibitionistic wishes and their defense by the ego and their punishment by the superego; an ego-alien symptom. Many subjects try to deal with this affliction by avoiding or restricting their speech; the subjects do not stutter when they are alone. The symptom usually increases in intensity when the subject talks to an authority figure.

Fenichel (1945) described the symptom, as one which resulted from a conflict between antagonistic tendencies. Though he consciously intends to speak, he must of necessity have some unconscious reason for not doing so. The subject's unconscious motive can only be determined where there is a recognition (on the part of the analyst) of the stimulus that has produced the stuttering. Thus, it is possible to recognize in analysis that "occasional stammering may be due to the unconscious instinctual significance of the thing the person is going to say." In severe cases, Fenichel insisted, "the function of the speech itself represents an objectionable instinctual impulse."

For example, a patient of Eidelberg's (1954), who stammered from the age of seven, consciously connected it with the experience of seeing another child in school have a bowel movement in his pants, and who also stammered. Further analysis revealed that this experience represented a screen memory for an earlier experience which occurred when he was four years old, at which time he saw his younger sister, then two years old, covered with feces. His id reaction may be expressed: "I want to eat feces." His ego defense was a mobilization of the opposite instinct fusion, so that the original sexual wish became aggressive: "I hate feces and want to get rid of them." However, both wishes remained present in his unconscious, so that he continually oscillated between them. Both impulses were repressed and their presentation was displaced to speech. As a result, the patient played with his words as he had wanted to play with his feces. To expiate any feelings of guilt, his superego accepted the stammering as punishment. The narcissistic mortification of acknowledging that he did not have the power to keep his feces was denied by an acceptance of his inability to control his speech. His total personality mildly resented the stammer, but also obtained some aggressive and exhibitionistic satisfaction through it.

Although stammering and stuttering are localized in the mouth, they should not be referred to as examples of oral regression, because the related unconscious content represents libidinal and aggressive anal-exhibitionistic impulses.

Related Concepts: CONVERSION AND CONVERSION SYMPTOMS; EXHIBITIONISM; SLIPS OF THE TONGUE.

REFERENCES

Eidelberg, L., *An Outline of a Comparative Pathology of the Neuroses.* IUP, pp. 161–162, 1954.
Fenichel, O., *The Psychoanalytic Theory of Neurosis.* Nor, pp. 311–313, 1945.

ADDITIONAL READINGS

Freund, H., "Psychopathological Aspects of Stuttering." *PT*, 7, 1953.
Glauber, I. P., "Freud's Contributions on Stuttering: Their Relation to Some Current Insights." *JAPA*, 6, 1958.
Krout, M. H., "Emotional Factors in the Etiology of Stammering." *ASP*, 31, 1936.
Scripture, E. W.: *Stuttering and Lisping.* Mac. 1912.
    "Treatment of the Stuttering." *Lancet*, 1, 1923.

1951

STIGMATA. Historically, the concept is of clerical origin and refers to the magical belief that the crucifixion wounds of Christ could be transferred to the faithful by fervent prayer. Psychodynamically, the concept is defined as a nonorganic syndrome of hysterics such as anesthesia, parasthesia, etc. These may be typical conversion symptoms, but the bleeding neurodermatitis of the palms is a psychosomatic disorder and not a pure conversion symptom. The swelling, hyperemia and abnormal sensations have been equated with genital excitement and masturbation along with punishment for forbidden sexual impulses. The identification with the crucified Christ is patently masochistic, but may also subserve other strivings and defensive needs. The hands are typically associated with instinctual temptations and prohibitions, and itching in particular may revive masturbatory conflicts. Excoriation punishes the guilty hands while continuing in a disguised form the masturbatory activity. Exhibitionism and defenses against it play an extremely important role. The bleeding hands may be flaunted just as the crucifix is displayed to the worshippers. Castration anxiety is alleviated by displacing fantasies of genital injury and identification with the menstruating female genital, from the genital to the masturbating hand. The hand is sometimes jokingly referred to as a girl or vagina by the male onanist, and as a penis by the female. The bloody hands, the identification with crucifixion, indicate the power of a punitive superego to "cut" the offending arm.

The skin is the physical boundary between the self and the outer world and may represent both the self and the object. It is an organ of perception, of object contact, a potential erogenous zone, and can assume the role of an organ of symbolic expression.

The hands themselves participate in symbolic gestures, in all types of self and object interaction, and are particularly suited to the frequent development of psychogenic dermatitis.

Ferenczi (1919) noted that the stigmata represented a displacement of an erotic zone (usually the genitals) onto the affected organ. Repressed impulses find their substitute expressions in a change in physical function. There is objective change in the tissues: hyperemia, swelling and bleeding. The hyperemia and swelling may represent erection, the bleeding and wounds can refer to female functions and the castrated state.

Needles (1943) described this phenomenon as one resulting from destructive wishes and related the case of a patient who developed stigmata during the course of his analysis. The patient was found to have had strong latent homosexual tendencies and, as a consequence, his self-punishment took a somatic form, spontaneous bleeding of the palms of his hands.

Related Concepts: HYSTERICAL CONVERSION; SOMATIZATION.

REFERENCES

Ferenczi, S., 1919, *Further Contributions to the Theory and Technique of Psychoanalysis*, BB, pp. 110–117, 1952.
Needles, W., "Stigmata in the Course of Psychoanalysis." Q, 12:23–39, 1943.

1952

STRANGULATED AFFECT. Freud and Breuer (1893), in studying and treating conversion hysteria, hypothesized that a normal discharge of emotion—in action, word and thought—was inhibited, and the affect was thus "strangulated"; i.e., it was forced to seek a substitute discharge through somatic pathways, creating the symptomatology of conversion hysteria.

The essential idea of strangulated affect was later carried over into the concept of repression, which supplanted it in analytic theory.

Related Concepts: REPRESSION; SCREEN MEMORY.

REFERENCE

Freud, S., & J. Breuer, 1893, "Studies on Hysteria." *SE*, 2:17, 1955.

ADDITIONAL READINGS

Freud, S.: 1893, "On the Psychical Mechanism of Hysterical Phenomena: A Lecture." *SE*, 3, 1962.
1925, "An Autobiographical Study." *SE*, 20, 1959.

1953

STRUCTURAL (TOPOGRAPHIC) APPROACH. Freud (1923), in devising the structural (or topographic) approach,* divided the total personality into three systems—the id, the ego, and the superego. The id is considered to be the seat of often contradictory wishes (instincts and drives), "the kingdom of the illogical" (Freud, 1940). Completely unconscious, the id is interested in the discharge of instinctual tension. The actual discharge usually takes place through the conscious part of the ego, but it may also be accomplished through the unconscious part of the ego. The activity of the id is governed by the so-called primary process, in which there is no recognition of good and bad, of yes and no, of time and space. The id has no connection with the external world, but opens towards the ego.

Under the influence of the external world, part of the archaic id becomes the ego, which examines and deals with the external world, controls motility, and serves as an honest broker between the id and the external world and the superego. The ego is partly conscious, partly preconscious, and partly unconscious. It is mainly interested in achieving an orderly discharge of the tensions originating in the

---

* Freud originally, in "The Interpretation of Dreams" (1900), used the term *topographic* (*topisch*) in connection with the concept of the systems *Ucs.*, *Pcs.*, *Cs.* Later, in "Two Encyclopedia Articles" (1923), he referred to the id, ego, and superego as the *topographic* division. Today some analysts use *topographic* in the former sense; others, in the latter. In order to avoid further confusion, two suggestions are offered: (a) drop the word *topographic* entirely, and use *systematic* when referring to the unconscious, conscious, etc., and *structural* when referring to the division into id, ego, and superego; or (b) use *topographic* only to refer to the division into id, ego, and superego, as indicated by Freud (1940) in "An Outline of Psycho-Analysis."

id, and in dealing with the stimuli from the external world. The ego may try to eliminate the unpleasure of increased tension by a wish to discharge it (pure pleasure principle). When wishing alone is unable to provide this discharge, the ego may utilize an external object and a motoric act, or the ego may decide not to discharge the instinctual tension and to instead endure the unpleasure (reality principle).

The superego, derived from the ego, represents the moral part of the personality. It consists of the conscience and ego-ideal. The superego may be partly conscious, partly unconscious, and partly preconscious. Identification with the parents—of their superegos—is fundamental in the formation of the superego. In the normal individual, the admonitions and prohibitions which constitute the so-called infantile superego have been completely assimilated and represent ego-syntonic concepts of ethical behavior, rather than dicta to be blindly obeyed. Sexualization of the superego is a term introduced by Freud (1924) and refers to the superego which is interested in punishing the individual (perhaps instead of guiding him toward morality).

Under normal conditions, the presentations of the three parts of the personality are cathected by secondary narcissistic or neutral energy. But under pathological conditions, according to Eidelberg (1954), they may be cathected by objectual energy. Eidelberg also suggested that the ego be considered as divisible into three parts: the central ego, which represents the honest broker; the presentation of the body; and the presentation of the sense organs. Consequently, in addition to the three libidinal types described by Freud (1931), two others may be suggested: the athletic type, in which most of the libido cathects the presentation of the body, and the sensuous type, in which most of the libido cathects the presentation of the sense organs.

Hartmann (1964) evaluated the value of the explanatory term, the *structural approach*, as follows: "The essential importance of constructs for the coherence of the psychoanalytic system (or whatever we choose to call it) can be gathered already from the brief outline I have given in the first part of this discussion. Theories, or hypotheses of a different order, connect them with observational data. That these constructs, which are introduced because of their explanatory value, cannot be directly defined in terms of observational data, but that inferences from the constructs can be tested by observation, has long been known in psychoanalysis. Still, some of these constructs seem particularly suspect to many critics of analysis. An occasional lack of caution in the formulation of its propositions, or Freud's liking for occasional striking metaphors has led to the accusation against analysis of an anthropomorphization of its concepts. But in all those cases a more careful formulation can be substituted which will dispel this impression.

"There is, then, the question whether and in what sense such constructs are considered 'real'; and, more specifically, the question has often been asked whether and in what sense Freud considered constructs like libido, the 'system unconscious,' and the substructures of personality in the sense of structural psychology, as real. He said that the basic concepts of science form the roof rather than the foundation of science and ought to be changed when they no longer seem able to account for experience; also that they have the character of conventions. But he certainly thought that what he meant to cover by these basic concepts had effects which could be observed. He was in no danger of confusing concepts with realities; he was a 'realist' in a different sense. He does not seem to have thought that 'real' means just 'the simplest theoretical presentation of our experiences,' but rather that those basic concepts pointed to something real in the ordinary sense of the word."

Related Concepts: DYNAMIC APPROACH; ECONOMIC APPROACH; METAPSYCHOLOGY; SYSTEMATIC (QUALITATIVE OR DESCRIPTIVE) APPROACH.

REFERENCES

Eidelberg, L., *An Outline of a Comparative Pathology of the Neuroses.* IUP, 1954.
Freud, S.: 1923, "The Ego and the Id." *SE*, 19:19–39, 1961.
     1924, "The Economic Problem of Masochism." *SE*, 19:169–170, 1961.
     1931, "Libidinal Types." *SE*, 21:215–222, 1961.
     1940, "An Outline of Psycho-Analysis." *SE*, 21:48, 1940.
Hartmann, H., *Essays on Ego Psychology.* IUP, p. 344, 1964.

1954

SUBLIMATION is the basic change which takes place in the original instinctual aim with respect to the external object and, as well, to the *form* of the instinctual gratification. In this, it represents instinctual vicissitudes which are, perhaps, the result of successful repression. Such a result permits the individual to avoid the damming up of his instinctual energy by obtaining a pleasant discharge.

Psychoanalysis is able to analyze only what does not make sense and is harmful to the patient. The aim is to make conscious what was unconscious. Sublimation, therefore, refers to the infantile changes which are transformed into valuable acts. Finally, it cannot be denied that all individuals have their sets of values, and, therefore, consider some activities as higher than others. Consequently, the ability to talk (a change in form and in aim) may be considered a sublimation of the original urge to cry, as with an infant, or it may refer to an example of aim-inhibited instinct.

Sublimation and aim-inhibited instincts are modifications, which, under the influence of the ego and superego, allow for mature gratifications, instead of the original infantile ones. For instance, interruption ordinarily would be experienced as a frustration. In an aim-inhibited instinct, this is not so. Feelings of tenderness, while derived from pregenital and genital sexual drives, are not necessarily dependent on "physical" sexual gratification. According to Freud (1905), the aim of an instinct is full discharge with the help of an external object. However, in general, enduring object relations become possible, independent of fulfillment of the original need. Aim-inhibited drives do not follow the pattern of relatively slow build-up and quick discharge; more constant and prolonged discharge is often possible. Rapid fluctuations in drive tension are less characteristic. Destructive instinct may also be aim-inhibited. For example, sarcasm may be an expression of an aim-inhibited wish to devour and bite. We may differentiate between the form of the discharge (eating) and the external object (food).

Some authors maintain that an aim-inhibited instinct requires countercathexis. Sublimated drives may allow relatively full discharge of the drive cathexis; aim-inhibited drives do not. Hartmann (1964) noted: "Looked at from this point of view (with all its implications for substitute gratification and aim-inhibited expression), it became possible to draw a rather comprehensive picture of the correlations between a person's needs on various levels, his emotions, his ways of solving problems. . . . This, of course, also emphasizes the comparative freedom from reactive rigidity, the comparative independence from, and variety of, possible responses to outer and to inner stimuli that we attribute to man to a greater extent than to other species."

Freud (1923) defined sublimation as a process which takes place as the result of the transformation of object-libido into narcissistic libido. Thus, what takes place leads to the rejection of the sexual aim and represents a step toward sublimation.

When the aim of being happy cannot be achieved, different paths may be used by individuals to achieve at least a partial happiness. Inherited factors interfere with the aim of achieving happiness and some individuals can only eliminate unhappiness by becoming psychotics or addicts.

Related Concepts: AESTHETIC PLEASURE; INSTINCT (INSTINCTUAL DRIVE).

REFERENCES

Freud, S.: 1905, "Three Essays on Sexuality." *SE*, 7: 156, 238–239, 1953.
　　　　1923, "The Ego and the Id." *SE*, 19:30, 1961.
Hartmann, H., *Essays on Ego Psychology.* IUP, p. 73, 1964.

1955

SUCCESS NEUROSIS. This concept applies to people who having achieved social and economic success and having every means at their command to enjoy life still complain of various neurotic difficulties. Their first signs of nervous disturbance occur when they begin to accumulate wealth—after they have established their economic security, which puts them in a position to be the main supporter of their parents and siblings. Adult success revives the repressed guilt feelings of childhood and adolescence, the early drives and desires of being better than father or brothers which creates chaotic feelings resulting in neurotic illness. Unconsciously, financial success equals the realization of oedipal wishes; the rivalry with father and brothers revives their castration fears and narcissistic mortifications.

These patients show masochistic character trends and regressive tendencies. Their ego becomes passive and ineffectual; they are overwhelmed (partly) by their guilt feelings and their need to suffer.

They are similar to the type of patient Freud described (1916) as being "wrecked by success." They differ from the type Freud described in being able to tolerate a limited success (polycrates complex).

In the cases cited by Lorand (1950), all the patients showed the same history: they came from very poor homes, suffered early childhood deprivations, and even hunger. All of them were self-made men. In their childhood, their father encouraged and expected them to earn and contribute their meager earnings to the upkeep of the home. They were not allowed to save up any money; it was all taken away by their father. In other words, they could not have the possessions their father had.

Related Concepts: CHARACTER NEUROSIS; MASOCHISM.

REFERENCES

FREUD, S., 1916, "Some Character Types Met With in Psychoanalytic Work." *SE,* 14, 1957.
Lorand, S. *Clinical Studies in Psychoanalysis.* IUP, pp. 245-254, 1950.

ADDITIONAL READING

Szekely, L., "Success, Success Neurosis and the Self." *M,* 33, 1960.

1956

SUFFOCATION FEARS often accompany hysterical conversion symptoms; such fears generally involve the sexualization of the respiratory function. However, the fear of suffocation is not solely a sign that warded-off impulses involve respiratory eroticism; the reverse may also be true: respiration may acquire an erotic quality only after, and because, anxiety has been connected with sexual excitement.

Fenichel (1945) described psychogenic breathing disturbances as "anxiety equivalents." In his view, these equivalents are perceived by the subject as fear of suffocation.

In bronchial asthma, the asthmatic seizure is a cry of help directed toward the mother. Alexander (1941) noted: "The asthmatic attack is a reaction to the

danger of separation from the mother. . . . [It] is a sort of equivalent of an inhibited and repressed cry of anxiety or rage." With the asthmatic, the parent (usually the mother) is fantasied as already introjected; there are conflicts arising between the ego and the patient's respiratory apparatus which represent the introjected object.

The fear of suffocation may also arise from the displacement of a sexual feeling from the lower part of the body to the upper. In the case of Dora, who suffered from fits of coughing (among other symptoms), the original perception of the older man's penis pressed against the lower part of her body (she was then fourteen) was repressed and replaced by the more "innocent" sensation localized in her throat and chest. [Freud, 1905.]

Related Concepts: BRONCHIAL ASTHMA; CONVERSION AND CONVERSION SYMPTOMS.

REFERENCES

Alexander, F., "Psychogenic Factors in Bronchial Asthma." *PSM,* 1941.
Fenichel, O., *The Psychoanalytic Theory of Neurosis.* Nor, pp. 250, 322, 1945.
Freud, S., 1905, "Fragment of an Analysis of a Case of Hysteria." *SE,* 7:41-42, 1953.

1957

SUGGESTION denotes the ability of some individuals to make others deny their own inner and external perception (or their importance) and, instead, to accept as true the external order rather than their own convictions. Freud and Breuer used suggestion in cathartic hypnosis by ordering the hypnotized patient to remember the repressed traumatic material. Later, Freud, with the help of the basic rule and a thorough interpretation of the patient's resistance, succeeded in obtaining the repressed material without the use of any other form of direct suggestion. In order to overcome this resistance, the patient had to accept the rule of free association as a method leading finally to a complete cure. In a number of cases, suggestion had a therapeutic affect, but the disappearance of symptoms led to a transference to the therapist. In analysis, the transference (positive as well as negative) has to be recognized and eliminated. Freud (1923) considered suggestion as being based on erotic attachment.

Related Concepts: HYPNOSIS; TRANSFERENCE.

REFERENCES

Freud, S.: 1920, "Beyond the Pleasure Principle." *SE*, 18:32, 1955.
1921, "Group Psychology and the Analysis of the Ego." *SE*, 18:127–128, 1955.
1923, "Two Encyclopedia Articles." *SE*, 18: 237, 1955.

ADDITIONAL READINGS

Jones, E., "The Action of Suggestions in Psychotherapy." *JAbP*, 5, 1910–1911.
Lossey, F. T., "The Charge of Suggestion as a Resistance in Psycho-Analysis." *IntJPsa*, 43, 1962.

1958

SUICIDE. Freud (1920) assumed that the ability to commit suicide required an energy which was at first directed against another person. Thus, one could refer to suicide as self-murder.

Under certain conditions, the human being who often lives in fear of death may decide to commit suicide instead of suffering agonies of pain because of illness or torture. This decision indicates that he regards death as the lesser evil. No one can say exactly how much pain "justifies" a suicide. From an analytical point of view, suicide represents a danger for the depressed and the melancholic patient. It appears to be the result of an intrapsychic conflict which is often aroused by such environmental factors as loss of the love object.

In melancholia an excessively harsh, sadistic superego turns against the self and succeeds in driving the person to death. The impoverished ego identifies with an ambivalently loved introjected object, treats itself as this object and turns against itself all the hostile impulses originally directed against the introjected object. In addition, the narcissistic mortification "I cannot eliminate what produces pain" is denied by the patient's ability to terminate his life.

Fenichel (1945) described suicide as an attempt by the ego to "appease the superego by submissiveness." The intended change cannot be achieved because the superego "has become inordinately cruel and lost its ability to forgive." In examining the case of the suicide of a depressed patient, Fenichel observed, from the point of view of the superego, "a turning of sadism against the person himself." From the point of view of the ego, the suicide was an expression of the unbearable pressures that must be appeased at all cost. In other suicidal acts, there was, as it were, a rebellious attitude expressed. The subject "murders" the original imago (infantile) incorporated into the superego.

Related Concepts: DEPRESSION; MELANCHOLIA.

REFERENCES

Fenichel, O., *The Psychoanalytic Theory of Neurosis.* Nor, pp. 400–401, 1945.
Freud, S., 1920, "'A Case of Homosexuality in a Woman." *SE*, 18:162, 1955.

ADDITIONAL READINGS

Adler, A., "Selbstmord." *JIndP*, 14, 1958.
Friedman, P., "Sur le Suicide." *RFPsa*, 8, 1935.
Milner, M., "A Suicidal Symptom in a Child of Three." *IntJPsa*, 25, 1944.
Sadger, J., "Ein Beitrag zum Problem des Selbstmordes." *PsaP*, 3, 1928–1929.

1959

SUNDAY (WEEKEND) NEUROSIS is characterized by an outbreak of depression or anxiety, or both, on a non-working day. The day represents a change from the week's normal activity to which the neurotic responds as threatening. The normal object relationships are different, as are the external precipitating factors. The neurosis may be associated with the play activity of childhood, the emergence of infantile wishes which are otherwise repressed. The resulting depression serves in the guise of a substitute defense; the resulting withdrawal makes the normal participation associated with weekend activities impossible (or difficult). It may result, as well, in increased oral envy, with the feeling that other persons are getting the narcissistic supplies which they cannot obtain, and may thus account for the complaints which are sometimes expressed.

Ferenczi (1952) noted that a neurotic attitude toward the weekend may also be *specifically* determined by actual childhood events, such as family outings, visiting the relatives, which arouse primal-scene fantasies, masturbatory fantasies, etc. The child's external object relationships may have changed on such a day (or a holiday); for instance, the presence of the father, separation from a teacher, reunions with divorced parents, etc. In analysis, the Sunday neurosis is sometimes associated with the patient's separation from the analyst. As a result, there is a reactivation of feelings of anxiety and of object loss.

Related Concepts: ANXIETY; DEPRESSION.

REFERENCE

Ferenczi, S., *Further Contributions to the Theory and Technique of Psychoanalysis.* BB, p. 174, 1952.

1960

SUPEREGO is denotative of that part of the total personality which consists of the ego-ideal and the conscience; i.e., the goal toward which the individual strives and those incorporated inhibitory forces from the outer world that have been internalized. In this, the superego is the heir to the oedipus complex, arising only after that complex has been deposed. As a result of the dissolution of the oedipus complex, the superego is abandoned and the image of the parent is established in the individual. While the child is growing up this image becomes more impersonal, because it represents not only the actual parent but other people the child considers to be authorities (Freud, 1933).

The superego is partly conscious, partly preconscious, and partly unconscious. It is cathected either by secondary narcissistic libido or destrudo, or neutral libido and destrudo. Under pathological conditions, the superego may be cathected by object libido and destrudo (sexualization of the superego).

"Sexualization of the superego" is a concept introduced by Freud (1924) to describe a process through which the superego engages in sadistically punishing the individual, perhaps torturing him, instead of encouraging him to accept and assimilate those ethical standards which he finally considers ego-syntonic (moral masochism).

In many neuroses, the superego appears excessively severe, but psychoanalysis can only decrease this severity by helping the patient eliminate those infantile wishes which require such a severe superego. However, the superego of a patient, after a successful analysis, is not eliminated, nor should it be substituted for by the ego.

The superego appears to play a greater role in certain neuroses, as in phobias, obsessional neuroses and melancholia, than it does in conversion neuroses. As a result of an id regression, there is also a regression in the superego; it appears that in obsessional neurosis and in melancholia the superego keeps on punishing the patient (Freud, 1923).

Glover (1939) described this agency of the mind, as follows: "During the pre-genital phases of infancy the child has passed through instinctual crises leading to the abandonment in turn of oral, excretory and other forms of infantile sexual interest. Now the more completely the instinct is abandoned, the more likely it is that an effective control system has been set up in the mind. Theoretically any system that instigates the inhibition of instinct performs in however rudimentary a manner, a super-ego function. The earlier the function, the more it is concerned with primitive instinct. It is possible therefore to subdivide the super-ego into *layers representing historical phases of the infantile struggle to master primitive forms of instinct.* As has been indicated the main groups of *infantile* instinct are concerned with love and aggressivity respectively. These vary in quality, intensity and distribution in the different phases of early childhood. And there are numerous combinations (fusions) of infantile sexuality and aggressiveness. Since the majority of these impulses are concerned with hate of parental objects who are both loved and feared they cannot and may not be gratified, and tend to lead to the abandonment of that particular object. It is reasonable to assume that, although in early infancy it is not very well organised, a kind of super-ego reaction develops for each phase. Although it cannot be regarded as a psychic institution, it is safe to say that it represents a *nucleus* of a super-ego system. Thus owing to the early primacy of *oral* love and hate we can say that one of the earliest nuclei of super-ego formation is an *oral nucleus.* This means that ego-phantasies of oral sadism (devouring, biting the mother or breast) arouse an inner conviction that a talion oral punishment is threatened (being devoured by a 'wild object'). And we know from study of depressive cases that the appropriate affect induced by this opposition is one of depression. In the case of later phases of love and hate, there is less need for speculation and hypothetical reconstruction. Clinically one can observe that excretory (*anal, urethral*) interests and their corresponding phantasies are controlled by what Ferenczi called 'sphincter-morality'. Study of normal character shews many reactions derived from this phase. These can now be described as a result of the activity of a substantial *nucleus* of the super-ego, the *anal super-ego*. Pathological formations dating from this period can be easily detected during the analysis of cases of obsessional neuroses."

Related Concepts: CONSCIENCE; CONSCIOUS; PRE-CONSCIOUS; STRUCTURAL (TOPOGRAPHIC) APPROACH.

REFERENCES

Freud, S.: 1923, "The Ego and the Id." *SE*, 19:55, 1961.
　　1924, "The Economic Problem of Maso-chism." *SE*, 19:169, 1961.
　　1933, "New Introductory Lectures on Psycho-Analysis." *SE*, 22:63–65, 1964.
Glover, E., *Psycho-Analysis.* SP, pp. 59–60, 1939.

1961

SUPERSTITION is denotative of those magical acts which can influence the future or the magic knowledge of things to be avoided because they can be influenced by magical mechanisms. Freud (1901) argued that it stemmed from those unconscious motivations in chance and in faulty actions which were disposed of by displacing them to the outer world. Freud did not believe in superstition, and assumed that certain phenomena represented a grati-fication of unconscious wishes. Later, in 1933, he suggested that it was animism which partly succeeded in surviving, being disguised as a superstition.

Freud (1913) regarded the instinctual repression as a basis of civilization. He thought that even the savages succeeded, with the help of various taboos, in controlling their original wishes.

Related Concepts: ANIMISM; MAGIC; RELIGIOUS FAITH.

REFERENCES

Freud, S.: 1901, "The Psychopathology of Everyday Life." *SE*, 6:257–258, 1960.
　　1913, "Totem and Taboo." *SE*, 13:97–99, 1955.
　　1933, "New Introductory Lectures on Psycho-Analysis." *SE*, 22:165–166, 1964.

1962

SUPERVALENT denotes an excessively intense idea which cannot be resolved by any effort of thought, either because, as Freud (1905) noted, "it itself reaches with its roots down into the uncon-scious, repressed material, or because another unconscious thought lies concealed beneath it." The latter he identified as directly contrary to the supervalent one.

Freud illustrated its pathological character in the case of Dora. She was disposed to believe (quite rightly) that her thoughts about her father needed to be judged in a special way. She was critical of herself for criticizing her father's relation with Frau K., a criticism connected with her unconscious jealousy.

Related Concepts: MEGALOMANIA; PARANOID CONDI-TION (STATE).

REFERENCE

Freud, S., 1905, "Fragment of an Analysis of a Case of Hysteria." *SE*, 7:54, 62–63, 1953.

1963

SUPERVISION. Each candidate is required to analyze at least four patients under supervision before graduating from a psychoanalytic institute.* Once a week or twice a month, the candidate dis-cusses his case with the supervisory analyst. The supervisory analyst (who has never seen the patient) tries to separate the errors resulting from a lack of experience from those caused by the candidate's own unconscious problems. These "blind spots" are not analyzed by the supervisory analyst; the candidate is encouraged to analyze them for himself, or to mention them to his training analyst.

It is obvious that the technique is not uniform, for each candidate is encouraged to develop his own personal approach to the patient. The basic rules of Freudian psychoanalysis are, of course, subsumed.

The minimal standards for supervision are given by Lewin and H. Ross (1960), as follows: "(1) To instruct the student in the use of the psychoanalytic

---

* Minimum of 150 hours in the U.S.

method. (2) To aid him in the acquisition of therapeutic skill based upon an understanding of the analytic material. (3) To observe his work and determine how fully his personal analysis has achieved its aims. (4) To determine his maturity and stability over an extended period of time. . . .

"The rule that the supervisor should be someone who was not also the student's personal analyst is generally followed. In the early days of institute training, the lack of teaching manpower and the prestige of leaders sometimes operated in the other direction, but only in Budapest, where first the leadership of Ferenczi and then emulation lengthened his shadow into an institution, has it been a normal procedure to have the student's analyst also be his supervisor."

Related Concept: TECHNIQUE OF PSYCHOANALYSIS.

REFERENCE

Lewin, B., & H. Ross, *Psychoanalytic Education in the United States.* Nor, pp. 257–258, 1960.

1964

SUPPRESSION is a preconscious and conscious psychical process, in which ideas and affects are deliberately eliminated from consciousness. In this they become preconscious and are recoverable, though in some cases the endopsychic censor may intervene between the preconscious and conscious systems. This concept originated with Freud's (1900) systematic approach; it largely disappeared after the introduction of the structural approach (in 1923). In the latter system, the concept of repression is an unconscious process wherein ideational elements are relegated to the unconscious, unavailable to conscious recall. The term suppression was used by Freud in a general sense, particularly in his early writings, to designate a repudiation. Freud (1900) used the term suppression as a synonym for repression in his early writings. Later, in 1923, he differentiated between the elimination of ideas from the elimination of affects and referred to these latter mechanisms as dream distortions.

The term suppression is still characteristically retained in describing the suppression of affects, in which the idea is retained in consciousness while the associated affect is subdued. It might more correctly be said to be inhibited.

Related Concepts: DENIAL (DISAVOWAL); REPRESSION.

REFERENCES

Freud, S.: 1900, "The Interpretation of Dreams." *SE,* 5:467–468, 1953.
     1923, "The Ego and the Id." *SE,* 19:23–28, 1961.

1965

SYMBIOSIS is denotative of a biological condition in which two subjects live in a close spatial and physiologically reciprocal dependent relationship. This condition is characteristic of the infant's postnatal relationship to its mother. The source of this postnatal mother-child symbiosis is found in the reciprocal wishes and defenses between the subjects, as well as in their biological and psychological needs. The object relationship of this symbiotic condition occurs when the infant first becomes aware of the need-satisfaction which is obtained through repeated experiences of gratification and frustration which attend feeding, fondling, etc. The infant gradually learns to separate wish from action, and, thus, to separate the self from that of his mother. He learns, in brief, to give up his infantile omnipotence. He learns to make this distinction because he discovers that wishing alone will not gratify his needs.

In the symbiotic psychosis, on the other hand, the mental representation of the mother is not separated or differentiated from the self because of regression to the symbiotic phase of development. When confronted with separation or independence from the mother, the illusion of symbiotic oral omnipotence is threatened and disintegrative panic may occur. The peculiar hypercathexis of one part of the body seen in many symbiotic children often corresponds to a particular overstimulation which occurs during the parental symbiotic relationship. The child may be treated as an appendage of the parental body.

In a focal symbiosis, it is usually the smaller or weaker partner who remains functionally dependent in a specific area on the active response of the other partner. The focal symbiotic relationship exists in respect to the functioning of a special organ or body area. This is frequently seen in twins or special sibling relationships. The symbiosis may therefore be global or focal, superficial or intensive, and may have different pathological implications for each symbiont. Symbiotic ties may occur in neuroses, but are more common in psychoses, perversions and psychosomatic disorders, where symbiotic transference may predominate in the therapeutic relationship.

Symbiosis is a normal phase in infantile development and can facilitate further maturation, but fixation to this phase of development may lead to marked pathological disturbance in body image, ego boundaries, and identity. The symbiosis may be consciously perceived or unconsciously operative and in the mutualism of two different organisms acting as object for the other there is a prototype for later intimate relationships. Pollock (1964) noted: "We might ask what is it that is internalized or introjected in these instances of symbiotic neurosis. We speak of internal objects, introjects, imagos, internalized images, and the like. It is my contention that what is internalized is the experience and relationship that the individual had with the pertinent external figure over a long period of time and in relation to particular needs and wishes. The experience may be a series of encounters, some positive and some negative, some meaningful and some insignificant; in other words what is utilized for internalization is the multiple relationships with meaningful objects as well as the results of such interactions. The resulting internalization and neutralization of both libidinal and aggressive energy contributes to structuralization. In analytic therapy, the analyst-patient relationship, operating initially under the aegis of the basic or primary transference, facilitates the regression and reliving of the old internalized relationships with the analyst. In the symbiotic neurosis, the transference demands for repetition of the old relationship or even of a currently continuing relationship with a real figure are not gratified. Through interpretation, but by his presence also, the analyst becomes a new kind of introject that neutralizes the effect of the older one and finally is assimilated as an identification. Different levels and varieties of symbiotic interactions will obviously result in different transference manifestations and demands of the analyst at different times."

Related Concepts: AUTISM; EGO BOUNDARIES; PARASITIC SUPEREGO.

REFERENCE

Pollock, G. H., "On Symbiosis and Symbiosis and Symbiotic Neurosis." *IntJPsa*, 45:27, 1964.

1966

SYMBOLIZATION is the unconscious process in which emotional values are displaced from one object to another, so that repressed wishes may achieve a measure of disguised satisfaction, i.e., the conscious mind is entirely ignorant of the fact that symbols have been employed. The principal significance, therefore, of all symbols are the primary ideas which they represent through the existence of some factor common to the presentation of the repressed idea which it represents. Symbol formation, in this formulation, consists of a displacement from an idea of primary instinctual interest onto an idea of less instinctual interest, and thus represents a means for overcoming (at least partially) the repression, and of giving expression, even in its altered form, to repressed material. In this, the symbol allows for a partial satisfaction and also at the same time represents a defense of the primary idea.

Symbolization first drew notice in terms of its function within the dream. Freud (1900) recognized early that the analyst's understanding of the meaning of the symbol is not sufficient to translate the content of a manifest dream into a latent one. He pointed out that an analyst requires the help of the patient whose associations play a decisive role in the interpretation. He also noted that symbolism plays a great role not only in dreams but also in the study of all unconscious material.

With the introduction of the second theory of instincts, many analysts agreed that, in addition to erotic wishes, aggressive wishes were also expressed in dreams. Fenichel (1945) noted: "The symbol is conscious, the symbolized idea is unconscious. . . . Symbolic thinking is vague, directed by the primary process."

The symbol indicates or represents two or more ideas or objects which differ from a sign. In the content of speech, the important meaning is guessed. However, one of the main characteristics of the symbol is the fact that it is not identical with the object it represents. In psychoanalysis, the decisive meaning of the symbol is unconscious. The symbol is permitted to become conscious because, instead of being recognized as representing two or more ideas or objects, it is regarded by the neurotic as being an object by itself and thus he denies the presence of the repressed object.

As noted, the symbol owes its main significance to the primary idea for which it stands and denies. The fact that the essential element in symbolic representation is always that part which is repressed and onto which the greatest amount of cathexis is attached, explains why energy always flows from the primary idea to the symbol and never in the reverse direction. Conscious awareness of the meaning of the symbol is usually accompanied by repugnance and disbelief. Symbols are usually sensorial and concrete, whereas the idea they represent may be abstract. Symbols have a relative constancy of meaning, both for the individual and the race, even exhibiting a remarkable ubiquity among different races and different cultures, and in widely different historical periods. Their possible variations are usually very small and are independent of individual conditioning factors. Symbols are linguistically connected to the primary idea for which they stand. From a genetic standpoint, symbolism and symbolic ways of thinking represent the outgrowth of a more primitive form of thought, from both an ontogenetic and phylogenetic standpoint, and are, therefore, particularly common in regressive states and under circumstances which facilitate regression, such as sleep, dreams, fatigue, and neurotic and psychotic states.

The greatest number of symbols pertains to the male and female genitals, a fact which has been explained on the basis of the particular repression to which the sexual function is subjected, as well as by the particular importance of sexual cults in early civilization. [Jones, 1916.]

Related Concepts: DREAMS; THINKING; WORDS.

REFERENCES

Fenichel, O., *The Psychoanalytic Theory of Neurosis.* Nor, p. 48, 1945.
Freud, S., 1900, "The Interpretation of Dreams." *SE*, 5:684, 1953.
Jones, E., 1916, *Papers on Psycho-Analysis.* HPI, pp. 87–144, 1949.

ADDITIONAL READINGS

Arlow, J. A., "Notes on Oral Symbolism." *Q*, 24, 1955.
Berna, J., "Die 'Réalisation symbolique' in der Kinderanalyse." *P*, 9, 1956.
Caruso, I. A., "Über die Symbollehre als psychosomatischer Beitrag zur Erkenntnistheorie." *ZPSM*, 1, 1955.
Glover, E., *Psycho-Analysis.* SP, 1949.
Groen, J., "Der Symbolisierungszwang." *Im*, 8, 1922.
Jones, E., "The Mantle Symbol." *IntJPsa*, 8, 1927.
Kanner, L., "The Tooth as a Folkloristic Symbol." *R*, 15, 1928.
Lorand, S., "The Mantle Symbol." *IntJPsa*, 10, 1929.
Milner, M., "Aspects of Symbolism in Comprehension of the Not-Self." *IntJPsa*, 33, 1952.
Riviere, J., "Phallic Symbolism." *IntJPsa*, 5, 1924.
Rorschach, H., "Zur Symbolik der Schlange und der Krawatte." *C*, 2, 1912.
Rubinfine, D. L., "Perception, Reality Testing and Symbolism." *PsaStC*, 16, 1961.
Seidenberg, R., "Changes in the Symbolic Process During a Psychoanalytic Treatment." *JNMD*, 127, 1958.
Spielrein, S., "Selbstbefriedigung in Fussymbolik." *C*, 3, 1913.
Stekel, W., "Der Mantel als Symbol." *C*, 3, 1913.
White, W. A., "Symbolism." *R*, 3, 1916.

1967

SYMPTOMATIC ACT is a seemingly accidental and unmotivated action, which actually expresses an unconscious intention and its defense. The so-called symptomatic acts are different from parapraxes, because they do not represent any meaning and appear to be without importance. However, similar to parapraxes, they require a careful analysis of the factors responsible for their occurrence. [Freud, 1916.]

A symptomatic act is ego-syntonic, but its analysis reveals both an unconscious intention and the presence of opposing forces. A tendency that has been warded off, either by repression or suppression, finds a distorted expression in action which is counter to the opposing conscious wish. Many symptomatic acts that are habitual (such as playing with a watch chain or fiddling with clothing) are often masturbatory equivalents.

Jones (1911) cited the example of a physician who kept an old-fashioned monaural stethoscopy on his desk, placed between himself and his patients.

When asked about it, the doctor said that it had no meaning, but analysis yielded a different explanation. "Our doctor placed his straight stethoscope (symbolizing the penis) between himself and his women patients exactly as Sigurd (in the Nibelungen Saga) placed his sword between himself and the woman he was not to touch. The act was a compromise formation: it satisfied two impulses. It served to satisfy in his imagination the suppressed wish to enter into sexual relations with any attractive woman patient, but at the same time it served to remind him that the wish could not become reality. It was, so to speak, a charm against yielding to temptation."

Related Concept: PARAPRAXIS.

REFERENCES

Freud, S.: 1916, "Introductory Lectures on Psycho-Analysis." *SE*, 15:61, 1963.
Jones, E., "Beitrag zur Symbolik im Alltagsleben." *C*, 1:96–98, 1911.

ADDITIONAL READINGS

Fenichel, O., *The Psychoanalytic Theory of Neurosis*. Nor, 1945.
Hart, H. H., "The Eye in Symbol and Symptom." *R*, 36, 1949.
Lustman, S. L., "Defense, Symptom, and Character." *PsaStC*, 17, 1962.

1968

SYNTHESIS. This construct was employed by Jung (1909),* and others, to denote the reformation of those constituent elements that compromise the mental life of the patient. "The synthesis is . . . not so satisfactory as the analysis; in other words, from a knowledge of the premises we could not have foretold the nature of the result" (Freud, 1920). It was Freud's contention that the patient's development could not only be traced from its final outcome backwards.

Once the various wishes and demands (and their defenses) become conscious, a better compromise between these tendencies can be achieved. Freud (1919) felt that if the analyst succeeded in exposing the neurotic defense mechanisms, and if the patient was prepared to face the truth instead of repressing or denying it, or both, and to recognize the anachronistic aspects of his problems, the patient could arrive at a better solution than the one for which the unconscious ego must be blamed. At the same time, it cannot be denied that what Freud (1920) called the "human influence"—the positive transference and the patient's identification with the image of the therapist—helps the patient to achieve a quicker solution of his conflicts. The passive role the analyst plays is, in part, a restriction placed upon him to avoid selecting a solution which he personally would prefer and thus advising his patients to follow his example. Instead, the analyst has to insist that the patient decide for himself what appeals to him after his blind spots have been eliminated.

Many analysts compare analytical therapy with the resetting of a badly-healed fracture. Once the conditions for the ideal healing have been restored, natural forces can take over. A temporary split in the ego is necessary for the isolation and elimination of what cannot be assimilated. Psychotics often become psychotic because they cannot tolerate a split within and prefer instead to have a conflict between themselves and the external world.

Freud's warning regarding therapeutic ambition obviously does not mean that he was not interested in curing the patient. He was aware that some of his pupils might—pushed by their therapeutic ambition—try to achieve a therapeutic change without eliminating the basic causes of the neurosis. It is well known that, probably as a result of the transference, such changes may take place in the beginning of the analysis. Freud always insisted that analytical research and analytical therapy could not be separated and that consequently therapeutic change, after the unconscious material had become conscious and was worked through and assimilated, represented proof of the correctness of the analytical explanation.

Related Concepts: PSYCHOANALYSIS; THERAPY.

REFERENCES

Freud, S.: 1919, "Lines of Advance in Psycho-Analytic Therapy." *SE*, 17:160, 1955.
    1920, "Beyond the Pleasure Principle." *SE*, 18:18, 1955.

---

* See Edward Glover's *Freud or Jung*. Nor, 1950.

ADDITIONAL READING

Silbermann, I., "Synthesis and Fragmentation." *PsaStc*, 16, 1961.

1969

SYSTEMATIC (QUALITATIVE OR DES-CRIPTIVE) APPROACH. Freud (1900) originally divided the psyche into the system unconscious and the system conscious-preconscious. He assumed that neurosis resulted from a conflict between the unconscious and the conscious. In addition to the systematic approach, which was also referred to as a qualitative or descriptive approach, separating conscious from unconscious and secondary from primary process, Freud introduced the structural approach, dividing the total personality into three parts, the id, ego and superego. [Freud, 1923.]

Related Concepts: DYNAMIC APPROACH; ECONOMIC APPROACH; METAPSYCHOLOGY; PRECONSCIOUS; STRUCTURAL (TOPOGRAPHIC) APPROACH.

REFERENCES

Freud, S.: 1900, "The Interpretation of Dreams." *SE*, 5: 610–611, 1953.
1923, "The Ego and the Id." *SE*, 19:19–39, 1961.

T

2000

TABOO, on the one hand, means sacred and consecrated, but, on the other, it means uncanny, dangerous, forbidden and unclean. Freud (1913) expressed the dual-meaning of the concept when he termed it "holy dread." The word *taboo* appears to unite positive and negative aspects; it perhaps represents what was originally desired and later prohibited. The father ruling the primal herd, in this view, is a tyrant who keeps the females for himself and prohibits their use by the sons for sexual satisfaction. Whatever its origin, it does involve the primitive prohibition which is imposed from without (by an authority) directed against the strongest desires of man. Freud compared this state with the obsessional prohibition exhibited by neurotics. He found that the taboo appeared to represent two contradictory ideas, something which is desired and something one is afraid of. Freud thought that it might have indicated a historical development, something similar to a reaction formation, indicating a desire which had to be rejected.

Thus, the wish and its prohibition are both repressed (ambivalence) and the desire to violate the taboo is mobilized (the attraction of the forbidden). Whenever the individual breaks the taboo, he discovers the presence of aggressive pleasure connected with its defiance coupled with the danger of external punishment or with the feeling of remorse. In this, it may be thought of as a precursor to the formation of the superego.

Related Concepts: ANIMISM; ATTRACTION OF THE FORBIDDEN; INCEST; OMNIPOTENCE OF THOUGHT; TOTEM.

REFERENCE

Freud, S., 1913, "Totem and Taboo." *SE*, 13:4, 18, 34–35, 67, 1955.

2001

TEACHING ANALYSIS. The presentation of material collected in analysis permits the instructor to offer a schematic presentation of the dynamic factors involved. The instructor cannot prove that the unconscious exists, for it is based on heuristic assumptions. He can, however, present those derivatives which stem from the patient's unconscious life and, further, reveal those resistances which are brought into the open as a result of the analytical situation. These phenomena, together with those conscious elements which characterize the patient—his voice, his voluntary and involuntary gestures, his ideas—can be presented in the form of a case history to the student in an analytical institute.

The form of this presentation and the need to protect the patient's identity does not allow for continuously recorded data. The case history, as presented, is generally used to illustrate a given factor, a typical happening in the analytical treatment. Though the student cannot verify the data presented, he may accept it subject to future confirmation. Its scientific validity can be verified either in terms of his own behavior or in the behavior of other patients under analysis.

Most institutes offer reading courses, lecture courses, seminars, clinical conferences and continuous case seminars. However, the student's training analysis, in which he faces his own unconscious, is regarded as the most valuable learning process.

The value systems of individual psychoanalysis manifest themselves also in the principles for the selection of candidates for psychoanalytic training. The standards applied for the selection almost invariably contain the following criteria: (a) independent and reliable superego; (b) ability to maintain object relationships; (c) devotion to the pursuit of the science of human behavior, with an ability to "unlearn" as well as to learn; (d) interest in research or teaching; and (e) absence of psychosis, psychopathy, perversion, etc. To this must be added the inherent "gift" for psychoanalytic therapy and the knowledge of psychiatry, [Lewin and Ross, 1960.]

Related Concepts: SUPERVISION; TRAINING ANALYSIS.

REFERENCE

Lewin, Bertram D., & Helen Ross, *Psychoanalytic Education in the United States.* Nor, p. 300, 1960.

2002
TECHNIQUE OF PSYCHOANALYSIS.
Freud (1910), in all his suggestions on technique, stressed the fact that the proper mastery of subject could only be obtained through clinical experience and not from books. This experience, coupled with the therapist's own analysis, was the governing condition for the practice of psychoanalysis. He termed the technique a simple (?) one. He noted, in 1912: "It consists simply in not directing one's notice to anything in particular and in maintaining the same 'evenly-suspended attention' . . . in the face of all that one hears."

More specifically, he recommended in 1915 that the therapist assume a position behind the patient— a position that would facilitate the free associative process, "to prevent the transference from mingling with the patient's associations." This physical "isolation" permits the analyst to give himself over to his own unconscious associative processes; and, further, the patient receives no hint of what the analyst's interpretation might be from the nonverbal communication inevitable in a face-to-face relationship.

During the first interview, the analyst will try to make a diagnosis of the illness and attempt to determine whether the patient is suitable for the analytic treatment. The patient will try to make up his mind as to whether he wants to be analyzed, and whether this analyst is the person in whom he has confidence. In many cases, it may be advisable to see the patient a few times before reaching an agreement of what should be done. Some analysts like to take detailed notes concerning the life and the illness of the patient. Others are more flexible and are willing to wait until the patient has unburdened himself before collecting facts (e.g., the number of siblings). As noted, there is some variance as to the relationship which is to be established during the initial period. In addition, some analysts like to engage in theoretical speculations about the dynamic structure of the patient whom they have seen; others consider such an approach harmful.

Independently of this, however, a differentiation must be made early between the normal conscious attitude of the patient towards his analyst and his irrational demands. While it is true that the patient *transfers* his infantile wishes to others, most authors agree that the analytic situation facilitates the mobilization of repressed emotions. If properly handled, a differentiation is made between the patient's adult feelings and the infantile emotions he tries to hide.

In order to deal successfully with the unconscious problems of the patients, it is not sufficient to know the genetic cause of a symptom. To cure a patient, the analyst must be able to evaluate the *quantitative* importance of the various unconscious elements, to show the patient not only what he does not know but what he violently refuses to recognize. Many interpretations are accepted and remain therapeutically without value, because they are used by the patient to hide some other even more unpleasant material. The inability to measure the phenomena involved should not be used as an excuse to neglect an *estimation* of the relative importance of the various infantile wishes with which the patient is dealing, to differentiate between the repressed and the repressing factors. The analyst mobilizes the infantile wishes of the patient—as distinguished from other objects the patient has to deal with—because of the free and uncritical flow of associations present in the analytic situation.

This discharge of tension takes place only verbally and is not the final goal of analysis. To the contrary, the analyst will try after his patient has verbalized his infantile ideas to show him why they don't make sense *today*. Furthermore, the patient and the analyst will have to find out how these infantile wishes are to be modified to make their conscious gratification possible.

As the patient knows very little about the personality of his analyst, it is possible to show the patient whom he has in mind when he talks about his analyst. While it is true that a successful analysis is impossible as long as the patient remains detached and cool, it is equally true that he has to recognize and to renounce the infantility of his emotions and the archaic character of his object relations in order to be freed of his "bound" infantile wishes.

It must not be forgotten that the work of an analyst is more like the work of a surgeon than that of a pathologist. Analysis is not a post mortem, for while it is impossible to cure a patient without hurting him he should not be exposed to any unnecessary pain. To be frank does not mean to be rude. With some patients, bluntness may be the "tool"; with others, politeness. Some analysts discuss only the pathology with their patients. They feel that a discussion of the patient's normal reactions represents a waste of time. Nonetheless, it seems, that an understanding of the pathological nature of a phenomenon is possible only by comparing it with a normal one. It is easier for a patient to recognize his neurotic traits if the analyst shows the patient that he, along with others, is capable of functioning in a healthy fashion. A discussion of the positive aspects of his personality may be used to protect him from the shock connected with a disclosure of his neurotic character traits. The fact that the analyst approves of parts of the patient's personality shows the patient that his doctor is not an enemy. With some patients—the so-called moral masochists—there is a resentment at external praise. The analyst's partial approval of their behavior may mobilize an explosive reaction which then can be used to illuminate their intolerance of success. In some cases, the analyst's aggressive countertransference appears to be responsible for his avoidance in mentioning the patient's positive aspects.

During the session, the analyst is to "turn his own unconscious like a receptive organ towards the transmitting unconscious of the patient." Just as the patient must relate everything that comes into his mind, so the analyst is directed to put himself in a position to make use of everything that is said (or done). The analyst is, thus, in a position to use his own unconscious as an instrument in the analysis. To fulfill this aim, the analyst must not tolerate any resistance in himself which might hold back from his consciousness what has been perceived by his unconscious.

Resistance

The patient's first symptom or symptomatic act, or both, may be of special importance. They indicate the nature of the complex which governs the neurosis. Nonetheless, the interpretation connected with positive transference must remain uncommunicated until this transference has become a resistance. It is precisely an examination of resistance and transference, as Freud (1912) noted, that comprises analysis and little else. When the resistance has been overcome, the unconscious desires which were repressed are made conscious. The resistance is that part of the patient's personality which resents the basic aim of the analysis; namely, to undo the repression and to make unconscious wishes— their gratification and their frustration—conscious.

In translating the unconscious into the conscious, Eidelberg (1954) noted, the analyst usually finds—in addition to dammed-up infantile wishes— narcissistic mortifications which have been caused by the patient's internal or external "enemies." This condition is illustrated in the history of a patient whose mother closed his nostrils in order to force him to open his mouth so that he might be fed. He succeeded in denying this external narcissistic mortification by inflicting an internal mortification on himself; namely, by blaming himself for those things for which he did not want to blame others. In addition, some recognition must be given to the phenomena of *acting out* and *acting in*. Whenever the patient "acts" instead of "talks," his analysis becomes impossible. Finally, an examination should be made of the resistances which result from the fear of being overwhelmed by instinctual demands (with their resultant discharge) and the resistances caused by fear or frustration and rejection. For example, a female patient was afraid to verbalize her sexual wishes to avoid being seduced by the analyst, but, at the same time, she was also afraid that he wouldn't which would indicate his rejection.

Psychoanalysts who complain about the resistance of their patients sometimes forget that without this resistance analytic treatment would be impossible. The resistance indicates the presence of repressed material, and represents the dynamic factor which has to be utilized in order to transform the original infantile wishes into mature behavior. If the patients were not disgusted and horrified by their recognition that part of them has remained unchanged, that it does not participate in the development of their personality, there would be no therapeutic changes. Whenever the analyst is prepared to believe that the patient has accepted the presence of his infantile wishes, failing to understand that the patient's acceptance wards off the acknowledgement of other more dangerous wishes (which the patient tries to hide), he runs the risk of underestimating the strength of the patient's resistance.

While it is true that resistance is the name given to the power which interferes with the analytic work, it is necessary to remember that this resistance is the result of the so-called historical misunderstanding. After the analyst has succeeded in arousing doubts in his patient's mind about the validity of the arguments used in the defense of his resistance, he will be able to persuade him to investigate the unconscious factors responsible for this resistance. Most patients refuse to face their unconscious because they believe that facing and recognizing unconscious impulses *means giving in to their gratifications*.

Transference

At the beginning of treatment, many patients are under the impression that analysis will cure them by helping them to "unburden" themselves. They anticipate that they will find a friendly father confessor who will listen patiently, encourage and reassure them. They are surprised when they discover that the analyst—although friendly and patient—expects them to have the courage to open up that part of their personality which they have kept secret from others and from themselves. When the proper time arrives, the analyst will try not only to give the patient his empathy and in-

tellectual understanding but will also try to "shock" the patient—to provide an emotional experience necessary for cure. Such an emotional experience will usually take place only if the patient has established a workable transference to the analyst, and is prepared to participate emotionally in the critical appraisal of his unconscious.

The resistance often uses the mechanism of transference as its weapon to interfere with the progress of analysis. In this, the patient unconsciously strives to avoid the insight which the cure demands. The transfer of unconscious infantile wishes to the person of the doctor facilitates their admission into consciousness. After this transference takes place, the analyst will have to indicate to the patient that what he experienced in the present actually had its reference in the past, and, thus, was a repetition of a childhood experience, *and an attempt to deny it*.

As Ferenczi and Rank (1925) pointed out, the transference is an intermediate goal of analysis: the replacement of the manifest neurosis by a transference neurosis. It proceeds from this that the analyst is thus provided a means by which to help the patient penetrate into his own unconscious. The analyst tries to compel the patient to fit these emotional impulses into the nexus of the treatment and to understand them in the light of their psychical value.

Countertransference

Some analysts use the term *countertransference* for those feelings the analyst experiences toward his patients, while others prefer to speak of countertransference only when repressed infantile wishes are involved. The "ideal" analyst should be free from all these infantile emotions, but experience shows that this goal is difficult to achieve, and that analytic work may mobilize unconscious wishes which otherwise might have remained dormant. Whenever a circumstance like this occurs, the analyst should be able to recognize it and either analyze it himself or ask a colleague to do it for him.

Eidelberg (1954) provided the following example: "A male patient suffering from ejaculatio praecox was in treatment with a female analyst. She forgot her appointment with the patient on two occasions just at the time when his condition began to improve. She analyzed her parapraxis and discovered that her patient's restored erection had mobilized her own penis envy, still unsolved. The improvement in her patient was attendant upon the continuation of his analysis, and meant for her that she would be having sexual intercourse with a woman through her unconscious identification with the patient. She fought against this forbidden homosexual satisfaction by mobilizing an unconscious hostility against the patient. After she had recognized the cause of her trouble, she managed to finish his analysis successfully."

Elsewhere, Eidelberg (1958) added: "The masochist's need of punishment becomes understandable if he discovers the crimes he keeps on commiting in his unconscious. Like other neurotics, he does not differentiate in his unconscious between wishes and actions. Consequently, whenever he has a hostile wish, he develops a feeling of remorse instead of a feeling of guilt. In other words, instead of rejecting his prohibited infantile wish, he gratifies it partly, with the help of his neurotic character trait, and he needs punishment to free himself from this consequent feeling of remorse. Whereas a normal person, after recognizing the presence of an aggressive wish may reject this wish, aided by the feeling of guilt, and feel proud of his moral achievement, the neurotic reacts to his wish as if this wish represented an act, and he is therefore unable to remain moral. Instead, he has no other choice but to accept punishment for the presence of his hostile wishes. . . .

"The masochist is interested in changing his analyst into a sadist and a voyeur. In some cases, it is not easy to avoid being thus seduced, and therefore an unrelenting watch over the analyst's emotions should be encouraged. Many analytic interpretations are not helpful because they refer only to the infantile scene and avoid the transference situation. Not only what the analyst says, but also how he says it, his tone of voice, and the choice of his words, are often the cause of success or failure in the analysis of all patients, but appear to be even more important in dealing with masochists."

REFERENCES

Eidelberg, L.: *An Outline of a Comparative Pathology of the Neuroses.* IUP, pp. 81–82, 1954.
     "Technical Problems in the Analysis of Masochists." *JHH*, 7:108–109, 1958.

Ferenczi, S., & O. Rank. *The Development of Psychoanalysis.* NMDP, 1925.
Freud, S.: 1910, "The Future Prospects of Psycho-Analytic Therapy." *SE*, 11:145, 1957.
     1912, "A Note on the Unconscious." *SE*, 12:264, 1958.
     1915, "Paper on Technique." *SE*, 12:111–112, 115, 134, 138, 1958.

ADDITIONAL READINGS

Buxbaum, E., "Technique of Child Therapy—A Critical Evaluation." *PsaStC*, 9, 1954.
Eissler, K. R., "Notes on Problems of Technique in the Psychoanalytic Treatment of Adolescents. With Some Remarks on Perversions." *PsaStC*, 13, 1958.
Fierz-Monnier, H. K., "Methodik und Technik in der Praxis der Analytischen Psychologie." *P*, 8, 1954.
Goerres, A., "Die Technik der Psychoanalyse." *P*, 9, 1955–1956.
Klein, M., "The Technique of Analysis of Young Children." *IntJPsa*, 5, 1924.
Sharpe, E. F., "The Analyst—Essential for the Acquisition of Technique." *IntJPsa*, 11, 1930.

2003

TELEOLOGY (FINALITY) is a hypothesis which presupposes the "fact" of being directed toward or shaped by a purpose. The concept of the aim of an instinct, the elimination of unpleasure and the gain of pleasure, represents the final or teleological approach; e.g., we eat in order to obtain pleasure, on the other hand, the concept of the source of an instinct represents a causal approach: e.g., we eat because we are hungry.

Hartmann (1964) noted: "The kind of 'teleological' interpretation, which is also used in psychoanalysis, and, above all, in Adler's individual psychology, in which mental processes are understood in terms of their goals which may either be set consciously, or are unconscious—all this does not contradict a causal explanation. To view a process within a teleological framework can generally in biology be a valuable methodological principle—'the indication of the totality of relationships, of purposiveness facilitates the first causal connection between parts and whole'."

This teleological approach is discussed by the eminent biologist Mainx, (1955), as follows: "The teleologists distinguish between 'efficient causes' and 'final causes,' in which they regard 'final causality' (in the sense of aim or purpose causality) as an essential characteristic of fundamental biological processes. A statement formulated according to empirical science—'The state B follows regularly on the state A'—is customarily interpreted in such a way in ordinary language that A is called the 'cause' of B. Nevertheless, nothing at all is altered in the statement and its empirical testability if we call B the 'cause' of A. Only in the case of human actions is it otherwise, in so far as the state B, intended by the acting human being, is already consciously present as an aimed-at goal; and it is the knowledge of this connection which permits us so to transform the above statement that we include this fact in the definition of the state A."

Related Concept: CAUSALITY.

REFERENCES

Hartmann, H., *Essays on Ego Psychology*. IUP, p. 402, 1964.
Mainx, F., "Foundations of Biology," in *International Encyclopedia of Unified Science*. UCP, 1:72–73, 1955.

2004

TELEPATHY, according to Freud (1927), denotes the alleged fact that an event that occurs at a specific time comes more or less simultaneously into the consciousness of a person who is spatially distant, without any known method of communication coming into play. The term was introduced by F. W. H. Myers in 1882, but the phenomenon had been reported since ancient times.

More recently, there have been several large-scale "scientific" inquiries into these occurrences. The longest of these, in point of origin, was carried out by the Society for Psychical Research in England, beginning in the last century, while the most recent investigation (1964) was conducted by the Amsterdam Society for Parapsychological Research—a census of spontaneous parapsychological phenomena. Since 1930, J. B. Rhine and his associates at the Parapsychological Laboratory of Duke University have experimentally studied telepathic communication using "free" and "standardized"

materials. In France, R. Warcollier and his colleagues (until 1960) investigated this phenomenon utilizing thousands of "free" drawings and "random" images as their instrumentality. To date, no conclusive evidence has been offered by these experiments which would substantiate a claim for its occurrence.

A number of psychoanalysts—M. Balint, H. Deutsch, J. Ehrenwald, J. Eisenbud, W. H. Gillespie, I. Hollos, E. Servadio, etc.—have contributed to a psychological-psychoanalytical theory of telepathy; in particular, as it regards the possible telepathic occurrences in an analytical setting. These investigations have shown that the patient's telepathic dream, or phantasy, must be analyzed within the framework of a particular transference-countertransference situation in that phase of the analysis. Servadio's (1958) conclusions are of particular interest: "We may very well imagine situations in which the individual feels utterly prevented from conveying the meaning of a transference aspect or reaction of his, unless he temporarily reverts to an *immediate* kind of communication, or, better still, to a 'communion' of some sort, implying regressive non-singleness, and a sudden merging in a non-individualized, unconscious Gestalt; that, is, unless he can enact what is often also called 'thought-transference'."

In general, an extremely precise, "complementary" configuration of the problems of both analyst and patient has thus been found, which the patient seems to have perceived through extrasensory channels, to reveal unknowingly, as it were, the attention and the love the patient craves from the analyst. In or out of analysis, telepathy may be considered to be a regressive unconscious attempt to establish or to reestablish psychological relations to external objects without the help of the sense organs under conditions of emotional need or stress. In this view, telepathy has nothing to do with a wireless-like kind of transmission; there is nothing intellectual or superior about it. It is not influenced by distance; at least no physical support for this belief has been found to date. Its contents can be distorted by the primary process, as they occur in dreams and other mental processes which involve the participation of the unconscious.

Related Concept: OCCULT.

REFERENCES

Freud, S., 1927, "The Future of an Illusion." *SE*, 21:36–39, 1961.

Servadio, E., "Telepathy and Psychoanalysis." *Journal of The American Society For Psychical Research*, 52:132, 1958.

ADDITIONAL READINGS

Brunswick, D., "A Comment on E. Servadio's 'A Presumptive Telepathic-Precognitive Dream During Analysis'," *IntJPsa*, 38, 1957.

Ehrenwald, J., *New Dimensions of Deep Analysis. A Study of Telepathy in Interpersonal Relationships*. G&S, 1955.

Eisenbud, J., "Analysis of a Presumptively Telepathic Dream," in G. Devereux *Psycho-Analysis and the Occult*. IUP, 1953.

Roheim, G., "Telepathy in a Dream," in G. Devereux, *Psychoanalysis and the Occult*. IUP, 1953.

2005

TEMPERATURE EROTICISM. Cutaneous contact and temperature, as well as pain and other stimuli, are potential sources of erogeneous stimulations which, when combined with early eroticism, according to Fenichel (1945), form an essential part of the primitive receptive sexuality.

The pleasure of feeling warm and the unpleasure of feeling cold are part of sensations which characterize the oral period, and conditions involving a fixation at, or a regression to, the oral stage of libidinal development can result in symptoms involving temperature eroticism. Fenichel reported the case of a woman with severe anxiety who was unable to go to bed at night unless she took a hot drink and sat on a radiator to obtain its warmth; both are identified as substitute love objects.

Abraham (1910) described the following case history, in part: "The sensation of heat described by this patient, and, as will be shown, by others, too, is a normal accompaniment of sexual excitation. It had been transferred in his case from masturbation to the dream-state. It is worth noting that he blushed very easily. As soon as he came among people his extraordinarily excitable sexual phantasy became active and expressed itself physically as a wave of heat. It should not surprise us to find that this increased flow of blood also accompanied his phantasies of activity, since, as we know, they represented his unconscious sexual phantasies.

Even in the early stage of his 'exalted' phantasies he used to notice an 'under-current' of coldness and anxiety besides the rising heat; and in the final stage the feeling of coldness dominated. In general, therefore, the feeling of heat used to appear when he wished to push forward to sexual activity, while the feeling of coldness used to come on when his instinctual emotions had changed into anxiety and the tendency to repression had obtained the upper hand once more."

Related Concepts: EROTOGENIC ZONES; SKIN EROTICISM; STIGMATA.

REFERENCES

Abraham, K., 1910, "Hysterical Dream-States." *SPA*, p. 105, 1942.

Fenichel, O., *The Psychoanalytic Theory of Neurosis*. Nor, pp. 69–70, 390, 1945.

2006

THANATOS, according to Freud (1940) is a primary instinct aimed at the return of the organism to an inorganic state. The presence of Thanatos can be detected only by studying it in its various fusions with its counterpart Eros. It is questionable whether pure Thanatos, in fact, produces psychological derivatives. It would seem, however, that it does produce two so-called secondary instincts: (a) aggressive instinct fusions and (b) sexual instinct fusions. The quantity of Thanatos in the former is greater and plays the greater role; in the latter, Eros plays the greater role.

For some reason, Freud refused to name the energy of the destructive instinct. However, two of his pupils, Federn and Weiss, suggested *mortido* and *destrudo*, respectively. It is not clear whether the term destrudo refers to the aggressive fusion or to the energy of the pure Thanatos. It is also not clear whether libido refers to the energy of pure Eros or to the energy of the sexual instinct fusion. While it is true that the fusions of Eros and Thanatos appear to be responsible for our lives, the presence of sexual and aggressive instinct fusions which the individual tries to gratify at the same time with the same object leads to neurotic conflicts (Eidelberg, 1948).

Freud referred to Thanatos as being silent and

suggested that it produces psychological derivatives only when directed towards the external world. "So long as that instinct operates internally, as a death instinct, it remains silent: it only comes to our notice when it is diverted outwards as an instinct of destruction." This statement may contradict Freud's descriptions of such psychological derivatives as feelings of guilt, remorse and anxiety in which the aggression is discharged against the self. It seems that in those examples that it is not the pure Thanatos but the aggressive instinct fusion that is being discharged, and it is also questionable whether our muscles used in fighting can be regarded as gratifying the pure Thanatos and not the aggressive instinct fusion.

Hartmann (1964) discussed its historical importance, as follows: "Of course, there is also the historical fact that in those years which were, in spite of all, years of his greatest creativity, Freud developed three comprehensive theories simultaneously. There was, in adddition to his new ideas on psychic structure, the introduction of aggression as a primary drive on the same level as sexuality— and neither of these theories is more speculative than are many others in analysis; they are interrelated in more than one way. But there are also the far-reaching biological speculations on Eros and the death instinct. These differ from the two other theories, which are part of empirical psychology, in their sweep, and also in their difficulty of validation. The three theories are not always considered separately, and the speculative character which Freud himself attributed to the Eros-Thanatos theory might have cast its shadow on the two others. It is highly interesting that at the same time when Freud, on the level of biological speculation, tried to account for the 'phenomena of life' by the interplay of the two primordial drives, he *accentuated* for the purposes of empirical psychology the relative independence of the noninstinctual forces of the ego. Obviously, we are confronted here not only with two different terminologies. but also with two different levels of theory formation. It is not always easy to see clearly what refers to one and what to the other, though their distinction is essential."

Related Concepts: AGGRESSION; EROS; REPETITION COMPULSION.

REFERENCES

Eidelberg, L., *Studies in Psychoanalysis*. IUP, pp. 135–137, 1948.
Freud, S., 1940, "An Outline of Psycho-Analysis." *SE*, 23:149–150, 1964.
Hartmann, H., *Essays on Ego Psychology*. IUP, pp. 294–295, 1964.

2007
THEMATIC APPERCEPTION TEST (T.A.T.) is a *projective* instrument that is used as a diagnostic tool to elicit the thoughts, attitudes and feelings of the subject which lie behind the disguise of making up a story. The test consists of ten picture cards for women, ten for men, and ten for men and women. Unlike the Rorschach, with which it is often administered, there is no quantitative scoring technique. The themes that recur in more than one picture are noted down by the examiner: an analysis is made of the prevailing emotional tone of the narrative, of the subject's identification with the characters, of his strivings and needs, and of his conflicts and defenses.

In all, twenty cards are presented to the subject, accompanied by the question, "What do you see?" The story which is given by the subject would, for normals, deal with the content of the picture card in terms that would usually incorporate characters of the same age and sex. The content of the card would normally be consistent with the characterization offered by the subject.

The test is based principally on the assumption that the subject will deal with the picture and its elements in terms of what Murphy (1947) calls "the conception of the self." The general feeling tone (the affective level) is usually fairly consistent through the twenty cards. "The T.A.T.," according to Murphy, "permits, then, among other things, the gathering of data about the identifications, the affective level, and the relative strengths of the various needs of the individual. It provides a direct introduction to individual autisms, individual projections. And since unconscious needs receive considerable attention, the test serves the purpose of psychoanalytic free association."

Related Concepts: DEFENSE MECHANISMS; IDENTIFICATION.

REFERENCE

Murphy, G., *Personality*. HBP, pp. 671–672, 1947.

2008

THERAPY. The task of the analyst consists—in the main—of making conscious to the patient previously held unconscious material and in uncovering and overcoming the resistances which are employed in their maintenance. The analyst shows the patient what he refuses to see, and unmasks his unconscious wishes; he helps the patient to use rejection and sublimation instead of repression. [Freud, 1919.]

The basic rule of analysis is free association: the patient is required to tell all that comes to mind, without censorship, and without consideration of its pertinence. Nothing is to be excluded: not the names of his friends or the secrets of others, dreams or daydreams, etc. The analyst is interested in knowing all that the patient knows, for it is through this process that the analyst discovers those mental phenomena of which the patient may not be aware.

In the course of analysis, the patient transfers those repressed infantile wishes responsible for his problems onto the person of the analyst, who thus becomes a representative of infantile objects. Thereafter, the analyst assists the patient in his recognition of what was traumatic in infancy, and the defenses which served to keep the wishes repressed.

The patient knows very little about the personality of his analyst. Thus it is possible for the analyst to show the patient whom he has in mind when he talks about the analyst. A successful analysis is impossible as long as the patient remains detached: the patient has to renounce the infantility of his emotions and the archaic character of his object relations if he is to be freed of his "bound" infantile wishes.

Some analysts discuss only the pathology with their patients. They feel that a discussion of the patient's normal reactions represents a waste of time. Nonetheless, it seems that an understanding of the pathological nature of a phenomenon is possible only by comparing it with a normal one. It is easier for a patient to recognize his neurotic traits if the analyst shows him that he, along with others, is capable of functioning in a healthy fashion. A discussion of the positive aspects of his personality may be used to protect him from the shock connected with a disclosure of his neurotic character traits. The fact that the analyst approves of parts of the patient's personality shows the patient that his doctor is not an enemy. With some patients—the so-called moral masochists—there is resentment of external praise. The analyst's partial approval of their behavior, however, may mobilize an explosive reaction which then can be used to illuminate their intolerance of success. In some cases, the analyst's aggressive countertransference appears to be responsible for his avoidance in mentioning the positive aspects of the patient's behavior.*

During the session, the analyst is to "turn his own unconscious like a receptive organ towards the transmitting unconscious of the patient." Just as the patient must relate everything that comes into his mind, so the analyst is directed to put himself in a position to make use of everything that is said (or done). The analyst is, thus, in a position to use his own unconscious as an instrument in the analysis. To fulfill this aim, the analyst must not tolerate any resistance in himself which might hold back from his consciousness what has been perceived by his unconscious. [Freud, 1915.]

Therapy cannot be considered as purely an intellectual process. While it is true that patients are cured by finding out what they have kept unconscious, the treatment does not consist in arguing and reasoning alone. As noted, strong positive and negative emotions develop which are directed toward the analyst. The patient must be able to differentiate the real analyst from the one he creates in his transference fantasy; only then can he be analyzed successfully. Further, the patient's reluctance to discuss certain problems because of conscious or unconscious resistances must be dealt with. Only patients who are able to grasp the meaning of the resistance and are willing to analyze it can be cured.

----

* Therapy is not a post mortem, for while it is impossible to cure a patient without hurting him, he should not be exposed to any unnecessary pain. To be frank does not mean to be rude. With some patients, bluntness may be the tool; with others, politeness.

Neither the analyst nor the patient should be surprised that from time to time all explanations which are communicated and accepted by the patient appear to be completely forgotten. The patient refuses to accept responsibility for his neurosis, insisting that he should not be blamed for his symptoms because he does not like them. While it is true that he does not like the suffering caused by his illness, the patient prefers it to the conscious recognition of his problems. Although it often interferes with his gain of pleasure, the patient's neurosis does give him a partial discharge of his instinctual tension and often protects him from panic.

The patient in therapy should not expect his analyst to answer his questions or to offer him sound advice. On many subjects, the patient may be better informed than his analyst. Furthermore, a solution which appears to be good for one person may be bad for another. However, there is one bit of advice which the analyst gives his patients when he undertakes to analyze them. The analyst tries to persuade them to use a conscious method in dealing with their problems instead of an unconscious one.

The analyst has something to offer to each of the four parts of the patient's personality; to the id, a better means of discharge for its tension; to the ego, a better control of the other parts of his personality; to the superego, a better morality with a resulting decrease of tension between the ego and the ego-ideal; and to the sense organs, a better chance of finding and accepting a suitable external object. Obviously, a patient who is satisfied with the status quo and wants only to be left in peace is not suitable for analysis.

The analyst who is interested in removing his patient's unhappiness is aware of course that there are also other causes of unhappiness in addition to neurosis. The therapist may find it advisable to explain to the patient that analysis can only remove the suffering due to illness. It appears probable, however, that once the unconscious defense mechanisms are eliminated, the patient's chance of becoming happy will increase.

Related Concepts: HYPNOSIS; PSYCHOANALYSIS; SUGGESTION.

REFERENCES

Freud, S.: 1915, "Papers on Technique." *SE*, 12:111–112, 115, 134, 138, 1958.
    1919, "Lines of Advance in Psycho-Analytic Therapy." *SE*, 17:159, 160, 1955.

ADDITIONAL READINGS

Fairbairn, W., & D. Ronald, "On the Nature and Aims of Psycho-Analysis." *IntJPsa*, 41, 1960.
Frosch, J., "Special Problems of Psychoanalytic Therapy." *AnSurvPsa*, 1, 1950.
Glover, E., "Therapeutic Criteria of Psycho-Analysis." *IntJPsa*, 35, 1954.
Loewald, H. W., "On the Therapeutic Action of Psycho-Analysis." *IntJPsa*, 41, 1960.
Lorand, S.: & W. A. Console, "Therapeutic Results in Psycho-Analytic Treatment Without Fee." *IntJPsa*, 39, 1958.
    "Psycho-Analytic Therapy of Religious Devotees." *IntJPsa*, 43, 1962.
Nacht, S., "The Non-Verbal Relationship in Psychoanalytic Treatment." *IntJPsa*, 44, 1963.
Nunberg, H., "Evaluation of the Results of Psycho-Analytic Treatment." *IntJPsa*, 35, 1954.
Roth, N., "The Aim of Psychoanalytic Therapy." *PT*, 9, 1955.
Szasz, T. S., "On the Theory of Psycho-Analytic Treatment." *IntJPsa*, 38, 1957.

2009

THINKING is defined by Freud (1923) as an experimental kind of acting, carried out with a small expenditure of energy, which is related to perceptual elements in time. In this, thinking secures a delay in the motoric discharges and controls the access to motility. As such, it is essential to reality testing and is closely related to the primary and secondary processes.

It would seem that a successful inhibition—which is at first external and, at a later time internal—gives rise to mental activity. This activity implies the utilization of external and internal stimuli, their perception and evaluation; it involves the storing of memories (mneme system), remembering and planning. All these functions require a small discharge of instinctual energy—probably, narcissistic libido and narcissistic destrudo. In thinking, there is an acceptance of the external limitation of the power present in internal reality. [Freud, 1933.]

Related Concepts: ACTION (ACT); LANGUAGE.

REFERENCES

Freud, S.: 1923, "The Ego and the Id." *SE*, 19:19, 23, 25–26, 55, 1961.
  1933, "New Introductory Lectures in Psycho-Analysis." *SE*, 22:170, 1964.

ADDITIONAL READINGS

Arlow, J., "The Psychoanalytic Theory of Thinking." *JAPA*, 6, 1958.
Freud, S., "Studies on Hysteria." *SE*, 1, 1964.
Hanfmann, E., "Analysis of the Thinking Disorder in a Case of Schizophrenia." *ANP*, 41, 1939.
Inman, W., "Clinical Thought-Reading." *IntJPsa*, 39, 1958.
Keiser, S., "Disturbances of Ego Functions of Speech and Abstract Thinking." *JAPA*, 10, 1962.
Marcinowski, J., "Vom finalen und vom kausalen Denken in der Psychologie der Neurosen." *ZPt*, 8, 1935.
Sperling, O., "Thought Control and Creativity." *JHH*, 8, 1959.

2010

THRESHOLD SYMBOLISM is a term used by Silberer (1911) to describe a dream image which symbolizes the state of waking up. Freud (1900)* warned against overuse of the concept of functional phenomena, and emphasized that dream elements expressing a state of mind did so in an overdetermined sense, rather than a primary one. He admitted that Silberer had presented examples which indicated that part of the manifest content of the dream was connected with the desire to awaken.

The concept of threshold symbolism has been used rarely in recent years. Grotjahn's article, written in 1942, proved the exception to the rule: he appeared to agree with the concept of "functional" symbols. In discussing Grotjahn's article, Fliess (1953) flatly stated that there were no special "functional" symbols. Falling asleep and waking up are at times and in part experienced and therefore subject to thought as represented in the dream. This approach deprives "threshold symbolism" of any particular meaning.

Related Concepts: AUTOSYMBOLISM; HYPNAGOGIC PHENOMENON; SYMBOLIZATION.

---

* Added to the original work in 1914.

REFERENCES

Fliess, R., *The Revival of Interest in the Dream.* IUP, p. 98, 1953.
Freud, S., 1900, "The Interpretation of Dreams." *SE*, 5:504, 1953.
Grotjahn, M., "The Process of Awakening," *R*, 29:1–19, 1942.
Silberer, H., "Symbolik des Erwachens und Schwellensymbolik überhaupt." *Y*, 3:621–660, 1911.

2011

TIC is an involuntary motor automatism, usually with abrupt, repetitive involuntary movement of an interconnected group of muscles. They are differentiated from transient autoerotic habits, repetitive mannerisms and compulsions. The tic is a neurotic symptom, probably a conversion of oral wishes. Abraham (1921) noted: "The tic first mentioned in psycho-analytic literature (*Studien über Hysterie*, 1895) was a clicking tic, by means of which the patient wished unconsciously to awaken her sick father who had just fallen asleep. A purpose directed against his life is undoubtedly expressed in this case. One of my patients suffering from *tic général* made snapping movements with his fingers, while at the same time he threw his arm forward with an aggressive gesture. The tic which takes the form of making grimaces has an obvious hostile significance. Many more examples of this kind can be adduced.

"Other tics, particularly coprolalia, show their anal origin quite clearly, as Ferenczi has pointed out. Some—for example, the whistling tic—are derived directly from anal processes (*flatus*). Here the patient carries out his hostile and degrading purposes by anal means."

In children, symptomatic tics may be observed in the process of crystallization; "habit movements" in the process of becoming more involuntary indicates a degree of internalization of the conflict. Tics may be single and isolated or part of a tic syndrome, the *maladie des tics*. The tic syndrome consists of a generalized diffuse motor automatism which may appear in intermittent and migratory crops of tics or may inundate the entire neuro-muscular apparatus in such a way as to cause a paroxysmal motion which may be mistaken for chorea. The tic may appear within the context of neuroses or psychoses.

The tic represents the symbolic expression of conflict in body language, and contains elements of discharge, gratification and punishment. A forbidden motor impulse finds its outlet through an unrecognized and quick repetitious gesture or movement in a displaced set of muscle groups. Autoerotic habit movements are neither so vigorous nor so spasmodic, and are regular in their sequence of muscular contractions as are the true tics, though there may be transitions between autoerotic actions and tics. The tic may frequently represent a masturbatory conflict.

The ego of the patient with multiple tics usually displays impulsivity, hyperkinesis, oversensitivity, impatience and an inability to tolerate frustration. The ego is not in full control of the muscular apparatus; it has dissociated part of it because of the danger of uncontrolled instinctual discharge. Childhood illness, involving locomotion or occurring at the time of learning to develop independent motility, may predispose the subject to tics. The mothers of children suffering from this disorder have been described as over-protective, vindictive, and intolerant of any manifestation of phallic aggression or exhibitionistic tendencies in their sons. While the tic defends against an overwhelming instinctual impulse, it is at the same time an attempt to project an internalized conflict into the outer world and the paroxysms may represent the inner struggle and the attempt to discharge the unbearable affecto-motoric tensions. The inhibited affective movements may never have been expressed by the patient, especially in a traumatic situation or may represent a state of emotional excitement in another person with whom the patient has made an hysterical identification. The tic may repeat the struggle with ambivalently introjected objects represented by the muscles themselves, and may serve as a communication to objects by means of gesture and mimicry. This may be particularly true of facial tics, since facial expressions may communicate affect and mood. There is a fixation to the omnipotence of magical gestures, with representation of doing and undoing, impulse and punishment.

The anal orientation of patients with the tic syndrome reveals itself in the frequent coughing, swearing, and coprolalia or obscene speech which may be pervasive. Prognosis in the treatment of the tic patient depends upon the degree of invasion of the ego and the remaining ego assets which are conflict free.

Related Concepts: CONVERSION AND CONVERSION SYMPTOMS; IMPULSE.

REFERENCE

Abraham, K., 1921, "Contribution to a Discussion on Tic." *SPA*, p. 324, 1942.

ADDITIONAL READINGS

Aarons, Z. A., "Notes on a Case of *Maladie des Tics*." *Q*, 27, 1958.
Gerard, M. W., "The Psychogenic Tic in Ego Development." *PsaStC*, 2, 1946.
Klein, M., "Zur Genese des Tics." *Z*, 11, 1925.
Mahler, M., "A Psychoanalytic Evaluation of Tic in Psychopathology of Children." *PsaStC*, 3–4, 1949.
Peck, M. W., "Two Cases of Major Tic." *JNMD*, 58, 1923.
Reich, W., "Der Psychogene Tic als Onanieäquivalent." *ZSW*, 11, 1925.
Sadger, J., "A Contribution to the Understanding of Tic." *Z*, 2, 1914.

2012

TOILET TRAINING is the process of teaching the child to urinate and defecate in the toilet and not in his clothes. Unfortunately, training is frequently attempted in a manner and at a time which is not coordinated with the child's developmental pattern. From approximately the second year of life to the fourth, the child's chief interest is the retention and expulsion of feces. He regards his excrement as a valuable creation, a prized personal possession, which he has to slowly learn to relinquish. Under normal conditions, the child will learn to give up his interest in feces, sublimating the energy into such activities as painting, playing in the sand, being clean and orderly, etc. If the child is not permitted to slowly give up his anal interests, and a traumatic pressure is experienced, he may use the mechanism of repression (or denial) in an attempt to eliminate this interest from his conscious mind. The repressed, unconscious anal wishes may continue to dominate his life and produce various defense mechanisms. Since the anal wish is not conscious, it cannot be given up, and a continuous expenditure of energy is required to maintain it in its state of repression (countercathexis). The character trait provides a mechanism for accomplishing this continuing act of repression. [Freud, 1931.]

E. Geleerd (1944) noted: "Mothers often have a tendency to train their children quite early, especially when they have observed the regularity of the bowel function in the first few months. To their great distress, this regularity breaks down at the period of life when the elimination becomes an important source of pleasure to the infant. Investigation of children and adults with an obesssional or compulsion neurosis has shown without exception that this mental illness has important roots in the conflict between the desire to derive pleasure from elimination and the mother's insistence of toilet training."

Some authors view the toilet training conflicts as instrumental in the formation of an infantile conscience, a forerunner of the superego. "When asked to evacuate the bowels under certain conditions only, the child experiences the conflict between 'should' and 'would like to.'" [Fenichel, 1945.] Toilet training is the second important parental prohibition to be introjected. Good toilet habits that turn bad, or bad toilet habits that are continued past the age of two, may be a sign of unhappiness or illness. They may coincide with parental absence or the birth of a sibling.

Clinical Example

The patient was overly clean, compulsively neat, fussy, pedantic, and obstinate. Such an adult would have discovered in the course of his analysis that these traits were a reaction formation against an unresolved infantile anal wish to play with feces; he would then be able to give up his childish wishes since he would no longer require his unconscious defenses. The defecation and the mobilization of any such wish, he would have learned, caused him to anticipate parental displeasure: he had introjected his mother's prohibitions, substituting the wish, "I want to be overly clean," for his original anal wish, "I want to be dirty."

Related Concepts: ANAL PHASE; OBSESSIVE-COMPULSIVE NEUROSIS.

REFERENCES

Fenichel, O., *The Psychoanalytic Theory of Neurosis.* Nor, pp. 102, 305, 1945.
Freud, S., 1931, "Female Sexuality." *SE*, 21:223–246, 1961.
Geleerd, E., "Mothering, Feeding and Toilet Training in Infants." *BMC*, 8:182, 1944.

2013
TOLERANCE OF TENSION denotes the ability to experience unpleasure without seeking its immediate removal. The simple reflex is the pregenitor of the automatic discharge of the external stimulus. As a result of the inhibition of the motoric reaction, the stimulus becomes conscious and is discharged by the total, conscious action of the individual. In this, a longer or shorter toleration of the experience of tension is endured, and the instant discharge (omnipotence of thought) is given up.

In overcoming the feelings of infantile omnipotence the immediate gratification is given up: this act constitutes the first crucial step in the toleration of tension. It stems from an adult acceptance of the need for planning rather than for impulsive action, for anticipatory rather than for immediate gratification. Freud (1924) pointed out that while pleasure is often connected with a discharge of a tension, and unpleasure with its increase; in some cases, an increase of tension produces pleasure, and a decrease, unpleasure.

In addition to individual differences, the intensity of feeling interferes with the ability to wait, to suspend a decision, and to execute the required discharge. This tolerance of unpleasure should not be confused with masochism. The normal individual seeks pleasure but is willing to wait; the masochist wants pain and humiliation. The normal individual is willing to take risks and endure defeats while seeking victory; the masochist is sure to obtain the defeat he provokes.

Ella Sharpe (1930) reflects upon the analytic attitude of the analyst, as follows: "Tolerance emerges out of an acquaintance with one's own unconscious. A capacity for kindly scepticism and suspension of judgement is the accompaniment of a curiosity that has been purged of the infantile elements.

"One would expect, as a result of this special interest and orientation towards human life, that a person capable of acquiring a specialized technique in dealing with human nature would have a technique above the average in ordinary human contacts. It may well be that a person with capacity for this has been hindered by internal difficulties, but these difficulties being removed, the would-be technician must surely be a technicain in general before being one in particular. We are talking of psychology in *practice*, as an art, not as knowledge of theories. A practical technician cannot be an adept with human material in the laboratory and continually make gross errors in human contacts in the outside world. The capacity to get on to understanding terms in the external world with types of people differing from one's self, the capacity to sustain and maintain friendly relationships in spite of stresses and differences, are indicative of essential qualifications for acquiring a special technique for a special object.

"Whatever qualification is necessary in the way of knowledge of pathological states of mind, the future technician will have gained his knowledge of human nature not only in the consulting-room, but in actual living. He will also have ranged to some extent through some pathway of literature; biography, history, fiction, poetry or drama. In some field of literature he will have met, in addition to his actual contacts with people, phases of life and conduct that will have given him that broad general sympathy with life and people which no textbook of scientific principles can ever inculcate.

"I will give you a specific application of what I mean by knowledge of life and living as a necessary part of the equipment of a psycho-analyst. A physician correlates a description of symptoms with his deeper knowledge of anatomy, physiology and organ functions. He gets from the patient all the data that can be obtained. The data from the analysand has to be elicited in many forms. The unconscious has to be inferred from its representations. The more we are versed in forms of representation the quicker we shall be in understanding what is represented. Technique stands a chance of being more subtle whenever we have a first-hand knowledge of the things a patient is talking about. We proceed from end-result to origin, from preconscious to unconscious.

"Take as an example the following: a patient halts in the train of thought she is expressing. She says: 'I'm suddenly interrupted by thinking of Portia, not that Portia, but Brutus' Portia. I won't think of her, I don't like her.' The patient reverts to her original line of thinking. Now, if I know the history of Brutus' Portia, I know at once the unconscious theme towards which the resistances are directed. I know there is a correlation between the conversion symptoms of this particular patient and the fact that Brutus' Portia inflicted on herself a wound for a special purpose. The patient has unconsciously, with unerring instinct, selected a representation of her own unconscious psychology. If I do not know the role of this Portia in the play, I shall be slower in getting on to the track of the unconscious motivation. Take another example of the same kind. The patient suddenly thinks of the words 'Like a worm i' [in] the bud.' She repeats the phrase several times. She cannot recall the context, nor why the words were said. If I remember that the context is, 'She never told her love,' then I have at once the clue to the unconscious theme."

The toleration of tension permits the individual to give up those acts which are in accord with the unpleasure-pleasure principle for those of the reality principle: to remember, plan, and anticipate. The tolerance of tension requires that the individual be capable of enduring this dammed-up object-libido, and narcissistic libido, i.e., to experience unpleasure without his seeking to remove it immediately.

Related Concepts: INFANCY; OMNIPOTENCE OF THOUGHT; REALITY PRINCIPLE; UNPLEASURE-PLEASURE PRINCIPLE.

REFERENCES

Freud, S., 1924, "The Economic Problem of Masochism." *SE*, 19:160, 1961.
Sharpe, E. F., 1930, "The Technique of Psycho-Analysis," in *Collected Papers on Psycho-Analysis.*" HPI, pp. 12–13, 1950.

2014

TORTICOLLIS denotes a torsion-like spasmodic contraction of the muscles of the neck which results in a rotation of the chin and drawing of the head to one side. While the condition may be neurologically caused, many cases are psychogenic, and represent a special type of tic.

The muscles of the head and neck are particularly utilized in the expression of emotions in perceptual contact with the external world. During the development and integration of motility, this vital function may be impaired by an unconscious conflict (mobilization of the opposite) or through displacement, resulting in the symbolic expression. The muscular dystonia is often related to (a) warded-off bodily sensations and (b) repressed motor satisfactions in different muscle groups, or both. Spasms of the anal or genital zones may be substituted to spasms in other muscle groups, including the head and neck.

Torticollis, as with other tics, has the compromise function of being both a defense against translating an impulse into action and of simultaneously effecting discharge of the impulse. In the case of an eight-year-old girl described by Mittelman (1957), the torticollis represented looking only with the eyes and head instead of turning the whole body; it represented a denial of responsibility for the act—turning the head and then looking away—both motivated by the desire to see her step-father's genitals. She had also the wish not to see, to reject a feared object, and to search out and to avoid punishment.

Torticollis is frequently close to compulsion neurosis and occurs in predisposed impulsive individuals with strong elements of defense against threats to the body. The unconscious ego utilizes the regressive language of magical gestures. Stiffness of the head and neck frequently represents both erection and the punishment for masturbation. [Mahler, 1949.]

Related Concepts: Conversion and Conversion Symptoms; Motility; Tic.

REFERENCES

Mahler, M., "Psychoanalytic Evaluation of Tics." *PsaStC*, 3, 1949.
Mittelman, B., "Motility in the Therapy of Children and Adults." *PsaStC*, 12, 1959.

2015

TOTEM denotes a practice which governs all social and religious institutions in various primitive societies; that group or clan which takes its name from its totem. The totem may be an animal, a plant, or a force of nature which incorporates tribal prohibitions. The totem, Freud (1913) noted, stands first of all for all tribal ancestors of the clan. Wherever a totem exists, it is usually connected with the prohibition of having sexual relations with a member of the same totem. Thus, whether strictly enforced or not, its aim is the de facto prevention of incest.

The clan members show respect for the totem by not killing it, if it is an animal, or not gathering it and cutting it up if it is a plant. The totem is distinguished from a fetish in that it always incorporates a class of objects or a species of animals. Whatever its nature, it is always regarded with superstitious respect. Freud (1939) noted that totemism represented a primitive form of religion which aimed at the partial repudiation of instinctual demands.

Abraham (1913) discussed totemistic attitudes which appear in the mental life of the child. "Certain products of children's phantasy bear an extraordinary resemblance to the totemistic system of primitive peoples. A child who often openly displays an ambivalent attitude towards its father or mother, will frequently displace its feelings from them on to a certain animal or class of animals, or sometimes on to several such classes. It shows interest and love for this animal which is equivalent to a totem. But in its day dreams and night dreams the same object plays the part of an anxiety-animal. If the child develops a phobia, as so often happens, it is this animal which is usually the object of its anxiety. In not a few cases the animal retains its significance even later on, and appears in the phobias of adult neurotics just as it does in children.

"I have made a considerable number of observations relative to this, though I cannot given them in detail in this place. I shall select one or two only on which to base the remarks which follow. In the first place, the ambivalence of their attitude towards their totem (the feared animal) is obvious to many of the patients themselves. One of my cases, a woman who suffered from a slowly progressive hebephrenia, gave me, with that freedom from inhibition which is characteristic of such patients, most precise and instructive information concerning this and other important points of individual totemism. In her case the fly played the main part as an anxiety-animal. On one occasion she volunteered the information that her feelings towards flies were 'full of love', but that at the same time she had an impulse to kill them.

"It is also important to note that especially in dreams a particular animal may often represent not only the father (or mother) but the patient himself. In a dream of this kind which I came across, three generations—the father of the dreamer, the dreamer himself, and his son—were all represented by the same symbolic animal—the dog. This corresponds to the very common hereditary totemism of primitive peoples.

"I next refer to another individual parallel to the primitive totemic cult. This is concerned with plant-totemism, which, though rarer than animal-totemism, is occasionally observed. A neurotic who was constantly fleeing from his incestuous desire for his mother, showed in his waking phantasies and in his dreams all the phenomena of tree-totemism. In the garden of a small château where he lived as a boy there was a very large old tree which he regarded with religious awe; he used to pray to it and receive oracles from its rustling sounds. His defence against his incestuous wishes was associated with severe anxiety. He was pursued by continual unrest and could not settle down anywhere. In his waking dreams he seemed to be a tree standing in the parental garden, surrounded by other trees (his relatives) near the big oracle tree (his father), and to have taken firm root there. It seems to me that the repression of his incestuous desires demanded extraordinary measures so that his parents could not be symbolized by an animal. They had to be symbolized by a tree, which is sexually undifferentiated. This may throw some light on the totemism of certain primitive tribes, where the totem is not, as in most cases, an animal, but a plant.

"When we view infantile animal phobias and neurotic totemic symptoms we are struck by one fact which has hitherto found little or no consideration. In some of these cases the totem is a four-legged animal whose size and strength make it at once clear why it should be identified by the child with the mighty father. But in a considerable number of cases we find that the anxiety-animal is the smallest kind of animal known to the child, such as flies, wasps, butterflies, caterpillars, etc. The same thing occurs in a number of neurotics. The actual dangerousness of such animals is not a sufficient explanation of this form of infantile totemism, for only certain of them are at all injurious; others are quite harmless, and the child is able to kill them without risk. According to the evidence of my psycho-analyses of neurotics there seems to be a simpler and better explanation. These animals have the characteristic of making a sudden appearance. They approach all of a sudden, touch the human body unexpectedly, and disappear with equal rapidity. Of course individual determinants enter into every case. For instance, in one of my patients the wasp had replaced another animal, the tiger. The colour and markings of the wasp reminded the patient of the tiger, and its buzzing could represent the tiger's roar, which latter sound was associated with the child's dread of the deep, threatening voice of his father when he was angry. This patient spontaneously said that the sound of a wasp flying about with its threatening buzz was associated in his mind with feelings of rage. My psycho-analytic experience leads me to believe that small animals have a manifold significance. They represent the father who surprises the child by suddenly appearing near it or by alarming it with a threatening voice. It is also characteristic of these animals that they disappear quickly and can be killed more easily than big ones. Thus these small flying animals indicate on the one hand the dangerous power of the father, but serve on the other as an expression for the child's ideas of getting rid of him. These are the same animals that we meet with in mythology as 'spirit animals'. Patient E, whom we have already often mentioned, gave me quite freely considerable information about the infantilism which still persisted in him, and drew my attention among other things to his ambivalent attitude towards flies. He said that he used to amuse himself with killing flies and wasps in his childhood."

Related Concepts: ANIMISM; FETISHISM; OMNIPOTENCE OF THOUGHT; TABOO.

REFERENCES

Abraham, K., 1913, "Restrictions and Transformations of Scopophilia in Psycho-Neurotics; With Remarks on Analogous Phenomena in Folk-Psychology." *SPA*, pp. 226–229, 1942.

Freud, S.: 1913, "Totem and Taboo." *SE*, 13:2, 1955.

    1939, "Moses and Monotheism." *SE*, 23:119, 1964.

2016

TRAINING ANALYSIS. Originally, Freud suggested that each future analyst analyze himself. Later, he realized that an analysis by another analyst was preferable. This view has been accepted by all psychoanalytic institutes; students attend lectures only after an analysis has been completed or fairly advanced. Lewin and H. Ross (1960) discussed this problem, as follows: "Regardless of formulation, theory, and minor points of difference, in the psychoanalytic institutes the student is pragmatically a patient. He is operationally a kind of 'neurotic' person, even if not classifiable. In its earliest days, psychoanalysis was rather conventional in its concept of normality and accepted the current 'disease-entity' criteria of medical thought. For the time being, so far as 'normal' persons are concerned, psychoanalysts must use one of two heuristic assumptions. Either there exist 'normal persons' (this is different from a purely ideal concept of 'normality'), who are different from 'neurotic persons.' Or alternatively, the proposition would read, 'Everyone is somehow neurotic, symptoms or no symptoms in the classical sense.' There are, in other words, at least two interpretations of Freud's remark that he thought he was analyzing hysterics but found the whole world on his couch. Certainly the alternative assumption above is the one consciously held by the majority of psychoanalysts, and it is the working assumption of all when they deal practically with the education of psychoanalytic students."

Basically, didactic analysis is similar to therapeutic analysis. However, there are three aspects which make it different:

a. Motivation: The patient who seeks therapeutic analysis wants to be cured; the candidate wants to learn. The student undergoes analysis to learn from first-hand experience the basic concepts of psychoanalytic technique, and to free himself from unconscious blind spots which would otherwise interfere with his work.

b. Professional Discretion: This covers all subject communication. However, the analyst conducting the didactic analysis—with the permission of the candidate—has to report to the educational committee about his progress. Such a report is carefully drafted to protect the private life of the candidate; his neurotic problems which may interfere with his

ability to become a psychoanalyst are nonetheless considered.

c. Evaluation: The training has to evaluate the candidate's professional qualifications; other members of the educational committee also evaluate the candidate's qualifications. The evaluation is based on the candidate's freedom from a severe neurosis, successful completion of his own didactic analysis, and his psychological ability and empathy.

Originally, this training analysis was less formal and largely consisted of a self-analysis of the candidate's own dreams, as well as a study of the literature. Freud (1915) originally thought that the future analyst should prepare himself for his task by analyzing his own dreams. Later, he modified his views, suggesting that the analyst should be analyzed, and that even after his analysis has been terminated, self-analysis should be continued, or, at a later date, it should be reinstituted with a colleague (every five years on the average). [Freud, 1937.]

Related Concepts: SUPERVISION; THERAPY.

REFERENCES

Freud, S.: 1915, "Recommendations on Analytic Technique." *SE*, 12:116–117, 1958.
     1937, "Analysis Terminable and Interminable." *SE*, 23:216–253, 1964.
Lewin, B., & H. Ross, *Psychoanalytic Education in the United States.* Nor, pp. 49–50, 1960.

ADDITIONAL READINGS

Calef, V., Reporter, "Training and Therapeutic Analysis." *JAPA*, 2, 1954.
Ekstein, R., "Termination of the Training Analysis Within the Framework of Present Day Institutes." *JAPA*, 3, 1955.
Schultz-Hencke, H., "Noch Einmal die Lehranalyse." *P*, 6, 1952.

2017

TRANSFERENCE is the patient's cathexis to the presentation of the analyst of the mneme of previous "imagos," principally of the parents. When a patient experiences a positive transference in analysis, as Freud noted (1912), he "is dominated at that moment by an association which is concerned with the doctor himself or with something connected with him." The patient sees in the analyst the return of some important figure of his childhood or of his past, and transfers to him those feelings and reactions that applied to the model.

The conscious wish to be analyzed is a requirement for all patients who want to be involved in the analytic situation. It has to be augmented, however, by those unconscious factors which lead to the transference phenomenon. To this must be added the factor that only those patients who are willing to talk instead of acting—who will tolerate the absence of instant gratification—are suitable for analysis. Freud noted that the positive transference is to be analyzed only if it produces resistance, while the negative transference, because it endangers the continuation of the treatment, is to be isolated at once and thereafter demonstrated to the patient. It is this technique which enables the patient to discover the cause, whether conscious or unconscious, of his transference. It is the transference itself, which appears to stem only from those who suffer from repressed infantile wishes, that permits the analysis itself. Consequently, the love object of a normal person, who is free of infantile wishes, can be separated from that of a neurotic.

In analyzing the transference, the analyst, with the cooperation of the patient, has to discover the kind of infantile wish reponsible for the transference at a given moment: whether sexual or aggressive, or both; whether oral, anal or phallic. The objects the analyst represents, the instinctual aim of this infantile wish (to devour, etc), must also be uncovered.

Eidelberg (1960) provided the following example: A patient who remained silent for a long time was reminded by the analyst that he was supposed to say whatever went through his mind. The analyst added that many patients have trouble in bringing up critical (negative) thoughts concerning the analyst. Encouraged by this remark, the patient admitted that he considered quitting his treatment because he had discovered that his analyst was a show-off. As the analyst was not offended by this accusation, but inquired on what basis he had arrived at this judgment, the patient said, "You have a great many books on Napoleon. Twenty-four altogether."

The verbalization of these critical thoughts appeared to produce doubts in the patient's mind about the correctness of his accusation. He anxiously asked: "Are you making fun of me because of what I said?" On being reassured by the analyst that the patient is always right even if his words appear to contradict the rules of logic and that the patient is, therefore encouraged to seek additional explanations for his accusations, the patient remembered that at the age of nine his father gave him a book about Napoleon. "He said he had just finished reading it, and I remembered how shocked I was when I discovered that the pages of this book—which he had just told me he'd read and enjoyed—weren't even cut! I realized then—I should have before—that my father was a liar and a show-off."

While most analysts reserve the term transference for the phenomenon taking place in analysis, it cannot be denied that similar occurrences happen outside of the analytical situation; in analysis, however, it is possible to closely examine the emotions connected with repressed wishes, and to separate them from these wishes. These emotions are expressed in fantasies, actions, and attitudes, and are often associated with errors in perception and judgment. While traces of past experience may be found in almost every manifestation of the human personality, the role of the past is convincingly demonstrable in transference. This is especially if the psychoanalyst has adhered to the rule of neutrality and has served as a screen onto which the patient may project his infantile wishes. For example, a woman who came for analysis in the evening was almost convinced that following her session, the analyst would receive a visit from his sweetheart. She based this on the "appearance" of the analyst. Further analysis showed that she was re-experiencing the jealousy which she felt as a child when she had to go to bed in the evening and knew that her parents would make love once she was gone. She had cast the analyst in the role of her father, aided by a misjudgment of the analyst's appearance.

Freud (1905) first described transference as "new editions and facsimiles of the tendencies and fantasies which are aroused and made conscious during the process of analysis," whereby, "the person involved is replaced by the physician." Ferenczi (1909) recognized that this phenomenon manifests itself in all human relationships, and can be both heterosexual and homosexual. In 1912, Freud distinguished positive from negative transference, further dividing the former into a friendly and erotic type, and described transference neurosis. In 1920, Freud recognized transference as being partly caused by the repetition compulsion. In 1938, Freud finally stressed (a) the ambivalence of transference, (b) the reincarnation of figures from childhood in the person of the analyst, and (c) the analyst as a new superego.

Clinical Example

Abraham (1919) illustrated the behavior of a narcissistic patient, characterizing the transference as an identification (narcissistic rather than anaclitic object choice). "In place of making a transference the patients tend to identify themselves with the physician. Instead of coming into closer relation to him they put themselves in his place. They adopt his interests and like to occupy themselves with psycho-analysis as a science, instead of allowing it to act upon them as a method of treatment. They tend to exchange parts, just as a child does when it plays at being father. They instruct the physician by giving him their opinion of their own neurosis, which they consider a particularly interesting one, and they imagine that science will be especially enriched by their analysis. In this way they abandon the position of patient and lose sight of the purpose of their analysis. In particular, they desire to surpass their physician, and to depreciate his psycho-analytical talents and achievements. They claim to be able to 'do it better'. It is exceedingly difficult to get them away for preconceived ideas which subserve their narcissism. They are given to contradicting everything, and they know how to turn the psycho-analysis into a discussion with the physician as to who is 'in the right'.

"The following are a few examples: A neurotic patient I had not only refused to associate freely but to adopt the requisite position of rest during the treatment. He would often jump up, go to the opposite corner of the room and expound, in a superior and didactic manner, his self-formed opinions about his neurosis. Another of my patients displayed a similar didactic attitude. He actually said straight out that he understood psycho-analysis better than I did because it was he and not I who had the neurosis. After long-continued treatment he once said, 'I am now beginning to see that you

know something about obsessional neurosis'. One day a very characteristic fear of his came out. It was that his free associations might bring to light things that were strange to him but familiar to the physician; and the physician would then be the 'cleverer' and superior person of the two. The same patient, who was much interested in philosophical matters, expected nothing less from his psycho-analysis than that science should gain from it the 'ultimate truth'."

Related Concepts: DISPLACEMENT; HATE; LOVE; PROJECTION.

REFERENCES

Abraham, K., 1919, "A Particular Form of Neurotic Resistance Against the Psycho-Analytic Method." *SPA*, pp. 306–307, 1942.
Eidelberg, L., *Take Off Your Mask*, Py, pp. 144–146, 1960.
Ferenczi, S., 1909, "Introjection in the Neuroses." *SPsa*, pp. 35–42, 1916.
Freud, S.: 1905, "A Case of Hysteria." *SE*, 7:116, 1953.
　　　　　1912, "The Dynamics of Transference." *SE*, 12:100–102, 1958.
　　　　　1920, "Beyond the Pleasure Principle." *SE*, 18:21, 1955.
　　　　　1938, "An Outline of Psycho-Analysis." *SE*, 23:144–205, 1964.

ADDITIONAL READINGS

Abse, D. W., & J. A. Ewing, "Transference and Countertransference in Somatic Therapies." *JNMD* 123, 1956.
Adler, G., "Der transpersonale Aspekt der Übertragung." *P*, 1955.
Bibring-Lehner, G., "A Contribution to the Subject of Transference Resistance." *IntJPsa*, 17, 1936.
Fleming, J., "Observations on the Defenses Against a Transference Neurosis." *Ps*, 9, 1946.
Fox, H. M., "Effects of Psychophysiological Research on the Transference." *JAPA*, 6, 1958.
Freud, S., 1915, "Observations on Transference Love." *SE*, 12, 1958.
Glatzer, H. T., "Handling Transference Resistance in Group Therapy." *R*, 40, 1953.
Ivimey, M., "Development in the Concept of Transference." *Psa*, 4, 1944.
Jacobson, E., "Transference Problems in the Psychoanalytic Treatment of Severely Depressive Patients." *JAPA*, 1954.
Kanzer, M., "The Transference Neurosis of the Rat Man." *Q*, 21, 1952.

Lagache, D., "Quelques Aspects du Transfert." *RFPsa*, 15, 1951.

Leach, D., Report on Panel, "Technical Aspects of Transference." *JAPA*, 6, 1958.

Nacht, S.: "Thoughts on Transference and Counter-Transference." *RFPsa*, 13, 1949.

    "Technical Remarks on the Handling of the Transference Neurosis." *IntJPsa*, 38, 1957.

Rappaport, E., "The Management of an Erotized Transference." *Q*, 25, 1956.

Reich, W., "Zur Technik der Deutung und der Widerstandsanalyse. Über die gesetzmässige Entwicklung der Übertragungsneurose." *Z*, 13, 1927.

Rothenberg, S., "Transference Situations in an Hour of Analysis." *R*, 32, 1945.

Saul, L., "The Erotic Transference." *Q*, 31, 1962.

Sechahaye, M., "The Transference in Symbolic Realization." *IntJPsa*, 37, 1956.

Servadio, E., "Transference and Thought Transference." *IntJPsa*, 34, 1956.

Silverberg, W. V., "The Concept of Transference." *RFPsa*, 18, 1954.

Slavson, S. R., "Transference Phenomena in Group Psychotherapy." *R*, 37, 1950.

Spitz, R., "Transference: the Analytical Setting and its Prototype." *IntJPsa*, 34, 1956.

Sterba, R. F.: "Über latente negative Übertragung." *Z*, 13, 1927.

    "Zur Theorie der Übertragung." *Im*, 22, 1936.

Stern, A., "On the Nature of the Transference in Psychoanalysis." *NYMJ*, 107, 1918.

White, W. A., "The Mechanism of Transference." *R*, 4, 1917.

Winnicott, D., "On Transference." *IntJPsa*, 34, 1956.

Zetzel, E., "Current Concepts of Transference." *IntJPsa*, 34, 1956.

2018

TRANSFERENCE AND SEX. In most cases, the patient is able to transfer his infantile wishes to the analyst, regardless of the analyst's sex. The analyst may, therefore, represent members of the patient's family or any other persons connected with his repressed infantile wishes. The fact that the analyst represents the infantile object helps the patient to recognize that he is repeating what was traumatic in infancy. The patient learns to recognize and to analyze what at first appeared in analysis as a rigid repetition of his infantile experiences. In some cases, a change from a male to a female analyst (or vice versa) has to be made, either at the beginning or during the course of the analysis. This usually occurs when the analyst realizes that his sex interferes with the progress of analysis.

Eidelberg (1948) noted that the general rule in analysis—to have the patient's libido concentrated upon the analyst—may not always be advisable; in fact, just the opposite may be required to lessen the tension caused by the patient's homosexual trends, to make the patient more analysable. This was accomplished in the case of a male paranoid patient by advising him to have sexual relations with women.

Freud (1920) described the case of a female homosexual where he decided to terminate the treatment. The unconscious wish of revenge made the analysis impossible. Freud transferred this patient to another analyst.

As a result of the modification of analytical technique, cases similar to Freud's, showing a strong negative resistance, were analyzed without transferring the patient to an analyst of the other sex.

Related Concepts: AGGRESSION; COUNTERTRANSFERENCE; RESISTANCE.

REFERENCES

Eidelberg, L., *Studies in Psychoanalysis*. IUP, 1948.

Freud, S., 1920, "The Psychogenesis of a Case of Homosexuality in a Woman." *SE*, 18:164, 1955.

2019

TRANSFERENCE-LOVE, according to Freud (1915), is composed of earlier reactions, including infantile ones, which are transferred to the imago of the analyst; it has the appearance of *genuine* love. It is different from normal love, because it takes place independently of the person of the analyst. In addition, it leads to resistance, and it tends to decrease the reality testing.

As a result of analysis, the analyst will have to prove to the patient that all these feelings are actually determined by his compulsion to repeat his unresolved infantile conflicts. Freud expressed the opinion that positive feelings which may appear either as tender or erotic desires could only be analyzed when they begin to be used as resistance. Only patients who are willing to accept analytical abstinence, to forego the gratification of the wishes connected with the person of the analyst and are willing to analyze the unconscious cause of such wishes, can be successfully treated.

In the beginning of an analysis, the positive transference permits the patient to tolerate the unpleasure connected with giving up his resistance against the consciousness of his infantile feelings in order to please the analyst. A number of temporary improvements in the beginning of analysis are referred to as being caused by a manifestation of the positive transference, not by basic changes of the repression. After a time, however, the positive transference begins to form a transference-resistance. The patient becomes frustrated and disappointed because the analyst does not gratify his positive wishes. Freud pointed out that such a gratification, although desired by the patient, would destroy his chances of recovery and lead to a disappointment.

In a successful analysis of transference-love, the infantile character of this love will be demonstrated in a concrete and decisive manner: oral, anal and phallic desires will be exposed as hidden behind what appears to be genital maturity. The infantile omnipotence, the need for instant gratification, the confusion between internal and external reality, and the intolerance against the recognition of the infantile narcissistic mortification will be exposed and, finally, when all the infantile needs are recognized and rejected, the patient will acquire an ego-syntonic superego. As a result, the patient will refrain from using the analyst as a projection of his infantile superego.

In normal love, the object selected is either what the subject needs, or what is similar to the subject. Freud pointed out that these two forms of object selection (the anaclitic and narcissistic type) are usually mixed together in varying proportions. If the object is similar to the subject, this similarity may lead to competition and, finally, to conflict. A man who marries a woman who is similar to him, or if he becomes similar to her, or makes her similar to him, may in actuality be married to a competitor. This does not mean that the love-object should be completely different from the subject or that a certain amount of similarity between the two should be considered undesirable. How much difference between the two is required cannot be expressed in a mathematical formula.

Related Concepts: ACTING IN; ACTING OUT; COUN-TERTRANSFERENCE.

REFERENCE

Freud, S., 1915, "Observations on Transference-Love (Further Recommendations on the Technique of Psycho-Analysis III)." *SE*, 12:162, 168, 169, 1958.

ADDITIONAL READING

Jekels, L., & E. Bergler, "Übertragung und Liebe." *Q*, 18, 1949.

2020
TRANSFERENCE NEUROSIS refers to two different concepts: (a) a group of neurotic symptoms—conversion hysteria, compulsion neurosis, and anxiety hysteria, to name several; and (b) neurotic phenomena which are mobilized by the analysis itself and develop by reason of transference but which are distinguishable from it. The first concept (a) is little used today. It was first introduced by Freud (1917) to distinguish, from a practical point of view, those disorders which analysis could successfully deal with from those with which it could not (psychoses, psychopathic personalities, and narcissistic neuroses—for instance). In general, it (a) identified a group of disorders in which a therapeutic alliance was possible.

The second (b) use of the concept identifies a neurosis which has *replaced* the original. In this, it differs from the transference, for the behavior replacing the earlier neurotic symptom is more pathological; more extensive and coherent. Reich (1949) distinguished between transference and transference neurosis, as follows: "What makes transference particularly important is the fact that the essential part of the neurosis make their appearance only in the transference. For this reason, the dissolution of the 'transference neurosis' which gradually takes the place of the original neurosis, becomes one of the essential tasks of analytic technique. The positive transference is the main vehicle of the treatment. However, it is not the therapeutic factor in itself, but the most important prerequisite for establishing those processes which finally—independent of the transference—lead to cure."

Freud (1912) described transference neurosis as a condition in which the patient unconsciously strives to avoid the insight which the cure demands and "seeks to discharge his emotions regardless of the reality of the situation." In 1925, Ferenczi and Rank described the intermediate goal of psychoanalysis as the replacement of the manifest neurosis by a transference neurosis. The resolution of the latter takes place by consistently translating the unconscious material in all its expressions, thereby interpreting not only the meaning of the analytic situation but also reconstructing the infantile experience. Melanie Klein (1932) saw in the transference neurosis a reenactment of oral as well as phallic conflicts and emphasized the projection of an archaic superego and of the image of the good and bad mother on the analyst. Silverberg (1948) compared the transference neurosis with the traumatic neurosis by assuming that it was an attempt to learn by a series of rehearsals how not to be helpless or powerless in a situation which was originally so.

Related Concepts: NARCISSISM; TRANSFERENCE.

REFERENCES

Ferenczi, S., & O. Rank, *The Development of Psychoanalysis*. NMDP, 1925.
Freud, S.: 1912, "The Dynamics of Transference." *SE*, 12:105, 1958.
1917, "General Theory of the Neurosis." *SE*, 16: 299, 1963.
Klein, M., *The Psychoanalysis of Children*. Nor, 1932.
Reich, W., *Character-Analysis*. OIP, p. 119, 1949.
Silverberg, W. V., "The Concept of Transference." *Q*, 17:309–310, 1948.

2021

TRANSIENCE denotes the impermanence of external objects and the feeling of anticipation of their loss, a factor which interferes with pleasure, and which results from a revolt of the psyche against mourning. In discussing this phenomenon, Freud (1916) identified it as a factor where the mind instinctively recoils from anything that is painful (mourning); thus the enjoyment of beauty is interfered with by the thought of its transience.

It seems that the normal individual is not frightened by the danger of eventual object-loss; indeed, that such a possible loss—its anticipation—increases his ability to enjoy the object here and now. Those with a special adhesiveness of libido, with a consequent psychic inertia, rebel against the transience of everything that is mortal and fight against the recognition that whatever is born must eventually die, and they thus try to eliminate the suffering of mourning by avoiding object relationships.

Related Concepts: MOURNING; OMNIPOTENCE OF THOUGHT; PSYCHIC INERTIA.

REFERENCE

Freud, S., 1916, "On Transience." *SE*, 14:305–307, 1957.

2022

TRANSIENT EGO-IDEAL. In the therapeutic process, as transference revives the repressed and forgotten early emotional attachment to objects, the patient re-experiences his early hunger for love. This revived feeling brings about a fresh libidinal cathexis to the person of the therapist. Lorand (1962) suggested the concept *transient ego-ideal*; he identified the therapist's role as a need-satisfying transient object to the patient. In this transference relationship, the analyst supplies narcissistic and libidinal gratifications which were not given in early infancy and childhood, and so can correct the early, forbidding, severe, persecuting parental ego-ideal. In this the analyst supplies the permissive and loving constituent of the superego which was originally defective.

The repetition of earlier experiences—preoedipal, oedipal and postoedipal manifestations—are directed toward the analyst, who serves in the role of transient ego-ideal: the preoedipal, oedipal and postoedipal mother. In the transference, the patient relives his infantile ungratified hunger for love and his inability to tolerate frustration. In the therapeutic process a toleration can be built up. Here the synthesizing influence of the transient ego-ideal (the analyst) between constituent parts of the superego plays an important role.

Related Concept: SUPEREGO.

REFERENCE

Lorand, S., "Psycho-analytic Therapy of Religious Devotees." *IntJPsa*, 43:50–56, 1962.

2023

TRANSVESTITISM is a perversion in which the male and female wear clothing suitable to their opposite sex. The "role" which is assumed sometimes leads to a genital discharge, which often is only possible under the condition of the disguise. Others obtain some nongenital pleasure, or at least relief from unpleasure, by wearing such clothing. Analytical investigation reveals that this disguise is necessary to permit the individual unconsciously to play both roles at the same time and to gratify, in this manner, the male and female desires and to avoid the narcissistic mortification, "I cannot have a vagina and a penis at the same time," by accepting the narcissistic mortification, "I have to depend on my disguise." [Eidelberg, 1954.]

Related Concepts: BISEXUALITY; PERVERSION.

REFERENCE

Eidelberg, L., *An Outline of a Comparative Pathology of the Neuroses.* IUP, p. 204, 1954.

ADDITIONAL READINGS

Berman, L., "Perception and Object Relation in a Patient with Transvestitism Tendencies." *IntJPsa*, 34, 1953.

Deutsch, D., "A Case of Transvestitism." *PT*, 8, 1954.

Fessler, L., *A Case of Post-Traumatic Transvestitism. AP*, 1934.

Friend, M. R., L. Schiddel, B. Klein & D. Dunaeff, "Observations on the Development of Transvestitism in Boys." *Ops*, 24, 1954.

Grotjahn, M., "Transvestite Fantasy Expressed in a Drawing." *Q*, 17, 1948.

Thoma, H., "Männlicher Transvestitismus und das Verlangen nach Geschlechtsumwandlung." *P*, 11, 1957.

2024

TRAUMA is an experience which the individual cannot assimilate and, therefore, he eliminates the memory of this experience from consciousness by repression. It may arise from an external danger, as in war neurosis, or from internal assaults (such as pain or instinctual tension), which may lead to an internal narcissistic mortification. Freud (1916–1917) emphasized the economic aspects of the massive over-stimulation and the helplessness of the ego in his concept of trauma. It was his contention that the patient, as it were, had not finished with the traumatic event, "as though he were still faced by it as an immediate task which had not been dealt with." In this, it shows "an *economic* view of mental processes." That is, the psyche is presented with a stimulus of a certain quantity within a short period of time that cannot be "dealt with or worked off in the normal way," resulting in some instances—e.g., traumatic neuroses—in permanent damage in the way in which the energy operates.

The total personality's sudden loss of control over internal or external reality (narcissistic mortification) is accompanied by the emotion of terror, which, if overwhelming, results in paralysis and the use of a defense such as denial or repression. Finally, a self-created narcissistic mortification is often substituted for the original one to preserve control and preclude terror, serving, in the repression of the original mortification. [Eidelberg, 1957.] "In pathological cases, knowledge of a narcissistic mortification is repressed or denied, and consequently the infantile omnipotence is preserved by a neurotic defense mechanism. Not being able to control his instinctual demands, the patient may prefer to create the illusion of being dominated by the external world, thereby avoiding recognition of his weakness when faced with his id. Certain forms of intolerance, either with ourselves or others, may be due to failure to eliminate this infantile omnipotence." [Eidelberg, 1954.]

Related Concepts: ANXIETY; FIXATION.

REFERENCES

Eidelberg, L.: "An Introduction to the Study of Narcissistic Mortification." *PQ*, 31: 657–668, 1957. *An Outline of a Comparative Pathology of the Neuroses.* IUP, p. 38, 1954.

Freud, S., 1916–1917, "Introductory Lectures on Psycho-Analysis." *SE*, 16: 274–275, 1963.

ADDITIONAL READINGS

Bergen, M. E., "The Effect of Severe Trauma on a Four-Year-Old Child." *PsaStC*, 13, 1958.

Eidelberg, L., "A Second Contribution to the Study of the Narcissistic Mortification." *PQ*, 33, 1959.

Freud, S., 1926, "Inhibitions, Symptoms and Anxiety." *SE*, 20, 1959.

Gero-Heymann, E., "A Short Communication on a Traumatic Episode in a Child of Two Years and Seven Months." *PsaStC*, 10, 1955.

Kahn, M., & R. Masud, "The Concept of Cumulative Trauma." *PsaStC*, 18, 1963.

Meyer, F. M., "Ein Traum eines Morphinkranken." *PtPrx*, 2, 1935.

Murphy, W. F., "Character, Trauma, and Sensory Perception." *IntJPsa*, 39, 1958.

Nunberg, H., "Über den Traum." *PsaVkb*, 1957.

Stern, M. M., "Trauma and Symptom Formation." *IntJPsa*, 38, 1958.

2025

TRAUMATIC NEUROSIS denotes a syndrome occurring as an aftermath of sudden shock or fright or prolonged exposure to overwhelming stimulation. Clinical manifestations include: anxiety; limitations of various ego functions; emotional outbursts; insomnia; repetition in thought, speech or fantasy of the traumatic situation; and repetitive dreams in which the traumatic event is reproduced. In addition to these, psychoneurotic symptoms may also occur. Repetition of the traumatic situation in thought, speech, fantasy, or dreams is an expression of the repetition compulsion in its most undisguised form. The symptoms result from the relative incapacity of the ego to discharge or bind the tensions created by the excessive stimulation; they represent belated attempts at mastery (Fenichel, 1945). The psychoneurotic symptoms, when they occur, may represent drives which have broken through the defensive barrier as a result of withdrawal of cathexis from preexisting defensive functions, the energy being used, instead, in the service of mastering the trauma, thus upsetting the equilibrium between repressing forces and repressed impulses. In other instances, the traumatic event may serve to screen early repressed memories, in which case the psychoneurotic symptoms represent regressive attempts at mastery of early traumata. Traumatic neurosis is the only neurosis which is not caused by an infantile repressed wish. [Freud, 1920.]

During World War II, for example, soldiers were brought back from the front suffering from a syndrome that has, elsewhere, been called "war neurosis," a type of traumatic neurosis. Here, conversion symptoms were frequently seen, as well as other neurotic symptoms, and transient schizo-phrenic reactions were not uncommon. These neurotic and psychotic episodes generally ran a brief course and then the symptoms disappeared, soon after the affected soldier was removed from the danger area. An especially severe and prolonged form of traumatic neurosis—one which tends to persist for many years after the traumatic situation has ended—is seen among the survivors of Nazi concentration camps.

Freud (1919) thought that in the traumatic neurosis the patient was fighting the external world or part of his ego, whereas in ordinary transference neurosis, he was fighting his id.

Related Concepts: REPETITION COMPULSION; TRAUMA; WAR NEUROSIS.

REFERENCES

Fenichel, O., *The Psychoanalytic Theory of Neurosis*, Nor, pp. 117–128, 1945.

Freud, S.: 1919, "Introduction to Psycho-Analysis and War Neuroses." *SE*, 17:210, 1955.

1920, "Beyond the Pleasure Principle." *SE*, 18:12–14, 31–33, 1955.

ADDITIONAL READINGS

Murphy, W., "A Note on Trauma and Loss." *JAPA*, 9, 1961.

Sperling, O., "The Interpretation of the Trauma as a Command." *Q*, 19, 1950.

2026

TRAUMATIC NEUROSIS AND DREAMS. The dreams in traumatic neurosis usually end in the generation of anxiety, and, in this sense, it may be said that the function of the dream has failed; i.e., the defense mechanisms implicit in the dream have failed. In repeating the traumatic situation in their dreams, Freud (1917) noted, when they can thereafter be submitted to analysis, they reveal a correspondence to "a complete transplanting of the patient into the traumatic situation." Even so, as Freud later (in 1920) pointed out, the dreams which occur as the result of infantile traumas do not serve the function of fulfilling the wish because they arise "in obedience to the compulsion to repeat." They arise so as to bind the traumatic impressions, and, in this, they obey the compulsion to repeat.

Related Concept: DREAMS.

REFERENCES

Freud, S.: 1917, "Introductory Lectures on Psycho-Analysis." *SE*, 16:274–275, 1963.
    1920, "Beyond the Pleasure Principle." *SE*, 18:32–33, 1955.

2027

TRIAL ANALYSIS. It was Freud's custom when he knew little about a patient to take him provisionally for a period of one or two weeks. He felt that if the case had to be dismissed in this period the patient would be spared the distressing impression of failure and futility. Certain cases which were difficult diagnostic problems might be studied during the provisional analysis in a way in which no ordinary consultation or examination would allow. Freud was particularly concerned about possible schizophrenics being misdiagnosed as obsessionals and mistakenly put into psychoanalytic treatment.

Freud tried in the beginning of his work to isolate those symptoms or character traits which might interfere with the analysis. Later (1913), he suggested a short trial analysis, in which the patient learned a little about psychoanalytical technique, and the analyst, about the patient's resistances.

In a sense every psychoanalysis is a trial analysis. There is a tentativeness to the contract, an avoidance of lengthy discussions of diagnosis and prognosis and the probable length of treatment is left open. To inform the patient that he is "on trial" may sound too threatening and may color the spontaneous transference at the outset of treatment.

Related Concepts: TECHNIQUE OF PSYCHOANALYSIS; TRANSFERENCE.

REFERENCE

Freud, S., 1913, "On Beginning the Treatment (Further Recommendations on the Technique of Psycho-Analysis I)." *SE*, 12:123–125, 1958.

ADDITIONAL READING

Menninger, K., *Theory of Psychoanalytic Technique.* BB, 1958.

2028

TRIAL IDENTIFICATION denotes the transient introjection of an object, which is then projected back onto the object by the subject, a process that permits the analyst, according to Fliess (1942)—who first employed the term—to "square a perception from without with one from within." The so-called "born psychologist's keenness in sizing up his patients depends essentially on his ability to put himself in the latter's place, to step into his shoes, and to obtain in this way an inside knowledge that is almost first hand."[*]

In this formulation, the power to make trial identifications is seen as part of the normal ego function to establish object-relationships wherein the subject "samples" what it is like to be the object. Fliess identifies this "as a basic part of the gift of empathy" which occurs without loss of identity, the ability to think, see and feel what others experience. It occurs without countertransference difficulties.

Related Concepts: COUNTERTRANSFERENCE; EMPATHY.

REFERENCE

Fliess, R., "The Metapsychology of the Analyst." *Q*, 11:212, 214, 1942.

2029

TURNING ROUND UPON THE SUBJECT'S OWN SELF, one of the vicissitudes an instinct may undergo, is a mode of defense against the instinct. Examples of this process are seen in two pairs of opposites: in sadism and masochism and in scopophilia and exhibitionism. The "turning around of an instinct against the subject's own self" is made self-evident if masochism is considered the counterpart of sadism (directed toward the subject's own ego) and that exhibitionism includes the scopophilic pleasure of looking at one's own body.

Freud (1915) noted that the wish to humiliate and inflict pain appears at first at the masochistic stage. Only if the masochist changes into a sadist does his aim include not only to control but to humiliate (in identification with the humiliated object, the sadist gratifies his unconscious masochistic wishes).

---

[*] Italics removed.

The vicissitudes of the scopophilic component instincts are described as follows: at first, the child looks at an external object, then, he looks at himself; and, finally, he begins to develop the wish to be looked at.

Eidelberg (1948) suggested that instinctual vicissitudes should be separated from neurotic defense mechanisms: "The instinctual vicissitudes are oriented to the future and the outside world. 'Since I have suffered a narcissistic mortification and an instinctual inhibition,' the ego seems to say, 'I shall attempt, through appropriate change in my behavior, to achieve instinctual gratification and remove the narcissistic mortification.'

"Neurotic defense mechanisms are directed to the past and to the inner life. 'It is not true,' the ego says, 'that I have suffered a narcissistic slight and that I must endure an instinctual inhibition.'

"The instinctual vicissitudes are conscious or can become conscious processes; the neurotic defense mechanisms are unconscious. The instinctual vicissitudes are plastic and adjust themselves to new situations; the neurotic defense mechanisms are rigid.

"We define as instinctual vicissitudes those changes which instincts or instinct fusions undergo when the constitutionally determined disposition is subjected to external influences."

Related Concepts: ACTIVITY AND PASSIVITY; DEFENSE MECHANISMS; IDENTIFICATION; INSTINCTUAL VICISSITUDES.

REFERENCES

Freud, S., 1915, "Instincts And Their Vicissitudes." *SE*, 14:129–130, 1957.
Eidelberg, L., *Studies in Psychoanalysis.* IUP, p. 117, 1948.

2030

TYPICAL DREAMS, according to Freud (1900), are those which are dreamt alike by everyone and which appear to have the same meaning for all because they presumably arise from the same source in every case. It was Freud's contention that such dreams presented a number of difficulties. "The dreamer fails as a rule to produce the associations which would in other cases have led us to understand it, or else his associations become obscure."

Typical dreams may be divided into two categories: (a) those which have the same meaning; and (b) those which appear to have the same meaning but, with the help of the patient's associations, show a completely different meaning.

Related Concept: RECURRENT DREAMS.

REFERENCE

Freud, S., 1900, "The Interpretation of Dreams." *SE*, 4:241; 5:385, 685, 1953.

U

ULCERATIVE COLITIS. Nonspecific, idiopathic ulcerative colitis is a disease of the large bowel: it manifests itself in attacks of abdominal cramps and bloody diarrhea, commonly associated with fever, anorexia, and weight loss. The onset is generally sudden. The course of the illness is characterized by spontaneous remissions and exacerbations, often leading to chronic illness and surgery; in some cases it may be fatal. Murray (1930) pioneered in the psychiatric investigation of this disease. The studies of Sullivan and Chandler (1932) and of Daniels (1940) in this country, and Cullinan (1938) and Wittkower (1938) in England left no doubt about the significance of emotional factors in the origin and course of this illness.

M. Sperling (1960) described ulcerative colitis as an organ neurosis with pregenital conversion symptoms based on specific unconscious fantasies and conflicts in persons predisposed to such a reaction by a specific mother-child relationship in early life. She considered the variations in the severity of the somatic manifestations and the variations in the personality structure of the patients with ulcerative colitis as being determined by the levels of fixation. "Dependent upon whether there is a predominantly oral or anal fixation, there will be a greater or lesser diffusion between the libidinal and destructive energies. The psychological equivalents of the somatic manifestations in ulcerative colitis can range from melancholic depression and paranoid schizophrenia to perversion psychopathy."

Clinical Example

A thirty-eight-year-old patient had a fantasy that she was conceived orally through a mixture of feces and urine and was delivered anally. The onset of the ulcerative colitis six months prior to her marriage coincided with the onset of sexual activities with her fiancé and with the birth of an older friend's baby. After these fantasies were revealed, there was a dramatic improvement in her condition. The anal bleeding stopped for the first time in twelve years. Some of the dynamics of the colitis could now be understood as an omnipotent way of giving anal birth to a baby which was conceived orally by a combination of urine and feces. In the session following this interpretation, the patient announced that she had a dream the night before and wanted to make an amendment to the interpretation of the anal birth theory, namely, that she did not think that it meant birth of a full-term baby but that it probably represented a miscarriage. In her dream a cousin told her that she had a miscarriage and that it was all over the floor of the bathroom. The floor was covered with blood. She asked her cousin why she did not have it on the toilet; why she did it on the floor, and the cousin replied that she could not reach the toilet. [Sperling, 1960.] This dream indicated the presence of infantile anal-sexual and aggressive wishes.

Related Concepts: ANOREXIA NERVOSA; OBESITY.

REFERENCES

Cullinan, E., "Ulcerative Colitis: Clinical Aspects." *M*, 2:1351–1356, 1938.

Daniels, G., "Treatment of Ulcerative Colitis Associated with Hysterical Depression." *PSM*, 2:276, 1940.

Murray, C., "Psychogenic Factors in the Etiology of Ulcerative Bloody Diarrhea." *AJMS*, 180:239, 1930.

Sperling, M., "Unconscious Phantasy Life and Object-Relationships in Ulcerative Colitis." *IntJPsa*, 41:450–455, 1960

Sullivan, A., & C. Chandler, "Ulcerative Colitis of Psychogenic Origin." *Yale Journal of Biology and Medicine*, 4:779, 1932.

Wittkower, E., "Ulcerative Colitis: Personality Studies." *M*, 2:1356, 1938.

ADDITIONAL READINGS

Cushing, M. M., "The Psychoanalytic Treatment of a Man Suffering with Ulcerative Colitis." *JAPA*, 1, 1953.

Engel, G. L., "Studies of Ulcerative Colitis. I. Clinical Data Bearing on the Nature of the Somatic Process." *PSM*, 16, 1954.

Margolin, S., "Symposium on Psychotherapy in Medical and Surgical Hospitals." *BAPA*, 8, 1952.

Sperling, O.: "Psychosomatic Medicine and Pediatrics." in E. Wittkower & R. Cleghorn, *Recent Developments in Psychosomatic Medicine*. P&S, 1954.

Spitz, R., "The Psychogenic Diseases in Infancy, an Attempt at Their Etiologic Classification." *PsaStC*, 6, 1951.

2101

UNCANNY. The "repetition compulsion" of the uncanny* recalls the sense of helplessness experienced in some dream states. As the compulsion to repeat appears to dominate the unconscious, it is not surprising that whenever such a compulsion becomes conscious it is regarded as being uncanny. [Freud, 1919.]

The uncanny is most commonly identified in terms of coincidences associated with untoward events, at once frightening but, as well, old and familiar. The circumstances which appear to be familiar, that have been repressed, are again

---

* Freud pointed out that the word consists of two parts: *heimlich* and *un*. "Heimlich" appears to be the opposite of "unheimlich" which means *homely*, *secretive*. But it also belongs to two sets of ideas: it may mean *agreeable* but also something which should be *avoided*.

expressed in terms of the "compulsion to repeat," and are powerful enough to interfere with the pleasure-unpleasure principle.

The feeling of the uncanny depicted in literature must be separated from that experience in reality. It is not altogether surprising that a creative writer may describe a situation which could produce the feeling of the uncanny in such a manner that it produces laughter. Oscar Wilde in *The Canterville Ghost* succeeded in permitting the reader to identify with the children who, unafraid of the ghost in the haunted castle, made fun of him.

Case History

A young resident was asked by his chief to examine a certain problem and to write a paper about it. After completing it, the resident showed the paper to his chief who accepted it but suggested a better introduction which he dictated to the resident. The resident did not want to use the introduction, but kept quiet, accepted it, and went home. Two days later, he noticed that he had lost the paper and realized that this loss represented his resistance against having to add this introduction. He was ashamed to admit this to his chief and decided to tell a lie. He said that he had left the manuscript in the chief's office. Expressing his surprise, the chief tried to remind the resident that he had taken the paper with him when he left the office, but finally went with the resident to seek the lost manuscript in his office. The chief and the resident were both surprised to find the paper on the desk. While the chief had to admit that he forgot that the resident left without the manuscript, the resident had an experience of the uncanny. He was partly pleased that the paper had been found and that he no longer had to lie about it; he was also somewhat frightened by his parapraxis which succeeded in changing a conscious lie into the truth.

Related Concepts: AESTHETIC PLEASURE; NARCISSISTIC MORTIFICATION; NIRVANA PRINCIPLE; REPETITION COMPULSION.

REFERENCE

Freud, S., 1919, "The Uncanny." *SE*, 17:220, 238, 249, 1955.

2102

UNCONSCIOUS. Initially, many authors criticized Freud for using the term *unconscious* in connection with mental phenomena, because they thought that mental activity could only be conscious, and they suggested that he refer to nonconscious phenomena connected with psychic elements as *psychoids.* Freud rightly rejected this suggestion, because, with the discovery of psychoanalysis, he found a psychological method through which he was able to change unconscious phenomena into conscious phenomena. He originally regarded neurosis, and such phenomena as dreams and parapraxes, as being a result of a conflict between an unconscious wish and a conscious inhibition of such a wish. Later, however, he (1933) recognized that the defense of the wish was also unconscious, and he then introduced the structural approach to psychoanalysis.

Two kinds of unconscious are recognized. The first can easily become conscious and belongs therefore to the system *Cs.* The second belongs to the system *Ucs.* and can only become conscious after the censorship separating the two systems has been eliminated.

Today we assume that the whole id, part of the ego, and part of the superego are unconscious. We are able to examine the unconscious only after we have succeeded in overcoming the conscious and unconscious resistance.

In analyzing neurotic manifestations, dreams, or parapraxes, psychoanalysts should differentiate between the material which was repressed and became unconscious, and the power reponsible for this repression, which belongs to the ego and is usually referred to as countercathexis.

Freud assumed that only ideas may be repressed, and, therefore, he denied the presence of unconscious feelings and affects. However, some authors, pointing out that the discharge of the unconscious wishes may take place in the ego, consider the possibility of unconscious feelings. The feelings are neither conscious nor unconscious. Whenever they become attached to the word-presentation they become conscious, not through the word-presentation, but directly. [Freud, 1923.]

Related Concepts: CONSCIOUS; STRUCTURAL (TOPO-GRAPHIC) APPROACH; SYSTEMATIC (QUALITATIVE OR DESCRIPTIVE) APPROACH.

REFERENCES

Freud, S.: 1923, "The Ego and the Id." *SE*, 19:22–23, 1961.

    1933, "New Introductory Lectures on Psycho-Analysis." *SE*, 22:71, 1964.

ADDITIONAL READINGS

Burkamp, W., *The Causality of the Psychic Process and the Unconscious Regulations of Actions.* Spr, 1922.
Eidelberg, L., *An Outline of a Comparative Pathology of the Neuroses.* IUP, 1954.
Freud, S.: 1915, "The Unconscious." *SE*, 14, 1957.
    1916, "Introductory Lectures on Psycho-Analysis." *SE*, 15, 1963.
Hartmanns, E. von, "Law of Associations Guided by Unconscious Purposive Ideas." *Z*, 1, 1913.
Sachs, H., "The Breakthrough of the Unconscious." *Z*, 6, 1920.
Strachey, J., "Some Unconscious Factors in Reading." *IntJPsa*, 11, 1930.

2103

UNCONSCIOUS ACTION. Freud originally assumed that the system *Ucs.* was without access to action, to motility, and that unconscious stimuli became conscious in order to obtain a discharge. In introducing the structural approach, he (1923) recognized that the discharge of instinctual energy is possible without the help of the system *Ucs.*; the ego, which is in charge of motility, was thereby assumed to be partly preconscious and partly unconscious. Consequently, some discharge of instinctual wishes may take place on a preconscious or unconscious level; e.g., as in dreams, parapraxes, and neurotic symptoms and character traits. Dreams and parapraxes do become conscious after the discharge has taken place, and the discharge itself takes place before the instinctual wish and its defense have become conscious. The same is true of neurotic phenomena. [Freud, 1933.] Thus, Freud's original concept, wherein all neurotics suffer from an increased tension due to their inability to discharge dammed up impulses as long as they are unconscious, would seem to require revision. It may rightly be assumed that some of the impulses and their defenses are discharged, even though the impulse has remained unconscious. The ego often recognizes that partial discharge has taken place; it is not aware, however, of what has actually been discharged. For example, a patient whose dream is accompanied by a nocturnal emission appears to discharge part of his instinctual energy without awakening; i.e, without the help of the system of the conscious.

Related Concepts: PARAPRAXIS; UNPLEASURE-PLEASURE PRINCIPLE.

REFERENCES

Freud, S.: 1923, "The Ego and the Id." *SE*, 19:23, 1961.

1933, "New Introductory Lectures on Psychoanalysis." *SE*, 22:70–79, 1964.

2104

UNCONSCIOUS AFFECTS. Freud originally assumed that affects could not become unconscious; he reasoned that the discharge of psychic energy responsible for the affect could take place only in the system *Cs.* Even after the introduction of the structural approach, however, he continued to maintain that affects do not become unconscious, believing that *unconscious* affects were the result of the vicissitudes they had undergone; i.e., the affect was transformed into anxiety or was suppressed and prevented from developing at all. The recognition on the part of many analysts, however, that all discharges are controlled by the ego was offered in support of the thesis that the affect may be present in the unconscious part of the ego, which would seem to be consistent with the structural approach introduced by Freud. [Freud, 1923.]

Related Concepts: CONSCIOUS; EGO; PRECONSCIOUS; UNCONSCIOUS.

REFERENCE

Freud, S., 1923, "The Ego and the Id." *SE*, 19:23 1961.

2105

UNCONSCIOUS EMOTIONS AND FEELINGS. Freud (1923) believed that instinct fusions produce two kinds of derivatives: ideas and affects. While Freud maintained that only ideas could become conscious, some analysts reasoned that

feelings and emotions could also be considered as being localized in the unconscious part of the ego, a concept that would seem to be consistent with Freud's structural approach.

Fenichel (1945) noted: "There are tensions in the organism which, were they not hindered in their discharge and development by blocking countercathexes, would result in specific sensations, feelings, or emotions."

Related Concepts: CONSCIOUS; EGO; ID; PRECONSCIOUS; STRUCTURAL (TOPOGRAPHIC) APPROACH; SUPEREGO; SYSTEMATIC (QUALITATIVE OR DESCRIPTIVE) APPROACH; UNCONSCIOUS.

REFERENCES

Fenichel, O., *The Psychoanalytic Theory of Neurosis.* Nor, pp. 17, 161, 1945.

Freud, S., 1923, "The Ego and the Id." *SE*, 19:23, 1961.

2106

UNCONSCIOUS SIGNIFICANCE OF SPEECH. The function of speech, according to Freud (1940), brings the thoughts and ideas in the ego into a firm connection with the memory traces of visual and auditory perceptions. With the acquisition of speech a decisive step is taken toward the development of reality testing; it allows for a more precise communication with objects and for trial actions by way of anticipation (Fenichel, 1945). Inhibitions of speech—from mutism, stuttering and slips of the tongue to occasional lapses stemming from a given situation—interfere with these normal processes and are thus classed as clinical symptoms resulting from repression or other pathogenic causes.

The style of speech, the choice of words and the metaphors employed are all influenced by the developmental history of the ego and of the instincts. It may communicate an infantile mode of defense; it may have libidinal and aggressive connotative characteristics, it may be equated with bodily activities such as milk, feces, urine, semen, etc. In hysterical aphonia, the tongue may be cathected and serve as a phallic symbol. Words may acquire the significance of introjected objects, e.g., the conflict between the object and ego is expressed as a conflict between the patient and his speech production. Speech may have an exhibitionistic, narcissistic meaning in terms of attacking, seducing or charming the object and may be especially threatening where there is a fixation to the omnipotence of words. Obscene words, since they retain much of their original magical significance, may arouse defensive maneuvers. Affective speech may be inhibited, as well, where there is an intolerance of affect, and result in halting or incomplete productions. This may result, as Fenichel points out, from an obsessive tendency to doubt everything and to prepare for action instead of acting, which in severe cases may lead to a kind of paralysis. If it is due to a defect in the function of the superego (which is primarily introjected through the auditory sphere), the capacity to make a decision may be impaired; the fear of aggressive feelings may overwhelm the subject. When these functional disorders of speech are more than simple inhibitions, they are typical examples of pregenital conversion neuroses.

In slips of the tongue, as Eidelberg (1948) noted, a phrase or word that was to have been spoken is interfered with and results in another word or phrase taking its place. This "substitution" has both a conscious and unconscious significance; the latter represents a gratification of infantile instinctual wishes emanating from the id and the unconscious part of the ego which sets up a defense to prevent the unconscious wish from achieving satisfaction. This defense is two-fold: the instinct fusion pressing for satisfaction is turned against the self, and the opposite type of instinct fusion is mobilized. An analysis of the word or phrase which is eliminated should not be overlooked. Jones (1957) noted: "Eidelberg had now written a paper pointing out that the conscious intentions were often not 'harmless', and that the slip of the tongue or pen could be determined by ego-syntonic reactions against them—in other words, the reverse mechanism to that described by Freud."

In the psychoanalytic situation, speech serves as a means of discharge and as a binding of affects. Verbalization substitutes discrete discharges for more global ones, which may lead to overt destructive acts or to illness. The act of speech objectifies certain of the inner processes and strengthens the function of the reality principle. In this, it promotes integration and leads to psychoanalytic insight.

Related Concepts: NEOLOGISM; SLIPS OF THE TONGUE.

REFERENCES

Eidelberg, L., *Studies in Psychoanalysis*. IUP, pp. 161, 1948.
Fenichel, O., *The Psychoanalytic Theory of Neurosis*. Nor, pp. 46, 47, 182; 1945.
Freud, S., 1940, "An Outline of Psycho-Analysis." *SE*, 23:162, 1964.
Jones, E., *The Life and Work of Sigmund Freud*. HPI, 3:213, 1957.

2107

UNDISGUISED DREAMS. Freud (1900) divided all dreams into three parts: (a) undisguised dreams which expressed the infantile wish without disguise, (b) those dreams where the disguise was partial, and (c) those which showed a complete disguise.

Freud reported the case of a nineteen-month-old child who had been kept without food all day after the onset of an attack of vomiting. "During the night after this day of starvation she was heard saying her own name in her sleep and adding: 'Stwawbewwies, wild stwawbewwies, omblet, pudden!' She was thus dreaming of eating a meal and she laid special stress in her menu on the particular delicacy of which, as she had reason to expect, she would only be allowed scanty quantities in the future."

Related Concepts: ANXIETY; DEFENSE MECHANISMS.

REFERENCE

Freud, S., 1900, "The Interpretation of Dreams." *SE*, 5:643, 674, 1953.

2108

UNDOING is a defense mechanism which eliminates the feeling of conscious or unconscious remorse by the use of a magical gesture which annuls the forbidden act. Eidelberg (1954) cited the following case history: "A patient suffered from the obsession that any male person touching him would die. This obsession was a defense against his ambivalence: 'I want to destroy father,' and, 'I want to love father.' The resulting inability to make up his mind was eliminated by shifting responsibility onto the external object: 'It is not true that I want to destroy. The truth is that they destroy themselves by touching me.' This solution, although it partially satisfied his aggression and his infantile megalomania, produced a feeling of remorse. Accordingly, the patient tried to avoid being touched, but while traveling on the bus, he was often unable to do so. In order to save the life of the individual who touched him, and preserve the illusion of his infantile omnipotence at the same time, he would have to return home and wash his hands.

"Undoing is often connected with obsessional neuroses, forming part of a 'biphasic' symptom. While a normal person will try to avoid feelings of remorse and make up for wrongs he may have committed, the neurotic tries to eliminate his 'crimes' by the magic gesture of undoing."

Undoing is a mechanism most often used by obsessive-compulsive neurotics, who confuse their aggressive wishes with actions. Undoing is connected with the compulsion to repeat; the repetition means to carry out the same act free of its original unconscious meaning or with an opposite unconscious meaning. For example, a latent homosexual who initially expressed his homosexual desires by sitting on the left side of a theatre, might, in order to undo the first act, deliberately sit on the right side of the theatre. Sublimations may be utilized in undoing (e.g., philanthropy and exaggerated kindness). The mechanism of undoing is based on the patient's conviction that his hostile wishes are gratified by thinking and not by acting (infantile omnipotence).

Related Concepts: OMNIPOTENCE OF THOUGHT; REACTION FORMATION; REMORSE.

REFERENCE

Eidelberg, L., *An Outline of a Comparative Pathology of the Neuroses.* IUP, p. 112, 1954.

2109

UNPLEASURE is defined by Freud (1923) as a heightening of the instinctual tension. The normal individual avoids or eliminates unpleasure and strives toward the gaining of pleasure. Every unpleasure ought thus to coincide with a height-

ening, and every pleasure with a lowering, of tension due to stimulation. Under certain conditions, however, as in the stimulation of the erotogenic zones, an increase of tension may produce pleasure (called forepleasure). He noted, in 1924: "The state of sexual excitation is the most striking example of a pleasurable increase of stimulus of this sort, but it is certainly not the only one." Among others, he noted that changes of rhythm were to be differentiated as being partly responsible. Except for the instant elimination of unpleasure which does not (as a rule) lead to pleasure, a certain amount of unpleasure was to be tolerated in order to obtain pleasure at a later time (reality principle).

Freud (1939) offered a structural explanation, noting that *only* unpleasure takes place when the instinctual renunciation occurs for internal reasons; and, further, "in obedience to the superego, it has a different economic effect." A substitutive satisfaction, a yield of pleasure, takes place in the ego. It has, as it were, "brought the superego the sacrifice of an instinctual renunciation."

Unpleasure* may be caused by sensations which originate from internal or external sources. It functions as a signal and alerts the individual to the need for a reduction in tension which has increased above a certain threshold and, thus, has served to produce the feeling of unpleasure. Anna Freud (1936) suggested the term "fore-unpleasure" for the concept of anticipated unpleasure.

Eidelberg (1962) suggested, however, that it may be better to designate this discharge of tension as *instinct satisfaction* and to reserve the concept *pleasure* for those gratifications which take place when the object is pleasing to, and in a form appealing to, the total personality. Nailbiting, for instance, does not produce pleasure, though it does lead to a discharge of aggressive tension. He concluded: "Finally, it may be noted that while the repetition compulsion appears to be beyond the pleasure principle, it is compatible with the unpleasure principle. The fact that in a traumatic neurosis the patient repeats the original traumatic experience in his dreams does not represent the gratification of infantile sexual wishes but removes by an active repetition what was passively suffered,

___

* From the German word *Unlust*; not to be confused with pain, one form of unpleasure.

the unpleasure of the narcissistic mortification of having been overwhelmed by an external aggressor."

Whenever the individual plans to discharge the tension responsible for the feeling of unpleasure, he may also experience the feeling of forepleasure, which is characterized by the presence of increased instinctual tension. Unpleasure may also result from a decrease of instinctual tension below a certain threshold (e.g., the elimination of fatigue by resting, in which the instinctual tension increases). In addition, unpleasure may be experienced when the total personality is overwhelmed and forced to submit to an external or internal stimulus, as is the case in narcissistic mortification.

Masochism appears to contradict the pleasure-unpleasure principle. A further investigation nonetheless reveals that the masochist accepts certain self-provoked unpleasures in order to avoid those unpleasures over which he has no control. In addition, the unpleasure the masochist is interested in is not the unpleasure caused by an increase or decrease of instinctual tension but the unpleasure connected with the experience of an unjust and humiliating narcissistic mortification. [Eidelberg, 1959.]

Related Concepts: LAW OF CONSTANCY; NIRVANA PRINCIPLE; PLEASURE PRINCIPLE.

REFERENCES

Eidelberg, L.: "Humiliation in Masochism." *JAPA*, 7:274–283, 1959.
　　　　"A Contribution to the Study of the Unpleasure-Pleasure Principle." *PQ*, 36:312–316, 1962.
Freud, Anna, *The Ego and the Mechanisms of Defence.* IUP, p. 155, 1936.
Freud, S.: 1923, "The Ego and the Id." *SE*, 19:22, 1961.
　　　　1924, "The Economic Problem of Masochism." *SE* 19:160, 1961.
　　　　1939, "Moses and Monotheism." *SE*, 23:116–117, 1964.

2110
UNPLEASURE - PLEASURE PRINCIPLE.
Mental processes strive toward the gaining of pleasure and the avoidance of unpleasure,* in which

————

* From the German word *Unlust*; not to be confused with pain, which appears to be only one form of unpleasure.

the *pure* pleasure principle is assumed to control the infant's life in utero.* Unpleasure may be caused by sensations from either internal or external sources. It functions as a signal for the individual to reduce the dammed-up tension, which has increased above a certain threshold to produce the feeling of unpleasure. [Freud, 1905.]

Later, Freud (1923) modified this concept. "We interpret unpleasure as implying a heightening and pleasure a lowering of energic cathexis," by recognizing that, under certain conditions (stimulation of erotogenic zones), an increase of instinctual tension may produce forepleasure. It appears that the normal individual avoids or eliminates unpleasure, unless it is necessary to endure it in order to obtain better or safer pleasure in the future. Whenever the individual anticipates and plans the discharge of the tension responsible for the feeling of unpleasure, he may also experience the feeling of forepleasure, which is characterized by the presence of increased tension.

At first, Freud regarded the discharge of tension as being identical with pleasure. He (in 1920) defined man's goal as the disappearance of unpleasure or the experience of pleasure. Later, he (1930) noted: "There are *two* sides to this striving, a positive and a negative." In other words, the unpleasure-pleasure principle represents not one but *two* goals. While some individuals are interested both in eliminating unpleasure and in gaining pleasure, others may be primarily concerned either with attaining pleasure (whatever the risks may be) or with avoiding unpleasure (following the rule of safety first). Consequently, individuals may be divided into two types: some may be more interested in avoiding unpleasure, others in gaining pleasure.

It may be better to refer to the discharge of tension as *instinct gratification*, reserving the word *pleasure* for the gratification which takes place with objects pleasing to, and in a form appealing to, the total personality. Nailbiting, for example, does not produce pleasure, although it does discharge aggressive tension.

————

* It is questionable whether the human embryo experiences pleasure; the embryo probably reacts with unpleasure whenever his instinctual equilibrium (which he maintains with the help of his mother) is threatened. It appears that the newborn discovers the sensation of pleasure only after a few weeks or months.

Unpleasure may also result from a decline of instinctual tension below a certain threshold (e.g., fatigue, which is eliminated through rest in which the instinctual tension increases).

As Eidelberg (1962) noted, unpleasure may also be experienced when the total personality is overwhelmed and forced to submit to an external or internal stimulus (narcissistic mortification). Further, as Freud (1924) pointed out, masochism appears to contradict the unpleasure-pleasure principle; deep analysis, however, shows that the masochist accepts certain self-provoked unpleasure and thus avoids unpleasure over which he has no control.

Related Concepts: INSTINCT (INSTINCTUAL DRIVE); PLEASURE PRINCIPLE.

REFERENCES

Eidelberg, L., "A Contribution to the Study of the Unpleasure-Pleasure Principle." *PQ*, 36:312–316, 1962.
Freud, S.: 1905, "Three Essays on Sexuality." *SE*, 7:178, 183, 234, 1953.
　　　1920, "Beyond the Pleasure Principle." *SE*, 18:7, 1962.
　　　1923, "The Ego and the Id." *SE*, 19:22,1961.
　　　1924, "The Economic Problem of Masochism." *SE*, 19:158–161, 1961.
　　　1930, "Civilization and Its Discontents." *SE*, 21:76, 1962.

2111

URANISM is a rarely used synonym for homosexuality, usually in the male; first employed by Karl Heinrich Ulrichs in 1862. The term is derived from the mythical figure of Aphrodite Urania, the source of heavenly love between males, in contrast to physical and earthly love, of whom Plato (1941) wrote: "The son of the heavenly Aphrodite . . . is sprung from a mother in whose birth the female has no part, but she is from the male only; this is that love which is of youths only. . . . Those who are inspired by this love turn to the male."

Related Concepts: LATENT HOMOSEXUALITY; OVERT HOMOSEXUALITY.

REFERENCE

Plato, *The Symposium*. TP, 3:304, 1941.

2112

URINATION is the act of micturition; the need to urinate and its gratification, originally a derivative of an ego instinct.

In contrast to the sexual instinct which aims at the preservation and continuation of the species, the ego instincts only serve the individual. At first, they were considered by Freud (1905) to be free of libido. However, in his paper on narcissism, Freud (1914) modified his views and expressed the opinion that ego instincts, too, contained libido— a different libido from that of sexual instincts. This libido was referred to as *ego-libido* or *narcissistic libido*. In addition, Freud (1933) introduced the concept of the *phallic* stage in libidinal development, which replaced the original term *genital*. Phallic referred to the fact that the little boy and the little girl regard the penis or the clitoris, respectively, as their sexual organ. When the genital stage takes place (in puberty) the penis becomes the organ capable of producing sperm. In the girl, the onset of menstruation leads to the discovery of the genital role of the vagina; the development of the breasts helps the girl to overcome her penis envy and to accept the mature feminine role.

In many neurotics, the genital stage is not psychologically reached and, consequently, the unconscious wish to urinate or to be urinated on occurs, and interferes with normal sexual intercourse. As a result, various neurotic defenses appear: impotence, frigidity and humiliation of the love object.

In spite of the fact that the emission of sperm can take place only after the onset of puberty, Freud maintained his original opinion: the penis in boys and the clitoris in girls was capable of producing some kind of sexual feelings, a precursor to later genital feelings. Finally, the wish for a penis is renounced and the wish for a baby from father appears instead. The boy uses his penis for the purpose of urination, and to obtain exhibitionistic pleasure from the act. The girl is unable to compete successfully with the boy (e.g., in urinating while standing up), but does receive some sexual stimulation from her clitoris and the labia. It may be that the quantitative difference in the amount of erotic gratification available in the phallic stage is responsible for the fact that masturbation at this stage takes place, or at least is more often visible in boys than in girls. The difference between the penis and the clitoris may lead to the feeling of inferiority in a girl because she may regard the clitoris—which is smaller and refuses to grow—as an inferior organ and may develop penis envy.

On the basis of clinical material Freud (1932) assumed that being able to urinate and thus to quench fire was responsible for man's inability to preserve it in prehistoric times and, for a time, women were relied upon to do so. It was his contention that the urge to quench fire by urinating on it represented a homosexual tendency and that the primitive was unable to control these tendencies.

One may perhaps venture the suggestion that fire produced fear in the primitive and a feeling that he wanted to eliminate this fear by quenching the fire with his urine. Consequently, the urge to urinate could be considered as a defense against the dangers connected with fire, not only as an external danger but as an internal danger connected with his passions.

Independent of whether the urge to urinate on the fire represented a homosexual aggression or a defense against the danger connected with fire, it had to be inhibited or controlled. The "taming" of fire may thus be compared to the taming of a domestic animal and represented a step along the road primitive man took toward the formation of society. As the human being had for a long time to rely on the preservation of fire because he was unable to produce it, the urge to urinate and quench the fire represented a severe danger.

Related Concepts: Crying (Weeping); Nocturnal Enuresis; Phallic Stage.

REFERENCES

Freud, S.: 1905, "Three Essays on the Theory of Sexuality." *SE*, 7:217, 1953.

　　　1914, "On Narcissism: An Introduction." *SE*, 14:76, 1957.

　　　1932, "The Acquisition and Control of Fire." *SE*, 22:187–189, 190, 1964.

　　　1933, "New Introductory Lectures on Psycho-Analysis." *SE*, 22:98–99, 1964.

V

2200

VAGINA DENTATA is a fantasy in which the vagina is imagined (consciously or unconsciously) to possess teeth, a potentially dangerous, biting (castrating) organ. The vagina is equated with the mouth, a phenomenon also frequently found in the unconscious fantasy life of frigid women. The vagina may unconsciously represent a biting mouth, especially when there is pronounced penis envy and revenge castration impulses toward the partner, with a wish to bite off and incorporate his penis. The idea of teeth in the vagina may also be used as a denial (disavowal) of "female castration, with the teeth representing a penis (an internal phallus) and a denial that the female does not possess a penis." In men, vagina dentata fantasies are most frequently accompanied by castration anxiety, which is reinforced by their fear of retaliation for sadistic attitudes towards the breast. [Lorand and Feldman, 1955.]

Related Concepts: CASTRATION COMPLEX; FRIGIDITY; IMPOTENCE.

REFERENCE

Lorand, S., & S. Feldman, "The Symbolism of Teeth in Dreams." *IntJPsa*, 36:135–156, 1955.

ADDITIONAL READING

Lorand, S., "Contribution to the Problem of Vaginal Orgasm." *IntJPsa*, 20, 1939.

2201

VAGINAL FATHER is denotative of a symptom in males who have a conscious or unconscious wish to possess a vagina. The behavior of such subjects shows strong, feminine, motherly attitudes, especially in choosing a mate and, later, in their relationships to their children. There is an unconscious fixation to the "female penis" fantasy, the counterpart of the "male having a vagina." Characteristically, their behavior in social, sexual and family relationships shows a strong rivalry with women. In marriage they take over wifely duties; they serve as both father and mother to their children; and in their social life they are rather withdrawn in their relationships with men. In their dreams, they endow themselves with a vagina, at times dreaming about intercourse with a man. Frequently, they and their analyst are pictured as having breasts in their fantasies and dreams. Unconsciously, and to a great degree consciously, there is a strong identification with both the pre-oedipal and oedipal mother. There is a constant need to be loved; yet, they behave passively and submissively. Moreover, the early homosexual trend to transform the stern father into a more loving one is conspicuously present. They cannot stand not being loved (narcissistic mortification); their aggression is completely repressed and hidden by a constant smiling, compliant, superficially jovial behavior. [Lorand, 1939.]

They are very much like the Ngallunga tribe described by Róheim (1945). Here, in the initiation ritual, the initiator (an older man) shows his sub-incision hole to the youngsters. The aim of the

465

ritual is to separate the younger men from their mothers and aggregate them to the father's group. They are offering an artificial vagina instead of a real one.

Related Concepts: IDENTIFICATION; PENIS ENVY.

REFERENCES

Lorand, S., "The Role of the Female Penis Fantasy in Male Character Formation." *IntJPsa,* 20:171–182, 1939.
Róheim, G., *The Eternal Ones in Dreams.* IUP, pp. 155–177, 1945.

2202

VAGINISMUS is a painful spasm of the vagina, usually during coitus; a common cause of dyspareunia or painful intercourse. Vaginismus is caused by a spasm of the musculature of the vaginal introitus, which makes the insertion (or removal) of the penis very difficult or impossible. It may interfere with intercourse or serve as a mechanism which prevents the penis from escaping; the penis may represent feces and, at the same time, vaginismus may express revenge for castration.

Vaginismus may also serve the purpose of sadistically disappointing the partner; it may even represent a denial of the very existence of the vagina. The superego may permit various forms of petting and manipulation of the external genitalia, but not penetration. The symptom may be an outgrowth of the earlier masturbatory struggle in the oedipal phase, which may have resulted in an active rejection of feminine receptivity. Pregnancy fears and object relations fixated on an incestuous, sadomasochistic, or symbiotic level, along with the other complex factors in frigidity, may play a role. Abraham (1920) cited an example in which vaginismus superseded a symptom of hysterical adduction of the thigh (making intercourse impossible) whenever the woman was approached by her husband.

The inability to withdraw the penis from the vagina, because of spastic contraction of puborectal bundles of the levator ani (upper vaginismus), and possible spasm of the bulbocavernosus, is called *penis captivus.* The notoriety of this condition and the many jokes about it are out of keeping with its rarity, its innocuousness and the ease with which it can be corrected. Popular interest partly reflects male castration anxieties, which correspond with the fantasy of the vagina dentata, and the castration wish of the female. In both cases, the penis captivus fantasy reveals underlying primitive oral and anal fantasies with sadistic and masochistic components, or both.

Related Concepts: CASTRATION COMPLEX; FRIGIDITY; IMPOTENCE; PENIS ENVY.

REFERENCE

Abraham, K., 1920, "Manifestations of the Female Castration Complex." *SPA,* p. 355, 1940.

2203

VALUE consists of those shared cultural standards which are embodied in the moral, aesthetic and cognitive precepts of a society as measured in the individual attitudes, desires and needs of its members. The value standards of the society are perpetuated to the degree that its moral precepts are incorporated into the superego. The superego, then, is the representative of the parents and educators who superintended the actions of the individual in his first years of life. It perpetuates their function and their precepts almost without change. The ego-ideal (part of the superego) represents the positive goal the individual strives to achieve, and the conscience, with the help of feelings of guilt, the avoidance of certain immoral acts.

Though Freud (1932) believed that psychoanalysis was in no position to create a philosophy of life, he nonetheless recognized that it could not ignore those value judgments which determined much of the individual's social feeling. In this, undue repression lead to unsocial attitudes; the end-state of every neurosis. On the other hand, social demands played an important part in the creation of neuroses by imposing ever greater restrictions on direct gratifications. These restrictions then became internalized, inherited, and self-imposed—a view that became prominent in Freud's later writings on sociology. [Jones, 1955.]

Other psychoanalysts concurred as to the need to incorporate "value" in their schematization of individual behavior. Flugel (1945) believed that truth, goodness and beauty were absolute values. Marjorie Brierley (1947) identified integration as the highest value. H. D. Jennings White (1939) pointed out the dependence of the individual's intrinsic values upon the particular course taken in mental development. Sperling (1950) believed that there were no absolute values, and that such a belief was an illusion in the service of the gratification of one's exhibitionism. Hartmann (1964) viewed the concept of value, as follows: "One should beware of overemphasizing terminological questions in this field so little known to use; it might prove practical to include in the concept of ego interests, besides this one, other groups of ego tendencies of an otherwise similar nature, the aims of which do not center around the self; for instance, those which affect the outer world not only indirectly, in the sense just outlined, but whose aims are centered around other persons or around things; or those which are striving toward aims, originating in the superego but taken over by the ego, aims that center around values (ethical values, values of truth, religious values, etc.); and finally, interests of the ego in mental functioning itself (e.g., in intellectual activity) might also be included."

Related Concepts: EGO; ETHICAL APPROACH; SUPER-EGO.

REFERENCES

Brierly, M., "Notes on Psychoanalysis and Integrative Living." *IntJPsa*, 28:58, 1947.

Flugel, J. C., *Man, Morals and Society*. IUP, p. 11, 1945.

Freud, S., 1932, "New Introductory Lectures on Psycho-Analysis." *SE*, 22:158, 1964.

Hartmann, H., *Essays on Ego Psychology*. IUP, p. 136, 1964.

Jones, E., *The Life and Work of Sigmund Freud*. HPI, 2:244, 1955.

Sperling, O., "The Interpretation of the Trauma as a Command." *Q*, 19:352–370, 1950.

White, H. D., *Goals of Life*. CWD, 1939.

2204

VERBALIZATION is the ability to express ideas, feelings and emotions in words. Most analysts assume that, as a result of the inhibition of the primary process by the secondary process, a damming up of psychic energy takes place, which produces the sensation of unpleasure. As a result of this tension, the infant begins to use his body to express the unpleasure from which he suffers. Presently, he learns that in addition to crying and shouting he may indicate his needs by words. In other words, the cathexis of psychic energy which occupies the thing-presentation partly shifts to the word-presentation. The child learns to speak, to communicate to others (and to himself) his reaction to external and internal stimuli. Thus, the word which represents an idea connected either with an instinctual need or with a required external object is discovered, and, presently, the complicated pattern of verbalization becomes established.

The concrete stimulus from inside or outside which is responsible for the feeling that informs the individual of his needs changes first into a word (i.e., to a concrete object). Finally, the child discovers that—in addition to the presentation of a specific object, a concrete stimulus, and its verbal expression—an abstract concept (an abstract platonic idea) may be created. Such an abstract idea does not depend on internal or external stimuli. This abstract idea represents a change from a descriptive to an explanatory method. It does not cover a particular object or a specific stimulus; it refers to all objects or all stimuli belonging to a certain group. Consequently, the word "chair" does not refer to one chair but to any object which may be considered to be a chair. [Freud, 1923.]

Related Concepts: MAKING FACES; MANNERISM.

REFERENCE

Freud, S., 1923, "The Ego and the Id." *SE*, 19: 22–23, 1961.

2205

VERTIGO is a symptom experienced by some individuals when subjected to the sensation of rotation or of vertical movement (e.g., in an elevator). It may be confused with states of disequilibrium of varying degrees and may accompany various types of organic illness. True vertigo is frequently accompanied by nystagmus and past-pointing reaction and may be followed by attacks of nausea and emesis. The syndrome is a symptom-complex, consisting of vertigo, vomiting, and the perceptive type of tinnitus and deafness. Psychosomatic factors have been frequently indicated in vertigo syndromes, but a thorough neurological and physical examination is always indicated.

According to Weiss and English (1949), psychosomatic vertigo belongs to the group of vasomotor disturbances including blushing and fainting which represent pathological anxiety responses. Such symptoms are invested with symbolic meaning related to unconscious intrapsychic conflict. Instinctual impulses early become linked to motility and equilibrium. The affective accompaniment of both repressed sexual excitement and hostility may be expressed in vertigo. For example, a woman who daydreamed about street-walking would suffer attacks of dizziness, numbness, and tingling in her extremities instead of consciously experiencing any associated sexual excitement. By interfering with motility, vertigo defends against the translation of forbidden impulses into action. The illness is a punishment for the forbidden ideas and feelings. The more primitive and desomatized types of anxiety response are more likely to result in vertigo and other vaso-motor disturbances than circumscribed anxiety reactions which are experienced on a primarily mental level.

Related Concept: SOMATIC COMPLIANCE.

REFERENCE

Weiss, E., & O. English, *Psychosomatic Medicine.* Sau, pp. 688–698, 1949.

2206

VIRGINITY TABOO. The teleological meaning of the hymen, despite the study by scientists as to the function of this organ, remains largely a mystery; it retains its uniqueness because its destruction must occur before the female can function sexually as a mature individual. Defloration has remained a privilege that has been reserved for the husband—if only in a nominal sense—and still functions to keep the woman in sexual bondage. Its apparent intent was to restrict the woman's sexual aim: to warrant that her possession would continue undisturbed, apart from other enticements from the outside, and to insure that she had not been impregnated by another. Thus, its practice insured that the first act of marriage was preceded by what Freud (1918) called "certain precautionary measures." The husband was protected from the expectation associated with a dangerous situation, from a perpetual apprehensiveness that was characteristic of persons suffering from neurosis. An explanation for the universality of this phenomenon was found by Freud in the works of E. Crawley* (and others). In this, he draws attention to the fact that with the primitive "the taboo of virginity is part of a large totality which embraces the whole of sexual life."

As with all taboos, they are set up to protect the primitive man from some expected danger. The taboo against women thus follows the rule of avoidance. It stems perhaps from man's fear of "being weakened by the woman, infected with her femininity," as Freud called it. This restriction is akin to that situation in pathological cases in modern women wherein the danger aroused through the defloration consists in drawing her hostility down upon herself, a phenomenon that is characteristic of those women who are frigid. In this, defloration may mobilize the woman's aggression.

The primitive, according to J. G. Frazer,[†] appeared to display a different attitude toward defloration; instead of regarding it as a privilege the husband is entitled to, a priest or a stranger performed the act. This custom did not mean that the primitive did not attach importance to defloration but it did indicate that he was afraid of the result of a defloration (spilling of blood). Some primitives separated the act of defloration from the act of sexual intercourse; some combined both acts. [Freud, 1913.]

Related Concepts: ATTRACTION OF THE FORBIDDEN; TABOO.

REFERENCES

Freud, S.: 1913, "Totem and Taboo." *SE*, 13:120, 1955.
    1918, "The Taboo of Virginity (Contributions to the Psychology of Love III). *SE*, 11:197, 198, 203–204, 205, 1957.

---

* *The Mystic Rose*, London, 1902.
† *The Golden Bough*, London, 1911.

W

2300

WAR NEUROSIS is a traumatic neurosis precipitated by a war-time experience; the disturbance is variously called *shell shock*, *battle fatigue*, and *combat neurosis*. As in many other traumatic neuroses, it may have a superficial relationship to a precipitating, if catastrophic, event. War neurosis differs from peacetime traumatic neurosis in that a conflict arises between two ego-ideals, the customary one and the one the war has compelled the soldier to build; he may be afraid to lose both.

Freud noted, in two letters* to Jones (1955): "It is a question of a conflict between two ego ideals, the customary one and the one the war has compelled the person to build. The latter is concerned with relations to new objects (superior officers and comrades) and so is equivalent to the cathexis of an object; it might be called a choice of object not consonant with the ego", that is, the previous ego. "Thus a conflict comes about just as in ordinary psycho-neuroses."

The difference is that the so-called peacetime ego-ideal is strong but surprised; and the war-time, prepared but weakened. "In this way the war neurosis is a case of internal narcissistic conflict within the ego, somewhat analogous to the mechanism of Melancholy."

Related Concepts: REPETITION COMPULSION; TRAUMATIC NEUROSIS.

---

* October 27, 1918; February 18, 1919.

REFERENCE

Jones, E., *The Life and Work of Sigmund Freud*, HPI, 2:283–285, 1955.

ADDITIONAL READINGS

Appel, J., "Incidence of Neuropsychiatric Disorders in the U.S. Army in World War II." *APJ*, 102, 1946.
Kaufman, M., "Ill Health as an Expression of Anxiety in a Combat Unit." *PSM*, 9, 1947.
Young, J. C., "Two Cases of War Neurosis." *M*, 2, 1922.

2301

WAYWARD YOUTH is a classical work by Aichhorn (1925) on the treatment of delinquency, describing the influence of education on juvenile behavior. He suggested that the introduction of adult models were needed to strengthen and to alter the child's superego. In classical psychoanalysis transference is used to get the patient to remember or to repeat repressed traumatic experiences. Aichhorn modified the analytical technique and showed how the transference could be used in the treatment of psychopaths. His technique was based on the recognition that the psychopath's ego-ideal was defective and had to be replaced with the help of his identification with the psychoanalyst.

In classical psychoanalysis, the positive transference the patient makes to overcome his resistance—to accept the unpleasure connected with the memory of the repressed infantile wishes—is accomplished in order to please the psychoanalyst. Whenever negative transference is present the analyst has, by correct interpretation, to eliminate it and prove to the patient that he is not the hostile object of which the patient is afraid. In comparing the two, the classical one used by Freud in the analysis of neurotics and Aichhorn's technique, it must be noted that the therapist dealing with delinquents has to play a much more active role and cannot offer himself passively to the projections of the child.

Related Concept: PSYCHOPATHY.

REFERENCE

Aichhorn, A., 1925, '*Wayward Youth.*' V, 1935.

2302

WELTANSCHAUUNG is defined by Freud (1933) as "an intellectual construction which solves all the problems of our existence uniformly on the basis of one overriding hypothesis, which, accordingly leaves no question unanswered and in which everything that interests us finds its fixed place."

He pointed out that psychoanalysis is unable to offer a psychoanalytical Weltanschauung, because, being a science—a branch of biology—it has to adhere to what could be called a scientific Weltanschauung, which offers little if compared to religion and various philosophical systems.

Religion gives us an answer about our origin, promises ultimate happiness (in this, or the other world), and offers an ethical code of behavior. However, religion restores our peace of mind only under the condition that we are willing to believe its credo. In spite of church dictates, such men as Galileo and Copernicus learned to use their reasoning power and thus great progress was made in the natural sciences. As a result, other scientists were encouraged to devise methods applicable to their fields of investigation. Freud, for instance, introduced the causal approach to psychoanalysis. Nonetheless, as N. Hartmann noted (from M. Hartmann [1956]), there is a *hiatus irrationalis* which separates psychological from physiological phenomena. Alois Dempf (1955) stated that the history of philosophy was possible, but that a systematic philosophy was not. He also noted that

there is a tendency to formulate a materialistic monism out of physics and an idealistic one out of anthropology.

The danger of religion is due to our tendency to confuse the realm of what can be examined by our reason with what can only be experienced by our emotions. Whether God created this world may appear doubtful, but no one would care to negate that many of us have the need to believe in Him. Therefore, human beings may be considered responsible for the creation of the concept of God. Freud regarded religion to be an illusion and the main threat to our reasoning power. To this, he added that art, too, is an illusion. It may be difficult to accept this judgment, for he himself belonged to that small minority capable of aesthetic experience. Are we to consider painting, books and other art works as not existing in external reality? This is obviously not what Freud had in mind. It seems that the word *illusion* refers to our emotional reaction to a work of art.

Related Concepts: ILLUSION; OMNIPOTENCE OF THOUGHT; RELIGIOUS FAITH.

REFERENCES

Dempf, A., *Die Einheit der Wissenschaft.* Stuttgart: W. Kohlhammer, p. 170, 1955.
Freud, S., 1933, "New Introductory Lectures on Psycho-Analysis." *SE*, 22:158–160, 172, 181–182, 1964.
Hartmann, M., *Einführung in die allgemeine Biologie.* SG, p. 117, 1956.

2303

WET DREAM is connected with a nocturnal emission, and occurs more often in males than in females. Such a dream occurs often under conditions of genital abstinence; the manifest content is usually erotic and pleasant. However, some patients report nonerotic and unpleasant manifest dreams culminating in a climax.

In erotic dreams, the patient appears to experience forepleasure, but usually awakens when the climax occurs. The dream, with the help of forepleasure and perhaps fore-unpleasure, helps the patient remain asleep. The same takes place in the so-called obliging dreams, in which the patient first experiences gratification of his hunger and thirst; however, in a second phase, because the gratification is provided in a "hallucinatory manner" and is thus unable to eliminate the unpleasure connected with the instinctual tension, the patient wakes up.

Clinical Example

A patient dreamed the following: he was smaller than his wife, was standing in front of her, and both of them were nude. He was kissing her vagina and finally had an emission. He woke up and at first had the impression that the whole floor was covered by his semen which looked yellow, like pus.

The patient suffered from a partial difficulty in potency and required the active help of his wife to introduce his penis into her vagina. The day before the dream occurred, he brought up material indicating that he would like to be an infant and to bite his mother's breast.

The unconscious wish of the patient, which appears to be responsible for this dream, was an aggressive desire to bite off his mother's breasts and to devour them. This id wish was warded off by the unconscious ego which succeeded in mobilizing the opposite instinct fusion and changed its aggressive content into a sexual one. Consequently, the biting was changed into kissing. In addition, again as a result of an unconscious defense, the passive wish "I want to devour and swallow her breasts," was changed into the active aim of wanting to give her sperm. However, the original aggressive emotion was not completely eliminated and, consequently, in spite of the manifest erotic content, the patient awoke in terror, and had the impression that the sperm was changed into pus for a few moments. The superego helped the ego in warding off the aggressive wish. Instead of a feeling of guilt—or rather, remorse—in connection with the desire to bite off the breast of the woman in his arms, the feeling of shame was experienced. "I cannot have sexual intercourse; my semen is like pus." Finally, the original narcissistic mortification was derived, "I cannot control my aggressive wishes to bite my mother," by accepting the narcissistic mortification of being unable to introduce the penis into the vagina and unable to produce semen.

Related Concepts: FOREPLEASURE; OBLIGING DREAMS.

REFERENCE

Eidelberg, L., *An Outline of a Comparative Pathology of the Neuroses.* IUP, p. 121, 1954.

2304

WILD PSYCHOANALYSIS* denotes an interpretative or suggestive action that does not correspond to the technical rules and scientific precepts of Freudian psychoanalysis. It was Freud's (1910) contention that a scientific orientation was necessary to achieve an understanding of the nature of the origin and dynamics of the patient's behavior. The technical procedures, on the other hand, are no less important. Otherwise, a study of the literature—of its scientific data—would be cure enough.

Case History

A divorcee who was suffering from anxiety was advised by her physician who thought he was using Freudian analytic techniques that she could eliminate her anxiety by returning to the husband, or by masturbating, or by taking a lover. She was unable to resolve her problem, however "good" her doctor's advise.

Related Concept: TECHNIQUE OF PSYCHOANALYSIS.

REFERENCE

Freud, S., 1910, "'Wild' Psycho-Analysis." *SE*, 11:221–227, 1957.

2305

WIT IN DREAMS. Freud (1900) accounted for the presence of wit in dreams, explaining that the peculiar pathological conditions under which dreams were constructed made it possible, independently of whether the individual was witty or not while awake. For example, the fact that Freud's dreams often appeared to be witty, he explained, was due to his unconscious being able to become partly conscious with the help of the dream-work.

Related Concept: DREAMS.

---

* A distinction, however, should be made between *wild* psychoanalysis and *modified* psychoanalysis.

REFERENCE

Freud, S., 1900, "The Interpretation of Dreams." *SE*, 4:298, 1953.

2306

WOLF MAN. Perhaps the most important case history reported by Freud (1918), the Wolf Man—as he later was called—was treated during two separate periods, the first (1910–1914) lasting almost four years, and the second (1919) about four months. Twelve years later the patient developed hypochondriacal delusions and was treated by a student of Freud's, Ruth Mack Brunswick. The patient returned to her two years later, and she continued to treat him at various times for several years.

When the patient first came to Freud he was twenty-three years old. He was unable to dress himself or to perform most of the simple acts of life. His subsequent analysis disclosed that he suffered from a number of disorders: (a) hysterical conversion symptoms, his constipation; (b) anxiety hysteria, his wolf phobia, to which must be added his subsequent fear of lions and other animals; (c) obsessional neurosis, his piety and alternating blasphemous thoughts; and (d) anorexia, his appetite disturbances.

Witnessing the primal scene (or its reconstruction) had an important influence in the patient's early development. It lay at the base of his earliest memories and was a confirmation of Freud's belief in the existence of infantile sexuality, a confirmation of an earlier case, that of Little Hans. Instinctual behavior of a sexual origin was no longer confined to lower animals, but was confirmed in man.

His phallic interest first appeared at the age of two-and-a-half, when his genitals began to play a part. The patient remembered at this time his beloved nursemaid, Grusha, whom he saw kneeling on the floor with a pail and broom beside her, scolding or teasing him. To this must be added the screen memory of the butterfly, its yellow-striped wings opening and closing, which the patient related unconsciously to a later memory of a storehouse where pears were stored (in his language pears were called grusha).

Further analysis revealed that his choice of love objects was dependent upon the same condition and was connected with his compulsion, starting from the primal scene and going on to the scene with Grusha. All his love-objects were surrogates for this one person, for the debased love-object, which were brought to life in the memory of the maid scrubbing the floor. To this must be added the fact that Grusha was his first mother surrogate. The Grusha scene, and the screen memory which preceded it, revealed the significant element which was lacking in the patient's memory.

His later seduction by his sister disturbed and diverted his genital development. It offered him a passive sexual aim, which under the castration threat from his Nanya, broke down and so accounted for his regression to an earlier, sadistic-anal stage. His sadism was thus transformed to a great extent into the masochism which was its passive counterpart. His masochism dominated his fantasies and was accompanied by a phobia toward animals who were treated as representations of small children. At four, then, the activation of the picture of the wolf reestablished his genital organization, but it could not be maintained, and through a process Freud identified with a repression, this new element occurred in the form of the subsequent phobia.

Leaving the phobia aside, an investigation of his hysterical conversion symptoms—his constipation—may now be considered. "A portion of the homosexual impulse," Freud observed, "was retained by the organ concerned in it . . . his bowel."

The hysterical constipation was caused by the erotization of his anus, resulting from his identification with his mother. Thus, the infantile wish to have anal intercourse with his father was partly gratified and partly warded off by his constipation. This case illustrates the necessity of differentiating between the localization of a symptom and the resulting regression to an earlier, infantile stage of development. In this case, for example, the constipation was not the result of the regression to the anal stage. Although the patient had, in addition, such a regression, it was responsible for his obsessional neurosis and not for his constipation. The regression to the phallic stage was responsible for the constipation.

Finally, the structure of his obsessional neurosis may be investigated. The wolf phobia was replaced by his obsessional piety, a transformation that was provoked by his acquaintanceship, through his mother's agency, with the doctrines of religion. In these ceremonials he could identify with Christ, who also loved his father, and in this way drain off his deepest sexual feelings, already present in the form of unconscious homosexuality. At the same time, he could experience the masochistic pleasure associated with Christ's sacrifice on the cross to the honor of his divine father.

As noted, the wolf man developed a hypochondriacal delusion many years after the successful completion of his analysis. Ruth Mack Brunswick (1928) who successfully analyzed this delusion, claimed modestly that no new material was discovered but that the patient's father fixation (transference) was worked through. She suggested that the material was not new for the analyst but perhaps was new (emotionally) for the patient. She assumed that the remnant of transference produced the delusion; a hole in his nose, accompanied by the feeling that life was unbearable. It is evident from Ruth Brunswick's paper that this symptom represented a gratification of his wish to have a vagina (identification with the oedipal mother). The nose may have been selected for the localization of this symptom because it represented his penis; therefore, his symptom showed the condensation of his bisexuality.

Related Concepts: CONVERSION AND CONVERSION SYMPTOMS; HYPOCHONDRIASIS; PHOBIA.

REFERENCES

Brunswick, Ruth M., "A Supplement to Freud's History of an Infantile Neurosis." *IntJPsa*, 9:439–476, 1928.

Freud, S., 1918, "From the History of an Infantile Neurosis." *SE*, 17:95–96, 106–107, 112–115, 117–118, 121, 1955.

ADDITIONAL READING

Gardiner, M., "A Letter from the Wolf-Man." *BPAP*, 3, 1953.

2307

WORD ASSOCIATION TEST, introduced to psychology by Wundt, gained significance with the work of Jung* in 1903. A word (termed the 'stimulus-

---

* Jung, C. G., *Studies in Word-Association*, London, 1918.

word') was called out to the subject and he replied as quickly as possible with some other word that occurred to him (the so-called 'reaction'), his choice of this reaction not being restricted by anything. The points to be observed were the *time* required for the reaction and the *relationship*—which might be of many different kinds—between the stimulus-word and the reaction-word.

The experiment which Jung carried out acquired its value from the fact that the reaction to the stimulus-word could not be a chance one but must be determined by an ideational content present in the mind of the reacting subject. Freud (1901) had previously investigated the basic assumptions of psychic determinism, and demonstrated that a number of actions which were unmotivated (or thought at that time to be so) were to the contrary strictly determined. He took as his example failures of memory, slips of the tongue and the mislaying of objects, and showed that none were chance events, but, rather, in every case, possessed of a disturbing ideational content—a complex—that could be brought to light.

Jung applied Freud's ideas in developing the association test, and confirmed certain of Freud's conclusions. Under certain conditions, Jung experimentally demonstrated the presence of repressed material in what he called "affective complexes." He was thus able to "prove" that the reaction to a stimulus-word was not due to chance but was determined by its ideational content present in the mind of the subject.

Related Concept: PSYCHIC DETERMINISM.

REFERENCE

Freud, S., 1901, "Psychopathology of Everyday Life." *SE*, 6:254, 1960.

2308

WORD SALAD is a disorder of thinking and language as observed in deteriorated, severely ill schizophrenics who have undergone marked regressive alterations of ego function and who display primitive and distorted modes of speech. The patient may progress from loosened associations to irrelevancies, to incongruous, incomplete, fragmentary, illogical utterances that may become totally disorganized and unintelligible. Stereotyped phrases and styles, neologisms, unusual personal symbolism, confusion between symbol and referent may eventually give way to a jumble of words that have no apparent structure or meaning. [Noyes and Kolb, 1963.]

The relevancy and meaning of the schizophrenic's *word salad* may be extremely difficult to detect or decipher; it nonetheless has an internal meaning to the patient in terms of his fantasies and wishes. Condensation, displacement symbolism, lack of logic and syntax are clear indications of the primary process dream-like character of schizophrenic language. The patient's associations are largely directed by his internal preoccupations; the apparently formless word salad is actually molded by unconscious conflicts and an inability to resolve these conflicts without massive personality regression and disintegration. Word salad is invariably associated with other schizophrenic thought disorders, Bellak (1958) noted that these include loss of capacity for abstraction, loss of figurative and metaphorical language, inability to generalize, and the classical loosening of associations. The word may be confused with its symbolized object or may be eventually treated as an object in itself, changing its meaning and attributes. If visual and auditory sensory images replace ideas and concepts, communication may become exceedingly difficult.

Related Concepts: NEOLOGISM; PRIMARY PROCESS; UNCONSCIOUS SIGNIFICANCE OF SPEECH.

REFERENCES

Bellak, L., ed., *Schizophrenia*. Log, pp. 115–118, 1958.
Noyes, A., & L. Kolb, *Modern Clinical Psychiatry*. Sau, pp. 336–338, 1963.

2309

WORDS, according to Freud (1923), are verbal residues of auditory perceptions and of visual stimuli; while they are consciously connected with object presentations or inner perceptions, the cathexis comes from the id. Above all, it is the principle form of communication with others and with oneself.

Freud divided the object presentations into "thing" presentations and "word" presentations. It may be proper to suggest that when the word-presentations are concerned with abstractions of originally concrete objects or feelings, one abstraction may lead to other abstractions. In this, the perceptual apparatus plays no part. Originally, words represented concrete objects or sensations. The former were perceived through the sense organs and the latter through inner perceptions. In the primitive, as Freud (1933) noted, the magical nature of words is "derived from their overevaluation of their own intellectual operations, from their belief in the 'omnipotence of thought.'" Words were originally spells, acts of magic, and, to some degree, they still retain this power. With the obsessional patient, for instance, this "omnipotence of thought" is a demonstrable symptom; there is a separation between the presentation of feeling and the word presentation (isolation).

In schizophrenics, their play with words commonly centers on some part of their body, so that Freud (1915) spoke of *organ language*. Such patients treat the words as though it were a part of the primary process, employing both condensation and displacement. In renouncing the cathexis of objects, they retain a cathexis with the designating word. In a description of a case, Eidelberg (1948) noted: "[The patient] had the idea that the minute observations of the various words and letters represented symbolically a sexual play with the various parts of a beautiful woman's body."

Related Concepts: AFFECT; INHIBITION.

REFERENCES

Eidelberg, L., *Studies in Psychoanalysis*. IUP, p. 57, 1948.
Freud, S.: 1915, "Papers on Metapsychology." *SE*, 14:201, 202, 1957.
  1923, "The Ego and the Id." *SE*, 19:20, 23, 52, 1961.
  1933, "New Introductory Lectures on Psycho-Analysis." *SE*, 22:165, 1964.

ADDITIONAL READING

Rycroft, C., "An Enquiry into the Function of Words in the Psycho-Analytical Situation." *IntJPsa*, 39, 1958.

2310

WORKING THROUGH. Freud (1914) pointed out that the analyst cannot expect that the patient will give up a resistance immediately after this resistance has been pointed out to him. The young analyst may have the tendency to assume that it is sufficient to point out a resistance to the patient in order to have it eliminated. In fact, a long time is required before the patient can assimilate what he has learned, and without this assimilation it is impossible to help the patient.

Related Concept: TECHNIQUE OF PSYCHOANALYSIS.

REFERENCE

Freud, S., 1914, "Remembering, Repeating and Working-Through (Further Recommendations on the Technique of Psycho-Analysis II)." *SE*, 12:155–156, 1958.

ADDITIONAL READINGS

Greenacre, P., "Re-Evaluation of the Process of Working Through." *IntJPsa*, 37, 1956.
Novey, S., "The Principle of 'Working Through' in Psychoanalysis." *JAPA*, 10, 1962.

2311

WRITER'S BLOCK designates the inability to function as a creative writer. It does not involve the motoric function of the hand but is an interfering phenomenon that affects the mental ability to produce creative work.

Various unconscious factors may be responsible for this professional inhibition. The writer's analysis usually discloses that the creative activity has become connected with infantile repressed wishes (e.g., identification with the preoedipal mother, the wish to have a baby). In addition to oral material, anal and phallic, sexual and aggressive, exhibitionistic and scopophilic wishes are responsible for this inhibition.

Fenichel (1945) did not differentiate writer's block from writers' cramp. It was his view that all types of inhibitions may form the basis for a "block." In our present day society, working may lead to success and to the consequent fear of it, reawakening the oedipal fears and threats of having to compete with the father for the love of the mother. Fenichel also pointed out that "working" may have the qualities associated with the unconscious wish to be a slave, achieving the status of a forbidden act.

Case History

Donald developed the symptom that forced him to seek help because his writing became more and more an outlet for his unconscious wish to rape. By writing, he gratified his desire to force his readers to submit to what he wanted to have them read, and his pen unconsciously became the penis of the brute who ravishes an unwilling woman. At the same time, writing symbolized being raped by the publishers who, by paying him, were able to force him to write what they wanted.

It is true that originally Donald's writing had represented a defense against listening, because listening meant being raped by others. Writing let him avoid the company of others for a time. But eventually what put a stop to his writing was the frustrated wish to rape and be raped. As in all such instances, once a normal function of the body is used for the discharge of infantile wishes, it becomes blocked either by fear or by other paralyzing emotions. These are the punishments inflicted by our conscience which is not fooled by the ostensibly innocuous conscious meaning of what we are doing. [Eidelberg, 1961.]

Related Concepts: PREOEDIPAL MOTHER ATTACHMENT; WRITER'S CRAMP.

REFERENCES

Eidelberg, L., *The Dark Urge*, Py, p. 129, 1961.
Fenichel, O., *The Psychoanalytic Theory of Neurosis*. Nor, p. 183, 1945.

2312

WRITER'S CRAMP is defined as an ego-alien conversion symptom characterized by an impairment of the ability to use a writing instrument. The impairment is often caused by a painfully cramped hand. Eidelberg (1948) provided the following case history: A municipal clerk, fifty-one, suffered from writer's cramp (and agoraphobia). The patient's first wife was dead. He divorced his second, but his third marriage was "satisfactory."

The onset of his illness, however, occurred a year after his third marriage.

The arrival of writer's cramp so late in life indicated that there was a causal relationship between the patient's symptoms and his third marriage. This proved to be the case. The patient's present wife was frigid; his sexual pleasure was not as great as it had been in his previous sexual relationships. Part of his ungratified libido had thus cathected his hand by way of compensation. It occurred to the patient that the hand was used for masturbation and, thus, played the part of the vagina.

His wife's frigidity and aversion to coitus blocked the usual gratification of the passive instinctual wishes that normally takes place through identification with the woman. Through phallicization the hand became a female genital organ, while the pencil or pen took over the role of the penis. This phallicization led to a disturbance of the ego function of the affected member.

Analysis showed that the symptom was intended to gratify the patient's unconscious aggression against his wife. The symptom also represented unconscious exhibitionism. Since writing had acquired a sexual significance for the patient, i.e., it had become a kind of publicly displayed coitus with himself, the writing function had to be inhibited. After the symptom was formed it was used to gratify unconscious exhibitionism by arousing attention in the patient's associates. Finally, the symptom represented partial identification with the friend of the patient's foster father who had tried to seduce the patient to homosexual intercourse, and who had been retired prematurely because of his writer's cramp. Finally, the symptom represented a punishment by the superego for the gratification of his bisexuality.

Related Concepts: STAMMERING (STUTTERING); TIC; WRITER'S BLOCK.

REFERENCE

Eidelberg, L., *Studies in Psychoanalysis.* IUP, pp. 70, 81, 93, 1948.

ADDITIONAL READINGS

Eidelberg, L., "The Genesis of Agoraphobia and Writer's Cramp." Z, 22, 1936.
Jokl, R., "On the Psychogenesis of Writer's Cramp." Z, 8, 1922.

X

2400

XENOPHOBIA denotes a hatred of anything or anybody foreign or different; a character trait. According to Freud (1915), the first object-relation of the infant is referred to as primary identification. Whatever is different from the child is at first hated; it is loved when the child comes to recognize that part of the external world is a source of pleasure. At first the infant hates the external world and only slowly is he able to find out those external objects which he can use as sources of pleasure.

When the purely narcissistic stage is given up, the child learns that he may love some external objects because they are pleasurable; others, he may hate and want to destroy.

Related Concepts: HATE; LOVE; POLARITIES.

REFERENCE

Freud, S., 1915, "Instincts and Their Vicissitudes." *SE*, 14:136–137, 1957.

Y

YAWNING is usually observed in people who are getting tired or sleepy. It is characterized by a deep inspiration and decreases the intensity of hearing. Neurotic yawning may be used as an unconscious defense against the danger of being overwhelmed by infantile sexual or aggressive, or both, instincts. Ferenczi (1912) noted: "I noticed with one patient that he yawned with striking frequency. I then remarked that the yawning accompanied just those analytic conversations whose content, since it was important to him although disagreeable, would more suitably have evoked interest than boredom. Another patient who came to treatment soon after this brought me what I believe to be the solution of this peculiar phenomenon. She also yawned often and at inappropriate times, but in her case the yawning was sometimes accompanied with a flow of tears. That gave me the idea that these patients' yawning might be a distorted sign, and in both cases the analysis confirmed my surmise. The censorship effected in both cases the repression of certain disagreeable emotional states that were aroused through the analysis (pain, grief), but it was unable to bring about a complete suppression, only a displacement of the movements of expression, one that was enough, however, to conceal from consciousness the real character of the emotional state. On turning my attention, after these observations, to the movements of expression with other patients as well, I found that there are other forms of 'expression displacements.'"

Clinical Example

In the case of a woman patient who "had to yawn whenever she contemplated meeting her lover," Eidelberg (1954) noted, "analysis disclosed that her yawning was a defense against her sexual wishes. In this case, the ideas and emotions representing her sexual desires remained unconscious, and her yawning appeared to mean: 'I am not interested in seeing my lover. Instead of satisfying my sexual urge, I want to endure it, get tired, and sleep.' At the same time the inability to control her yawning represented an internal narcissistic mortification which she was willing to accept in order to deny a possible narcissistic mortification by her lover, who could have rejected her. Under normal conditions, the anticipation of meeting the man she loved would produce the desire to satisfy sexual urges, but she made an 'unconscious decision' against such satisfaction by mobilizing the wish to sleep."

Related Concept: DISPLACEMENT.

REFERENCES

Eidelberg, L., *An Outline of a Comparative Pathology of the Neuroses.* IUP, p. 109, 1954.
Ferenczi, S., 1912, "Transitory Symptom-Constructions During the Analysis." *SPsa*, pp. 209–210, 1916.

Z

ZOOERASTY denotes those sexual practices which occur between a human subject and an animal object; a perversion. The practice may lead to sexual gratification or be directed toward the masturbation (or its attempt) of the animal. Male subjects have attempted rectal, vaginal and oral penetrations of sheep, dogs, etc.; females have had pets perform cunnilingual and other perverse sexual acts.

According to Lorand (1950), the pervert is involved in avoidance and flight from mature heterosexual relationships. Invariably there is guilt over incestuous wishes and oedipal aggression. The animals are displaced substitutes for the infantile incestuous object, the parent or loved sibling. As in the case of phobia, the totemistic thinking of the child makes such displacement from person to animal a simple solution, in which both anxiety and guilt can be avoided. The animal is a silent partner who will not reveal the forbidden act and who can be omnipotently controlled. Dangerous wishes against the parent may be safely discharged while preserving the vital object relations. The history of the pervert may show that actual animal games were played with the parent; or there was direct observation of animals having intercourse in which the patient identified with the animal partner, a representation of the primal scene. The archaic superego in these patients precludes mature sexual gratification with a heterosexual partner. It also may invite actual or symbolic dangers of castration from a biting or kicking attack by the animal partner. Primarily, however, the animal is utilized as a source of reassurance against the danger of retaliatory castration and serves as an attempt to return to genital contact after fleeing such contact with human genitalia.

As with other perversions, there is usually a profound disappointment in the childhood objects, such that idealized image of the good parental object may be projected onto the animal partner. The animal is then seen as steadfast, loyal, benevolent, and gratifying rather than denying or withholding. This correspondence to immature object relations is a form of pregenital regression with accompanying sadomasochistic and homosexual fantasies. Such fantasies may at times be safely acted out with animals, an activity that would not be permitted by the superego and ego in relation to human objects.

Lorand (1956) demonstrated that the conscious and unconscious fantasy concomitant with such a perverse act is of profound importance in elucidating the underlying structure of the perversion. Those individuals who are fixated to sexual gratification with animals are exceedingly immature, incapable of assuming adult responsibilities, highly ambivalent and fearful of humans, and have a markedly narcissistic orientation. There is no true consideration for their partner, and, indeed, their partner may be an externalization of their own animal nature and a disguised acting out of a masturbatory withdrawal.

In addition to the oedipal repression subserved by the animal perversion, more primitive defenses of denial and projection are functionally important in the perverse ego organization. Like a mascot, the animal partner may be a magical fetish which protests against object loss and castration, thereby narrowly permitting sexual gratification.

Related Concepts: COMPULSIVE MASTURBATION; IMPULSE; PERVERSION.

REFERENCES

Lorand, S.: "Indecision as an Escape; Necrophilia and Sodomy," in *Clinical Studies in Psychoanalysis.* IUP, pp. 226–235, 1950.
"The Therapy of Perversion," in *Perversions, Psychodynamics and Therapy.* RH, pp. 290–307, 1956.

2601
ZOOPHOBIA is a fear of animals, especially common in children. Given further ego maturation, it may disappear under favourable external circumstances. Where the phobia is confined to one or to a few animals, the specificity and limitation represents the successful binding and delimiting of inner fears which have been projected outward to represent both the temptation and punishment for forbidden instinctual wishes. Generally, what is feared is unconsciously wished for, having a specific unconscious meaning. Even in those situations where there has been an actual serious attack by an animal, the structuralized and internalized phobia cannot be explained on the basis of the traumatic event. Invariably the experience is interpreted unconsciously as the materialization of an instinctual wish, frequently sadistic, or the punishment for such aggressive design. [Fenichel, 1945.]

The best studied cases of animal phobia are those of Little Hans and the Wolf Man. According to Freud (1926), Little Hans was grappling with his oedipal wishes: in resolving his ambivalence to his father, he projected his hostility and castrating wishes onto the horses. The father remained a love-object and the horses (who could be readily avoided) became the feared objects. The Wolf Man was afraid of being devoured, a phobia which also concealed the expression of a castration anxiety.

In this, the inverted oedipal complex and the passive feminine attitude toward the father was associated with the acceptance of castration. To submit as a female to his father in the primal scene meant to be castrated. Here, too, there was an adaptive advantage, for the wolves were to be seen only in picture books or zoos, both readily avoidable.

Displacements to animals is easily made by children who show traces of totemic thought. For them the adult belongs to the category of the big animal who has enviable attributes but may become dangerous. Here, Freud did not miss the contribution of the real parental behavior in the choice of a phobia. In the case of Little Hans, for instance, his father used to play horses with him. It is also likely that the father of the Wolf Man used to pretend to be a wolf and jokingly threaten to gobble him up.

In assessing the severity and importance of what are deceptively simple animal phobias, both genetic and dynamic, as well as structural and adaptive viewpoints are vital. A phobia of all animals is far more constricting and disruptive to functioning than the phobia of a single animal. The Wolf Man's fear of being totally devoured proved to be far more serious than Little Hans' fear of his finger being bitten off. The structure of the phobia must be compared with the structure of the total personality of the phobic patient. Regression of ego function and the evaluation of danger may be of far more pathogenic significance than libidinal regression or the regressive representation of castration through oral sadism. For example, the fear of being devoured may, according to Lewin (1950), represent the wish to be eaten as part of an oral triad and may sometimes be associated with the fear of loss of identity and the primitive wish for fusion with the mother.

Related Concept: TOTEM.

REFERENCES

Fenichel, O., *The Psychoanalytic Theory of Neurosis.* Nor, pp. 198–199, 213–214, 1945.
Freud, S., 1926, "Inhibitions, Symptoms and Anxiety." *SE,* 20:101–110, 1959.
Lewin, B., *The Psychoanalysis of Elation.* Nor, pp. 104–107, 1950.

Bibliography

The following list contains all the books and papers referred to in the text of this work through 1963, including the complete psychological writings of Sigmund Freud.

AARONS, Z.

"Notes On a Case of Maladie des Tics." *Q*, 27, 1958.
"A Study of Perversion and an Attendant Character Disorder." *Q*, 28, 1959.

ABEL, K.

Über den Gegensinn der Urworte. Leipzig, 1884.

ABRAHAM, E.

"On the Process of Projection." *ZPsychol*, 10, 1951.

ABRAHAM, H.

"Twin Relationship and Womb Fantasies in a Case of Anxiety Hysteria." *IntJPsa*, 34, 1953.
"A Contribution to the Problems of Female Sexuality." *IntJPsa*, 27, 1956

ABRAHAM, K.

"Beiträge zur Kenntnis des Delirium Tremens der Morphinisten." *CNP*, 25, 1902.
"The Psycho-Sexual Differences Between Hysteria and Dementia Praecox." *SPA*, 1942.
1910, "Hysterical Dream-States." *SPA*, 1942.
"Remarks on the Psychoanalysis of a Case of Foot and Corset Fetishism." *Y*, 2, 1910.
"Psychoanalysis of an Obsessional Neurosis." *BPV*, 1911.
"Über die Beziehungen zwischen Perversion und Neurose. Referat über die erste von Freud's *Drei Abhandlungen zur Sexualtheorie*." *BPV*, 1911.

"Aus der Analyse eines Falles von Grübelzwang." *BPV*, 1912.
"Beobachtungen über die Beziehungen zwischen Nahrungstrieb und Sexualtrieb." *BPV*, 1913.
1913, "Restrictions and Transformations Scotophilia in Psycho-Neurotics; With Remarks on Analogous Phenomena in Folk-Psychology." *SPA*, 1942.
1916, "The First Pregenital Stage of the Libido." *SPA*, 1942.
"Einige Belege zur Gefühlseinstellung Weiblicher Kinder gegenüber den Eltern." *Z*, 4, 1917.
1917, "Ejaculatio Praecox." *SPA*, 1942.
"Dreikäsehoch; zur Psychoanalyse des Wortwitzes." *Im*, 5, 1918.
1919, "A Particular Form of Neurotic Resistance Against the Psycho-Analytic Method." *SPA*, 1942.
1920, "Manifestations of the Female Castration Complex." *SPA*, 1942.
1920, "The Narcissistic Evaluation of Excretory Processes in Dream and Neurosis." *SPA*, 1942.
"Technisches zur Traumdeutung." *BPV*, 1920.
1921, "Contribution to a Discussion on Tic." *SPA*, 1942.
1921, "Contributions to the Theory of the Anal Character." *SPA*, 1942.
"Manifestations of the Female Castration Complex." *IntJPsa*, 3, 1922.
1922, "The Spider as a Dream Symbol." *SPA*, 1942.
"Vaterrettung und Vatermord in den neurotischen Phantasiegebilden." *Z*, 8, 1922.
"Anfänge und Entwicklung der Objekliebe." *BPV*, 1923.

"Ein Beitrag zur Prüfungssituation im Traume." *BPV*, 1923.

—— & H. Deutsch, "Über Phantasien der Kastration durch Beissen." *BPV*, 1923.

"Zum Introjektionsvorgang bei Homosexualität." *BPV*, 1923.

1924, "The Influence of Oral Erotism on Character-Formation." *SPA*, 1942.

1924, "A Short Study of the Development of the Libido, Viewed in the Light of Mental Disorders." *SPA*, 1942.

1925, "Character-Formation on the Genital Level of the Libido." *SPA*, 1942.

"The Influence of Oral Eroticism on Character Formation." *IntJPsa*, 6, 1925.

"Character Formation on the Genital Level of Libido-Development." *IntJPsa*, 7, 1926

"The Psychological Relations Between Sexuality and Alcoholism." *IntJPsa*, 7, 1926.

"Über Charakteranalyse." *Al*, 1926.

1927, "The Female Castration Complex." *SPA*, 1942.

ABSE, D.

—— & J. Ewing, "Transference and Countertransference in Somatic Therapies." *JNMD*, 123, 1956.

ACKERMAN, N.

"Paranoid State With Delusions of Injury by 'Black Magic'." *BMC*, 2, 1938.

ACKNER, B.

"Depersonalization: I. Etiology and Phenomenology; II. Clinical Syndromes." *JMS*, 100, 1954.

ADAMS, W.

"The Masochistic Character: Genesis and Treatment." *BPAP*, 9, 1959.

ADATTO, E.

"Ego Reintegration Observed in Analysis of Late Adolescents." *IntJPsa*, 39, 1958.

ADLER, A.

"Beitrag zur Lehre vom Widerstand." *C*, 1, 1911.

"The Feeling of Inferiority and the Striving for Recognition." *PRSM*, 20, 1927.

ADLER, G.

"Der Transpersonale Aspekt der Übertragung." *P*, 1955.

AICHHORN, A.

"Wayward Youth." *Im*, 1935.

ALBINO, R.

"Defences Against Aggression in the Play of Young Children." *M*, 27, 1954.

ALEXANDER, F.

"Kastrationskomplex und Charakter; eine Untersuchung über passagere Symptome." *Z*, 8, 1922.

"The Castration Complex in the Formation of Character." *IntJPsa*, 4, 1923.

"Dreams in Pairs and Series." *IntJPsa*, 6, 1925.

"Neurosis and the Whole Personality." *IntJPsa*, 7, 1926.

"Diskussion zur Laienanalyse." *Z*, 13, 1927.

"The Neurotic Character." *IntJPsa*, 11, 1930.

Psychoanalysis of the Total Personality. NMDP, 1930.

"Psychogenic Factors in Bronchial Asthma." *PSM*, 1941.

—— & J. French, *Psychoanalytic Therapy.* RP, 1946.

Fundamentals of Psychoanalysis. Nor, 1948.

"Analysis of the Therapeutic Factors in Psychoanalytic Treatment." *Q*, 19, 1950.

"The Psychosomatic Approach in Medical Therapy." *APPO*, 2, 1954.

—— & H. Visotsky, "Psychosomatic Study of a Case of Asthma." *PSM*, 17, 1955.

"Two Forms of Regression and Their Therapeutic Implications." *Q*, 25, 1956.

"A Case of Phobia of Darkness." *R*, 44, 1957.

ALLEN, R.

Elements of Rorschach Interpretation. IUP, 1954.

ALLENDY, R.

"Le Complexe d'Oedipe." *Esprit Nouveau.*, 1924.

ALLINSMITH, W.

"Conscience and Conflict: The Moral Force in Personality." *CD*, 28, 1957.

ALLPORT, G.

—— & L. Postman, *The Psychology of Rumor.* HH, 1947.

"The Roots of Religion." *PastoralPsychol*, 5, 1954.

ALMANSI, R.

"Applied Psychoanalysis: Religion, Mythology and Folklore." *AnSurvPsa*, 4, 1953.

"The Face-Breast Equation." *JAPA*, 8, 1960.

ALPERT, A.

—— & S. Krown, "Treatment of a Child with Severe Ego Restrictions in a Therapeutic Nursery." *PsaStC*, 8, 1953.

"Reversibility of Pathological Fixations Associated With Maternal Deprivation in Infancy." *PsaStC*, 14, 1959.

ALTSCHULE, M.

"Adrenocortical Function in Anorexia Nervosa Before and After Lobotomy." *NewEngJmed*, 248, 1953.

ANDREAS-SALOME, L.

"Narzissmus als Doppelrichtung." *Im*, 7, 1921.

"The Dual Orientation of Narcissism." *Q*, 31, 1962.

ANGEL, A.

"Einige Bemerkungen über den Optimismus." *Z*, 20, 1934.

ANSBACHER, H.
"Fetishism: An Adlerian Interpretation." *PQ*, 32, 1958.

APPEL, J.
"Incidence of Neuropsychiatric Disorders in the U.S. Army in World War II." *APJ*, 102, 1946.

ARIETI, S.
"The Processes of Expectation and Anticipation." *JNMD*, 106, 1947.
"Some Basic Problems Common to Anthropology and Modern Psychiatry." *AmAnthrop*, 58, 1956.
American Handbook of Psychiatry. BB, 1959.

ARLOW, J.
"Ego Psychology." *AnSurvPsa*, 1, 1950.
"Applied Psychoanalysis: Religion." *AnSurvPsa*, 2, 1951.
"A Psychoanalytic Study of a Religious Initiation Rite: Bar Mitzvah." *PsaStC*, 6, 1951.
"Psychoanalytic Studies in Psychosomatic Medicine." *AnSurvPsa*, 3, 1952.
"Psychodynamics and Treatment of Perversions." *BAPA*, 8, 1952.
"Masturbation and Symptom Formation." *JAPA*, 1, 1953.
"Notes on Oral Symbolism." *Q*, 24, 1955.
"On Smugness." *IntJPsa*, 38, 1957.
"The Psychoanalytic Theory of Thinking." *JAPA*, 6, 1958.
"The Structure of the Déjà Vu Experience." *JAPA*, 7, 1959.
—— & C. Brenner, "The Concept of Regression and the Structural Theory." *Q*, 29, 1960.
"Ego Psychology and the Study of Mythology." *JAPA*, 9, 1961.

ARONSON, G.
"Delusions of Pregnancy in a Male Homosexual with Abdominal Cancer." *AnSurvPsa*, 3, 1952.

AUFREITER, J.
"Psycho-Analysis and Consciousness." *IntJPsa*, 41, 1960.

AUSUBEL, D.
"Negativism as a Phase of Ego Development." *Ops*, 20, 1950.
Theory and Problems of Adolescent Development. G&S, 1954.
"Relationships Between Shame and Guilt in the Socializing Process." *PsycholRev*, 62, 1955.

AXELRAD, S.
—— & L. Maury, "Identification as a Mechanism of Adaptation." *AnSurvPsa*, 2, 1951.
"Comments on Anthropology and the Study of Complex Cultures." *PsaSS*, 4, 1955.
"On Some Uses of Psychoanalysis." *JAPA*, 8, 1960.

AZIMA, H.
—— & E. Wittkower, "Anaclitic Therapy Employing Drugs: A Case of Spider Phobia With Isakower Phenomenon." *Q*, 26, 1957.

BACON, C.
"The Role of Aggression in the Asthmatic Attack." *Q*, 25, 1956.

BADEL, D.
"The Repetitive Cycle in Depression." *IntJPsa*, 43, 1962.

BAK, R.
"Psychodynamics of Fetishism." *BAPA*, 8, 1952.
"Fetishism." *JAPA*, 1, 1953.

BALINT, M.
"A Contribution on Fetishism." *IntJPsa*, 16, 1935.
"Eros and Aphrodite." *IntJPsa*, 19, 1938.
"Primary Narcissism and Primary Love." *Q*, 29, 1960.

BALLY, G.
"Zur Frage der Behandlung schizoider Neurotiker." *Z*, 16, 1930.
"Das Inzestmotiv." *P*, 1, 1947.
"Das Schuldproblem in der Psychotherapie." *Schweiz-ANP*, 70, 1952.

BANDLER, B.
"Evaluation of Therapeutic Results: A Symposium." *IntJPsa*, 29, 1948.

BANDURA, A.
—— & R. Walters, *Adolescent Aggression*. RP, 1959.

BARAHAL, H.
"The Psychopathology of Hair-Pulling (Trichotillomania)." *R*, 27, 1940.
"A Psychoanalytic Approach to Schizophrenic Anxiety." *PQ*, 32, 1958.

BARBARA, D.
Stuttering: A Psychodynamic Approach to Its Understanding and Treatment. Julian Press, 1954.

BARRETT, W.
"Penis Envy and Urinary Control; Pregnancy Fantasies and Constipation; Episodes in the Life of a Little Girl." *Q*, 8, 1939.

BARRON, F.
"An Ego-Strength Scale Which Predicts Response to Psychotherapy." *JconsultPsychol*, 17, 1953.

BARTEMEIER, L.
"Schizoid Personality and Schizophrenia." *WarMed*, 1, 1941.
"A Psychoanalytic Study of Pregnancy in an 'As-If' Personality." *IntJPsa*, 35, 1954.

BAUDOUIN, C.

Psychoanalysis and Aesthetics. D, 1924.
"Ein Fall von Kleptomani ." *PsaP*, 4, 1930.
"La Réactivation du Passé." *RFPsa*, 14, 1950.

BAUMEYER, F.

"Bemerkungen zu Freuds Krankengeschichte des 'Kleinen Hans'." *PraxKinderpsychol.* 1, 1953.
"Der Fall Schreber." *P*, 9, 1955.
"The Schreber Case." *IntJPsa*, 37, 1956.

BEACHE, F.

"Psychosomatic 'Phenomena in Animals.'" *PSM*, 14, 1952.

BECK, A.

—— & M. Hurvich, "Psychological Correlates of Depression: I. Frequency of 'Masochistic' Dream Content in a Private Practice Sample." *PSM*, 21, 1959.

BEHN-ESCHENBURG, H.

"The Antecedents of the Oedipus Complex." *IntJPsa*, 16, 1935.

BEIER, E.

—— L. Gorlow, & C. Stacey, "The Fantasy Life of the Mental Defective." *JmenDef*, 4, 1951.

BEIN, E.

"Zur Aktivanalytischen Therapie der psychischen Impotenz." *ZSW*, 17, 1931.

BELL, A.

"Some Observations on the Role of the Scrotal Sac and Testicles." *JAPA*, 9, 1961.

BELLAK, L.

"The Concept of Projection." *Ps*, 7, 1944.
"On the Etiology of Schizophrenia (Dementia Praecox). A Critical Review of the Literature of the Last 10 Years." *JNMD*, 105, 1947.
The Tat and Cat in Clinical Use. G&S, 1954.
"An Ego-Psychological Theory of Hypnosis." *IntJPsa*, 36, 1955.
Schizophrenia. Log, 1958.

BENDER, L.

"Childhood Schizophrenia." *AmJOrthopsychiat*, 17, 1947.

BENEDEK, T.

"Dominant Ideas and Their Relation to Morbid Cravings." *IntJPsa*, 17, 1936.
"Dynamics of the Countertransference." *BMC*, 17, 1953.
"Toward the Biology of the Depressive Constellation." *JAPA*, 4, 1956.

BERES, D.

"Vicissitudes of Superego Functions and Superego Precursors in Childhood." *PsaStC*, 13, 1958.
"The Unconscious Fantasy." *Q*, 31, 1962.

BEREZIN, M.

"Enuresis and Bisexual Identification." *JAPA*, 2, 1954.

BERG, C.

"Fear—Normal and Abnormal." *MedPr*, 227, 1952.

BERGEN, M.

"The Effect of Severe Trauma on a Four-Year-Old-Child." *PsaStC*, 13, 1958.

BERGLER, E.

"Zur Problematik der Pseudo-Debilität." *Z*, 18, 1932.
—— & L. Eidelberg, "Der Mammakomplex des Mannes." *Z*, 19, 1933.
"Zur Problematik des 'oralen' Pessimisten demonstriert an Christian Dietrich Grabbe" *Im*, 20, 1934.
—— & L. Eidelberg, "Der Mechanismus der Depersonalisation." *Z*, 21, 1935.
"Bemerkungen über einer Zwangsneurose in ultimis. Vier Mechanismen des narzisstischen Lustgewinns im Zwang." *Z*, 22, 1936.
"Preliminary Phases of the Masculine Beating Fantasy." *Q*, 7, 1938.
"Contribution to the Psychoanalysis of Déjà Vu." *Q*, 11, 1942.
"Hypocrisy: Its Implications in Neurosis and Criminal Psychopathology." *JCP*, 4, 1942-1943.
"A New Approach to the Theory of Erythrophobia." *Q*, 13, 1944.
"Psychopathology of the 'First Impulse' and 'First Thought' in Neurotics." *PQSup*, 21, 1947.
"Boredom of Anticipation (Pseudo-Boredom)." *Samiksa*, 4, 1950.
"The Battle of the Conscience." *R*, 1953.

BERGMAN, P.

"An Analysis of an Unusual Case of Fetishism." *BMC*, 11, 1947.
—— & S. Escalona, "Unusual Sensitivities in Very Young Children." *PsaStC*, 3, 1949.

BERLINER, B.

"The Role of Object Relations in Moral Masochism." *Q*, 27, 1958.

BERMAN, L.

"Depersonalization and the Body Ego With Special Reference to the Genital Representation." *Q*, 17, 1948.
"Countertransferences and Attitudes of the Analyst in the Therapeutic Process." *AdvPsychiat*, 1953.
"Perception and Object Relation in a Patient with Transvestitism Tendencies." *IntJPsa*, 34, 1953.
"The Obsessive-Compulsive Neurosis in Children," in L. Bender *A Dynamic Psychopathology of Childhood.* CCT, 1954.
"Some Problems in the Evaluation of Psychoanalysis as a Therapeutic Procedure." *Ps*, 18, 1955.

BERNA, J.
"Kinderanalyse eines Aggressiven." *P*, 9, 1955.
"Die 'Réalisation Symbolique' in der Kinderanalyse."
P, 9, 1956.

BERNE, E.
"Concerning the Nature of Communication." *PQ*, 27,
1953.

BERNFELD, S.
"Über Faszination." *Im*, 4, 1928.
—— & S. Feitelberg, "Über psychische Energie, Libido
und deren Messbarkeit." *Im*, 16, 1930.
"Die Gestalttheorie." *Im*, 20, 1934.

BERNSTEIN, I.
"The Role of Narcissism in Moral Masochism." *Q*,
26, 1957.

BETTELHEIM, B.
—— & E. Sylvester, "Delinquency and Morality."
PsaStC, 5, 1950.

BHASKARAN, K.
"Some Somatization Patterns in Reactive Depression. A
Preliminary Report." *JNMD*, 21, 1955.

BIBRING, E.
"Klinische Beiträge zur Paranoiafrage." *Z*, 15, 1929.
"The Conception of the Repetition Compulsion." *Q*,
12, 1943.
"Das Problem der Depression." *P*, 6, 1952.
"The Mechanisms of Depression," in P. Greenacre,
Affective Disorders. IUP, 1953.

BIBRING, G.
"Über eine orale Komponente bei männlicher Inver-
sion." *Z*, 25, 1940.
—— T. Dwyer, D. Huntington, & A. Valenstein,
"Glossary of Defenses." *PsaStC*, 16, 1961.
—— T. Dwyer, D. Huntington, & A. Valenstein,
"A Study of the Psychological Processes in Pregnancy
and of the Earliest Mother-Child Relationships."
PsaStC, 16, 1961.
"A Contribution to the Subject of Transference Resis-
tance." *IntJPsa*, 17, 1936.

BIEBER, I.
"The Meaning of Masochism." *PT*, 7, 1953.
"The Psychosomatic Symptom," in J. Wortis, *Basic
Problems in Psychiatry.* G&S, 1953.

BIERMAN, J.
"Necrophilia in a Thirteen-Year-Old Boy." *PQ*, 31,
1962.

BIERMANN, G.
"Geständnis- und Wiederholungszwang im Sceno-Test."
ZdiagnPsychol, 3, 1955.

BING, J.
—— F. MacLaughlin, & R. Marburg, "The Metapsy-
chology of Narcissism." *PsaStC*, 14, 1959.
—— & R. Marburg, "Narcissism." *R*, 3, 1962.

BION, W.
"Notes on the Theory of Schizophrenia." *IntJPsa*, 35,
1954.
"Development of Schizophrenic Thought." *IntJPsa*, 37,
1956.
"Language and the Schizophrenic." *NewDirPsa*, 1958.
"On Hallucination." *IntJPsa*, 39, 1958.
Experiences in Groups and Other Papers. BB, 1961.

BIRAN, S.
"Der Unterschied Zwischen Phobie und Angsthysterie."
APPO, 3, 1955.

BIRD, B.
"Depersonalization." *AMAANP*, 80, 1958.

BIRD, H.
—— & P. Martin, "Countertransference in the Psychotherapy of Marriage Partners." *PS*, 19, 1956.

BIRNBAUM, K.
"Krankhafte Eifersucht und Eifersuchtwahn." *Sexual-
probleme*, 7, 1911.

BJERRE, P.
"Zur Impotenzfrage." *PtPrx*, 1, 1934.

BLANCHARD, P.
"Psychoanalytic Contributions to the Problem of Reading Disabilities." *PsaStC*, 2, 1947.

BLANK, H.
"Depression Hypomania, and Depersonalization." *Q*,
23, 1954.

BLANK, L.
"The Difference Between Thinking and Acting Pathologically With Implication for Projective and Psychoanalytic Techniques." *AmPsych*, 12, 1957.

BLAU, A.
"In Support of Freud's Syndrome of 'Actual' Anxiety
Neurosis." *IntJPsa*, 33, 1952.
"Nocturnal Enuresis." *JAMA*, 154, 1954.
"A Unitary Hypothesis of Emotion: I. Anxiety, Emotions
of Displeasure, and Affective Disorders." *Q*, 24, 1955.

BLEULER, E.
"Antwort auf die Bemerkungen Jungs zur Theorie des
Negativismus." *Y*, 3, 1911.
The Theory of Schizophrenic Negativism. NMDP, 1912.
Textbook of Psychiatry. Mac, 1924.
"Die Mneme als Grundlage des Lebends und der
Psyche." *Die Naturwissenschaften*, 21, 1933.
Dementia Praecox, or the Group of Schizophrenias.
IUP, 1950.

BLITZSTEIN, N.

"Amphithymia, Some Syndromes of Elations and Depressions." *ANP*, 36, 1936.

BLOS, P.

"Prolonged Adolescence: The Formulation of a Syndrome and Its Therapeutic Implications." *Ops*, 24, 1954.
"Preoedipal Factors in the Etiology of Female Delinquency." *PsaStC*, 11, 1957.
On Adolescence. Mac, 1962.

BLUM, H.

"Colour in Dreams." *IntJPsa*, 45, 1964.

BLUMGART, L.

"A Short Communication of 'Repression.'" *R*, 4, 1916.

BLUMSTEIN, A.

"Masochism and Fantasies of Preparing to be Incorporated." *JAPA*, 7, 1959.

BOEHM, F.

"Sexual Perversions." *IntJPsa*, 2, 1921.
"Die Heilung eines Exhibitionisten." *ZPSM*, 2, 1955-1956.

BOLTERAUER, L.

"Contribution to the Psychology of Fanaticism." *IntJPsa*, 33, 1952.

BONNARD, A.

"The Mother as a Therapist in a Case of Obsessional Neurosis." *PsaStC*, 5, 1950.
"The Metapsychology of the Russian Trials Confessions." *IntJPsa*, 35, 1954.
"Some Discrepancies Between Perception and Affect as Illustrated by Children in Wartime." *PsaStC*, 9, 1954.

BORNSTEIN, B.

"A Case of Cured Stupidity, Report on a Psychoanalytic Case History." *PsaP*, 4, 1930.
"Psychogenesis of Pseudodebility." *Z*, 16, 1930.
"Enuresis und Kleptomanie als passagere Symptome." *PsaP*, 8, 1934.
"Clinical Notes on Child Analysis." *PsaStC*, 1, 1945.
"The Analysis of a Phobic Child. Some Problems of Theory and Technique in Child Analysis." *PsaStC*, 3-4, 1949.
"On Latency." *PsaStC*, 6, 1951.
"Fragment of an Analysis of an Obsessional Child. The First Six Months of Analysis." *PsaStC*, 8, 1953.
"Masturbation in the Latency Period." *PsaStC*, 3, 1953.

BOSE, G.

The Concept of Repression. Calcutta: Bose, 1921.
"Genesis of Homosexuality." *Samiksa*, 4, 1940.
"The Paranoid Ego." *Samiksa*, 2, 1948.
"Ambivalence." *Samiksa*, 3, 1949.

BOUVET, M.

"Resistance and Transference." *RFPsa*, 23, 1959.

BOVEN, W.

Anxiety. D&N, 1934.

BOWLBY, J.

"The Abnormally Aggressive Child." *New Era*, 19, 1938.
"Separation Anxiety." *IntJPsa*, 41, 1960.
"Note on Dr. Max Schur's Comments on Grief and Mourning in Infancy and Early Childhood." *PsaStC*, 16, 1961.
"Processes of Mourning." *IntJPsa*, 42, 1961.

BRAIN, W.

Diseases of the Nervous System. IUP, 1948.

BRANCH, C.

"Schizophrenia and Related Problems." *JNMD*, 127, 1958.

BRAUTIGAM, W.

"Analyse der Hypochondrischen Selbstbeobachtung. Beitrag zur Psychopathologie und zur Pathogenese mit Beschreibung einer Gruppe von Jugendlichen Herzhypochondern." *Nervenarzt*, 27, 1956.

BRENNER, C.

"An Addendum to Freud's Theory of Anxiety." *IntJPsa*, 34, 1953.
An Elementary Textbook of Psychoanalysis. IUP, 1955.
"A Reformulation of the Theory of Parapraxes." *BPAP*, 5, 1955.
"Psychopathology of the Masochistic Character: Illustrative Cases." *JNMD*, 123, 1956.
"The Nature of Development of the Concept of Repression in Freud's Writings." *PsaStC*, 12, 1957.
"The Concept 'Preconscious' and the Structural Theory." *BPAP*, 9, 1959.

BRIERLEY, M.

"Die Affekte in der Theorie und Praxis." *Z*, 1936.
"Notes on Metapsychology as Process Theory." *IntJPsa*, 25, 1944.
"Notes on Psychoanalysis and Integrative Living." *IntJPsa*, 28, 1947.

BRILL, A.

"Diagnostic Errors in Neurasthenia." *MRR*, 36, 1930.
"Necrophilia." *JCP*, 3, 1941.
"Basic Principles of Psychoanalysis." *Q*, 18, 1949.

BRODSKY, B.

"The Self-Representation, Anality, and the Fear of Dying." *JAPA*, 7, 1959.

BRODY, E.

—— & F. Redlich, "Psychotherapy With Schizophrenics: A Symposium." *AnSurvPsa*, 3, 1952.

"Superego, Introjected Mother, and Energy Discharge in Schizophrenia: Contribution from the Study of Anterior Lobotomy." *JAPA*, 6, 1958.

BRODY, M.
"The Meaning of Laughter." *Q*, 19, 1950.
"Transference and Countertransference in Psychotherapy." *R*, 42, 1955.
"Clinical Manifestations of Ambivalence." *Q*, 25, 1956.

BRODY, S.
"Self-Rocking in Infancy." *JAPA*, 8, 1960.
"Some Aspects of Transference Resistance in Prepuberty." *PsaStC*, 16, 1961.

BROMBERG, N.
"Round Table: Intellectual Inhibitions and Environmental Pressures." *BAPA*, 8, 1952.

BROSIN, H.
"The Psychiatric Aspects of Obesity." *JAMA*, 155, 1954.

BROWN, B.
—— & M. Nyswander, "The Treatment of Masochistic Adults." *Ops*, 26, 1956.

BROWN, F.
"The Present Status of Rorschach Interpretation." *JAPA*, 5, 1957.

BRUCH, H.
"Obesity in Childhood and Personality Development." *Ops*, 11, 1941.
"Obesity in Relation to Puberty." *JPediat*, 19, 1941.
"The Psychology of Obesity." *CJM*, 31, 1950.
"Parental Education or the Illusion of Omnipotence." *Ops*, 24, 1954.
"The Role of Emotions in Obesity." *State of Mind*, 21, 1957.
"Developmental Obesity and Schizophrenia." *Ps*, 21, 1958.
"The Importance of Overweight." *JAPA*, 6, 1958.
"Obesity," in *The Pediatric Clinics of North America*. Sau, 1958.
"Transformation of Oral Impulses in Eating Disorders; A Conceptual Approach." *PQ*, 35, 1961.

BRUNSWICK, D.
"A Comment on E. Servadio's 'A Presumptive Telepathic-Precognitive Dream During Analysis.'" *IntJPsa*, 38, 1957.
"The Physiological Viewpoint." *IntJPsa*, 41, 1960.

BRUNSWICK, R.
"Die Analyse eines Eifersuchtswahnes." *Z*, 14, 1928.
"A Supplement to Freud's History of an Infantile Neurosis." *IntJPsa*, 9, 1928.
"The Analysis of a Case of Paranoia (Delusions of Jealousy)." *JNMD*, 70, 1929.

"Ein Nachtrag zu Freuds Geschichte einer infantilen Neurose." *Z*, 15, 1929.
"The Pre-Oedipal Phase of the Libido Development." *Q*, 9, 1940.

BRY, T.
"Acting Out in Group Psychotherapy." *IntJgrpPt*, 3, 1953.

BRYAN, C.
"A Slip of the Tongue." *IntJPsa*, 4, 1923.

BUCHENHOLZ, B.
"Pleasure, Preliminary Report of an Investigation." *JNMD*, 123, 1956.

BUNKER, H.
"American Psychiatric Literature During the Past Hundred Years," in *One Hundred Years of American Psychiatry*. CUP, 1944.
"Repression in Pre-Freudian American Psychiatry." *Q*, 14, 1945.
"Psychoanalysis and the Study of Religion." *AnSurvPsa*, 2, 1951.
"Tantalus: A Preoedipal Figure of Myth." *Q*, 22, 1953.

BUNNING, E.
Theoretische Grundfragen der Physiologie. Stuttgart: Piscator Verlag, 1949

BURKAMP, W.
The Causality of the Psychic Process and the Unconscious Regulations of Actions. Springer, 1922.

BURLINGHAM, D.
"Child Analysis and the Mother." *PQ*, 4, 1935.

BURSTEIN, A.
"Primary Process in Children as a Function of Age." *ASP*, 59, 1959.

BUXBAUM, E.
"Exhibitionistic Onanism in a Ten-Year-Old." *Q*, 4, 1935.
"Activity and Aggression in Children." *Ops*, 17, 1947.
"Technique of Child Therapy—A Critical Evaluation." *PsaStC*, 9, 1954.
Report on panel: "The Psychology of Adolescence." *JAPA*, 6, 1958.
"Hair Pulling and Fetishism." *PsaStC*, 15, 1960.

BYCHOWSKI, G.
Psychotherapy of Psychosis. G&S, 1952.
"The Problem of Latent Psychosis." *JAPA*, 1, 1953.
—— M. Klein, S. Nacht, H. Rosenfeld, W. Scott, & E. Zetzel, "Symposium on 'Depressive Illness.'" *IntJPsa*, 41, 1960.
"The Psychoanalysis of the Psychotic Core." Psychiatric Research Report 17, American Psychoanalytic Association, November, 1963.

BYCHOWSKI, G.

"The Ego of Homosexuals." *IntJPsa*, 26, 1945.
"Escapade: A Form of Dissociation." *Q*, 31, 1962.

CALEF, V.

Reporter, "Training and Therapeutic Analysis." *JAPA*, 2, 1954.

CAMERON, N.

"Introjection, Reprojection and Hallucination in the Interaction Between Schizophrenic Patient and Therapist." *IntJPsa*, 42, 1961.

CAMPBELL, C.

"Hallucinations: Their Nature and Significance." *P*, 9, 1929-1930.
"Clinical Studies in Schizophrenia: A Follow-Up Study of a Small Group of Cases of Deterioration With Few Special Trends." *AJP*, 99, 1943.

CANTRIL, H.

The Invasion From Mars. PUP, 1940.

CARP, E.

"Zur Psychoanalytischen Auffassung der Hypochondrie." *ZNP*, 115, 1928.

CARROLL, E.

"Acting Out and Ego Development." *Q*, 23, 1954.

CARUSO, I.

"Über die Symbollehre als Psycho-Somatischer Beitrag zur Erkenntnistheorie." *ZPSM*, 1, 1955.

CASEY, R.

"The Psychoanalytic Study of Religion." *ASP*, 33, 1938.

CASUSO, G.

"Anxiety Related to the 'Discovery' of the Penis: An Observation." *PsaStC*, 12, 1957.

CHRISTOFFEL, H.

"Exhibitionism and Exhibitionists." *IntJPsa*, 17, 1936.
"Male Genital Exhibitionism," in S. Lorand *Perversions: Psychodynamics and Therapy.* RH, 1956.

CLAR, W.

The Psychology of Religion. Mac, 1958.

CLEMENS, J.

Zur Psychologie des Exhibitionismus. VS, 1933.

COHEN, F.

"The Relationship Between Delusional Thinking and Hostility. A Case Study." *PQ*, 30, 1956.

COHEN, N.

"Countertransference and Anxiety." *OutPsa*, 1955.

COLM, H.

"Phobias in Children." *PPR*, 46, 1959.

CORIAT, I.

"A Note on the Medusa Symbolism." *AmIm*, 2, 1941.

CREMERIUS, J.

"Die Bedeutung der Oralität für den Altersdiabetes und die mit ihm verbundenen depressiven Phasen." *P*, 11, 1957.

CROCE, B.

Aesthetic. NP, 1904.

CRONIN, H.

"Phallic Symbolism in a Narcissistic Neurosis." *R*, 20, 1933.

CROWLEY, R.

"Psychoanalytic Literature on Drug Addiction and Alcoholism." *R*, 26, 1939.

CULLINAN, E.

"Ulcerative Colitis: Clinical Aspects." *M*, 2, 1938.

CUSHING, M.

"Psychoanalytic Treatment of Ulcerative Colitis." *BAPA*, 8, 1952.
"The Psychoanalytic Treatment of a Man Suffering With Ulcerative Colitis." *JAPA*, 1, 1953.

CUTLER, R.

"Countertransference Effects in Psychotherapy." *JconsultPsychol*, 22, 1958.

DAI, B.

"Obsessive-Compulsive Disorders in Chinese Culture." *SocProbl*, 4, 1957.

DALLY, P.

—— & W. Sargant, "A New Treatment of Anorexia Nervosa." *BMJ*, 1, 1960

DALMAU, C.

"Post-Oedipal Psychodynamics." *R*, 44, 1957.

DANIELS, G.

"Treatment of Ulcerative Colitis Associated With Hysterical Depression." *PSM*, 2, 1940.

DARWIN, C.

The Expression of the Expression of Emotions in Man and in Animals. Mur, 1873.

DATTNER, B.

"An Historical Slip." *C*, 1, 1911.

DAVIDSON, A.

—— & J. Fay, "Phantasy in Childhood." *JAPA*, 4, 1956.

DAVIDSON, H.
"The Psychosomatic Aspects of Educated Childbirth."
NYSJM, 53, 1953.

DAVIS, H.
"Anorexia Nervosa." *E*, 25, 1939.

DeFOREST, I.
"Love and Anger, Two Activating Forces in Psychoanalytic Therapy." *Ps*, 7, 1944.

DEMARTINO, M.
Dreams and Personality Dynamics. CCT, 1959.

DEMENT, W.
"Dream Recall and Eye Movement During Sleep in
Schizophrenics and Normals." *JNMD*, 122, 1955.

DEMPF, A.
Die Einheit der Wissenschaft. Stuttgart: W. Kohlhammer, 1955.

DESMONDE, W.
"Eros and Mathematics: Some Speculations." *AmIm*,
14, 1957.

DEUTSCH, F.
"Zur Bildung des Konversionsymptoms." *Z*, 10, 1924.
On the Mysterious Leap From the Mind to the Body.
IUP, 1959.

DEUTSCH, H.
"Über die Pathologische Lüge." *Z*, 8, 1922.
"Okkulte Vorgänge während der Psychoanalyse." *Im*,
12, 1926.
"Über Frigidität." *Z*, 15, 1929.
"On Female Homosexuality." *Q*, 1, 1932.
Psychoanalysis of the Neuroses. HPI, 1932.
"Über einen Typus der Pseudoaffektivität." *Z*, 20, 1934.
"A Discussion of Certain Forms of Resistance." *IntJPsa*,
20, 1939.
The Psychology of Women. G&S, 1, 1944.
—— & J. Eisenbud, "Telepathy in Psychoanalytic Treat-
ment." *Tomorrow*, 1, 1953.
"Paper Read at Edward Bibring Memorial." *BML*, 1959.
"Psychoanalytic Therapy in the Light of Follow-Up."
JAPA, 7, 1959.

DEUTSCHE, D.
"A Case of Transvestitism." *PT*, 8, 1954.

DEUTSCHE, F.
—— M. Kaufman, & J. Waller, "Anorexia Nervosa:
A Psychosomatic Entity." *PSM*, 2, 1940.

DEVEREUX, G.
"The Social and Cultural Implications of Incest Among
the Mohave Indians." *Q*, 8, 1939.

"Applied Psychoanalysis: Social Sciences." *AnSurvPsa*,
2, 1951.
(ed), *Psychoanalysis and the Occult.* IUP, 1953.
"Primitive Genital Mutilations in a Neurotic's Dream."
JAPA, 2, 1954.
"Acting Out in Dreams: As a Reaction to a Break-
Through of the Unconscious in a Character Disorder."
PT, 9, 1955.
A Study of Abortion in Primitive Societies. JP, 1955.
"A Primitive Slip of the Tongue." *AnthropQuart*, 30,
1957.
"The Significance of the External Female Genitalia and
of Female Orgasm for the Male." *JAPA*, 6, 1958.

DOLLARD, J.
—— & N. Miller, *Social Learning and Imitation.* YUP,
1941.

DRIESCH, H.
"Bewusstsein und Unterbewusstsein." *Dtschemed-
Wschr*, 48, 1922.

DUDLEY, G.
"A Rare Case of Female Fetishism." *IntJSexol*, 8,
1954.

DUNBAR, F.
Synopsis of Psychosomatic Diagnosis and Treatment.
Mos, 1948.

DUNN, C.
"Anorexis Nervosa." *Lancer*, 1, 1937.

DURKIN, H.
"Acting Out in Group Psychotherapy." *Ops*, 25, 1955.

EDEL, M.
—— & A. Edel, *Anthropology and Ethics.* CCT, 1959.

EHRENWALD, J.
*New Dimensions of Deep Analysis. A Study of Telepathy
in Interpersonal Relationships.* G&S, 1955.

JOKL, R.
"On the Psychogenesis of Writer's Cramp." *Z*, 8, 1922.
"Bemerkung zur Physiologie der in der Hypnose sugge-
rierten Sinneseindrücke." *ZNP*, 1928.
"Die Empfindung Nass und Trocken," in *Zeitschrift für
die gesamte Neurologie und Psychiatrie.* Berlin: Verlag
von Julius Springer, 1928
"The Perception of Wet and Dry." *ZNP*, 3, 1928.
"On the Mechanism of the Imitative Gesture." *JPN*, 46,
1928-1929.
"On the Humiliation of the Love Object." *Z*, 20, 1934.
"A Suggestion for a Comparative Theory of the Neur-
oses." *IntJPsa*, 16, 1935
"The Genesis of Agoraphobia and Writer's Cramp." *Z*,
22, 1936.
"A Contribution to the Study of the Masturbation
Fantasy." *IntJPsa*, 26, 1945.
"A Contribution to the Study of Wit." *R*, 32, 1945.

"Psychoanalysis of a Case of Paranoia." *R*, 32, 1945.

Take Off Your Mask. IUP, 1948.

"In Pursuit of Happiness." *R*, 33, 1951.

"A Contribution to the Study of the Phenomenon of Resistance." *PQ*, 26, 1952.

"A Discussion of Dr. Wexler's Paper ('The Structural Problem in Schizophrenia: The Role of the Internal Object')," in *Psychotherapy With Schizophrenics*, ed. E. B. Brody and F. C. Redlich. IUP, 1952.

"Dynamics and Therapy of Homosexuality." *BAPA*, 8, 1952.

Studies in Psychoanalysis. IUP, 1952.

"Neurosis: a Negative of Perversion?" *Q*, 28, 1954.

An Outline of a Comparative Pathology of the Neurosis. IUP, 1954.

"Analysis of a Case of a Male Homosexual," in *Perversions, Psychodyanmics and Therapy*, ed. S. Lorand & M. Balint, RH, 1956.

"Neurotic Choice of Mate," in *Neurotic Interaction in Marriage*, V. W. Eisenstein, ed. BB, 1956.

"An Introduction to the Study of Narcissistic Mortification." *PQ*, 31, 1957.

"Psychoanalyse einer Psychopathin." *P*, 12, 1958.

"Technical Problems in the Analysis of Masochists." *JHH*, 7, 1958.

"Humiliation in Masochism." *JAPA*, 7, 1959.

"Schizoid Character." *JHH*, 8, 1959.

"A Second Contribution to the Study of the Narcissistic Mortification." *PQ*, 33, 1959.

—— & J. N. Palmer, "Primary and Secondary Narcissism." *PQ*, 34, 1960.

"A Third Contribution to the Study of Slips of the Tongue." *IntJPsa*, 41, 1960.

The Dark Urge, Py, 1961.

"A Contribution to the Study of the Unpleasure-Pleasure Principle." *PQ*, 36, 1962.

"Ein Beitrag zum Studium der asthetischen Lust." *P*, 10, 1962.

EISENBERG, L.

"School Phobia: A Study in the Communication of Anxiety." *P*, 114, 1958.

EISENBERG, S.

"Time and the Oedipus." *Q*, 25, 1956.

EISENBUD, J.

"Analysis of a Presumptively Telepathic Dream," in G. Devereux *Psycho-Analysis and the Occult*. IUP, 1953.

"Behavioral Correspondences to Normally Unpredictable Future Events." *Q*, 23, 1954.

"Time and Oedipus." *Q*, 25, 1956.

EISENSTEIN, V.

(ed), *Neurotic Interaction in Marriage*. BB, 1956.

EISLER, E.

"Regression in a Case of Multiple Phobia." *Q*, 6, 1937.

EISNITZ, A.

"Mirror Dreams." *JAPA*, 9, 1961.

EISSLER, K.

"Some Psychiatric Aspects of Anorexia Nervosa." *R*, 30, 1943.

"Remarks on the Psychoanalysis of Schizophrenia." *AnSurvPsa*, 2, 1951.

"Notes Upon the Emotionality of a Schizophrenic Patient and Its Relation to Problems of Technique." *PsaStC*, 8, 1953.

"Notes Upon Defects of Ego Structure in Schizophrenia." *IntJPsa*, 35, 1954.

"An Unusual Function of an Amnesia." *PsaStC*, 1955.

"Some Comments on Psychoanalysis and Dynamic Psychiatry." *JAPA*, 4, 1956.

"Notes on Problems of Technique in the Psychoanalytic Treatment of Adolescents. With Some Remarks on Perversions." *PsaStC*, 13, 1958.

"The Function of Details in the Interpretation of Works of Literature." *PQ*, 28, 1959.

"Notes on the Environment of a Genius." *PsaStC*, 14, 1959.

"On the Metapsychology of the Preconscious: a Tentative Contribution to Psychoanalytic Morphology." *PsaStC*, 17, 1962.

Goethe, a Psychoanalytic Study. WUP, 1963.

EKMAN, T.

"Phaenomenologisches und Psychoanalytisches zum Problem des Mitleids." *Z*, 26, 1941.

EKSTEIN, R.

"Language of Psychology and of Everyday Life." *PsycholRev*, 49, 1942.

"Termination of the Training Analysis Within the Framework of Present Day Institutes." *JAPA*, 3, 1955.

—— J. Wallerstein, & A. Mandelbaum, "Countertransference in the Residential Treatment of Children; Treatment Failure in a Child with a Symbiotic Psychosis." *PsaStC*, 14, 1959.

ELKISCH, P.

—— & M. Mahler, "On Infantile Precursors of the 'Influencing Machine.'" *PsaStC*, 14, 1959.

ELLIS, H.

Psychology of Sex. GCB, 1954.

ENGEL, G.

"Studies of Ulcerative Colitis. I. Clinical Data Bearing on the Nature of the Somatic Process." *PSM*, 16, 1954.

Psychological Development in Health and Disease. Sau, 1962.

ERIKSEN, C.

"Psychological Defences and 'Ego Strength' in the Recall of Completed and Incompleted Tasks." *ASP*, 49, 1954.

ERIKSON, E.

Childhood and Society. Nor, 1950.
"The Dreams, Specimen of Psychoanalysis." *JAPA*, 2, 1954.
"The Problem of Ego Identity." *JAPA*, 4, 1956.
Identity and the Life Cycle. IUP, 1959.

EVANS, W.

"Evasive Speech as a Form of Resistance." *Q*, 22, 1953.

FAERGEMAN, P.

"Fantasies of Menstruation in Men." *Q*, 24, 1955.

FAIRBAIRN, W.

"A Revised Psychopathology." *IntJPsa*, 22, 1941.
"Endopsychic Structure Considered in Terms of Object Relationships." *IntJPsa*, 25, 1944.
"Object Relationships and Dynamic Structure." *IntJPsa*, 27, 1946.
"Considerations Arising Out of the Schreber Case." *M*, 29, 1956.
"On the Nature and Aims of Psycho-Analysis." *IntJPsa*, 41, 1960.

FALSTEIN, E.

"Juvenile Alcoholism: A Psychodynamic Case Study of Addiction." *Ops*, 23, 1953.

FARRELL, B.

"Morals and Religion." *The Listener*, 21, 1956.

FEDERN, P.

"Die Geschichte einer Melancholia." *Z*, 9, 1923.
"The Ego-Cathexis in Parapraxis." *Im*, 19, 1933.
"The Four Statutes of Compulsive Neurosis." *Z*, 19, 1938.
Ego Psychology and the Psychoses. BB, 1952.
"Ego Psychology and the Psychoses." *AnSurvPsa*, 4, 1953.
"Depersonalization." *RevPsicoanal*, 11, 1954.

FEIGENBAUM, D.

"Analysis of a Case of Paranoia Persecutoria: Structure and Cure." *R*, 17, 1930.
"Notes on the Theory of Libidinal Types." *Q*, 1, 1932.
"On Projection." *Q*, 5, 1936.
"Depersonalization as a Defence Mechanism." *RevPsicoanal*, 11, 1954.

FELDMAN, A.

"Zola and the Riddle of Sadism." *AmIm*, 13, 1956.

FELDMAN, H.

"The Illusion of Work." *R*, 42, 1955.

FELDMAN, S.

"On Blushing." *PQ*, 15, 1941.
"Mannerisms of Speech; a Contribution to the Working Through Process." *Q*, 17, 1948.
"Contributions to the Interpretation of a Typical Dream: Finding Money." *AnSurvPsa*, 3, 1952.
"A Syndrome Indicative of Repressed Oral Aggression." *Samiksa*, 7, 1953.
"Crying at the Happy Ending." *JAPA*, 4, 1956.
"Blanket Interpretation." *PQ*, 27, 1958.
Mannerisms of Speech and Gestures in Everyday Life. IUP, 1959.
"Blushing, Fear of Blushing, and Shame." *JAPA*, 10, 1962.

FENICHEL, O.

"Hysterien und Zwangsneurosen Psychoanalytische Spezielle Neurosenlehre." *IntPV*, 19, 1931.
"Perversionen, Psychosen, Charakterstörungen." *IntPV*, 19, 1931.
"The Scoptophilic Instinct and Identification." *IntJPsa*, 18, 1937.
"Zur Oekonomie der Pseudologica Phantastica." *Z*, 24, 1939.
"Psychoanalysis of Anti-Semitism." *AmIm*, 1, 1940.
The Psychoanalytic Theory of Neurosis. Nor, 1945.
"A Contribution to the Psychology of Jealousy." *OF-CP*, 1, 1953.
"Defense Against Anxiety, Particularly by Libidinization." *OF-CP*, 1953.
"On the Psychology of Boredom." *OF-CP*, 1953.
"Organ Libidinization Accompanying the Defense Against Drives." *OF-CP*, 1, 1953.
"Respiratory Introjection." *OF-CP*, 1953.
"The Counterphobic Attitude." *OF-CP*, 1954.

FERBER, L.

Report on Panel: "Phobias and Their Vicissitudes." *JAPA*, 7, 1959.

FERENCZI, S.

1908, "The Analytic Interpretation and Treatment of Psychosexual Impotence." *SPsa*, 1916.
1909, "Introjection and Transference." *SPsa*, 1916.
1911, "On Obscene Words." *SPsa*, 1916.
"Goethe über den Realitätschwert der Phantasie beim Dichter." *C*, 1912.
1912, "On the Part Played by Homosexuality in the Pathogenesis of Paranoia." *SPsa*, 1916.
1912, "Transitory Symptom-Constructions During the Analysis." *SPsa*, 1916.
"Lachen." *BaustPsa*, 4, 1913.
1913, "Stages in the Development of the Sense of Reality." *SPsa*, 1916.
1914, "The Ontogenesis of the Interest in Money." *SPsa*, 1916.
Sex in Psycho-Analysis. GP, 1916.
"Denken und Muskelinnervation." *Z*, 1919.
"Die Nacktheit als Schreckmittel." *Z*, 1919.
1919, "Sunday Neuroses." *SPF*, 2, 1950.
1921, "Weiterer Ausbau der aktiven Technik." *Z*, 7, 1921.
—— & O. Rank, *The Development of Psychoanalysis.* NMDP, 1925.

1925, "Psychoanalysis of Sexual Habits," in *Further Contributions to the Theory and Technique of Psychoanalysis*. HPI, 1926.
"Bausteine für Psychoanalyse." *IntPV*, 1927.
"The Principles of Relaxation and Neocatharsis." *SPF*, 3, 1930.
"Geburt des Intellekts." *BaustPsa*, 1931.
"Autoplastic and Alloplastic Adaptation." *IntJPsa*, 30, 1949.
Further Contributions to the Theory and Technique of Psychoanalysis. HPI, 1950.
"Stages in the Development of the Sense of Reality." *SPsa*, 1950.
Psychoanalysis of Sexual Habits. BB, 1952.

FESSLER, L.

A Case of Post-Traumatic Transvestitism. AP, 1934.

FEUER, L.

Psychoanalysis and Ethics. CCT, 1955

FIERZ-MONNIER, H.

"Methodik und Technik in der Praxis der Analytischen Psychologie." *P*, 8, 1954.

FINE, R.

Freud: A Critical Re-Evaluation of His Theories. DM, 1962.

FINK, H.

"Sexual Taboos in Modern Marriage." *Realife Guide*, 1, 1957.
"Momism and Incest." *Realife Guide*, 2, 1959.

FISCHLE-CARL, H.

"Tagträume und Wachphantasien." *Al*, 1957.
"Zur Behandlung der Paranoia." *Al*, 1958.

FISHER, C.

—— & I. Paul, "The Effects of Subliminal Visual Stimulation on Images and Dreams: A Validation Study." *JAPA*, 7, 1959.
"Psychosomatic Medicine." *ProgNeurolPsychiat*, 11, 1956.
"Dreams, Images and Perceptions. A Study of Unconscious-Preconscious Relationships." *JAPA*, 4, 1956.

FISHER, S.

"Body Image and Asymmetry of Body Reactivity." *ASP*, 57, 1958.

FLEMING, J.

"Observations on the Defences Against a Transference Neurosis." *Ps*, 9, 1946.

FLIESS, R.

"Metapsychology of the Analyst." *Q*, 1942.
"Countertransference and Counteridentification." *JAPA*, 1, 1953.
The Revival of Interest in the Dream. IUP, 1953.

"The *Déjà Raconté:* A Transference-Delusion Concerning the Castration Complex." *Q*, 25, 1956.
"Phylogenetic versus Ontogenetic Experience. Notes on a Passage of Dialogue Between 'Little Hans' and His Father." *IntJPsa*, 37, 1956.

FLUGEL, I.

"The Death-Instinct, Homeostasis, and Allied Concepts." *IntJPsa*, 1953.

FLUGEL, J.

Man, Morals and Society. IUP, 1945.
"Psychoanalysis and Morals." *YPBsa*, 2, 1946.
"The Taboo of the Bosom." *IntJSexol*, 8, 1955.

FOULKES, S.

—— & E. Anthony, *Group Psychotherapy. The Psycho-Analytic Approach*.
"On Introjection." *IntJPsa*, 18, 1937.

FOWLER, H.

A Dictionary of Modern English Usage. Revised by Ernest Gower. LCP, 1965.

FOX, H.

"Body Image of a Photographer." *JAPA*, 5, 1957.
"Effects of Psychophysiological Research on the Transference." *JAPA*, 6, 1958.
"Narcissistic Defenses During Pregnancy." *Q*, 27, 1958.
"The Theory of the Conversion Process." *JAPA*, 7, 1959.

FRAIBERG, S.

"A Critical Neurosis in a Two-and-a-Half Year Old Girl." *PsaStC*, 7, 1952.
"On the Sleep Disturbances of Early Childhood." *RevPsychoanal*, 15, 1958.

FRANK, G.

"The Literature on Countertransference: A Survey." *IntJgrPt*, 3, 1953.

FRANK, J.

"Treatment Approach to Acting-Out Character Disorders." *JHH*, 8, 1959.

FREEDMAN, A.

"Observations in the Phallic Stage." *BPAP*, 4, 1954.
"Countertransference Abuse of Analytic Rules." *BPAP*, 6, 1956.
"The Feeling of Nostalgia and Its Relationship to Phobia." *BPAP*, 6, 1956.

FREEMAN, L.

Fight Against Fears. Crown, 1951.

FRENCH, T.

"Defense and Synthesis in the Function of the Ego. Some Observations Stimulated by Anna Freud's *The Ego and the Mechanisms of Defense*." *Q*, 7, 1938.

FRENKEL-BRUNSWIK, E.

"Social Tensions and the Inhibitions of Thought." *SocProbl*, 2, 1954.

FREUD, A.

"The Relation of Beating Phantasies to a Day Dream." *IntJPsa*, 4, 1923.

Introduction to the Technique of Child Analysis. NMDP, 1928.

"Psychoanalysis of Children," in C. Murchison, *Handbook of Child Psychology.* Cl, 1931.

"Indications for Child Analysis." *PsaStC*, 1, 1945.

The Ego and the Mechanisms of Defense. IUP, 1946.

"Aggression in Relation to Emotional Development: Normal and Pathological." *PsaStC*, 3–4, 1949.

"Certain Types and Stages of Social Maladjustment." *YBPsa*, 5, 1949.

"Clinical Observations on the Treatment of Manifest Male Homosexuality." *Q*, 20, 1951.

"An Experiment in Group Upbringing." *PsaStC*, 6, 1951.

"A Connection Between the States of Negativism and of Emotional Surrender." *IntJPsa*, 33, 1952.

"The Mutual Influences in the Development of Ego and Id: Introduction to the Discussion." *PsaStC*, 7, 1952.

"Some Remarks on Infant Observation." *PsaStC*, 8, 1953.

"The Problem of Aggression, of Its Relation to Normal and Pathological Development." *Harefuah*, 50, 1956.

"Adolescence." *PsaStC*, 13, 1958.

"Discussion of Dr. John Bowlby's Paper." *PsaStC*, 15, 1960.

FREUD, S.

1891, "Aphasie," in A. Villaret, *Handwörterbuch der Gesamten Medizin.* Stuttgart: Enke, 1, 1888–1891.

1893–1895, "Studies on Hysteria." *SE*, 2, 1955.

1893, "On the Psychical Mechanism of Hysterical Phenomena: A Lecture." *SE*, 3, 1962.

1894, "The Neuro-Psychoses of Defence." *SE*, 3, 1962.

1895, "Obsessions and Phobias: Their Psychical Mechanism and Their Aetiology." *SE*, 3, 1962.

1895, "On the Grounds for Detaching a Particular Syndrome from Neurasthenia Under the Description 'Anxiety Neurosis.'" *SE*, 3, 1962.

1895, "A Reply to Criticisms of My Paper on Anxiety Neurosis." *SE*, 3, 1962.

1896, "The Aetiology of Hysteria." *SE*, 3, 1962.

1896, "Further Remarks on the Neuro-Psychoses of Defence." *SE*, 3, 1962.

1896, "Heredity and the Aetiology of the Neuroses." *SE*, 3, 1962.

1897, "Abstracts of the Scientific Writings of Dr. Sigmund Freud." *SE*, 3, 1962.

1898, "The Psychical Mechanism of Forgetfulness." *SE*, 3, 1962.

1898, "Sexuality in the Aetiology of the Neuroses." *SE*, 3, 1962.

1899, "Screen Memories." *SE*, 3, 1962.

1900, "The Interpretation of Dreams." *SE*, 4–5, 1953.

1901, "Autobiographical Note." *SE*, 3, 1962.

1901, "The Psychopathology of Everyday Life." *SE*, 6, 1960.

1904, "Freud's Psycho-Analytic Procedure." *SE*, 7, 1953.

1905, "Fragment of an Analysis of a Case of Hysteria." *SE*, 7, 1953.

1905, "Jokes and Their Relation to the Unconscious." *SE*, 8, 1960.

1905, "Psychical (or Mental) Treatment." *SE*, 7, 1953.

1905, "Psychopathic Characters on the Stage." *SE*, 7, 1953.

1905, "On Psychotherapy." *SE*, 7, 1953.

1905, "Three Essays on the Theory of Sexuality." *SE*, 7, 1953.

1906, "Preface to Freud's Shorter Writings." *SE*, 3, 1962.

1906, "My Views on the Part Played by Sexuality in the Aetiology of the Neuroses." *SE*, 7, 1953.

1906, "Psycho-Analysis and the Establishment of the Facts in Legal Proceedings." *SE*, 9, 1959.

1907, "Delusions and Dreams in Jensen's Gradiva." *SE*, 9, 1959.

1907, "Obsessive Actions and Religious Practices." *SE*, 9, 1959.

1907, "The Sexual Enlightenment of Children." *SE*, 9, 1959.

1908, "Character and Anal Erotism." *SE*, 9, 1959.

1908, "Civilized Sexual Morality and Modern Nervous Illness." *SE*, 9, 1959.

1908, "Creative Writers and Day-Dreaming." *SE*, 9, 1959.

1908, "Hysterical Phantasies and Their Relation to Bisexuality." *SE*, 9, 1959.

1908, "On the Sexual Theories of Children." *SE*, 9, 1959.

1909, "Analysis of a Phobia in a Five-Year-Old Boy." *SE*, 10, 1955.

1909, "Family Romances." *SE*, 9, 1959

1909, "Notes Upon a Case of Obsessional Neurosis." *SE*, 10, 1955.

1909, "Some General Remarks on Hysterical Attacks." *SE*, 9, 1959.

1910, "The Antithetical Meaning of Primal Words." *SE*, 11, 1957.

1910, "Five Lectures on Psycho-Analysis." *SE*, 11, 1957.

1910, "The Future Prospects of Psycho-Analytic Therapy." *SE*, 11, 1957.

1910, "Leonardo Da Vinci and a Memory of His Childhood." *SE*, 11, 1957

1910, "The Psycho-Analytic View of Psychogenic Disturbances of Vision." *SE*, 11, 1957.

1910, "Shorter Writings." *SE*, 11, 1957.

1910, "A Special Type of Choice of Object Made by Men (Contributions to the Psychology of Love I)." *SE*, 11, 1957.

1910, "'Wild' Psychoanalysis." *SE*, 11, 1957.

1911, "Formulations on the Two Principles of Mental Functioning." *SE*, 12, 1958.

1911, "The Handling of Dream-Interpretation in Psycho-Analysis." *SE*, 12, 1958.

1911, "Psycho-Analytic Notes on an Autobiographical Account of a Case of Paranoia (Dementia Paranoides)." *SE*, 12, 1958.

1911–1915, "Papers on Technique." *SE*, 12, 1958.

1911–1913, "Shorter Writings." *SE*, 12, 1958.

1912, "Contributions to a Discussion on Masturbation." *SE*, 12, 1958.

1912, "The Dynamics of Transference." *SE*, 12, 1958.

1912, "Recommendations to Physicians Practising Psycho-Analysis." *SE*, 12, 1958.

1912, "On the Universal Tendency to Debasement in the Sphere of Love (Contributions to the Psychology of Love II)." *SE*, 11, 1957.

1912, "A Note on the Unconscious in Psycho-Analysis." *SE*, 12, 1958.

1912, "Types of Onset of Neurosis." *SE*, 12, 1958.

1913, "The Claims of Psycho-Analysis to Scientific Interest." *SE*, 13, 1955.

1913, "The Disposition to Obsessional Neurosis." *SE*, 12, 1958.

1913, "An Evidential Dream." *SE*, 12, 1958.

1913, "Introduction to Pfister's *The Psycho-Analytic Method*." *SE*, 12, 1958.

1913, "Observations and Examples from Analytic Practice." *SE*, 13, 1955.

1913, "The Occurrence in Dreams of Material from Fairy Tales." *SE*, 12, 1958.

1913, "Preface to Bourke's Scatologic Rites of All Nations." *SE*, 12, 1958.

1913, "On Psycho-Analysis." *SE*, 12, 1958.

1913, "The Theme of the Three Caskets." *SE*, 12, 1958.

1913, "Totem and Taboo." *SE*, 13, 1955.

1913, "Two Lies Told By Children." *SE*, 12, 1958.

1914, "Fausse Reconnaissance ('Déjà Raconté') in Psycho-Analytic Treatment." *SE*, 13, 1955.

1914, "The Moses of Michelangelo." *SE*, 13, 1955.

1914, "Observations on Transference-Love (Further Recommendations on the Technique of Psycho-Analysis III)." *SE*, 12, 1958.

1914, "On the History of the Psycho-Analytic Movement." *SE*, 14, 1957.

1914, "On Narcissism: An Introduction." *SE*, 14, 1957.

1914, "Remembering, Repeating and Working Through (Further Recommendations on the Technique of Psycho-Analysis II)." *SE*, 12, 1958.

1914, "Some Reflections on Schoolboy Psychology." *SE*, 13, 1955.

1915, "A Case of Paranoia Running Counter to the Psycho-Analytic Theory of the Disease." *SE*, 14, 1957.

1915, "Instincts and Their Vicissitudes." *SE*, 14, 1957.

1915, "On Transience." *SE*, 14, 1957.

1915, "Papers on Metapsychology." *SE*, 14, 1957.

1915, "Repression." *SE*, 14, 1957.

1915, "Thoughts for the Times on War and Death." *SE*, 14, 1957.

1915, "The Unconscious." *SE*, 14, 1957.

1916, "Part II. Dreams." *SE*, 15, 1963.

1916, "Part I. Parapraxes." *SE*, 15, 1963.

1916, "Shorter Writings." *SE*, 14, 1957.

1916, "Some Character Types Met with in Psychoanalytic Work." *SE*, 14, 1957.

1917, "A Childhood Recollection from *Dichtung und Wahrheit*." *SE*, 17, 1955.

1917, "A Difficulty in the Path of Psycho-Analysis." *SE*, 17, 1955.

1917, "Part III. General Theory of the Neuroses." *SE*, 16, 1963.

1917, "A Metapsychological Supplement to the Theory of Dreams." *SE*, 14, 1957.

1917, "Mourning and Melancholia." *SE*, 14, 1957.

1917, "Introductory Lectures on Psycho-Analysis." *SE*, 15, 1963.

1917, "Transformation of Instinct as Exemplified in Anal Erotism." *SE*, 17, 1955.

1918, "From the History of an Infantile Neurosis." *SE*, 17, 1955.

1918, "The Taboo of Virginity (Contributions to the Psychology of Love III)." *SE*, 11, 1957.

1919, "A Child Is Being Beaten: A Contribution to the Study of the Origin of Sexual Perversions." *SE*, 17, 1955.

1919, "Introduction to Psycho-Analysis and the War Neuroses." *SE*, 17, 1955.

1919, "Lines of Advance in Psycho-Analytic Therapy." *SE*, 17, 1955.

1919, "On the Teaching of Psycho-Analysis in Universities." *SE*, 17, 1955.

1919, "Preface to Reik's Ritual: Psycho-Analytic Studies." *SE*, 17, 1955.

1919, "Shorter Writings." *SE*, 17, 1955.

1919, "The 'Uncanny.'" *SE*, 17, 1955.

1920, "Beyond the Pleasure Principle." *SE*, 18, 1955.

1920, "The Psychogenesis of a Case of Homosexuality in a Woman." *SE*, 18, 1955.

1920–1922, "Shorter Writings." *SE*, 18, 1955.

1921, "Group Psychology and the Analysis of the Ego." *SE*, 18, 1955.

1921, "Psycho-Analysis and Telepathy." *SE*, 18, 1955.

1922, "Dreams and Telepathy." *SE*, 18, 1955.

1922, "Some Neurotic Mechanisms in Jealousy, Paranoia and Homosexuality." *SE*, 18, 1955.

1922–1925, "Shorter Writings." *SE*, 19, 1961.

1923, "Dr. Sandor Ferenczi (On His 50th Birthday)." *SE*, 19, 1961.

1923, "The Ego and the Id." *SE*, 19, 1961.

1923, "The Infantile Genital Organization: An Interpolation into the Theory of Sexuality." *SE*, 19, 1961.

1923, "Josef Popper-Lynkeus and the Theory of Dreams." *SE*, 19, 1961.

1923, "Remarks on the Theory and Practice of Dream-Interpretation." *SE*, 19, 1961.

1923, "A Seventeenth-Century Demonological Neurosis." *SE*, 19, 1961.

1923, "Two Encyclopedia Articles." *SE*, 18, 1955.

1924, "The Dissolution of the Oedipus Complex." *SE*, 19, 1961.

1924, "The Economic Problem of Masochism." *SE*, 19, 1961.

1924, "The Loss of Reality in Neurosis and Psychosis." *SE*, 19, 1961.

1924, "Neurosis and Psychosis." *SE*, 19, 1961.

1924, "The Resistances to Psycho-Analysis." *SE*, 19, 1961.

1924, "A Short Account of Psycho-Analysis." *SE*, 19, 1961.

1925, "An Autobiographical Study." *SE*, 20, 1959.

1925, "Josef Breuer." *SE*, 19, 1961.

1925, "Negation." *SE*, 19, 1961.

1925, "A Note Upon the 'Mystic Writing-Pad.'" *SE*, 19, 1961.

1925, "Preface to Aichorn's Wayward Youth." *SE*, 19, 1961.

1925, "Some Additional Notes on Dream-Interpretation as a Whole." *SE*, 19, 1961.

1925, "Some Psychical Consequences of the Anatomical Distinction Between the Sexes." *SE*, 19, 1961.

1926, "Address to the Society of B'Nai B'rith." *SE*, 20, 1959.

1926, "Inhibitions, Symptoms and Anxiety." *SE*, 20, 1959.

1926, "The Question of Lay Analysis." *SE*, 20, 1959.

1926, "Psycho-Analysis." *SE*, 20, 1959.

1926, "Shorter Writings." *SE*, 20–21, 1959.

1927, "Fetishism." *SE*, 21, 1961.

1927, "The Future of an Illusion." *SE*, 21, 1961.

1927, "Humour." *SE*, 21, 1961.

1928, "Dostoyevsky and Parricide." *SE*, 21, 1961.

1928, "A Religious Experience." *SE*, 21, 1961.

1929, "Some Dreams of Descartes: A Letter to Maxime Leroy." *SE*, 21, 1961.

1930, "Civilization and Its Discontents." *SE*, 21, 1961.

1930, "The Goethe Prize." *SE*, 21, 1961.

1931, "Female Sexuality." *SE*, 21, 1961.

1931, "Libidinal Types." *SE*, 21, 1961.

1931–1936, "Shorter Writings." *SE*, 22, 1964.

1932, "The Acquisition and Control of Fire." *SE*, 22, 1964.

1932, "My Contact with Josef Popper-Lynkeus." *SE*, 22, 1964.

1933, "New Introductory Lectures on Psycho-Analysis." *SE*, 22, 1964.

1933, "Sandor Ferenczi." *SE*, 22, 1964.

1933, "Why War?" *SE*, 22, 1964.

1935, "The Subtleties of a Faulty Action." *SE*, 22, 1964.

1936, "A Disturbance of Memory on the Acropolis." *SE*, 22, 1964.

1937, "Analysis Terminable and Interminable." *SE*, 23, 1964.

1937, "Constructions in Analysis." *SE*, 23, 1964.

1937–1938, "Shorter Writings." *SE*, 23, 1964.

1938, "A Comment on Anti-Semitism." *SE*, 23, 1964.

1939, "Moses and Monotheism." *SE*, 23, 1964.

1940, "An Outline of Psycho-Analysis." *SE*, 23, 1964.

1940, "Splitting of the Ego in the Process of Defence." *SE*, 23, 1964.

Psychoanalysis and Faith: Dialogues with the Reverend Oscar Pfister. BB, 1963.

FREUND, H.

"Psychopathological Aspects of Stuttering." *PT*, 7, 1953.

FRIEDEMANN, M.

"Anagoge, Übertragungsträume." *PtPrx*, 2, 1935.

FRIEDJUNG, J.

"Ein Beispiel einer kindlichen Phobie." *C*, 2, 1912.

FRIEDMAN, L.

"Defensive Aspects in Orality." *IntJPsa*, 34, 1953.

"Psychoanalysis and the Foundation of Ethics." *JPhilos*, 53, 1956.

FRIEDMAN, P.

"Sur le Suicide." *RFPsa*, 8, 1935.

FRIEND, M.

"Problems of Early Ego Development (Panel)." *AnSurvPsa*, 2, 1951.

—— L. Schiddel, B. Klein, & D. Dunaeff, "Observations on the Development of Transvestitism in Boys." *Ops*, 24, 1954.

FRIES, M.

"Psychosomatic Relationships Between Mother and Infant." *PSM*, 6, 1944.

—— & P. Woolf, "Some Hypotheses on the Role of the Congenital Activity Type in Personality Development." *PsaStC*, 8, 1953.

"Some Factors in the Development and Significance of Early Object Relationships." *JAPA*, 9, 1961.

FROMM, E.

"Faith as a Character Trait." *Ps*, 5, 1942.

The Forgotten Language: An Introduction to the Understanding of Dreams, Fairy Tales and Myths. G, 1957.

FROMM-REICHMANN, F.

"Psychoanalytic Psychotherapy with Psychotics. The Influence of the Modification in Technique on Present Trends in Psychoanalysis." *Ps*, 6, 1943.

"Basic Problems in the Psychotherapy of Schizophrenia." *Ps*, 21, 1958.

FROSCH, J.

"Special Problems of Psychoanalytic Therapy." *AnSurvPsa*, 1, 1950.

—— & B. Wortis, "Contribution to the Nosology of Impulse Disorders." *AJP*, 3, 1954.

"Transference Derivatives of the Family Romance." *JAPA*, 7, 1959.

FRUMKES, G.

"Impairment of the Sense of Reality as Manifested in Psychoneurosis and Everyday Life." *IntJPsa*, 34, 1953.

FUCHS, E.

"Neid und Fressgier." *PsaP*, 7, 1933.

FURRER, A.
"Eine Indirekte Kinderanalyse." *PsaP*, 3, 1929.

GAINES, C.
"Psychoanalysis and Faith." *NAmerRev*, 219, 1924.

GARDINER, M.
"A Letter From the Wolf-Man." *BPAP*, 3, 1953.
"A Fleeting Phobia in a Girl of Three." *BPAP*, 4, 1954.
"Feminine Masochism and Passivity." *BPAP*, 5, 1955.

GARDNER, G.
"The Therapeutic Process. II. The Therapeutic Process From the Point of View of Psychoanalytic Theory." *Ops*, 22, 1952.
"The Origin and Nature of Aggressive Behavior." *DAM*, 1955.
Report on panel: "Problems in Early Infancy." *JAPA*, 3, 1955.

GARMA, A.
"Vicissitudes of the Dream Screen and the Isakower Phenomenon." *Q*, 24, 1955.
"The Unconscious Images in the Genesis of Peptic Ulcer." *IntJPsa*, 4–5, 1960.

GARTNER, P.
"Analytische Deutung einer 'Flucht in die Gesundheit'." *PsaPrx*, 1, 1931.

GAUPP, R.
"Zur Lehre von der Paranoia." *Nervenarzt*, 4, 1947.

GELEERD, E.
"The Analysis of a Case of Compulsive Masturbation in a Child." *Q*, 12, 1943.
"Mothering, Feeding and Toilet Training in Infants." *BMC*, 8, 1944.
"A Contribution to the Problem of Psychoses in Childhood." *PsaStC*, 2, 1946.

GERARD, D.
"Intoxication and Addiction. Psychiatric Observations on Alcoholism and Opiate Drug Addiction." *QJSA*, 16, 1955.

GERARD, M.
"Child Analysis as a Technique in the Investigation of Mental Mechanisms. Illustrated by a Study of Enuresis." *P*, 94, 1937.
"The Psychogenic Tic in Ego Development." *PsaStC*, 2, 1946.

GERARD, R.
"The Biology of Ethics," in I. Galdston, *Society and Medicine*. IUP, 1955.

GERO, G.
"Zum Problem der Oralen Fixierung." *Z*, 24, 1939.
"An Equivalent of Depressional Anorexia," in P. Greenacre, *Affective Disorders*. IUP, 1953.

Gero, G. & L. Rubinfine, "On Obsessive Thoughts." *JAPA*, 3, 1955.
"Sadism, Masochism and Aggression: Their Role in Symptom Formation." *Q*, 31, 1962.

GERO-HEYMANN, E.
"A Short Communication on a Traumatic Episode in a Child of Two Years and Seven Months." *PsaStC*, 10, 1955.

GERSON, A.
"Über den Selbstmord." *ArchKrimin*, 76, 1924.

GESSMANN
"Das Problem der Überwertigkeit." *ZNP*, 64, 1921.

GILL, M.
—— & M. Brenman, *Hypnosis and Related States*. IUP, 1959.
Topography and Systems in Psychoanalytic Theory. IUP, 1963.

GILLESPIE, W.
"The General Theory of Sexual Perversion." *IntJPsa*, 37, 1956.
"The Structure and Aetiology of Sexual Perversion," in S. Lorand, *Perversions: Psychodynamics and Therapy*. RH, 1956.

GILMAN, L.
"Insomnia in Relation to Guilt, Fear, and Masochistic Intent." *ClinPath*, 11, 1950.
Insomnia and Its Relation to Dreams. L, 1958.

GINSBURG, S.
"Concerning Religion and Psychiatry." *Child Study*, 30, 1953.

GIOVACCHINI, P.
"Resistance and External Object Relations." *IntJPsa*, 42, 1961.

GITELSON, M.
"On Ego Distortion." *IntJPsa*, 29, 1958.

GLATZER, H.
"Handling Transference Resistance in Group Therapy." *R*, 40, 1953.
"Acting Out in Group Psychotherapy." *PT*, 12, 1958.
"Analysis of Masochism in Group Psychotherapy." *IntJgrPt*, 9, 1959.
"Notes on the Preoedipal Phantasy." *Ops*, 29, 1959.

GLAUBER, I.
"Freud's Contributions on Stuttering: Their Relation to Some Current Insights." *JAPA*, 6, 1958.

GLAUBER, P.
"Observations on a Primary Form of Anhedonia." *PQ*, 18, 1949.

GLICKSBERG, C.
"Depersonalization in the Modern Drama." *The Personalist*, 39, 1958.

GLOVER, E.
"Notes on Oral Character Formation." *IntJPsa*, 6, 1925.
"On Child Analysis (Symposium Contribution)." *IntJPsa*, 8, 1927.
"The Etiology of Alcoholism." *ProcRSM*, 21, 1928
"Common Problems of Psychoanalysis and Anthropology." *Man*, 32, 1932.
"A Note on Idealization." *IntJPsa*, 19, 1938.
"The Psychoanalysis of Affects." *IntJPsa*, 20, 1939.
The Psycho-Pathology of Prostitution. London: Institute for the Scientific Treatment of Delinquency, 1945.
Psychoanalysis. SP, 1949.
Freud or Jung. AU, 1950.
"Therapeutic Criteria of Psycho-Analysis." *IntJPsa*, 35, 1954.
The Technique of Psychoanalysis. IUP, 1955.
On Early Development of the Mind. IUP, 1956.
Selected Papers on Psychoanalysis. IUP, 1956.

GLUECK, B.
"The Ego Instinct (Symposium on the Relative Roles in Psychopathology of the Ego, Herd and Sex Instincts)." *JAbP*, 16, 1921.

GOERRES, A.
"Die Technik der Psychoanalyse." *P*, 9, 1955–1956.

GOJA, H.
"Halluzinationen eines Sterbenden." *Z*, 6, 1920.

GOLDFARB, W.
"The Significance of Ambivalency for Schizophrenic Dissociations." *JclinPsychopath*, 6, 1944.

GOLDSTEIN, K.
"Zum Problem der Angst." *ZPt*, 2, 1929.

GOLPERT, H.
"Der Traum als Ausdruck." *Nervenarzt*, 20, 1949.

GORDEN, L.
"Incest as Revenge Against the Pre-Oedipal Mother." *R* 42, 1955.

GORDEON, R.
"The Phenomenon of Abreaction." *JNP*, 3, 1923.

GORDON, A.
"Obsessive Hallucinations and Psychoanalysis." *JAbP*, 12, 1917.
"Illusion of 'The Already Seen' (Paramnesia) and of 'The Never Seen' (Agnosia)." *JAbP*, 15, 1920.

GOTTESMAN, A.
"The Preoedipal Attachment to the Mother; A Clinical Study." *IntJPsa*, 39, 1958.

GRABER, G.
"Onanie und Kastration." *PsaP*, 2, 1927–1928.
"Die Widerstandsanalyse und ihre therapeutischen Ergebnisse." *ZPt*, 11, 1939.

GRANT, V.
"A Case Study of Fetishism." *ASP*, 48, 1953.
"Paranoid Dynamics. A Case Study." *P*, 113, 1956.

GRAUER, D.
"How Autonomous is the Ego?" *JAPA*, 6, 1958.

GRAVES, R.
Adam's Rib. New York: Thomas Yoseloff, 1955.

GREEN, G.
The Daydream, a Study in Development. ULP, 1923.

GREENACRE, P.
"The Eye Motif in Delusion and Fantasy." *P*, 5, 1926.
"The Predisposition to Anxiety." *Q*, 10, 1941.
"Conscience in the Psychopath." *Ops*, 15, 1945.
"The Biological Economy of Birth." *PsaStC*, 1, 1946.
"Special Problems of Early Female Sexual Development." *PsaStC*, 5, 1950.
"Respiratory Incorporation and the Phallic Phase." *PsaStC*, 6, 1951.
(ed), *Affective Disorders: Psychoanalytic Contributions to Their Study*. IUP, 1953.
"Certain Relationships Between Fetishism and Faulty Development of the Body Image." *PsaStC*, 8, 1953.
"Fetishism and Body Image." *PsaStC*, 8, 1953.
"Further Considerations Regarding Fetishism." *PsaStC*, 10, 1955.
Swift and Carroll: A Psychoanalytic Study of Two Lives. IUP, 1955.
"Re-Evaluation of the Process of Working Through." *IntJPsa*, 37, 1956.
"The Childhood of the Artist." *PsaStC*, 12, 1957.
"Early Physical Determinants in the Development of the Sense of Identity." *JAPA*, 6, 1958.
"The Relation of the Impostor to the Artist." *PsaStC*, 13, 1958.
"Play in Relation to Creative Imagination." *PsaStC*, 14, 1959.
"Further Notes on Fetishism." *PsaStC*, 15, 1960.
"Regression and Fixation? Considerations Concerning the Development of the Ego." *JAPA*, 8, 1960.

GREENSCHPOON, R.
"A Famous Case of Compulsive Neuroses." *R*, 24, 1937.

GREENSON, R.
"On Boredom." *JAPA*, 1, 1953.
"Forepleasure: Its Use for Defensive Purposes." *JAPA*, 3, 1955.
"Phobia, Anxiety and Depression." *JAPA*, 7, 1959.
"Empathy and Its Vicissitudes." *IntJPsa*, 41, 1960.

GREGORY, J.

"The Dream of Frustrated Effort." *P*, 4, 1923.
"The Nature of Laughter." *P*, 4, 1923.

GREIG, A.

"Child Analysis." *Q*, 10, 1941.

GRIEG, J.

The Psychology of Laughter and Comedy. D, 1923.

GRINBERG, L.

"Aspectos magicos en la transferencia y contratransferencia. Identificacion y contra-identificacion proyectivas." *RPsi*, 15, 1958.
"On A Specific Aspect of Countertransference due to the Patient's Projective Identification." *IntJPsa*, 43, 1962.

GRINKER, R.

"A Comparison of Psychological 'Repression' and Neurological 'Inhibition.'" *JNMD*, 89, 1939.
—— & J. Spiegel, *Men Under Stress*. Bl, 1945.
"War Neuroses or Battle Fatigue." *JNMD*, 101, 1945.
"Brief Psychotherapy in Psychosomatic Problems." *PSM*, 9, 1947.

GROEN, J.

"Der Symbolisierungszwang." *Im*, 8, 1922.
"Psychosomatische Forschung als Erforschung des Es." *P*, 4, 1951.

GROSS, O.

"Zur Differentialdiagnostik Negativistischer Phänomene." *PNW*, 37, 1904.
"Die Affektlage der Ablehnung." *MPN*, 32, 1912.

GROTJAHN, M.

"The Process of Awakening." *R*, 29, 1942.
"Psychoanalytic Contributions to Psychosomatic Medicine—A Bibliography." *PSM*, 6, 1944.
"Transvestite Fantasy Expressed in a Drawing." *Q*, 17, 1948.
Beyond Laughter. Bl, 1957.

GUNTRIP, H.

Personality Structure and Human Interaction. The Development Synthesis of Psychodynamic Theory. IUP, 1961.

HAAS, W.

"Über Echtheit und Unechtheit von Gefühlen." *ZPsychopath*, 2, 1914.

HADLEY, E.

"The Origin of the Incest Taboo." *R*, 14, 1927.

HALL, G.

"Thanatosphobia and Immortality." *AJP*, 25, 1915.

HANFMANN, E.

"Analysis of the Thinking Disorder in a Case of Schizophrenia." *ANP*, 41, 1939.

HARLEY, M.

"Some Observations on the Relationship Between Genitality and Structural Development at Adolescence." *JAPA*, 9, 1961.
"The Role of the Dream in the Analysis of a Latency Child." *JAPA*, 10, 1962.

HARNIK, J.

"Nachtrag zur Kenntnis der Rettungsphantasie bei Göthe." *Z*, 5, 1919.
"Die Mitwirkung des Ichs in der Psychogenese der Giftsucht — und was daraus für die Therapie folgt." *ZPt*, 6, 1933.

HARRIS, I.

"Typical Anxiety Dreams and Object Relations." *IntJPsa*, 41, 1960.

HARRISON, I.

"A Clinical Note on a Dream Followed by Elation." *JAPA*, 8, 1960.

HARRISON, T.

(ed), *Principles of Internal Medicine*. Bl, 1950.

HART, H.

"The Eye in Symbol and Symptom." *R*, 36, 1949.
"Masochism, Passivity and Radicalism." *R*, 39, 1952.

HARTMANN, H.

"Ein Fall von Depersonalization." *ZNP*, 74, 1922.
"Kokainismus und Homosexualität." *ZNP*, 95, 1925.
Die Grundlagen der Psychoanalyse. Leipzig: Thieme, 1927.
"Gedächtnis und Lustprinzip. Untersuchungen an Korsakoffkranken." *ZNP*, 126, 1930.
—— & E. Stengel, "Studien zur Psychologie des induzierten Irreseins." *AP*, 95, 1931.
"Psychoanalysis and Psychology." *PsaT-IUP*, 1944.
—— E. Kris, & R. Loewenstein, "Comments on the Formation of Psychic Structure." *PsaStC*, 2, 1946.
—— E. Kris, & R. Loewenstein, "Notes on the Theory of Aggression." *PsaStC*, 3-4, 1949.
"Comments on the Psychoanalytic Theory of the Ego." *PsaStC*, 1950.
—— & S. Betlheim, "On Parapraxes in the Korsakow Psychosis," in *Organization and Pathology of Thought*. CUP, 1951.
"Contributions to the Metapsychology of Schizophrenia." *PsaStC*, 8, 1953.
"Notes on the Reality Principle." *PsaStC*, 11, 1956.
Ego Psychology and the Problem of Adaptation. IUP, 1958.
—— & R. Loewenstein, "Notes on the Superego," in *The Psychoanalytic Study of the Child*. IUP, 1962.
Essays on Ego Psychology. IUP, 1964.

HARTMANN, M.

Einführung in die allgemeine Biologie. Berlin: Walter de Gruyter & Co., 1956.

HARTMANNS, E. VON
"Law of Associations Guided by Unconscious Purposive Ideas." *Z*, 1, 1913.

HATTINGBERG, H. VON
"Analerotik, Angstlust und Eigensinn." *Z*, 2, 1914.
Über die Liebe: eine ärztliche Wegweisung. Munich: Lehmann, 1936.

HAVENS, L.
"The Placement and Movement of Hallucinations in Space: Phenomenology and Theory." *IntJPsa*, 43, 1962.

HAWKINS, M.
"Psychoanalysis of Children." *BMC*, 4, 1940.

HAYAKAWA, S.
Language in Action. HB, 1939.

HEIDER, F.
"The Function of Economical Description in Perception." *Psych Issues*, 1, 1959.

HEILBRUNN, G.
"Fusion of the Isakower Phenomenon With the Dream Screen." *Q*, 22, 1953.
"The Basic Fear." *JAPA*, 3, 1955.
"Comments on a Common Form of Acting Out." *Q*, 27, 1958.

HEIMAN, M.
(ed), *Psychoanalysis and Social Work.* IUP, 1953.

HEIMANN, P.
"A Contribution to the Problem of Sublimation and Its Relation to the Processes of Internalization." *IntJPsa*, 23, 1942.

HELLWIG, A.
"Zur Psychologie des Aberglaubens." *Zrheinwestphal-Volksk*, 8, 1913.

HENDRICK, I.
"Ego Defense and the Mechanism of Oral Ejection in Schizophrenia: The Psychoanalysis of a Pre-Psychotic Case." *IntJPsa*, 12, 1931.
"The Ego and the Defense Mechanisms: A Review and a Discussion." *R*, 25, 1938.

HERMANN, I.
"Randbemerkungen zum Wiederholungszwang." *Z*, 8, 1922.
"Psychoanalyse und Logik: Individuell-logische Untersuchungen aus der Psychoanalytischen Praxis." *IntPV*, 1924.
"Das Ich und das Denken." *Im*, 15, 1929.

HEYER, G.
"Hypnose und Notzucht." *ZSW*, 15, 1928.
"Die Polarität, ein Grundproblem im Werden und Wesen der Deutschen Psychotherapie." *ZPt*, 7, 1934.
"Erythrophobie." *Hippokrates*, 20, 1949.

HILL, L.
"Anticipation of Arousing Specific Neurotic Feelings in the Psychoanalyst." *AnSurvPsa*, 1951.

HILTNER, S.
"Religion and Psychoanalysis." *R*, 37, 1950.

HINRICHSON, O.
"Über das 'Abreagieren' beim Normalen und bei den Hysterischen." *ZNP*, 16, 1913.

HITSCHMANN, E.
"Paranoia, Homosexualität und Analerotik." *Z*, 1, 1913.
"Diskussion der Laienanalyse." *Z*, 13, 1927.
"Die Zwangsbefürchtung vom Tode des gleichgeschlechtlichen Elternteils." *PsaP*, 5, 1931.
"Psychoanalysis of Compulsion Neuroses." *ZNP*, 1932.
"Freud's Conception of Love." *YBPsa*, 1953.

HOFFER, W.
"Einleitung einer Kinderanalyse." *PsaP*, 9, 1935.
"Diaries of Adolescent Schizophrenics (Hebephrenics)." *PsaStC*, 2, 1946.
"Development of the Body Ego." *PsaStC*, 5, 1950.

HOFSTUTTER, P.
Über eingebildete Schwangerschaft. Vienna: Urban & Schwarzenberg, 1954.

HOLLANDER, M.
"Prostitution, the Body, and Human Relatedness." *IntJPsa*, 42, 1961.

HOLLITSCHER, W.
"The Concept of Rationalization." *IntJPsa*, 20, 1939.

HOLT, R.
"A Critical Examination of Freud's Concept of Bound vs. Free Cathexis." *JAPA*, 10, 1962.

HOOP, J.
"Über die kausalen und verständlichen Zusammenhänge nach Jaspers." *ZNP*, 68, 1921.
"Über Autismus, Dissoziation und Affektive Demenz." *ZNP*, 97, 1925.

HORNEY, K.
"On the Genesis of the Castration Complex in Women." *IntJPsa*, 5, 1924.
"Discussion on Lay Analysis." *IntJPsa*, 8, 1927.
"The Dread of Women." *IntJPsa*, 13, 1932.
New Ways in Psychoanalysis. Nor, 1939.
"Inhibitions in Work." *Ps*, 7, 1947.

HORTON, D.

"The Function of Alcohol in Primitive Societies. A Cross-Cultural Study." *QJSA*, 4, 1943.

HSU, H.

"An Experimental Study of Rationalization." *JAbP*, 44, 1949.

HUG-HELLMUTH, H.

"On Female Masturbation." *C*, 3, 1912.

HYROOP, M.

"The Factor of Omnipotence in the Development of Paranoid Reactions." *PT*, 5, 1951.

INMAN, W.

"A Psycho-Analytical Explanation of Micropsia." *IntJPsa*, 19, 1938.
"Clinical Thought-Reading." *IntJPsa*, 39, 1958.

ISAACS, S.

"Criteria for Interpretation." *IntJPsa*, 20, 1939.
"An Acute Psychotic Anxiety Occurring in a Boy of Four Years." *IntJPsa*, 24, 1943.
"Notes on Metapsychology as Process Theory: Some Comments." *IntJPsa*, 26, 1945.
"The Nature and Function of Phantasy." *IntJPsa*, 29, 1948.

ISAKOWER, O.

"A Contribution to the Pathopsychology of Phenomena Associated With Falling Asleep." *IntJPsa*, 19, 1938.
"On the Exceptional Position of the Auditory Sphere." *IntJPsa*, 20, 1939.
"Spoken Words in Dreams." *Q*, 23, 1954.
"Analyzing Instrument." Minutes of Faculty Meeting, New York Psychoanalytic Institute, November, 20, 1963. Mimeograph Copy.

IVIMEY, M.

"Development in the Concept of Transference." *Ps*, 4, 1944.
"The Narcissistic Type in Psycho-Analysis." *Ps*, 11, 1951.

IZNER, S.

"On the Appearance of Primal Scene Content in Dreams." *JAPA*, 7, 1959.

JACOBSON, E.

"Beitrag zur asozialen Charakterbildung." *Z*, 16, 1930.
"Depression: the Oedipus Conflict in the Development of Depressive Mechanisms." *Q*, 12, 1943.
"The Child's Laughter; Theoretical and Clinical Notes on the Function of the Comic." *PsaStC*, 2, 1946.
"Contribution to the Metapsychology of Cyclothymic Depression," in *Affective Disorders*, P. Greenacre ed. IUP, 1953.
"The Self and the Object World." *PsaStC*, 9, 1954.

"Transference Problems in the Psychoanalytic Treatment of Severely Depressive Patients." *JAPA*, 1954.
"Denial and Repression." *JAPA*, 5, 1957.
"Depersonalization." *JAPA*, 7, 1959.
"The 'Exceptions': An Elaboration of Freud's Character Study." *PsaStC*, 14, 1959.

JARVIS, V.

"Clinical Observations on the Visual Problem in Reading Disability." *PsaStC*, 13, 1958.

JARVIS, W.

"When I Grow Big and You Grow Little." *Q*, 27, 1958.
"Some Effects of Pregnancy and Childbirth on Men." *JAPA*, 10, 1962.

JEKELS, L.

"Analerotik." *Z*, 1, 1913.
"A Case of Slip of the Tongue." *Z*, 1, 1913.
"Eine Tendenziöse Geruchhalluzination." *Z*, 3, 1915.
"Mitleid und Liebe." *Im*, 22, 1936.
—— & E. Bergler, "Instinct Dualism in Dreams." *Q*, 9, 1940.
"A Bioanalytical Contribution to the Problem of Sleep and Wakefulness." *Q*, 14, 1945.
—— & E. Bergler, "Übertragung und Liebe." *Q*, 18, 1949.
"The Psychology of Pity." *SPJ*, 1952.
"On the Psychology of Comedy." *TDR*, 2, 1958.

JELGERSMA, G.

"Projection." *IntJPsa*, 7, 1926.

JELLIFFE, S.

"The Mneme, the Engram and the Unconscious. Richard Semon: His Life and Work." *JNMD*, 57, 1923.

JELLINEK, E.

"Phases of Alcohol Addiction." *QJSA*, 13, 1952.

JOHNSON, A.

—— & S. Szurek, "Collaborative Psychiatric Therapy of Parent-Child Problems." *AmJOrthopsychiat*, 12, 1942.
"Some Etiological Aspects of Repression, Guilt and Hostility." *Q*, 20, 1951.
"Factors in the Etiology of Fixations and Symptom Choice." *Q*, 22, 1953.

JOKL, R.

"Discussion der 'Laienanalyse." *Z*, 13, 1927.
"Der Widerstand gegen die Psychoanalyse." *WMW*, 1, 1930.

JONES, E.

"The Action of Suggestion in Psychotherapy." *JAbP*, 5, 1910–1911.
"An Example of the Literary Use of a Slip of the Tongue." *C*, 1, 1911.
"The Psychopathology of Everyday Life." *PPsa*, 1913.

"Mother-Right and the Sexual Ignorance of Savages."
IntJPsa, 6, 1925.
"Introductory Memoir." *IntJPsa*, 7, 1926.
"Child Analysis." *IntJPsa*, 8, 1927.
"The Early Development of Female Sexuality." *IntJPsa*,
8, 1927.
"The Mantle Symbol." *IntJPsa*, 8, 1927.
"Fear, Guilt and Hate." *IntJPsa*, 10, 1929.
"The Phallic Phase." *IntJPsa*, 14, 1933.
"The Psychopathology of Everyday Life." *PPsa*, 1938.
Papers on Psycho-Analysis. WW, 1948.
"The Phallic Phase." *PPsa*, 1950.
The Life and Work of Sigmund Freud. HPI, 2, 1953.
"Psychoanalysis and Religion." *PsaVkb*, 1957.

JOSEPH, E.

"An Unusual Fantasy of the Manner in Which Babies
Become Boys or Girls." *Q*, 29, 1960.

JUNG, C.

Studies in Word Association (*1910*). New York, 1914.
*Psychology of the Unconscious: A Study of the Trans-
formations and Symbolisms of the Libido.* KP, 1916.
Two Essays on Analytical Psychology. London: Balliere,
Tindall & Cox, 1928.

KAHN, M.

—— & R. Masud, "The Concept of Cumulative Trauma."
PsaStC, 18, 1963.

KANNER, L.

"The Tooth as a Folkloristic Symbol." *R*, 15, 1928.
"Irrelevant and Metaphorical Language in Early Infan-
tile Autism." *P*, 103, 1946.
Child Psychiatry. CCT, 1957.

KANZER, M.

"Repetitive Nightmares After a Battlefield Killing."
PQ, 23, 1949.
—— & S. Tarachow, "Arts and Aesthetics (Part 6)."
AnSurvPsa, 1, 1950.
"Manic-Depressive Psychoses with Paranoid Trends."
IntJPsa, 33, 1952.
"The Transference Neurosis of the Rat Man." *Q*, 21,
1952.
"The Metapsychology of the Hypnotic Dream." *IntJPsa*,
34, 1953.
"Observations on Blank Dreams with Orgasms." *Q*, 23,
1954.
"The Communicative Function of the Dream." *IntJPsa*,
36, 1955.
"Gogol—a Study on Wit and Paranoia." *JAPA*, 3, 1955.
"Acting Out, Sublimation and Reality Testing." *JAPA*,
5, 1957.
"Contemporary Psychoanalytic Views of Aesthetics."
JAPA, 7, 1957.
—— & L. Eidelberg, "The Structural Description of
Pleasure." *IntJPsa*, 41, 1960.

KAPLAN, L.

"Animism and Narcissism (A Psycho-Analytic Study),"
JSP, 1, 1923.

KAPP, R.

"Sensation and Narcissism." *IntJPsa*, 6, 1925.

KARPE, R.

"Die Abstillung als Versagung." *PsaP*, 11, 1937.

KARPMAN, B.

"From the Autobiography of a Liar; Toward the Clarification of the Problem of Psychopathic States." *PQ*,
23, 1949.
"Aggression." *Ops*, 20, 1950.

KASANIN, J.

"Neurotic 'Acting Out' as a Basis for Sexual Promiscuity in Women." *R*, 31, 1944.
"The Psychological Structure of the Obsessive Neuroses." *JNMD*, 99, 1944.

KATAN, M.

"Schreber's Delusion of the End of the World." *Q*, 18,
1949.
"Further Remarks about Schreber's Hallucinations."
IntJPsa, 33, 1952.
"Schreber's Pre-Psychotic Phase." *IntJPsa*, 34, 1953.
"Schreber's Hereafter." *PsaStC*, 14, 1959.

KATZENSTEIN-SUTRO, E.

"Über einen Fall von Pubertätsmagersucht." *Schweiz-
medWschr*, 83, 1953.

KAUFMAN, I.

"Some Etiological Studies of Social Relationships and
Conflict Situations." *JAPA*, 8, 1960.

KAUFMAN, M.

"Projection, Heterosexual and Homosexual." *Q*, 3, 1934.
"Religious Delusions in Schizophrenia." *IntJPsa*, 20,
1939.
"Ill Health as an Expression of Anxiety in a Combat
Unit." *PSM*, 9, 1947.

KEHRER, F.

"Über Hypochondrie." *ZPt*, 2, 1929.

KEISER, S.

"The Fear of Sexual Passivity in the Masochist." *IntJPsa*,
30, 1949.
"A Manifest Oedipus Complex in an Adolescent Girl."
PsaStC, 8, 1953.
"Orality Displaced to the Urethra." *JAPA*, 2, 1954.
"Disturbances in Abstract Thinking and Body-Image
Formation." *JAPA*, 6, 1959.
"Disturbances of Ego Functions of Speech and Abstract
Thinking." *JAPA*, 10, 1962.

KEMPER, W.

"The 'Rule of Abstinence' in Psychoanalysis." *P*, 8, 1955.

KESTENBERG, J.

"On the Development of Maternal Feelings in Early Childhood; Observations and Reflections." *PsaStC*, 11, 1956.

"Vicissitudes of Female Sexuality." *JAPA*, 4, 1956.

KHAN, M.

—— & R. Masud, "Clinical Aspects of the Schizoid Personality: Affects and Technique." *IntJPsa*, 41, 1960.

KLEIN, M.

"The Technique of Analysis of Young Children." *IntJPsa*, 5, 1924.

"Zur Genese des Tics." *Z*, 11, 1925.

Psycho-Analysis of the Child. HPI, 1932.

"A Contribution to the Psycho-Genesis of Manic Depressive States." *IntJPsa*, 16, 1935.

The Psychoanalysis of Children. HPI, 1937.

"Mourning and Its Relation to Manic-Depressive States." *IntJPsa*, 21, 1940.

"Notes on Some Schizoid Mechanisms." *IntJPsa*, 27, 1946.

Contributions to Psycho-Analysis. 1921–1945. HPI, 1948.

"A Contribution to the Theory of Anxiety and Guilt." *IntJPsa*, 29, 1948.

"On the Criteria for Determination of a Psycho-Analysis." *IntJPsa*, 31, 1950.

Envy and Gratitude. A Study of Unconscious Sources. BB, 1957.

"On the Development of Mental Functioning." *IntJPsa*, 39, 1958.

KLUCKHOHN, C.

"Ethical Relativity: Sic et Non." *JPhilos*, 1955.

KNIGHT, R.

"Postgraduate Course in Psychiatry for Physicians." Unpublished Lectures to Nonpsychiatrist Physicians. Menninger Clinic, 1935.

"Psychotherapy in Acute Paranoid Schizophrenia with Successful Outcome: A Case Report." *BMC*, 3, 1939.

"Introjection, Projection and Identification." *Q*, 9, 1940.

"The Relationship of Latent Homosexuality to the Mechanisms of Paranoid Delusions." *BMC*, 4, 1940.

"Intimidation of Others as a Defense Against Anxiety." *BMC*, 6, 1942.

—— & C. Friedman, eds., *Psychoanalytic Psychiatry and Psychology: Clinical and Theoretical Papers.* IUP, 1954.

KOHLER, A.

"Psychische Faktoren bei Gewichtsverschiebungen." *ZpsychosomMed*, 3, 1957.

KOHLER, J.

"From Matriarchy to Patriarchy." *DerTag*, 1919.

KOHUT, H.

"Clinical and Theoretical Aspects of Resistance." *JAPA*, 5, 1957.

"Death in Venice, by Thomas Mann. A Story About the Disintegration of Artistic Sublimation." *Q*, 26, 1957.

"Introspection, Empathy, and Psychoanalysis: An Examination of the Relationship Between Mode of Observation and Theory." *JAPA*, 7, 1959.

"Beyond the Bounds of the Basic Rule. Some Contributions to Psychoanalysis." *JAPA*, 8, 1960.

KOLANSKY, H.

"Treatment of a Three-Year-Old Girl's Severe Infantile Neurosis: Stammering and Insect Phobia." *PsaStC*, 15, 1960.

KOLB, L.

"Psychiatry." *AnRevMed*, 7, 1956.

KOURETAS, D.

"Sur un cas de Névrose à Base d'Envie du Penis." *RFPsa*, 14, 1950.

KOVACS, S.

"Introjektion, Projektion und Einfühlung." *C*, 2, 1912.

KRAMER, P.

"Early Capacity for Orgastic Discharge and Character Formation." *PsaStC*, 9, 1954.

"On Discovering One's Identity. A Case Report." *PsaStC*, 10, 1955.

KRAPF, E.

"The Social Therapy of Schizophrenia." *P*, 12, 1958.

KRAUSE, M.

"Defensive and Nondefensive Resistance." *Q*, 30, 1961.

KRIS, E.

"Zur Psychologie der Karikatur." *Im*, 20, 1934.

"The Psychology of Caricature." *IntJPsa*, 17, 1936.

—— & E. Gombrich, "The Principle of Caricature." *M*, 17, 1938.

"Probleme der Ästhetik." *Z*, 26, 1941.

"Danger and Morals." *Ops*, 14, 1944.

—— & A. Kaplan, "Aesthetic Ambiguity." *PPR*, 8, 1948.

"On Preconscious Mental Processes." *PQ*, 19, 1950.

"Ego Psychology and Interpretation in Psychoanalytic Therapy." *Q*, 20, 1951.

"Some Comments and Observations on Early Auto-erotic Activities." *PsaStC*, 6, 1951.

Psychoanalytic Explorations in Art. IUP, 1952.

"The Psychology of Caricature." *PEA*, 1952.

"Psychoanalysis and the Study of Creative Imagination." *BullNYAcadMed*, 29, 1953.

"New Contributions to the Study of Freud's 'The Interpretation of Dreams': A Critical Essay." *JAPA*, 2, 1954.

The Origins of Psychoanalysis. BB, 1954.
"Neutralization and Sublimation: Observations on Young Children." *PsaStC*, 10, 1955.
"The Personal Myth." *JAPA*, 4, 1956.
"Some Comments and Observations of Early Auto-erotic Activities." *PsaStC*, 1962.

KRIS, M.
Child Analysis in Psychoanalysis Today. IUP, 1944.
"The Use of Prediction in Longitudinal Study." *PsaStC*, 12, 1957.

KROEBER, A.
"Totem and Taboo: An Ethnologic Psychoanalysis." *AmAnthrop*, 22, 1920.
"Totem and Taboo in Retrospect." *Soc*, 45, 1930.
Anthropology, Race, Language, Culture, Psychology, Prehistory. HB, 1948.

KRONFELD, A.
"Zur Psychologie des Süchtigseins." *PtPrx*, 2, 1935.

KROUT, M.
"Emotional Factors in the Etiology of Stammering." *ASP*, 31, 1936.

KUBIE, L.
"A Critical Analysis of the Concept of a Repetition Compulsion." *IntJPsa*, 20, 1939.

LAFORGUE, R.
"De l'angoisse à l'orgasme." *RFPsa*, 4, 1930–1931.
"Les Resistances de la fin de Traitement Analytique." *RFPsa*, 6, 1933.
The Relativity of Reality; Reflections on the Limitations of Thought and the Genesis of the Need of Causality. NMDP, 1940.

LAGACHE, D.
"Quelques Aspects du Transfert." *RFPsa*, 15, 1951.

LAMPL-DE GROOT, J.
"The Pre-Oedipal Phase in the Development of the Male Child." *PsaStC*, 2, 1946.
"Re-Evaluation of the Role of the Oedipus Complex." *IntJPsa*, 33, 1952.
"On Defense and Development: Normal and Pathological." *PsaStC*, 11, 1957.

LANDAUER, K.
"Paranoia." *PsaVkb*, 1926.
"Die Onanieselbstbeschuldigungen in Psychosen." *PsaP*, 2, 1927–1928.
"Die Ich-Organisation in der Pubertät." *PsaP*, 9, 1935.

LANTOS, B.
"Analyse einer konversionshysteria im Klimakterium." *Z*, 15, 1929.

LEACH, D.
Report on Panel, "Technical Aspects of Transference." *JAPA*, 6, 1958.

LEUBA, J.
"Introduction to the Clinical Study of Narcissism." *RFPsa*, 13, 1949.

LEVIN, A.
"The Oedipus Myth in History and Psychiatry; A New Interpretation." *Ps*, 11, 1948.

LEVINE, J.
—— & F. C. Redlich, "Failure to Understand Humor." *Q*, 24, 1955.

LEVY, K.
"Simultaneous Analysis of Mother and Child." *PsaStC*, 15, 1960.

LEWIN, B.
"Anal Erotism and the Mechanism of Undoing." *Q*, 1, 1932.
"Sleep, the Mouth and the Dream Screen." *Q*, 15, 1946.
"Inferences from the Dream Screen." *IntJPsa*, 29, 1948.
The Psychoanalysis of Elation. Nor, 1950.
"Phobic Symptoms and Dream Interpretations." *Q*, 21, 1952.
"Reconsiderations of the Dream Screen." *Q*, 22, 1953.
"Sleep, Narcissistic Neurosis, and the Analytic Situation." *Q*, 1954.
"Dream Psychology and the Analytic Situation." *Q*, 1955.
—— & H. Ross, *Psychoanalytic Education in the United States.* Nor, 1960.
"Reflections on Depression." *PsaStC*, 16, 1961.

LEWINSKY, H.
"Boredom." *BJEP*, 13, 1943.

LEWIS, H.
"The Effect of Shedding the First Deciduous Tooth Upon the Passing of the Oedipus Complex of the Male." *JAPA*, 6, 1958.

LEWIS, N.
—— & H. Yarnell, *Pathological Fire Setting.* NMDP, 1951.

LICHTENSTEIN, H.
"Identity and Sexuality: A Study of Their Interrelationship in Man." *JAPA*, 9, 1961.

LIDZ, T.
"The Family Environment of the Schizophrenic." *P*, 13, 1959.

LIND, J.
"The Dream as a Simple Wish-Fulfillment in the Negro." *R*, 1, 1914.

LINDNER, S.

"Das Saugen an den Fingern, Lippen, etc. bei den Kindern (Ludeln)." *PsaP*, 8, 1934.

LINN, L.

"Trauma and Denial." *BAPA*, 8, 1952.

"The Role of Perception in the Mechanism of Denial." *JAPA*, 1, 1953.

"The Discriminating Function of the Ego." *Q*, 23, 1954.

A Handbook of Hospital Psychiatry. A Practical Guide to Therapy. IUP, 1955.

"Some Developmental Aspects of the Body Image." *IntJPsa*, 36, 1955.

"Psychoanalytic Contribution to Psychosomatic Research." *PSM*, 20, 1958.

"Some Comments on the Origin of the Influencing Machine." *JAPA*, 6, 1958

LIPTON, S.

Report on Panel, "Aggression and Symptom Formation." *JAPA*, 9, 1961.

LOEWALD, H.

"Hypnoid State, Repression, Abreaction and Recollection." *JAPA*, 3, 1955.

"On the Therapeutic Action of Psycho-Analysis." *IntJPsa*, 41, 1960.

LOEWENSTEIN, R.

"Un cas de jalousie pathologique." *RFPsa*, 5, 1932.

"Phallic Passivity in Men." *IntJPsa*, 16, 1935.

"Conflict and Autonomous Ego Development During the Phallic Phase." *PsaStC*, 5, 1950.

"Some Remarks on the Role of Speech in Psychoanalytic Technique." *IntJPsa*, 37, 1956.

"A Contribution to the Psychoanalytic Theory of Masochism." *JAPA*, 5, 1957.

LOFGREN, L.

"A Case of Bronchial Asthma with Unusual Dynamic Factors, Treated by Psychotherapy and Psycho-Analysis." *IntJPsa*, 42, 1961.

LONDON, L.

"Psychopathology of Erythrophobia (Blushing)." *SouthernMedSurg*, 1945.

—— & F. Caprio, *Sexual Deviations.* Washington: The Linacre Press, 1950.

LOOMIE, L.

—— H. Victor, & M. Stein, "Ernst Kris and the Gifted Adolescent Project." *PsaStC*, 13, 1958.

LORAND, S.

"A Horse Phobia: A Character Analysis of an Anxiety Hysteria." *R*, 14, 1927.

"The Mantle Symbol." *IntJPsa*, 10, 1929.

"Fetishism in Statu Nascendi." *IntJPsa*, 11, 1930.

"Contribution to the Problem of Vaginal Orgasm." *IntJPsa*, 20, 1939.

"The Role of Female Penis Fantasy in Male Character Formation." *IntJPsa*, 20, 1939.

"Anorexia Nervosa; Case." *PSM*, 5, 1943.

Clinical Studies on Psychoanalysis. IUP, 1950.

—— & S. Feldman, "The Symbolism of Teeth in Dreams." *IntJPsa*, 36, 1955.

"The Therapy of Perversions," in *Perversions: Psychodynamics and Therapy.* RH, 1956.

"Dream Interpretation in the Talmud (Babylonian and Graeco-Roman Period)." *IntJPsa*, 38, 1957.

Book Review, New Directions in Psycho-Analysis, M. Klein *et al.* eds. *IntJPsa*, 38, 1957.

"Resistance." *Q*, 27, 1958.

—— & W. Console, "Therapeutic Results in Psycho-Analytic Treatment Without Fee." *IntJPsa*, 39, 1958.

"Psycho-Analytic Therapy of Religious Devotees." *IntJPsa*, 43, 1962.

LOSSEY, F.

"The Charge of Suggestion as a Resistance in Psycho-Analysis." *IntJPsa*, 43, 1962.

LOW, B.

Psycho-Analysis. A Brief Account of the Freudian Theory. AU, 1920.

LUBIN, A.

"A Boy's View of Jesus." *PsaStC*, 14, 1959.

LUNDHOLM, H.

"Repression and Rationalization." *M*, 13, 1933.

LUSTMAN, S.

"Psychic Energy and Mechanisms of Defense." *PsaStC*, 12, 1957.

"Defense, Symptom and Character." *PsaStC*, 17, 1962.

LYND, H.

On Shame and the Search for Identity. HB, 1958.

MACALPINE, I.

—— & R. Hunter, "The Schreber Case. A Contribution to Schizophrenia, Hypochondria, and Psychosomatic Symptom Formation." *Q*, 22, 1953.

MACCURDY, J.

"The Pathology and Treatment of Insomnia in Fatigue and Allied States." *JAbP*, 15, 1920.

McDOUGALL, W.

"A New Theory of Laughter." *P*, 2, 1922.

"Instinct and the Unconscious. *JAbP*, 20, 1925.

McELROY, R.

"Psychoneurosis, Combat-Anxiety Type." *AJP*, 101 1945.

MAEDER, A.

"Zur Frage der Teleologischen Traumfunktion. Eine Bemerkung zur Abwehr." *Y*, 5, 1913.
"Heilung einer Hundephobie bei einem 7-jährigen Knaben." *ZKinderpsychiat*, 10, 1943.

MAHLER, M.

"Pseudo Imbecility: A Magic Cap of Invisibility." *Q*, 11, 1942.
Child Analysis: Modern Trends in Child Psychiatry. IUP, 1945.
"Psychoanalytic Evaluation of Tics." *PsaStC*, 3, 1949.
"On Child Psychosis and Schizophrenia: Autistic and Symbiotic Infantile Psychoses." *PsaStC*, 7, 1952.
—— & P. Elkisch, "Some Observations on Disturbances of the Ego in a Case of Infantile Psychosis." *PsaStC*, 8, 1953.
"Autism and Symbiosis, Two Extreme Disturbances of Identity." *IntJPsa*, 39, 1958.
"On Sadness and Grief in Infancy and Childhood. Loss and Restoration of the Symbiotic Love Object." *PsaStC*, 16, 1961.

MAINX, F.

"Foundation of Biology," in *International Encyclopedia of Unified Science.* UCP, 1, 1955.

MALAMUD, W.

"The Application of Psychoanalytic Principles in Interpreting the Psychoses." *R*, 16, 1929.

MALINOWSKI, B.

"Psychoanalysis and Anthropology," Letter to the editor. *Nature*, 1923.
"Psychoanalysis and Anthropology." *P*, 4, 1923–1924.
"Mutterrechtliche Familie und Oedipus-Komplex." *Im*, 10, 1924.
Sex and Repression in Savage Society. KP, 1927.

MALLET, J.

"Contribution to the Study of Phobias." *RFPsa*, 20, 1956.

MANCHEN, A.

"Denkhemmung und Aggression aus Kastrationsangst." *PsaP*, 10, 1936.

MANNHEIM, R.

"Allmacht der Gedanken bei Kindern." *PsaP*, 2, 1927–1928.

MARCINOWSKI, J.

"Die Erotischen Quellen der Minderwertigkeitsgefühle." *ZSW*, 4, 1918.
"Vom finalen und vom kausalen Denken in der Psychologie der Neurosen." *ZPt*, 8, 1935.

MARCOVITZ, E.

"The Meaning of Déjà Vu." *Q*, 21, 1952.

MARCUS, E.

"Zum 'Lust und Realitätsprinzip'." *C*, 4, 1913.

MARCUSE, M.

"Das Bettnässen (Enuresis Nocturnal) als Sexualneurotisches Symptom." *ZSW*, 11, 1924.

MARGOLIN, S.

"Symposium on Psychotherapy in Medical and Surgical Hospitals." *BAPA*, 8, 1952.

MARKUSZEWICZ, R.

"Beitrag zum Autistischen Denken bei Kindern." *Z*, 6, 1920.

MARMOR, J.

"Orality in the Hysterical Personality." *JAPA*, 1, 1953.
"Some Comments on Ego Psychology." *JHH*, 7, 1958.

MASSERMANN, J.

"Psychodynamisms in Anorexia Nervosa and Neurotic Vomiting." *Q*, 10, 1941.

MATTE BLANCO, I.

"On Introjection and the Processes of Psychic Metabolism." *IntJPsa*, 22, 1941.

MAYER, F.

"Freud und Adler im Licht der Aesthetik." *ZPt*, 4, 1931.

MEAD, M.

"Cultural Contexts of Puberty and Adolescence." *BPAP*, 1959.

MEINERTZ, J.

"Psychologie, Existenz, Anthropologie." *P*, 1953.

MENG, H.

"Neurasthenie, Neuropathie, Psychopathie des Kindesalter." *PsaVkb*, 1926.
"Das Problem der Onanie von Kant bis Freud." *PsaP*, 2, 1927–1928.
"On the Psychology of the Instinctual Narcissist." *PsaP*, 9, 1935.
"On the Problems of Neuroses, Psychology of Psychoses, Endocrine System." *P*, 13, 1959.

MENNINGER, K.

"Reversible Schizophrenia." *P*, 1, 1922.
Love Against Hate. HB, 1942.
Theory of Psychoanalytic Technique. BB, 1958.

MENNINGER, W.

"The Treatment of Chronic Alcohol Addiction." *BMC*, 2, 1938.
"Psychoanalytic Principles in Psychiatric Hospital Therapy." *SouthernMedJ*, 32, 1939.
"Alcoholism: A National Emergency." *MennQ*, 1, 1957.

MEYER, F.

"Ein Traum eines Morphinkranken." *PtPrx*, 2, 1935.

MICHAELS, J.

"Enuresis—a Method for Its Study and Treatment." *Ops*, 9, 1939.

Disorders of Character: Persistent Enuresis, Juvenile Delinquency and Psychopathic Personality. CCT, 1955.

MILLET, J.

Insomnia: Its Causes and Treatment. New York: Greenberg, 1938.

MILNER, M.

"A Suicidal Symptom in a Child of Three." *IntJPsa*, 25, 1944.

"Aspects of Symbolism in Comprehension of the Not-Self." *IntJPsa*, 33, 1952.

MITSCHERLICH, A.

"Lust und Realitätsprinzip in ihrer Beziehung zur Phantasie." *P*, 6, 1952.

"The Individual in Anxiety. A Word on the Mass Reactions of our Time." *DAW*, 11, 1956.

MITTELMAN, B.

—— & H. Wolff, "Emotional Factors in Gastric Neurosis and Peptic Ulcer; Experimental Studies." *PsycholBull*, 37, 1940.

"Motility in Infants, Children, and Adults: Patterning and Psychodynamics." *PsaStC*, 9, 1954.

"Motor Patterns and Genital Behavior: Fetishism." *PsaStC*, 10, 1955.

"Motility in the Therapy of Children and Adults." *PsaStC*, 12, 1957.

"Intrauterine and Early Infantile Motility." *PsaStC*, 15, 1960.

MOLONEY, J.

"Fear is the Most Dangerous Contagion in the World." *Child-FamDig*, 1958.

MONEY-KRYLE, R.

The Development of the Sexual Impulses. HB, 1932.

MOORE, B.

"Congenital vs. Environmental: An Unconscious Meaning." *JAPA*, 8, 1960.

Report on Panel, "Frigidity in Women." *JAPA*, 9, 1961.

MORGENTHALER, W.

"Erinnerungen an Hermann Rorschach, Die Waldauzeit." *SchweizZPsychol*, 1958.

MULLER-BRAUNSCHWEIG, C.

"The Girl's First Object Cathexis in Relation to Penis Envy and Femininity." *P*, 13, 1959.

MURPHY, G.

Personality. HBP, 1947.

MURPHY, W.

"Narcolepsy—A Review and Presentation of Seven Cases." *P*, 98, 1941.

"Character, Trauma, and Sensory Perception." *IntJPsa*, 39, 1958.

"A Note on Trauma and Loss." *JAPA*, 9, 1961.

MURRAY, C.

"Psychogenic Factors in the Etiology of Ulcerative Bloody Diarrhea." *AJMS*, 180, 1930.

MURRAY, J.

"Narcissism and the Ego Ideal." *JAPA*, 12, 1964.

NACHT, S.

"Thoughts on Transference and Counter-Transference." *RFPsa*, 13, 1949.

"Essai sur la peur." *RFPsa*, 16, 1952.

"The Ego in Perverse Relationships." *IntJPsa*, 37, 1956.

"Technical Remarks on the Handling of the Transference Neurosis." *IntJPsa*, 38, 1957.

"The Non-Verbal Relationship in Psychoanalytic Treatment." *IntJPsa*, 44, 1963.

NEEDLES, W.

"Stigmata in the Course of Psychoanalysis." *Q*, 12, 1943.

NELKEN, J.

"Analytische Beobachtungen über Phantasien eines Schizophrenen." *Y*, 4, 1912.

NIEDERLAND, W. G.

"Three Notes on the Schreber Case." *Q*, 10, 1951.

"Jacob's Dream." *JHH*, 3, 1954.

"The Earliest Dreams of a Young Child." *PsaStC*, 12, 1957.

"Early Auditory Experiences, Beating Fantasies and Primal Scene." *PsaStC*, 13, 1958.

"The Psychoanalysis of a Severe Obsessive-Compulsive Neurosis." *BPAP*, 8, 1958.

"The 'Miracled-up' World of Schreber's Childhood." *PsaStC*, 14, 1959.

"Schreber—Father and Son." *Q*, 28, 1959.

"The First Application of Psychoanalysis to a Literary Work." *Q*, 29, 1960.

Panel Discussion on Narcissism. *JAPA*, 10, 1962.

"Further Data and Memorabilia Pertaining to the Schreber Case." *IntJPsa*, 44, 1963.

"A Psychoanalytic Inquiry into the Life and Work of Heinrich Schliemann," in *Drives, Affects and Behavior.* IUP, 1965.

NOVEY, S.

"The Principle of 'Working Through' in Psychoanalysis." *JAPA*, 10, 1962.

NOYES, A.

—— & L. Kolb, *Modern Clinical Psychiatry.* Sau, 1963.

NUNBERG, H.

"The Feeling of Guilt." *Q*, 3, 1934.
"Homosexualität, Magie und Aggression." *Z*, 22, 1936.
"Evaluation of the Results of Psycho-Analytic Treat-
  ment." *IntJPsa*, 35, 1954.
*Principles of Psychoanalysis—Their Application to the
  Neuroses.* IUP, 1955.
"Über den Traum." *PsaVkb*, 1957.
—— & E. Federn, *Minutes of the Vienna Psychoanalytic
  Society.* IUP, 1963.

ODIER, C.

"A Literary Portrayal of Ambivalency." *IntJPsa*, 4, 1923.

OLDEN, C.

"About the Fascinating Effect of the Narcissistic
  Personality." *AmIm*, 2, 1941.
"On Adult Empathy With Children." *PsaStC*, 8, 1953.

OLINICK, S.

"Questioning and Pain, Truth and Negation." *JAPA*, 5,
  1957.

OPHUIJSEN, J.

"Mededeelingen over het Fetischisme." *NTvG*, 1928.

OSTOW, M.

Report on Panel, "Theory of Aggression." *JAPA*, 5, 1957.

PAPPENHEIM, E.

—— & M. Sweeney, "Separation Anxiety in Mother and
  Child." *PsaStC*, 7, 1952.

PARIN, P.

"Gegenübertragung bei verschiedenen Abwehrformen."
  JPsa, 1960.
—— F. Morgenthaler, & G. Parin-Matthey, *Die Weissen
  denken zu viel.* Zürich: Atlantic Verlag, 1963.

PARKIN, A.

"On Fetishism." *IntJPsa*, 44, 1963.

PAVENSTEDT, E.

"The Effect of Extreme Passivity Imposed on a Boy in
  Early Childhood." *PsaStC*, 11, 1956.

PAYNE, C.

"Some Freudian Contributions to the Paranoia Problem." *R*, 1, 1914.

PAYNE, S.

"The Fetishist and His Ego," in *The Psychoanalytic
  Reader.* IUP, 1948.

PECK, M.

"Two Cases of Major Tics." *JNMD*, 58, 1923.

PELLER, L.

"The Concept of Play and Ego Development." *IntJPsa*,
  1954.
"Libidinal Phases, Ego Development and Play." *PsaStC*,
  9, 1954.
"Reading and Daydreams in Latency. Boy-Girl Differences." *JAPA*, 6, 1958.

PENROSE, L.

"Some Psychoanalytical Notes on Negation." *IntJPsa*, 8,
  1927.

PETO, A.

"The Fragmentizing Function of the Ego in the Transference Neurosis." *IntJPsa*, 42, 1961.

PFEFFER, A.

Alcoholism. G & S, 1958.
"A Procedure for Evaluating the Results of Psychoanalysis." *JAPA*, 7, 1959.

PFEIFER, S.

"Der Traum als Hüter des Schlafes." *Z*, 9, 1923.
"Repeated Slips of the Tongue During Analysis." *Z*, 9,
  1923.

PFISTER, O.

"Psychoanalyse und bildende Kunst." *PsaVkb*, 1926.
"Die Rolle des Unbewussten im philosophischen Denken." *Dialectica*, 1949.

PHILLIPS, L.

—— & J. Smith, *Rorschach Interpretation: Advanced
  Techniques.* G&S, 1953.

PIAGET, J.

The Moral Judgment of the Child. HB, 1933.
The Child's Conception of Physical Causality. HB, 1934.

PICHON, E.

"Rêve d'une femme frigide." *RFPsa*, 6, 1932.
"Death, Anxiety, Negation." *Evolutpsychiat*, 1, 1947.

PICHON-RIVIERE, A.

"Dentition, Walking, and Speech in Relation to the
  Depressive Position." *IntJPsa*, 39, 1958.

PIOTROWSKI, Z.

Perceptanalysis. Mac, 1957.

PLATO

The Symposium. TP, 1941.

PLAUT, A.

"Aspects of Consciousness." *M*, 32, 1959.

POND, D.

"Narcolepsy." *JMS*, 98, 1952.

POSINSKY, S.
"The Death of Maui." *JAPA*, 5, 1957.
"The Problem of Yurok Anality." *AmIm*, 14, 1957.

POTZL, O.
"Zur Metapsychologie des 'Déjà Vu.'" *Im*, 12, 1926.

PRAGER, D.
"An Unusual Fantasy of the Manner in Which Babies Become Boys or Girls." *Q*, 29, 1960.

PRINCE, M.
"The Mechanism and Interpretation of Dreams." *JAbP*, 5, 1910.

PUTNAM, J.
"Psychoanalyse und Philosphie." *C*, 3, 1913.

RADO, S.
"Das Problem der Angst in seinem Verhältnis zur Psychoanalytischen Libidotheorie." *ZSW*, 10, 1923.
"Eine Traumanalyse." *Z*, 9, 1923.
"The Economic Principle in Psychoanalytic Technique." *IntJPsa*, 6, 1925.
"The Problem of Melancholia." *IntJPsa*, 9, 1928.
"Psychoanalysis of Pharmacothymia." *Q*, 2, 1933.

RAGLAN, L.
"Magic and Psychoanalysis." *Man*, 41, 1941.

RAMZY, I.
—— & R. Wallerstein, "Pain, Fear, and Anxiety: Study in Their Interrelationships." *PsaStC*, 13, 1958.

RANGELL, L.
"A Treatment of Nightmares in a Seven-Year-Old Boy." *PsaStC*, 5, 1950.
"The Analysis of a Doll Phobia." *IntJPsa*, 33, 1952.
"The Psychology of Poise." *IntJPsa*, 37, 1954.
Report on Panel, "The Dream in the Practice of Psychoanalysis." *JAPA*, 4, 1956.
"The Nature of Conversion." *JAPA*, 7, 1959.
"The Scope of Intrapsychic Conflict: Microscopic and Macroscopic Considerations." *PsaStC*, 18, 1963.
"Structural Problems in Intrapsychic Conflict." *PsaStC*, 18, 1963.

RANK, B.
—— & D. MacNaughton, "A Clinical Contribution to Early Ego Development." *PsaStC*, 5, 1950.

RANK, O.
Der Künstler; Ansätze zu einer Sexualpsychologie. H, 1907.
"A Contribution to the Study of Narcissism." *Y*, 3, 1911.
"Beiträge zur Symbolik in der Dichtung." *Z*, 2, 1914.
The Trauma of Birth. NMDP, 1914.
Art and Artist: Creative Urge and Personality Development. TP, 1932.

RAPAPORT, D.
—— & R. Schafer, "The Rorschach Test: A Clinical Evaluation." *BMC*, 9, 1945.
"On the Psychoanalytic Theory of Thinking." *IntJPsa*, 31, 1950.
"The Autonomy of the Ego." *BMC*, 15, 1951.
"On the Psychoanalytic Theory of Affects." *IntJPsa*, 34, 1953.
"The Theory of Ego Autonomy: A Generalization." *BMC*, 22, 1958.
—— & M. Gill, "The Points of View and Assumptions of Metapsychology." *IntJPsa*, 40, 1959.

RAPAPORT, J.
"A Case of Necrophilia." *ClinPath*, 4, 1942–1943.

RAPPAPORT, E.
"The Management of an Erotized Transference." *Q*, 25, 1956.

RASCOVSKY, A.
"Beyond the Oral Stage." *IntJPsa*, 37, 1956.

RASCOVSKY, M.
—— & A. Rascovsky, "On Consummated Incest." *IntJPsa*, 31, 1950.

REDL, F.
"'Pansexualismus' und Pubertät." *PsaP*, 9, 1935.

REDLICH, F.
"The Psychiatrist in the Caricature." *Ops*, 20, 1950.
Psychotherapy with Schizophrenics. IUP, 1952.

REICH, A.
"Narcissistic Object Choice in Women." *JAPA*, 1, 1953.
"A Character Formation Representing the Integration of Unusual Conflict Solutions into the Ego Structure." *PsaStC*, 8, 1958.

REICH, W.
"Über Spezifität der Onanieformen." *Z*, 8, 1922.
"Der Psychogene Tic als Onanieäquivalent." *ZSW*, 11, 1925.
"Der Triebhafte Charakter; eine Psychoanalytische Studie zur Pathologie des Ichs." *IntPV*, 1925.
"Zur Technik der Deutung und der Widerstandsanalyse Über die gesetzmässige Entwicklung der Übertragungsneurose." *Z*, 13, 1927.
"Die Funktion des Orgasmus zur Psychopathologie und zur Soziologie des Geschlechtslebens." *NeueArb*, 6, 1927.
"Über kindliche Phobie und Charakterbildung." *Z*, 16, 1930.
"Die Charakterologische Überwindung des Oedipus-Komplexes." *Z*, 17, 1931.
Character-Analysis: Principles and Technique for Psychoanalysts in Practice and in Training. OIP, 1945.
Character Analysis. OIP, 1949.

REIFF, R.

—— & M. Scheerer, *Memory and Hypnotic Age Regression, Developmental Aspects of Cognitive Function Explored Through Hypnosis.* IUP, 1959.

REIK, T.

"Die 'Allmacht der Gedanken' bei Arthur Schnitzler." *Im*, 2, 1913.
"Arthur Schnitzler als Psycholog." *RvHSIm*, 3, 1914.
"Aesthetik, Literatur, Kunst." *Y*, 6, 1914.
"Fehlleistungen im Alltagsleben." *Z*, 3, 1915.
"Zur Analerotik." *Z*, 3, 1915.
"Some Remarks on the Study of Resistances." *IntJPsa*, 5, 1924.
"Geständniszwang und Strafbedürfnis; Probleme der Psychoanalyse und der Kriminologie." *IntPV*, 1925.
"Zur Psychoanalyse des Mitleids." *PsaP*, 2, 1927–1928.
"Das Schweigen," in *Wie man Psychologe wird. Al*, 1928.
Listening With the Third Ear. FS, 1948.
Dogma and Compulsion: Psychoanalytic Studies of Religion and Myths. IUP, 1951.
The Creation of Women. George Braziller, Inc., 1960.

REXFORD, E.

"Child Psychiatry and Child Analysis in the United States." *JCPs*, 1, 1962.

RICHARDSON, H.

"Love and Psychodynamics of Adaptations." *R*, 43, 1956.

RICHARDSON, G.

—— & R. A. Moore, "On the Manifest Dream in Schizophrenia." *JAPA*, 11, 1963.

RICHTER, H.

"The Basis of Masochism." *Nervenarzt*, 25, 1954.
"Object Relationship in Schizophrenia." *Nervenarzt*, 29, 1958.

RIESE, W.

"On Exhibitionism." *DtschZges*, 18, 1932.

RIOCH, D.

"Certain Aspects of 'Conscious' Phenomena and Their Neural Correlates." *P*, 111, 1955.

RITVO, S.

—— & S. Provence, "Form Perception and Imitation in Some Autistic Children: Diagnostic Findings and Their Contextual Interpretation." *PsaStC*, 8, 1953.
Report on Panel, "Object Relations." *JAPA*, 10, 1962.

RIVIERE, J.

"The Castration Complex." *IntJPsa*, 5, 1924.
"A Castration Symbol." *IntJPsa*, 5, 1924.
"Phallic Symbolism." *IntJPsa*, 5, 1924.
"Jealousy as a Mechanism of Defense." *IntJPsa*, 13, 1932.

"A Character Trait of Freud's," in J. M. Sutherland, *Psycho-Analysis and Contemporary Thought.* HPI, 1958.

ROBBINS, B.

"Consciousness, Central Problem in Psychiatry." *PT*, 1, 1956.

ROBINSON, V.

(ed), "Sexual Anesthesia," in *Encyclopedia Sexualis.* DR, 1936.

ROCHLIN, G.

"The Disorder of Depression and Elation." *JAPA*, 1, 1953.

ROHEIM, G.

The Eternal Ones in Dreams. IUP, 1945.
"Masturbation Fantasies." *PQ*, 20, 1945.
"The Magical Function of the Dream." *IntJPsa*, 30, 1949.
Psychoanalysis and Anthropology. IUP, 1950.
"Mythology of Arnhem Land." *AmIm*, 8, 1951.
"The Anthropological Evidence and the Oedipus Complex." *AnSurvPsa*, 3, 1952.
"Telepathy in a Dream," in G. Devereux, *Psychoanalysis and the Occult.* IUP, 1953.
Magic and Schizophrenia. IUP, 1955.

ROMANO, J.

(ed), *Adaptation.* CorUP, 1949.

ROMM, M.

"Transient Psychotic Episodes During Psychoanalysis." *JAPA*, 5, 1957.

ROOSE, L.

"The Influence of Psychosomatic Research on the Psychoanalytic Process." *JAPA*, 8, 1960.

ROOT, N.

"A Neurosis in Adolescence." *PsaStC*, 12, 1957.

RORSCHACH, H.

"Zur Symbolik der Schlange und der Krawatte." *C*, 2, 1912.

ROSEN, V.

"On Mathematical 'Illumination' and the Mathematical Thought Process: A Contribution to the Genetic Development and Metapsychology of Abstract Thinking." *PsaStC*, 8, 1953.
"Strephosymbolia: An Intrasystemic Disturbance of the Synthetic Function of the Ego." *PsaStC*, 10, 1955.
"Abstract Thinking and Object Relations: With Special Reference to the Use of Abstraction as a Regressive Defense in Highly Gifted Individuals." *JAPA*, 6, 1958.

ROSENFELD, H.

"Notes on the Psychopathology of Schizophrenia." *P*, 10, 1956.
"An Investigation into the Psycho-Analytic Theory of Depression." *IntJPsa*, 40, 1959.

ROSENMAN, S.
"Pacts, Possessions and the Alcoholic " *Im*, 12, 1955.

ROSNER, A.
"Mourning Before the Fact." *JAPA*, 10, 1962.
"The Aim of Psychoanalytic Therapy." *PT*, 9, 1955.
"On the Mechanism of Hysterical Conversion." *PT*, 11, 1957.
"Manifest Dream Content and Acting Out." *Q*, 27, 1958.

ROTH, N.
"The Aim of Psychoanalytic Therapy." *PT*, 9, 1955.
"On the Mechanism of Hysterical Conversion." *PT*, 11, 1957.
"Manifest Dream Content and Acting Out." *Q*, 27, 1958.

ROTHENBERG, S.
"Transference Situations in an Hour of Analysis." *R*, 32, 1955.

ROWSON, A.
"Accident Proneness." *PSM*, 6, 1944.

RUBINFINE, D.
"On Denial of Objective Sources of Anxiety and 'Pain.' " *YBPsa*, 9, 1953.
"Perception, Reality Testing and Symbolism." *PsaStC*, 16, 1961.
"Maternal Stimulation, Psychic Structure, and Early Object Relations; With Special Reference to Aggression and Denial." *PsaStC*, 17, 1962.

RUFFLER, G.
"The Analysis of a Sado-Masochist," in S. Lorand, *Perversions: Psychodynamics and Therapy*. RH, 1956.

RUSSELL, B.
Dictionary of the Mind. PL, 1952.

RYECROFT, C.
"A Contribution to the Study of the Dream Screen." *IntJPsa*, 32, 1951.
"A Detective Story. Psychoanalytic Observations." *Q*, 26, 1957.
"An Enquiry into the Function of Words in the Psycho-Analytical Situation." *IntJPsa*, 39, 1958.
"The Analysis of a Paranoid Personality." *IntJPsa*, 41, 1960.
"Beyond the Reality Principle." *IntJPsa*, 43, 1962.

SACHS, H.
"Eine Fehlhandlung zur Selbstberuhigung." *Z*, 3, 1915.
"The Breakthrough of the Unconscious." *Z*, 6, 1920.
"Zur Genese der Perversionen." *Z*, 9, 1923.
"Agieren in der Analyse." *Z*, 15, 1929.
"Psychotherapy and the Pursuit of Happiness." *AmIm*, 2, 1941.

SACHS, L.
"A Case of Castration Anxiety Beginning at Eighteen Months." *JAPA*, 10, 1962.

SADGER, J.
"Ein Fall von Multipler Perversion mit Hysterischen Absenzen." *Y*, 2, 1910.
"Über den Sado-Masochistischen Komplex." *Y*, 5, 1913.
"A Contribution to the Understanding of Tic." *Z*, 2, 1914.
"Ein Beitrag zum Problem des Selbstmords." *PsaP*, 3, 1928–1929.

SALFIELD, D.
"Depersonalization and Allied Disturbances in Childhood." *JMS*, 104, 1958.

SAUL, L.
"Inferiority Feelings and Hostility." *P*, 108, 1951.
"A Note on Exhibitionism and Scopophilia." *AnSurvPsa*, 3, 1952.
"The Ego in a Dream." *Q*, 22, 1953.
The Hostile Mind. RH, 1956.
"Technique and Practice of Psychoanalysis." *L*, 1958.
—— & A. Beck, "Psychodynamics of Male Homosexuality." *IntJPsa*, 42, 1961.
"The Erotic Transference." *Q*, 31, 1962.

SAUSSURE, R. de
"Mechanisms of Defence and Their Place in Psycho-Analytic Therapy: Discussion." *IntJPsa*, 35, 1954.
"The Metapsychology of Pleasure." *IntJPsa*, 40, 1959.

SAVITT, R.
"Extramural Psychoanalytic Treatment of a Case of Narcotics Addiction." *JAPA*, 2, 1954.
"Psychoanalytic Studies on Addiction: Ego Structure in Narcotic Addiction." *Q*, 32, 1963.

SCHACTER, N.
"The Nightmare: Its Psychosomatic Constellation." *RFPsa*, 23, 1959.

SCHAFER, R.
Psychoanalytic Interpretation in Rorschach Testing. G&S, 1954.

SCHEIDLINGER, S.
Psychoanalysis and Group Behavior. Nor, 1952.

SCHIFFER, I.
"The Psycho-Analytic Study of the Development of a Conversion Symptom." *IntJPsa*, 43, 1962.

SCHILDER, P.
"Über Elementare Halluzination des Bewegungssehens." *ZNP*, 80, 1923.
—— & O. Isakower, "Optischräumliche Agnosie und Agraphie." *ZNP*, 11, 1928.

"Über Neurasthenia." *Z*, 17, 1931.
The Image and Appearance of the Human Body. IUP, 1950.
Introduction to a Psychoanalytic Psychiatry. IUP, 1951.
The Nature of Hypnosis. IUP, 1956.

SCHMALTZ, G.
"The Problem of Exhibitionism (Case Report, Symbolism and Theory)." *P*, 6, 1953.

SCHMIDEBERG, M.
"On Fantasies of Being Beaten." *R*, 35, 1948.

SCHMIDL, F.
"Psychoanalysis and History." *Q*, 31, 1962.

SCHNEIDER, D.
The Psychoanalyst and the Artist. IUP, 1954.

SCHNEIDER, E.
"Experimentelle Magie." *Z*, 7, 1921.
"The Origin of Pavor Nocturnus in a Child; An Addendum." *PsaP*, 2, 1927–1928.

SCHREBER, D.
Memoirs of My Nervous Illness. William Dawson, 1955.

SCHULTZ-HENCKE, H.
"Die Struktur der Psychose." *ZNP*, 175, 1943.
"Noch einmal die Lehranalyse." *P*, 6, 1952.

SCHWARTZ, L.
"An Interpretation of the Emotional Needs of the Adolescent." *VTB*, 16, 1941.
"Psychosomatic Aspects of Cardiospasm With Case Presentation." *Samiksa*, 3, 1949.

SCOTT, W.
"A Note on the Psychopathology of Compulsive Phenomena in Manic Depressive States." *IntJPsa*, 27, 1946.
"On the Intense Affects Encountered in Treating a Severe Manic Depressive Disorder." *IntJPsa*, 28, 1947.
"Notes on the Psychopathology of Anorexia Nervosa." *M*, 21, 1948.

SCOTTLANDER, F.
"Phobie; eine Untersuchung über die Hintergründe der Neurose." *P*, 1, 1947.

SCRIPTURE, E.
Stuttering and Lisping. Mac, 1912.
"Treatment of the Stuttering." *Lancet*, 1, 1923.

SEARL, M.
"The Flight into Reality." *IntJPsa*, 10, 1929.

SEARLES, H.
"Anxiety Concerning Change, as Seen in the Psychotherapy of Schizophrenic Patients—With Particular Reference to the Sense of Personal Identity." *IntJPsa*, 42, 1961.

SECHEHAYE, M.
Symbolic Realization; a New Method of Psychotherapy Applied to a Case of Schizophrenia. IUP, 1951.
"The Transference in Symbolic Realization." *IntJPsa*, 37, 1956.

SEGAL, H.
"A Psychoanalytic Approach to Aesthetics." *IntJPsa*, 33, 1952.
"A Necrophilic Phantasy." *IntJPsa*, 34, 1953.
"A Note on Schizoid Mechanisms Underlying Phobia Formation." *IntJPsa*, 35, 1954.

SEIDENBERG, R.
"Changes in the Symbolic Process During a Psychoanalytic Treatment." *JNMD*, 127, 1958.

SELIGMAN, C.
"Anthropology and Psychology: A Study of Some Points of Contact." *JRoyAnthropInst*, 54, 1924.
"The Unconscious in Relation to Anthropology." *BJP*, 18, 1928.
"Anthropological Perspective and Psychological Theory." *JRoyAnthropInst*, 62, 1933.

SERVADIO, E.
"Psychoanalyse und Telepathie." *Im*, 21, 1935.
"The Lure of the Forbidden." *IntJPsa*, 34, 1953.
"Psychoanalyse und Telepathie," in G. Devereux, *Psychoanalysis and the Occult*. IUP, 1953.
"The Role of the Pre-Oedipal Conflicts." *RFPsa*, 18, 1954.
"A Presumptively Telepathic-Precognitive Dream During Analysis." *IntJPsa*, 36, 1955.
"Transference and Thought Transference." *IntJPsa*, 34, 1936.
"Telepathy and Psychoanalysis." *JASPR*, 4, 1958.

SEYLER, C.
"Slips of the Tongue in the Norse Sagas." *IntJPsa*, 36, 1955.

SHANDS, H.
"Anxiety, Anaclitic Objects, and the Sign Function: Comments on Early Developments in the Use of Symbols." *Ops*, 24, 1954.

SHARPE, E.
"The Analyst—Essential Qualifications for the Acquisition of Technique." *IntJPsa*, 11, 1930.
"Survey of Defence Mechanisms in General Character Traits and in Conduct-Evaluation of Pre-Conscious Material." *IntJPsa*, 11, 1930.
"Anxiety: Outbreak and Resolution." *IntJPsa*, 12, 1931.

"Technique in Character Analysis." *IntJPsa*, 12, 1931.

"Variations of Technique in Different Neuroses. Delusion, Paranoid, Obsession, Conversion Types." *IntJPsa*, 12, 1931.

Collected Papers on Psycho-Analysis. HPI, 1950.

"Psycho-Physical Problems Revealed in Language: An Examination of Metaphor," in *Collected Papers on Psycho-Analysis.* HPI, 1950.

SHENGOLD, L.

"Chekhov and Schreber: Vicissitudes of a Certain Kind of Father-Son Relationship." *IntJPsa*, 42, 1961.

SHEPPARD, E.

—— & L. Saul, "An Approach to a Systematic Study of Ego Function." *Q*, 27, 1958.

SHERMAN, M.

"Clues to the Third Ear." *R*, 46, 1959.

SHINDLER, W.

"Exhibitionistic 'Acting-Out' and Transference in Family Group-Therapy." *ZDiagPsychol*, 5, 1957.

SIEGMAN, A.

"The Psychological Economy of Déjà Raconté." *Q*, 25, 1956.

SILBERER, H.

"Report on a Method of Eliciting and Observing Certain Symbolic Hallucination-Phenomena." *OrgPath*, 1909.

"Symbolik des Erwachens und Schwellensymbolik überhaupt." *Y*, 3, 1911.

Probleme der Mystik und ihrer Symbolik. H, 1914.

SILBERMANN, I.

"A Contribution to the Psychology of Menstruation." *IntJPsa*, 31, 1950.

"Two Types of Preoedipal Character Disorders." *IntJPsa*, 38, 1957.

"Synthesis and Fragmentation." *PsaStC*, 16, 1961.

"The 'Jamais' Phenomenon in Reference to Fragmentation." *Q*, 32, 1963.

SILVERBERG, W.

"The Schizcid Maneuver." *Ps*, 10, 1947.

"The Factor of Omnipotence in Neurosis." *Ps*, 12, 1949.

"The Concept of Transference." *RFPsa*, 13, 1954.

"Acting Out Versus Insight: A Problem in Psychoanalytic Technique." *Q*, 24, 1955.

SILVERMAN, S.

"Ego Function and Body Language." *BPAP*, 1960.

"Ego Functions and Bodily Reactions." *JAPA*, 10, 1962.

SIMMEL, E.

"Doktorspiel, Kranksein und Arztberuf." *Z*, 12, 1926.

"Zum Problem von Zwang und Sucht." Report, Fifth General Medical Congress for Psychotherapy, Baden-Baden, 1930.

"Der Coitus Interruptus und sein Gegenstück, der Coitus prolongatus." *Z*, 18, 1932.

"Alcoholism and Addiction." *Q*, 17, 1948.

SINGER, M.

"Fantasies of a Borderline Patient." *PsaStC*, 15, 1960.

SLAVSON, S.

"Transference Phenomena in Group Psychotherapy." *R*, 37, 1950.

SOCARIDES, C.

"The Development of a Fetishistic Perversion: The Contribution of Preoedipal Phase Conflict." *JAPA*, 8, 1960.

SOKOLNICKA, E.

"Analysis of an Obsessional Neurosis in a Child." *IntJPsa*, 3, 1922.

SOLMS, W.

"Zur Frage der Monomanien. III. Dipsomanie, Kleptomanie, Pyromanie." *WienZNervenh*, 11, 1955.

SOLNIT, A.

—— & M. Stark, "Mourning and the Birth of a Defective Child." *PsaStC*, 16, 1961.

SOLOMON, J.

"Active Play Therapy." *Ops*, 8, 1938.

"Active Play Therapy, Further Experience." *Ops*, 10, 1940.

An Introduction to Projective Techniques, Anderson & Anderson, eds. PH, 1951.

A Synthesis of Human Behavior. G&S, 1954.

"Nailbiting and the Integrative Process." *IntJPsa*, 6, 1955.

SONNENFELD, K.

"Hand Kissing and Hand Fetishism." *JSexolPsychoanal*, 1, 1923.

SPERBER, A.

"Über das Auftreten von Hemmungen bei Tagträumen." *Im*, 16, 1930.

SPERLING, E.

"The Interpretation of the Traumas as a Command." *Q*, 9, 1950.

SPERLING, M.

"A Psychoanalytic Study of Ulcerative Colitis in Children." *Q*, 15, 1946.

"The Analysis of the Exhibitionist." *IntJPsa*, 28, 1947.

"A Contribution to the Psychodynamics of Depression in Women." *Samiksa*, 4, 1950.

"Mucous Colitis Associated with Phobias." *Q*, 19, 1950.

"Animal Phobias in a Two-Year-Old Child." *IntJPsa*, 34, 1953.

"Food Allergies and Conversion Hysteria." *Q*, 22, 1953.

"Psychosis and Psychosomatic Illness." *IntJPsa*, 36, 1955.

"Pavor Nocturnus." *JAPA*, 6, 1958.

"A Study of Deviate Sexual Behaviour in Children by the Method of Simultaneous Analysis of Mother and Child," in *Dynamic Psychopathology in Childhood*, L. Jessner and E. Pavenstedt, eds. G&S, 1959.

"Unconscious Phantasy Life and Object-Relationships in Ulcerative Colitis." *IntJPsa*, 41, 1960.

SPERLING, O.

"Zur Kasuistik und Auffassung der Narkolepsie." *DtschZNervenheilk*, 102, 1928.

"Alkoholismus und Sexual-Erziehung." *Sexualnot und Sexualreform*, 1931.

"On Appersonation." *IntJPsa*, 25, 1944.

"The Interpretation of the Trauma as a Command." *Q*, 19, 1950.

"Illusion, Naïve or Controlled." *AnSurvPsa*, 2, 1951.

Report on Round-Table, "Intellectual Inhibitions and Environmental Pressures." *BAPA*, 8, 1952.

"Psychosomatic Medicine and Pediatrics," in E. Wittkower & R. Cleghorn, *Recent Developments in Psychosomatic Medicine*. London: Pittman & Sons, 1954.

"Failure of Leadership." *PsaSS*, 1955.

"A Psychoanalytic Study of Social-Mindedness." *Q*, 24, 1955.

"Psychodynamics of Group Perversions." *Q*, 25, 1956.

"A Psychoanalytic Study of Hypnagogic Hallucinations." *JAPA*, 5, 1957.

"Thought Control and Creativity." *JHH*, 8, 1959.

"Exaggeration as a Defense." *Q*, 32, 1963.

SPEYER, N.

—— & B. Stokvis, "The Psychoanalytic Factor in Hypnosis." *M*, 17, 1938.

SPIEGEL, L.

—— & C. Oberndorf, "Narcolepsy as a Psychogenic Syndrome." *PSM*, 8, 1946.

"A Review of Contributions to the Psychoanalytic Theory of Adolescence: Individual Aspects." *PsaStC*, 6, 1951.

"Acting Out and Defensive Instinctual Gratification." *JAPA*, 2, 1954.

"Comments on the Psychoanalytic Psychology of Adolescence." *PsaStC*, 13, 1958.

"The Self, the Sense of Self, and Perception." *PsaStC*, 14, 1959

SPIELREIN, S.

"Über den psychologischen Inhalt eines Falles von Schizophrenie (Dementia Praecox)." *Y*, 3, 1911.

"Selbstbefriedigung in Fussymbolik." *C*, 3, 1913.

"The Manifestations of the Oedipus Complex in Childhood." *Z*, 4, 1916.

"Verdrängte Munderotik." *Z*, 6, 1920.

SPITZ, R.

"Wiederholung, Rhythmus, Langeweile." *Im*, 23, 1937.

"Hospitalism." *PsaStC*, 1, 1945.

"Anaclitic Depression. An Inquiry Into the Genesis of Psychiatric Conditions in Early Childhood." *PsaStC*, 2, 1946.

"Relevancy of Direct Infant Observation." *PsaStC*, 5, 1950.

"The Psychogenic Diseases in Infancy, an Attempt at Their Etiologic Classification." *PsaStC*, 6, 1951.

"Authority and Masturbation: Some Remarks on a Bibliographical Investigation." *Q*, 21, 1952.

"The Primal Cavity: A Contribution to the Genesis of Perception and Its Role for Psychoanalytic Theory." *PsaStC*, 10, 1955.

"Transference: the Analytical Setting and Its Prototype." *IntJPsa*, 34, 1956.

No and Yes, IUP, 1957.

"Some Early Prototypes of Ego Defenses." *JAPA*, 9, 1961.

"Autoerotism Re-Examined: The Role of Early Sexual Behavior Patterns in Personality Formation." *PsaStC*, 17, 1962.

SPRAGUE, G.

"Regression in Catatonia." *JNMD*, 91, 1940.

"Deeper Levels of Regression." *PQ*, 16, 1942.

SPRINCE, M.

"The Development of a Preoedipal Partnership Between an Adolescent Girl and Her Mother." *PsaStC*, 17, 1962.

STÄRCKE, A.

"Rechts und links in der Wahnidee." *Z*, 2, 1914.

"Ein einfacher Lach- und Weinkrampf." *Z*, 5, 1919.

"The Reversal of the Libido-Sign in Delusions of Persecution." *IntJPsa*, 1, 1920.

"Aanvullende mededeelinger bij de Demonstratie eener Artistieke Productie." *NTvG*, 65, 1921.

"The Castration Complex." *IntJPsa*, 2, 1921.

"Conscience and the Role of Repetition." *IntJPsa*, 10, 1929.

STEIN, M.

"Premonition as a Defense." *Q*, 2, 1953.

"The Adolescent and His Parents." *Child Study*, 1955.

Reporter, "The Problem of Masochism in the Theory and Technique of Psychoanalysis." *JAPA*, 4, 1956.

STEINER, M.

"Die Bedeutung der femininen Identifizierung für die männliche Impotenz." *Z*, 16, 1930.

STEKEL, W.

"Über einen Perückenfetischisten." *C*, 1, 1911.

"Goethe über einen Fall von Konversion." *C*, 2, 1912.

"Der Mantel als Symbol." *C*, 3, 1913.

"Ein Fall von larvierter Onanie." *C*, 3, 1913.

"Parapathie und Phimose." *PsaPrx*, 1, 1931.

STENGEL, E.

"Zur Lehre von den transcorticalen Aphasien." *ZNP*, 1936.

"Air-Raid Phobia." *M*, 20, 1944.
Review, *The Nature of Hypnosis* by P. Schilder. *IntJPsa*, 37, 1956.
"The Treatment of Depressions." *JMS*, 1958.

STEPHEN, A.

"Impotence." *M*, 15, 1936.

STEPHEN, K.

"Introjection and Projection: Guilt and Rage." *M*, 14, 1934.

STEPHENS, D.

"Anorexia Nervosa: Endocrine Factors in Undernutrition." *JCE*, 1, 1941.

STERBA, E.

"Nacktheit und Scham." *PsaP*, 3, 1929.
"Analysis of Psychogenic Constipation in a Two-Year-Old Child." *PsaStC*, 3–4, 1949.

STERBA, R.

"Über latente negative Übertragung." *Z*, 13, 1927.
"Zum oralen Ursprung des Neides." *PsaP*, 3, 1928.
"Das Schicksal des Ichs im therapeutischen Verfahren." *Z*, 20, 1934.
Handwörterbuch der Psychoanalyse. IntPV, 1936.
"Zur Theorie der Übertragung." *Im*, 22, 1936.
"Zwei Arten der Abwehr." *PsaP*, 10, 1936.
"Die Aggression in der Rettungsphantasie." *Z*, 25, 1940.
"The Abuse of Interpretation." *Ps*, 4, 1941.
"Metapsychology of Morale." *BMC*, 7, 1943.
"On Spiders, Hanging, and Oral Sadism." *AmIm*, 7, 1950.
"Character and Resistance." *AnSurvPsa*, 2, 1951.
—— & E. Sterba, "The Anxieties of Michelangelo Buonarroti." *IntJPsa*, 37, 1956.

STERN, A.

"On the Nature of the Transference in Psychoanalysis." *NYMJ*, 107, 1918.

STERN, E.

"Zum Problem der Spezifizität der Persönlichkeitstypen und der Konflikte in der Psychosomatischen Medizin." *PSM*, 4, 1957.

STERN, M.

"Trauma and Symptom Formation." *IntJPsa*, 39, 1958.
"Blank Hallucinations: Remarks About Trauma and Perceptual Disturbances." *IntJPsa*, 42, 1961.

STEVENSON, I.

—— & H. Ripley, "Variations in Respiration and in Respiratory Symptoms During Changes in Emotion." *PSM*, 14, 1952.

STODDART, W.

"A Pun Symptom." *IntJPsa*, 10, 1929.

STORCH, A.

"Die Welt der beginnenden Schizophrenia und die archaische Welt. Ein Existenzial-Analytischer Versuch." *ZNP*, 127, 1930.

STORFER, A.

"Samples From a *Dictionary of Psychoanalysis*." *Z*, 10, 1924.

STRACHEY, J.

"Some Unconscious Factors in Reading." *IntJPsa*, 11, 1930.
"The Nature of the Therapeutic Action of Psychoanalysis." *IntJPsa*, 15, 1934.
"The Emergence of Freud's Fundamental Hypotheses." *SE*, 3, 1962.

STRAUSS, A.

"Unconscious Mental Processes and the Psychosomatic Concept." *IntJPsa*, 36, 1955.

STRAUSS, H.

"Epileptic Disorders." *AHPsa*, 1959.

STUNKARD, A.

"Obesity and Denial of Hunger." *PSM*, 21, 1959.

SUGAR, N.

"On the Question of Mimic Affirmation and Negation." *Z*, 26, 1941.
"Zur Frage der unbewussten Verständigung und der 'Ansteckenden' Fehlhandlung." *Z*, 26, 1941.

SULLIVAN, A.

—— & C. Chandler, "Ulcerative Colitis of Psychogenic Origin." *Yale Journal of Biology and Medicine*, 4, 1932.

SULLIVAN, H.

"The Oral Complex." *R*, 12, 1925.
"The Onset of Schizophrenia." *P*, 7, 1927.

SYLVESTER, E.

"Analysis of Psychogenic Anorexia and Vomiting in a Four-Year-Old Child." *PsaStC*, 1, 1945.

SZALAI, A.

"Die 'Ansteckende' Fehlhandlung." *Z*, 19, 1933.

SZASZ, T.

"Factors in the Pathogenesis of Peptic Ulcer." *PSM*, 11, 1949.
"Oral Mechanisms in Constipation and Diarrhoea." *BAPA*, 6, 1950.
"A Contribution to the Psychology of Bodily Feelings." *Q*, 26, 1957.
"On the Theory of Psycho-Analytic Treatment." *IntJPsa*, 38, 1957.
Pain and Pleasure: A Study of Bodily Feelings. BB, 1957.
"The Role of the Counterphobic Mechanism in Addiction." *JAPA*, 6, 1958.

SZEKELY, L.
"Success, Success Neurosis and the Self." *M*, 33, 1960.

SZUREK, S.
"Teaching and Learning of Psychoanalytic Psychiatry in Medical School." *Q*, 26, 1957.

TAMM, A.
"Prophylaxe und Behandlung der Onanie." *PsaP*, 4, 1930.

TANNENBAUM, S.
"Orgasm in the Female." *JSexolPsychoanal*, 2, 1924.

TARACHOW, S.
"A Psychosomatic Theory Based on the Concept of Mastery and Resolution of Tension." *R*, 32, 1945.
"The Syndrome of Inhibition." *PQ*, 21, 1947.
"Mythology." *AnSurvPsa*, 1, 1950.
"Applied Psychoanalysis: Comedy, Wit and Humor." *AnSurvPsa*, 2, 1951.
"Judas the Beloved Executioner." *Q*, 29, 1960.

TAUBER, E.
—— & M. Green, *Prelogical Experience. An Inquiry Into Dreams and Other Creative Processes*. BB, 1959.

TAUSK, V.
"Zur Psychologie der Kindersexualität." *Z*, 1, 1913.
"Kleider und Farben im Dienste der Traumdarstellung." *Z*, 2, 1914.
"Bemerkungen zu Abraham's Aufsatz," in *Über Ejaculatio Praecox*. *Z*, 4, 1916.
"Über eine besondere Form von Zwangsphantasien." *Z*, 4, 1916.
"Compensation as a Means of Discounting the Motive of Repression." *IntJPsa*, 5, 1924.
"On the Origin of the 'Influencing Machine' in Schizophrenia." *Q*, 2, 1933.
"On Masturbation." *PsaStC*, 6, 1951.

TAYLOR, W.
"Behavior Under Hypoanalysis and the Mechanism of the Neurosis." *JAbP*, 18, 1923.

TESLAAR, J. VAN
"Religion and Sex, an Account of the Erotogenetic Theory of Religion as Formulated by Theodore Schroeder." *R*, 2, 1915.

THOMA, H.
"Männlicher Transvestismus und das Verlangen nach Geschlechtsumwandlung." *P*, 11, 1957.

THOMPSON, C.
"Analytic Observations During the Course of a Manic-Depressive Psychosis." *R*, 17, 1930.

TILLMAN, C.
"Detecting Schizoid and Pre-Schizophrenic Personalities." *BMC*, 5, 1941.

TOMAN, W.
"Family Constellation as a Character and Marriage Determinant." *IntJPsa*, 40, 1959.

TRAIN, G.
"Flight into Health." *AJPT*, 7, 1953.

TRIDON, A.
Sex Happiness. Re, 1938.

TRILLING, L.
"Art and Neurosis," in *The Liberal Imagination*. V, 1950.

UEXKULL, T. VON
"Möglichkeiten und Grenzen psychosomatischer Betrachtung." *Nervenarzt*, 26, 1955.

VALENSTEIN, A.
Report on Panel, "The Psychoanalytic Concept of Character." *JAPA*, 6, 1958.

VAN DER HEIDE, C.
"A Study of Mechanisms in Two Cases of Peptic Ulcer." *PSM*, 2, 1940.

VARENDONCK, J.
The Evolution of the Conscious Faculties. Mac, 1923.

VORWAHL, H.
"Erwartung und Eintreffen der Menstruation im Seelenleben der Mädchen." *PsaP*, 5, 1931.

WAELDER, R.
"The Principle of Multiple Function, Observations on Over-Determination." *Q*, 5, 1936.
Basic Theory of Psychoanalysis. IUP, 1960.

WALDER, J.
"Analysis of a Case of Night Terror." *PsaStC*, 2, 1946.

WALDHORN, H.
"An Assessment of Analyzability." *Q*, 39, 1960.

WALL, J.
"Anorexia Nervosa." *BullNYAcadMed*, 32, 1956.

WECHSLER, D.
"The Incidence and Significance of Fingernail Biting in Children." *R*, 18, 1931.

WEGROCKI, H.
"A Case of Number Phobia." *IntJPsa*, 19, 1938.

WEINBERG, S.
Incest Behavior. Cit, 1955.

WEINER, I.
"Father-Daughter Incest." *Q*, 36, 1962.

WEISMANN, A.
"Essays Upon Heredity and Kindred Biological Problems." *CP*, 2, 1892.

WEISS, E.
"A Contribution to the Psychological Explanation of the 'Arc de Cercle'." *IntJPsa*, 6, 1925.
"Regression and Projection in the Super-Ego." *IntJPsa*, 13, 1932.
"Psychosomatic Aspects of Hypertension." *JAMA*, 120, 1942.
"Clinical Aspects of Depression." *Q*, 13, 1944.
"Projection, Extrajection and Objectivation." *Q*, 16, 1947.
—— & O. English, *Psychosomatic Medicine*. Sau, 1949.

WEISSMAN, P.
"Ego and Superego in Obsessional Character and Neurosis." *Q*, 23, 1954.
"Pregenital Compulsive Phenomena and the Repetition Compulsion." *JAPA*, 4, 1956.
"The Childhood and Legacy of Stanislavsky." *PsaStC*, 12, 1957.
"Some Aspects of Sexual Activity in a Fetishist." *Q*, 26, 1957.
"Characteristic Superego Identifications of Obsessional Neurosis." *Q*, 28, 1959.
"The Psychology of the Critic and Psychological Criticism." *JAPA*, 10, 1962.

WEIZSÄCKER, V. VON
"Two Types of Resistance." *P*, 4, 1950.

WENZL, A.
Die Philosophischen Grenzfragen der modernen Naturwissenschaft. WK, 1954.

WEXLER, H.
"Fate Knocks." *IntJPsa*, 40, 1959.

WHEELIS, A.
The Quest for Identity. Nor, 1958.

WHITE, H.
Goals of Life. CWD, 1939.

WHITE, R.
"What Is Tested by Psychological Tests?" in *Relation of Psychological Tests to Psychiatry*. G&S, 1952.
"The Schreber Case Reconsidered in the Light of Psychosocial Concepts." *IntJPsa*, 44, 1963.

WHITE, W.
"Hallucinations." *JNMD*, 31, 1904.
"Symbolism." *R*, 3, 1916.
"The Mechanism of Transference." *R*, 4, 1917.

WIEDEMAN, G.
"Survey of Psychoanalytic Literature on Overt Male Homosexuality." *JAPA*, 10, 1962.

WILSON, G.
"The Analysis of a Transistory Conversion Symptom Simulating Pertussis." *IntJPsa*, 16, 1935.

WILSON, R.
"A Case of Anorexia Nervosa With Necropsy Findings and a Discussion of Secondary Hypopituitarism." *JclinPath*, 7, 1954.

WINNICOTT, D.
"Primitive Emotional Development." *IntJPsa*, 26, 1945.
"On Transference." *IntJPsa*, 34, 1956.
Psychoanalysis and Contemporary Thought." G, 1959.

WINTERSTEIN, A.
"Drei Fälle von Versprechen." *C*, 2, 1911.
"Fear of the New, Curiosity and Boredom." *PsaB*, 2, 1930.
"On the Oral Basis of a Case of Male Homosexuality." *IntJPsa*, 37, 1956.

WISDOM, J.
"On a Differentiating Mechanism of Psychosomatic Disorder." *IntJPsa*, 41, 1960.
"Comparison and Development of the Psycho-Analytical Theories of Melancholia." *IntJPsa*, 43, 1962.

WITTKOWER, E.
"Ulcerative Colitis: Personality Studies." *M*, 2, 1938.

WOLBERG, L.
"The Problem of Self-Esteem in Psychotherapy." *NYSJM*, 43, 1943.
Hypnoanalysis. G&S, 1945.
"A Mechanism of Hysteria Elucidated During Hypnoanalysis." *Q*, 14, 1945.
"Hypnosis in Psychoanalytic Psychotherapy." *ProgPT*, 2, 1957.

WOLFENSTEIN, M.
"A Phase in the Development of Children's Sense of Humor." *PsaStC*, 6, 1951.
"Children's Understanding of Jokes." *PsaStC*, 8, 1953.
"Mad Laughter in a Six-Year-Old Boy." *PsaStC*, 10, 1955.

WOLFF, M.
"Sexuelle Neugierde eines kleinen Mädchens." *PsaPrx*, 3, 1933.
"The Problem of Neurotic Manifestations in Children of Preoedipal age." *PsaStC*, 6, 1951.
"On Castration Anxiety." *IntJPsa*, 36, 1955.

WRIGHT, H.

"A Contribution to the Orgasm Problem in Women." *IntJSexol*, 3, 1949.

WULFF, M.

"Beiträge zur infantilen Sexualität." *C*, 2, 1912.

"Zur Psychogenität des Asthma bronchiale." *C*, 3, 1913.

"Über einen interessanten oralen Symptomenkomplex und seine Beziehungen zur Sucht." *Z*, 18, 1932.

YATES, S.

"Phobias. II." *M*, 11, 1932.

YAZMAJIAN, R.

"Slips of the Tongue." Presented at Mid-Winter Meeting of the American Psychoanalytical, December 6, 1963.

"Verbal and Symbolic Processes in Slips of the Tongue." Presented at State University Downstate Medical Center, Division of Psychoanalytic Education, November 6, 1963.

"Color in Dreams." *Q*, 33, 1964.

YOUNG, J.

"Study of a Severe Case of Obsessional Neurosis." *M*, 1, 1921.

"Two Cases of War Neurosis." *M*, 2, 1922.

ZELIGS, M.

"Acting In: A Contribution to the Meaning of Some Postural Attitudes Observed During Analysis." *JAPA*, 5, 1957.

ZETZEL, E.

"The Concept of Anxiety in Relation to the Development of Psychoanalysis." *JAPA*, 3. 1955.

"Current Concepts of Transference." *IntJPsa*, 34, 1956.

ZIWAR, M.

"Aggression and Intercostal Neuralgia, a Psychosomatic Study." *EJP*, 1, 1945.

ZULLIGER, H.

"Psychoanalysis and the Form-Interpretation Test." *IntJPsa*, 31, 1950.

"Angst in der Spiegelung des Tafein-Z-Tests." *Zdiag-Psychol*, 2, 1954.

ZUTT, J.

Psychiatrische Betrachtungen zur Pubertätsmagersucht Klin. Weschr, 24–25, 1946.

ZWERLING, I.

"The Favorite Joke in Diagnostic and Therapeutic Interviewing." *Q*, 24, 1955.

Index

A

Abraham, Karl, 24, 100, 322, 376, 392
  on abnormal thinking, 9-10
  biography of, **1-8**
    character of, 7
    member of Vienna Society, 159
  on introjection, 205-6
  masochistic patient of, 140
  most important contribution of, 2
  on nocturnal enuresis, 272-73
  on optimism, 283-84
  on penis envy, 300
  on psychosexual development
    oral stage, 2, 3, 284, 285-86, 320
    postambivalent stage, 317-18
  pregenitality, 320-21
    stages of anal phase, 31
  on sexual inhibition, 392
    frigidity, 166, 167, 189, 466
    impotence, 124, 188-89
  on spider symbolism, 413-14

on temperature eroticism, 435
theory of psychosis of, 351
    manic-depressive psychosis, 229-30
    megalomania, 243
    melancholia, 243-44
  on tics, 439
  on totemic behavior, 443-44
  on transference, 447
Abraham, Max, 4
Abreaction, **8,** 52, 62, 379
Absence, **8-9,** 44
Abstinence, 342, 385
  from alcohol, 23
  from drugs, 16
  rule of, **384,** 448
  sexual, *see* Sexual abstinence
Abstract thinking (ideas), **9-10,** 151, 395, 467, 474
  affects and, 19-20
  as behavioral derivative, 273
  conscious, 458
  preconscious, 319
  unconscious, 126
Abulia, **10**
Academy of Child Psychiatry, 70

Accident proneness, **11,** 286
Acrophobia, **11,** 311
Acropolis (Athens), 104
Acting in, **11,** 378, 384
Acting out, **11-12,** 25, 185, 221, 378, 384
  accident proneness as, 11
  by alcoholics, 23
  destructive, 204-5
Action (acts), **12,** 365, 368
  during sleep, 19
  thought and
    equation, 234, 282, 283
    ideas translated into action, 372
    regression to thought from action, 366
    thought as experimental action, 438
    thought substituted for action, 46
  types of
    accidental, 295
    mob, 237
    normal, 252
    raptus, **364**

Page numbers in **boldface** refer to main entries

Action, types of *(Continued)*
  reflex, **370-71**
  symptomatic, **426-27**
  trial, 9, 98, 411
  unconscious, **457-58**
Active therapy, **13-14**
  active play therapy, *see* Play
    therapy
  of Ferenczi, 143-44, 164
Activity, **12-13,** 228
  inhibition of, 252
  lack of, 283-84
  as neurotic predisposition, 71
  passivity and 12-13, 21, 81,
    231-32, 297
  activity changed to passivity,
    366
  activity precedes passivity, 397
  adolescent roles, 17
  conflict between, 79
  flexible utilization of, 370
  love as both, 225
  masochistic and sadistic
    representation, 386
    in oral pessimism, 284
    passivity changed to activity,
      87, 188
    passivity substitutes for
      activity, **14**
    as polarities, 315
    roles of, in relaxation, 373
    in turning against self, 95
  from preoedipal mother
    fixation, 241
Actual neuroses, **14-15,** 38, 179
    341, 400
  abandonment of theory of, 267
  See also Anxiety neurosis;
    Neurasthenia
Adaptation, **15-16,** 45, 183, 303
  genetically determined, 36, 408
  prevented by illusions, 186
  to reality, 368, 372
  See also Alloplastic adaptation;
    Autoplastic adaptation
Adaptational approach, 342
Addiction, **16,** 93, 298, 320, 400,
    419
  addicting drugs, 113-14, 154-55
  alimentary orgasm and, 25
  as ego-syntonic trait, 124

euphoria and, 133
  to masturbation, **238-39**
  projective diagnosis of, 384
  See also Alcoholism
Adler, Alfred, 163, 369
  Freud's relationship with,
    159-60
  individual psychology of, 192,
    433
  theory of self-assertion of, 198
Adolescence, **16-18,** 70, 354
  action of component instincts
    during, 77
  delinquency in, 469-70
  identity during, 410
  instinctual aims of, 242
  masturbation during, 237, 238,
    274
  See also Puberty
Aerophagia, **18**
Aesthetic pleasure, **18-19,** 46, 130
  ambiguity in, 27
  as forepleasure, 150
  from humor, 76, 81-82,
    175, 211, 355
  illusion as essential to, 186
  from looking, 393
Aesthetics, 8, 216, 374, 383, 392,
    466
  analyst's knowledge of, 442
  breast envy and, 58
  psychoanalysis applied to,
    41-42, 344, 345
  role of illusion in, 470
Affection, *see* Love
Affective complexes, 473
Affects, **19-20,** 207, 375, 440
  affective transformation, 253
  as behavioral derivatives, 273
  deprivation of, 266
  discharge of, 62, 215
  discrepancy between thought
    and, 389
  of dreams, 109
  isolation of, 365
  of pain, 291
  postponement of, 362
  in promiscuity, 333
  as substitute for action, 46
  synonym for, 126

types of
    ambiguous, 26
    anxiety as, 37
    strangulated, 340, 417; *see
      also* Repression
    unconscious, 8, 19-20, **458**
  See also Emotions; Feelings
Agent provocateur, **20**
Aggression, **21-22,** 50, 53, 74,
    129, 173, 291, 373, 429
  Abraham's work on, 2
  activity as synonym for, 13, 21
  aggressive instinct-fusion, 198,
    199, 328, 339, 377-78,
    435-36; *see also* Destrudo
  ambivalence and, 27, 28, 93,
    324
  anxiety and, 37, 38, 39, 61
  civilization and, 72, 73, 343
  crying and, 89
  as destructive force, 162
  fear of aggressive fighting, 204
  forms of
    anal, 31, 405-6
    deneutralized, 319
    healthy, 318
    infantile, 25, 316-17, 371,
      422
    internalized, 228
    mutism, 253
    neutralized, 390, 413, 425
    nonneutralized, 354
    oral, 285, 403, 471
  paranoid, 88
  phallic, 308
  phobic, 310
  visual, 305
  imitation of, 187-88
  love changed to, 293
  manifestations of
    conversion, 59
    death instinct, 130
    doctor game, 107
    dreams, 110, 350, 425
    hair pulling, 171
    hypochondriasis, 180
    impotence, 124
    nailbiting, 283
    oedipal, 241, 263
    raptus actions, 364

ritual, 383
slips of the tongue, 27
wit, 176
see also Anger; Destruction;
Hatred; Hostility; Rage;
Revenge
masochistic provocation of,
232, 233, 268
measurement of, 133
pregnancy and, 323
respiratory discharge of, 379
responses to feeling or acts of
blushing, 55, 132
curbing of, in altruism, 26
denial in necrophilia, 261
fear, 396, 401, 411
frigid, 166-67
masturbation as defense
against, 237
projection, 388
punishment in nightmares,
271
reaction formation, 312
remorse, 72, 374, 398, 460
repression, 316, 380
transformation to masochism,
289
against self, *see* Self—aggression
against
simultaneous gratification of sex
drive and, 43, 315, 363,
369, 385, 393
subjects of
alcoholics, 23-24
analysts, 85, 86
homosexuals, 140, 142
narcissistic types, 221
obsessional neurotics, 366
superego, 123
ulcer patients, 301, 302
See also Death instinct
Aggressivization, *see* Sexualization
—aggressivization and
Agnosia, **20-21,** 39
Agoraphobia, 120, 136, 185, 252,
310, 311
Aichhorn, August, *Wayward
Youth,* **469-70**
Aim inhibition, **22-23,** 35, 72, 292,
419

delay of discharge and, 98, 99
discharged in humor, 81
under hypnosis, 178, 179
in love, 224, 225, 257, 409
neutralization and, 271
of oedipal wishes, 307
relaxation and, 373
of scopophilic and epistemophilic instincts, 130
Alcoholics Anonymous, 24
Alcoholism, **23-25,** 210
Abraham's explanation of, 2, 24
as marital problem, 231
rationalization of, 23, 24, 364
Alexander, Franz, 143, 420
dream theory of, 111, 291
short-term therapy of, 404, 405
Alimentary orgasm, 24, **25**
Alloplastic adaptation, **25-26**
alloplastic identification, 185
Ferenczi on, 16
Almansi, R. J., 137
Altruism, **26,** 107, 127, 225
in love, 257-58
social mindfulness as, 409
Ambiguity, **26-27**
Ambition, 285
Ambivalence, 26, **27-28,** 93, 459
Abraham's contribution to
understanding of, 6-7
oral, 27, 284-85, 301, 317, 324
postambivalent phase, **317-18**
roles of
in depression, 378
in melancholia, 205-6, 244
in obsession, 365, 366, 369,
383
in paranoid state, 293
in perversion, 304
in taboos, 429
sexual, 265
solution of, 225
toward spiders, 413
totemic, 443, 444
of transference, 447
Ambivalent oscillation, 27, **28-29,**
93, 412
defense against, 279
Amenhotep IV, King of Egypt, 3
Amentia, **29,** 172

American Association of
Psychiatric Clinics for
Children, 70
American Board of Psychiatry and
Neurology, 70
American Psychoanalytic
Association, 145
Amnesia, **29,** 271, 365
after raptus actions, 364
alcoholic, 23
after hypnosis, 178
infantile, *see* Screen memories
paramnesia, **292-93,** 376
Amphimixis, **29-30**
Amsterdam Society for
Parapsychological
Research, 434
Anaclitic dependence, **30,** 115
Anaclitic depression, **30**
Anaclitic object choice, 30,
184-85, **277-78**
in love, 225, 409, 449
Anaesthesias, 153-54, 416
in intercourse, 194
vaginal, 166, 274
Anagogic interpretation, **30-31**
Anal (anal-sadistic) phase, **31-32,**
169, 175, 191, 220, 383,
386, 416
Abraham's analysis of, 2, 31,
321
in cloaca theory, 74
discovery of, 158
ingredients of
aggression, 31, 405-6
ambivalence, 93, 285, 317
attachment to mother, 325
frustration, 213
identification, 136, 201
inferiority feelings, 192
instinctual aims, 199
obesity, 277
passive-receptive longing, 297
introjection and, 205
as origin of tics, 439
penis envy rooted in, 300
regression to, 31, 180, 224, 232,
351, 366, 371, 380, 472;
see also Anal wishes
revival of conflicts of, 323
toilet training during, 440-41

Anal wishes, 25, 124, 366, 403
  obsessional neurosis due to, 71,
    279
  pseudo-hypersexuality and, 335
  renounced in sphincter control
    and morality, 412-13
  roles of
    in attitudes toward money,
      248-49, 380, 402, 412
    in boredom, 58
    in bronchial asthma, 59
    in choice of a mate, 231
    in compulsive washing, 120
    motivation for sacrifice, 385
    in ulcerative colitis, 455
  types of
    erotic, 379
    exhibitionistic, 102, 106
    submissive, 369
Analysis, *see* Hypoanalysis;
  Psychoanalysis
"Analysis of a Phobia in a
  Five-Year-Old Boy"
  (Freud), 223; *see also*
  "Little Hans"
"Analysis of Urethro-Anal Habits,
  The" (Ferenczi), 144
Analytic insight, 13, **32**, 320, 347
Analyzing instrument, **32**
Ananke (fate), **33**, 312, 374
Angel, Anny, 284
Anger, 115, 395
  intolerance of, 301
  unconscious, 95
  See also Rage; Resentment
Anhedonia, **33**
Animism, **33-34**, 194, 329-30, 392,
  423
"Anna O." (case history), 155-56
Anorexia nervosa, **34-35**, 277, 472
Anterograde amnesia, 29
Anthropology, *see* Psychoanalytic
  anthropology
Anticathexis, *see* Countercathexis
Anticipation, **36-37**, 64, 132, 411,
  450
  in forepleasure and
    fore-unpleasure, 151, 340,
    460
  free will and, 152
  in illusion, 186

as inner reality, 340
role of, in shame, 404
See also Anxiety
Anti-Semitism, 165, 170, 175, 388
  Abraham's encounters with, 4
Antithetical meanings, **37**
Anxiety, 37-38, 59, 162, 173, 236,
  265, 331, 382, 471, 472
  of analyst, 86
  at birth, 52
  drugs and, 113, 114
  forms of
    fore-unpleasure, 151
    instinctual, 242, 342
    nocturnal, 271, 299
    normal vs. neurotic, 196-97
    objective, anticipation as, 36
    persecutory and depressive,
      294
    phobic, 266, 375
    schizophrenic, 390
    separation, 277
    signal, 342, 380, **405**
    social, 80
    transformed libido, 14
    See also Castration anxiety
  fragmentation and, 151
  psychoanalytic approaches to
    active therapy, 14
    anthropological, 361
    catharsis, 62
    structural, 342
    systematic, 341
  reassurance against, 368, 369
  responses to, 370
    avoidance, 201
    intimidation as defense, 203-4
    intolerance, 301
    projection, 389
    raptus actions, 364
    repetition compulsion, 374
    vertigo, 468
  results of
    alcoholism, 24
    inability to relax, 373
    prevention of sleep, 177
    repression, 380
    sexual inhibition, 194
  roles of
    in anhedonia, 33
    in decompensation, 92

in depersonalization, 102,
  103
in hypochondriasis, 180
in pyromania, 357
in temperature eroticism, 435
in weekend neurosis, 421-22
  sexualization and
    aggressivization of, **401-2**
  sources of
    deviation from ritual, 382
    dreams, 111, 112, 452
    fantasies, 140, 167, 322, 362
    homosexuality, 149, 194, 196
    masturbation, 237
    return of repressed material,
      267
    threats to barriers, 49
  See also Fear
Anxiety neurosis, **38-39**, 268, 299
  as actual neurosis, 15, 400
  with neurasthenia, 266
Anxiety state, **39**, 49
  of "'Little Hans," 67, 223
  stage fright as, 415
Aphanisis, **39**
Aphasia, **39**
  agnosia as, 20, 39
Apperceptive distortion, **39-40**
Appersonation, **40**, 138, 409
Applied psychoanalysis, **40-42**,
  343, 344-45, 466
  Abraham's contribution to, 3
Arc de cercle, **42**
Arlow, Jacob A., 97
Art, *see* Aesthetics
As-if personality, **42-43**
Asthma, bronchial, **58-59**, 353-54,
  420
Athletic types, 65, 221, 418
Attraction of the forbidden, **43**, 73
Authority problems, 10, 369, 415
  adolescent, 17
  in child analysis, 69
Autism, 43, 389, 436
Autobiography (Freud), 154, 156
Autoeroticism, **43-44**, 243, 257,
  401, 440
  of alcoholics, 24
  fantasies of, 52
  fixation on, 351
  during puberty, 355

Page numbers in **boldface** refer to main entries

rhythmic activities as, 381-82
See also Masturbation;
Narcissism
Autohypnosis, **44-45**
Automatic obedience, **45,** 139
Automatism, **45-46,** 364
tics as, 45, 439
Autonomy, **46,** 412
ego, 19, 118
precedes autoplastic adaptation,
15
primary, 75
Autoplastic adaptation, 15-16,
46-47
autonomy precedes, 15
autoplastic identification, 185
Autosymbolism, **47**
Avoidance, **47-48,** 93, 148, 403
of conflicts, 292
of insight, 432, 449
masochistic, 314
of narcissistic mortification, 47,
93-94, 192, 210, 295, 314,
407
of pain, 48, 118, 201
phobic, 131, 268, 309-10, 312
of suffering, 175
of unpleasure, 307, 315, 381,
461
Azima, H., 114

B

Bak, R., 147
Barriers, **49-50,** 303
Basic rule, *see* Free association
Baumeyer, F., 391
Beating fantasies, **51-52,** 232, 312
Bed-wetting, *see* Enuresis
Bellak, L., 39-40, 474
Benedek, T., 103
Bentham, Jeremy, 313
Bergler, Edmund, 55, 232, 284
on day residues, 92
on déjà vu, 97
on depersonalization, 102
describes breast complex, 58
Bergson, Henri, 76
Berlin, 1, 4-6, 154, 158

Berlin Psychoanalytic Society, 1,
5-6
Bernays, Martha, 152, 154,
156-57, 158
Bernays, Minna, 157, 158
Bernheim, Hippolyte, 178
Bestiality (zooerasty), 304,
481-82
Beyond the Pleasure Principle
(Freud), 158, 188
Bibring, E., 103, 244
Binet, Alfred, 146
Bioanalysis, 143
Birth trauma, **52-53,** 79, 191
Bisexuality, **53-54,** 231-32, 376,
476
Abraham's study of, 2
activity reflects, 12-13, 21
adolescent, 17
biological (hermaphroditism),
300, 301
as cause of repression, 51, 365
cloaca theory and, 74
in competitive jealousy, 209
discoverer of, 158
hypochondriacal (psychosomatic) symptoms of, 179,
353, 473
in homosexuality, 217
in negative Oedipus complex,
263
overt, 288
sociological, 231
See also Phallic mother; Phallic
woman; Vaginal father
Blau, A., 15
Bleuler, Eugen, 159, 218
Abraham and, 4-5
coins term ambivalence, 27
coins term autism, 43
on schizophrenia, 121, 265, 389
Blindness, hysterical, 224, 346
Blos, P., 17
Blum, H., 75
Blumgart, L., 145
Blushing, **54-55,** 119, 435, 468
fear of (erythrophobia), 55,
131-32, 311, 415
Body, self-observation of, 397
Body ego, 65, 118, 395

Body image, **55-56,** 309, 395, 399
Body language, **56-57,** 216
organ language, 474
psychosomatic, 352
tic as, 440
See also Mannerisms
Boehm, Felix, 5
Bohr, Niels, 63
Bonaparte, Marie, 344
Borderline cases, **57,** 124, 218,
400
Boredom, **57-58,** 373, 382
Bornstein, Bertha, 69
Brain, W. R., 296
Breast complex, **58,** 300, 306,
324-25
Breast envy, **58,** 247, 263, 326
in preadolescence, 17
Bremen, 3-4
Brenner, C., 381
Breuer, Josef, 50
Freud's collaboration with,
155-56, 157, 158, 178, 439
discovery of abreaction, 8
discovery of catharsis, 62
discovery of strangulated
affect, 417
divisions of hysteria, 379
function of autohypnosis, 44
origin of psychoanalysis, 340,
341
use of suggestion, 420
Brierley, Marjorie, 467
Brill, A. A., 5, 145, 261
as Freud's translator, 346
Bronchial asthma, **58-59,** 353-54,
420
Brooding, 10, 130, **278-79**
Bruch, H., 227
Brücke, Ernst, 153
Brunswick, Ruth Mack, 134, 179,
293, 472, 473
Budapest, 141-42, 145, 424
Burghölzli (Zurich), 5
Buxbaum, Edith, 171
Bychowski, G., 132
on introjects, 204-5
on latent psychosis, 218
on primitive superego, 330
on psychotic core, 354

C

Campbell, C. M., 390
Cannibalism, 18, 317, 321, 362, 369
  causes slip of the tongue, 345-46
  manic-depressive, 228, 229
  in melancholia, 244, 260
Caprio, F., 274-75
Caricature, **61**
Carmichael, H. T., 298
Castration anxiety, 38, 39, **61,** 176, 217, 220, 301, 361, 415
  associated with mothers, 325
  bisexuality and, 54, 232
  in blushing, 55, 132
  as characteristic of phallic stage, 307-8
  over circumcision, 388
  in daydreams, 91
  defense against
    avoidance, 403
    denial, 284, 305, 308
    eating as defense, 277
    reaction formation, 198
  menstruation as reminder of, 245, 324
  pity and, 312
  pregnancy and, 323
  prototype of, 191
  of Rat Man, 365
  reassurance against, 369
  results of
    fetishism, 146-47
    hair pulling, 171
    impotence, 124, 125, 188
    misogyny, 247
    pseudodebility, 334
  of Schreber, 391
  with vagina dentata fantasies, 465, 466
Castration complex, **62,** 166, 191, 367, 481-82
  as cause of enuresis, 272
  Oedipus complex and, 281, 289
  penis envy and, 299
  spider symbolism in, 413, 414
  threefold outcome of female, 289
Castration threats, 61, 223, 472

deferred obedience to, 96
denial of, 270
Oedipus complex and, 106-7
primal scene connected with, 327-28
produce sexual inhibition, 400
from superego, 123
Catatonic schizophrenia, 144, 389
  mutism in, 253
  symptom of, 45
Catharsis, 8, **62-63,** 340
Cathexis, **63,** 94, 205, 307, 373, 418, 474
  as basis of economic approach, 339
  blending of, 78
  delusions and, 99
  deprivation of, 207
  displacement of, 306
  forms of
    anticathexis, *see*
      Countercathexis
    attention, 45
    decathexis, 389
    fantasy (introversion), 149, **206,** 303
    hypercathexis, 399, 424
    recathexis, 351, 389
  intensity of, 224
  lowering of energetic, 461
  in obesity, 277
  shifts in, 355, 397
  subjects of
    ego, 118, 119, 121, 122
    ego functions, 17
    libido, 63, 94, 98-99, 125, 172, 179, 222, 243, 257, 260, 284, 302, 326, 328, 389, 394, 395, 401, 418
    of superego, 422
  withdrawal of, 14, 29, 253, 272, 303, 396
Causal approach, 50, **63-64,** 152, 313, 470
  final, *see* Teleological approach
  See also Psychic determinism
Censorship, 57, **64-65,** 318, 424
  of dreams, 64, 113
  freedom from, 50, 91; *see also*
    Free association
  of id, 183

Central ego, **65,** 118, 221
Character neurosis, **65-66,** 76, 304, 343
  denial in, 352
  destiny neurosis compared to, 105
  schizoid, **388-89**
Character traits, 66-67, 90, 341, 453
  Abraham's studies of, 2-3
  function of, 342-43
  neurotic, 47, 76, 79, 83-84, 93, 119, 124, 148, 267, 268, 278, 304, 312, 366, 400, 431, 457
  optimistic, 284
  oral, 285-86
  phallic, 305
  reaction formation as cause of, 366
  xenophobia as, 477
  See also Ego-alien traits;
    Ego-syntonic traits; Phallic
    character; Phobic
    character; Psychotic
    character
Charcot, Jean Martin, 20, 153, 155
Child analysis, **67-70**
  simultaneous with mother
    analysis, **405-6**
  See also "Little Hans"
"Child Analysis in the Analysis
    of the Adult" (Ferenczi), 144, 146
Child Guidance Clinics, 70
"Child Is Being Beaten, A"
    (Freud), 51
Child psychiatry, **70-71**
  play therapy, 13, 68-69
  short-term, 404-5
  See also Child analysis
Choice
  freedom of, 338
  of localization of a symptom, 224
  neurotic
    choice of a mate, 231
    choice of neurosis, 65, **71-72,** 80, 221, 298, 360

Page numbers in **boldface** refer to main entries

object, *see* Anaclitic object choice; Narcissistic object choice

Chronic alcoholism, 23-24

Civilization, **72-73;** *see also* Psychoanalytic anthropology

Civilization and Its Discontents (Freud), 35, 343

" 'Civilized' Sexual Morality and Modern Nervous Illness" (Freud), **73**

Clark University (Worcester, Mass.), 141, 155, 161

Claustrophobia, **74,** 311

Climax, *see* Orgasm

Clitoris, 192, 462-63
  frigidity and, 62
  as penis, 107, 309

Cloaca theory, **74**

Coitus, 251, 271, 273
  defloration, 468
  first, 119
  an illicit act, 226
  inhibition over, *see* Sexual inhibition
  invitation to, 42
  masochistic stimulation for, 232
  monogamous, 369
  between parents, *see* Primal scene
  promiscuous attitude toward, *see* Nymphomania; Promiscuity
  in psychoanalytic anthropology, 240, 241
  role of aggression in, 21-22
  scopophilia in, 351
  See also Orgasm; Prostitution; Rape

Coitus interruptus, 14-15, 38, 266

Colitis, ulcerative, 353, 405-6, **455-56**

Collective unconscious, **75,** 361

Color, 360
  in dreams, **75-76,** 110

Color responses, 383

Comic quality, **76**

Command negativism, 265

Committee, secret, 163-65

Commonwealth Fund Program for the Prevention of Delinquency, 70

Comparative approach, 195-97, 360
  to pathology of neuroses, **76-77**

Competition (rivalry), 199, 209, 225
  between fathers and sons, *see* Oedipus complex

Complexes, 375, 391, 473; *see also* Breast complex; Castration complex; Oedipus complex; Polycrates complex

Compliance, 412, 413
  social, **408-9**
  somatic, **410-11**

Component instincts, **77-78,** 147, 148, 198, 200
  in maturation, 401
  in perversion, 77, 270, 289
  sadism and masochism as, 386
  scopophilia as, 392

Compromise formations, 116, 288, 345

Compulsion, 25, 185, 190, 262, 287, 298
  automatism in, 45
  component instinct in, 270
  counter-compulsion, 143
  decompensation for, 92
  as defense, 346, 365
  destructive, 204
  doubt dispelled by, 28
  erotic reality as, 44
  masturbation equivalents constitute, 326
  reaction formation in, 135
  to rebel, 369
  rhythm in, 381
  severe superego in, 173
  See also Mania; Obsession; Obsessive-compulsive neurosis; Repetition compulsion

Compulsive masturbation, **78,** 95, 238, 239
  erotomania and, 274, 387
  of pyromaniacs, 357

Compulsive-obsessive neurosis, *see* Obsessive-compulsive neurosis

Compulsive (obsessive) thinking, 9, 382

Condensation, **78-79,** 113, 203, 211, 265, 382, 474
  of bisexuality, 473
  as primary process mechanism, 329

Conflicts, 77, **79,** 244, 312, 441
  ambivalence, *see* Ambivalence
  avoidance of, 292
  drugs and, 115
  expression of, 457
    acting out, 23
    body language as, 56, 440
    impotence, 400
    repression, 375
    in speech, 403, 411, 458-59, 474
    symbolic, 383
    transference neurosis, 450
    vertigo, 468
  external, 427
    absence of, 25-26
    interpersonal, 249
    as projected internal conflict, 336
    psychopathic, 348, 349
    with society, 72
  freedom from, 402
  growth of humor and, 176
  over identification, 136
  independent of traumas, 340-41
    masturbatory, 237
  metaphoric hints at, 246
  need for reassurance and, 369
  neurotic, 77, 80, 337, 372, 428, 435
  nuclear neurotic, 199, 267
    pathoneurotic, 298
    psychotic vs., 268, 351-52
    of Rat Man, 365
  Oedipal, *see* Oedipus complex
  of parasitic superego, 296
  results of
    frigidity, 166
    maladjustment, 228
    mutism, 253
    neurosis, 80, 337, 428

Conflicts, results of *(Continued)*
  nightmares, 271
  parapraxis, 294, 295
  perversion, 270
  phobia, 310
  reading disturbances, 367
  rebelliousness, 369
  recurrent dreams, 111
  regression, 301, 371
  revenge, 380
  revival of conflicts, 323
  stage fright, 415
  war neurosis, 469
reworking of early, 372
short-term therapy for, 404
solution of internal, 162
sources of
  imbalance of polarities, 315
  monogamy, 73
  neurotic symptoms, 148, 194
structural, 79, 267
"Confusion of Tongues Between
  Adults and the Child"
  (Ferenczi), 144
Congenital (connate)
  characteristics, **79-80;**
  see also Heredity
Conscience, **80,** 122, 242, 363,
  466
  fear of, 123
  infantile, 441
  in melancholia, 243
  of moral masochists, 232
  in promiscuity, 333
  punishment by, 413, 475
  undifferentiated ego, 204
Conscious (consciousness), **80-81,**
  178, 251, 340-41, 348,
  429, 475
  affects and, 19-20
  conflict of, 79, 337
  defense mechanisms and, 95
  elimination of, 261
  forces acting on
    censorship between precon-
      scious, unconscious and,
      64-65, 318
    dissociation, 8, 346, 365;
      see also Absence
  expansion, 114
  resistance, 377

functioning of id and, 183
ingredients of
  gratification, 387
  identification, 201-2
  instinctual vicissitudes, 200,
    454
  mental phenomena, 245
  perception, 302, **303,** 359
  perversions, 270
  symbolization, 425, 426
neurotic, xvii
  "loss of consciousness," 322
  obsessional neurosis, 365
as part of ego, 118, 251-52, 338
psychoanalytic approaches to
  dynamic, 345
  structural, 417-18
  systematic, 246, 318-19, 345,
    428
  qualitative, 342, 359
  raptus actions and, 364
  removal of impulse from, *see*
    Repression; Suppression
  speech functions and, 412
  storage of memories and, 121
Constancy, law of, 105, 176, **219,**
  266, 338, 387
Constipation
  hysterical, 180, 195, 224, 472
  of speech, 403
Construction, 203
"Contra-Indications to the
  Active Psychoanalytic
  Technique" (Ferenczi),
  143
Control, **82,** 287
  as ego function, 12, 82, 90, 117,
    183, 302, 362, 372, 395,
    438, 458
  loss of, *see* Narcissistic
    mortification
Convenience dreams, 109
Conversion, **82-83,** 93, 216, 314,
  439
  blushing as, 132
  bronchial asthma as, 59
  leap from psychic to somatic,
    247, 334
  motility contrasted to, 252
  pregenital, 459
  of psychic excitement, 56

as psychosomatic disturbance,
  353
Conversion hysteria, *see*
  Hysterical conversion
Conversion symptoms, 15, 71,
  82-83, 93, 221, 267, 268,
  442
  arc de cercle as, 42
  blushing as, 55, 119
  body language and, 56
  bronchial asthma and, 59
  or erotic types, 298
  imitation and, 187
  impotence as, 125
  nocturnal enuresis as, 272
  regression in, 334
  stigmata as, 416
  of war neurosis, 452
  writer's cramp as, 475
Coprophagia (coprophagy), **83,**
  277
Coprophilia, **83-84,** 199
Coriat, Isador H., 305
Countercathexis (anticathexis),
  49, **84,** 98, 189-90, 267,
  333, 390
  aggressive, 26-27, 310
  of aim-inhibited drives, 22-23,
    373, 419
  as defense, 295, 346-47
  diminution of, 372, 373
  essence of, 82
  frustration due to, 195
  against id, 65, 242
  in perversion, 304
  in reaction formation, 366
  in repression, 84, 95, 377, 378,
    441, 457
  resistance against, 120
  in shamelessness, 404
  unconscious, 375
Counterphobia. **84,** 260, 305, 369,
  402, 404
Countertransference, 50, **85-86,**
  134, 342, 431, 432-33, 453
  as analytic variable, 32
Crawley, Ernest, *The Mystic
  Rose,* 468
Creativity, **87-88,** 151, 372
  linguistic, 216, 475
  narcissistic source of, 259

relaxation prior to, 373
studies of, 41
test of, 384
Crime, 336, 360, 380, 383
    arson, 364
    criminal law, **218-19**
    juvenile, 469-70
    punishment for mental, 233
    theft, 348
    See also Prostitution
Criticism, **88**, 158, 165, 292
    of Adler, 160
    anticipation of, 132
    artistic, xv
    in dreams, 10
    of Ferenczi, 143-44, 146
    of Freud, xiv, xvi, 20, 88, 126,
        165, 292, 457
    guilt over, 398
    self-criticism, *see* Self-criticism
"Critique of C. G. Jung"
    (Abraham), 3
Croce, Benedetto, 81, 216
Cross section of neurosis, **88-89**
Crucial alcoholism, 23
Cruelty, *see* Sadism
Crying, *see* Weeping
Culture, *see* Psychoanalytic
    anthropology
Curiosity, **90**, 285, 441
    arousal of, xvi, 404
    sexual, *see* Sexual curiosity

D

Dalldorf (Berlin), 4-5
Dams, 401
Darwin, Charles, 54, 235, 236
Daudet, Alphonse, *Le Nabab,* 376
Day residues, 12, 75, **91-92,** 110
Daydreams, **91**, 150, 299, 468
    excessive, 44
    prelogical thinking in, 323
    See also Fantasies
Death instinct, *see* Thanatos
Death wish, 310, 365
    ambivalence due to, 28
    denial of, 376
    of Freud, 153

nirvana principle connected
    with, 387
roles of
    in anorexia nervosa, 34
    in depression, 103-4
    in melancholia, 244
    in necrophilia, 261
Deautomatization, 46
Decompensation, **92**
Defeat (failure), 259, 386, 405
    masochistic, 232, 233, 235, 251,
        264, 441
    neurotic provocation of, 262
    See also Success
Defense hysteria, 379
Defense mechanisms, 31, **92-96,**
    109, 144, 242, 288, 331,
    427
    assimilation of, 364
    character, 66-67
        phobic character, 312
    classification of, 266
    countercathexis of, 378
    ego's attitude toward, 270
    inner identification in, 202
    instinctual vicissitudes and, 200,
        454
    of nymphomaniac, 274
    objects of
        conscious recognition, 14, 93
        curiosity, 90
        emotion, 126
    in regression, 371, 372
    responsibility for, 118
    results of
        interference in choice of
            mate, 231
        paresis, 296
        perversion, 304
        pseudo-hypersexuality, 335
        psychopathic defenses, 349
    as threat to sexuality, 401
    traced to repression, 316
    types of
        appersonation, 40
        counterphobia, 84
        depersonalization, 102
        ego-syntonic, 123
        impotence, 124
        jamais phenomenon, 209
        laughter, 218

masturbation, 237
masturbation fantasies, 240
micropsia, 247
mutism, 253
narcolepsy, 261
overeating, 277
perversion, 135-36
primary and secondary, 93
projective identification, 332
rationalization, 268
yawning, 479
see also Ambivalence;
    Ambivalent oscillation;
    Avoidance; Conversion;
    Denial; Derealization;
    Displacement;
    Exaggeration; Fixation;
    Inhibition; Introjection;
    Isolation; Negation;
    Projection;
    Pseudoidentification;
    Reaction formation;
    Repression; Reversal into
    the opposite; Turning
    against self; Undoing
Defenses, 23, 162, 341, 348, 351,
    372
    absence of, 390
    breakdown of, 92
    in conversion, 83
    language and
        body language, 56
        slips of the tongue, 407, 412
        speech functions, 411-12
    neuropsychoses of, **266-67**
    objects of
        ambivalence, 279, 459
        bisexuality, 54
        breast complex, 300
        effect of drugs, 115
        ego-alien impulses, 364
        homosexuality, *see*
            Homosexuality—defenses
            against
        masturbation, 171
        return of repressed material,
            267
        submission, 265
    sexualization of, 202
    strength of, 268

Defenses *(Continued)*
varieties of
adolescent, 17
aesthetic pleasure, 19
anal, 31
anorexia nervosa, 35
arc de cercle, 42
boredom, 57, 58
bronchial asthma, 59
caricature, 61
censorship, 64
compulsion, 346, 365
crying, 89
delusion, 100, 293
erotic transference, 130
fetishism, 135-36, 147, 304,
392-93
hallucinations, 171
impotence, 188
oral, 295
phobia, 310
psychosis as, 389
regression, 371
secondary, 379-80
shame, 404
torticollis, 443
totemic behavior, 444
urination as, 463
Deferred reaction, **96-97**
deferred obedience, **96**
Déjà raconté, **97,** 103
Déjà vu, **97-98,** 103
Delay of discharge, 82, **98,** 368;
373, 395
Delibidinization (desexualization),
98-99, 107
deaggressivization and, 72, 271,
339
as sublimation, 258
Delusions, **99-100,** 135, 206
gratification through, 236
illusion contrasted to, 186
projective diagnosis of, 384
psychiatric approach to, 337
varieties of
autoplastic, 46, 185
belief in omnipotence, 282
of fusion, 121
of grandeur, **100**
hebephrenic, 174

hypochondriacal, 179, 472,
473
of influencing machine, 193
jealous, 210
manic-depressive, 228, 229
melancholic, 243-44
nihilistic, 272
of observation, **101**
paranoid, 99-101, 272, 292,
293, 357, 389, 391
of persecution, 100, **101,** 243,
293, 391
Dementia praecox, *see*
Schizophrenia
Dempf, Alois, 470
Denial (disavowal), 24, 93-94,
101-2, 228, 279, 400
anticipation in, 36
forms of
hysterical, 346
negation, 94, **262-63**
obsessional, 317
psychotic, 102, 269, 336, 354
inferiority based on, 193
objects of
aggression against breast, 289
breast envy, 306
castration, 62, 171, 227, 309,
465
castration anxiety, 284, 305,
308
cause of conflicts, 352
childhood experience, 432
curiosity, 90
death, 29, 370
death wish, 376
exhibitionism, 393
femininity, 223
guilt, 347, 348
infantile omnipotence, 397
inhibition, 298
narcissistic mortification,
259, 279, 283, 378, 399,
416
perception, 93, 101, 200, 347,
420
scopophilia, 136
sensation, 398
superego, 350
truth, 363
unpleasure, 368

roles of
in anorexia nervosa, 34
in elation, 125, 133
in fetishism, 146-47
in nymphomania, 274
in perversion, 270
in pseudodebility, 334
in reassurance, 369
as source of neurosis, 315
unsuccessful, 93
Dependence, 96, 297, 301, 331
anaclitic, **30,** 115
denial of, 102
infantile, 191
on love-object, 280
in mass psychology, 179
wish for, 265
See also Addiction
Depersonalization, **102-3,** 130,
193
psychopathic, 350
Depression, 103-4, 268, 320, 331,
373, 422
Abraham's analysis of, 1
of alcoholics, 23
anaclitic, **30**
anticipation in, 36
with decompensation, 92
drugs alleviate, 114
menstrual, 245, 324
metaphors of, 246
narcissistic object choice and,
185
need for punishment in, 262
normal, 228
over object-loss, 252-53
in oral pessimism, 284
raptus actions with, 364
resistance with, 377-78
role of superego in, 363
suicidal, 362, 421
See also Manic-depressive
psychosis
Derealization, 94, 102-3, **104**
Descartes, René, 330*n*
Descriptive (qualitative,
systematic) approach, 63,
251, **428**
development of, 341
to need for punishment, 262
psychiatric, 337

to resistance, 377
to suppression, 424
to total personality, 246-47, 318-19
Desexualization, *see* Delibidinization
Destiny (fate) neurosis, 11, **104-5,** 374
Destruction, 162, 292, 362
  aim-inhibited, 22, 419
  ambivalence and, 27, 317, 459-60
  delusions of, 272
  fantasies of, 229, 254
  by fire, 357
  in hatred, 173
  instinct of, 198, 339
  introjects and, 204-5
  of raptus actions, 364
  See also Destrudo; Suicide; Thanatos
Destrudo, 21*n*, 59, 89, 118, 198, 381
  anal phase of, 31
  cathexis of, 63, 94, 179, 243, 257, 302, 394, 395
  conflict of, 79
  confusion over meaning of term, 435
  countercathexis of, 84, 310
  developmental stages of, 169, 220, 308
  in hypochondriasis, 179-80
  manifestation of, 130
  in masturbation, 44
  mourning and, 252
  object and narcissistic, 185, 257, 258-59, 302, 310, 328, 339, 393, 402, 422
  oral component of, 285
  quantity of, 312
  source of, 293
Determinism, *see* Causal approach; Psychic determinism
Deuterophallic stage, **105,** 334
Deutsch, Felix, 56, 162-63
Deutsch, Helene, 5, 76, 434
  describes as-if personality, 42
  on pseudologia fantastica, 336
  theory of destiny neurosis of, 105

Development of Psychoanalysis, The (Rank and Ferenczi), 143
Deviation, *see* Sexual perversions
Dictionary, psychoanalytic, **344**
Dictatorial ideas, 347-48
Disavowal, *see* Denial
Discharge, **105-6,** 183, 359
  as behavioral derivative, 273
  delay of, 82, **98,** 368, 373, 395
  in forepleasure, 313
  interferes with pleasure principle, 367
  methods of
    laughter, 61, 218
    rage, 362
    tears, 89
  objects of
    affects, 62, 215
    aim-inhibited drives, 22-23
    instinct-fusions, 328
    instincts in id, 387
    pent-up emotions, *see* Abreaction
    psychic energy, 12, 14, 218, 338, 373, 457-58
  types of
    abnormal, 44
    motoric and secretory, 245
Displacement, 56, 94, **106,** 211, 278, 312
  as characteristic of phobias, 310, 482
  expression, 479
  objects of
    ambivalence, 443
    cathexis, 306
    instinct-fusion, 360
    instinctual energy, 14
    language, 474
    oral wishes, 285
    resistance, 12
    sexual curiosity, 10
  as primary process mechanism, 329
  roles of
    in blushing, 55, 132
    in crying, 89
    in dreams, 78, 111, 113
    in neurotic fear, 139
    in ritual, 383

  in stammering, 416
  in stigmata, 417
  sublimation as, 134
  onto substitute, 67, 224, 266, 292
  symbolization as, 425
  upward, 181
Dissociation, 177, 316
  of consciousness, 8, 346, 365; *see also* Absence
  of ego identity, 132
"Dissolution of the Oedipus Complex, The" (Freud), **106-7**
Distortion, 57, 366
  apperceptive, **39-40**
  dream, 64, 366, 434
Doctor game, **107,** 375
"Dora" (case history), **107-9,** 186, 394, 410-11, 420, 423
Doubt, compulsive, 279, 365, 366, 411
Dramatization therapy, 404
"Dream and Myth" (Abraham), 3
Dream-screen, **113,** 349
Dream-state, 322
Dream-work, 34, 110, **113,** 471
  autosymbolism as, 47
  color in, 75
  modifies affect, 109
Dreams, 1, 20, **109-13,** 119, 262, 401, 407, 434
  Abraham's studies of, 3
  of anal birth, 455
  of children, 68
  components of
    breast envy, 326
    color, **75-76,** 110
    condensation, 78, 265-66
    day residues, 12, 75, **91-92,** 110
    egotism, 122
    feelings, 110, **139-40**
    intellectual activity, 111, **201**
    metaphors, 216, 246
    motility, 111, **252**
    periodicity, 381
    regression, 372
    repetition compulsion, 375
    spider symbolism, 413-14
    symbols, 425, 439

Page numbers in **boldface** refer to main entries

Dreams, spider
     symbolism *(Continued)*
     totem animals, 443, 444
     wish to castrate, 348-49, 350
     wit, 112, 203, **471-72**
     see also Language—in dreams
   hallucinations and, 172, 177,
     371
   interpretations of
     anagogic, **30-31**
     dream as hallucinatory
       omnipotence, 356
     dream as inner reality, 340
     dream as language of
       unconscious, 41
     dynamic, 345
   moral responsibility and, 111,
     251
   pair of, 111, **291,** 407
   somatic stimuli and, 109-11,
     411
   as source of déjà vu, 97
   traumatic neurosis and, 111,
     452-53
   types of
     ambiguous, 26, 27
     blank, 280-81
     homosexual, 88, 92, 110,
       140, 278, 306
     nightmares, **271-72, 299**
     obliging, 111, **278,** 470-71
     promiscuous, 333
     prophetic, 280
     recurrent, 75, 111, **370**
     typical, 111-12, **454**
     undisguised, 112, **459**
     wet, 458, **470-71**
   of ulcer patient, 301
   See also Daydreams; Freudian
     theories—dream theory
Drive, instinctual, *see* Instinct
Drugs, 75, **113-16,** 176
   alcohol used as, 23
   Freud's work with cocaine,
     154-55
   Ostow on, 113-16
   tension discharged through, 238
   See also Addiction
Duke University, Parapsychologi-
   cal Laboratory of, 434
Dunbar, F.. 11

Dynamic approach, 79, **116,** 162,
     202, 246, 334, 342, **345-46**
   to paranoid state, 293
   to rituals, 383
   to schizophrenia, 389
Dynamic conflict, 79

E

Economic approach, 79, **117,** 162,
     202, 246, 312
   to anticipation, 405
   psychic energy as focus of, 117,
     339, 342
   quality and quantity of drive in,
     359-60
   to resistance, 377-78
   to schizophrenia, 390
"Economic Problem of
     Masochism" (Freud), 360
Economical conflict, 79
Education, 157, 217
   of Abraham, 4-5
   of Ferenczi, 141
   of Freud, 153
   linguistic, 215
   modern theory of, 201
   psychiatric
     child psychiatry, 70
     empirical, 442
   psychiatric vs.
     psychoanalytic, 337
     psychoanalytic, 219, 396-97;
       see also Teaching of
       analysis; Training analysis
     supervision requirement,
       423-24
   psychoanalysis applied to, 41,
     344
   resistance as problem of, 265
   sexual, 24
   strictness in, 45
"Effect on Women of Premature
     Ejaculation in Man, The"
     (Ferenczi), 142
Ego, **117-19,** 162, 175, 206, 406
   of alcoholics, 23-24
   behavioral derivatives in, 273
   countercathexis and, 84, 267

   development of, 384, 395, 397,
     411, 482
     adolescent, 17, 242
     infantile, 25
     inhibited, 34-35
     integrated, 332
   dreams and, 75, 110
   education theory regarding, 201
   effect of drugs on, 113, 114-15
   fixation of, 148
   hate in, 173
   I and non-I elements of, 137
   inferiority feelings and, 192
   masochism, morality and, 250
   of mourner, 252-53
   as partly conscious, 19, 338,
     457
   of patient with multiple tics,
     440
   polarity of external world and,
     315
   primary gain to, 329
   processes of
     compromise, 288, 316, 345,
       349, 394
     resistance, 142, 329, 341,
       377, 394
     response to introjects, 204
     see also Ego functions
   psychoanalytic approaches to
     adaptational, 342
     comparative, 195
     dynamic, 344, 345
     ego-resistance, 142, 329, 341,
       377, 394
     gains for ego, 438
     interpretation as, 202-3
     quantitative, 360
     systematic, 345
     topographic, 161, 251-52,
       338, 342, 345, 351,
       417-18, 460
   psychotic, 351, 354, 372
     manic-depressive, 228-29
     paranoid, 88-89
     schizophrenic, 100, 333,
       389-91
   quality and, 359
   regression of, 371-72, 396
   relationship to, to total
     personality, 338

appeasement of superego, 421

communication between id and ego, 183

conflicts, 79, 244, 267, 268, 270, 351, 375

defense against superego, 61

help from superego, 471

isolation from id and superego, 398

libido in ego, 174

narcissistic libido, 260

organized part of id, 247

superego as ego, 363

reward for, 381

roles of
in bisexuality, 53, 54
in catharsis, 62
in exaggeration, 135
in depression, 103, 363
in hysterical materialization, 181
in inhibition, 193-94
in mystic union, 253-54
in obesity, 277
in oceanic feeling, 280-81
in phobic character, 312
in sacrifice, 385
in slips of the tongue, 407-8
in traumatic neurosis, 452

self and, 118, **119-20**, 395, 396

sense organ perception and, **120-21**

sensorium and, **120**

split of, 146-47, 333, 397, 427

stability of, 370

varieties of
body, 65, 118, 395
central, **65**, 118, 221
introego, **204**
normal, 230
perverse, 481
pleasure, *see* Pleasure ego
primitive, 254
psychopathic, 349-50

Ego-alien traits, 40, 93, 106, **119**, 475

depersonalization as, 102

hatred as, 135

jamais phenomenon as, 209

neurotic, 65, 66-67
impulsive traits, 364
neurotic symptoms, 123-24, 415
obsessive-compulsive neurosis, 279

of superego, 119, 123, 205, 250, 347, 410

Ego and the Id, The (Freud), 162, 215, 247

Ego boundaries, **121,** 139, 166, 354
in appersonation, 40
dissolution of, 272
in elation, 125
extension of, 184

Ego formation, 55
Abraham's theory of, 2-3, 6-7
nuclear theory of, 274

Ego functions, 19, 65, 84, 121-22, 313, 319, 333
automatism and, 45-46
cathexis of, 17
effects on
disturbance by déjà vu phenomena, 97
effect of tranquilizers, 114
impoverishment of, 66
maturity of, 241-42
regression of, 371, 372, 473, 482
roles of
in delay of discharge, 98, 368, 373, 395
in identity, 399
in reassurance, 369
in schizophrenia, 389-90
in slips of the tongue, 412
sexualization of, 243, 390, **402**
varieties of
abstract thought, 9
adaptation, 15
anticipation of danger, 36
autonomy, 46
censorship, 64
control, 12, 82, 90, 117, 183, 302, 362, 372, 395, 438, 458
freedom, 152, 287
intentionality, 302
mobility, 251

mobilization of barriers, 49
nondefensive, 271
perception, 303
pregenital, 320
reality testing, 121, 215-16
repression, 375
self-observation, 397
see also Language; Thought

Ego-ideal, 35, **122,** 123, 144, 438, 466
in anhedonia, 33
division of, 364
formation of, 17
in mania 125,
leaders as, 296
love object as, 184
in melancholia, 243
primitive, 330
role of, in humor, 176
substitute, 178
transient, **450**
wartime, 39, 469

Ego instincts (self-preservative drives), 15, 75, 98, **122-23,** 173, 197-98, 292, 315, 402
conflicts of, 341
energy of, 339
function of, 257
libidinal character of, 161, 222, 282
of narcissistic types, 221
sexual instinct vs., 462

Ego strength and weakness, 82, 120, **123,** 135
normal, 273, 287
in perversion, 270
projective identification and, 333
in psychosis, 351

Ego-syntonic traits, 67, 79, 88, 106, 119, **123-24,** 134, 270
in character neurosis, 65, 66
due to fixation, 148
in impulse neurosis, 189-90
masturbation fantasies as, 239
masturbatory equivalents and, 321, 426
of normal action, 252
in perversion, 136, 147, 304, 316, 393

Page numbers in **boldface** refer to main entries

Ego-syntonic traits *(Continued)*
  phobic, 312
  in psychotic character, 354
  of rationalization, 364
  of speech, 295, 403
  of superego, 250, 410
Ego types, 65
Egoism, 257-58
Eidelberg, Ludwig, 16, 43, 187,
    191, 404, 451
  on alloplastic adaptation, 25-26
  bisexual patient of, 53-54
  on blushing, 55, 119
  on breast complex, 58, 324-25
  on day residues, 92
  on defense mechanisms, 93,
    200, 331
    denial, 102, 352
    depersonalization, 102
    displacement, 106
    introjection, 94, 205
    projection, 331-32
    pseudoidentification, 335-36
    reaction formation, 366
    repression, 380
    undoing, 459-60
    yawning, 479
  on ego-alien symptoms, 119
  on emotions
    anticipation and, 405
    envy vs. jealousy, 129, 210
    theory of happiness, 173
    theory of humiliation, 175
  on Freud, 88, 152-66
  on inhibition, 475-76
    frigidity, 166, 393-94
    impotence, 124, 432-33
    inhibition of motility, 252
    inhibition of reading, 403
  instinct theory of, 368
    breakthrough of instinctual
      demand, 366
    compromise formations of
      instincts, 288
    death instinct, 435
    instinctual aim, 199
    instinctual vicissitudes, 200,
      454
    pregenital instincts, 387
    sexual vs. aggressive
      instincts, 21-22

    theory of libido, 185, 222,
      339
  "Introduction," ix-xiii
  on kleptomania, 213
  on marriage, 73, 231
  on masturbation
    adult masturbation, 237
    masturbation fantasies,
      239-40
    pregenital masturbatory
      equivalents, 321-22
    as self-rape, 363
  on normality, 273
  perceptual theory of, 120-21
  personality divisions of, 65,
    118, 221
  on perversions, 270, 304-5,
    306-7, 352, 393
    homosexuality, 289
    transvestitism, 451
  on phallic character, 305, 306-7
  psychoanalytic anthropology of,
    241
  on psychosexual development
    oral stage, 285, 324
    preoedipal stage, 324-26
  on rape, 363
  on regression, 371
  theory of activity of
    acting in, 11
    definition of active aim, 12
    feminine activity, 13, 232
  theory of humor of, 76, 81, 82,
    211, 218
  theory of identification of, 136,
    185-86, 201-2, 328
  theory of language of, 474
    slips of the tongue, 295,
      407-8, 412, 459
    stammering, 416
    writers' inhibitions, 475-76
  theory of masochism of, 140,
    232, 233, 235, 250-51,
    262, 264, 433, 461
  theory of narcissism of, 257,
    258-59, 260, 282-83, 451
  theory of neuroses of, 366,
    460-61
    bronchial asthma as neurosis,
      59

    character neurosis, 66, 352,
      388
    neurotic anxiety, 197
    neurotic choice, 71, 231, 298
    neurotic remorse, 374, 398
    obsessional brooding, 278
    psychopathy, 347-51
    theory of phobia, 310-11, 352
  theory of pleasure of
    forepleasure, 150, 313
    pleasure-unpleasure
      principle, 313-15, 367-68,
      460-61, 462
  theory of psychosis of, 352
    psychotic character, 354
  view of psychoanalytic
    approaches of
    comparative, 76, 360
    quantitative, 360
    structural, 192, 418
  view of psychoanalytic session
    of, 431
    analyst's empathy, 127
    countertransference, 432-33
    division of analytic material,
      88-89
    erotic transference, 131
    method of investigating
      symptoms, 286
    strength of resistance, 120
    transference, 446, 448
  view of repetition compulsion
    of, 374
Eisenbud, J., 280, 434
Eissler, K. R., 41, 390
  on anorexia nervosa, 34-35
  on oceanic feeling, 281
Eitingon, Max, 5, 159, 163, 165
Ejaculatio praecox, 85, 119,
    124-25, 188-89, 432-33
  Abraham's study of, 2, 6
  as common phenomenon, 194
Ejaculatio retardata, **125,** 188, 189
Ekstein, R., 12
Elation, 36, **125**
  manic, 228-29
  sustained, *see* Euphoria
Electro-therapy, 155, 156
Ellis, Havelock, 43-44, 156
Embryology, 320-21
Emotional insight, **126**

Emotions, **125-26,** 152, 188, 245
  adolescent, 355
  of analysts, xvi
  discharge of pent-up, *see*
    Abreaction
  in phantom limb sensations, 309
  unconscious, 126, **458**
  See also Affects; Feelings;
    specific emotions
Empathy, **126-27,** 453
Endopsychic perception, **127-28,**
  247
Energizing drugs, 114-16
Energy, psychic, *see* Psychic
  energy
Engel, G., 56
England, 434, 455
  Freud's exile in, 165-66
English, O., 468
Entitlement, narcissistic, **128**
Entropy, **128**
  negative, 63, 297
Enuresis (bed-wetting), 246, 265,
  357
  nocturnal, 124, **272-73,** 289,
    300
Envy, **128-29,** 236
  jealousy contrasted to, 129, 210
  negation of, 263
  oral, 421
  projection of, 316
  visual defense against, 247
  See also Breast envy; Jealousy;
    Penis envy
Epileptic personality, **129-30**
Epinosic gain, *see* Secondary gain
Epistemophilic instinct, **130**
Erikson, Erik, 17, 410, 412
  psychoanalytic anthropology of,
    36, 344
Eros (life instinct), **130,** 161, 198,
    342, 435, 436
  activity and, 13
  in adaptation, 15
  in aggression, 21
  in constancy principle, 219
  creativity connected with, 87
  energy of, *see* Libido
  fate vs., 33
  fusion of, 267, 328
  institutionalization of, 35

loss of function and, 180
  mixture of thanatos and, 360
Erotic transference, **130-31;**
    see also Transference-love
Erotic types, 117, 221, 360
  characterization of, 65, 71, 174
  conversion hysteria of, 80
  parapraxes of, 407-8
  symptoms of, 79, 124
Eroticism, 80, 366
  respiratory, **379,** 420
  sexuality and, 400
  skin, **406**
  temperature, **435**
  urethral, 189, 357, 403
  See also Autoeroticism, Libido;
    Love; Sexuality
Eroticization, *see* Sexualization
Erotogenic zones, 77, **131,** 220,
  291
  in coprophagia, 83
  forepleasure from, 150, 313,
    461
  infantile, 191, 192
  as masturbation equivalents,
    239
  oral zone, 108, 320
  resexualization of, 181
  skin as, 406
  as source of component
    instincts, 198
Erotomania, 274-75, 387
Erythrophobia, 55, **131-32,** 311,
  415
Escapades, **132**
Ethical approach, **132-33,** 466-67
Euphoria, 16, **133-34;** *see also*
    Nirvana principle;
    Oceanic feeling
Eunuchoidism, 298
Evaluation
  of analyst in training, 445
  of physiological data, 245
  of psychoanalytic therapy,
    134-35, 344
Exaggeration, 94, **135**
Exhibitionism, 50, 77, 87, 132,
  135-36
  damming of, 239
  developmental stages of, 169,
    199

  anal, 31, 416
  oral, 285
  as perversion, 304
  responses to
    change, 95
    defense of, 102
    defenses against, 42, 59, 404
    denial, 393
    displacement, 106
    shamelessness, 404
    stage fright, 415
    sublimation, 367
  roles of
    in blushing, 55
    in enuresis, 272
    in hair pulling, 171
    in hallucination, 172
    in hysterical paralysis, 83
    in joke telling, 74
    in kleptomania, 213
    in phallic character, 305
    in phobia, 310
    in tears, 89
    in theft, 350
    in writer's cramp, 476
  scopophilia paired with, 95,
    102, 392, 393, 453-54
External ego, 65, 118
External identification, 40, **136,**
  185, 187
Extrasensory perception, *see*
  Occult phenomena
Extroversion, 303

F

Face-breast equation, **137**
Faces, making of, **227-28**
Failure, *see* Defeat
Faith, *see* Religious faith
Family romance, **137-38,** 303
Fanaticism, **138**
Fantasies, 20, 56, **138-39,** 209,
  236, 283, 340, 362, 384,
  395, 398
  acting out of, 481
  from dream-pairs, 407
  flight into, **148-49,** 370
  hallucinogens produce, 114
  leap into, 247

Fantasies *(Continued)*
  relaxation therapy and, 373
  repression of, 97, 307, 327, 373,
      400
  roles of
    in anxiety, 38
    compensation for frustration,
        167
    in hysterical materialization,
        181
    in penis envy, 299
    in pseudologia fantastica, 336
    in psychosomatic
        disturbances, 352
    in reality principle, 367
    in ritual, 383
    in slips of the tongue, 407
    substitute for action, 46
    in temperature eroticism, 435
  sphincter control of, 422-23
  subject matter of
    anal birth, 455
    coitus cum matre, 217
    death, 261
    destruction, 229, 351
    penis captivus, 466
    phallic mother, 308, 325, 414
    pregnancy, 277, 323
    primal scene, 367
    vagina dentata, 58, **465,** 466
  subjects of
    alcoholics, 24
    feminine men, 297
    pyromaniacs, 357
    Schreber, 391
    ulcer patient, 302
    Wolf Man, 472
  tolerance of, 373
  types of
    beating, **51-52,** 232, 312
    coprophagic, 83, 277
    family romance, 137-38
    infantile, 1, 274, 333
    masochistic, 140
    oedipal, 237, 324
    omnipotent, 330
    paranoid, 293, 351
    preconscious, 319
    premonitory, 253
    primal, **327**
    primordial, 361

    rape, 363
    rat, 139, 365
    rebirth, **370**
    rescue, **376-77**
    respiratory introjection, **379**
    sadistic, 51, 149, 239, 293,
        357, 365, 422
    schizophrenic, 253-54, 351,
        389
    spider, 413
    totemic, 443, 444
    see also Daydreams;
        Masturbation fantasies
Fantasy cathexis (introversion),
    149, **206,** 303
Fascination, **139**
Fate (Ananke), **33,** 312, 374
Fate neurosis, *see* Destiny neurosis
Father complex, 391
Fathers, 88, 178, 244, 278, 288
    in beating fantasies, 312
    in case histories
      of Dora, 107-9
      of Little Hans, 67, 71, 99,
          196, 223-24, 482
      of Rat Man, 365
      of Wolf Man, 472-73, 482
    death of, 96
    hatred of, 324-25, 386
    identification with, 45, 53,
        184-85, 241, 281, 308, 386
    as secondary figures, 52
    totems of, 444
    vaginal, **465-66**
  See also Oedipus complex;
      Patriarchy; Primal
      parricide; Primal scene
Fear, xvi, **139,** 199, 463
  anxiety contrasted to, 37
  interaction of rage and, 362
  objects of
    aggression, 396, 401, 411
    aphanisis, 39
    conscience, 123
    death, 277, 287, 294, 362,
        421
    fighting, 204
    free association, 447
    id, 102
    instincts, 396
    introjection, 333

    pregnancy, 323
    punishment, 72, **93,** 348
    rape, 363
    retaliation, 380
    sexuality, 274
    success, 475
    suffocation, **420**
    women, 326
  paralytic, 305
  roles of
    in frigidity, 166
    in narcissistic mortification,
        259
  secondary, 379-80
  as source of menstrual disorders,
      324
  as source of resistance, 378
  stage fright, 311, **415**
  structural approach to, 342
  weeping as sign of, 89
  See also Anxiety; Intimidation;
      Phobias
Federn, Paul, 21*n,* 121, 143, 159
Feelings, 19, 228, 406*n*
  absence of, 102; *see also*
      Anaesthesias
  in dreams, 110, **139-40**
  unconscious, 126, **458**
  See also Affects; Emotions;
      Sensations
Feigenbaum, D., 145
Feldman, S. S., 55, 216, 230, 465
Feminine masochism, **140,** 234
Femininity, 223, **231-32,** 323, 468
  activity or passivity of, 12-13,
      21, 231, 297
  beating fantasies and, 51-52
  object choice and, 30, 277-78,
      401
  See also Menstruation
Fenichel, Otto, 76, 215, 257, 274,
    345
  on automatic obedience, 45
  on compulsive thinking, 9
  on congenital characteristics,
      79-80
  concept of eroticism of
    skin eroticism, 406
    temperature eroticism, 435
  on coprophagia, 83
  on coprophilia, 84

on countertransference, 85
on delusions of persecution, 101
describes suicide, 421
ethical theory of
    judgment preceding action,
        12, 37
    moralization, 364
on flight into fantasy, 148-49
on flight into reality, 150
on hunger for stimuli, 176
on impotence, 125, 287, 387
on making faces, 227-28
on masturbation
    addicts, 238
    compulsive, 387
    equivalents, 326
    fantasies, 239
    infantile, 192
    masochistic, 406
on passive-receptive attitudes,
    298
on petrifaction, 305
on phallic mother, 90
on pseudoimbecility, 334
on psychogenic illness
    breathing disturbances, 420
    bronchial asthma, 58-59
    menstrual disorders, 324
    narcolepsy, 261
on raptus actions, 364
on relaxation, 82, 373
on respiratory introjection, 379
on sacrifice, 385
on self-assertion, 198
on sublimation, 99, 362
on suppression of sensation, 398
on symbolization, 425
theory of alcoholism of, 24
theory of body image of, 55
theory of identification of,
    126-27, 187, 254, 330, 379
theory of imitation of, 187
theory of language of, 403
    body language, 56, 352
    speech functions, 411, 416
    stammering, 415-16
    unconscious meaning of
        speech, 458, 459
    writers' inhibitions, 475
theory of neurosis of

counterphobia, 84, 369, 402,
    404
description of claustrophobia,
    74, 311
erythrophobia, 131-32
impulse neurosis, 189-90
neurosis as negative of
    perversion, 269-70
neurotic boredom, 57
neurotic periodicity, 381
obsessive rituals, 382-83
phobic character, 312
pseudo-hypersexuality, 335
role of reassurance, 369
schizoid character, 388
traumatic neurosis, 452
zoophobia, 482
theory of psychosis of
    borderline psychosis, 57
    description of megalomania,
        243
    hebephrenia, 174
on tics, 89
on toilet training, 441
view of anti-Semitism of, 388
Ferenczi, Sandor, 44, 97, 232, 439
on adaptation, 15-16, 46-47
on automatic obedience, 45
biography of, **140-46**
    member of Vienna Society,
        146, 159
    secret committee
        membership, 163-64
    as teacher, 141, 144, 145, 424
connects money with anality,
    248-49
dream theory of, 203, 356
on impotence, 400
on latency period, 217
on omnipotence, 282, 356
as originator of term
    protopsyche, 334
on parasitic superego, 296
psychoanalytic theory of
    active therapy, 13-14,
        143-44, 164
    goal of transference, 432
    relaxation technique, 373-74
    transference outside analysis,
        446
on purified pleasure ego, 355-56

sphincter morality of, 412-13,
    423
on stigmata, 417
theory of alcoholism of, 24, 210
theory of neurosis of
    theory of hysteria, 181
    transference neurosis, 432,
        450
    weekend neurosis, 421-22
on yawning, 57-58, 479
See also specific works
Fetishism, 83, **146-47**, 306, 482
    Abraham's study of, 2
    as defense, 135-36, 147, 304,
        392-93
    hair pulling and, 171
Finality, *see* Teleological approach
Fine, R., 374
Fischer, K., 19
Fisher, C., 303
Fixation, 53, 57, 94, **147-48**, 198,
    247, 297
    avoidance indicates, 47
    as cause of neurosis, 267
    due to narcissistic scar, 260
    on early developmental stages,
        371
    anal, 380
    narcissistic, 282
    oral, *see* Oral fixation
    phallic, 80, 309
    pregenital, 199, 270, 354
    preoedipal, *see* Preoedipal
        mother attachment
    objects of
        component instincts, 77
        incestuous object, 124, 400
        phallic mother, 17, 325
        trauma, *see* Traumatic
            neurosis
    oedipal, *see* Oedipus complex
    roles of
        in anhedonia, 33
        in neurotic choice of a mate,
            231
    synonym for, 339
    See also Fetishism
Flechsig, P. E., 391
Fliess, Wilhelm, 37n, 40, 153, 156,
    346
    Abraham's allegiance to, 3, 5

Fliess, Wilhelm *(Continued)*
 on empathy, 126-27, 453
 Freud's friendship with, 157-58
 on functional symbols, 439
Flight, 179, 196
 into fantasy, **148-49,** 370
 into health, **149**
 into illness, **149-50,** 266, 273,
  329, 351
 into reality, 25, 149, **150,** 185
Flugel, J. C., 288, 316, 395-96,
  466-67
Focal symbiosis, 424-25
Forbidden, the, *see* Taboos
Forepleasure, 135, **150-51,** 313,
  393, 399, 404
 anticipation in, 36, 340
 becomes unpleasure, 18
 component instincts in, 77
 in dreams, 109, 470
 epistemophilic, 130
 in humor, 19, 81, 211
 inhibition toward forms of, 194
 olfactory stimuli to, 200
 before removal of unpleasure,
  461
 in skin eroticism, 406
Fore-unpleasure, 109, **151,** 340,
  460
Fowler, H., 355
France, 153, 434
Fragmentation, 15, **151-52**
Frazer, Sir James George, *The
 Golden Bough,* 468
Free association (basic rule),
  50-51, 142, 420, 430,
  436-37
 difficulty in, 152
 fear of, 447
 psychoanalytic theory
  discovered from, 156
 psychopathic attitude toward,
  347
 relaxation for, 82
 substitute for, 68, 69
 technique of, 50, 344
Free will, **152,** 338
Freiburg, Moravia, 4, 152, 153
Freud, Amalie (Sigmund's
  mother), 153
Freud, Anna, 88, 162, 342

on altruistic surrender, 26
on avoidance, 47-48, 118
concept of maladjustment of,
  228
on educational theory, 201
as her father's nurse, 163
on identification, 127, 187-88
on isolation, 207
on neurotic inhibition, 193-94
on play therapy, 67-68
on psychosexual maturation,
  242
 adolescence, 17, 354-55
 period of negativism, 264-65
on Rorschach Test, 384
theory of revenge of, 380
on unpleasure, 36, 151, 460
Freud, Jakob, 152-53
Freud, Julius, 153
Freud, Martha Bernays, 152, 154,
  156-57, 158
Freud, Sigmund, 470
 biography of, **152-66**
  medical career, 107, 153
 case histories of
  Anna O., 155-56
  case of displacement, 106
  sadistic patient, 386
  see also "Dora"; "Little
   Hans"; "Rat Man";
   Schreber Case; "Wolf
   Man"
 most important contributions
  of, 162
 on obscurity, xii
 pupils and colleagues of, ix,
  xvii, 21*n*, 40, 41, 76,
  156-61
  Abraham as, 1, 2, 3, 5, 6,
   163-64
  Brill as, 346
  Brunswick as, 472
  collaboration with Breuer;
   see Breuer, Josef—Freud's
   collaboration with
  conflicts between, 3
  criticism of Freud, 88, 158
  defections, 52, 141, 156, 158,
   159-61, 163, 164-65
  Ferenczi as, 141, 143, 144,
   145-46, 163-64, 373

  Fliess as, 157-58
  Koller as, 154-55
  psychoanalytic anthropology
   of, 36, 344
  secret committee, 163-65
 theories of, *see* Freudian
  theories
 See also specific works
"Freudian slips," *see* Slips of the
  tongue
Freudian theories, ix, xiv-xix, 45,
  207, 227, 237, 243, 309,
  437
 of abstract thought, 9, 438, 458
  supervalent ideas, 423
 aesthetic, 19
 of amphimixis, 29-30
 on analytic session
  access to sublimation, 292
  basic rule, 50-51, 340
  concept of analyzing
   instrument, 32
  function of transference, 158,
   427, 445-47
  negative therapeutic
   response, 263-64
  psychoanalytic technique,
   430, 431
  role of sublimation, 99
  role of working through, 32,
   475
  rule of abstinence, 384
  source of transference, 226
  theory of resistance, 339,
   377, 431
  transference-love, 448-49
  transference neurosis, 447,
   449-50
 anthropological, **35-36,** 40, 130,
  132-33, 174, 343-44, 369
  animism, 33-34
  concentration on patriarchy,
   240
  fire quenched by urination,
   463
  function of civilization, 72-73
  introduction of, 343
  lack of inhibition, 340
  mass psychology, 235-36,
   372
  need for revenge, 380

olfactory stimuli in, 245
origin of anti-Semitism, 388
origin of taboos, 279, 429
primitive language, 474
primitive man, **329-30**
progress of mankind, 186
racial memory, 361
role of incest, 190
role of sacrifice, 385
source of omnipotence of
    thought, 282
source of primal fantasy, 327
theory of collective
    unconscious, 75
totems, 443
universal virginity taboo, 468
of anxiety, 61, 191
    anxiety neurosis, 38, 267
    anxiety state, 39
    neurotic anxiety, 38, 236
    signal anxiety, 405
of applied psychoanalysis,
    40-41, 343
of body image, 55
of castration
    castration anxiety, 61, 191
    castration complex, 62, 281
of cathexis, 63, 461
    anticathexis, 84
of character traits, 67, 366
cloaca theory, 74
of complexes, 375
    castration complex, 62, 281
    Oedipus complex, 281,
        307-8, 355
    Polycrates complex, 316
of consciousness, 80-81, 245,
    303, 318-19, 337-38, 359
of criminal psychoanalysis,
    218-19
critics of, xiv, xvi, 20, 88, 126,
    165, 292, 457
of defense mechanisms
    avoidance, 47
    conversion, 82-83, 93
    definition of denial, 101-2
    derealization, 104
    negation, 94, 262-63
    projection, 99, 331
    reaction formation, 95, 399,
        401, 409

repression, 375-76, 379
of deferred reactions, 96
development of, 340-41
dream theory, 106, 109-12, 158,
    203, 254, 337, 457
    amentia compared to dreams,
        29
    anagogic interpretation,
        30-31
    analysis of analyst's dreams,
        396
    autosymbolism, 47
    condensation, 78, 266
    conflicts, 79
    day residues, 91-92, 110
    daydreams, 91
    distortion in dreams, 64, 366
    dream as language of
        unconscious, 41
    dream censorship, 64, 113
    dream symbols, 425, 439
    dreams of phallic mother,
        306
    egotism of dreams, 122, 258
    feelings in dreams, 140
    hallucination in dreams, 172
    immorality of dreams, 251
    importance of theory, 162
    intellectual activity in
        dreams, 201
    latent dreams, 26, 109, 110
    motility in dreams, 252
    nightmares, 271, 299
    obliging dreams, 278
    recurrent dreams, 370
    repetition of trauma in
        dreams, 452
    role of absurdity, 10
    somatic stimuli and dreams,
        411
    typical dreams, 454
    undisguised dreams, 459
    verbalization in dreams, 414
    wit in dreams, 471
of emotion
    description of layers of
        jealousy, 209-10
    mourning, 253
    remorse, 374
    unconscious emotion, 458
of entropy, 128

ethical, 404, 470
    concept of morality, 249-50,
        251
    ethical approach to
        psychoanalysis, 132-33
    role of religion, 374
    system of values, 466
    value judgments, 134
of family romance, 138
of fantasies
    beating fantasies, 51-52
    fantasy cathexis
        (introversion), 206
    discovery of rebirth fantasy,
        370
    rescue fantasy, 376
of fate, 33
on form of therapy
    interaction of psychiatry and
        psychoanalysis, 337
    lay analysis, 219-20
    self-analysis, 396-97
    short-term therapy, 404
    training analysis, 445
    trial analysis, 453
    wild psychoanalysis, 471
of free will, 152
of frustration, 167
of hypnosis, 178, 179
of hysteria, 20, 29, 56, 71,
    107-9, 150, 153, 155-56,
    172, 216, 346, 366, 379,
    410-11
of idealization, 184
of identification, 118, 184
    primary, 328, 477
of illusional phenomena, 392
    delusions, 99-101
    hallucinations, 172
    theory of illusion, 186
of imitation, 187
of impotence, 188, 248, 287, 400
of inferiority, 193
instinct theories, 64, 75, 84,
    160, 161-62, 197-200
    aggressive instinct, 21, 73,
        301, 308, 317
    anal phase in, 31
    component instincts, 77, 135,
        386, 392
    controversy over theory, 27

Freudian theories, instinct
theories *(Continued)*
development of libido, 191
ego instincts, 122-23, 161,
173, 257, 282, 315, 339,
402
epistemophilic instinct, 130
erotogenic zones in, 131
identification of ego, 118
instinct as myth, 254
instinct of primary
masochism, 328
instinctual aims, 22, 35, 198,
199, 419
instinctual gratification, 387
instinctual need, 200
instinctual vicissitudes, 200,
375, 393
instincts maintain constancy,
219
Jung's disagreement, 159
life and death instincts, 130,
294, 328, 342, 435-36
limits on instinctual
sublimation, 81
location of libido in, 222, 389
manifestation of sexual
instinct, 225
oral phase and, 285
position of psychic energy,
339
projection of superego, 99
quality and quantity of
instinct, 359-60
reversal into the opposite, 95,
200, 375
revision, 88
role of activity and passivity,
12-13, 14, 21, 297
role of affects, 19
role of anxiety, 37, 38
role of barriers, 49-50
role of central ego, 65
role of conscience, 80
role of desexualization, 98-99
social instincts, 409
theory of ego, 119, 120, 121,
195, 215
theory of id, 183, 247, 338
theory of superego, 422

two instinctual derivatives,
126, 267
of language
agnosia, 20, 39
ambiguity, 26-27
antithetical meanings, 37
aphonia, 410-11
language of unconscious, 41
magical, 474
reading, 367
sexualization, 403
slips of the tongue, 295, 407,
473
speech functions, 411, 412,
458
unconscious significance,
458, 459
verbalization, 467
of marriage, 230, 231
of mass psychology, 235-37,
372
of memory, strength of, 247
methodology, 344, 345
of misogyny, 248
of narcissism, 100, 128, 351
characterization of
narcissistic mortification,
259
description of narcissistic
gain, 258
narcissistic scar, 260
of neurosis, 49, 135, 174, 236,
238, 267-70, 337, 389, 400
actual neurosis, 14-15, 179,
267
anxiety neurosis, 38, 267
character neurosis, 66
choice of neurosis, 71, 80
comparative pathology, 76
destiny neurosis, 104-5
development of neurosis, 273
development of theory, 156,
161
gain in neurosis, 329, 394
housewife neurosis, 108
importance of theory, 162
localization of neurotic
symptoms, 224
narcissistic neurosis, 260, 351
neurasthenia, 266, 286

neuropsychoses of defense,
266
neurotic anxiety, 38, 236
obsessional neurosis, 279,
282, 285, 286, 365-66
organic nature of neurosis,
245
predisposition to neurosis, 80
psychosomatic symptoms,
352-53
role of abstinence, 9, 14
role of avoidance, 47
role of ego-syntonic
formations, 123-24
success neurosis, 420
symptom formation, 295
systematic approach, 428
theory of phobias, 11, 190,
311
transference neurosis, 447,
449-50
traumatic neurosis, 147-48,
452
war neurosis, 469
of neutralization, 271
nirvana principle, 272, 374, 387
of occult phenomena, 280
déjà phenomena, 97
telepathy, 434
of oceanic feeling, 280
origin of, 155-56, 340-41
of overdetermination, 286
of paresis, 296
of penis envy, 129, 299-300
perceptual, 302-3, 359
endopsychic perception,
127-28
self-observation, 397, 398
of perversions, 135-36, 404
fetishism, 146-47, 171,
392-93
masochism, 140, 189,
232-33, 250
polymorphic perversion,
316-17, 392
of pleasure and unpleasure,
374, 387
definition of unpleasure, 460
forepleasure, 150, 313
pleasure principle, 173, 313,
356

Page numbers in **boldface** refer to main entries

pleasure-unpleasure
principle, 106, 314, 315,
461-62
purified pleasure ego, 355-56
quality of tension and, 360
tolerance of unpleasant
tension, 441
of polarities, 315
of preconscious, 318-19, 337-38,
359
of primal scene, 327-28
of primary process, 329, 395
of problem of masturbation, 238
of psychosexual maturation,
400-1
adolescence, 17
anal phase, 31, 321, 412,
440-41
deuterophallic stage, 105
genital phase, 169, 400, 401,
462
latency period, 217, 401
oral stage, 284-85
phallic phase, 307-8
polymorphic perversion,
316-17
preoedipal phase, 324, 325
protophallic stage, 334
of psychosis, 268-69, 351
introduction of term
paraphrenia, 294, 389
paranoid state, 293
theory of mania, 125, 229,
357
theory of melancholia, 205-6,
243
theory of paranoia, 172, 272,
391
theory of schizophrenia, 389
of punishment, 175, 370
of quality, 359-60
of reality
psychic reality, 340
reality principle, 313, 367,
368
of reflex acts, 370-71
of regression, 371, 372
of remorse, 374, 398
of repetition compulsion,
374-75, 382, 452, 456

of sexuality, 400-1
bisexuality, 53, 54, 217, 263,
288
development of theory, 156
masculinity and femininity,
231-32, 323, 401
overt homosexuality, 288-89,
409
of sexualization and
aggressivization, 402, 403
of sleep, 406-7
sociological, 409-10, 466
of suicide, 421
of superstition, 423
of symptomatic acts, 426
theoretical approaches
comparative, 76-77
deterministic, 338, 346, 473
dynamic, 116, 345
economic, 117, 246, 359-60
ethical, 132-33
first use of causality, 63-64,
470
quantitative, 359-60
scientific *Weltanschauung,*
392, 470
structural, 246-47, 345, 351,
417-18, 424, 457, 458
systematic, 428
teleological, 320, 367
of time, 78
of transience, 450
of traumas, 451
birth trauma, 52
infantile amnesia over
traumas, 393
traumatic effect, 10, 20, 29,
174
traumatic neurosis, 147-48,
452
of two object choices, 277-78
of unconscious, 50, 262, 294,
313, 318-19, 457-59
broadens field of psychiatry,
337
critique of, 126, 457
"kingdom of the illogical,"
183
language of unconscious, 41
negation in, 94
role of affects, 19-20, 458

structural approach, 337-38,
457
theoretical formulation, 158,
457
unconscious action, 457
unconscious becomes
conscious, 81, 457
of wit, 76, 81-82, 175, 203, 211,
218, 355
Frigidity, 24, 93, **166,** 189, 190,
210
case history of, 131
comparative approach to, 76-77
conditional, 166
degrees of, 194
fantasies with
fire fantasies, 357
vagina dentata, 465
as marital problem, 231, 476
masochism and, **166-67,** 234
in nymphomania, 274-75
orgastic, 287
penis envy produces, 62, 166,
465
reaction to defloration in, 468
screen memory with, 393-94
vaginismus as, 466
Frosch, J., 357
Frustration, 118, **167,** 245, 322
of activity, 14
countercathexis as source of,
195
forms of
oral, 137, 289, 324
sacrifice, 385
sexual, 130, 301
traumatic, 297-98
impulsivity and, 190, 274
mirrored in metaphors, 246
projection of, 42
response to feeling of
guilt, 72
masochistic nullification, 235
rage, 361-62
undoing, 380
visual defense, 247
results of
change in libido, 222
establishment of reality
principle, 357
kleptomania, 213

Page numbers in **boldface** refer to main entries

Frustration, results of *(Continued)*
    pseudoidentification, 336
    psychosomatic suicide,
      353-54
    resistance, 378
    role of, in neurotic development,
      273
    toleration of, 373, 387
Future of an Illusion, The
    (Freud), 35, 343-44

G

Garma, A., 301-2
Geleerd, E. R., 78, 441
Genetic approach, 162, 293, 342
Genetics, *see* Heredity
Genital phase, **169,** 221, 285, 308,
    400, 401
    Abraham's analysis of, 2, 3
    in adolescence, 17, 355
    failure to reach, 462
    form of love during, 225
    instinctual aims of, 199
    menarche at, 245
    morality of, 371
    orgasm as characteristic of, 287
    as postambivalent stage, **317-18**
    pseudo-hypersexuality in, 335
    See also Phallic phase
Gestures, *see* Mannerisms
Gill, M., 359
Glauber, P., 33
Glover, Edward, 194, 285, 333,
    371
    on Abraham, 1-8
    on active therapy, 144
    on communication between id
      and superego, 183
    concept of idealization of, 364
    defines psychosomatic, 352
    describes superego, 422-23
    on development of ego, 118
    on frustration, 167, 362
    nuclear theory of, 274
    on rage, 362-63
Glover, James, 5
Grabbe, C. D., *Hannibal,* 280
Grandeur, 23, 158, 228, 277
    delusions of, **100**

in humor, 175
primitive, 330
Gratification, *see* Satisfaction
Graves, Robert, 235, 240-41, 255,
    333-34
Greenacre, Phyllis, 41, 55, 399
    theory of fetishism of, 147, 171
Greenson, R., 57, 58
Grief, 2, 209; *see also* Brooding;
    Melancholia; Mourning;
    Remorse
Grinberg, L., 332
Grinker, R., 404
Groddeck, Georg, 183
Grotjahn, M., 176, 439
Group paranoia, **170**
Group psychology, *see* Mass
    psychology
"Group Psychology and the
    Analysis of the Ego" (Freud),
    35, 343
Guilt, 103, 245, 341-42, 365, 373,
    398-99, 404
    beating fantasies and, 51
    in dreams, 92, 110
    freedom from, 231
    in inferiority feelings, 192, 381
    remorse vs., 374, 398
    response to
      denial, 347, 348
      nailbiting, 283
      projection, 95, 331
      punishment, 97, 262
      sexual inhibition, 194
    role of, in anorexia nervosa, 34
    role of, in sacrifice, 385
    sources of
      aggression, 401
      anthropological, 361
      exhibitionism, 415
      fear of retaliation, 380
      fantasies, 167
      frustration, 72
      hatred, 173
      masturbation, 237, 238
      perception from superego,
        302
      success, 316
      superego, 381
    in success neurosis, 419-20

varieties of
    alcoholic, 23, 24
    criminal, 219
    hysterical, 150
    masochistic, 233, 234, 250,
      314
    obsessional, 236, 279
    oedipal, 324
    paranoid, 89, 99-100
    secondary, 379-80
    See also Remorse

H

Habituation, 16
Hair pulling, **171**
Haizmann, Christopher, 96
Hall, G. Stanley, 161
Hallucinations, **172-73,** 266, 271,
    313
    autoplastic, 46, 185
    with delusions, 101
    hallucinatory-magical
      omnipotence, 356, 367
    hypnagogic, 177
    negative, 172
    pseudohallucinations, **335**
    psychotic, 109, 266, 335, 356,
      389
      amentia and, 29
      gratification, 351
      hebephrenic, 174
      megalomaniacal, 243
      paranoid, 172, 351
Hallucinogenic drugs, 114, 133
Happiness, **173,** 280, 419
    marital, 230-31
    religious promise of, 470
    as result of analysis, 438
    over reward, 381
    See also Elation; Euphoria
Hartmann, Heinz, 55, 338, 342,
    343
    on adaptation, 15
    on aim-inhibited drives, 22, 419
    analysis of relaxation by, 373
    on automatism, 45-46
    concept of masculinity of, 232
    on delay of discharge, 98
    on ego functions, 402

Page numbers in **boldface** refer to main entries

on free will, 152
on heredity, 75
on impotence, 287
on insight, 201, 320
on neutralization, 271, 302
on normality, 273
on paranoia, 170
perceptual theory of, 302, 368
on pleasure principle, 313
on precocious maturation, 241-42
on primary and secondary autonomy, 46
psychoanalytic theory of causality, 64
economic approach, 117, 202, 339
interpretation, 202
methodology, 344-45
prediction, 320
structural approach, 418
teleological approach, 433
on reality, 368, 372
on social compliance, 408-9
on thanatos, 436
theory of cathexis of countercathexis, 84, 98
ego cathexis, 118, 119
theory of schizophrenia of, 389-90
value system of, 134, 467
Hartmann, Max, 128, 470
Hartmann, N., 470
Hatred, **173**, 184, 386, 388
ego-alien, 135
for external world, 315, 477
love changed to, 366, 391
for men, 247-48
projection of, 331-32, 378
secondary, 379-80
of self, 133, 326, 331, 362-63
transfer of, 324-25
for women (misogyny), **247-48**, 289, 307
See also Ambivalence; Anti-Semitism
Hayakawa, S. I., 216
Health, 251, 287
flight into, **149**
See also Illness; Normality
Hebephrenia, **174**, 389, 443

Heine, Heinrich, "The Baths of Lucca," 355
Heredity (genetics), 71, 148, **174**, 183, 361, 389, 419
as cause of alcoholism, 24
as cause of hysteria, 20
as cause of peptic ulcers, 300-1
determines adaptation, 36, 408
genetic theory of humor, 176
hereditary collective unconscious, 75, 361
hereditary obesity, 277
inherited incest taboo, 190
predisposition to homosexuality in, 288
psychiatric reliance on, 337
as source of neurosis, 296, 341
as source of primal fantasy, 327
See also Congenital characteristics; Genetic approach; Instinct; Libidinal types
Hermann, I., 323
Hermaphroditism, 300, 301
Herodotus, 316
Hoffer, W., 55
Hoffmann, Heinrich, *Struwelpeter*, 327-28
Homosexuality, 85, 198, 248, 271, 304, 320, 348
active and passive, 142
aim-inhibited, 409
alcoholism and, 23, 210
anxiety over, 149, 194, 196
causes of
breast envy, 58, 306
defense, 147
negative Oedipus complex, 263
penis envy, 300
component instinct in, 270
defenses against
fetishism, 304
nymphomania, 274-75
promiscuity, 333
result in rebelliousness, 369
undoing, 95
disposition to, 26
fantasies of, 370, 383, 391, 481
intimidation and, 204
narcissistic object choice in, 30, 225, 277, 288

in paranoia, 293, 391
phallic pride and, 308
platonic, 108
primitive, 463
at puberty, 355
in transference, 446, 448
vaginal-father symptom in, 465
of Wolf Man, 472, 473
See also Latent homosexuality; Overt homosexuality
Horney, Karen, 199
Horton, D., 24
Hostility, 85, 199, 231, 261
forms of
destructive, 354
negative therapeutic reaction, 263, 347, 349
negativism, 265
paranoid, 293
punishment, 233
objects of
fathers, 67, 71, 99, 196, 223-24
men, 77, 300
parents, 380
psychoanalytic principles, 346
projected, 268, 269, 332-33, 362
as response to defloration, 468
responses to
pain, 173, 209
remorse, 234, 259
Hostilodynamics, **174-75**
Humiliation, 74, **175**, 189, 345, 350, 404, 415
fantasies of, 239-40
infliction of, *see* Sadism
masochistic, 175, 232-33, 235, 314, 453
over menstruation, 245
through punishment, 140
sphincter morality and, 413
undoing of, 380
Humor, 7, 46, **175-76**
forepleasure in, 19, 81, 211
See also Comic quality; Wit
Hunger, 382, 395, 398
for love, 297
for stimuli, **176-77**
tensions due to, 362

Hypersexuality, pseudo-, 274, **335,** 387

Hypnagogic phenomena, **177,** 206, 335

Hypnoanalysis, 50, 153, **177**

Hynoid hysteria, 379

Hypnoid state, 8, **177-78,** 341

Hypnosis, **178-79,** 204, 298, 340, 364, 382
  autohypnosis, **44-45**
  as short-term therapy, 404
  as source of parasitic superego, 296
  use of suggestion in, 420
  wish for, 331

Hypochondriasis (hypochondria), 129, **179-80,** 193
  as actual neurosis, 15
  delusional, 179, 472, 473

Hysteria, 26, 65, 83, 135, 144, 223, 298, 337, 366
  agent provocateur of, 20
  Breuer and Freud's studies of, *see* Breuer, Joseph—Freud's collaboration with
  case history of, **107-9,** 186, 394, 410-11, 420, 423
  of erotic types, 221, 360
  forms of
    body language, 216
    claustrophobia, 74
    conversion, *see* Hysterical conversion
    hysterical amnesia, 29, 365
    mass, **237**
    neuropsychosis of defense, 266
    retention, **379**
  hallucinations with, 172
  predisposition to, 71
  psychosis in relation to, 2
  rationalization in, 364
  repression in, 93, 365
  symptoms of, 8, 20, 42, 44, 56, 150, 153, 155-56, 196, 236, 353, 410-11
  of Wolf Man, 472

Hysterical (phallic) character, **306-7**

Hysterical conversion (conversion hysteria), 44, 45, **180**

narcolepsy as, 261
predisposition to, 80
secondary gain in, 394
strangulated affect in, 417
symptoms of, 195, 224, 240, 472; *see also* Paralysis—hysterical

Hysterical materialization, 180, **181**

I

Id, 65, 84, 110, **183-84,** 247, 258, 382, 404
  control of, 62, 372
  discharge of instincts in, 387
  ego and, 117, 118, 123, 135
  fixation of, 148
  fragmentation in, 151
  hatred in, 173
  instinct-fusion in, 273, 360
  interpretation of, 202
  Klein's use of term, 294
  libido in, 174
  processes of
    cathexis, 359
    compromise, 288, 316, 345, 349
    conflict, 79, 267, 268, 270, 351, 375, 394
    perception, 302
    primary processes, 329
    primitive thought, 323
    resistance, 339, 377
    secondary processes, 395
  psychoanalytic approaches to
    dynamic, 345
    gains for id, 438
    quantitative, 360
    topographic, 161, 251, 338, 342, 345, 389, 417-18
  roles of
    in bisexuality, 53, 54
    in bronchial asthma, 58-59
    in ego-alien symptoms, 119
    in inhibition, 194
    in neurosis, 452
    in perception, 398
  sequestration of, 399

types of
  adolescent, 17, 242
  id of erotic types, 221
  paranoid, 88
  psychopathic, 349-50

Idealization, **184,** 224, 364

Ideas, *see* Abstract thinking

Identification, 35, 36, 59, 123, **184-86,** 198, 362, 370, 399, 418, 481
  as basis of emotion
    love, 224, 225
    pity, 312
    pride, 327
  of hypnotic subject, 178, 179
  imitation and, 187-88
  in individual psychology, 192
  objects of
    analyst, 388
    dead persons, 379
    deities, 253-54, 473
    fantasies, 239, 240
    frustrating object, 167
    leaders, 236
    patients, 85, 86
    persona, 303
    phallus, 305, 306, 307, 309
    ungiving parents, 380
    weeping person, 89
  in oral period, 301
  regression to, 260
  roles of
    in altruism, 26
    in bisexuality, 53
    in envy, 128
    in fascination, 139
    in humor, 81
    in mass hysteria, 237
    in melancholia, 244
    in rape, 363
    in sadism, 386
    in scopophilia, 393
    in sublimation, 99
    in writer's cramp, 476
  varieties of
    anal and urethral, 413
    external, 40, **136,** 185, 187
    feminine, 124, 132, 140, 179, 180, 231, 234, 240; *see also* Mothers—identification with

hysterical, 109, 186, 394, 440
internal, 40, 185, **201-2**
masculine, 166; *see also*
    Fathers—identification with
masochistic, 232, 233, 363,
    416
mutual, 410
pregenital, 144
primary, 45, 185, 284, **328,**
    477
projective, *see* Projective
    identification
pseudoidentification, 42,
    185-86, **335-36**
secondary, 186, **394**
social, 409
transference as, 447
transient, 354
trial, **453**
See also Empathy
Identity, 43, 75, 396, **399,** 410
adolescent, 17
dissociation of, 132
ideational and perceptual, 356
loss of, 125, 152, 415, 482
Illness, physical, 92, 122, 153, 206,
    298, 440
of analysts
    Abraham, 4*n,* 6
    Ferenczi, 145-46
    Freud, 162-63, 165
déjà vu during, 97
euphoria during, 133
as expression of tension, 56, 216
Ferenczi's concern with, 144
flight into, **149-50,** 266, 273,
    329, 351
menstruation viewed as, 324
as negative therapeutic reaction,
    264
regression as result of, 372
self-observation in, 397
varieties of
    bronchial asthma, **58-59,**
        353-54, 420
    categorization of, 245
    functional, 286
    narcolepsy, **261**
    peptic ulcer, **300-2**
    syphilis, 296

ulcerative colitis, 353, 405-6,
    455-56
See also Hypochondriasis;
    Psychosomatic disturbances
Illusion, 23, 135, **186-87,** 236, 392
aesthetic, 470
ambivalence and, 27, 28
of appersonation, 40
of free will, 152
hallucination contrasted to, 172
of omnipotence,
        see Omnipotence
See also Delusions;
    Hallucinations
Imitation, **187-88,** 252
Impotence, 45, 185, **188-89,** 190,
    203, 248, 471
Abraham's study of, 2
bisexuality and, 53-54
degrees of, 194
denial due to, 94, 102
effected by woman, 309
Ferenczi's concern with, 142,
    400
forms of
    ejaculatio praecox, *see*
        Ejaculatio praecox
    ejaculatio retardata, **125,** 188,
        189
    orgastic, 152, **287,** 387
inner identification in, 202
as marital problem, 231
masochism and, **189,** 234, 251
as neurotic symptom, 386
Impotentia ejaculandi, 125, 188-89
Impulses, **189-90,** 372, 387, 432
of alcoholics, 23, 24
discharge of unconscious, 457
disorders of, 25, 357
elimination of, *see* Repression;
    Suppression
perverse, 401
raptus, 364
Incest, 156, 188, **190-91,** 373, 444
acrophobia and, 11
fantasies of, 51, 370
fixation on, 124, 400
Jung's theory of, 161
spider as symbol of, 413, 414
taboo against, 35, 166, 190
See also Oedipus complex

Incorporation, 16, 236, 246, 263,
    297
defenses against, 373
failure in, 262
oral, 57-58, 229, 261, 284, 301,
    324, 394, 403
reincorporation, 277
replacement of, 320
Indecision, *see* Ambivalent
    oscillation
Individual (Adlerian) psychology,
    192, 433
Individuality, loss of, 236
Inertia, psychic, **339-40,** 450; *see*
    also Fixation
Infancy, 43, 49, **191-92,** 362, 381
psychosexual development
    during, *see* Libidinal
    phases; Polymorph
    perverse behavior
symbiosis in, 424-25
Infantile amnesia, *see* Screen
    memories
Infantile masturbation, **192,** 307
Inferiority feelings, 89, 175,
    192-93, 245, 381
compensation for, 159, 327
defense against, 100
of eldest child, 153
from narcissistic scar, 260
in penis envy, 62, 107, 300, 307,
    463
of perverts, 304
Influencing machine, **193**
Inhibition, 75, 79, 148, **193-95,**
    298
forms of
    anorexia nervosa, **34-35,** 277,
        472
    intellectual, 334, 399
    linguistic, *see* Language—
        disturbances of moral,
        see Morality
    normal vs. pathological,
        195-96
    phobic, 268
    sexual, *see* Frigidity;
        Impotence; Sexual
        inhibition
as function of superego, 422
lack of, 340

Page numbers in **boldface** refer to main entries

Inhibition *(Continued)*
  objects of
    aggression, 324
    discharge of energy, 395
    instinctual aims, *see* Aim
      inhibition
    motility, 252
    primary process, 467
    will, 10
    wit, 176
  as source of thought, 438
  sources of, 403
    ambivalence, 366
    obsessional brooding, 278
    shame, 217
"Inhibitions, Symptoms and
    Anxiety" (Freud), 162,
    195-97
Insanity, *see* Psychosis
Inman, W. S., 247
Insight, 202, 230
  analytic, 13, **32**, 320, 347
  avoidance of, 432, 449
  emotional, **126**
  intellectual, **201**
Insomnia, **197**, 407
Inspectionism, *see* Scopophilia
Instinct (instinctual drive), 2, 17,
    197-98, 379, 382, 396
  Abraham's conflict with his, 7
  control of, 82, 118, 121
  denial of, 397
  etiology of, 41
  gratification of, *see* Satisfaction
  instinct-fusions, 273, 310, 317,
    328, 339, 355, 357, 360,
    366, 371, 377-78, 412,
    416, 422, 435; *see also*
    Aggression; Libido
  located in id, 183, 338, 387
  phases of instinctual thrust, 354
  types of
    active and passive, 12-13, 14,
      21
    aggressive, *see* Aggression
    component, *see* Component
      instincts
    death, *see* Thanatos
    human social, **409**
    instinctual energy, *see*

Destrudo; Libido; Psychic
    energy
  of knowledge, *see*
    Epistemophilic instinct
  life, *see* Eros
  of looking, *see* Scopophilia
  nonsexual, 122
  of personality, *see* Ego; Id;
    Superego
  of self-assertion, **198-99**
  self-preservative, *see* Ego
    instincts
  sexual, *see* Libido
  See also Freudian theories—
    instinct theories
"Instincts and Their Vicissitudes"
    (Freud), 246
Instinctual aims, 198, **199**, 242,
    402
  inhibition of, *see* Aim inhibition
Instinctual need, **200**
Instinctual vicissitudes, **200-1**,
    225, 375, 389, 393, 399,
    453-54
Instinctualization, 9, 34, 45-46,
  of smell, **199-200**
Intellectual activity, 99, 285
  in dreams, 111, **201**
Intellectual insight, **201**
Intelligence, 98, 135, 304
Intentionality, 302
Intercourse, *see* Coitus
Interfering tendency, 295
Internal identification, 40, 185,
    201-2
Internalization, 56, 98, 425, 466;
    see also Introjection
*International Journal of Psycho-
    Analysis,* 142, 143
International Psychoanalytic
    Association, xvii-xix, 141,
    337
  Abraham as officer of, 5-6, 8
  first congress of, 160
  Jung resigns from presidency
    of, 3, 159
Interpretation, **202-3**
Interpretation of Dreams, The
    (Freud), 160, 161, 246, 417n
  on paramnesia, 292

publication of, 159
Intimidation, **203-4**, 227, 362
*Introductory Lectures on
    Psychoanalysis* (Freud),
    161
Introego (undifferentiated ego
    conscience), **204**
Introjection, 16, 86, 90, 94, 200,
    205-6, 235, 308, 421
  anal, 249, 366
  of anxiety, 188
  in bronchial asthma, 420
  in depression, 103
  interaction between projection
    and, 332-33
  in introego, 204
  introjection of, 459
  manic-depressive, 228-29
  melancholic, 243-44, 259
  psychotic, 268, 354
  respiratory, **379**
  of sources of pleasure, 356
  in symbiosis neurosis, 425
  transient, 453
  See also Identification
Introjects, **204-5**, 330, 381
Introversion (fantasy cathexis),
    149, **206**, 303
Inversion, *see* Homosexuality
Isakower, O., 32, 206, 215-16
  dream theory of, 111, 414-15
Isakower phenomenon, **206-7**
Isolation, 199, **207**, 265, 322
  of affect, 365
  as defense mechanism, 93, 94,
    227, 279
  Freud's period of, 157
  megalomaniacal, 243
  produces autism, 43
  as psychoanalytic technique,
    430

J

Jackson, John Hughlings, 39
Jacobson, Edith, 55-56, 103, 327
Jamais phenomenon, **209**
Jarvis, V., 367

Jealousy, **209-11,** 237, 300, 348, 446
  alcoholic, 23, 210
  envy contrasted to, 129
  paranoid, 95, 293, 331
  pathological, 105, 185, 202
  repression of, 71
  sibling rivalry as, 153
  See also Envy
Jekels, Ludwig, 92, 312
Jelliffe, Smith Ely, 145
Jellinek, E., 23
Jensen, W., 127-28
Jews, *see* Anti-Semitism
Joke, *see* Humor; Wit
Jones, Ernest, 39, 191, 220, 299, 469
  on Abraham, 1, 4, 5, 7, 8, 164
  on committee members, 164, 165
  edits psychoanalytic journal, 142, 143
  on Eidelberg, 295, 412, 459
  errors of, concerning Ferenczi, 144, 145-46
  on Freud, 157-58
    childhood, 153
    cocaine episode, 154, 155
    family relationships, 157
    Freudian sociology, 466
    his tolerance of criticism, 88
    Jung's relationship with Freud, 159
  psychoanalytic anthropology of, 36, 344, 426
  on secondary defenses, 379-80
  as secret committee member, 163
  on Stekel, 160-61
  on symptomatic acts, 426-27
  on two phallic stages, 105, 334
  in Vienna Society, 159
Jung, Carl Gustav, 45, 206, 361, 427
  Abraham and, 1, 5
  concept of persona of, 303
  defection of, 159, 161, 163
  employs anagogic interpretation, 30
  employs word association test, 473

K

Kahane, Max, 159, 356
Kanner, L., 43, 70
Kanzer, M., 12, 161-62
Kaplan, A., 27
Kardiner, Abram, 344
Keller, Helen, 248
Kielholz, Arthur, 24
Klein, Melanie, 5, 293, 294, 308, 450
  play therapy of, 67-69
  theory of projection of
    central Kleinian theory, 331
    projective identification, 332-33
Kleptomania, 190, **213,** 300
Knight, R. P., 24, 92, 203-4, 293
Kohut, H., 11, 176
Kolb, L. C., 24, 474
Koller, Carl, 154-55
Königstein, Leopold, 154, 155
Kräpelin, Emil, 389
Kris, Ernst, 41, 42, 55, 271, 320, 343
  on aesthetic pleasure, 19, 27
  on caricature, 61
  on personal myths, 303
  view of preconscious of, 319
  view of regression of, 372

L

Laforgue, R., 373
Lamartine, Alphonse de, *Jocelyn,* 376
Landauer, K., 17
Language (speech), **215-16,** 265, 318, 351, 370, 384, 446
  Abraham's affinity for, 1, 4
  disturbances of, 335, 411-12, 458
    aphonia, 410-11
    reading, 278, 376, 403
    stammering, 403, **415-16**
    word salad, **473-74**
    writers' inhibitions, 78, 353, 402, **475-76**
    see also Aphasia; Mutism; Slips of the tongue

  in dreams, 9
    spoken, 111, **414-15**
  functions, of, **411-12,** 416, 458
  improvement in use of, xvi
  innate symbols of, 75
  meanings of
    antithetical meanings, 37
    unconscious significance, **458-59**
  neologisms in, **265-66,** 474
  reality of, 50, 340
  role of, in abreaction, 8
  sexualization and
    aggressivization of, **402-3**
  sublimated use of, 419
  of unconscious, 41, 361
  varieties of
    ambiguous, 26-27
    metaphoric, 216, **246,** 474
    obsessional, 382
    psychoanalytic, 344
    schizophrenic, 389, 390, 473-74
    see also Body language
  See also Verbalization; Word association test; Words
Latency period, 106, **217,** 307, 309, 401
  avoidance of pain in, 201
  character formed during, 242
  ego in, 17
  origin of term, 158
  as postoedipal phase, 318
  prepubertal stage of, 354
Latent homosexuality, 95, **217-18,** 307, 417
  in dreams, 88, 92, 110, 140
  scapegoating in, 388
  as threat to mature sexuality, 401
Latent psychosis, **218**
Laughter, 74, 76, 89, **218**
  discharge of energy through, 61
  as pleasure, 81, 82
Laws
  of constancy, 105, 176, **219,** 266, 338, 387
  criminal, **218-19**
  scientific, 345
  of the talion, 381
Lay analysis, 145, 219-20

Page numbers in **boldface** refer to main entries

Leadership, 236, 369, 372
  absence of, 237
  of group perversion, 296
  of psychotic character, 354
LeBon, Gustave, 80, 236
"Leonardo da Vinci and a
      Memory of his Childhood"
      (Freud), 3, 306
Levey, H. B., 302
Lewin, Bertram D., 113, 133, 430,
      482
  on oceanic feeling, 280-81
  on standards for supervision,
      423-24
  on training analysis, 445
Libidinal phases (infantile
      sexuality), 34, 191,
      220-21, 225, 400-1
  Abraham's studies of, 1, 2, 3
  boredom and, 58
  conflicts over sexuality in, 342
  discovery of, 156, 162
  as first phase of instinctual
      thrust, 354
  polymorphic perversion in,
      316-17
  rage reactions in, 362
  rescue fantasy and, 376
  speech functions and, 411
  See also Anal phase; Genital
      phase; Oral phase; Phallic
      phase; Pregenitality
Libidinal types, 66, 117, 270,
      221-22
  conflicts of, 79, 80
  ego-syntonic traits of, 67, 79,
      124
  mixed, 174
  neurotic choice of, 65, 71
  See also Erotic types;
      Narcissistic types;
      Obsessional types
"Libidinal Types" (Freud), 360
Libidinization, *see*
      Delibidinization;
      Sexualization
Libido (libidinal energy, sexual
      instincts), 81, 89, **222,**
      272, 336, 375, 381, 450
  of alcoholics, 23
  ambivalence toward, 27, 28

confusion over meaning of
    term, 435
decrease in amount of, 184
deneutralized, 319
developmental phases of
  adolescent, 242
  anal, 31
  infantile, *see* Libidinal phases
  narcissistic, 44, 99, 118, 138,
    173, 222, 257, 258-59,
    260, 271, 284, 302, 326,
    328, 339, 393, 394, 401,
    402, 409, 419, 422, 462
  oral, 277, 284-85
diagnosis of disturbances of,
    384
effect of drugs on, 115-16
ego instincts and, 122, 341
fixations of, 53
forces acting on
  frustration, 72
  inhibition, *see* Sexual
    inhibition
  neutralization, 425
  regression, 396
  repression, 21, 37, 61, 316
  transformation, 14-15, 37,
    38, 258
male, 232
manifestations of, 130, 225
mobile, 339
of mourners, 252, 253
non-Freudian concepts of
  Adler's, 160
  Jung's, 159
predisposition of, 71
processes of
  cathexis, 63, 94, 98-99, 125,
    172, 179, 222, 243, 257,
    260, 284, 302, 326, 328,
    389, 394, 395, 401, 418
  conflict, 79, 341
  countercathexis, 84, 366
  discharge, 373, 395
  gratification, *see* Sexual
    satisfaction
  instinct-fusion, 198, 199,
    377-78
  withdrawal, 170, 179, 244,
    260, 351, 389, 390, 391
  of psychotics

    manic-depressives, 229
    megalomaniacs, 243, 351
    schizophrenics, 100, 389,
      390, 391
  Róheim redefines, 39
  roles of
    in anhedonia, 33
    in hypochondriasis, 179-80
    in identity, 399
    in introversion, 206
    in rituals, 383
    in social instincts, 409
  source of, 293
  See also Eros; Eroticism; Love;
    Sexuality
Life instinct, *see* Eros
Lindner, S., 191, 192
Linton, Ralph, 344
Lipps, T., 57
Listening with the third ear, **223**
"Little Hans" (case history), 96,
    99, **223-24**
  phobia of, 67, 71, 138, 196,
    310-11, 482
Localization of symptoms, 180,
    224
Loewenstein, R., 55, 271, 343
London, L., 274-75
Lorand, Sandor, 11, 34, 344*n*,
    450, 465
  criticizes Kleinian theory, 294
  on Ferenczi, 140-46
  on perversion, 481
  on success neurosis, 420
Love (affection), 16, 89, **224-25,**
    243, 312, 342, 363, 384,
    477
  anorexia nervosa and, 34, 35
  antithetical meanings of, 37
  capacity for
    incapacity, 333
    loss of capacity, 252
  changed to hate, 366, 391
  as criterion of normality, 273
  dread of loss of, 221
  elation due to, 125
  gained through sacrifice, 385
  humiliation and, 175
  ingredients of
    altruism, 257-58
    happiness, 173

Page numbers in **boldface** refer to main entries

idealization, 184
need for, 450
hunger as, 297
intensified, 199
paranoid, 293
renunciation of demand for
love, 26
in postambivalent phase, 317
refusal to give, 124
in relaxation technique, 373
of self, 133, 326, 331; *see also*
Narcissism
from superego, 369
varieties of
adolescent, 17, 410
all-embracing, 280
anaclitic, 278, 281, 409, 449
punishment as love, 233
see also Transference-love
See also Ambivalence;
Eroticism; Libido
Lure of the past, **225-26**

M

McDougall, W., 198, 236
Magic, 181, **227,** 228, 366, 443
in alcoholic's thinking, 23
of cave paintings, 41
in dark glasses, 132
hypnosis and magical thinking,
178, 179
in imagery, 61
infantile omnipotence and, 356
of language, 253, 411, 459, 474
in neurosis, 142, 148, 227, 279,
282
revenge as, 380
science and, **392**
spiders as magical omens, 413
of stigmata, 416
in undoing, 95, 227, 371, 380,
383, 384, 459-60
See also Religion; Superstition
Mahler-Schoenberger, M., 334,
443
on infantile psychosis, 43, 121,
390
Mainx, F., 21, 297, 433-34
Making faces, **227-28**

Maladjustment, **228,** 384
Malinowski, Bronislaw, 35-36,
241, 344
Mammary complex, *see* Breast
complex
Mania, 115, 260, 282, 387
forms of
kleptomania, 190, **213,** 300
nymphomania, **274-75,** 300
persecution, 105, 185, 202
pyromania, **357**
see also Megalomania
ingredients of
celebration, 229, 363
conflict, 79
elation, 125
glorified instinctual activity,
364
shamelessness, 404
Manic-depressive psychosis, 80,
125, **228-30**
Abraham's concern with, 2, 5
oscillation of mood in, 381, 382
Mannerisms (gestures), 215, 216,
230, 245
magical, 181, 356, 443
omnipotence of, 415
symbolic, 417
See also Tics
Marcovitz, Eli, 97
Marriage, **230-31,** 306-7, 364,
369, 475-76
of Abraham, 4, 5
conflicts resulting from, 73
of Ferenczi, 142
of Freud, 156-57
origin of monogamous, 334
of ulcer patients, 301-2
virginity taboo and, 468
Masculine protest, 159-60
Masculinity, 21, 184, **231-32,** 386
as active state, 12-13, 231, 297
beating fantasies and, 51-52
object choice and, 30, 277-78,
401
virginity taboo and, 468
Masochism, 50, 77, 213, **232-35,**
237, 262, 304, 350, 441
accident-proneness due to, 11
avoidance of unpleasure in, 461
countertransference and, 433

as feminine trait, 297
negative therapeutic reaction
and, 234, 250-51, 260,
263-64
pleasure-unpleasure principle
and, 234, **314-15**
rebelliousness in, 369
role of humiliation in, 175,
232-33, 235, 314, 453
roles of
in altruism, 26
in dreams, 140
in fantasies, 51-52
in rape, 363
in sacrifice, 385
in stigmata, 416
in success neurosis, 420
seeking of anxiety in, 402
self-esteem and, 234, **397**
sexual inhibition and
frigidity, 166-67, 234
impotence, **189,** 234, 251
sources of
defense, 147
pain, 291, 406
subjects of
humorists, 176
hypnotic subject, 296
ulcer patients, 301
Wolf Man, 472, 473
varieties of
feminine, **140,** 234
moral, 232-33, 234, **250-51,**
268, 370, 422, 431
primary, 234, **328-29,** 386
See also Sado-masochism
Masochistic mechanism, 234, **235**
Mass hysteria, **237**
Mass (group) psychology, 179,
235-37, 343, 372
rituals in, 383
scapegoating in, 388
See also Leadership
Masturbation, 184, 204, **237-38,**
383, 471
of animals, 481
autoerotism and, 44
castration threats and, 62
as cause and result of neurosis,
9
coitus equated with, 124

Masturbation, *(Continued)*
  as displacement, 106
  frequent, 116
  of frigid patient, 77
  masochistic stimulation for, 232
  menstrual evidence of, 324
  punishment for, 416, 443
  response to
    blushing, 132
    defense against, 171
    projection, 89
    response to prohibition, 367
  of sadistic patient, 386
  types of
    anal, 403
    compulsive, *see* Compulsive
      masturbation
    excessive, 15, 266, 274
    infantile, **192,** 307
    normal, **274**
Masturbation addicts, **238-39**
Masturbation equivalents, 238,
    272, **239,** 426
    pregenital, **321-22**
    prephallic, **326-27**
    rhythmic activities as, 381-82
Masturbation fantasies, 172, 177,
    238, **239-40,** 251, 322, 333
  bisexuality and, 54
  masochistic, 167, 189, 234, 406
  of rape, 363
  sadistic, 149
  sado-masochistic, 386
  of satyrs, 387
Matriarchy, 235, **240-41,** 254,
    333-34
Maturation, 115, **241-43,** 382
  affects body image, 55-56
  of awareness of self, 395
  delusional phase of, 293
  frustration and, 167
  masturbation and, 237-38
  period of negativism in, 264-65
  sense of humor and, 176
  toilet training coordinated with,
    440
  See also Adolescence; Anal
    phase; Freudian theories—
    of psychosexual
    maturation; Genital phase;
    Latency period; Libidinal

phases; Oedipal stage; Oral
    phase; Phallic phase;
    Postambivalent phase;
    Postoedipal period;
    Pregenitality; Preoedipal
    stage; Puberty
Megalomania, **243,** 293, 330, 351
  infantile, 460
  schizophrenic, 100, 389
Meisl, Alfred, 248
Melancholia, 65, **243-45,** 252-53,
    282, 394, 422
  alimentary orgasm and, 25
  ambivalence and, 27-28
  change of mood in, 381
  conflict in, 79
  depression contrasted to, 103
  Freud's work on, 2
  introjection in, 205, 259
  manic-depressive psychosis and,
    229-30
  as narcissistic neurosis, 260,
    268, 351
  oral fixation in, 94, 147, 285
  phallic mother in, 306
  role of self-hatred in, 362-63
  suicidal, 421
  tranquilizers affect, 114-15
Memory, 126, 202, 281, 295, 303,
    473
  delay of discharge facilitates, 98
  forms of
    dreams, 109
    inner reality, 340
    perception, 120, 302
    primal, 327
    racial, **361**
    screen, *see* Screen memories
  loss of
    abreaction compared to
      fading of memory, 8
    blanking out of sexual
      memory, 298
    see also Amnesia
  range of, 178
  remarkable feats of, 43
  repression of, 375
  roles of
    in anticipation, 36
    in anxiety, 38
    in dreams, 75

    in fantasy, 138
    in impotence, 400
    in jamais phenomenon, 209
  storage of, 121; *see also* Mneme
    system
  stripping of affect of, 207
Menninger, Karl A., 72
Menstruation, 242, **245,** 381, 416
  disturbances of, 34, 245, **323-24**
  fetish for coitus during, 304
  onset of, 199, 354
Mental phenomena, *see* Psychic
    phenomena
Metaphoric language, 216, **246,**
    474
"Metapsychological Supplement
    to the Theory of Dreams,
    A" (Freud), 246
Metapsychology, 118, **246-47,**
    319, 399, 407
  of dreams, 111
  of drugs, 114-15
  Freud's writings on, 161-62
  period of, 341-42
Meyer, C. F., *Die Richterin,* 40
Meynert, Theodor, 29, 153
Micropsia, **247**
Micropsychophysiology, **247**
Micturition, *see* Urination
Misogyny, **247-48,** 289, 307
Mittelman, B., 443
Mneme system, 120, **248,** 337, 438
Money, 106, **248-49,** 382, 402
  miserliness toward, 84, 248,
    380, 412
Moral masochism, 175, 232-33,
    234, **250-51,** 268, 370,
    422, 431
Moral responsibility, 153, 413
  dreams and, 111, **251**
Morality, **249-50,** 357, 379, 385,
    438
  development of, 215
  of perverts, 304
  regression of, 371
  religious, 374
  role of conscience in, 80
  sense of justice in, 317
  sphincter, **412-13,** 422
  See also Ethical approach;
    Taboos; Values

Page numbers in **boldface** refer to main entries

Moralization, 364
Morgenthaler, W., 344
Mortido, *see* Destrudo
Mortification, *see* Narcissistic
    mortification
Moses and Monotheism (Freud),
    35, 40, 344
Mothers, 34-35, 144, 147, 244,
    299, 440, 450
  of alcoholics, 24
  ambivalence toward, 26
  in case histories
    of Dora, 108
    of Little Hans, 71, 96, 223-24
    of Wolf Man, 472, 473
  in criminal fantasies, 229
  favorite child of, 153
  identification with, 53, 180,
    184, 188, 210, 217, 231,
    241, 281, 289, 295, 308,
    388, 465, 473; *see also*
    Primary identification
  of paranoids, 88
  of primal horde, 236
  as primary figure, 52
  simultaneous analysis of child
    and, **405-6**
  in symbiotic relationship, 424
  See also Matriarchy; Oedipus
    complex; Preoedipal
    mother attachment; Primal
    scene
Motility, **251-52**, 387, 440, 442
  alloplastic, 25, 185
  control of, 117, 183, 438
  in dreams, 111, **252**
  inhibition of, 402
  interference with, 468
  regression of, 372
  ritualized, 382
Motivation for analysis, 445
Mourning, 162, 205-6, **252-53**,
    363, 450
  anticipation in, 36
  by melancholics, 27
  perverse, 261
  regression as aid in, 372
  weeping as, 89
"Mourning and Melancholia"
    (Freud), 246
Murphy, G., 383, 436

Murray, C., 455
Murray, J. M., 128
Mutism, 108-9, **253**
Myers, F. W. H., 434
Mystic union, **253-54**
Mythology, 36, 226*n*, 249, **254-55**
  Abraham's studies of, 1
  castration in, 328
  distortion in, 336
  dreams and, 112
  Graves' studies of, 240
  heroic, 235-36
  personal, **303**
  petrifaction in, 305
  phallic woman in, 306
  precursor of, 330
  psychoanalysis applied to, 41,
    344
  spiders in, 413
  spirit animals in, 444
  virginal goddesses in, 247-48
  See also Religion

N

Nailbiting, **283**, 460
Narcissism, 221, 225, 228, **257-58**,
    326, 397
  conquest of, 318
  fascination with, 139
  gratification of, 370, 387, 393
  impotence related to, 125,
    188-89
  in nuclear theory, 274
  pride rooted in, 327
  primary and secondary, 100,
    257, 297, 330, 354
  primitive, 330
  at puberty, 355
  reassurance in, 369
  regression to, 44, 45, 260, 272,
    282, 372
  in resistance, 378
Narcissistic entitlement, **128**
Narcissistic gain, **258-59**
Narcissistic mortification (loss of
    control), 14, 43, 66, 123,
    200, 234, **259-60**, 342,
    374, 421
  abreaction and, 8
  of alcoholics, 23, 24

  altruism and, 26
  causes of
    forced defecation, 249
    helplessness, 167
    humiliation, 175
    lack of knowledge, 130
    lack of penis, 299, 307
  death wish prevents, 244
  in depression, 103, 104
  external, 59, 95, 99, 101, 110,
    151, 238, 253, 283, 322,
    331, 363, 378, 431, 479
  gratification from elimination
    of, 387
  infantile, 198, 282-83, 399
  laughter and, 218
  masturbation fantasies and, 167,
    239, 240
  in menstruation, 245
  overcoming of, 90, 259
  phallic character and, 305
  response to, 366, 416, 454
    anal regression, 380
    avoidance, 47, 93-94, 192,
      210, 295, 314, 407
    formation of psychosis, 148
    infantile amnesia, 393
    introjection, 205
    magical elimination, 142
    negation, 263
    obsessive denial, 279
    projection, 336
    protection, 132
    repression, 89, 259, 283
    stripping of affect, 207
    sublimation, 370
    substitution of another
      mortification, 16, 77, 102,
      106, 451, 471
    unpleasure, 233, 314, 461
  revival of, 267
  as trauma, 451
Narcissistic need, **260**
Narcissistic neurosis, 2, **260**, 268,
    341, 351
Narcissistic object choice, 30,
    184-85, **277-78**
  of bisexuals, 53
  of homosexuals, 30, 225, 277,
    288
  mixture of anaclitic and, 449

Narcissistic object
    choice, *(Continued)*
    parental love based on, 225
    in transference, 447
Narcissistic omnipotence, *see*
    Omnipotence
Narcissistic scar, **260-61**
Narcissistic tranquility, 113-14,
    116
Narcissistic types, 66, 117, 221,
    240, 298, 408
    characterization of, 65, 174
    ego-syntonic traits of, 67, 79,
    124
    neurotic choice of, 71, 360
Narcolepsy, **261**
Necrophilia, **261-62,** 304
Need, 369, 370
    instinctual, **200**
    for love, *see* Love—need for
    narcissistic, **260**
    for punishment, 97, **262,** 316,
    369; *see also* Guilt;
    Masochism
    for revenge, 380, 381
Needles, W., 417
Negation, 94, **262-63**
Negative Oedipus complex, 51,
    187, **263,** 307-8, 310, 376
    in bisexuality, 53
    due to castration complex, 62
    latent homosexuality and, 217
    misogyny results from, 247
    role of blushing in, 55
    of Wolf Man, 179, 180, 224,
    263
Negative therapeutic reaction,
    263-64, 341
    of masochists, 234, 250-51, 260,
    263-64
    of psychopaths, 347, 349
    of transference, 128, 142, 158,
    446-47, 469-70
Negative tropism, **264**
Negativism, **264-65**
Neologisms, **265-66,** 474
Neurasthenia, 9, 238, **266,** 286,
    299
    as actual neurosis, 15, 400
Neuropsychoses of defense,
    266-67

Neurosis (psychoneurosis), 87,
    94, 156, **267-69,** 397, 447
    Abraham's concern with, 1, 2
    Adler's theory of, 160
    amnesia linked to, 29
    exchange of, in marriage, 231
    gain in, 377
    primary (paranosic), **329,**
    394
    secondary (epinosic), 63,
    329, 370, 380, **394**
    hides impotence, 188
    ingredients of, 351
    ambivalence, 27, 365, 366,
    369, 383
    anxiety, 37-38
    confusion of realities, 150,
    186, 245
    condensation, 78
    denial, 102, 363
    failure to reach genitality,
    462
    fore-unpleasure, 151
    hallucinations, 335, 371
    identification, 184
    inhibition, 75, 193-94
    introversion, 206
    jamais phenomenon, 209
    maladjustment, 228
    masturbatory equivalent, 322
    mutism, 253
    negativism, 265
    omnipotent feeling, 142, 282,
    398
    passive-active polarity, 315
    passive-receptive attitudes,
    298
    penis envy, 62
    periodicity, 381
    primal fantasies, 327
    pseudo-hypersexuality, 335
    pseudologia fantastica, 336
    rationalization, 65, 123, 268,
    364
    rebellion, 369
    remorse, 374, 398
    self-assertion, 199
    sublimation of scopophilia,
    10
    temporary regression, 246
    totemic, 444

latency period and, 217
of libidinal types, 221
mass psychology and, 236-37
nuclear complex of, 224, 230
psychoanalytic approaches to,
    437-38, 445
    comparative, **76-77**
    cross section of neurosis,
    88-89
    neurosis as negative of
    perversion, 135, 147,
    269-71, 304
    structural, 351, 389
    systematic, 428
of Rank, 164
rigidity of, 148
role of aesthetic pleasure in, 19
sources of, 71, 389
    abstinence, 9
    coitus interruptus, 266
    conflict, 77, 80, 337, 351,
    428, 457
    disturbance of genital
    function, 287
    failure of abreaction, 52
    fear of aphanisis, 39
    fixation or regression, 267,
    401
    hereditary, 296, 431
    incestuous wishes, 190
    Oedipus complex, 281, 307
    precocity, 242
    seduction, 341
    social demands, 466
    trauma, 174
    unsuccessful repression, 375
treatment of
    abreaction as cure, 8
    incurable neurosis, 251, 260
    process of analysis, xvi-xvii
    projective diagnosis, 384
    psychiatric, 336, 337
two instinct-fusions discharged
    in, 328
varieties of
    borderline, 57
    bronchial asthma, 58-59
    depression as, 103
    housewife, 108
    impulse, 189-90
    infantile, 342

insomnia, 197
masochistic, 314-15
narcissistic, 2, **260**, 268, 341, 351
observational, 413
parapathy, 294
pathoneurosis, **298**
success, **419-20**
Sunday (weekend), **421-22**
symbiotic, 425
ulcerative colitis, 455
see also Actual neuroses; Anxiety neurosis; Character neurosis; Compulsion; Destiny neurosis; Hypochondriasis; Hysteria; Moral masochism; Obsession; Phobias; Psychopathy; Transference neurosis; Traumatic neurosis; War neurosis
See also Character traits—neurotic; Choice—neurotic; Conflicts—neurotic; Freudian theories—of neurosis; Neurotic symptoms
Neurotic symptoms, 47, 65, 102, 190, 195, 242, 270, 386, 457
ambiguity and, 26, 27
analyzable, 40
discharge drive-energy, 329
ego-syntonic formations and, 123
flight into health and, 149
Freud's own, 157
localization of, 224
psychoanalytic approaches to
comparative, 76, 196, 360
first symptom, 431
quantitative, 360
short-term therapy, 404
structural, 195, 267
teleological, 63
role of penis envy in, 300
sources of
castration complex, 62
conflict, 79, 268
defenses, 93

repressed infantile wishes, 9, 199, 267, 342-43, 379
revival of conflict, 323
sexual inhibition, 400
of specific neuroses
actual neuroses, 15
anxiety neurosis, 38
traumatic neurosis, 452
symptom formations, 295, 392
varieties of
autoplastic, 46, 185
compromise, 184, 394
compulsive doubt, 279
impotence, 400
inability to relax, 373
inferiority feelings, 193
nailbiting, 283
nocturnal, 299
paralysis, 252
psychosomatic, 352-53
repetitive, 382
stammering, 415
tics, 439
Neutralization, 98, **271**, 302, 425
failure in, 262, 390
See also Psychic energy—neutral
"New Introductory Lectures on Psychoanalysis" (Freud), 320*n*
New School for Social Research (N.Y.C.), 142, 145
New York Psychoanalytic Society, 145
New York Society of Clinical Psychiatry, 145
Niederland, W. G., 260-61, 281, 391
Nietzsche, Friedrich, 160, 223
Nightmares (pavor nocturnus), **271-72, 299**
Nihilism, **272**
Nirvana principle, 219, **272,** 374
Nocturnal emissions, 110, 140, 386, 458, 470
overly frequent, 15
Nocturnal enuresis, 124, **272-73,** 289, 300
Normal masturbation, **274**
Normality, **273,** 445
of Abraham, 7, 8
appearance of, 65-66

marriage and, 230-31
maturity and, 242
"Nosology of Male Homosexuality, The" (Ferenczi), 142
Noyes, A., 24, 474
Nuclei, **274**
Nunberg, H., 370, 413
Nymphomania, **274-75,** 300

O

Obedience, 236
automatic, **45,** 139
deferred, **96**
Oberndorf, C., 144-45
Obesity, 116, **277**
Object choice, *see* Anaclitic object choice; Narcissistic object choice
Objective data, 302
Obliging dreams, 111, **278,** 470-71
Oblivescence, 362
Observation
delusions of, **101**
of self, 215, **397-98**
See also Scopophilia; Voyeurism
Obsession (obsessional neurosis), 65, 268, 285, 286, 314, 337
anality in, 31, 441
fixation points of, 44
ingredients of
compulsive thinking, 9
defense mechanisms, 93, 94
denial, 317
guilt and remorse, 236, 279, 374
helplessness, 152
isolation, 207
omnipotence, 282, 474
reassurance, 369
sexualization of thought, 403
strict superego, 366, 422-23
tactic of disappointment, 166
undoing, 459-60
leap into, 247
precocity as cause of, 242
predisposition to, 71
projective diagnosis of, 384

Obsession obsessional
  neurosis, *(Continued)*
quantitative approach to, 360
roles of
  character neurosis, 66
  neuropsychosis of defense,
    266
subjects of
  analysts, 86
  Rat Man, 365-66
  Wolf Man, 180, 224, 472-73
with washing, 84, 119-20
See also Compulsion; Obsessive-
  compulsive neurosis
Obsessional brooding, 130, **278-79**
Obsessional types, 117, 124, 221,
  360
anxiety hysteria of, 71, 80, 298
avoid slips of the tongue, 408
characteristics of, 65, 174
Obsessive-compulsive neurosis,
  82, 148, 207, **279,** 365-66
repetitive symptoms of, 382
rituals in, 227, 382-83
self-observation in, 397
Occult phenomena, **279-80**; *see
  also* Animism; Déjà
  raconté; Déjà vu; Magic;
  Superstition; Telepathy
Oceanic feeling, 254, **280-81**
Oedipus complex, 164, 166, 207,
  209, 247, **281-83,** 289,
  309, 371, 383
adolescent, 354, 355
anthropological roots of, 35,
  240, 241
case histories of
  Little Hans, 67, 99, 223-24,
    366
  Rat Man, 365
  Wolf Man, 473
after father's death, 386
identification and, 180, 184-85
influences on
  drugs, 115
  preoedipal mother
    attachment, 324
  primal scene, 327
  puberty, 169, 184
ingredients of
  blushing, 55

guilt over oedipal fantasies,
    237
  incest, 190
  rescue fantasy, 376
severe trauma, 303
  triumph, 277
Jones supports theory of, 36
metaphors based on, 246
as origin of superego, 249-50,
  307, 308, 422
outcome of
  anorexia nervosa, 34
  dissolution of complex,
    106-7, 220
  estrangement, 137
  genital sexuality, 401
  inhibition of creativity, 475
  perversion, 481
  phobia, 310
  promiscuity from oedipal
    fixation, 333
  rebelliousness, 369
  rejection of feminine
    receptivity, 466
  satyriasis, 387
  success neurosis, 419
  successful resolution of
    complex, 225
  wish for a child, 323
perversion and, 270
preadolescence as period of, 17
sacrifice and, 385
See also Negative Oedipus
  complex; Postoedipal
  period; Preoedipal stage
Omnipotence, 29, 33-34, 95, 100,
  270, **282-83,** 297, 354,
  364, 392, 407
anthropological roots of, 330
as component of disturbance,
  398
  addiction, 16
  manic-depressive psychosis,
    228-29
  masochism, 233, 234
  megalomania, 243
  nymphomania, 274
  obsession, 366
  perversion, 304
conflicts over, 380
defined, 191, 282

destruction of, 43
in ego regression, 371
fantasies of, 149, 277
of fathers, 45
humor related to, 76, 81, 211
hypnosis and, 178, 179
magical-hallucinatory, 356,
    367
oral, 424
preserved by pride, 327
punishment affects, 175
relinquishing of, 44, 87, 441
responses to
  belief in, 383
  denial, 397
  fascination, 139
  projection, 279
symptoms resulting from
  aerophagia, 18
  impotence, 124
  inferiority feelings, 192-93
  mutism, 253
three stages of, 142
undoing and, 460
of words, 411, 415, 474
"On Narcissism" (Freud), 161
"On the History of the Psycho-
  Analytic Movement"
  (Freud), 144, 160
Onanism, *see* Masturbation
Onychophagia (nailbiting), **283,**
  460
Optimism, 17, 36, 125, **283-84**
of Abraham, 6, 7
normal, 228
oral, 283, 373
Oral fixation, 34, 285, 301, 351
alcoholism as, 23, 24
in melancholia, 94, 147
Oral pessimism, **284**
Oral phase, 169, 191, 220,
    284-86, 395
Abraham's analysis of, 2, 3,
    284, 285-86, 320, 321
anal phase contrasted to, 31
discovery of, 158
homosexual development in,
    289, 304
identification in, 136, 201
  primary, 285, 328
  secondary, 186, 394

ingredients of
  ambivalence, 27, 284-85,
    301, 317, 324
  attachment to mother, 325
  conflict, 450
  fantasies, 379
  frustration, 213, 362
  inferiority feelings, 192
  instinctual aims, 199
  obesity, 277
  oral nucleus of superego, 422
  overindulgence, 411
  passive-receptive longing,
    297
  skin eroticism, 406
optimistic character molded in,
  283
regression to, 34, 103, 125, 147,
  238, 244, 301, 351, 435;
  see also Oral fixation; Oral
  wishes
results of
  menstrual disorders, 324
  penis envy, 300
  reading disturbances, 367
revival of conflicts of, 323
Oral wishes, 13, 124, 169, 421,
  482
in addiction, 113
of analysts, 86
attitude toward money as, 249
in bronchial asthma, 59
in choice of a mate, 231
in face-breast equation, 137
as motivation for sacrifice, 385
in nymphomania, 274
response to
  conversion, 439
  defense of wish, 295
  mutism, 253
  pseudo-hypersexuality, 335
  repression, 108, 285
  sublimation, 285, 367
varieties of
  manic-depressive, 228-29
  necrophilic, 261
  oral incorporation, 57-58,
    403
  oral-sadistic, 99, 283, 284,
    285, 335, 403, 471
  submissive, 369

    see also Cannibalism
Organ language, 474
Organic phenomena, **286-87,** 351;
    see also Illness
Orgasm (climax), 152, **287**
  alimentary, 24, **25**
  delay in reaching, 125
  in erotic dreams, 470
  of fetishist, 146
  heterosexual vs. homosexual,
    325
  lack of emotion with, 188
  of perverts, 304
  during rape, 363
Orgastic impotence, 152, **287,** 387
Ostow, Mortimer, 113-16
Overdetermination, **288,** 320
Overt homosexuality, 53, 111,
    137, **288-90,** 409
  due to breast envy, 58, 306
  fixation to phallic mother in,
    325
  in preadolescence, 17

P

Pain, 162, 266, **291,** 451
  avoidance of, 48, 118, 201
  breaks psychic barrier, 49
  coitus associated with, 194
  in envy, 129
  over hostility, 173, 209
  infliction of, *see* Sadism
  of mourning, 253
  narcotic relief from, 113-14,
    154
  pleasure from, 406
  seeking of, 262
  suicide as result of, 421
  thanatos as cause of, 180
  tolerance of, under hypnosis,
    178
Pair of dreams, 111, **291,** 407
Palmer, J. N., 257, 258-59, 328
Panic, 236
Pansexualism, **292**
Paralysis, 186, 252, 299, 305
  hysterical, 83, 153-54, 180,
    204-5, 224, 253
  of speech, 459

syphilitic, 296
Paramnesia, **292-93,** 376
Paranoia, 24, 128, 138, 194, 448
  case history of, *see* Schreber
    Case
  delusional, 99-101, 272, 292,
    293, 357, 389, 391
  fixation-points of, 44, 351
  group, **170**
  hallucination in, 172, 351
  of hypnotic subjects, 179
  material gained from analysis
    of, 88-89
  as narcissistic neurosis, 260
  as paraphrenia, 294, 389
  phobia contrasted to, 269
  projection in, 95, 266, 268, 331,
    389, 391
Paranoid condition (state), 26,
    193, **293**
Paranoid-schizoid position, **294**
Paranosic (primary) gain in
    neurosis, **329,** 394
Parapathy, **294**
Paraphrenia, 44, **294,** 389
Parapraxis, 119, 162, 251, 262,
    294-96, 401, 456
  ambiguity and, 26, 27
  applied psychoanalysis and,
    40-41
  dynamic approach to, 345
  ejaculatio praecox as, 85
  forgetting as, 432-33
  psychic determinants of, 346-47
  slips of the tongue as, 295, 407
  source of, 457
Parasitic superego, **296**
Parapsychology, *see* Occult
    phenomena
Parathymia, 229-30
Paresis, 133, **296-97,** 404
Parin, P., 85, 344
Paris, Freud's studies in, 153
Parricide, 241
  primal, 35-36, 229, 330, 385
Passive-receptive longing,
    297-98
Passivity, 15, 132, 176, **297,** 301,
    404
  activity and, *see* Activity—
    passivity and

Passivity *(Continued)*
  of analysts, xvi
  due to castration anxiety, 305
  as neurotic predisposition, 71
  paranoid, 88-89
  repetition of passive role, 374
Past, 36
  lure of, **225-26**
Pathognomy, **298**
Pathoneurosis, **298**
Patriarchy, 235, 236, 240-41,
      255, 333
  Jewish, 254
Paul, I. H., 303
Pavlovian therapy, 14
Pavor nocturnus, *see* Nightmares
Pedophilia, 304
Peller, L. E., 318
Penis captivus, 466
Penis envy, 107, 109, 192, 232,
      245, **299-300**
  affects masturbation, 238
  in analyst, 85, 433
  desire for children and, 129,
      323
  disturbance due to, 62
  in frigidity, 62, 166, 465
  in phallic stage, 220-21, 307,
      463
  of phallic woman, 309
  psychopathic, 348-51
Peptic ulcers, **300-2**
Perception, 245, 248, **302-3,** 371,
      395, 474
  as component of psychic
      apparatus, 337, 338
  denial of, 93, 101, 200, 347, 420
  ego and, **120-21**
  fantasy vs., 149
  hallucinogens distort, 114
  nonpathological distortion of,
      39-40
  of psychic qualities, 359
  regression in, 372
  roles of
    in body image, 55-56, 309
    in dreams, 75, 110, 111, 252
    in flight into reality, 150
    in projection, 331
    in reading, 367
    in reality principle, 368

  in thinking, 438
  types of
    accidental, 295
    endopsychic, **127-28,** 247
    extrasensory, *see* Occult
        phenomena
    olfactory, **199-200**
    preconscious, 81
    self-observation, 215, **397-98**
    visual, abnormality of, **247**
    see also Feelings; Sensations
  See also Hallucinations;
      Illusion; Insight;
      Scopophilia; Voyeurism
Perceptual consciousness, 302,
      303, 359
Perfectionism, 23
Periodicity, 158, 272, **381-82,** 411
Persecution, 158, 193
  delusions of, 100, **101,** 243,
      293, 391
  paranoid, 88, 179
  persecution mania, 105, 185,
      202
Persona, **303**
Personal myths, **303**
Perversions, *see* Sexual
      perversions
Pessimism, 17, 228
  Freud's alleged, 6, 161
  oral, **284**
Petrifaction, **305**
Pfister, Oskar, 146, 375
Phallic character, **305-6, 306-7,**
      369
Phallic mother, 17, 90, 300, **306,**
      324
  fantasy of, 308, 325, 414
  homosexual partner as, 289
  of ulcer patients, 301, 302
Phallic phase, 103, 169, 220-21,
      307-8, 462-63
  Abraham's analysis of, 2
  aggressive, 310
  cloaca and, 74
  fixation of, 80, 309
  ingredients of
    attachment to mother, 325
    conflict, 450
    envy, 128, 299
    frustration, 213

  identification, 136, 201
  inferiority feelings, 192, 463
  instinctual aims, 199
  masturbation fantasies, 237
  narcissistic mortification, 380
  obesity, 277
  sadism, 386
  as oedipal stage, 106, 307-8
  regression to, 32, 71, 180, 224,
      232, 351, 366, 371, 380,
      472; *see also* Phallic wishes
  revival of conflicts of, 323
  two stages of, **105, 334**
Phallic pride, 307, **308-9**
Phallic wishes, 42, 124, 132, 169,
      350, 403
  attitudes toward money as, 249
  hysteria due to, 71, 224
  toward mothers, 299
  pseudo-hypersexuality and, 335
  roles of
    in bronchial asthma, 59
    in choice of a mate, 231
    in dreams, 110
    in enuresis, 272
    in phobia, 310
  submissive, 369
Phallic woman, **309,** 465; *see also*
      Phallic mother
Phantom limb, **309**
Phenomenological approach, 377
Philosophy, 41, 470; *see also*
      Aesthetics; Ethical
      approach; Morality;
      Values
Phobias, 148, 190, 268, 279,
      298, **309-12,** 314
  active therapy for, 14, 143
  analyzable, 40
  childhood, 35
  of intercourse, 194
  projection in, 74, 95, 132, 269,
      310, 331
  projective diagnosis of, 384
  psychosis contrasted to, 352
  repression in, 375
  traumas determine, 10
  types of
    acrophobia, **11,** 311
    agoraphobia, 120, 136, 185,
        252, 310, 311

Page numbers in **boldface** refer to main entries

claustrophobia, **74,** 311

counterphobia, **84,** 260, 305, 369, 402, 404

erythrophobia, 55, **131-32,** 311, 415

inhibition as, 193

totemic, 443-44

xenophobia, 236, **477**

see also Zoophobia

Phobic character, 23, **312**

Pichler, Hans, 162-63

Pity, 23, 89, 139, **312-13,** 316

Play therapy, **13,** 67-69

Playfulness in art, 19

Pleasure, 24, 120, 224, 334, 373

as goal, 371

of reality principle, 367

polarity of unpleasure and, 315

self equated with, 356-57, 396

sources of

orgasm, 287

perversion, 304

repetitive rhythmic actions, 382

warmth, 297

varieties of

aggressive, 21, 22

functional, 258

masochistic, 232, 402

narcissistic, 387, 393

sadistic, 385, 386

see also Aesthetic pleasure; Forepleasure

See also Unpleasure

Pleasure ego, 121, 125, **355-57**

Pleasure principle, 9, 173, 219, **313-14,** 319, 356

in alloplastic adaptation, 25

automatism and, 46

beyond, 460

component instincts and, 77

id serves, 183

need for punishment and, 262

of normal action, 252

other principles related to

expression of nirvana principle, 272, 387

replacement by reality principle, 121, 367-68

see also Nirvana principle; Unpleasure-pleasure

principle

primary process connected with, 329

pure, 323, 418

quantity of tension in, 360

religion linked to, 280

Polarities, **315**

Pollock, G. H., 425

Polycrates complex, **316,** 420

Polymorph perverse behavior, 147, **316-17,** 392

Positive tropism, **317**

Postambivalent phase, **317-18**

Postoedipal period, **318**

Preconscious, 20, 81, 302, **318-19,** 359, 412

censorship between unconscious, conscious and, 64-65, 318, 424

conflict of, 79, 337

functions of, 118

automatizing, 193

ingredients of

automatic activity, 45

gratification, 387

verbal images, 246

part of ego as, 19, 183, 251-52

psychoanalytic approaches to

preconscious as analyzing instrument, 32

structural, 338, 342, 345, 417-18

systematic, 246, 318-19, 337, 345, 428

Precocity, 241-42

Prediction, **319-20**

Pregenital masturbatory equivalents, **321-22**

Pregenitality, 169, 171, 270, **320-21**

ambivalence in stage of, 27

component instincts during, 77

conversion neurosis during, 412

fixation on, 199, 270, 354

form of love during, 225

introego and, 204

metaphors based on, 246

origin of superego in, 144, 422

regression to, 128, 199, 401, 481

revival of fantasies of period of, 323

as source of menstrual disorders, 324

See also Anal phase; Oral phase; Phallic phase

Pregnancy, 131, **323,** 455

fantasies of, 277, 323

fear of, 166

repressed wish for, 83

unconscious wish for, 18, 181

Prelogical (primitive) thinking, **323**

Premenstrual disorders (tensions), **323-24**

Preoedipal mother attachment, 188, 324, **325-26,** 387

activity results from, 241

defense of, 293

of homosexuals, 288-89, 304

misogyny results from, 247

persistence of, in women, 281, 289

as precursor of morality, 250

surrogate, 229

Preoedipal stage, 171, 270, 303, **324-25,** 376

promiscuity rooted in, 333

regression to, 354-55, 371

Prephallic masturbation equivalents, **326-27**

Prepuberty, 354

Pride, 129, 221, **327**

phallic, 307, **308-9**

Primal fantasy, **327**

Primal parricide, 35, 36, 229, 330, 385

Primal scene, 99, 176, 299, **327-28,** 386

deferred reaction to, 96

fantasies of, 367

identification and, 180, 184, 481

re-creation of, 261

Primary (paranosic) gain in neurosis, **329,** 394

Primary identification, 45, 185, 284, **328,** 477

Primary masochism, 234, **328-29,** 386

Primary processes, 29, 117, **329,** 364, 389, 395, 425, 434

Primary processes *(Continued)*
 barriers and, 49
 exploration of, 341
 govern id, 183
 immediate discharge in, 339
 inhibition of, 467
 metaphoric language and, 246
 neologisms conform to laws of,
  265
 regression to, 227, 371
 systematic approach to, 428
 transition to secondary from,
  323, 372
 unconscious and, 319, 337
Primitive peoples, *see*
  Psychoanalytic
  anthropology
Primitive superego, **330**, 383
Primitive (prelogical) thinking,
  323
"Principle of Relaxation and
  Neocatharsis, The"
  (Ferenczi), 44
Prodromal alcoholism, 23
Progerism, **331**
Progressive amnesia, 29
"Project for a Scientific
  Psychology" (Freud),
  246, 272*n*
Projection, 24, 90, 94, 110, 235,
  331-32, 362, 436
 of analyst, 397
 countertransference and, 86
 objects of, 378
  blame for impotence, 387
  frustration, 42
  incestuous wishes, 156
  jealousy (envy), 209-10, 316
  masturbation wishes, 89
  omnipotence, 279
  rage, 362
  sources of unpleasure, 356
 omnipotence results from, 142,
  282
 origin of, 396
 roles of
  in altruism, 26
  in delusions, 99-100, 101
  in face-breast equation, 137
  in micropsia, 247
  in nymphomania, 274

 in pseudoidentification,
  335-36
 in rationalization, 364
 in transference neurosis, 450
 tic as method of, 440
 types of
  nonpathological, 39-40, 95
  phobic, 74, 95, 132, 269, 310,
   312, 331
  pregenital, 320
  psychotic, 79, 95, 102, 266,
   268, 269, 293, 331, 351,
   389, 390, 391, 397
  see also Scapegoat
   mechanisms
Projective identification, **332-33**
 counteridentification, **332**
Projective tests, 40; *see also*
  Rorschach Test; T.A.T.
Promiscuity, 231, 274-75, **333-34**
Prostitution, 140, 375, 397, 468
 Ferenczi's concern with, 141,
  142
 frigidity and, 167
 of psychopath, 350
Protophallic phase, 105, **334**
Protopsyche, **334**
Pseudodebility (pseudoimbecility),
  334-35
Pseudohallucination (illusion),
  335
Pseudo-hypersexuality, 274, **335,**
  387
Pseudoidentification, 42, 185-86,
  335-36
Pseudologia fantastica, **336**
Psychiatry, **336-37**, 430
 dynamic, 341
 as threat to psychoanalysis, 220
 See also Child psychiatry;
  Hypnoanalysis;
  Psychoanalysis
Psychic apparatus, 2, **337-38**, 339,
  371
Psychic determinism, **338**, 340,
  346-47, 473
Psychic (mental) energy, **339**, 366
 of aggressive drive, 21
 bound, 50, 63, 319, 395
 in countercathexis, 84

 discharge of, 12, 14, 218, 338,
  339, 395, 398, 457-58
 as focus of economic approach,
  117, 339, 342
 in introjection, 94
 metaphoric reflection of, 246
 neutral (indifferent), 271, 293,
  319, 371, 373, 402
 objectual, 418
 reality principle requires, 368
 as source of unpleasure, 387
 withdrawal of, 99, 205, 406-7
 See also Destrudo; Libido;
  Tensions
Psychic inertia, **339-40,** 450; *see
  also* Fixation
Psychic (mental) phenomena,
  245-46, 286, 341
 blankness as, 322
 reflex acts ad, 370-71
 See also Psychic apparatus;
  Psychic determinism;
  Psychic energy; Psychic
  inertia; Psychic reality
Psychic reality, 156, 245, 251, **340**
Psychical Research, Society for
  (England), 434
Psychoanalysis, xiv-xix, **340-43,**
  372
 components of analytic session
  analyst's empathy, 126-27
  autoplastic identification, 185
  déjà raconté, 97
  mutual language, 215
  role of criticism, 88
  see also Catharsis;
   Countertransference; Free
   association; Recovery
   wish; Resistance;
   Transference; Working
   through
 contributions to
  Abraham's most important, 2
  Ferenczi's, 140-41, 146
  Freud's most important, 162
  Jung's, 159
 education in, *see* Education—
  psychiatric; Supervision;
  Teaching of analysis;
  Training analysis
 "English School" of, 396

Page numbers in **boldface** refer to main entries

evaluation of, **134-35,** 344
father of, *see* Freud, Sigmund
forms of
    lay analysis, 145, **219-20**
    training, 397, 430, **445**
    trial analysis, **453**
    wild, **471**
    see also Applied
        psychoanalysis; Child
        analysis; Self-analysis
freedom as result of, 338
impossibility of, for normal
    personalities, 230
interaction of psychiatry and,
    337
law and, **218-19**
limitation of, 87
organizations of, 1, 5-6, 145;
    see also International
        Psychoanalytic
        Association; Vienna
        Psychoanalytic Society
origin of, 155-56, 340-41
as science and art, xiv-xvi
shortening of process of, 13-14,
    341, 404-5
theoretical approaches to, *see*
    Adaptational approach;
    Causal approach;
    Comparative approach;
    Descriptive approach;
    Dynamic approach;
    Economic approach;
    Ethical approach; Genetic
    approach; Psychic
    determinism; Quantitative
    approach; Structural
    approach; Teleological
    approach
Psychoanalytic anthropology, xiv,
    35-36, 40, 130, 265, 331,
    343-44
of alcoholic primitives, 24
animism in, 33-34, 329-30
as applied psychoanalysis, 41
development of language in, 215
ethics in, 132-33
fire quenched by urination in,
    463

on function of civilization,
    72-73
magical language in, 474
matriarchy in, 235, 240-41
mystic union founded in, 254
origin of mass psychology in,
    235-36
racial memory in, **361**
revenge in, 380, 381
symbolization in, 426
theory of collective unconscious
    in, 75
totems in, 443-44
vaginal father in, 465-66
See also Freudian theories—
    anthropological
Psychoanalytic dictionary, **344**
Psychoanalytic methodology, 143,
    344-45
Psychoanalytic technique, 341,
    369, **430-33,** 437-38, 442
for analyzing perverts, 304-5
approach to mass psychology
    as, 236
basic rule of, *see* Free
    association
causal, 63
classical, as inadequate for
    children, 68
Ferenczi's contribution to, 144
modification of, 448
    relaxation principle as,
        373-74
    for treatment of delinquents,
        469-70
    for treatment of psychopaths,
        347
nonconformity to, 471
pathognomy, 298
of prediction, 319-20
projective counteridentification
    interferes with, 332
of Rank, 52
use of tranquilizers as, 114
See also Abreaction; Analytical
    insight; Analyzing
    instrument; Interpretation;
    Play therapy
Psychodynamics, *see* Dynamic
    approach
Psychogenesis, **346**

Psychological tests
    Rorschach, **383-84,** 436
    Thematic Apperception,
        436-37
    word association, 159, **473**
"Psychology of the Mass and
    Analysis of the Ego," *see*
    "Group Psychology and
    Analysis of the Ego"
Psychoneurosis, *see* Neurosis
*Psychopathology of Everyday
    Life,* The (Freud), 88,
    346-47
Psychopathy, 45, 343, **347-51,** 362
as ego-syntonic behavior, 124
as need for punishment, 262
"Psychosexual Impotence in
    Man" (Ferenczi), 142
Psychosis, 25, 105, 135, 185,
    268-69, 351-52, 359, 419
active therapy for, 14
forms of
    amentia, **29,** 172
    borderline, **57**
    delusional, 99, 174, 206, 228,
        229, 243-44; *see also*
        Paranoia—delusional
    hallucinatory, *see*
        Hallucinations—psychotic
    infantile, 43, 121, 390
    latent, **218**
    symbiotic, 424, 425
    see also Hebephrenia;
        Manic-depressive
        psychosis; Melancholia;
        Paranoia; Paranoid
        condition; Paraphrenia;
        Schizophrenia
incidents of, 410
ingredients of
    conflict, 79, 228, 372
    denial, 102, 269, 336, 354
    elation, 125
    jamais phenomenon, 209
    metaphoric language, 216,
        246
    micropsia, 247
    mutism, 253
    neologisms, 265
    pseudologia fantastica, 336

Page numbers in **boldface** refer to main entries

Psychosis,
    ingredients of *(Continued)*
    rage, 362
    regression, 372
    self-observation, 397
    split of ego, 427
    tics, 439
lack of control causes, 148
of narcissistic types, 221, 360
nightmares and, 271
projective diagnosis of, 384
psychiatric treatment of, 336-37
symptoms of, 44, 93, 102
    automatic obedience, 45
    delusions, 100, 101
    hallucinations, 172
    of latent psychosis, 218
    negativism, 265
    nihilism, 272
    projection, 331
    schizophrenic, 389
See also Freudian theories—of
    psychosis
Psychosomatic disturbances,
    352-53, 384, 425
effect of hypnosis on, 178
penis envy as cause of, 350
peptic ulcer as, 300
stigmata as, 416
vertigo as, 468
See also Hypochondriasis
Psychomatic suicide, **353-54**
Psychotherapy, *see* Therapy
Psychotic character, 124, **354**
Psychotic core, **354**
Puberty, 17, 77, 106, **354-55,** 401
    ego defenses at, 53
    fantasy during, 138
    genital phase and, 169, 221
    identity during, 410
    instinctual strength at, 242
    neurosis at onset of, 184, 386
    penis size at, 217, 298
    pseudo-hypersexuality at, 335
    regression during, 372
    sexual inhibition at, 281
    sulkiness at, 265
Punishment, 92, 288, 311, 429
    agents of
        conscience, 413, 475

superego, 123, 279, 415, 418,
    476
for aggression, 132
castration connected with, 307,
    314, 328
delusions and, 99-100
in depression, 103
over discharge of tension, 367
in dreams, 111, 271, 370
fantasies of, 51-52, 232, 239,
    365
forms of
    acrophobia, 11
    anorexia nervosa, 34
    divorce, 307
    pathoneurotic, 298
    petrifaction, 305
    revenge, 380
    slips of the tongue, 295
    stammering, 416
    stigmata, 416-17
    torticollis, 443
    vertigo, 468
    see also Sadism
as humiliation, 175
need for, 97, **262,** 316, 369; *see
    also* Guilt; Masochism
for parent's death, 96
provocation of, 213, 226, 237,
    316, 363, 385
for rage, 362
reaction to
    anticipation, 36
    avoidance, 334
    fear, 72, 93, 348
    fore-unpleasure, 151
    masochistic satisfaction,
        232-34, 250, 304
    sexual inhibition, 400
Puns, 61, **355**
Purified pleasure ego, **355-57**
Pyromania, **357**

Q

Qualitative approach, *see*
    Descriptive approach
Quality, 342, **359**
Quantitative approach, 202, 262,
    359-60, 430

Question of Lay Analysis, The
    (Freud), 219

R

Racial memory, **361**
Rado, Sandor, 5, 24, 25, 296
Rage, 250-51, 264, 353-54, **361-63**
Rangell, L., 56
Rank, Otto, 143, 344, 411
    in secret committee, 163, 164-65
    theories of
        birth trauma, 52
        controversial, 1, 3
        transference neurosis, 432,
            450
    in Vienna Society, 159, 164
Rapaport, D., 82, 384
Rape, 274, **363-64,** 369, 386
    anal, 402
    discovery of, 241
    fantasies of, 239-40
    reaffirms masculine power, 254
    unconscious wish to, 475
Raptus actions, **364**
"Rat Man" (case history), 139,
    365-66
Rationalization, 192, 232*n*, **364-65**
    of alcoholics, 23, 24, 364
    neurotic, 123, 268, 364
        character neurosis, 65
Reaction
    abreaction, **8,** 52, 62, 379
    deferred, **96-97**
    See also Negative therapeutic
        reaction
Reaction formation, 84, 95, 235,
    366-67, 371, 386, 413
    in compulsion neurosis, 135,
        383
    of doctors, 107
    forms of
        altruistic, 26
        crying, 89
        excessive cleanliness, 84
        excessive pride, 327
        pity, 312
        shame, 272, 399
        shamelessness, 404
        social identifications, 409

neurotic use of, 93
objects of
anal wishes, 441
castration anxiety, 198
curiosity, 90, 399
rage, 362
revenge, 381
sibling rivalry, 225
unpleasure, 401
racial memory of, 361
replaces perversion, 52
Reading, 278, **367,** 403
Reality, 252, 315, 354, 370, 398
break with, 351, 389
denial of, 94, 269, 279
development of sense of, 142
discovery of, 355-56
"erotic," 44
flight from, 179
flight into, 25, 149, **150,** 185
illusion and, 186
internal becomes external, 50
loss of control over, *see*
Narcissistic mortification
neurotic vs. psychotic relation
to, 268
overestimation of inner, 282
psychic, 156, 245, 251, **340**
relativity of, **372-73**
removal from, 322
Reality principle, 9, 36, 313, 314,
319, **367-68,** 442, 460
alloplastic adaptation and, 25
frustration and, 167, 357
functioning of, 123
as part of adaptation, 15, 16
pregenital, 320
secondary processes and, 395
Reality testing, 15, 46, 100, 178,
196, 382
as action, 12
communication as tool for, 411
compromise with, 253
disappearance of, 172
as ego function, 121, 215-16
fantasy reduction due to, 138
impairment of, 243, 372
in psychosis, 102, 269, 351
results in split of libido, 222
role of thought in, 9, 438
in schizophrenia, 390

smell as, 200
Reassurance, 368-69, 402, 481
Rebelliousness (defiance), 202,
369, 412, 413
against authority figures, 10, 17,
369
Rebirth fantasy, **370**
Reconstruction, 203
Recovery wish, **370**
Recurrent dreams, 75, 111, **370**
Reductionism, 41
Reflex act, **370-71**
Regression, 151, 273, 285, 333,
351, 370, **371-72,** 422, 473
causes need for revenge, 381
dynamic approach to, 345
to early developmental phases,
366
anal, 31, 180, 224, 232, 351,
366, 371, 380, 472; *see*
also Anal wishes
magic-hallucinatory
omnipotence, 356
narcissistic, 44, 45, 260, 272,
282, 372
oral, 34, 103, 125, 147, 238,
244, 301, 351, 435; *see*
also Oral fixation; Oral
wishes
passive-receptive phase, 297
phallic, 32, 71, 180, 221, 298;
see also Phallic wishes
phase of alimentary orgasm,
25
pregenital, 128, 199, 401, 481
forms of
catatonic, 389
fascination, 139
homosexual, 53
hypnotic, 178
lure of the past, 226
most pathogenic, 482
symptomatic, 167
to identification, 185
of love, 225
to magic gestures, 181
metaphoric thinking in, 216,
246
in obsession, 365, 366
in perversion, 270
preoedipal, 354-55, 371

to primary processes, 227, 371
to primordial states, 254
to protopsyche, 334
regressive masturbation
equivalents, 239
relationship between rhythm
and, 382
response to
avoidance, 236
deneutralization, 271
fluctuation in
self-presentation, 396
formation of neurosis, 267
formation of tics, 144
neurotic choice of a mate,
231
production of phantom limb,
309
symbolization in, 426
Reich, Wilhelm, 190, 287, 344
theory of phallic pride of, 308-9
on transference neurosis, 449
Reik, Theodor, 5, 41-42, 253
Jewish myths examined by,
254-55
on listening with the third ear,
223
Reitler, Rudolf, 159
Rejection, 265, 268, 398, 404
as mature mechanism, 375
provocation of, 27, 397
sexual, 24, 131, 348, 350, 378
Relativity of reality, **372-73**
Relaxation, **373**
Relaxation principle, **373-74**
Religion, 25, 129, 226n, 254-55,
354, 366
of Abraham's family, 4
behavioral code due to, 133
forms of
matriarchal, 235, 240
obsessional, 473
paranoid, 357
totemic, 190, 443
Freud's investigation of, 35
as illusion, 186
ingredients of
identification, 236, 473
racial memory, 361
ritual, 382, 383, 385
stigmata, 416

Page numbers in **boldface** refer to main entries

Religion,
  ingredients of *(Continued)*
  taboos, 316, 334
 origin of
  geographic origin, 281
  precursor of religion, 33-34
  source of religion, 280, 330
 Weltanschauung of, 470
 See also Anti-Semitism;
  Religious faith
Religious faith, 10, 161, 370, **374**
Remorse, 89, 103, 228, **374,** 429,
  459-60
 over aggression, 72, 374, 398,
  460
 over death, 28, 96, 244, 259
 elimination of, 262
 guilt vs., 374, 398
 over masturbation, 363
 in obsessional neurosis, 236,
  279
 role of, in masochism, 140,
  233-34, 314
Repetition compulsion, 87, 173,
  341, **374-75**
 affects marriage, 231
 of alcoholics, 24
 automatism related to, 46
 counterphobia related to, 84
 discoverer of, 158
 fixation due to, 148, 339
 imitation as, 187
 rhythmic nature of, 381, 382
 transference and, 226, 374-75,
  447, 448
 in traumatic neurosis, 374-75,
  452, 460-61
 of uncanniness, 456
 undoing related to, 460
Repressed material, return of, 149,
  223, 267, **379-80,** 382
 cause of, 95
 negation of, 94, 262
Repression, 118, 142, 151, 162,
  235, 365, **375-76,** 377
 absence of, 348
 Adler's denial of, 160
 anthropological application of,
  36
 avoidance of, 99
 bisexuality as cause of, 51

body language and, 56
boredom and, 57
condemnation replaces, 292
conversion and, 82-83
countercathexis in, 84, 95, 377,
  378, 441, 457
endopsychic perception of,
  127-28
first, 74
first observation of, 341, 417
forms of
 instinctual vicissitude, 200
 normal, 273
 primary and secondary, 95,
  375
 suppression, 424
mechanism of, 72
objects of, 397
 anal wishes, 31, 440-41
 breast complex, 58, 306
 coprophilia, 83
 early commands, 96
 fantasies, 97, 307, 327, 373,
  400
 hostility, 71
 incestuous wishes, 190
 "incompatible idea," 20, 379
 libido, 21, 37, 61, 316
 masturbation, 237-38, 239,
  274, 326
 narcissistic mortification, 89,
  259, 283
 Oedipus complex, 107, 281,
  307, 309
 oral wishes, 108, 285
 preoedipal stage, 241
 scopophilic and
  epistemophilic wishes, 366
 sensation, 398
 sensory perception, 200
 sexual curiosity, 399
 slips of the tongue, 408
 trauma, 148
other defense mechanisms
  compared to, 94, 101
resistance as indicator of, 432
results of
 defense mechanisms, 316
 inferiority, 193
 neurosis, 199, 267, 315, 365
 paranoid hallucinations, 351

parapraxis, 347
prevention of sense of
 identity, 399
stammering, 416
roles of
 in impotence, 400
 in paramnesia, 292
 in perversion, 269-70
 in reaction formation, 366
 in scapegoating, 388
 in sleep, 407
 in symbolization, 425
traumatic neurosis and, 452
unsuccessful, 92-93, 372, 375
"Repression" (Freud), 246
Repression resistance, 377
Rescue fantasy, **376-77**
Resentment, 23, 85, 93
Resistance, 40, 50-51, 81, 162,
  341, 373, **377-78,** 420, 456
 barriers and, 50
 castration complex in, 62
 displacement of, 12
 neurotic, 2
  character neurotic, 66
  hysterical, 379
  obsessional neurotic, 207
  psychopathic, 347, 350
 to new psychoanalytic concepts,
  xix
 period of childhood, 264-65
 pleasure from overcoming of, 22
 psychoanalytic approaches to,
  377-78, 431-32, 446
  countertransference and, 86
  destruction, xvi, 342
  in evaluation of therapy, 134
  interpretation, 88, 202-3, 341
  measurement, 339
  overcome by hypnosis, 156,
   177
  resistance due to erotic
   transference, 131
  working through, 32, 230,
   377, 475
 role of rationalization in, 364
 to self-analysis, 396
 strength of, 120
 transference-love and, 448-49
 types of
  censorship, 183

criminal, 219
ego-resistance, 142, 329, 341, 377, 394
id-resistance, 339, 377
superego-resistance, 377
transference-resistance, 377, 449
See also Acting in; Acting out
Respiratory eroticism, **379**, 420
Respiratory introjection, **379**
Responsibility, *see* Moral responsibility
Retention hysteria, **379**
Retroactive amnesia, 29
Retrograde amnesia, 29, 271
Retrogressive amnesia, 29
Return of repressed material, *see* Repressed material, return of
Return to the womb, 356, 370, 407
Revenge, 109, 215, **380-81**, 448
as abreaction, 8
for castration, 465, 466
kleptomania as, 213
Reversal into the opposite, 95, 200, 375, 390
Reward by the superego, 115, **381**
Rexford, E., 70
Rhine, J. B., 434
Rhythm and periodicity, 272, **381-82**
Ribot, Théophile, 33
Rituals, 36, 344, 366, **382-83**, 410
obsessive-compulsive, 227
Reik's studies of, 41-42
sacrificial, 385
Rivalry, *see* Competition
Rivière, Joan, 396
Róheim, Géza, 36, 41, 344, 465-66
Rorschach, Hermann, 383
Rorschach Test, **383-84**, 436
Rosen, V., 14
Rosenman, Stanley, 24
Ross, Helen, 423-24, 430, 445
Rule of abstinence, **384**, 448
Russell, Bertrand, 129, 133

S

Sachs, Hanns
Freud, Master and Friend, 154

as secret committee member, 163, 165
in Vienna Society, 159, 160
Sacrifice, **385;** *see also* Scapegoat mechanism
Sadism (cruelty), 77, 107, 194, 288, **385-86,** 433
fantasies of, 51, 149, 239, 293, 357, 365, 422
forms of
anal, *see* Anal phase
masochism as, 232, 386, 453
oral, 99, 283, 284, 285, 289, 301, 321, 323, 324, 335, 367, 386, 403, 422, 471
phallic, 386
religious, 236
healthy retention of, 317, 318
identification with, 233, 363
as masculine quality, 297
objects of
mothers, 71
self, 362
projected, 293
roles of
in intercourse, 327, 363
in nymphomania, 274
in sexuality, 324
in shamelessness, 404
subjects of
superego, 148, 228, 233, 250, 279, 301, 302, 386, 421, 422
witty people, 176
Wolf Man, 472
Sado-masochism, 261, 271, 387, 481
in impotence, 125, 386
Salzburg, Austria, 159, 160
Sarcasm, 22, 419
Satisfaction (gratification), 115, 118, 334, 373, **387**, 395, 432
of addicts, 16
of adult wishes, 384
in character neurosis, 65, 66
of component instincts, 77
as elimination of need, 200
forms of, 199
active and passive, 232
altruistic, 26

excessive, 148
narcissistic, 370, 387
pathoneurotic, 298
see also Sexual satisfaction; Sublimation; Substitution
of others' wishes, 354
pleasure vs., 460
psychogenic symptoms due to, 353
sources of
act of looking, *see* Scopophilia; Voyeurism
fantasy, 138
gain in neurosis, 329
humor, 81-82
masochism, 250-51
neurotic symptoms, 196
sexualization, *see* Sexualization
unwillingness to renounce, 377
Satyriasis, **387**
Saul, Leon J., 174, 399
Savitt, R. A., 16
Sarwer-Foner, G., 114
Scapegoat mechanisms, **387-88**
Schafer, R., 384
Schilder, P., 14, 102, 309
Schizoid character, **388-89**
Schizophrenia (dementia praecox), 194, **389-90**
Abraham's concern with, 2, 5
classes of
hypnotic, 204
latent, 218
potential, 57
symbiotic, 121
transient, 452
see also Catatonic schizophrenia; Hebephrenia; Paranoia
effect of drugs on, 114, 115
ingredients of
autism, 43, 389
autoerotism, 243
break with reality, 351, 389
entitlement, 128
fanaticism, 138
hallucination, 335, 389
mystic union, 253-54
negativism, 265
projective identification, 333

Schizophrenia,
 ingredients of *(Continued)*
  stereotypes, 381
  word salad, 473-74
 manic-depressive psychosis
  and, 228
 misdiagnosis of, 453
 paraphrenia as, 294, 389
 symptoms of, 44, 45, 100-1, 389
Schizophrenic surrender, **390-91**
Schreber, Daniel Paul, *Memoirs
 of My Nervous Illness,* 391
Schreber Case (case history), 254,
 351, 389, **391-92**
 publication of, 40
Schrödinger, Erwin, 21, 128
Science, 58, 90, 285, 286, 297, 374
 empirical, 434
 ethics of, 133
 as illusion, 186
 laws of, 345
 magic and, **392**
 psychoanalysis as, xiv-xvi, 51,
  447
 psychoanalysis applied to, 41
 views free will, 152
 xenophobia of, 236
Scopophilia (inspectionism), 77,
  132, 328, **392-93**
 blocking of, 310
 in blushing, 55
 defenses against, 59, 136
 desexualization of, 99
 developmental stages of, 169,
  199
 in doctor game, 107
 in enuresis, 272
 epistemophilic instinct
  contrasted to, 130
 exhibitionism paired with, 95,
  102, 392, 393, 453-54
 oral, 285
 origin of, 248
 punishment for, 305
 shame over, 399
 sublimation of, 9-10, 367
 in theft, 350-51
 See also Voyeurism
Screen memories (infantile
 amnesia), 292, 341,
 393-94, 416

anagogic interpretation of, 31
in personal myths, 303
See also Dream-screen
Secondary (epinosic) gain, 192,
 230, 261, 310, 319
 in neurosis, 63, 329, 370, 380,
  394
Secondary identification, 186, **394**
Secondary processes, 117, 265,
  329, 364, **395**
 barriers and, 49
 delay of discharge and, 98, 395
 inhibit primary processes, 467
 source of, 337
 systematic approach to, 428
 transition from primary to, 323,
  372
Sedative drugs, 16, 113
Seduction, 148, 331, 378, 472
 by leader, 296
 repression of, 207
 theory of infantile, 156, 266,
  316, 327, 340, 341
Self, 369, **395-96,** 436
 aggression against, 103-4, 185,
  310, 381-82, 436
  in anticipation, 405
  autocastration, 237, 364
  rape, 363
 ego and, 118, **119-20,** 395, 396
 love and hate for, 133, 326, 331,
  362-63
 non-self vs., 55, 357, 395-96
 pleasure equated with, 356-57,
  396
 preoccupation with, 43, 389,
  436
 society and, **410**
 turning against, *see* Turning
  against self
 See also Depersonalization
Self-analysis, 341, **396-97**
 by analysts, xix, 85, 445
 of Freud, 157-58, 341
Self-assertion, instinct of, **198-99**
Self-criticism, 173, 243-44, 379
 absence of, 347, 349, 352, 354
 in depression, 377-78
 of Dora, 423
Self-esteem, 125, 198, 364, 370,
  415

of alcoholics, 23, 24
excessive, 243, 253
heightened feelings of, 25
loss of, 381
masochism and, 234, **397**
phallic pride as, 308
See also Pride
Self-observation, 215, **397-98**
Self-pity, 23
Self-preservative drives, *see* Ego
 instincts
Self-reproach, 27, 205, 243-44
Sensations, **398;** *see also* Feelings
Sense of guilt, *see* Guilt
Sense of identity, *see* Identity
Sensorium, **120**
Sensory perception, *see* Perception
Sensuous types, 65, 221, 418
Sequestration, **399**
Servadio, E., 226, 434
Sexual abstinence, **9,** 73, 470
 actual neuroses due to, 14-15,
  38
Sexual curiosity, 10, 62, 367,
  399-400; *see also*
  Scopophilia; Voyeurism
Sexual excitement, 11, 271, 287,
  435, 460, 468
 drugs affect, 114
 as erotic transference, 131
 during menstruation, 245
 projection of, 74
 See also Component instincts
Sexual inhibition, 24, 194, 280,
  400
 feminine, *see* Frigidity
 masculine, *see* Impotence
 at puberty, 281
Sexual intercourse, *see* Coitus
Sexual instincts (drive), *see* Libido
Sexual organs, *see* Clitoris; Penis
 envy; Vagina
Sexual perversions, 93, 271, **304-5,**
  343, 392-93
 causes of
  denial, 352
  drugs, 115
 component instincts in, 77, 270,
  289
 defense of, 335
 inhibition alternates with, 194

neurosis as negative of, 135, 147, **269-71,** 304
promiscuity linked with, 333
symbiosis in, 425
unpleasure over, 401
varieties of
adult masturbation as, 237
group, 296
infantile, 52
oral, 285
transvestitism, 304, **451**
see also Coprophilia; Exhibitionism; Fetishism; Homosexuality; Masochism; Nymphomania; Sadism; Necrophilia; Polymorph perverse behavior; Satyriasis; Scopophilia; Voyeurism; Zooerasty
Sexual satisfaction (libidinal gratification), 8, 22, 42, 278, 373, 387
as central part of life, 280
of frigid women, 62
marital, 73
narcissism in, 257-58
partial, 72
simultaneous aggressive and, 43, 315, 363, 369, 385, 393
See also Coitus
Sexual seduction, *see* Seduction
Sexual traumas, 5, 6, 20
Sexual wishes, *see* Anal wishes; Oral wishes; Phallic wishes
Sexuality, 17, 274, 301, 330, **400-1**
ambivalence toward, 265
beginning of, concealment of, 29
denial of, 34
development of Freud's theory of, 156
Ferenczi's theory of, 143, 146
infantile, *see* Libidinal phases
latent, *see* Latency period; Latent homosexuality
promiscuous, 231, 274-75, **333-34**
pseudo-hypersexuality, 274, **335**
relationship of neurosis to, 365
sadistic concepts of, 324
transference and, **448**

See also Bisexuality; Eroticism; Femininity; Homosexuality; Masculinity; Pansexualism
Sexualization (libidinization), 53, 232, 239, 243, 362
aggressivization and
of anxiety, **401-2**
deaggressivization and desexualization, 72, 271
of defenses, 202
of ego functions, 390, **402**
of speech, **402-3**
of thinking, 278, **403**
desexualization, *see* Delibidinization
resexualization, 181
of superego, 233, 243, 370, 418, 422
of thinking process, 34, 130, 365
Shame, 175, 316, 379, **404,** 471
blushing due to, 54-55
crying and, 89
over enuresis, 272
in inferiority feelings, 192
inhibitory function of, 217
in sphincter morality, 413
as source of impotence, 400
Shamelessness, 135, **404**
Sharpe, Ella F., 85-86, 246, 441-42
Short-term therapy, 13, 52, **404-5**
Siegman, A. J., 97
Signal anxiety, 342, 380, **405**
Silberer, Herbert, 30-31, 47, 177, 439
Silbermann, I., 151, 209
Silverberg, W. V., 450
Simmel, Ernst, 5, 238
Simplex schizophrenia, 389
Simultaneous analysis of mother and child, **405-6**
Skin eroticism, **406**
Sleep, 19, 229, 398, **406-7,** 479
as autoplastic adaptation, 46
disturbances of, 386
dreams prolong, 109-10, 407
drugs to induce, 113
as regression, 356, 372
relaxation for, 82
semiconscious state preceding, 177, 206

walking during, 251, 299
See also Dreams; Insomnia
Slips of the tongue, 88, 345-46, 403, **407-8,** 412, 459, 473
ambiguity in, 27
as parapraxis, 295, 407
resistance to analysis of, 120
two determinants of, 288
unawareness of, 19
as wish fulfillment, 262
Social compliance, **408-9**
Social instinct, human, **409**
Social mindfulness, **409**
Society, 9, **410**
Sociology, psychoanalysis applied to, 41, 344, 466
Sodomy, *see* Homosexuality; Zooerasty
Solomon, J. C., 13, 283, 331
on tropism, 264, 317
Somatic compliance, **410-11**
Somatic stimuli and dreams, 109-11, **411**
Sorrow, *see* Grief
Speech, *see* Language
Sperling, M., 271, 299, 455
on psychosomatic suicide, 353-54
on simultaneous analysis of mother and child, 405, 406
Sperling, O., 24, 138, 177, 296
on appersonation, 40
on ego boundaries, 121
on exaggeration, 94, 135
sociology of, 409
value system of, 467
Sphincter control, 125, 166, **412**
Sphincter morality, **412-13,** 422
Spiders, **413-14**
Spiegel, L., 395
Spitz, R., 30, 381-82, 406
Stage fright, 311, **415**
"Stages in the Development of the Sense of Reality" (Ferenczi), 142
Stammering (stuttering), 403, **415-16**
Stein, M., 253
Stekel, Wilhelm, 159, 173, 294
defection of, 160-61, 163
Stengel, E., 170

Page numbers in **boldface** refer to main entries

Sterba, E., 404

Sterba, R. F., 344, 413

Stern, Adolf, 145

Stigmata, **416-17**

Stimuli, 120, 395
  boring, 57
  hunger for, **176-77**
  internal, 259, 398, 438
    dreams and somatic, 109-11, **411**
    external vs., 116
  olfactory, 200
  qualitative change in, 359
  response to
    denial, 101-2
    derealization, 94
    ego's response, 118
    emotion as, 126
    protection against stimulus, 49-50, 92
    sensation, 398
  verbal expression of, 467

Storfer, A. J., 344

Strachey, Alix, 5, 101, 118

Strachey, James, 177-78, 263, 359, 392*n*
  on Breuer, 156, 178
  critique of Freud by, 195
  on metapsychology, 246
  on psychic determinism, 346
  on secondary processes, 395

Strangulated affect, 340, **417;**
  see also Repression

Strauss, H., 129

Structural (topographic)
    approach, 65, 202, 312, 337-38, 359, **417-18,** 457, 458
  to conflicts, 79, 267
  development of, 161, 246-47, 319, 342
  to inferiority feelings, 192-93
  to mental phenomena, 371
  to motility, 251-52
  to psychosis and neurosis, 351, 389-90
    to suppression, 424
  to unpleasure, 460

Studies on Hysteria (Breuer and Freud), 156, 439

Stuttering (stammering), 403, **415-16**

Subconscious, *see* Preconscious; Unconscious

Sublimation, 35, 123, 162, 308, 372, 376, 401, **419**
  after analysis, 292
  character traits formed by, 366
  forms of
    displacement, 134
    neutralization, 271
    normal, 273
  ingredients of
    abreaction, 8
    catharsis, 62
    cathexis, 23, 419
  as instinctual vicissitude, 200
  Jung's contribution to theory of, 159
  during latency, 217
  limits on, 81
  modern education and, 201
  objects of
    aggression, 72
    anal wishes, 31, 169, 440
    anxiety, 402
    breast envy, 58
    fantasies, 138
    homosexuality, 409
    masculine strivings, 300
    oedipal wishes, 307
    oral wishes, 285, 367
    perversion, 52, 304
    pregenital wishes, 169
    rage, 362
    sadism, 386
    scopophilia, 9-10, 99, 392
    sexual curiosity, 399
    sibling rivalry, 225
    undoing, 95
  origin of term, 158
  pleasure from, 368
  roles of
    in art, 87, 90
    in narcissistic gain, 258
    in reading, 367
    in recovery wish, 370
    in undoing, 460

Substitution, 22, 35, 279, 373, 406
  for breast, 324, 325
  for family romance, 303

linguistic, 294-95, 412

locus of, 460

mastery of mechanism of, 362

for mourned object, 253

of passivity for activity, 14

for penis, 299, 300

See also Masturbation equivalents

Success, 251, 283, 475
  of Freud, 152-53
  intolerance of, 189, 233, 264, 316
  therapeutic, 320
  See also Defeat

Success neurosis, **419-20**

Suffocation fears, **420**

Suggestion, **420-21**

Suicide, 40, 108, 244, 254, 282, 362, **421**
  psychosomatic, **353-54**
  as raptus action, 364
  responsibility for, 377-78

Sunday (weekend) neurosis, **421-22**

Superego, 25, 65, 162, 247, 309, 382, **422-23**
  aerophagia gratifies, 18
  anaclitic depression and, 30
  analyst as, 447
  analytic gains of, 438
  analytic material on, 88, 89
  blushing and, 55
  development of, 137, 370, 388, 395
    adolescent, 17, 242
    infantile, 72, 205, 410
    maturity, 241
  fixation of, 148
  functions of, 341, 366, 414
  compromise, 258, 268, 288, 316, 345
    control of curiosity, 90
    defined, 422
    in identity, 399
    moralization, 364
    perception, 302
    perpetuation of parental values, 466
    reward, 115, **381**
    sexualization of functions, 243

language and, 215
of manic-depressives, 228-29
origin of, 144, 249-50, 307, 308,
    410, 412-13, 422, 429
of perverts, 270, 393
projection of, 99-100, 101, 336,
    450
psychoanalytic approaches to
    development of superego,
    388
    dynamic, 345
    ethical, 132
    quantitative, 360
    superego-resistance, 377
    topographic, 161, 338, 342,
        417-18, 460
quality of, 359
regression of, 371, 422
relationship of, to other instincts
    of personality, 117, 123,
        135, 338, 422
    communication between id
        and superego, 183
    conflicts, 79, 244, 267, 268,
        375, 394
    ego defense against superego,
        61
    ego helped by, 471
    fusion with ego, 357
    isolation of ego, 398
    libido in superego, 174
    superego as ego, 363
roles of
    in altruism, 26
    in bisexuality, 53
    in dèjà vu, 97
    in depersonalization, 102
    in dreams, 75, 111, 414-15
    in ego-alien symptoms, 119,
        476
    in elation, 125
    in fate neurosis, 104-5
    in impotence, 124
    in pathoneurosis, 298
    in phobia, 310, 312
    in reassurance, 369
    in ritual, 383
    in shame and shamelessness,
        404
    in vaginismus, 466
sequestration of, 399

severity of, 173, 281, 366, 422
as source of guilt, 398
submission to, 402, 421
two parts of
    conscience, 80, 122
    ego-ideal, 122, 176
types of
    archaic, 380, 384, 386, 413,
        450, 481
    defective, 23, 411, 450, 459
    external, 415
    parasitic, **296**
    primitive, **330**, 383
    psychopathic, 347, 348,
        349-50
    sadistic, 148, 228, 233, 250,
        279, 301, 302, 386, 421,
        422
Superstition, 227, 346-47, 366,
    383
    animistic, 34, 423
    See also Magic
Supervalent ideas, **423**
Supervision, **423-24**
Suppression, 397, 398, **424;** *see
    also* Denial; Repression
Surrender
    altruistic, 26
    schizophrenic, **390-91**
Symbiosis, 43, **424-25**
Symbolism, 56, 143, 177, 417
    autosymbolism, **47**
    Jung's theory of, 161, 361
    linguistic, 216, 278, 361, 367,
        475
    ritualistic, 383
    spider, 413
Symbolization, **425-26**
Symptomatic acts, **426-27**
Symptoms, 44, 167, 246, 318, 357,
    381
    conflicts due to, 148
    effect of drugs on, 115
    localization of, 180, **224**
    method of investigation of, 286
    pathognomy of, 298
    of specific disturbances
        conversion, *see* Conversion
            symptoms

hysteria, 8, 20, 56, 150, 153,
    155-56, 196, 236, 353,
    410-11
    neurosis, *see* Neurotic
        symptoms
    phobia, 310
    psychosis, *see* Psychosis—
        symptoms of
    psychosomatic disturbances,
        350
two determinants of, 288
varieties of
    acrophagia, 18
    anorexia nervosa, 34-35
    brooding, 130
    compromise, 386
    depersonalization, 102
    discharge as, 105
    ego-alien, 118-19
    ejaculatio praecox, 124
    hair pulling, 171
Synthesis, 82, **427-28**
Systematic approach, *see*
        Descriptive approach

T

Taboos (prohibition, the
        forbidden), 23, 343, 369,
        393, 400, 408, **429**
    attraction of, **43,** 73
    on becoming godlike, 316
    as first moral restriction, 34
    incest, 35, 166, 190
    on knowledge, 403
    lure of, 226
    against odors, 200
    origin of, 279, 334
    of touching, 207
    virginity, **468**
Talion, law of the, 381
Tarachow, S., 261
T.A.T. (Thematic Apperception
        Test), **436-37**
Tausk, Viktor, 193
Taylor, E. B., 33
Teaching of analysis, xv, **429-30**
    by Abraham, 1, 5, 6
    by Ferenczi, 141, 144, 145, 424
Tears, *see* Weeping

Technique of psychoanalysis, *see*
    Psychoanalytic technique
Teleological approach (finality),
    21, 63, 64, 116, 313, 367,
    433-34
    role of present in, 320
    to virginity, 468
Telepathy, 280, **434-35**
Temperature eroticism, **435**
Tensions, 118, 362, 373, 396
    anticipation of, 342
    discharge of, 11, 98, 105-6, 110,
        183, 367, 387, 457-58
    emotion as, 125
    freedom from, 373
    of forepleasure, 150
    of fore-unpleasure, 151
    homeostasis and, 116
    illness as expression of, 56, 216
    as instinctual energy, 63
    mirrored in metaphors, 246
    premenstrual, **323-24**
    quantity of, 360
    spontaneous release from, 8
    tolerance of, 190, 342, **441-42**
    unpleasant, 59, 259, 313-14,
        315, 359, 441, 460-62,
        467, 471
Thalassa: A Theory of Genitality
    (Ferenczi), 143
Thanatos (death instinct), 130,
    161, 173, 198, 222, 342,
    435-36
    in adaptation, 15
    in aggression, 21
    biological negation of, 30
    in constancy principle, 219
    energy of, *see* Destrudo
    fate vs., 33
    fusion of, 267
    institutionalization of, 35
    introduction of theory of, 160
    Klein's use of term, 294
    mixture of eros and, 360
    nirvana principle connected
        with, 272
    pain resulting from, 180
    passivity and, 13, 15
    as primary instinct, 122
    as primary masochism, 328

repetition compulsion linked to,
    87, 374
Thematic Apperception Test
    (T.A.T.), **436-37**
Therapy, 23, 126, 369, **437-38**
    drug, 115-16
    electro-therapy, 155, 156
    emotional insight in, 126
    negative reaction to, *see*
        Negative therapeutic
        reaction
    See also Active therapy;
        Hypnoanalysis; Play
        therapy; Psychiatry;
        Psychoanalysis; Short-term
        therapy
Thought (thinking), 98, 129,
    438-39
    action and, *see* Action—thought
        and
    disappearance of, 322
    discrepancy between affects
        and, 389
    disorder of, 473-74
    in dreams, 111, 201
    errors of, 295
    forms of
        abstract, *see* Abstract thinking
        creative, 372
        obsessive (compulsive), 9,
            382
        prelogical (primitive), **323**
        primary-process, 295, 389
        rational, maturation of, 242
        symbolic, *see* Symbolism;
            Symbolization
        see also Intellectual activity;
            Intellectual insight
    impairment of alcoholic's, 23
    as mental phenomenon, 245
    omnipotence of, *see*
        Omnipotence
    reality and, 340, 368
    sexualization of, 34, 130, 365
        aggressivization and, 278,
        403
*Three Essays on the Theory of
    Sexuality* (Freud), 143,
    160
Threshold symbolism, **439**

Tics, 89, 144, **439-40**
    as automatism, 45, 439
    torticollis, **442-43**
Time, 63, 286
    concept of, **78**, 412-13
    See also Past
Toilet training, 106, 380, 405,
    440-41
    castration anxiety and, 61
    first repression during, 74
    produces sexual inhibition, 400
Tolerance of tension, 190, 342,
    441-42
Tolstoy, Leo, *Anna Karenina*,
    230-31
Tongue, slips of the, *see* Slips of
    the tongue
Topographic approach, *see*
    Structural approach
Torticollis, **442-43**
Totem and Taboo (Freud), 35,
    161, 343
Totems, 35, 190, **443-44,** 481, 482
    in manic celebration, 229
Train, G. J., 149
Training analysis, 397, 430, **445**
Tranquility, narcissistic, 113-14,
    116
Tranquilizers, 114-16
Transference, 40, 50, 126, 134,
    178, 280, 326, 342, 430,
    431, 432, 437, **445-48**
    acceptance of interpretation
        during, 341
    Breuer's fear of, 156
    delusion due to, 179
    elimination of, 420
    forms of
        countertransference, *see*
            Countertransference
        erotic, **130-31;** *see also*
            Transference-love
        negative, 128, 142, 158,
            446-47, 469-70
        repetition compulsion as, 226
        symbiotic, 425
    as human influence, 427
    incapacity for, 351
    ingredients of
        spider symbolism, 413
        wish for recovery, 370

manipulation of, 373, 404, 405
reassurance and, 369
sex and, **448**
in specific therapies
    hypnoanalysis, 177
    play therapy, 13, 68-69
    of Rank, 52
subjects of
    psychopaths, 347
    schizoid character, 388
    Wolf Man, 473
transference remission, 149
Transference-love, **448-49**
    countertransference-love, 85
    See also Erotic transference
Transference neurosis, 161, 206,
    432, **449-50**
    failure to develop, 260
    repetition compulsion in,
        374-75, 447
    resolution of, 341
Transference-resistance, 377, 449
Transience, **450**
Transient ego-ideal, **450**
"Transitory Symptom-Formation"
    (Ferenczi), 142
Transvestitism, 304, **451**
Traumas (shock), 62, 297-98, 437,
    451-52
    barriers to, 49
    conflict independent of, 341
    forms of
        birth, **52-53,** 79, 191
        preoedipal, 171
        sexual, 5, 6, 20
        visual, 75
        see also Narcissistic
            mortification
    hypnoanalysis of, 177, 340
    relaxation therapy for, 373
    repetition of, 374-75, 381, 382
    results of
        avoidance, 47
        compulsion, 346
        determination of phobias and
            abulias, 10
        fixation, 94
        hysteria, 153, 236, 266, 340,
            341, 379
        impotence, 400
        infantile amnesia, 393

misogyny, 247
neurosis, 174
personal myths, 303
phallic character, 307
primal parathymia, 229-30
psychosis, 389
regression, 371
sources of
    pain, 291, 451
    sexual inhibition, 400
weeping over, 89
Traumatic neurosis, 144, 381, 451,
    452
    anxiety state as, 39
    dreams and, 111, **452-53**
    as fixation, 147-48
    repetition compulsion in,
        374-75, 452, 460-61
    See also War neurosis
Trial analysis, **453**
Trial identification, **453**
Trobriand Islanders, 35-36
Tropism, **264, 317**
Trotter, Wilfred, 236
Turning against self, 56, 95, 354,
    377, 390, **453-54**
    masochism as, 386
    as instinctual vicissitude, 200,
        375
"Two Encyclopedia Articles"
    (Freud), 246
Typical dreams, 111-12, **454**

U

Ulcerative colitis, 353, 405-6,
    455-56
Ulcers, peptic, **300-2**
Ulrichs, Karl Heinrich, 462
Uncanniness, 102, 193, 271, 375,
    456
    spiders produce feeling of, 413,
        414
Unconscious, xvi-xvii, 50, 237,
    251, 429, **457**
    of analyzing instrument, 32
    collective, **75,** 361
    components of
        defense mechanisms, 454
        feelings, 140

gratification, 387
identification, 201-2
masturbation fantasies, 240
memory, 248
narcissistic mortification,
    259-60
symbolization, 425, 426
thing- and object-
    presentations, 9
countertransference and, 85-86
defense mechanisms and, 94-95
dissociation of, 346
in dream-work, 113
interaction of conscious and,
    340
    censorship between
        preconscious and, 64, 318
    separation, 377
    unconscious becomes
        conscious, 81, 457
as part of ego, 118, 123, 251,
    338, 457
processes of
    conflict, 79, 337
    language, 41, 361
    primary, 329, 337
    rationalization, 364
psychoanalytic approaches to,
    340-41, 430-33, 437-38
    analyst's unconscious, 431,
        437
    deterministic, 346-47
    dynamic, 345
    hypnosis, 178
    Klein's use of term, 294
    play therapy, 69
    structural, 338, 342, 345,
        417-18, 457
    systematic, 246, 318-19, 337,
        345, 428
psychopathic, 348-49
as source of neologisms, 265-66
of ulcer patient, 301
See also Freudian theories—of
    unconscious
"Unconscious, The" (Freud), 161,
    246
Unconscious action, **457-58**
Unconscious affects, 8, 19-20,
    458

Page numbers in **boldface** refer to main entries

Unconscious emotions and
     feelings, 126, **458**
Unconscious significance of
     speech, **458-59**
Undisguised dreams, 112, **459**
Undoing, 135, 262, 374, 398,
     459-60
  magical, 95, 227, 371, 380, 383,
     385, 459-60
  neurotic use of, 93, 279, 374
United States, 164, 165, 434
  Ferenczi's trips to, 141, 142,
     144-45
  Freud's lectures in, 141, 155,
     161
  Koller's practice in, 155
Unpleasure, 120, 188, 371, 396,
     460-61
  avoidance of, 207, 315, 381
  in character neurosis, 66
  elimination of, 78, 173, 387
  expectation of, 36
  goal of elimination of, 367
  polarity of pleasure and, 315
  in repetition compulsion, 374
  resistance against, 377
  sources of
     dreams, 411
     forepleasure, 18
     lack of excitation, 176
     perverse impulses, 401
     symptoms, 93, 353
     unsuccessful discharge, 105-6
  tension and, 59, 259, 313-14,
     315, 460-62, 467
     in dreams, 471
     quantity of tension, 359
     tolerance of tension, 441
  types of
     anxiety, 37
     boredom, 57
     chronic, 33
     infantile, 191, 356-57
     masochistic, 232, 233
     see also Fore-unpleasure;
        Pain
Unpleasure-pleasure principle,
     106, 219, 272, 313-15,
     387, 442, 456, **461-62**
  abandonment of, 340
  division of, 367-68

dynamic approach to, 116
masochism and, 234, **314-15**
quality and, 359
repetition compulsion in,
     460-61
Uranism, **462**
Urethral eroticism, 189, 357, 403
Urination, 257, 381, **462-63**
  control of, 412
  as expression of contempt, 287
  See also Enuresis

V

Vagina, 32, 54, 199
  in cloaca, 74
  as organ of gratification, 62
Vagina dentata, 58, **465**, 466
Vaginal father, **465-66**
Vaginismus, **466**
Values, **466-67**; see also
     Evaluation
Verbalization, 320, **467**; see also
     Language
Vertigo, **467-68**
Vienna, 143, 145
  as Freud's home, 153-58, 163,
     165
Vienna Psychoanalytic Society, 41,
     146, 155, 160-61, 365
  business agent for, 164
  business meetings of, 160
  formation of, 159
  Anna Freud in, 163
Virginity taboo, **468**
Vomiting, 285, 335, 467
  with anorexia nervosa, 34
  hysterical, 83, 181, 224, 394
  with pregnancy, 323
Voyeurism, 75, 83, 415, 433
  as perversion, 304

W

Waldhorn, H. F., 370
Wandsbek, Germany, 154, 156-57
War neurosis, 296, 451, 452, **469**
  Abraham's paper on, 6
  as anxiety state, 39
Warcollier, R., 434

Wayward Youth (Aichhorn),
     469-70
Weekend (Sunday) neurosis,
     421-22
Weeping (crying), **89**, 215, 246,
     355, 396
  as abreaction, 8
  aggression expressed in, 199
  defense against, 218
  manic-depressive psychosis
     traced to, 228
  as signal, 356, 387
  sublimation of, 419
  with yawning, 57, 479
Weismann, August, 29-30
Weiss, E., 468
Weissman, P., 204, 413
Weltanschauung, 345, **470**
  scientific, 392, 470
Wenzl, Aloys, 63
Wet dreams, 458, **470-71**
White, H. D. Jennings, 467
Whole responses, 383
Wild psychoanalysis, **471**
Wilde, Oscar, *The Canterville
     Ghost,* 456
Will
  free, **152**, 338
  inhibition of, 10
  to power, 160
Winkelman, N. W., 114
Winterstein, Alfred von, 58, 344
Wish fulfillment, 50, 91
  in dreams, 109, 111, 112, 262,
     371
  See also Satisfaction
Wit (jokes), 10, 27, 175, **211**,
     345
  classification of jokes, **73-74**
  comic quality, **76**
  content and form of, **81-82**
  in dreams, 112, 303, **471-72**
  pun as, 61, **355**
  sexual aggression in, 403
  as sublimated anxiety, 402
  See also Humor
Withdrawal syndrome, 16, 114
Wolberg, L. R., 177, 404
"Wolf Man" (case history), 196,
     263, **472-73**, 482
  deferred reaction of, 96

evaluation of therapy for, 134
hypochondriacal delusion of,
179, 472, 473
hysterical conversion of, 180,
472
as latent homosexual, 217, 472,
473
localization of symptom of, 224
rebirth fantasy of, 370
structural approach to, 195
Woodruff, Lorand Loss, 30
Word association test, 159, **473**
Word salad, **473-74**
Words, **474;** *see also* Language
Working through, 32, 62, 377,
475

of gestures, 216, 230
as part of abreaction, 8
World War I, 164, 365
Abraham's service in, 6
effect of, on Freud, 161
Ferenczi's service in, 142-43
Wortis, B., 357
Writer's block, 402, **475**
Writer's cramp, 78, 353, **475-76**
Wulff, M., 379
Wundt, Wilhelm, 473

Xenophobia, 236, **477**

Y

Yawning, 57, **479**
Yazmajian, R., 75, 407, 408

Z

Zooerasty (bestiality), 304,
481-82
Zoophobia, 443-44, **482**
of Little Hans, 67, 71, 138, 196,
223, 310-11, 366, 482
of Wolf Man, 180, 263, 472,
482

Page numbers in **boldface** refer to main entries